A

Philip E. Lilienthal

■   ■   ■

B O O K

The Philip E. Lilienthal imprint
honors special books
in commemoration of a man whose work
at the University of California Press from 1954 to 1979
was marked by dedication to young authors
and to high standards in the field of Asian Studies.
Friends, family, authors, and foundations have together
endowed the Lilienthal Fund, which enables the Press
to publish under this imprint selected books
in a way that reflects the taste and judgment
of a great and beloved editor.

The publisher gratefully acknowledges the generous contribution to this book
provided by the
Chiang Ching-Kuo Foundation for International Scholarly Exchange
and by the
Philip E. Lilienthal Asian Studies Endowment
of the University of California Press Associates,
which is supported by a major gift from Sally Lilienthal.

The Victorian Translation of China

不以文害辭，不以辭害志，以意逆志，是爲得之。

JAMES LEGGE'S CREDO AS A TRANSLATOR

Therefore those who explain the Odes, may not insist on one term so as to do violence to a sentence, nor on a sentence so as to do violence to the general scope. They must try with their thoughts to meet that scope, and then we shall apprehend it.—*The Chinese Classics,* "The Works of Mencius," V, part I, iv. 2 (1861).

The Victorian Translation of China

James Legge's Oriental Pilgrimage

Norman J. Girardot

UNIVERSITY OF CALIFORNIA PRESS

Berkeley   Los Angeles   London

Excerpt from A. R. Ammons's "Corsons Inlet," copyright © 1963 by A. R. Ammons, from *Collected Poems 1951–1971* by A. R. Ammons. Reprinted by permission of W. W. Norton & Company, Inc.

Excerpt from Debra A. Castillo's *The Translated Word,* © 1984, reprinted with permission of the author.

University of California Press
Berkeley and Los Angeles, California

University of California Press, Ltd.
London, England

© 2002 by The Regents of the University of California

Library of Congress Cataloging-in-Publication Data
Girardot, N.J.
   The Victorian translation of China : James Legge's Oriental pilgrimage. / Norman J. Girardot.
     p.   cm.
"The Philip E. Lilienthal Asian studies imprint."
   Includes bibliographical references and index.
   ISBN 0-520-21552-4 (alk. paper)
   1. Legge, James, 1815–1897. 2. Missionaries—China—Biography. 3. Missionaries—Great Britain—Biography. I. Title: James Legge's Oriental pilgrimage. II. Title.
BV3427.L42 G57   2002
266'.02342051'092—dc21
[B]   2001027444

Manufactured in the United States of America
11   10   09   08   07   06   05   04   03   02
10   9   8   7   6   5   4   3   2   1

To my mother and father, and to Kay

Fear God, and keep his commandments: for this is the whole
duty *of man. For God shall bring every work into judgment,
with every secret thing, whether* it be *good or whether* it be *evil.*

ECCLESIASTES 12:13–14

*It is well said, in every sense, that a man's religion is the chief
fact with regard to him. A man's, or a nation of men's. By
religion I do not mean here the church-creed which he professes,
the articles of faith which he will sign and, in words and
otherwise, assert; not this wholly, in many cases not this at
all. . . . This is not what I call religion, this profession and assertion; which is often only a profession and assertion from the out-
works of the man, from the mere argumentative region of him, if
even so deep as that. But the thing a man does practically believe
(and this is often enough* without *asserting it even to himself,
much less to others); the thing a man does practically lay to
heart, and know for certain, concerning his vital relations to this
mysterious Universe, and his duty and destiny there, that is in
all cases the primary thing for him, and creatively determines all
the rest. That is his* religion; *or it may be, his mere scepticism
and* no-religion: *the manner it is in which he feels himself to be
spiritually related to the Unseen World or No-World; and I say, if
you tell me what that is, you tell me to a very great extent what
the man is, what the kind of things he will do is.*

THOMAS CARLYLE, *ON HEROES AND HERO WORSHIP,* 1841

*So we return briefly to the original myth. The Sacred Scripture
represents for many the myth of an absolute text, yet the fall from
Eden guaranteed its corruption and the fall from Babel, its unintelligibility. How can it be absolute when it exists in various
forms and is subject to the errors of chance that befall human
texts? Can those sacred texts be considered in any way infinite, or
only susceptible to infinite imperfect interpretations? Sacred
Scripture also falls subject to the penalties of Babel; it has no one
name, no one language. The words that compose it are doubly,*

triply metaphorical. The word of God is mediated through a human word, translated into human languages, further mediated by the distance separating man from a direct relationship to the things of the world. Translated from one language to another, always with a slippage of meaning. Which, if any, language was the original word of God?

DEBRA A. CASTILLO, *THE TRANSLATED WORD*, 1984

CONTENTS

ILLUSTRATIONS

PREFACE

The history of the Victorian Age will never be written: We know too much about it. For ignorance is the first requisite of the historian—ignorance, which simplifies and clarifies, which selects and omits, with a placid perfection unattainable by the highest art. . . . It is not by the direct method of a scrupulous narration that the explorer of the past can hope to depict that singular epoch. If he is wise, he will adopt a subtler strategy. He will attack his subject in unexpected places; he will fall upon the flank, or the rear; he will shoot a sudden, revealing searchlight into obscure recesses, hitherto undivined. He will row out over that great ocean of material, and lower down into it, here and there, a little bucket, which will bring up to the light of day some characteristic specimen, from those far depths, to be examined with a careful curiosity.

LYTTON STRACHEY, *EMINENT VICTORIANS*, 1918

MY LEGGE WORK

The origins of this work go back several decades to the time when I was finishing a book on the "early Taoism" in the ancient Chinese texts known as the *Laozi/Lao Tzu*, more popularly called the *Daode jing* (The book of the way and its power), and the *Zhuangzi/Chuang Tzu* (The book of Master Zhuang/Chuang). As a counterpoint to my findings about the "myth and meaning" of the Daoist image of chaos *(hundun/hun-tun)*, I made a special effort in the concluding paragraphs of that book to refer to James Legge's quaint Victorian revulsion over the Daoist deification of the principle of chaotic "misrule."[1] The long and twisting journey that led to the writing of this book actually stems from that earlier work's overly capricious estimation of Legge's curious Victorian inability to embrace what I saw at the time as the wonderfully anarchic Daoist vision. Needless to say, I have come to perceive more fully my own quaintness in these matters and, as a comparativist at the start of the twenty-first century, my own ironic indebtedness to James Legge and the Victorian translation of China.

I had no idea that my discovery of the Daoist fascination with a mythic chaos would, in its own strange way, anticipate a kind of postmodernist academic and popular passion for the "secret order" of chaos in the human understanding of reality.[2] What I did know at that time, in the 1970s, was that sinological and comparative scholars were finally discovering the significance of the Daoist tradition, and religion in general, for a fuller and more accurate understanding of Chinese civilization. Casting about for a new research and writing project, I became increasingly intrigued with the idea of dealing with some of the more blatant misconceptions about Daoism (e.g., the distinction between an early and "pure" Daoist philosophy and a later "corrupt" Daoist religion) and Chinese religion (e.g., the assumption that Confucian China was special in relation to all other civilizational traditions because of its largely nonreligious and mythless nature) that seemed so prevalent in mainstream scholarship associated with sinology and the comparative history of religions during the first half of the twentieth century. I must also confess that I was fascinated with the idea of writing a biographical study as a break from the kind of conventional textual analysis and interpretation that had consumed my energies during my apprenticeship as a scholar.

These interests came together in relation to the Victorian missionary-scholar James Legge, who seemed to be an important, if perhaps somewhat stuffy, foundational figure for the discursive history of Western distortions about China, the "great tradition" of Confucianism, and the nature of Chinese religion and unreligion. A biographical study of Legge also had the potential for being an interesting and (perhaps) entertaining story of Victorian, Evangelical, and Orientalist prejudice. I imagined at that time, therefore, a narrative that dealt both with the issue of how someone like Legge (as a representative of conventional missionary apologetic and amateur sinological opinion) could have been so foolishly wrong about Daoism and how a more enlightened tradition of so-called critical interpretation (coming to fruition only in the 1960s and 1970s) associated with the comparative history of religions finally managed to get it right. After some preliminary archival explorations, it became clear that there were copious primary sources for Legge's biography and that, even better, he had a very close and productive relationship with Max Müller, the reputed father of the "comparative science of religions," at Oxford University in the latter part of the Victorian era. This juxtaposition of Legge and Müller, sinology and comparative religions, the *Chinese Classics* and the *Sacred Books of the East,* convinced me that I had found a worthwhile and potentially provocative scholarly project. I was furthermore under the simplistic impression that a study of this kind would make for a relatively short and focused biographical work, no doubt something that could easily be completed in a few years of concerted archival research and conscientious writing. Certainly there could not be that much to a work that seemed to be mostly a digest of Legge's shortcomings as a hopelessly biased missionary-scholar who only found fulfillment in the more academically rigorous and secular practices of Müller's new humanistic science of comparison.

Everything I imagined or thought at that time has proven to be almost completely naive or wrong. As I plunged into the archival chaos of Legge's life and Victorian cultural history, it became increasingly obvious that I could take nothing for granted about Legge, Müller, missionary tradition, sinology, academic history, or the comparative science of religions. This realization and the serendipity of archival research were truly exciting, but my relatively short and manageable project had now taken on a life of its own. By the mid-1980s, therefore, I was overwhelmed with mountains of research notes and archival materials from four continents and I found myself collaborating with a scholar also dedicated to Legge's checkered legacy. My little biographical study of a few years' duration had become a massive intercontinental enterprise entering into its second decade of ever-expanding research. Instead of a chronicle of how someone like Legge could have been so horribly mistaken about the whole matter of China, Chinese classical texts, Confucius, Daoism, and religion in general, I came to appreciate that the story was much more interestingly complicated, ambiguous, and discursively transformative than I could ever have foreseen.

Because of these realizations early in my Leggian labors, I decided not to pursue a straightforward "womb to tomb" biography of Legge (1815–1897). Rather, I wanted as much as possible to use the prism of Legge's life and works to get at the Victorian foundations of the modern Western perception of China and religion. My concern was to explore the rise of two particular and peculiar disciplinary traditions associated with the appearance of the "human sciences" in the nineteenth century: sinology or (more accurately) sinological Orientalism and the comparative science of religions. It seemed that a careful and contextualized examination of these "quite unimportant" and "formidably remote" scholarly disciplines would help in the understanding of some of the most important intellectual and religious changes at the end of the Victorian period.[3] These were changes profoundly associated with tectonic shifts in the cultural-social landmass and the arrival of the modern world—involving such matters as the incremental secularization of public life, the emerging relativistic climate of comparison and pluralism regarding *other* religions and cultures, the curricular and structural transformation of education in both the natural and humanistic sciences, the progressive professionalization of academic life, the implicit cultural imperialism of the Orientalist disciplines, the changes in the worldwide missionary movement, the one-sided encounter of a so-called progressive West with a retarded Orient, and so on. More than the chronicle of a relatively obscure Victorian sage, the story I had to tell was directly expressive of a whole set of profound transformations in the Western discourse about the otherness of the Orient and of non-Christian religion during the nineteenth century.

What better figure than Legge to get at the foundations of professional sinology, and who better than Max Müller (1823–1900) to examine the origins of the academic discipline known as comparative religions? Each was associated with the major canonical work of the nineteenth century in his respective field: the Chinese or Confucian *Classics* in the case of sinology and the *Sacred Books of the East* in comparative religions. Even more interesting is that they were professorial colleagues and collaborators at Oxford University from the 1870s to the end of the century. Indeed, much of the story of the changing intellectual and religious climate during the last years of the Victorian period can be found embedded in the relationship of James Legge and Max Müller at Oxford and in their monumental production of the *Sacred Books of the East* (in which the *Chinese Classics* were transformed into the *Sacred Books of China*).

Legge becomes in this way a pivotal figure for examining some of the most portentous intellectual and religious developments at the end of the nineteenth century. To deal responsibly with these events meant, however, that I would have to adopt the contextualizing and intertextualizing methods of cultural history with a simultaneous biographical focus on the rich details of Legge's career at Oxford University (1876–1897). This is not to say that the earlier phases of Legge's long life—that is, his formative upbringing in Scotland and London (1815–1839) and his active missionary career in Malacca and Hong Kong (1840–1873)—were insignificant and unrelated to later developments. That is clearly not the case, and careful attention must be paid to the entire trajectory of Legge's life. Nevertheless, my primary focus in this work is on Legge's life as it relates to Oxford University, Max Müller, and Victorian tradition at the end of the century. For this reason, I have included in this study only a short prologue, which, as supplemented by the much fuller transitional chapter "Pilgrim Legge and the Journey to the West" (chapter 1) and other recent biographical works (especially those of Lauren Pfister), sets the context for Legge's early hyphenated career as a missionary-pastor-educator-scholar, his eventual separation from the London Missionary Society, and his cultivation of a pioneering academic career as a sinological Orientalist and comparativist at Oxford.[4]

Although this book was not conceived of as a simple biography, it demanded that I pay meticulous attention to the complicated biographical and intellectual nuances of both Legge and Müller's overlapping lives, as well as to the dramatically changing nature of higher academic life at Oxford. Seeking both cultural breadth and biographical depth, I have operated with the principle that a balanced understanding of a changing historical situation calls for an examination of the smallest details associated with the interrelated dynamics of particular cultural and personal factors. Moreover, I believe that it is the finding of God *and* the Devil in the fuzzy fractal patterns of biographical and textual details that is crucial to a study of this sort. This has resulted in a work of considerable length that fits into no easy disciplinary categories, but to accomplish what I set out to do has required such an expansive format. At the end of my story about these matters, it is my hope that I have given both God and the Devil their due.

A HORRID MESS

Throughout this work, I have taken to heart Lytton Strachey's acerbic admonition about the devilishly dark and furtively humorous sides of Victorian characters, especially stereotypically good and wholesomely godly missionaries like Legge. But I am also acutely sensitive to recent debunking criticism of the great Bloomsbury debunker of eminent Victorian figures and all attempts at a biographical art relying on an overly "direct method of a scrupulous narration" (see the epigraph to this preface).[5] I have found myself following more in the footsteps of contemporary biographical masters such as Richard Holmes (Shelley), Richard Ellman (Oscar Wilde), and, for that matter, Michael Holroyd (the massively indefatigable biographer of the apostle of sarcastic biographical brevity, Strachey), whose exhaustive approach to the reconstruction of past lives still respects Strachey's passion in *Eminent Victorians* for shooting "a sudden, revealing searchlight into obscure recesses" of Victorian pretension and phoniness. More significantly, these biographers combine both a hermeneutic of suspicion *and* a hermeneutic of trust. They trust in the human and rhetorical importance of constructing a boggy discursive tale that copiously overflows the terse "little bucket[s]" of Strachey's critical imagination.

Despite Strachey's righteous, and amazingly influential, bluster about these matters, the Victorians themselves were not so oblivious to the darker demands of biography. Even Thomas Carlyle, the great Victorian expositor of the heroic man thesis of history, was not reluctant to mock the standard devout biography: "How delicate, decent, is English biography, bless its mealy mouth."[6] Nonetheless, I must admit that the one existing biography about my subject, *James Legge Missionary and Scholar,* written by Legge's spinster daughter Helen Edith Legge, provides ample grist for the Stracheyian mill. This work is a prime example of the primly pious testimonial or "funereal portrait" mode of Victorian biography that, as ordinarily compiled by a grieving widow or other close relative, was made up of a cavalierly edited collection of letters, cuttings, journals, and other family materials arranged in a loose chronological order. Strachey could easily have been thinking of Helen Edith's commemorative volume (as well as Georgina Müller's even more effusive two-volume assemblage about her husband, Max, published in 1901) when he mocked all such "literary abominations" for their "ill-digested masses of material, their slipshod style, their tone of tedious panegyric, their lamentable lack of selection, of detachment, of design."[7]

Published by the Religious Tract Society in 1905, Helen Edith Legge's biography is, to quote her niece Dominica Legge, a "horrid mess" that overemphasizes the "ever-abounding enthusiasm" of the missionary side of Legge's career (only one of the fourteen chapters is devoted to the Oxford years!) and almost totally neglects (or suppresses) the dramatically controversial and significantly transgressive aspects of Legge's scholarly, religious, political, and educational work.[8] Helen Edith cannot be legitimately criticized for failing to produce an intellectual biography of her father, but within the limited purview of testimonial writing of the period, her gross manipulation of the documents—even to the point of editorially transcribing, excerpting, camouflaging, altering, losing, or (perhaps even) destroying some of these materials—needs to be known and censured.[9] For all her attempts to promote and protect the precious legacy of her father, Helen Edith managed to accomplish exactly the opposite by making Legge out to be too much of a plaster saint, too much the stereotypical heroic, ever-stalwart, "gracious and strong" London Missionary Society agent and "herculean" translator of the Chinese classics.[10] Given the intervening war years and the publication of Strachey's definitive attack on all such prissy Victorian efforts, the existence of Helen Edith's well-intentioned, but hopelessly insipid, biography has tended only to ensure the continuing obscurity of its subject.

A SUBTLER STRATEGY?

In response to Strachey's cynical advice, there has in recent decades been a broad interdisciplinary and revisionary resurgence of both Victorian biography in particular and Victorian studies in general.[11] These developments put the lie to Strachey's overly precious dictum that "we know too much" to write the "history of the Victorian Age." Such history or, better, multiple microhistories, is being written and rewritten now—precisely because, with a doubling of the original irony, much more is known about the Victorians than was ever dreamed by Strachey's generation. Today no one really objects to Strachey's platitudinous comments about a historian's "ignorance" of the past, but most of the best Victorian biographers would argue that it makes all the difference in the world to know as much as possible about one's subject, to dig deeply and broadly in primary sources, to be sensitive to interdisciplinary perspectives on the era in question, and to cast a net widely into the vast sea of cultural context. It is always imperative to be fiercely and intelligently selective, but knowing what to include and exclude is, in the end, significantly affected by the thoroughness and depth of the scholarly research.

It has become all too obvious that Strachey was himself a clever methodological fraud. For all his apparent "careful curiosity" and wicked honesty, he actually and lazily tended to rely on a small number of convenient secondary sources for his portraits in miniature. We are left, then, with the rapidly fading image of a consummate historian and exquisite literary stylist whose genius rested on his ability to reduce vast mountains of documentary material to a few deliciously pithy anecdotes and events. The reality is that Strachey seems to have operated with little firsthand familiarity with the trees, but this deficiency never hindered his talent for holding on to, and blithely foisting upon others, all sorts of witty preconceptions about the forest.

Another aspect of Strachey's "intellectual dishonesty" and "breathtaking disingenuousness" is related to his emphasis on always "lay[ing] bare the facts" of the case "dispassionately, impartially, and without ulterior intentions."[12] For Strachey, who reveled in his own predilections for ridicule, to claim to be motivated solely by calm objectivity reaches astonishing heights of absurdity. It is far more honest to agree with Janet Malcolm that the strange art of biography is, by its very nature, a "flawed genre in which the pose of fair-mindedness, the charade of even-handedness, the striking of an attitude of detachment can never be more than rhetorical ruses."[13] I have no qualms about generally agreeing with Malcolm's observation but, just as I have qualified my understanding of Strachey, so also should I say that surely the game of biographical "fair-mindedness" and "detachment" is a matter of the degree of self-consciousness about the ambiguity and flux of knowledge concerning a person and a period. What is particularly interesting is that the period I am writing about in this book deals directly with the curious history of the transformation of theological partiality and the institutionalization of the secularized ruses of academic, scientific, and comparative "objectivity" in the human sciences.[14]

I do believe that some rough narrative structure following the primary way stations of Legge's life is rhetorically advantageous—even if this narrative line is not always very direct, scrupulous, or complete. My sense of design for this work was, consequently, to produce a biographical study responsive to the cultural history of the last part of the nineteenth century (particularly from 1873, when Legge leaves China forever). Accordingly, I have taken the liberty of punctuating the chronological narrative with substantial blocks of textual and contextual analysis. I make no apology for this method because Legge's evolving identity, like that of so many of the great Victorians, is primarily defined by his relation to texts and contexts— particularly by his Scottish Nonconformist upbringing; by his engagement with native Chinese heathens and converts, conservative missionaries, British merchants, and Oxonian dons; and by the complex intertextual and translational interplay among all manner of "Western" and "Eastern" texts classified as classics and scriptures. I freely admit, then, to the difficulties inherent in any kind of serious biographical study, no matter how focused and delimited. Instead of Strachey's "little bucket," which has proven to be more of an unscrupulous personal conceit than any kind of real methodology, I have preferred to lower more and larger buckets, sloppy with context and leaking excessive details, as I rowed out over the great ocean of material. My approach is by no means a subtler strategy with respect to these biographical issues, but it is more complete and more responsive than the approach of either Strachey or Helen Edith Legge to the always ambivalent and fluidly transformational nature of a human life.

MY GUY

The bottom-line question for biographers is whether they ended up liking their subject. To answer this is not as straightforward as it might seem because there is always a natural tendency to justify the many years of unappreciated drudgery in obscure archives. Thus it better well be that "my guy" turns out to be historically weighty, surprisingly colorful, and outstandingly worthwhile. But the my-guy question is a little more complicated than this because there is also a post-Stracheyian, and very human, urge to pile up dirt at the expense of amiability. It is all to the good, then, if your guy, especially someone from the Victorian era, turns out to be an inveterate bed wetter or a secret onanist (as was one of Legge's own political heroes, the liberal prime minister William Gladstone). Woe to the biographer saddled with someone too blandly virtuous, without even a wink and a nudge of sexually salacious or morally duplicitous behavior.

I confess to having had a few fears along these lines. Nonetheless, the saving grace of this work, and an affirmation that light is forever compromised by the dark, is that I always had the wonderfully petty self-deceptions of academic and religious persons to contemplate. Müller is an especially arch instance of this principle. But I also found that Legge's own virtue was hardly bland or pure. Most of all, he struggled with the demons of "godly" pride and prejudice, afflictions that plagued many China missionaries and Oxford professors driven by a transcendental faith and a prophetic ambition. Moreover, his seemingly conventional goodness and sturdy diligence were more than humanly qualified and shadowed by his sometimes socially awkward single-mindedness; his battle with his own youthful arrogance in Malacca and Hong Kong; his stubborn independence when in confrontation with missionary, educational, and political authorities; his Scottish country-bumpkin simplicity and lack of cynical sophistication; his Evangelical righteousness and bourgeois devotion to his scholarly work; his overly hearty and often patronizing patriarchal approach to familial and interpersonal intercourse; his willingness to risk public censure and ridicule in the name of transcultural intellectual conviction and moral principle; his sometimes unbearably long-winded Sabbath-culture habits of preaching and praying; his admitted deficiencies as a philosopher and poet; and his hesitant appreciation for the "sympathetic comprehensiveness" of the comparative approach. While never self-important in the virtuoso Müllerian manner, he did not suffer fools gladly—whether High Church Anglicans or anyone else from the realms of sectarian religion, commerce, politics, or

the university. It could even be said that Legge had more meaningful intercourse with certain Chinese heathens and quasi-Christians (among them,
his first co-translator and religious colleague, Ho Tsun-sheen; his later literary collaborator on the Chinese classics, Wang Tao; and Hong Rengan,
the "Shield King" of the Taiping rebellion) than with some Oxonian Christians (such as Benjamin Jowett and the nameless Anglican officials at Oxford who frustrated his plans for burying his second wife).

Legge was virtuous, but not unsullied. Whatever his deficiencies, it seems
that he was not a typical Stracheyian hypocrite even though it could be argued, from either a Victorian Evangelical or Chinese Confucian point of
view, that a kind of ritual hypocrisy or ceremonial respect for propriety is always the necessary "homage that manners pay to morals."[15] It was the turn-
of-the-century Stracheyian "Bloomsbury chic" ethic (as an extension of the
earlier aesthetics of decadence in the 1890s) that, in a kind of ultimate secularized totalization of Protestant middle-class values, elevated individual
"authenticity" and autonomy over any ritualized obligation and duty to others. From this perspective, the "basic flaw" of the Victorians was their "weakness for religion" and their foolish emphasis on the interconnection of religious convictions, ritual manners, moral principles, and codified laws.[16]
We see here some of the roots of the common suspicion among academic
historians of the twentieth century that Victorian missionaries or ex-
missionaries like Legge must necessarily, because of their religiosity, be
morally and intellectually flawed. By the same token, it could be argued
that the fundamental flaw of religion and the hypocrisy of relating manners
and morals made the even more thoroughly secularized turn-of-the-century
sinological Orientalists and comparativists emphasize the essentially agnostic (or nonreligious/a-religious) and unmodern nature of Confucius and
Confucianism. Confucius or Kongzi may not have worn religion on his
sleeve, as did many Victorians, but (like Roman Catholics and Victorians in
general) he was notoriously susceptible to the hypocritical equation of the
outer display of social ceremony with individual virtue. This seems to be a
reasonable inference deriving from the traditional Western interpretation
of a hypothetical Confucius and Confucianism.[17]

ACCESSIBLE DISCOURSE

Finally, I want to say that that this book is manifestly an *academic* work. This
declaration means that I have not avoided various theoretical and technical
matters, nor have I been reluctant to analyze the Leggian scholarly corpus in
considerable detail. I have sought to make my discussion as scholarly responsible and contextually rich as possible, but I have also struggled to make
the whole work accessible to a broad multidisciplinary audience. I have
tried, therefore, to avoid the seductive temptations of postmodernist jargon
and an overly politicized reliance on abstract theory. I have also refrained

from a Saidian-style Orientalism that would hegemonically interpret all Orientalist texts and persons in terms of strictly one-sided power relations.[18] Too often forgotten is that the actual practice and reception of Orientalism are "often fragmentary, transformative, unreflective, anecdotal."[19] In the case of the Western sinological view of China, in particular, the modifying influence of the self-image of the Chinese literati (the Ruists or Confucians) and the commentarial tradition cannot be underestimated. China spoke back to its powerful interlocutors from the very beginning of its checkered encounter with European civilization. To be sure, native intellectuals at the end of the Qing dynasty had assimilated much of the Western modernist rhetoric of science and progress, but they regularly modulated, resisted, challenged, and transformed this discourse in relation to traditional Chinese prerogatives.

I have not hesitated to employ various critical notions and tropes when pertinent to the deconstructive slant of my discussion, but I have attempted to use common expressions for the more esoteric "lit-crit" terminology. Edward Said (unlike some of his disciples) is a rather good example of this accessible style of scholarship: *Orientalism,* while impressively theoretical and brilliantly literate, deals with specific texts and cultural productions in a generally readable and gracefully supple academic vernacular. Perhaps the best model for what I am attempting in this book is seen in the impressively insightful and suggestive work by Said's mentor, Raymond Schwab. Published in 1950, *La Renaissance orientale* is an authentic masterpiece of intellectual history and cultural analysis. It is an academic work that is highly erudite and technical, yet written with great literary verve and passion.[20] It is also a work that deals with concrete persons as seriously as it does with texts and intertextual discourse—something that has been missing from much contemporary scholarship. The real fascination of a work like this is the opportunity to observe the incremental and often contradictory transformations of a person responding to cultural forces of diverse origin and ambivalent logic. The particular value of watching Legge's life unfold within its multiple cultural contexts (Scotland, England, Hong Kong, China, Oxford) is that his story of a "mind in transition" helps to set the stage for the modern and postmodern understandings of China and religion in the twentieth and twenty-first centuries. Finally, however, my Legge work has simply and most meaningfully resulted in a tale that has been good to tell and to think.

For all of my strictures about Strachey's biographical minimalism and my own belief in the culturally constructed nature of human identity, I basically sympathize with the spirit of his observation that "human beings are too important to be treated as mere symptoms of the past."[21] It is this factor that, along with the accompanying cultural discourse and intertextual contextualizing, I hope I have captured and communicated in this biographical study.

ACKNOWLEDGMENTS

The Master said, "In my dealings with men, whose evil do I blame, whose goodness do I praise, beyond what is proper? If I do sometimes exceed in praise, there must be ground for it in my examination of the individual."
JAMES LEGGE, *THE CONFUCIAN ANALECTS, THE CHINESE CLASSICS*, 1893

Drawing upon archives located on three continents, this is a work that has taken many years to complete. To be truthful, it has been an all-consuming project that has really taken much too long to bring to fruition. Starting out as a solo project in the early 1980s, it eventually became a collaborative project with Dr. Lauren Pfister of Hong Kong Baptist University. For various reasons, the collaborative process floundered and I therefore must take sole responsibility for this book. Despite these difficulties, I profited greatly from the collaborative relationship. Both of us were positively transformed by the intensity of our long collaboration, and both of us, I believe, have now been empowered to write a book that flows from our deepest convictions. It took two Legges to walk the path leading to this book, even if in the end it must stand on one.

The prolonged and complicated production of this book also suggests that I have been helped by an especially large number of individuals and institutions. Feeling some acute end-of-my-tether exhaustion, I might well be tempted to rely on only a general statement of hearty thanks to all who assisted me along the seemingly interminable way. It is better, however, that I gird up my psychic loins and honor the spirit of the ancient Chinese master by properly performing the ritual duty of acknowledging those who have played a special role in this enterprise. Some have given much, while others have committed smaller acts of benevolence. All have made a difference, and all deserve an excess of praise.

Most of all, I am deeply appreciative for the diligence of my assistants—Jia-pei and Jan-ming Hou in Bethlehem, Pennsylvania (now residing in Indiana). At Lehigh University, I additionally thank the ever-patient staff of the Inter-Library Loan Office of the University Libraries; Nancy Sutton and Marian Gaumer of the Religion Studies Department Office; the former deans John Hunt and Jim Gunton of the College of Arts and Sciences; Mary Jo Hill of the Office of Research, and Kathleen Gallagher; and Professors Michael Raposa, David Pankenier, and Robert Phillips, always supportive colleagues and friends. I am also very appreciative of various small grants from the Lehigh Faculty Research Fund that came along at crucial points in the protracted research for this work. Others in the United States deserving of acknowledgment include Kathleen Lodwick at the University of Pennsylvania, Allentown; John Lundquist, the Susan and Douglas Dillon Chief Librarian of the Oriental Division at the New York Public Library; Eric Ziolkowski at Lafayette College, Easton, Pennsylvania; the staffs of the University of Pennsylvania Library in Philadelphia, Pennsylvania, at the Pitt Theological Library at Emory University in Atlanta, Georgia, and at the Harvard Yenching Library; and the staffs of Butler Library and the Asian Studies Library at Columbia University. I want, moreover, to thank those in the special collections library of the College of William and Mary, the American Bible Society archives, the Historical Society of Pennsylvania, and the Rutgers University library archive.

For services and kindnesses rendered during several visits to the United Kingdom, I want expressly to thank the British Museum Library, Dr. Williams's Library, the School of Oriental and African Studies Library, University College Library (the Archives of Routledge & Kegan Paul Ltd.), the National Register of Archives, the Royal Asiatic Society, and the Council for World Missions, all in London; the Bodleian Library, the Oriental Institute, the Taylor Institution Library, the Corpus Christi College Archives, Mansfield College Library, Manchester College Library, Somerville College Library Archives, New College Library Archives, the Oxford University Press Archive, and the Centre for Oxfordshire Studies in Oxford; the University of Cambridge Library (including the Bible Society Archive and the Jardine Matheson Archive); and the University of Birmingham Special Collections. In Scotland, I acknowledge the help of the library in New College at the University of Edinburgh and the University Archive at Edinburgh, the archives of the Free Church of Scotland College on the Mound in Edinburgh, the National Library of Scotland, and the King's College Archive at the University of Aberdeen.

Beyond the always courteous and conscientious general staff of these institutions, I would like especially to recognize the uniquely gracious help of Rosemary Seton at the School of Oriental and African Studies Library, Steven Tomlinson at the Bodleian Library, Alma Jenner at the Mansfield College Library, Jill Hughs at the Taylor Institution Library, Peter Foden at the Oxford University Press Archive, Alan Jesson at the Bible Society Archive in Cambridge, Arnott T. Wilson of Edinburgh University library, and Myrtle Anderson-Smith of the Special Collections at King's College Library at the University of Aberdeen. Special thanks also to Dr. R. Gary

Tiedemann and Professor Timothy Barrett of the History Department at the School of Oriental and African Studies; Dr. K. M. Elisabeth Murray, great-granddaughter of James Murray of the *Oxford English Dictionary;* Dr. Alan Chard at Oxford and Dr. Sarah Allen at the School of Oriental and African Studies and now affiliated with Dartmouth College; and Professor Andrew Walls at the Centre for the Study of Christianity in the Non-Western World at Edinburgh University. Miss Viola Wyatt and Mrs. Margaret Olopanu are additionally to be thanked for their warm hospitality while I was in Oxford. Also at Oxford, I acknowledge the encouragement of the current incumbent in Legge's Chinese chair (now called the Shaw Professorate), Professor Glen Dudbridge. In Hong Kong, I appreciate the thoughtful help of the historians Lau Tze Yui and Timothy Man Kong Wong. In Beijing, I thank Jeffrey Bohrer for his perspicacious guidance concerning Chinese trains and cabs, on the wind-swept paths up Taishan, and in the Confucian forest in Qufu; also especially helpful was Dr. Tang Yi of the Institute for Study of World Religions at the Chinese Academy of Social Sciences in Beijing. Information and correspondence with Professor Eric Sharpe of the University of Sydney filled in details about the history of comparative religions. Gillian Bickley in Hong Kong helped in several important ways regarding illustrative materials. Lastly, I acknowledge the fact that Diane LaBelle allowed me to use her blue drafting pencil at a crucial stage in the correction of the manuscript.

I also want to thank my various editors who have supported me during my long Leggian journey—particularly Edward Dimendberg (now at the University of Michigan) and, at the University of California Press, Sheila Levine and Laura Harger. Most treasured in this regard is Frances Bowles, my heroic and patient copyeditor.

I (along with Lauren Pfister) owe a very special debt of gratitude to the National Endowment for the Humanities Special Projects Division for a grant for "interpretive research" (Grant Number RO-22494) that, in conjunction with supplemental funding and support from the Chiang Ching-Kuo Foundation and the Pacific Cultural Foundation in Taiwan, made this a feasible undertaking. Because of these awards and the assistance of our respective institutions, we were able to devote two uninterrupted years of labor to the Legge project. This work would still lie cybernetically fallow in my hard drive if it were not for the blessed gift of time offered by these fellowships. Moreover, as an aging scholar who grew up writing dissertations and books on primitive electric typewriters, I would like to give praise to my word processor (WP 6.1; now 8.1) and to the communicative glories of e-mail and the electronic transference of text files.

Finally, I would like to say that my one strong regret is that Professor Dominica Legge, the great-granddaughter of James Legge and a formidable linguistic scholar in her own right, is not alive to see the completion of this work. She was my first exposure to the Legge family and, throughout the month of April 1983, she gave freely of herself and of her personal materials not yet deposited in the Bodleian Library. Beyond the excitement of being made privy to a whole body of new archival materials was the inspiration of her own persevering spirit. There was also, of course, her wonderfully lively and uncensored testimony concerning the whole "horrid mess" of Helen Edith Legge's biographical methods. Though in her eighties, Dominica Legge carried on in an independent way that would have pleased her great-grandfather.

Two other parties to the legacy of James Legge deserve my special thanks: Ewen and Mae McDonald of Huntly, Aberdeenshire, in Scotland, who warmly opened their home and gave me some real insight into the Legge family homestead, and Christopher and Judith Legge and their family in London. Without any hint of suspicion or censure of what I was doing, Christopher (the grandson of James Granville Legge) and his son, James, graciously shared their family memorabilia. They have continued to be helpful and supportive in the very best of unmeddlesome ways. In this regard, I am deeply grateful to James Legge the Younger, who, in the midst of his own career at Christ Church College, Oxford, was kind enough to prepare the elaborate family genealogy used in this book.

I am quite prepared to accept full responsibility for any blunders remaining in this work. On the other hand, I would surely appreciate it if any of the above (knowing and unknowing) facilitators were willing—in a supererogated application of Confucius's silver rule of reciprocity—to accept some culpability in these matters. The allusion to discursive interaction and corporate guilt is admittedly a distortion of the Chinese principle, but it is offered here in the interests of drawing attention to the fact that, on occasions such as this, I am primarily engaged in a ritual of "praise and blame." Let me also say that I hereby accept all blame for indulging in too many (irresistible) Leggish puns. To avoid any last charges of unfilial behavior, I conclude by saying that, without a special dispensation from my family, none of this would ever have come to pass. They were truly joyful when it seemed that Legge would finally be put to rest. I fully concur with their sentiments.

NOTE TO THE READER
ON TRANSCRIPTION AND ROMANIZATION

Confucius said: "I hate a semblance which is not the reality."
JAMES LEGGE, *THE WORKS OF MENCIUS, THE CHINESE CLASSICS*, 1895

Things are seldom what they seem.
W. S. GILBERT, *H.M.S. PINAFORE*

I do not presume that readers of this book are missionary historians, sinologists, Victorian scholars, historians of religion, or—God forbid!—comparativists of any kind. I would like to believe (naively, no doubt) that my account of James Legge's transcultural pilgrimage will be of interest to a broad range of academic specialists and even to the proverbial intelligent general reader with some interest in biography, China, and the intellectual history of the Victorian era. The problem is that readers from a particular academic field cannot be expected to know very much, if anything at all, about any other disciplinary area. As seen from the discussion that follows, a certain methodological provincialism and disciplinary isolation are unusually prominent within the fields of sinological Orientalism and the comparative history of religions—two neglected orphans in the history of the human sciences during the nineteenth and early twentieth centuries. The singularity of sinology and comparative religions, I hasten to add, does not make them any less important than other humanistic disciplines. These disciplines, along with the whole controversial issue of missionary tradition, actually have some special interest precisely because of their historical and methodological strangeness in relation to the mainstream of academic discourse in the West.

Given these extra- and interdisciplinary considerations, as well as the technical nature of much that follows, I want to explain some of the writing conventions used throughout this book. The first issue has to do with the most common problem associated with writing about China—that is, the special linguistic and historical difficulties of transcribing Chinese characters, which are not alphabetical, into accessible Western forms that preserve some semblance of accurate pronunciation. This is the problem of dealing with the romanization of Chinese words in relation to several specialized

systems of transcription (for the English-speaking world since the turn of
the century, this refers to the older Wade-Giles system and, since the 1970s,
the pinyin system). For anyone not privy to some of the peculiar rules of
these systems (e.g., the nonaspirated consonants and *j* sound in the Wade-
Giles and the initial *q, x, zh,* and *c* in pinyin), the pronunciation of Chinese
words can be a forbidding and often laughable exercise. Although there is
no easy solution to these difficulties, I append below a brief pronunciation
guide to pinyin romanization and refer the reader to the fourteenth edition
of the *Chicago Manual of Style* (Chicago: University of Chicago Press, 1993)
for a table converting Wade-Giles and pinyin, and vice versa.

These problems are made even more complicated for this book when it
is appreciated that the nineteenth century was a period when the principles
of the disciplinary transcription of Chinese were emerging in relation to
the whole history of the imperialistic involvement of Western nations in
China (a history that was expressly grounded in comparative and philological issues). Furthermore, in the case of English transcription, this history
involves the contributions of two consul-scholars directly associated with
James Legge—namely, Thomas Wade and Herbert Giles. Indeed, a fully
nuanced history of Chinese romanization systems (particularly the system
associated with the hyphenated linkage of two supercilious and irascible
sinological figures like Wade and Giles, and the politically correct implications of using pinyin) would make a wonderfully suggestive case study in the
intellectual and political ambiguities of Western Orientalism. With regard
to this book, I have primarily employed pinyin romanizations (thus, for example, *Daoism* rather than the more usual *Taoism*) along with, where historically appropriate, Wade-Giles and sometimes the original, and often
not easily decodable, nineteenth-century transcriptions. This usage is complicated by variations in South Chinese dialectical pronunciation and by
Legge's use of at least three different transcription systems during his long
career: his 1861–1872 procedures, Max Müller's system for the *Sacred Books
of the East,* and, in 1893–1895, a modified Wade system. The pinyin system
is, after all, the convention officially adopted and promoted by the People's
Republic of China and is also, in a somewhat awkward way, more linguistically accurate. A case could be made that terms like *Tao* and *Taoism,* or, for
that matter, *Confucius* and *Confucianism,* have, after roughly 150 years of
common usage, become English words and should be left inviolate. It is the
critical concern of this book, however, to examine the historical legacy that
gave rise to such presumptions.

I have left Chinese proper and place names untranslated. Some long-
familiar romanized place names that originated in the nineteenth century
have, however, been retained (e.g., Peking for Beijing and Canton for
Guangzhou). Some personal names (e.g., those of Legge's student, co-
translator, and religious colleague, Ho Tsun-sheen/He Jinshan, and of the

three "Chinese boys" who were baptized in Scotland, Lee Kim-lin, Song Hoot-kiem, and Ung Mun-sou) have also been left in the form most commonly used by Legge. Titles of Chinese texts are initially given in their romanized form (using the original nineteenth-century transcriptions where necessary) and pinyin and, thereafter, in a translated form, for example, *Shoo King/Shujing* (The book of historical documents). Wherever appropriate, I use Legge's often standard translation of titles.

In response to the imperialistic and Orientalistic assumptions traced in this book, I have departed from standard sinological practice in one outstanding case. I refer to my preference for using the romanized form, Kongzi (or often also Master Kong), for the common Latinate name of Confucius (as well as Mengzi for Mencius, Laozi for Lao Tzu, Zhuangzi for Chuang Tzu, and so on). In like manner, and for reasons of alerting my readers to the fact that even seemingly innocent names, words, and phrases may disclose a whole history of linguistic colonialism, I have preferred to use the quasi-romanized forms, Ruist (for *ruren*) and Ruism (for *rujiao* or *rujia*), for the manufactured Western expressions "Confucian" and "Confucianism." The fuller rationale for following such nonstandard conventions will become evident in the course of my discussion. (I am not, however, the first to use this kind of terminology; see especially the brilliant and controversial work by Lionel Jensen, *Manufacturing Confucianism: Chinese Traditions and Universal Civilization* [Durham and London: Duke University Press, 1997].) Here let it be said only that, although "Confucius" is a Latin phonetic transcription, first popularized by the Jesuits in the seventeenth and eighteenth centuries, of a rather rare honorific title *(kongfuzi)* for the ancient Chinese sage, the terms *Confucian* and *Confucianism* represent second-order abstractions that correspond to no actual Chinese expressions or historical entities. In a work that has so much to do with the sometimes pathetic, but always revealing, drama of the Protestant term question, I have tried to be especially sensitive to all such terminological issues related to transliteration and translation.

For reasons of readability, I have purposely avoided most abbreviations in the text. Other technicalities of theory, method, and vocabulary related to the various disciplinary fields dealt with in this book (especially missionary history, Victorian cultural history, Scottish ecclesiastical history, the history of British higher education, Orientalism and sinology, comparative religions, translation studies, and the general history of the human sciences in the nineteenth century) have been kept to a minimum (see the Bibliographical Note at the end of the book). I believe that, in the final analysis, all forms of human expression are certainly rhetorical (broadly conceived), but this does not mean that all written discourse about discourse in the past has to read like a postmodernist manifesto. Another way to say this is to borrow from Jean and John Comoroff *(Of Revelation and Revolution),* who note that "meaning may never be innocent, but it is also not merely reducible to the postures of power." The dynamics of individual human motivation and intention still count for something, even within a hermeneutics of suspicion.

GUIDE TO THE PRONUNCIATION OF PINYIN ROMANIZATION

Vowels		*Consonants*	
a	as the *a* in *father*	b	as the *b* in *be,* aspirated
ai	as the *i* in *bite*	c	as the *ts* in *bits*
ao	as the *ow* in *cow*	ch	as the *ch* in *church*
e	as the *a* in *America*	d	as the *d* in *do*
ei	as the *ei* in *weigh*	g	as the *g* in *go*
i (yi)	as the *ee* in *meet;* when *i*	h	guttural, as in the Scottish
	occurs after *c, ch, r, s, sh, z,*		*loch*
	or *zh,* it sounds more like	j	as the *j* in *jeep*
	the *e* in *her*	k	as the *k* in *kind,* aspirated
ian	as *yen*	l	as the *l* in *light*
ie	as the *ere* in *here*	m	as the *m* in *mouse*
o	as the *o* in *or*	n	as the *n* in *nose*
ou	as the *oa* in *boat*	ng	as the *ng* in *sing*
u	as the *u* in *flute*	p	as the *p* in *par,* aspirated
ü	as the German umlaut *ü*	q	as the *ch* in *cheese*
ui	as *way*	r	as the *r* in *pleasure*
uo	as the *wa* in *wash*	s	as the *s* in *sister*
		sh	as in English
		t	as the *t* in *top*
		x	as the *sh* in *shore*
		y	as the *y* in *silly*
		z	as the *ds* in *suds*
		zh	as the *j* in *judge*

The Strange Saga of Missionary Tradition, Sinological Orientalism, and the Comparative Science of Religions in the Nineteenth Century

Biography, as Heinrich Simon . . . said, is the best kind of history, and the life of one man, if laid open before us with all he thought and all he did, gives us a better insight into the history of his time than any general account of it can possibly do. Now it is quite true that the life of a quiet scholar has little to do with history, except it may be the history of his own branch of study, which some people consider quite unimportant, while to others it seems all-important. This is as it ought to be, till the universal historian finds the right perspective, and assigns to each branch of study and activity its proper place in the panorama of the progress of mankind towards its ideals. Even a quiet scholar, if he keeps his eyes open, may now and then see something that is of importance to the historian.

MAX MÜLLER, *MY AUTOBIOGRAPHY*, 1901

THE BEST KIND OF HISTORY

Friedrich Max Müller, the most famous comparative philologist and Orientalist of the nineteenth century, once self-servingly quoted a historian's observation that, in many ways, "biography . . . is the best kind of history." The life of a single person, "if laid open before us with all he thought and all he did, gives us a better insight into the history of his time than any general account of it can possibly do." One problem with this methodological principle seems, however, to be the case of the "quiet scholar" who apparently has "little to do with history," except for "the history of his own branch of study, which some people consider quite unimportant, while to others it seems all-important." This judgment is, as Müller says, "as it ought to be" until "the universal historian" finds the right comparative perspective, "and assigns to each branch of study and activity its proper place in the panorama of the progress of mankind towards its ideals." The point is that the life and discipline of "even a quiet scholar"—and Müller was quite typically thinking of himself—may have some general cultural and historical significance, especially if that scholar had the good sense to respond to the changing times and "keeps his eyes open."[1]

But Müller, a prolific academic entrepreneur and a well-connected counselor to the British nobility, was hardly a "quiet scholar." A much better test of the principle concerns his more unassuming Oxonian colleague, the ex-missionary and professor of Chinese James Legge. I cannot pretend to be Müller's "universal historian," but I do believe that a fully contextualized life of a seemingly quiet missionary and humble scholar such as Legge gives us a revealing perspective on the larger panorama of Victorian cultural history, if not the nineteenth-century "progress of mankind towards its ideals." In the course of his long life as a transcultural pilgrim in Britain and Asia, Legge was someone who kept his eyes open, his religious outlook broad, his translator's pen active, and his moral sensibilities acute.

The trick of this kind of biographical procedure is always to "lay open"—like a comparative anatomist spilling out the internal organs with a scalpel—all a person "thought and all he did" in relation to the larger cultural carcass of the period. Important social developments, intellectual transformations, institutional changes, and religious upheavals are all part of the panorama associated with Legge's long life. So also do we discover that the various realms of activity and study closely identified with Legge—the Protestant missionary enterprise, the emergence of sinological Orientalism, and the creation of the comparative science of religions—are not so completely trivial in relation to the larger pageant of Victorian history. It is not that these pursuits can be seen as "all-important," but rather that they become interesting precisely because of their relative obscurity and strangeness amid the other emergent human sciences in the nineteenth century. Meaning and importance both depend, as Müller and Michel Foucault would say on quite different methodological grounds, in "finding the right perspective."

REMOTE AND STRANGE

The Western study of Chinese culture and its institutions, that hermetically specialized field within the larger domain of Orientalism known as "sinology," has always been a peculiar discipline. From its beginnings with the Jesuits and French Enlightenment *philosophes* in the seventeenth and eighteenth centuries, down through its crystalization as a professional academic discipline in the nineteenth century, sinology has reflected and refracted the changing attitudes of the Western encounter with the otherness of Chinese tradition. The checkered history of this intercourse has often been a one-sided intellectual and cultural exchange that, until roughly the end of the nineteenth century, when secularized academic institutions prevailed, was primarily a record of the changing fortunes of the Roman

Catholic and Protestant missionary enterprises. But, unlike some other Oriental traditions and, by definition, the illiterate or "savage" cultures, the native Chinese literati class and traditional commentaries were present to guide and adjust Western views on the meaning of the ancient textual tradition, particularly when those views were rooted in the somewhat common classical and commentarial prejudices of European and Chinese scholar-ministers.[2]

In the nineteenth century, when the common philological and racial "brotherhood" of the Indo-European traditions became an article of intellectual and imperial faith, China's remarkable linguistic and cultural isolation, its "formidable solitude," as Raymond Schwab rightly put it, became even more of a factor in the retarded development of sinological Orientalism as an academic discipline, even more of a unrecognized instance of an imperial Western science unwittingly in collusion with traditional Ruist or Confucian forms of Chinese cultural mythology.[3] The discovery of the Aryan equation of Europe and India at the end of the eighteenth century, and its scholarly efflorescence in the field of comparative philology in the next century, meant that the professionalized study of Chinese language and literature in the nineteenth century was not as advanced, or as academically and institutionally privileged, as were either Indological or Semitic Orientalism. In an address to the Royal Asiatic Society in the late nineteenth century, Max Müller, the great Indologist and tireless promoter of Victorian Orientalism, said that the problem was that there were "no intellectual bonds"—no linguistic, spiritual, or social kinship—that united Europe and China. Sinology was therefore in the nineteenth century destined to remain a marginal discipline, a "quite unimportant" branch of study "confined to a very small number of scholars."[4] Professional sinology, or sinological Orientalism, was in this way a largely peripheral discourse within the newly emerging academic salons of international Orientalism in the nineteenth century, disciplinary organizations best exemplified by the tradition of regular scholarly congresses that, beginning in Paris in 1873, met in the great imperial capitals of the Western world.

The impoverished situation of sinological Orientalism was unlikely to change in the nineteenth and early twentieth centuries because the West, as Müller in a flight of quasi-racist rhetoric once declared, "received nothing from the Chinese." "There is," he emphasized, "no electric contact between the white and the yellow race." Despite the monumental productions of James Legge's *Chinese Classics* and *Sacred Books of China* (for Müller's own *Sacred Books of the East* series), the fact was that, according to Müller's authoritative estimate in the 1890s, China had "not been brought near to our hearts." The ever-present and essential difference was that, to use Müller's words again, "China is simply old, very old—that is, remote and strange."[5] Unlike the philological principles linking India and Europe, there was no real linguistic or intellectual premise for a sympathetic understanding of China, no real basis for any kind of convincing comparative similitude. As Zhang Longxi has said, China in the nineteenth century became for the West the "image of the ultimate other."[6]

QUITE UNIMPORTANT BRANCHES OF STUDY

Along with the obdurate strangeness of the Chinese language, the special cultural singularity of China was shown by the seemingly unreligious and nonmythological nature of its authoritative texts. The ancient Chinese documents appeared very much unlike the richly imaginative, and epically dynamic, religious literature of Hinduism and Hellenic tradition — or, for that matter, the theistic and prophetic drama of the Semitic biblical traditions. This contrast was particularly striking when the lushly mythological Vedic hymns of ancient Aryan India or the dramatic tales of Greek mythology were compared with the "prosy and dosy" literature of the great or high tradition of Chinese Confucianism attributed to the ancient moral philosopher and sage educator known to the West as Confucius. In the nineteenth century, when the comparative sciences of philology and history became the foundations for the imperious intellectual mission of the human sciences, the unclassifiable Chinese language and the seemingly religionless, mythless, and agnostic Chinese civilization were the primary factors contributing to the special isolation, distortion, and handicapped nature of sinology as one of the newer disciplines of the universal science of Orientalism. During this same period in the mid- and late nineteenth century, the old certitude in the static exclusivity and superiority of the Christian tradition—as well as the general study of religion and religions—was undergoing dramatic changes that would lead both to the emergence of a new science of comparative religions and, after the turn of the century and the First World War, to this fledgling discipline's mostly marginalized and contested status within the more fully secularized academy.

Sinology and comparative religions may well be the two most peculiar, and orphaned, offspring of the human sciences in the nineteenth and early twentieth centuries. It is for this reason that these two academic disciplines share a certain kind of disciplinary alienation and have often been found, even within institutions of higher learning, to be "quite unimportant branches of study." The very set-apart strangeness of the two disciplines—in relation to their separate histories in the nineteenth century, their mutual involvement in the transformations of the Protestant missionary movement, and their controversial appropriation of the comparative method, and in terms of their brief convergence in the so-called sacred books produced by Max Müller and James Legge—makes them ideal vehicles for getting at some important issues of Victorian cultural history. Moreover, the tense relationship of missionary tradition with Orientalistic disciplines such as sinology and the rise of sympathetic, impartial, or comparative approaches to the study of non-Christian religion and civilization is a sorely neglected aspect of this history. An analysis of the interrelated traditions of the Protestant missionary movement, sinological Orientalism, and the comparative science of religions—as mirrored in the life and work of James Legge—is consequently an excellent way to study larger cultural changes at the end of the nineteenth century. These are changes that directly anticipate the emergence of the modern world of the twentieth century and, in diverse and devious ways, continue to distort Western and Chinese perceptions of each other.

COMPARING RECENT DEVELOPMENTS

A fuller awareness of the history of sinological strangeness is made all the more interesting and relevant by the simple fact that the specialized study of Chinese cultural institutions, especially traditions that can be loosely identified as philosophical and religious, has undergone a quiet revolution in recent decades, especially since the 1960s and 1970s. There are many examples of these often revisionary, and frequently interdisciplinary, developments, but let me mention only the explosion of archaeological information; the application of new interdisciplinary methodologies and the dramatic reevaluation of earlier interpretations of the ancient tradition; the growing realization of the importance of religion throughout Chinese history and for all aspects and levels of Chinese society; the fuller incorporation of Chinese literature into the comparative study of world literature; the advances in the study of the Daoist tradition and in the nature and significance of a sinified Buddhism; the heightened appreciation of popular traditions; sweeping reconsiderations of Confucius, Confucianism, and neo-Confucianism; reexaminations of the whole meaning of *modernization* and *westernization* in relation to Chinese tradition; and so on. As a result of these developments, the very definition, classification, and understanding of Chinese *religion, philosophy,* and, for that matter, Chinese *culture* and *civilization*— as well as the ambiguous meaning of artificial categories such as "Confucianism" and "Daoism"—have been radically transformed by sinological specialists and comparative scholars.[7]

Prevailing scholarly assumptions about Chinese tradition, ancient and modern, are being questioned and often overturned, even to the extent that hoary methodological debates dating back to the nineteenth century are being resurrected and fought once again—often with little awareness of their historical precedents. One instance of these revisionary turns that directly harks back to positions staked out during the last part of the nineteenth century concerns the reassertion of comparativistic and diffusionist theories arguing for multicultural, especially Western Asiatic and perhaps even Indo-European, sources for the Chinese language and civilization.[8] China's wholly unique linguistic and cultural tradition was a basic article of polygenetic faith for both secularized Western and chauvinistic native Chinese scholars ever since the old comparativistic approach was definitively quashed after the turn of the century. Now, however, it is becoming increasingly probable that traditional Chinese civilization, which was never purely monolithic in its origins or cultural development, will only be fully and fairly known comparatively in relation to its complex interaction with other ancient traditions.[9]

THE NEGLECT OF NINETEENTH-CENTURY BRITISH ORIENTALISM

This shifting situation in the overall study of Chinese affairs, coupled with theoretical perspectives emphasizing the constructed nature of all cultural representations and the complex interconnections of Western imperialism, the missionary movement, academic Orientalism, and the creation of the human sciences, dramatizes the need for a careful reevaluation of the history of Western forms of knowledge concerning China. Considerable work along these lines has been done on the Jesuit and Enlightenment fabulations of China during the seventeenth and eighteenth centuries.[10] After years of studied neglect, there also have been some, albeit only partially successful and modestly influential, efforts in recent decades to rethink the historical and intracultural significance of the nineteenth-century and early-twentieth-century Protestant missionary experience in China.[11] Surprisingly, however, little serious attention has been given to the formative significance of the nineteenth century for the emergence of the Western humanistic discipline of sinology in relation to missionary tradition and the rise of other human sciences such as comparative philology, comparative religions, folklore studies, and anthropology.

This oversight is particularly unfortunate because it is in the nineteenth century, more than in either the seventeenth or eighteenth century, that the definitive constellation of factors responsible for the institutionalization of sinology as one of the various European disciplinary traditions of Orientalism is witnessed. These developments were first and most powerfully in evidence in France, but as a result of the growing Anglo-American confrontation with China throughout the century, there was after midcentury an increasingly important British contribution to sinology in particular and to Orientalism in general. The general importance of British tradition in the latter half of the century is most obviously related to the worldwide sway of British imperialism. But several other factors contributed directly to the British role in the gradual professionalization of sinology as one of the fledgling disciplines of Orientalism. These factors include, among other considerations, the changing forms of the Anglo-American Protestant missionary enterprise and the influence of liberal Evangelical theology (exemplified by Legge's brother, George, and his father-in-law, John Morison); the often contradictory, but always entrepreneurial and sometimes philanthropic, evolution of British commercial and political interests in China; the ever-branching development of the Royal Asiatic Society (mainly, in China, the North China Branch in Shanghai, which was periodically under the tutelage of exceptional figures such as Alexander Wylie, Henri Cordier, and Joseph Edkins) and the appearance of various English-language treaty-port journals in China devoted to the study and comparative analysis of Chinese tradition (e.g., *Chinese Repository, China Review, Chinese Recorder,* and the *Journal of the North China Branch of the Royal Asiatic Society*); a greater experiential (or "field experience") familiarity with China that came from living in the country and having to contend practically with the Chinese language; and the more concerted development of the pragmatic tools of transcultural intercourse such as dialectical dictionaries, grammars, systems of linguistic transcription or romanization, primers, and texts. Finally, we must take into account—and Legge is an exemplary embodiment of these factors—a kind of Scottish Enlightenment, Nonconformist Protestant, Germanically Romantic, and broadly pietistic intellectual spirit that, coupled with the religious and commercial outreach of the British empire, was related to the emergence (roughly after midcentury) of the new historiographic and comparative sciences of human civilization. What is observed at the end of the century is the belated academic maturation and professionalization of the British (principally Scottish and English) and American style of amateur scholarship that, as promoted by the spectacular advances of British imperialism and its academic embodiment in London, Oxford, and Cambridge, selectively drew upon other nationalistic modes of intellectual production and secular proclamation—particularly the French-Jesuitical Enlightenment tradition of rational analysis and the newly conceived Germanic institutions of academic research (i.e., the Ph.D. traditions of *Wissenschaft* that have influenced all Western institutions of higher learning down to the present day).

This relatively brief British era of sinological Orientalism during the last part of the nineteenth century depends primarily on the emergence of a remarkable group of hyphenated missionary- and consul-scholars who, after starting out in the grand tradition of the British and American amateur scholar, went on to become professional or semiprofessional sinologists. Of all those who can be included in this diverse and truly impressive (but largely neglected) group (Sir John Francis Davis, Robert Morrison, Elijah Bridgman, Samuel Wells Williams, Alexander Wylie, John Chalmers, Ernst Eitel, Joseph Edkins, Edward Parker, Thomas Wade, Ernst Faber, W. A. P. Martin, and Herbert Giles), James Legge was by far the most important and paradigmatic.[12] By the 1870s, English-language scholarship concerning China, which was initially grounded in the often "listless" dilettantish speculations of missionaries and civil servants operating within Chinese coastal enclaves, had temporarily surpassed the armchair scholarship of the early French academicians in Paris. Legge epitomizes these developments and more than any other single scholar contributes to the late nineteenth-century canonization of a specialized body of translated knowledge about the classical or Confucian nature of traditional Chinese civilization.

For all of these reasons, the last quarter of the nineteenth century was the pivotal period for the explicit establishment of sinological Orientalism as a new academic discipline throughout Europe and America. It was at this time that a reluctant British ascendancy in the newly professionalized circles of sinological scholarship and comparativistic Orientalism was apparent, a brief intellectual hegemony resting largely on the sturdy shoulders of James Legge and Max Müller and their monumental outpouring of translations, books, and articles. It is possible, therefore, to speak of a Leggian epoch of sinology—from 1873 (when Stanislas Julien died in Paris and James Legge arrived back in England) to 1897 (when Legge died in Oxford and Édouard Chavannes reestablished the grandeur of the French tradition)—that shaped significant aspects of the later disciplinary tradition.[13]

A QUIET SCHOLAR

Biographies that privilege individual intentionality, whether of quiet scholars or loud politicians, have in recent decades been seen as deceptive sources for cultural history. Much caution is called for when dealing with the so-called authoritative implications of persons or authors in relation to cultural productions, but at the same time I do not totally renounce the semi-Carlylian significance of "great" individuals in the history of discursive fabulation. It could be argued that I cannot have it both ways, but a close reading of the life and work of figures such as James Legge and Max Müller convinces me that an honest and full interpretation of either individual lives or of cultural history requires a dual hermeneutic that respects the ambiguous interaction of human identity and intentionality with culture while, at the same time, taking into account the variously constructed and transformative cultural incarnations of personality. Furthermore, in James Legge, the quiet missionary and scholar, I am dealing with someone who— in the Evangelical Christian sense of "pilgrim's progress" and in the classical Confucian sense of the constant ritual cultivation of character—kept his eyes open to the otherness of Chinese texts and persons and his moral antennae sensitive to the changing times. Consciously and unconsciously, he clearly participated in many events "of importance to the historian."

The problem is that Legge's wide-eyed, open-minded, and morally sensitive involvement in the changing shapes of Victorian history has been mostly overlooked and ignored. Arguably the greatest of the nineteenth-century sinologists, he is today vaguely, if at all, remembered only as the heroically industrious missionary-scholar who earnestly, but turgidly, translated the Confucian classics. The simple biographical facts of his long life (1815–1897)—a Nonconforming Scottish Congregationalist of the "middling classes" stationed in Malacca and Hong Kong for the London Missionary Society (1839–1870) and later the first professor of Chinese at Oxford (1876–1897)—seem to reveal not so much a historically significant figure but rather another tedious Victorian patriarch with an uncompromising dedication to a jealous God and to a "too-industrious scholarship." Even worse is that Legge's claim to fame as a quiet sinological scholar was often seen as the work of a *mere* translator lacking, as the French Durkheimian sinologue Marcel Granet said quite incorrectly, any "rules to guide it."[14]

There is a massive literature devoted to the Christian missionary movement in China, but most of the early studies concerned with the nineteenth century were either conventional overviews of Protestant missionary history from an apologetic perspective or biographical accounts with a narrow denominational orientation. For various reasons that will become manifest in this study, Legge was often overlooked or slighted by orthodox missionary historians; more secular historians tended to see Legge as only another, somewhat more liberal, example of the typical missionary insensitivity to Chinese culture. Never enough of a conventional missionary for missionary historians, Legge was at the same time too closely identified with the missionary enterprise to be taken seriously by later secular scholars. A careful examination of Legge's career shows, however, that both missionary commentators and academic historians have been guilty of perpetuating an overly stereotypical understanding of the nineteenth-century missionary experience in China.

It has, then, been James Legge's fate to be yet another "forgotten Victorian sage" memorable only as an anachronistic monument of steadfast evangelical piety and quaintly wholesome dutifulness—or, in Legge's own characteristically humble self-appraisal, a "moderate Calvinist" with a "habit of working."[15] There have even been misgivings about Legge's abilities as a translator. He is usually praised as a meticulous textual scholar who carefully weighed native exegesis, but he has also been severely criticized for what has been perceived as his blatantly intrusive missionary bias, his totally uncritical philological and historical methods, his overly slavish devotion to the Song dynasty commentarial tradition of the great Ruist philosopher-statesman Zhu Xi, and his obvious reliance on native informants such as Wang Tao who did all the hard textual work. His English renderings have furthermore been disparaged for their stiffly formal style and the antiquated use of mock archaic language and syntax to convey a classical remoteness of time and place.[16] Given Legge's primary identification as a translator (and commentarial exegete), I have paid close attention to the way in which the whole neglected issue of translation as a primary mode of transcultural representation and interpretation is embedded within a nested set of historical contexts, ideological presuppositions, and rhetorical strategies.

Depicted as an overly "sane and sober" translator-transmitter of the Confucian Five Classics *(Wu jing)* and Four Books *(Si shu)*, Legge has not ordinarily been seen as a creative participant in what the Anglican theologian Charles Hardwick called in 1855 the "portentous agitation" of the new forms of critical humanistic discourse and the overall disinterested, sympathetic, or comparative spirit that were beginning to emerge in Britain during the mid-Victorian period.[17] Legge was, it seems, someone who partially identified with Confucius, who simply and modestly "believed in and loved the ancients." Like the ancient Chinese master, he was just "a transmitter, not a transformer"—not, to use Legge's own translation of this famous line from the *Analects,* a "maker or originator."[18]

FINDING THE RIGHT PERSPECTIVE

To correct this legacy of amnesia and distortion, it is necessary to approach the circumstances of Legge's life from the broadest possible framework relating to the history of Evangelical and Dissenter religiosity, Victorian missionary tradition, British imperialism and Hong Kong colonialism, the liberal transformation of British higher education, the emergent scholarly traditions of Orientalism and sinology, and the rise of the academic sciences of comparison. On the Chinese side of things, the curiously synergistic factors of Qing dynasty imperialism, Manchu racism, and the self-propagated valorization and sometimes strident Occidentalism of the Ruist scholarly class should not be forgotten. The documentary record of Legge's long odyssey in Asia and Europe, spanning almost all of the nineteenth century, reveals a richly complex and liminal portrait of a cultural pilgrim whose life—somewhat like those of Thomas Carlyle, Benjamin Jowett, or Max Müller—reflected much of the intellectual and religious controversy, and many of the significant institutional transformations, of the Victorian era. My concern will be to find, borrowing again from Müller, the right kind of comparative perspective on these matters—a perspective that, if no longer demonstrative of the progress of human knowledge, is nevertheless successful in assigning "each branch of study" to "its proper place" in the complicated rhetorical panorama of cultural discourse.

Legge's unique position within the nineteenth-century history of missions in China is related to several factors. First, it may be noted that

Legge's Scottish background gave him a kind of special freedom and flexibility for rethinking the character of Chinese culture. This involved such factors as his earnest Sabbath-culture upbringing; his early study of the Latin and Greek classics; his exposure to the Aristotelian common sense tradition of Thomas Reid and Dugald Stewart at King's College, Aberdeen; his unusual openness to interpersonal relations with native Chinese of all classes; his Nonconformist liberality and Evangelical sense of moral duty; his appreciation of Jesuit scholarship; and his awareness of new developments in Protestant biblical criticism and Germanic historical criticism. Secondly, Legge developed approaches to Chinese religion and philosophy that initiated new authoritative standards for the translation, interpretation, and evaluation of these traditions. It was primarily because of these efforts (building, of course, on the earlier Jesuit enterprise) that the authoritative Chinese literary tradition of the Ruist scholar-bureaucrats came to be known as "Confucianism" in the West. Legge's achievements as a translator have been acknowledged, but the historical scope and intellectual depth of his Chinese scholarship are still not adequately appreciated. Legge not only mastered the ancient canonical texts of both the Ruists and Daoists, but also worked through available commentarial traditions in a way that undermines the charges that he was mostly dependent on the philological expertise of his Chinese assistants and that he was only a blind follower of Zhu Xi's twelfth-century opinions.

Legge's enduring historical significance, both as a textual transmitter and cultural transformer during his own era and with regard to his impact on subsequent missionary and academic discourse concerning Chinese tradition, is most importantly linked with the two greatest textual productions of nineteenth-century sinological Orientalism: Legge's monumental English-language edition of the *Chinese Classics* (the eight-volume first edition published in Hong Kong in 1861–1872 and the five-volume second and partially revised edition published in Oxford in 1893–1895) and his rendition, while at Oxford, of the *Sacred Books* of Confucianism and Daoism (in six volumes published between 1879 and 1891) for Müller's celebrated *Sacred Books of the East* series, which was published in fifty volumes between 1879 and 1902. Though now dated in style and deficient from various technical perspectives, these massive translations of and extensive interpretive commentary on the Confucian and Daoist classics are still being reprinted as the standard Western-language versions of these ancient texts.[19]

Almost no attention has been given to the convergence of Legge's evolving intellectual concerns with the perspectives of the comparative science of religions promulgated by Legge's Oxonian mentor, Max Müller. During his Oxford years, Legge's views gained a new degree of tolerance, comprehensiveness, and synthetic consistency—developments that were anticipated by his early terminological investigations in the 1850s concerning the

Chinese names for God, but are most prominently traced in his 1877 paper on the relation of Confucianism and Christianity and in his full-scale comparative treatment of the *Religions of China* in 1880. During his tenure as the professor of Chinese at Oxford, Legge's sinological evaluations of Chinese tradition changed significantly, more explicitly revealing his concern for an "impartial but not neutral" approach to Confucianism and his growing respect for the moral and "religious" nature of Master Kong and the tradition associated with him. As a full-time sinological scholar with comparative interests, Legge's assessments of important figures such as the Ruists Master Meng, Zhu Xi, and Han Yu, and the Daoists Laozi and Zhuangzi—as well as of Buddhist materials and other important historical and literary texts—became more precise and interconnected with his overall grasp of the Chinese language and literature. Moreover, by virtue of Legge's authoritative comparative identification of certain traditional Chinese texts as "sacred books," traditions such as "Confucianism" and "Taoism" were for the first time included in the newly conceived, and hierarchically ordered, history of "world religions."[20] These two Chinese traditions became what Legge's colleague and editor, Max Müller, classified as the "higher" traditions making up what were called the six Oriental "book religions" (i.e., Hinduism or Vedic-Brahmanism, Buddhism, Jainism, Zoroastrianism or Parsiism, Confucianism, and Daoism).

There is an important interpretive twist in Legge's formulation of the "classical" and "sacred" texts associated with Confucianism and Daoism. Unlike some academicians and missionaries who simply read out of these traditions only what they (and their communities) sought, Legge located a Chinese fundamentalist who had already set out a similar comparativist discourse concerning "higher" and "lower" Chinese traditions. His cultural model was the famous scholar-poet Han Yu of the Tang dynasty, the initiator of an orthodox line in Ruist intellectual criticism and the master of an intolerant sarcasm meant to dislodge powerful Chinese attractions to "superstitious" traditions such as Buddhism and Daoism.[21] Legge clearly felt that his own "impartial but not neutral" comparativism was justified by Han Yu's Confucian precedent, yet he was selectively transmitting translated visions of Confucianism and Daoism (as well as some limited profiles of Buddhism) that were *both* Chinese and Western in rhetorical formulation and intellectual conceptualization. In this sense, for example, the standard emphasis on the early, pure, philosophical, or classical Daoism associated with Laozi and Zhuangzi was in part a Ruist or Confucianized way of distinguishing the later ritualistic, corrupt, and heterodox Daoist religion, and in part a recasting of the overall Daoist tradition in the Müllerian, comparativist, Protestant, and Orientalist developmental pattern of world religions.

Legge should also be remembered for his distinctive, and generally enlightened and liberally transgressive, contributions to the early colonial history of Hong Kong. He was not only actively and creatively involved in various religious issues (e.g., the rancorous term question debates, which concerned the best way to translate the biblical God into Chinese, and the gradual emergence in Protestant circles of more comparativistic, accommodationist, and social-gospel missionary methods), but was also directly engaged in various controversial aspects of social practice (e.g., the creation of a new system of nonsectarian general education for the Chinese of the colony) and political policy (e.g., his public criticism of government policies on opium, gambling, and the Taiping rebellion). In addition to these activities in Hong Kong, he played a noteworthy, though almost totally forgotten, role in the liberalization of Oxford University during the last quarter of the nineteenth century. He was, for example, actively involved in the religious and intellectual emergence of Nonconformity in Oxford, the establishment of the professorial system, the promotion of a new multicultural curriculum and examination system, and the establishment of women's education at Somerville College.

TRANSLATING A TRANSLATOR

From the very start of his career in Malacca in 1840, Legge was already a missionary-educator-scholar who sometimes went against the grain of traditional missionary methods and theories. As a professor of Chinese at Oxford, he was someone who was never satisfied with a conventional academic life either in the Müllerian mode of Orientalist entrepreneur or in the Benjamin Jowett style of university baron. Legge characteristically preferred the quiet life of the scholarly translator, transcultural transmitter, and educational transformer to the noisy machinations of the missionary or academic politician. In both vocations, as missionary and professor, he was especially the consummate translator of Chinese texts into classical and sacred books of interest to the West—an educational enterprise that contested ordinary missionary standards of religious sympathy, social propriety, textual decipherment, and cultural representation. From the very beginning, his new version of, and commentary on, the Confucian classics was intended both for native Chinese students and the overall cultivation of a cross-cultural discourse with the West. Legge's *Chinese Classics* not only challenged many European presuppositions about the nature of Chinese civilization (albeit using Western terms and categories), but also challenged the status quo of conventional native Chinese scholarly opinion and the endemic Occidentalism of the Qing-period Ruist bureaucrats.

Legge was therefore not just a heroic exemplar of an earlier and mostly moribund age. He was more of a hyphenated and transitional agent who facilitated the passage from the earlier amateur tradition of Chinese studies to the later era of professionalized academic sinological Orientalism. He productively straddled the divide between the ardently antagonistic evangelism of the traditional Protestant mission and the more sympathetic and accommodationist approach associated with the new academic science of religion. As someone with a foot firmly planted in both conservative and liberal camps, Legge was old-fashioned, but it is more accurate to say that his emotional and intellectual evolution anticipates, parallels, and, to some degree, promotes a broader cascading set of interrelated changes that set the stage for a modern discourse within the academy and the missionary movement at the turn of the century. These changes are directly connected with important transformations in the sympathetic comprehensiveness of Protestant missionary policy and in the relentlessly textual, culturally insulated, and largely Confucian, classical, or "great tradition" bias of later mainstream sinology in Europe and America.

More than anyone else in the Victorian period, it is Legge who, by selectively borrowing from Müller's comparative science of religion and native Chinese commentarial traditions, effectively translated the religious mission of Protestantism in China into the idealized hermeneutical mission of academic sinological Orientalism. Nor must it be forgotten that the touchstone for Legge's own hyphenated missiological and sinological labors relied on his intensely reciprocal face-to-face encounters with Oriental texts and heathen persons. These were dutiful moral transactions that often challenged the popular presuppositions of conventional missionary theology and the fashionable excesses of comparative academic scholarship.

ORIENTALISM AND ORIENTALISMS

Bringing Legge out from behind the clouds of neglect and distortion shows that his pilgrim's passage from an early evangelical missionary career to the new, more secular, academic sciences of sinology and comparative religions participates in, and contributes to, some of the most significant religious and intellectual changes during the Victorian era. Thus a deeper appreciation of Legge's transcultural and transformative career in relation to both the peculiar nature of sinological Orientalism and comparative religions constitutes a critical test of some of Edward Said's more sweeping generalizations and aggressive formulations about the intellectual colonialism of Orientalism in the nineteenth century. This issue concerns the degree to which it is not only possible, but also crucial, to distinguish among different types of Orientalism (e.g., sinological, Indological, Islamic, Semitic, and so on, as well as important national variations) and the extent to which the process of cross-cultural intercourse can be reduced to some monolithic scheme of Western domination.[22] Furthermore, the specific example of sinological Orientalism raises the important question of how certain Asian elite traditions influenced and transgressively appropriated various Western forms of Orientalism.

A prismatic analysis of Legge as a hyphenated missionary-scholar and as a sinological comparativist is of special interest for the way in which it is an embodied instance of the canonization and objectification of native texts that is not just a heavy-handed Western imposition of Orientalistic categories of knowing in the Saidian sense. We will want to examine the possibility that an overly cynical and one-sided emphasis on the intrusion of the Western imperialistic mission in the Orient (whether religious, commercial, political, or scholarly) may, in fact, prevent us from taking into account the revisionary reception and transformation of that mission in specific Asian traditions. Most of all, a balanced approach to the whole issue of Orientalism and the little-appreciated matters of Manchu Sino-Imperialism and Ruist/Confucian Occidentalism will lead to a more fully ambiguated understanding of Chinese and Western transcultural interaction and translation.

THE RIGHT TIME FOR RETROSPECTION

More than one hundred years have passed since the end of the Leggian era of sinology, and the time is ripe for a detailed examination of Legge's influence on the ways, and intertextual byways, by which the West has made sense and nonsense of Chinese tradition. That the appropriate time has arrived for such a substantial retrospective evaluation of the cultural significance of Legge's career and monumental textual productions in sinology and comparative religions is strongly suggested by recent attempts at producing more definitive and accurate versions of the "basic texts" of ancient China.[23] These new translations will definitely be more stylistically in tune with current academic fashion. Such works will also, no doubt, be more technically sound and textually sophisticated, for it is indeed possible to make some real progress in establishing philologically, or recovering archaeologically, the best critical (and/or earliest) versions of an ancient text. But the insinuation that new modern or postmodern editions will necessarily overcome the deficiencies of the early nineteenth-century sinologists is certainly naive.

New scholarly translations of ancient Chinese literature should be welcomed, as there is much to be gained from such efforts. The issue is not, however, so much one of simple philological accuracy or historical truthfulness, but the more convoluted hermeneutical issue of a translator's interpretive fidelity and transgressive challenge to the prevailing cultural discourse. After all, each age gets pretty much the classics, sacred books, or basic texts it most fervently wants and secretly desires. The salvific qualification here is "pretty much," but the overall point is still not insignificant. Translation is typically a visceral "sense by sense" operation where the meaning discovered is largely a confabulation of current ways of knowing. There is all the more reason and rhetorical compulsion, therefore, to try to locate and understand our own disciplinary progenitors and traditions, along with their submerged desires and hidden intertextual connections. One way to begin this task is to come to a fuller understanding of important nineteenth-century textual translators, cultural transformers, and "quiet scholars" such as James Legge.

Missionary Hyphenations
West and East, 1815-1869

Q. 39. What is the duty which God requireth of man?
 A.   The duty which God requireth of man is obedience to His revealed will.
Q. 40. What did God at first reveal to man, for the rule of his obedience?
 A.   The rule which God at first revealed to man for his obedience was the moral law [Rom. 1:14, "the law written in their hearts"].

SHORTER CATECHISM OF THE WESTMINSTER ASSEMBLY:
WITH PROOFS FROM THE SCRIPTURES, 1684

A SMALL TOWN GATHERED IN A HOLLOW

At the prompting of his sons and daughters in the spring of 1896, James Legge sat down in his Oxford study to record the fading memories of his long and productive life. The patriarch of a large family and the aging patron of sinological Orientalism in the Western world, he felt the sad chill of his waning years but was happy to comply with his children's wishes. His emotions were certainly affected by an awareness that his days were numbered and also by his own desire to reflect on the sinuous turnings, if not "every secret thing," in his life's journey. No doubt, as with every other important juncture in his life, he believed that he had both an earthly and a heavenly duty to register his pilgrim's passage as a father, Christian, missionary, and scholar. This autobiographical document, and several other sources from his early life, gives us some clues for understanding the critical permutations in his life as an ordained agent of the London Missionary Society, as a missionary-pastor-scholar in Hong Kong, and as a sinologist-Orientalist-comparativist at Oxford. These hyphenated transitions not only trace out the dynamic trajectory of Legge's own career but also reflect a much larger imbricated set of cultural, religious, and intellectual changes emerging during the Victorian era.

Unfortunately, the eighty-one-year-old professor never completed his "Notes of My Life." The memoirs somewhat mysteriously break off at the threshold of his thirty-year career in Hong Kong, that brash colony of the

British imperial and commercial mission established in 1842 as a result of the first Opium War with China. Legge does, however, give us a revealing portrait of his earliest years as a "middling class" boy from a small town in Scotland, his studies at King's College in Aberdeen, his "conversion experience" as a young man, his decision to dedicate his life to the foreign missions under the tutelage of the London Missionary Society, and his initial experience as a twenty-five-year-old missionary at the Anglo-Chinese College in the exotic Asian outpost of Malacca.[1] His narrative often seems to follow a standard Evangelical plot as celebrated in various mid–nineteenth century novels written by George Macdonald (1824–1905), another famously independent Scotsman and Dissenter from the same small town as Legge. This was the paradigmatic coming-of-age story that told of an exceedingly earnest "young academic boy" from a provincial town in Scotland who, after adventurously going off to see the larger cosmopolitan world of England and London as a young man, finally finds the righteous Christian God in his heart of hearts. This kind of affirmation then leads to a lifelong struggle with many of the more conventional, and sometimes hypocritical, forms of society and religion.[2] For Legge and the piously resolute characters of Macdonald's novels, the deepest realization of a true Christian was an "obedience to God" rooted in the moral law—that "natural law," as Saint Paul, Dugald Stewart, Thomas Carlyle, and Max Müller would variously have it, "written in the heart of man."[3]

Access to the World

James Legge—the youngest of the four sons (George, John, William, and James) of a successful draper, Ebenezer Legg[e] (1770–1848; see figure 1)—was born on December 20, 1815. The place of his birth was Huntly, a "small town gathered in a hollow" of heath and fir-covered mountains situated at the fork of the peat-darkened Deveron and Bogie Rivers in Aberdeenshire, Scotland.[4] The year of his birth is most notably remembered for the Duke of Wellington's final defeat of Napoleon at the battle of Waterloo and the subsequent swift ascendancy of British imperial fortunes throughout the world. Legge was born at a time that represents, as one historian puts it, the misshapen "birth of modernity"—an expression that alludes to the increasingly radical, international, and all-encompassing "access to things" (exotic ideas, texts, artifacts, art works, architecture, machines, religions, and cultures) ushered in by the new industrial age and the growing military, commercial, and political hegemony of the Western world.[5] The sense of portentous civilizational "progress" associated with the increased exposure to, and dominion over, the otherness of the world can, in fact, be specifically connected with the self-consciously enlightened and liberal advances in education, communication, industry, technology, reli-

Figure 1. Ebenezer Legg[e] (1770–1848). Painting by Andrew Geddes,
ca. 1820. Reproduced courtesy of the Legge Family Collection.

gion, and social policy associated with Scottish tradition at this time, especially within the burgeoning middle class of merchants and professionals. It
is not insignificant, therefore, that Legge was born into a "well-off" mercantile family that at the start of the nineteenth century was prospering
through the rapid expansion of the bleaching and linen trades in Huntly.[6]
   The wee gray granite town of Huntly in the hinterlands of northeast
Scotland was already, in the early years of the nineteenth century, regionally famous for sending its sons out to the foreign missions. William Milne
(1785–1822), who, with Robert Morrison (1782–1834), also from the
London Missionary Society, established the first Protestant mission to
China, came from Huntly, as did other well-known missionaries who went
to India and Africa. Huntly's larger religious and global destiny was particularly associated with its so-called Missionar Kirk, a prominent Congrega-

tionalist church that included as active members the Legge family and other "energetic," and often Whiggishly liberal, businessmen of the locality.[7] The significance of this legacy for James Legge is due both to his upbringing within the stern Calvinistic religiosity of the Missionar Kirk and to the overall romantic belief that, even in a small provincial town, enterprising Christians could productively participate in a heroic, and divinely ordained, mission to the entire world. Legge vividly remembered the sometimes overly fastidious practice of religion within his household and the Missionar Kirk. He also recalled that, as a heaven-sent sign of his future career, he had discovered in his father's library a copy of one of William Milne's missionary pamphlets written on exotic glossy paper in the seemingly indecipherable script of the heathen Chinese.[8]

The Huntly Tradition

In these diligent boys who traced their origins to Huntly and its environs, there seemed to be some propensity in the blood for spiritual and intellectual outreach—or perhaps, as some local Aberdeenshire amateur ethnographers would have it, a potent maltlike distillation of spirit and mind that came from imbibing the cold, dark, and peaty waters of the rivers that define the region. Whether a reflection of the Missionar Kirk's openness to the exotic realms of heathendom, the general independence of the Evangelical tradition of dissent in Scotland, the progressive traditions of the Scottish universities and middle class, the distinctive Germanizing tendencies of Scottish literary tradition exemplified by Walter Scott (1771–1832) and Thomas Carlyle (1795–1881), the Whiggish political sentiments of new periodicals such as the *Edinburgh Review* (founded in 1802), or the proud poetic spirit of bardic verse and clan mythology associated with Robert Burns (1759–1796), it is worth knowing that, in addition to various notable missionaries and the maverick novelist, poet, and mystic George Macdonald, the Huntly region produced several pioneers in the study of alien forms of religion.[9]

This regional tradition is exemplified by the liberal Christian convictions and groundbreaking scholarly work of two other sons of Huntly and vicinity, James Hastings (1852–1922) and William Robertson Smith (1846–1894).[10] Both Hastings and Smith were ordained Dissenting ministers (Hastings was of the Free Church and Smith was of the Free Scottish Church) and, like James Legge, went on to promote a new scholarly sensibility and "comparativist mentality" toward the study of non-Christian religions.[11] This mentality was a discursive sensibility in British intellectual circles in the last third of the nineteenth century that involved a complex mixture of liberal trends in evangelical apologetics associated with the missionary movement, elements of eighteenth-century Deistic rationalism and "natural religion," the tradition of Scottish common sense philosophy (especially via Thomas Reid and Dugald Stewart), the so-called higher philological criticism of the Bible (these factors having especially a Germanic and academic pedigree), the comparative historical sciences associated with the "enormous antiquity" of sacred books (again having German and also French origins), and the evolutionary or speculative comparativism associated with the new ethnographic study of what were held to be uncivilized folk and savages.[12]

These were all components in what, by the end of the century, can be identified in different ways and degrees with Max Müller's freshly proclaimed "science of religion" and with what Edward Tylor (1832–1917) called the new "anthropological" study of cultural development. Many of these ideas had emerged previously in French Enlightenment and German Romantic circles, but the formative developments in the creation of a new academic discipline named the *comparative* or *scientific* study of religions were primarily, during the last third of the nineteenth century, occurring in Britain as a result of the work of Müllerian Orientalists and comparativists, the Tylorian school of anthropology (popularly epitomized by James Frazer's *Golden Bough,* 1890), the all-encompassing and "agnostic" science of social progress advocated by Herbert Spencer (1820–1903), the folklore movement and the concern for "natural history," the prolific work of brilliant literary generalists such as the earlier Thomas Carlyle and the later Andrew Lang (1844–1912), and the often overlooked contributions of a Nonconformist and Broad Church group of academic scholars and editors (which included the sinological Orientalist Legge, the philosophical theologian Andrew Martin Fairbairn, and the Unitarian comparativist J. Estlin Carpenter at Oxford, as well as Robertson Smith and James Hastings).[13]

At the end of his life at Cambridge University, Robertson Smith was an Islamicist and Hebrew scholar who was notorious for his general editorship of the revolutionary ninth edition of the *Encyclopedia Britannica* and, by virtue of his major work on the *Religion of the Semites* (1889), for his contributions to a new sociology of religions.[14] Smith's career has an interesting resonance with Legge's intellectual evolution in the last quarter of the century, when both men were engaged in battles with conservative sectarian factions over the ostensibly heretical turn of their scholarship. James Hastings has a similar significance for the emerging comparative science of religions and its association with liberal forms of evangelical dissent. Hastings did not possess Robertson Smith's linguistic and theoretical genius, but he was a courageous and tireless editorial promoter of more comprehensive approaches to the study of world religions. This is especially apparent in his groundbreaking *Dictionary of the Bible,* which emphasized critical exegetical approaches to the scriptures, his creation of the influential periodical known as the *Expository Times* (1889), and his justly famous multivolume *En-*

cyclopedia of Religion and Ethics (1908–1921). At the beginning of the twentieth century, it is this last work that, along with Müller's *Sacred Books of the East*, largely defined the fledgling science of religions.

The Great Commission

Much of the passionate commitment to the Protestant missionary agenda throughout the world in the early part of the nineteenth century stems from earlier waves of religious revival at the end of the previous century, pietistic movements that were particularly strong among the nonconforming sects of Methodists, Presbyterians, Baptists, and Congregationalists in Britain and led to the formation of the London Missionary Society in 1795.[15] Devoted to the realization of the New Testament's "great commission" to convert the greater heathen world (Matt. 28:19–20), the Protestant missionary movement was primarily driven by an Evangelical recognition of sinful guilt and by the dutiful cultivation of a Christian character that comes from faithfully responding to God's "call" for salvation (as proclaimed by the Pauline epistle to the Romans). The missionary movement in the nineteenth century was consequently motivated by a complex set of theological, psychological, and sociological factors that emphasized the urgency of God's biblical commandments for personal and international conversion and the special affinity of Protestant Christianity, moral renewal, mental maturation, economic development, social advancement, and civilizational progress. It was the "whole duty of man" not only to secure one's personal salvation but also to work for the Christian regeneration of the entire world.

An ominous extension of these principles is linked with various pressing concerns about the imminent millennial fulfillment of Christ's commission, beliefs that colored much of the missionary movement throughout the nineteenth century. One version of these expectations that characterized Legge's missionary agenda (as well as his brother George's theology of universalism) was the marvelously flexible theological idea of postmillennialism.[16] Founded on the belief that the second coming of Christ would occur only after the appearance of a universal millennial civilization established on earth through reformative human efforts (associated by the end of the century with the secularized theology of the social gospel), this was a theory of progressive individual and social conversion that lent itself to the more liberal missionary policies favoring the Christian accommodation with, or fulfillment of, the best or purest aspects of heathen religion and morality.[17]

Sabbath Culture

The Missionar Kirk in Huntly in the early part of the nineteenth century upheld the fundamental commitments of Evangelical Protestantism, but as a Congregationalist church it also dissented from the national Church of

Scotland (i.e., the Presbyterian church as distinct from the Anglican church of England) and asserted its staunch independence from any overseeing ecclesiastical or sectarian authority.[18] Especially characteristic of the Calvinistic religious temper in Legge's church during the time of his upbringing was an emphasis on learning and living the commandments of God as compactly summarized in the *Shorter Catechism of the Westminster Assembly* of 1684.[19] It was the practical struggle of translating these textually deposited principles into the overall texture of life that mattered most profoundly—that is, the constant work of a godly life as embodied in an intense Sabbath-culture regime of religious practice, moral edification, and education.[20] Identified as ultra-Sabbatarian, the Missionar Kirk observances on Sunday were meant to be a concentrated manifestation of a Christian life dedicated to God that gave structure and meaning to the totality of one's life, including the zealousness of business, educational, and domestic activities during the week. Indeed, the members of the Missionar Kirk were notorious throughout the area for the righteous rigor and interminable length of "their church-going habits."[21] On the Sabbath frivolous secular activities (even recreational walks or reading) were banned and the entire day was devoted to a series of lengthy church services and sermons, Sunday school for the children, family scriptural study, and individual prayer.

The protracted fervor of the Sunday services in the Missionar Kirk is graphically illustrated by a passage found in George Macdonald's novel *Alec Forbes of Howglen* (1865). Clearly modeled on Macdonald's own experiences in the Huntly kirk, this passage begins its description of a typical Sabbath with the minister's first lengthy sermon of the day, which stressed a "terrible chapter of denunciation out of the prophet Isaiah." After a long, standing prayer, the words of the Hebrew psalmist were invoked regarding "the wicked" who would "be turned into hell" along with "all the nations that forgot God." Then another sermon, lasting for several hours, melodramatically and meticulously depicted the fate of the wicked. These extended sermonic condemnations concluded with more long prayers and scriptural readings, interludes of more joyful hymnal singing, and a final benediction. Given the patriarchal sternness and guilt-ridden sense of damnation associated with these services, it can well be imagined along with Macdonald that the participants, especially the children, would leave church and shamefully make their way through the dark streets of the gray town of Huntly, creeping home as if they were entering "into the Outer Darkness."[22]

The general accuracy of Macdonald's portrait is confirmed by Legge's own description of his churchgoing as a boy. Although he did not remember these services as being "invested . . . with a repulsive garb," he says that his father's religion seemed in "error on the side of strictness." The problem in the Legge household in Huntly was that "the voice of Moses was allowed . . . too often to overpower the voice of Christ."[23] It is evident that Legge's general liberality of religion, especially as tempered by his experience with Chinese heathens who did not always seem to dwell within the Outer Darkness, was initially affected by his, and his older brother George's, reaction against the overly narrow and condemnatory elective Calvinism of his early years in Huntly. As he tells us on several occasions in later life, his basic theology progressively became a kind of "moderate Calvinism" that foreswore the excruciating scrupulosity of his childhood Sabbatarianism and affirmed the possibility of a universal salvation of all the races of humankind.

Legge says that he found increasingly that the righteous strictness of the Sabbath culture within the Missionar Kirk congregation, and even some of the teachings of the Westminster Confession, was becoming "strange and distasteful" to his "moral nature." Relating a boyhood instance of this estrangement and his awareness that the "simple sincerity" and religious certainty of the kirk most often allowed "no rebound to a preference of different views," he tells of the time he dared to wonder if "children and those who died very young" might not "all [get] to heaven." He was quickly admonished by a member of the kirk who assured the young Legge that only those "from a' eternity eleckit" will come to "everlasting life." According to this "Old Calvinist," whose views were ratified by Legge's older brother John, there was no way to be sure that infants and children are "amang the eleckit." Legge remarks that he was not satisfied by the unbending certainty of these views, but these troubles soon evaporated like "the morning cloud or early dew."[24] While ephemeral in his youth, these very same clouds of moral doubt would reappear more vigorously in later life as he pondered the degree to which both British infants and Chinese heathens could be included among God's "eleckit."

Despite his sensitivity to some of the overly austere and morally compromising aspects of the Calvinist dispensation during his youth, a generalized Sabbath-culture approach to social and religious life had a salutary influence on Legge's overall career as a missionary, educator, and scholar in Hong Kong and Oxford. It was always the more positive implications of a Sabbath-culture approach to life that overwhelmed any lingering meanness of spirit. Thus Legge's characteristic emphasis on disciplined rituals of self-rectification within the home, school, and church made all the difference in these matters of election and salvation. Most of all, this was for Legge (as it was for his brother George) a perspective based not on the condemnation of those beyond the pale of God's redemption but on a more moderate, genial, natural, and comprehensive application of the moral law.

School and Sublimity

Legge did not know about his real mother (Elizabeth Cruickshank Legge, 1781–1817, who died for unspecified reasons) until he was seven or eight years old.[25] He makes perfunctory references to his "good" stepmother (Barbara Spence Legge, who married Ebenezer two years after Elizabeth's death), but he plainly grew up in a predominantly patriarchal world where attention to conscientious self-improvement and sturdy perseverance was paramount. Education, religious, moral, and secular, was the most important method for personal advancement in the world, and Ebenezer Legge, having himself received only a smattering of formal learning, conscientiously promoted the schooling of his four sons—two of them, George and James, going on to graduate with M.A. degrees from King's College, Aberdeen.[26] With regard to his boyhood education, briefly at the Dissenters' school and then at the more rigorous parish school in Huntly, James tells us that he was at first not particularly studious, much preferring the more robust and rambunctious pursuits of hiking, fishing, swimming, and bird-nesting (a popular activity of amateur natural history that involved birdwatching and the observation and collection of different kinds of nests and eggs).

It was, however, during one of his youthful rambles to the small seaside town of Buckie in the north of Banffshire that he first became aware of the divine expansiveness of nature, the human mind, and God. While viewing the tumultuous sea break upon the rocks below the coastal cliffs of Buckie, he remembers that he was "thrilled through [his] whole being." As these waves of emotion filled him, the "idea of sublimity" arose "in [his] soul," which was then immediately followed by the reflection: "This is grand and I understand it, but there is that within me, which is grander and greater than this."[27]

For Legge this boundless reverie of his boyhood spirit providentially pointed toward his own later voyages by distant oceans and foreign languages to the remotest outposts of the world and literature. This kind of rapturous experience, along with the natural thrills of bird-nesting and the special friendship of a childless neighbor, Old Susie, who had befriended him and filled his imagination with Walter Scott's novels and the adventures of Robin Hood, was Legge's fondest memory of his early years, certainly more so than anything he recounts about his earliest home life, churchgoing, or formal schooling. Even as a stout-hearted and carefree "laddie" from the Scottish countryside, it was his exposure to all of the expansive strangeness of God's creation through nature and texts that stirred his heart and mind.[28] The God of his fathers was a stern and demanding God, but also a strangely mesmerizing presence hidden in the wild excesses of nature, the intricate diversity of animal life, and in a surrogate mother's dramatically recited tales. The same signs of God's universal presence that were revealed by the uplifting wisdom of the Hebrew Psalms and the moral universality of the Latin and Greek classics, he would come to decipher in the strange Chinese texts of his later years.

Version Making

Legge did not discover and cultivate his scholastic talents until he entered the Latin classes at the Huntly parish school at the age of twelve. His ability to memorize quickly the Psalms and the *Shorter Catechism* had already hinted at his potential as a student, but it was not until his special prowess for translating Latin surfaced that he seemed destined for an intellectual vocation involving the ministry or teaching. The "great business" of learning Latin at this time was the regular practice of version making, which perfected his proficiency for rapidly translating back and forth from Latin and English, a practice that drew upon certain standard or classical Latin texts such as Caesar, Sallust, Horace, Virgil, and Ovid. Quickly marked as academically gifted, Legge followed in his brother George's footsteps and in the spring of 1829 was sent to the grammar school in Aberdeen in preparation for securing a bursary for attending the university. Living away from home for the first time in his life, Legge tells us that he enjoyed his relative independence (he lodged at the home of his step-mother's brother) and guiltily partook of diversionary amusements in Aberdeen, especially several popular though illicit theatrical productions. But the young Legge was duty-bound and he applied himself to his studies, paying particular attention at this time to the works of George Buchanan (1506–1582) and to cultivating his "rare" facility for writing in Latin.[29]

This was a period of adolescent physical and emotional turmoil. In addition to various recreational temptations and a severe leg wound, Legge was almost crushed to death under a platform during a political rally in Aberdeen just a week or so before he was to take the bursary examination for the second time. It was during his recuperation from these accidents that he perfected his amazing talents for translating Latin in the form of version making, especially making use of Buchanan's Latin rendition of the Hebrew Psalms and his history of Scotland, the *Rerum Scoticarum Historia*. Having adopted what would become his lifelong habit of early rising to pursue his studies, Legge says that he practiced by turning an English translation of Buchanan's history into Latin and then comparing it with the original: "In this way I acquired great readiness in writing Latin. It was easier for me to write a letter in Latin than in English."[30] Buchanan's work may be seen as more than a simple practice text for Legge's version making. Buchanan anticipated the nineteenth-century emergence of more critical approaches to the use of ancient sources and the writing of a Scottish national history—methods that were complemented by Dugald Stewart's common sense concerns for a universal humanity and the writing of a "conjectural history" that combined empirical study and inductive reason. It is in this way that Buchanan's work on the Psalms and his concern for understanding ancient Scottish tradition would provide Legge with an important analogue for understanding the clannish aspects of Zhou-period history as found in the

Chinese classical texts (especially the *Book of Historical Documents* and the *Book of Poetry*). The Latin version making of the Hebrew Psalms and the text-critical methods appropriate for understanding ancient Scottish national history suggest that Buchanan's works were Legge's first primer in translation and philological method.[31]

A Good Grind

In November of 1831, when he was only a few weeks short of his fifteenth birthday and still recovering from his brush with death, Legge won the coveted first bursary (which amounted to only £20 per session) for King's College, Aberdeen. Etched in his memory at this time was an offhand comment that he would perhaps become the very first first-bursar also to win the Huttonian Prize as the outstanding graduate of Aberdeen University.[32] No first-bursar had ever done so and, as seen by his frequent allusions to the prize, Legge made this special scholastic distinction his goal during his college years. His description of his college experience (1832–1835) in Aberdeen indicates that he made steady progress toward the prize, easily securing first-place passes in classical languages and doing surprisingly well in other subjects such as chemistry, mathematics, natural philosophy, and moral philosophy (particularly the Scottish school of the philosophy of common sense associated with Thomas Reid and Dugald Stewart).[33] While attending extracurricular student functions, he also came to realize his complete incapacity for singing and dancing. Some sixty years later, he defensively remarked that these defects "unfitted" him for social intercourse and perhaps also, because of his lack of a "good" musical ear, accounted for his lifelong difficulty in "acquiring the 'tones' in the different colloquial dialects" of China.[34] Admitting that he was still sometimes attracted to popular entertainments such as the theater and novel reading, Legge's retrospective sketch of his student career shows him dutifully perfecting the habits of the adept academic grind, skills of resolute perseverance that would serve him well in his struggles with Chinese literature and in his life as an Oxford professor. As he wrote to his brother George at this time: "I must exert myself."[35]

Looking to excel in his studies and to make good on his chances of winning the Huttonian Prize, Legge devoted his vacations in Huntly to preparing for the next academic sessions in Aberdeen, paying special attention to mathematics. which he knew would be crucial in the examinations. It was also during one of these interim periods in Huntly that, while traveling in the countryside, he tells of an experience of the "beauty of nature" that renewed the powerful sense of sublimity experienced in his early boyhood when he first saw the sea at Buckie.[36] During another summertime in Huntly, Legge remembers an incident that presaged his later life as a missionary in Oriental lands. Significantly enough, his intellectual

Figure 2. The Reverend George Legge, L.L.D, of Leicester (1802–1861).
Engraving, probably by J. Cochrane, *Evangelical Magazine* 27 (1849).

confidant and brother George (see figure 2), who had recently taken up a
ministry in a Congregationalist church in Bristol, England, was visiting at
this time. Reminiscing with George and his father at the family graveyard in
Dumbennan about the mother he never knew, he had an eerie feeling
about the future direction of his life. Here on a mound by his mother's
grave his father told of her vow that their oldest child, George, should go on
to dedicate his life to the church ministry. Even more poignant was that
Legge remembers his father also suggesting that he would have "liked one
of his sons to become a Missionary." Anticipating the explicit decision "to
become a Christian" that would come several years later, Legge says that he
was haunted at this time by the increasingly powerful idea that it might be
his "duty to take on [himself] the vows of a Missionary to some heathen
people." Feeling the pressures of Victorian familial piety in the presence of

his prosperous father and academically accomplished brother, and the spectral haunting of his unknown mother, he recalled another sure sign of his future vocation—his boyhood discovery in his father's library of Milne's Chinese treatises. A tangible sense of destiny came over him and he vividly recalled the fabulously cryptic inscriptions and "silky feeling of the thin yellowish paper" of Milne's pamphlet, wondering "how it was to be read, and what its contents could be."[37]

Becoming a True Christian

Legge's growing sense of prophetic destiny was triumphantly reinforced by his successful graduation as the Huttonian prizeman of 1835. But, having attained this cherished goal, he was left with the quandary of not knowing exactly what to do with the rest of his life. The M.A. graduate had grown into a big-framed young man with a ruddy complexion, angular yet modestly handsome facial features, and an unruly shock of curly reddish hair. The twenty-year-old Legge also displayed the proud posture and anointed arrogance of a privileged Scots youth poised to take on a career beyond the confines of Huntly and Aberdeen. Quite consciously modeling his life on the course taken by his ordained brother George, Legge may to some degree have been speaking also of himself when he described his brother as "not the meekest of men," often coming "into collision with individuals and parties."[38]

Because of his scholastic achievements, Legge was offered an academic appointment at King's College (i.e., a position that would have led to his assumption of the chair of humanities, which focused on the Latin classics), but inasmuch as it presupposed his entry into the ministry of the established Presbyterian Church of Scotland, he was understandably reluctant, as he put it, "to turn from the principles of my father and brothers merely for the temporal advantages which such a step would bring me."[39] Equally important in this decision was his growing conviction that it was his duty to follow the dictates of a spirit disposed to heroic wandering. As in the case of his brother George, the greater worlds of England, London, and all of heathendom beckoned. This was clearly a time ripe for dramatic decisions and lifelong commitments. It is not surprising, therefore, that the educationally accomplished and somewhat headstrong Legge from the Missionar Kirk in Huntly would focus his attention on the opportunities afforded by the "Congregational ministry at home" (as undertaken by George) or "the service of the London Missionary Society abroad" (as suggested by his dead mother's prophecy and the subliminal prompting of Milne's mysterious Chinese treatise).

In the characteristic pattern of evangelical young men seeking to divine their destinies in the face of pressing ancestral responsibilities, heady psychosexual emotions, and vocational uncertainties, Legge recognized that the crux of his dilemma hinged on the "great subject of religion." It depended on his finding the courage to make an existential or personal commitment to "becoming a true Christian." Remembering this threshold phase of his religious conversion some sixty years after the fact, Legge says that "I had much religious knowledge, was well acquainted with the Scriptures, and had read many books on Theology, yet neither in heart nor life was I a real follower of Christ." There was still no lifelong commitment to God's commandments. As he declared at this crucial juncture: "I had not taken His yoke upon me, and was not habitually learning of Him; I had not got the peace, which He and He alone could give, and I dared not to desire to be a minister of His Gospel either at home or abroad."[40] It is the ritualized Evangelical response to competing desires that is noteworthy here—that is, the intellectually and emotionally seamless linkage of heavenly destiny, righteous duty, habitual learning, and the "one needful thing" of religious, moral, social, and sexual peace.

Like any significant initiatory transition during a confusing period of life, Legge's conversion required some preliminary wandering in the wilderness before he was able to achieve a "settled condition." Seeking guidance and direction, he decided at first only to follow "the example" of his brother George and to venture out into the "wide world" of England, traveling south to London and Leicester (where George lived), and then taking a teaching position in Blackburn, Lancashire. While he was in London and Leicester, young Legge's religious longings grew in response to the preaching of the popular Congregationalist minister Thomas Binney and other famous Nonconformist preachers such as the Congregationalist Edward Miall and the Baptist James Mursell. This was a time when the constraints on Nonconformists in England were hotly debated, the unfairness of many of the established practices (such as restrictions on marriage and burial, and exclusion from matriculation at Oxford and Cambridge) reinforcing his attachment to the liberal politics of the day and, as a Scotsman and Dissenter, his feelings of marginality in relation to the greater English society. It was at this time also that Legge was prone to engage in public debates with those who infringed upon his youthful, but increasingly righteous, religious sensibility, an especially memorable example of this being his combative encounter with a "Roman Catholic bully" in Leicester.[41]

While teaching mathematics in Blackburn, Legge found the nerve to declare personally and publicly his allegiance to the Congregationalist Church, "thus accomplishing a purpose which had been floating in [his] mind for some years." He refers to this action as bringing him "an exhilaration of the spirit," but it also appears that his formal church membership was somewhat anticlimactic given the continuing vocational crisis of his life.[42] The fulfillment of his desire to become a "true Christian" came about only in his subsequent decision to study for the Congregationalist ministry and to join the ranks of missionaries being sent out to the far reaches of the world by the London Missionary Society. Traveling back home between school sessions in Blackburn, Legge was, he says, impressed by the revivalistic fervor of religion in Huntly at that time and felt personally "drawn more and more to the foreign field." These feelings quickly led to his decision to leave his teaching position and, in September of 1837, after spending some time with his brother in Leicester, he began studying for the ministry in London at the Congregationalist Highbury Theological College, from which George had graduated some years earlier.[43]

Beginning Chinese

Given his degree from Aberdeen and that (as his brother George accurately observed) "study [was] with him a habit," Legge was able to complete the four-year course of study at Highbury in two years.[44] Cultivating the study of Hebrew along with his special strengths in Latin and Greek, Legge remarks that he was exposed at this time to the "higher study" of the New Testament, learning exegetical principles and critical methods that would carry over into his work with the Chinese texts. Despite some resistance from his mentors at Highbury who felt that a high level of education better fitted one to become a successful minister at home than abroad (the prevailing prejudice holding that such intellectual attainments were not necessary for work among heathens), Legge stubbornly committed himself to the foreign missions.[45] Accepted by the London Missionary Society after some unfounded concern over his physical health (one doctor detecting "a tendency to consumption"), he was nominated for the mission station at Malacca, "especially to assist in the Anglo-Chinese College there." Along with his growing Christian commitment was always, it seems, his emotional attraction to those saffron pages of cryptic Chinese characters found in his father's library.

This assignment to the Chinese-speaking outpost of Malacca must have deeply confirmed his feelings of divine destiny. Not only was he being sent to the very place where William Milne of Huntly once composed the "silky yellow" pages he had fondled in his father's library, but so also did he find himself actually studying Chinese with Milne's son in London under the tutelage of Samuel Kidd (1799–1843), another missionary who had once served in Malacca and was recently appointed to teach Chinese at University College. Beginning in 1838 the studies that would forever change his life, Legge fondly recalls that Kidd was a "very competent teacher." Even though the textbooks were few (including Robert Morrison's dictionary and translation of the New Testament, a copy of the *Analects,* and a few of Milne's Chinese tracts), he says that he enthusiastically threw himself into the work at hand, finding it particularly helpful to have mastered the use of radicals in the location of characters in a Chinese dictionary.[46]

Figure 3. Mary Isabella Legge (née Morison; 1816–1852).
Engraving, probably by J. Cochrane, *Evangelical Magazine* 31 (1853).

Marriage and Ordination

The rapid culmination of all these developments came from the "settled peace" brought about by Legge's formal ordination on May 25, 1839, and his marriage, some five days later, to Mary Isabella Morison (1816–1852; see figure 3), the daughter of John Morison, a socially and ecclesiastically prominent Congregationalist minister in London and the well-known editor of the *Evangelical and Missionary Magazine*. Particularly revealing of his newly converted and vocationally committed condition is the examination Legge took at the time of his ordination, administered by a Mr. Philip as a representative of the London Missionary Society, his Chinese professor Samuel Kidd, his brother George, and his future father-in-law, Dr. John Morison. Although this ordination exam was mostly a pro forma exercise, Legge's state of mind and heart regarding the "great work of religion"—or what was then the "truth present to [his] mind"—are conveniently summarized by his recorded confession of faith and vocation at this time. Structured as formal answers to a set of four basic questions ("What leads you to conclude that you are a Christian?" "What induced you to devote yourself to the work of a missionary among the heathen?" "What are the doctrines which you believe to be contained in the Holy Scriptures?" and "How do you purpose to exercise your ministry among the heathens?"), this document deserves some careful inspection.[47]

Some fifty-seven years later, in "Notes of My Life," Legge remembered that there was one aspect of his youthful ordination credo that required no qualifying emendation or apology. The "few sentences" that he recalled were the following: "My views are prevailingly what are usually denominated evangelical. But I do not profess myself of any school or party. I would not subscribe to any creed. I have never seen the book of any theologian to whose sentiments and to whose mode of exhibiting them I might not object."[48] These pointed excerpts from such a long examination document (more than thirty handwritten pages) attest to the fact that Legge's character was consistently marked by a proud religious, intellectual, and moral independence. This principled questioning of all conventional schools and parties is the thematic skein that runs throughout the various hyphenations and transitions punctuating his long career.

Though Dead She Spoke

At the outset of his ordination examination Legge immediately alluded to the haunting incident in the churchyard cemetery at Dumbennan when he felt his mother whispering to him from the grave—"though dead she . . . spoke." What she said to him "from heaven" referred not just prophetically to his chosen vocation as a missionary, but also concerned her painful reproach for the sin and neglect of his early life. It was this maternal spirit issuing forth from the family sepulcher—as a kind of feminine counterpoint to the patriarchal confines of his upbringing and an act of ghostly communication and judgment that evokes a connection with the most ancient of Chinese ancestral traditions—that he recognized as one of the most important "stirrings of conscience" in his early life.[49] This experience, along with his subsequent religious encounters while teaching at Blackburn and his brooding meditation on the Pauline epistles (especially Romans, Philippians, and Hebrews), led to the definitive "Christian alteration" of his character. He indicates that this conversion of mind and heart then quickly engendered a "desire to be rendered useful in salvation" as a missionary.[50]

Knowing that his own conversion came about through the intervention of "another agent" (his mother's uncanny intercession and the saving faith communicated through the scriptures), Legge suggests that missionaries were, so to speak, the external spiritual agents necessary for the operation of faith among the heathens. He was therefore divinely obliged to take up the vocation of a missionary and help, in a postmillennial sense, "to speed the second coming." Characteristically for Legge, the duty to become a missionary was premised on the principle of moral reciprocity. Like Paul during the apostolic period, missionaries "must" act as God's agents to the whole world. This is a response called forth by the realization that Christ's sacrificial death and love can be fully accomplished for humankind only through the evangelical actions of all Christians. Strangely in keeping with the memories of his mother's spectral communication, Legge indicates that his convictions about becoming a missionary were most strongly ratified by a prolonged "trance state" that he experienced while recuperating from a severe illness during his college years in Aberdeen. Careful to indicate that this trance was probably nothing more than a "natural occurrence," he says that he felt that his future life would be "occupied with the engagements of missionary labours."[51]

The Grand Object of Mission

Legge concluded his examination by offering some brief reflections on the missionary methods he intended to use among the heathens. While he knew that his views would be "liable to very considerable modifications" once he entered into the mission field, he nonetheless outlined an agenda that emphasized the importance of a "perfect acquaintance with [the Chinese] language or languages." His "grand object" was "to speak and write as a Chinaman" so that the heathen nation "may be saved." It would be necessary to get ready for such an encounter in the way a general prepared for battle. Although he invoked the common tropes of martial engagement associated with Protestant missionary apologetics, Legge states that it was important to know far more than the material resources of the enemy. An intellectual and personal communication with heathens was required, and this, in turn, demanded an immense sacrifice of much labor and time. For Legge, this meant that missionaries to the Chinese must undertake a close "examination of their history, their philosophy, their religion and their poetry." At the same time, a resolute missionary must cultivate a "familiarity with [Chinese] customs and manners" that can come about only as a result of "many years' unceasing toil."

Before he had ever met a heathen Chinese face to face, Legge declared that a meaningful missionary intercourse would require more than a "mere" mastery of "terms and phrases." More important was the existential "manner and form" of the exchange between a missionary and a Chinese. Most of all, he believed that while he "may speak *from* the heart," he must also be able to "speak *to* the heart." This implied that he must "obtain a perception" of the "genius," or distinctive character, of the Chinese language and people. The mission of linguistic translation and religious conversion was fundamentally in this way a mutually educative process of moral transformation or, to borrow from the evangelical idiom, a procedure of "sanctification" for both the Christian pilgrim and the Chinese heathen. Crucial to the whole missionary enterprise in Legge's youthful estimation was the differential equation of translation and conversion—that is, the possibility of attaining some real reciprocity between European and heathen languages and between Christian and Chinese persons.[52]

Legge's emphasis on conversion through a prolonged linguistic and moral translation that comes about through a "perfect" learning of the literature and character of the heathen was not generally characteristic of missionaries at the time. Though often associated with the better-educated missionaries of the London Missionary Society, especially those who worked with so-called civilized heathens such as "Hindu" Indians and "Confucian" Chinese, a concern for the slower methods of translation and education, implying some degree of understanding of and respect for non-Christian scriptures and persons, was not common to missionaries more convinced of the prophetic inevitability and imminence of a global Christianity. As suggested by David Livingstone, the typical foreign missionary of the period was often a "dumpy sort of man with a Bible under his arm" who believed in the almost magical efficacy of the promulgation of the Christian scriptures and the inexorable advance of European civilization.[53] An emphasis on the importance of self-learning and native education, an appreciation for the "measlies" of heathen language and literature, and a moral imperative to speak both to and from the heart was mostly the prerogative of those missionaries, frequently from a Scottish background, who had some substantial formal education in academic and theological subjects.[54] Another saving grace in these matters is that, again unlike Livingstone's dumpy missionaries, most of whom had an almost total lack of ironic perspective on the world or themselves, Legge actually possessed a "pawky" sense of humor. This was a trait that fortunately became more pronounced in his later life, especially after he had wearied of the mean-spirited seriousness of various religious and academic squabbles.

TO DARK SINIM INCITED

Far, far had he gone, in the freshness of youth,
By love to dark Sinim incited;
Had valiantly master'd her language uncouth,
And her sons to a Saviour invited. . . .

J. D. H., "THE MISSIONARY," LINES ON THE DEPARTURE OF DR. L[EGGE],
BY AN EVANGELICAL CLERGYMAN, *EVANGELICAL MAGAZINE,* 1848

White Calico

In August of 1839 James Legge, his new wife, Mary Isabella, and two other missionary colleagues, William Milne and Benjamin Hobson, left London

on the sailing vessel *Eliza Stewart* for the almost five-month voyage to the exotic climes of Malacca, the former Dutch colonial outpost ceded to the
British in 1824. Located in the straits between Sumatra and the Malay
Peninsula in the vicinity of Singapore and Penang, this European and Asiatic settlement had been chosen by John Morrison, the pioneering missionary to China, as the site of the Anglo-Chinese College. Because the Chinese mainland was closed to foreigners with either mercantile or religious
interests, Morrison established the college as the London Missionary Society's "ultra Ganges" station for educating young overseas Chinese in Christian and Chinese literature and for preparing a corps of missionaries for
eventual service in China proper.

Legge made good use of his time on board the *Eliza Stewart* by working
assiduously on his Chinese lessons, memorizing whole books of the Bible,
and ministering on Sundays to the other passengers and the sometimes
heathenish British crew. Amid these activities and the general fascination
and fear of being on a ship upon the open seas, there was one small incident that stands out as a telling commentary on the young Legge's heightened sense of divine destiny and his increasingly inflated estimation of his
own self-worth. In a letter home to her mother, Mary Isabella Legge remarked that after only a few weeks into their voyage, "dear James doffed his
clerical habiliments, and made his debut in white calico." With some be-
musement, Mary Isabella says that Legge, decked out "in white from head
to foot, with . . . a broad-brimmed straw hat," was the very picture of a "West
Indian" plantation master.[55]

Mary Isabella was careful to qualify this unflattering comparison by
stressing that her husband's habits of dress did not truly reveal "the inner
man." However, the very fact that Legge's wife saw fit to comment on his
sudden sartorial transmutation once he was free from the restrictions of
the English class system and en route to heathen people crying out for
the Lordly yoke of salvation hints at some immodest motivations. Like
many other middle-class missionaries and merchants seeking heroic self-
aggrandizement in foreign lands, Legge was acting out a typical Victorian
drama of psychological and social wish fulfillment. This kind of transformation among ambitious young men when first being sent out to conquer
and convert the world is evident among many evangelical missionaries of
the nineteenth century whose social and religious "humbleness" seemed
quickly to disappear once they left home for less civilized nations.[56]

Painful Events in Malacca

A propensity for pious hauteur among missionaries fresh to the field was
often coupled with an extreme impatience with the methods and results of
the existing missionary enterprise. This psychological complex was dis-

turbingly evident in the twenty-four-year-old Legge's initial reaction to the missionary situation in Malacca. He himself only alludes to some "painful events" connected with his disappointment over the meager educational accomplishments of the few Chinese students at the Anglo-Chinese College (which seemed too lax in its educational and religious standards) and his inability to get along with the resident principal, John Evans.[57] Evans was dismissively described by Legge as a "tall and stout" man of mock "magisterial appearance and manners" who had no particular intellectual distinction (especially in comparison with the impressive erudition and linguistic achievements of Dr. Walter Medhurst, whom Legge met in the Javanese city of Batavia on his way to Malacca).[58] Even worse than the deficient educational program of the college was that Evans seemed overly concerned with the hasty baptism of ill-prepared Chinese. (Many of the male students at the college were discovered to be members of the Triad Society in Malacca!) He also appeared to be mismanaging the financial operations of the mission—a charge that was sure to command the attention of the society's directors back in London. In like manner, Evans found Legge to be "aloof," "moody and despondent" (due, it was said, to his "too hard" language study of the Hokkien dialect in a tropical climate), and harboring an arrogantly critical attitude toward his surroundings and colleagues.[59]

Whether the brashly callow but university-educated Legge (see figure 4) or the older and more experienced but self-educated Evans was more to blame in this conflict of temperament and policy is not entirely clear from the written record preserved in the London Missionary Society archive, but it was not long before Evans requested to leave the mission field. Even before he could prepare for his journey home, however, he suddenly died of cholera. With Evans's disgrace and demise, Legge assumed full responsibility for the mission station and college. During his swift ascendancy at the mission station, Legge showed no particular guilt over his complicity in Evans's tragic end. Such pangs of conscience would emerge only later in Legge's missionary career, when he himself experienced the pricks of criticism and self-doubt.

The Seeds of Hyphenation

One other evocative incident early in Legge's tenure in the "barbarian luxuriance" of tropical Asia was his first exposure to Chinese religious practices (see figure 5). While in Batavia on his way to Malacca, Legge was taken by his host, the senior missionary agent and translator Walter Medhurst, to a Daoist temple in the Chinese quarter of the city. Happening upon a "great service being performed to the Queen of Heaven, a famous goddess specially worshipped by sailors" (the reference here is to the popular South Chinese cult of Tianshang Shengmu, "Holy Mother of Heaven," or Tian-

Figure 4. The Reverend James Legge, D.D., president of the
Theological Seminary in Hong Kong. Engraving, probably by J. Cochrane,
Evangelical Magazine 36 (1858).

hou, "Consort of Heaven"), Legge says that he was instantly reminded of
"the worship in Jerusalem of an idol with the same appellation, so graphically described and strongly condemned in the 44th chapter of Jeremiah"
(referring to the worship of a "queen of heaven" that was the Babylonian-
Assyrian goddess Ishtar). He approvingly noted that Medhurst engaged in
a "noisy" debate with a crowd of worshipers in the temple. Although Medhurst loudly denounced the "folly" of the service, Legge meekly noted (not
knowing enough spoken Chinese at this time to be anything more than a
mute observer) that there was no diminishment of ceremonial enthusiasm
in the temple. Medhurst would say in his defense only that the Chinese were
particularly clever in argumentation and that, most sadly, Christian missionaries never seem to be "able to touch and quicken their consciences."[60] This
is a remarkable observation in light of the fact that the two European missionaries had absolutely no compunction about abruptly disrupting and imperiously dismissing the temple service. To condemn the folly of the tradi-

THE IDOL INVOKED.—*Vide page* 44.

Figure 5. Missionary image of a Chinese temple. Engraving, *Evangelical Magazine*
(also known as the *Missionary Magazine and Chronicle*) 20 (1842).

tion because of some vague biblical comparisons with ancient Israelite
"idolatry" was understandable given the belligerent missionary theology of
the period, but it was certainly no less foolish than the clever and one-sided
disputations of the Chinese worshipers.

Legge's youthful insensitivity to the missionary activities of his own European colleagues in Malacca and his religious and moral numbness to the
ritual expressions of Chinese religion are broadly characteristic of Protestant missionary attitudes. What is arresting about Legge is, however, that he
spent the rest of his multifaceted career working against these darker im-
pulses of missionary character and method. The sins of pride he perpe-
trated against Evans would be absolved only in the course of the gradual
maturation of his moral sensibility as he confronted the failures of his own
missionary labors in Hong Kong (evidenced by the sluggish pace of con-
versions, the difficulties of educating young Chinese as "true Christians,"
and a growing native Chinese antipathy toward the missionary enterprise).
These changes also became more manifest as he learned to understand and
respect his Chinese acquaintances as much, or more so, than some of his
more contentious missionary colleagues who were caught up in the sectarian rancor of the term question (concerned with the amazingly tenacious
problems of translating the Bible into Chinese) and many of his fellow Eu-

ropean colonists who were singularly motivated by commercial interests. The narrowness and intellectual imprudence of his understanding of Chinese religion and literature would change as he plunged more deeply into the broad currents of the ancient Chinese "classics"—particularly as his comparative frame of reference came to encompass all of the world's "sacred books."

The seeds for this transforming moral growth and religious-intellectual hyphenation were planted during Legge's last few years in Malacca, before the whole missionary enterprise was triumphantly moved to Hong Kong and the other treaty port enclaves "notched into the flesh" of China in the aftermath of the first Opium War (1839–1842). It was in Malacca that he met three young Chinese who would greatly affect his life as a missionary and scholar for many years afterward. These were the Anglo-Chinese college students Ung Mun-sou (variously Ung A-sou, Ung Ah-sou, Ng Asou, Ng Mun-sow), Lee Kim-lin (Lee Kim-leen), and Song Hoot-kiem (Song Hoot-kiam), who would eventually accompany Legge back to Britain, where they would be baptized in Huntly. These "Chinese boys, lads, or youths," as they came to be called by the British press, were Legge's prize specimens of converted heathens and the future hope of an Asia best Christianized by a native clergy.

The Great Story of the Classics

The other Chinese person who played a major role in Legge's early missionary career was Ho Tsun-sheen, an older and more advanced student at the college in Malacca who produced Legge's first collaborative literary translation. This work was a translation of a popular Chinese historical romance that was published in 1843 as *The Rambles of the Emperor Ching Tih in Keang Nan*.[61] The title page of this work identifies the translator as a certain Tkin Shen, most probably Legge's precocious student Ho Tsun-sheen, who would go on to become a prominent Chinese Christian pastor and theologian in Hong Kong. (Ho's name was variously romanized: Ho Tsun-shin, Ho Fuk-tong, Ho Yeung, and, it seems, [Ho] Tkin Shen.)[62] Evidencing more humbleness toward Ho than he ever showed to Evans, Legge was careful to say that he only revised Ho's English translation, basically pursuing the translation as an exercise for improving his own command of the written language.

Most important is that the preface to this work makes reference for the first time to what would be Legge's major accomplishment in life, the translation of the Chinese classics. Legge says that "it occurred" to him sometime in 1841 or 1842 that it would be worthwhile to bring out "an edition of the 'Four Books and Five Kings,' the Gospels, as they have been called, and

Pentateuch of China, accompanied with a translation and notes, which might serve as a standard work to the foreign student of Chinese literature, and lay open to the general reader the philosophy, religion, and morals of that singular people."[63] Another eighteen years would pass before he would start to realize this plan, but it is apparent that the overall project of the *Classics* was already gnawing at his consciousness in the early 1840s.

Doubtlessly these thoughts occurred to Legge because of his initial misgivings about the intellectual preparedness of missionaries in Malacca and his own university-trained appreciation of the moral perspicacity of the pagan classics from Rome and Greece. He may also have been influenced by Walter Medhurst's interest in the ancient Chinese literature associated with the so-called Confucian school. Furthermore, as seen in his ordination exam, Legge's ideas about an extensive translation program fit with the apologetic need to understand one's adversary through a mastery of the relevant languages and literature. "Knowing the enemy" was the tried and true principle of the Pauline missionary strategy, a policy vigorously promoted in the nineteenth century by the Anglo-American and Evangelical Protestant sense of worldwide manifest destiny. Remarkable also is that Legge's first public statement about the Chinese classics appeals to their general educational merit and, in describing them as the Chinese "Gospels and Pentateuch," makes an implicit accommodationist judgment about the religious nature of these heathen texts. Thus from the very outset of his career, Legge tended to justify his labors as a missionary converter and scholarly translator in relation to the basic literary and philosophical import of Chinese classics.

It was the literary and historical narratives told by these works (similar stories being told by the Mediterranean classics and by the heroic tales of Scotland) that were intrinsically compelling for the "foreign student." For the directors of the London Missionary Society, however, heathen texts were interesting only as "indirect" tools for conversion. There was already in this way an evident hyphenation entering into Legge's sense of himself as an educated missionary with scholarly, as well as simply religious or apologetic, concerns and satisfactions. This whole shift in Legge's intellectual and emotional passions regarding China was most strikingly ratified in the diary he kept during the time of his first furlough home from Hong Kong (1845–1848). In dialogue with himself in this intimate journal, he suggests that his fascination with China was not just because it groaned for conversion. Rather, there was the basic scholarly and philosophical attraction of knowing the other simply for the sake of its own otherness. The ancient Chinese tradition was the repository of a "great story" that deserved to be translated, known, and appreciated in its own terms. For Legge—and here there are clear echoes of Buchanan, Scott, Stewart, Carlyle, and his brother

George—it was therefore necessary to pursue the story of alien civilizations with the "eyes of a philosopher" whose "mind demands to be satisfied as to its language, its history, its literature, and its moral and social state."[64]

Legge's increasingly lopsided conjunction of apologetic and philosophical-literary reasons for translating the Chinese classics is one of the crucial factors that led to his eventual withdrawal from missionary activity in Hong Kong (after 1867) and his assumption of a new public identity as a professional sinologist at Oxford in 1876. Sometimes stubbornly righteous to a fault, Legge did not consistently emphasize the apologetic or utilitarian importance of these works in relation to his administration of the missionary station in Hong Kong. He was also never willing to compromise the early-morning hours he devoted to his classical translations, saying only that he had purposefully trained himself to work with very little sleep so that he would always have a full working day available for his "direct" missionary duties. Despite his herculean efforts to balance his missionary and scholarly activities, Legge's dual life in Hong Kong, his civic endeavors in the colony, and his increasing fame as a translator after the first volume of the *Classics* appeared in 1861 led to tensions with his superiors at the London Missionary Society—particularly the powerful secretary of the society, Arthur Tidman.

Hong Kong in the 1840s

The opening of China that resulted from the Opium Wars led to the creation in 1842 of the British crown colony of Hong Kong on a relatively desolate bit of land within the Pearl River estuary leading to Canton, the major city in South China. Realizing the special opportunities this new territory afforded missionaries, Legge was quick to move the London Missionary Society operations to the colony of Hong Kong, arriving there in the summer of 1843. It was here in this new boisterous outpost of the British empire that missionaries, merchants, and politicians must have felt the special thrill of prophetic fulfillment. At the time, one of the most widely discussed biblical prophecies (Isa. 49:12: "Lo, these shall come from afar, / and lo, these from the north and west, / and these from the land of Sinim") was liberally interpreted to refer to China.[65] As Legge said, there was a heady sense wafting through the thick humid air of Hong Kong that God was using the "British to show forth his glory" and that at last the time had arrived for the fulfillment of the Great Commission.[66]

During his early years in Hong Kong, Legge busied himself primarily with the establishment of the new missionary station and rapidly reconstituted the old Anglo-Chinese College as a theological seminary for a small number of promising Chinese students (including his prize pupils, Ung Mun-Sou, Lee Kim-lin, and Song Hoot-kiem, who had followed their teacher to Hong Kong). As the Chinese and European population of the colony grew, Legge was increasingly concerned with the cultivation of a permanent Chinese Christian congregation and with the creation of a chapel for Nonconforming colonists (established in 1845 as the Union Church with Legge as the first pastor). His helpmate, Mary Isabella, cared for their new family (Eliza Elspeth was born in 1840 and Mary Isabella in 1842; another child died in infancy in 1843) and generally took responsibility for maintaining an English home within what was perceived by the Europeans as the dank and feverish island colony. Legge was also proud that his wife learned some Chinese and found time to conduct a Christian school for Chinese girls.

A Question of Terms

Amid all of these activities, Legge's special work as a translator continued in both a strict utilitarian sense (recalling his first exposure to Milne's silky treatises in his father's library, he was now producing a series of Chinese-language Christian tracts) and in a more indirect literary mode (his ongoing work on the Chinese classics, labors that were promoted by Medhurst's new translation of *The Shoo King or Historical Classic* in 1846). Always pragmatic about the publication of his scholarly work, Legge paid special attention to the establishment of a mission press in Hong Kong capable of printing Chinese-language materials with movable metal type. Having already gained a considerable reputation as a Chinese scholar, he was duly appointed to a distinguished group of missionaries of various denominations and nationalities who were charged with producing a generally acceptable Chinese-language rendition of the Bible, the so-called Delegates' Version.[67]

Meeting for the first time in Hong Kong on August 12, 1843, the delegates from the treaty port cities took up the difficult and delicate task of organizing their work on the new translations. Legge and the older Medhurst were appointed to a committee charged with deciding the controversial issue of which Chinese terms should be used for the translation of the word *God*. In the early 1840s the tendency was to side with John Morrison's preference for *shen* (generally meaning spirit or spiritual beings), and Legge supported this position at this time. The learned Medhurst, however, had come to the decision (based on his careful study of the Chinese classics, the fruit of which was published in 1847 as his *Dissertation on the Theology of the Chinese*) that the ancient classical terms *di* and *shangdi* were best suited as translations for the monotheistic God of the Israelites and Christians, a choice that echoed the earlier findings of the Jesuits.[68]

It was this term question first raised in these meetings that would provoke the Protestant equivalent of the Jesuitical rites controversy in the seventeenth and eighteenth centuries and lead to a series of furious and never fully resolved debates throughout the rest of the nineteenth century.[69] These were hotly contested disputations not only because they tended to polarize basic sectarian and nationalistic differences among the various missionary factions, but also because the possibility of finding the Christian God already terminologically present in Chinese texts threatened much of the antagonistic exclusivity of traditional evangelical missionary theology. Translation was consequently recognized as a dangerous two-edged sword that potentially fostered the religious and intellectual conversion of both Christians and heathens. At the center of these debates was the issue that would eventually motivate much of Max Müller's science of religions: the realization that the study of Oriental texts documented the terminological comparability of Christianity with other religions. Although it was found to be the most advanced and fulfilled religious tradition, Christianity was on the verge of being classified as only another of the religions of the world.

Good and Bad Boys

It was not long before Legge's intense schedule of missionary and scholarly work led to a breakdown in his health. After fighting various bouts of fever with leeching and bleeding during the years of 1844 and 1845, he decided to return home for the recuperative effects of the more "vigorous" northern European climate.[70] This was not, however, to be a routine furlough from the mission field. Legge obviously wanted to capitalize on the triumphalist feelings at this time that the whole Anglo-American Protestant missionary enterprise was very close to the rapid conversion of darkest Sinim. As the prophet Isaiah had predicted, the time of fulfillment was at hand.

With more than his health in mind, Legge arranged for a return that would highlight his own successes in Hong Kong and would generally stimulate public interest and financial contributions to the China mission. What better way to accomplish these ends than to bring a part of the exotic Orient back to Britain as a kind of traveling cabinet of curiosities? In addition to his wife and two young daughters, he therefore brought a Chinese nurse to help with the children (Jane A-sha) and, although he had not received the express consent of the London Missionary Society, he also brought the three "Chinese lads" who had been with him since his days in Malacca. Ung Mun-sou and the two older Chinese, Lee Kim-lin and Song Hoot-kiem (the three were apparently in their late teens or early twenties at this time), would in fact become "objects of considerable interest" in Britain.[71]

Leaving Hong Kong in the winter of 1845, Legge's exotic party arrived in England on March 28, 1846, and rapidly made its way to Scotland. These "interesting strangers" were then enrolled in Legge's old parish school in Huntly under the conscientious tutelage of the Reverend John Hill. Regularly pursuing their education for the next year and a half, the three Chinese behaved with "uniform correctness" and acquired sufficient scriptural knowledge to make them "proper subjects" for Christian baptism.[72] They were consequently christened in Huntly on October 15, 1847, in front of a large and enthusiastic assembly. Most important, as emphasized by several published accounts from the period, these "Chinese converts" would certainly prove to be "very useful in propagating Christianity among the vast population of China, to which they, as Chinamen, will have free access through the length and breadth of the land, while the labours of our foreign Missionaries are limited to those places opened by the arrangements with [the] Government."[73]

Three months before his return to Hong Kong, Legge made a grand tour of the salons, lecture halls, and chapels of Manchester and London to show off his new converts dressed in traditional Chinese garb, their long pigtails dangling impressively behind them.[74] It was soon said that all of London was witnessing the "first fruits to Christ of the Chinese mission in modern times."[75] Among the more memorable of these staged events was the climactic public service held at Craven Chapel on Tuesday evening, February 8, 1848, at which one of the Chinese addressed the assembly "in admirable English."[76] A day later, the religious and political significance of Legge's Chinese converts was ratified by a special audience in Buckingham Palace with Queen Victoria and Prince Albert. As reported by the *Illustrated London News,* the queen "evinced great interest in the Chinese youths, and asked many questions, which it was highly gratifying to Dr. Legge to answer."[77] The young men themselves beamed with enigmatic Chinese-Christian smiles (see figure 6) but seemed to have said nothing directly to the divinely regal lady.

Legge must have felt a rush of special gratification at what had been accomplished and a keen sense of anticipation as he set out again for the mission field. These emotions are graphically depicted by the famous painting that was commissioned to memorialize the "remarkable" events surrounding the "Conversion and Baptism of three natives of China" (and the subsequent engraving published in the *Evangelical Magazine* of 1849; see figure 7).[78] This image deserves some special scrutiny because allegorically it sums up the whole Victorian missionary encounter with China at this moment of swollen expectations and paternalistic confidence. Dr. Legge, solemnly seated at the left of the picture, is shown as the very epitome of a dignified Victorian father patiently instructing his youthful but studious charges. The faces of his three alien pupils glow with quiet confidence and each of them manifests a single-minded devotion to the "great truths of Christianity" contained in the scriptures held in their hands. The composition of the picture seems designed to suggest that the three Chinese are no

Figure 6. "Chinese Youths Recently Introduced to the Queen." Identified as *(left to right)* Lee Kim-lin, Song Hoot-kiem, and Ung Mun-sou. Engraving, *Illustrated London News,* April 22, 1848.

longer under the dark thrall of heathenism and have, in fact, "happily embraced" the Christian faith.[79] This central tableau, which denotes the future hope of the Chinese nation, is underscored by the right side of the picture, where a drawn curtain prophetically reveals the coming purgation that will destroy the old imperial tradition in China.

This is a stereotypical portrait of a Victorian colonial patriarch who has patronizingly instructed a backward and still-childlike people in the progressive ways of Christian civilization. Nevertheless, it is remarkable that the portrayal of the individual Chinese students is mostly devoid of the stock characteristics of the "Chinaman." Their shaded faces even have a vague Caucasoid appearance (compare, for example, the more prominent noses in the *Evangelical Magazine* engraving with the flatter and more Mongoloid features seen in the *Illustrated London News* picture). Because these Oriental heathens had experienced the transforming power of the Christian faith, they were apparently shown with "likenesses" that were quasi-European and therefore particularly "striking and impressive."[80]

Given the symbolic power of the three Chinese students and their potential as native clergy for spearheading the conversion of China, we can well imagine how devastating it was when in 1856 the Chinese seminary in

Figure 7. The Reverend James Legge with Chinese students in the Theological
Seminary, Hong Kong. *Left to right:* Legge, Lee Kim-lin, Song Hoot-Kiem, and Ung
Mun-sou. Engraving by J. Cochrane, *Evangelical Magazine* 27 (1849), after a
painting (28 inches × 39 inches) by H. Room. Reproduced courtesy of the
London Missionary Society/Council for World Mission archive.

Hong Kong was closed in utter failure. None of the seminary's seventeen
students went on to become a preacher, but even more hurtful to Legge
must have been the realization that his three special Chinese converts, who
had been baptized in Huntly and had met the queen of England, had now
irrevocably turned away from service to the church. Because they spoke English, Song and then Lee were tempted into business and other secular activities. Much worse was that Ung Mun-sou, who had seemed the most
promising of the three, fell into criminal activities involving theft and the
Hong Kong underworld.[81]

Hong Kong in the 1850s

During the long sea voyage to Hong Kong in 1848, Legge notes in his diary
that he had redoubled his scholarly efforts to master ancient Chinese literature. Perhaps because the eventual and even rapid conversion of China
seemed assured, he now appears more forthcoming about his desire "to be

distinguished among sinologues." Drawing upon his version-making practices when he was a schoolboy in Aberdeen, he says that his motto in learning Chinese was *Nulla dies sine linea* (Not a day without lines). It was his daily habit therefore to translate passages back and forth from Chinese and English. "Let me labour at it," he says, "till it becomes as simple a matter with me to write a little story in Chinese as in English."[82]

Feeling revitalized in body and spirit from his time in Britain, Legge immersed himself in his missionary and scholarly work back in the colony of Hong Kong. In the early 1850s, he reentered the term question battle still being waged among the missionary delegates responsible for producing a new common translation of the Bible. At some point during the previous few years he had decisively changed over to the Shangdi position—an alteration that was specifically prompted by his reaction to the American William J. Boone's strident arguments for the Shin-ite position and bitter attack on Medhurst's case for Shangdi.[83] Legge weighed into the fray with two long scholarly treatises that set forth his philological, philosophical, and theological reasons for accepting the truth of the Shangdi perspective: *An Argument for Shang Te as the Proper Rendering of the Words Elohim and Theos, In the Chinese Language: with Strictures on the Essay of Bishop Boone in Favour of the Term Shin* (published in 1850) and *The Notions of the Chinese Concerning God and Spirits* (appearing in 1852).

These works show that Legge's understanding of the terminological questions was moving in the direction of a more liberal and sympathetic interpretation of Chinese tradition, especially in light of the Ruists' impressive morality and, as implied by the Shangdi school, by the quasimonotheism that seemed embedded in the ancient classical texts. At the very least, the scholarly erudition of these works demonstrates that Legge was well on his way to becoming a recognized sinologue not just among his missionary colleagues but also among academic Orientalists based in Paris (especially the formidable Stanislas Julien, who had assumed Abel Rémusat's position at the Collège de France). Legge also tells us that at about this time—given his close study of Chinese texts and his field experience with the Chinese people—he was very favorably impressed by Frederick Denison Maurice's protocomparativistic work, *The Religions of the World and Their Relations to Christianity,* published in 1847.[84] For Legge, understanding and respect for Chinese tradition were preferable to the immediate and total condemnation so often recommended by conventional missionary policy.

Darkness and Light

The passion of Legge's scholarly work during this period seems in many ways a response to the fact that he was dealing with a number of deeply disturbing events in his personal life. He suffered the deaths, in rapid succession, of his father on May 3, 1848, his infant daughter, Anne Murray, on September 10, 1848, and his friend and tutor to the Chinese converts, John Hill. Most calamitous, however, was the premature and tragic death of his thirty-six-year-old wife, Mary Isabella, in the early morning of October 17, 1852. Having suffered for several months with a series of wasting illnesses, she died in her husband's arms while giving birth to a stillborn child. Legge's only solace was that she seemed to give evidence on her deathbed that her suffering spirit had been "released from its earthly house only to be with Christ in paradise."[85]

These grievous events, along with the upsetting failure of the Chinese seminary and the outbreak of hostilities between Britain and China toward the end of 1856 (a seemingly minor incident involving the Chinese boarding of the British flagship *Arrow* in the Canton harbor led to warfare lasting to 1860), caused Legge to bury his sorrows in steady work. Significantly, his devotion to the projected translation of the Chinese classics was now, as he was completing his study of the Four Books and related commentaries, becoming more focused. By 1856, he had secured a promise from Joseph Jardine, the wealthy and influential owner of the Jardine Company, the leading opium merchants in the China trade, to cover the publication costs for the classics. Some months later, in 1857, as he prepared for another furlough home to attend his children and marshal support from the London Missionary Society for his scholarly labor, he printed a "Specimen of the Chinese Classics," an eleven-page pamphlet (see figure 8) that sets out most of the technical conventions he would follow when the volumes started to appear four years later. Each page of this sample translation of chapter 1 of the *Analects* had a three-tiered arrangement of the Chinese text, the translation, and his commentarial notes. All of this was to be accompanied by a "Prolegomena and a Critical and Exegetical Commentary"; the only thing missing were the "copious indexes" of words and phrases he would ultimately append to each of his volumes.[86]

Another promising, though ambiguous, ray of light at this time concerned the evangelical Christian traits associated with the Chinese visionary Hong Xiuquan and his cataclysmic Taiping rebellion (1850–1864). Throughout much of the 1850s the Taiping movement was seen by many missionaries, including Legge, as an exciting step toward the fulfillment of biblical prophecy.[87] Hong Xiuquan's revelations were, in fact, said to have come from Shangdi, which was taken as the Chinese name for the Christian God. Legge was directly involved in these events through his close association from 1854 to 1857 with Hong Rengan (also known as Hong Yi-sien, Hung Jin, and Hung Yan), a younger cousin of Hong Xiuquan, who became the influential Shield King of the Taiping movement when it established its base of operations in Nanjing. Along with Ho Tsun-sheen and Wang Tao, Hong Rengan was remembered by Legge as one of the most intelligent and impressive Chinese he had ever met. It was yet another bitter

SPECIMEN

OF

THE CHINESE CLASSICS;

WITH A TRANSLATION: PROLEGOMENA: AND A CRITICAL
AND EXEGETICAL COMMENTARY.

BY

JAMES LEGGE, D.D.,

Of the London Missionary Society.

HONGKONG:

Figure 8. Specimen of the *Chinese Classics* by James Legge, D.D. Cover *(above)* and page 1 *(right)* of the *Confucian Analects,* Book I. Appears by permission of the Library of the School of Oriental and African Studies, University of London (Council for World Mission archive, South China/Incoming/Box 6 [1858]).

CONFUCIAN ANALECTS.

BOOK I.—HEŎ URH.

不　不　亦　自　說　時　　　論
亦　知　樂　遠　乎　習　子　學　語
君　而　乎　方　。　之　曰　而　
子　不　　來　有　不　學　第
乎　慍　節　不　朋　亦　而　一
。　。　人　　節　　

CHAPTER I. The Master said, "Is it not pleasant to learn with a constant perseverance and application?

"Is it not delightful to have friends coming from distant quarters?

"Is he not a man of complete virtue, who feels no anger and dissatisfaction, though men may take no note of him?"

TITLE OF THE WORK.—論語.—'Discourses and Dialogues,' that is, the discourses or discussions of Confucius with his disciples and others on various topics, and his replies to their inquiries. Many chapters, however, and one whole book, are the sayings, not of the sage himself, but of some of his disciples. The characters may also be rendered *Digested Conversations*, and this appears to be the more ancient signification attached to them, the account being that, after the death of Confucius, his disciples collected together and compared the memoranda of his conversations which they had severally preserved, digesting them into the twenty books which compose this work. Hence the name 論語, 'Discussed Sayings,' or 'Digested Conversations.' I have styled the work 'Confucian Analects,' which is more descriptive of its character than any other name I could think of.

HEADING OF THIS BOOK.—學而第一. The two first characters in the book are adopted as its heading. This is similar to the custom of the Jews, who name many books of the Bible from the first word in them. The sixteen chapters of this book are occupied, it is said, with the fundamental subjects which ought to engage the attention of the learner.

1. THE WHOLE WORK AND ACHIEVEMENT OF THE LEARNER, FIRST PERFECTING HIS OWN KNOWLEDGE, THEN DELIGHTED WHEN HIS FAME ATTRACTS LIKE-MINDED INDIVIDUALS, AND FINALLY COMPLETE IN HIMSELF. 子 at the commencement means Confucius. 子, 'a son,' is also the common designation of males—especially of virtuous men. It is used in conversations in the classics, in the same way as our 'Sir.' When it follows the surname, it is equivalent to our 'Mr,' or may be rendered—'the philosopher,' 'the scholar.' Often, however, it is more convenient to leave it untranslated. When employed *before* the surname, it indicates that the party spoken of was the master of the writer, as 子沈子, 'my master, the philosopher 沈.' Standing single and alone as in the text, it denotes Confucius, *the* philosopher, or rather *the Master*. 學 is interpreted by Choo He, as meaning 效 'to imitate;' it means to make, in whatever way, the acquirements and attainments of others our own. 習 is the rapid and frequent motion of the wings of a bird in flying, used for 'to repeat,' 'to practise.'

pill for Legge to determine that, by the end of the decade, Hong Rengan, along with the rest of the Taiping movement, had become politically corrupt and religiously demonic.[88] It was not until 1865 that the Manchu government in Peking, with foreign assistance, was able to suppress the movement once and for all.

Treaties and Troubles

In 1858 and 1860 treaties were signed in Tientsin and Peking by China and the combined British and Western powers, thereby ending the awful hostilities that began so trivially in Canton in 1856. The Chinese imperial government had been humiliated and foreigners, including missionaries, were for the first time permitted to travel in the interior of the country. Even more important from the missionary perspective was that Christians (whether European or native Chinese) were allowed to propagate Christianity freely and were assured tolerance in the practice of their faith. These developments seemed to give further evidence of the impending collapse of the Peking government and the eventual triumph of Christianity throughout the Land of Sinim. Yet again a darker and more ambivalent reality frustrated the prophetic expectations of the Protestant missionaries. In particular, the treaty provisions of tolerance served only to provoke a greater resistance among Chinese officials and a popular revulsion against the now legally sanctioned methods of Christian evangelization. This situation led to sporadic eruptions of Chinese violence against both foreign and native Christians. Legge was personally affected by these outbreaks, so that in 1860 and 1861 he was severely distressed by a series of bloody assaults against a native Christian community in the small town of Poklo in southern China. These events culminated in the killing of Ch'ea Kim-kong (Ch'ëa Kim-kwong, Che Jinguang), an esteemed Chinese Christian acquaintance of Legge's from Hong Kong and the first Chinese "Protestant martyr."[89]

These troubling developments, along with the disappointment associated with the Taiping movement, were accentuated by the disheartening statistics on the relative paucity of actual Chinese converts. The London Missionary Society pioneered in the new statistical science and was faced with numerical results that too often seemed to require constant explanation and interpretive finesse, especially in consideration of the money and manpower expended on the China mission. From Legge's more realistic in-the-field and gradualist perspective, however, the society had not done enough to support either his direct evangelical or indirect scholarly efforts in South China. For most of the late 1850s and 1860s, he was therefore regularly pleading with the directors to assign more missionaries to the Hong Kong station and for some minimum encouragement of his translation project. In the early 1860s, after the death of his brother and theological mentor George (who died on January 24, 1861) and the publication of the first volume of his *Chinese Classics (The Confucian Analects),* he threw himself even more fully into his indirect methods and was frequently involved with educational and civic matters in the colony.[90]

HONG KONG IN THE 1860s:
TEXTS AND TERMINATIONS

Patient steady work was [James Legge's] motto, and he persevered in such work, preaching in chapels, teaching in schools, superintending a printing-press and type-foundry for printing Chinese Bibles and tracts, and burning the midnight lamp over his translations and commentaries of the Chinese Classics.

E. J. EITEL, "THE PROTESTANT MISSIONS OF HONGKONG,"
CHINESE RECORDER, 1876

Originally, it is known, each advance in Oriental studies proceeded from the expansion of Christendom among Mohammaden and heathen peoples. Already for a long time now Oriental science almost everywhere has withdrawn and headed in other directions than those of missions and missionaries, attaining an independent status for itself. This is less often the case with East Asia. By far most of the men who have devoted and continue to consecrate their lives to research of the Chinese cultural system have been and are Christian messengers. Westerners have to thank them in particular for information about East Asian lands. The history of Chinese literature in Europe is therefore intimately bound up with the history of missions, and, if one is not satisfied with piecemeal work, it will be impossible to deal with the one without mentioning the other.

KARL FRIEDRICH NEUMANN, *SINOLOGUES AND THEIR WORKS,* 1847

Standing on the Peak

The colony of Hong Kong was thriving in the 1860s and had achieved a population of more than a hundred thousand Asians and Europeans. In many ways, it was already a city that seemed to combine the best and worst from the East and West. Regardless of the industrious religiosity of the Protestant missionary community, Hong Kong was a place spawned and nurtured by the opium trade and was a notorious resort for both Chinese and European thieves and pirates. To use Jan Morris's words, Hong Kong was always a blatantly "louche and lascivious city . . . obsessed with money and chicanery . . . set up as a clearing house for Indian and European goods on way to China." The city in this sense often exemplified the worst excesses of a rapacious commercialism devoid of any Christian varnish. But even though Hong Kong in the nineteenth century was predominantly a "garrison town of pirates and racketeers, prostitutes, gamblers, and confidence men," there were others—both Europeans and Asians—who went against the grain of this "bitter, brilliant, grasping place."[91] One of these counterpoints was the whole conjoined tradition of missionary work and sinological scholarship that, as seen in the progressively hyphenated character of a man like Legge, never fully capitulated to a guilt-free religious, intellectual, and moral hypocrisy. What was meaningful and moral for Legge seemed always to be found in what was *between* all received categories and definitions.

The changes that Hong Kong was undergoing in the 1860s and 1870s are illustrated in a talk given by Legge less than a year before his final departure from the colony.[92] Presented as a public lecture at the City Hall, this talk, "The Colony of Hong Kong," is a fascinating insider's perspective on the "amazing growth" of Hong Kong from its war-booty origins in January 1841 down to the time of Legge's address in the early 1870s. With a mixture of nationalistic hubris and biblical critique, Legge began with the observation that, as a long-term inhabitant of the colony, he felt the thrill of "Britannia standing on the Peak" and looked down "with an emotion of pride on the great Babylon which her sons have built." Reminiscing about his first experience of the hills overlooking the harbor, hills that reminded him of his native Aberdeenshire, Legge recalled the early "atmosphere of disease" and fever (a "miasma set free from the ground which was everywhere being turned up") that had plagued the colony and had morbidly affected his own family.[93] Proudly declaring that the climate and mortality rate were now "quite as good as they would be in London," he went on to say that the overall problem of "law and order" in the colony had improved greatly. Though things were better, he emphasized his belief, considered by many to be "too visionary and utopian," that the police force should include a Chinese contingent.

Legge surveyed important historical events down to the time of his address—alluding to the notorious poisoned bread incident of 1857 (he remarks in passing that he had become friends with Cheong A-lum, the baker convicted of the premeditated poisoning of Legge himself and a large segment of the European community) and to his efforts on behalf of the Hong Kong central school system. Referring to the late 1860s and early 1870s, he noted that the advance of spectacular mechanical devices (such as the telegraph and Suez Canal), as well as numerous wars and revolutions throughout Europe, America, India, and Africa, underscored a situation of "almost unparalleled change all over the world." Japan was making impressive progress and even China seemed to be "really moving." Legge was moreover encouraged to find that developments in China, though slow, seemed to be largely self-generated. The clear implication was that Christianity and British civilization were only the proximate, and not the necessary, agents in China's arousal. Unqualified contempt for China must be replaced with "respect for the country and its people." From Legge's increasingly outspoken perspective, therefore, Britain should renounce the continuing opium traffic as a corrupt "phantom of the past." Commenting on the missionary enterprise (and the tendency of the secular media to link opium and missionaries as the two great problems of British and Chinese relations), he concluded by stressing that the missions, despite various problems, were "commanded by God." But he really made only a meager defense of missionaries while acknowledging "abuses" that should be "proved, punished, and forbidden."

The public reception given to Legge's address supports the judgment that by the end of the 1860s he was identified more as a scholar-sinologue and public figure than as a conventional missionary agent. As recorded in the *North-China Herald,* "loud applause" accompanied the introduction to his presentation when it was pointed out that "it was almost impossible to place a just value on the labours which Dr. Legge had given to the world." His scholarly work on the Chinese classics meant that he stood "at the head of Sinologues, and . . . had done more to give Western nations an idea of China and the Chinese than twenty travellers." Most of all, said the *Herald,* his translations had done more "than twenty missionaries."[94] This was not a conclusion that would be comforting to the directors of the London Missionary Society back in England.

Filthy Heathens and Victorian Purity

During his trip home to Britain in 1859, Legge married for a second time, taking Hannah Mary Johnston (1822–1881) as his wife in a ceremony in London. Hannah Mary was seven years younger than Legge and had only recently been widowed. Like Mary Isabella, Hannah was from a clerical and socially well-to-do Dissenting family. Unlike Mary Isabella, however, Hannah seemed much less constitutionally adapted to life in Hong Kong and did not attempt to conduct, as Isabella had done, a school for native Chinese girls. Hannah was more than satisfied with taking care of the children (which in the 1860s was Legge's second family of Helen Edith, James Granville, Thomas Morison, and Anna Georgina; Hannah Mary also had an older daughter, Marian, by her former husband), running the domestic and social affairs of the imposing Mission House, and commanding a large battalion of Chinese nurses, cooks, and coolies.

Hong Kong had grown immensely in population and wealth, and the pretensions of its European masters had expanded in kind. This kind of social puffery is seen in what was described as Legge's "demeanor of a bishop" when presiding over meetings and is also suggested by Hannah Mary's self-satisfied rule over the manorial Mission House and by her concomitant inability to cope emotionally with the human and cultural "filth" of China. James Legge had assumed a prominent role within the colony and, despite the taint of Nonconformity, the Legge family enjoyed considerable prestige. As the one responsible for maintaining the ordered peace and cultural purity of the household in the midst of the chaotic Orient, Hannah devoted herself to her domestic empire, plainly relishing those social occasions that called for some special show of British hospitality to her European guests and subservience from her Chinese attendants.

The ability of the British to re-create a perfect simulacrum of upwardly mobile middle-class life is witnessed in many of the procedures of missionary families in the treaty port cities in China. Thus the kind of genteel Victorian existence associated with the London Missionary Society's Mission House in Hong Kong ("a noble structure . . . quite equal to a nobleman's mansion in England"; see figure 9) is portrayed by a revealing letter about a typical day in Hannah Mary Legge's domestic routine in the 1860s. Hannah Mary's epistle depicts a household that was kept "as English as possible" in order to uphold her acutely self-conscious standards of gracious hospitality and ritual propriety. This kind of life came complete with a contingent of native servants, or "boys" as they were "invariably called," and involved frequent opportunities for formal dining, along with all the accoutrements of English teas and entertaining, tiffin and croquet.[95]

Inasmuch as this kind of life was not attainable by an ordinary Dissenting household back home, there is a slight note of guilt in Hannah's letter.[96] She apologetically explained that, though some might say this lifestyle was not appropriate for a missionary, the maintenance of a full-fledged British way of life should be taken as a lesson for "filthy" heathens in the superiority and "cleanliness" of Christian civilization. At the same time, such standards of domestic and moral purity functioned as lessons for the unruly elements within the diverse European community. As Hannah Mary said elsewhere, the foul nature of the heathen was most fully revealed in the "squalid wretchedness" of Chinese religion, especially as manifest in the "dirt and smoke and odour" of the "infantile" rites observed in a temple or "Joss House."[97]

The travel writer Henry Knollys might have had Hannah Mary in mind when, in his fussy (and hardly unbiased) portrait of English life in China, he discussed some of the problems with missionaries in the colony of Hong Kong. He found that the Protestant missionaries all too often seemed to postpone "the interests of their religious calling to the furtherance of their worldly prospects." It was their "unhumble strife for social status" that was at the root of many of these problems, and this was a striving for which the missionary wives were "habitually responsible." Going on to a fuller analysis of the "missionary question," Knollys noted that for the typical missionary the prospects of missionary life were very attractive. Given an assured and liberal income from the missionary societies (for Legge it was £300 per year with generous supplements for children), the missionary was able to live "in a condition of affluence which would be unknown to him elsewhere; a luxurious house with luxurious appliances and table, coolies to carry him about, and an ample margin of [Hong Kong] dollars."[98]

A Dream Fulfilled: The Chinese Classics

By far the most important event during these busy years in Hong Kong was Legge's publication in 1861 of the first volume of the *Chinese Classics* (see figure 10) and his steady production of the succeeding volumes every few

Figure 9. Drawing of the London Missionary Society Mission House, Hong Kong, ca. 1860s–1870s. Reproduced courtesy of the Legge Family Collection.

years afterward. The fact that volume 1 of this edition comprised the *Lunyu* (The digested sayings) of the Master Kong—or as Legge, drawing upon the model of the Latin classics, entitled his translation, *Confucian Analects*—and two other of the classical Four Books, the *Daxue* (The great learning) and the *Zhongyong* (Doctrine of the mean), was certainly no accident. It also was not simple chance that caused Legge to open his *Classics* with the *Analects*. This meant that he was not following the traditional Ruist ordering of the classics (which began with the *Yijing* [The book of changes], a work that Legge found impenetrable) or the Four Books (which the famous Song scholar Zhu Xi arranged from the shortest to the longest: *The Great Learning, The Doctrine of the Mean, The Analects,* and *The Mencius*).[99]

Based on his comments in the 1840s, it was obvious that Legge's plan for translating the Chinese classics would focus on the "Great Story" told by the history of Chinese literature and religion.[100] In keeping with the story of the Christian scriptures, in which the Old Testament was fulfilled by the revolutionary good news of the New Testament, Legge clearly saw the ancient Five Classics of Chinese literature culminating in the later Four Books, which enunciated a moral message curiously similar to that found in the four Gospels. Always smarting from the London Missionary Society's charges that his scholarly interests were too indirect, Legge found a way to combine the society's apologetic concerns with his own scholarly passions. To begin the *Classics* with the *Analects* and two other of the Four Books, quickly followed by *The Works of Mencius,* which in Legge's judgment was the most morally astute of these texts, was a strategy with both a pragmatic and philosophical justification.

A Want of Divine Greatness

For Legge it was also critical to start with the text that, like the Gospels' account of Christ, told the story of Confucius as the model sage for all later Chinese classical tradition. Much of Legge's prolegomena to the first volume of the *Classics* is consequently devoted to a critical examination of the "Life of Confucius" in implicit comparison with the sacred biography of the Christian founder. Legge's discussion of the Chinese master indicates that he had done his historical and philological research in Chinese and European sources with great care (his bibliography and notes show that he was well apprised of native Chinese commentarial scholarship, especially Zhu Xi and Mao Qiling at this time, and was using the so-called modern critical edition of the Four Books by Ruan Yuan, 1764–1849),[101] but more revealing of Legge's hyphenated state of mind at the time, and a gloss on the overall missionary perspective, was his evaluation of Confucius or Kongzi's "greatness" in relation to the divine figure of Christ and the achievements of Christian civilization. It is in this sense that Legge found Kongzi's teachings to be lacking in the theistic

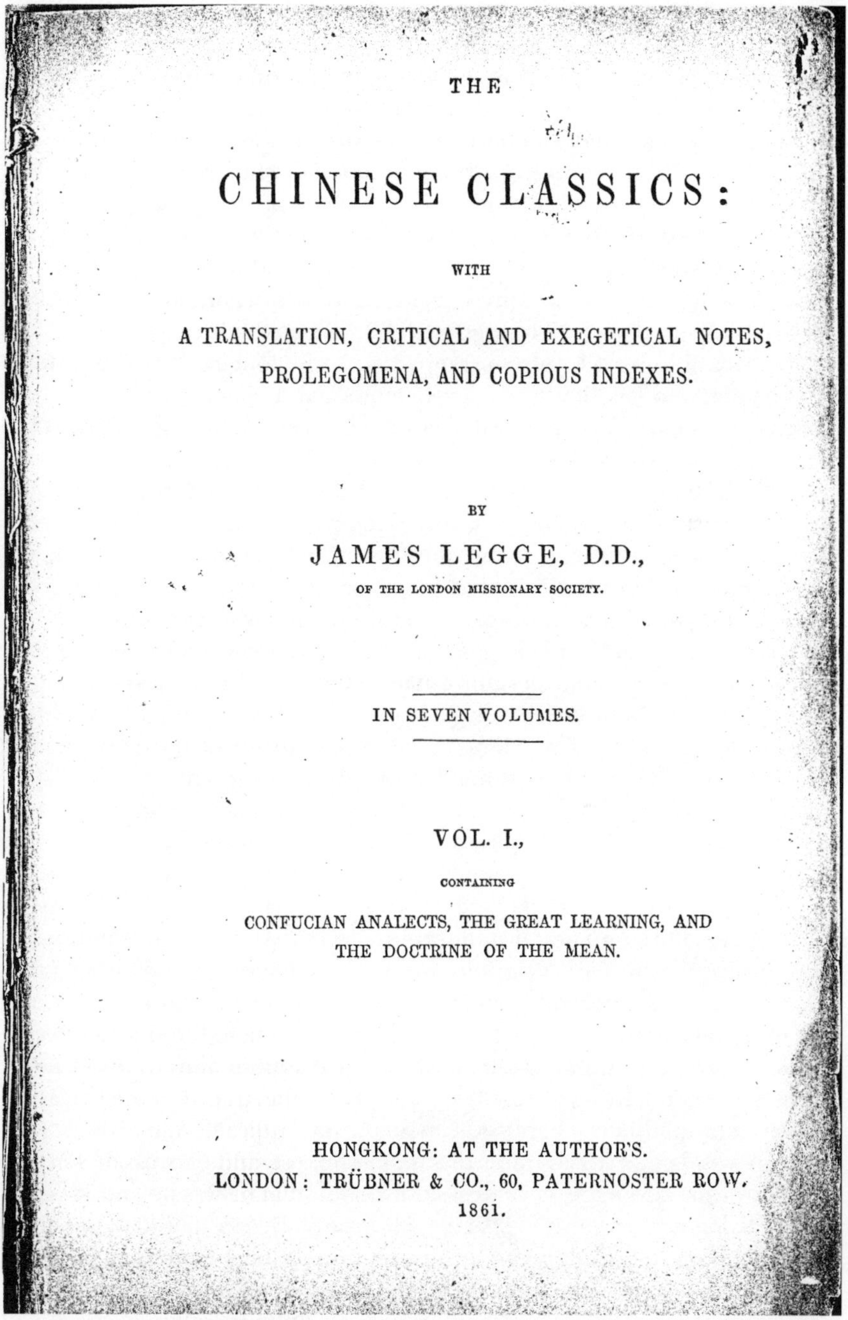

THE

CHINESE CLASSICS:

WITH

A TRANSLATION, CRITICAL AND EXEGETICAL NOTES,
PROLEGOMENA, AND COPIOUS INDEXES.

BY

JAMES LEGGE, D.D.,
OF THE LONDON MISSIONARY SOCIETY.

IN SEVEN VOLUMES.

VOL. I.,

CONTAINING

CONFUCIAN ANALECTS, THE GREAT LEARNING, AND
THE DOCTRINE OF THE MEAN.

HONGKONG: AT THE AUTHOR'S.
LONDON: TRÜBNER & CO., 60, PATERNOSTER ROW.
1861.

Figure 10. Title page of the *Chinese Classics* by James Legge, D.D., volume 1
(Hong Kong: At the Author's, 1861).

beliefs he found in the Five Classics (referring here to *di, shangdi,* and *tian,* found in the *Historical Documents* and *Poetry*) and lacking any concern with "spiritual" matters. He decided that Confucius (and Mencius even more so) had much to say that was exemplary about moral development and ethical relations, but that he was fundamentally "unreligious" if not "irreligious." (It should be noted that the term *agnostic* had not yet been coined by Thomas Huxley.) Furthermore, it was the influence of the Master's unreligion that caused later generations of Chinese to respond so unfavorably to the "ardent religious feeling" displayed by evangelical Protestantism.[102]

The overall tone of Legge's examination of Kongzi in 1861 is decidedly antagonistic and his final judgment stands out as harsh and insensitive. Hoping that he had not been unfair to the Chinese sage, Legge concluded that, after "long study," he was "unable to regard [Confucius/Kongzi] as a great man." The reason for this was that Kongzi "was not before his age, though he was above the mass of the officers and scholars of his time. He threw no new light on any of the questions which have a world-wide interest." Especially damning was that he "gave no impulse to religion" and showed "no sympathy with progress." Although the Master's influence had "been wonderful" in China, Legge can only deduce that "it will henceforth wane." It was his opinion therefore that "the faith of the nation in [Confucius] will speedily and extensively pass away."[103]

The rest of James Legge's long career, once he was able to put some of his compromising hyphenations behind him, represents a struggle to amend the severity of his initial understanding of Master Kong. In fact, one of the first serious scholarly reviews of the *Classics,* in the *Edinburgh Review* in 1869, criticized the uncharitable "injustice" of Legge's views. Challenging academic criticism of this kind, more so than laudatory articles appearing in pious denominational publications, prodded Legge into important modifications of his early opinions and was one factor, among others, that led to his long scholarly pilgrimage of atonement—culminating in his revision of the prolegomena to the *Analects* for the second edition published in Oxford in 1893. Another of the arbiters of the comparative immorality of Legge's views on Kongzi may be Wang Tao (see figure 11), a classical scholar and nominally a baptized Christian who began his eleven-year relationship with Legge shortly after the appearance of volume 1 of the *Classics.* Wang was one of Legge's greatest admirers, judging his classical scholarship as "wide and extensive."[104] Legge felt similarly toward Wang, respecting his literary knowledge and accepting him as a professional colleague and personal friend—the kind of close association with native Chinese that often led Legge to reassess some of his harsher judgments about China and Confucian teachings. However, the sympathetic enlargement of his opinions regarding the "greatness" of Master Kong seems to have been most profoundly promoted by his own reaction to the sectarian prejudice con-

Figure 11. The Legge family with Wang Tao, in Dollar, Scotland, 1869.
Left to right: Marian, J. L., Thomas, Hannah, Helen Edith, Anna, James, and
Wang Tao. Reproduced courtesy of the Legge Family Collection.

nected with the continuing term question and to the nagging injustice of
the London Missionary Society's attitude toward his translation project.

Translating for the Hundredth Man

In the mid-1860s, when Legge was furiously working on the complicated
Book of Historical Documents, his first translation from the ancient Five Clas-

sics, the ever mounting intensity of his scholarly work again became his way of coping with various personal and familial difficulties (involving some of his own health problems, but primarily having to do with Hannah Mary's chronic malaise and inability to continue living in the colony), as well as his usual frustrations with the London Missionary Society. At about this time, he began working out his own theory and method of scholarly translation, an issue that would follow him when, a decade later, he started to produce the *Sacred Books of China* for Max Müller at Oxford. As he said in 1867, when he was initiating his translation of the *Book of Poetry,* a diligent translator must always work as if he were writing for the "hundredth man" who cares about the meticulous technical details of scholarship ("99 out of 100 do not care for critical notes"). Only in this way will a translation have "permanent value" and constitute "something that will be referred to hundreds of years hence." This is the kind of labor Legge found "very absorbing" even though (and here he displays a sensitivity to an emerging Victorian hierarchy of intellectual production in which some scholars were in danger of being dismissed as *mere* translators) the mind has not, to quote his convoluted prose, the "exhaustion of prolonged original thought such as is produced in building the lofty rhyme or elaborating the philosophical discussion, or even in writing the three volume novel."

Legge took consolation from the fact that his commentarial efforts required "a constant mental exercise" of a "minute and accurate discrimination" that "now and then . . . throw[s] light on general topics." His concern was philosophical, historical, and philological: that is, "to find the place of China in the scheme of universal history and thought." There is no attempt to state the ordinary missionary justifications for his scholarship. His rationale and motivation were primarily scholarly, keeping in mind that scholars also had a sacred mission to know the "great story" of other nations.[105] In a letter to his wife in 1866, he showed his familiarity with current theories of comparative philology and Orientalism. Discussing the origin of the different races based on the newly fashionable study of linguistic roots, he remarked that it may well be possible to show that "Jews, Aryans, and Chinese," if not Africans, were "all descended from a common ancestor." But whatever the case, he flatly declared that "no conclusion from scripture" should be allowed to "stand in the way of scientific investigations and inductive conclusions."[106] "Knowing the enemy" was leading Legge to the unnerving realization that the real nemesis of understanding was to be found in an overly pious neglect of the small "details" of language and history.

The standard "know thine enemy" rationale Legge gave to the London Missionary Society to justify his scholarly work was part of a larger, and gradually expanding, set of reasons that were more in keeping with the purely scientific concerns of academic and secular Oriental scholarship. In the late 1860s, the philosophical and philological motivations for translating the classics were probably more important than the conventional missionary explanations he offered to the London Missionary Society. More and more Legge was affirming the necessary scholarly expansion of traditional missionary and apologetic methods for transforming China. In the decades of the 1860s and 1870s, this was a dangerously liberal view of "universal history" that was not shared by many working missionaries.

I Care for Naebody and Naebody Cares for Me

By the end of the 1860s, Legge had altered his working relationship with the London Missionary Society. By so doing he decisively, yet discreetly and quietly, brought closure to many of the hyphenated tensions affecting his career as a missionary-scholar. He did not officially resign or retire from the society, but requested, at the time of his penultimate return to Britain in February 1867, to be no longer employed as an active missionary agent.[107] Thus before his last return to Hong Kong in 1870, he made special arrangements with the Union Church to provide him with a full-time salary as pastor, thereby releasing him from his regular responsibilities for overseeing the mission station in Hong Kong. He also arranged with the London Missionary Society board to continue to use the press for his *Classics*—stressing the society's complete freedom from any financial liability.

Legge tells us that he insisted upon such an arrangement both because of his frustrations with the board's insensitivities to his needs in the field and because of the cool, and at times outrightly suspicious and disapproving, attitude of some board members, particularly Arthur Tidman, toward his "special work" of translating the classics.[108] As far back as 1857–1858, Tidman, then the influential secretary, was writing "his dear brother" Legge about the board's "unanimous" concern that "in prosecuting the translation of the Chinese Classics your time and attention not be so far engaged as to render it impracticable for you to exercise an adequate supervision over the entire Mission in Hong Kong, and also to take your full part in such missionary labours as may be practicable in that Colony." Despite their concerns about the impractical apportionment of his labor in the mission field, the board members did officially approve Legge's translation project. But their grudging support was qualified by two new stipulations in 1858. First, there was a more formal reiteration of the provision that "the expense of printing at the Mission Press" would be borne strictly by the "liberality" of Legge's "generous friend" (Jardine) without any demands upon the society. Second, as Tidman's letter stated, "the Directors were desirous to ascertain whether those sentiments of Confucius which are at variance with Christian truth, would be accompanied by annotations in refutation of the one and in confirmation of the other."[109]

Given Legge's tireless attention to all of his missionary duties, and his careful relegation of his translation work to the late evening and early morning hours, these suspicions and unneeded advice voiced by the directors of the society in London during his second furlough home (1858–1859) must have been extremely galling. Unfortunately, there is only an edited version of Legge's response to Tidman.[110] Thanking the society for its support, he notes that he would have preferred the board to have worded the resolution differently. After all, his "service of nearly twenty years would have justified and might have prompted a concurrence that should have worn no aspect of grudging." Addressing the key issue of his comparison of Confucianism and Christianity in his translations, he indignantly declared that "it was unnecessary thus to school me in the way in which I should execute what I have taken in hand." He could "afford to smile" when "the same thing was mentioned by some of the members of the Eastern Committee," but now, "when it comes to me repeated by you [Tidman], as an important part of an official communication, I hardly know how to take it."[111]

The sadness of the board's officious questioning of Legge's work is that, despite his "smiling" retort, it inevitably compromised his identity as a missionary and fueled his frustrations with the bureaucratic and sectarian shortsightedness of church organizations. Already in 1858, therefore, he writes that "no one is so well aware as I am of my many deficiencies as a missionary, and of my much unprofitableness in the past." At this time, he declares that he has "no wish but to end [his] days as a missionary." However, as he says in 1864 while procuring the type for the third volume of his *Classics,* he was still feeling the "cool shoulder" of Tidman and was prompted to think of the refrain "I care for naebody and naebody cares for me."[112]

This continuing estrangement, aided and abetted by other instances of negligence and misunderstanding, clearly colored the relationship between Legge and the London Missionary Society down to the late 1860s. By the time of his return to England in 1867, it led to his resolve to return to Hong Kong, but not in "the service of the Society," in order to complete the publication of the *Chinese Classics.* Asking for special permission to use the society's press for the *Classics,* he made it clear that whatever the society's actions, he would not "come out again [to China] as a missionary." Carefully disclaiming any feelings of "animosity," and ritually acknowledging that "the Society has had abler agents," he concluded his letter by affirming that he had always "kept the great object of my mission before my mind."[113] But the issue at this time was how he weighted the scholarly and apologetic aspects of his mission and its "great object."

When Legge wrote the London Missionary Society in 1867 concerning his intentions, the board was under the new secretariat of Joseph Mullens (who took over in 1866; he indicated that he had already heard rumors of Legge's desire to sever relations with the society). Mullens tried to ameliorate the situation by addressing some of Legge's grievances about his "Chinese volumes." Admitting that many statements made to Legge were "unjustifiable" and that he was "badly used," Mullens defensively claimed that it was all a misunderstanding caused by an "individual [Tidman]," not by the board (private board minutes indicate that this is not an entirely truthful statement). What Mullens really meant is that the board, as it was then constituted, would not criticize Legge's devotion to the *Classics*. No doubt influenced by the positive recognition coming to the society because of Legge's growing fame as the translator of the *Chinese Classics,* Mullens's face-saving letter goes on: "Things were written to you that touched your self-respect; but they were written by an individual [Tidman] whose prejudices and predilections are no longer the guide of this Society—not one Director of the Society would endorse the sentiments and expressions which so stirred you. Everyone deeply regrets that such things were ever said at all."

Pleading with him to reconsider his decision to end his active missionary career with the society, Mullens neatly, and sanctimoniously, turns the moral tables on Legge by saying, "Do not, my dear friend, visit upon us who disapprove that injustice an evil in which we had no share. You have now been a missionary of the Society nearly thirty years. You have attained the highest position as a Chinese scholar. This is deeply felt here—I tell you frankly, that in the whole range of the Society's officers and missionaries, *no one,* (except Moffat) [Robert Moffatt] stands higher than yourself."[114] But Legge had dealt with the society long enough to mistrust any smooth overtures of reconciliation. He therefore insisted on the arrangement of disengagement he was proposing for his final stay in Hong Kong (1870–1873), an arrangement that would maintain cordial public relations with the society but would allow him to focus his energies on the *Classics* and on pastoring at the Union Church.

Although Legge's translations of the *Chinese Classics* could be taken as materials "best adapted to be forged into weapons of spiritual warfare," there was a growing suspicion among many missionaries that his work was doing more to promulgate the "great story" of Orientalism among Europeans than to Christianize the Chinese. As was evident throughout the rest of the nineteenth century, the London Missionary Society board, as well as other sponsoring agencies, had good reason to be worried. Not only was the whole missionary movement changing, but the whole scholarly mission to translate and know the Orient was being taken over by academic, as well as more secular and "unreligious," disciplines associated with the comparative sciences of man—changes in the production and control of knowledge that, during the last quarter of the nineteenth century, were largely promoted by Max Müller at Oxford. Legge's identification as a "missionary" with the London Missionary Society was, from the very beginning of his career, central to his understanding of himself as a "Good Christian" pilgrim. However, at the beginning of the 1870s, a time of sweeping change throughout the world, he was poised at the threshold of assuming a new scholarly identity and academic mission.

Minds Bent on Learning

The sublimated hurt of Legge's relationship with the London Missionary Society, his own self-doubt as a missionary, and his dismay over the sectarian pettiness of the term question were all factors in the 1860s and 1870s that pushed Legge to reconsider the "greatness" of Confucius/Kongzi and also, it seems, to find some more humbling degree of personal identification with the Chinese master as a failed transformer and successful scholar-educator. The ancient Chinese master Kong was, it is fair to say, a textual educator-transmitter more than anything else and was also, like Legge, someone who unjustly suffered the bitter fruit of misunderstanding and failure in his public mission. Legge's own transcultural journey, spawned by ritual duty and sustained by the hard-won moral insight of experience and learning in the encounter with the otherness of China and the obtuseness of the London Missionary Society, gave him a method and morality for understanding Kongzi and the Chinese tradition that went beyond the uncharitable and confrontational approach he outlined in 1861. Indeed, Legge's pilgrimage to North China in 1873 suggests that he was starting to interpret his own life in the light of a more empathetic and revisionary understanding of the Chinese master's journey toward virtue and wisdom.

The Reverend Doctor Legge and Master Kong were partial failures in their original careers as men of mission seeking to convert the unbelievers around them, and both were mostly ignored or denigrated by their political superiors. Both came to see that, despite early problems of pride and various failures, they could still contribute to the transformation of human nature (in both the public and private sense) through their work as scholars, translator-transmitters, and teachers of the ancient classics. And for both of them, the challenge of their lives was "to be unrecognized" for the vocation they originally embraced, and "yet remain unembittered." That was, as Master Kong taught, the hard moral lesson of achieving fulfillment as a "superior man"—or, as Legge would understand it, the difficult task of building a fully "Christian" character. It is the lifelong cultivation of this lesson that both Kongzi and Legge could agree is central to the "whole duty of man."

In the Leggian "analectical" transcription of the *Lunyu,* Master Kong says of himself that "at sixty, my ear was an obedient organ for the reception of truth." In like manner, as he approached his sixtieth year, James Legge's own ear was obediently becoming attuned to the difficulties of truth in a transcultural context involving a confrontational intercourse between foreign persons and texts. Legge had every good reason to feel that he had reached a real turning point in his life as, upon his return to Hong Kong in

1870, he had, by accepting the Union Church pastorate, terminated his official missionary duties and salary. Furthermore, by virtue of his scholarly labors during his last decade in the colony, he had started to place ancient Chinese literature within the "great story" of world history. For the first time, therefore, China was becoming a fit subject for the new Victorian sciences of comparative analysis. Just as Thomas Carlyle portrayed the blasphemous "Mahomet" or Mohammed as a heroic "great man," Legge was now in the process of conceiving Confucius as a cultural hero worthy of respect and emulation. Ultimately Legge would suggest that the Chinese master could be understood as a kind of prophetic founder or reformer of the ancient Chinese theistic religious system.

With the death of Stanislas Julien in 1873, Legge became the single most influential translator-interpreter of China for the Western world. The prominence of the Ruist classics in their Leggian embodiment within European and American scholarly circles served to extend and crystalize the old Jesuitical and Enlightenment stereotype of China as quintessentially classical and Confucian. At the same time, Legge's *Chinese Classics* were giving strong evidential meaning to the general Orientalist idea of China as a great, though retarded and unreligious, civilization mired in the ancient past. Whereas ordinarily—to quote his nephew, John Legge—"the tawny-faced, oblique-eyed grinning Mongolian" was "not redolent of the aroma of lettered culture," Legge's *Chinese Classics* documented China's place within the "universal history of man." Even more amazing, and something truly at the heart of Legge's transformative impact on Victorian religious and intellectual tradition, was that the ancient accomplishments of Chinese civilization, though sharing in some primordial revelation told of in the Bible, were self-generated and came about "untouched by the light of Divine Revelation and unmodified by contact with other people."[115] The awareness of China's isolation and "formidable solitude" was connected with the daunting realization that, even without the special divine knowledge provided by the Old and New Testaments, the ancient Chinese were aware of the "true God" and practiced a morality of the silver rule. The *Chinese Classics* therefore opened polygenetic horizons of universal history and religion that went beyond the family resemblances already detected, on the higher or scientific basis of comparative philology, among the so-called Aryan traditions.

Legge's decision to break his regular association with the London Missionary Society during his last sojourn in Hong Kong and China is in keeping with the overall pattern of his life up to that time as a willfully independent evangelical Scotsman and as a boldly hyphenated missionary-scholar. Even as Legge would eventually translate the ancient Chinese master into the moral paragon and cultural hero "Confucius," so also did these same Chinese texts gradually transform the "Good Christian," Legge. Both Legge and Kongzi ended up living strangely resonating lives because both men were interpreted by discursive paradigms (Evangelical Christian and Ruist) that valorized the gradual ritual struggle of character cultivation. To borrow from the biographical paradigm established in the *Analects* (II.iv.6), it may be said that, "at fifteen" Kongzi and Legge were resolutely "bent on learning." "At thirty," both of them "stood firm" (too firm, at times!) on the moral and spiritual principle in their hearts. At the age of forty, they had "no doubts" about their life's work as teacher-commentator-transmitters of ancient texts. And both could also clearly affirm that by the age of fifty, they "knew the decree of heaven"—even if there might be some serious disagreement concerning the terminology *(tian, shangdi)* and meaning of such a celestial commission.

After years of wandering exiled from kith and kin and having little permanent success in converting others to their ways of healing the world, both the missionary-scholar James Legge and the minister-sage Confucius would eventually return home to find, at around sixty years of age, that they were able to hear—sometimes uncomfortably and with great sadness—the strong small voice of human reciprocity. Both ultimately left their active careers of mission to the greater world to accept the pathetic joys and indirect influence of editing and propagating neglected collections of ancient texts. Both had the wisdom in the last part of their lives to devote themselves "to the completion of their literary labours."[116] Like Master Kong, the missionary-scholar Legge was learning a great moral lesson that comes only from the study of classical texts and in the transformative passage of a human life. This was the difficult struggle to become humble and wise, accomplishments, hyphenations, and revisions that come only in the course or *dao* of a human life. Most of all, it was moral discernment that was the secret of both philosophical knowledge and existential conversion. As the *Analects* said in Legge's translation, it is the ability of a "superior man" at the age of seventy "to follow what his heart desires without transgressing what is right." The extent to which James Legge was able to achieve this grace and wisdom when he surpassed the age of seventy remains to be seen.

CHAPTER ONE

Pilgrim Legge and the Journey
to the West, 1870-1874

And therefore, good Christian, come a little way with me [Good-Will], and I will teach thee about the way thou must go. Look before thee; dost thou see this narrow way? THAT is the way thou must go; it was cast up by the Patriarchs, Prophets, Christ, his Apostles; and it is as straight as a rule can make it: This is the way thou must go.

But said Christian, Is there no turnings nor windings, by which a Stranger may lose the way?

Good-Will. Yes, there are many ways butt down upon this, and they are crooked and wide: But thus thou mayest distinguish the right from the wrong, that only being straight and narrow. . . . Then Christian began to gird up his loins, and to address himself to his Journey. So the other [Good-Will] told him, that by that he was gone some distance from the Gate, he would come at the House of the Interpreter, at whose door he should knock, and he would shew him excellent things. . . .

Sir [Interpreter], said Christian, I am a man that am come from the City of Destruction, and am going to the Mount Zion; and I was told by the Man that Stands at the Gate, at the head of this way, that if I called here, you would shew me excellent things, such as would be an help to me in my Journey.

JOHN BUNYAN, *THE PILGRIM'S PROGRESS*, 1678

A PILGRIM'S PROGRESS

In the spring of 1873, thirty years after he first arrived as a missionary in the newly created colony of Hong Kong, James Legge prepared to leave his prophetic Land of Sinim. It was time to leave. Fifty-eight years old and completing a culminating three-year obligation to the Union Church and the *Chinese Classics* in Hong Kong, where, as the residents said, "only the temporary was permanent,"[1] the Reverend Doctor was more than ready to go home to Scotland and rejoin his long-suffering wife and family. A good but irrevocably hyphenated Christian missionary, he stood again at a pilgrim's gate of departure. Although he wistfully thought of returning to the colony to complete his sinological publications, he seems to have known that he would never return to this strange Oriental land.

Never much of a mass converter of the heathen Chinese, Legge had by this time proven his missionary credentials as a compassionate minister and educator to the Chinese community and his scholarly mettle as a translator and transmitter of Chinese traditions. However, he was in some ways more of a transformer of Westerners to a vision of a classical China than he was a converter of Chinese to the Christian gospel. Moreover, because of the hegemony of Western ways of knowing throughout the nineteenth century, some of Legge's understandings of the ancient Chinese tradition actually ended up rebounding on China's own understanding of itself, an act that had the effect of reinforcing an already existing self-image among the elite Ruist class of Chinese scholar-officials known to the West as Confucians. Indeed, Legge's perception of some Chinese texts as classics was guided by the age-old stream of Ruist commentary communicated to him by native teachers and traditional exegetical texts.

As the most important nineteenth-century inheritor of the humanistic tradition of sinological understanding initiated by Matteo Ricci and the Jesuit missionaries of the seventeenth and eighteenth centuries, Legge had permanently altered the meaning of the ancient Chinese sage known as Confucius (Kongzi, Master Kong, Kong Qiu, Zhongni; rarely, it seems, Kongfuzi) and such key Chinese terms as *Lunyu* (Digested conversations, Discourses and dialogues, or, as canonically standardized by Legge, the Horatian-sounding Analects), *ru* (the Confucians, scholars, or literati), and *jing* (classic, authoritative text, or, eventually, sacred book) for the West. Already in early Jesuit scholarship honorific and unusual titles such as "Kongfuzi" had been transformed in Latin translation into a name (Confucius) for a kind of quasi-Renaissance classical hero associated with a literate philosophical tradition of elevated moral teachings known as Confucianism (i.e., the *rujiao*, "teachings of the scholars or literati," or *rujia*, "school of the literati"—neither of which refers specifically to Kongzi as a founder-originator). With the triumph of Legge's Protestant evangelical episteme in the nineteenth century, this kind of Jesuitical and Enlightenment terminology took on a new set of more overtly sanctified and universal meanings. The moral paragon known as Kongzi, Master Kong, or Confucius assumed the aura of a Carlylian "great man" or a Protestant "religious reformer-founder" of an ancient theistic religious system called Confucianism.[2]

Ways Crooked and Wide

Given everything that had transpired in the previous three decades in Malacca and South China, it is safe to say that Legge's final departure from Hong Kong in 1873 was no simple leave-taking. This was not just another temporary furlough from the trials and tribulations of the foreign mission field; nor was it a typical retirement from an active life dedicated to missionary and scholarly work, to family, and to the church. Rather, Legge was embarking upon a final journey back to the West that was, in many ways, a pilgrim's passage home freighted with nostalgia about past frustrations and with hope about future possibilities. As the distillation of all that he had experienced as a proudly conscientious missionary-scholar, single-minded domestic patriarch, enlightened but stubborn educator, compassionate yet demanding pastor, and concerned colonial citizen, the events of his last months in China represent a singularly important transition to a new life and a new academic mode of being.

Legge was betwixt and between old evangelical certainties and new moral doubts, between an old theological apologetic and new—more ambiguously sympathetic, comprehensive, and comparative—ways of knowing the otherness of Chinese texts and persons. In keeping with his fervent Christian belief in the dynamic character of Evangelical conversion and the "fourfold" process of fulfilling human nature, Legge was entering into what he would have called another crucial "transitional" phase in his life, a liminal or interstitial zone separating different cultures, vocations, and beliefs. Legge successfully negotiates "ways crooked and wide" during this transitional year only by seeking a pilgrim's guidance, so to speak, from John Bunyan's allegorical Good-Will and Interpreter. The famous translator was in the process of being translated—a process involving significant rituals of physical translocation and permanent psychological transformation.[3] In the spirit of Bunyan's good Christian wayfarer, Legge would therefore "gird up his loins" and address himself fully to his long journey home to the West. There are many "excellent things" to be found by a good Christian who does his duty to man and God.

Legge's gradually more sympathetic understanding of Master Kong and the ancient classics was tempering his overall awareness of himself, religion, morality, and humanity—as well as enlarging his methods of textual translation and personal intercourse. Ever since the time of the Anglican bishop J. W. Colenso's embarrassing capitulation to African doubts about the Old Testament, it was a Victorian canard to believe that a prolonged exposure to the exotic, and especially an overly sympathetic appreciation of the native point of view (which by the end of the 1880s was equated with an overabundance of tolerant "indifferentism" and an overindulgence in the new comparative science of religions) tended to produce a person who was only hopelessly, pathetically, and comparatively religious.[4] Moncure Conway, an American Unitarian living in London and an erstwhile lay disciple of Max Müller's new science of comparative religions, recognized that the infamous Bishop Colenso, who had given "heed to the awakened doubt of the dark-skinned 'heathen' he went out to convert," was very much a "typical figure of the new generation" in the last part of the nineteenth century. Most curious in this regard is that Conway immediately goes on to identify another typical figure of the Colenso generation, another missionary who paid attention to the heathen—namely, Professor James Legge of Oxford

University.[5] Conway leaves us with the suggestion that Legge, like Colenso, had drunk too deeply and too long from the forbidden elixirs of accommodation and compromise.

A Considerable Emotion of Sorrow and Regret

Separated from his wife and children for more than three years and not far from his sixtieth birthday, Legge was tormented by pangs of homesickness and by sporadic physical infirmities—not the least of which were bouts of physical exhaustion, partial deafness, and, even more frightening, an episode of nocturnal sleepwalking and falling. But these were largely minor ailments of body and spirit and he was still, as the self-styled amanuensis of nineteenth-century sinology, Henri Cordier, observed at this time, a robustly vigorous "big man." A tall, corpulent, and rudely colored Scotsman, Legge had, according to the carefully discerning Cordier, the "air of a gentleman farmer."[6]

Legge's last three years in Hong Kong gave him the blessed opportunity to focus his ministerial energies on his pastorate to the English congregation at the Union Church (where he often had to conduct as many as four separate services on Sunday; he also met regularly with colonial soldiers, English prisoners, and Chinese prisoners) and to concentrate his scholarly talents on his "special work" of translation. Despite the difficult separation from his family, he tells us that those years in Hong Kong passed quickly—particularly because, in addition to his work at the Union Church, he was constantly preoccupied with his "studying and publishing."[7] Always noted for a ploughman's "habit for work," he had labored with earnest, though sometimes rather stolid, passion as a full-time pastor of the Union Church that he had founded back in 1843. During the last three years he expressly set himself the goal of rebuilding the congregation, which had diminished in the face of his previous divided responsibilities, the ignominious failure of a pastor appointed from London, and the sometimes halfhearted concern of the London Missionary Society.[8]

Legge's sermons from this period reveal "a considerable emotion of sorrow and regret" about his missionary career and the overall success of the China mission.[9] In contrast with the usual triumphalism of his earlier preaching, his Union Church sermons in the early 1870s sounded the discouraging theme that the "progress of Christianity" in China was "tardy." Or, as he once said from a postmillennialist perspective, "the result is not what we should of ourselves have expected from the representations of scripture as to the design of Christianity and the promise of its triumph." The problem of how to account for this "want of success" was clearly weighing heavily on Legge—as it was for many other frustrated missionaries at this time. He admitted that he might be accused of depicting the situation in "too gloomy colours." But ever righteous, he can only say that he "must speak according to the conviction of [his] heart."[10]

In one of these sermons, Legge (following his brother George's views) defends the proposition that the real "uniqueness" of the Gospel is, in counterdistinction to "other religions," which are "all exclusive," to be found in its "impartiality" and "universality." Christianity knows, as he put it, "no system of class legislation" and, although "political and social changes have always accompanied the spread of Christianity," it cannot be directly equated with any particular form of government or social system. Such sociopolitical developments and reform are "things that must occur in the progress of society," not because Christianity necessarily causes them or disrupts traditional societies. Indulging in a bit of typical Victorian anti-Semitism, he remarks that it was precisely the "spirit of pride and exclusiveness" of the Jews that led them to reject a gospel open to "people for all nations." And because of this vanity, "they themselves were crushed beneath the wheels of the Chariot of the Gospel."[11]

The crux of Legge's last sermons at the Union Church is the issue of repentance and the purgative journey necessary to achieve the moral character and personal integrity of a "disciple of Christ." Remarkable is his acute sense of the difficulty, if not the impossibility, of living up to the fullness of "Christian character," especially on the part of those who are merely "hanging on to the congregation" and those who "stood aloof" from the Christian fellowship of the communion services. Given the tenor of the times within the British empire, and the increasingly acute Victorian "crisis of faith" after midcentury, it is significant that Legge mentions his awareness of a "worldliness of heart" and a "current of unbelief" within the Union congregation and in the larger European community.[12] From the very beginning of the colony, there was what one commentator called the "frequent spectacle of European irreligion" and a "very prevalent" desecration of the Sabbath.[13]

These and other indications suggest that Legge was working out a new self-definition that acknowledged, incorporated, and transcended his partial failures as a missionary and preacher. His experience of the Orient was inexorably reorienting his identity from that of a hyphenated missionary-scholar to what was now coming to the fore in academic circles: a "scientific" and "impartial" professional scholar of China known as a "sinologist." This new profession was not just a variation of the traditional Victorian figure of the "gentleman scholar" or "man of letters," but for the first time within British academic circles was a new vocational option within the vast disciplinary sea of Orientalism.[14] Legge's one real and unquestioned success during his years in China was, after all, as an educator and a scholar. Whereas he worried about his "deficiencies" as a missionary and preacher, Legge was now being affirmed by Stanislas Julien in Paris and others as the *facile princeps* of sinological Orientalists.[15]

Legge's Middle Path

Legge first received international recognition for his Chinese scholarship in the *British Quarterly* in 1867 and a few years later in the *Edinburgh Review,* the oldest, best-known, and most influential of the Whiggish literary reviews published in Great Britain. But the strongest public validation of Legge's new identity as a sinologue is found in Ernst Johann Eitel's long analysis of "The She King [the Book of Poetry]," the very first article in the inaugural volume of the new scholarly China coast publication known as the *China Review* (1872–1901).[16] Eitel was himself a hyphenated missionary-scholar in Hong Kong whose career was also moving in a more scholarly and secular direction. Drawing upon his background as a German with a Ph.D. degree from Tübingen, his editorship of the *China Review* was already setting new critical standards for Chinese scholarship.[17] Furthermore, in 1879, a few years after Legge became the first professor of Chinese at Oxford, Eitel left the London Missionary Society to continue his editorship and to enter into a career as the Inspector of Schools in Hong Kong and the private secretary to the colonial governor, Sir John Pope Hennessy.[18]

Eitel's review was the first balanced appraisal of Legge's work from the standpoint of the best academic or critical scholarship of the day. In this sense, it was noteworthy that Eitel felt that Legge had actually surpassed the French academicians: "there is not a foreigner in China or out of it, whose acquaintance with the classical lore of the Flowery Kingdom can compete in extent of range, thoroughness and solidity with that of the Rev. Dr. Legge." Moreover, in comparison with the more confrontational tone in the prolegomena to the *Analects,* Legge's later work on the *Book of Poetry* showed a more mature and impartial scholarship. His "acquaintance with the Chinese textbooks and commentaries" had "deepened and grown more intimate." So also had his "judgment of the value of Chinese thought" impressively "mellowed and ripened by years of experience."[19]

Eitel was particularly well acquainted with the latest Germanic "higher criticism" concerned with philological sources (i.e., what Eitel calls *Quellenstudium,* involving both comparative linguistic and historical research methods). Noting earlier European editions of the *Book of Poetry* (primarily Father Lachmarme's version published in 1783 and its later redactions; Sir John Davis's rendition was only a "paraphrase"), he therefore commends Legge's attention to the "history, variations, and mutilations of the text" for showing as much "pedantically minute research as [Constantin von] Tischendorff ever gave to his recension of the sacred text of the New Testament."[20] Eitel remarks that Legge's translation was "eminently faithful to the original" and was based "on sound etymological principle and clear conception of what French critics generally call the 'spirit' of the language." Eitel said, however, that he could "not shut [his] eyes against a certain rigid stateliness, almost amounting to prosy heaviness and quaintness." These were unfortunate qualities that, according to Eitel, "characterized Dr. Legge as a translator in his previous publications and come out more strongly here where he is dealing with quaint poetical effusions which he was not enthusiast enough to admire very highly."[21]

Eitel also correctly noted that, "as a commentator," Legge upheld a "perfectly independent position." More so than in his earlier volumes, he had "not adopted the views of any particular school of Chinese commentators." As the leading censor of "amateur Sinologues" who indulge too wildly in comparative speculation linking China with the Aryan language and tradition, Eitel was pleased to see that Legge had not "delivered himself . . . to any of the modern factions of European Sinologues." Comparing the "critical spirit" of the Zhu Xi school with the "old conservative school" that favored "allusive or allegorical hermeneutics super-imposed on the text," Eitel found that Zhu Xi, though "cramped" as is "every Chinese critic by an undue admixture of national vanity," represented a "system of interpretation based on the true hermeneutic principle" that attacked old beliefs with the "weapons of rationalistic criticism" and located "the meaning of every single Ode or passage in an Ode" in the "text itself."[22] Most impressive for Eitel was that Legge was not "captivated" by either Chinese school and maintained his own "exegetical impartiality." Agreeing with Wang Tao's assessment of Legge's critical independence, Eitel says that, with a "dry sly humour," he "supplements the views" of the one with the other or "leaves the question at issue."[23]

Legge's textual methods had the additional virtue of standing "in the middle" of the European debates between the "conjectural-emotional" school (associated with the Aryan comparativism of Joseph Edkins and Max Müller) and the "sober critical" school that applied mathematical and astronomical tests to textual questions (associated with John Chalmers in China). Praising Legge's ability to avoid both the "misty halo of fanciful conjecture" and the "cold blasts of negative criticism," Eitel nevertheless found him too trusting of the chronology of the *Book of Poetry*. Whereas Legge felt that *"in the whole"* the Chinese text preserved "a truthful outline of what actually happened," Eitel more radically believed that the *Book of Poetry* was an orally transmitted compilation only recorded and edited "within a few centuries of the time of Confucius."[24]

Ascending a Peak

During his last years in Hong Kong, Legge burned "the mid-night lamp" and honed his sinological skills not only on his translation of the controversial *Book of Poetry* (1871), but also on the formidable *Spring and Autumn Annals* and *Zuo's Commentary* (1872). As his expertise and confidence grew, Legge put more and more effort into the commentarial and historical sources for his translations (crucially assisted by Wang Tao's extensive digests of native commentary) and the volumes expanded in size and in the time required for their completion.[25] As he learned, the work of translation involved more than the "slovenly and unscholarly practice" of paraphrase. Critical for any translation was the development of hermeneutical methods of philological and historical interpretation, tools that in Legge's estimation must draw upon the best Chinese and Western traditions of textual analysis but also require refinement by each individual scholar.[26]

Legge described his actual working routine as primarily a matter of plodding perseverance: "page gets trotted off after page—it is just like ascending [a] peak—if you stand at the bottom and dwell on the distance and the steepness of the ascent, the feet almost refuse to move." At times, he says that "the toil seems too great to be undertaken," but you simply must "gird up your loins and go at it, you pant and groan and perspire—but ere long the summit is attained."[27] In 1873 Legge had not yet translated all of the traditional Five Classics, but he had established a base camp very near the summit.[28] Writing in the preface to his rendition of the *Spring and Autumn Annals* dated September 26, 1872, he noted that he still had the "so very voluminous" *Record of Rites* and the "so sui generis" *Book of Changes* to translate and annotate. Only then would the task which he had undertaken so many years ago "be fully accomplished." Although he had to return to England, he declared that he would "not allow anything to interfere with the completion" of his "labours upon them" and may even have contemplated returning to Hong Kong to ensure their publication.[29]

A New Era in Hong Kong

During his last three busy, yet domestically forlorn, years in Hong Kong, Legge more than fulfilled his twin commitments to the Union Church and the Confucian classics. He felt comfortable in telling his wife back in Dollar, Scotland, that "in the two objects which I had in view I was entirely successful." Concerning his literary labors, he goes on to say that "it is much to have got off out of my hands the fourth and fifth volumes of the Classics." Taking pride in the increased sophistication of his scholarship in these most recent volumes, he also claims to her, and this is a judgment that would be repeatedly challenged by critics of his time and later, that he had attained a style of translation that did "not leave much to be desired." He is happy to note that "the ruins of Union Church have been built up again, and the congregation handed over to Mr. Lamont [the new pastor] in a thoroughly satisfactory state."[30]

Beyond his pastoral duties at Union Church, Legge devoted much time to ministering to the European and Chinese communities. This involved, among other activities, making hospital calls to the sick and dying, cultivating the sparse sprouting of the native Christian churches, and preaching both to colonial soldiers and to Chinese prisoners. As a concerned elder statesman and wise sage, he also played a prominent and often outspoken role in the civic and intellectual life of Hong Kong, a city that was now one of the most commercially vigorous, architecturally ostentatious, and intraculturally complex outposts of the British empire in the East. No longer the dreaded "grave of Europeans," Hong Kong as a prosperous and civilizationally auspicious beacon of Victorian colonial policy epitomized the increasingly aggressive nature of Western commercial and political imperialism toward China in the last third of the nineteenth century. The Victorian saying was that, by acquiring Hong Kong, Great Britain "had cut a notch in the body of China as a woodsman cuts a notch in a great oak he is presently going to fell."

Writing in 1873 after five years spent in Hong Kong and wandering through China, the pioneering British photographer John Thompson remarked that the city of Victoria in the colony of Hong Kong, with "its splendid public buildings, parks and gardens, its docks, factories, telegraphs and fleets of steamers," could now be "fairly considered" as the "birthplace of a new era in eastern civilization." This "new era" as concretely exemplified in Hong Kong was primarily to be seen in its glorious fulfillment of the classic "imperial social arrangement" that complemented the usual British class structure with an expansive middle-class Victorian world "complete with cricket games, rabbit hunting and fancy dress balls." The wondrous grace of the British colony was that it was a place where reputations among the colonial inhabitants depended as much on appearance and self-made wealth as on inherited status. The increasingly large Chinese population in the colony was, on the other hand, "treated as a degraded race of people." As the Reverend George Smith of the Anglican Church Missionary Society reported, individual Chinese were "not permitted to go out into the public streets after a certain hour in the evening without a lantern and a written note from their European employer, to secure them from the danger of apprehension and imprisonment till the morning."[31]

Straightforward and Honest Men

In contrast with the general contempt directed toward the Chinese of the colony, Legge evinced an increasing, although halting and modulated, empathy toward Chinese acquaintances in the colony and toward Chinese historical figures he was encountering in his literary work. His charitable instincts were still often compromised by the apologetic need to demonstrate the absolute superiority of Christianity, but there were clear signs of intellectual and moral amelioration. In a lecture delivered at the City Hall on "Two Heroes of Chinese History," he favorably compared the ancient qualities (the virtues of social order, filial piety, royal duty, sympathy with human misery) of two Chinese feudal figures (Duke Hwan of Ts'e [Qi Huangong] and Duke Wan of Ts'in [Qin Wengong]) with the Carlylian heroism seen in English and Scottish tales.[32] The rather mean lesson he drew from this observation was that "morally and socially" the condition of the Chinese "is much the same" as it was in the days of its feudal heroes. The problem is one of political progress that, in the absence of "heavenly revelation," has never breathed "new life into the spirit of the people." As to whether or not the heavenly revelation of a Christian era was dawning for China, he seemed less sanguine, saying only that he must "leave it with Him" who "holds the heart of everyman in His hands." It is up to individual Christians to be "heroes of the highest style" and exemplify "real Christian principle" in their lives.

More poignant is that at the very beginning of this lecture, Legge describes a conversation he once had with "a well known Chinese gentleman" who was "sending one of his sons to England to be educated." Responding to the father's concern that his son be made a "straightforward and honest man," Legge said that he "could not guarantee that he would have those qualities unless he became, what his father was not, a Christian about whom there could be no mistake." What is interesting is that the father, while having no great objections to his son's becoming a Christian, replied as a good comparativist by saying: "I have also seen a great deal of what you call Christians, and of Parsees, Mahometans, and Jews as well; and I have come to the conclusion that straightforward, honest men are about equally rare among them all." Reacting to the Chinese gentleman's unexpected frankness, Legge retorts that he quickly "controverted his opinion, from which I vehemently dissented." He then somewhat lamely added that "straightforwardness and honesty" are attributes "more hopefully" looked for among "people whom we call Christians" than among "the other classes which he mentioned, and much more than among his countrymen." The qualifying term "hopefully" is the most revealing word used in this response and suggests, despite Legge's tart protestation, some creeping comprehension of the Chinese father's point.

Seeking Justice

Legge's difficulty in seeing any connection between the heroic greatness of past and present Chinese was further tested by a stinging review of the *Chinese Classics* appearing in the *Edinburgh Review,* the most famous literary journal of the time. Though published in 1869, this article apparently did not come to Legge's attention till sometime in the early 1870s.[33] Published anonymously (although the author can now be identified as the Anglican cleric the Very Reverend Charles Henry Butcher, who spent many years in Shanghai as a consular chaplain and then dean of the Shanghai Cathedral), it is a provocative overview of British attitudes toward China and Confucius—especially Legge's "unjust" and "abrupt unfriendliness" to the ancient Chinese master.[34] Butcher's review begins by praising Legge's "elaborate and conscientious translation" of the *Analects,* which should help to overcome some of the European "indifference to the Flowery Land."[35] But it quickly moves on to consider a vexatious "fault" in Legge's biography of the Master Kong: "He [Legge] is possessed with a passion the very converse of that which usually besets biographers. The more closely he examines his hero the less he likes him. Familiarity appears almost to have bred contempt. The intimacy which has lasted for twenty-one years ends in coldness."

Butcher finds Legge's general conclusions about the Chinese sage ("after long study of his character and opinions, I am unable to regard him as a great man") distinctly distressing. Legge's attitude toward Confucius displays a "strain of abrupt unfriendliness which seems unjustifiable." Butcher, who was apparently of a Broad Church Anglican background, also notes that Legge seems to deem it his "duty" to be "always weighing Confucius in the balance of the sanctuary." The "sayings of the Chinese Sage are perpetually thrown into disadvantageous comparison with the lessons of the Founder of Christianity, and his shortcomings and deficiencies are exhibited with merciless minuteness." And this is "hardly fair." According to Butcher, there is yet another blatant inconsistency in Legge's analytical procedures. When it happens, therefore, that "on one or two important doctrines several very plausible points of agreement between Christ and Confucius may be alleged," Legge "will not endure it for a moment." Butcher particularly reacts to the "injustice" of this kind of overly antagonistic method where words "lose their wonted sense, and a resemblance as clear as the sun in heaven is to be pronounced a divergence as wide as the poles, rather than a single anticipation of Christianity shall be found in Confucius."

Butcher also criticizes Legge's "stigmatized" view of Confucius as " 'unreligious and unspiritual.' " Finding this conclusion "too sweeping and severe," Butcher develops a theory on these matters that to some extent echoes Legge's revised evaluations of the Chinese master's religiosity and Confucianism's degenerative religious history (i.e., his writings in 1877, 1879, 1880, and 1893). Thus Butcher argues that Confucius actually accomplished a moral and spiritual reformation of the ancient religion (involving ethics, monotheism, and the rejection of ritualistic idolatry and materialism), although the Chinese people at the time of this reform had a "carnal" mindedness exactly comparable to the "Jews of the reign of Ahaz" and the Roman Catholics of the Middle Ages.[36]

Butcher ends his searching analysis of Legge with the stock Orientalist supposition that the relative lack of true religious "spirituality" and sublimity in Confucius is most likely due to the evident fact that the Chinese were "notoriously deficient in imagination." Confucius certainly had "many virtues" of the "thoroughly practical kind," but he was himself "utterly devoid of imagination and faith" and seems "to have ignored the truth that this faculty is one of the most powerful instruments of moral good."[37] In the larger sense of the needed "regeneration" of this "most ancient and arrogant of nations," Butcher notes that China is seen too typically as only a "swathed mummy, a rigid petrifaction, or a corpse" waiting for the revolutionary "galvanic battery" of "Western science and enterprise." But Butcher argues for understanding and investigating China's own indigenous institutions before resorting to "indiscriminate" destruction and coercive revolution. Concluding in a way that reflects Legge's own evolving views, Butcher says that "if investigation precede revolution, we may ourselves learn many useful lessons and correct many false impressions."[38]

Butcher's critique had a powerful effect on Legge—especially as it touched upon his scholarly judgments and his acute sense of personal justice.[39] This review may even be seen as marking an important way station in Legge's journey as a transcultural pilgrim and sinologue—that is, as a powerful stimulus to his unfolding sense of duty to "sympathetic comprehensiveness" in scholarship and his affirmation of the moral worth of Oriental "great men" and "heroes." Instead of "speedily and extensively" passing away, Legge's faith in, and even partial identification with, a great and heroic Confucius/Kongzi (and Mencius/Mengzi) will only expand and deepen. These developments are symbolically underscored by Legge's ritual journey to the Altar of Heaven and the burial mound of Kongzi in North China and are most explicitly found in his later reflections on Confucius and Confucianism.

Legge ended up agreeing in many ways with Butcher's view that Confucius's ideal of the superior man (stressing humility, straightforwardness, virtue over comfort, law over sensual gratification, respectful loyalty, kindness, and justice) had "nothing paltry, nothing local, nothing mean" about it. There was a dawning recognition that, as Butcher suggests, Kongzi's value system was very similar to the ethical code of a Victorian gentleman. Furthermore, Legge also came around to the position shared by Butcher and Max Müller: that the Chinese master, who "first taught that the proper study of mankind is man," actually anticipated a moral and methodological sensibility comparable to the spirit of the newly emerging "human sciences." Legge and Butcher would concur that Western scholars, if they honestly want to appreciate the unfairness of the usual criticism of Confucius and Confucianism, need only "look at home."

A PILGRIM'S PASSAGE HOME

He bent his mind to find the Dragon Den,
Firmly resolved to climb the Vulture Peak.
Through how many states did he roam beyond his own?
Through clouds and hills he passed ten thousand times.
He now leaves . . . to go [home] to the west;
He'll keep law and faith to reach the great void.
JOURNEY TO THE WEST (XIYOU JI), TRANSLATED BY A. C. YU

Translated from darkness, he finds himself in a region of marvellous light.
JAMES LEGGE, "THE FOURFOLD STATE OF MAN," 1871

Roaming beyond Many States

On March 29, 1873, Legge boarded the French mail steamer *Tigre*, bound
for Shanghai, the first stop on his last passage home.[40] Some five months
later, he arrived in Dollar, Scotland, for the long-delayed reunion with his
wife and family. This was no ordinary homeward journey. It was surely not
the most expeditious route home as, even in the days of sailing vessels
forced to circumnavigate the horn of Africa, one could, as Legge did back
in the 1840s, travel between England and Hong Kong in about three
months. In the new era of rapid travel and communication that emerged
during the last half of the nineteenth century—the age of accelerated
transportation and cultural intercourse involving steamships, railroads, and
the telegraph—an ordinary journey between China and England followed
a westward route through the Indian Ocean and the newly opened Suez
Canal, and usually took about a month and a half. This was the route tra-
versed by Legge in his most recent round-trip voyages in 1867 and 1870.

Legge said that his extended itinerary was only motivated by his sentimental need to tour parts of China he had not previously visited, especially since
these were his last days in the East. He also felt the urge to complete a Jules
Verne–style *tour du monde*.[41] On another occasion, he said that he was
influenced by a desire to "compare" the north with the south of China.[42]
There is also a genuine sense in which Legge's final journey and round the
world circuit—encompassing such typical "scenes and sights" as the "squalid"
grandeur of Peking, the Great Wall, and the Ming Tombs, as well as a boat trip
along the Grand Canal and the Yangtze (even today a typical tourist's itinerary)—constitute one of the earliest depictions of foreign tourism in China.[43]

Recreational tourism was a new phenomenon of the Victorian era created by the worldwide dominion of the Western nations that, for the first
time, made the exotic generally accessible. Just as by midcentury it was
rightly said that the sun never set on the British empire, the protective light
of the "higher" civilizations illuminated previously "darkened" continents,

rendering them subject to the ever-insistent and classifying order of Western rule and inquiry. The whole world could now be swiftly and efficiently explored, measured, mapped, telegraphically networked, and toured. This situation came about—as a handmaiden to the utilitarian machinery of global commerce, warfare, and colonial settlement, as well as the general policy of missionary expansion—through the ever-expanding technologies of rapid transport and communication, the imposition of diplomatic rights of national recognition and free passage, and the changing traditions of middle-class leisure and sport in the nineteenth century.[44]

But Legge's prolonged trip throughout northern China and then home to the West via an eastward route through Japan and the United States was not a simple instance of a lingering farewell to an exotic land or a tourist's impulse to see the sights and to circumnavigate the globe. The destinations in question, destinations that were religiously and emotionally charged for Legge, are especially the three northern Chinese sites of the Altar of Heaven in Peking, the holy mountain of Tai in Shandong province, and the tomb of Confucius (and Mengzi/Mencius) in the town of Qufu (Ch'u-fu). All three of these are traditional sacred sites—the high holy places of the ancient heathen, and ongoing imperial, religion in China. In this sense, these sites are especially potent destinations for pilgrims mindful of how these places, in particular, link the present with the ancient Ruist and imperial traditions recorded in the classics. And Legge, more so than any other Westerner of the nineteenth century, was acutely aware that travel to these locations was tantamount to a journey in space that was also a trip back in time, back to the very wellsprings of all that had religious, moral, and historical significance in China.[45]

Changes Deep-Down in the Essence of the Soul

This was a voyage designed, both consciously and unconsciously, to validate and valorize Legge's own changing understanding of China. For a foreigner such as Legge to travel to these places, places that were the concrete embodiment of sentiments he had only abstractly encountered, translated, and transmitted in his *Chinese Classics,* had a special gravity (although he was not the first Westerner or, for that matter, the first Protestant missionary to visit any of these sites).[46] His destinations can be seen as stations in his own inward journey of self-translation, a journey to the heart of heathen darkness, to the very source of China's Confucian otherness. This was a journey that would have disturbing, even scandalous, implications for more conventional missionaries.[47]

As Legge once said, a human life "as the Christian conceives it" is best "compared to a voyage." It is, moreover, often "a tempestuous voyage, and with a poor skiff, and at times we may reel to and fro like a drunken man, and be at our wits end, with the storm around and destruction threatening." But, as he concludes, "skilful seamanship struggles with all of this, and when the tempest is over there are sunny skies, and shinning seas and here and there safe haven."

In his sermons on the "Fourfold State of Man," Legge often referred to the passage from lower to higher states of life as a "pilgrim's progress" that moves a human being from the "City of Destruction" to the "City of God" (passing from the "sinful" or "natural" state through the "transitional" and "regenerate" states to the "Christian state"). This is reminiscent of Bunyan's pilgrim, but Legge is also following the ideas of Bishop Joseph Butler.[48] It is the last, a "Christian state," a "change deep-down in the essence of the soul," that is manifest in such qualities as a "habitual self-improvement" and other moral qualities, along with a sense of "security and blessedness." Most of all, the change "must be manifest in a constant consciousness and a consistent life." The implication is that Legge saw himself as the inveterate pilgrim who is always approaching, but never fully attaining, the final state. His regular state of mind and character would probably best be described as the "regenerate" state, which, as he says by way of its relation with the natural and transitional phases, is equivalent to the "converted" state of having faith (which gives rise to repentance and the "renovation" of character). The point is that continuous change, and often backsliding, characterizes each stage of the process. There is always, as he put it, the problem of the constant "peccability of Christians."[49]

On to the Higher Civilization of Shanghai

Legge's travels in North China began with his arrival in Shanghai on April 2, 1873, and ended with his return to the city at the end of May. His time in Shanghai, the most fully hybrid Chinese-European city along the coast, neatly frames his pilgrim's tour through the Manchu capital of Peking and the largely unsullied hinterland of North China. By the early 1870s, Shanghai had already become the greatest of the treaty ports of China and was the crucial staging point for all ventures inland to northern or central China. Above all, Shanghai was a Chinese city transformed by foreign influence and entrepreneurship, a place where, even more than in Hong Kong, the commercial and cultural avarice of the Western powers was arrogantly displayed. Within the large foreign community, especially for those with business interests but also for many missionaries, there was a powerful Orientalist rationale for the Western transfiguration of Shanghai, a rationale largely couched in rhetoric that emphasized the city's exemplification of the higher civilizational progress and dynamism brought to China by the Western powers.

John Thompson's photographic images and accompanying description of the city in the early 1870s document the common British experience that, when arriving in Shanghai, it was easy to imagine that one "had been suddenly transported to one of [the] great English ports." This was an "illusion" fostered by the "crowd of shipping, the wharves, warehouses, and landing-stages, the stone embankment, the elegance and costliness of the buildings, the noise of constant traffic in the streets, the busy roads, smooth as a billiard-table, and the well-kept garden that skirts the river." All such constructions afforded comforting "evidence of foreign taste and refinement." Nevertheless, one had only to "drive beyond the foreign settlement to dispel the dream, and to find the native dwellings huddled together, as if pressed back to make way for the higher civilization."[50] Legge's own feelings about the spectacle of Shanghai were more ambivalent than Thompson's. Certainly he was less confident in the evidence of higher civilizational progress afforded by "foreign taste and refinement." Though impressed by the energy and bustle of the streets, noting the presence of more than seven thousand "passenger wheelbarrows," he also says that the famous Shanghai Bund seemed mostly a "display of the pride of civilized life and its vanity." It awakened in him "little complacency," even though "thousands of Chinese looked on with delighted admiration."[51]

The Squalor of Peking

After several days of meeting with missionary friends such as William Muirhead, Alexander Wylie, and the former American missionary and now diplomat Samuel Wells Williams, and partaking of the hospitality and political intrigue of the foreign community (at the time of the visit of the Russian Grand Duke Alexis), Legge left Shanghai and made his way by boat to Tianjin (T'ien-tsin; sometimes romanized as Teen-tsin in the nineteenth century), the river port city for Peking. From Tianjin he traveled overland by native mule cart and was subjected to the jarring disrepair of the roads and the ever-present "filth" of roadside hostelries instead of the relative luxury of the foreign steamships. Reaching the fabled city of Peking (see figure 12) for the first time in his life on April 16, 1873, Legge reports that his initial sight of this vast imperial capital of towers and pagodas, particularly the imposing outer and inner city walls, made a "grand impression" on him: "I never saw anything so imposing as that wall with its buttresses, gates, and towers, and I could understand how travellers, entering the city on horseback, have been known to dismount and shake hands while they congratulate one another on having reached a city of so noble an appearance."[52]

As with the illusion of Shanghai's "higher civilization," Legge's first vision of Peking proved to be a romantic "enchantment" that was quickly dissolved by the full realization that "dirt and dust everywhere abound." This was, moreover, not a matter of mere "dirt and dust" (the reality of which, given the dry wind and the loess soil, was a fact of life in traditional Peking) but rather—as was more typically Hannah Mary Legge's horrified reaction

Figure 12. Street scene, Peking. Photograph, ca. late 1860s, from John Thompson, *Illustrations of China and Its People,* vol. 4 (London: Sampson Low, Marston, Low, and Searle, 1874), plate 9.

to Chinese things unsanitized by European order—a case of "indescribable filth," "squalor," "ruin," and "decay."[53]

Staying within the Chinese city at the London Missionary Society head-quarters, where he was graciously hosted by the Edkinses and Dudgeons, Legge spent several busy weeks in Peking, noting at one point his several long talks with the rather stiff Thomas Wade at the British Legation.[54] Using the society's headquarters as his base, he toured various sites in and around the city, including the Great Wall, the Ming Tombs (where walking the "avenue of animals" he felt a "wantonness of barbaric grandeur"), the Summer Palace (burned by the French and British troops in 1860), the Great Bell Tower, the Palace of Harmony Lamasery, and among other attractions, the Confucian temple in Peking (viewing there, appropriately enough, a set of classics carved in stone). In the midst of describing these activities, at least in the long article written for popular consumption in *The Oriental,* Legge includes his reflections on the increasingly controversial "question of missionary success." Given the escalating Chinese hostility toward missionaries living in the interior of China since the time of the Tianjin Treaty and the statistics on the very meager number of converts attracted to Protestant Christianity, Legge comments that "there are some who are prepared to deny that any great results,

Figure 13. The Altar of Heaven, Peking. Photograph, ca. 1873, from John Thompson, *Illustrations of China and Its People* (London: Sampson Low, Marston, Low, and Searle, 1873–1874), plate 16.

if any Christian results at all, have yet accrued from the labours of Protestant missionaries in China." Others venture "to say that our plans are not the best, and we ourselves not the men, for so peculiar and difficult a field."[55]

The Altar of Heaven

While always supporting the general spirit of the "great commission" of foreign missions, Legge had good reason to feel that missionary policy was sometimes neither very effective nor entirely Christian. Given his frustrations about his own missionary career, he probably thought himself to be among those men not in the long run suited for such a special career. This was, after all, a field of endeavor made increasingly "peculiar and difficult" not just by Chinese hostilities and arrogance, but also by the antagonistic theology, insensitive methods, sectarian infighting, and nationalistic jealousies of the mission societies. Evidence of these feelings is especially seen in his visit to the hallowed grounds of the Altar of Heaven (see figure 13), an ancient structure situated in an enclosed park in the Chinese section of Peking three miles to the south of the Manchu imperial palace. It is this that Legge calls the "finest sight" in all of Peking.[56]

The imperial Altar and Temple of Heaven in Peking were the most important monuments to what Legge believed to be continuing sacrificial rituals of true monotheistic worship to Shangdi/Tian, a practice that, over the centuries and though reformed during the Ming dynasty, was clearly distorted by idolatrous elements. These rituals were, moreover, sadly restricted to the imperial household only. In keeping with his developing historical appreciation of Chinese religion, Legge understood the Altar of Heaven to be the single most powerful sign of China's original and reformed faith in the Divine. Furthermore, it was Legge's view that foreign mentors, missionaries, and scholars could help China reactivate its inherent ability for religious, moral, and civilizational progress in the Western Christian manner. What was needed for the salvation of China was not its complete capitulation to foreign treaties and terms, but its transformation and fulfillment through the use of existing native resources.

Accompanied by a small party of missionary associates, Legge visited the "most important of all the religious structures in China" on April 21.[57] This was, as Legge said, an event imbued with "much of a pilgrim spirit." Describing the triple circular terraces of the open-air altar, paved with blue-white marble and progressively 210, 150, and 90 feet in diameter, he says that, as he approached the structure, he "called to mind how the worship of the Supreme God had been maintained in China for—say 4,000 years, without any symbol of idolatry, on this and similar altars, according to the situation of the capital which has varied at different times." This spot was, as he emphatically declares, "holy ground" and he felt compelled to take his shoes "from off of [his] feet"—an extraordinary and provocative act for any Protestant missionary of this period. As he said in a letter to his wife: "I never felt under a more holy awe than when I was there."[58]

Legge described the traditional "worship" and "prayer" that took place at this site "under no roof and with no image of the Divine Being."[59] On the holiest day of the winter solstice, the emperor kneeled and bowed "before the spirit of God" and, laying his hand on the uppermost altar stone, performed the "principal prayer of the occasion" by acknowledging himself as God's priestly "servant or minister." These actions were then consummated by the "special burnt-offering" of a whole bull to Heaven (Tian/Shangdi). Although he does not explicitly make the point, his language suggests the similarity of these Chinese practices and the ancient Jewish Temple sacrifice.[60]

Legge's explanation of the altar and the imperial rites is generally accurate, but there was much disagreement at that time (and down to the present day) about whether or not these activities could legitimately be interpreted as expressions of monotheistic worship and prayer.[61] A. P. Happer, Legge's most vociferous critic and the influential American missionary editor of the *Chinese Recorder and Missionary Journal*, went out of his way to document what he felt was the idolatrous nature of the imperial rituals at the Altar of Heaven. Happer admitted the "striking resemblances" of the Chinese imperial practices with Mosaic sacrifices (although there was no awareness of the doctrine of atonement in China, "no idea of substitution of an innocent victim as a propitiation for the sins of the guilty"), due to "dispersion from the Tower of Babel via Noah." But contrary to Legge's views, the Chinese state religion had quickly substituted the objects of nature for the true God and fallen into an idolatry and deification of nature, especially dualistic sky and earth worship, identical to that seen in other heathen traditions.[62]

Before leaving the upper area of the altar, Legge says that he "gathered the party" and then, "join[ing] hands around the circular slab," they all proceeded to sing a Christian doxology:

> Praise God, from whom all blessings flow.
> Praise Him all creatures here below,
> Praise Him above, ye Heavenly host;
> Praise Father, Son and Holy Ghost.[63]

This impromptu liturgy engendered an inner prayer that Legge felt certain was shared by all of the others making up this peculiar choral union upon the stark heathen mound: "each praying in his heart that the time may soon come when the sovereign and people of China shall know God as He has been revealed to us by His Son."

This strange scene of shoeless Christian pilgrims singing Christian prayers at the Chinese Altar of Heaven powerfully evokes the plaintive disposition and comparativist temper of Alfred Tennyson's poem *In Memoriam:*

> And falling with my weight of cares
> Upon the great world's altar-stairs
> That slope through darkness up to God
> I stretch lame hands of faith, and grope,
> And gather dust and chaff, and call
> To what I feel is Lord of all,
> And faintly trust the larger hope.[64]

It is the "larger" intellectual and moral "hope," groping upon "the great world's altar-stairs," that leads from "darkness up to God." Such are the sentiments seemingly experienced by Legge kneeling in prayer at the pagan altar. He did not doubt the truth of his Evangelical God or Christianity, but his incredible actions at the Altar of Heaven, and his prayerful "larger hope," conspicuously challenged conventional missiological ways of knowing and evaluating non-Christian traditions.

Legge's behavior at the Altar of Heaven suggests a connection with the early Jesuit missionaries who accommodated traditional Chinese rituals, actions that in the seventeenth and eighteenth centuries scandalized more orthodox Catholic missionaries and the papacy. It is remarkable that, immediately after visiting the Altar of Heaven, Legge paid his respects at the old Portuguese cemetery in Peking where the tombs of the famous "Romish missionaries" (Ricci, Schaal, Lombard, Verbiest, and others) were found. Given the usual anti-Catholic bias of Evangelical missionaries, this was no trivial act, and Legge was certainly aware that he could be accused of some Jesuitical tendencies. While honoring the memory of the Jesuit pioneers, he was therefore careful to articulate his general antipathy to "popish" practices. He pointedly notes the "incense urns" and other symbols of syncretistic idolatry set before the tomb of Matteo Ricci.

Ascending China's Holy Mountain

Legge left Peking on May 1, accompanied by Joseph Edkins and Alexander Williamson. Going first to Tianjin, where they said farewell to Williamson, Legge and Edkins turned south into Shandong province. It was fitting that Edkins—small, lean, and gray-bearded (see figure 14)—was Legge's companion: both were Scotsmen, old acquaintances, and London Missionary Society colleagues, and both, over the years, had become increasingly involved with scholarship and what could be called a liberal and liberating pilgrim's approach to the problems of China's difference. Edkins was also a seasoned resident of the north who spoke fluent Mandarin, as Legge did not. Though eight years junior to Legge, Edkins was somewhat more acculturated to native ways, so that, for example, he "went in a good deal for Chinese food." Legge says that he had little liking for such food, except "in the matter of hardboiled eggs, bread, and sometimes a bowl of rice."[65]

Traveling by means of native carts (see figure 15) that were not "Milton's 'cany waggons light,' " the two wayfarers embarked upon the most arduous and alien part of their trip, passing through parts of China rarely visited by Europeans. Legge describes the traveling conditions and their "rough and ready" way of life:

> I have a mattress, which just fits into the bottom of the cart; but at the back of the vehicle is a box of stores, my traveling bag, a bundle of wraps, a canister of tea, and other odds and ends, and against these leans the mattress, which thus supports my back. On the front part of it, moreover, is my double blanket, folded so as to cover upon both sides as a buffer between my knees and the hard sides of the cart. On it I sit, and have my rug by me besides, which I find useful as a protection from the sharp air of the moon and from the sun later in the day, as his rays blaze on my protruding legs. My portmanteau is strapped on the cart behind outside. When we came to a halt for the night, all the baggage is carried inside, and my first business is to lay my rug on the *kang* or bedstead, over it the mattress, and then my blanket. That has never yet been too warm.

The two travelers eventually passed through the city of Dezhou (romanized by Legge as Tih-chow) and then, on May 11, they arrived in Jinan (romanized as Ts'e-nan), the capital of Shandong province. Legge liked much of the city, especially its fountains, but he was again struck by the material "decay" of Chinese cities unenlightened by Western ways of civic

Figure 14. The Reverend Joseph Edkins, B.A., D.D. *The Chronicle of the London Missionary Society* 7, no. 73 (1898): 8. Reproduced courtesy of the London Missionary Society/Council for World Mission archive.

maintenance. As he says, the "evil" of this kind of decadence seems to arise "from the want of a public spirit and municipal management of affairs as much as from a natural liking for dirt." China, it seems to Legge, "has no idea of carrying on the struggle with the natural progress of things to decay and dilapidation."[66]

Partly following the Grand Canal during this phase of the trip, the two travelers headed toward the ancient town of Confucius's birth and death. But before reaching the Chinese master's ancestral home, Legge once more played the role of religious pilgrim. The two wayfarers decided to ascend the four-thousand-foot-high Mount Tai (Taishan, called Tae by Legge), the "most famous" sacred mountain and "pilgrimage hill" in all of

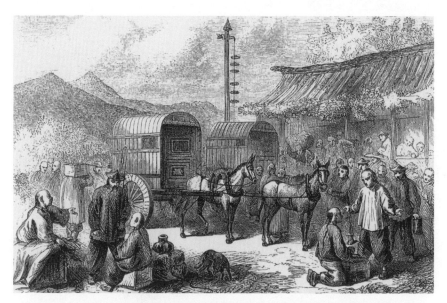

Figure 15. Chinese mule cart. Engraving from A. Williamson, *Journeys in North China, Manchuria, and Eastern Mongolia; With Some Accounts of Corea* (London: Smith, Elder, 1870), 1: frontispiece.

China (see figure 16).[67] As recorded in the Chinese classics, this mountain was an ancient site of imperial sacrifice and worship, as well as the locus of various other imperial and popular religious traditions. In the course of time, it had become one of the "principal seats of the Taouist [Daoist] superstition." This "most debased system" had a "temple of one of its principal deities on the very summit" and, a little below the summit and to the east, a popular temple devoted to a "Sacred Mother" who had the power to make women pregnant.[68] Not yet having much of an appreciation for either ancient Daoist literature or the living Daoist tradition, Legge makes only the most perfunctory comments. He says that he was "sad to see Confucianism so dishonored in relation to Taouism." The temples on the mountain, especially the one Confucian temple, were found to be filthy and "dilapidated" and the pilgrims appeared to be "utterly lost and degraded."[69]

Stopping at a hostelry before ascending the mountain, Legge records an incident of intercultural misunderstanding that was, he assures us, the "only one of the kind in the whole journey." After dinner, a "bevy of young ladies" was sent to the pious missionaries' rooms to entertain them with music and, as he delicately phrases it, to "help us otherwise to pass the time." Indignant, they "quickly sent them away" and informed the Chinese

Figure 16. Pilgrim's map of Taishan, ca. 1900. Drawing from Édouard Chavannes,
Le T'ai Chan (Paris: Ernest Leroux, 1910), facing page 4.

landlord of "the enormity of letting such questionable characters come about his establishment."

The next day, after hiring four men, Legge and Edkins were carried in mandarin style up the mountain in chairs, observing along the way an all-pervasive "idol worship." Legge says that he was especially bothered by the crowds of beggars and by a man, wearing a heavy cangue on his neck in penance for the sickness of his parents, who was slowly and painfully making his way up the thousands of steps leading to the top of the mountain. Feeling that "there was in his case the perversion of what was good," Legge says that he "tried to say something . . . of the one and only God, who hears and answers prayer, and of Christ, whose yoke," unlike the futility of the self-imposed purgative ritual of the Chinese cangue or of Romish penitential practices, "was easy." Legge does not tell us the outcome of this encounter, but the image of this bizarre situation that comes to mind is one of a gawky foreigner awkwardly descending from the elevated comfort of a sedan chair to offer some scraps of saving wisdom to a Chinese man trying desperately to complete his ritual of filial repentance. Speaking in halting Mandarin Chinese in a didactic manner reserved for heathens and Catholics, this presumptuous stranger proceeded to instruct the poor pilgrim in some of the fine points of evangelical theology. It can only be assumed that the Chinese penitent was more dumbfounded than enlightened by this well-intentioned but ludicrously insensitive message.

Standing on the Grave of the Great Sage

Leaving Mount Tai on May 15, the two stalwart sojourners had to pass through extensive poppy fields as they approached the "town of Confucius." Legge remarks on his "melancholy interest" in these fertile fields because, as a result of the "profitableness" of the burgeoning native opium business, they had been recently planted with opium poppies. "Our journey," he says, "brought the fact to light that the same thing is going on in Shan-tung [Shandong] and other eastern parts of the empire." Moreover, the poppy cultivation "all proceeds in defiance of the Government,—to the weakening of its authority, and the demoralization of the people. The problem of how China is to be delivered from the evil of opium-smoking becomes greatly complicated by it." The lesson he drew from this was not to justify the continuation of the British opium trade (the Chinese were now growing and trading it themselves). Rather, in keeping with Legge's Whiggish political bent as well as his Christian sentiments, he prophesies that while "China may crumble away, demoralized and disorganized by the growth of the [opium] habit," Great Britain will "find that a retribution overtakes it for its policy in regard to the opium traffic." Britain's judgment may come about "more slowly perhaps, but not less surely."

TOMB OF CONFUCIUS.

Figure 17. Mound tomb of Kongzi (Confucius), Qufu. Engraving from
A. Williamson, *Journeys in North China, Manchuria, and Eastern Mongolia; With
Some Accounts of Corea* (London: Smith, Elder, 1870), 1: 230.

Edkins observed that the poppy fields seemed a "thing of bad omen" and
a sad "sign of the time" as even the teaching of the Master Confucius "cannot sufficiently brace the moral energy of his countrymen."[70] With a sadness in their hearts as they entered the "country of Confucius," they approached the outskirts of the sage's holy city (Qufu) and first came across
the Konglin or Forest of Kong, which contained the graves of Kongzi and
his descendants.[71] Finding the grave site in the ancient forest, Legge says
that he immediately climbed to the top of Kongzi's burial mound (see
figure 17). Here he mused on the "remarkable man who lay beneath."
Haunted by the generations of Chinese who had stood at this very spot and
reminiscing in a comparative vein, he recalled his visit in 1846 to the island
of Saint Helena and the "open and empty grave of the first Napoleon." The

Carlylian historical question of "heroes" and "greatness" then arose in his mind: "Which of the two, Confucius or Napoleon, was the greater man?" Quickly answering his own rhetorical question, he surprisingly states that he is "inclined to give the palm to the Chinese sage. No other has had so lasting and profound an influence on such multitudes of his fellow-men, and some of the moral and social principles which he enunciated will never lose their value." Immediately identifying himself as a "Sinologue," Legge admits in the best critical manner that "notwithstanding the speculations and reasonings of myself and other Sinologues, it still remains to exhibit in a thoroughly satisfactory manner the characteristics of Confucius and of his teachings, which so powerfully affected his immediate disciples, and by which he continues to retain such a hold on the hearts and minds of all classes of the Chinese people." These are extraordinary statements given his published opinions in 1861 and directly forecast his revisionary estimate of Confucius's true "greatness" in his final Oxford edition of the *Classics* in 1893.[72]

There are other aspects of Legge's stay in the Qufu area that are in keeping with his growing appreciation of Kongzi and the contradictions of the tradition associated with him. Thus he notes his excursion to the temple of the famous executor of the "mandate of heaven," the Duke of Zhou, and his visit, on May 18, to the temple and burial site of the moral philosopher and second greatest sage of the Ruist literati tradition, Mengzi or Mencius. More pathetic was when the travelers discovered that, having switched from mule carts to wheelbarrows for transportation, their new "chairmen" were direct descendants of the great sage Kong. Legge can only remark that it was truly "something to think of that we, barbarians, should be wheeled along the country by descendants of the Sage." For Legge, the servile and illiterate condition of these men only served to illustrate the failures of the system of education in the Qing dynasty. "There is not," as Legge sadly observes, "a single free school for the benefit of Confucius's descendants."[73]

Shanghai and Japan

Returning to Shanghai by the Grand Canal and the Yangtze River, Legge was pleased to be able to indulge in his favorite pastime of bird-watching. He records his observations of cormorant fishing, as well as of cuckoos, larks, and crows—all of which prompted him to reflect on the seeming lack of any Chinese interest in "natural history." Legge notes that he had lost fourteen pounds during his arduous two-month trek. Moreover, although his health was good during the trip, he was weakened, after spontaneously "feasting on some Mulberry leaves," by a severe bout of diarrhea. With mock biblical guilt, he reports to his wife, "Retribution came, and I had continually all the afternoon to be quitting the barrow and running aside into the fields." He also says that, in contrast to the increasing talk about the hostility of the Chinese to foreigners, he had only the "highest praise" for the Chinese they encountered, even in places totally unfamiliar with foreigners. "Between Peking and Shanghae," he was astonished that, aside from being the "grazing stock" for the curious, he "did not see an angry look, and hardly heard an uncivil word."

Back within the European enclave of Shanghai and fresh from their tour of China's "holy land," the two scholarly pilgrims were invited by the North China Branch of the Royal Asiatic Society to speak about their travels. Meeting on a Monday, with learned men such as Alexander Wylie, Henri Cordier, and Thomas Kingsmill in attendance, both Legge and Edkins were specially recognized for their stature as sinological scholars in this bastion of British science overseas. Edkins spoke first, giving a substantial presentation on the "city of Confucius" they had just returned from. Legge was then introduced in a way that deferred to his special accomplishments as a distinguished "philological" and "historical" student of China. His "utterances" were said to "have a worth of their own" as, unlike so many in Shanghai, he was not "a novice come lately to China." He was described, in language that simultaneously affirmed and denied some of the common racial prejudices of the period, as a man who, having "made himself intimately acquainted with the literature of the Middle Kingdom," had no "preconceived notions of the mission of the Anglo-Saxon race" and was without "a tendency to treat all men who have not white faces as niggers."[74]

Within this Shanghai-based organization designed, like the overall European transformation of the city, to extend the enlightened dominion of Western commerce and technology, Legge's talk painted a basically unfavorable picture of the contemporary situation in China. Reflecting especially on conditions in the imperial city of Peking, he began his talk with some familiar comments on the incredible "filth" of the Chinese, comments that were received by this audience with knowing laughter. But the real brunt of his remarks had to do with the piteous state of the imperial government. Though he increasingly believed in China's archaic worth and intrinsic capacity for progressive change, he condemned the "incompetency of the present Government." Winning the appreciative applause of his audience, he concluded by noting that in present-day Peking there was "not the slightest symptom of any change coming over the spirit of the Government." Things were "going forward" not so much because of the Chinese themselves, but because of the general "progress of events" propelled by the Western powers. As for the Chinese, or more accurately their Manchu rulers (particularly the Dowager Empress Cixi at this time), he could only lament that "the spirit of the Government lags as far behind as it did thirty years ago."[75]

Leaving Shanghai and China forever on the morning of June 4, Legge landed the next day in Nagasaki, Japan, and, before heading out across the Pacific, spent the next few weeks touring Kobe, Osaka, Yedo, and Yokohama. In the several accounts of his voyage, Legge pays little attention to Japan, noting only some of the changes since his last visit in 1865 and briefly mentioning, for example, his trips to a Buddhist temple and to the grave of the famous forty-seven Ronin. Touring Yedo (later known as Tokyo), he says that, having an "impression of flimsiness," he did not think of it as a "great city." Nevertheless, it was extremely neat and clean when compared to the filthiness of Peking. Again the rhetoric of physical cleanliness and civic order alludes to a greater contrast with the civilizational backwardness of China. Instead of the "supineness" of the Chinese government, the Meiji-period Japanese had the good sense (after prodding from the Americans) to end their self-imposed isolation by establishing a parliamentary constitution and by embracing the lessons of Western industrial and military progress.[76]

An American Excursion

Departing from Yokohama on June 24, Legge boarded the American ship *Colorado* to make his way across the Pacific to the United States. On board were nearly a thousand Chinese passengers, thirty of whom were young men sent out by progressive factions within the Chinese government to learn English and Western science in American schools. The promise of change suggested by this Chinese mission to America, especially when compared with what Legge had just described in Shanghai as the hopeless "supineness" of the Chinese government, is striking. Legge, however, seems to have had no significant intercourse with the Chinese on board and his narrative abruptly jumps to his arrival in San Francisco on July 13.

After arriving in the United States, Legge traveled by train and horseback in the Yosemite Valley and in parts of the American Wild West. His most memorable experiences of the West were a spectacular grove of giant sequoia trees and the fantastic soaring peaks of the Yosemite Valley that rose up, he writes, like "the spires of a Cathedral." This encounter with the inspiring grandeur of nature stirred his Scottish soul and, as such experiences had done in the past, gave rise to feelings of divine sublimity, as well as to a more comparative historical sense of the relation between human traditions and their natural environments. The Yosemite Valley, which served as the last retreat of some American Indian tribes, reminded him of the kind of mountain fastness that sheltered "highland clan[s]" from "encroaching Saxons."[77] In the spirit of the Scottish nostalgia for highland "wilderness," Legge was still interpreting his travels as a kind of pilgrimage event—even here within a realm mostly untouched by civilization but nonetheless expressing something of a "natural theology" (i.e., in terms of religiousness of the experience of nature's sublimity) and a "classic" dimension (i.e., in terms of its historical connections).[78]

Just as Chinese religion (referring primarily to the tradition of Confucianism) could be understood in terms of its historical or developmental relationship with Christianity, so also did these experiences of nature posit a kind of universal natural religion or "natural supernaturalism" that lay beneath all historical forms of religion. This idea of a natural religion, originally connected with eighteenth-century rationalism and later romantic notions, was another one of the crucial factors associated with the emergence in the last third of the nineteenth century, especially in Britain, of the comparative science of religions. This is seen both in relation to some of Max Müller's theories of religious origins and by the charter associated with the creation of the famous Hibbert and Gifford lectureships.

Legge's other significant experience in the American West also bears on his increasing sensitivity to a comparative approach to religious experience and the history of religions. He made a special point of visiting Salt Lake City to attend a Mormon service at the Tabernacle. Legge's curiosity is a manifestation of a broader nineteenth-century fascination with Mormonism as a strange "new religion" and as a potentially dangerous corruption of Christianity similar, it would seem for anyone familiar with Chinese history, to the Taiping movement. Among other similarities, the Mormon and Taiping movements were founded on a new revelation to visionary founders in cultural settings radically different from the origins of Christianity. However, both claimed to disclose revolutionary "latter day" secrets that extended and fulfilled the Christian message. And both religions preached the establishment of a theocratic order licensing new social forms. Legge's reaction to the Mormon service he attended on Sunday, July 27, was not very favorable. He reports that, though the "music and singing [were] good," there was "little solemnity about the service." He was especially disappointed with the two speakers at the service. The first was Thomas Young, Brigham Young's eldest son, whom Legge judged to be "insincere" with "very little pith in what he said—a very lame vindication of Mormonism." The second speaker, Orson Pratt (a significant prophetic figure in the institutionalization of Mormonism), was more "intellectually able" and "blew the trumpets," but also "did not shine."[79] Although Legge does not draw out any of the broad implications of his visit to Salt Lake City, his pronounced interest in the Mormon community strongly recalls his old fascination with the religious reformation undertaken by the Taiping movement. And even though both his Taiping and Mormon experiences were disappointing, Legge truly believed in the prophetic possibility of religious reform, and by way of implication, in the emergence of a new global Christianity coming about through the renovation of strange cultural traditions and experiences.

The rest of Legge's cross-country American trip was conducted by railroad and, after rapidly passing through Chicago and Niagara Falls, he arrived in New York City on August 4. This phase of the trip was mostly unremarkable. He does, however, record his disappointment over not being able to meet with W. D. Whitney, a scholar of Sanskrit at Yale University and vociferous critic of Max Müller—a small incident that documents Legge's awareness of Müller and the increasingly controversial nature of his views. Concluding his pilgrim's tale, Legge quickly describes his departure from the port of New York on August 13 and his arrival in Liverpool, England, eleven days later.

A Mean Narrow Lane

After arriving in England, Legge hurried north to Dollar, Scotland. Here in this small town twenty-five miles northwest of Edinburgh as the crow flies across the Firth of Forth, he was at last reunited with his "dear Mama" (his wife, Hannah Mary), those of his children still at home (Thomas Morison, James Granville, Helen Edith, and Anna Georgina), and step-daughter (Marian Willetts). The story that can be told about this period—that is, the rest of 1873 down until 1875, when he moved to King Henry Road in London in anticipation of greater vocational transformations—concerns Legge's Dollar days of rejoicing in the bosom of his Scottish hearth and home. Given the scholarly focus of his work at this time, these were also long days of concentrated study, continuing translation, and editorial revision. In rural Dollar, Legge lived, to borrow from the *Analects* (VI.ix; *Chinese Classics*, vol. 1 [1893]), in a "mean narrow lane" far removed from the cosmopolitan life in the great metropolis of London and detached from the centers of scholarship at Edinburgh and the English universities. Nevertheless, his continuing literary activities kept him in touch with a greater community of readers interested in the exotic Orient. As he was entering his sixth decade, it seemed fitting that this time in his life would be a period of ancestral retreat and rustic withdrawal. He was at the end of his active career as a missionary and pastor, and, given the leisure of his retirement, there was plenty of time to complete the translations of the last of the Five Classics. There was, of course, the question of how these works would be published, but he had learned to trust in God and Shangdi, if not in the London Missionary Society. Most likely, given the relative success of his earlier *Classics* distributed in England by Trübner and Company, he assumed that the remaining translations would be published as part of Trübner's new Oriental Series.

Relations with the London Missionary Society

On January 9, 1874, the London Missionary Society board accepted James Legge's full retirement from "active foreign work." The board resolution of this date specifically mentions the society's "cordial" acceptance of "his request for a future recognition of his claims on the Society."[80] But Legge had already reestablished a friendly relationship with the society and, after his return to Britain in 1873 and his formal retirement as a missionary, he even agreed to serve as a board member on the society's Eastern Committee, which met several times a year in London (an arrangement that ended when he assumed his professorship at Oxford).[81]

The conservative and authoritarian nature of the ruling directorate of the society and its foreign missionary policy, especially concerning the relationship between missionary and scholarly prerogatives, would continue to be a factor in later developments associated with Legge's image among missionaries and the perceived dangers of comparative scholarship in the mission field. By this time Legge's "special work" as a translator and scholar had been independently and publicly vindicated, even to the point where he was now known less as a missionary, or even as a conjunctive missionary-scholar, than simply as the distinguished scholarly translator of the *Chinese Classics*. Ever since the death of Stanislas Julien in 1873 in Paris, Legge had become the premier sinologist within the intellectual world of Orientalism. This was a judgment ratified in 1875 by the august French Academy—and therefore, so to speak, for the whole learned world of sinological Orientalism—when it awarded Legge the first Prix Julien for his translation of the *Spring and Autumn Annals*.

Legge now thought of himself as a doubly hyphenated ex-missionary-scholar: a translator, scholar, teacher, Orientalist, and sinologue who happened to have been a missionary in an earlier part of his life. During this period in Dollar, even before his apotheosis as an Oxford professor, he was appreciated more by secular scholars than by his former missionary colleagues. But because of the fame he had attained for his scholarly work, the society seemed to find it advantageous to celebrate the accomplishments of its former missionary and to insinuate its ever stalwart support for the *Chinese Classics*. In its January resolution, therefore, the London Missionary Society carefully recorded its "affectionate regard for him personally and their high estimate of . . . [his] Christian principle, zeal and ability." Even more astonishing, given earlier tensions, was the society's belated affirmation of his "special work." No matter that it had never financially supported the *Classics* project (even insisting on guarantees that it would be entirely funded by the generous guilt-donations of Joseph and Robert Jardine) or that only a decade before it did not have such a lofty estimate of Legge's abilities as a missionary. Now when Legge no longer needed the blessing, it was quick to assert its gratitude and undying support. The society board thereby declared its "deep sense of the value of the linguistic service which he has rendered in opening up to the examination of foreign Christian and other students the higher literature of the Chinese thus offering an important aid in the promotion of missionary work among the higher as well as the lower grades of the Chinese people." This board, no doubt seeing itself as a "higher grade" of committee, concluded the resolution by expressing its desire for Legge's continued good health so that he may complete his work and win the "honour of our common Lord."[82] The irony of this mock sincerity on the part of the society would be especially apparent in the events surrounding the 1877 Missionary Conference in Shanghai and in the continued failure of the London Missionary Society and other missionary societies to make use of Legge's professorial services at Oxford. It seems that the missionary societies' "deep sense of the value" of Legge's linguistic services was largely a passing fancy. All of this no doubt brought a sly knowing smile to Legge's face.

A Revisionary Spirit

Even during his semiretirement in Dollar, Legge was intensely involved in many and sundry activities, including those that were expressive of the profound ministerial spirit of his life. These activities included periodic Sunday preaching by invitation, attendance at London Missionary Society Eastern Committee board meetings at the headquarters in London, and various kinds of public-spirited lecturing, both locally in Scotland and to the south in England (often having to do with China and general matters of education). He also became active in the politically controversial anti-opium movement in England.[83] Most of all, he continued his lifelong habits of daily study, his "great pleasure" during this period being that he could devote even the daylight hours to his beloved *Classics*. No longer did he have to eke out a few hours of study in the evening and early morning; no longer did he have constantly to justify his translations to an unappreciative missionary board.

All was not bliss. One discordant note was that he now had to be concerned about the income his scholarship was producing. Having officially resigned from active missionary service, his livelihood depended on his meager retirement funds and whatever additional money was forthcoming from his part-time ministerial activities and the sales of his translations.[84] He was never one to complain, but it is clear that money was always a concern for the Legge household. These concerns would be especially acute back home in a family used to the grand Mission House lifestyle of the Orient. Legge never made any substantial income from the original mission press printing of the *Classics*—which he wanted to put into the hands of missionaries as cheaply as possible and which were, after all, highly technical works unsuited to a general audience. Even though some royalties came in through the foreign sales of these books, he often seemed to be in debt to Trübner and Company, which distributed the *Classics* in England.[85] There was, however, a growing demand for books about Oriental and Chinese subjects (especially if they were classical or sacred texts) that were expressly written for a generally literate, though not necessarily scholarly, readership in both Great Britain and America. The extent of this interest is indicated by the appearance in the United States of a number of abridged pirated editions of the *Chinese Classics.*[86]

Because of the piracy problem, Trübner and Company advised Legge of the need to "produce a popular edition" of the *Chinese Classics* having the greatest general appeal. Taking this advice to heart, Legge busied himself with the preparation of new, more accessible and marketable versions of Confucius and Mencius. This meant the excision of the Chinese text and a general reduction of the elaborate explanatory apparatus. As Legge tells us in the preface to the Trübner edition of the *Life and Teachings of Confucius* published in 1875, his revisions were all done in relation to his "increased acquaintance with the field of Chinese literature." And although he admits that the actual "alterations," "additions," and "corrections" in the prolegomena, notes, and translations were relatively "few and unimportant," he emphasized that he had carefully reworked his original editions.[87]

But it is important to notice what was *not* changed in this revision of the *Analects.* Conspicuous (especially after his eulogy upon the Chinese sage's grave) is that this popular edition retained his concluding sentiments from 1861 concerning Confucius: "after long study of his character and opinions, I am unable to regard him as a great man." It seems, nonetheless, that Legge had become quite edgy about the question of Kongzi's "greatness," especially as this quality was for Legge always related to religious truth and moral virtue. His defensiveness about this issue was initially provoked by the *Edinburgh Review* in 1869, but is also suggested here by his pained reaction to the views expressed by a certain "Mr. Baker of Massachusetts," who produced one of the pirated American editions. Legge was irked that Baker criticized him for not recognizing that "Confucius was a most religious man" and that "the worship of God was more nearly universal in China than in the Theocracy of Israel" (quoting Baker from Legge's preface to the 1875 Trübner edition of the *Classics*). Yet, within a few years Legge himself would be adopting much of Baker's argument.

The Bonny Book of Poetry

Another important revisionary work of this period is Legge's collaborative production of a metrical version of the *Book of Poetry* or, as he called it on this occasion, the *Book of Ancient Poetry.*[88] The fact that the Chinese possessed a classical book devoted to rhymed poems or "psalms" that were originally sung as ballads, laments, or folk songs—and were expressive of the deepest social and religious emotions of early China—created a kind of comparative linkage with the "ancient poetry" of other traditions. For Legge, these connections would have included especially the Hebrew Psalmist tradition, as well as the Burnsian ballad tradition so important for any Scotsman. Because it was the subject of Max Müller's first great scholarly work, there is also some possibility that Legge was aware of the similarities with the heroic songs and epic sensibility of the ancient Indian *Rig-Veda*. Even though Legge did not directly refer to any of these traditions at this time, he was certainly aware of them and it is safe to assume that they influenced his determination to produce a translation of the Chinese poems in English verse. It seems he was also reacting to the criticism, by Eitel and others, of his original prose translation of the *Book of Poetry*.[89] But his immediate decision to produce such a work came about in the spring of 1874 at the prompting of his nephew, the Reverend John Legge, who was living in Victoria, Australia.

The problem of communicating the meaning and form of these poems relates directly to Legge's understanding of translation as a critical act of scholarship involving technical philological issues, interpretive hermeneutical issues, and literary style. The problem of making these poems more appealing and popular therefore was not necessarily a matter of making them any less accurate or precise. Legge was self-consciously trying to give a more literary feel to his translations while avoiding any violation of his standards of accuracy. For Legge, it was becoming obvious that stylistic form had as much to do with faithfulness in translation as any attempt at literal word-by-word congruency.

The problem was that Legge was overly sensitive to his stylistic shortcomings and tried to offset these weaknesses by drawing upon a group of poetic collaborators. He tells us that his original plan was to pool the efforts of his nephew, John Legge, and his cousin, James Legge of Staffordshire, along with the assistance of Alexander Cran of Fairfield and W. T. Mercer, an old friend from Hong Kong (and Oxford M.A.). As might be expected with such an unwieldy assemblage, Legge's collaborators were not able to follow through on their commitments to the project. The final product was three-quarters Legge's own work and was a rather incongruous blend of his old stiffly formal style accompanied by Scottish doggerel and some bits of sprightly rhyme.

Shadows of a Long Nightmare

Legge's own reflections on his career during this transitional period are found in an address he gave on October 5, 1874, at the installation of a certain E. J. Dukes as a missionary to Amoy.[90] The missionary nature of this event affects the overall tone of this talk, but it is a revealing, and at times an unusually candid, document of Legge's changing state of mind. He begins his talk by reminiscing about his own visit to Amoy in Fujian (Fukien) province back in 1852. Describing Amoy as "picturesque," he goes on to an illustrative anecdote that shows, as he puts it, the "way inferior creatures" are "more at home with the peoples of the East than with ourselves." The incident in question concerned a brood of swallows that never seemed to be bothered by the "constant stream" of Chinese going by their nest. Though admittedly "trivial," he drew the patronizing lesson that it was such "small matters" that "tended to maintain the earnest sympathy of my heart with the Chinese people and to sustain my purpose to declare to them the gospel of the grace of God." Moving on to a discussion of a Chinese rebel movement, which in 1853 had held Amoy for more than six months, he noted (in the evangelical spirit of "afflictive providence") the kind of "good" that "came out of the evil" of the movement. Thus the rebels destroyed many idols and temples and "many of the people became convinced of the vanity of idolatry."

More telling than these rather conventionally pious sentiments are Legge's comments about some of the factors affecting the success of the China missions. Referring to the darker issues of missionary activity in China, he concluded the address by describing the "fierce" term controversy, which "raged with violence" for five or six years back in the 1850s. Even more disheartening was his sad confession that within the ashes of this debate "there still glow the former fires." Recollecting that this debate "sometimes comes across me as the shadow of a long continuing nightmare," he depicted the controversy as a situation where "one party accused the other of making the scriptures teach, and of themselves preaching, idolatry; the second party retorted upon their opponents that they made the scriptures speak, and themselves preach, nonsense." The consequences were "disastrous" in that the debate created "mutual alienation among the missionaries," "astonishment" among native converts, and the "derision of the heathen."

THE ZEITGEIST OF THE 1870s:
FAITH IN HONEST DOUBT

The opening of China to the Western nations, and of the West to Chinese emigration and labor, are events as momentous in their religious as in their commercial and political bearings . . . [and] announce a new phase in the education of Christendom. It is as certain that the complacent faith of the Christian Church in itself as the sole depository of religious truth is to be startled and confounded by the new experience, as that the fixed ideas of that huge population which swarms along the great river-arteries of China, and heaps flowers in the temples of spirit-ancestors, and bows at shrines of Confucius and Fo, are to be astounded at the immense resources of the "outside barbarians," and their peculiar worship of Mammon and Christ.

SAMUEL JOHNSON, *ORIENTAL RELIGIONS,* 1872

> *There lives more faith in honest doubt,*
> *Believe me, than in half the creeds.*
>
> TENNYSON, *IN MEMORIAM,* 1850

Things Are on the Turn

The general state of world affairs in the late nineteenth century was one of rapid and dramatic change. Whether for good or ill, things were very much "on the turn" in both Legge's estimation and in the opinion of most nineteenth-century commentators.[91] The sense of change that was sweeping the world was in most instances viewed as a necessary and welcome product of the civilizational forces unleashed by the self-righteously aggressive "high imperialism" of the late nineteenth century. Like the gigantic Frankensteinian "galvanic battery" spoken of in the *Edinburgh Review* (see above, page 80), Western political, military, and commercial power—along with its handmaidens of science, technology, and, of course, Orientalist scholarship and the missionary movement—were in the process of shocking the Oriental corpse back to some semblance of life.

During the decade of the 1870s, Britain became self-conscious about the glory and burden of its global hegemony—a development symbolized by the proclamation on January 1, 1877, of Queen Victoria's status as empress of India. To borrow from Legge's imagery when he surveyed the accomplishments of Hong Kong, the situation was one of Britannia proudly standing upon the Himalayan heights to survey the amazing changes it had wrought throughout the Asian continent. At the same time there was a contentious scramble throughout the unclaimed reaches of the world for commercial markets and colonial possessions by other Western pretenders to global eminence. These indecorous developments would result in conflicts throughout the waning years of the Victorian age and climax in the worldwide cataclysms after the turn of the century. Building upon earlier advances, the 1870s were also an astonishing period of accelerating technological invention and industrial progress most brilliantly exemplified by the rapid appearance between 1876 and 1878 of the telephone, phonograph, and electric lamp. All of these political, commercial, and technological changes, pressed upon the entire world by the restless energy and nationalistic jealousies of Western nations, were epitomized by another singular event of the 1870s, the so-called Universal Exhibition of 1878 in Paris. Even more spectacularly than the first world exposition held in England's Crystal Palace in 1851, the Parisian event (as exemplified by its central symbol of the Eiffel Tower, engineered by Ferdinand de Lesseps, the builder of the

Suez Canal) celebrated and displayed the triumphs of "higher civilization" throughout the world.[92]

Just as machines became more and more the "measure of man," so also was there a growing urge to extend the principles of quantitative measurement, statistical analysis, and rational classification to the whole developmental history of human institutions and material culture, from savage and mechanically primitive cultures to the civil and literate, yet stagnant, societies of the East and to the complexly civilized and technologically sophisticated Western tradition.[93] This leads to a drive to display and document the newly accumulated material goods and intellectual booty of the imperial endeavor, both as a public act of self-aggrandizement and, coupled with the academic management of this new knowledge, as a fulfillment of middle-class Victorian desires for edifying entertainment. These cultural and emotional elements are seen in the aforementioned World Fairs, as well as in the whole phenomenon of traveling exhibitions, regional expositions, public foundations, libraries, and museums. The new museums (such as the Pitt-Rivers anthropological museum in Oxford, England, or the Musée Guimet of Asian religions in Lyons, France), in particular, can be seen as the "successors and spiritual legatees of the early nineteenth-century literary and philosophical societies." All of these developments—along with the new research universities, the new academic disciplines of both the natural and human sciences, new international learned organizations, societies, congresses, monumental publishing projects, journals, and encyclopedias—were expressive of the worldwide rationalization, quantification, and control of information during this period.[94]

The political and material changes wrought during this high imperial period are paralleled by a whole series of mutations in the overall fabric of European social, cultural, and intellectual life. These changes were especially significant within Victorian British tradition, which at this time was the political and commercial standard-bearer for the whole Western world. And from the 1870s onward in Britain, as Richard Altick has said, a "strong tide set in against the confident [religious] orthodoxies of the mid-Victorian period."[95] This turning away from conventional religiosity is seen in the pervasive currents of intellectual doubt, emotional trepidation, and spiritual ambivalence running throughout the last part of the Victorian era. These elusive alterations in Victorian religion are witnessed in the emergence of new alternative sources of faith and anxiety seen, for example, in the theological universalism of George MacDonald, psychic research (the British Society for Psychical Research was founded in 1882), Mme Blavatsky's esoteric theosophical movement (*Isis Unveiled* was published in 1877), Westernized forms of Buddhist mysticism (Edwin Arnold's *Light of Asia* appeared in 1879), and the popular "imperial Gothic" occult literature of the 1880s and 1890s (e.g., by Robert Louis Stevenson, Rudyard Kipling, Bram Stoker, Arthur Conan Doyle, Andrew Lang, and Rider Haggard).[96]

Unbelief Serving Belief

One important shift of values and ideals in the latter half of the century in Britain is related to changes in the old-fashioned evangelical spirit of hard work, moral earnestness, self-improvement, missionary zeal, and an education narrowly focused on the Bible and one's own sectarian beliefs. As David Newsome has argued, there is a "gradual abandonment of the ideals of godliness and good learning in the last half of the nineteenth century" in favor of a newly aggressive emphasis on the code of manly strength and physical cleanliness, honor-in-might gamesmanship, and hearty fair play. These developments have been called (most prominently by Charles Kingsley) the cult of "muscular Christianity." "Moral earnestness became *theumos*" or "the hearty enjoyment of physical pursuits" and the belief was fostered that "manliness and high spirits are more becoming qualities in a boy than piety and spiritual zeal."[97] In this context, all the vocational pursuits of a British gentleman, including missionary activity and scholarship, aspired to zealous pugnaciousness and manly fair play.

In the watershed period of the 1870s, or somewhat earlier, the godliness of the Evangelical Christian character "ceased to be an essential concomitant" with "good learning." Godliness came more to be identified with the aggressive spirit of muscular Christianity that could often lend itself to a truculent defense of old antagonistic pieties, especially when associated with the jellyfish "indifferentism" and effeminate "toleration" of the new science of religions or, in the case of the China mission, with the effete dangers of comparativism and "Leggism." At the same time, "good learning" was itself becoming generally comparative, secular, pluralistic, scientific, and agnostic—even as it tried to project a manly spirit of intellectual battle.[98]

Terms such as *secular* and *agnostic* (the latter coined by Thomas Henry Huxley in 1869) at this time did not necessarily indicate any rejection of religion, but often, as in the case of Legge, had more to do with an increasing frustration with the sectarian distortions of education and national life in general. Concurrent with these developments was the emergence of a disciplinary doubt, or critical spirit of nonparochial inquiry, appropriate to philological and historical issues of academic scholarship.[99] Legge's nonsectarian secularity and antidenominationalism with regard to education is well documented and goes back to the very beginnings of his career as an educator in Malacca and in Hong Kong. Eitel notes, for example, that Legge's reformation of the government schools in Hong Kong was essentially based upon "a Nonconformist liberation scheme which preferred secularism to episcopalianism."[100] The secularism of his Chinese scholarship is

seen most overtly in his condemnation of the nightmarish denominational-
ism of the term question debate.

There is *no* justification for ever calling Legge a religious agnostic.[101]
The real issue is Bernard Lightman's discovery that agnosticism in the last
quarter of the nineteenth century "owes a profound debt to an epistemological position put forward by a number of ardent Christian thinkers."[102]
Thus for many Victorians agnosticism represented a species of rational
scepticism rooted in Kantian principles, and it is found, most notably, in
the work of Thomas Huxley, Herbert Spencer, and Leslie Stephen. This
strain of agnosticism, it is true, often ended up as "an arm of an ideological
scientific naturalism" that was anti-Christian and atheistic. More commonly,
however, it was simply and generically nonreligious in the way that Legge
described Confucius in 1861. A certain agnostic spirit or disciplined doubt
can also be indirectly linked with Max Müller's science of religion (declared initially in his "Introduction to the Science of Religion" lectures at
the Royal Institution in London in March 1870) and, perhaps even more
surprisingly, with Henry Longueville Mansel's famous Bampton Lectures,
The Limits of Religious Thought (1858). Broad Church liberal scholars like
Müller and archconservative Anglican clerics like Mansel both wanted to
place unbelief and strategic doubt in the service of an ultimately fortified
belief in the higher truth of Christianity.

The irony of Mansel's position was that "in order to preserve the truth of
Biblical Christianity in the face of growing scepticism," he ended up both
affirming the infallibility of Christian scripture and doubting the role of reason in religious thought. This kind of logic depended on a pietistic or intuitionist position, supported in the case of Mansel by the "caricatured Kantianism" of the Scottish common sense philosopher William Hamilton.[103]
Müller's Kantianism, as modified by his own romantic comparativism and
Broad Church sensibility, was not concerned with defending conservative
Anglicanism or with a radical rejection of rationality, but is in its own way
no less intuitionist regarding the ultimate origin (linguistic response to nature), inner meaning (pure intuition of the "infinite"), and progressive development of religion (from lower to higher and universal, more purely
spiritual and ideally moral, forms).[104] Like Mansel (and Legge), Müller was
also basically dismissive of Romish, medieval, material, and ritual forms of
religion.

Though he was never very philosophically sophisticated, Legge, with his
youthful unwillingness to "subscribe to any creed," his grounding in the
Scottish common sense philosophy, the influence of his brother George's
liberal "theology of harmony" (where "doubt" was honored as a stepping-
stone to intellectual and religious maturity), and his gradual movement toward a Müllerian-style comparativism, evinced an implicit principle of
hermeneutical doubt in his scholarship. The disciplines of translation and

philological annotation in particular lend themselves to a pragmatic agnosticism toward any single, presupposed, or dogmatic meaning for foreign words and terms. As seen in the term question debate, Legge's protocomparativist inclinations and translator's questioning of the common missionary interpretation of heathen terms led to his scholarly faith in an ancient Chinese theism and an elevated Confucian moral system. This was a perfect instance of unbelief serving belief in the manner suggested by Mansel and Müller.

An Agnostic Zeitgeist

The famous Victorian poet, Oxford professor, and liberal cultural critic Matthew Arnold first used the German expression *Zeitgeist* in English to refer to the defining temper, genius, or spiritual essence of a cultural period. Even more significant is that, in Arnold's usage, this most Germanic of ghostly conceits was especially related to an increasingly critical, rational, secular, and academic approach to religion. As Arnold said, it was the late-Victorian Zeitgeist that was "sapping the proof from miracles."[105] This was the same spirit that Tennyson expressed in his famous poem *In Memoriam*—that is, giving literary sanction to a new kind of universal faith in a methodological doubt that "gropes" amid the "dust and chaff" found upon the altars of all the world's religions.

But such changes respecting a so-called crisis of faith in Britain at this time were not the result of any single cultural factor or some metaphysical and infectious *geist*. Rather, alterations in religious attitudes of this magnitude were the result of a dynamic constellation of individual, social, and cultural factors generating various moods, ideas, and practices regarding the nature and developmental history of religions. Collectively and rhetorically, these factors were expressive of the increasingly pervasive approaches, which were labeled "critical," "comparative," "scientific," and "evolutionary," to understanding the natural and human worlds.

As related to the changing patterns of belief and new ways of studying religion in England at the end of the century, this "higher critical" style involved a whole set of overlapping, and sometimes contradictory, elements. These elements included agnosticism and the growing traditions of rational skepticism and atheism, the emergence of a literate reading public and a vigorous periodical media, the nonsectarian bent of the national education movement, the secularization and professionalization of Oxford and Cambridge, and the comparativist mentality and Germanic research methods associated in England with both the broadly believing Müller and the more radically atheistic Herbert Spencer and Edward Tylor. Here also the role of Congregational Nonconformity in British political and intellectual life (e.g., Legge, A. M. Fairbairn, T. H. Green, and Robert F. Horton at

Oxford in the 1880s), along with Unitarians (J. Estlin Carpenter) and Broad Church Anglicans (in varying degrees, Müller, Frederick Denison Maurice, Charles Hardwick, Mark Pattison, Archibald Sayce, Arthur Stanley, Benjamin Jowett, and William Gladstone), is a significant factor in the liberalization of British religious scholarship along German lines and the comparativist spirit of the age.[106]

Prodigious Change Respecting Religious Systems

Many of these changes can be associated with the gradual transformation of British discourse about religion that was first announced in the nineteenth century by the "unshackling" of Thomas Carlyle's intellect—a transformation that, as Ruth apRoberts shows, involved a more contextualized, relativized, and pluralistic way of approaching the otherness of the non-Western world and non-Christian religions.[107] Carlyle's "driving impulse to investigate history" was very much like Legge's philosophical concern for the "Great Story" of China—both men's motivations being rooted in their fervent Scottish upbringing and the fierce independence and free will of their Calvinism.[108] Through a Germanic scholarship that was open to other literatures, heroes, and religions, Carlyle found "his way out of the parochialism of Christianity into the wider world of multiplicities of myth-making, where the many varied forms of religion are the most important and characteristic products of humankind."[109] Much the same could be said about Legge and his gradual adoption of a Müllerian-style comparativism. The intellectual and cultural movement from a parochial Christianity through a kind of protocomparativism to a full-blown comparative science of religions—developments in Britain (of many degrees and shades) stretching from Carlyle in the first part of the century to Müller, Tylor, Lang, Smith, Fairbairn, Hastings, Frazer, and others at the end of the century—is in many ways the basic paradigm for the Victorian "movement of mind" concerning religion. Quoting the philosopher Nelson Goodman, apRoberts defines this intellectual and emotional shift as a passage from faith in "unique truth and a world fixed and found" to an awareness of the bewildering diversity of "conflicting versions of worlds in the making."[110]

The Zeitgeist of the 1870s was the inclination to create a Zeitgeistian ghost of unbelief as a way of taming the complex experience of multiple worlds of meaning. Published between 1871 and 1872, George Eliot's novel *Middlemarch* expresses some of the basic tension between the older, Casaubon-like yearning for some absolute "Great General Truth" and the new German philological sciences of language and history, which insisted on the "diversity and uniqueness of cultures." And it was especially the "comparativist" concern for the "multiplicity and diversity of religions in history" that created "a problem for the orthodox worldview." Disturbing questions naturally arose: "Where does Christianity fit in among these diversities?" How can one ever discover a "binding theory that will bring [human] lives and Christian doctrine into a relation with the amazing past"?

In Britain such queries led, belatedly but relentlessly, from Carlyle to new liberal schools of historical theology, to the higher criticism of the Bible, to the different academic disciplines of Orientalism, and to the comparative science of religions and the *Sacred Books of the East*.[111] The real difficulty in dealing with these developments is that the "essential" nature, significance or insignificance, history, and future of religion and religions (along with the related category of culture) were the pivotal issues of Victorian intellectual and emotional life.[112] As Frederick Denison Maurice said in his *Religions of the World and Their Relations to Christianity*, the nineteenth century was the age when "a prodigious change" was taking place "in the feelings of men generally—of philosophical men particularly—respecting Religious Systems."[113] It was time, said the radical American transcendentalist Samuel Johnson, that "the older religions were studied in the light of their own intrinsic values."[114]

CHANGING MISSIONS:
RELIGIOUS, CIVILIAN, AND ACADEMIC

Whenever I have conversed on this subject with missionaries who have seen active service, they all agree that they cannot be converting all day long, and that nothing is more refreshing and invigorating to them than some literary or scientific work.

MAX MÜLLER, ADDRESS TO THE ARYAN SECTION,
SECOND INTERNATIONAL CONGRESS OF ORIENTALISTS, 1874

The mission of Christianity to the heathen is not only for the overthrow of many of their religious peculiarities, but quite as truly for the essential modification of its own.

SAMUEL JOHNSON, *ORIENTAL RELIGIONS*, 1872

The 1870s were a time when the ruddy blush of Western high imperialism was upon the face of the world, a visage that was now seen to be mottled by many racial hues. It was a time of change that expressed itself especially in terms of a mental shift involving the meaning and study of religions, a shift that I have broadly identified as the gradual unfolding of a comparativist mentality. The central intellectual issue of the 1870s down to the turn of the century was the problem of understanding what had been unexpectedly revealed about savage and Oriental worlds. And it was the discipline of philology, especially as developed by German and continental scholars familiar with Aryan or Semitic languages, that accentuated the power of the comparative method, ostensibly putting the new human sciences on a plane equal to what had been achieved in the natural sciences by Carolus Linnaeus's taxonomy, Georges Cuvier's anatomy, Charles Lyell's geology, and Charles Darwin's evolutionary natural history.

Comparative philology was intimately linked with the study of Oriental texts and the investigation of different world religions. Furthermore, the intertwined study of languages and religions, along with the application of evolutionary theory to the study of cultures, was the most characteristic concern of comparativism after midcentury in Britain. This obsession with the linguistic and cultural significance of religion, and with historical origins in general, is seen in developments within the various disciplines of Orientalism, and in the fields of anthropology (e.g., Edward Tylor and James Frazer), folklore (e.g., Edward Clodd and Andrew Lang), and sociology (e.g., Herbert Spencer and Robertson Smith). But the special Victorian fascination with religion is most fully expressed in Britain in the last third of the nineteenth century by Frederick Max Müller's creation of a whole new scholarly discipline. This was variously known as the science of religion, the comparative science of religions, or simply as comparative religion.[115]

The appearance of this new academic discourse can be precisely dated to the time in February and March of 1870 when Müller gave his famous lectures, "Introduction to the Science of Religion," to a large and enthusiastic audience at the Royal Institution in London. The response to Müller can be gauged by the fact that these lectures were promptly serialized for popular consumption in *Fraser's Magazine*. In 1873, they were published in book form and then went through several editions. What had Müller accomplished beyond giving a name to already existing attitudes and practices? He certainly was not the sole creator of a comparativist sensibility regarding religion. He was, however, a scholar of comparative philology and an Indological Orientalist at Oxford who became an enthusiastic promoter of a comparative approach to the study of religions. In this sense, he gave the fledgling science of religion an "impulse, a shape, a terminology, and a set of ideals."[116] More than any of his contemporaries (such Cornelis Tiele at Leiden University in Holland and Albert Réville in Paris), Müller had the celebrity and persuasiveness that established an influential public image for the new discipline. Müller was the one professional comparativist who recruited a "whole generation of scholars to his cause as editors, translators and commentators in his *Sacred Books of the East* enterprise."[117]

They Cannot Be Converting All Day Long

The last quarter of the century was also a turning point for the missionary ideal as related to all aspects of spiritual, intellectual, and material colonialism. This was a time when the old seamless alliance between the civilizing mission of political imperialism and the evangelical mission of Christianity was being publicly questioned by missionary-scholars such as Legge and by civil servants such as Thomas Wade and Rutherford Alcock. There was a growing awareness that missionary ideals and methods narrowly conceived in doctrinal terms were creating a "missionary problem" that actually retarded the progress of the Western nations in Asia. The perception of such a problem involved an overall shift toward a more secularly defined ideal concerning the civilizing mission of the West, an ideal in which the force of traditional religious proselytization was secondary to the revolutionary power of technology and science.[118]

These changes were associated with a redefinition of *mission* in commercial, political, and academic terms. In this way, the old evangelical missionary movement was challenged by newer methods of interaction with China suggested by Legge and later by the theology of the social gospel. So also did the secularization of national education and the cultivation of new scientific disciplines in the universities come to the fore in Britain and in foreign mission fields as the keys to personal transformation and national reformation. The real issue was, as it was for Master Kong and the Ruist tradition in China, the nature of education as the primary agency of moral civilization. From Legge's prophetic angle of vision, the scholarly and educational mission (whether at home among Christians or abroad among heathens) should strive for a secular avoidance of sectarian religion. Instead of sectarian creeds and rapid religious conversion, it was better to stress literature or the great stories of different religions by studying classics and sacred books in the Carlylian or Müllerian sense. As Müller humorously suggested, even missionaries cannot "be converting all day long." It was wise, therefore, to know that "literary or scientific work" was "refreshing and invigorating" in its own right and helped to further the missionary cause. Moreover, such scholarly and educational concerns might in the final analysis be the best way to promote the religious, moral, and civilizing aspects of the missionary ideal. This, according to Müller, was the "true missionary spirit."

Müller in Westminster Abbey

The tensions in the overlapping religious, civilizing, and academic understandings of the missionary ideal are portrayed in Max Müller's famous lecture on missions delivered in the evening of December 3, 1873—a lecture presented in the nave of Westminster Abbey in London, the ancestral sanctuary of the British royalty and poets. Like the Altar of Heaven in Peking, this was the sacred site of the Church of England's ritual administration of the heavenly mandate between God and his imperial agents on earth. There could not have been a more fitting venue for Müller's celebration of the "true missionary spirit" that was lifting the world onto a higher religious and civilizational plane.[119] Müller was reputedly the first layman to be invited to give a lecture in Westminster Abbey, an achievement facilitated by the dean of the abbey, Arthur Penrhyn Stanley. Stanley was Müller's old friend and colleague from Oxford and, along with Benjamin Jowett and Mark Pattison, was one of the leading liberal clerics of the Anglican Church.[120]

In a sermon delivered in the forenoon of the day on which Müller spoke, Dean Stanley gave his reasons for inviting Müller to speak on missions within the "sacred precincts" of Westminster Abbey. There were, as Stanley explains, seven reasons for the "peculiar circumstances" of Müller's lecture and the "greater confidence" in the future of Christian missions. In the first place, there was "the better knowledge of the Divine nature acquired by the extinction of the once universal belief that all heathens were everlastingly lost." Second was the scholarly satisfaction that came from "the increased acquaintance with the heathen religions themselves." Third and fourth were "the instruction which Christian missionaries have gained . . . from their actual experience in foreign parts" and "the recognition of the fact that the main hindrance to the success of Christian missions arises from the vices and sins of Christendom." Stanley's last three points concern the "testimony borne by missionary experience to the common elements of and essential principles" of Christianity, an "acknowledgment of the indirect influences of Christianity through legislation and civilization," and, in keeping with Müller's comparativist spirit, the "newly awakened perception of the duty of making exact, unvarnished, impartial statements" on the subject of heathen religions.[121]

Stanley emphasizes that the goal of mission can only be to "make better men and better citizens—to raise the whole of society by inspiring it with a higher view of duty, with a stronger sense of truth." This involves the "powerful conviction that only by goodness and truth can God be approached or Christ be served—that God is goodness and truth, and that Christ is the Image of God, because He is goodness and truth." If God is goodness and truth and these are qualities to some degree shared by the eight great literate religions (as Müller was to argue on the basis of the *Sacred Books*), then the danger is that there is no exclusive Christian means to either truth or justice. If, as Stanley says, the essence and object of Christianity, its stamp as the "supreme religion," is simply and only that it "produces characters" that in "truthfulness, in independence, in mercy, in purity, in charity" recall something of Saint Paul himself ("even as he recalled something of the mind which was in Christ Jesus"), then it does not take much to see that Christian exclusivity is particularly vulnerable to the moral purity of Confucius's life and teachings.

To claim in the face of comparative testimony concerning other religions and the "vices and sins of Christendom" that there was something uniquely and supremely Christian about the process of moral character formation (defined here in Protestant Victorian terms as a "reproduction of Paul") is to see how close nineteenth-century theological apologetic was to becoming hollow bluster. This is not the conclusion that Stanley comes to, but it is a thematic undertow of his sermon and his invitation to an unordained secular scholar such as Müller. For Stanley the lesson of means that flows from his discussion of the highest moral end of reforming human nature and instilling the duty to raise the whole of society is that any and all methods are legitimated—whether it be by "a short, sudden, electric shock" or "by a long course of civilizing, humanizing tendencies." It may come about through the agency of the Bible, but also by means of ancient classics or holy books, not all of which are necessarily Christian. It may come about through traditional evangelization, but it is just as likely (and really *more* likely) to be effected by the transformative processes of literary translation and secular education. But most of all, in Stanley's day it comes about through exposure to the civilizing machinery of colonialization: the "superiority of European genius, the spread of English commerce, the establishment of just laws, pure homes, merciful institutions."[122] For Stanley this means above all else that missionaries should be "tolerant" of many different modes of waging what John Bunyan called the "siege of man's soul."

Stanley's final theme points directly to Müller and also, in some ways, to the newly laicized Legge. While recognizing the important role of clergy in missions, Stanley also stresses the "agency of Christian laymen in this same work of evangelization." This is so in several ways (via the laws, literature, and influence of Christian Europe, via devout colonial magistrates or pure-minded merchants and soldiers), but is especially promoted by those laymen and scholars with a special comparative interest in the study of foreign cultures, languages, and religions—that is, in Stanley's rotund prose, those with "intelligent and far-seeing interest in labours, which, though carried on mainly by the clergy, must if they are to be good for anything, concern all mankind alike."[123] Ending with a prayer of manly faith in God's horror of intellectual narrowness, Stanley hoped that, by Müller's comparative efforts, a "more systematic form may thus be given to our knowledge, and a more concentrated direction to our zeal."[124]

The New Science

Coming now to Müller's evening lecture in the nave of the abbey, it is striking that he first appeals to the new "science of religion" that had been called into life—"a science which concerns us all, and in which all who truly care for religion must sooner or later take their part." This is, moreover, a science that he succinctly describes as a "careful study of the origin and growth" of religions and a "critical examination of the sacred books on which all of them profess to be founded" (that is, the eight historical or literate religions: the three religions, Jewish, Christian, and Mohammedan, of the Semitic races; the three of the Aryan or Indo-European races, the Brahman, Buddhist, and the Parsi; and the two Chinese systems of "Confucius and Lao-tse"). Each of these religious traditions must then be subjected "to a scientific classification, in the same manner as languages, apparently unconnected and mutually unintelligible, have been scientifically arranged and classified." This is a method that involves "a comparison of those points which all or some of them share in common, as well as by a determination of those which are peculiar to each."[125]

Based on these kinds of inductive procedures, Müller proposes a particular classificatory system that basically divides the eight traditions into "Non-Missionary and Missionary religions." This is, he says, a classification that "rests on what is the very heart-blood in every system of human faith." To explain this he first points out that the three religions of Judaism, Brahmanism, and Zoroastrianism "are opposed to all missionary enterprise." They are *"dying or dead"* (Müller's emphasis). Conversely, Buddhism, Mohammedanism, and Christianity have "a missionary character from their very beginning" and have therefore "life and vigor." All three of these missionary religions "want to convince" and "mean to conquer." It is this dynamic quality that "lifts them high above the level of the other religions of the world."[126] Not surprisingly, Müller finds that the highest of the high is Christianity, whose "very soul," like the imperial spirit of Western civilization and its colonial outreach, is "missionary, progressive, world-embracing." Notwithstanding Christianity's superiority, the evidence of comparative study shows that the "spirit" of truth and love is alive in the "hearts of the founders" of these three great religions. As the "life-spring of all religion," these abstractions of truth and love must, by their very nature, "plead . . . persuade . . . convince . . . and convert." Most of all, it is the spirit of love that openly accepts the deepest longings of all men and women. This is a spirit that echoes the famous refrain of Tennyson: "There lives more faith in honest doubts / Believe me, than in half the creeds."[127]

The Holy War of the Future

The "decisive battle for the dominion of the world" will be fought by the three living missionary religions of Buddhism, Mohammedanism, and Christianity. Here the statistical threat of the Asian excess of population comes to the fore. This is a result of the disturbing finding that, although "the number of Christians is double the number of Mohammedans," the Buddhist religion "occupies the first place in the religious census of mankind." It is among these three powers that "the Holy War of mankind" will "have to be fought, and is being fought at the present moment, though apparently with little effect. To convert a Mohammedan is difficult; to convert a Buddhist, more difficult still; to convert a Christian, let us hope, well nigh impossible."[128] But if the holy battle just envisioned seems a stalemate, "what then," asks Müller, "is the use of missionaries?"[129] In answering this question, Müller first insists on distinguishing between "parental" and "controversial" missionizing. It is only among the "uncivilized races" that it is appropriate for a missionary to act with a parent's love and authority. More difficult is the case of the "controversial missionary" who must "attack the faith of men brought up in other religions, in religions which contain much truth, though mixed up with much error." The difficulties in this case (such as in India and China) "are immense, the results very discouraging," and the conclusion to be reached is that controversial or antagonistic methods will hardly carry the day in the struggle among the major religions.[130]

There is, fortunately, a third option, which "has produced the most important results" and will allow for the "final victory." This method, as Müller describes it, stresses the peaceful coexistence of different religions. It is this kind of approach that, while abstaining from all direct confrontation, tends to bring out all "the best elements in each [religion], and at the same time keeps under all that is felt to be of doubtful value, of uncertain truth." For Müller the advantage of this method is shown by historical testimony: "whenever this has happened in the history of the world, it has generally led either to the reform of both systems, or to the foundation of a new religion."[131] The best contemporary example of this principle was the history of the reform Hinduism of Brahma-Samaj and recent schismatic developments inspired by Keshub Chunder Sen. Such a schism is disruptive and difficult but nevertheless is "a sign of life."[132]

Missions and Religious Miscegenation

Müller admits that Indian missionaries have not been very favorably disposed to the movement of Keshub Chunder Sen.[133] They have preferred rather to avoid the dangers of any kind of compromise or syncretistic grafting of religions. The missionaries to India, and this holds for China as well, wish only to "transplant . . . Christianity in its full integrity from England to India, as we might wish to transplant a full-grown tree."[134] Here let me only draw attention to Müller's choice of metaphors—that is, his appeal to a horticultural vocabulary of transplantation, grafting, crossbreeding, and hybrids. This is a kind of polite rhetoric that, in the vein of a growing social Darwinism, betrays contradictory racial emotions about both the dangers of miscegenation and the potential advantages of managed cross-fertilization or eugenics. As applied to religion, this kind of discourse refers to deep-seated Protestant fears of a syncretistic blending of religions that, as seen in Roman Catholicism's unhappy compromise with paganism, destroys the original purity of Christianity. Müller's suggestion is interesting because it seems to encourage some form of controlled interbreeding and "reciprocal sympathy" between religions. These kinds of metaphors, and related rhetorical logic, would constitute a common trope in the Victorian comparativist discourse about heathen religions.

For Müller the significance of Keshub Chunder Sen's movement is that it exemplifies the kind of powerful religious reform rising up in the nineteenth century (including the two movements personally witnessed by Legge—the Taipings and the Mormons). This phenomenon of reformation, from the perspective of Müller's spin on the Protestant principle, is the "most momentous in this momentous century." What this means, then, is that the "true missionary spirit" must allow for, tolerate, and even cultivate authentic native reform. By fostering this "spirit of truth and love, of forbearance, of trust, of toleration, of humility" toward heathen religions, missionaries will also at the same time overcome sectarianism and "forget [their] own small feuds."[135] The incongruity of this position is that, both theoretically and pragmatically, the most fully Christian approach to other religions is simultaneously the most humanistic and secular method (meaning here nonsectarian, not anti- or a-religious). Implicit also is Müller's developmental view of religion, including Christianity. Heathen religions, such as Hinduism, were being reformed in confrontation with Christianity, and Christianity was perpetually renewing itself in the dynamic Protestant spirit of reformation. All of these changing forms are but steps toward a universal religion of humanity that will eventually emerge out of the higher religion and global mission of nineteenth-century Protestant Christianity.

Less Doctrine, More Love

According to Müller, the final premise of missionary work is that the "fundamentals" of all true religion are not rooted in creeds but in the "love of God, and in our love of man." The danger to be avoided is, from this perspective, the problem of "too much faith—particularly when it leads to the requirement of exactly the same measure of faith in others." The "most valuable" lesson for a missionary is an interesting variation on the Confucian silver rule of human reciprocity—that is, missionaries must "learn to demand less from others than from themselves."[136] For all of his appeal to a new comparative science and a critical method, it is quite obvious that Müller's position is most reflective of his deep roots in German Protestant pietism and romantic idealism. It is the comparativist and Orientalist spirit within the context of the growing religious doubt of the late Victorian age, rather than any precise inductive method, that informs his conclusion that the best missionaries are secular-scientific scholars rather than sectarian-theological churchmen. The best missionaries may, in fact, be men of "literature, science, art, politics" who "are no longer Christian in the old sense of the word."

Müller's advice to missionaries (and at this time Legge probably would have agreed with much of the talk's spirit, if not all of its particulars) is that if Christianity "is to conquer in the Holy War of the future, it must throw off its heavy armor." What is wanted is "less of creeds, but more of trust; less of ceremony, but more of work; less of solemnity, but more of genial honesty; less of doctrine, but more of love."[137] These ideals represent a fairly conventional statement of Victorian evangelical morality applicable as much to secular as to religious life. Such essential and universal values can be associated with the academic life of liberal Oxford professors like Müller, a lifelong Orientalist scholar who surely fancied himself as "no longer a Christian in the old sense of the term." They would also be embodied to some degree in Legge's forthcoming career as a professor at Oxford, where, as an ordained Nonconformist minister and a retired missionary, he most probably, but awkwardly, conceived of himself as a Christian in both Müller's old and new senses of the term. Despite their differences, both Legge and Müller felt that Christian "love" should take precedence over creeds and sectarian dogmas.[138]

A Movement of Mind

As already seen in some of his lectures and sermons from the early 1870s, Legge was increasingly tentative about attributing social and political progress directly and exclusively to Christianity. This ambivalence contrasts with his earlier tendency to see all significant historical developments (the Taiping movement being the most egregious example) as providentially predetermined in relation to the "Great Commission." For Legge the "Great Story" of the "Land of Sinim" was becoming a narrative that, before biblical principles of exegesis were applied, had first to be understood on its own terms and in relation to its own resources. This represents a momentous shift from a biblically based conviction in the imminent mass conversion of the Chinese to a gradualist faith in secular educational methods and Oriental scholarship.

No absolute loss of Christian faith is implied in this shift. Rather, it is a matter of the newly conceived comparativist attitudes and methods substituting for narrowly literal formulas of biblical explanation. This kind of discursive "movement of mind" can be associated in Britain with Carlyle, Maurice, Hardwick, and Müller, but it also resonates with Legge's protocomparativist interests in the term question debate in China, his difficulties with the London Missionary Society, his experience as a translator of Chinese texts, his personal associations with various Chinese, and his pilgrimage to North China. This shifting intellectual and emotional perspective on Chinese texts and persons is additionally related to Legge's liberal postmillennialist theology wherein the universal coming of the kingdom of God is due to the human implementation of social justice and civilizational development.[139]

This Victorian "movement of mind" is often identified with the intellectual revolution fostered by Charles Darwin after the publication of *The Origin of Species* in 1859 and *The Descent of Man* in 1871. As Owen Chadwick and George Stocking have argued, however, Darwin is often more of a symptom of these changes than a causal factor. Thus the strain of social evolutionary thought in Victorian anthropology owes as much to James Cowles Prichard, common sense philosophy, and Scottish conjectural history as it does to Darwin.[140] Furthermore, both Carlyle and Müller's comparativism is fundamentally indebted to romantic Herderian ideas of *Entwicklung*.[141] Interesting also is that Darwin's own crisis of faith, and his movement away from orthodox religion, seems to have come about not so much because of his scientific discoveries about human development and natural selection, but because of what he had heard about non-Christian religions, especially Hinduism. The often debated "crisis of faith" of the late nineteenth century was as much indebted to the emergence of Orientalism and the comparative science of religions as it was to doubts arising from evolutionary biology, geology, and the natural sciences.[142] The multifaceted "movement of mind" called "comparative religions" was a central element in Legge's development as a scholar and sinological Orientalist. Even more broadly (and not often recognized), the spirit of comparativism significantly affected attitudes and methods throughout the foreign missions. Within the Chinese context of missions from the late 1870s to the turn of the century, this kind of scholarly comparativism is actually identified as a dangerous methodology called "Leggism."

There Are Other Worlds besides Our Own

The Scotsman James Legge, by virtue of his transcultural experience in China and his later life in the academic sinecure of Oxford, and the German Max Müller, as a result of his transnational career as an Orientalist scholar in exile in England, were strangers in a strange land. Both of them were engaged in a pilgrimage that encompassed—in different, yet ultimately convergent, ways—many of the concerns, ideals, questions, and doubts of the rapidly changing Victorian age. Each of their existential journeys was charged with missionary passion, and each of them played a role in transforming the very meaning of the academic mission to encompass the otherness of the Orient and its religions. Moreover, their final transfigurations, as well as their strategic alliance as foreigners or outsiders (as, respectively, a German Lutheran and a Scottish Nonconformist in an Anglican institution), and as professors, Orientalists, translators, editors, and comparativists, would come about at Oxford University, the oldest and most hallowed of initiatory sites in England for young men and learned sages.

For Müller, life at Oxford became—after his ignominious rejection for the Boden chair of Sanskrit in 1861 and after his decision to stay at the university in the mid-1870s—a matter of an increasingly ardent, and at times defensive, mission to promote the comparativist method of understanding language, myth, religion, and thought itself. As Müller proclaimed so boldly to the Congress of Orientalists in London in 1874, the "comparative spirit is the truly scientific spirit" of the age—adding in his unabashedly romantic way, "nay, of all ages!" "All human knowledge," he unhesitatingly asserts, "begins with the Two or the Dyad, the comprehension of two single things as one."[143]

Legge's life in the 1860s and 1870s was a gradual passage from his status as a Christian missionary to a hyphenated missionary-translator to a Congregational pastor and part-time scholar to a full-time sinological Orientalist. At the age of sixty and back home in Britain, Legge stood upon the threshold of a new professional identity and mission in life. As suggested by his growing sympathy for, and partial identification with, Confucius's own life passage, Legge was now prepared to be receptive to the truth of Müller's *Sacred Books* and ready, as the Chinese master recommends for those approaching the seventh decade of life, "to do as he pleased."

Despite admonishment from the London Missionary Society, Legge had long realized, like Müller, that "there were other worlds besides our own" (quoting Müller's address to the Congress of Orientalists of 1874). Furthermore, Legge instinctively knew that such a comparative awareness of literature and religion made all the difference in the world. As Müller said in 1874, the very "possibility of comparing, measuring, and understanding" is "implied in parallels." It is, as Legge also knew, the vision of some terminological and textual similitude bearing on language, religion, and morality, the comparativist perception of the dyad, that is the basis for all true translation and transcultural communication. Such an intellectual and social passage would, however, be accomplished only at an English and Anglican university that was in the throes of a profound institutional and social reformation.

Given Müller's concern for the deficiencies of Orientalism at Oxford, and because of the efforts of a self-appointed group of concerned merchants and politicians, the time would come when Legge, only a few years after his return home, would be anointed by Corpus Christi College and the university as the first professor of Chinese at Oxford. It was, moreover, the creation at Oxford University of a gigantic new translation enterprise—in an age of monumental textual projects—involving the ancient classics or sacred books of the whole Oriental world that would bring Legge and Müller together in a shared academic mission. This mission and meeting at (so to speak) John Bunyan's House of the Interpreter would continue to the end of the century and would prove to be the definitive intellectual and spiritual journey for both men.

CHAPTER TWO

Professor Legge at Oxford University, 1875-1876

Oxford is a microcosm of English intellectual life. . . . At Oxford men have been thinking what England was to think a few months later, and they have been thinking with the passion and the energy of youth. . . . It is characteristic of England that the exciting topics, the questions that move the people most, have always been religious, or deeply tinctured with religion. Conservative as Oxford is, the home of "impossible causes," she has always given asylum to new doctrines, to all the thoughts which comfortable people call "dangerous."

ANDREW LANG, *OXFORD: BRIEF HISTORICAL AND DESCRIPTIVE NOTES*, 1890

When Cardinal Newman in the latter part of his life visited Oxford, a distinguished company was invited to meet him. A generation had passed since he left Oxford. A friend who sat near him at table told me that Newman inquired of a master, "What changes have come over Oxford since I left?" The answer was, "Greater than I can enumerate; chiefly this, the university has been largely secularized."

MONCURE CONWAY, *AUTOBIOGRAPHY*, 1904

A MICROCOSM OF BRITISH INTELLECTUAL LIFE

This chapter begins and ends with an academic inauguration at Oxford University. The first of these, Max Müller's installation in 1868 in the new Chair of Comparative Philology, looks ahead to, and facilitates, the second: James Legge's assumption in 1876 of the first Oxford professorship of Chinese. Both of these initiatory events are related in terms of the increasing professionalization of academic Orientalism in Britain as a humanistic science, and both signal some of the profound changes occurring in English higher education in the 1850s and early 1870s. Promoted in the rapidly expanding periodical press of the period, these were nationalizing and liberalizing transformations of the ancient educational institutions of Oxford and Cambridge. In turn, these changes were directly associated with larger currents of cultural and social reform sweeping through English life during the late-Victorian era.[1] As Müller bluntly said in 1873 about the oldest and most famous of the English universities: "Oxford wants new life."[2]

Reforming Organized Torpor

For much of the first part of the century, Oxford was vainly recalcitrant in matters of educational reform when compared with continental institutions and the Scottish universities. However, by the turn of the century, and especially in the 1870s and 1880s, Oxford was at last seeking out new sources and methods of academic life. From the justly critical perspective of a German research scholar like Müller, Oxford had become too smugly complacent with its long-inherited traditions of gracious indulgence, religious conservatism, and intellectual sluggishness. As a closed corporation of the landed class and the established Anglican Church, Oxford was known more for its "organized torpor" than for its academic vigor or for its contributions to the life of a rapidly changing imperial nation.[3] This kind of vigilant traditionalism reflected the orthodox practice and prescribed study of religion. Oxford was but a microcosm of the larger situation in England, where the influence of radical intellectual and religious movements from the continent was long delayed, despite the fact that critical gusts of German academic scholarship were blowing into the sequestered British Isles throughout most of the century.[4] Living in the aftermath of John Henry Newman and the Tractarian Movement in the 1840s and 1850s, and the creeping religious liberalism of the infamous *Essays and Reviews* of the 1860s, Oxford University in the 1870s was in the midst of a rapid and far-reaching metamorphosis as an academic institution of secular learning. But even during this period of change, the reactionary Romish sentiments of Newmania, especially in the guise of various "spectral Puseyisms" (referring to the leading Oxonian Tractarian of the 1870s, Edward B. Pusey), still continued to scent the rarefied clerical atmosphere of certain ancient colleges.

The inaugurations of Müller and Legge are specific manifestations of the larger revolutions in the intellectual and social institutions of Western academic life. Müller's philological Orientalism, together with his new, comparative "science of religions" and Legge's "sinology," can therefore be associated with the emergence of a new constellation of disciplines and curricula at the end of the Victorian era (i.e., the natural sciences along with the linguistic and historiographic human sciences). The events surrounding the professorial and curricular acceptance of the German philologist Müller and the Nonconformist sinologue Legge are moreover directly related to the rapid professionalization, specialization, and secularization of academic life at Oxford in the last quarter of the century.[5]

The Ideal of Wissenschaft

These changes are related to the internal political struggle at Oxford to institutionalize, after the important English university reforms of the 1850s and 1870s, the new German academic ideal of *Wissenschaft* incarnate in the alien presence of Dr. Friedrich Max Müller (Ph.D., Leipzig). The rationale for academic life in the progressive Germanic sense was that only research scholarship, by virtue of its fastidious devotion to pure, essential, critical, disinterested, impartial, scientific, comparative, inductive, or analytical methods, could contribute to the various special branches, or newly classified species, of knowledge opened up by the relentless worldwide dominion of the Western nations in the nineteenth century.[6] At Oxford in the early 1870s the promotion of this kind of higher and purer academic goal meant primarily the promotion, within the growing liberal faction at Oxford under the symbolic tutelage of Müller, of the "endowment of research" and the overall transformation of undergraduate and faculty life.

"Endowment" in this new liberal sense referred primarily to the funded enhancement of the professorial system of university-based experts, or research scholar-professors, in specialized disciplinary fields distinct from the traditional collegial and tutorial emphasis on teaching an edifying classical corpus of ancient Greek and Latin texts. It was the methodical augmentation of a disciplinary body of knowledge ("knowledge for knowledge's sake" associated with a particular language, or language family, and its related literature), rather than teaching directed toward the cultivation of the moral character and social conscience of the student, that motivated research scholarship. Traditionally the emphasis on teaching the Mediterranean classical corpus could be justified by its contribution to the common molding of an efficient bureaucracy of educated civil servants (whether stationed at home or in the colonies). The endowment of research perspective, though not always intended as such by its supporters, favored a shift away from the teaching of undergraduates to the supposedly higher academic pursuit of pure research promulgated through graduate studies (which provided for a staff of research assistants), printed monographs, dictionaries, encyclopedias, museums, and other types of monumental compendia of specialized historical facts and classified artifacts. Because of the purer motivations of research for research's sake, this kind of activity was declared to be even more beneficial and virtuous than was traditional pedagogy for the imperial progress of Western civilization. Research professors, as distinct from clerical dons engaged in promulgating the vague Mediterranean generalities of a liberal education at the college level, were primarily concerned with understanding whole new bodies of knowledge and, by virtue of linguistic competence and historical insight, uncovering (classifying and preserving) new species of information, applying comparative principles, collecting artifacts, and translating texts from all times and places. Whereas the old tutorial system was by its very nature provincial in a religious and curricular sense, the new research disciplines took the whole world as their subject matter and, as modeled on the comparative philological methods promoted particularly by Sanskritic and Semitic Orientalists, sought to classify all cultural traditions, past and present, in relation to various evolutionary historical schema, a delimited set of philological families, and several hierarchically arranged biological races.

These new notions of pure research and science (whether natural or historiographic in form) were often antagonistic to the traditional pedagogy in the colleges. At the same time, these new ideas about the method and meaning of knowledge were rhetorically aligned with the traditional Oxford system of liberal education (traditionally referring to a curriculum focused on the study of the Mediterranean classical tradition) and competitive examinations (which privileged rote memorization and the facile "version-making" translation of the Latin and Greek classics to and from English). Social barriers were in this way redrawn along class lines that united the amateur scholars among the gentry with the newly emerging professional men of the middle classes. Boundaries were therefore "drawn between technology, with its artisan and commercial connotations, and the concept of 'pure' science as a pursuit fitted, like Latin and Greek, to train the minds of gentlemen" for the work of administering an empire.[7]

Much of the intellectual and emotional climate in England supporting these changes was a product of an age that, because of its imperialistic ambitions, had to confront the existence, and comparative truth, of other classics, other sacred books, and other strangely parallel worlds and cultures that were ancient, Oriental, or savage in nature. More practically speaking, the transformation of scholarship at Oxford was fundamentally related to important changes in English social history as the Oxbridge system of higher education became, often reluctantly, less of an elite clerical finishing school for noble Anglican families and more of a national institution concerned with the training of middle-class professional men from different, nonconforming religious backgrounds.

Oxford in the 1870s: So Much to Sift

In his inaugural lecture of 1868 that established the new humanistic discipline of comparative philology at Oxford, Max Müller insightfully noted that the ancient English universities traditionally supplied only what the empire "expected or demanded." And England, or rather English parents from either an upper- or middle-class background, "did not send their sons to learn Chinese or to study Cornish." There was "no supply where there was no demand" and the "professorial element in the university"—"the true representative of higher learning and independent research"—languished.[8] But it was only after the gradual professionalization of the professorate itself, the self-interested association of university prestige (as distinct from the authority of the colleges and tutors) with illustrious professorial ornaments, and the grudging acceptance of the new disciplines into the undergraduate examination system that a demand was created for nonclassical subjects and dons. Only then could English parents even partially justify their sons (and daughters after 1879, an event also involving Legge) studying the language and history of such exotically extravagant Oriental traditions as that of China—or, for that matter, even modern English history or the English language.

The comparative classification, evaluation, and assimilation of the increasingly abundant and bewilderingly diverse forms of new information pouring into the intellectual coffers of Paris, Berlin, London, and Oxford from all over the world necessitated the creation of new humanistic sciences and new methods of critical interpretation. Ultimately this resulted in the transformation of older forms of biblical, classical, and commentarial understanding associated with clerical training and led (beginning in the 1850s) to the establishment of a new class of university research scholars deployed and employed precisely because of their specialized ability to translate, critically decipher, and imperialistically control alien texts. "One of the great charms," as Müller put it, of these new sciences was that "there is so much to explore, so much to sift, so much to arrange." Moreover, to explore, to arrange, to sift, to classify, to order—such actions always implied in Müller's formulation of these matters an imperial "will to power" based on the oldest of martial principles: "divide and conquer [*divide et impera*]."[9]

According to Müller, the modern spirit of education should not hand down intact nor lay up, "as it were, in a napkin, the traditional stock of human knowledge." The really important academic task, even more than teaching, was the process of "constantly adding" to this stock of knowledge, "increasing it fivefold and tenfold."[10] Above all else, this required a devotion to "knowledge for its own sake" and a "chivalrous" commitment "to studies which command no price in the fair of the world" and "lead to no places of emolument in church and state."[11] Thus did Max Müller lay out a program for a new generation of scientific learning at Oxford.

A New Class of Scholar

There was a time in the recent past at Oxford when, as Müller said, "every kind of learning" was in the hands of the celibate tutors of the colleges. But now "other studies, once mere germs and shoots on the tree of knowledge, separated from the old stem and assumed an independent growth" (whether as the natural or humanistic sciences). The time had come to support, financially and politically, a new class of professional dons or secular fellows.[12] The problem was that at that moment in England (that is, in the late 1860s) no remunerative lifelong career in pure scholarship was really possible and "no father could honestly advise his son, whatever talent he might display, to devote himself exclusively to classical, historical, or physical studies." The tradition in England was still too much that of the amateur or gentleman scholar. Men with scholarly interests, even those with independent means, could not "devote more than the leisure hours, left by their official duties in church or state, to the prosecution of their favorite studies."[13] This, of course, also constitutes an apt description of Legge's hyphenated situation as a missionary-scholar, pastor-scholar, or amateur sinologist in the late 1860s and early 1870s.

The new professional class of university professors and their deputies—determined in relation to professional credentials and secular scholastic accomplishments rather than celibate status and clerical preferment—will "follow up new lines of study" and "devote [its] energies to work which, from its very nature [i.e., secular, not clerical], could not be lucrative or even self-supporting." This "class of independent workers" would devote itself to "original research." Research scholarship of this kind would involve not just translation pure and simple or the "acquisition of a scholar-like knowledge of other languages besides Greek and Latin" (as it did in Müller's reputation-making scholarship on the *Rig-Veda*), but, in a higher sense, the preparation of "critical editions of the classics" and, for those not committed to the physical sciences, "fearless" research into "the ancient history of mankind" and a "life-long occupation with the problems of philosophy." Lastly, but "not least," these scholars would be concerned with "a *real* [my emphasis] study of theology" or, more accurately, with the "science of religion."[14] For Müller, therefore, the methods and goals of the various new "research" disciplines are descriptively solipsistic and are all closely interrelated—especially the comparative sciences of philology, Orientalism, mythology, and religion.[15]

Only because of these developments would the greatest of the British universities be able, in the face of the threat of French and German advances in the academic colonization of scholarship, to "maintain the fame of English learning, English industry, and English genius in that great and time-honored republic of learning which claims the allegiance of the whole of Europe" or even (the rhetoric at this point reprising another of Müller's braying nays) the "whole civilized world."[16] In this way, England, "the wealthiest country in Europe," would be able to restore Oxford's grandeur "not simply as a place of education" immersed in an unwieldy mix of "spectral Puseyisms," Paterian aestheticism, Spencerian atheism, and Huxleyian agnosticism, but as a true "seat of learning."[17] The problem was that both from the Broad Church *Essays and Reviews* liberal position of Benjamin Jowett and from the more radically secular standpoint of Mark Pattison, Oxford had, since the end of the eighteenth century, remained too much of a "castle of indolence" that ridiculed new forms of Germanic scholarship and shied away from any critical approach to the crucial issues of religion in the singular and plural.[18]

A Dissipated Lizard

Mark Pattison, the intellectually formidable rector of Lincoln College who was once described as "a dissipated lizard with a cold," was the archetypal mordant scholar and ordained Oxonian cleric who "lived wholly" for research and study.[19] "Petrified by the sentiment of the infinite" glimpsed within the bewildering historical plenum of literature (what he called the *totum scribile* or all that had been written in the world), Pattison is the great Oxford exemplar of radical intellectual change and religious cynicism in the late nineteenth century.[20] As suggested in his *Memoirs,* Pattison's intellectual development was never a matter of an abrupt conversion; rather, it was more of a slow, gradual, transforming process of maturation—a process fictionalized in Mrs. Humphry Ward's best-selling novel, *Robert Elsmere.*[21] As he remarks in his *Memoirs* about his changing states of mind at Oxford: "I seemed to my friends to have changed, to have gone over from High Anglicanism to Latitudinarianism, or Rationalism, or Unbelief, or whatever the term may be."

But "this is not so," Pattison says, because "what took place with me was simple expansion of knowledge and ideas," a gradual "widening of horizons" concerning religion: from his boyhood Puritanism ("almost narrowed to two points—fear of god's wrath and faith in the doctrine of atonement") through Anglicanism and absquatulation to, slowly and finally, a comparativist perspective where "all religions appear in their historical light, as efforts of the human spirit to come to an understanding with that Unseen Power whose pressure it feels, but whose motives are a riddle." There was no sudden "conversion or change of view; I could no more have helped what took place within me than I could have helped becoming ten years older."[22]

Ransacking the Past

Pattison was one of the leaders in the "endowment of research" debate over the changing meaning of the university in the mid-1870s, a movement that peaked in a series of *Essays on the Endowment of Research* published in the very year of Legge's inauguration.[23] The authors of these reforming essays saw Müller as their hero and concluded the *Essays* with an extended extract from Müller's 1868 inaugural address. Aside from the overall concern for institutional reform, our attention is drawn to the specific methodological tone of several of the essays that sought, especially regarding the comparative and historiographical sciences, to combine the German academic spirit (which may be "too lax" or philosophically speculative in its methods) with some of the slow and steady empirical advantages of the "sober English mind."[24]

As Müller's new deputy, the Assyriologist and Anglican priest Archibald Sayce, makes clear in his discussion of the "historical sciences" for the *Essays,* the scholarly research of the human sciences needs to borrow from the "exact and cautious" habit of mind, and the "inductive and comparative method," coming from "the advances of physical science." It is this kind of sensibility that will set aside the "jealous exclusiveness of the old classical scholarship" and apply itself to all of the burgeoning new worlds of language, literature, and history.[25] In Sayce's view, history in the broadest sense is a kind of master comparativist discipline drawing together all of the other human sciences, such as comparative philology, ethnology, archaeology, comparative law, comparative literature, comparative philosophy, and comparative religions. The ideal for this new school of historians is that the "facts with which they deal would be compared, classified, and verified with the same rigour as the facts of chemistry or physiology."[26]

It was exciting for historians with this new comparativist sensibility to know that so many new worlds, beyond the old Mediterranean classical realm, had been opened up for exploration and dominion. Sayce's primary example of these new worlds and of the fact that "some of the most valuable facts" of linguistic science may be discovered in "a remote and barbarous idiom" is, most interestingly, the Chinese language—and yet "those only who have devoted their attention to the science of language can have any idea of the loss occasioned to it at Oxford by the absence there of a Chair of Chinese."[27] What is especially needed, says Sayce, is the "enthusiasm of the explorer and discoverer." "Further research," therefore, demands that new texts be "procured" and the "monasteries of the East," the "records of Brahmin and Buddhist temples," and the "mounds of Ninevah and Babylon" be "ransacked."[28] As to the advantages that will come from such an aggressive approach, Sayce says that the "decipherment of the sacred records of India, of Persia, of Egypt, and of Babylonia" have already "opened a new chapter in the history of Christianity and religion, and brought home to us a lesson of tolerance and brotherhood which cannot but influence our dealings with men of other creeds as well as the current of our own religious life." How such a rapacious attitude toward academic research would result in lessons of tolerance and brotherhood remained blithely unclear.

According to Sayce, the only truly appropriate place for the accomplishment of all this furious researching, comparing, and classifying is the university, with its enlarged corps of battle-hardened professors. "Universities," Sayce declares, "should be the place where the whole circle of existing knowledge is brought together and enlarged." This will involve a whole series of interrelated institutions, which collectively constitute an amazingly accurate description of the imperialistic agenda of the Western university ideal in the nineteenth and twentieth centuries:

First of all will come a numerous and well-endowed staff of professors, each regarded by competent experts as supreme in his own special subject, and accompanied by one or more assistant lecturers. Next we must have museums and galleries, filled with carefully selected specimens of art and science and furnished with all possible means for studying them. Then will follow collections of inscriptions and manuscripts. . . . Lastly [there will be] funds for scientific missions for excavating abroad, or for observing the manner of fast-perishing savages, as well as for the production of books of permanent value which shall embody the researches of eminent *savants*.[29]

The Jowler

The celebrated and intimidating Benjamin Jowett, "the Jowler," the imperious master of progressive Balliol College, was primarily responsible for setting the moderately liberal intellectual and political agenda for much of Oxford during the 1870s and 1880s. With good reason, some have called him, after Newman, the greatest and most influential Oxford figure of the nineteenth century. He was the one whose pithy Olympian command, "cease to drift," became the standard for an undergraduate education all too prone to lazy intellectual meandering. Jowett's liberal sensibilities are not only Broad Church but also broadly expressive of the comparativist perspective of religions expressed by his fair-weather friend and colleague Max Müller. Indeed, the liberal flavor of Jowett's comparativist sensibility is conveyed by an oft-told anecdote that, after hearing the Master of Balliol preach on non-Christian religions, a distinguished Indian visitor to Oxford "announced himself re-converted to Buddhism."[30] Müller, it is important to note, was much closer to Jowett's (and Arthur Stanley's) liberal Anglican position than to Pattison's more radical scepticism. Müller's science of language did not "unduly threaten religious faith"[31] and, as A. C. de Vooys has said, Müller remained "at heart a believer"—a pietistic and "sentimental Lutheran" who, in England, identified with the class-bound social and intellectual pretensions of Oxonian Broad Church Anglicanism.[32]

Jowett differed from both Müller and Pattison on the "endowment of research" debate at Oxford. The Jowler, unlike the Imperious German and the Dissipated Lizard, was coolly contemptuous of what he viewed as the "useless learning" associated with German-style research professorships. As a distinguished scholar of the Greek classics, Jowett still held onto the old tutorial ideal of a "liberal education" centered on the Mediterranean classics and stressing the character-building skills of translation, rote memory, rhetoric, and composition. This did not mean that he was opposed to new intellectual trends, innovative disciplinary areas, German-influenced critical methods, or—for that matter—the enhancement and expansion of the university professorate. He was even one of the supporters of the new professorial chair of Chinese established for Legge. Nor did Jowett oppose the introduction of new subjects and disciplines into the various college curricula: for example, he was one of the staunch defenders of T. H. Green's Hegelian approach to philosophy at Balliol College.

It was rather a matter of Jowett's reservations about a narrowly academic "knowledge for knowledge's sake" pedagogy at the undergraduate level. For Jowett, a liberal education should be "applied" to the difficult issues of the moral development and social engagement of human nature. In this educational context, the Greek and Latin classics had proven their worth. As a liberal traditionalist in educational matters, Jowett was not in principle opposed to the use of other subjects, especially if those other languages and literatures had edifying import or some kind of classical status. (Here it is worth noting that, inasmuch as he tried always to combine pure scholarship with very practical pedagogical concerns, Legge's conception of his professorial position at Oxford had more affinity with Jowett's views on these matters than with Müller's.)

Horton's Upheaval and Unrest

Another perspective that gives some clue to Legge's initial emotions about the academic environment he was entering at Oxford is seen in the autobiographical reflections of the Nonconformist theologian Robert Forman Horton. Horton was among the first of the dissenting Congregationalist undergraduates admitted after the University Tests Act in 1871, attending Oxford during the years that overlapped with the time of Legge's arrival there (1874–1878). From his evangelical outlook, Horton tells us that the late 1870s were a time of intellectual "upheaval and unrest" and, although Comtean positivism had not gained a strong hold in Oxford life, utilitarian, agnostic, and materialistic views were rampant. The "whole trend" before the contrapuntal influence of T. H. Green's Hegelian idealism in the 1880s was "against faith, not only against Christianity, but against Theism."[33] Furthermore, religious life at this time was still dominated by the High Church Puseyites, while the evangelical and Nonconformist presence was "genuine but feeble," tending toward an unattractive antiintellectualism and the "dissonance of dissent."[34]

Corroboration of Horton's views and further insight into a Nonconformist and Congregationalist evaluation of the religious situation are provided by the previously quoted "Oxonian" writing for the *Congregationalist* magazine in 1879.[35] From this observer's vantage point, Oxford tolerated all sorts of sins except the "wearing of dirty linen and [religious] enthusiasm." Oxford was in the throes of a "cold-blooded, analytical age" and was becoming thoroughly secular in both substance and emotion: "the university as a university is not religious, but painfully, hideously irreligious." Interestingly, this secular attitude is linked with a comparativist sensibility toward non-Christian religions: "there is a story of one of these 'leaders of thought,' that there came under his teaching a converted Mahomedian, whom, by an impartial appreciation of alien religions, he induced to return to his old faith." The punch line to this story is that the professor in question "justified the result by pleading 'that it did not matter, the man in question was not much credit to any religion!' "[36]

An Important Epoch

This story sounds suspiciously like a garbled variation on the anecdote recounted above about the redoubtable Jowler Jowett and the Indian visitor. More noteworthy, perhaps, is that there was apparently a popular mythicized narrative tradition about both the effects of comparativist thought and the exotic presence of various native Orientals at Oxford. With regard to the latter issue, we know that by the end of the decade—due to the general attractiveness of Oxford for Orientals living under British rule, but also because of Orientalist scholars such as Müller, Monier Williams, Legge, Sayce, and a young A. A. Macdonell, who were drawing strange disciples and visitors—there was a tiny Asian presence at Oxford. An interesting example of this alien faction is the extended presence of two Japanese Buddhist students who studied Sanskrit and Chinese texts at Oxford with both Müller and Legge in the 1870s and 1880s.[37]

For anyone within the British Isles (except perhaps the Scots, who were rightfully proud of their own more liberal tradition of university education), it was self-evident that whatever was instituted at Oxford ("one of the most celebrated universities during the Middle Ages and in the modern history of Europe") would reverberate throughout much of the Anglo-American world of higher education—if not throughout all of Europe and the "whole civilized world." In this sense, Müller observed in 1868 that the "foundation of a professorial chair in the University of Oxford"—positions in new disciplinary fields such as comparative philology or in newly specialized forms of Orientalism such as sinology, for instance—"marks an important epoch in the history of every new science."[38]

The Honored Republic of Learning

To appreciate the epochal implications of Legge's inauguration, it is crucial to investigate the overall rationale for Oriental studies developed in Müller's inaugural address in 1868 on behalf of the chair of Comparative Philology. Müller's talk sets the context for several critical institutional reforms at Oxford, changes that he himself both fomented and benefited from. "Fortunately," as Müller said, ever since the reforms of the 1850s, Oxford had started to enter into the modern era in the "honored republic of learning." This was marked by the fact that "the funds originally intended, without distinction, for the support of 'true religion and useful learning,' are now again more equally apportioned among those who, in the age in which we live, have divided and subdivided the vast intellectual inheritance of the Middle Ages." This address is also significant for containing the first recorded allusion to the contested establishment of sinological Orientalism as one of the newer nooks and crannies in "the boundless field of human knowledge" at Oxford.[39]

The Boden Chair Affair

On October 27, 1868, Friedrich Max Müller—resident of Oxford for more than twenty years and an elected fellow of the austerely prestigious All Souls College—stood in the speaker's well of the Sheldonian Theatre, the oddly handsome circular arena designed by Christopher Wren that was ringed by the busts of classical patriarchs and was the site of many famous and infamous Oxonian orations. Those addresses were often controversial presentations concerned with matters of the mind and spirit, but, even more frequently, they turned on heated issues of academic politics. The intertwined intellectual and political significance of the setting could hardly be lost on Müller since this was the location of the most severely traumatic disappointment in his career at Oxford.

Some seven years earlier, Müller was decisively defeated—as he tactfully put it in his autobiography, "for financial, theological, or national reasons"—in the convocational voting (open to all graduates of Oxford and in 1868 numbering around four thousand members) for the Boden chair of Sanskrit. His ignominious failure to secure the Boden professorship and its particularly generous emoluments (£1000 a year) was one of the pivotal events in Müller's scholarly life and puts the lie to his claim that he never had any interest in worldly success. No matter how much he protested otherwise, Müller was constantly haunted by this rejection. It was, after all, a humiliating event, debated in the *Times* of London as much as in Oxford itself, and one that he personally interpreted as irrevocable proof of his status as a German intruder at Oxford.

As Müller is careful to indicate, the decision was not made on scholarly grounds but in relation to the "express desire" of Colonel Joseph Boden, of the East India Company, "to provide efficient missionaries for India."[40] It almost seems at times, and his famous lecture at Westminster Abbey (see pages 113–19) is one specific example of this, that Müller is constantly driven to show how his incumbency would have lived up to the spirit, if not exactly the letter, of the chair's stipulations concerning missionaries. We know, therefore, that, while he was clearly stretching the point, Müller felt that the new comparativist disciplines were crucial to the developmental fulfillment of Christianity's true mission to the world.

Müller's difficulties in securing the Boden chair are similar to the issues complicating the relationship between the London Missionary Society and an agent such as Legge, who spent so much time translating the Oriental classics. The question in both cases was one of which approach, apologetic and antagonistic or scholarly and comparatively sympathetic, was more efficient in transforming literate heathen peoples such as the Indians or the Chinese. Which was more effective? Was it the controversial conversion of natives (so effective with illiterate, so-called savage traditions) through the fluent use of the spoken vernacular and a determined dissemination of a wholly unique and singularly salvific Bible? Or did it depend on methods, such as those employed by Müller and Legge, that took seriously the principle of identifying cultures through translation and comparison, even to the point that literate traditions such as the Indian and Chinese were perceived to have ancient scriptural traditions? Müller and Legge would say that preference must be given to an approach that recognizes the superiority of the Christian Bible but, at the same time, acknowledges and respects the wisdom and truth found in the bibles of the literate Eastern civilizations.

It must have been galling for Müller to know that the Boden chair went to Monier Monier-Williams, a former evangelical Anglican missionary to India who had only a meager scholarly reputation and, most damaging from the standpoint of Müller's critical philological science, little appreciation of ancient Sanskrit classics such as the *Rig-Veda*. In fact, Müller and Monier-Williams both engaged in a healthy contempt for each other's person and scholarship. This mutual antipathy reached such proportions that, in partial response to the constant denigration of his scholarly abilities (e.g., Müller's fury, and proffered resignation, over an honorary award given to Monier-Williams) and Oxonian accomplishments (such as, for example, the endowed establishment of the Indian Institute), Monier-Williams launched an angry public attack on the comparative science of religions and Müller's pet project of the *Sacred Books of the East*. Even at the time of the convocation election for the chair, Monier-Williams proudly stood on the amateur's side of "practical" English scholarship, opposed to Müller's Germanic and professional "endowment of research" approach. "Englishmen," said Monier-Williams, "are too practical to study a language [such as Sanskrit] very philosophically."[41]

Tall and strikingly handsome, with bright blue eyes, a musically resonant voice, poetic eloquence, expository power, metaphorical inventiveness, diplomatic manners, and an erect, somewhat military, bearing, Müller, already one of the most prolific and publicly renowned scholars in the British

Isles and on the continent, was only forty-five years old in 1868. As he stood in the Sheldonian to give his inaugural address for the newly created professorial chair in Comparative Philology, he could not help but feel that he had overcome the shadows cast by the Boden incident. This newly created university position was, as he says rather disingenuously in his autobiography, a great "honour" that he "had never even dreamt" of receiving and that he "certainly had never taken any steps" to secure.[42] These observations reveal an instance of the darker side of Müller's character in that he identifies his feigned disinterest in the Tylorian professorship with what, in his autobiography, he calls the real "secret" of his whole life. This secret is described as, on the one hand, his honest conviction or "faith" in comparative scholarship and, on the other hand, his mock-humble declaration of a "perfect indifference as to worldly success."[43]

Although he was eight years younger than Legge, Müller was very much the senior in their forthcoming relationship as professorial colleagues at Oxford and as fellow laborers on the monumental *Sacred Books of the East*. In the simplest sense this disparity was the result of Müller's seasoned familiarity with the arcana of academic life at Oxford. It also depended on Müller's creation and editorial direction, under the aegis of the Oxford University Press (where he sat on the overseeing board), of the *Sacred Books* project and his overall influence within the world of international Oriental scholarship. Even beyond the relatively narrow academic realm of universities, Orientalist congresses, and scholarly journals, Müller had achieved considerable public fame as a pioneer in, and as a popularizer of, various intellectual fields (especially for his work in Indian studies, comparative philology, comparative mythology, and most recently, in the mid-1870s, the comparative science of religion). By the end of the decade, many of Müller's views were passionately criticized and he was defensively embroiled in several celebrated battles, the most notable being those concerning his anti-Darwinian ideas about language origins and his theory of mythology.[44]

Compared with Müller, Legge was only a relatively obscure ex-missionary from the provincial lowlands of northeastern Scotland who had spent most of his life in the exotic hinterland of China. He was, moreover, an evangelical Nonconformist with the air of a "country farmer," which meant, even after the reforms of 1871 opened the ancient university to dissenters (that is, the Tests Act by which faculty and students were no longer required to sign a statement confirming their belief in the Thirty-nine Articles of the Anglican faith), that he would always be an outsider to much of the academic and social life at Oxford. Whatever renown Legge had attained as a sinological scholar beyond the London Missionary Society and other missionary circles was in precisely the area in which Müller was the acknowledged international master and arbiter—that is, in the translation and publication of the Oriental classics. Legge was never obsequious in his relationship with Müller, but it is clear that the old Scotsman felt indebted to his considerably more famous younger colleague.

Every Nook and Every Corner

As was the tradition on such inaugural occasions, Müller in 1868 carefully set out the historical background and academic justification for his new position. Even beyond what I have already discussed of his rationale, this meant that for Müller the study of comparative philology could be shown to be one of the best ways of reviving, on a more scientific and critical basis, the traditional Oxonian study of the Greek and Latin classics. But what is particularly salient is that he opens his lecture with a special plea for the need to look into "every nook and every corner in the boundless field of human knowledge." For Müller this specifically refers to the expansion of Oriental studies at Oxford. Orientalism as a new subject matter and discipline had not been totally ignored in England. Britain could hardly remain oblivious to the fabled East since, by the last quarter of the nineteenth century, it ruled one of the greatest Oriental empires of all time. Many of the great eighteenth-century pioneers in Sanskrit, such as William Jones and Henry Thomas Colebrooke, were, after all, British gentlemen scholars. Moreover, the *Asiatic Researches* established in Calcutta in 1788 could lay claim to being the first scholarly journal of Orientalism. At Oxford there were chairs in both Arabic and Sanskrit. Similar positions existed at Cambridge and at a few London colleges. For Müller it was incredible that, in a country having the greatest commercial and political interest in China (some £40,000,000 of trade per year by the late 1860s),[45] so little attention was paid to the newly emerging Orientalist science of sinology. Even though in London there were two Chinese positions (one of which was long vacant),[46] neither of the ancient universities of Cambridge and Oxford had a chair in Chinese—that "language which, from the very beginning of history, . . . seems always to have been spoken by the largest number of human beings."

Going on to provide a fuller intellectual rationale for the academic study of Chinese, Müller claims that a position is particularly called for "if we consider the light which a study of that curious form of human speech is intended to throw on the nature and growth of language." Furthermore, research on China and the Chinese language is justified "if we measure the importance of [China's] enormous literature by the materials which it supplies to the student of ancient religions and likewise to the historian who wishes to observe the earliest rise of the principal sciences and arts in countries beyond the influence of Aryan and Semitic civilization."[47]

Like a Never-Fading Photograph

Lastly, Müller declares that we should consider the "evidence which the Chinese language, reflecting, like a never-fading photograph, the earliest workings of the human mind, is able to supply to the student of psychology, and to the careful analyzer of the elements and laws of thought." Then, he says (and all of these are reasons extrapolated from claims associated with the study of comparative Aryan philology), we would "feel less inclined to ignore or ridicule the claims of such a language to a chair in our ancient university."[48] But few, if any, of these sweeping contributions to human knowledge ever came about—or were even attempted after the embarrassing collapse of the Turanian hypothesis, the demise of sinological Aryanism and Babylonianism, and the fading away of Leggian Shangdi-ism. These failures distinguish the special case of sinological Orientalism from other forms of Orientalism. During the nineteenth century, Orientalism in the most general sense, especially when conceived of as a particular method and comparativistic attitude, mostly fell under the Aryan rule of comparative philology and its handmaiden, Sanskritic or Indological studies.

Much of the unrealized potential for comparative theorizing in sinology is related to the unique stubbornness of what the great chronicler of Indological Orientalism, Raymond Schwab, called "China's linguistic instrument." The embarrassing and even laughable inability of nineteenth-century Chinese scholars to determine in any convincing way, as had been done for Sanskrit and the "familial" similarities of Aryan or Indo-European languages, some essential sameness beneath the strangely undulating surface of the Chinese language (both phonically and graphically) prevented sinology's entry into the mainstream of Orientalism and the comparative sciences. As Schwab suggests, it was the "formidable solitude" of the Chinese language and tradition, especially after the spectacular failures of various monogenetic theories of sino-Aryan and sino-Babylonian linguistic origins, that helped to render "the problem of equivalences among languages almost absurd." So also did the obdurate singularity of the Chinese tradition and the consequent emphasis on linguistic and cultural polygenesis—along with other dramatic disciplinary developments in the human sciences at the turn of the century—lead finally to the suppression of Müllerian-style comparativism.

Hebdomadal Ridicule

In his inaugural address, Müller mentions that a good deal of ridicule was directed against the claims of a Chinese chair at Oxford. What is interesting about this particular example of Oxonian derision is that Müller was alluding to an actual incident involving the Hebdomadal Council, the all-powerful intercollegiate ruling body of Oxford University. (Müller once lamented that he was never an elected member of this inner sanctum of Oxford political power.) It is also evident that he was referring to Legge (though he remains unnamed and with a mistaken national identity) when he notes that "an offer to found a professorship of Chinese, to be held by an Englishman whom even Stanislas Julien recognized as the best Chinese scholar of the day, has lately been received very coldly by the Hebdomadal Council of the University."[49] How this coldly received offer relates to the later successful effort initiated in 1875 is not exactly clear, although Legge's *Chinese Classics* were certainly known at Oxford by the late 1860s and he may even have been there in person when, in the winter of 1868, Wang Tao gave a public lecture at Oxford.[50] What is certain is that Max Müller was instrumental in Oxford's change of heart in 1875 and had been a supporter of Legge's scholarship since the first volume of the *Chinese Classics* was published.

Müller on "The Works of Confucius"

In 1861, at the time of his difficulties with the Boden chair, Müller wrote a review of what he called "The Works of Confucius," Legge's first volume of the *Classics*.[51] In light of the issues surrounding the Boden debacle and his Westminster lecture on missions, it is notable that Müller emphasizes the "usefulness" of missionaries who spend their "leisure hours" engaged in "scientific pursuits." The missionary movement, which "is spread over the whole globe," constitutes the "most perfect machinery that could be devised for the collection of all kinds of scientific knowledge."[52] Müller flattered Legge by identifying him with a hardy band of enlightened missionaries who were "pioneers of science"—an illustrious group that included the "Jesuit missionaries in India and China," the "Baptist missionaries at Serampore," Wilson and Moffatt, among others, in India, and "last but not least," Livingstone in Africa. Müller observes that Legge's work on the Chinese sage known as Confucius proves "what can be achieved by missionaries." "Even if he had not converted a single Chinese," he would, because of his scholarly efforts, have rendered "important aid to the introduction of Christianity into China."[53]

The rest of this review is mostly an unremarkable digest of Legge's career and his translation of Confucius or Kongzi's teachings. Of special interest is the selection of quotations from the Chinese sage, which suggests some of Müller's own ruling principles. Müller singles out passages that illustrate Kongzi's "tolerant spirit"; his "honest manliness"; his passion for knowledge, which, if "less profound than that of Socrates, is nevertheless full of good sense"; the humanistic wisdom of his particular way of phrasing the golden rule; and his "witness to the hidden connection between intellectual and moral excellence."[54] But Müller avoids any real discussion of Kongzi's religiousness or of Legge's views of the man and his legacy, remarking only in passing that "on subjects which transcend the limits of human understanding, Confucius is less explicit." Müller finds this silence or "reticence" "remarkable" in its own right when compared with "the recklessness with which oriental philosophers launch into the deep waters of religious metaphysics."[55]

AMATEURS AND PROFESSIONALS
IN THE HISTORY OF BRITISH SINOLOGY

We may smile, if we please, at the levity of the French, as they laugh without scruple at our seriousness; but let us not so far undervalue our rivals in arts and in arms, as to deny them their just commendation, or to relax our efforts in that noble struggle [of Oriental studies], by which alone we can preserve our own eminence.

WILLIAM JONES, "ON THE SECOND CLASSICAL BOOK OF THE CHINESE," 1799

Voguish "Ologies"

Eight years after Müller's rehearsal of the subject, the Sheldonian stage was set for a sinological drama to unfold for the first time at Oxford. The improbable protagonist in this event was James Legge. Standing at the same spot in the Sheldonian that Müller had stood, Legge in October of 1876 gave his own inaugural lecture as the new professor of Chinese. By this time, the climate in Oxford for Chinese studies and Nonconformists had changed from ridicule to diffident acceptance. To comprehend this belated and grudging acceptance of sinological Orientalism, some of the checkered history of British Chinese scholarship must be examined. Often lethargic throughout much of the first half of the nineteenth century, sinological scholarship in English can also be thought of in William Jones's terms as a "struggle" between the earnest gentlemanly "seriousness" of the British and the "higher," and more professionalized, Jesuitical "levity" of the early French academicians. The sober struggle waged by British missionary and gentleman scholars was a battle against the internalized inertia of the old ideal of the amateur and, more externally and nationalistically, a contest waged experientially in the field against the abstract scientific pretensions of Parisian *sinologues de chambre* such as Rémusat and Julien.

The overall history of Western sinology remains to be written. Part of the problem in producing such a history is directly related to the strangeness of sinological Orientalism in relation to the greater realm of Aryan and Semitic philology and Orientalism in the nineteenth century. But the problem is primarily rooted in the overall complexity of the historical record from both a European and an Asian point of view. The study of Chinese tradition is intertwined with the whole spotted chronicle of Western relations with all of Asia. Moreover, the specific Western encounter with the Middle

Kingdom has a long and complicated history that, though initiated by medieval European merchants and missionaries, begins in earnest only with
the brilliant multinational efforts of the Jesuits in the seventeenth and eighteenth centuries. The history of the intellectual involvement of the West
and the "curious land" of China has been impressively studied by Henri
Cordier, Donald Lach, Raymond Dawson, David Mungello, Étiemble, and
others (most recently, Lionel Jensen, Robert Bickers, and David Honey)
from the European point of view and by Jacques Gernet, Jerome Ch'en,
Paul Cohen, and Zhang Longxi from more of the Chinese perspective.[56]
Despite these efforts, and an abundance of substantial specialized studies
devoted to the early Jesuit mission, a full examination of the history of sinology as it relates to the "general intellectual history of the Western world" is
only now "getting under way."[57] Most unfortunate in this regard is that the
history of nineteenth-century sinology and its contextual relation with the
larger discursive currents of Orientalism, the comparative "humanistic sciences," and various nationalistic genres of scholarship have been largely neglected.[58]

The nineteenth century is especially important in relation to glacial
shifts in the epistemes of Western knowledge at the start of the century. As
Michel Foucault understands it, this involved a gradual movement away
from a mimetic representational approach to the understanding of experience (especially the natural world) to a developmental, historical, or comparative method of knowing the order (hierarchical classification) and
meaning (in terms of some originally pure essence, root, race, *Quelle*, family, ancestor, etc.) of things. The distinctive epistemological quality of the
nineteenth century was its focus on "man" (the patriarchal meaning intended in both a developmental and hierarchical sense) and the historical
methods, or comparative sciences, of studying the institutions of civilization
in relation to their origins and growth.[59] As the work of Schwab and Maurice Olender shows, Orientalism, comparative philology, Indology, and
Indo-European studies (along with, to some degree, Semitic forms of Orientalism)—more so than the late-blooming and largely isolated sinology—
had a special role to play in the unfolding of these new ways of knowing at
the start of the nineteenth century. Part of the reason for this is that a comparative and historical approach to understanding seemed to be powerfully
supported by the self-proclaimed success of the Aryan or Indo-European
hypothesis in comparative philology.[60] The situation regarding the so-
called Turanian or Chinese languages was in no way comparable when it
came to the crucial matter of comparison. The Chinese language, like sinology and most things about Chinese civilization at that time, maintained its
integrity by remaining singularly peculiar.

It is not until the 1870s that the study of Chinese texts became the professionalized Oriental science of sinology embracing Anglo-American tra-

dition and the rest of the Western world. Although the Parisian sinological tradition went back to the start of the century, it was only later that the specialized study of Chinese language and literature became a self-conscious academic discourse rooted in philological and comparative historiographical methods ministered by a multinational battalion of research scholars. Public manifestations of these developments were seen in the emergence of various new learned societies, journals, university positions, museums, and congresses throughout Europe and America. For the first time, the study of China established itself as an academic discipline or -ology beyond the enlightened academic salons of Paris.

These developments in the English-speaking world are reflected by a discussion, occurring in the mid-1870s, about the use of a new professional vocabulary of *sinologue* and *sinologist*. The *China Review,* which along with several other English-language journals produced in coastal enclaves in China was among the first true sinological journals, refers to a letter originally appearing in the February 13, 1876, issue of the general literary review known as the *Academy* that remarked on the fact that in intellectual circles the word *sinologue* was "coming into vogue." At the same time, the London *Times* was publicly notifying its readers of the imminent creation of an Oxford professorate of Chinese. Echoing nationalistic rivalries over the intellectual control of these new linguistic and literary worlds, the author of the letter in the *Academy* was concerned that since in "English we say philologist, etc. . . . ," the Gallic word *sinologue* should take on proper English dress and be altered to "Sinologist"—"in which form it is an excellent English word, well deserving of a place in our dictionaries."[61]

Another important sign is the appearance in 1878 of the first volume of Henri Cordier's massive, and constantly expanding, bibliography known as the *Bibliotheca Sinica.*[62] Knowledgeable about both continental and British scholarship, Cordier was the self-appointed, and indefatigable, chronicler of sinological productivity in the late nineteenth century, an accomplishment that reflects an understanding of disciplinary history primarily in terms of the categories and quantities of its discursive output.[63] Western translations of Chinese texts and other Western writings about China (stretching back to the Jesuits) could now be shown to be classifiable into different discrete developmental periods, topics, and methods (involving an alphabetic ordering of authors and a chronological ordering like that of the earlier, but flawed, *Bibliothèque de Ternaux-Compans,* as well as the more important and *"scientifique"* arrangement in terms of Cordier's five general divisions and fourteen subdivided topical categories for "La Chine proprement dite").[64]

Cordier's classification system helped to establish the parameters for the new science of sinology.[65] However, this kind of bibliographical work, and the special role it plays in the creation of a new academic discourse, is yet another characteristic example of the imperialistic thrust of the nineteenth-century classificatory episteme. Just as the nineteenth century was the great age of monumental textual anthologies and multivolume translations, critical compendia of different textual editions, gigantic encyclopedias, specialized professional journals, scientific societies and academies, "universal" expositions and historical museums, exotic dictionaries and other arcane tools of the discursive sciences, so also were vast second-order bibliographies such as Cordier's—that control, display, classify, compartmentalize, and quantify knowledge—another mark of the age. Again showing the shifting sands of prestige associated with certain kinds of scholarly production during this embryonic period in the history of the "human sciences," one could, as Cordier did, make a substantial scholarly reputation and career by assembling such weighty tomes.[66] Cordier's *Bibliotheca Sinica,* like Legge's translation of the *Chinese Classics,* went on to win in 1880 the coveted Prix Julien of the French Institute. This was before bibliographical work, like Leggian translation, became a *mere* propaedeutic to *real* scholarly research and interpretation.

The Leggian Epoch of Sinology

What can be called the Leggian epoch of sinology—that is, the period roughly from the ascendancy of Legge at Oxford in the 1870s to the end of the century and the revitalization of the French tradition under Édouard Chavannes—coincides with the Müllerian era of comparative Orientalism, which embraced the sciences of comparative philology and religion. The synergistic interrelationship of these exotic disciplines (Orientalism, comparative philology, comparative religion) and the stillborn emergence of sinological Orientalism give some fresh insight into several more general social and cultural issues during the late-Victorian period. So may the Müllerian and Leggian era of British Orientalism, comparativism, and sinology after the 1870s be distinguished from the earlier French eighteenth- and nineteenth-century epoch by the fact that academic developments in the last quarter of the nineteenth century were more institutionally and internationally formative than they were earlier. Despite the influence of the powerful French academicians Rémusat and Julien during the first part of the century, it is not until after the impact of Legge's *Chinese Classics* and Müller's *Sacred Books of the East,* the two greatest scholarly projects of Chinese translation and comparative Orientalism in the late nineteenth century, that the specialized fields of sinological Orientalism and the comparative science of religions achieve some disciplinary recognition within Western academic discourse.

New English-language periodicals (like the China-based publications of the Royal Asiatic Society, the *Chinese Expository, China Review,* and *Chinese*

Recorder) play a role in these developments as the first specialized sinological journals in the Western world. The *Journal asiatique,* though founded in 1822 by Rémusat, tended to focus its attention on Sanskritic and other Indo-European issues; the *Annales du musée Guimet* (1880) and the *Revue de l'Extrême-Orient* (1882, 1883, 1887) were really only precursors to Cordier's fully professionalized *T'oung Pao,* appearing in 1890.[67] French-language publications in sinology would reassert their privileged status after the turn of the century, but the dominance of the British empire at the end of the nineteenth century meant that English-language scholarship would eventually achieve linguistic hegemony within most political and academic realms.

In his magisterial study of intellectual developments on the continent, Schwab recognized that the mid-1870s represented a "boundary line" in the development of Orientalistic discourse related to India. By 1875 most of the significant revelations about Indo-European tradition had been made and the "classification of knowledge" and the academic "consolidation of a humanistic base" had been achieved (e.g., in 1868 the École des Hautes Études was founded in Paris and Indic studies were permitted into the curriculum). At this time, according to Schwab, a series of important publications appeared that essentially summed up the earlier "heroic age" of textual conquest and linguistic advance in the general Indo-European realm of Orientalism:

> Theodor Benfy's *Geschichte der Sprachwissenschaften Orientalischen Philogie in Deutschland (History of Linguistics and Oriental Philology in Germany)* appeared in Munich in 1869. In Paris a "Bibliothèque Oriental" was added in 1870 to a series entitled "Chefs-d'oeuvre de l'Esprit humain." In 1875 [*sic;* the correct date is 1879] the *Sacred Books of the East* series, edited by Max Müller, began to appear in England, making the texts available to everyone. And in 1876 James Fergusson published in London a *History of Indian and Eastern Architecture,* the third volume of his *History of Architecture in All Countries.*[68]

Schwab's list should be expanded to include other watershed works in the 1870s dealing with several new forms of Orientalism and comparative science. Thus Müller's first lectures on the comparative science of religions (1870) and the completion of Legge's first series of the *Chinese Classics* (1872) appeared at this time. In related developments, the Royal Anthropological Society was formed in 1871 and, in the same year, Edward Burnett Tylor published the first edition of his two-volume *Primitive Culture: Researches into the Development of Mythology, Philosophy, Religion, Language, Art, and Custom.* A few years later Herbert Spencer published his *Principles of Sociology.* We can also mention the publication, in America, of such popular works as Moncure Conway's *Sacred Anthology* (1873), Freeman Clarke's *Ten Great Religions* (1871), and Samuel Johnson's multivolume *Oriental Religions and Their Relation to Universal Religion* (*India* in 1872, *China* in 1877, *Persia* in 1885). These last-named American works, although equal, and in some cases superior (particularly Samuel Johnson's work), to many similar studies produced in Europe, were nevertheless mostly ignored by the Old World potentates of academic Orientalism and comparativism in Paris (J-P. A. Réville), in Holland (Cornelis Tiele), and especially in England (Müller).[69]

After midcentury, the growing scientific proficiency and practical knowledge of China-coast scholarship showed the deficiencies of the rationalistic logic of the French-Jesuitical methods as manifest in Julien's "relentless textuality" and dictatorial nastiness. As Cordier (a living bridge between the French and British traditions) accurately remarks, the significance of the 1870s and 1880s in the development of sinology was that, with the return from China of "glorious veterans" like Legge, there was, for the first time, a needed combination of a "practical knowledge" of China with the powerful library science and rationalistic critical attitude of the French tradition. Moreover, China was no longer so wholly isolated and, as graphically symbolized by Legge's observational tour of North China in 1873, there was a concomitant efflorescence of practical fieldwork disciplines such as archaeology, ethnography, folkloristics, and epigraphy in China.[70] Unfortunately, many of these new, more practical sinological Orientalists still tended to look to fashionable Indo-European theories (or to other, even more archaic sources such as Babylonian tradition) for solutions to the obdurate enigmas of the Chinese language and tradition. Despite, or sometimes because of, these efforts, China stubbornly maintained its strangeness.

Singular Listlessness?

Timothy Barrett has written an excellent analysis of what he views as the meager and apathetic history of British sinology—that is, its ever present "listlessness," a characterization borrowed from the early diplomat-scholar John Francis Davis. The problem is that Barrett's little book, for all its pithy and often witty virtues, denigrates the truly formidable significance of Anglo-American developments in sinological Orientalism during the last quarter of the nineteenth century—especially the period from 1873 to 1897, the Leggian epoch in Western sinology.[71] These too often overlooked developments include the accelerated, and self-motivated, professionalization of China-coast amateur scholars from missionary, diplomatic, and commercial backgrounds and the emergence of new specialized journals and a whole series of substantial publications concerned with technical philological matters (grammars, dictionaries, translations) and with new critical interpretive perspectives (comparative philology and other new comparative sciences applied to the study of religion, folklore, ethnography, and anthropology). The role that many China-coast figures (especially missionaries) played in the emergence of sinological Orientalism in the nineteenth century has been largely ignored (e.g., Alexander Wylie, John Chalmers, Joseph Edkins, Ernst Eitel, Ernest Faber, W. A. P. Martin, John Fryer, J. Dyer Ball). Even when figures such as Legge are mentioned, their missionary-tainted backgrounds often seem to prevent any awareness of their full historical and cultural importance. Specially debilitating for the comprehension of the British-American impact on late-nineteenth-century sinological Orientalism has been the common tendency to overlook the contributions of the pioneering English-language China-coast periodicals, the *Chinese Repository,* the *Celestial Empire,* the *Journal of the Shanghai Literary and Scientific Society, Notes and Queries on China and Japan,* the *Phoenix,* and, particularly, the *China Review* and the *Chinese Recorder.*[72]

A strong case can be made that the *Journal of the Shanghai Literary and Scientific Society* under the editorship of the American missionary Elijah Bridgman (it was established in 1858, a descendant of Bridgman's earlier *Repository* and the immediate precursor of the *Journal of the North China Branch of the Royal Asiatic Society*) and the *China Review* (the first issue appearing in July 1872) under Eitel were the first true sinological journals in the Western world. They were, at the very least, the first periodicals wholly devoted to China that were at the same time self-conscious about their so-called scientific mission.[73] The *Review* (along with, to a somewhat lesser degree, the *Recorder*) and the *Journal of the North China Branch of the Royal Asiatic Society* most fully express the secularizing and scientific tendencies of the period. The earlier *Journal of the Shanghai Literary and Scientific Society,* founded by Bridgman, represents a transitional stage where missionary and secular ("scientific and literary") interests were unapologetically combined in the great "battle" for knowledge about the Orient.[74] For Bridgman, the glory of China was the "abundance of work" and the biblical depths of hidden wisdom it offered to the earnest researcher.[75]

Earlier histories of sinology have been remiss in their appreciation of Legge and other pioneering nineteenth-century British and American hyphenated scholars. An especially telling example of this neglect is Barrett's perfunctory reference to the enduring nature of Legge's *Chinese Classics* and his failure even to mention the nature and significance of the Chinese volumes in the *Sacred Book of the East* series. Remarking that Legge produced a "basically sound corpus of work" that was "remarkable in its own time" and is "still useful today," Barrett concludes by saying that Legge was, with the "possible exception of Samuel Beal," the "first professional British scholar in Chinese studies to win an international reputation."[76] Barrett is hard pressed to do much more than suggest that Legge's tenure at Oxford marked a new sinological era "in some ways." Laying out just some of these ways has, however, proven to be a formidable exercise that belies the ordinary defamation of nineteenth-century British sinology.

ORIENTAL DISCOURSE IN THE 1870s:
ALL THAT IS IMPLIED IN PARALLELS

*Before all, a study of the East has taught us the same lesson which the Northern
nations once learnt in Rome and Athens, that there are other worlds beside our
own, that there are other religions, other mythologies, other laws, and that the
history of philosophy from Thales to Hegel is not the whole history of human
thought. In all these subjects the East has supplied us with parallels, and with all
that is implied in parallels, viz., the possibility of comparing, measuring, and
understanding.*

MAX MÜLLER, *SECOND INTERNATIONAL CONGRESS OF ORIENTALISTS,* 1874

The Congressional Spirit

The social and cultural development of Orientalism—and sinological Orientalism's retarded role in relation to the greater whole—is seen in the
newly institutionalized convocations, or multinational congresses, of Orientalists, which were being held for the first time in the 1870s.[77] These
meetings manifest not only the growing internationalism of Western scholarship but also, as seen in the pecking order of cities that hosted these congresses, the political and intellectual lines of force among the different European nations. The first International Congress of Orientalists met, under
the presidency of the French Japanologist Leon de Rosny, in Paris in 1873,
the year of James Legge's last departure from the Orient and the start of his
new career as a full-time sinological Orientalist.[78] Given the role played by
the French Academy in institutionalizing continental Orientalism in the
first part of the century, it was entirely appropriate that this newly flourish-
ing field, its ranks swollen as a result of the increased sway of Western imperialism, which simultaneously created new subjects for investigation and
established positions from which to manipulate and study these data, would
hold its inaugural session in Paris. But Great Britain was the leading Western imperial power in the latter half of the nineteenth century and it was
equally inevitable that the second congress would meet in London at the
Royal Institution in September 1874.[79]

In the 1870s, the great metropolis of London was the capital of an unprecedented global empire. As Samuel Birch put it in his inaugural address
to the second congress in 1874, London was a city connected with the East
"by a thousand ties, the interests of commerce, the spread of civilization,
missionary labours, and the duties of governing Oriental Dependencies of
various tongues and sites." This first Orientalist congress in London also signaled, after decades of listless amateurism when compared with the professionalized Oriental scholarship in France and Germany, the emergence, in
both a "practical" and "theoretical" sense, of a newly vigorous British scholarship in Orientalism and other humanistic sciences. Birch could rightly say

that London was now "distinguished for its extent as well as for its devotion to the study of the East."[80]

The meeting in London symbolized the passing of the torch of Oriental, comparative, and sinological accomplishment from the continent to England. This was a sinological passage, so to speak, from the Julien calendar to the Leggian epoch. The year of Legge's final return to England, 1873, is also the year of the great Julien's death in Paris.[81] What is important here is not just the temporary eclipse of the Parisian sinological tradition, but the demise of the old *sinologie de chambre* methodology in favor of practical field experience in the Orient and an ability to speak the living languages of China. Some of these changes in terms of the emergence of sinology as a distinct Orientalist field populated largely by hyphenated gentleman scholars, or returned and retired civil servants and missionaries, are shown by the personnel at the congress in London. The secretary to the congress was Robert K. Douglas, a recently returned consular official who now held a chair of Chinese studies at King's College in London. The inaugural address was given by another Englishman, the aforementioned Samuel Birch, an Egyptologist and sinologist who specialized in the study of Chinese Buddhism and held a position at the British Museum and at University College, London. But even more significant than these very few academic sinologists in England at this time was the regal presence of Max Müller as the presiding head of the Aryan section of the Congress, the largest and most politically potent group within the congress. In terms of what was to come, the absence of James Legge from this meeting was also noteworthy. Well known but without any public identity or income as a professional sinologist, Legge stayed away in the fastness of his Scottish retreat. He was not, however, forgotten at the congress and, if anything, some of the developments there can be seen to foster the creation of his chair at Oxford.

The Advance of Oriental Knowledge

Samuel Birch's brief inaugural talk sets the tone for the London meeting by linking the "spread of civilization" with the "advance of 'Oriental knowledge'" promulgated by the congress. This advance of "Oriental knowledge" is at the same time dependent on the march of empire because it provides for "improved facilities of access" and has provided scholars with an "immense quantity" of new materials and texts to analyze.[82] With a good deal of imperial pomposity, Birch rambles on to other topics related to the advancement of "Oriental knowledge"—such as, for example, the unrealistic promulgation of a "universal alphabet" designed to bring about philological unity in the East.[83] Two factors can be directly related to the institutionalization and discursive logic of this domain of knowledge. The first of these concerns the impassioned plea for accelerated excavations in the East "undertaken purely from a scientific point of view" so as to provide grist for the Orientalist and comparativist mill. The continued influx of newly plundered "monumental information" and the "discovery of fresh materials" were necessary "to stimulate the student." Without a constantly replenished supply of new facts, monuments, texts, languages, the "study languishes." The second factor is directly related to the global sway of Western imperialism at this time, the various linguistic-racial "families" of the world, the methods for gathering material facts and observable information from the past and present, and the swollen scholarly ranks of Oriental research. As Birch notes, the philological categories of "Semitic, Turanian, Aryan, and Hamitic" and the technical methods of archaeology and ethnology "embrace all the topics, linguistic and scientific, connected with the East." Yet all was not equal in this array of languages, races, and cultures: the "flood of light" thrown on the history of European languages made the Aryan section the "most favoured" of disciplines within "Oriental knowledge."[84]

Of all the Oriental sections and linguistic families, the so-called Turanian category, which included the Chinese language and traditions, was the most problematic. The Turanian grouping was already by this time understood as a basically arbitrary category having little of the comparative significance associated with the Indo-European family of language and race. Originally *Turan* meant only those countries bordering on ancient Iran or Persia, but in 1847 Baron Christian K. J. Bunsen, Müller's friend and mentor in England, proposed to use this term "for all languages of Europe and Asia which are neither Semitic nor Aryan." The identifying linguistic trait that links this incredibly diverse group of languages and makes them "one great family," like the Aryan, was said to be the primitive principle of "agglutination," which involved the simple addition (affixing or "gluing" on) of particles, prefixes or suffixes, to unchanged root words.[85] By the end of the decade, it was mostly agreed that the Chinese language did not really display the principle of agglutination.

An Empire of Learning

The dominant position of the Sanskritic or Indo-European field within Orientalism suggested by Birch is authoritatively underscored by the keynote address given to the Aryan section of the congress by Max Müller. Müller was the doyen of Sanskrit studies and comparative philology by virtue of his monumental four-volume edition of the *Rig-Veda* (see figure 18) and because of his special position at Oxford. Besides his renown in the newly emergent fields of comparative mythology and comparative religion, Müller was unquestionably the leading international spokesman for Orientalism in the last half of the nineteenth century.

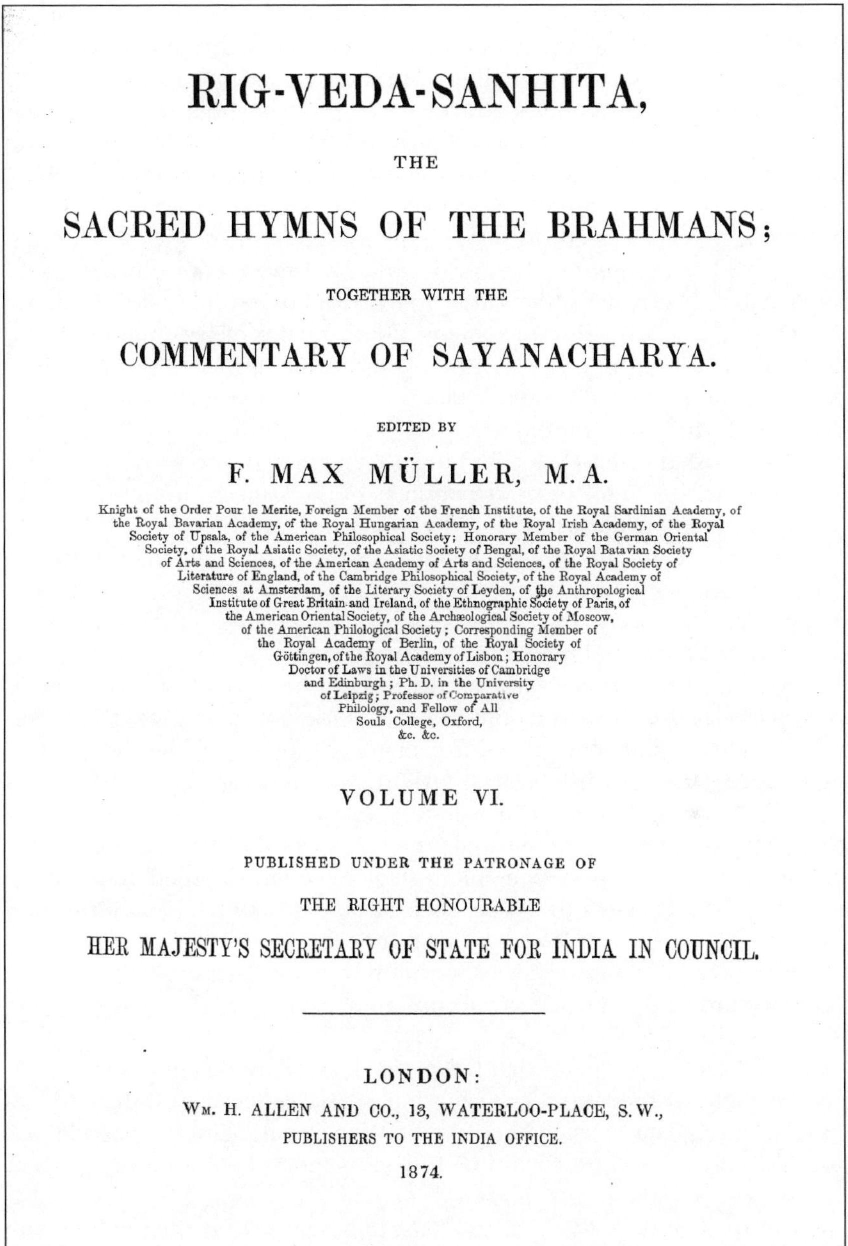

RIG-VEDA-SANHITA,

THE

SACRED HYMNS OF THE BRAHMANS;

TOGETHER WITH THE

COMMENTARY OF SAYANACHARYA.

EDITED BY

F. MAX MÜLLER, M.A.

Knight of the Order Pour le Merite, Foreign Member of the French Institute, of the Royal Sardinian Academy, of
the Royal Bavarian Academy, of the Royal Hungarian Academy, of the Royal Irish Academy, of the Royal
Society of Upsala, of the American Philosophical Society; Honorary Member of the German Oriental
Society, of the Royal Asiatic Society, of the Asiatic Society of Bengal, of the Royal Batavian Society
of Arts and Sciences, of the American Academy of Arts and Sciences, of the Royal Society of
Literature of England, of the Cambridge Philosophical Society, of the Royal Academy of
Sciences at Amsterdam, of the Literary Society of Leyden, of the Anthropological
Institute of Great Britain and Ireland, of the Ethnographic Society of Paris, of
the American Oriental Society, of the Archæological Society of Moscow,
of the American Philological Society ; Corresponding Member of
the Royal Academy of Berlin, of the Royal Society of
Göttingen, of the Royal Academy of Lisbon ; Honorary
Doctor of Laws in the Universities of Cambridge
and Edinburgh ; Ph. D. in the University
of Leipzig ; Professor of Comparative
Philology, and Fellow of All
Souls College, Oxford,
&c. &c.

VOLUME VI.

PUBLISHED UNDER THE PATRONAGE OF

THE RIGHT HONOURABLE

HER MAJESTY'S SECRETARY OF STATE FOR INDIA IN COUNCIL.

———————

LONDON:

Wᴍ. H. ALLEN AND CO., 13, WATERLOO-PLACE, S. W.,

PUBLISHERS TO THE INDIA OFFICE.

1874.

Figure 18. Title page of Max Müller's *Rig-Veda-Sanhita;* Müller's inverted pyramid
of honors. London: Wm. H. Allen, 1874.

Why should there be a congress of Orientalists? Müller suggests that the discipline needed to let the general public know that Orientalists were "really doing something"—especially as (and here we see a prescient comment on the emerging academic culture) there often seemed to be so much "wrangling and ill-natured abuse" at these "scientific tournaments." The reasons for Oriental congresses are really twofold. First, there was the need "to see where we are and to find out where we ought to be going." Second, such congresses were platforms that allowed scholars to tell the world what they "have been doing for the world" and, even more important, it would seem, "what, in return," Orientalists may "expect the world to do" for them.

Turning to a discussion of some of the problems of Orientalism in the last part of the century, Müller notes the dangers of "extreme specialization" and the absence of scholarly giants like Wilhelm von Humboldt, Franz Bopp, and Christian Bunsen, who were "never entirely absorbed or bewildered by special researches." The unspoken exception is Müller himself, who never hesitated to "trace vast outlines of the kosmos" in his own work. But what is noteworthy is that, for Müller, specialization necessarily leads to the need for "combined work carried out *viribus unitis* [by men united]." And an example of such cooperative work turns out to be what may be the first public reference to the famous project of the Sacred Books, here called the "Sacred Books of Mankind."[86]

Elaborating on the need to tell the world what Orientalists have been doing, Müller is disturbed by the fact that "Oriental studies still stand outside the pale of our schools and universities." And this is despite the fact that "during the last fifty years," Oriental scholarship has "contributed more than any other branch of scientific research to change, to purify, to clear, and intensify the intellectual atmosphere of Europe." In addition to this, Oriental studies have done more than any other to broaden the "horizon in all that pertains to the Science of Man." With a typical Müllerian flourish, he continued: "We have not only conquered and annexed new worlds to the ancient empire of learning, but we have leavened the old world with ideas that are already fermenting even in the daily bread of our schools and Universities."[87]

Müller stresses the point that the public lack of interest in things Oriental, especially in England, was dismaying precisely because "India and Europe are one." The "curtain between the West and the East has been lifted" and—slipping now into a kind of Indo-European triumphalism—these two worlds, "separated for thousands of years, have been reunited as by a magical spell, and we feel rich in a past that may well be the pride of our noble Aryan family." The "most vital element" of Western civilization came as light from the East in the ancient past (he enumerates, for example, language, alphabets, figures, weights and measures, art, religion, traditions, and nursery stories). Now there is a "new world" and the "barrier between the West and the East, that seemed insurmountable, has vanished." The dramatic outcome of this is simply that "the East is ours, we are its heirs, and claim by right our share in its inheritance."[88]

The Dyadic Science of Religion

The great lesson for all to learn from the study of the East is, in Müller's estimation, the simple and fundamental awareness that, like what was "once learnt in Rome and Athens," there "are other worlds besides our own, that there are other religions, other mythologies, other laws, and that the history of philosophy from Thales to Hegel is not the whole history of human thought." The importance of the East is that, in all these subjects, it has "supplied us with parallels, and with all that is implied in parallels, viz., the possibility of comparing, measuring, and understanding."[89]

The comparative principle is central to understanding in the most basic sense. Understanding "by parallels" is, for Müller, the key modality of human knowing. Furthermore, fields such as the comparative study of religions, an adjunct to comparative philology, was becoming one of the most exciting of the new human sciences. Here Müller gives one of his fullest definitions of the "comparative spirit," which is the "truly scientific spirit of [the] age, nay of all ages." The reason for this is that "an empirical acquaintance with single facts does not constitute knowledge in the true sense of the word." "All human knowledge," he says, "begins with the Two or the Dyad, the comprehension of two single things as one." He goes on: "If we may still quote Aristotle, we may boldly say that 'there is no science of that which is unique.' . . . As soon as the same fact is repeated, the work of comparison begins, and the first step is made in that wonderful process which we call generalization, and which is at the root of all intellectual knowledge and of all intellectual language." The "primitive process of comparison is repeated again and again" and then, appealing to comparative etymologies as his favorite source for getting at the "root" meaning of things, Müller concludes his dissertation on the "comparative spirit" by saying, "When we now give the title of *Comparative* to the highest kind of knowledge in every branch of science, we have only replaced the old word *intelligent* (i.e., interligent) or inter-twining, by a new and more expressive term, *comparative*."

Müller's conclusion touches upon three issues directly pertinent to James Legge (given Müller's special interest in Legge as a potential contributor to the *Sacred Books*). The first of these is Müller's renewed plea for a "patient study of the sacred scriptures of the world," which will be crucial for clearing up ideas about "the origin, the nature, the true purposes of religion." Most of all, there "can be no science of one religion, but there can be a science of many." Comparison is then the secret to the proper study of religion and depends primarily on the translation and availability of sacred books, all of which, except for the Christian scriptures, were written in Oriental languages. Far more important than the actual texts or materials is, as Müller says, the *"spirit"* of "perfect impartiality" in which they have been treated:

> The sacred books of the principal religions of mankind had to be placed side by side with perfect impartiality, in order to discern the points which they share in common as well as those that are peculiar to each. The results already obtained by this simple justa-position are full of important lessons, and the fact that the truths on which all religions agree far exceed those on which they differ, has hardly been sufficiently appreciated.

Legge was one of those bravely independent souls who appreciated this lesson and was on the threshold of teaching it to his fellow missionaries. As Müller recognized, this lesson would disquiet many not used to the unsettling truths of "parallels." For the great lesson to be learned is simply that "all religions spring from the same sacred soil, the human heart; that all are quickened by the same divine spirit, the still small voice." Finally, even though the external forms of religion may "change, may wither and decay, yet, as long as man is what he is and what he has been, he will postulate again and again the Infinite as the very condition of the Finite."[90]

The second factor concerns the "claims of Oriental studies on our public sympathy and support." He explains that he is referring to the great old English universities, especially Oxford—the "first University in what has rightly been called the greatest Oriental Empire"—where there is "hardly any provision for the study of Oriental languages" that approximates the coverage of even the smaller German universities. There were chairs of Hebrew and Sanskrit, but there was nothing "deserving the name of a chair" for the "modern languages of India, whether Aryan or Dravidian, for the language and literature of Persia, both ancient and modern, for the language and antiquities of Egypt and Babylon." Nor were there any positions for Turkish or for Chinese.[91]

Müller's third and last point brings the first two issues together and directly anticipates the appointment of Legge to the first chair of Chinese at Oxford. Toward the end of his address and after his discussion of the deficiencies of Orientalism at English universities, Müller declares that "Oriental studies owes much" to the missionary societies, which sent out "apostles of religion and civilization." Surely thinking of Legge, as well as of other distinguished missionary scholars, Müller emphasized that missionaries have often been "pioneers of scientific research." The best arrangement for missionary work is obviously, according to Müller, one that combined religious proselytization with serious scholarly research. As he so drolly had said in his lecture in Westminster Abbey, missionaries cannot be expected to "be converting all day long" and need the refreshment and invigoration of "some literary or scientific work." Recognizing the potential tension between missionary and scientific work, Müller concludes by observing that "some such connection with the Universities and men of science would raise [the missionary's] position."[92]

As Müller knew, an Oxbridge degree was an important, if not necessary, credential for a British parliamentary career, for the diplomatic service, and for colonial administration.[93] At the same time, men like Legge, returning from the mission field to new careers in universities, could help to promote the Western mission—at least in the civilizing, if not directly in the religious, sense of the word. Müller, who was ever conscious of public sentiment, did not stress the inevitable shift toward a more secularized understanding of the Western civilizational mission that comes about through explicitly humanistic and comparative methods. The great American comparativist Samuel Johnson quite forthrightly recognized that "the mission of Christianity to the heathen is not only for the overthrow of many of their religious peculiarities, but quite as truly for the essential modification of its own."[94] This is the lesson of the comparativist temperament associated with the professional Orientalist who quietly does the heroic work of civilization within the context of a university.

The Aryan Era of Sinology

By the 1870s, the grand agenda outlined by Müller in his congressional address had started to affect the study of China, but comparison in the nineteenth century, it must be kept in mind, was always more of a temperament or attitude of mind than a specific research technique. Even Müller was not always consistent about the meaning and method of comparison. Sometimes, he argued for a kind of biblical monogenesis concerning language, religion, and civilization; at others, he seemed to favor the more "anthropological" idea of polygenetic origins. In the area of sinological Orientalism these ambiguities were even more pronounced, so that it is possible to distinguish between a relatively sober and insular application of comparative principles (practiced by scholars such as Legge, Wylie, Eitel, Faber, Herbert Giles, Gustave Schlegel, Charles Harlez, and Henri Cordier) and other, more wildly enthusiastic and inclusive schools of sinological comparison. The first of the schools showing an obsessive infatuation with an unbridled comparativism can be called the sino-Aryan tradition of sinology, which can be roughly dated to the appearance of Joseph Edkins's infamous *China's Place in Philology* (1871) and had a relatively brief heyday during the decades of the 1870s and 1880s. This school, along with the rival sino-Babylonian school and earlier pan-Egyptian theories, eventually died a slow death by ridicule toward the end of the century.[95]

Aside from its attraction for folklorists and mythologists (such as N. B. Dennys and J. Dyer Ball), the sino-Aryan school is most distinctively associated with the work of the incredibly prolific and versatile missionary-scholar Edkins, the lesser labors of Thomas McClatchie, an Anglican cleric in Hong Kong, and Thomas Kingsmill, a civilian engineer and geologist in Shanghai who was active in the North China Branch of the Royal Asiatic Society.[96] As Eitel remarks, "Edkins aspires to be the Max Müller of Chinese philology and tries to do for the language of Cathay what Max Müller did for Sanskrit."[97] The Aryan school, as well as the Babylonian school emerging in the 1880s, basically upheld a quasi-biblical monogenetic theory of origins, an effort that hinged on the reduction of the Chinese language (religion, literature, civilization) to something other than itself. As Edkins himself said, the issue basically comes down to deciding whether "religion, language, and history are one in origin" or whether "there was more than one Adam" and "more than one commencement of civilizational arts."[98]

This reductive transformation of Chinese into some other primordial source language has appeal both from a religiously committed perspective such as Edkins's (who wanted to show the ultimate identity of Chinese with Aryan and Semitic roots and thus with a biblical theory of linguistic development) and from a more secular perspective such as Kingsmill's (who implicitly sought an ultimate validation of the linguistic, racial, and civilizational superiority of Aryan tradition).[99] As extreme versions of the idea of monogenetic primordiality, both perspectives soared well beyond Müller's comparative theories.[100] According to Eitel, who knew both Chinese and Sanskrit, Müller was "possessed with the modesty of true science" and considered it "impossible," even within the restricted sphere of the Aryan dialects, "to draw any conclusion as to the historical connection of races."[101] The tradition of Edkins, Kingsmill, and, most gratuitously, Thomas McClatchie, having no such Müllerian compunction or Leggian humility, was characterized by Eitel as the "conjectural-emotional school" of sinology.

Into the Aryan Kettle

For several decades, Eitel waged a running battle with the Aryan school in the pages of the *China Review*. The most notorious of Eitel's efforts was his discussion of amateur sinology, which ostensibly was a review of Ernst Faber's study of the literary and historical sources for Confucius and Confucianism. But Faber's work was only Eitel's springboard for a quaintly hilarious attack on "all forms of sinologic dillettantism [*sic*]" associated with Kingsmill, McClatchie, and Edkins.[102] This article also appraises the difficulties related to the professionalization of sinology during this period, a process that was retarded by an excessive attachment, on the part of the sino-Aryan sinologists in the field, to comparativism. It was this kind of methodology that was, after all, responsible for the professional status and scientific prestige of Indological Orientalism. In the case of sinological Orientalism, however, the results seemed to lead only to public derision and academic isolation.

As portrayed by Eitel, the problem was a comparativist "tendency observable of late among modern sinologues" that had become almost a "mental disease, chronic in some, intermittent in others." The principal symptoms of this "epidemic" were "ingenious speculation" and "hasty generalization" that usurped "the name of science," "a curious mixing up of supposititious facts and circular reasonings," and a "lofty contempt for detailed researches into the minutiae of antiquity" combined with a "general paralysis of the critical faculty."[103] It is important to recognize here that these traits of the amateur were the antithesis of everything more professionally represented in sinology by Legge's plodding methods. At the same time, Eitel gives the impression that the sino-Aryan comparativists had unfortunately and uncritically espoused the weaknesses of Müller the solar mythologist, and had forgotten the more cautious methods of Müller the Sanskritist and comparative religionist.

Eitel satirizes what he calls the "secret recipe of the amateur sinologist's method." This involves firstly (and here the target is especially Edkins) the taking of the names found in an ancient Chinese classic and, after stripping them of any "national and personal characteristics," throwing them "into an Aryan kettle," seasoned with the sun and moon, the five planets, and twenty-eight constellations. This brew is stirred until it becomes "thoroughly solar" and is then put into "Grimm's philological crucible" and fed "with chips from a German workshop." After simmering for a while, the Chinese words "change into Aryan surds and sonants" and "chopped Sanskrit-Chinese roots." At this point, the whole concoction may be dished up to the North China Branch of the Royal Asiatic Society or sent off to "the editor of the *China Review*."[104]

Eitel makes it clear that he has two other "amateur sinologues" in mind, McClatchie and Kingsmill. In the case of McClatchie, who had just published a "dirty minded" study of the *Yi jing* (The book of changes),[105] Eitel remarks that this breathtakingly hermetic analysis absurdly tried to prove that "the whole of the Yih-king" is only a Chinese transcript of the materialistic system of phallic idolatry "set up at Babel."[106] Alluding to Kingsmill, Eitel also refers to a recent "novel elucidation of the Shoo-king [The book of historical documents]," wherein most Chinese legends are found to be only unimaginative versions of Vedic myths of nature worship.[107]

More Subtle Weapons

The end result of Eitel's appraisal of the state of sinology was the need for an "excellent tonic" against all such "Aryan hallucinations." Not surprisingly, he was referring to the "more modest" and "critical" methods of scholars such as Legge and Faber, who take "nothing for authentic or reliable on the mere strength of popular opinion or tradition."[108] Especially commendable is Faber's use of Germanic *Quellenstudium,* which is concerned with a "microscopic test," or a more controlled comparative philological and historical consideration, of literary sources and their developmental interconnections within a single tradition. In the case of the study of Kongzi or Confucius, Legge had already produced an impressive translation of the *Analects* and a sketch of the great sage's life, but the most basic—critical, comparative, or scientific—work of understanding Kongzi and his *Quellen* was yet, according to Eitel, to be accomplished. The "unfulfilled desideratum" of a fully professional approach to Kongzi involved three basic issues: (a) the history of the age that produced Kongzi, (b) his precursors and epigones, and (c) the phases of development of Ruism. Only in this way—"with the more subtle weapons of Western science on the battle field of practical, speculative, and critical philosophy"—will Western scholar-soldiers be able to stand before native scholars without retreat or "blushing."[109]

Whether or not one entirely agrees with Eitel's analysis of the problem, it is true that the "foundations of a scientific study of Chinese" had not been laid as firmly as they had been in the study of Sanskrit.[110] The real problem is that, regardless of feelings about the mercurial Müller, in a more fundamental way "what [Barthold Georg] Niebuhr did for classical history or [Franz] Bopp for Aryan philology, has still to be inaugurated amongst the sinologues."[111] More amazing is that this "critical" and "comparative" philological understanding of Chinese linguistic and textual history was *never* fully accomplished in the nineteenth century. Nor did twentieth-century sinology prove itself to be any more perspicacious about the philological provenance and comparative implications of the Chinese language and tradition.

Part of the difficulty in this whole discussion is the disagreement over what constitutes a truly scientific or professional basis for sinological Orientalism. Is it a matter of the application of speculative comparativist methods, especially comparative philology, or the more delimited historical emphasis on sources, or *Quellen,* within single traditions? Both perspectives are concerned with "origins" as the basic premise of understanding, but they are not mutually exclusive. Putting aside the special extravagance of his hotly contested theories on comparative mythology, Müller himself could be said to uphold the basic premises of controlled *Quellenstudium* over any undisciplined cross-racial attempts at comparing different language families and civilizational traditions. Müller was always careful to distinguish himself from amateur theorists like John Chalmers, who indulged themselves too freely in "promiscuous conjectural knowledge."

The sound and fury generated by these debates, along with Legge's sinological elevation as an Oxford professor, at least indicated that there never was a time when, as one publication put it, "the study of Chinese was pursued with greater vigor." After the death of Julien, things never "looked more promising" with regard to the future of the science of sinological Orientalism, especially for several generations of English-speaking scholars with some direct practical experience in coastal communities in China.[112] This newfound vitality is seen in almost any "number of the *China Review*," a periodical, more than any other, that teemed "with proofs of the philological enterprise" and the "self-cultivated" professionalization of sinological methods among a growing number of gentleman scholars either in, or freshly returned from, the field.

Sinology's Place in Orientalism

Things looked promising in the 1870s for the ascendancy of sinology within the hierarchy of Orientalist science. It is clear, nonetheless, that sinology never became a full participant in the great comparativist adventures of the "Oriental Renaissance" in the nineteenth century. The discipline's continuing peripheral status is seen significantly in the relative neglect of East Asian materials when compared with the abundance of volumes devoted to Aryan texts in the *Sacred Books of the East* series. The marginality of sinology is also related to the battles described here—that is, the laughably unsuccessful efforts of the Aryan-era sinologists and the failure of any kind of convincing comparative philological understanding of the Chinese language. These problems were only exacerbated in the 1880s by a resurgent second wave of the sino-Babylonian era.

For other reasons, too, sinology lacks status: its general disciplinary isolation and academic impotence, its overly modest and conservative critical methods, its special indebtedness to the elitist Great Tradition worldview promulgated by native Chinese Ruist scholarship and commentarial tradition, its truncated and ultimately aborted interest in comparativism, and the characteristic emphasis on the "mere" translation of ancient classical and scriptural texts by the greatest professional practitioners of the nineteenth century. Sinological Orientalism after the turn of the nineteenth century tended to assert its own integrity as a discipline by flaunting the unique linguistic and civilizational singularity of its subject matter. China was worth studying precisely because it could not be studied like any other tradition, precisely because its literature and cultural institutions could not be easily or convincingly *compared*. China could never be understood in the Müllerian sense that "India and Europe" were said to be "One." The distinctive curse *and* blessing of sinological Orientalism was its endemic and obdurate strangeness.

Legge was not unsympathetic to the issues raised by the comparativistic daring of some of his colleagues in China (particularly his old friend and traveling companion Edkins). But he was only a mild comparativist of the Müllerian mold. Despite his appreciation of a comparative method and perspective, he instinctively drew back from extreme monogenetic theorizing, preferring more of an emphasis on the distinctiveness of individual language families and traditions. In response to Edkins's theologically loaded rhetorical question (was there more than one Adam, more than one commencement of civilization?), Legge, at this point in his evolution as a full-time professional scholar, would have answered, along with Müller, that there could well have been several Adamic progenitors of the races, several natural revelations (most powerfully seen in the *Chinese Classics*), and several independent civilizational centers. But neither Legge nor Müller believed that such views impugned the specialness of Christian revelation or the superior progress of Western civilization.

THE CHINESE CHAIR AT OXFORD

The foundation of a professorial chair in the University of Oxford marks an important epoch in the history of every new science.

MAX MÜLLER, "INAUGURAL LECTURE ON THE VALUE OF COMPARATIVE PHILOLOGY AS A BRANCH OF ACADEMIC STUDY," 1868

Scholarly Expectations

Legge does not indicate when he first became aware of the efforts of an endowment committee in London to found a chair on his behalf at Oxford. What is known is that, after about a year into his bucolic retreat in Dollar, Scotland, he moved his family south to England and, in 1875, took up residence at 33 King Henry Street in London. His move to the metropolis seems to have been motivated largely by his desire to facilitate the efforts of the endowment committee and to be available for meetings with officials at Oxford.

Legge never expected to become an Oxford professor when he returned to Britain in 1873 (before 1871 the appointment of a Nonconformist would have been impossible), but he was delighted when the possibility of such an appointment arose and he did everything he could to help the process along. He was willing to put up with some Oxonian high-handedness concerning the permanent funding of the position and uncomplainingly accepted a meager yearly income only roughly equivalent to what he had been receiving as a missionary in China (around £200 to £300 a year).[113] The only positive side to the financial negotiations was that he did not have to barter crassly for the position, as Thomas Wade had to do some years later at Cambridge by promising his collection of Chinese books to the university library.

By 1875, even before he was installed in Oxford, Legge had settled into his new identity as a full-time scholar. This was a year that was primarily devoted to scholarly activities such as his popularized or modernized revision of Mengzi (*The Life and Works of Mencius,* 1875) and his versified translation of the *Shi jing* or *Book of Poetry*—works that were now receiving the attention of stylish London literary reviews such as the *Spectator,* the *Academy,* the *Athenaeum,* and the *Pall Mall Gazette.*[114] His growing reputation as the greatest living sinologist and as the true inheritor of Stanislas Julien's sinological mantle, as well as his newfound celebrity within London literary circles, was solidified when in this same year Legge became the first recipient of the Prix Julien (carrying a monetary award of 1,500 francs) for his translation of the *Spring and Autumn Annals.*

Legge's scholarly activities also took the form of attending meetings of the Royal Asiatic Society in the city. In October 1875, before he was a regular member, he was asked to prepare a report on the history of Chinese philology and its present state, which was included in the society's annual address for 1875.[115] In the published proceedings of the society in which this report was presented, Legge is identified by his association with the recently deceased French academic master Julien—who, in 1867, "dedicated his 'Syntaxe Nouvelle' " to Legge and of whom he spoke as " '*Traducteur des classique chinois; l'un des plus éminents sinologues de nôtre époque.*' "[116] Legge is also for the first time publicly linked in print with Max Müller, it even being remarked, in a way sure to prick Müller's vanity, that Legge's *Classics* "will be a greater monument of labour than Prof. Max Müller's edition of the Veda."[117] This comparison would not escape the attention of Müller, who was acutely conscious of his own prestige and was highly appreciative of Julien's scholarship.

Legge's report on the state of Chinese philology is fascinating in several respects, especially as it gives some insight into his intellectual evolution at this time. Given the growing impact of comparative philology on Chinese studies as seen in the latest works of his old London Missionary Society friends John Chalmers and Joseph Edkins, and given his own recent correspondence with, and interest in, Max Müller, it is not surprising that he chose to discuss the peculiarities of the Chinese language and the influence of comparative philology. It is in fact a rehearsal for some ideas that he would expand in his inaugural lecture in 1876.

Dark Linguistic Abysses

Legge's report is a solid, if uninspired, synopsis of Western philological studies of the Chinese language at that time. Displaying his inherently straightforward, commonsense approach to scholarly matters, it documents his initial wavering attitude toward some of the more extreme comparative philological theories about Chinese. There is a clear effort to model him-self on Julien by adopting the French sinologue's extreme rationalistic re-serve and caution, though not his arrogant attitude, when approaching is-sues of translation and philological interpretation. An example of this critical discretion, emphasis on native sources, and avoidance of compara-tive speculation is seen in Legge's clear recognition of the new philological importance of phonetics in the approach to the study of the Chinese lan-guage and his wariness of any hasty identification of Chinese radicals or primitives with Indo-European root words.[118]

Especially revealing here—showing both the increasingly popular at-tempt to apply Aryan standards to Chinese even to the extent of absorbing it into some universalized Indo-European system of linguistic meaning—is Legge's respectful discussion of Edkins's endeavor to reconstruct the origi-nal sounds of archaic Chinese speech by making a study of different con-temporary dialects. Legge recognizes the importance of these philological efforts and basically demurs to Edkins's superior expertise on technical is-sues of dialect. Legge is, however, more tentative in his evaluations of Chalmers's pioneering work (*Origin of the Chinese,* 1866) in the increasingly fashionable science of "comparative philology" and Edkins's more sophisti-cated and controversial book *China's Place in Philology* (1871).[119]

Edkins's book, provocatively subtitled "An Attempt to Show That the Lan-guages of Europe and Asia Have a Common Origin," argues passionately, if not always very cogently, for the "radical identity" of all languages.[120] Em-bracing a position more extreme than any publicly taken by Müller, Edkins attempts to provide philological proof for biblical theories of an original lin-guistic unity. Legge admits "admiration" for Edkins's ideas, but also specifically notes the criticism and "doubt" of "some of the most eminent philologists of Europe." For Legge it is better to be an agnostic comparativist than to be a blind believer in the comparative unity of all languages. This is no ordinary doubt: When brought "to the brink of dark linguistic abysses" by Edkins, Legge was compelled to " 'linger shivering.' " These "dark linguistic abysses" are a bit like Mark Pattison's *totum scribile,* the bewildering totality of all languages or literature, which can only intimidate and frighten the puny efforts of translation, interpretation, and assimilation by the scholar.

Despite his shivering apprehension about such provocative, and ulti-mately unprovable, theorizing on the hidden grand unity of all languages, Legge does not completely side with the more agnostic critical position es-poused by Eitel, who in the spirit of his German Ph.D. is the most outspo-ken critic of unwarranted comparative speculation in sinology. Coming as close as he will ever come to speculating about ultimate philological ori-gins, Legge says only that, when the "root sounds of Chinese as exhibited in their phonetics" are compared with the "root sounds of the Semitic, Tu-ranian [note that he distinguishes between Chinese and Turanian], Sanscrit, and other systems of languages," then it "will *appear* [my emphasis] that the fathers of the different races speaking them all sat or lay around the same hearth, and could have oral communication with one another."[121]

Legge did not shiver at the thought of any kind of comparative method, but rather seems to recoil instinctively from the rush to speculative judgment unfounded in Chinese sources. He wants to distance himself from the "dark abyss" implied by the ultimate oneness of all languages—and, by way of implication, the primordial unity of all literatures, religions, and traditions. From the very beginning of his reflections on comparison, Legge draws back from overly grandiose efforts to reduce China—the Chinese language and everything else Chinese—to something other than itself. Legge is in the process of assuming a comparativist stance that, while broadly appreciative of some abstract ideal unity, most fundamentally respects—as do Goethe, von Humboldt, Herder, Carlyle, Bunsen, and Müller— the very real differences developmentally embedded in other languages, other races, other religions, and other literatures.

Legge's cautious comparativism would undergo various tentative expansions and contractions throughout his professorial career. But his comparative sensibility seems finally not to be directly or originally borrowed from Müller. It appears instead to have been derived from the cumulative impact of all the transformative experiences throughout his earlier career—that is, the influences of his Scottish heritage and education, his reading of Maurice's and Hardwick's meditations on world religions in the 1840s and 1850s, his own practical confrontation with the otherness of Chinese culture and persons, his protocomparative reflections on the dreaded term question, his translation of ancient Chinese literature, and his prayerful epiphanies at the Altar of Heaven and on the mound of Kongzi.

Corresponding Colleagues

By 1875 Legge must have been well aware of Müller's work in comparative philology and in comparative religions (no doubt he had read Müller before this, but there is no way to know for sure when this was—perhaps at the end of the 1860s, when he returned to England, perhaps when he visited Oxford in 1868 with Wang Tao).[122] Even more important is that at this time Legge began a personal association with Müller. It started with a letter sent on February 13, 1875, in which Müller praises Legge's *Chinese Classics* (they are "good because Julien said so" and he is not "lavish in praise"), mentions his plans for an anthology of sacred books, and invites Legge to meet him in Oxford on Friday.[123] We have no record of the actual meeting but may assume that they discussed the prospects of a Chinese chair at Oxford and Legge's contribution to the *Sacred Books of the East* series, still pending approval at the university and press.[124]

Legge was already concerned about his chances at Oxford, especially given the delicate questions of whether Oxford was willing to support such a chair and whether the university would be willing to have a Nonconformist in such a position. Legge's concern was not unfounded, and on February 27, 1875, he received a letter of inquiry from Dean Liddell of Christ Church College. Liddell was guardedly optimistic about Legge's suitability and mentioned, in a way that must have encouraged Legge, that he "must wait for Max Müller's opinion." Notwithstanding the reform of 1871, which opened Oxford to students and faculty of the dissenting faiths, the issue of the Nonconformity of a professor was still a sticky matter among university officials. In November, well after the endowment committee had entered into negotiations with Oxford, Liddell privately wrote Sir Rutherford Alcock (at this time chairman of the committee) to inquire "whether as a nonconformist minister [Legge] takes a strong party view of his duties or is not of strong sectarian tendencies." Alcock's reply is not extant, but given everything we know about Legge's outspoken antisectarian views, Liddell was no doubt satisfied on this count.[125]

The Committee of Endowment

Müller's encouragement and the possibility of finishing the Chinese classics by publishing them as a part of a monumental library of world classics were probably viewed by Legge as a prophetic vindication of his stubborn devotion to scholarship during his years in Hong Kong. He must also have taken special pride and satisfaction in learning that at this time a group of citizens had been formed to solicit an endowment for a new Chinese professorship. And this was no ordinary committee. Under the leadership of two old Hong Kong friends, James Banks Taylor and Alfred Howell, the assembly included various "London merchants who have to do with trade with China" (including Robert Jardine) and celebrated governmental figures such as Sir John Davis, the former governor of Hong Kong, and Sir Rutherford Alcock, at one time the minister plenipotentiary to China.[126] This was an exoneration of the man and his accomplishments that was publicly proclaimed and supported throughout the foreign community of China, in the pages of the London *Times,* and in the lecture halls of the Royal Institution in London— the very place where Müller had first lectured on comparative philology and the comparative science of religions. At the Royal Institution, Robert K. Douglas trumpeted Legge as the probable "first holder" of a "Chinese Professorship at the older University."[127]

Oddly enough, the actions of this committee, like the earlier patronage of Joseph Jardine, show the special role that secular philanthropic interests played in the support of Legge's scholarship. There is a kind of symbolic cord linking Joseph Jardine's midwifery at the birth of the *Chinese Classics* with Robert Jardine and the endowment committee's facilitating the consummation of Legge's labors as a translator. Meeting for the first time on Tuesday, April 20, 1875, in the boardroom of the Oriental Bank Corporation building in London, the committee laid its plans for raising an endowment sum of £3,000 that, it was understood, would be matched by an equal amount from existing Oxford sources (the goal was an annual endowment income of around £250). The minutes of this meeting also record that both Max Müller and Dr. H. G. Liddell (the dean of Christ Church College and a prominent supporter, along with Müller, of liberal reform at Oxford) had "unofficially intimated their approval" but indicated that, for Oxford's endorsement, sufficient external funds would be necessary. At the next two meetings (May 13 and October 19, 1875) the committee membership was expanded to include Robert Jardine and, after the October meeting, Sir John Davis; and Sir Rutherford Alcock took over as chair.[128] At the session in October, a letter was read from Dean Liddell supporting the committee's action and Legge, who had been invited to attend this meeting, was asked to speak on behalf of his candidacy.[129] Needless to say, Legge cordially assured the committee that he would "endeavour to prove worthy of the confidence shown in him" and said that he looked forward to the "beneficial results from the greater interest likely to be taken in China and the Chinese language if the action now proposed by the Committee were undertaken by the University of Oxford."[130]

Müllerian Machinations

At the same time that these negotiations were taking place, Max Müller was undergoing another of his periodic bouts of pique over his status at Oxford. Still feeling abused by his failure to secure the Boden chair fifteen years earlier, Müller was especially chagrined to discover that in the fall of 1875 Benjamin Jowett, and other liberals whom he considered his friends and colleagues, was proposing to confer an honorary D.C.L. degree upon the Boden professor, Monier-Williams, for his efforts on behalf of the Indian Institute.[131] Partially as a result of his personal antipathy toward Monier-Williams, but also because his plans for the new *Sacred Books* were still pending—in addition to his desire to return to his Sanskrit studies, as well as pangs of homesickness heightened emotionally by the death of his favorite daughter—Müller started to consider his retirement from Oxford and a return to a German-speaking country. More privately, and sometimes disingenuously, he reported to various confidants that he felt like a "nobody in the University; and when I see how I am treated, I really feel sometimes ashamed of myself, not for my own, but for my wife's sake."[132] To another friend he wrote that he was also fed up with the "clerical intrigues and petty jealousies" consuming so much of Oxford life.[133] "I am very tired," he reported to his old friend A. P. Stanley, dean of Westminster.[134] At this time, he was receiving attractive offers from various European universities, the most enticing coming from the University of Strasbourg. These may have been offers that he himself had solicited and orchestrated as a part of his political campaign at Oxford.[135]

These painful machinations at Oxford are the necessary context for understanding some of Müller's communications with Legge in the mid-1870s. Their initial epistolary contact in February 1875 was followed up with a meeting between them, and then in the following months there was a fairly active correspondence that expressed both Legge's fascination with Müller's interest in him and Müller's dark misgivings about his own situation at Oxford. On December 13, 1875, for example, Legge writes Müller from London that, although the university seemed close to approving a Chinese chair, he was chagrined to think that Müller would not be there.[136] Responding right after he had written his formal resignation from Oxford, Müller said, rather bitterly, "I looked forward to your arrival here with the greatest interest. Oxford wants scholars more than anything else, if it is not to diminish down to a mere High School! I had a very selfish interest too, for having lost Julien, I thought I should have in you a new guide *in rebus Sinicis*. All that is not to be ours." Müller concluded this missive by recalling his earlier desires for an expanded commitment to Orientalism at Oxford: "In spite of my not being able to enjoy your society here, I am truly glad that the Chair of Chinese is safe, and from all I hear, it will be established on a far better basis than I ventured to hope at first."[137]

The resolution of these matters came about during the first part of 1876 and overlapped with the finalization of Legge's position at Oxford. Publicly embarrassed (Müller personally circulated a printed notice of his resignation and an account of the situation appeared in the London *Times*) and politically pressured by Müller's proffered retirement (sent to the vice-chancellor on December 1, 1875), the councils of power at Oxford certainly knew that they were being manipulated.[138] They were nevertheless sufficiently motivated to arrange for the university press to support the *Sacred Books* project.[139] Müller's professorial chair was reconstituted (despite strained technical objections to the new arrangements from Charles Dodgson, alias Lewis Carroll, of Christ Church) in February 1876 by convocation vote, in such a way that he was free to devote all his time to his editorial chores on the *Sacred Books*.[140] Writing to his friend Arthur P. Stanley on February 21, Müller remarked that he was in the end "surprised by the true kindness" expressed to him by Jowett and others at Oxford. Equally important was the "offer of the University Press to print the translations of the Sacred Books of the World," a project, he correctly assumed, that would occupy him "for the rest of [his] life."[141]

Whatever his exact motivations, Müller was clearly the winner in the convoluted maneuvers among the power elite at Oxford. He was also at this
time at the height of his international public fame, political influence, and
social prestige. The cogency of many of his opinions would increasingly be
criticized. The fashionableness of his florid intellectual style and Broad
Church religiosity also would wane during the next few decades, but the
fact is that, to the end of the century, Müller was one of the most illustrious
and influential scholarly figures of the Victorian era (see the appendix to
this chapter). Toward the end of his life, however, Müller was in many ways
famous for being famous and had to suffer the indignity of being surpassed
in intellectual influence by rivals such as Edward Tylor and James Frazer.

Müller spent the rest of his very productive life in Oxford working assiduously on, among numerous other publications, his magnum opus, the *Sacred Books of the East*. During this period he also played a decisive role in the
academic normalization of Orientalism (and its various disciplines) and especially in the academic promotion and public popularization of the comparative science of religions. He was, furthermore, James Legge's constant,
if not intimate, professorial colleague, intellectual mentor, and editorial
overseer on the *Sacred Books* project. Too much the plain evangelical "middling class" Scotsman from the country to be truly a confidant of the intellectually urbane, poetically eloquent, politically manipulative, and socially
glib Müller, Legge nevertheless had a special relationship with the illustrious younger man.

Circular Arguments

The endowment committee's work culminated in a printed circular (entitled simply "Chinese Professorship at Oxford") that was used as the primary
means to solicit funds. Although deeming it "superfluous to adduce any
elaborate arguments," this document did give a basic explanation for the
proposed chair. Stressing the political, religious, and commercial advantages that would accrue from a "thorough knowledge of the language and
a familiar acquaintance with the classic authors of China," the committee
also addressed John Davis's old nemesis of British scholarly listlessness. Appealing to national pride, the circular emphasized how "strange" and "unaccountable" it was that "the country which [had] the largest interest in the
Far East—larger, indeed, than all other countries put together, and the
most richly endowed Universities in the world—should have been most
backward in promoting the study of Oriental languages generally, and of
Chinese in particular."[142] Despite the illustriousness of patrons such as Alcock and Davis and the fact that the marquis of Salisbury and the earl of
Derby each pledged £100, it took till May 1878, and only after substantial

contributions from the foreign community in China, to raise the full amount of £3,000.[143] In a way expressive of the endemic British lethargy concerning this issue, the Shanghai *North-China Herald* registered its "disappointment" at the "smallness of the amount" that had been raised in England and the "fewness of names" on the subscription list.[144]

On February 22, 1876, the London *Times* noted that Oxford had a total of 2,542 undergraduate students, 308 faculty masters qualified as members of Congregation (made up of residential faculty), and a "body of Professors" that remained unchanged, "although a Professor of Chinese is all but added to the list."[145] It took until April 1 for Liddell to write Alcock and report that Legge was "now a complete professor."[146] Even then not everything was fully consummated. In typical Oxonian fashion, there were still a few impediments connected with the formal addition of Legge's name to the list of university professors. The most important of these problems involved an embarrassing oversight concerning the need for Legge's formal matriculation in order to receive his M.A. degree by Decree of Convocation (the assembly open to all graduates); the ironing out of various financial details concerning emoluments from his fellowship at Corpus Christi College, the university, and the endowment; and, sadly, an unseemly battle to ensure the permanency of the endowment funds.[147] The only positive element in these last details of the professorship was the welcomed endowment on November 15, 1876, of the Davis Chinese Scholarship established by Sir John Davis to help overcome any continuing apathy toward Chinese studies on the part of undergraduates.[148] Unfortunately, listlessness in student interest and institutional support continued to prevail.

Endowed Frugality

The terms of the professorship were ultimately worked out and by the late summer of 1876 Legge was preparing for his official inaugural lecture in the Sheldonian Theatre at the start of the Michaelmas term in October. The general stipulations of the chair were fairly standard in that he was expected to be in residence at least six months of the year (between October 10 and July 1, the period covering the three terms of the Oxford academic year) and to offer several public lectures.[149] Given the thrust of Müller's concerns for the professorate and the concurrent reforming influence of the "endowment of research" faction at Oxford, the university most likely intended the new Chinese chair to be a research position. But Legge had a broader ministerial understanding of his professorial duties. Despite his love of scholarly research, there was still too much of the Christian missionary, Nonconformist minister, nonsectarian educator, and Confucian gentleman in his character to allow for a university career without a devoted commitment to the mission of teaching. From the very outset, therefore,

Legge was more than conscientious in fulfilling his contractual obligations to the chair. He was always actively engaged in the teaching of the Chinese language and tradition—even though he usually had very few students and often found himself appealing, mostly unsuccessfully, to various government and missionary agencies for additional warm bodies to teach.[150]

Although his professorial salary was not immense, Legge lived a graciously donnish, though demonstrably frugal, life.[151] His residence was at 3 Keble Terrace, a comfortable Victorian brick row house on the fringe of the more opulent residences in the University Parks and Norham Gardens area of north Oxford (where Müller lived). Having by the end of his life six children and fifteen grandchildren and having no other means than that which came from the "labour of [his] brain," he was never wealthy. Nor was he socially stylish or politically influential in the Müllerian sense of academic life at Oxford. Nonetheless, he always had, as he put it, "enough to make ends meet to the end."[152]

IN THE SHELDONIAN THEATRE:
I WAS AS ONE THAT DREAMED

During all the years I was in China, I often wished that there were Chairs for its language and literature in the great universities of this country. That I should myself occupy one of them did not enter into my thoughts. When this was first suggested, about eighteen months ago, I was as one that dreamed.

JAMES LEGGE, *INAUGURAL LECTURE*, 1876

Professorial Nonconformity

When James Legge, as a freshly designated fellow of Corpus Christi College, stood upon the Sheldonian stage to deliver his inaugural address on October 27, 1876, it appears that he was the very first ordained Nonconformist to lecture as a university professor at Oxford.[153] Beyond this simple but significant detail illustrating the changing circumstances at Oxford is also the fact that Legge stood for many other things largely foreign to the ancient spires and cloistered gardens of Oxford. A former missionary who had spent most of his life in China, a politically astute supporter of general education in Hong Kong, an outspoken opponent of the opium trade with Whiggish leanings, a learned scholar who was conversant with the Chinese classics as well as the writings of the Latin, Greek, and Hebrew traditions— Legge was all of these things, as well as a bucolic Scotsman with disarmingly unpretentious manners and a sober seriousness often leavened with puckish humor. He was someone who favored directness over academic haughtiness, pedantic obscurity, or cynical weariness. An exemplar of northern simplicity and the guileless evangelical earnestness of an earlier Victorian

Figure 19. Oxford's "Eastern Sages." *Left to right:* Archibald Sayce, Max Müller, James Legge, ca. 1879. Reproduced courtesy of Oxford University, Bodleian Library, G.A.Oxon. 4°416, number 902.

generation, Legge would never adopt Müller's entrepreneurial manner or, as the century wore on, rest comfortably with the growing Oxonian taste for the languid aestheticism of Walter Pater and Oscar Wilde.

Legge's Nonconformist sensibility and sinological expertise were unique to the donnish scene at Oxford and indicate that his presence in the Sheldonian was not just the inauguration of a new position, but was yet another sign of the commencement of a new intellectual and educational era at Oxford. Just as Müller brought the new worlds of Germanic and Orientalist scholarship to Oxford, so would Legge, both by himself and in collaboration with Müller, be instrumental in opening Oxford to yet other exotic realms of the mind, spirit, and gender. Legge, along with Müller and Archibald Sayce (an Assyriologist who was, after 1876, Müller's deputy in the comparative philology chair), signals therefore the dawn of the "Eastern Sages" at Oxford—an event that was waggishly captured in a caricature of this new breed of professorial creatures (see figure 19).[154] What is marvelous about this image is how it so deftly portrays popular conceptions of these three scholars in relation to their respective Gilbert and Sullivan–style costumes.

On the left is a caricature of Archibald Sayce depicting him in mock Egyptian garb, holding a hieroglyphic cartouche, the pyramids and a crescent moon in the background. In the middle, suggesting his prominence as the pivot of the Orientalistic sun and moon, is the cartoon Max Müller, gravely ludicrous as he stands barelegged in Hindu fakir's dress while holding a flute in one hand and a coiled snake in the other. Suggested here is that Müller had already been publicly burlesqued for his special blend of scholarly snake-charming and exotic humbuggery.[155] To the right, and facing his mentor Müller, is James Legge bedecked in a comic Chinaman's outfit (modeled, it seems, on an earlier caricature—see figure 23, below) complete with an absurd Qing-period pigtail hanging down to his knees, elevated block sandals, a high-peaked mandarin hat, and an incongruous Japanese-style parasol. A stock eight-tiered pagoda and the rising sun are seen behind this farcical Mikado mandarin.

This image obviously lampoons popular stereotypes of the Near and Far East and of the scholars known as professional Orientalists; it also suggests that at this time university professorships and Orientalism had attained a special academic prominence and that these three "Eastern Sages" were well-known Oxonian figures who invited parody. In terms of Oxford impressions of Orientalism during this period, it is also interesting that neither Monier-Williams as the professor of Sanskrit nor the professor of Islam were included in this cartoon pantheon of Eastern specialists. Part of the reason for this oversight seems to be that Orientalism, as a newly established academic discipline, was especially associated in England with the central influence of Max Müller, his comparative philological methods, and his close colleagues.

Beginning Again

Legge must have been beset by powerful waves of emotion as he prepared to give his first lecture as an Oxford professor in the Sheldonian Theatre. Profound thankfulness for God's attentiveness and a solemn determination to continue with his lifelong habits for concentrated early-morning scholarship and a daytime teaching ministry surely entered into his ruminations. Perhaps also there was a feeling of righteous pride given all he had gone through to reach such an elevated academic platform. Whatever the emotions and thoughts, the fact is that this was the beginning of a second career and second identity for James Legge (see figure 20).

At the age of sixty he was embarking on a journey that he had prepared for throughout his whole life, yet at the same time, he must have felt some trepidation knowing that he was but a feckless tyro when it came to the ancient academic world of Oxford. Still something of a country bumpkin in

Figure 20. James Legge in academic garb, Oxford, 1876. Photograph by Hills and Saunders, Oxford. Reproduced courtesy of the Legge Family Collection.

Oxford, he nonetheless had enough self-confidence in his own Noncon-formist conscience and scholarly abilities to march proudly into the *sanc-tum sanctorum* of English academic life. To borrow from his favorite stock of preacher's metaphors, he would most likely have to weather a new set of storms, sudden squalls, and prolonged tempests during his sojourn in Ox-ford. But for a true Christian pilgrim, such struggles would lead to a new phase of character building. Oxford presented Legge with an opportunity for a new mission—a more fully academic and secular mission fraught with dangers as distressing as anything encountered in heathen Hong Kong. For the courageous Legge, ever open to intellectual translation and personal transformation, these new circumstances were something to embrace joyfully.

At first glance, it seems strange that Legge's inaugural address does not deal in any detail with the *Chinese Classics,* Confucius, or—aside from touching upon the issue of the history and the immensity of Chinese literature— the religious content of Chinese tradition. In contrast with a lifetime of habits built up as a missionary, he seems to be consciously trying to underscore the distinctiveness of his new professorial and academic identity. As any aspiring comparativist schooled in the Müllerian point of view should do, Legge discusses the general reasons for the academic professionalization of sinology and the specific rationale for a chair at Oxford. Appropriately enough and by way of a further public identification with the Müllerian tradition of Orientalism, Legge begins his address by directly quoting Müller's observation made at his own inauguration: "The foundation of a professorial Chair in the University of Oxford marks an important epoch in the history of every new science."[156] Here it is important to heed the emergence of a new kind of social and political history—that is, the often pathetically petty machinations of academic life over specific disciplines, endowed chairs, and new positions. Worth noting in this regard is that, although both Müller and Legge dealt with the historical and theoretical grounds for their academic positions, Legge's approach was more personally folksy and pedagogically pragmatic than Müller's mostly triumphal rationale.

A Sinological Pedigree

Legge begins his address by certifying his scientific credentials and by establishing his pedigree in the emerging multinational discipline of sinology. He accomplishes this in several ways, the first of which deals with his understanding of the history of nineteenth-century sinological Orientalism. Admitting that his position was not the first Chinese chair in England, he dilates upon the role played by Robert Morrison, the first Protestant missionary to China and "the first Englishman that distinguished himself by his attainments in Chinese." Through Morrison's efforts in 1825, there was an attempt to establish the study of Chinese at one of the ancient universities. These efforts failed, but led to the brief existence (down to 1828) of a "Language Institution" in London.[157] Through the work of a "committee of gentlemen" in 1838 (Legge says "1837" in his autobiographical "Notes of My Life") not unlike his own endowment committee, University College of London, which had received Morrison's library after his death, appointed the Reverend Samuel Kidd—a London Missionary Society missionary back from the field in Malacca and Legge's first teacher—to a professorship of Chinese. Kidd was, as Legge says in "Notes of My Life," a "very competent teacher" who engendered his initial enthusiasm for the study of the language and the understanding of the Confucian *Analects*.[158] But upon Kidd's retirement in 1842 the chair was left vacant until assumed by Samuel Beal in 1873. The reason for this vacancy was, as Legge poignantly comments, "the want of students." In 1846 another Chinese position was established at King's College, London, which, though "too slenderly endowed," was filled continuously down until the present time. It was held at that time by Robert K. Douglas, whom Legge calls a "very able occupant."[159]

Legge's miniature history of British academic sinology ends abruptly on the sad note that, like the experience of Morrison, Kidd, and Beal, the "resort of students" to Douglas's position "has been small." In contrast with this kind of torpor, continental sinological studies, especially among the French, started early and underwent "assiduous cultivation." In particular, it was the "genius and inquiring spirit" of *sinologues de chambre* such as Jean-Pierre Abel Rémusat, Stanislas Julien, and the marquis d'Hervey de Saint-Denys (successive holders of the Collège de France chair) that established the greatness of the French academic tradition. In addition to this, the French had the good sense to establish a second institution in Paris, l'École spéciale des langues orientales vivantes, devoted to practical teaching (for diplomatic and commercial purposes), and employing scholars, of modern Asian languages such as Chinese, Japanese, Annamese, and Hindustani.

Despite the domination of textuality represented so tirelessly by Julien, who, as Legge notes here, "used to glory in the fact that he never in his Chinese studies enjoyed the assistance of a native of China,"[160] the later French tradition respected both the archaic and the contemporary, the dead and the living, the written and spoken sides of Oriental tradition. For all of his own emphasis on the ancient classics, Legge also clearly favored an approach to the understanding of China that incorporated both old and new aspects "of the linguistic and cultural tradition." To be sure, the archaic was the ground of being for sinological meaning, as it was for most Orientalists, historians, and anthropologists, but there was also a growing realization (based in many ways on the linguistic prowess of the hyphenated missionaries and civil servants in the field) that an awareness of the living written and oral languages, and access to China's own textual scholars, was crucial for a full understanding of the ancient texts. As exemplified by l'École spéciale des langues orientales vivantes and the Chinese field experience of his old friend Cordier, Legge argues for a sinological curriculum that would mesh the austere classicism of Julien with a more warm-blooded, and orally fluent, experience with the actual land and people of China. Julien, for all of his vaunted erudition, could not speak Chinese and, regardless of his protestations to the contrary, seemed to have a sneaking suspicion that even a lowly Protestant missionary-scholar such as Legge might be privy to dimensions of philological insight and sinological learning beyond anything available in Paris.

Going on to a rapid review of other European positions (in particular, Germany, Holland, Italy, and Russia; developments in the United States are notably excluded, even though in 1876 Yale University was installing Samuel Wells Williams as the first American professor of Chinese),[161] Legge concludes the first part of his address by emphasizing how "much less interest" had been shown in Great Britain when compared with the conspicuous "love" of Chinese "literature and science" in France. It is, consequently, his hope that the Oxford chair will contribute to a "better state of things" respecting sinological Orientalism in Britain. This "better state" of sinology is, after all, "required" by British relations with China concerning politics and commerce.[162]

The Religious Interest of the Chair

Legge also makes it clear that, because of the needed "protection and freedom of action" of the missionary societies, Britain has a clear "religious interest" in China, even though this interest does not, and should not, approximate the kind of patronage given to religion by Russia and France. A more extensive religious interest in China should be manifest among British churches, and Legge naively remarks that the creation of the Chinese chair at Oxford "ought to be warmly hailed by all who have the direction of our missionary societies." However, in a way that paralleled the diffidence of the government, there was very little actual support for the seemingly self-evident proposition that missionary agents "should be men that have been disciplined and trained by the fullest and most generous education." "Let them," says Legge, who was already thinking of the viability of his new position, begin their study of Chinese in Oxford or London and "at the same time have the opportunity of attending other classes to the extent at least which is deemed desirable for the young men intended for the civil service in India."

The obviousness of this principle was never truly ratified by the missionary societies, so that aside from being rebuffed by his own society, Legge was also mostly ignored by other groups like the Foreign and British Bible Society. The reasons offered for this refusal and lack of interest, both explicit and implicit, reveal a particular kind of evangelical fear that education would compromise the enthusiasm and purity of faith. Often it was said that young men would not have the patience to spend a year or two preparing for the field: "their enthusiasm would burn low and would be less effective . . . better to learn in the field."[163] Other, more implicit reasons seem to be the old Dissenting fears of education acquired within the camps of the established enemy, especially Oxbridge. Later there was also the suspicion, especially after 1877, that Legge as a "former missionary" was himself a dangerous mentor, someone tainted by a comparativist perspective and susceptible to heretical views on heathen religions.[164]

Reading, Writing, and Speaking

Discussing the practicality of teaching the written and spoken languages of China, Legge affirms his belief that it is entirely possible at Oxford to "make one's own whatever has been written or printed in Chinese, just as it is possible to learn here Greek, Latin, Hebrew, Arabic, or Sanskrit."[165] He also says that students in England could learn to express their thoughts "in writing in a style that will be intelligible to a native of any part of China"—even though that style of composition will never achieve the standards of elegance expected of a native scholar. Concerning spoken colloquial Chinese and the special problems of the different dialects, Legge notes that fluent idiomatic use of the language will come about only through "long and habitual intercourse" with native speakers. But this is really the case with any language and the only real peculiarity of Chinese is its tonal discrimination of words. With some implicit allusion to his own difficulties as a fluent speaker of some of the Chinese dialects, he remarks that tones need not be a "serious obstacle" if, like children, one can "mingle freely and without much *mauvaise honte* among the natives." He adds that his own children "always chattered freely in Chinese before they attained to speak anything like accurate and grammatical English." Referring to the special problems created by the Chinese dialects, he stressed the special status of the Mandarin dialect, which is "spoken over a greater part of the country than any other" and the need therefore for students to give it their "chief attention." Referring again to the French practice, he alludes to the desirability of having a native assistant, who speaks Mandarin "purely," attached to his Chinese chair—a desire never realized during his tenure.

My Idea of a University

Having provided a "good *raison d'être*" for the usefulness of the Oxford chair, Legge devoted the rest of his lecture to a more elevated scholarly consideration of sinological Orientalist scholarship and philological science.[166] Always the Scottish common sense realist, and not without good political instincts and a knack for self-preservation, Legge was careful, throughout the first half of his talk, to underscore the practical service the position could render to the nation; but there was a broader context of intellectual and educational change at Oxford that must also be addressed. Evident are not only Müller's conceptions of the humanistic sciences, but also the broader "endowment of research" debate taking place at this time at Oxford. What is certain is that both ideals, purity and practicality, theory and action, were necessarily interconnected for Legge.

Because these intellectual and practical issues were formative factors in the social history of higher education throughout the rest of the Victorian period, Legge's ideas deserve some attention. Dividing his discussion into two parts, he first addresses the issue of the history and literature of China. Here it is obvious that his educational ideal was really as much Ruist or Confucian (as well as Riccian and, broadly, in the liberal Nonconformist sense of mission) as it was Müllerian, Jowettian, or, for that matter, Newmanian. For Legge, the "idea of a University" was that it should be an institution devoted to the "promotion" of *both* "learning and education." This means that the university, as an institution of scholarly learning, can never be exclusively interested in research and the advancement of knowledge for its own sake. Rather, it must live up to the "duty of imparting to its youth the highest knowledge which the age enjoys on all subjects belonging to the culture of the mind and the formation of the character." For Legge, interestingly, this proposition was immediately illustrated by an appeal to the "Chinese philosopher Mencius [Mengzi]," who said that the "delight" of the most noble and high man "is to have under him the most talented youths of the kingdom, and to teach and nourish them." This is, says Legge, "a delight which hardly any individual can enjoy, but it is largely the privilege of a great University like this." It was clearly a special pleasure for Legge to be in such a privileged position. There is a fitting parallel here since, just as Mengzi was a controversial moral advocate in kingly courts at the end of the Warring States period in ancient China, so also was Legge at the end of the Victorian era a champion of sinology among the educationally and socially privileged in Oxford.

Chinese History and Literature

After establishing the principle of education as the cultivation of mental and moral character, Legge takes up the issue of the advancement of knowledge via the "researches of science" and the need for an enlarged view of the "number and range of subjects embraced in the field of study."[167] Oriental subjects such as the history and literature of China should be among these new subjects since—even though they "have not affected" Western tradition "as those of Greece and Rome have done, to say nothing of the Semitic nations"—they "will be found rich in interest and instruction." Legge then reinforces this tepid proposition by making the point that the Chinese people's unique isolation, like that of the ancient Britons, gives them some special interest.

Even more significant is that, from the most ancient period, China had already achieved a "state of high civilisation" with a "very various literature" and "social principles of great strength and virtue." There "should be," therefore, "lessons of the greatest value to be learned from the study of Chinese history." Legge finishes this line of thought by giving his own convoluted version of Müller's rhyming comparative axiom of "he who knows one, knows none." "We cannot," says Legge, "know humanity as we ought to do, as in these days we feel that we must do, without [China]." Digressing on some of the salient characteristics of Chinese literature, Legge notes that, from the earliest period, it had "a stamp of genuineness and credibility such as no other ancient literature exhibits." Throughout this long history, the Chinese people produced a "vast ocean" of literature dealing with all manner of subjects. Moreover, some of these works, especially those concerned with "questions of moral and social interest," are discussed with "a sobriety and good sense that are refreshing" even for European inquirers.

With these advantages in view, Legge was in effect following Matthew Arnold's ideas about "literary" and "cultural" matters. Legge thereby defines sinology as the "exploration and unfolding of the stores of Chinese literature." This is a task that, given the remarkable abundance of documents, is only in its infancy. Legge is careful to note that "perhaps more than a beginning" had already been made in sinological Orientalism—and here he is clearly thinking of his own "exploration and unfolding" of the literary and religious narratives found in the *Chinese Classics*. There can be no weeping on the part of the sinologist, Orientalist, or "philosophic thinker" because the time is far distant when, "in travelling through history, ancient and modern, from Egypt and Europe, on through India, and arriving [lastly, it is implied] in China," there will be "no more worlds of thought and deeds to be conquered." There will always be other worlds of thought and deed, besides our own, to know and vanquish. Furthermore, Legge basically identifies these "other worlds besides our own" with what we can know—in a Carlylian, Arnoldian, and Müllerian sense—through the translation, philological analysis, and comparative interpretation of ancient literary texts and their history. In this way, the meaning of the basic civilizational institutions such as religion, politics, and commerce is absorbed into the comparative history or Great Story of world literatures.

Philological Considerations

For Legge at this juncture in his intellectual pilgrimage, Müllerian philological considerations about the "nature of the Chinese language, and especially of the written language," are found to be crucial for an understanding of Chinese history and literature, as well as for an overall critical science of sinological Orientalism.[168] This conclusion follows from the central role that translation and the philological analysis of words play in dealing with any kind of foreign language, but it is also suggested by the distinctive nature of the Chinese language. From a comparativist standpoint, Chinese is unquestionably "unique among the other languages of mankind." Because of its uninflected monosyllabism, argues Legge, it differs from the Aryan and Semitic language families. Contrary to earlier theories once held by Müller, Legge makes it clear that Chinese must be distinguished from the Turanian languages because it has "none of the agglutination" that characterizes that family. Furthermore, if the most ancient humans spoke monosyllabically ("and I suppose there is not one among us who does not believe that they did so"), then, even if Chinese is not exactly a "relic of the earliest human speech," it still seems "to be more akin than any other existing language to what that speech was." This kind of broad comparative speculation concerning ultimate origins marks a significant departure from Legge's previous scholarly proclivities.

Another illustration of the Chinese language's primitive similitude, if not primordial character, is its failure to analyze words into elementary sounds and to develop a representational system of alphabetical signs—even after contact with Sanskrit. Instead, the Chinese written language is based on the simple, yet clever, use of pictorial and phonetic symbols; most words or characters are the result of a systematic combination of *both* kinds of signs. Legge then remarks that, although the philological study of Chinese grammar was retarded when compared with the Aryan languages, it has now "been attained to" and a Chinese book can be "translated into English with as much certainty as a Greek or Latin one."

With typical Victorian confidence in intellectual progress and the prowess of philological methods, Legge reiterates his conviction that "there is now . . . little difficulty or uncertainty in the interpretation of the most ancient Chinese documents." Having been in the thick of a prolonged, and soon to be rekindled, war over the interpretation of Chinese classical terms for God—a nightmarish battle of interpretation that went back to the time of the first Jesuits in China—Legge might have expressed more reservation on this issue. Because he does not, it may well be that this is another instance of his growing faith in a comparativist sensibility and scholarly methods coming from his newfound identity as a professional sinologist, as an Oxford professor, and as Müller's collaborator. Legge seems to feel that academic secular scholarship solved many problems that, previously, in a more sectarian missionary context, were insoluble.

Legge agreed with Julien's observation that, whatever its apparent primitive nature, the Chinese language was fully capable of treating "all the subjects, scientific or literary, that exercise the human spirit." There is no intellectual or poetic poverty inherent in Chinese that would make it "impossible to conceive of a Chinese Parliament or Debating Society." As

Legge says in relation to his own personal experience (thinking, perhaps, of his Chinese associates Ho Tsun-sheen and Hong Rengan): "I have listened to triumphs of oratory in China as great as ever I have known in this country."

Despite European advances in the "mastery of Chinese," the real comparative, critical, analytical, and scientific work was yet to be done: "we understand the working of the machine . . . it remains for us to take it to pieces, and see the principles on which it was built." Only through the use of comparative philological methods will it be possible to reconstruct some of ancient Chinese social history and to "throw light on the origin of words." Even more than in his report for the Royal Asiatic Society in 1875, Legge is sympathetic to some of Edkins's speculative considerations about the " 'conditions of those times anterior to linguistic history.' " This prelinguistic period, according to Edkins (but also influenced by some of Müller's more controversial notions concerning the "ding-dong" origin of language),[169] was a time " 'when language was a true idealism.' " " 'Every word' " was " 'the clear and expressive sign of some natural sound, and the human sensations, in the hour of their juvenile freshness and truthful sharpness, were assisted in the formation of language by an intellectual faculty which only acted in accordance with the unartificial laws of nature.' "[170] These are, however, Edkins's and not Legge's views. Backing away from the biblical appeal of Edkins's speculations, Legge can only say, rather wanly, that this kind of analysis "will demand equally caution, ingenuity, and persistence."

Granting the application of some assiduous caution, Legge indicates that it may be possible to bring sinology into the "field of comparative philology." But he makes it clear that the solitude of sinology will continue with respect to Orientalism since it is "impossible" for Chinese to "ever play the part in this which Sanskrit has done." It is, as Legge puts it, the "unique character" of the language that resists absorption into the greater speculative schemes of comparative science. Despite this, he echoes his earlier report to the Royal Asiatic Society and says that, if it is possible to reconstruct Chinese phonetic "root words," then we may discover "an amount of agreement between [language families] sufficient to justify the belief that the fathers of all [the] different races sat or lay around the same hearth, and had oral communication with one another." In contrast with the half century of groundbreaking comparative work already devoted to Aryan languages, serious comparative philological analysis of Chinese, according to Legge, dates only to Chalmers's *Origin of the Chinese* and Edkins's treatise *China's Place in Philology*. Hinting along with Eitel that the findings of these two missionary-scholars were too "amateurish," Legge adds the comment that other professional European sinologists, such as Professor Gustave Schlegel of Leiden, have recently "pursued the subject." Legge no longer seems to shiver in the face of the dark and cold abysses of meaning conjured up by his earlier report, but he nevertheless maintains his cautious hesitancy toward this kind of scholarship.

Legge's inaugural address can be read as a muted prolegomena to his own future speculative ventures in the comparative philology of the Chinese language and religion. This is suggested, for example, by the appearance during this period of several lectures devoted specifically to technical philological and disciplinary matters—that is, in addition to his inaugural lecture and earlier Royal Asiatic Society report, a talk in 1878 on "The Nature and History of the Chinese Written Character" and, in the same year, his address at the Congress of Orientalists in Florence entitled "The Present State of Chinese Studies." After 1878, Legge drew away from this kind of philological discussion. No doubt part of his reluctance to pursue the more daring forms of philological and comparativist theorizing was related to the pressure to finish his contributions to the *Sacred Books of the East*. As he also freely admitted elsewhere, he was basically a "prosy and dosy" translator who, in his own simple but sure way, was temperamentally unsuited to the romantic indulgence and philosophical bravado demanded by a Müllerian-style science of comparative philology. Legge embodied a kind of prudent spirit of sympathetic concern for the plurality of religion, but resisted the siren call of methods that tended to destroy the singularity of China's otherness. Generally he rejected the kind of theological comparison that entertained difference only as a way of returning to the same. For Legge it was always best, as he says in his inaugural lecture, to avoid any "foregone conclusion." He preferred to affirm that "the maxim for each inquirer must be *festina lente* [make haste slowly]."[171]

The Goodness of Scholarship

Legge concludes his inaugural lecture with a few, rather perfunctorily optimistic, comments on the Chinese government, which, because it was "rousing itself to put an end to the national isolation," might actually be "stirred" to send some of its young men to England for a general education (as it had to the United States).[172] More interesting are his autobiographical reflections on his previous career as a missionary and how he ended up on the stage of the Sheldonian.[173] Noting that he had been less than a year in the East when he realized that "all of the classical books of the Chinese" covered "the whole field of thought through which the sages of China had ranged," he had devoted almost twoscore years of his life to the study of Chinese literature. Having produced eight heavy volumes of translation, he still had two other Confucian classics to complete in order to bring his original "plan" to fruition (which may require "three or four, perhaps, five additional volumes"). Legge declares at this point that he "never wavered" in his conviction that this kind of scholarly undertaking was "good, and even necessary to the success of missionary labour in China." What is hinted at here by the "and even" qualification and comma-ed caesura is that it is really the intrinsic goodness of the scholarly work itself—the knowing and telling of the Great Story—that is the primary, if not exclusive, justification for his work. He publicly confesses that, as his scholarship proceeded, "it came to engross my time more and more, and interfere with the prosecution of direct missionary work both in preaching and teaching." Knowing the background and subtext for this statement, we understand just how truly revelatory and emotionally charged it is and how much he had changed in terms of his own public image and self-identity. He was now prepared to substitute the scholarly mission of professorial sinology and university teaching for the "direct missionary work of preaching and teaching."

Contrary to what some at Oxford may have thought when Legge was proposed for the professorship—that he could not help but continue in the unsophisticated and unscholarly ways of an evangelical missionary—he had truly been translated and transformed. He had, indeed, gone further in the direction of a newly professionalized and liberally secular sense of education than had many Oxonians who were still clinging to the old orthodox habits of the established church and the Mediterranean classics. Like Müller and other progressive reformers at Oxford (including, in different ways and to different degrees, Jowett, Pattison, Liddell, and Green), Legge had fully committed himself to the "exploration and unfolding" of "other worlds besides our own." There is even a sense in which Legge, in his own quietly resolute way, was at least as intellectually liberal as Müller and was, in some ways, actually more radical than the peripatetic Max concerning certain social and political issues.

Legge's new identity as a university professor had its own kind of goodness and purity that he was grateful to partake of. The duties of scholarship have their own justification, which—like the higher acts of duty to God and family, if not to missionary societies and sectarian dogma—calls for faith and dedication. As the new professor of Chinese he will, "with God's help," do all he can do "to justify" his appointment. This will involve both research and teaching and an overriding concern to keep the chair "practically useful." Both the ancient Confucian Masters Kong and Meng would have heartily approved Legge's sagely understanding of an educational mission that necessarily combined pure research with a civic and moral practicality.[174]

Terminal Rites

In June, at the end of the academic year, it is a tradition at Oxford to celebrate the Encaenia—an annual commemoration of the founders and benefactors of the university and a time for the bestowal of honorary degrees. Concerned both with termination and commencement, this ceremony is memorable for the chancellor's procession of robed dons who parade from the High Street to the Sheldonian Theatre. Also remarkable, especially during the Victorian era, was the licentious spirit of spring release and renewal. This aspect of these academic rites was especially the prerogative of the rowdy assemblage of undergraduates who, while sitting in the balcony of the Sheldonian, were given license, before the arrival of the official procession, to mock the solemnity and pomposity of the occasion.[175]

Professor Legge most probably first marched in an Encaenia procession during the spring of 1877 (perhaps in the manner suggested in the appendix to this chapter).[176] For Müller and Legge the previous academic year had been a special turning point in their lives. For Müller the events of the past year led to a commitment to Oxford and England that would last to his death in 1900. At the same time, these events created the circumstances that gave life to the enormous *Sacred Books of the East* project, an enterprise that would consume him to the very end of his days. It was this massive project, designed to make the most authoritative Oriental texts available to scholars and other sympathetic parties, that became the defining focus in his life as an Orientalist and comparativist.

Even more than Müller, Legge would have felt the special poignancy of being back in the Sheldonian after his inaugural lecture at the start of the academic term. The autumnal rites of inauguration were a solemn ratification of his newly elevated status, whereas now he was joyfully celebrating the successful completion of his first academic year as a university professor. Full of intense emotions and only vaguely aware of the raucous laughter of students, Legge marched again into the Sheldonian—Oxford's first Nonconformist professor, the first professional sinological Orientalist at the ancient English universities, and Müller's first collaborator in the gigantic undertaking of the *Sacred Books,* the foundational documents for the new comparative science of religions.

Despite the pandemonium, Legge must have felt some renewed sense of ministry and mission within this setting. As a good philological scholar and Latinist, he would have known that the Latin word *encaenia* could refer to the spring anniversary festival of the dedication of a temple or church, especially the Temple of Jerusalem. Having left the religious vocations of missionary and preacher, he was now in the process of discovering that his new dedication to a more secular and academic professorial life was also an act that reaffirmed his faith in the mission of learning and the ministry of education. This was, moreover, an initiatory realization and transformative lesson of life that was, as he knew so well by now, as much Chinese and Confucian as it was English, Scottish, or European.

Long-Continuing Nightmares

Given his perspicaciousness with regard to the lessons learned on his pilgrim's journey in China, Legge was most probably content with his new lot in life, but at the same time, sensed the envy and hatred that always lurks in the hearts of those who have not traveled so far. The blessings that came from a transcultural transformation (whether the bridged traditions be Eastern and Western, religious and secular, or missionary and academic) inevitably brought also the danger of being misunderstood and rejected by those who were left behind nursing old class resentments, theological differences, sectarian tensions, and nationalistic prejudices.

Legge's honeymoon was short lived. Already spring storm clouds of missionary resentment were rumbling in condemnation of the new professor of Chinese at Oxford. Only one month before his inaugural Encaenia, the first general conference of Protestant missionaries in Shanghai had found heretical implications in Legge's paper comparing Confucianism and Christianity. An initial explosion of anger was vented at the conference, but it was only later that the full significance of the condemnation in Shanghai was felt back home within missionary and scholarly circles. Legge generally had every right to believe that, after such a long and committed career as a missionary, he could now quietly close out his years as a scholar sequestered within the academic enclave of Oxford. But the more he devoted himself to the comparative methods of sinological Orientalism, the more he would be haunted and taunted by old missiological nightmares and new terminological specters.

Caricatures of Max Müller and James Legge at Oxford

FRIEDRICH MAXIMILIAN MÜLLER: KNOWN TO THE MANY

There is no better way to characterize Max Müller's unique significance within Victorian intellectual and social circles during the 1870s than to consider his caricatured image and biography published in the February 6, 1875, issue of the stylish London periodical *Vanity Fair* (see figure 21).[1] Honored by governments and national academies, Müller at the age of fifty-one was now, as the title of this series of articles indicates, one of the truly notable Men of the Day. He had just "concluded his great work, and given to the world the last volume of his 'Rig-Veda-Sanhita' which will remain to all time a monument of his erudition and a storehouse for Sanskrit students." In 1875 he was also publishing the fourth volume in the first series of his collected essays, *Chips from a German Workshop*. Müller's name was very much in the air, a result of the seemingly endless stream of publications (books as well as more ephemeral writings in journals and literary reviews) and his well-known, and often controversial, public lectures on the comparative science of religions. During this period, also, he was notably engaged in a series of public debates with Charles Darwin over the origin of language. Many of these accomplishments were known only by a few fellow scholars who cared about such arcane matters; but as *Vanity Fair* makes clear, Müller was that rare kind of public intellectual in an age of increasing specialization who was truly "known to the Many."[2]

In addition to his scholarship, Müller carried on an exceedingly active social life, hobnobbing with assorted literary figures, politicians, the social elite of London, and the royal family. He was often invited to Buckingham Palace for tête-à-tête sessions with the crown prince Albert. As noted in the *Vanity Fair* article, he lived within "grand ducal spheres" and was "a man of

Figure 21. Max Müller, "The Science of Language." Drawing by Ape (pseudonym), *Vanity Fair*, February 6, 1875.

the world moving in good Society, the guest and sometimes the host of Royalties." He was, furthermore, "very highly valued" in English society because he fortunately, or quite strategically, chose to marry the well-connected, and intellectually poised, Georgina Grenfell.[3] All things considered, he was one of the most celebrated and socially prominent scholars in the Western world, honored even more lavishly in Europe than in England. The Royal Academy of Turin declared him to be among an excruciatingly select (though now mostly forgotten) group of six "living immortals" in the realm of scholarship, the others being Victor Cousin, Adilfe Thiers, August Böckh, Theodor Mommsen, and G. Grote.[4]

The satiric engraving entitled "The Science of Language" by the caricaturist styled "Ape" suggests much of the spirit of Müller's international fame as a scholar and society figure, as well as deftly and cynically suggesting Müller's faith in the science of his own self-importance. The aura of intellectual composure and social hauteur is hinted at by the overall demeanor of the image. This is no flagrant comic jape, but a more subtle portrait of a man who is very serious about being taken seriously. The figure is elegantly turned out with a handsome frock coat, his hands folded in confident repose. Most fittingly prominent and overbearing is the great cerebral head that, with furrowed brow, perched spectacles, and a slightly pursed smile, nods knowingly in silent contemplation, it would seem, of the secrets of language, religion, and social position. He is, after all, the "one man who knows everything about every language."

The "Men of the Day" commentary accompanying this caricature of "Frederick Maximilian Müller, LL.D." is by the pseudonymous Jehu Junior, "jehu" being a humorous biblical allusion to a "furious driver" or "coachman" who runs in the fast track of the social or literary world.[5] The opening paragraph of this miniature biography perfectly captures the essential Müller and deserves full quotation.

> Never was there a man with so many learned titles or with so good a claim to them as Max Müller. He is a glorified Dryasdust of the most successful kind. He is the one man who knows everything about every language. He has written libraries, and in order to do so has achieved work which would do credit to universities. Most of his books are of that high order which nobody will read and most people will never hear of; yet he is known to the Many, and indeed is one of the few of those who have trodden the higher and more thorny paths of science whose names command respect even from the vulgar.[6]

Going on to a fairly balanced short recitation of the life of this German poet's son, the *Vanity Fair* article highlights Müller's precocious publication of Sanskrit fables at the age of twenty-one, his early dalliance with German poetry and literature, his studies with the great Orientalist Eugène Burnouf in Paris, where he first devoted himself to a mastery of the *Vedas,* and his arrival in 1846 in England to edit Sanskrit manuscripts found only in London and at the Bodleian in Oxford.

Eventually settling in Oxford, he was able to publish, through H. H. Wilson's encouragement and the financial support of the "unjustly-maligned East India Company," the first massive volume of his edition of the *Rig-Veda* (and Sanhita commentary) in 1854, and went on to become an Apostle for the Science of Language in England. Unsuccessful in his candidacy for the Boden chair of Sanskrit, his talents were finally recognized by the creation in 1868 of a new professorship in comparative philology. Insinuating that suspicions about his political loyalties were not completely unfounded, our ever-observant Jehu Junior notes that, although Müller had "become very English," he had "not ceased to be intensely German." A defender of German unity, he was often a kind of "unavowed Ambassador of Prussia in England."

AN ASSEMBLY OF DONS

Despite lingering reservations about his Nonconformity, Oxford easily accepted Legge into the ranks of the professoriate. It even appears from extant graphical testimony that he rather quickly and seamlessly faded into the crowlike mass of tottering dons, ceremoniously cloaked in black gowns and mortarboards (see figure 22). The precise occasion for this "assembly of dons" is uncertain (an Encaenia procession?), but several observations can be made. The first of these is simply that, although the picture may be roughly dated to the late 1870s (1877 or perhaps, according to one suggestion, 1879), the location can be precisely identified as the west side of Radcliffe Square with Brasenose College to the right and Saint Mary's Church looming in the background. Not all of the dons in the picture can be distinguished, but a distinct hierarchy of authority and influence is clearly suggested by the processional. Thus the figures, mostly professors and university officials, who are individuated in the immediate foreground take on an aura of special importance in the academic and political scheme of things.

It is in keeping with the social history of the period to recognize that Max Müller is shown front and center exhibiting a self-satisfied smile of scholarly fame and academic influence. There is some small controversy over exactly which figure is Professor James Legge, but it seems most likely that his rather dour visage is seen in the third rank of figures, standing immediately in front of the Brasenose archway and looking across to the Radcliffe Camera. Putting all of these factors together, we have in this picture an evocative representation of academic society at Oxford in the late 1870s. Most of all, it suggestively illustrates the rising fortunes of the professoriate, the pivotal role of Müller at the highest levels of university life, and the tertiary but quite significant and distinguishable presence of Legge in relation to university affairs. The important point here is that, even at the start of his university career, Legge was not totally lost within the dark, nondescript flock of other dons.

JAMES LEGGE: A GREAT GUN OF OXFORD

What was Legge's reception as an "Eastern Sage" in greater Oxford? What was his image, if any at all, on the city streets among students, more traditionally minded faculty and staff, merchants, and townsfolk? Beyond the

Figure 22. "An Assembly of Dons." The circled figure most likely is Legge. Drawing, Shrimpton and Son, Oxford, ca. 1879. Reproduced courtesy of Oxford University, Bodleian Library, Falconer Madan, G.A.Oxon 4°414, number 595.

photograph of Legge in his academic robes (see figure 20), an image was produced at the time of his appointment that provides us with a popular comic visualization of the new professor of Chinese. This caricature (see figure 23; number 381 in the Falconer Madan set of Oxford Caricatures) is a wonderfully fey, Gilbert and Sullivan cartoon portrait of one of the newly appointed "Great Guns of Oxford." It also seems to be the source for the later depiction of Legge as an Eastern Sage (see figure 19).[7]

This picture is instructive for what it discloses about a whole nested set of rather typical racist preconceptions and imperialistic attitudes—sentiments that were prevalent at that time because of the inaugural presence of an official Chinese diplomatic delegation in England. Playing upon a rather

Figure 23. James Legge as one of the "Great Guns of Oxford." Drawing, Shrimpton and Son, Oxford, ca. 1879. Reproduced courtesy of Oxford University, Bodleian Library, Falconer Madan, G.A.Oxon 4°413, number 381.

raw sense of comic relief concerning the guise and demeanor of a "heathen Chinee" and a Nonconformist professor, Legge is shown in what may be a Tylorian Institution lecture hall elevated, in the manner of an actor on a stage, on two decorated boxes. To his right is a chinoiserie teapot standing on a table covered with mockly ornate brocade embroidered with two mock

Chinese characters.[8] On his left, like theatrical props, are a painted fan and, incongruously in the background, a multitiered miniature pagoda.

Most striking in this overall tableau is the central "heathen Chinee" figure of Legge, who is bareheaded, with bushy eyebrows, prominent nose, muttonchop sideburns, a sly Cheshire-cat smile, and a ridiculously long queue, which he holds in an outstretched hand. Wearing a mandarin-style long-sleeved tunic with an odd, and distinctly un-Chinese, four-in-hand ribbon tie drawing together his Victorian collar and a kind of shoulder cope (perhaps a sly reference to evangelical or clerical garb), he displays a porcelain teacup and saucer in his right hand. Appended to the bottom of the drawing is an anonymous bit of doggerel verse that suggests that Legge's professorial lectures were only comic explanations of the dark and vain ways of the "peculiar Chinee." What is fascinating about this picture is the suggested link between the "heathen Chinee" and Legge's own exotic nature as a Chinese professor and as a Nonconformist preacher. At an Oxford that was becoming "curiouser and curiouser" (not just because of the peculiar legacy of Charles Dodgson and other traditional Oxford eccentrics) in its acceptance of "many worlds besides our own," even the humorous depiction of such Orientalistic and professorial peculiarities reflected a growing awareness and acceptance of a changing situation at the university and within the wider culture.

MAX MÜLLER: A GREATER GUN OF OXFORD

Another perspective on Legge's situation at Oxford is brought out by comparing his portrait as a "Great Gun" with the image of one of the greatest of all guns at that time—Oxford's own "Chip from a German Workshop," Max Müller. In figure 24, Müller is shown, without any comic-opera paraphernalia, standing, it would appear, on the High Street outside All Souls College, with the spire of Saint Mary's rising above his right shoulder. The dating of these images is problematic, but again it appears that this print was produced around 1875–1876. Most likely, it appeared at the time of the renegotiation of his professorship, the finalization of his editorship of the *Sacred Books,* and his most satisfying triumph over his enemies and fairweather colleagues such as Benjamin Jowett. As suggested by this image and the "Assembly of Dons" picture (see figure 22), Müller was now at the height of his personal prestige and political power at Oxford. Even though he was never a member of the Hebdomadal Council, Müller was among the elite power brokers at the university, the Bodleian, the Tylorian Institution, and the university press. He had by this time, despite his disingenuous protestations, gone from being a German outsider to an ultimate university insider.

GREAT GUNS OF OXFORD.   A CHIP FROM A GERMAN WORKSHOP.

Figure 24. Max Müller, "A Chip from a German Workshop." Drawing, Shrimpton and Son, Oxford, ca. 1875–1876. Reproduced courtesy of Oxford University, Bodleian Library, Falconer Madan, G.A.Oxon 4°413, number 220.

As befits someone known throughout Oxford for his erudition and influence, Müller is shown in a grave, vaguely haughty manner, dressed in his academic gown, holding a book (doubtlessly meant to be one of his own) in his right hand, and standing outside All Souls College, one of the bases of his Oxonian eminence. The only slightly satirical element in this caricature is the exaggerated, almost platform-size mortarboard he is wear-ing—suggesting possibly the inflated sense of his own self-importance as parodied in the earlier *Vanity Fair* caricature.

Whatever the satirical subtleties suggested, the obvious point is that Müller, unlike the incomparably less academically significant Legge, is not someone to be immediately or frivolously burlesqued as a peculiar Eastern Sage, ridiculous Hindu snake charmer (see figure 19), or comic Oriental-ist. He was, as we know, subject to such mockery (outside Oxford in *Vanity Fair*, but also within the university when academic and intellectual fashions start to pass him by or when, as in the "Eastern Sages" image, he is specifically identified as a foppish Orientalist or exotic Indological fakir), but here the emphasis is less satirical than it is corroborative of his elevated position within the Oxford hierarchy of power. Whereas Müller was adept at playing the foreigner while drinking from the wellsprings of power, Legge—a ruddy Scots Nonconformist who also had the misfortune of being that rarest of all exotic birds, a sinologist—remained awkwardly on the margins of academic politics at Oxford.

CHAPTER THREE

Heretic Legge:
Relating Confucianism and Christianity,
1877-1878

In [Chinese] records and conduct, we observe a high degree of piety and reverence for divine things. . . . But as we approach Confucius, a great and mournful change appears. The name of God is not even mentioned by him. . . . His was a system of secularism, pure and simple. . . . We are persuaded that Dr. Legge in his annotations upon the Chinese Classics will fully endorse these opinions.
WILLIAM MUIRHEAD, *CHINA AND THE GOSPEL,* 1870

NOTHING PURE AND SIMPLE

The new professor of Chinese quickly became known at Oxford for his staunch devotion to exotic scholarship and for his quaint appearance and uncompromising routines. Even though he was now in his sixties, Professor Legge maintained his ruddy complexion and a full head of unruly hair complete with bushy side locks, much of which had turned from an iridescent reddish hue to a silvery white. Always a creature of duty and habit, he persevered with his lifelong routine of concentrated study in the wee hours of the day, rising at three or four A.M., after only a few hours of sleep, and working through the early morning. This unyielding practice, going back to his youth, would continue for the next twenty-one years, almost to the very day of his death.

Such epic doggedness of intellectual labor was definitely not the norm for many faculty or students at that time. Helen Edith Legge tells us that all of Oxford was "amazed" at Legge's "simplicity" and his incredible dedication to odd hours and strange Oriental books.[1] James Murray, arriving in 1878 to edit the monumental *Oxford English Dictionary* and having a similar simplicity of character and a corresponding passion for unrelenting labor, remarked that it was best to disguise any penchant for "real work" at a place as "fastidious and otiose" as Oxford. Murray, a close friend of Legge and a fellow Nonconformist, went on to observe that, at Oxford (quoting "one of the most widely known men in Oxford," quite possibly Max Müller), "even men who work do it in secret and pretend openly to be merely men of the world."[2] This kind of sophisticated guile was not at all in keeping with the earnest evangelical character of either Legge or Murray.

192

Described at this time as "very Scottish in appearance" (particularly with his hearty complexion, blue eyes, shock of white hair, and full sideburns) and having a "striking country look," Legge became known for his mildly eccentric and absent-minded ways around town. He never, for example, seemed to get used to "new-fangled things" like trains, and it was said that, on those occasions when he went into London, the "entire railway staff was mobilized" to see that he was "safely put into the train."[3] Drawing upon eye-witness accounts, Dominica Legge reports that her grandfather was especially forgetful of his appearance and sometimes startled people on the street as he rushed to college sessions attired in his black academic gown and an incongruous red fez.[4] This was, however, a time of high eccentricity at Oxford—consider, for example, such transcendently peculiar characters as Charles Dodgson, Oscar Wilde, William Spooner, John Ruskin, and Henry Acland. Legge, in such company, was hardly peculiar.[5]

Hannah Legge's Lament

Legge's first half-decade at Oxford was a time of his own relative good health (he complained only of a few minor attacks of eczema and, in common with Müller, suffered sporadic pangs of gout) and, even more thankfully given his earlier separation from his family, a period of special domestic happiness shared with his wife, children, and grandchildren.[6] After her chronic ill health and inability to endure the rigors of colonial life in Hong Kong, Hannah Mary Legge (see figure 25) was especially delighted to bask in the relative grace and social prestige of an Oxford professor's wife. Legge himself says that, after they arrived in Oxford from the hinterlands of China and Scotland, Hannah "enjoyed the society and intellectual life of the place exceedingly." Up to the time of her sudden and premature death in 1881, she "was fond of meeting many of the accomplished, scholarly, and thoughtful men about the University"—including those who, like James Murray, became family friends and other more curious souls such as the introverted photographer, mathematician, tutor at Christ Church, and immortal creator of *Alice in Wonderland*, Charles Dodgson (better known to posterity as Lewis Carroll).[7]

The Legges and the Müllers did not commingle socially. The Müllers—given Max's aristocratic pretensions, Georgina's prominent family, and their Broad Church allegiance—moved within a significantly more elevated social world. For Legge and Murray, both of them simple Nonconformists and active fellow members of the George Street Congregational Church in Oxford, it "was not easy to gain an entree to University circles."[8] The colleges and their common rooms were snobbishly exclusive and, as Elisabeth Murray points out with respect to her grandfather, it was quite "possible for even a Professor or a scholar of European fame to live for years in the city without making the acquaintance of the leaders of the University."[9]

Figure 25. Hannah Mary Legge (née Johnston; 1822–1881), ca. 1870s.
Photograph by John Burton and Sons. Reproduced courtesy of the Legge Family
Collection.

While portraying her as an "ardent" wife, loving mother, and "careful
housekeeper," Legge also recalls that Hannah Mary "maintained a vigilant,
if not always a calm, outlook on the progress of public events, and the developments of philosophical thought whenever they entered into the
sphere of theology."[10] All things considered, Legge was chiefly pleased to

discover that, in contrast with her earlier hypochondria, his wife's "health too was better on the whole than it had been in any other place, with the exception perhaps of London."[11] Here Legge's understated qualification that Hannah's views were not always so "calm" most probably disguises a deeper element of strain within the relationship.

The bliss of their first few years in Oxford was short-lived. Hannah Mary's usual despondency and religious scrupulosity reasserted itself and, as her husband said, she "became dissatisfied more and more" with Oxford culture as "a very inferior and unreliable thing, compared with religion" and was afraid of "the children being over-stimulated intellectually." Given Hannah's acute sensitivities, it may also be that the inevitable social friction between plain and simple evangelicals like the Legges and Broad Church establishment sophisticates like the Müllers was a further element in Hannah's rejection of Arnoldian culture at Oxford. Repudiating various "developments of philosophical thought" and such Oxford options as Ritualism (it "disgusted" her), Latitudinarianism (it "afforded no spiritual nourishment"), Unitarianism (it made "truth a lie"), and Antisupernaturalism (it was only "a pretentious and unsubstantial meteor"), she was particularly "shocked" by the notion of Conditional Immortality, which she found "degrading to humanity and dishonouring to God."[12]

No doubt influenced by her feverishly difficult years amid the "filth" of heathen Asia and, perhaps, affected by the disturbing comparativist implications of her husband's work and his association with the arch Latitudinarian Müller, Hannah Mary was often morbidly pained by the thought of "what was to be the condition of the multitudes who pass away from life and had not welcomed and obeyed the message of the Gospel." Thoughts such as these led to bouts of uncertainty, but in the end she always came back to an intensely Calvinistic affirmation of an "atoning Saviour" and an agonized concern for her own salvation and that of her children.[13]

As Legge says in a way that reflects as much on himself as his wife: "In the course of years, while living in Hong-kong, she came to be more, or perhaps I should say less, of a moderate Calvinist than she had been." Most of all, and here it would seem part of her spiritual and physical difficulty in coping with the "damned" otherness of heathen worlds, children, and her own psyche, Legge remarks that he "could never induce her to throw Calvinism, as an attempt to compress the thoughts and ways of the Infinite and Eternal God within the limits of a human, erring logic, overboard altogether." Unfortunately, she could not be content, as he was (and we need to be alert to the hint of Victorian patriarchal condescension here), "with the facts of the Gospel, without an attempt to formulate them."[14]

The picture that is painted here is one that suggests that, while the Victorian patriarch and Oxford professor Legge was going about his important masculine business of scholarship and teaching ("nay," as Müller would have put it, the manly "battle" of such activities!), his wife was given to morose religious brooding about the state of her own, and her children's, soul and felt increasingly dependent on her daily spiritual practice of an intensely private "communion with God." Now Legge carefully, and rather patronizingly, says that Hannah's spiritual exercises showed "no inanity" and "no stupidity," but it is clear that he felt that these practices fed her propensity for looking at the "dark side of things" and were related to her "frequent illnesses and states of prostration."[15]

Far better, says Legge—the moderate Calvinist, Müllerian comparativist, and nonsectarian pragmatist—would it have been for her to have heeded his advice that "she needed to believe in God as the God of love." But also, adds Legge, she should more optimistically "believe in man, which she would do when she believed more unhesitatingly in God."[16] The intriguing incongruity of this situation is that, on the one hand, the intensity of Hannah's religiosity and private devotions caused her to believe all the more hesitatingly and tormentedly. Her husband's methodological comparativism and educational secularism, on the other hand, seemed only to reinforce his unhesitating belief in God's fundamental goodness and Scripture's essential truth.

Hannah Mary's problems in adjusting to the darkly unnerving cultures of China and Oxford serve to dramatize the fact that there was nothing so very plain and simple about the country bumpkin Chinese professor and his family in Oxford. Even Legge's typical patriarchal attitudes toward his wife were offset by his championing of higher education for women at Oxford and his unhesitating devotion to his daughters' upbringing. Helen Edith seems to have been especially favored by her father. After the death of Hannah, Helen Edith, who was only in her late teens at the time, assumed control of the household on Keble Terrace. It appears that, in some ways, Helen Edith's rise within the family hierarchy led to a kind of matriarchal rule of Legge's daughters over his sons and of the daughters of Hannah over those of Mary Isabella.

The Politics of Opium

Even if he did not have access to the highest circles of Oxford society and was something of a scholarly cram, Legge's extracurricular activities while in Oxford were varied and provocative. As seen from his active civic life in Hong Kong, Legge was by no means a political innocent. And when back in England he continued to engage in public, and often unpopular, causes. He was clearly not, as some said at Oxford, as "simple as a child."[17] One manifestation of this was his outspoken involvement in the increasingly contentious political debate over Britain's opium policy. A founding member of the Anglo-Oriental Society for the Suppression of the Opium Trade, Legge continued to voice his position that the opium trade was "a curse to China and a disgrace to Britain."[18]

The opium trade debate in Britain at this time was directly linked with the growing controversy over the desirability of promoting missionary traffic in China. This quite public and heated discussion implies (again relatively and comparatively) that it was neither opium nor Christianity per se that was at fault. Both could be used as either a drug or a medicine, and the root of the problem was the ethnocentrically arrogant attitude and selfish ways in which both were sold to the Chinese public. To some extent, it was the immoral commodification of Christianity (success being statistically measured in terms of gross units of converts) that catered to the darker side of human nature (whether Western or Asian) and, as with opium, led only to a revulsive reaction on the part of many Chinese (whether the literati or the lower classes).

These activities were given an added dimension by the fact that in 1876 the Chinese government for the first time established an official embassy in England. The initial delegation was led by Guo Songtao (Kuo Sung-t'ao) (1818–1891), a well-connected member of the Hanlin Academy and a progressive official (see figure 26). Guo lived between two worlds, becoming notorious among many Chinese. Just as Legge's ideas about the comparative worth of Confucianism or Ruism as a moral (and even "religious") system brought him rejections from his fellow missionaries, so also did Guo get into trouble for his heretical view that Western civilization was "morally equivalent" to Chinese civilization.[19]

On February 12, 1877, at the time of the Chinese New Year, Guo says that "Professor Legge came to visit" the embassy in London and "spoke about opium," reportedly saying that "England calls itself a nation of benevolence and justice and yet shows itself on this issue lacking in these two virtues." That is why, says Guo, Legge and his "gentry" friends in England "have formed a Society to eliminate the evils of opium." Furthermore, Legge is said to have recommended to the Chinese that if they, "the ambassadors, speak eloquently in the Upper House [of Parliament] and request the prohibition of opium," then they "need have no fear, for the English themselves will help [them] as much as possible."[20]

Legge's own writings indicate that this account is basically an accurate description of the meeting.[21] What should be appreciated is the courageousness of Legge's stance at this time (leading to public taunts of his being a "sentimentalist, goose, and fanatic") and especially his willingness to make personal contact with agents of the Chinese government on English soil. Such actions were by no means the ordinary behavior of a university professor from Oxford concerned with "pure research" and serve to show that his Nonconformist, ministerial, and missionary background gave him a broader, more Christian *and* Ruist conception of his educational duties as a scholar with a social conscience. It was his "whole duty" as a gentleman of the professional classes to take the actions he did.

Figure 26. Guo Songtao, the Chinese ambassador to Great Britain, ca. 1870s. Engraving from J. D. Frodsham, *The First Chinese Embassy to the West: The Journals of Kuo Sung-t'ao, Liu Hsi-hung, and Chang Te-yi* (Oxford: Clarendon Press, 1974), reprinted by permission.

Education in China

Another example of the cosmopolitan complexity of Legge's activities, his Christian and Ruist sense of duty to the common good, and his openness in promoting unpopular views is seen in an address on "Education in China" he gave to a local committee of the Central Elementary School shortly after his arrival in Oxford.[22] Reflecting on his early, and controversial, espousal (going back to the late 1830s and early 1840s) of a system of nonsectarian national education, he says that he could only rejoice in the "thoroughly undenominational" nature of the new Central Elementary School. These comments lead significantly to his observations on traditional Chinese education, which, for all its "defects," should be admired. It should be esteemed precisely because of its moral content and (he implies) because of its "thoroughly undenominational" focus on the national welfare.[23] In

Legge's estimation, a national education open to all classes and denominations should avoid the prescription of any set creeds, dogmas, or ecclesiastical organizations (a practice Oxford itself initiated only in 1871).

How could Legge feel that a pedagogical and "nondenominational"
affirmation of a monotheistic God necessarily lent some special sanction
and irresistible force to ethical practice—especially as traditional Chinese
society was arguably no less moral than British society? Even though Legge
at this time was coming to the conclusion that Chinese Ruists clearly had
a strong moral—and, to some degree, religious—tradition (particularly
in the ancient period given the unsullied testimony of the *Classics*), they
were still—even in the face of his mellowed experience, and comparative
evaluation, of ancient Chinese texts, the Altar of Heaven, and Chinese
acquaintances—*less* moral, on balance, than Christians were. The very fact
that Legge was struggling with the perspectival relativity of these issues indicates how far he had moved beyond the ordinary evangelical missionary
position. That Chinese were still less moral than Christians was becoming
harder and harder to maintain when confronted with the evil of the opium
issue and the pleading of righteous Chinese officials.

A Miserable Scantiness of Audience

Legge's sense of duty to his new educational vocation at Oxford was more
conscientious and vigorous than that of many other professors at the university, some of whom would have been perfectly happy to avoid completely
the bothersome encumbrance of courses and lectures. As indicated by his
inaugural address, Legge's "idea of a university" necessarily coupled serious
scholarly research with dedicated teaching. But knowing something already
of his scholarship and research, we need to pay some attention to the nature and extent of Legge's teaching activities at Oxford (see appendix B for
a list of Legge's Oxford lectures and courses). A later occupant of the Oxford chair of Chinese has indicated that the extent and nature of Legge's
teaching was mostly unknown: "How many pupils Legge taught is not
known. Nor is there any record of what he taught them."[24] This situation is
compounded by some nineteenth-century accounts: "Dr. Legge, the learned
occupant of the newly created Chinese Chair at the University of Oxford,
was unable to boast of a single student."[25]

As Algernon Steadman's guide to late-nineteenth-century Oxford
claims, the university strove "to imbue the student with the highest form of
culture" and "to teach him the best that has been thought and written by
the best minds on the highest subjects." Concerned with "producing noble
tendencies rather than commercial results," Oxford aimed, says Steadman,
"at humanizing the man rather than turning him out a professional expert." In this way, a student could enter into the "great struggle of human

life." The reality of student interests at Oxford was rather different from
what this noble credo would lead us to believe. The truth of the matter is
perhaps best suggested by the "collection of rules of conduct" given to each
student, along with a Latin copy of the University Statutes, upon matriculation. It is in these rules of daily life that special care is taken "to caution" students "against wearing boots, carrying bombarding implements, smoking,
and playing marbles on the steps of the Bodleian."[26] Even after the reforms
of the 1850s and 1870s and the trend-setting example of Benjamin Jowett's
academically competitive Balliol, it was an open question (as the Oxford
novels of the period also colorfully indicate) whether "there was any intellectual life at all" among Oxford students. After all, the undergraduates
mostly led a "life of amusement, consisting of a long holiday, scarcely broken
by the slight labour of getting up enough facts to pass their examinations."[27]

For those students actually disposed toward a more studious approach to
their college years, it was still doubtful that there would be much interest in
the "public lectures" given by university professors. Such lectures were, first
of all, not "useful for the Schools" (i.e., the examination system for graduation) and were open to the distractions of a "mixed" audience (i.e., including females).[28] As Müller once observed, "The young men are encouraged
in each college to attend the lectures delivered by the tutors, and are given
to understand that professorial lectures 'do not pay' in the examinations."
Moreover, the exams are "chiefly in the hands of the college tutors."[29]

In such an environment it is not surprising that professorial courses and
lectures by the Eastern Sages, which did not increase one's chances as a
"pass-man," would be known for the "miserable scantiness of their audiences."[30] It is entirely possible therefore that during his first few terms
(Michaelmas 1876 and Hilary 1877) at Oxford, Legge (whether to his
courses or public lectures, or both, is not clear) did not attract any students,
but it is demonstrably the case that this situation did not prevail. The *China
Review* was therefore "pleased" to learn that in the Trinity term (1877)
there were "now a few students giving attendance to Chinese studies" (the
course at this time involved the study of elements of Chinese grammar,
readings in the *Analects,* and the Chinese version of the Gospel of John).[31]

Actual attendance figures for lectures are given in an interesting survey
article in the *Edinburgh Review,* in which the overall institution of university
professorships at Oxford is discussed.[32] In general, the writer is dubious of
professors who were required to teach but all too often had "no audiences."
Whatever audiences there were too often included few real students and
too many "ladies and strangers." Claiming that "as a body" the professoriate
was "disliked" for its inflated endowments, desultory teaching, and devotion to obscure languages like "Sanskrit and Chinese," the writer goes on to
give the attendance statistics for the lectures of the forty-five university professors, among whom is the professor of Chinese with an "average atten-

dance of 4."³³ This is indeed a meager number, but it is not very different from the statistics for the other professorial lectures at that time or, for that matter, for the Chinese chair in the twentieth century.

Because of the Davis Chinese Scholarship (which paid £50 per annum for two years), we know that from the very beginning there was at least some monetary incentive to take up Chinese even if one did not have real aspirations toward a civil service, missionary, or sinological career. From university records it is clear that the scholarship, although sometimes vacant, was usually taken advantage of, and that there were a dozen or so Davis scholars from the late 1870s to the time of Legge's death.³⁴ Interestingly enough, some of Legge's examinations for the scholarship are extant and it is possible to get an idea of his pedagogical interests and techniques. On March 16, 1877, for example, the London *Times* published a notice on the Davis Scholarship competition and included a description of the examination to be administered: "the nature of the Chinese written characters; the Radicals or Classifiers, under which the characters are arranged in defining dictionaries; the first two books of the Confucian Analects; the first chapter of St. John's Gospel in what is called 'The Delegates' Version'; the names and dates of the Chinese dynasties; and the composition of easy sentences in Chinese."³⁵

Unfortunately, none of the Davis scholars achieved any real status in Chinese studies and, unlike Rémusat and Julien, who cultivated a number of students who went on to become distinguished sinological scholars, Legge's British students were mostly pedestrian, if not exactly listless. Beyond his peripheral contact with Müller's two Japanese students, Legge could really boast only of the Austrian Arthur von Rosthorn (1862–1945) as a serious sinological disciple. Coming to Legge as a graduate student from Vienna, Rosthorn was an accomplished scholar and went on to a prominent diplomatic career, publishing extensively on ancient Chinese society, religion, and philosophy as well as on the work of his mentor, Legge, and on Max Weber's sociological studies of China.³⁶

Regardless of his few students, Legge threw himself into his courses and was fondly remembered for his care and devotion to teaching.³⁷ His regular elementary and advanced courses on Chinese language and literature, as well as his varied public lectures each academic year (except during a few terms when he was ill in the 1880s), give a sense of his educational methods and the evolving scope of his scholarly interests.³⁸ Regarding his teaching methods, it is clear that he attempted to combine some study of grammatical and philological principles with a primary focus on reading varied Chinese texts. These texts spanned a very broad range of time and genre— ranging from the ancient Confucian classics to Daoist texts such as the classic *Zhuangzi* (The book of the Master Zhuang) and the popular medieval *Ganying pian* (Tractate of actions and their retributions), from the dynastic histories to the Kangxi Edict (along with its several supplements), and from Han Yu's elegant essays and Zhu Xi's stately commentaries to traditional poetry and Ming novels such as *Xiyou ji* (Journey to the West).[39]

Legge's emphasis as a teacher was upon reading and understanding the classical language (generically *wenyen*—including some of its stylistic variations such as different kinds of poetic diction and Han Yu's *guwen*), but at the same time we are struck by the breadth of his reading materials and the fact that the more practical aspects of composing and speaking the modern Mandarin vernacular were also taught. It is also worth noting that his changing course readings often, if not always, corresponded with his public lectures and the evolution of his research interests as a scholar and translator—thus the progression through ancient Ruist texts (especially the *Lunyu* or *Analects* and the *Mengzi* or *Mencius)* into the later Ruist writings of the dynastic historians, as well as the works of Han Yu and Zhu Xi, heterodox Buddhist and Daoist texts, and poetry and other literary works. Despite the fact that in the language courses the most recurrent texts are the *Analects* and *Mencius,* the topics for the courses and lectures cannot be narrowly identified as only Ruist in nature. His efforts concerning Daoism are especially noteworthy and can be considered a typical example of the Orientalist urge to define and distinguish the classical, ancient, or pure textual expressions of Asian traditions.

Legge's newfound career as a sinological scholar and teacher led to a broadening of his awareness of the strange literary riches of the Chinese tradition. In many ways, this involved an interesting stretching of the Orientalistic (and to some degree the Ruist or Confucian) categories of classic and sacred books, along with their corollary implications of ancientness and purity, to include other traditions. It also tended to reinforce an emerging set of presuppositions associated with sinological Orientalism. Thus, while Chinese literature beyond the Ruist classics was often found to be grotesque and tedious, it did not seem to contain the extremities of sexual licentiousness, mythological fancy, and bloodthirsty superstition found in other literatures (especially the ancient Aryan epic literature of India and Greece). Although Legge as a missionary had already encountered some of the strange worlds of Chinese literature (e.g., his very first translation, with Ho Tsun-sheen, of the historical novel *Zhengde xia Jiangnan* as *The Rambles of the Emperor Ching Tih in Keang Nan*), his ability to explore the totality of heathen literature was positively enhanced by his new vocation as a professional scholar. Unfettered by the sectarian concerns and theological predispositions of missionaries, Legge now had the freedom to cultivate his faculty for "sympathetic comprehensiveness."

Sympathetic Comprehensiveness

The most insightful recognition of Legge's new academic position and its "enhanced faculty" of vision is found in an anonymous article, "The Professorship of Chinese at Oxford," appearing in the July 28, 1877, issue of the Shanghai *North-China Herald,* one of the leading organs for British commercial interests in China. Adopting a cynically realistic tone, the writer questioned whether "many students will gather at the Doctor's feet" because Oxford undergraduates may, given the aestheticism of Walter Pater and Oscar Wilde, cultivate "a taste for Blue Pot, but they will not allow the Book of Odes to take the place of Homer."[40]

The author of this article correctly predicts that Legge, who was certainly the "right man" at the "right place," will have great difficulty in attracting students to the study of Chinese and will be in the same position as Stanislas Julien, who, "as no one ever attended his lectures, was devoutly believed to be an inoffensive lunatic" laboring "under an insane desire to teach a stove to speak Chinese." Even though this anecdote is faulty in several respects (Julien was hardly "inoffensive" and he would have been more concerned with getting the stove to read classical Chinese than he would have been in having it speak), it accurately suggests that Legge's professional reputation as a university professor and sinological Orientalist would depend less on his having students than on his scholarly publications and his penetration "into the inner circle of Sinologues" once ruled so ruthlessly by Julien.

Most interesting, however, is that the writer is so sensitive to the important intellectual disparity between the missionary and the professorial Legge, noting shrewdly that the "intellectual atmosphere of a great University is very different from that of a Mission." At Oxford, this difference involves "a sympathy with the progressive and ever-moving thought of Europe," which "must influence the Professor." In particular, the anonymous author finds evidence for this kind of influence in Professor Legge's recently published paper on "Confucianism in Relation to Christianity," a lecture originally presented in absentia at the first general meeting of Protestant missionaries in Shanghai in May 1877, and considered by some in the audience as advancing patently heretical views. It is worth noting that, in light of the article in the *North-China Herald* and of the implications of heresy that were read into the paper because of its consideration of Confucianism *in relation to* Christianity and which provoked such high-handed censorship by the authorities at the conference, Legge's identity as a "former missionary" takes on a "world of suggestion."

In the spirit of the earlier chastisement of Legge's approach to Confucius found in the *Edinburgh Review* (see pages 78–80), the writer makes the point that, "formerly," Legge had too much of the annoying missionary habit of "always finding fault with the great sage for not attaining unto that clearness of moral perfection which is found in men enlightened by Christianity." The obverse was just as disconcerting: "When any resemblance to the Gospel precepts was found in the Classics, he was only too anxious to explain it away." At Oxford everything had changed in Legge's approach to such interpretive matters. "Now," the *Herald* said, "we see a far better spirit prevalent." As attested to by his new comparative publication on the relation of Confucianism and Christianity, Professor Legge betrays for the first time an "enhanced faculty of sympathetic comprehensiveness with the varied culture of the time." This, according to the *Herald,* was in keeping with the intellectual climate of a university, not the parochial environment of the seminary or missionary society.

A Never-Wavering Great Man

These changes of comprehensiveness did not come about just because Legge was now at Oxford. They are as much related to his evangelical temperament and the transformative experiences of his missionary career as they are to any kind of "far better spirit prevalent" at Oxford. But this far better spirit of "sympathetic comprehensiveness with varied culture" was truly characteristic of only a relatively small, albeit increasingly influential, liberal Broad Church faction at Oxford especially associated in the 1870s with Müller, Pattison, Sayce, and Jowett. Later in the 1880s and 1890s these liberal currents would be greatly enhanced by the growing Nonconformist presence at Oxford (including Legge, Horton, James Murray, Green, and Fairbairn). Much of academic society at Oxford, even in the 1870s, was far more preciously parochial and clerically petty than evangelical missionary groups such as the London Missionary Society.

Because of his own transcultural experiences as a missionary in China and as a translator of Chinese texts, Legge truly was the right person at the right time to arrive at Oxford and take advantage of the new liberalizing currents (i.e., curricular expansion, methodological diversification, religious secularization, and the vocational professionalization of higher education in England). As Müller made clear in his inaugural address in 1868, it was the increasing religious tolerance and sympathy for intellectual comprehensiveness at an institution dedicated to the training of men for the work of a global empire that led to the creation of positions in such formerly outlandish subjects as comparative philology and Chinese.

Legge would suffer the slings and arrows of conservative missionary accusations and resentments, both public and private, as a result of various controversial works published while at Oxford—especially the paper on Confucius and Christianity (1877), his first translations for Müller's *Sacred Books* (1879), and a book on the general subject of Chinese religions (1880). These works, which trace out Legge's changing intellectual trajectory and collectively solidify his new identity as a sinological Orientalist, also finalize his bittersweet relationship with the organized missionary movement. It is true, as Helen Edith Legge says, that Legge "never wavered" in his "belief in Missions."[41] But what she does not recount is that, while her father remained prophetically committed to the broad revolutionary ideals and practical civilizational importance of the Christian mission to China, the murmurs of missionary censure led him to stand apart from any further official involvement in organized missionary activities. An example of his more qualified support of missions after 1877 is seen in the general conference on foreign missions held in Mildmay Park, London, in October 1878, at which time Legge reiterated his belief in the eventual "complete success" of the missionary movement. However, during his remarks at this conference Legge also described his troubling interview with Guo Songtao in London, and it became clear that, for Legge, the success of missions was contingent on a new and more sympathetic approach to China. By the late 1880s, Legge often refused to participate in missionary conferences that perpetuated outmoded methods and triumphalistic views.

Helen Edith's biography makes it seem as if the only difference between the early missionary-Legge and the later professor-Legge was that, with respect to missions, he emphasized even more the need for missionaries in the field "to become acquainted" with heathen literature and religions.[42] The fact that Legge had arrived at a position that was considerably more radical than this, implying the need for a significant comparativist revision of conventional missionary policy and practices respecting heathen religions, is totally avoided by Helen Edith. This omission was made in spite of the fact that many conservative missionaries in China were very much aware of the alarming implications of Professor Legge's latest scholarship from Oxford.

Some missionaries were even prepared to equate the pernicious effects of various, although not always equivalent, things such as "Romish accommodationism," "comparative religions," "indifferentism," and "syncretism" with a general intellectual attitude called "Leggism."[43] It is possible to trace a direct line in the nineteenth-century Protestant missionary movement from the scandal in 1877 of Legge's Shanghai paper down to the controversial surfacing in 1893 of accommodationist triumphalism at the Parliament of Religions in Chicago and the eventual secular transformation and indigenization of Christian missions after the turn of the century (particularly the so-called social gospel movement).

Most incredible of all is that Helen Edith Legge completely neglects to mention the scandal of the 1877 paper and its aftermath involving the continuing missionary outrage over the *Sacred Books of China,* published in 1879, and the *Religions of China* (1880). Contrary to the sanitized image put forward in *James Legge Missionary and Scholar,* Legge was never just the ever-faithful London Missionary Society agent and prosaically plodding scholar-translator. The uncensored record depicts someone who played a formative, and sometimes transgressive, role in the intertwined nineteenth-century history of Protestant missionary tradition, sinological Orientalism, and the comparative science of Chinese religions.

Points along the Trajectory

A quick glance at Legge's public lectures at Oxford before the traumatic events in Shanghai during May of 1877 brings to light a number of common themes regarding his enhanced "faculty of sympathetic comprehensiveness" and his evolving understanding of Confucianism. During the Hilary term 1877 he gave a lecture, entitled simply "Confucius," that amounted to a trial run of some ideas published later in his Shanghai paper; a few months later (in March) he followed this with a public talk, "Mencius/Mengzi," that was also devoted to a basically positive, almost Pauline, assessment of the Second Sage of Confucianism.[44] The lecture on Mencius begins with a stirring overture to the "advance of the West" and the relative "stationariness" and "retrograding" of the East—a condition that will be rectified only by the uplifting influence of "truly Christian" representatives from the West. This kind of rhetoric represents no more, and no less, than typical boilerplate Victorian progressivist ideology common to missionaries, politicians, and scholars. Legge's introduction of these ideas is still sermonically couched in a theology of God's providence and Christian atonement, themes that someone like Müller would have avoided in a university lecture. But such apologetic theologizing in the course of a academic lecture, whatever the subject, was by no means unusual at Oxford at that time.

Regarding the Orient's need for the stimulus of Western progress (whether Christian or civilizational was moot), there was not much difference between missionaries in China and dons at Oxford. An enhancement of comprehensiveness is seen in the degree to which a non-Western and non-Christian tradition is capable of building upon its own original and inherent resources or, because of its utter depravity, must be totally reconstituted. Interestingly, in this lecture, Legge makes a special point of rejecting popular racist pronouncements on civilizational development, pronouncements that were often associated with Müllerian theories of Aryan superiority.[45] As Legge says, the belief that progress was "an affair of race" and that the "Turanian and the negro" were not capable of Aryan achievements is disproved by the "early progress" of the Chinese: "the pleading of *race* [Legge's italics] seems to be all in favour of the Aryan now; it would have been all against him, if it had been agitated 2,500 years ago."[46]

The wondrous adaptability of the Orientalist perspective is seen here. Depending on one's scholarly persuasion and personal temperament, Orientalism allowed the comparative philologist, Indologist, or sinologist to have it both ways—that is, to affirm the contemporary retardation of Asian civilizations while disallowing or allowing (as the case may be, and the distinction was primarily one of the difference between "civilized" and "savage" traditions) for an essential or original capacity for progress that was manifest in the ancient past. It seemed obvious that Europe was the modern inheritor of the dynamic epic spirit of the ancient Indians and Aryans. For China, however, there was no contemporary continuation of the archaic Chinese capacity for progressive civilizational change, and it was incumbent upon the West to apply the electrodes of galvanic resuscitation.

Imperial Comprehensiveness

Another series of public lectures from this period dealt with the subject of "Imperial Confucianism." (The first three lectures were given during May, Trinity term 1877, and overlapped therefore with the presentation in absentia in Shanghai of the infamous paper comparing Confucianism and Christianity.) This four-part lecture is, on the surface, a rather monotonous, point-by-point discussion of the "sweet reasonableness" of the famous sixteen maxims of the Emperor Kangxi's Sacred Edict of 1670 (along with its later "amplification" and "paraphrase").[47] More interesting is to try to read between the lines of these talks to see what they say about Legge's own evolving views on Ruism. Aside from the fact that he clearly chose the edict for pedagogical purposes (i.e., as a brief specimen of Chinese prose using both literary and colloquial idioms), there is a sense in which these lectures rehearse his experience of contemporary "imperial Confucianism" back at the Altar of Heaven in Peking and raise many of the comparativist issues that he had provocatively set out in his paper "Confucianism in Relation to Christianity."

One other reason for the nineteenth-century fascination with these maxims is that they approximate so much of the tone and content (the "European good sense") of Victorian middle-class morality—that is, the value of patriarchal filial piety, which may be compared with the Fifth Commandment; generosity and peacefulness toward kindred and neighbors; the importance of industry and thrift; the need for general and advanced education; the promulgation of laws; the significance of manners and propriety; and the prohibition against false accusations.[48] Legge allows that "falsehood is, probably, more common among them than among ourselves," but the surprising thing is said to be that these principles are not the "drivellings of dotage," as are those of some other Orientals.

Legge's muted reflections on the Sacred Edict in his first three lectures suggest that the fundamental issue of deciding between the relative morality of Europeans and Chinese is still very much of a problem for him. Especially poignant in this regard is the fact that the fourth and last lecture given at the Sheldonian Theatre on November 28, 1877, was attended by the Chinese ambassador to England, Guo Songtao. Here was someone who really put the rhetoric of European incomparability and the issue of moral reciprocity to the test—someone who was highly appreciative of European civilization and ethical values but, as Legge knew so well from their tense encounters concerning opium, would countenance no automatic presumption of moral superiority on the part of his British hosts.[49]

Given the implications of having Guo in the audience, Legge's last lecture is somewhat of a disappointment in that he devotes much of it to the remaining four maxims (and they tend to be unremarkable and rather dull—i.e., having to do with sheltering deserters, paying taxes, suppressing thievery and robbery, and controlling animosity and anger to preserve life), which call forth nothing very arresting in his interpretive discussion. The only thing of consequence is the conclusion, which is ostentatiously lavish in its general praise of the maxims. They are, he says, "fine examples of high principle," which show the "highest human wisdom" and "justify the highest encomiums that have been passed on." This praise is immediately qualified by the stereotypical, though understated and abbreviated, observation that ultimately something more is "needed than the highest human wisdom to make a nation truly good and great." What is especially fascinating and atypical here is that this qualification is itself qualified with a revealing allusion to Legge's own sensitivity to the charge of "Christian bigotry" overtly leveled against him by the *Edinburgh Review* and *North-China Herald* critics and more indirectly, though more powerfully, by Guo Songtao.

Legge's defense of his conclusions is not, interestingly enough given the tribulations in his life, exclusively Christian or theologically apologetic. In the paper "Confucianism in Relation to Christianity," written at the same time that he was working on these lectures, he did end with a specific appeal to Christian principles. Here at Oxford his plea concerns more of the Müllerian impartial scholar's method. This is something of a "let the chips fall where they may" defense of his judgment about China's relative deficiencies in goodness and greatness—a defense that is in its own disguised way as intrinsically apologetic as any theological argument. Some of Guo Songtao's own reaction to Legge's obloquies were actually recorded. It is hardly surprising to learn that Guo, as a Ruist scholar trained in the arts of rhetorical discourse, was less than swayed by Legge's scholarly rationalization for the ethical gradient favoring the West.

Seeing Ourselves as We See Others

The fact that Legge was not the only one to take steps in the direction of a more sympathetic comprehensiveness toward the heathen Chinese is delightfully illustrated by the appearance at this time of a very broad, but knowledgeable, "turn-about" satire on the British understanding of Chinese tradition. This controversial work was doubtlessly influenced by the recent European travels of such Chinese scholars as Wang Tao and the establishment of a resident Chinese embassy in Great Britain, but, from the testimony of internal evidence, it also clearly reflects the influence of the growing secularist and comparativist sentiment in the foreign community in China and within scholarly circles in Britain. The work in question was published in London in 1876 and is suggestively entitled *Some Observations upon the Civilization of the Western Barbarians, Particularly of the English; Made During a Residence of Some Years in Those Parts.* This book purports to be a translation by a pseudonymous John Yester Smythe, Esquire, of Shanghai, of the observations recorded by a "mandarin of the first class" improbably known as Ah-Chin-Le. The actual author is John B. Swasey, of which little is known besides his name and the fact that he clearly possessed considerable knowledge of China.[50]

A satire on what could be called a kind of comic Occidentalism, this is an unexpectedly extensive work covering many traditional Orientalist subjects transposed and translated into an English setting, complete with fragments of mock Chinese terminology included within a technical apparatus of parenthetical brackets. It is most appropriate therefore that the very first chapter in the book is concerned with "The Religion and Superstitions of the English," which, with delicious irony and full appreciation of a Ruist or Confucian method of reciprocal cultural understanding, opens with a discussion of the fact that "the worship of the Supreme Lord of Heaven (Chang-ti) is not unknown to these Barbarians, though degraded by many superstitions." Turning the missionary discussion of Confucius upside down, our pseudonymous Mandarin of the First Class observes that the originally pure worship of the Supreme Lord was degraded by the appearance, some five hundred or six hundred years after "Confutze," by a new sect of devotees who "asserted that they had among them a Son of Heaven . . . called Christ."[51]

Referring to the dismal sectarian squabbling that so bothered Legge, the perceptive Ah-Chin-Le remarks, "Each Sect denounces every other; and, so far is the contention carried, that the teaching of the people is lost sight of; the special Superstition of a Sect being held by its adherents far more important than merely 'Secular' teaching! . . . Each Sect dislikes and denounces every other; and the members of all damn to everlasting torments the whole human race but themselves!"[52] Our erstwhile Occidentalist continues by noting that it is impossible "to make intelligible the countless vagaries of the Sects." Even more disturbing is that "they all fight under the same Christ-God, whom they all address, among other titles, as the 'Prince of Peace' (Tchu-pe). They all profess to follow His precepts, one of which is to love all men, even enemies." Furthermore, says our amazingly candid spectator, the precepts of the Christ-God are written in "Sacred Books" not unlike the Chinese classics. While the Christ sects "go on damning each the other," each of them nevertheless swears its oaths upon the same Sacred Books and "resort[s] to them for the unchangeable rules of belief and practice."[53]

This blunt Swiftian humor cut close to the bone but, nonetheless, the book seems to have disappeared beneath the placid surface of conventional piety with only a slight ripple. The perceptiveness of this little work is seen in its self-conscious awareness of what could be described as the discursive inertia of a particular kind of hegemonic consciousness. Here this problem is more simply and intelligibly identified in the Voltairean sense of the difficulty of changing superstitious beliefs "rooted in fears." Especially with regard to matters "wherein the imagination has chief power, and nothing can be *known*," it is the case that "even honest men of wisdom fear radical changes." Such "men of wisdom," whether Chinese or English, "prefer to bear inconveniences, and dread the effect of *new doctrines* upon ignorant masses."[54]

This is a more honest and "comprehensively sympathetic" appraisal of superstitious beliefs than is seen in an otherwise enlightened article in the *North-China Herald* that attempted to set some of the "tail-cutting craze" among Chinese in a comparative context.[55] While stressing the "queer" and "fantastic" nature of these stories, the *Herald* had the uncommon good sense to realize that "in odd corners of Great Britain and Ireland, the queerest observances are practised and the most eccentric beliefs entertained." Unlike the more astute and amusing Ah-Chin-Le, this reporter undercut his own good sense by then suggesting that in the Orient "absurd" opinions and practices are "carried on by the educated classes, by the courtiers and the statesmen, by the priesthood and the men of letters, by the wealthy merchants and the men of leisure and culture." "In England and America," in contrast, the belief in "demons, witches, charms, and omens is restricted almost entirely to ignorant rustics and the neglected masses in the great towns." Shortly after this statement was printed in Shanghai, the Society for Psychical Research was established in England and the *Oxford Magazine* was publishing accounts of various ghostly occurrences among the elite and educated.

THE CHINA MISSION: GREAT AND MOURNFUL CHANGES

The most grievous charge we bring against [Confucius] . . . is his irreligious spirit. He falls far beneath the ancient sages in this respect. . . . The effect of all this we need not say has been of a vitiating and depraving kind. . . . It cannot be denied that the moral character and secularism of Confucius have had an injurious effect upon the Chinese from age to age. Not only is he wanting in the

elements of true greatness, and not only is his system defective in relation to
spiritual and Divine things, but both his precepts and his practices are chargeable
with results, that show their nature and operation in the untruthfulness and
ungodliness of the Chinese.

WILLIAM MUIRHEAD, *CHINA AND THE GOSPEL,* 1870

Missionary Failures and Fruits

While Legge was in Oxford dutifully adjusting himself to his new academic circumstances, the Protestant missionary movement was undergoing a traumatic adaptation to a rapidly changing situation in China. What
made this situation so complex and difficult was that the earlier missionary pioneers in China, such as Legge and Samuel Wells Williams, were
leaving the field and were often taking up other vocations at home. The
new and inexperienced missionaries going abroad were having to deal
with a China that was simultaneously more accessible (i.e., inland China
was opened to missionaries as a part of the Tianjin Treaty of 1858 and
1860) and more hostile to the presence of foreigners, especially missionaries.[56] There were also continuing problems of sectarian and nationalistic squabbling among the missionary societies, a situation that in the
1870s led directly to the revival of the dreadful term question.[57] Much of
the internecine turmoil within the Protestant missionary world in China
at this time was related to disturbing questions of self-doubt connected
with charges that the movement had basically failed. Both in China and
back at home, there was an increasingly vocal chorus of secular critics who
ridiculed the tiny number of Chinese converts and, for reasons of commercial and political stability, called for a reduction of missionary operations. According to these critics, irresponsible missionary activity was the
single most important cause for anti-Western animosity among the Chinese people.[58]

Samuel Johnson and Confucius

A good example of this kind of criticism is found in the masterful synthesis
of nineteenth-century sinological scholarship making up the China volume
(1877) of *Oriental Religions and Their Relation to Universal Religion,* by the radical American evolutionary transcendentalist thinker Samuel Johnson.[59]
Johnson devotes a whole section of this thousand-page book to "missionary
failures and fruits."[60] In the face of the "almost infinitesimal harvest" of converts, Johnson claims that a "confession of failure" on the part of the Protestant societies was unavoidable. According to Johnson, the reasons for this
failure are not due to a lack of opportunity, but have much to do with the
cultural insensitivity and isolation of Protestant missionaries when compared with their more indigenized Catholic counterparts. In addition to

this, there is the problem of an evangelical theology that emphasizes "natural depravity," a concept that was "absolutely irreconcilable with the organic life of the [Chinese] nation."[61]

Johnson also points out the inanity of Christians who condemn the hopeless superstition of heathens and yet practice a kind of incredible "fetichism [fetishism]" or "bibliolatry" involving an "enormous expenditure of money, machinery, and labor in printing and circulating Bibles." It is, in fact, the "logic of the Christian" that often constitutes "an impenetrable barrier" to a "rationalistic people like the Chinese." As Johnson says, learned Chinese "readily detect the absurdity of an attempt to absorb all their own sober historical traditions into the sacred books of a people of whom they never heard, upon the pretence that this people has been miraculously illuminated to furnish the criterions of truth and duty."[62] Digressing on other problems of the organized Protestant effort in China (including the "prolonged and hopeless disputes" of sects and translators over the name of God), Johnson understandably stresses the "prodigious" presumption of claiming an "exclusive [Christian] ownership in the way of salvation." Then raising the issue that so exercised Legge, Johnson remarks that Christians were clearly "unfit" to be "instructors in benevolence" to the Chinese.[63]

Concluding this section in a way that would have pricked Legge's sensibilities, Johnson says that the real "fruit" and "service" of the missionaries was not in their proselytizing efforts, but in the more hyphenated and "secular" scholarly work of individual missionaries like Legge, Marshman, Milne, Medhurst, Edkins, Eitel, Chalmers, and Faber.[64] These active and former missionaries are the authentic agents of civilizational progress in both a physical and morally spiritual sense. And in a very special way it was the intellectual, linguistic, and spiritual work of these men as cross-cultural communicators of the best of the Western and Oriental traditions that was the source of their transformative power. This is because the scholarly translation projects of such men both "enlighten the minds and heal the bodies of the Chinese by Western science and make known the literature of this hitherto unknown people to the world." This, Johnson implies, is the real work of conversion. Therefore, the crowning glory of the missionary movement was not the promulgation of religion or theology. Rather, it was the transmission of medicine and science to the Orient and the diffusion of Chinese literature and Oriental wisdom to the West.[65] This is clearly an understanding of missionary work that anticipates the later liberal commitment to the social gospel. Given his "universal" perspective on "those deeper ethical and spiritual processes which run beneath all special faiths or systems,"[66] it is not astonishing to learn that Johnson was an "ardent and devoted admirer of Confucius" and, when comparing him with Buddha and Jesus, "gives preference" to the Chinese sage and his rational social morality and sober spirituality.[67] Instead of the "supreme enemy" of Christianity and all true religion, Johnson in effect found Confucianism to be the closest thing imaginable to a kind of Oriental transcendentalism.

Painful and Profound Respect

While Johnson's massive work was mostly ignored by scholars and was understandably spurned by missionaries, it was reviewed by Legge in the influential literary periodical known as the *Academy*.[68] This review is fascinating both in terms of what Legge does and does not say in his evaluation of Johnson's views on China and the missionary movement. Legge notably manifests real sympathy for the book even though he is dismayed by certain aspects of Johnson's position (e.g., his rationalistic antisupernaturalism; while rejecting the old notion of Chinese atheism, and agreeing with Legge that Shangdi was the ancient Chinese God, Johnson did not believe that the Chinese language had a word "capable of rendering the service required for the 'Bible-God' ").[69] Johnson often seems to betray an ungentle "spirit of animosity" toward Christianity in his book, but Legge states that he is left with the strong impression that Johnson "is an earnestly religious man" and that his work "will amply repay study." Furthermore, though discouraged by Johnson's pantheistic tendencies, Legge approves of his rejection of the frequent claims that Chinese tradition, particularly Confucianism, was wholly irreligious or atheistic. Affirming what he calls the unique "supernatural element" in Jesus' life, Legge does admit, however, that he finds Johnson's preference for Confucius over Jesus "painful."

Most personally revealing is Legge's discussion of Johnson's views on "missionary failures." Carefully pointing out that "Sectarian Protestants" could easily show "that their success is grotesquely understated," Legge provocatively concludes that "it will be well for them to weigh all that [Johnson] has said about them and their procedures, and 'be taught even by an enemy.' " Regardless of various criticisms and qualifications, this review is a positive appreciation of what Legge calls in his conclusion a "powerful volume" of "vast research" and "profound thought."[70] The fact that Legge takes a public position (albeit in a scholarly journal unlikely to be consulted by missionaries in China) in partial sympathy with both Confucius and Johnson as the "supreme enemies" of the missionary movement in China shows just how much his new professorial identity and the events in Shanghai (see pages 214–18) have loosened his mind and pen about such matters.[71]

Extrapolating from Legge's "enhanced faculties for sympathetic comprehensiveness" wherein one can "be taught even by an enemy," it would seem that the problem of missionary failure and self-doubt, what one Nonconformist publication called the "decline of holy zeal," has some significant connection with the growing comparativist "spirit of the times."[72] This "decline" or, better, transformation, of the missionary spirit in the 1870s and 1880s is, according to the *Congregationalist,* a phenomenon that seemed especially to affect "earnest missionaries" returning home "after long years of peril and of labour."[73]

The problem from the conservative point of view was that "missionary zeal will never develop under the eclectic view of religion that regards Christianity only as one of several systems, each of which has characteristic excellences of its own, possibly the best of all, but yet having no more right to be regarded as the one truth than any of the rest." Such "eclectic views" as these lead necessarily to a diminishment of the "aggressive work" of missionaries and muscular Christians.[74] The *Congregationalist's* characterization of the "eclectic view" was never exactly Legge's position on these matters (nor was it Müller's), but most comparativist perspectives, whether extreme or moderate, were tarred with the same brush. Such approaches were also typically contrasted with what conservative missionaries took to be the more orthodox, muscular, and aggressive approach to Oriental traditions. This kind of contentious contrast was very much in evidence at the Shanghai missionary conference that resulted in a sharp polarization between Legge's sympathetic revisionary comparison of Confucianism and Christianity and the more conventional antagonistic position of "Christian Manliness."

The Shanghai Missionary Conference, 1877

The need for a general meeting of all Protestant missionaries in China was directly related to the prevailing problems in the missionary movement: the haunting sense of self-doubt and failure, the heated sectarian and nationalistic disputations reflected in the revival of the term question, the generational change of missionary personnel in the field, the growing hostility of the Chinese, the waning of public and governmental support back home, and the development of reforming sentiments among evangelical missionaries concerned about the great famine in China in 1876–1877.[75] By far the most important issue was the need for a general reassessment of missionary policy and practices in light of both the rapidly changing situation in China (changes that were perceived as involving great dangers and significant opportunities) and, as I have tried to show, the changing intellectual situation with respect to the "eclectic," "sympathetic," "comprehensive," or comparative evaluation of Oriental religions.

The first published proposal in 1874 for a "'general conference' of all the missionaries in China" stressed that, in addition to various practical and sectarian issues, "one of the most momentous questions" was the "basic problem of attitude which Christianity assumes towards heathen systems."

This specific problem was obviously related to the term question as well as to other practical issues such as a common translation or "Union Bible," Sabbatarian questions, the possible role of ancestor rites in Christian worship, the place of the Chinese classics in education, and the effectiveness of conversion through traditional colporteurage methods. In the discussion of the proposal in the *Chinese Recorder,* the conventional position on these overall issues was said to be epitomized by those who "still publicly state that Confucius [was] certainly in hell."[76]

The circulation of the conference proposal gave rise to a considerable internal debate among the resident missionaries in China, with the liberal faction, represented in print by Alexander Williamson, the London Missionary Society agent and Legge's old acquaintance in North China, strongly favoring such a general meeting. In light of the contemporaneous emergence of the international congresses of Orientalists and other attempts to professionalize and organize occupations with various kinds of expert knowledge, it is notable that, among other arguments, Williamson specifically argues for such a "general conference" on the basis that missionaries should be "capable of meeting like the other sciences."[77]

The question of whether to hold the proposed conference was put to a general vote, with two-thirds of the Protestant missionaries in China favoring such a meeting (the count was 110). Given this kind of sentiment, a Committee of Arrangements (consisting of the English Presbyterian Carstairs Douglas, the American Presbyterian Calvin W. Mateer, the London Missionary Society's William Muirhead, the American Presbyterian John Butler, and the London Missionary Society's Alexander Wylie) was formed to plan the meeting, raise the necessary funding, send out invitations to speakers (despite his absence from the field, Legge was one of the first to be invited to present a paper), and resolve some difficulties that had already emerged. The most disturbing of these difficulties was, not surprisingly, the long-standing problem of the term question.[78]

With the Committee of Arrangements in the hands of what was perceived to be a liberal Shangdi faction, the Shin-ite group demanded representation and a special joint committee was formed to try to reach a workable plan for dealing with the cantankerous term perplex at the conference (the Shin-ite committee members included the Anglican bishop John Shaw Burdon and the Americans John Nevius, a Presbyterian, and Henry Blodget, a Congregationalist). The compromise decision reached by this group was, after much righteous argument and bluster, to decide not to make a decision—that is, they agreed to prohibit discussion of the issue at the conference and thereby maintain the "spiritual tone" at the proceedings.[79] This decision to ban a topic that had engendered so much emotion over the years, and was central to most of the key religious and intellectual issues of mission policy, was marvelously naive and was, as it turns out, the immediate context for the great controversy that would arise out of the reading of Legge's paper on the second day of the conference.

The conference met for a total of thirteen consecutive days, from May 10 through 24, in Temperance Hall in Shanghai and, according to contemporary missionary accounts, was declared to be a "great success."[80] This assessment is certainly exaggerated, and it is best simply to focus on a description of the overall event. Attracting an average of about 120 to 150 missionaries and guests on most days (who were about equally divided between British and Americans, with a scattering of other nationalities), the conference opened with a unified worship service and an organizational meeting that, given nationalistic tensions, diplomatically elected both American (Robert Nelson of the American Episcopal Church) and British (Carstairs Douglas of the English Presbyterian Church) chairmen to oversee the proceedings.

On the second day of the conference, the first full day of scheduled presentations, Legge's paper was read in session by William Muirhead.[81] Other papers, including Edkins's talk on Daoism and Buddhism, were also given, and there were discussions of the day's presentations. In the discussion of Legge's paper it seems that very little was said or, as reported by one eyewitness, little was said that was to the point. It was not until the next to the last day of the conference, after much closeted indignation and stifled anger, that, as the official proceedings would have it, the issue of Legge's paper came up and "a resolution proposed by Rev. S.L. Baldwin to omit the essay and discussion on Confucianism from the published record" was passed "without dissenting voice."[82] The resolution (number 8 of the conference) tersely and inaccurately says that the only reason for the action taken was because of the prior agreement to avoid all discussion of the term question and that, given his ignorance of this stipulation, the omission of his paper imputed "no fault" to Dr. Legge.[83]

The official actions, and the reasons given for those actions, were mostly an attempt to whitewash a much more complex and nasty situation that involved Legge's paper and a larger nested set of sectarian fears, nationalistic jealousies, and theological disagreements all coming to a head at that time. The darker side, or terminological terror, of the whole affair is suggested by the *China Review*'s description of the session on the twelfth day, when the resolution on Legge's paper was proposed.[84] Saying that the supposed vote "without dissenting voice" on the resolution was both a sham and the "shame of the Conference," the *Review* claims that Legge's opponents were "secretly whipped up to attend in full force" and overwhelm any liberal support for his views. At the very least, the account in the official *Records* is severely and suspiciously truncated. This, along with the *Review*'s description, strongly suggests that the vote was manipulated and, in this sense, was designed to find "fault" with Legge and all that he stood for. It was, as the *Re-*

view rightly says, "a vote which was uncharitable as a studied insult to Dr. Legge, and intolerant as an anathema of truths which no argument would have sufficed to refute."[85] The reference to anathemas hurled in Legge's direction was more than just rhetoric, although again this was a side of the whole affair that many missionaries preferred to keep to themselves.

The actual accomplishments of the conference were more show than substance. Aside from the roars at Legge and the liberals, the conference mostly ended with puffs of scented smoke and a bureaucratic squeak. The puffs of smoke included an increased conscientiousness about compiling statistics to prove more scientifically the success of missionary activities and the issuance of various innocuous resolutions, manifestos, and appeals.[86] Often these actions amounted to no more than renewed pleas for more missionaries because, as one unanimous resolution put it, "we want China emancipated from the thraldom of sin in this generation."[87] The bureaucratic squeak was the creation of yet more committees assigned to deal with various unresolved problems and tasks—for example, the inevitable Term Committee (dominated by American Shin-ites) charged to "harmonize divergent views," as well as committees concerned with the production of a common (Union) Bible and other issues.[88] Not unexpectedly, one of the final actions of the conference was to recommend the convening of another general conference.

If not a "complete success," the conference was at least a partially successful holding operation by the never monolithic conservative faction within the missionary movement. Legge—and all that a symbolic Leggism, Confucianism, and comparativism could be said to represent, especially in terms of the growing fears and uncertainties over the altered situation in China and the changing attitude of missionaries prone to be too intellectual, too eclectic, too tolerant, too secular, too universal, and too comparative—was successfully silenced and the forces recommending a radical reassessment of missionary methods were held at bay. This would be, however, a hollow triumph. From this point on to the end of the century, general missionary policy increasingly moved in a more liberal and secular direction. The liberal position would never completely triumph over conservative evangelical mission methods, but it was generally the case that, after the turn of the century (and especially as ratified by the 1910 World Conference of Missionaries in Edinburgh), the liberal theology of the "fulfillment" theory, the "social gospel," and "indigenization" was in ascendancy.[89]

Silence Is Golden

Aside from the conservative missionary tendency to distort, dismiss, or downplay the Legge incident at the time of the general conference, there is the larger issue of the complete suppression of Legge's paper a year later in the published proceedings.[90] As would be said today, the effective silencing of this event shows the admirable "damage control" in the media achieved by conservative missionary "spin doctors"—so much so that Helen Edith Legge and Lindsay Ride's biographies make no mention of the incident or its profound implications for the missionary movement and Legge's career.[91] This is not to say that the affair was not widely known in China. The event and its significance were furiously debated in various China-based periodicals at the time of its occurrence, but the full import of the situation surrounding Legge's paper was not generally appreciated back in the missionaries' home countries. Furthermore, by the time the official proceedings were published in 1878, and despite the circulation of a printed version of the paper by Legge's friends,[92] the incident had been largely excised from the public memory.

Eitel's sinologically oriented *China Review* even drew attention to the fact that Legge's paper did not appear in the published conference *Records* and pointedly condemned such petty manipulations of the historical record.[93] But Eitel's scholarly and secular audience was not very concerned with the sectarian infighting of missionaries chronicled so faithfully in the *Recorder* (keeping in mind that the *Review* sponsored its own sinological and Orientalistic battles). It was the sanitized version of the conference that was mostly communicated to the public back home by reviews of the *Records of the General Conference* in popular church-related publications such as the *Congregationalist.*[94]

DEFECTIVE, NOT ANTAGONISTIC: "CONFUCIANISM IN RELATION TO CHRISTIANITY"

> *Let no one think any labour too great to make himself familiar with the Confucian books. So shall missionaries in China come fully to understand the work they have to do; and the more they avoid driving their carriages rudely over the Master's grave, the more likely are they soon to see Jesus enthroned in his room in the hearts of the people.*
> JAMES LEGGE, "CONFUCIANISM IN RELATION TO CHRISTIANITY," 1877

Rudely Driven Carriages

How is it that Legge's short paper, presented in Shanghai in 1877, "Confucianism in Relation to Christianity" (twelve printed pages of text), was so threatening to the established missionary order in China? In what way was this paper a turning point in the history of the Protestant missionary movement? First, it should be recognized that this unusual little document appeared during a year replete with other events portending significant change in Victorian society. Queen Victoria was crowned as the empress of India in 1877, an event that ratified the global dominance of the British empire, but this was also the year that another liberal Evangelical, William Robertson Smith (see pages 20–22), resigned his position as a professor at the Free Church Divinity College of the University of Aberdeen in protest over the formal charges of heresy brought against his discussion of the Bible in the new ninth edition of the *Encyclopedia Britannica*.[95]

At first perusal, Legge's Shanghai paper appears to be a fairly conventional expression of nineteenth-century missionary apologetic scholarship of the "fulfillment" genre.[96] It does not have any particular stylistic elegance, compelling rhetorical ebullience, or keen philosophical flair like that seen in Müller's and Robertson Smith's writings. Furthermore, although this paper is effectively organized and communicates much of the plain and straightforward charm of the author's personality, it often seems obtrusively judgmental. To evaluate "Confucianism in Relation to Christianity" in this way, however, is to fail to appreciate just how radical the paper was in the 1870s. Despite the defensive apologetic in the last few pages, the overall thesis, argument, and pretext of the paper, along with its nuanced subtext, were truly disturbing for many in the assembled audience of Protestant missionaries in China. It is Legge's final warning against carriages "rudely" driven "over the Master's grave," and various pointed qualifications about Jesus' eventual enthronement in China, that make all the difference.

The problem was not so much that Legge dared to mention the tabooed term question in the course of the paper (there is only a passing reference to the terms for God in one section of the paper), but that he was publicly building a case for a broad attitudinal shift in the overall terms of the missionary movement. The challenge of Legge's views comes from the fact that they allude to the changing circumstances in China—a situation in which the natives were increasingly vocal, and even violent, in their dealings with missionaries. The crisis for the Protestant missionary movement was not just that the natives were talking back or that the Chinese had realized that the "free gift" of the gospel and Western civilization always came with strings attached. What was most disturbing was that some missionaries, especially "former missionaries" such as Legge, were now really listening to what the heathens had to say (or had anciently said in their classical literature) and were finding various "relations" or "parallels" with Christian tradition.[97] The realization that the relationship between missionaries and the Chinese had to take on more of the characteristics of a two-way conversation carried with it the potential danger of a reciprocity that could lead to the conversion of Christians as much as it could win over heathens. This conversational or dialogical approach to missionary activity was the comparative method recommended by Müller in his lecture in Westminster Abbey.[98]

A Calm and Dispassionate Mind

At the very outset of "Confucianism in Relation to Christianity," Legge apologizes to his "dear brethren" at the missionary conference for writing "at the last moment hurriedly," even though he had been invited to contribute a paper almost a year and a half earlier.[99] Confessing that his new professorial duties—duties "perhaps not more important" than his responsibilities to the conference, "but yet more pressing"—had kept him "very busy." The result is that his present effort "may not be so complete and well digested" as he had wished. This is a polite way of saying that he was really more interested in his duties as an dispassionate scholar in Oxford than in contending with the sectarian passions of missionaries assembled in Shanghai.

Suggestive of Legge's altered vocational circumstances and changing state of mind is that, after a few obligatory comments on the satisfactions of a missionary career, he raises various "doubts" about the benefits of a general conference of Protestant missionaries. After all, as he candidly says, the "history of ecclesiastical councils and conferences in the past is not encouraging." But with the conference soon to convene in Shanghai, it is Legge's hope for those in attendance that, "where there has been a difference of opinion and practice on some important subjects, if you cannot be of the same mind and the same judgment about them, you may be able to agree to differ."[100] With an acute sense of the effect his paper may have on missionaries not always inclined to listen sympathetically to another's point of view, whether other missionaries or heathen Chinese, Legge recommends that the conference participants should, above all, strive "to maintain a calm and dispassionate mind." Missionaries should always, says Legge, heed Saint Paul's counsel to the Philippians: "Do all things without murmurings and contentions."

Supplementing the Old Testament

Legge begins his comparative deliberations by describing Confucianism as "the subjects set forth in what are styled the Confucian books—the *Five King* more especially and the *Four Shu*." He then remarks that he will eschew the subjects of national history and physical speculation in the classics even though he hints that he has recently found a "clue" to the enigmatic natural philosophy of the *Yi jing* (The book of changes). "We are not," he says, "to look for truth on questions of natural and physical science" in the Confucian classics. Neither should we "presume" to find such truths in the "Scriptures of the Old and New Testaments." Legge's passing reference to the *Yi jing* is not as innocuous as it might seem, for already in 1876 Thomas McClatchie had translated it only to discover an incredible dualistic cosmogony wherein the classical Shangdi was a "filthy hermaphroditic monad" not unlike Bel, Baal, Jupiter, and Priapus. McClatchie's "key" to the mysteries of the *Yi jing* was the method of "comparative mythology," which not only showed the obscene nature of the god Shangdi but also documents the fact that *shen* or *shin* means "god or gods" and not just "spirit." For Mc-Clatchie the *Book of Changes* confirmed above all the "exact parallel between the Stoics and the Confucians."[101]

The subjects that are crucial to Legge's "special theme" of relating Confucianism and Christianity are "the religious and moral teachings in the Confucian books." These teachings will be examined in the classics in relation to three doctrinal issues: (1) God and other objects of worship, (2) human nature and a future state, and (3) human moral and social duties. Legge's "three heads" represent his minimum definition of religion and indicate his very Protestant focus on textual, conceptual, and ethical issues. Ritual seems to come into the picture only as a secondary (and often corrupting) response to religious beliefs—hence the actions of worshiping God and spirits, the funereal practices associated with the affirmation of a future life, and the moral actions and ritual customs of civilized social intercourse that express the best prompting of the human heart.

In his discussion of Confucian ideas about God—a subject of concern from the very beginning of his classical studies—Legge says that he "feels increasingly that missionaries ought to congratulate themselves that there is so much in Confucianism about God."[102] That this statement was more rhetorical than substantive is indicated by the fact that he immediately launches into a digest of his views on the terms for God in Chinese *(di, shangdi, tian)*, a subject that was sure to stir up dissension. But this discussion of terms takes up only two relatively brief paragraphs and is by no means, as the conference vote to censure his paper implied, the focal point of the whole paper. From Legge's perspective it was necessary to refer briefly to the idea and terminology of God if he were to discuss at all the assigned topic of Confucianism. That the condemnation of Legge's paper masked deeper dissention and fears is indicated by the unchallenged delivery of several other conference papers that dealt at considerable length with the term question.

The particular quandary of the so-called term question was that it depended too much on what progressive scriptural scholars of the period called the "lower criticism" of individual words and texts. What was significant about the newer forms of textual criticism from Germans such as Julius Wellhausen, Max Müller, and Ernst Eitel was the recognition that precise questions about the philological meaning of particular terms or words could be decided only in relation to a "higher," more comprehensive and interpretive context of meaning. This broader and more developmental framework of meaning required the historical and comparative analysis of terms within the context of an overall textual tradition (involving dating, determination of variant editions, *Quellenstudium* and form analysis, discriminations of parallels and universals, and naturalistic explanations of miracles and the supernatural).[103]

Despite Müller's growing influence, Legge was never a practitioner of the more extreme interpretive forms of "comparative philology" or "higher criticism." To the end of his life, he held on to a belief in the supernatural, the reality of miracles in the New Testament, and the unique historicity of Jesus' life. Legge's approach in his Shanghai paper is, nonetheless, illustrative of some aspects of the "higher criticism." Already in 1850 and 1852 he was employing protocomparative etymological, philological, and religious arguments that drew upon the lower criticism of his seminary training and the higher classical scholarship associated with his university career at Aberdeen. In this 1877 paper it is abundantly clear that a sympathetic appreciation and higher understanding of the comparative "religiousness" of Confucianism goes beyond the philological discussion of individual terms. The most intriguing manifestation of this higher interpretive sensibility in the first section of his paper is the suggestion that the best method for bringing the Chinese to an understanding of the Christian God was to "supplement" what the Confucian classics already said about God, an operation that reflects the Christian completion of the Jewish Old Testament.[104]

Just as a Christian is enriched by the study of the Hebrew scriptures, so also may one rejoice in, and learn from, the passages about *di* and *shangdi* in the ancient Chinese books. What is so significant about this "Judaistic tendency"[105] to compare the Confucian classics and the Old Testament is that we see Legge laying the groundwork for his translations in Müller's *Sacred Books of the East*. The Chinese classics are no longer authoritative or "classical" in the sense of the purely heathenish Greek and Roman classics. Rather, they are now being assigned to a new category of meaning—they are now seen as full-fledged religious scriptures or bibles. They are the Sacred Books of China and can be related to the definitive Holy Book or Bible.

Legge next addresses the apparent problem of having texts that know of God and the worship of God yet, at the same time, refer to a "universally practiced" ancestor worship ("more than anything else . . . the religion of the Chinese"). Part of the difficulty is that the Chinese classics "do not take us back to a time when the religion of China was a pure monotheism." But Legge's real method for dealing with this problem is to make use of the fundamental Protestant interpretive ploy that saw the development of idolatrous forms of worship (like the Roman Catholic cult of the dead) as a "corrupt and depraving admixture" of the original purity of divine worship.[106]

In the course of time, and through the "co-operating influences of Taouism and Buddhism," an incredible "mass of superstition and idolatry" grew up and led the masses of Chinese astray. More important is that the

Chinese emperor, as the high priest of the people, maintained a true worship to the one God. According to Legge, the Great Plan in the *Book of Historical Documents (Shu jing)* shows, moreover, that the reverence paid the ancestors and other spirits "did not detract from faith in Him and dependence on Him, as the Supreme Ruler of men."[107] Legge's conclusion is that the emperors of China have always worshiped one God and that the other *"imaginary* [my emphasis] spiritual beings," though inferior to the High God, may "act the part of mediators between the worshipper and Him." This false worship of inferior spirits is "contrary to Christianity, just as the Roman Catholic worship of saints and angels is contrary to it." For this reason, ancestor and spirit worship must be condemned, but there is every possibility that, even after Christianity is known throughout China, such practices will linger "just as traces of the Popish errors" have persisted in England and other Protestant countries. Comparatively speaking, therefore, the supplemental and revolutionary fulfillment of Chinese religion will parallel the Christian fulfillment of Judaism and the Protestant purification of Catholic tradition.[108]

Human Nature

Legge's second topic, the Confucian understanding of human nature, is presented equally positively. Starting with the idea that in the classics "man is a creature of Heaven or god," Legge is especially concerned to show how Mengzi's affirmation of the goodness of human nature is not necessarily in conflict with the Christian doctrine of human sinfulness. As he explained in 1861, he believes that the second greatest Confucian, Mengzi or Mencius, is referring to the ideal state of human nature in the "same way" that Bishop Butler does in his *Sermons.*[109] So, while the Confucian teaching is incomplete and presumptuous (asserting that the ancient Chinese sages "had always been perfectly virtuous"), Legge is convinced that Mengzi "did very great service to the cause of truth and virtue among his countrymen." Missionaries must, therefore, "supplement" Confucian ideas of human nature by instructing the Chinese on "the contrariety of the actual man to the ideal, on which neither Confucius nor any Chinese thinker before or after him could throw light." Considering the fact that the Chinese ambassador to England, Guo Songtao, was an invisible member of Legge's audience, this amounts to a weak and self-serving presumption that Christians know more about the problems of moral contrariety than do Confucians.

Legge also took up the questions of Confucian beliefs about immortality and future retribution. Regarding the first issue, he simply notes that Confucianism may "not teach the immortality of man, but neither does it deny it." This, then, is but another instance of Confucianism's being, like the Pentateuch and Judaism, "defective" but not "antagonistic to Christianity."

As to the question of future retribution, Confucianism again is clearly defective (since retribution works itself out in this life or in one's descendants). With respect to the objection that Buddhism introduced notions of retribution into Chinese religious tradition (particularly ideas of hell—the missionary word being derived from a Buddhist source), Legge says only that "Buddhism is antagonistic to Christianity as Confucianism is not, proceeding from an entirely different view of the system of the universe." Despite the real deficiencies of Confucianism, it is no more "antagonistic to Christianity than the greater portion at least of the Old Testament." The implication is that the Confucian classics might actually be superior in some ways to the Jewish Bible—an inference that was sure to test the patience of many in the Shanghai audience.[110]

Pushing Back the Feelers

"The teaching of Confucianism on human duty," Legge boldly declares, "is wonderful and admirable." It is not "perfect." Nor does it begin from the premise of the "first and great commandment" of love, but "on each of the last three of the four things which Confucius delighted to teach,—'letters, ethics, devotion of soul, and truthfulness,' his utterances are in harmony with both the Law and the Gospel." The fact that Confucianism now seems to have anticipated *both* the Pentateuchal Law and the higher Christian truth of the gospels raises the relational stakes. Driving this point home and thinking that "all the members of the Conference will be very much of one sentiment" regarding these issues, Legge declares that "a world ordered" by these Confucian principles "would be a beautiful world."[111]

After mentioning the wonderful beauty of the "five human relations," "benevolence and righteousness," and the "exhibition of the power of example," Legge discusses Confucius's "negative form" of the Golden Rule in a way that amends his earlier views.[112] Thus there are passages in the *Zhongyong* (The doctrine of the mean) that show that "he understood it as a positive rule, and held that it was then only fulfilled, when the initiative was taken in carrying it into practice." He reinforces this by extending his original 1861 discussion of Mengzi, in which he concluded that "heathen man" in China may be *"a Gentile without the law,"* but nevertheless *"is still a law to himself* [Legge's italics]." He says now that this "Mencian" principle, which "the apostle Paul affirms" (Rom. 2:14–15) applies to *all* of Confucianism. It is this that shows how the ancient Confucian texts can be considered more as sacred books than just as classical works. "No moral teacher of Greece or Rome" has such a "grand . . . illustration of the averment."[113]

In light of these "not mean" moral sentiments, Legge suggests that "the highest point of Christian morality ['to return good for evil'] was, at it were, pushing its feelers backward into Chinese society in the 5th or 6th century before our era." The fact that the great Chinese sage was unable to give the highest morality "a welcome into his breast" will certainly, he says, be regretted by "all the members of the Conference." In a way that rubs incongruously with his earlier concern about maintaining a "calm and dispassionate mind," Legge then reiterates the judgment he made in 1861 criticizing "the passionless character of Confucius's notices of the events that he is chronicling, and the ways in which he fails to discharge the duty of a truthful historian."[114]

Earthy Edification

Moving rapidly to his conclusion, Legge remarks that the practical outcome of his reflections is that "missionaries should endeavour not to exhibit themselves as antagonistic to Confucius and Confucianism." This flies in the face of the aggressive or muscular stance of missionary policy, but he is careful to identify his methods with the apostolic procedures of Saint Paul. At the same time, Legge is inclined to a belief that goes well beyond any of his previous judgments: namely, that "Confucius—not to specify others—was raised up by God for the instruction of the Chinese people."

In this way, the idea of prophecy in relation to China has come full circle in Legge's thought. Instead of the old triumphalist notions of the Land of Sinim, which seemed to call for the total obliteration of the native heathenism, Legge has arrived at an unprecedented, and even shocking, accommodationist position that suggested that certain ancient Chinese sages were prophets "raised up by God." The fact that the ancient Chinese communication with God was incomplete and that it fell into grave errors of worship "need not," says Legge, "interfere with our admitting that those men were *specially* [my emphasis] helped by God, that He might keep up some knowledge of Himself, and of the way of duty among the millions of their race." The startling, and even heretical, nature of these statements is the insinuation that the Chinese actually had access, like the Jews, to a "special" revelation of Divine Sovereignty.

From the standpoint of Legge's own conceptual categories, it is most likely that the hint of "specialness" concerning the Chinese and Confucius cannot be directly equated with his theological understanding of the uniquely miraculous revelation given to Moses and Jesus. His earlier reference to the Pauline principle of Romans 2:14–15 is probably the key to Legge's conception of the "special" prophetic nature of Confucianism. Thus, the Chinese have been without the law (that is, without the special miraculous revelation of the Mosaic covenant in the Pentateuch), but have become a "law unto themselves" because of "natural revelation" and the prudential and theistic wisdom of the ancient classics (keeping in mind the emergent protocomparativism in Legge's 1852 treatise on terms).

Sensing that he had gone beyond the bounds of theological propriety with his suggestion that Confucius could in some fashion be regarded as "a man sent of God," Legge draws back to what he believes to be the less disturbing proposition that missionaries should make "the best use they can of what is good and true in the Confucian system." In the spirit of Saint Paul's idea that the Old Testament was a kind of "schoolmaster to lead us to Christ," so also could Confucianism "be made to serve a similar purpose with the Chinese." The difficulty is that even these seemingly mild suggestions intimate that the Protestant mission to China should really be reconstituted in educational terms.

The root problem with this supplementary educational method of teaching the "doctrine of the Cross" is, as Legge admits, the problem of awakening "in the minds of the Chinese a sense of sin." The very need for a relational or comparative approach among missionaries, which is secular to the extent that it avoids sectarian parochialism and an antagonistic approach, may be the factor that plays too much into the hands of the "cold and unspiritual" earthiness and "prevailing secularism" of Confucianism in the nineteenth century. Legge has little practical advice to offer to his former missionary brethren as to how this problem is overcome, except to say that the "deeper, richer truth" of Christ must be unfolded in a kind of tough love approach involving "prayers and pain."

Legge then mentions a conversation on missions that he had "not very long ago" with "one of the ablest and most learned men in England, a very broad churchman, and perhaps something more." It was the opinion of this unnamed learned gentleman that missionaries find "a more excellent way" that avoids "collision with the existing heathen religions" and speaking ill of their great teachers. Legge reports that he responded by defending missionary methods and their willingness to "recognize whatever was good and true in the heathen religions." Nevertheless, his unnamed conversation partner remained "unconvinced."

This abrupt response clearly goaded Legge's conscience. It may well be that the poignancy of this incident, coming at the very end of Legge's little comparative treatise, is explained by the strong possibility that the "able and learned" gentleman (who was "perhaps something more"!) was no other than Max Müller, someone who would have had every opportunity and reason to discuss missionary methods with Legge at Oxford. Legge tells us, therefore, that it is this conversation—along with, we presume, the encounters with Guo Songtao, the questioning of missionary methods by Johnson, the criticism of his own fairness and sympathetic comprehensiveness by reviewers of his earlier work, and the testimony of his own experiences back in China—that led him to a new self-reflexive "muse[ment]" on antagonistically confrontational and comparatively sympathetic methods of dealing with heathen systems. His first reflections amount to a rather standard dismissal of the syncretistic notion that Christianity could be "tacked on to" or could "absorb into itself" any heathen religion. From the Protestant point of view concerned with the purity of ancient Confucianism and a pristine Christianity, this was the great corrupting sin of Roman Catholicism and its analogical way of responding to pagans and heathens. It is in this sense that Legge says that missionaries "have not merely to reform," but rather must "revolutionize" in the radical sense of the Protestant reformation (exemplified most fully and aggressively in the Scottish tradition by John Knox). The true reformation of a "people's religion" cannot, after all, be "brought about without heat and light."[115]

In addition to his earlier judgments of Confucius's prophetic role among the Chinese and the "specialness" of the revelation in the Confucian classics, Legge asserts that Confucianism "is not antagonistic" to Christianity in the way that the "atheistic" Buddhism and the "pantheistic" Brahmanism are. It is nonetheless a system "bounded by earth and by time." The difficult, "impartial but not neutral" paradox of this position is that ultimately even the most sympathetic missionary cannot help but "pull down Confucius from his elevation"—especially when confronted by the "want of any deep sense of sin" and "any glow of piety."[116] These observations surely grow out of Legge's self-reflections explaining, expanding, correcting, and justifying some of his earlier judgments about the Chinese master Kong. This is a process of transformative self-understanding that will come to fruition only in the later production of the *Sacred Books of China* for Müller and in the Oxford revisions of the *Chinese Classics*.[117]

All of this is the critical context for Legge's words of advice to his former missionary colleagues in China. First (and the subtext here concerns the London Missionary Society's suspicions about his own work on the classics), he emphasizes that no missionary should "think any labour too great to make himself familiar with the Confucian books." Second (and he must have been thinking of his own pilgrimage by rude cart to Kongzi's ancestral grave, his humbling encounters with Guo Songtao, and his unnamed conversational partner at Oxford), missionaries must "avoid driving their carriages rudely over the Master's grave."

THE AFTERMATH: MURMURINGS AND CONTENTIONS

A missionary of the Puritan type is as much offended by being asked to make allowance for the pagan's reverence for a hill side plateau or a shady grove, as John Knox would have been outraged if he had been desired to show respect for a chapel of the Virgin Mary or the oratory in which were treasured the relics of a Saint! To the modern evangelist everything that belongs to the old cult has to be remorselessly torn down, and every feeling, however deep rooted and innocent, connected with nature worship has to be rooted out. Of course, from his peculiar standing point, the missionary is right. The only question is whether missionaries with more cultivated sympathies and wider knowledge than the existing societies send out would not effect more good.

NORTH-CHINA HERALD, SHANGHAI, 1879

Beware of being caught in the measlies of Chinese learning.

ROBERT NELSON, *CHINESE RECORDER*, 1877

Caught in the Measlies

Legge's short paper, and the resulting controversy over policy and methods, represents a turning point in missionary history.[118] Fortunately, it is possible to examine some of the secret inner history of this event and to fit the issues of Leggism and comparativism into a larger understanding of missionary policy in China. This kind of examination is feasible because there are not only published documents that allude to these closeted matters, but also an even more revealing deposit of confidential letters dealing with Legge's so-called heresies.[119] As Legge himself seemed to know, "murmurings and contentions" would most probably overwhelm any dispassionate consideration of a paper proposing a comparative appreciation of Confucius and Confucianism. As he also knew, it was his new prestige as an Oxford professor and sinological Orientalist, someone "caught in the measlies of Chinese learning," that made his views all the more influential and threatening.[120]

There is a considerable body of published material (articles, reviews, and "letters to the editor"), mostly within the missionary community, that expresses the darker side of the Legge affair. Most important is a long article in the May–June 1877 issue of the *Chinese Recorder and Missionary Journal* by Robert Nelson, an American Episcopalian missionary, a Shin-ite supporter in the revived term question, and one of the chairs of the Shanghai conference.[121] Nelson's published article, which is almost as long as Legge's original paper, was written as a defense of the actions taken by the conference under his co-chairmanship. Saying that the primary objection to the paper was that it "introduced the term question sideways" on the pretext of a discussion of Confucianism, Nelson insists that the decision to withdraw the paper from the published proceedings was only to "preserve the harmony of the conference" and to avoid any "great confrontation" or "catastrophe" involving Legge's supporters in China, the "Shang-ti men."

Nelson's claim that he was concerned merely to maintain harmony within the missionary community is contradicted by the content of his essay, which, in the name of "right reason" and "established truth," amounts to a sweeping attack on Legge's "indefensible and unsound" views—an attack that was sure to stir up a "great controversy." There is no doubt that Nelson was charging Legge with heresy (as the letters he received in response document; see pages 231–33), although the word itself was never used in the article. The length and intensity of Nelson's discussion also show that the term question was only the terminological tip of a much greater tangled mass of social, religious, intellectual, and emotional problems within the missionary movement. Most of all, it is apparent that the strong feelings against Legge were motivated by fear: As Nelson says, Legge's views were extremely dangerous and could "cause trouble."

Recalling Damnable Behavior

Nelson's argument begins with what he calls the "logical" objections to Legge's view that Shangdi can be considered "our God, the true God." According to Nelson, Legge is the first to make such a blatantly "rash statement" and, despite his stature as an Oxford professor and the "measlies" of his sinological expertise, offers no real proof for this disquieting assertion. The emotional nature of these issues is shown by Nelson's sudden reference to Legge's shocking liturgical performance at the Altar of Heaven during his visit to North China in 1873 (Nelson specifically refers to the shoeless Legge singing the doxology at the base of the altar). Clearly the scandalous implications of Legge's actions in Peking had been stewing within the missionary community for the past four years; allusions to these actions were made repeatedly among Shin-ite, and mostly American and Anglican, missionaries.

According to Nelson and Happer, Legge's worshipful actions toward Tian in Peking were shockingly illogical and inconsistent.[122] This is because, Nelson claims (on the basis of both missionary and native sources), the Chinese "never understood Tien as God" and were given to "contemptuous atheism and humanitarianism." The contradiction of Legge's paper was his claim that the Chinese both knew God and yet remained heathens by worshiping many gods and spirits. In the spirit of Longobardi's condemnation of Ricci, Nelson insinuates that Legge was in danger of reviving the old Jesuitical heresy of accommodationism, another dangerously sympathetic approach to heathenism that was linked to the original "term and rites controversy." Even though ancestral rites were debated at the Shanghai conference in a way similar to that used by the early Jesuits and Dominicans,[123] the issue of heresy within the Protestant context was much more exclusively an issue of faith, belief, doctrine, and terms, rather than of works or ritual action.

An even more serious theological problem is that Legge rejects the "principle of the essential unity of the Godhead." It is logically and theologically untenable to claim that the Chinese religion can display a "monotheism and a polytheism at the same time." Although Nelson's overall critique is mostly based on an accurate accounting of Legge's position, this is one instance where the desire to find fault overwhelms the stated facts of the matter.[124] As we know, Legge's understanding of the mixed nature of the Chinese worship of the "true God" and multiple inferior, or intermediary, divinities (all of whom Legge carefully labels as "imaginary") was based on his comparison of this situation with the emergence of the corrupt syncretism of Roman Catholicism in Christian history. But Nelson's First Commandment objection to all of this is that the "true God is One" and, echoing Bishop Boone's position from the 1850s, cannot be "just a *chief* god."

The Shame of a Supplementary Christianity

Nelson says that Legge is particularly "unsound" when he suggests that Mencius's idea of goodness does not conflict with Christianity. Furthermore, no appeal to Bishop Butler will help. The problem is Legge's insufficient Pauline emphasis on the "fallen and corrupt" depravity of human nature, which can only be changed by the divine atoning action of Christ.[125] Even if one understands Mencius to be referring only to an ideal goodness, the problem is that he still implies that change is possible through "human perfectibility." The failure to condemn Confucianism for its humanistic presumption of perfectibility (even though, in his 1861 discussion of Mencius, Legge is quite clear on Confucianism's not providing the means for moral rectification) is, according to Nelson, Legge's greatest affront to accepted Christian truth.

Other prominent missionaries continued to expand Nelson's attack on Legge for his "incorrect" views of the Confucian "doctrine" of human nature and his willingness to mix the poison of Chinese heathenism with the honey of Christianity.[126] Writing in the late 1880s, the American Devello Z. Sheffield specifically identified Legge as the initiator of a whole trend of "boneless" theology seeking "compromise" with Confucianism. These "liberal Christians," such as Legge, Alexander Williamson, and Ernst Faber— along with their "jellyfish" guides in compromise, Max Müller, Samuel Johnson, and James Freeman Clarke—want only to "water down" the true severity of biblical theology and make heathen religions into "false allies" of Christianity. The problem with such men is that they are "too compassionate" and favor an "unnatural fellowship" with heathenism that resembles the corrupt papist "baptism" of heathenism in the Middle Ages. Liberals like Legge who fail to see that Christianity must "smite" the heathen are particularly dangerous because they often pose as "authoritative interpreters" of Oriental religion, and yet "stand in the outer circles of Christianity."[127]

Profoundly disturbing for Nelson is Legge's recommendation that Christianity must "supplement" Confucianism. Such a conception of missionary
methods suggests that Christianity is actually secondary to the great work already accomplished by the quasi-prophetic wisdom of Confucius and the
Confucian classics. Related to this is Legge's troubling attempt to "pull
down the Old Testament to the level of Confucianism." For Nelson and
other conservative missionaries, the real problem is that Legge's relational
approach gives "favour to rationalistic views" that will only "damage pure
Christianity." Nelson does not tell us what this "pure Christianity" is, but he
does not hesitate to say that any "exaltation of Confucianism" and a "practical disparagement of Christianity" can only "help the enemies of missionaries among Chinese and foreigners." While missionaries should not be
timid in condemning Confucianism when the "sin of righteousness" shows
up, Nelson correctly interprets Legge as suggesting that "sins of righteousness" weigh heavily on both sides of the Occidental-Oriental divide. But, as
Nelson recognizes, if "Christianity is only a little better than Confucianism,"
then "why is there any need of missions?" In the holy war for the reformation of China, are not educators and scholars, professors and scientists, engineers and doctors more important than missionaries? These are the questions that will echo throughout the rest of the century among both
Westerners and Chinese.

Private Damnations

Nelson's article had the effect of fomenting both a public and private confrontation between conservative and liberal elements within the missionary
movement in China. The public side of the debate took the form of a further intensification of the already resurgent term question. The private side
of the conflict is found in various personal letters written to Nelson in response to his "very clear and manly" broadside against Legge.[128] What
makes this private correspondence significant is that, besides the very candid anti-Legge letters (ten separate letters by American Episcopalian, Presbyterian, Baptist, and Methodist missionaries, as well as support from the
"English Bishop of China," no doubt John Shaw Burdon, and "other English clergy"[129]), we also have a pro-Legge epistle by Edkins and, most interestingly, a copy of Legge's own reply to Nelson. Even though the American origination of many of these letters is partially explained by Nelson's
own nationality and natural circle of friends, there is more than a hint of
larger sectarian and nationalistic tensions.[130]

There is no point in discussing the individual letters in any detail, but it
is important to know that several writers bluntly condemn Legge's views as
"sins against sound doctrine" and "insidious heresies."[131] One general
characteristic of these letters is the extreme sensitivity manifested toward

Legge's status as a Chinese scholar—after all, "the errors of a man of such reputation for learning are far more mischievous than the errors of a common man, that do not reach so many ears, nor come with the weight of authority."[132] Another defining trait in these letters is the recognition that this whole controversy went well beyond the single issue of the term question and referred, as R. H. Graves of the American Baptist Missionary Union put it, to the emergence of a troublesome "tendency" among missionaries. This was the Leggian tendency "to gain favor for Christianity by assimilating its statements as much as possible to Chinese systems with which . . . most of the native teachers will sympathize." As another letter by T. P. Crawford revealingly indicates, the "real point of conflict between missionaries in China is not 'terms' but *doctrines* [Crawford's italics]."[133] The passion of these letters also indicates that the Leggian position on many of these matters was winning a considerable number of converts from among the more liberal missionaries.[134]

Given the touchiness among the missionaries about natives becoming privy to internal missionary dissent, it is revealing to see that one letter specifically warns of the "harm" that a reported Chinese-language translation of Legge's essay would cause among learned Chinese.[135] Related to the social and intellectual dynamics of missionaries vis-à-vis the secular world of foreigners in China is also the evocative observation that the sinologically oriented *China Review* will most likely "be severe" in dealing with Nelson's attack on Legge's paper, a comment which Nelson explains is due to the fact that the *Review* "is edited by a partisan of Dr. Legge."[136] This is an accurate evaluation of the more scholarly and secular attitudes expressed in Eitel's *Review* and serves only to dramatize the emerging polarization between the conservative missionaries (as seen especially in Happer's *Recorder*) and the hyphenated missionary-scholars.

A Straw Man

The only response from Legge's supporters in this collection of letters is found in a few "postscript" comments by Legge's old fellow pilgrim, Joseph Edkins. For Edkins, the whole affair was having a chilling effect on missionary relations, and especially relations with "friends from afar" like Legge, since from now on, "no one will feel sure that he is not going to be tried for heresy."[137] Legge's own reply is less a rejoinder to Nelson than a brief and weary expression of his unwillingness to continue the dispute. He makes it clear, however, that the whole incident is not really the "controversy about the terms" because he does not enter into it at any length in his paper. He then mounts a brief defense of his position, which turns out to be a reiteration of the Müllerian scholar's credo of impartial and sympathetic comparativism. Thus, as Legge declares, he "lost all sight" of himself in the paper and "had regard simply to the facts of the case and to [his] deductions from them being logical." Finally, disclosing some element of anger, Legge observes that Nelson's whole essay was too much an effort to set up, and knock down, a "straw man." Saying only that he will not sleep any "less soundly" because of being made out an "incorrect theologian," Legge concludes abruptly by sarcastically remarking that he is not "unversed in the true nature and position of Christianity."[138]

Slouching toward the Termination

The publicly stated reason for the censorship of Legge's conference paper had to do with the revival of the seemingly endless term question. But much of the emotion connected with this issue and the overall Legge affair is related to the fact that by the late 1870s there were clear signs that the Shangdi position, and all that it implied by way of a more sympathetic appreciation of Chinese tradition, was in ascendancy. Moreover, the constant recycling of the same arguments meant that the whole issue was losing its value as an "intellectual amusement"—and for those who mostly relished it as an opportunity for "sarcastic flings," this realization was perhaps the real death knell.[139]

A good review of the overall term question at this time in all of its solemn and silly glory is seen in a discussion, no doubt by Eitel, of John Chalmers's pamphlet published in 1876 and entitled *The Question of Terms Simplified*.[140] Although adopting a liberal perspective on these matters, the reviewer provides a helpful digest of the two phases of the nineteenth-century Protestant controversy. The first phase dates back to the late 1840s and early 1850s and led to the unfortunate production of several separate versions of the Chinese Bible. "Only lately" have the "smoldering embers of discord burst anew into flame." The new battle was, according to Eitel, caused by Thomas McClatchie's "desertion of the Shangti side on mythological grounds of his own imagination." Discovering from his translation of the *Book of Changes* that Shangdi was not God but a "hermaphroditic monad," McClatchie suggested that Shangdi missionaries were actually fostering "a system of Priapism."

Eitel's only comment on McClatchie's fecund and lascivious imagination was to observe, on the basis of a prize essay contest for Chinese Christians, that intelligent natives mostly "approve of Shangti." It was Chalmers's suggestion that the whole confused issue might be resolved, or at least "simplified," by the use of strict philological criteria of the lower-criticism variety. These criteria should, moreover, be independently applied by scholars who were capable of doing so because all too often native assistants told their missionary employers only what they wanted to hear. While not denying the significance of Chalmers's suggestion, Eitel makes the more insightful observation that the term question really betrays a "deeper root than that of philological ignorance." It is, as he puts it, the "essence of Protestantism" to allow every individual to think for oneself.[141]

Eitel's final judgment was that it was probably foolish to think that some kind of unity among "militant" Protestants could be achieved on either "lower" philological or other "higher" critical grounds. Eitel's keen discernment of the situation is borne out by the subsequent history of the Protestant term debate, an issue that gradually died down with a lingering whimper rather than with any decisive cry of victory or defeat. As Eitel already recognized, the debate would eventually "solve itself when native Christians" were able to "assert their own convictions." Legge's liberal and liberating arguments relating Confucianism and Christianity did not end the term controversy, but it may be said that the enhanced attitude of sympathetic comprehensiveness among missionaries eventually, and as a practical rather than a logical matter, enabled Chinese Christians to make up their own minds without the domineering oversight of their Western mentors. Among native Chinese Christians in the twentieth century, there was a decided preference for Shangdi but no real resolution of the debate.

Extending the Feelers of Leggian Comparativism

The disturbances unleashed by Legge's brief paper on the relation between Confucianism and Christianity continued to grow and expand throughout the rest of the nineteenth century, sending ramifying feelers outward into other areas associated with the missiological and sinological understanding of Chinese tradition. Legge's first volume for Müller's *Sacred Books* and his own *Religions of China,* examined in the next two chapters, demonstrate that the issues raised in 1877 engaged both liberal missionaries and secular scholars. The spread of these ideas at this time is also seen in Ernst Faber's scholarly writings and in Edkins's publication in 1878 of *Religion in China,* a work that grows out of, and vastly extends, the spirit of Legge's Shanghai conference paper. Alexander Wylie, one of the oldest and most distinguished of the hyphenated missionary-scholars, explicitly recognized that Edkins's book, like Legge's work, dramatized the way in which the different religions of the world were "now being summoned before the bar of science." It is a "comparative view" that insists upon calling all religions "to pass a competitive examination" that, in the end, can only find Chinese religion "wanting" the leaven of Christianity. According to Wylie, it is works like these that are "indispensable" to missionaries and "students of comparative religion."[142]

CHAPTER FOUR

Decipherer Legge:
Finding the Sacred in the *Chinese Classics*,
1879-1880

Translation is a difficult art, and scholars, particularly those who know the lan-
guage from which, or the language into which, they translate as well as their own,
consider a good translation almost impossible. I have had some experience in
translating, and I know something of the treatment which translators may expect
from conceited critics. The Sacred Books of the East, translated by myself and a
number of friends, the best scholars I could find, have not escaped that kind of
pedantic criticism. Impartial and honest critics have recognized the difficulties
under which scholars labour in translating, often for the first time, ancient
texts. . . . There are some critics who think they have done their duty if they can
discover a few flaws in a translation, though they cannot even appreciate the
labours and the brilliant though silent discoveries of a first translator. The work
that has to be done by a first translator of an ancient text is often the work of a real
decipherer.

MAX MÜLLER, *AULD LANG SYNE*, 1898

TREES MAY FALL

On October 15, 1877, Professor and Mrs. Legge strolled down Broad Street
in Oxford to observe the havoc unleashed the day before by a violent wind
storm. Walking past the Sheldonian Theatre, they made their way over to
the High Street, where they were amazed to see the massive roots and limbs
of ancient oak trees ripped from the grounds around Magdalen College.
Unable to resist the temptation to draw a homiletic lesson from this natural
disaster, Legge tells us that he was reminded of a Chinese ode: "While leaf
and branch still vigorous grow, / A tree may fall! / And what that fall has
wrought, / Its roots uptorn the course will show."[1] "So it was," says Legge,
that the outward appearance of aggressive good health may only disguise a
weakened system of roots. In this way a top-heavy and secretly weakened
tree will be uprooted and dashed asunder by the first swift winds of confrontation and change.[2]

The fact that Legge was at this time finishing up his new abridged translation of the *Book of Poetry* for the first published volumes of Müller's *Sacred*

Books of the East may account for the Chinese maxims springing to his mind even before the proverbial wisdom of the Bible. Whatever the reasons for his preferential selection of the Chinese saying, this small incident tends to reinforce his earlier conclusion that the teachings of the Confucian classics may often be related to the proverbial and providential wisdom of the Sacred Scriptures.[3] Just as the Holy Bible is universally applicable to all aspects of human life within, prophetically speaking, all the nations of the world, so also is it suggested here, in a meager but evocative way, that the Chinese classics potentially have an authority and sacred omniscience that extend even to the interpretation of random natural events in Oxford, England, during the late nineteenth century.

Keeping in mind that this incident was coming at the start of Legge's second full academic year at Oxford, and immediately after the tempestuous struggle over "relational" matters at the missionary conference in Shanghai, I may be permitted even further poetic license concerning the providential toppling of gnarled oaks by sudden external forces and covert internal changes. One tree that had definitively fallen was simply Legge's familiar reliance on interpretive formulas and rhetorical tropes drawn from the Mediterranean classics and the singularly sacred Bible of Western tradition. Another related and more substantial tree that surely had fallen, both because of gradual inner transformations and the abrupt recent turbulence of the Shanghai affair, was Legge's old uncontested identification with the organized Protestant missionary movement and its customary antagonistic approach to Chinese heathenism, especially the tradition known as Confucianism.

Although by no means uprooted, the biblically tested trunk of evangelical missionary policy and methods in China were themselves bending in the face of the newly insistent winds of comparison stirred by Legge the sinological Orientalist at Oxford and by other missionary-scholars in the field. In the same sense, the comparative, scientific, critical, and humanistic study of religions, whether Western or Oriental, was emerging for the first time as a vigorous public issue within Victorian life in Britain. The staunch old tree of theological apologetic based strictly and absolutely on the Bible was on the verge of falling to higher forms of critical method within the academies of elevated learning in England, as it had already succumbed to liberating winds in continental Europe.[4] As Müller would have said, it was an occurrence that was bound to happen because of external intellectual and social forces that brought the Western world into a fateful confrontation with multiple other Oriental worlds. In addition to this, and despite continuing appeals for an unabashedly antagonistic approach to the Orient, the increasing secularity of the universities and the increased "sympathetic comprehensiveness" directed toward Oriental religions were progressively weakening the roots of the older theology.

The Hibbert Lectures

The public emergence of a more scientific and comparative method of studying religion in Victorian tradition is seen in the inaugural series of Hibbert Lectures given by Max Müller in April 1878, at the Charter House at Westminster.[5] Created by a trust established by the Unitarian Robert Hibbert, this controversial lectureship was devoted to topics approached from the standpoint of "scientific theology," a method that was inspired by Müller's famous lectures on the "science of religion" earlier in the 1870s. In keeping with the spirit of Müller's comparative approach, and, for that matter, Legge's study relating Confucianism and Christianity, these lectures were intended "to promote comprehensive learning and thorough research in relation to religion as it appears to the eye of the scholar and philosopher, and wholly apart from the interest of any particular Church or system."[6]

Sensitive observers of the period recognized that the Hibbert Lectures, like the even more celebrated Gifford Lectures in 1888 (inaugurated, appropriately enough, in Glasgow by Müller), were an "important indication of a change in public opinion on a matter of grave consequence." Not so long before, all religions, save Christianity, had been "regarded with unmixed and absolute disfavour . . . [and] were considered to be irredeemably and hopelessly false." It was in the current enlargement of the "theological horizons" of studying the "Gentile religions" in a comparative or relational way that contrasted so much with the earlier view. Such an expansion of sympathetic comprehensiveness in the study of all religions was more advanced within the "liberal schools" of Germany, France, and Holland but, as one contemporary commentator said, the institution of the Hibbert Lectures would "doubtless assist Englishmen of science to systematize their opinions."[7]

Whereas several academic chairs in the "comparative science of religions" had been established on the continent by the end of the 1870s, no such positions had been created in the relatively more conservative religious climate of Victorian England. In this sense, the Hibbert Lectures could be said—using the words of the third Hibbert lecturer, Ernest Renan—to "form in some sort a Chair of the Comparative History of Religions, but a Chair which is occupied every year by a new Professor, who speaks only of that which he has made the subject of special study."[8] Given his reputation as the father of the science of religion, it was no accident therefore that Müller would be the first incumbent in the Hibbert lectureship, the start of the series even being delayed for two years so that the illustrious scholar could serve as the inaugural lecturer.[9]

English and Scottish universities were notably reluctant to create positions in comparative religions, the first such named positions arising only in the next decades at Victoria University, Manchester, and at the Congregationalist Mansfield College and the Unitarian Manchester College located in Oxford. Despite (or perhaps because of) Müller's reputation as the founding figure of the comparative science of religions and his influence on the endowment of Oriental research, the ancient colleges of Oxford University throughout the nineteenth century never saw fit to create a position in comparative religions.[10] In a very real sense, therefore, the popularization and academic promotion of this new science in the British Isles came about because of the well-publicized institution of the Hibbert and Gifford lectureships.[11] In both cases the lectures, which often attracted large, enthusiastic audiences and generated much controversy in the public press, were published as books and were widely disseminated.[12] Moreover, those invited to give the Hibbert and Gifford Lectures made up a stellar roster of the most famous international scholars of religion, distinguished because of their academic and scholarly attainments rather than because of any particular clerical training or status (unlike those giving the more celebrated Bampton Lectures at Oxford).[13]

Regardless of the different scholars enlisted and the breadth of topics represented, neither the Hibbert nor the Gifford Lectures included any sinological Orientalist speaking on China in the broadly philosophical and historical way of, for example, Müller on Hinduism, Renan on Roman Catholicism, Rhys Davids on Buddhism, Sayce on Babylonian religion, or Tylor and Lang on "savage" religion. This glaring exception only serves to underscore, yet again, the relative insularity and strangeness of sinological Orientalism in the nineteenth century and the tendency to overlook Legge because of his tainted background as a missionary, his unsophisticated country character and evangelical simplicity, his admitted lack of philosophical profundity, his scholarly persona as only a diligent translator, and his liabilities as someone at once too old in body and mind and too outdated in style and method.

It is, nonetheless, tempting to think that the *North-China Herald* may have had Legge in mind when it commented on the need for the Hibbert Lectures to be given by "some competent Sinologue" who might "at last" give an "intelligent account of the religious beliefs of China in their relation to other creeds."[14] Unfortunately, as the *Herald* rightly notes, the state of Chinese scholarship, when compared with other Orientalist disciplines, was mostly "divided" and "unsatisfactory." Even recent contributions to the study of Chinese religions that were "based on sound principles and conceived in a proper spirit" (thinking here, perhaps, of Legge's 1877 conference paper or Edkins's 1878 *Religion of China*) were nevertheless too "sketchy and imperfect." The problem was that "no sooner is an attempt made to clear the ground, than we have some publication issued by a sinologue, who pursues antiquated methods and listens to authorities discredited and superseded twenty years ago, which throws everything into hopeless confusion again."[15] It was this kind of situation that Legge's 1880 book, *Religions of China*, conceived in a "proper" Müllerian spirit, was designed to address.

The Man Is the Child

Müller's Hibbert Lectures on the growth of Indian religion are also significant for their uncompromising discussion of a developmental approach to the study of religions that, because "there is no distinction in kind between [heathen religions] and our own religion," could be legitimately applied to the history of all religions, including Christianity. "No doubt," as Müller colorfully put it, "the man is different from the child, but the child is the man and the man is the child, even the very suckling." "We can hardly believe it," yet, says Müller, "the fact is there, and so it is in the growth of religion."[16]

Müller wanted to bring his audience to an appreciation of the "true, *historical* value" of the ancient Hindu religion from a perspective that was not "exclusively European or Christian." The truth is that Müller's strictly "scientific" and "historical point of view" concerning the ancient "value" and subsequent degenerate "growth" of Hinduism was hardly impartial, or even much less evangelical or classically Protestant than the approach of many current and former missionaries. To some extent, the "difference" between the traditional missionary apologetic and Müller's new science was basically a matter of the terminological translation or transposition from a theological to an "impartial" secular rhetoric. The terms of the relationship were changed, but in some important ways the structure, logic, and triumphalistic outcome of the operation were mostly the same. As Müller himself tells us, his real aim was not just to enlighten his Western audience, but to undertake a real educative *mission* to modern-day India.[17]

At the risk of being misunderstood by both his European and Indian audience, Müller spoke as the bearer of a two-pronged message to the "Hindus of his age." He wanted to warn Hindus of the danger of, on the one hand, "undervaluing or despising the ancient national religion" and, on the other, of the greater dangers of "overvaluing" and "interpreting" later Hinduism "as it was never meant to be interpreted." From this point of view— a perspective broadly in keeping with Legge's relational view of ancient Confucianism and its later need for "revolutionary" supplementation and completion—the ancient sacred books of "Hinduism," especially the *Upanishads*, may be admired and some of the teachings retained, but the "right way" of development in the future will require real religious change and reformation.[18]

An Academic Life

The "right way" for James Legge at this juncture was to increase his commitment to academic life. Beyond his regular courses and lectures during the next few years, this meant his special dedication to Müller's *Sacred Books of the East* project, the first volumes of which were scheduled to appear in

1879. Legge was particularly thankful for Müller's invitation to participate in the project and also for his help in establishing the Chinese position at Oxford. The invitation to contribute to Müller's project not only gave Legge a chance to realize his original pledge to complete the translation of the basic canon of Chinese classics (requiring the publication of the *Book of Changes* and *Record of Rites* to finish his version of the Five Classics and Four Books), but also allowed him to expand his conception of the sacrality of the classical Chinese tradition and to venture into new, and manifestly more strange and heterodox, realms of Oriental religiosity.

By the start of 1878 Legge was finishing up his revised translations of the *Book of Historical Documents* and *Book of Poetry,* as well as completing a new translation of the *Xiao jing,* the *Book of Filial Piety,* for his first contribution to Müller's series.[19] But, as Legge says in a letter to his stepdaughter, he was already in the summer of 1878 getting up at four o'clock in the morning to work three or four hours on a very different kind of Chinese religious classic promised for the *Sacred Books.* This was the so-called bible of the Daoist tradition known as the *Daode jing,* the "obscurest book," as Legge says, "ever written."[20] Inasmuch as this text was associated with what Western sinologues were then starting to call "Taoism," the most blatantly "corrupt" form of superstition encountered by the missionaries and the Ruist elite in modern China, we can see how far Legge had progressed in the enhancement of his "sympathetic comprehensiveness."

Another aspect of Legge's increased identification with the academic profession of Orientalism was his first-time participation in an international congress of Orientalists. Appointed as the presiding head of the Chinese Section of the fourth congress held in Florence, Italy, at the end of September 1878, Legge mentions that, although he could not speak Italian, he made his opening remarks to the assembled Orientalists in classical Latin, a language that he was still fluent enough in to impress the attending Orientalists, most of whom were in the habit of showing off their linguistic skills. Given the intellectual and social evolution of this era, it is also noteworthy that Legge's contribution to the conference, "On the Present State of Chinese Studies and What Is Wanted to Complete the Analysis of the Chinese Written Characters," was designed to accent his developing philological interests and his concern for the increased professionalization and methodological sophistication of sinology as an Orientalist discipline.[21]

Despite its brevity, Legge's talk in Florence was an insightful discussion of the apparent pictographic nature of Chinese written characters and the analytical confusion in European sinology concerning the philological significance of the so-called radicals (or roots) found in Chinese defining dictionaries and the more linguistically relevant six classes of written symbols. In this presentation, as with some of his earlier philologically oriented papers, Legge is refining his views on the deficiencies of those studying Chinese philology (and he names here both Edkins and Chalmers) with an eye to the kind of breakthrough (especially having to do with the distinction between the more graphic or pictorial Chinese symbols and the strictly phonetic alphabetic systems) that would equal the advances in the comparative philology of Aryan languages achieved by Bopp, the Grimms, and other Indo-European Orientalists.

Legge makes it clear that, unfortunately, he does not yet possess the "spiritual discernment" necessary for such a breakthrough.[22] Legge never did achieve this discerning vision toward the philological lineage of Chinese. In fact, Legge, and most of his other sinological contemporaries, basically gave up the scientific *and* spiritual quest for any convincing comparative philological discernment of the Chinese language in its own terms. For some, the comparative philological problem was merely transposed onto another framework of originary linguistic and civilizational meaning, usually Aryan or Babylonian. The "formidable solitude" of Chinese continued largely unaffected by Western sinological speculation throughout the rest of the nineteenth century, a situation that started to change in the twentieth century only with the greater appreciation of native Chinese linguistic scholarship (as Legge was strongly recommending) and the pioneering philological work of Western sinologists such as Bernhard Karlgren.[23]

As a part of his trip to Florence, Legge spent some time traveling throughout Germany, Switzerland, and France. Most of these travels were devoted to simple sightseeing. However, given all of the transformations in his life up to this time, we are not really shocked to discover that he also went out of his way to visit, no doubt arranged through the efforts of Müller, Renan and his family in France. Although Müller described his old friend and Orientalist cohort as "a little foggy and sometimes clouded by his language," Renan was the most renowned and controversial exemplar in all of continental Europe of a liberal approach to the history of religions.[24] It was one thing to have met with the sinologue Julien in Paris, but a meeting with the archradical Renan would have been beyond the pale for the earlier Legge of the London Missionary Society, no matter how scholarly or liberal he was as a missionary.[25]

A Revolution in Kind

Legge's commitment to his new professorial identity and to the university community at Oxford did not preclude the continuation of his lifelong dedication to the mission of general education and to the reformation of certain aspects of Victorian civic and social life. Back in England after many years of involvement in the civic life in Hong Kong, Legge continued his support for national education, his backing of a higher education shorn of sectarian religious tests, and his public championing of an anti-opium policy. Another outstanding example of Legge's devotion to a more secular kind of mission is seen in his direct participation in the foundation of women's higher education at Oxford. Along with such maverick figures as the novelist Mrs. Humphry Ward and the Hegelian don T.H. Green, Legge was a member of the provisional committee for the establishment of Somerville College in Oxford that met in February 1879. After the incorporation of the college in 1879 (Lady Margaret Hall, an Anglican college, was founded at the same time), he also served, from 1881 to 1883, on the first College Council alongside other prominent Oxford evangelicals, among them Robert Horton and Andrew Martin Fairbairn.[26]

The provisional committee, with the prompting of Legge, made a special point of disallowing any kind of religious tests for admission to Somerville and set the rule that the membership of the ruling council should include an equal number of women and men. Furthermore, on the question of religious discipline at Somerville, Legge was instrumental in drafting the final compromise rule stipulating that, instead of compulsory college chapel, students would only "be expected . . . to attend a place of worship chosen by themselves or their parents."[27] All of these accomplishments, it should be said, were achieved in spite of powerful opposition from a mixed lot of conservative and liberal dons, including the High Church Pusey and the very Broad Church Müller and Jowett (both of whom were more comparatively broad in intellectual than in social and political matters).[28]

These actions are an excellent exemplification of Legge's evolving spirit of mission, a way of active social engagement that, in this case, challenged conventional practices restricting female education. Compared with Müller, Legge—the evangelical country Scotsman and former missionary—was often the more transgressive figure in contesting oppressive Victorian social forms. Legge did not leave any records of his reasons for promoting higher education for women, but it seems plausible that—in addition to his long-standing interest in educational issues, his evangelical commitment to self-cultivation on the part of both men and women, and perhaps his awareness that young women were in the majority at many professorial lectures at Oxford[29]—he was also responding to the presence of several strong and influential women in his own life. I refer to his two wives, whose intelligence burned brightly even without the benefit of higher education, and to several of his quite independent daughters, especially Helen Edith and his stepdaughter Marian. In fact, it sometimes seemed that he favored Helen Edith over his two sons. The tradition of Somerville College as a training ground for a host of formidably intelligent and brilliantly accomplished British women is very much in keeping with the strong feminine element that often seemed to underlie Legge's mostly traditional, and often patronizing, patriarchal manner.

The Very Reverent Max Müller

Legge gives us a glimpse into his changing state of mind about the study of religion and his increasingly close working association with Müller in a rare fifteen-page essay entitled "Professor F. Max Müller." Existing only in a blurred handwritten copybook that is ignored in Helen Edith Legge's work, this document (which was most likely given as a public lecture to a general audience, perhaps a church group), can be dated from internal evidence to 1879, the very year that the first three volumes of the *Sacred Books of the East* appeared and that Legge's reputation was forevermore publicly linked with the acclaimed progenitor of the comparative science of religions.[30] Coming so close after the whole Shanghai incident, which condemned his theology and methods, this text takes on added significance as a public declaration of Legge's new scholarly faith and methodological sympathies.

Beginning his reflections by briskly reviewing the professor's early life, Legge stresses the groundbreaking importance of Müller's 1860 lectures on the "science of language," his monumental multivolume edition of the *Rig-Veda* with the Sanhita commentary, his lectures in the early 1870s on the comparative science of religions, and his amazingly diverse essays collected under the general title of *Chips from a German Workshop*.[31] Legge draws one important conclusion from this material: "[T]here is no religion without God, or, as St. Augustine expressed it[,] that 'there is no false religion which does not contain some elements of truth.'" For Legge this is a finding that is very much embodied in his own three key comparativist publications in 1877, 1879, and 1880 and "ought never to have been doubted"—although the debate over the existence of a savage or heathen High God in the late 1870s was only beginning to pass from the missionary context of the term question to the equally contentious, confused, and mean-spirited context of the fledgling sciences of man (including the comparative science of religions, anthropology, sociology, ethnology, and folklore).

The most interesting part of the essay comes in the last few pages where Legge discusses his own perspective on the "results at which [Müller] had arrived." Legge begins by referring almost wistfully to Müller's persuasive and "elegant" writing style that, while betraying a poet's sensibility, only enhances the powerful "train of logic" running throughout his work. Interesting also is the discussion of Müller's controversial theory of roots, which stood in stark opposition with the Darwinian view of language origin, a position that dramatized Müller's posture as a religious radical who nevertheless offered comforting support to religious faith and the superiority of

Christianity. Restricting himself mostly to a descriptive presentation of philological roots as the four hundred or five hundred "general ideas" intrinsic to human nature in its original (and divinely created) state, Legge seems sympathetic to Müller's theories while avoiding any mention of what some critics had designated as his inherently silly "ding-dong" theory of resonating root sounds called forth by the primordial response of human beings to the natural world.

Anyone responsive to intellectual debate and academic scholarship in England at that time would be aware of the very prominent criticism of Müller's comparative philological and mythological theories, and Legge carefully implied in this essay that final conclusions respecting issues of language origin were premature and probably impossible. It was best therefore to take a guarded approach to all such matters and to refrain from further inquiry until Müller had a chance to answer some of his more vociferous critics. The irony of this situation is that, with the publication of Legge's first contributions to the *Sacred Books of the East*, Müller for several years found himself responding to more of Legge's missionary critics back in China than to his own antagonists in England.

Legge ends his essay with a fascinating discussion of Müller's views on the comparative science of religions. Understandably sensitive to this topic given his own recent Shanghai experience, Legge prefaces his discussion with the assertion that, despite the accusations of some critics, Müller was (as, it is implied, he was also) indeed "very reverent." For Legge the important point of the "relational" or "comparative" approach to religion is that, far from being heretical or unchristian, it was the recommended strategy of early Christian apologists such as Paul. In this sense, Legge (recalling the liberal theological views of his brother George) makes it clear that comparative religion—as an inductive science of the universality, essential truth, and historical growth of religion—is a crucial weapon in the encounter with other religions and in the battle with "modern infidelity."

Legge then states his general agreement with three comparativist lessons derived from Müller's 1865 "Lectures on the Vedas." The first of these lessons is the principle of the purity of origins or, as it is put in this essay, that "religion in its most ancient form is generally free from later blemishes."[32] The second lesson is that there is "hardly any religion which does not contain some truth, some important truth." This essential, and usually disguised, truth hidden in ancient texts (whether discovered in the sacred books of Hinduism, Buddhism, Confucianism, or Daoism) is most often a "sufficient" means "to enable those who seek" the Christian lord "to feel after Him and to find Him" (here quoting a Pauline phrase from Acts 17). The third lesson, derived from a conscientious attention to a comparative study of religions, is that we "learn to appreciate better what we have in our own religion." Invoking the Pauline argument yet again, Legge notes that "no one who has not examined patiently and honestly the other religions of the world can know what Christianity really is."

To say sincerely along with Saint Paul that one is not "ashamed by the Gospel of Christ" (Rom. 1:17) is premised here—by both Müller and Legge—on an honest comparative appreciation of other religions. Appropriately enough, Legge concludes his essay by embracing the words of Müller's preface to the publication of his *Lectures on the Science of Religion* in 1873:

> That study [of comparative religions or theology], I feel convinced, if carried on in a bold, but scholar-like, careful, and reverent spirit, will remove many doubts and difficulties which are due entirely to the narrowness of our religious horizon; it will enlarge our sympathies, it will raise our thoughts above the small controversies of the day, and at no distant future evoke in the very heart of Christianity a fresh spirit, and a new life.[33]

The "fresh spirit" and "new life" that animate this accord with Müller's plea for an enlargement of sympathies that rises above the "small controversies of the day" is unquestionably the fact that Legge was gratefully engaged in what was to be the crowning glory of the comparativist enterprise in the nineteenth century, the *Sacred Books of the East*. As Legge says, the "present year [1879] should witness the publication of the first three volumes of the series" superintended by Müller for the Oxford University Press. One of these volumes will be Legge's new rendition of the classical books of *Historical Documents, Poetry,* and *Filial Piety* as "texts of Confucianism" that were now understood as select examples of the newly designated *Sacred Books of China.*[34] At this time, Legge notes that Müller contemplated a series of twenty-four volumes appearing at the rate of about three volumes a year. But as he correctly predicts, the series "will extend . . . over many more than 24 volumes" and will lead to "momentous practical results."

NO DISTINCTION IN KIND:
THE *SACRED BOOKS OF THE EAST*

The more I see of the so-called heathen religions, the more I feel convinced that they contain germs of the highest truth. There is no distinction in kind between them and our own religion. The artificial distinction which we have made, has not only degraded the old revelations, but has given to our own almost a spectral character. No doubt the man is different from the child, but the child is the man and the man is the child, even the very suckling. We can hardly believe it, yet the fact is there, and so it is in the growth of religion.

MAX MÜLLER, LETTER TO A.P. STANLEY, 1878

Most of my English critics say "Les Bibles de la humanité ne sont pas amusantes." Certainly not! They are not amusing; on the contrary, they are the very saddest books to read. But they must be read, they must be meditated on, if we want to know what kind of creature homo sapiens is.

MAX MÜLLER, LETTER TO E. RENAN, 1883

An Enlargement of Theological Horizons

The surest sign of what the *North-China Herald* called the "enlargement of theological horizons" on matters of "grave consequence" is seen in the appearance in 1879 of three volumes of sacred books culled from the textual worlds of Asia being explored by Oriental scholars. This gigantic enterprise under the general editorship of Max Müller was no mere dilettantish anthology of the "gems of oriental wisdom," but would constitute a veritable library of complete, or close to complete, texts making use of the most advanced Oriental scholarship of the day and sanctioned by the most famous learned institution in all of the Western world. The first volumes were published in 1879, but the production of the whole series known as the *Sacred Books of the East* continued until after the turn of the century (forty-nine volumes of scriptures and an additional index volume, 1878–1910).[35] Müller's *Sacred Books* project, which initially involved a battalion of twenty of the best Oriental scholars in the world, was a massive editorial undertaking and truly one of the great scholarly monuments of an age known for its vast literary productions.[36] Even though it did not exactly constitute the "Oriental renaissance" of Western civilization hoped for at the beginning of the century, it at least signaled at the end of the century the more complete institutionalization of Orientalism and the comparative method within the Western academic world.

The *Sacred Books* can be equated with several other enormous team efforts involving the Oxford University Press at this time: the new revised translation of the English Bible from original sources (initiated in 1870 at Cambridge University and appearing more than ten years later), Jowett's multivolume edition of the Greek classics, and James Murray's *Dictionary of the English Language* (which became the *Oxford English Dictionary* in 1895, begun by Murray in 1878; the first volume appeared in 1884 and the last in 1928).[37] Projects like these (unlike other, more commercial projects undertaken elsewhere, such as the *Encyclopaedia Britannica,* Chambers's *Cyclopedia,* and Leslie Stephen's *Dictionary of National Biography,* which appeared in sixty-three volumes between 1885 and 1900)[38] may not always realize a profit sufficient to offset the costs of production, but, as Müller told the Delegates of the University Press, such undertakings were wholly justified as crucial contributions to the "advancement of sound learning and science," not to mention providing rewarding work for junior scholars beginning their careers.[39]

As Müller argued the case with his fellow Delegates of the press, and this seems to be a turning point in the publishing policy of university presses in the English-speaking world, it would be well for Oxford "to draw a line between two classes of books." One category would be those works published for profit as "booksellers"; the other class would be "for the encouragement of scientific works" requiring the special approval and oversight of the "Delegates of the University Press." This last category of exceptional noncommercial works designed for the "advancement of sound learning" would moreover receive a uniquely prestigious imprint as Clarendon Press books.[40]

At least three of these immense projects (the revised edition of the Bible, the *Sacred Books*, and Murray's dictionary) reflect an important nineteenth-century shift in the meaning and methods of knowing. This change can be characterized as a movement from individual scholarship to the necessarily cooperative efforts of a team of professional academic scholars (what Müller calls the method of *viribus unitis*). Much of this newly bureaucratized and entrepreneurial approach to knowledge was prompted by the profusion of new information, texts, and artifacts flooding into the capitals of the great imperialistic nations, especially London, but it also had to do with the growing sense of the need for a more progressive, professional, scientific, specialized, and academic mission to the entire world. Just as the Protestant mission to the heathen world was distinguished from other more crassly commercial and military operations by its officially more disinterested concern for moral and religious progress, so also is there a sense in which the increasingly secularized academic establishment maintained the integrity of its educational mission by its self-proclaimed devotion to a specialized research scholarship requiring international disciplinary cooperation (i.e., the "congressional spirit" discussed above; see pages 145–53) and gigantic publishing ventures that were theoretically "non-commercial" in nature. The fact of the matter was that the publishing of the Bible—as of Murray's dictionary and Jowett's classical editions, if not all of Müller's *Sacred Books*—was a steady source of income for the press and the university.[41]

One Bible and Many Translations

The potentially threatening recognition of the existence of many bibles or sacred books can be related to a revisionary scholarly climate in late-Victorian tradition concerning the extreme plurality of the translations of, and the multiple Protestant interpretations of, the One Holy Bible. This situation is most obviously seen in the controversial effort in England at this time to produce, by academic committee, a new authorized revision of the English Bible based on the original languages and the new higher critical scholarship. The intention was that this revised translation would replace the standard King James version, a cooperatively produced translation that had achieved a special authoritative status and venerable quasi-sacrality in the Victorian world. This revisionary climate is also seen in China, where the conference of Protestant missionaries in Shanghai in 1877 turned its attention away from Legge only to sponsor a renewed, though ultimately unsuccessful, effort at attaining a single Union Bible in various Chinese dialectical forms (especially classical Chinese, the so-called easy classical, and Mandarin vernacular languages). Coming in the wake of more than a half century of denominational rivalry, terminological debate, and several contested translations, this was, for the rest of the century, mostly a doomed effort.[42]

From a Protestant perspective the salvific power of Christian revelation—unlike the Hebraic, Islamic, and, to some degree, the Roman Catholic idea of revelation, which depended on the integrity of a single sacred language (Hebrew, Arabic, Latin)—could be fully and totally communicated only in multiple, and changing, vernacular translations within particular traditions. This suggests that the One Holy Bible should be understood as a culturally sensitive, and constantly expanding, discursive mosaic made up of a potentially endless number of different, yet overlapping, textual versions. Such a view has scriptural license in Western tradition since, after Babel, the Hebrew Bible itself says that there can no longer be just one race, one language, one translation, or even one Bible. The oneness of the biblical revelation will henceforth be refracted through a translated historical plurality of different tongues and written languages—even within a single linguistic tradition. In Oriental traditions, as the etymology of the Chinese term *jing* for "authoritative text," "classic," or now "sacred book" suggests, such a text is not a single thing, but the divinatory skein or "warp in the weaving" of a larger and constantly expanding commentarial and discursive fabric.[43]

Moreover the passionate Evangelical bibliolatry of the Protestant missionary movement led to an ever-increasing, and often bewildering, proliferation of polyglot Bibles: English, German, Zulu, Latvian, Hindi, Cherokee, Manchu, Japanese, and so on (as famously documented in the constantly updated lists of hundreds and hundreds of translations maintained by the British and American Foreign Bible Societies). Each of these was theoretically a translation of the One Bible, but at the same time each was only a translated version of some original texts that were themselves but translations of other translations and, penultimately, the written transcriptions of even more fluid oral traditions. It is impossible, therefore, to say which version (no matter how far back one is able to go with regard to ancient biblical texts) is absolutely the original, pure, definitive Bible amid the infinite sliding spectrum of endless versions of versions, multiple translations of other translations and transcriptions, and written distillations of oral traditions.

This historically contextualized, intratranslationally transformative, and open-ended intertextual fluidity was, of course, the brunt of much of the

German higher criticism and idealistic hermeneutics, especially as applied to the ancient Jewish testamental scriptures. It was not explicitly articulated as such, but the implication was that, although ultimate Truth might be singular and timeless, it could be known only in terms of its multiple historical manifestations—the most ancient, critically and philologically determined, texts, however, coming closest (comparatively speaking) to some originally pure and singular revelation. This was but another way of saying what Müller had been suggesting all along in the Herderian spirit of German romanticism: Truth is known interpretatively only by virtue of a comparative method that makes use of the translated and transformative nature of all historical and textual information. The One could only be known in its developmentally plural manifestations. All knowledge was in this sense a translated and constantly transformed knowledge. So also was knowing in this way intrinsically comparative or relational in nature and method.

The disturbing confusion of multiple revisions, critical versions, and so-called authorized translations of the Christian Bible in Victorian England is complicated further by the transcultural problems of translation and interpretation arising in the comparative study of other Oriental traditions. To take the Leggian instance of China, the issue is simply that there may be one final, highest, or most complete revelation of God in the Christian New Testament, but the existence of Oriental classical literature testifies to the presence of many other, completely different holy bibles or sacred books. These other scriptural works were found to be crude and incomplete when compared with the Christian scriptures, but they could nevertheless be considered as authoritative deposits of religious and moral wisdom or even as authentic fragments of an ancient divine revelation to Oriental civilizations. From the relativizing perspective of a translator and comparativist, as was Legge, the ancient Chinese already possessed a partial or natural revelation from God, which needed supplementation and fulfillment in the way that the Christian New Testament completed the Old Testament of the Hebrews.

What is suggested here is that the higher Christian revelation can—by means of translation—be added to the existing Chinese scriptures, thereby providing the Chinese with a new degree of divine truth necessary for their future salvation and civilizational progress. At the same time, the translation of the Chinese sacred books into a Western language leads to the implicit creation of a larger and more complete transcultural scripture that reestablishes some of the lost primordial unicity of both the Oriental and Christian writings. This leads to the conclusion that, in principle, the complete revelation of the Divine (the Müllerian developmental perception of the Infinite) is fully recognized only in the total collection of scriptures from throughout the world. Even when an assemblage such as the *Sacred Books* fails to include the Old and New Testament for fear of offending pious feelings of exclusivity, it is clearly insinuated by Müller that, no matter how special, advanced, and fulfilled any one scripture may be, they are all, in their sheer multiplicity and developmental historicity, fundamentally alike "in kind" and essentially "one."

Mere Translation

Müller's cooperatively produced *Sacred Books*, like the collective effort to revise the English Bible from original languages, was above all a project that depended upon, and valorized, the craft of translation and the specialized mastery of difficult and obscure written languages. Yet these projects implied that translation by itself was mostly a lower-order philological skill (an aspect of the "lower criticism"),[44] the fruit of which, no matter how technically accurate and stylistically graceful, only provided for a more accessible compilation of raw texts, data, or facts. In this sense, translations made texts available for the higher critical operations of historical interpretation. They provided grist for the hermeneutical mill of comparative analysis that extracted the interstitial meanings hidden by the metaphorical husks of individual words.

The highest order of scientific Oriental scholarship ideally involved the personal mastery of the original languages of all the texts one was working with, but more practically speaking, such philological breadth and skill, even for someone as linguistically gifted as Müller or Legge, was impossible. Only those with the higher critical skills of historical analysis and theoretical induction (like Müller, himself, of course) were fully and truly capable of the humanistic science of comparison. Legge's identification with Müller and his participation in the production of the *Sacred Books of the East* were, in this sense, a two-edged sword. Translating for the *Sacred Books* was an honor and an elevation of his scholarly prestige as a sinological Orientalist, but since that scholarly activity was all or most of what he came to be known for academically, he ran the risk of being identified as *only*, or *merely*, a translator—someone who did not really advance human knowledge. Sadly, it often seemed to be Legge's fate to be taken, by Orientalists, as a mere translator and, by missionaries, as too much of a heretical comparativist.

Many Worlds and Many Bibles

The proximate cause for Müller's *Sacred Books of the East* was the incredible explosion in the nineteenth century of information about new Oriental and savage worlds. The exploration, classification, and management of these new realms of meaning, particularly the Oriental traditions, called for some appropriate, impartial, and scientific scholarly response. What better reaction than to sift, edit, translate, compare, and publish the textual deposits of these strange, though historically important, civilizations? As vampires needed blood to live (Bram Stoker's *Dracula* would arrive in England by the end of the century), so also did practicing Orientalists crave texts on which to hone their professional skills and to further their careers among the academic undead.

As the political, commercial, and intellectual ransacking of these new worlds intensified during the last quarter of the nineteenth century, the growing scholarly consensus coming from the newly professionalized academic fields of Orientalism was that, despite superficial appearances, there really was "no distinction in kind" (anciently and essentially) between the Western Bible and some other authoritative texts associated with "high" Oriental civilizations, such as those of India and China. Most convincing in this regard was the scriptural and sacred quality perceived in Indo-European texts. The hyphenated family linkage between the Indian and European traditions was admittedly a theoretical philological construct, but, in time and through the cumulative sanction of scholarly iteration, what was made up as a useful methodological fiction became a complex linguistic, historical, and racial fact.

Protestant Sacredness

Much of the prestige of Sanskritic, Indo-European, or Aryan studies at this time was derived from Müller's impressive work on the original text of the *Rig-Veda,* the oldest of the Indian scriptures.[45] But Müller's editorial emphasis on critically capturing, preserving, and canonizing some ancient, definitive, and original "writtenness" of the *Rig-Veda* really did violence to the Brahmanical insistence on the oral nature of Vedic tradition. As Wilfred Cantwell Smith has said, Müller's overall sense of the normativity of sacred books and his turning of the "Hindu *Veda* into a written book is an entrancing instance of nineteenth-century Western cultural imperialism, here quietly imposing the Western sense of 'scripture.' "[46] The English word *scripture* was used only for the sacred scripture of the Old and New Testaments down till the eighteenth century. In the nineteenth century, terms such as *scripture*—as well as *sacred writing, holy book,* or even *bible*—were for the first time used in a generic and pluralistic way. As William Graham indicates, it was especially Müller's *Sacred Books* that sanctioned the notion that many different Oriental texts functioned as "scriptures in ways analogous to the Hebrew and Christian bible."[47]

From the perspective of the Müllerian Orientalist, the *Vedas* were the most ancient of the Indian classics. Since they possessed "power, authority, unicity, and divine inspiration," they were unmistakably a collection of "holy," "sacred," or "religious" scriptures. At the very least, the mythological and religious nature of the early and later Vedic texts seemed obvious when compared with the infinitely more prosaic Chinese classics and the moot religiosity of Kongzi. This judgment concerning the authentic sacredness or profound religiosity of the Indian classics (especially in reference to the philosophical purity and elevated metaphysics of the *Upanishads,* selections from this work making up Müller's very first volume for the *Sacred Books*) seems to hinge on an amorphous set of Evangelical Protestant assumptions about history, religion, and the special importance of scripture *(sola scriptura)* and individual moral regeneration.[48] In addition to a rather obvious anti-Catholic perspective on the general history of religions, priests, and ritual, these mostly unspoken criteria included, for both Müller and Legge, an emphasis on reified religious beliefs, doctrines, and moral codes embedded in scriptures and conscience; stress on a monotheism unsullied by intermediary spiritual beings; the importance of nonpetitionary prayer and worship; the need for a radical spiritual transformation of human nature and an ongoing self-cultivation; and the authoritative role of individual religious founders, prophets, and reformers.

A Kind of Canonical Sanction

Interestingly, Müller's most explicit criterion for designating something as a sacred book did not depend so much on the book's specific doctrines or on some self-assertion of divine origin or revelation ("it was soon found that very few, if any, of the books themselves put forward that claim"). It was rather a matter of texts that had been canonically chosen as authoritative by their respective traditions. "We agree," Müller says, "to treat as Sacred Books all those which had been formally recognized by religious communities as constituting the highest authority in matters of religion, which had received a kind of canonical sanction, and might therefore be appealed to for deciding any disputed points of faith, morality or ceremonial."[49] The real issue here is that the "authoritative status and normative uses of scripture as a defining characteristic" in the comparative study of religion are clearly derived from a Protestant "concern with the sources of the authority of its tradition and the nature of the normative character of its Scripture."[50]

Legge's revisionary translations and more relational reconsideration of the ancient Chinese classics documented the normative nature, moral greatness, and authentic Protestant sacredness of an almost prophetlike Confucius and the anciently pure monotheistic tradition of worship and ethical behavior known by Western sinologues as Confucianism. It was Legge's steady conviction in the monotheistic belief of the classics and his changing views of the religiousness of the Chinese Sage and his eponymous tradition (concerning worship, human nature, the afterlife, morality, and postmortem retribution) that were leading to a reformation of Protestant missionary policies and allowed for the definitive incorporation of Confucianism into the hallowed ranks of Müller's eight great "book religions."

For the first time a strong, evidential case could be made for the sympathetic relational study of particular ancient Chinese texts as not just authoritative classics like the Greek and Roman texts, but as truly sacred books, scriptures, or bibles.[51] It is in this sense that the events of 1879 represent a turning point in the fortunes of the comparative science of religions and another crucial step in Legge's own intellectual evolution as a sinological translator and comparativist. The year 1879, therefore, witnessed the publication of the first three volumes of the *Sacred Books of the East.* These included Müller's own translation of selected *Upanishads* as the first volume, with Georg Bühler's translation of the *Sacred Laws of the Aryas* in the second volume, and Legge's Chinese sacred books, the *Book of Historical Documents,* the *Book of Poetry,* and the *Book of Filial Piety,* as the third volume.

We see, like Legge in quoting his ode, that another mighty oak, weakened from within and violently buffeted from without, was on the verge of falling. I refer to the further weakening of regnant Western ideas about Confucianism as simply an authoritative, but outdated, nonreligious, and desiccated classical tradition and the habitual tendency to condemn heathen traditions. To say that the Confucian classical texts were sacred, scriptural, and even biblical for Oxford academicians such as Legge and Müller is to valorize the tradition in such a way that it now had some universal religious and moral significance, no matter how developmentally incomplete. Just as, in 1877, Legge had related Confucianism and Christianity on religious and moral grounds, so now these new publications—under the disturbing title of the *Sacred Books of the East* and the impressive imprint of the Oxford University Press, publishers of the revised edition of the English Bible—were raising the relational stakes even higher. It was hard enough for traditional missionaries in the field and resolute conservative Christians at home to put up with the affront of the Chinese classics and other ancient heathen texts; now they were being asked to swallow the even more outrageous proposition that there was "no distinction in kind" among the bibles of the world, including *the* One Bible. Truly troubling to conservative sensibilities was the underlying rationale of Müller's project that certain Oriental texts, and now Chinese Confucian and Daoist texts as well as the more obvious Hindu and Buddhist scriptures, were sacred in a way somehow comparable with, if not as complete as, the One Holy Bible.

For missionaries active in China who were already incensed over Legge's audacious Shanghai conference paper, his contribution to Müller's *Sacred Books* two years later served only to broadcast his apostasy around the world. These were, then, matters no longer restricted to private correspondence and the relatively tiny and closed worlds of the *Chinese Recorder, China Review,* and the *North-China Herald.* Rather, the tide of opinion had turned in such a way in China and throughout European Christendom that only a counterattack at the highest levels would suffice. It is in this sense that one of the first, and most prolonged and belligerent, assaults on the *Sacred Books* came about, along with several lengthy critiques by A.P. Happer in the *Chinese Recorder,* as a broadside specifically directed against Legge's prerogatives as a translator for Müller's series. This attack was organized by John Shaw Burdon, the obstreperous Anglican bishop of Hong Kong and, besides appearing in papers throughout the foreign communities in China, was featured prominently in the London *Times* for the general delectation of learned society.

A Profane History of the Sacred Books

To gain some perspective on the role that Legge's initial contribution to the *Sacred Books of the East* played in the reception of the overall series, it is necessary to go back and briefly reconstruct some of the history of this project that was justifiably called by contemporaries one of the major scholarly and religious achievements of the nineteenth century.[52] As Archibald Sayce said in a review of the first volume, the publication of the *Sacred Books* was an event that was truly a "significant sign of the age." At no other time in Britain would it have been possible to study religion with the "dispassionate interest" and comparative methods of science and to publish the results "at the expense of a University supposed to be the stronghold of narrow orthodoxy."[53]

Documenting the inception, editorial negotiations, and prolonged production of the *Sacred Books* turns out to be more difficult than it might first appear. Aside from Müller's preface to the first volume of the *Sacred Books* and the discussion in his *Lectures on the Science of Religion* (as well as one or two other articles directly addressing the question of the sacred books),[54] there are few extended discussions of the rationale for, and process of, producing the series in Müller's extant public or private papers. Even more frustrating is that nineteenth-century publishing records are notoriously ephemeral and, unfortunately, the Oxford University Press archive is only a minor exception to this rule.[55]

The problem in writing even an opuscular history of the *Sacred Books* as a cultural artifact is indicated by the fact that it is not at all clear when Müller first conceived of the idea for such a project or when the series was finally approved by the press. Müller's idea for such an undertaking, a work that he will call the "opus magnum" of his later life, most certainly came into being in the early 1870s, when he was still smarting from the humiliation of having been passed over for the Boden chair of Sanskrit and was taking only partial consolation in his position as the professor of comparative philology.[56] The approval of the series even became a rather crass bargaining chip in the negotiations that led to Müller's renewed commitment, early in 1876, to Oxford University. From this indirect evidence, it seems that the

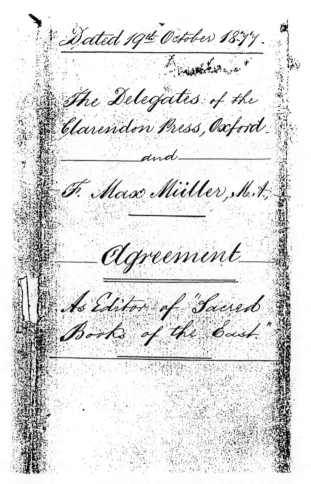

Figure 27. Cover page of Max Müller's contract for the *Sacred Books of the East*, 1877. Reproduced courtesy of the Oxford University Press archive, Oxford.

press, after being assured of financial support from the Indian government, officially sanctioned the publication of the *Sacred Books* sometime during the fall of 1877 (see figure 27).[57]

From the Eastern Flowerets to the Sacred Books

It has been said that the first actual reference to the *Sacred Books* is found in a letter to Legge written in 1875, but Müller had already discussed this kind of project in his remarks in London at the Congress of Orientalists in 1873.

In the broadest theoretical sense, the unformulated gleam in the progenitor's eye may be perceived in Müller's meandering discussion of the small "aristocracy" of canonical "book religions" in his "Lectures on the Science of Religion" (the particular talk in question being the "Second Lecture" given on February 26, 1870, and published in 1873).[58] Müller's address at the congress also provides us with a crucial clue as to the actual inception of the *Sacred Books* project for, as he said at that time, "a patient study of the Sacred Scriptures of the world is what is wanted at present more than anything else, in order to clear out ideas of the origin, the nature, and the purposes of religion." It is at this point in his talk that he specifically refers to the just published *Sacred Anthology* by Moncure Conway, an American Unitarian churchman and gentleman living in London.[59] Conway reports in his *Autobiography* that he sent the first published copy of the *Sacred Anthology* to Müller who was, at that time, preparing his remarks for the forthcoming congress.[60]

While Müller himself was loath to admit publicly to such a vulgar American influence, Conway proudly claims (in 1904, after Müller's demise) that it was the great popular success of his meager, and admittedly dilettantish, anthology of topically arranged "Eastern flowerets" and "Oriental gems of wisdom" that was the spark for Müller's monumental scholarly project designed to provide a more "discriminating" public with scholarly translations of complete texts, flowerets along with "brambles and thorns."[61] Conway, in fact, says that Müller, in the course of inquiring about the financial support for the *Anthology,* privately told him that "the interest in Oriental literature stirred up by the anthology inclined him [Müller] to undertake the publication of the 'Sacred Books of the East.' "[62] Basking in the glory of Müller's reputation, Conway confesses at the end of his life that he was "carrying into my closing days the reflection that my 'Sacred Anthology' contributed something to the publication of the 'Sacred Books of the East,'—the chief religious achievement of the nineteenth century."[63]

Müller would most probably have known of J.-P. G. Pauthier's earlier "portable Asia for the curious" known as *Les Livres sacrés de l'Orient* (appearing in Paris in 1852; six years later an expanded edition called *Les Livres sacrés de toutes les religions sauf la Bible* was published) and, as Schwab remarks, Müller's title was "no doubt" a direct translation from Pauthier.[64] But Pauthier's work was done in the nascent years of nineteenth-century French Orientalism and, even though he was more determinedly scholarly than Conway was, he was widely denounced as a incompetent charlatan by Julien and others.[65]

There is, in other words, some real plausibility in Conway's claim to have been the immediate catalyst for Müller's *Sacred Books.* This conclusion is strengthened by the fact that Müller wrote a favorable, and quite influential, review of the *Anthology* for the *Academy.*[66] This review almost reads as a preliminary brief for his own proposal to the Oxford University Press (as was his address the year earlier to the Congress of Orientalists), entitled in his preface to volume 1 of the *Sacred Books* a "Program of Translation of the Sacred Books of the East." Though undated, Müller's prospectus was clearly written sometime shortly after this review, that is, in late 1874 or early 1875. As Müller says, the incredible response to Conway's work illustrating the "sympathy of religions" (where "sympathies far outweigh the differences") proves the "wide interest in a subject hitherto strangely neglected." Noting the scholarly deficiencies of Conway's anthology, its "purely practical character," and its tendency to present too much of a "glowing account" of the Oriental scriptures, Müller concludes in a way that indicates his own plans to step into the breach: "We trust that his book will arouse a more general interest in a long-neglected and even despised branch of literature, the Sacred Books of the East."[67]

Petrifactions of Bygone Ages

Müller's prospectus for the *Sacred Books*—entitled *The Sacred Books of the East, Translated, with Introductions and Notes, By Various Oriental Scholars, and Edited by F. Max Müller*—was dated October 1876 in its printed form as a circular and was used for negotiating with potential translators and for informing the curious about his scholarly endeavors.[68] This circular—along with the embryonic comments in the *Introduction to the Science of Religion*, the actual preface to the first volume and the address to the 1873 Congress of Orientalists, and the review of the *Sacred Anthology*—is the most important document for understanding Müller's original rationale and plan for the first twenty-four-volume set of Oriental bibles.

Before examining the substance of the prospectus, I should draw attention to Müller's introductory comments to the version printed in volume 1 of the series (and there called a "Program of a Translation"). It is in these remarks that Müller airs his editorial difficulties in securing the best Oriental scholars and in getting his contributors to carry through on their agreements with him.[69] As he says, recalcitrance, illness, domestic affliction, and "even death" took their toll. The most loyal and faithful of all the contributors, and the only one to make all of the deadlines, was the aged, but always hardy and ever-diligent, Legge.[70] Müller also faced the additional problem of working with native scholars whose cooperation he "particularly desired to secure." Initially contracted Indian scholars such as Rajendralal Mitra and R. G. Bhandarkar were unable to fulfill their commitments and, out of the final list of twenty contributors, only two were non-Western scholars, one Indian (Kashinath Trimbak Telang) and the other Japanese (J. Takakusu).[71]

The argument presented in the prospectus is interesting first of all for its defense of the academic Orientalist proposition originally developed in the

Lectures on the Science of Religion and in the congress talk. Müller's contention was that, aside from their aesthetic appeal to the dilettante or their theological interest to the missionary (who, like a general, uses them to know thoroughly an enemy), the real importance of the *Sacred Books* is to be found in their general character as the "oldest" records marking "the beginning of . . . documentary, in opposition to purely traditional, history." In this way, these materials are not only historically valuable for their religious views, but also for their information "on the moral sentiments, the social institutions, [and] the legal maxims of some of the most important nations of antiquity."[72]

Some nations may have an ancient literature or an oral tradition (such as the national epics of the Greeks or the heroic tales of the Celts, Germans, and Slavs), but few have left anything that explicitly "deserves the name of Sacred Books." Thus the Homeric hymns have no particular sacred or canonical national sanction and, with his typical anti-Catholic bias flying, Müller says that the sacred literature of ancient Roman Italy was more of a "liturgical rather than of a purely religious kind" (taking it for granted that something liturgical or ritualistic will necessarily be less than purely—or protestantly—religious). Other ancient though extinct traditions, such as those of the Egyptians and Babylonians, may have some literature that merits consideration as authentic sacred books but, according to Müller, these traditions were still too imperfectly known to allow for meaningful comparative study.[73] There were too few reliably translated texts.

Müller reaches the conclusion that, putting aside the Hebrew and Christian scriptures (and he does not explain here why they are excluded, the implication being that his readers do not need to have such an obvious exception spelled out), there are only six "great and original religions which profess to be founded on Sacred Books, and have preserved them in manuscript." These make up what in 1870 Müller called in his *Lectures on the Science of Religion* the small "aristocracy of real book-religions in the history of the world":[74] the religions of the Brahmans and those "founded" religions of "Buddha, Zarathustra, Khung-fu-tze, Lao-tse, and Mohammed."[75]

Discussing the reasons that Orientalists had not already produced "complete," "trustworthy," and "readable" translations of the major sacred books, Müller indicates that one important factor was simply that, in many cases, there was much additional philological work to be done in the "critical restoration of the original texts." Some of the best scholars preferred to wait before indulging in the "mere translation" of complete texts. Ever the practical-minded intellectual, however, Müller argues for the necessity of scholars, or teams of scholars, making a "certain sacrifice" of their specialized philological researches "to render the general results already obtained accessible to the public at large."[76]

Exceptions Obscene and Leggian

Müller remarks on how difficult it was to find the funds necessary for a subject that excites only the "theoretic" rather than the "historical interest" of the public. Unlike the support for Conway's popular *Anthology* of homiletic and platitudinous "flowerets," which gave the public what it wanted to hear, Müller's collection of "complete" sacred books could not count on "a circulation large enough to make it a matter of private enterprise and commercial speculation." The problem was that the inclusion of *complete* sacred books would not cater to the vulgar taste for pious snippets of Oriental wisdom. The sacred books, while containing much that is beautiful and sublimely gemlike, also include much that is "extremely childish, tedious, if not repulsive." In addition to this, they harbor passages that were blatantly obscene by Victorian standards and, as he notes in the extended preface to volume 1, the excision of the nasty bits of sexual license was the only general exception to his rule of completeness.[77]

There was one other exception that had nothing to do with obscenity, but rather with Legge's abridgment of one of his translations of the Chinese sacred books. It is in the spirit of the principle of completeness that we witness Müller, in several letters, trying to convince Legge to avoid using only selections from the *Book of Poetry* for his initial contribution to the *Sacred Books:* "Critics would at once lay hold of it, and say that we had left out things likely to throw discredit on the early religions, etc."[78] In the end, Legge published only a partial version of the *Book of Poetry,* albeit together with complete new translations of the *Book of Historical Documents* and the *Book of Filial Piety.*[79]

According to Müller's prospectus, the significance of these complete Oriental works is entirely academic since "no one but the historian will be able to understand the important lessons which they teach." Because the general educated public will be unable to appreciate the historical importance of such texts, it is the task of academic institutions with a higher academic purpose of advancing research and science to step into the breach and fund these projects. Support for the publication of collections of exotic Oriental texts can only be justified on scientific grounds that are the same as those of a university's recognizing "the duty of collecting and exhibiting in Museums the petrifactions of bygone ages, little concerned whether the public admires the beauty of fossilised plants and broken skeletons, as long as hard-working students find there some light for reading once more the darker pages in the history of the earth."[80]

The prospectus concludes with a statement of Müller's specific publication agenda, which, at the time he was writing, involved a series of no more than twenty-four volumes to appear over a period of eight years. While his stated intention in the twenty-four volumes was to cover the six book religions with an eye to the usefulness and completeness of individual texts and with as much balance and breadth as possible, it also seems evident that he was consciously creating a plan that would necessitate the continuation of the series and the engagement of his editorial services for the rest of the century. Like the argument for "collecting and exhibiting" the sacred books or "broken skeletons" of bygone ages so that "hard-working students" may have something to do, we see that much of the rationale for such non-commercial and strictly "historical" projects concerns the furtherance of academic careers.

Selections for the Hard-Working Student

Regarding the individual volumes and the relative weighing of the different book religions, we need to consider Müller's original plans—in 1876 and in his revised schedule of selections made in 1879—with respect to the number and type of texts to be included in the series. Concerning the Brahmanical works, Müller remarked that he was independently publishing a scholarly translation of the Vedic hymns so that only a "freer" rendition of selected hymns was required for the *Sacred Books*.[81] Of more concern to Müller was a selection of principal *Upanishads,* which he calls "theosophic treatises of great interest and beauty." Considering their philosophical and historical importance (in both Indian history and the history of Western Orientalist scholarship), it is not surprising therefore that a collection of the *Upanishads* became Müller's initial contribution to the *Sacred Books* and the very first volume of the series. As spelled out in his revised plan, the Brahmanic texts would also include various law books in prose and poetry and later works such as the celebrated *Bhagavadgītā* and the popular *Vayu-purana.*

Admitting the difficulty of selecting texts from the immensity of Buddhist literature, Müller emphasized the need for works from both the Pali and Sanskrit collections. As noted in his revised plan, these would be supplemented by some Chinese Mahayana documents. Zoroastrian texts would include the *Zend-Avesta* along with a few Pahlavi and Parsi documents. Jain literature, while outside the scope of the series in 1876, is included in the revised agenda in the form of some selected Prakrit *sūtras.* As for Islam—or "Mohammedanism" as it was often called at that time as a "founded" religion like "Christianity," "Confucianism," or "Buddhism"—"all that is essential," says Müller, is a "trustworthy translation of the *Koran.*"

In 1876, Müller mentioned his hope, based on Legge's advice, to give key texts from both the Five Classics (the "King" or *Wu jing*) and the Four

Books (the *Si shu*) in "highest authority" among the "followers of Khung-fu-tzu"—specifically referring to the need for "entire" versions of the books of *Historical Documents, Poetry, Changes, Filial Piety,* and the *Record of Rites,* along with the *Analects* and *The Works of Mencius (Mengzi).* Neither of these last two texts found their way into the *Sacred Books.* They were, however, included in the revised 1893–1895 Oxford edition of Legge's original Hong Kong version of *The Chinese Classics.* Already in 1870, in the "Lectures on the Science of Religion," Müller was insistent on the inclusion among the six great Oriental religions of "Tao-sse" (1870) or "Taoism" (1879), the "system" founded by Laozi. In 1876 Müller says that "we require only a translation of the Tao-teh King with some of its commentaries" along with, "may be," some later text "to illustrate the actual operation of its principles." By 1879 these requirements will be stipulated by both Müller and Legge as a translation of the *Daode jing* (called the *Tao and Its Characteristics* in the 1891 edition of the *Sacred Books*), the *Zhuangzi,* and the *Ganying pian (The Tractate of Actions and Their Retributions),* a medieval text illustrating the "actual operation" of popular morality. By 1891, when the two volumes of the sacred books of Daoism appeared in the series, these texts were supplemented, in volumes 39 and 40 of the *Sacred Books,* by various commentarial works and selected short "mystical canons" from the so-called corrupt later tradition.

It seems probable that Legge's growing interest in Laozi was prompted by Müller's influential comments in the *Lectures on the Science of Religion* and his desire to include them among the *Sacred Books.* What also seems apparent from the expanded set of texts included in the published volumes (and from his "relational" discussion of Daoism in his 1880 *Religions of China*) is that, once his interest had been provoked, Legge grew increasingly engaged in the sympathetic study of the Daoist classics. In many ways, it is Müller and Legge's incorporation of Taoism within the boundaries of the *Sacred Books,* defined in relation to the religious purity of the ancient classical texts of the *Laozi* (the *Daode jing*) and the *Zhuangzi,* that establishes this Chinese tradition for the first time in mainstream Victorian consciousness.[82]

We must also take notice of both what has been called the "relentless dominance of textuality" in the Orientalist worldview and Müller's overwhelming Aryan or Indo-European bias in compiling the *Sacred Books.*[83] In the culminating set of forty-nine volumes, the Indian religions made up thirty-three volumes—that is, twenty-one Vedic-Brahmanic volumes, two Jain volumes, and ten Buddhist volumes (only one of which, volume 19, was devoted to a Chinese Buddhist text and two others included Mahayana texts influencing East Asian tradition). To this must be added the eight volumes of Persian or Zoroastrian texts, which gives a grand total of forty-one out of forty-nine volumes (more or less, depending on how a few of the Buddhist volumes are counted) that could be generally classified as belonging to "Indo-European" tradition.[84] Trailing weakly along at the end

came the two-volume translation of the Islamic Koran and Legge's six volumes devoted to Confucianism and Daoism.

Aside from the flagrant slighting of the rich textual heritage of Islam
(particularly the *Hadith* traditions), the most egregious case of shortsightedness concerns the completely inadequate and distorted representation of
East Asian religious traditions. As seen from the numerical breakdown of
texts, the non-Aryan traditions of Asia receive not only less coverage than
do the Brahmanical and Buddhist texts but also less than the Persian Parsi
scriptures do. Note, for example, the total exclusion of texts referring
specifically to Japan, Korea, or to any of the traditions of Southeast Asia and
the failure to give any balanced selection of East Asian Buddhist texts. The
fact that Vajrayana materials were generally excluded is not unexpected
given the endemic bias against ritualistic and corrupt traditions.

The Sublime and the Vulgar

Müller's 1879 "Preface to the Sacred Books of the East" supplements the
case for the *Sacred Books* made in his earlier prospectus. Much of the first
part of the preface expands on the rule of completeness and the "more
scholarlike" and historical need to include that which is "fresh, natural, simple, beautiful, and true" along with that which contains "so much that is not
only unmeaning, artificial, and silly, but even hideous and repellent."[85]
Here he develops an interesting theory of oral and textual transmission designed to answer the perplexing problem of how sacred texts, so full of an
authentic "divine afflatus," can have such a "mixed character" of the sublime and the repulsive.[86]

Müller's explanation of the amalgamation of the religiously (and
morally) pure and corrupt in authoritative sacred texts was "not entirely to
[his] own satisfaction." Having registered this qualification, it is clear that
his theory of the gradually corrupted, and periodically reformed, transmission of oral and written tradition is itself made up of an unwieldy mixture
of euhemeristic, "disease of language," and "priestly influence" elements—
all of which collectively amount to a combined reworking of various Reformation and Enlightenment perspectives on religious development. In the
process of the handing down of a tradition, especially by word of mouth or
by means of ceremonial acts, there was always the danger of linguistic confusion, forgetfulness of original circumstances, and the liturgical or priestly
valorization of some basically trivial or superstitious custom.[87]

What makes Müller's reflections interesting is that, while he clearly feels
that the "wild confusion of sublime truth with vulgar stupidity" is more of a
problem for the Oriental scriptures than for the Jewish and Christian scriptures, there is, finally, no "distinction in kind." In his emotional conclusion,
Müller does not hesitate to suggest that it is ridiculous to believe that all

Oriental people were "forsaken of God" while Westerners "are His chosen people." "We must not forget," he says, "that there are portions in our own sacred books, too, which many of us would wish to be absent, which, from the earliest ages of Christianity, have been regretted by theologians of undoubted piety, and which often prove a stumbling block to those who have been won over by our missionaries to the simple faith of Christ."[88] This is a point that not only harks back to Müller's *Lectures on the Science of Religion* and his missionary talk at Westminster Abbey, but would also strike a chord with that former missionary of "undoubted piety," James Legge.

A Proper Use of Translation

The other especially noteworthy aspect of Müller's preface to the *Sacred Books* is his elaboration of a theory of translation to account for the practical and philosophical problems of "rendering ancient thought into modern speech."[89] It is worth following the exposition of these points since it becomes increasingly obvious that Legge, especially in his special "rapport" with the peculiar *Book of Changes* and his growing appreciation for the esoteric classic, the *Daode jing (The Book of the Tao and Its Characteristics)*, is drawing upon some of Müller's ideas. In his work for the *Sacred Books,* Legge seems to be quite self-consciously expanding his identity as a scholar who was more of a "real decipherer" than a "mere translator."

Müller first cautions his readers about the "difficulties in making a proper use of translations." His concern is to disabuse his audience of the notion that one needed only to read the sacred books in translation "in order to gain an insight into the nature and character of the religions of mankind." Part of this criticism is also directed against the overly hasty methods of amateur philosophers and self-styled anthropologists who, without knowing the languages, believe that they can generally classify all religions after having studied a few savage tribes or having glanced at the accounts of various travelers and missionaries.[90]

It is best to study the sacred books in their original languages, and to study them with great care. But translations have their place as long as they are approached with a "scholarlike spirit" and an unwillingness to accept too quickly prevailing "general assertions" about this or that Oriental text. Even more important when using translations is the recognition that what looks "at first sight" as completely unintelligible or ridiculous is not necessarily "devoid of all meaning." Müller illustrates this point with reference to the empathy needed to appreciate the legitimate meditative and religious significance of the famous opening of the *Chandogya Upanishad,* which recommends a "one-pointed" mental concentration on the syllable *Om*—a notion that would seem mostly absurd or impossible to a Victorian used to constant mental activity.[91]

In a way that will have a direct bearing on Legge's own attempt to penetrate the perplexing enigmas of the *Book of Changes* and the Daoist texts, Müller concludes that for a translator or a reader of translations caution and sympathy are always called for in attempting to understand ancient Oriental texts. It is not so much that Oriental sacred books possess truth, he says, but that they display the developmental process in the unfolding of religious truth throughout the nations of the world: "Even behind the fantastic and whimsical phraseology of the sacred writings of the Hindus and other Eastern nations, there may be sometimes aspirations after truth which deserve careful consideration from the student of the psychological development and the historical growth of early religious thought, and that after careful sifting, treasures may be found in what at first we may feel inclined to throw away as utterly worthless."[92]

Müller's parting advice concerns the problems of translating an Oriental text, so widely removed from the Victorian age in time and "sphere of thought," in the same way that one would translate "a book written a few years ago in French or German." This is an undertaking that admits of the "most partial success only" even as one's knowledge of the ancient Oriental language grows more intimate, but he believes that a careful scholar-translator can achieve accurate and meaningful results. The real issue for Müller is primarily the stylistic question of whether or not the translator may be permitted to do some violence to the target language "rather than to misrepresent old thoughts by clothing them in words which do not fit them?"[93] For seasoned translators like Müller, the answer is assuredly and always a matter of choosing the "smaller evil" when "the choice lay between sacrificing idiom or truth." A reader of the *Sacred Books,* says Müller in a way that surely speaks for Legge as well, should "not expect too much from a translation." Stylistic problems in translations are always semantic problems and as "easy as it might be to render word by word," a translator must focus on the more difficult issue of rendering "thought by thought."

Müller illustrates this principle of translation by referring to his adoption of "self and Self," instead of the more usual "soul, mind, or spirit," as terms "least liable to misunderstanding" when translating the key Upanishadic term of *ātman*.[94] While Müller argues for using the most "adequate" term in English for the Sanskrit whenever possible, he also recommends retaining a Sanskrit word "rather than use a misleading substitute in English" (the example he offers is the word *sat* meaning something like the "subtle essence or root of everything").[95] The crucial point is that "it would be wrong to smooth down [the] strangeness [of the *Upanishads*] by clothing them in language familiar to us, which, because it is familiar, will fail to startle us, and because it fails to startle us, will fail also to set us thinking."[96] Müller makes it clear that his reflections on translation really amount to an argument for the comparativist spirit of empathetic comprehensiveness in both the translator of texts and the reader of translations. The implication is that only by achieving some degree of "thought by thought" empathy, as a translator or reader, for the ideas contained in ancient Oriental texts is it possible to achieve some real appreciation of the "half-religious" and "half-philosophical" utterances found in the *Sacred Books of the East*. It is not enough to say that such works are simply "strange, or obscure, or mystic"; surely Plato or Bishop Berkeley are "strange" until "we have identified ourselves with [them]."

The *Sacred Books* must be "judged from within," and never from without. It is therefore the original, and often opaque, authorial meaning, or essential intention, that must be empathetically uncovered or understood. In accomplishing this, "we need not become Brahmans or Buddhists or Taosze [*daoshi;* Daoist priests] altogether, but we must for a time, if we wish to understand, and still more, if we are bold enough to undertake to translate their doctrines." In commencing this most profound transformative operation of translation and comparison, we (i.e., the translator and the reader of translations) discover that "[w]e cannot separate ourselves from those who believed in these sacred books. There is no specific difference between ourselves and the Brahmins, the Buddhists, the Zoroastrians, or the Taosze. Our Powers of perceiving, of reasoning, and of believing may be more highly developed, but we cannot claim the possession of any verifying power or of any power of belief which they did not possess as well."[97]

These words might almost be taken as the interpretive credo of the comparative humanistic sciences at the end of the nineteenth century. Translating and understanding strange Oriental texts depends on a new kind of pietistic transcendental faith that impartially seeks to uncover what is always essentially or symbolically "hidden" in the documents that make up the developmental history of religions—that is, "something that could lift up the human heart from this earth to a higher world, something that could make man feel the omnipresence of a higher Power, something that could make him shrink from evil and incline to good." The lesson here, a lesson that Legge had been progressively embracing in his own distinctive Evangelical and Scottish common sense way, is that we "must draw in every religion a broad distinction between what is essential and what is not, between the eternal and the temporary, between the divine and the human."[98]

A Motto, Figurehead, and Flag

As an observation on the overall comparativist spirit embodied in the *Sacred Books,* we should take special notice of what Müller considered the general epigram for the whole series. Included by Müller "in the very nick of time" as the epigraph to volume 1, this is the long quotation from the seventeenth-century Anglican divine Bishop Beveridge. Müller had the good fortune to receive the quotation from a English socialite, Lady Welby, who "just happened to find" a copy of the bishop's "Private Thoughts" and, believing that it might console Müller in his battles with critics who claimed that a comparative approach to religion and the very idea of the sacred books of the East would discredit Christianity, sent it on to him in Oxford right at the time he was finishing up the first three volumes for the press.[99] Wiring the binder to stop work so that the new epigraph could be included, Müller says that the quotation came as a "bolt out of the blue." Hauntingly, and uncharacteristically for his time and office, the bishop spoke of the need for a "diligent and impartial enquiry into all the religions" (see appendix A). This was "exactly what was wanted" as a "motto, figure-head, or flag" for the overall project of the *Sacred Books*.[100] This is a motto that also has special pertinence for James Legge's own journey as a "diligent and impartial" decipherer of the *Sacred Books of China*.

THE WORK OF A REAL DECIPHERER:
THE *SACRED BOOKS OF CHINA*

God will be His own interpreter. China, separated from the rest of the world, and without the light of revelation, has played its part, and brought forth its lessons, which will not, I trust, be long without their fitting exposition.

JAMES LEGGE, PROLEGOMENA, *THE CHINESE CLASSICS*, VOL. 3, 1865

When we think of the undiscriminating ignorance with which in former times Christian teachers confounded together under one uniform condemnation the debasing superstitions of African Fetish worshippers, the civilised philosophy of Confucius, the intricate mythology of India, the sublime monotheism of the Koran—and when we compare this with the exact and profound acquaintance which European scholars have gained of the Sacred Books, of the varying ceremonies, of the shades of religious sentiment in all these different races, an acquaintance sometimes far exceeding that which is possessed by the natives themselves—is it possible not to see that some corresponding change must take place, in fact has already taken place, in great measure from the coarse unreasoning attacks which were the unavoidable weapons of our earlier missionaries, to whom all these things were unknown.

NORTH-CHINA HERALD, 1879

Prefatory Observations

Legge's volume 3 of the *Sacred Books* appeared, along with volumes 1 and 2, in the late spring of 1879. Designated as the *Sacred Books of China*, part 1, *The Texts of Confucianism*, this volume included a revised rendition of the complete *Book of Historical Documents* (with asterisks attached to passages "embodying, more or less distinctly, religious ideas") and an abridged revision of the *Book of Poetry* containing only "the religious portions" of the text.

In addition to these revised texts, volume 3 also contained a totally new translation of the *Book of Filial Piety*, an important text that was not one of the Five Classics or Four Books, but was nonetheless included in other canonical groupings and was one of the first texts so honored by the Han dynasty.[101] Each of these texts was preceded by an extensive philological and historical introduction that was mostly a revised adaptation of his earlier prolegomena (except for the completely new introduction to the *Filial Piety*).[102] An examination of these introductory comments to the newly entitled *Sacred Books of China* in relation to Legge's earlier prolegomena to the same books in the *Chinese Classics* will show how Legge's metamorphosis as a professor and comparativist was affecting his primary activities as a translator and "decipherer" of Chinese tradition. Nevertheless, the best way to evaluate the introductions to individual texts is to compare them with Legge's general preface to volume 3, which he completed in April 1879 after the introductions and the translations had gone to the press. His "prefatory observations" on this occasion are particularly striking because they lay out some of his evolving methods of translation, philological scholarship, and comparative analysis.

Two of the Three

Legge begins his preface with an extremely abbreviated discussion of Buddhism. This was the one tradition of the "three religions" that was most problematic for him—both because of its original foreignness within the context of Chinese history and because he had never really attempted any serious translations of Chinese Buddhist texts. Although he eventually developed some technical expertise on Buddhism and published a translation of a famous Chinese Buddhist pilgrim's narrative (see below, pages 409–14), he is content here to mention only a few odd bits of information about the introduction of Buddhism into China and the translation of the Buddhist canon into Chinese.[103]

More important is the treatment of Daoism, which comes toward the end of his prefatory comments.[104] Given its "native origin" and the classical purity of the ancient text known as the *Tao-teh King* (or *Daode jing*, and translated here as *The Classic of Tao and Virtue*) attributed to the semifabulous sage known as Laozi, Daoism was more attractive to Legge than Buddhism was. Legge's comments at this time, though relatively sparse when compared to his discussion of Confucianism, demonstrate his growing intellectual sympathy and professional interest in this tradition, a trend that would continue throughout the next decade.[105]

The kind of living Daoism that Legge had encountered firsthand in China was mostly dismissed and ignored as a corrupt tradition that came about "in the course of time" through a syncretistic borrowing and process of mythological exaggeration, from the earlier classical text of Laozi, from later forms of Confucianism, and especially from the imported Buddhism. This popular Daoism retained "a morality of a high order in some respects" (hence the reason for singling out the popular *Ganying pian* for translation as *A Tractate of Actions and Their Retributions*), but it was basically "a system of grotesque beliefs and practices, ministering to superstition, and intended to refine and preserve the breath of life."[106]

The preface also shows that a new terminological question—that is, the meaning and translation of *dao*—was becoming a significant concern for Legge at this time. Very much in keeping with Müller's reflections on the translation of esoteric Oriental terms, Legge claims that the most sensible proposals for dealing with *dao* were either to leave it untranslated or to use "the Way, Reason, and the Word" as "thought by thought" transcriptions. He says that he was sorely tempted to translate it "by the Word in the sense of the Logos," but goes on to state that this "would be like settling the question which I wish to leave open, viz. what amount of resemblance there is between the Logos of the New Testament and this Tao, which is its nearest representative in Chinese." As seen in his subsequent considerations of this new term question (see below, pages 427–30), Legge tries several other possibilities before arriving at the conclusion that *dao* is best left untranslated.

Confucianism before Confucius

Most of the preface is taken up with a detailed consideration of Confucianism and the nature of its classical literature. Briefly discussing this tradition as the "religion of China par excellence" and the first of the "three religions," Legge stresses the foundational issue so dear to Western observers— that this is a tradition "named from the great sage who lived in the fifth and sixth centuries B.C."[107] Interestingly enough, Confucianism predates Confucius or Kongzi—which is a convenient finding that allows Legge to argue for the original or essential theistic religiosity of Confucianism even if the words of Confucius himself, as recorded in the *Analects,* were devoid of any specific appeal to the divine.[108] For Legge, "Confucianism" was the extremely ancient "system" of religious belief and reverent worship of the Chinese people that was not created, but only transmitted and morally reformed, by the Master Kong. This process seems similar therefore— although Legge does not make the comparison explicit here—to the emergence of Christianity as a religion named for Christ but prefigured in the ancient Hebrew scriptures.

Chinese books before Confucius do not "profess to contain any divine revelation," but "the references in them to religious views and practices are numerous." These documents are the crucial sources for constructing "an outline of the early religion of the people."[109] Leaving this historical outline of archaic Chinese religions to another time, Legge occupies himself with an annotated listing of the works making up the authoritative canon known as the Five Classics.[110] From this discussion it is clear that, although Legge had mastered most of the lower philological techniques practiced by both traditional Western and Chinese scholars, he had not fully embraced the higher, more radically historical and skeptical, methods (e.g., the text-critical methods of Julius Wellhausen or the Neibhurian *Quellenstudium* recommended to him by Eitel). Nor was he a practitioner of the speculative comparative methods of mythological analysis favored by some of the more radically modern Orientalists, folklorists, and anthropologists of the day. In this sense, some of Legge's views must be seen as old-fashioned by the most progressive Western (and Chinese) standards of the period.

The Book of Historical Documents

An example of Legge's approach to textual matters is seen in relation to his work on the *Book of Historical Documents,* the classic having, as he says, the "greatest importance." Legge must have been aware that eighteenth-century Chinese "evidential criticism" had shown significant sections of the *Documents* to be forgeries; and he was demonstrably sensitive to the fact that "the earliest chapters were not contemporaneous with the events which they describe."[111] Despite his awareness of the need to approach his material with a healthy degree of methodological agnosticism, he nevertheless made use of the old-text version (which included forged material), continued to believe in an exaggerated antiquity of the oldest parts of the text (and in the general credibility of the text's chronology back to the "twenty-fourth century B.C."), and affirmed the historicity of the sage kings Yao, Shun, and Yu even though he believed the events recorded about them had the "savour" of "legendary tales."[112]

This is not to say that Legge was unaware of the composite and contested nature of the text. Native Chinese criticism had already alerted him to many of these issues. Moreover, Legge makes a point of critically examining the sources for the *Documents* to see if there were "sufficient proofs of the composition in ancient times of such documents as it contains, and of their preservation, so that they could be collected in a sort of historical canon."[113] Impressive also is Legge's attempt to use astronomical data to verify the genuineness of some of the chronology found in the early documents. He therefore used a star chart (drawn up by an Oxonian colleague, C. Pritchard, the Savilian Professor of Astronomy) to verify the presence of culminating stars at the equinoxes and solstices around the time of Yao's accession to the throne—i.e., 2357 B.C. On this basis, it was Legge's rather sophisticated, though flawed, conclusion that, while the events recorded in the Yao section of the *Documents* were probably more legend or myth than history, it could be argued that "the compiler of [the Yao section] had before him ancient documents, and one of them must have contained the facts about the culminating of the stars."[114]

Myth and Non-Myth in Chinese Literature

Although mythology (Legge prefers to say "legend") is often rooted in actual historical events and personages and may make use of amazingly precise astronomical observations, Legge is reluctant to read his documents as consisting of material that is overly legendary, fabulous, mythological, made up, or fictional in nature. His reluctance is to some degree conditioned by the egregious failures of the sino-Aryan methods of "comparative mythology" and the general ridicule of Müller's theories of comparative mythology in the late 1870s. Much of the problem was simply that so much mythological theory at that time was based on comparative philological theory rooted in the study of Indo-European languages or on anthropological speculations about nonliterate savage tribes. The Chinese texts maintained their singularity with regard both to comparative philological and comparative mythological issues.

Even more important for Legge was his belief that the historicity of the Confucian scriptures approximated that seen in the Hebrew scriptures. Moreover, much of ancient Chinese history from the ninth century B.C. seemed to have astronomical confirmation (especially regarding the verification of references to eclipses). Even as late as 1892, after being criticized for an overly reverent attitude toward the coherence and factuality of the Chinese classics, Legge held onto the notion that the Chinese chronology of the classics was as accurate and convincing as almost anything seen in the Bible. As he said to an audience at the Royal Asiatic Society in London, the "existence of Yao, Shun, and Yu is not to be doubted. I could as soon doubt the existence of Abraham and the other Hebrew patriarchs in our Sacred Scriptures." Personages before the time of Yao (such as Fuxi, Shenneng, and Huangdi) were said on the authority of Ma Tuanlin to be only the "wild reveries of Taoist speculation."[115]

As we know from his continuing defense of the historicity of the Gospels and of Jesus' miracles, Legge purposely adopted an exclusionary and apologetic theory that did not allow for the application of the idea of myth to either the Christian or Confucian bibles.[116] No doubt this reflected his resistance to the conclusions of many comparative mythologists who were suggesting (along with Müller) that any trace of myth in a document tended to mean that the events and personages were entirely fictitious, imaginative, or reflective of linguistic maladies. Such a radically reductionistic conclusion—that figures such as Mohammed, Buddha, and Laozi, or even Kongzi, Moses, and Jesus, evaporated into the mists of archaic mythic musement—was too much to accept for someone of Legge's evangelical convictions, no matter how liberal he was on many other issues.[117]

Even though twentieth-century scholarship in China and the West convincingly shows that the accounts of Yao, Shun, and Yu are almost entirely based on a mythic structuring of events, there was much good sense in Legge's cautious approach to comparative mythological theory at the time he was writing.[118] There is no reason to believe that the discovery of legendary or mythic elements in an ancient text necessarily meant that the document had no astronomical, chronological, or real historical significance. It was a defensible position (in keeping with what Legge called the "stomach of our common sense") to distinguish among figures in ancient texts that were more or less legendary and mythic in nature.[119] There are, as Legge argues, significant differences in the degree of historicity in the traditional sacred accounts of figures such as Jesus and Kongzi on the one hand and the more overtly, or superstitiously, mythicized Siddhartha and Laozi on the other.

This is an interesting twist on another kind of argument concerning the specialness or strangeness of Chinese bibles when compared to all other scriptures—except, oddly enough, the so-called nonmythological Christian Bible. The two great exceptions to the corrupting influence of mythological thought in the history of religions were, from this point of view, the Christian and Chinese scriptures. Like the assumed special historicity of Hebrew and Christian scriptures when compared with the wildly imaginative, grotesque, and salacious mythology of other sacred books (especially Indian literature), the Confucian canon seemed to possess a dryly historical, prosaically moral, and expressly nonprurient nature that gave it, for someone of Legge's pietistic Victorian sensibility, a degree of pure religiousness and morality that came closest to the One Holy Bible. Once the Leggian quest for the theistic foundations of the Chinese classics became obsolete, it was still a convenient fiction of Western academic sinology to maintain the specialness of ancient Chinese literature in terms of its purely nonmythological, and therefore mostly nonreligious, nature.[120]

The Religious Content

Legge does not explicitly discuss in any synthetic way the religious content of the *Book of Historical Documents* in either the preface or introduction to the 1879 edition. This is curious because he does include such a synoptic analysis in the prolegomena to his 1865 edition of the *Documents,* and we would think that at this time, given his growing comparative interests, he would be even more candid and expansive in his evaluation of the ancient Chinese "knowledge of God."[121] That he is not more outspoken in this manner suggests that he preferred, in the aftermath of the Shanghai fiasco, to let the documentary texts speak for themselves.

In 1879, Legge was content "to call the attention of the reader to passages" that "more or less distinctly" embodied "religious ideas" by attaching an asterisk to them.[122] Since even a quick perusal of the new translation registers the many starred and, ostensibly, religious passages, it can be said that this version, even more than the earlier edition, makes an especially strong case for the pervasiveness of "religious ideas" and the consequent nature of this text as an authentic "sacred book."[123] The prominence of the asterisked passages sprinkled so liberally with an upper-case "God," or a theistic "Heaven," who blesses and punishes his people, cannot help but communicate the idea that the *Documents,* despite the obvious presence of various tutelary deities and the practice of ancestor worship, include a kind of theology of history, the "dominion of heaven" *(tianming)* doctrine.[124]

As reflected in his discussions of the *Book of Changes,* the *Book of Filial Piety,* and the *Record of Rites (Li ji),* Legge now views the Chinese "ritual books" more scientifically and comparatively as manifestations of the historical development of the Confucian religion. Furthermore, he now often views such latter-day ritual practices of divination and filial piety as repositories of significant moral, social, and religious meaning. This represents a notable change from the views expressed in 1865, when he confessed bleakly that, regarding something so blatantly "superstitious" as divination, it was "difficult to understand how the really great men of ancient China could have believed in it."[125] In 1879 it was not so much a matter of the "really great men of ancient China" believing in it, but an insinuation of Legge's own scholarly belief in its significance for an understanding of Chinese religious history.[126]

The Book of Poetry

Legge ranks the *Book of Poetry* as "second" only to the *Book of Historical Documents* in terms of antiquity and importance. Like the *Documents,* the *Poetry* is made up of diverse materials dating over a period from the early to the late Zhou dynasty (i.e., roughly from the first millennium to the fifth century B.C.E.; Legge argues that five poems are from the Shang). The long introduction is mostly a revision of his original prolegomena to the 1871 edition of the *Poetry,* but, as is often the case with Legge's revisions, there were just enough subtle changes to indicate his active rethinking of many key problems of decipherment. One good example of this, and something that again illustrates Legge's sympathy for Müller's theory of translation and interpretation, is a new paragraph stating his concurrence—and, he supposes, the agreement of most other "western Sinologist[s]"—with Zhu Xi's hermeneutical principle that interpreters "must find the meaning of the poems in the poems themselves, instead of accepting the interpretation of them given by we know not whom, and to follow which would reduce many of them to absurd enigmas."[127] Finding the meaning of apparent unmeaning is, as both Zhu Xi and Müller were suggesting, a matter of a translator-decipherer-commentator's discovering what was already symbolically hidden in the words and text.

The unstated parallel in both the 1871 prolegomena and in this introduction is the degree to which the ritual ceremonies seen in the "Odes of the Temple and the Altar" (which have elements of a sacrifice and a communal feast) are similar to priestly Hebrew rituals found in the Old Testament (particularly as seen in the Psalms).[128] So also does Legge unexpectedly suggest—in almost the manner of Robertson Smith—that the seasonal sacrifices ultimately had a sociological rationale in that they "were designed mainly to maintain the unity of the family connexion."[129] Functioning as a religious sanction, they were also "intimately related to" the Confucian moral duties of filiality.

Switching the order of paragraphs, Legge concludes his 1879 discussion with the passage he began with in 1871. This pertains to the "incidental" attention the Book of Poetry pays to the "worship of God." Seen most fully in the Book of Historical Documents, these sacrificial practices were intended to "serve Shang-Ti" and were "rendered by the sovereign" on altars at the time of the summer and winter solstices. These ceremonies were not alluded to in the Book of Poetry, but it is with respect to the reference to other "sacrifices to God" that Legge makes a small, but not insignificant, alteration. In 1871 he referred to the "divided opinion" of native Chinese scholars as to the existence of such passages in the Poetry. Now he drops the qualifying phrase to stress the "intimation" of such divine worship in two places in the fourth part of the Book of Poetry.[130]

The Book of Changes

Regardless of his inherent conservatism in technical philological issues, Legge by no means always accepted orthodox native opinion. A good example of this is his discussion in the 1879 preface of the "obscure and enigmatical" Yi jing, or the Book of Changes, a translation that became the standard English title of this work.[131] In keeping with iconoclastic native criticism, he explicitly rejects the claim that the Book of Changes is the "most ancient of all the Chinese classics." He does, however, accept the tradition that King Wen and his son, Duke Zhou, were the "authors of the text of the Yi." At the same time, he seems to accept the historical reality of the mythical culture hero Fuxi, who was traditionally dated to the "thirty-fourth century B.C."[132]

Anticipating his complete translation of the Book of Changes in volume 16 of the Sacred Books, Legge remarkably does not simply dismiss or condemn what Thomas McClatchie and other missionaries often saw as the most bizarrely heathen and symbolically licentious of the Chinese classical works.

Even though this text was connected with the idolatrous practice of divination and other "superstitious" activities, Legge says that it nonetheless touches, albeit "in a fragmentary manner," upon "many metaphysical, physical, moral, and religious matters." In this way, the "student of it"—and this statement is certainly self-referential—"is gradually brought under a powerful fascination."[133]

The Books of Ritual and Filial Piety

Legge says that the *Record of Rites,* which is only one of a class of "ritual books," does not "throw so valuable a light on the ancient religion of China as the older Shu and Shih" (the books of *Historical Documents* and *Poetry*). Special caution is always called for when using such ritual texts to assess the ancient religion. This is because they represent Han-period compilations that "sometimes put ideas of their own into the mouth of the sage [Kongzi], and made additions to the writings which were supposed, correctly or incorrectly, to have come from his immediate disciples." Despite these problems, Legge for the first time affirms the extreme value of these texts for understanding ancient Chinese "sacrificial worship" and the "ideas underlying it."[134]

The *Book of Filial Piety,* which unreliably purports to come from Confucius himself, may also be considered in the genre of the later ritual texts. In keeping with a Müllerian perspective on these matters (i.e., the evolutionary historical relationship among texts such as the *Rig-Veda, Brahmanas, Upanishads, Bhagavadgītā,* and *Puranas*), Legge claims that these later texts illustrate the developmental history of the ancient Chinese religion—that is, the passage from the earliest sacrificial "worship of God" to the gradual dominance of ancestral worship and a kind of religion based on the "cardinal virtue of Filial Piety."[135] Legge makes it clear that he believes an ethics based primarily on filial piety is "open to criticism in many respects."[136] At the same time, he suggests that these ancestral rituals and the related system of filiality were deserving of respectful attention and serious study. Celebrated by the Chinese as "the fundamental principle of human virtue," filial piety could also be sociologically understood as a "great source of social happiness and the bond of national strength and stability."[137]

Terminal Judgments

Legge concludes his preface to the first volume of the *Sacred Books of China* with a long excursus (pp. xxii–xxx) justifying another of the subtle but significant changes in his translation of the *Book of Historical Documents.* Aside from the starred passages signaling the "religious portions" and his use of a "larger apparatus of native commentaries," Legge says that he "wrote out" the whole of this version "afresh," but with hardly any "substantial" changes from his original translation in 1865. One of these very small changes—in 1879 he leaves the character *di* untranslated when applied to the ancient sage emperors Yao and Shun; in 1865 he had translated it as "emperor"—has, however, a bearing on his evolving ideas about translation and his views on the history of Chinese religion. Inasmuch as the term *di* in his estimation specifically refers to "God" or the Divine, Legge suggests that the two ancient heroes of Yao and Shun were, in the course of time, divinized in a way not unlike the process of euhemerization seen in other traditions.[138] As Legge says, it was by "a process of deification" that "the title of Ti came to be given, in the time of the Kau [Zhou] dynasty, to the great names, fabulous and legendary, of antiquity." And "thus," it was "applied to the heroes Yao and Shun."[139]

More important than this seemingly minor alteration is what Legge does *not* change regarding the other and more significant instances of *di* in this version of the *Documents* as a sacred book. He comments that, after much study and reflection, he had not "wavered" in the conclusion he came to more than twenty-five years ago: that "Ti [Di, Shangdi] was the term corresponding in Chinese to our 'God.'" Given this constant conviction through the years, he notes that he has rendered the special terms of *di* and *shangdi* "by 'God' in all the volumes of the Chinese classics thus far translated and published."[140]

What is extraordinary in 1879 is Legge's confession that he actually hesitated before continuing this practice in his first volume for the *Sacred Books of the East*. Showing his sensitivity to Müller's principles of accurate yet impartial "thought by thought" translation, Legge says that it was his understanding that contributors to the *Sacred Books* should "give translations of those texts without any colouring in the first place from the views of the translators." Recalling his embroilment in the long nightmare of the term dispute, and its most recent flare-up in Shanghai, Legge pointedly ponders whether or not his "own view of Ti, as meaning God" had primarily grown up "in the heat" of the controversies in China. He then explicitly states the perspectival dilemma of translation regarding *di* and the existence of a classical Chinese "high god" in a way that is as succinct and aptly problematic today as it was in his day. As he rhetorically puts it: "a reader, confronted everywhere by the word God, might be led to think more highly of the primitive religion of China than he ought to think. Should I leave the names Ti and Shang Ti untranslated? Or should I give for them, instead of God, the terms Ruler and Supreme Ruler?"[141]

Legge responds to his own query by rehearsing various philological theories to account for the divine implications of the "personal names" Di and Shangdi and, by association, Heaven or Tian. Here is the real reason for his careful consideration of *di* in relation to Yao and Shun and for honoring other Chinese emperors (e.g., Huangdi). It was necessary to explain this term's special usage (as a term of "deification") to overcome objections that it does not always mean "God" or the Divine. Calling these terms "personal names" is also an important categorical shift from Legge's argument in 1850 in which he maintained that both terms were "relative terms," rather than generic words or personal names in relation to grammatical usage.

"Being satisfied as to the proper signification of Ti as God," Legge concludes that he could not, except for the case of Yao and Shun, see his way to adopt the course of leaving it untranslated or to render it as "Ruler" or "Supreme Ruler." He was driven to Müller's principle of translating "thought by thought" rather than "word by word." His determination "to retain the term God for Ti and Shang Ti" in the *Sacred Books of China* was in this way rooted not only in theology but also in his scholarly integrity as a translator and in his role as a "real dicipherer." For Legge the English word (or "idea") of "God" fit "naturally into every passage where the character [*di*] occurs in the old Chinese classics," save in the exceptions already noted. It is therefore by virtue of his inductive judgments as a scholarly commentator-translator-decipherer, rather than as someone giving a missionary "colouring" to his work, that he can say that "I can no more translate Ti or Shang Ti by any other word but God than I can translate *zan* [*ren*] by anything else but man."[142]

THE INTERMINABLE QUESTION

If we look but steadily into those black Chinese eyes, we shall find that there, too, there is a soul that responds to a soul, and that the God whom they mean is the same God whom we mean, however helpless their utterance, however imperfect their worship.

MAX MÜLLER, *LECTURES ON THE SCIENCE OF RELIGION*, 1870

Reformers and Rumpers

None of the ideas expressed in the first three volumes of the *Sacred Books* was particularly startling for Orientalists or the learned public in Oxford, London, Berlin, or Paris. Legge's admitted hesitation in the face of the special problems of translating *di* and *shangdi* as "God" would, however, give license to his enemies back in Shanghai, Hong Kong, and Peking. Indeed, the missionary reaction to Legge's contribution to the *Sacred Books* represents yet another spasm of the ever-present term question, a convulsive groan that publicly linked Legge's heretical tendencies with Müller and the new comparative science of religions. The apocalyptic nature of the ongoing battle for the soul of the Protestant missionary movement in China is shown in the biting overview of the seemingly "interminable question" published at this time by John Chalmers.[143] He identifies three parties in the overall debate. One of these is the "Romanist" party, which has successfully made up its own word for the Christian God (i.e., Tianzhu). The Protestant parties include the Shangdi party or, as he calls them here, the "Reformers," made up of "all Germans, all English and Scotch Presbyterians, all Wesleyans and London missionaries." It is this group that is epitomized by the position taken by Legge. The third group is the Shin-ite party, which is composed mostly of Americans and followers of the Church of England. The different factions within this group, although often at war with one another, generally agreed in their hatred of the Reformers who heretically sanction the use of idolatrous terms such as *di* and *shangdi* and find significant religious and moral values in Confucianism.

Chalmers calls the Shin-ite party the "Rumpers" because they were, at that time, a "diminished body . . . much in need of a Cromwell." Two prominent members of the Rumpers actually aspired to the mantle of Cromwell (or Bishop Boone), and as Chalmers would have it, "conspired together" to revive the fortunes of the Shin-ite persuasion by embarrassing Legge and suppressing, once and for all, the dangerous comparativist implications of the Reform party. The first of these erstwhile Cromwells was A. P. Happer, the American Baptist editor of the *Chinese Recorder,* who published in his own journal, under the pseudonym of "Inquirer," a long public letter (also published as a pamphlet) to Müller condemning Legge's contribution to the *Sacred Books.*[144] The other conspirator was the Anglican bishop of Hong Kong, John Shaw Burdon, who organized, a few months after Happer's letter was published, another open circular letter to Müller vigorously criticizing Legge's new *Sacred Books of China.*[145]

This new flurry of furious accusations for the first time brought the implications of the earlier Shanghai affair out into the open in the foreign community in China and among the educated public in England. Even though he was writing from a biased position, Chalmers was correct in supposing that these terminological issues involving China reflected larger currents of change in the missionary movement and in the study of Oriental religions. Rejoicing in the "spirit" of these transformations and in the "cause of truth," Chalmers also accurately predicted that Happer's and Burdon's attacks on Legge and their appeal "to Max Müller and men of his stamp" would "in the end lead to a result which the appellants do not anticipate."[146]

Colored and Uncolored Translations

Happer's long and meandering letter in the *Chinese Recorder* opens with the criticism that the translations in volume 3 of the *Sacred Books* were "very seriously coloured" by Legge's distorted and predetermined view that the Shangdi of the Chinese classics was "the true God, the Jehovah of the Sacred Scriptures."[147] In Happer's estimation, Legge is concerned only with giving his own gloss on Chinese beliefs and does not adequately present the

Shin-ite position or the native Chinese understanding of the ancient terms. The intense emotional edge of Happer's position is indicated by his indignant observation that Legge had revealed his personal depravity on these matters by his notoriously blasphemous actions at the Altar of Heaven in Peking back in 1873.[148]

For Happer the whole debate was not an issue of terms or translation, but more fundamentally a matter of the obvious "facts" of Chinese religious belief and practice. And the clearest fact of all for Happer was the patently idolatrous nature of Tian. Thus Tian (and by extension Di and Shangdi) was only the crude deification of the material sky that was often dualistically paired with the deified physical earth. In this sense, the "chief god of the Chinese is a false god" and cannot be equated with the one true God of the Jews and Christians. What is worth noting here is that, even though Müller had already rejected the validity of using a classificatory system of "true and false religions," Happer ignorantly believed that Müller would be receptive to the old apologetic argument that the "general consent" of history held that all ancient nations, save the Jews, "worshipped false gods."[149]

More effective than Happer's critique of Legge, and more cleverly designed to sway Müller, was the circular letter signed by twenty-four missionaries in China that was forwarded to Müller by the Anglican bishop of Victoria, Hong Kong, John Shaw Burdon.[150] Although there was a distinctly disreputable side to his character, Bishop Burdon's self-estimation knew no bounds and he was, at that time, an influential figure in the missionary community in China. He was also an experienced ecclesiastical politician with a known dislike of Nonconformists and the "reforming" Shangdi-ites.[151] He was, in other words, someone to be reckoned with, and it was this circular letter, rather than Happer's earlier and more theologically effusive letter, that Müller felt compelled to answer.

Instead of claiming, as Happer did, a privileged awareness of the "facts" of Chinese religion and invoking theological theories about the deification of the material heavens and the origins of false religions, the circular letter wisely stressed issues of procedural fairness. Cutting to the heart of the matter, the letter appealed directly to Müller's "enlightened and liberal" integrity as a scholarly editor dedicated to impartial methodological fairness. In the circular letter more so than in Happer's missive, therefore, the basic argument against Legge is that his translation of *shangdi* as "God" is more of his own one-sided "interpretation" than an "uncoloured" translation. Since Legge's "interpretation of the term has been denied by persons as thoroughly qualified as himself to form a judgment on the subject" and the overall issue is a "still open" question, it was wrong for Müller, so "fearless in his love of truth," to give, in effect, his "imprimatur" to a partisan and unproven opinion.[152]

Müller's favoritism is said to be even more unjustified by the questionable claim that the Leggian position represents "the view of a very small number even of those who prefer to use 'Shang-ti' to make known the true God to the Chinese."[153] And it is this observation that shows that the letter writers' real concern is with a comparativist approach that, by suggesting that a heathen god such as Shangdi may be the same as the Jehovah of the Christian scriptures, dares "to think," as Legge put it in his preface, "more highly of the primitive religion of China than we ought to think." This last assertion by Burdon and his cohorts is something that was best kept to themselves as they, like Happer, did not seem to be aware that already in 1870 Müller had declared his high regard for a primitive Chinese theism.

From the very beginning of Müller's proclamations on the comparative science of religions as it applied to China, the issue was not the absence of any authentic religiosity, but more of a matter of uncovering the real theistic *meaning* of ancient Chinese religious tradition. For Müller in the *Lectures on the Science of Religion,* the basic inductive fact of early Chinese history was therefore that "the God whom they *mean* is the same God whom we *mean,* however helpless their utterance, however imperfect their worship."[154] It is this characteristic comparativistic emphasis on the real or essential, though symbolically cloaked, "meaning" of Chinese religion that allowed for, and even necessitated, an interpretive translation of certain terms over a merely literal translation (where *shangdi* means Supreme Ruler or Emperor) or a "transferred" translation (where the Chinese term is left unchanged).

Happer and Burdon have a point in their observation that most native Ruist commentators failed to perceive any kind of monotheistic meaning in the ancient texts and that a literal or "transferred" translation of *shangdi* would be the most truly impartial way to render this contested term.[155] In this sense, interpretations of *shangdi* as a "false god" or the "one, true God" are both impositions that ultimately derive from a similar kind of hierarchical and essentialized hermeneutical perspective. On the basis of the available textual evidence and native testimony, neither "meaning" can be definitively proven to be a pure "fact" or the single absolute and transcendental "truth" about ancient Chinese tradition.

Memento Mori

On November 1, 1880, Legge prepared a thirty-page response to some of the more conspicuous charges leveled against him. Understandably reluctant to become again a "controversalist" in the term question, he felt that, as his honor as a translator and scholar had been questioned, he had to produce a public response.[156] He tells us that the "strictures" on his scholarly methods in "Inquirer's letter" gave him "real distress" and "provoked" him into vindicating his views.[157] Müller, the acknowledged international arbi-trator of academic Orientalism, had, after all, helped Legge to secure his position at Oxford and had trusted his scholarly reputation enough to com-mission his contributions to the *Sacred Books*. It was one thing to have silently endured the aspersions of conservatives at the Shanghai confer-ence; it must have been exceedingly vexing for him to suffer such vocifer-ous missionary criticism directed against his first major work as an Oxford professor and as a collaborating colleague of the illustrious Max Müller.

Nothing specifically indicates that Legge was estranged from Müller dur-ing the months between Happer's initial epistolary assault and Müller's final reply in mid-December. Nevertheless, there is some indirect evidence that Müller was more circumspect in his relationship with Legge. This cool-ness is vaguely insinuated by the long delay of Müller's response even after Legge's letter, and more strongly intimated by Legge's distinctly guarded references to Müller in his private correspondence during this period. Per-haps the most direct suggestion of Legge's strained association with Müller is seen in a letter to Alexander Wylie in which Legge describes a meeting with Müller in Oxford in late November.[158] It was at this meeting with a cor-dial, though carefully observant, Müller that Legge found himself defend-ing his position on *shangdi* with the visiting Japanese minister Mori Arinori. Mori took the position that it was better to "transfer the word God phonet-ically to Chinese." After the meeting where nothing was resolved, Legge sent Mori a copy of his published letter to Müller as a fuller explanation of his views on the matter.

A few days later, Müller forwarded a letter to Legge from Mori, who, after giving Legge's letter "prolonged thought," came to the conclusion that "Dr. Legge is right."[159] As Legge tersely says at this point, "I expect this will have considerable weight with M.M. The judgment of a Japanese will be more prised than that of a more competent Englishman."[160] The accuracy of Legge's surmise is reinforced by the fact that it was only now, immediately after Mori's letter rather than after Legge's own letter of explanation, that Müller prepared his defense of Legge's contribution to the *Sacred Books*.

The Symbolic Theology of the Classics

Legge's weary November letter was directed primarily to Happer's charges and was circulated as a printed pamphlet. Adopting a tone of righteous in-dignation, Legge had no qualms now about referring quite openly to the "theology of the Chinese classics."[161] As seen from the views expressed in the *Religions of China,* these most recent attacks tended only to drive him even further into the camp of the comparative science of religions. Legge is, at first, pained to point out that the oft-quoted principle of avoiding any kind of translation "coloured" by the personal views of the translator was

not so much Müller's "rule" but Legge's own self-imposed, and fully rationalized, methodology as a sinologist. This was, moreover, a personal rule that
he had followed from the very beginning of his career as a translator and,
contrary to Happer's assertion, his translation of *di* and *shangdi* as "God"
was approved by a "majority of Chinese scholars."

The heart of Happer's argument (as it was of McClatchie's more erotic
understanding of these same matters) was that the belief and worship of Tian
was a idolatrous deification of the visible sky; and that, therefore, this "fact"
put the lie to any Chinese belief in the one true God. But, as Legge says, the
Chinese use of Tian is fundamentally the same as the English use of
"Heaven" to mean the idea or thought of "God." The crux of the issue for
Legge is precisely what Happer wanted to exclude—that is, not what may be
believed about the corruption of Tian in later history (as a Müllerian "disease
of language" perhaps), but "whether the Chinese may not have intended at
first to designate the true God by the visible Heaven as a symbol."[162]

Here for the first time, Legge enunciates a Müllerian-style theory concerning the original "symbolic" power of sensible language to express the
ideal concept or thought of the "shrouded" Divine, "nameless Something,"
"Unknown," or "Infinite."[163] The actual process, says Legge, "which formed
the nexus between the names of sensible objects and the concepts of the
mind is a thing shrouded from us at this distance of time from the infancy
of our race." Nonetheless, the "structure" and symbolic content of the Chinese character *tian* ("made up of two simple characters, which mean 'The
Great One'") hint that there was a "transference of Thien [*tian*], the name
of the sky, to denote the concept of God" as originally expressed by the
"personal names" of *Di* and *Shangdi*.[164] Unfortunately, he documents this
theory with only a loose accumulation of textual evidence (e.g., passages
concerning Chinese forms of prayer; the testimony of some native commentators; and a detailed, but rather convoluted, discussion of various
compound expressions using *tian* and *di*).[165] For Legge, this textual material shows that, before the deification of the visible heaven, there "must
have been" an originally pure "idea of deity in the minds of the worshippers." He concludes that the name for the original "idea of Deity was Ti;
the process of deification was by styling Heaven Ti, and intensifying the title by
the addition of Shang into Shang Ti."[166]

Going on to an almost rhapsodic discussion of *di* and *shangdi,* Legge suddenly alludes to his feelings of triumph and pain concerning the nature of
Chinese religion. Asserting again his claim to have discovered "more than
thirty years ago" the significance of *di* as God, Legge, with a rare display of
rhetoric and emotion, strongly affirms his convictions concerning an ancient Chinese monotheism. Truly "surprised" by the "tumult" his views
caused among some missionaries in China, he says that he will not temper
his scholarship to suit his enemies. Like Saint Paul, who must tell the hard

truth to friends and enemies, he declares that his "conclusions are correct."[167]

Perhaps the most daring expression of Legge's comparativist faith at this point is his explicit claim that, more so than other nations, the ancient Chinese had a special affinity with the ancient Hebrew tradition. Because the Chinese have "kept the monotheistic element prominent . . . down to the present time" and lack only an awareness of God's "self-existence" (as the Hebrew word *Jehovah* expresses), it is the special privilege of missionaries and scholars "to quicken" the Chinese to a full appreciation of God and "to testify" to them "as Moses was commissioned to do to the children of Israel, 'I AM—Shang Ti, the self-existent—hath sent me to you.' "[168] It may well be that, in making this statement, Legge is still holding onto a fundamental distinction between *shangdi* as the "idea of the true God" and the Hebrew divine terminology of *Jehovah* meaning "self-existent." Nonetheless, the clear import of the rhetorical style employed here suggests a congruence of divine names in the broad Müllerian sense.[169]

The rest of Legge's letter is a rather anticlimactic review of the term question. Restating his objections to the use of *shen,* which "properly" means "spirit," Legge also expresses his sympathy for the alternative use of Tianzhu, an artificial term used traditionally by the Roman Catholics and by a small, but growing, group of Protestants fed up with the ridiculous polarization of the other two camps. At the very end of this letter, Legge observes that, at one time in his life, he believed the term question to be "the most important controversy in the world." He now views such matters with more detachment and even suggests that he has attained a state of mind, and sympathetic comprehensiveness, superior to the sectarian pronouncements of missionary theology. For Legge, as it was for other aspiring academic Orientalists, the authoritative judge of most issues pertaining to general Oriental belief, philological scholarship, and interpretive theory was the imperious pope of the comparative sciences, Max Müller. "Rejoic[ing]" that such a great scholar had been called in to render his "judgment" on these agitated questions, Legge confidently waited for Müller's reply.

Papal Blessings

Legge was forced to wait for Müller's verdict to the point where his collegial patience must have been sorely tested—especially when we consider that it was Legge, and not Müller, who had looked "steadily" into "black Chinese eyes" and discovered the idea of God there. It was more than a month and half later, in mid-December, before Müller took pen in hand to address the tempest provoked by Legge's contribution to the *Sacred Books.* Given everything that had transpired, including a notoriety that had now spread to the pages of the London *Times,* it must have been heartening for Legge to see that Müller responded with a ringing endorsement of Legge's position.[170] Müller's reply was very much a vindication of Chalmers's prediction that Legge's missionary foes were only making trouble for themselves and for the viability of traditional missionary approaches to Oriental religions.

The tone of Müller's reply is that he is writing in support of his own position as the proprietary editor of the *Sacred Books* and as a theoretically disinterested promoter of the new comparative science of religions. This is understandable given the fact that both Burdon's and Happer's letters appealed directly to Müller's honor as an editor and scholar, but it is still curious that, even though the outcome of his reply is an endorsement of Legge's views, Müller nevertheless seems to avoid discussing Legge's specific arguments in any detail. I may be reading too much into Müller's benign neglect, but I cannot refrain from the suspicion that Müller sometimes adopted a vaguely patronizing attitude toward his older, and rather old-fashioned and less philosophically sophisticated, colleague.[171]

Müller indicates that he wished to deal particularly with the charge of "unfairness" implied by Burdon's letter. Although he had expressed his own belief that *shangdi* meant God as early as 1852, he readily admitted that it was "by no means easy to give a decisive answer" to the question of whether this term should necessarily be translated as "God" in a scholarly series like the *Sacred Books.* Despite his initial uncertainty, Müller declares himself in complete agreement with Legge's position that Shangdi in the "ancient scriptures" is a "name intended for the true God." Thus even though these same scriptures sometimes make use of a mythological language "inapplicable to the Supreme Ruler of the Universe," this only goes to show that the "sacred texts of no nation, not even of those of Jews and Christians, are entirely free from child-like, helpless, poetical, and what are called mythological expressions."[172]

Müller's most important point is basically to restate his own arguments as adapted by Legge's letter of November 1. From this point of view, words such as *heaven* or *Tian* originally functioned as metaphors for the pure idea of Divinity; only later in the course of time did they experience the partial degradation of mythological language. He suggests that Happer would definitely "not say that the Chinese, alone of all nations on earth, had never any word for God at all." This is because Happer himself admits that the Chinese "deified the sky" and, granting this, "how could people deify the sky or anything else without possessing an idea and a word for deity?" Even more decisive for Müller is the case to be made for the universality of the divine ideal and therefore against the specious classification of false gods and religions. As Müller rhetorically asks: "Are there any who still believe in the actual existence of false gods, or of gods not quite true?" For Müller, if not for Legge, all such individualized references to different gods (such as Bel, Jupiter, Varuna, Shangdi, and by way of inference, Jehovah) are but imperfect expressions or personal names of the one infinite God-idea. It is the recognition of the plurality of names for the Deity "as preserved in the ancient languages of the world" that displays the basic developmental pattern of religious history—that is, the "gradual growth of human thought and human language in their endeavour to find better and better names for what after all admits of no name."[173] But even in the relatively advanced religion of the Old Testament there may be, as there was in ancient China, the residual use of anthropomorphic, metaphorical, and mythological terms for Divinity.

It is the symbolic principle of the ideal sacred meaning hidden in all religions (the Infinite) that is central to the application of Müller's comparative science. He therefore declares that he undertook the publication of the *Sacred Books* in the spirit of Saint Augustine, echoing Saint Paul, who said "that there is no religion without some truth in it." In this way, Müller especially wanted "to make missionaries see that, hidden beneath a fearful amount of rubbish, and worse than rubbish, there are grains of gold to be found in every book that has once been called sacred by human lips." It is this remarkably open-ended belief in the possibility of finding something of value, something of the sacred, some idea of the Divine or Infinite, in every human tradition, whether Aryan or Turanian, that constitutes the methodological creed of "real dicipherers" such as Müller and Legge.

The Pauline Paradigm

This comparativists' creed represents the articulation of a new and more purely academic mission to translate, classify, and understand the languages and civilizations of the world. Yet at the same time—as both Müller and Legge knew well—this principle represents only a superficially secularized restatement of the Pauline methods of transcultural communication employed in ancient Athens. As recounted in the New Testament, it was on Mars's Hill, in a pagan city, that Paul has the sympathetic comprehensiveness not "to break the altar of the unknown God." But it was also Paul's impertinent greatness—in a sense as an Orientalist interpreter-decipherer—to presume that he knew more of the real, or hidden, meaning of Greek religion than the Athenians themselves: "'Whom ye ignorantly worship, Him declare I unto you.'"[174]

The political nature of the Pauline rhetorical paradigm is beautifully illustrated by the liberal American missionary John Ross, who generally favored a Leggian emphasis on the "whole duty of man" in missionary work. This implied the need for the "wise utilization of Confucianism" as a kind of "spiritual pablum" to break down the prejudice of the Chinese toward

Christianity. Confucianism becomes the "thin edge of the wedge of Christian truth," which, if used properly and selectively, will "gradually drive
home the whole body of truth." For Ross, this "thin edge" methodology is
primarily understood as an unsentimental application of Paul's methods on
Mars's Hill. According to Ross, the important lesson to learn from this biblical model is the need to adapt one's method to the circumstances at hand
and especially to be, as Paul was, "crafty" and as "wise as a serpent."[175]

It is this kind of serpentine guile, strategic tolerance, and hidden interpretive arrogance written into the heart of the Pauline paradigm that is
championed by missionaries (whether conservative or liberal) and comparative scholars (whether Orientalists, historians, or anthropologists).[176]
More than a simple matter of secretly shared universal values, Paul's story is
too often the tale of a velvet glove of outward sympathy masking an iron fist
of religious and interpretive domination. The Pauline narrative was ubiquitous in Victorian discourse about cross-cultural relations precisely because
it allowed for, and sanctioned, a camouflaged passage from the theological
absolutism of the traditional missionary enterprise to the accommodationist and supplementarian approaches to the liberal-secular values of the social gospel and, finally, to the ostensibly impartial and scientific approaches
of academic Orientalist scholarship.

CHAPTER FIVE

Comparativist Legge:
Describing and Comparing the Religions
of China, 1880-1882

[The study of the ancient religions of mankind], I feel convinced, if carried on in a bold, but scholar-like, careful, and reverent spirit, will remove many doubts and difficulties which are due entirely to the narrowness of our religious horizon; it will enlarge our sympathies, it will raise our thoughts above the small controversies of the day, and at no distant future evoke in the very heart of Christianity a fresh spirit, and a new life.

MAX MÜLLER, *INTRODUCTION TO THE SCIENCE OF RELIGION*, 1873

The study of [the Oriental religions] continues to be a duty, full of interest and importance. The results of it will throw light on the religious nature and wants of man, and show how adapted Christianity is to supply those wants and satisfy that nature. They will even help to give us, I believe, a better understanding of Christianity itself, and a more vivid apprehension of its doctrines.

JAMES LEGGE, *RELIGIONS OF CHINA*, 1880

DOUBTS AND DIFFICULTIES

The new decade of the 1880s was a bridge between the dutifulness of the earlier Victorian age and the coming cultural decadence of the 1890s and the global conflagrations after the turn of the century. A transitional period for the summing up and partial closure of earlier controversies, this decade, along with the last years of the century, witnessed the unfolding of new, more complicated and even more deadly, conflicts of body, mind, and spirit. The 1880s were the beginning, therefore, of a self-conscious fin de siècle time for the survival of the fittest in academic and professional circles. In the broadest sense, this period saw the drawing of an ambiguous line of demarcation between what was archaic and religious and what was modern and secular in Western tradition.

Among many material and cultural innovations, the 1880s witnessed the first practical utilization of telephones, electric lights, and vaccination; the invention of gasoline engines, typewriters, and linotype machines; and the discovery of radio waves. There was also an increasing literacy at all levels of British society and the zenith of agnosticism and atheism was reached among both the highly educated and the urban laboring classes—

developments that were paralleled by the new social activism of the Salvation Army and the emergence of the scientific supernaturalism of the Society for Psychical Research. This was a period during which there were, among many other notable social and cultural developments, continued efforts for the fuller emancipation of women in all walks of life; the steady progress of professionalization in higher education, public life, and organized sports, which led to the further retreat of the gentleman amateur ideal in England; the epoch-ending deaths of Disraeli and Carlyle in 1881 and Darwin in 1882; the ascendancy of Oscar Wilde's aesthetic dandyism, Herbert Spencer's sociology, Edward Tylor's evolutionary anthropology, William Gladstone's liberal politics, and Rudyard Kipling's and John Robert Seeley's high imperialism.[1]

The contentious thunder of religious conflict, especially in the protracted and clamorous war of the "natural" and "historic" sciences with traditional Protestant belief that was initiated in England in the 1850s, continued to rumble. By the decade of the eighties, however, the fractious roar of religious debate had mostly quieted down to a dull drone that affected, but did not overwhelm, most aspects of Victorian intellectual life. As in the sudden and protracted skirmish over Legge's translations for Müller's *Sacred Books*, passions connected with the validity and unique superiority of conventional Christianity were close to the surface and could erupt, in either agreement or dissent, at any moment. Unsettled feelings of confusion and doubt were especially felt when Victorian Christianity was comparatively confronted with the strange, yet hauntingly familiar (and linguistically familial), worlds of meaning made available by philological science, higher historical criticism, and the translations of sacred Oriental literature.

Such was the enthusiasm for things exotic and Oriental throughout the 1880s that there was, for example, an incredible popular infatuation with Edwin Arnold's heroic poetic biography of the Buddha (*The Light of Asia*, first published in 1879 but republished many times in Britain and America throughout the next decade)[2] and a more restricted, but ardent, interest in Mme Helena Petrovna Blavatsky and Colonel Henry Steel Olcott's esoteric quasi-Buddhist theosophy. These popular enchantments, as well as other more ephemeral and marginal productions, were culturally significant indicators of the climate of opinion in England at this time but, as Müller would constantly remind his more "scholar-like" audiences, they were also prime specimens of the despised "gems of Asian wisdom" genre.[3] These works were not to be equated with the bold and careful examples of the new comparative science of religions found in the complete, spiritual warts and all, translations of the *Sacred Books*.

In Europe and the United States during the last few decades of the nineteenth century, "comparative religions"—along with all of its attendant "doubts and difficulties"—reached new heights of interest among the general public and achieved increased professional acceptance among Orientalist scholars, folklorists, anthropologists, liberal theologians, and intellectuals of all sorts.[4] This was a trend that—as subsequently epitomized by the phenomenal popular success of James Frazer's erudite, but religiously debunking, *Golden Bough* (appearing in several different versions and editions between 1890 and 1922), and by the academic prestige of James Hasting's scholarly, though still reverent, *Encyclopedia of Religion and Ethics* (twelve volumes, 1908–1921)—would continue roughly until after the First World War.[5]

Novel Sentiments of the Decade

The emotional and intellectual temper of the 1880s in Oxford is evoked by the pious but progressive religious concerns found in Mrs. Humphry Ward's best-selling novel *Robert Elsmere* (1888) and by the languid aesthetic passions depicted in *Marius the Epicurean* (1885), an influential historical novel by the Brasenose College don and classicist Walter Pater. *Robert Elsmere* was a controversial and widely discussed roman à clef of changing religious views at Oxford and in Britain toward the end of the century—a veritable *Middlemarch* of the late-Victorian age. As illustrated by the transformations of the Oxford-educated cleric Robert Elsmere, the work's namesake and protagonist, this expansive and evocative three-volume novel was especially expressive of the liberal—both Broad Church Anglican and progressive Nonconformist—emphasis on equating "true" or "universal" religion with a socially engaged moral conscience. At an important turning point in the novel, Henry Grey, a character clearly modeled on the Oxonian philosopher Thomas Hill Green (see figure 28), summarily announced to the confused Robert Elsmere:

> The thought of man, as it has shaped itself in institutions, in philosophies, in science, in patient critical work, or in the life of charity, is the one continuous revelation of God! Look for Him in it all; see how, little by little, the Divine, indwelling force, using as its tools—but merely as its tools!—man's physical appetites and conditions, has built up conscience and the moral life; think how every faculty of the mind has been trained in turn to take its part in the great work of faith upon the visible world! . . . Learn to seek God, not in any single event of past history, but in your own soul,—in the constant verifications of experience, in the life of Christian love.[6]

These sentiments—particularly for a certain kind of concerned Christian and intellectual—were related to a "loss of faith" in the laissez-faire improvement of the lower classes within the great industrialized cities of England. At Oxford this kind of socially conscious religiosity and reform-

Figure 28. Thomas Hill Green, Fellow of Balliol College, Oxford, ca. 1880s.
Photograph from R. L. Nettleship, *Memoir of Thomas Hill Green*
(London: Longmans, Green, 1906), frontispiece.

ing mentality was inspired by Green, the evangelical moral philosopher
and "saintly" Balliol don, and other Oxford Idealists (such as Arnold
Toynbee and Benjamin Jowett), as well as by broad-minded Noncon-
formists such as Robert Horton, Andrew Martin Fairbairn (head of the
Congregationalist Mansfield College in Oxford; see figure 29), J. Estlin
Carpenter (head of the Unitarian Manchester College in Oxford), and

Figure 29. The Reverend A. M. Fairbairn, Principal of Mansfield College, Oxford, ca. 1880s. Photograph by Elliot and Fry, from W. B. Selbie, *The Life of Andrew Martin Fairbairn* (London: Hodder and Stoughton, 1914).

James Legge.[7] The attractiveness of Green for undergraduates was, in particular, the "union in him of the speculative and the practical." For Green—as for Legge and other educated Nonconformists of the period— it was necessary to affirm the connection between intellectual or spiritual ideals and practical ethical action.[8]

For some of these figures—such as Jowett, Fairbairn, Carpenter, and Legge—this kind of moral conscience and civic-mindedness was coupled with an interest in, from either a professional or a personal perspective, a careful comparative study of, and relative tolerance toward, Oriental religions and other peoples. As suggested by the climactic encounter between Robert Elsmere and Henry Grey in Ward's novel, the conclusions drawn from the comparative study of world religions, among other considerations of the higher historical criticism (exemplified by the Mark Pattison–

like antagonist known as Squire Wendover in *Robert Elsmere*), inexorably led to "doubts and difficulties" concerning conventional religious beliefs. More positively, these same considerations led sensitive and still devout men and women to see religion in its purer, and more essentially evangelical, meaning as the progressive unfolding of human moral consciousness.[9]

As we know from Legge's continued affirmation of New Testament supernaturalism, not all liberal evangelicals interested in the comparative science of religion would go as far as the Greenish or Müllerian rejection of miracles and their endorsement of the "scholar-like," yet "bold," belief that the total life history of the world, in the past and as projected progressively into the future, was the "one continuous revelation of God."[10] Nonetheless, all of the various shades of "scholar-like" comparativism, on a sliding scale from "reverent" to "irreverent," at this time generally agreed on the important reforming mission of the comparative study of Oriental religions. The difference was really a matter of the qualitative degree of moral insight among the various religions (whether a silver or a golden moral rule), or a developmental issue having to do with the point at which, in the historical scheme of things, the "life of Christian love" completed, fulfilled, and replaced Buddhist compassion or Confucian filiality. All agreed that the future was to be largely an unfolding of the "higher" values of Christian civilization, but at the same time all also tended to agree that an exposure to Oriental religions could, to use Müller's words as quoted by Legge, "evoke in the very heart of Christianity a fresh spirit, and a new life" that would rise above "the small controversies of the day."[11]

Walter Pater's *Marius the Epicurean* is a counterpoint to *Robert Elsmere* and represents a moment in the history of British thought and sensibility when "the repudiation of revealed religion by men of culture and intellectual leadership" coincided with a sometimes contradictory interest in the profane stylistic purity and iconographic religiousness of art and literature.[12] Whereas for Ward and Green, religion and true Christianity were to be found primarily in moral conscience and social action, Pater's work was a radical extension of Matthew Arnold's view that the essence of religion was expressed most fully and fervently in creative acts of pure linguistic or cultural production—performances of artistic artifice that did not necessarily have any moral significance or socially redeeming qualities.

Pater's "arts for art's sake" aestheticism in this sense contributed greatly to the decadent movement of Wilde, Aubrey Beardsley, and Algernon Swinburne at the end of the century and anticipates the irreverent modernist and secularist conviction in the irrelevancy of traditional religion. More than the vague but still "reverent spirit" of Green's Hegelian idealism,

Müller's Kantian comparativism, or Legge's sinological comprehensiveness, it is the decadent rejection of conventional religious belief and morality that lends itself to the broader, disinterested scientific and secular movement. It is this movement that renounced the academic legitimacy of orthodox personal belief and disenfranchised the study of religion and morality within the university.[13]

Müller's Depression

Within the learned world in Britain at this time it was becoming obvious that the conflict between religion and science had somewhat diminished. Individual battles over these issues, such as the controversies involving Legge and Müller, still flared periodically, but the larger war in British universities and in other circles of educated opinion was gradually being won by the forces of secular impartiality and methodological agnosticism. Science, especially in its naturalistic usage as an inductive and value-free method of experimental knowledge, was on the verge of triumphing decisively over theological forms of knowledge in institutions of higher learning and among the lay professions.

This victory, secured most definitively and hegemonically in European and American universities after the First World War, was the fulfillment of a naturalistic and materialistic understanding of science—a rationalistic epistemology and reductionistic modus operandi that revived the enlightened skepticism of the eighteenth century and excluded the kind of romantic and idealist tradition of the "human sciences" espoused by Max Müller and other early practitioners of the comparative sciences of philology and religion.[14] This kind of epistemological shift was, furthermore, not just benignly a-religious but—as it often was in the eighteenth century and as exemplified variously in the nineteenth century by the work of Auguste Comte, Herbert Spencer, Edward Tylor, and James Frazer—was more often than not aggressively irreverent and antireligious. These developments, especially within the increasingly secular academies of higher learning, also involved a general repudiation of idealistic presuppositions and comparative methods in philology and religion that sought to discover and classify hidden roots or symbolic meanings.

This move toward a more naturalistic scientific approach to humanistic knowledge was originally sparked in Oxford during the late 1860s by Müller's own revolutionary promotion of the Endowment of Scientific Research in English higher education. The fact that the professional and specialized academic understanding of "science" and "comparison" in relation to the study of human institutions was bypassing Müller in favor of Mark Pattison's style of skeptical rationalism—or the even less reverent Tylorian anthropological and Spencerian sociological approaches—only shows that, for all his celebrity at this time, Müller was increasingly viewed as old-fashioned and even vaguely supercilious. This progressively less deferential attitude toward Müller, at least on the part of fashionable undergraduate opinion at Oxford, is seen in various articles published during the 1880s and 1890s in the *Oxford Magazine*.[15]

Müller stubbornly ignored many of the more vicious personal attacks and seemed mostly oblivious to any deterioration of his academic authority and intellectual reputation. But, despite the outward show of confidence in his own scholarly immortality, there were various psychosomatic signs at this time that indicate that Müller was afflicted by a considerable degree of inner doubt and difficulty. The most suggestive hint of this is found in a letter dated January 1, 1880, in which, in the course of discussing a "long illness" involving a "troublesome liver," Müller reveals that his greatest problem had to do with a prolonged mental "depression" that, try as he might, he could not subdue: "One has no appetite, either physical or mental, and when one hopes it is passing away, the misery begins again."[16]

The fear of being branded an intellectual humbug and has-been was exacerbated by various other difficulties in Müller's scholarly life during the early 1880s. One of these unwanted problems was the prolonged altercation over the first of the *Sacred Books of China*. This is suggested by the simple fact that Müller's confession of a severe depression was communicated in a letter to the German sinologist Victor von Strauss und Tornay, a leading critic of Legge's first published translations for Müller. At about the same time and despite his handsome stipend from Oxford University Press, Müller was privately complaining about the "heavy burden" of his editorship—a situation that was made even more difficult by the need to defend Legge's surprisingly controversial volume, as well as the scholarly integrity and academic value of the whole *Sacred Books* series.[17]

The ordeal of Müller's life during the early 1880s was also affected by other disputes involving his controversial Hibbert Lectures, his support of Renan's visit to London and Oxford as the Hibbert Lecturer of 1880,[18] his exceptionally active schedule of multifarious public talks and scholarly meetings, and his solicitous, but frustrating, tutoring of Sanskrit with two Japanese Buddhist students at Oxford (Bunyiu Nanjio and Kenjiu Kasawara). Most bothersome of all, although he pretended to be above such petty concerns, was his increasingly embattled defense of his scholarship in the face of continuing attacks by the ubiquitous intellectual gadfly Andrew Lang and the fiercely tenacious American Sanskritist William Whitney.[19] These troubles were, moreover, aggravated by the depressing realization that, especially within the university, Tylor's anthropological—what Müller called the "ethnographic" or "theoretical"—approach to "savage religion" was winning more academic converts than was Müller's more romantically historiographic science of "book-religions."[20]

The Perfect Manhood of the Aryan Mind

This constant fighting over the methods and meaning of the humanistic sciences of comparison must have been upsetting to Müller's scholarly equilibrium and may even suggest some of the context for Müller's "wasting his time" in the early 1880s on a new English translation of Immanuel Kant's *Critique of Pure Reason*.[21] Defending the amount of time he was spending on his translation of the *Critique*, Müller admitted that he could not "explain it fully." His primary justification was that, despite the efforts of Hegelian idealists such as T. H. Green at Balliol, the utilitarian "English philosophy" was "still anti-Kantian" and that was like "anti-Copernican astronomy."[22] Müller hoped to show the English what all of continental Europe knew—that Kant, "construed" correctly, was the "*Lingua franca* of modern philosophy."[23]

For Müller, Kant's significance was also directly connected with the intrinsic progress and prowess of the Aryan tradition. The reason for this is that "while in the Veda we may study the childhood, we may study in Kant's Critique of Pure Reason the perfect manhood of the Aryan mind." "In the Veda," says Müller, "we see how the Divine appears in the fire, and in the earthquake, and in the great and strong wind which rends the mountain. In Kant's Critique the Divine is heard in the still small voice—the Categorical Imperative—the I Ought—which Nature does not know and cannot teach."[24] It is here that Müller's pietistic German heritage and Aryan Kantian Imperative find some strained Aristotelian affinity with Legge's Scottish common sense philosophy, his Wordsworthian poetic naturalism, and his dutiful evangelical affinity for the non-Aryan moral commands of the Confucian sacred books.[25] In this sense, both Müller and Legge were "still reverent" comparativists with a broadly similar, if certainly not identical, philosophical and metaphysical basis for their prophetic confidence in the progress of reason and religion.

In the Early 1880s

While Müller struggled with depression, Kant, and his editorial duties during the first few years of the 1880s, Legge was caught up in the tedious imbroglio over his first volume for the *Sacred Books of China*, and had also to contend with various infirmities of body and spirit. For someone who had just turned sixty-five most of Legge's health problems were relatively minor (such as his periodic bouts of gout and eczema), but he also suffered in June 1881 the tragic sudden death of his second wife, Hannah Mary, the "dear mama" to four of his children. Before the terrible trauma of Hannah Legge's premature death and despite the miniature tempest over his *Sacred Books of China*, Legge carried on with his professional and domestic life in his usual dutiful way. Various photographs from this period show a pros-

Figure 30. The Legge family at Oxford, ca. 1870s–1880s. *Left to right:* James, Helen Edith, Hannah, Marian, Anna, J. L., and Thomas. Photograph by Hills and Saunders, Oxford. Reproduced courtesy of the Legge Family Collection.

perous paterfamilias. In these staged images he comes across as a proud professor, patriarch, and "Papa" who doted benevolently on his children and grandchildren and basked in their respect and devotion (see figures 30–32).

A representative instance of Legge's more mundane habits at this time is that, when responding to a query on an article appearing in the London

Figure 31. James Legge with his daughters and grandchildren, Oxford, ca. 1890s: James, Helen Edith, Anna, and the Hunt and Collier children. Reproduced courtesy of the Legge Family Collection.

Times, he answered like the stereotypical comic Scotsman, saying that, instead of reading the *Times* every day as do most educated men in the city, he was "content" with "a cheap and brief newspaper." "I only go out to look at 'The Times,'" he says, "when I have knowledge that there is something of a peculiar nature likely to interest me in it."[26] This letter and his other extensive correspondence during this period shows that he had become something of a public factotum in Britain for all manner of learned and frivolous inquiries having to do with the curious Chinese. An example of this is a minor incident that appeared in the *Times* as well as in the more specialized *China Review* concerning what Legge called an impossibly "ridiculous" Chinese inscription found on one of the terra-cotta vases unearthed by Heinrich Schliemann at the site of the ancient Greek city of Troy.[27]

As the Western powers started—militarily, economically, and scientifically—to capitalize on their dominion over countries and archaeological sites throughout the entire world, such supposed discoveries and decipherments linking distant Oriental civilizations with the West were becoming more and more frequent. These findings, whatever their actual value, gave evidence of a growing climate for diffusionist speculation, espe-

Figure 32. *Legge in Repose in His Oxford Study*, ca. 1880s–1890s. Drawing, ink, artist unknown. (Ref. MS 380476/no.51.) Appears by permission of the Library of the School of Oriental and African Studies, University of London.

cially in terms of the ultimate "Western" origins of Oriental civilizations. After various phases of quasi–Tower of Babel theorizing about the possible Israelite, Egyptian, and Indo-European origin of things Chinese, the 1880s proved to be the "Babylonian era" of sinological Orientalism.[28] Furthermore, many of these developments directly involved Legge's second contribution to the *Sacred Books*—his interpretive translation of the enigmatic *Book of Changes*.

While diligently maintaining his regular academic duties amid the swirl of controversy over his first Chinese sacred books, Legge continued his involvement in Nonconformist activities at the university and at home (especially with the creation of a Nonconformists Union and the Congregationalist Mansfield College). The "Year Book" of the George Street Congregational Church in Oxford shows that Legge attended Sunday services regularly, contributed generously to various church and charitable funds (except, it is worth noting, to the yearly collection supporting the London Missionary Society), and, according to the "Church Records," diligently presided in the early 1880s over a series of special deacons' meetings charged with the difficult task of obtaining a new minister for a church with such a formidable congregation (besides Legge, James Murray and Andrew Martin Fairbairn were also members) and in a city with such an intellectual tradition. Legge proposed several outstanding candidates, including the brilliant young Oxford graduate Robert Horton, but his efforts were to no avail. Given his lack of success in these matters, the death of his wife, and his growing sense that his "association with the deacons was hindering rather than promoting the settlement of a pastor," he retired in November of 1881 from further involvement in official church affairs.[29]

Legge's courses for 1880–1881 mainly stressed the Four Books, Chinese historical writings, the Delegates' Version of the Chinese Bible, principles of composition, and, for the first time, readings of Fa Xian's Buddhist travelogue. During the first few years of the new decade Legge's primary scholarly labors consisted in his new translation of the *Book of Changes* for Müller and his production, as the outcome of a series of public lectures, of an expansive popular portrait of the native Chinese religions, published in 1880 as the *Religions of China*. This work stands out from Legge's more usual translations and commentary as his only attempt at a full-length interpretive synthesis in an explicitly comparative mode.

THE *RELIGIONS OF CHINA*

It is indeed a wonderful fact to think of, that a worship of the one God has been maintained in the vicinity of their capitals by the sovereigns of China almost continuously for more than four thousand years. I felt this fact profoundly when I stood early one morning by the altar of Heaven, in the southern suburb of Peking. It was without my shoes that I went up to the top of it; and there around the central slab of the marble with which it was paved, free of flaw as the coerulean vault above, hand in hand with the friends who accompanied me, I joined in singing the doxology.

JAMES LEGGE, *RELIGIONS OF CHINA*, 1880

Of religion, too, as of language, it may be said that in it everything new is old, and everything old is new, and that there has been no entirely new religion since the beginning of the world. The elements and roots of religion were there as far back as we can trace the history of man; and the history of religion, like the history of language, shows us throughout a succession of the new combinations of the same radical elements. An intuition of God, a sense of human weakness and dependence, a belief in a Divine government of the world, a distinction between good and evil, and a hope of a better life,—these are some of the radical elements of all religions. Though sometimes hidden, they rise again and again to the surface. Though frequently distorted, they tend again and again to their perfect form. Unless they had formed part of the original dowry of the human soul, religion itself would have

*remained an impossibility, and the tongues of angels would have been to human
ears as sounding brass or a tinkling cymbal.*
        MAX MÜLLER, *CHIPS FROM A GERMAN WORKSHOP*, VOL. 1, 1867

Shoeless at the Altar of Heaven

The first epigraph to this section yet again indicates that the controversies
surrounding Legge's work at this time often made reference to his fateful
pilgrimage in 1873 to the Altar of Heaven in Peking. That provocative
event was something that Legge continually, and almost liturgically, invoked as a touchstone experience validating the maverick scholarly direction of his early missionary life (going back particularly to his philological
and textual discoveries in 1850–1852, in which he maintained that
shangdi was the conceptual equivalent of the Hebrew and Christian God)
and also giving sanction to his latter-day mission as a professional academic and sinological Orientalist.[30] Much of Legge's later work, particularly his interpretive evaluations of Chinese religion, seems to flow out of
that epiphanic experience at the Altar of Heaven in northern China. It
was this daring act—and the unforgettable image of the shoeless Legge
bowed in praise of the Divine on the steps of the heathen Chinese altar—
that most rankled the theological sensibilities of conservative missionaries
back in China. For some, A.P. Happer in particular, there was almost an
obsessive fixation on the incident and a concern that Legge's scholarship—
whether translations for the *Sacred Books* or interpretive essays such as his
Shanghai paper—was forever and blasphemously compromised by the
comparativist attitude revealed by his actions at that rude pagan sanctuary
in Peking.

This kind of judgment could be applied, most of all, to Legge's *Religions
of China: Confucianism and Taoism Described and Compared with Christianity,* a
work that was originally given as a series of lectures during the spring of
1880 and then published in book form later that same year. No longer an
abbreviated and cautiously labeled "relational" essay as was his 1877 Shanghai paper, this much fuller work was now subtitled in a way that indicated
Legge's straightforward intent to "describe and compare" Confucianism,
Daoism, and Christianity. The *Religions of China*—in book form more than
three hundred pages in length—was nothing less than Legge's attempt to
work out interpretively the embryonic implications of his terminological
findings published in 1850 and 1852, his pilgrimage in 1873 to northern
China, his 1877 Shanghai paper, and his 1879 preface to the *Sacred Books of
China*.[31] This monograph includes an especially detailed decipherment of
Confucianism along with the important added dimension of a sympathetic
discussion of the "philosophy and religion" of the tradition called "Taoism."

Whereas Confucianism and Buddhism had both been recognized as specific types of Oriental religion by this time in Europe and America, Daoism was only then, in the late 1870s and through the 1880s and 1890s, entering into Western consciousness as a textual object.

A Pioneering Study

Legge no doubt seized upon the invitation to give his "Religions of China" lectures to a Presbyterian group in London as a welcome opportunity, within a respectably conventional venue, for a full-scale response to his critics and antagonists. Seemingly taking Müller's confidence in him as a "real decipherer" rather than just a "mere translator" to heart, Legge eschewed translation to produce his longest and most coherent inductive interpretation of Chinese religious tradition, now notably understood in terms of an indigenous historical plurality of the "Confucian" and "Taoist" religions. Buddhism, the other of the traditional "Three Teachings," was ostensibly not discussed at length because it was originally a foreign importation into China. Furthermore, Legge simply had not yet seriously studied Chinese Buddhist literature.[32]

The *Religions of China,* along with Legge's writings in 1850–1852 and two other shorter, and later, comparative studies (*Christianity and Confucianism Compared in Their Teaching of the Whole Duty of Man* [1883] and "Confucius the Sage and the Religion of China" [1889]),[33] constitutes the most important synthetic statement of Legge's evolving "spiritual discernment" of Chinese religious tradition. More than the "disappointing" and unrealized promise of Ernst Faber's *Introduction to the Science of Chinese Religion* (1879),[34] the *Religions of China* also represents the first full-blown attempt to apply the methods of a Müllerian-style comparative science of religion to Chinese tradition.

Though almost completely outdated in relation to the present-day scholarly understanding of Chinese religion, and a discouraging confirmation of Legge's dogged analytical skills and stolid style, the *Religions of China* is nevertheless a pioneering work in the Western study of Chinese religions. A best-selling book that went through several British and American editions, it was the benchmark sinological statement on its subject until the appearance of J.J.M. de Groot's more anthropologically informed and descriptively rich *Religious System of China* (six volumes, 1892–1910) and Édouard Chavannes's amazingly erudite monographs combining ethnography, textual analysis, and historical criticism (e.g., *Le T'ai Chan,* 1910). Despite its sometimes annoying weaknesses and apologetic indulgence, this is a work that deserves our careful attention—for what it says and does not say, comparatively and relationally, about Chinese religions as well as for its particular rhetorical demeanor and theological bias. Legge's *Religions of China* is unquestionably a significant document in the meager disciplinary history of nineteenth-century sinological Orientalism.

Things Admitted by All

The *Religions of China,* originally presented as the Spring Lecture for the Presbyterian Church of England, was delivered at the Presbyterian College, Guilford Street, London. The traditional Protestant evangelical expectations for these lecturers were considerably different from, for example, the expectations for the pointedly iconoclastic "scientific theology" and "natural religion" of the Hibbert and (later) Gifford Lecture series. It is in this churchly context that the basic refrain of "no distinction in kind" uttered by Müller as the high priest of comparativism is ameliorated in favor of Legge's own more apologetic theological stance on these matters.[35] As Legge rhetorically asks toward the end of his analysis in the *Religions of China:* "And now the train of my reasoning has brought us face to face with the question:—Is the difference between Christianity and the religions of China in kind and not merely in degree? Is it THE religion while each of them is merely a religion?"[36]

The necessary answer to such artificial questions would be obvious to Legge's Presbyterian audience and, for all of his "sympathetic comprehensiveness" toward Chinese religion, he does not hesitate to give them the "foregone conclusion" they wanted to hear.[37] For Legge, the issue becomes one of the reasoned affirmation of the "supernatural" and the traditional gospel accounts of the miracle of the "resurrection of Christ."[38] It is still the general theological worldview, if not the ethics, of the Westminster Confession of his childhood that is operant here.[39] The supernaturalistic metaphysics and anti-Humian "evidence" for New Testament miracles are the factors that for Legge, rather than for Müller, put Christianity on a plane infinitely higher than all other religions.[40] Legge suggests that there is a real difference "in kind" that goes beyond "mere degree." Given the nature of his audience and his own religious convictions, we should not be surprised to discover that part of this last section is a triumphalistic inventory of how Christianity is "incomparably greater" than are the religions of China.

Legge obviously feels a need to maintain his intellectual independence in relation to some positions held by Müller and the even more audacious American generalist scholar and transcendentalist Samuel Johnson. As we already know by virtue of Legge's suspiciously positive review of Johnson's brilliant comparative work on the Orient and "universal religion" (see pages 213–14), there was always the danger that Legge would be too closely identified with this "greatest enemy of Christian missions." Legge makes a special effort therefore to repudiate the "insubstantial hope" that by the "eclectic process" of comparatively adding together the important truths of the different religions, we may "frame a universal religion that will supersede Christianity itself."[41]

What is really interesting is that Legge seems, almost willfully, to compromise some of the hard exclusivity of his answers to various catechismal queries about the kindred similarities and defining differences among religions. A careful examination of this section of the book shows that he actually softens the need to reject Müller's principle of "no difference in kind." Thus Legge only modestly affirms, in the course of a long and somewhat convoluted discussion of the supernatural and miracles, the safe and conventional response that everything hinges on the uniqueness of the Christian miracle of resurrection. In the wake of his roundabout profession of a traditional faith in the singularity of Christ, he also manages to stake out the unexpectedly provocative position that *both* Confucianism and Daoism, in the purity of their foundational, classical forms if not in their corrupt later manifestations, share some essential kinship, some "divine stamp," with Christianity. These Chinese traditions are in this way fundamentally akin to the ancient Israelite religion that needed to be "fulfilled" and "completed" by the coming of Christ. One of the really distinctive aspects of the *Religions of China*, when compared with Legge's earlier writings, is its explicit, and repeated, comparison of Confucianism and the Israelite religion as described in the Hebrew sacred books or Old Testament. Legge had hinted at such a troubling analogy before (originally in *Notions of the Chinese Concerning God and Spirits* [1852][42]), but never had the correlation been so outspoken and exact, even to the extent, in some ways, of favoring the Chinese "Old Testament" to the Hebrew scriptural dispensation. As Legge declares, "all" of them—that is, "Christianity, Confucianism, and Taoism"—"allow the element of the supernatural, all assert the fact of revelation, all acknowledge the existence of God." No matter how it is qualified, this assertion does, then, suggest a similarity of "kind" that is intrinsically related to the historical question of the "purity" and "degree" of the "divine stamp" on the Chinese religions. Legge even has the nerve to say that "[o]n each of these points there are great differences in the three religions when we go into detail; but the things themselves are admitted by them all."[43] I need only underscore the principle that "the things themselves"—the essential religious ideas and universal moral ideals—are what finally should count in the comparative enterprise as conceived by Müller.

The Path of Duty

Legge's views are really more subversive than they might first appear. The *Religions of China* should therefore be read in a way that teases out some of its disguised qualities. The seemingly bald finality of Legge's claim that the "record" of the *Sacred Books* shows us the "most important distinction" between Christianity and the Chinese religions is less than unequivocal. The distinction is simply that "THEY [the Chinese religions of Confucianism and Daoism] are of men and by man,—not without God indeed, but with Him only as all things are included in the circle of His knowledge and ordination; IT [Christianity] is of God, and by God, specially revealed to make known the path of duty and the way of life."[44] The problem with this formulation of natural and special revelation is apparent and is the cause of the dilemma that gnawed at Legge's conscience as a Christian missionary and as a comparativist scholar. It is the human moral issue, or what might be legitimately thought of as the humanistic or Confucian issue of the social transactions "of men and by man," that is at stake.

At the very end, Legge raises two "practical issues" that go to the heart of the moral matter and are clearly related to his rejection of the Calvinistic theology of the *Shorter Catechism*. The first of these practical ethical issues is the presumptive conclusion, granting that the "true Christian is the highest style of man," that "only" the Chinese "adoption of Christianity . . . will enable the people to hold their own, and lift them up in the social scale." Even though he says that he has come to "think highly" of the "actual morality" and "intellectual capacity" of the Chinese—indeed, "more highly . . . than many of our countrymen do"—he declares that "their best attainments in moral excellence . . . are not to be compared with those made by docile learners in the school of Christ."[45] The second "practical" moral issue undercuts the inevitability of the conclusions Legge had just drawn about the superior moral excellence practiced by the "docile learners in the school of Christ." This issue is the crucial evangelical issue of embodied moral character and the actual behavior of men and women in the visible world. Although Legge does not make the connection here, this is also the crucial Confucian issue as well. It is this problem that raises the increasingly heated missionary question of why Christianity had not triumphed in China. From Legge's postmillennialist theological perspective—and equally from a Müllerian comparativist standpoint—the answer cannot be that "God's purpose slumbers," but rather that the current failure has to do with the moral deficiencies of individual Christians and "so-called Christian nations."[46]

The tragic dilemma is that—in relation to the "divisions" among churches, the "inconsistencies and unrighteousness" of missionaries, and the "selfishness and greed" of the commerce and policy of Christian nations—Christians "must blame themselves" for the failure of Christianity in the Orient. The ultimate practical issue can consequently only be one that is a "path of duty of men and by man." This, in the final analysis, reestablishes the fundamental moral kinship of Christianity and the Chinese religions and again raises the quandary of whether Christianity can be comparatively and honestly judged as morally superior. It is this most human of issues—and the difficulty, if not the impossibility, of definitively weighing the relative moral worth and ethical "progress" of different "persons," "religions," and "nations"—that gives pause to Legge's deliberations about the justifications for a religious and scholarly mission to the Orient.

Just as Legge was arriving at some cautiously confident conclusions about the imminent triumph of missions in China (such as during the early years of the Taiping rebellion or in relation to later developments in Poklo) or the absolute superiority of Christianity in relation to all other religions (as in his earlier sermon, "The Land of Sinim," delivered in 1859), some unexpected person or event would intervene to sow doubt and confusion. Although partly an outcome of his more profound comparative appreciation of the Chinese classical texts and sacred books, the most powerful and creative form of this ambiguity was provoked by Legge's ritual pilgrimage in northern China and his practical encounters with various living representatives of Chinese tradition.[47] This kind of existential moral quandary is also seen in Legge's concluding "musement" in his 1877 Shanghai paper (see page 226). But ever since his return to England, it was especially epitomized by his several challenging personal exchanges with Guo Songtao over the morality of Britain's opium policy.

Which Is the Better?

The *Religions of China* ends with Legge's retelling the story of his "conversation with His Excellency Guo Songtao, the former Chinese ambassador, soon after he arrived in London in 1877." I have already referred to Guo's account of this meeting (see page 197), and here Legge's own poignant version of the incident is seen. The crux of the conversation was, according to Legge, the Chinese ambassador's insistent question about which of the two countries, England and China, was "better" from a "moral standpoint" of "benevolence, righteousness, and propriety?" Legge says that, "after some demur and fencing," he replied, "England"—an answer that amazed and befuddled Guo. "I never saw a man more surprised. He pushed his chair back, got on his feet, took a turn across the room, and cried out, 'You say that, looked at from the moral standpoint, England is better than China! Then how is it that England insists on our taking her opium?' "[48] The fact that these are the very last words in the *Religions of China* and that Legge chooses to conclude his comparative analysis with a story of an unanswered question about the relative morality of different traditions is surely noteworthy. At the end of the comparative enterprise is not catechismal certitude or more evidence for the "foregone conclusion" of Christian superiority, but a moral question that, from both an earnest Evangelical and an earthy Confucian standpoint, leaves all easy apologetic or theoretical answers hanging.

To be fair to Legge, the comparative question of national morality does not rest (as Legge carefully phrases it for Guo) on the issue of an existing "Christian England," but on "England" in relation to its own partial Christianity and moral diversity. Viewed from a Evangelical standpoint, this issue had both a prophetic and moral poignancy alluding to both China and England. As a Nonconformist, Legge normally would distinguish between England in general and a Christian England, whereas we would not expect Guo to do so on his own. This is an important consideration because the moral force of Guo's question hinges on the issue of opium and this was, for Legge, a matter that could be used to characterize a truly Christian position on English national policy. Even as early as 1861 Legge had challenged British imperialistic policy involving military force, an act that was for him, like his condemnation of the opium trade, a prophetic challenge to the often tragically compromised, immoral, and fundamentally non-Christian ruling factions in Britain.

More so than the philosophical and poetic Müller, Legge ploddingly brings the comparative question back to the practical and experiential issue of building moral character and living up to one's theological and ethical duty. Legge's practical bent as primarily an indefatigable translator-commentator-decipherer, rather than as a mesmerizing thinker-philosopher-scientist, is also suggested by his preference, after his apologetic and philosophical resources were exhausted in his more analytical works, for invoking the anecdotal testimony of his own life and answering unresolved questions with other difficult questions. His motivations are, to be sure, part and parcel of his Scottish Dissenter tradition, which stressed the importance of a true Christian's prophetic and pragmatic responsibility to confront evil wherever it may be found abroad or at home. At the same time, these convictions were clearly stretched by his newfound moral comprehensiveness as a professor and comparativist. Legge thereby manages to maintain his own moral integrity as a Christian and comparativist scholar while, at the same time, responding to, and respecting, the meaning and moral worth of "the things themselves." This unusual toleration and respect for the ambiguity engendered by a dialogical encounter with the heathen otherness of a person, text, or tradition is a scholarly duty that seems to define the comparative method for Legge as much as the "whole duty of man" (Ecclesiastes) describes the path of moral responsibility for a faithful Jew and Christian.

En Rapport *with the Chinese Fathers*

Because much of *Religions of China* is an elaboration of various descriptive and analytical factors already discussed in relation to Legge's writings in the late 1870s, I will highlight only those issues that are new and distinctively expanded or altered. This means that some passing attention should be paid to the book's first two sections devoted to Legge's evolving understanding of his favorite topic of Confucius and Confucianism. Also important is the surprisingly sympathetic third section on the Daoist system. His views in this work are the crucial foundation for his later translations of, and discussions about, the Daoist texts and tradition (especially his two-volume translation in 1891 of the *Texts of Taoism* for Müller's *Sacred Books*).

Legge begins his investigation of Ruist tradition by making it clear that Master Kong must be considered to have been a "religious teacher" and that the tradition associated with his name has the primary characteristics of a revealed religion, especially with regard to its ancient monotheistic doctrine and worship. Most important here is his explication of ideas that were only vaguely hinted at previously—one of the most important of these being the more precise definition of "Confucianism" as, first, the "ancient religion of China" and, only secondarily, as "the views of the great philosopher himself, in illustration or modification of it." For the first time, Legge makes it explicit that, in this respect, Confucianism is "pretty much as when we comprehend under Christianity the records and teachings of the Old Testament as well as those of the New."[49]

Responding to various articles in specialized sinological journals such as the *China Review* that argued for the nonreligious and skeptical nature of both Confucius and Confucianism, Legge enters into a elaborate descriptive presentation of the evidence for an ancient Chinese "doctrine and worship of God." In fact, the whole first section of *Religions of China* is taken up with his elaborate defense of this proposition, many of the particulars of which were already present in his writings going back to the 1850s. Until his appointment as a professor at Oxford, Legge's views were largely identified, even by missionary friends such as William Muirhead, with the position that found the Chinese sage Confucius, and the Confucian tradition, to be basically nonreligious or a-religious, if not skeptical, agnostic, or antireligious. "Religion," after all, had to do with the "relation between man and a living God" and was not just a "system of morals intended for the government of human society"—although it was clearly that also.[50] Based on this understanding, most of the first two lectures were devoted to an explication of the ancient Chinese belief in a monotheistic God and in the practices of "worship" and "prayer" that, despite inevitable corrupting factors, maintained the "relation between man and a living God." None of this, to be sure, was completely new to Legge (see, e.g., his *Notions of the Chinese Concerning God and Spirits* [1852] and his 1877 Shanghai paper), but it is interesting to see how he now develops these ideas with the explicit academic methods of comparative philology and religion.[51]

For the first time, Legge specifically appeals to the Müllerian evidence of philological roots that go back "to a period long anterior to the composition of the most ancient Chinese books." Legge says that he is attempting to determine some of the foundational ideas of the "fathers of the Chinese people" by studying Chinese "primitive characters" in the same way that "Aryan philologists" tried "to give us pictures of the earliest Aryan life" based on Sanskrit root words. Despite his caution concerning the "difficult and uncertain" quest for roots, it is clear that Legge has decided at last to try his hand at a comparative philological analysis of Chinese that built upon his early terminological studies in 1850–1852, something he has only hinted at and drawn back from before (in, e.g., his papers for the *Royal Asiatic Journal* and for the Congress of Orientalists in Florence).[52]

Legge is even bold enough to suggest, without any real discussion, that an analysis of Chinese roots in relation to the "pictures and ideagrams" of the "primitive written characters" has a distinct advantage over the more phonetically dependent Sanskrit. The hidden "meaning" of the Chinese "primitive characters" can consequently be deciphered without any "reference to the names by which they have been called." And, as he adds, "according to the sentiment of the line in which Tennyson condenses two well-known lines of Horace: 'Things seen are weightier than things heard,' "[53] Legge is remarkably enthusiastic about the possibility that this mostly untested, and increasingly ridiculed, method of analyzing the Chinese language will "put us *en rapport* with the Chinese fathers fully five thousand years ago." Indicating that the results obtained may in the long run be even more important that those derived from the less visually aided study of Sanskrit, Legge indulges in the uncharacteristically overwrought and typically Müllerian observation that "from no other source do we obtain information so important and reliable concerning what we may call the religion of infant man."[54]

After all of this dramatic buildup, it is disappointing to discover that what Legge sees hidden, after "some toilsome digging," in a select group of "primitive written characters" (not surprisingly, *tian* for "heaven or sky" and *di* for "God," but also *qi* for "spirits," *shi* for "revelation," *gui* for "manes [ghosts] of the departed," and *bu, gua,* and *kau* as three interrelated terms for "divination") is nothing very new or particularly exciting. It is the term question revisited, only now gussied up with some "comparative philological" nomenclature. In this sense, the conclusion from Legge's philological quest mostly tends to corroborate what he already knew from the classics as early as the 1850s: that the primordial religion of the ancient Chinese people was an amazingly pure monotheism.[55]

With the "results derived from the primitive characters," Legge gives several new interpretive twists to his subject. One of these findings is simply that now the ancient Chinese monotheism could be extended as far back as "five thousand years ago" and that this original monotheistic religion did not appear to have been "henotheistic" in the way that Müller described the ancient

Vedic religion. This fundamentally pure monotheism was, nonetheless, subject to the corrupting influence of "nature worship" and "superstitious divination." Here Legge is particularly exercised to counter Cornelis Tiele's classification of the "old religion of China" as an "animistic religion" having a "fetishist tendency" that was "combined into a system before it was possible for a regular mythology to develop out of it."[56] For Legge, animistic spirits in ancient China were worshiped only because of "the relation that they are supposed to sustain to the worshippers, and to the Supreme Spirit, or God."[57]

Based on his study of the oldest of the classics (especially the *Book of Historical Documents,* the *Book of Poetry,* and the *Book of Changes*), Legge had already come to the conclusion that the early historical development of the ancient religion, particularly from the period of the primitive characters down to the "twenty-third century B.C.," shows the emergence of a kind of "twofold worship" tradition—that is, worship of the High God (Shangdi/Tian) by the ruler of the state and the worship of the ancestors by the heads of families. Much of his historical discussion—especially concerning the period of Yao, Shun, and Yu recounted in the *Book of Historical Documents* and the *Book of Poetry*—is only a more elaborate presentation of this basic thesis, now fleshed out with additional classical quotations and methodological observations concerning henotheism, animism, fetishism, and a kind of Müllerian "disease of language" problem involving the Zhou period usage of the dualistic expression "Heaven and Earth."[58]

Legge stresses that the Chinese are especially impressive for having "guarded against" the usual mythological corruption of the expression "Heaven and Earth" and the imperial worship at the twin Altars of Heaven and Earth in Peking. As in his terminological writings from the 1850s, Legge declares that one of Confucius's primary contributions toward maintaining the purity of the ancient religion was to have declared clearly that the solstitial sacrifices to Heaven and Earth were "those by which we serve Shang Ti."[59] Even though the "dualistic name" of Heaven and Earth "unfortunately" continued throughout the rest of Chinese history, the imperial traditions of prayer preserved the purer spirit enunciated by Confucius. This was a tradition of prayerful thanksgiving that was, according to Legge, found in the solstitial ceremonies of the Ming and Qing emperors. These prayers were also, it seems, Legge's primary justification in 1873 for singing the Christian doxology upon the Altar of Heaven in Peking.

Interpreting the Most Mysterious of Classics

Legge then turns to an unusually lengthy digression on the "mysterious" *Book of Changes (Yi jing)* in relation to the issues of imperial worship and the apparent duality of Heaven and Earth. At this time, he was already working on a translation of the *Changes* (as well as the *Liji* or *Record of Rites*[60]) for

Müller's series. He wanted to take advantage of this occasion to answer the charges of the hypereclectic Canon McClatchie (whom he refers to as "M'Clatchie"), who claimed that the *Book of Changes,* more than any other of the classics, showed the blatant polytheistic, idolatrous, and pornographic nature of ancient Chinese religion. Identifying his position with that of Matteo Ricci, Legge still seemed to be in the midst of his own self-administered exorcism of the dark, nightmarish specters of the term debate. At the same time, he was proving to himself, and other professional sinological skeptics such as Eitel, that an appeal to Müllerian comparative methods need not necessarily result in McClatchie's patently silly and smutty conclusions (see pages 370–71).[61]

"What do we find in the Yi?" Legge's fullest answer to this question, an issue that still puzzles sinological scholarship, is given in his translation and commentary in volume 16 of the *Sacred Books of the East,* which appeared in 1882. In the *Religions of China,* the answer is largely a matter of, first of all, realizing that the *Book of Changes* is not the oldest of the classics, an honor reserved for parts of the *Book of Historical Documents* and *Book of Poetry.* Furthermore, Legge admits that, given this text's divinatory purpose and symbolic system of lines, "a reader must be prepared for much in it that is tantalizing, fantastic, and perplexing." The process of change indicated by the lines of the text is, however, a process symbolizing the principle of generalized "antinomies" in natural and human life—not, as McClatchie would have it, of a ruling "sexual antinomy."[62] Legge has to admit that the *Changes* is a work of "strange physical speculation, constructed so as to serve the purpose of divination, and affords us little help in studying the subject of religion." This practice of divination was, moreover, the manifestation of a superstition that "had infected the minds of the earliest fathers," a matter shown both by the early texts and by a more sober philological analysis of the Chinese "primitive characters."

Despite this superstitious element, Master Kong sensibly gave the text a "moral and ethical character" and explained the linear figures in relation to the processes of seasonal change, which, in their whole yearly passage, "crown" Shangdi as the Lord and Master of Nature. The true hidden meaning of the mysterious *Book of Changes* is, as interpreted by Kongzi's reforming "religious" vision, the operation of the spiritual power of divinity in physical and human nature. And this is, according to Legge when he "first apprehended [Confucius or Kongzi's] meaning," an understanding of the text that powerfully alludes to the "words of the apostle Paul, 'The same God worketh all in all.' "[63]

Protestant Proclivities of Solstitial Worship

The rest of this section is devoted to an extended portrait of the imperial prayers at the solstitial services since the time of the Ming dynasty down until the late nineteenth century. The important point in all of this is not the ritual performance of the services, but the empathetic fashion in which Legge narrates the activities at the specially privileged altars.[64] The other significant issue is the detailed set of conclusions Legge draws from these imperial practices. The first, and most critical, of these conclusions is that "the original monotheism of the Chinese remains in the state worship of to-day." Whatever "uncertain polytheism" might have emerged at various times in the long course of Chinese history was "swept away from the impe-rial worship soon after the middle of our fourteenth century, immediately on the rise of the Ming dynasty, whose statutes have supplied us with a se-ries of such remarkable prayers." (In *Notions of the Chinese Concerning God and Spirits* [1852], he referred to these changes as the Ming "reform.") Equally remarkable is the obvious inference that the Ming imperial purification of Chinese worship, no matter what continued at the more vul-gar levels of society, was tantamount to a kind of Protestant purification of the Chinese state religion two centuries before a similar transformation of Christianity in Europe. Implying that the Chinese religion had suffered degradation in the same way that Christianity had suffered the corruptions of Roman Catholicism, this view also suggested that China, which had ex-perienced a self-generated reformation, was capable—with a little con-certed help from its Western friends and mentors—of religious and civi-lizational progress.[65]

A second conclusion very much in keeping with this conspicuous Protes-tant paradigm is that, for Legge, the solstitial services had to be understood as prayerful "oblations," or freely given burnt offerings, rather than as any type of ritualistic "propitiatory sacrifices" made with the expectation of some certain return on one's ritual investment. The offerings at the altars were, according to Legge, "tributes of duty and gratitude" and not expres-sions of a crass "sense of guilt." Most of all, and even though they did not harbor the "idea of substitution," these sacrificial practices expressed an al-most Evangelical "feeling of dependence" over and against any indulgent sense of Catholic contrition, ritual reciprocity, or priestly mediation.[66]

The third major conclusion is that the Chinese emperor, in the course of practicing the solstitial ceremonies, expressed the collective obligations to God of his dynastic line and of "all the millions of his subjects." Although he was performing the "highest act of worship in the religion of China," the emperor should not be considered as a "High Priest." Moreover, from the earliest periods in Chinese history on down to the present, there was never any priestly class or special category of ritual specialists like the Indian Brah-mans. In China, the closest approximation of a "clerical body" was the literati—the Ruist class or composite group of "Confucian" scholar-bureaucrats—an elite body that was more ministerially concerned with the educational, moral, and civic implications of ritual forms than with the religious efficaciousness of ritual. In Legge's estimation, the emperor, when presiding over the state worship at the Altars of Heaven and Earth, was acting very much like a Protestant "minister of religion," who expresses the "highest ideas of God" and acknowledges "the dependence of all upon Him." A "minister of religion" obligatorily acts "as the parent and representative of the people, and not as a priest."[67] There is even a suggestion that the Chinese state religion was actually purer than Hinduism, Roman Catholicism, and perhaps the ancient Israelite religion, each of which relied on the ritual practices of priests. The Chinese religion (meaning primarily, for Legge, the theistic primordial "Confucianism"), despite its deficiencies, had avoided the abominations of priests and, as exemplified by the purified religion of the Ming dynasty, was surprisingly Protestant and ministerial in spirit.

Ancestor Worship

In the second major section of the *Religions of China,* Legge took up the "worship of the dead" as the other, and more generally popular, aspect of the "bifurcated" Chinese religion of Confucianism. Whereas the "worship of God" was the exclusive ministerial responsibility of the emperor, ancestor worship had "always been the practice of all the Chinese people." What is worth noting is Legge's rudimentary effort to frame his discussion of ancestor worship in relation to an etiological story of religious devolution. Thus in the beginning, as "testified to by the primitive written characters," the worship of God was "the first, and for a time, probably, the only worship."[68] "By-and-by" things changed in the sense that people began to worship individual spirits associated with the multiple dimensions of the natural world collectively "conceived to be the manifestation of God." Then "it came about" that the worship of God and the subordinate nature spirits was the sole prerogative of the king or emperor. While all of the people recognized the one God, they were "debarred from the worship of Him." Their instincts for worship thwarted, they sought out the only available alternative: "[T]here remained for them the worship of their ancestors."[69]

   The causal linkages in this narrative are vague, to say the least, but it was this sort of just-so theorizing, rooted either in the metaphors of a devolution from some primordial monotheism or in the storied images of a gradual evolution toward monotheistic belief, that was at the heart of the comparative enterprise fostered either by Müller's science of religion or by Tylor's and Frazer's anthropology. Legge's sketchy account of the "by-and-by" emergence of ancestor worship is not any less convincing than many of the other nineteenth-century versions of the early history of heathen religions— although it must be said that Legge's very tentative grasp of the social dynamics and ritual significance of ancestor worship would have profited from

the more descriptively elaborate and conceptually sophisticated, if not necessarily more accurate, totemistic views held by early sociological pioneers
such as his fellow Scotsmen Robertson Smith and John McLennan.[70]

Entering into a long discourse on the nature and importance of "filial
piety" in the ancient tradition, especially as valorized by Kongzi, Legge
makes the point (in line with common Ruist interpretations of the ancestral
rites) that the ongoing tradition of ancestor worship is best thought of as an
expression of the "fundamental duty" of the virtue of filiality. It is this basic
moral principle that, as Legge concludes from his study of the *Book of Historical Documents* and the *Book of Poetry,* is the primary motivation for the
emergence, powerful emotional appeal, and social functionality of the worship of the dead in Chinese tradition.[71] Believing that there was much that
was "pleasing" about the practice of filial worship, Legge also concluded
that, as the only "channel" for the "flow of religious feeling" among the people, it was made into a "religion" that stood "side by side" with the "higher
worship" of God. In this way, the influence of ancestor worship was "injurious" since it "tended to produce the superstition of tutelary spirits" with its
accompanying "defect" of the inability of the common people to maintain
the elaborate rites. It was this defect, says Legge, that eventually drove the
people "into the arms of the Taoists and Buddhists, becoming the victims
especially of Taoist superstition." The "good and admirable" feelings of
filial piety originally associated with the practice of ancestor worship were
then corrupted by the Daoist priests who, in a way again remarkably similar
to the practices of Roman Catholic priests, demanded payment for the de-
liverance of the dead trapped in "a sort of purgatory."[72]

The Glow of Affection

Legge then turned to a more positive appreciation of filial piety—that is,
the original motivation and abiding justification for the practice. At its best,
and contrary to much traditional missionary opinion on this matter, the
virtue of filial piety in China expresses the spirit of Moses' Fifth Commandment: "Honour thy father and mother, that thy days may be long in the
land which Jehovah thy God giveth thee."[73] The whole issue finally comes
down to the evaluation of one's practical experience with the Chinese people. Legge therefore remarks that his old missionary antagonist, M. T. Yates,
who had written the position paper on ancestor worship for the Shanghai
conference, found the Chinese to be the "most unfilial" and "disobedient
to parents" of "all the people of whom we have any knowledge." Legge
pointedly says that his experience in China was decidedly otherwise: "I am
thankful I have not to endorse this representation."

In the end, the question for Legge becomes whether or not there is "reason to think that the worship of the spirits . . . had or has now a beneficial,

a moral and religious influence?" He first of all admits that, as a good Protestant Christian, he can only "smile" at the Catholic *ex opere operatis* "idea of the service having power to bring the spirits to the tablets from wherever they are." Regardless of this reservation, the essential meaning of ancestor worship, as shown by philological and historical analysis, is the activity of a "sincere worshipper striving to recall his fathers, and dwelling on their virtues, till he feels the glow of affection, and resolves to be good as they were." The comparison remains unstated, but there is an obvious parallel here between the "glow of affection" and moral motivation brought about by Chinese ancestor worship at its best and the mostly middle-class Evangelical understanding of Victorian patriarchal sentiment and familial obligations.[74] Even though it is insinuated more than asserted, this kind of sympathetic comparison also represents a distinct step beyond anything Legge had previously suggested regarding the meaningful religiosity (as related especially to the imperial worship of God at the altars in Peking) and morality (concerning particularly the influence of filial piety and ancestor worship) of Chinese tradition. If his 1877 Shanghai paper was offensive to many missionaries for dwelling too much on the "terms" of an archaic Chinese monotheism, here he has only compounded his transgression by rescuing ancestor worship from the pit of superstitious idolatry and heathen immorality.

The Whole Duty of Morality

Legge's next major topic only reinforced these conclusions by reiterating an interpretive theme that had preoccupied him from the very beginning of his translations of the Four Books. This is the issue of the Chinese "doctrine of man"—"especially as to his nature, his duty, and his destiny." According to Legge's understanding of Chinese tradition, it is the basic "duty" of all human beings, as intelligent creatures of God and as assisted by the government of kings and the teaching of sages, to comply with their inner moral nature.[75] The fullest exposition of the ideal goodness of human nature and its proneness to go astray is to be found in the works of Mencius, which Legge discusses in relation to how this sage's views anticipate "every important point" insisted upon by the famous eighteenth-century theologian Bishop Butler (this is an abbreviated version of the discussion of Mengzi in the prolegomena to the *Chinese Classics* [1861], vol. 1).

There is nothing new about this discussion of the ideal conception and real defect of Chinese morality, but Legge does elaborate on his earlier analysis by introducing an extended investigation of the practical "course of human duty as laid down by the sages raised up by Heaven."[76] This "course of human duty" takes on special significance in the light of my running reflections on Legge's underlying pragmatic concern for the experiential evidence of moral progress derived from a comparative assessment of the actual behavior of individuals and nations. It directly relates, in other words, to the comparative ethical aporia suggested by Legge's rhetorical decision to end these lectures with the Chinese ambassador's obdurate questions about the morality of the English nation.

Most important in Legge's analysis of the "whole duty of man in the religion of China" are the sagely teachings about the "five constituent relationships of society" (i.e., the relations of ruler to subject, father to son, husband to wife, elder brother to younger brother, friend to friend). The chief defect with this mostly admirable teaching (particularly the Confucian ideas about "friendship" and mutual helpfulness) is the failure to say anything about the human duty to worship God. According to Legge, the other major problem with traditional social life in China was the relative inferiority of women, a situation sadly dramatized by the continuing practices of concubinage, female infanticide, and foot-binding. These three problems were treated with a fairness and refreshing lack of distorted exaggeration unusual for the period.[77]

The Whole Duty of Comparison

In the concluding pages to his discussion of the "Confucian religion" Legge turns to the question of the life and influence of the ancient Chinese sage known in the West as Confucius. As suggested by his earlier investigations of the prehistoric religion of "twofold worship" and its "rules of social duty," Legge believed that Kongzi "did not originate the religion of his country." Legge even concludes that the Chinese Master Kong himself made very few changes in the essence of the ancient religion and did not "modif[y] its records" very significantly.[78] Legge did not seem to believe that Kong's role in establishing the "Confucian religion" was as creatively formative as that of other religious founders such as Buddha, Mohammed, or especially and uniquely Christ. Kongzi may be best understood as a kind of prophetic-inheritor, reforming-transmitter, or purifying-moralist of the archaic religion. He was, says Legge, a "messenger from God to his countrymen for good."[79] No matter how "great and wonderful" Kongzi was in the Carlylian sense, it is the ancient—pre-Confucius—religion of China that was "still greater and more remarkable."[80] For all of Legge's trust in experience over abstraction, his method of analysis, as now influenced by Müller's idealistic comparative science, privileges the purity of the original doctrinal or catechismal meaning of the tradition over any later biographical confusions, conceptual contradictions, and moral defects introduced by individual human agents (Christ being the special "supernatural" exception to this rule). Legge admits here that his reason for naming the ancient "national religion" of China "Confucianism" is really only a matter of his own scholarly license "vindicat[ed]" by the state patronage of the sage in the Han dynasty and the present-day "imperial prayer" in ritual homage to him in Peking.[81]

The ordinary charges against the Chinese master were that his moral system was atheistically based and that his ceremonialism and social etiquette were fundamentally insincere and coldly formalistic. As Legge's London Missionary Society colleague William Muirhead put it in 1870 (after considering the evidence found in Legge's translations of, and commentary on, the classics), Confucius was fundamentally "irreligious." Legge found Kongzi at least partially guilty of some of these charges in 1861, but here he presents us with a brief biographical portrait of the master as a basically "great and wonderful" religious, moral, and scholarly figure. The biography in the *Religions of China* seems at first to be only an abridged version of the earlier and "fuller" account found in his 1861 prolegomena to volume 1 of the *Chinese Classics*. Even more than the delicately nuanced reworking of his 1861 prolegomena for the 1893 Oxford edition of the *Classics*, Legge in the *Religions of China* alters his earlier biography in a way that significantly changes the tenor of that work.[82] Legge is clearly showing his listeners and readers that, in the practice of the "whole duty" of scholarly comparison as taught by Müller, he has fully assimilated the lessons of sympathetic comprehensiveness and empathetic fairness.

Gold and Silver

Examples of this ameliorative process are numerous, but I will cite only Legge's revised opinion concerning the "memorabilia" of the master's personal characteristics. "At one time" when he "compared" these Chinese accounts with "the different style of [the] gospels," Legge says that he "was offended by them." Now he reports that he has "long learned" to "welcome" rather than to condemn them—even though the Chinese portraits of Kongzi (found both in the *Analects* and the *Record of Rites*) were for the Victorian literary sensibility not as effective or felicitous as the narrative style of the Christian gospels was.[83] Legge makes it clear that he has learned to be more scientifically "dispassionate" and comparatively equitable in his evaluations of heathen individuals and traditions—a lesson that was strongly recommended to him by the *Edinburgh Review*.[84]

Another example of Legge's revisionary state of mind is his discovery that Kongzi's "greatest achievement" in morality was his formulation of the "golden rule" of positive reciprocity—not just the comparatively less enlightened inverted or silver principle of earlier evaluations.[85] Likewise, concerning his earlier views about the Chinese master's "coldness" of religious temperament in "the avoiding of the personal name of Ti, or God," Legge is willing to give Kongzi the benefit of the doubt. Therefore, in a curious, but typical, coupling of Evangelical righteousness and Victorian authoritarianism, Legge here allows for the possibility that, since "the public worship of God was restricted to the sovereign," Confucius must have "felt himself fettered and did not care to use the personal name."[86] Legge also surmises that the most famous of all passages used to document Kongzi's nonreligious nature ("To give one's self to the duties due to men, and while respecting spiritual beings, to keep aloof from them, may be called wisdom," *Analects* VI.xxii) may mean nothing more than his warning to his disciples about the "superstitions" to which spirit worship may lead.

Lest he appear to be overly forgiving of Kongzi, Legge makes a point toward the end of this section (as well as throughout the fourth, and most overtly apologetic, section of the book) of reiterating two factors that lower his estimation of the ancient sage. The first of these is that Laozi actually bettered Kongzi in the realm of morality by stressing the supererogated and Christlike "return of good for evil" rather than the other sage's "return of justice." The second issue is the disturbing question of Kongzi's "concealment" of historical truth in his scholarly work on the *Spring and Autumn Annals.* Acknowledging that the issue may more properly be the hermeneutical question of "what is truth" rather than the Chinese sage's own duplicity, Legge—now a dutifully conscientious professor with an academic code of ethics rather than a righteous missionary following the Mosaic decalogue— still comes to the conclusion he came to in the fifth volume of the *Chinese Classics* (1872): that the Master Kong is sometimes untruthful and "misrepresents events he is writing about."[87]

In the final analysis and after carefully debunking the extravagant claim that Kongzi had predicted that a "true saint" was coming "from the west,"[88] Legge notably modifies the assessment of the master that he made in 1861 in a way that directly anticipates the conclusion he reached in 1893 about Kong as a "very great man." Legge therefore says here that "K'ung [Kong] was a great and wonderful man," but includes the reservation (absent in 1893) that the ancient religion was more important than the man. As he indicated elsewhere, Confucius too much "left men to the uncertain gropings and vague monitions of natural religion." He had no "gift or aptitude for anything like theology."[89] It is, then, for Legge the religious system of "Confucianism" that is "still greater and more remarkable" than Confucius himself.[90]

A Pure Philosophy and a Corrupt Religion

The American sinologist Herrlee Glessner Creel in 1970 used the basic question "What is Taoism?" for the title of an influential book on the Daoist tradition; the very same query opens section three of Legge's *Religions of*

China. The simple interrogatory congruence of these two titles aside, Creel's answer to the question was astonishingly similar to that proposed by Legge almost one hundred years earlier.[91] As Legge put the matter in the *Religions of China:*

> Taoism is the name both of a religion and a philosophy. The author of the philosophy [Laozi] is the chief god, or one at least of the chief gods, of the religion; but there is no evidence that the religion grew out of his book [the *Daode jing*]. It was impossible, indeed . . . for it to do so in many of its aspects. Any relation between the two things is merely external, for in spirit and tendency they are antagonistic.[92]

A full scholarly awareness of Daoism and its apparent "antagonistic" nature came late to the overall enterprise of sinological Orientalism. Thus the difficult definitional and historical question of "what is Taoism?" was only dimly coming into Victorian consciousness in the 1870s and 1880s. This attention came about both because of a wave of new translations, especially of classics such as the *Daode jing* (the Book of the *dao* and its characteristics) and *Zhuangzi* ([Book of the] Master Zhuang), and the emergence of fresh interpretations that went beyond early Jesuit and French Enlightenment efforts to define Daoism as the Rationalist tradition.[93]

The question to be asked about the perennial query of "what is Taoism?" really comes down to asking how sinologists from Legge to Creel (with the important exception of several French scholars in the first half of the twentieth century who availed themselves of the *Daozang* or Daoist canon) could have gotten the answer so horribly distorted and lopsided, so grotesquely a corrupt gloss on this exceedingly rich and complex tradition. The answer to this hermeneutical question about questions is largely a matter of the powerfully persuasive interpretive framework about Daoism that emerged in nineteenth-century sinological discourse. Furthermore, since Legge is the dominant voice of professionalized sinological Orientalism in the late nineteenth century—precisely when "Taoism" was first being authoritatively named, defined, and explained for a Victorian audience—we may assume that Legge's way of translating and interpreting the hidden meaning of the tersely enigmatic *Daode jing* and the later popular tradition will loom large in the development of a particular kind of Orientalistic logic about the antagonistic pure and corrupt forms of Daoism. The definitive moment for the creation of this amazingly pervasive logic can even be identified with Legge's 1891 translations of the Daoist sacred books for Müller's series. But the *Religions of China* is a kind of trial run of Legge's mature ideas about philosophical and religious Daoism, concerns that along with his work on

Buddhism would occupy much of his attention throughout the decade of the 1880s.

The Corrupt Religion

Legge in the *Religions of China* first takes up the popular, but "gross," religious forms of Daoism. By so doing, he leaves us with the impression that he is purposely saving the best for the last. He begins with a description of the mostly repugnant "superstitions" of the later religious tradition and culminates with an exposition of the original philosophy concerned with the cultivation of the "highest and purest" aspects of human nature.[94] Acknowledging that the Daoist religion, though considered a "heterodox tradition" by the Qing government, was legally tolerated and officially regulated, Legge gives us a clue to his overall interpretation of the tradition when he opens his discussion with a reference to the "popes of Taoism" (describing a kind of apostolic succession from the first *tianshi* or Heavenly Master, Zhang Daoling, in the first century C.E.) and its priestly system of "ecclesiastical gradations of rank and authority."[95]

These locutions concerning "popes," "grossness," and "corruption"— along with the antagonistic rhetorical structure of the overall discussion— draw attention to the underlying antipapist bias seen in much of the nineteenth- and twentieth-century Orientalist discussion of Daoism.[96] The nineteenth-century comparative analysis of Oriental religious history often mirrored the Reformation myth that Protestantism was primarily a profound cleansing of Roman Catholic ritual corruption and a return to the cognitive purity, elevated spirituality, and golden rule morality of the original religion of Christ.[97] This interpretive perspective especially applies to the dangerous problem of syncreticism and, as Legge says here, the freedom of Protestant Christianity from any "depraving admixture" of inferior worship such as that found in Romanism.[98]

In keeping with his concern for the origins and developmental history of the Chinese religions, Legge suggests that the inception of Daoist superstition—as distinct from "the Tao Teh King, of the sixth century B.C.," that savors neither "of superstition [n]or religion"—cannot be precisely determined. He nevertheless links the emergence of superstitious religion to the corruptions of the primordial monotheism that, after the hiatus of Kongzi and Mengzi, became pervasive during the degenerate reign of the first emperor, Shi Huangdi. For the most part, these "tendencies to superstition" were promoted, as with the case of ancestor worship, by the fact that the people were officially "debarred from communion" with the High God and therefore sought solace in inferior, and often dangerous, beliefs and practices.[99] Becoming even more bizarre and diffuse in the later Han dynasty (especially those involving the emperor Wudi and magical beliefs in immortality and various alchemical practices), these superstitions were eventually organized into a religious system with an ecclesiastical organization, popes, priests, iconography, liturgy, and scriptures. This primarily came about through the "overmastering influence" of Buddhism, which entered China from India in the first century C.E.[100]

These foundational borrowings from Buddhism clearly manifest Daoism's bastardized nature. Even worse in this regard was the "gross" hybrid temple pantheon of Daoism in which "Chaos [*hundun*]," "that unspiritual God and miscreator," was ranked as one of the great gods.[101] Legge also blames the increasing idolatry of the Confucian state religion on the Buddhist and Daoist tendency "to multiply idol-deities indefinitely."[102] Especially disturbing for Legge is that his revered "personal name" for God, Di, is actually "given to scores of the Taoist deities." One can only conclude, says Legge, that "no polytheism could be more pronounced, or more grotesque, with hardly a single feature of poetic fancy or aesthetical beauty."[103]

Queer Practicality

For Legge, the only redeeming quality of the Daoist religion was its moral teaching as expressed by extremely popular tracts such as the *Ganying pian* (Tractate of actions and their retributions). Although often "queer and grotesque," these works contain much good practical advice blending basic moral precepts from all three of the traditional teachings. There is, nevertheless, a queerly distorted aspect of the moral system that Legge identifies as a "recent development." This is the belief, syncretistically shared with Buddhism and based on the Indian idea of "metempsychosis or transmigration," in an afterlife retribution. Sadly these ideas include a purgatorial system (the Ten Courts of Justice) that is manipulated by the "mercenary purposes" of the priests in the flagrantly indulgent manner of the Roman Catholic clergy.[104]

After an inventory of other "grotesque" practices (demonology, magical exorcism, and geomancy), Legge concludes by honestly admitting that "much research" on the religion was still required. He believed, however, that popular Daoism was clearly a crudely degenerate religion "begotten by Buddhism out of the old Chinese superstitions." Though it thrived in spite of opposition from state Confucianism, Legge felt certain that it was destined to collapse in the face of the progress of "real science" and Christianity.[105] This progressive improvement and regeneration of China will come about only if the Western representatives of real science and Christianity "act according to the golden rule of Confucius, and do to the Chinese as we would have them do to us, and according to the still grander maxim of Laotsze, overcome their evil by our good."[106]

The Pure Philosophy

The *Religions of China* is remarkable for Legge's overwhelming identification of the early Daoist philosophy with its "only text-book"—the ancient *Daode jing* (or Book of the *dao* and its characteristics), which has "come down to us from the pencil of Lao-tsze, its author." From a realm of grotesque darkness and fear we enter into a region of the purer and more ethereal light of the classics and sacred books of old, that territory of meaning so effectively colonized by Müller's Orientalist science of comparison. This movement back in time to the purity of the *Daode jing* is also for Legge a remembrance of experiences he had more than thirty years earlier as a missionary back in China. A memory that stayed with him till this time was the "case of one Taoist dignitary who visited him" in Hong Kong: "He told me that his study of the tao of Lao-tsze for fifty years had convinced him of his impotency to attain to its ideal, and he had almost resigned himself to despair, hopeless of finding some truth for which his heart yearned." Only after reading some Christian tracts did the scales fall from his eyes and he accept the "revelation of God in Christ."

Because of experiences like this, Legge concludes that when the "professors" (rather than the "priests" or "popes"!) of religious Daoism "confine themselves to the study of the Tao Teh King, and cultivate the humility and abnegation of self which are there so strongly inculcated, they are more prepared than the Confucian literati to receive the message of the gospel."[107] It is this kind of emotional recognition—here provoked by the wistfully nostalgic memories of an old Evangelical missionary-scholar—that in many ways lies behind the obsessive Western fascination with a "philosophical," "classical," or "mystical" Daoism associated with the singularly enchanting and morally uplifting ancient "text-book," "bible," or "sacred book" known as the "Tao Teh King."

The Author and His Text-Book

Legge begins his discussion of the early tradition with an "historical account" of the "old mystic and moralist" Laozi, the "author" of the *Daode jing* and the reputed older contemporary of Kongzi. Legge evinces some hesitation over various fantastic hagiographical elements and composite details in his assessment of the extant reports about the shadowy "Old Boy" (such as the meeting between him and Master Kong). Nonetheless, he affirms the traditional commentarial views of Laozi's authorship of the *Daode jing* ("there is no reason for us to doubt that the book which he wrote at the request of Yin Hsi . . . was the Tao Teh King which we still possess") and the dating of the text to the sixth century B.C.E.[108] (The old-fashioned nature of these views from both a native Chinese and Western perspective on higher criticism would give rise to a prolonged sinological battle between Legge and Herbert Giles, a young British scholar who was a harbinger of a more "modern" and destructive approach to critical questions about the authorship, historical provenance, and literary coherence of ancient texts.)

A clue to Legge's fledgling interpretation of the *Daode jing* is suggested by his surprising comparison of the text with the Sermon on the Mount. This comparison obviously drew attention to the extreme brevity of the two texts, but it also seemed to suggest some broad congruence of moral vision (the emphasis on humility) and style (the parabolic form). Despite these affinities, Legge generally rejected earlier attempts to find the Christian trinity or the name of Jehovah in the *Daode jing*.[109] In this way, Legge agreed with Julien and Müller in rebuffing such influential allegorical interpretations of the text on the philological, historical, and comparative grounds of "false parallels." This shows how far Legge had come from the days when, from the standpoint of missionary apologetics, everything of value in Oriental tradition was prophesied, anticipated, prefigured, or allegorically symbolized by the Christian Bible. But it may be argued that a Müllerian comparative detection of some hidden historical patterns, philosophical essences, categorical similarities, philological roots, or stylistic structures in ancient Oriental texts was not really so very different from the Jesuitical unveiling of occult Christian allegories. The rhetorical structures were basically the same, and it was mostly a matter that the hidden theological "meanings" were only transposed by the "science of comparison" onto a more universally "impartial" or "essential" frame of reference.

The Drift and Aim of a Glorious Dreamer

On the key issue of the difficult meaning and translation of "Lao-tsze's grand theme" of *dao,* Legge in 1880 adopts the sensible position that—as a mysterious power, attribute, or "way" of acting rather than a personal being—the term was best left untranslated. As to the "things that are taught in the book" about the *dao* and its power, Legge remarks that he is not quite confident that he had completely "cracked the shell" of meaning. Reminding his listeners of his method of repeatedly "translating afresh" a text and "transcribing at the same time the original and the happiest portions of Chinese commentary on it," he says that he always works in a way that allows the "meaning and spirit [to] soak gradually into the mind." Despite the fact that he was then working on his third translation of the *Daode jing,* he says that he was "still waiting for more light on many chapters."[110]

It would take Legge another decade of careful reiterative translation and commentarial reflection to illuminate more fully the meaning of this text. Nevertheless, in the *Religions of China,* he pragmatically proceeds with a partial explication based on his belief that he has "attained to the practical drift and aim" of the text. He briefly enumerates seven key ideas of which I need mention only his evident intellectual and emotional resonance with the moral implications of themes such as "emptiness" and "receptivity"; "freedom from preoccupation"; "unselfish usefulness"; the "three precious things" of compassion, economy, and especially humility; and "returning good for evil," an elevated moral sentiment that was "new to China and originated with Lao-tsze."[111] The only regretful note in this litany of virtue is Legge's frustration over the hermitlike rejection of "the progress of knowledge and society." For a good Victorian dedicated to the progressive social missions of Christianity, civilization, and education, this shows that Laozi, for all the partial but "glorious" appeal of some of his ideas, was "after all only a dreamer."[112]

Taking up Robert Douglas's observation that "Lao-tsze knew nothing of a Personal God," Legge, after some fairly strained exegesis of several problematic passages, comes to the not very surprising double-negative conclusion that he does "not feel called on to admit that Lao-tsze did not believe in God."[113] The overall conclusion that he draws about the classical Daoism of the *Daode jing* is that, "while the existence of God is not denied," there is "no inculcation of religion in the book." For all of its terse mystery, this text has primarily a philosophical or humanistic focus on the cultivation of the "highest and purest" aspects of human nature without any expressed dependence on, or concern for, the "worship" of some supernatural power—whether God, Dao, or spirits. The real "mystery" is how the practices of the incredibly "base religion described in the former part of the lecture" could in any way be identified, "as they are," with Laozi and his "system of thought." For Legge, this is a kind of term question that remained totally "inexplicable."[114]

COMPARING COMPARISON:
THE STIGMATA OF TOLERATION

We had occasion to notice, a few months ago, the very marked change which is taking place in the Missionary mind with regard to the Heathen philosophers and teachers. There was a time, as well all remember, when it was the fashion to condemn to indiscriminate perdition, Plato, Confucius, Zoroaster, Sakymouni, and Mohammed. The toleration which we find in Dante was not shown by Protestant Preachers. . . . The danger now seems to be that the students of the Classics will begin to find too much in them. For years they were stigmatized as the cause of Chinese stagnation, and as the insurmountable barrier which blocked the road of Progress; and we must not all at once change the note, and belaud the sacred books with a praise as undeserved as was the censure which we first bestowed on them. It is equally untrue to say that Confucius wrote sentences of unsurpassed wisdom, as that he was a pernicious propagator of error, whose writings and whose body alike deserve to be burned. Just at this moment, critics seem disposed to run from the extreme of reviling to the extreme of encomium.

NORTH-CHINA HERALD AND SOUTH-CHINA AND COASTAL GAZETTE, 1882

I have often been pained to the quick by the misrepresentations of the Confucian system on missionary and other platforms, which only show how little the speakers have entered into the Spirit of our ninth commandment. They bear such an amount of false witness that I am content for the most part to keep away from missionary meetings, and run the risk of being stigmatized as having lost my interest in the great missionary work.

JAMES LEGGE, "THE BEARING OF OUR KNOWLEDGE OF COMPARATIVE
RELIGIONS ON CHRISTIAN MISSIONS," 1886

The Wholeness of Human Duty

The last section of the *Religions of China* is devoted to an extended comparison of Confucianism and Daoism with Christianity. This is an exercise that takes the form of a largely apologetic dissertation on the human "defects" of the Chinese religions and the necessity for their completion in the supernaturally based religion of Christ.[115] What we have not explored is Legge's justification for his particular approach to comparison. Regarding the "dispassionate" but ultimately judgmental nature of his general procedure, Legge says simply and honestly: "I cannot make my mind a *tabula rasa* in regard to the faith in which I was brought up, and which, in mature years, after not a little speculation and hesitancy, I embraced for myself, with an entire conviction of its truth." This "impartial but not neutral" principle, arrived at after "not a little speculation and hesitancy," can be said to be Legge's particular application of Bishop Beveridge's axiom of a "diligent and impartial enquiry into all religions," which Müller used as the motto for the *Sacred Books*. This principle is complemented by a variation on a theme struck in Legge's sermons during his last days in Hong Kong that the more "a man possesses the Christian spirit, and is governed by Christian principle, the more anxious will he be to do justice to every other system of religion, and to hold his own without taint or fetter of bigotry."[116] For Legge, reared in the Scottish familial wisdom of the Bible and the Westminster Confession, it is above all the Ninth Commandment that qualified all efforts at an honest Christian approach to the understanding of, and intercourse with, other people and nations: "Thou shalt not bear false witness against thy neighbor." The very fact that the Chinese could be viewed as "neighbors" rather than as just damnable "heathens" represents a decisive step in the direction of new habits of comparative thought stressing some degree of sympathetic comprehensiveness.

What, then, was the fuller content of the Christian spirit and principle? It was, as Legge most clearly articulates in a later essay, the "whole duty" of Ecclesiastes 12:13 to "fear God and keep his commandments." Central to the comparative enterprise were the Old and New Testament rule to "love thy neighbour as thyself" and especially Christ's (and Laozi's!) golden command to love one's enemies.[117] As always, it was Paul who expressed most poignantly the whole duty of the comparativist when, "looking abroad on the various forms of belief in the world," he counseled Christians to "prove all things and hold fast that which is good."[118] The duty of holding fast to the moral implications of any comparative situation involving intercultural intercourse is more important than the individual terms of the comparison.

This comparativist principle translates into Legge's own personal "grief" over the "ignorant" and "incautious assertions of writers who think that apart from [the] Christian Scriptures there are no lessons for men about their duties, and that heathendom has in consequence never been anything but a slough of immoral filth and outrageous crime." For Legge this betrays not only a profound ignorance of heathen tradition, but also an obliviousness to the central commandments preached by the Bible and Christianity—especially loving one's neighbor and not bearing false witness.[119] Legge's strongest statement of "pain" in this regard is his incredible, but understandable, admission in 1886 that because of the "misrepresentations" and blatant "false witness" about Confucianism by missionaries, he was mostly "content" to avoid "missionary meetings and run the risk of being stigmatized as having lost [his] interest in the great missionary work."[120] Doubtless the intensity of feeling expressed here is not just due to the general calumny toward Confucianism by many missionaries, but also includes the sting of personal invective and condemnation directed specifically against Legge's own comparative views on these matters.

An important addendum to the Christian duty of comparison "without taint or fetter of bigotry" is suggested by Legge's observation that, despite the unique "organic unity" of the Christian Scriptures,[121] a scholar must search the sacred books fairly and diligently, using "all legitimate methods of criticism and interpretation." Very much in the spirit of Robertson Smith's defense of the higher criticism when applied to the Bible, Legge is not reluctant to say:

> The books of the Old and New Testaments have come down to us just as the Greek and Roman and Chinese classics have done, exposed in the same way to corruption and alteration, to additions and mutilations. The text of them all has to be settled by the same canons of criticism; the meaning of the settled text has to be determined by similar or corresponding processes of construction. The fact that we have in the Christian scriptures a revelation does not affect the method of their study.[122]

A Catechism without Answers

Legge's application of the comparative method of studying the Chinese religions is clearly indebted to Müller, but is not identical to that practiced by the Oxonian master of scientific comparison. Part of this difference is the result of factors predating Legge's awareness of Müller—such as, for example, Legge's own progressive transformation of his Scottish Nonconformist heritage and his early philological scholarship in terminological matters of translation (especially as seen in the *Notions of the Chinese Concerning God and Spirits* [1852]). Another seeming difference was Müller, Samuel Johnson, and Bishop Beveridge's more radically "impartial" stance that, in theory at least, was less prone, after the work of descriptive analysis was completed, to a rush to judgment concerning the "foregone conclusion" of Christian superiority. In practice, there was really very little that separated Müller's theoretical and scientific procedures from Legge's more frankly apologetic and Evangelical methods.

There is, however, one significant difference that should be emphasized here—namely, the degree to which Christianity was conceived of as a completely perfect or perfected religion. Like other religions, Christianity was subject to historical change, but it was the view of theologians and comparativist scholars such as Legge, on the one hand, that, as a "religious system," Protestant Christianity could not really be improved or become any more perfect. For those who generally espoused this view and feared any kind of hybridization of religion, the perfection of Christianity as a religious system did not, of course, mean that individual Christians, Christian communities, or even "Christian nations" need not constantly improve their actualization of Christ's perfect rule. Idealist scholars such as Müller and Johnson, on the other hand, often took the position that the superiority and "higher" status of Christianity in relation to all other religions at the end of the nineteenth century did not preclude the fact that Christianity itself, through a principle of radical syncretistic development and pluralistic incorporation, must undergo further progress, fulfillment, and completion.

At stake here is the degree to which one must remain open to the transgressive probability that other individuals, nations, or religions may actually raise disturbing questions about the finality, perfection, and morality of the Christian tradition itself (including its seemingly perfect "religious system" as much as its obviously imperfect individual, social, and national realizations of the system). What is so fascinating about Legge is precisely his honest hesitation concerning these matters—a raising of unanswered, and perhaps unanswerable, comparative moral questions such as that posed at the very end of the *Religions of China* (see pages 304–5). Whatever his old-fashioned catechismal certitude about the essential finality and doctrinal perfection of Christianity, Legge was never quite so sure about judgments made in the light of a comparative assessment of the actual practice of Christian and Chinese morality. But for Legge this kind of final pause, hesitation, or methodological caesura was also clearly an important aspect of the "whole duty" of a true comparativist and Christian prophet-minister-scholar-teacher.

Knowing Both Men and Systems by Their Fruits

Perhaps the most direct and effective statement of the dilemma of moral certitude is to be seen in Legge's *Christianity and Confucianism Compared in Their Teaching of the Whole Duty of Man,* a lecture first published as a pamphlet for the Religious Tract Society in 1883. A reworking of many of the themes seen in the *Religions of China,* the *Whole Duty of Man* focuses on the specific issue of "duty" that links both Confucianism and Christianity. This treatise is particularly interesting because of its conclusion, which echoes, and expands upon, the interrogatory doubt that rhetorically closed the *Religions of China.*[123] Legge ends his 1883 discussion with the observation that, no matter how convincing the "evidence of facts," there is always the practical need "to weigh the moral condition of the Chinese people as compared with our own." He admits that comparing "men and systems" by their actual goodness or moral "fruits" is easier said than done. Especially "difficult," is, as he puts it, the possibility "of doing so in an even balance."[124]

Legge goes on to say that there is much to "like" and "even to admire" about the Chinese.[125] Most of all, it is the "teaching of human duty" in Confucianism that has "done much for them." This is so much so that Legge revealingly declares: "I thought of them better, both morally and socially, when I left them, than when I first went among them, more than thirty years before." Now it is true that the Chinese are "very much less enlightened," "less capable of comprehensive views," "more conservative," and "more superstitious" than Westerners are. Nevertheless, they "deserve our esteem," says Legge, and we should always remember the real comparative lesson: that "they measure foreigners from their own standpoints, weighing them as well as they can in the balances of 'benevolence, righteousness, propriety, wisdom, and sincerity.' "[126]

Despite his admission that the "nations of Christianity come far short of the standard of duty and character" that Christians "ought to be aiming after," Legge rather limply asserts that the "fruits of Christianity" are "incomparably better than those of Confucianism."[127] The implication is that the fruits of Christianity are to be judged superior to the "conservative" Confucianism because of the salvation it offers to individuals and because it directly furthered the dynamic progress of Western civilization. No matter how jaded and mixed were the results of the ameliorative effect of Christianity on civilizational development, it seemed clear that the spirit of Christianity was the inner engine of constant moral improvement and social betterment in the West. From this perspective, it is the forceful Christian mis-sionary impulse, or "aggressive character of Christianity," that is the prime motivation for social and political progress. The real difference between the two traditions comes down to the tersely pat formulation that "Confu-cianism tends to make men satisfied with what they are, while true Chris-tianity makes them dissatisfied that they are not better."[128]

The Mystery of Comparison

Intermixed with the rhetorical flourishes about Christian incomparability in the finale to the *Whole Duty of Man* is the other, more ambiguous and hes-itant, issue of the unfathomable "mystery" of why "so great a portion of mankind be still non-Christian" in defiance of the aggressive Christian pur-suit of "a new moral world." It is here that the comparativistic warning of the Sermon on the Mount ("Judge not, that ye be not judged") particularly applies. In "all [the] intercourse" with heathen peoples, therefore, it is al-ways best to recognize that no Christian can truly judge another person or nation, even heathen people or traditions, until he is satisfied that "he has realized 'a new moral world' in himself."[129]

What is left unsaid here is that this methodology involves a lifelong task of character building, which, as both Legge and Confucius knew so well, al-ways depends on the give and take of reciprocal social intercourse. It refers to a process of personal cultivation that is never complete in this life. In the meantime—that is, within the methodological space created by the strate-gic pause or hesitancy before any final judgments—there is the prospect of hearing some of the unanswerable moral questions asked by foreigners and heathens. There is the transgressive possibility that Christians may be changed by Confucians just as much as the other way around. And at least with regard to James Legge himself—formerly a missionary and now a com-parativist professor who has undergone a steady pilgrim's transformation of intellect and attitude—this is surely the case.

The "whole duty" of understanding the other is, from this oblique per-spective of "not a little hesitancy," a matter of the degree to which honest doubt and sincere ambiguity about one's own religious stance and moral position is allowed into the formula of comparative analysis. For Legge this becomes an issue of how much the rule of Christ, "whatsoever ye would that men should do unto you, even so do ye also unto them," is applied to in-tercultural intercourse. Legge's unstated, or unconsciously repressed, corollary is that this same principle of reciprocity, whether in its silver or golden version, is also at the crux of the Confucian approach to human re-lations. It was, as Guo Songtao reminded him, a question of the "weighing of foreigners" in the "balances of 'benevolence, righteousness, propriety, wisdom, and sincerity.' "[130] The fundamental uncertainty of the results of this dual reciprocity is the real mystery raised by the difficult duty of candidly comparing one person or tradition with another. Interestingly enough, this was a lesson sometimes more fully appreciated by the Nonconformist Legge and the Confucian Guo Songtao than by the great academic master of comparative Orientalism, Müller.

QUESTIONS OF MORALITY

Comparative religion . . . has not done much harm; it has been merely a fresh element thrown into the bubbling cauldron of infidelity.

A STUDENT, *CHINESE RECORDER*, 1882

[Hannah Mary Legge] was nervous and apprehensive of evil, looking at the dark side of things rather than at the bright. I used to tell her that she needed to believe in God as the God of Love, and as conducting a loving providence, and also to believe in man, which she would do when she believed more unhesitatingly in God.

JAMES LEGGE, *THE LATE MRS. LEGGE*, 1881

The Facile Princeps *of Sinology*

Writing his stepdaughter Marian Willetts Hunt early in the year of 1881, Legge mentioned, amid tidbits of domestic information, that he was busy at work on his translation of the *Book of Changes* for Müller. He was also very pleased to tell her that his publisher, Hodder and Stoughton, had just reported to him that the *Religions of China* was selling well, some 1,250 copies having been sold since its appearance about a year earlier. His good fortune in this regard was offset by the discovery that his book was reprinted in the United States by Charles Scribner's Sons, who, so typically at this time, sought no permission or agreement with his English publishers. Despite the considerable frustration and lost remuneration as a result of this and other pirated editions of his work (especially in America and in the coastal communities of foreigners in China), Legge stoically comments that he at least had the satisfaction of getting his book more widely circulated. For this reason, he could only rejoice in the blessings that the new decade was bringing.[131]

Legge's pleasure over the modest popular success of the *Religions of China* was heightened by the fact that this work was, for the first time, displaying his abilities as a comparativist and not just as a mere translator. But he must have taken even greater satisfaction from knowing that, after the missionary condemnation of his views, his most forthright and comprehensive comparative statement about the Chinese religions was well received by the book-buying public. The periodical press mostly tended to praise Legge's general scholarship and findings, although no one thought his philological speculations particularly impressive or groundbreaking.[132] The *China Review* commended the book as the product of "mature study" by the "*facile princeps* among Classic Sinologists." According to this reviewer (no doubt Eitel), who ignored the book's philological analysis, the old boy Legge sometimes showed himself to be "too trusting of authorship" and overly confident in the "authenticity" of ancient Chinese chronology and the testimony of native critics. But the *Review* was especially thankful for the book's convincing demonstration of the "religious element" in Confucianism and the Chinese belief in a "Supreme Being"—billed here as "James Legge's greatest service to Sinology." Though "not disposed to place Confucius so high as [Legge] places him," the reviewer appreciated the emphasis on the comparative "moral effects" of the different religions and the willingness to study all aspects of a tradition such as Daoism, no matter how superstitious and repugnant.[133]

The most balanced secular appraisal of Legge's views in the *Religions of China* is found in the stylish and widely read London literary weekly the *Spectator*.[134] Giving Legge credit as a real "authority" on matters Chinese, the anonymous spectator approved of the descriptions of Confucianism and Daoism, as well as the attempt to overturn the assumption that China was a land totally devoid of religion, "properly so called." But Legge was taken to task for indulging in "too much common-place Christian apology" and for recommending that Christianity should simply "supplant" the "coldness of Confucianism" and the lotus-eating "terrors of Taoism." According to the *Spectator,* it would be "better to lead [the Chinese] back to the wisdom of their own fathers."[135] The *Spectator,* nonetheless, recognized that Legge's views, regardless of the apologetic residue, were far in advance of those of most missionaries in China who tended to believe that "Chinese minds" were "absolutely blank in religious matters." Alluding to the term question revived by the debate over Legge's translations for Müller's *Sacred Books,* the reviewer insightfully realized that these issues "go deeper than a mere question of translation" and right "to the root of missionary work." Legge was congratulated for generally following the enlightened comparative methods of Müller and Saint Paul with respect to heathen religions.[136]

Generally suspicious of Legge's real motivations, church-sponsored publications were most often disturbed by Legge's open identification with the influential "comparative religion" camp associated with Müller. Legge's old nemesis, A.P. Happer, did not fail to register his objections to the *Religions of China,* actually praising the eighteenth-century papal bull against the Jesuits and all others, like Legge, who would dare to compromise on issues concerning heathen religions.[137] As editor of the *Chinese Recorder and Missionary Journal,* Happer also seems to have encouraged articles opposing the comparativistic and Leggian approach to Chinese religions.[138] At first, this takes on the narrow character of the ever-simmering term question debate, but later in the 1880s and 1890s (after Happer had stepped down as editor) the red flag of "terms" and "translation" in the *Recorder* was mostly raised within the *Spectator*'s deeper context of meaning concerning the theoretical and practical issues of a comparative approach to Chinese religions. Throughout the next two decades there is an extensive, and at times furious, debate in the pages of the *Recorder* over the theological and tactical relations between Christianity and heathen tradition. This debate is initially associated with Legge's writings and then becomes more generally identified with broad Leggian attitudes and the overall methods of "comparative religions."[139]

A Bubbling Cauldron of Infidelity

The linkage of Legge's views with the growing "dangers" of the comparative science of religions is seen in a long semisarcastic review in the *Recorder* by an anonymous "Student" of Müller's *Sacred Books*.[140] This article specifically accuses Legge of aiding and abetting Müller's devious stirring of the "bubbling cauldron of infidelity" by placing heathen books "in the same category" as the Christian Scriptures. Though Legge is unnamed, there is no doubt who the "distinguished Western scholar" helping Müller is: "a missionary having retired from missionary work, he was subsequently invited at home, to a professorship of the language and literature of the people among whom he had laboured as a missionary. He accepted the position." Even more transparent is the Student's tattletale observation that this unnamed former missionary "was spoken of by the people among whom he had been a missionary thus; He, knowing the superior excellency of the system he had learned in the heathen, had left preaching the gospel to them, that he might make known that system to his countrymen."[141] The suggestion that Legge had actually become an academic missionary of Confucianism to the West has, of course, some real merit—although reverse proselytization was hardly the conscious intent of Legge's latter-day incarnation as a professional sinological Orientalist and comparative scholar. Various articles in the *Chinese Recorder*—especially our Student's conclusion that a certain sinological professor's tactics could only harm the missionary movement and "lower the regard of the Holy Bible"—were largely a distortion of Legge's real position as a professor and comparativist. Such extreme views, nonetheless, accurately reflect the mistrust and fear inspired among the more traditional China missionaries by Legge and comparativism.

This anxious distress continued within missionary circles in China until after the turn of the century. Beyond the Student's concern that Christianity would be seen as only one among many world religions, there was the suspicion that the Leggian principle of "completing" or "fulfilling" Confucianism really concealed the possibility of a syncretistic grafting or blending with Christianity. Such an ameliorated Confucianism also dangerously lent itself to the further "vamping up" of new bastardized religions (e.g., Mme Blavatsky's quasi-Buddhist theosophy and Keshub Chunder Sen's Christian-Hinduism).[142] Even journals at home, such as the *Congregationalist,* were at this time detecting a "decline" in the aggressive "holy zeal" that should motivate missions, a decline that was particularly attributed to the "spirit of the times," which favored a comparative or "eclectic view of religion."[143]

To Believe in Man

Despite continued missionary complaints about his work and methods at the beginning of the new decade, Legge took solace from the fact that he had, after all, conducted himself in Müller's "bold, careful, scholar-like" manner. Furthermore, as he would assuredly add, he always behaved in a fully reverent manner. He had, as he always had throughout his life, done his whole duty as a Christian and as a scholar—convictions that seemed ratified by his more cosmopolitan critics, if not by the guardians of traditional missionary theology writing for the *Chinese Recorder.* Legge was no ordinary Scots Calvinist, but rather, as he often reminded his wife, someone who in the course of his long life had increasingly learned "to believe in man" because of his belief in the intrinsic goodness of God's providence.[144] To some degree, therefore, he had actually adopted something of a Confucian or Mencian vision of human nature.

Wrapped in the protective mantle of his family, local congregation, and university, Legge began the new decade doing what he loved most of all—teaching his classes, lecturing, and working, always working, on new translations of the *Sacred Books of China.* The first few months of the new year of 1881 were an especially blissful period: By this time, he had successfully established himself as the leading sinological Orientalist in the Western world, as an influential figure in the comparative study of Oriental religions, and as an active reforming member of the Oxford University community. Never one of the nattering nabobs of university politics like Müller, he was, in his own quietly conscientious way, a significant figure in various academic and religious circles.

Most comforting of all was the general happiness of his domestic life. His stepdaughter Marian had recently married and had already given her parents a new grandson, Colin. His son Tom, always his "mother's pet," was a bright and active boy who was now attending Trinity College at Oxford. The younger son, James Granville, would matriculate at Queen's College.[145] His two daughters who were still at home, Anna and especially his favored Helen Edith, continued to brighten the hours falling between the long sessions of work in his study. But Legge took the greatest comfort in knowing that, as the new year of 1881 began, his young wife (she was fifty-one, fourteen years younger than her husband) and "dearest Hannah," who had been susceptible to bouts of brooding despondency and sickness, had now entered into a more positive frame of mind and body.[146] She seemed to be content at last in overseeing her children's upbringing and with her own intensely private religious devotions. She also seemed to enjoy, on the whole, the busy social life of an Oxford don's wife.

A Shadow from the Dark Valley

Such unsullied bliss was not to continue for long. As Legge put it in his haunting postmortem letter to Hannah's brother, "a shadow from the dark valley" fell upon Hannah on May 1. At that time, she became aware that "a small tumour was forming in her left breast." While neither James nor Hannah at first felt any great alarm, it quickly became clear that the growth (*cancer* had not yet entered into the medical lexicon) had progressed to the point where Hannah was feeling a numbness in her left arm. By the end of May, Legge arranged for them to go to London so that she could be examined by an "eminent" medical practitioner, only identified here as a "Mr. Lister" (clearly the famous Joseph Lister, 1827–1912, founder of the antiseptic method).[147] Deciding that immediate action was necessary, Lister and his assistant proceeded with a full-scale mastectomy on a chloroformed Hannah in London on the afternoon of Friday, June 17—an operation that, as Lister assured the family, "would not be attended with danger."

The operation went well and for several days Hannah seemed to be slowly recuperating. On Sunday, Lister gave Legge permission to return home to Oxford to take care of some outstanding business. Legge tells us that he spent part of that day in the recovery room with Hannah. He was cheered by her ability to eat more normally but, at the same time, vaguely troubled by her talk of not being able "to realize the presence of Christ." Still he thought that he would soon be able to bring her back to Oxford, and as he says here: "I told her so with a kiss." In a way that he afterward recognized as an omen, he says that "she kissed me in return and smiled, but looked sad. Alas! Alas!"[148] Seeing her once more before he left for Oxford on June 20, Legge says only that she complained of some slight "inward pain" but insisted he go on home to Oxford, sending Helen Edith to her on Thursday. Only afterward did he guiltily hear that, as he left her room, she called out to him with a plaintive and almost inaudible "Darling!"[149]

Arriving home at Keble Terrace in Oxford that evening, Legge occupied himself with unattended correspondence and in the afternoon of the next day gave a lecture to two missionary students who had been studying Chinese with him since the beginning of April. Then on June 21 a telegraph arrived from Lister urgently requesting his return to London. Frantically catching the train and arriving back in London that evening, Legge found that Hannah's "inward pain" had shown itself to be a severe peritonitis that had quickly overwhelmed her, leaving her unconscious and with a "death rattle in her throat." Successfully relieved of the cancerous growth, Hannah died from an internal infection, a result that may actually have some relation to Lister's acclaimed efforts in perfecting aseptic surgical techniques. Struck dumb by the scene before him, Legge painfully says that, within several minutes of his arrival, Hannah's breath became more rapid and then stopped; "she had drawn her last breath." It was "ten minutes past eleven," on June 21, 1881—exactly twenty-two years and twenty-seven days after they were married in London.[150]

Begging a Grave

Legge was devastated by the all-too-sudden and premature death of his cherished wife and by his guilt over leaving her bedside to go to Oxford at the time of her greatest need. It was in a traumatic and ambiguous crisis such as this, like the other darkly unexplainable and tragically premature death of Mary Isabella Legge while in childbirth in Hong Kong some thirty years previously, that funeral rituals take on an extraordinary emotional, social, and spiritual importance. For someone of Legge's Dissenting religious sensibilities and evangelical conviction in Christ's nonsectarian rule of love, the whole sorry matter of Hannah's death and encumbered burial has therefore a pathos that goes to the very core of his lifelong struggle with, and hesitancy over, the catechismal certitude and "false witness" of conventional apologetic theology, his divided life as a missionary-scholar-educator in China, the folly of denominational disagreements, and his transformative comparative judgments about the significant religiosity of ritual traditions within Chinese tradition (funeral rites being a key aspect of the Confucian tradition).

The aftermath of Hannah Legge's death is not a pretty story. In a most profound way, the ensuing events truly ambiguate, yet again, that most important comparative question about the moral superiority of the Christian religion and the just administration of its funeral rituals. Wanting to go along with his daughters' wishes that their dear Mama be buried in Oxford at the cemetery of Holywell in the center of the city, Legge made arrangements for her coffin to be transported by train back home to Oxford. He knew in the pit of his stomach that there might be problems with Holywell because they would have to get special permission for a Nonconformist burial in an Anglican cemetery.

Depositing the coffin in the room behind his study in the house on Keble Terrace on Thursday, June 23, Legge went off to arrange for the funeral and burial on Saturday. He was pathetically unsuccessful in getting permission to use Holywell cemetery from the Anglican vicar of Saint Mary's, who was disturbed by Legge's Nonconformity and the precedent it might create for others in his family.[151] Legge indicates that by this time he was "despising" himself for "begging a grave" in such a sad and humiliating way. The final blow was that, after arranging for a burial site at Saint Sepulchre's cemetery in the parish of Saint Giles (the parish where their home in Oxford was located), he discovered on the day of the internment, in a pouring rain, that the cemetery chapel was locked and closed to their funeral party. Again the issue was the "pitiful" sectarian matter of his family's outsider status as Nonconformists.[152]

Legge's grief-stricken reflections on his wife in his letter to her brother in Australia are touching and remarkable in several ways. It is fascinating to discover that Hannah had sequestered several "when I die" letters for her children, dispensing pious sentiments and practical advice (especially concerning the children's moral training, an approach that Legge was wholly in agreement with).[153] Even more morbidly interesting is Legge's revelation that she had actually written two more "To my dear husband when I die" letters at other times, a too-frequent practice that spoke to her Calvinistic tendency to look "at the dark side of things rather than at the bright."[154]

Putting aside the question of how Legge's descriptions of Hannah's "perfect Christian womanhood" and "tendency to despondency" reflect on the authoritarian and patriarchal context of middle-class Victorian families and gender roles, I conclude this chapter with some consideration of how these mournful events must have sorely tested his assumptions about his acceptance at a "reformed" Oxford ostensibly open to all classes and creeds. After all that had transpired, he was still, in a sense, a heathen among the orthodox Christians. And just as his old Chinese acquaintances and beloved Chinese books forced him constantly to return to the impossible question of comparative morality, so also might we imagine that these gravely hypocritical machinations by the most officially established, and smugly educated, of British Christians ("undocile learners in the School of Christ") would secretly reinforce his questioning of the "foregone conclusion" of a superior Christian character and code. Here was strong evidence that the actualization of the "whole duty of man," one's propensity to hold fast to the good or right thing, was not an inevitable product of higher Christian breeding or civilization.

The events of June 1881 surely dashed any illusions Legge might have had about his situation and status at Oxford. Nevertheless, he finally knew the real provenance of his own duty as an Evangelical Christian and comparativist scholar. Certainly much wiser about the darkly duplicitous ways of the world, he was still profoundly reverent. Most of all, he recognized that his sacred responsibility was primarily to himself, to his children and grand-

children, to the continued reform of the religious and intellectual environment in Oxford, to his translations of Oriental books, to the hard and sometimes disheartening moral truth of comparative religions, and to God. He
was now content to stand mostly aloof from the petty sectarian bickering
among Protestant missionaries and from the constant squabbles of academic politics at Oxford. Whatever battles he would gird his loins for in the
future would be, therefore, largely internal contests conducted within his
own heart and mind, as well as a whole series of more public, but mostly
technical, sinological conflicts with other professional Orientalist scholars.
Instead of prolonging his parochial disagreements with missionaries in
China or university authorities in Oxford, Legge would focus his remaining
energies on the difficult moral problems of transcultural understanding.

CHAPTER SIX

Translator Legge:
Closing the Confucian Canon,
1882-1885

*Therefore those who explain the Odes, may not insist on one term so as to do violence
to a sentence, nor on a sentence so as to do violence to the general scope [zhi, meaning "will, determination, intention, purpose"]. They must try with their thoughts to
meet that scope, and then we shall apprehend it.*
JAMES LEGGE, "THE WORKS OF MENCIUS," *THE CHINESE CLASSICS*, VOL. 2, 1861

*In the study of a Chinese book there is not so much an interpretation of the charac-
ters employed by the writer as a participation of his thoughts;—there is the seeing of
mind to mind.*
JAMES LEGGE, PREFACE TO THE *YI KING, THE SACRED BOOKS OF THE EAST*,
VOL. 26, 1882

APPREHENDING THE SCOPE

Remorseful and alone in Oxford, James Legge suffered various ailments of
body and spirit in the months after his beloved wife's premature death and
undignified burial. Legge's malaise, a combination of headache "attacks"
and an unidentified general "sickness," continued throughout the fall of
1881 and into the new year of 1882. Neither a brief trip in September of
1881 to Germany for the Fifth International Congress of Orientalists in
Berlin, nor tea at the Mark Pattisons' and games of bagatelle at home with
his children, could help him forget the hurt of his head and heart.[1] These
lingering aggravations were obviously connected with Legge's profound sadness over his wife's death and with his righteous, yet impotent, anger about
the insulting circumstances of her burial in Oxford. He had already felt the
sting of condemnation by many of his old missionary brethren back in China
for his unconventional views on heathen religion. And now, after more than
half a decade as a professor of Chinese, he was faced with the excruciating
realization that, at a moment of acute personal pain calling for the broadest
latitude of religious practice and moral compassion, he and his family were
rebuffed by fellow Christians at Oxford.[2] Unceremoniously made to feel like
an outcast during the most important crisis in his life since his return from

China, Legge was forced to reassess his relationship with his newly adopted home, a home that he and his family had come to love and revere.

It was not easy for a middle-class family from the northern Scottish countryside and the remote Oriental colonies to resist the temptation to bask in the ancient glory of a donnish life at Oxford, and there were clear signs that Legge's children enjoyed the prestige and privilege of their Oxonian sinecure.[3] For Legge himself, who had experienced more of the fickleness of human associations—whether European or Chinese, Christian or Confucian—and the dangers of self-aggrandizement by virtue of office or location, these temptations were less seductive. Given his comparativist sensitivity to the religious and ethical relativity of any existential situation in life, Legge knew very well that all human institutions, Oxford University as well as the Hanlin Academy in Peking, required progressive moral rectification coupled with far-reaching religious, social, and political reform. This attitude was, moreover, illustrative of the spirit of T. H. Green's evangelistic and quasi-Nonconformist concern for linking speculative philosophical and religious ideals with practical moral and social action—lessons that needed application at Oxford and in the urban slums of London.[4]

Rites of Closure and Reform

Legge's aggrieved feelings and aggravated thoughts in the early 1880s led to his redoubled commitment, even as he approached his seventh decade of life, to a Greenian-style concern for religious freedom and national education at Oxford and for the disinterested and comparative reformation of historical knowledge coming from scholarly work on Oriental literature and from other academic labor. Having dedicated himself from the very beginning of his missionary career to apprehending the scope of Chinese texts and now, after embarking upon a professorial mission, appreciating more fully the scope of his own ambiguous situation at Oxford, Legge found solace, firstly and most characteristically, by throwing himself into the hard work of completing his translations of the Chinese canon of Confucian classics.

The next few years, from 1882 to 1885, would witness the fulfillment, after almost a half century of effort, of Legge's original pledge to translate all of the texts included in the most hallowed Ruist collections of authoritative Chinese texts, the so-called Five Classics and Four Books.[5] This was a project concluded just as several other monumental Victorian ventures were either seeing renewed life (such as the *Encyclopedia Britannica* and the *Sacred Books*) or just getting under way (e.g., the first A–Ant fascicle of the *Oxford English Dictionary* appeared in 1884 and the first volume of the *Dictionary of National Biography* in 1885). These long-awaited rites of closure involved the publication of Legge's pioneering decipherment of the enigmatic *Book of Changes* and his meticulous two-volume rendition of the immense *Record of Rites* for Max Müller's continuing *Sacred Books of the East* series (the sixteenth, twenty-seventh, and twenty-eighth volumes). During this same period, Legge faithfully conducted his Chinese classes and, as always, resolutely continued to offer public lectures at the Taylorian Institution during the spring and fall terms at Oxford (notably at this time on pre-Han history, on the *Daode jing* [The book of the *dao* and its characteristics], and on Fa Xian's travels).[6]

The extreme paucity of students attending his Chinese classes was a continuing concern (averaging, it seems, between two and five students, including the Davis scholarship recipients),[7] but, inasmuch as further pleading with the missionary societies for students was mostly unproductive, Legge seemed resigned to his lot as a teacher of the very few.[8] The one ray of light in all of this was that Legge had the satisfaction of attracting his first, and only, real sinological disciple: the young Austrian scholar Arthur von Rosthorn, who studied classical texts at Oxford from 1882 to 1886.[9] In addition to these pedagogical efforts, Legge was at this time struggling to perfect his rendition of the ancient *Book of the Dao and Its Characteristics*—along with the *Book of Changes,* the most "obscure" of Chinese texts—which was scheduled to appear in the recently approved second series of Müller's *Sacred Books.*

Children of an Alien Faith

During the early 1880s Legge also had the special satisfaction of helping Bunyiu Nanjio, one of the two Japanese Buddhist monks who had come to Oxford to study Sanskrit with Müller, publish an Oxford Clarendon Press edition of the *Catalogue of the Chinese Translation of the Buddhist Tripitaka, the Sacred Canon of the Buddhists in China and Japan.* Appearing in 1883, this was the first work printed at the Oxford University Press with a new set of Chinese type matrices acquired from the Chinese government through Legge's efforts.[10]

The tragic side of these transcultural efforts to assist the Japanese Buddhist recovery of its own Sanskrit heritage was that the other monk, Kenjiu Kasawara, after years of diligent training in Oxford with Müller and Legge, died shortly after his return to Japan in 1883. The "strange pathos" of his untimely death was indicated by the *Oxford Magazine,* which, after paternalistically recalling "that little body, whom many of us may remember to have seen silently gliding about Oxford so short a while ago," commented on the "patience, kindness, generosity of the Master [Müller], who had unwittingly drawn these children of an alien faith [Bunyiu Nanjio and Kenjiu Kasawara]" to Oxford. These "diligent" representatives of an alien religion, older than Christianity and "outnumbering the Catholic Church itself," had come "across seas and lands to sit at [Müller's] feet" and to "spell out, through two languages, their way back to the authentic fountains of their own spiritual force!" But an important question remained: "Is all the effort wasted?" Surely here too, said the *Magazine,* we may trust "the larger hope."[11]

In keeping with Müller's observations on reforming movements in the Orient and the "attempts to found selective systems based upon a fusion of the religions of the Christian conquerors and the conquered heathen," the *Oxford Magazine* recognized that there was always the reverse danger that the Christian religion would be crassly modified by the "spell" of the Orient exemplified by Edwin Arnold's Victorian Buddhism and Mme Blavatsky's eclectic Mahatmas. But these syncretistic possibilities were "too shocking" and absurd to contemplate seriously, and our anonymous *Oxford Magazine* commentator was content to rest with the "larger hope" of the "Christian conquerors."

Rites of Accomplishment

Legge's monumental productions as a translator and his increasingly celebrated reputation as the premier Western sinologist gave him an elevated stature and identity within the realm of academic scholarship that went beyond his tentative social and religious acceptance at Oxford. The perfect ritual symbol of his renown as a scholar and Orientalist came about in April of 1884 when he was chosen to receive an honorary degree at the extraordinary academic ceremonies celebrating the tercentenary of Edinburgh University. Marching alongside such giants of the Victorian era as the illustrious Frenchmen Louis Pasteur, who had conquered viral disease (a "short man with a gray moustach [*sic*]"), and Ferdinand de Lesseps, who promoted and built the Suez Canal ("an old man with white hair and that indescribable Frenchy military look"); the American James Russell Lowell; the anthropologist Sir John Lubbock; the innovative physician Sir James Paget—and, of course, Oxford luminaries such as Jowett, Liddell, and Müller—Legge, the simple country Scotsman and former missionary, must have felt a special swell of satisfaction.

Helen Edith Legge, who as a young girl attended these "splendid" ceremonies in Edinburgh, writes that the procession was an especially "marvellous" affair and was enthusiastically cheered by the assembled audience. She even makes a point of telling us that she felt a unique thrill as her father marched by in full academic regalia and when the famous Max Müller, coming somewhat afterward in alphabetical order, actually turned and nodded at her. Helen Edith says only that Müller's gesture caused her to blush like a "glowing coal"—a telling acknowledgment of Müller's status as academic royalty and as a special acquaintance of the Legge family.[12]

An Oxford Union of Nonconformists

At this time Legge also renewed his efforts on behalf of nonsectarian religious freedom and the acceptance of Nonconformity at Oxford. This took the form of a growing movement to reform some of the defects of the Oxford system by promoting the organized presence and influence of Nonconformist activity among undergraduates and faculty (at the beginning of the 1880s it was estimated that there were approximately two hundred Nonconformists as resident or nonresident students and perhaps only six proclaiming Nonconformist dons).[13] One important manifestation of his interest was Legge's participation in the founding of an Oxford University Nonconformists' Union devoted to supporting Dissenting ideas and an evangelical lifestyle in the face of the overweening authority of the established Church and the dangerous allure of fashionably decadent currents of skepticism, agnosticism, atheism, and Comtism.

An inaugural meeting of interested students took place on May 10, 1881, in the New College rooms of the controversial young Nonconformist tutor Robert F. Horton, with Legge and other prominent Dissenting faculty in attendance. By November of that same year, Professor James Bryce of Oriel College was named president of the small but enthusiastic new organization, with Legge and T.H. Green agreeing to serve as vice-presidents. From the minutes of the group, it appears that the union was a forum for presenting and discussing liberal religious and social ideas in the Greenian mold. Examples of these concerns are seen in the talks given on "Social Wreckage: Its Causes and Cure" and "The Problem of Life in East London," as well as in the papers that Legge himself read to the group on "The Use and Abuse of Mission" and "The Progress of Christianity and Why It Has Not Been Greater."[14]

Aside from a few absences due to illness, Legge took a particularly active role in union meetings down to 1886 when the organization was effectively supplanted by the creation of Mansfield College, a new independent Congregationalist institution at Oxford under the direction of Andrew Martin Fairbairn, the leading Congregationalist theologian and intellectual during the last part of the nineteenth century.[15] Throughout the rest of the decade, Legge continued to play an important role in charting the fortunes of Nonconformity as embodied by the fledgling Mansfield College, both by means of his close association with Fairbairn and by virtue of his presence on various important Mansfield College committees.

Regarding the Nonconformists' Union, it seems that Legge, raised in the long-winded traditions of Scottish sabbatarianism, was, for undergraduate tastes of the 1880s, overly enthusiastic in his piety. At the very beginning of the union, Legge volunteered to offer a prayer at the start of each session but, after only three regular meetings, it became clear that there was growing opposition among the students to the old Scotsman's extemporaneous offering of the opening invocation. At the Tuesday evening meeting on November 21, 1882, this whole issue came to a head and the student motion that "a collect be used in opening the meetings instead of extempory prayer" was passed by a vote of fourteen to five.[16] We are not told what so bothered the undergraduates about these opening prayers, but given everything known about Legge's ministerial loquaciousness and sometimes painfully earnest piety, it probably had something to do with an old-fashioned evangelical preacher's penchant for equating the effectiveness of a prayer with its length.[17]

Christmas at the Sheldonian

Despite the increased visibility of Nonconformity within Oxford academic and social life in the 1880s, the acceptance of Dissenting religion, as also the progress of women's education, was frustratingly gradual and dishearteningly erratic. Almost every advance was fought and begrudged by conservative religious factions at the university. And where there were no dramatic encounters, the residual forces of establishmentarian religious and social assimilation generally tended to lessen the passion of Dissenting resentments. The most famous example of the problems associated with the acceptance of Nonconformity in the 1880s—an issue that had theoretically been resolved by the reforms in the early 1870s—was the contretemps over Robert Forman Horton's proposed appointment in 1883 as an examiner in the university exams on the Rudiments of Faith and Religion (primarily a test of biblical knowledge, but also involving the Thirty-nine Articles of the Anglican faith). Nominated by the new vice-chancellor, Benjamin Jowett, and another liberal churchman and provost of Queen's College, Dr. John Magrath, and approved by the congregation of dons, Horton was eventually rejected in December 1883 by a convocation of all Oxford M.A.s who were greatly agitated by the possibility of a Dissenter's examining students in Anglican theology.[18]

As Horton was aware, the real issue in this fight was the fear that Dissenting Nonconformity and the forces of academic liberalism were making too many brazen demands upon the prerogatives of the established Church at Oxford, especially concerning its inner sanctum of orthodox theology. Control of the examination system was, after all, the central mechanism for exercising power over undergraduate life. In this sense, the religious and political conservatives were pleased that the final vote caused the dreaded Nonconformist Horton to depart from Oxford forever. Shortly afterward, the divinity exam in faith and religion was abolished for all undergraduate degrees.

This tiny, and typically Oxonian, tempest was in its own way a significant event in the struggle for religious freedom and for the progressive nationalization and academic secularization of Oxford University. The evidence for Legge's direct involvement in the Horton affair—or at least what was evidently his well-known symbolic identification with the salient issues and

Figure 33. "Christmas at the Sheldonian Theatre," 1883. *Left to right:* John Magrath, Benjamin Jowett, James Legge, and Robert Horton. Reproduced courtesy of University of Oxford, Bodleian Library, Falconer Madan, G.A.Oxon 4°417, number 1027.

leading dramatis personae—is dramatized by an extant caricature published by Shrimpton and Sons and mockingly entitled "Christmas at the Sheldonian Theatre Under the Experienced Management of Mr. B. BJ. W. TT" (see figure 33). This beguiling image (the kneeling Jowett is fitting the slipper to the ugly stepsister Horton's foot under the watchful eye of the other ugly stepsister, Legge, in formidable female garb; Anglicanism is shown as the banished Cinderella) draws upon the added controversy of Jowett's proposal to use the Sheldonian for theatrical productions and shows satirically how prominently Legge was identified with the disruptive presence of Nonconformity and the powers of liberalism. The cartoon depiction suggests more than any available discursive account that Legge was clearly a well-known and formidably disruptive figure in various reforming aspects of academic life at Oxford. Indeed, this characterization of Legge's stern visage and queenly drag recalls very much Ernst Eitel's telling comment that, with regard to the politics of educational reform in Hong Kong, Legge assumed very much of the practiced and commanding demeanor of an Anglican bishop.

THE RENEWAL OF THE *SACRED BOOKS OF THE EAST*

Look at the sciences of Language, of Mythology, of Religion. What would they be without the East? They would not even exist. We have learnt that history does not necessarily proceed from the present to the past in one straight line only. The stream of history runs in many parallel branches, and each generation has not only fathers and grandfathers, but also uncles and great-uncles. In fact, the distinguishing character of all scientific research in our century is comparison. . . . The mere lesson that we are not the only people who have a Bible, that our theologians are not the only theologians who claim for their Bible a divine inspiration, that our Church is not the only Church which has declared that those who do not hold certain doctrines cannot be saved, may have its advantages, if rightly understood.

MAX MÜLLER, "FORGOTTEN BIBLES," *NINETEENTH CENTURY,* 1884

If Rightly Understood

The early 1880s were a time of accelerated scholarly and social activity for Max Müller. Faint intimations of Müller's eventual eclipse as one of the pillars of Victorian intellectual tradition were already on the horizon, but it seems that, aside from a prolonged bout of despondency, Müller was mostly oblivious to such dark omens. In the early years of the decade, he busied himself with various new and old projects (e.g., his controversial *India— What Can It Teach Us?* and his revised edition of the *Introduction to the Science of Religion,* published in 1882), but was primarily concerned with winning the necessary approval from the university press to continue the *Sacred Books of the East* series. Müller always seemed to know that the production of the *Sacred Books* was a project that, along with his beloved edition of the *Rig-Veda,* would guarantee his scholarly immortality—whatever the viability of, among other products of his never-tiring pen, his mythological theories or his anti-Darwinian speculations about language origin. And even though many of his theoretical positions are more interesting than it was fashionable to admit in twentieth-century scholarship, his instinct about his own future reputation in this regard was largely correct.

The original agreement with the Clarendon Press of the university called for the completion of a first series of twenty-four volumes in 1884. Inasmuch as the volumes were appearing pretty much on time and because, despite persistent complaints from conservative critics, the series had already won an abundance of praise for Müller and the press, there was really very little doubt that a second and final series would be authorized. Müller was always confident that, "if rightly understood," the *Sacred Books* would be renewed till the end of the century. Furthermore, though subscriptions for the entire set of volumes were relatively few, some individual volumes had sold quite well considering their formidable scholastic pedigree (so-called best-sellers from the initial series were Müller's volume on the *Upanishads,* the *Koran,* the *Bhagavad Gita,* some of the Buddhist Pali volumes, and Legge's Chinese volumes).[19]

Because of his own dedication to the *Sacred Books* series and to Müller's editorship, Legge took the initiative in writing Müller in November 1881 to see if he, Legge, would be receiving a new contract to finish the volumes he had originally promised for the overall series.[20] With his soon-to-be consummated translation of the *Book of Changes,* Legge's original agreement with the press would be fulfilled and he was especially hopeful to have the opportunity to publish all the Confucian books mentioned in Müller's original prospectus. This required only the publication of the *Record of Rites* (which would take "more than one volume of 450–500 pages") and, in addition to the Daoist sacred books, another "Confucian volume" to accommodate the promised Four Books and portions of the Song philosophers. Legge was generally able to fulfill his dream, although the expected fourth Confucian volume never materialized as part of the *Sacred Books* series. Legge, in fact, never produced any translations of the Song philosophers, but a revised edition of the Four Books was published in 1893 and 1895 as a part of the Oxford University Press's reissued five-volume set of the *Chinese Classics.*[21]

A General Wish That the Series Continue

The key document in the renewal of the series of the *Sacred Books* is the letter Müller wrote in 1882 to Henry Liddell, dean of Christ Church College at that time and secretary to the Delegates of the University Press.[22] Beginning with an account of his "stewardship" of the project, Müller proudly informed the Delegates that, despite ongoing difficulties with various contributors and a slow start, the series was on schedule. He made it clear that, by the end of 1884, "all the great religions of the East" will have been "fairly represented." Entering into the heart of his appeal, he emphasized that twenty-four volumes could not, however, "possibly give an adequate idea even of the more important of the Sacred Books of the East" ("meaning by Sacred Books none but those that have received some kind of canonical sanction").

Müller then explains his self-styled "courageous" decision to begin the series with the "obscure" and sometimes "repellent" *Upanishads.* Interestingly, part of his justification is that, because Buddhism was "of late" occupying so much public attention, it was important to make available those texts that "embody the first germs of Buddhism in its historical development out of Brahmanism." He also defensively notes that the reason his translation differed "so widely from previous translations" was "chiefly due" to his "keeping [himself] as much as possible independent of native commentators, who, though indispensable and extremely useful, are so much under the spell of the later systematic Vedanta philosophy, as often to do violence to the simpler thoughts of ancient poets and philosophers."[23]

Discussing the status of some of the other book religions included in the series, Müller was gratified to mention that the new translation of the Koran seemed to have "raised quite a new interest in a work which was often supposed to be unreadable except in Arabic." And the Confucian works by Legge were, says Müller, in the "very best hands," guardedly adding, in light of the earlier missionary furor, that the volume of the *Book of Historical Documents* and the *Book of Poetry* had proved acceptable, if not to missionaries, then to European and native scholars. Müller furthermore remarks that Legge's "forth-coming translation of the Yi King is looked forward to with the highest interest." As it turns out, this was an understatement: The translation of the *Book of Changes* for the *Sacred Books* touched off a scholarly controversy among rival Orientalists over the terms and context of translation every bit as emotional as the debate among missionaries about Legge's first volume for the series.

"Among Oriental scholars and students of ancient religions," says Müller, there "is a general wish that the Series should be continued." The one sensitive issue is, as Müller puts it, that the *Sacred Books* were not "more attractive and more popular" in nature. Rehearsing his worn and ready arguments from the original prospectus, Müller again rests his case on the scholarly and historical need for publishing "complete" translations that include both the beautiful and the repulsive. In contrast to the instant gratification sought by vulgar seekers after gems of Oriental wisdom, the scholarly extraction of scattered "nuggets of gold" from the complete *Sacred Books* will be "all the more precious" precisely because they are "hidden under so much rubbish" and "so much detritus of early thought."

The bottom line in Müller's argument is the question of the bottom line—that is, the financial status of the series. In this regard, Müller was pleased to note that, though never intended as a "commercial speculation," the series so far had enjoyed a financial success sufficient to cover the substantial publishing expenses involved and even (as he was "surprised" to learn) to ensure the press "a fair margin for profit by the sale of copies still on hand." The only sore point indicated is that, although Müller himself was appreciative of the "generous" remuneration given to him as editor (apparently around £200 per annum), he was embarrassed to receive so many complaints about the meager honorarium paid to the translators (it appears to have been around £100 per volume, no matter how much time was involved),[24] remarking that the "youngest clerk in the India Office receives more than we pay to these scholars." But the passing nature of these comments leads us to see them as mostly a pro forma complaint. Nothing was ever done to sweeten the financial agreements with the translators in the second series of volumes and, as Legge knew so well, the press was ruthless in docking honorariums for corrections made in the page proofs.[25]

In Müller's less than humble estimation, there was no conceivable reason that the press should not carry on the work. And given Müller's cozy relationship with the Board of Delegates of the press, his entrepreneurial talents as a career academician, and his prestige as a luminary of All Souls, there is every reason to believe that there was little suspense about the final, and very affirmative, decision. But Müller was not about to leave the outcome to chance.

Remembering Forgotten Bibles

There is another document that is important for the history of the *Sacred Books* and for setting the context for Legge's *Book of Changes* (1882) and his *Record of Rites* (1885), two works that span the first and second series of Müller's library of Oriental scriptures. This is the popular, but substantial, article entitled "Forgotten Bibles" that Müller published in 1884 upon the occasion of the completion of the first series of twenty-four volumes of the *Sacred Books* series.[26] The interest of this article is that it represents a rationale for the second series of translations that is sensitive to some of the newer methodological issues associated with the anthropological or Tylorian tradition (called here the "theoretical school") in the comparative study of religions. Since it is this less reverent anthropological school that by the end of the century was largely superseding the Müllerian, Orientalist, or historical school in the study of alien traditions, Müller's views on these matters should be examined with some care.

Noticeable is Müller's habit of drawing attention to his own wisdom and bravery in undertaking such a difficult and consuming enterprise. Leading a "noble army of martyrs" in the cause of Oriental scholarship, Müller reiterates much of his old elitist academic justification for producing yet more "complete" volumes of Oriental "babbling." The reason now, as in 1879, is "historical" in that the Oriental scriptures are the crucial documents for studying the origin and development of religions throughout the world. But as Müller notes here, a new criticism had entered into the fray with regard to the worth, or lack of such, of a comparative approach to the developmental history of religion relying on the study of the ancient bibles of Oriental peoples. From the new, and increasingly more influential, anthropological point of view, the problem was that the approach of the *Sacred*

Books was "purely" historical without the more philosophically sophisticated evolutionary perspective of those who study religion in relation to "psychophysiological experiments" or from "the creeds of living savages."[27] Müller primarily has Edward Tylor in mind in this discussion of the "theoretic" or "synthetic" (also equivalent to "constructive" and "a priori") school.[28] Just the year before, Tylor had been appointed to a post at the University Museum at Oxford and, with the publication in 1881 of *Anthropology: An Introduction to the Study of Man and Civilization* and his "Lectures on Anthropology," which were published in *Nature* in 1883, his approach was reaching new heights of acceptance and influence in academic circles concerned with the history, but even more crucially and fundamentally with the evolutionary or primitive prehistory, of the so-called savage religions.[29]

The Theoretical Temptation

Based on what he considered his more careful and evidential analytic approach to historical facts preserved in written documents, Müller says that his school in the study of religion was particularly sensitive to the lessons learned from the methods of comparative philology. This science, first of all, "takes language as it finds it" and only then analytically traces it back through written sources as a "language family" (he still refers here to the three primary families of Aryan, Semitic, and Turanian). The analytical process is akin to the tracing of a flower or fruit back to its seed by observing different preserved specimens of the growth cycle. In philological analysis this method results in the discovery of the essential linguistic roots of a language, which are but "metaphor[s]" for the "medium" of homologous analysis and for those "ultimate" facts that resist "all further analysis."[30] According to Müller, the theoretical school claims that it is necessary only to watch a child imitate sounds to know how languages arise. The fallacy here, and Müller's point is as well taken at this time as it was when he argued the antievolutionary point with Darwin himself, is that interjections or imitations "explain words which really require no explanation" (e.g., "crashing, cracking, creaking, crushing, scrunching") whereas "real words" (i.e., root words "expressive of general concepts" such as man, tree, name, law) are left hanging. The theoretical school simply takes it on its own theoretical faith that "real words" evolved out of the interjectional vocabulary.[31]

The same problems accrue in the comparative science of religions when one is considering the differences "between the historian and theorist." Assured that all human beings were originally "savages" or "children," the Tylorian theorist insists that the origin of religion—and its psychodevelopmental agencies of "animism, personification, and anthropomorphism"—

can only be understood by studying the lives of children and savages. Granting infantile behavior at any stage of civilizational development, the question remains for Müller how the core religious "idea" of the "infinite," or the essential concept of a monotheistic god, could have simply evolved out of childish notions of animism. "However strange it may seem to us," the "chief lesson" from the study of "savage tribes" was, according to Müller, that "the perception of the Unknown or the Infinite was with many races as ancient as the perception of the Known or the Finite, that the two were, in fact, inseparable."[32] But Müller withdraws from a full discussion of these issues, preferring to say only that we must guard against the easy temptation "to throw contempt or ridicule" on the theoretical school.[33]

The rest of the article is devoted to a restatement of Müller's tried and true arguments for his historical school as exemplified by the *Sacred Books*—arguments that show Müller's historical method to be just about as theoretical and synthetic as anything speculatively proposed by Tylor and company. That a reconstructed and hypothetical linguistic root or some kind of archaic henotheism is any more factual than are interjectional words or animistic beliefs in terms of the original condition of language and religion is problematic, to say the least. Both positions were products of rival discursive traditions affirming either a "still reverent" idealistic philosophy (rooted in a belief in a creator God or some transcendent category of the mind) or a more atheistic and materialistic faith that found the source of religious ideas in a postulated evolution of human consciousness.

Despite the silliness of the nomenclature, the rationalistic and reductionist evolutionary genre of "bow-wow" and "pooh-pooh" interjectional theories about language origins eventually had the rhetorical edge over Müller's romantic and still reverent "ding-dong" notions of primordial linguistic resonance.[34] Many of Müller's final theoretical efforts seemed to be in response to the threatening views of the theoretical school and were often directed toward an idealistic understanding of the seamless—logical, essential, or spiritual—relation between pure thought and actual language, concepts and words, Logos and history (e.g., his *Science of Thought* [1888] and parts of his 1888–1892 Gifford Lectures).

No Books, No Popes

Putting aside the questionable issue of which school was more truly theoretical or factual, we need to appreciate the cogency of Müller's position. It was his firm belief that he had something definite and "authoritative" to hold onto—that is, the written-down and preserved documents of forgotten bygone eras now translated, remembered, and analyzed. From this perspective, anthropologists of Tylor's bent were only deceiving themselves by thinking that they could project present-day reports about illiterate "Red

Indians, Africans, or Australians" back into the distant past. They should wait, as the linguistically adept Müller condescendingly remarked, till they "know at least their languages."[35] In contrast to this, the comparative "study of book-religions, if we once have mastered their language, is easier, and admits of more definite and scientific treatment than that of native religions which have no books, no articles, no tests, no councils, no popes."[36] It is astonishing to find Müller actually commending the presence of councils and popes, but his strategic willingness to do so here serves only to accentuate how strongly he felt about the relative triviality of so-called savage traditions for understanding the origin and development of human institutions.

This devaluing of living savage traditions, seemingly devoid of any written-downness or recorded "history," lends itself to the general neglect of the popular and folk, or the more apparently oral and ritual, traditions of the common people, the masses, within highly literate traditions such as India and China.[37] Even when such popular living traditions clearly had "books, articles, tests, councils" or even "popes," as did the Heavenly Masters tradition of Daoism practiced in South China in the nineteenth century, it was preferable to examine the essential and classical meaning of the religion in relation to its ancient written-down bibles. Inasmuch as Legge was a fellow traveler, if not a full-scale disciple, of the Müllerian school, we see this bias toward living popular or folk religion exemplified by his general approach to Chinese religions, his *Religions of China* being the most obvious example. We also witness the roots of a basic "present versus past" or "context versus text" bifurcation of subject matter, method, and mood associated with, on the one hand, the academic disciplines of anthropology and, on the other, the comparative history of religions. This is a situation that persists down to the present day.

A More Modest Anatomical Method

Müller's contention, noting again his need for a pretense of humility, was that the superiority of the historical school is found in its "more modest" methods. The "true disciples of the historical school" should consequently carry on their important work of "publishing and translating the ancient records of the great religions of the world" without regard for "the sneers of those who do not find in the Sacred Books of the East what they, in their ignorance, expected." Lapsing into a typically excessive stylistic display, Müller remarks that anthropologists with such a theoretical sneer—"who no doubt would turn up their noses at a kitchen-midden, because it did not contain their favourite lollypops"—can only be pitied.[38]

Müller's last metaphorical image for the methods of the historical school is that of the technique and determination of "comparative anatomy." Just as comparative anatomists had to overcome the squeamishness of the public toward the gruesome but ultimately life-giving work of dissecting the human carcass, so also must students of comparative religion have the fortitude to transform the "shudder" of revulsion toward alien religions, and the analytical dismemberment of all religion, into an attitude of tolerance and disinterested scholarly curiosity. By such a procedure, sympathetic students of religion will "see all that is good and all that is bad in various forms and phases of ancient faith." Such students "must be blinder than blind if they cannot see how the comparative anatomy of those foreign religions throws light on the questions of the day, on the problems nearest to our own hearts, on our own philosophy, and on our own faith."[39] It was the fear that such procedures, whether of the more agnostic theoretical or of the residually reverent historical schools, would throw too much compromising light on the Christian faith that caused so many conservative Victorians to resist aggressively the lure of comparison. Their quite legitimate concern was whether the analytical dissection was being performed on a dead or living body. The first kind of operation could—theoretically—lead to knowledge. The other most definitely resulted in murder. From a conservative theological perspective, it was better to defer to doctrine than deliberately to dissect.

In many ways, however, the findings of the comparative sciences of the nineteenth century, both of the naturalistic and humanistic variety, had already irrevocably moved the academic study of religion away from a "muscular" Evangelical theology and an established biblical creed toward a more anatomical scrutiny of religion. Comparatively speaking, this involved more of a relativized awareness of, if not always respect for, the sometimes strangely familiar religious survivals of savages and the haunting metaphysical and moral homologies of forgotten Oriental bibles. The increasing Victorian appreciation of the Confucian sacred books and the holy life of the compassionate Buddha was a powerful instance of these developments.

Toward the end of the Victorian era the Christian religion was not completely moribund in higher education. But as an established and privileged way of knowing within the academy, it was entering the last phases of its long slide into academic oblivion, a process of secularization that was consummated after the First World War. This accelerating secular drift in universities led to some eleventh-hour reactionary defenses of traditional theology that are splendidly exemplified in Oxford by the Boden Professor's, Monier-Williams, comically pugnacious attacks on Müller and the whole "effeminate" enterprise of the *Sacred Books*. This fear of religious miscegenation was associated with images of a flaccidly liberal "indifferentism," which, among ever-vigilant conservative churchmen, demanded a kind of militant homophobia directed against a limp-wristed scholarship proclaiming the universality of religions and the significance of the Oriental *Sacred Books*.

Iconographical Comparisons

A symbol of these protracted transformations may be seen in the juxtaposition of several fascinating popular images of Western imperial power and transcultural religious awareness. The first of these was a popular portrait of Queen Victoria reading the Bible, which was inscribed with the legend "The Secret of England's Greatness." Another was the well-known painting by Thomas Jones Barker, *Queen Victoria Presenting a Bible in the Audience Chamber at Windsor* (see figure 34).[40] These were images that concisely summed up the Christian and civilizing mission of British imperialism during the Victorian age. The contrasting event comes about from the fact that Max Müller was officially permitted to present to the British queen and Empress of India a special set of the *Sacred Books of the East*—an event that summons up the image of the most powerful potentate of the century dutifully examining the heretofore forgotten bibles of the Orient alongside a piously worn King James Version of the Christian scriptures. What better symbol for the newly enlarged sympathies and pluralistic mission of Oriental scholarship as a royally sanctioned handmaiden to the British empire?[41] The event resonates with another episode, almost a half century earlier, the queen's audience in 1849 with the young missionary Legge and the three "Chinese boys" who were recent converts to Christianity (see page 46). In the 1880s, the queen is presented with the aged professor Legge's translations of the Chinese sacred books, along with other Oriental works, that signal a progressive intellectual conversion of Western missionaries (whether religious or secular) to a more sympathetic and comparative approach to heathens.

Somewhat later toward the end of the century in China a group of "lady" missionaries headed by the English Baptist Timothy Richard presented the Chinese dowager empress with a large-type Delegates' Version translation of the New Testament, specially bound and in a silver casket. To make sure that the translation (using Shangdi for God) was felicitous enough for an empress, Wang Tao, who, as it is said in accounts of this event, was instrumental in the original preparation of the Delegates' Version, was especially consulted.[42] There is not a little here of what Samuel Johnson called the Evangelical propensity for a superstitious kind of bibliolatry that, in this case, implied the possibility of wondrous things happening for Christ if the redoubtable old dowager empress would but take a peek at the greatest story ever told. But such a dramatic outcome was not forthcoming, and it was finally admitted that there was only the untrustworthy word of the Chinese Foreign Office that the gift of the Christian Testament actually

Figure 34. *Queen Victoria Presenting a Bible in the Audience Chamber at Windsor*, 1861. Painting, oil on canvas (66 inches × 84 inches), by Thomas Jones Barker. By courtesy of the National Portrait Gallery, London.

reached the empress. Given these ambiguous results, it seems that this small, but ripely evocative, event was quickly forgotten.

EN RAPPORT WITH CHANGE: TRANSLATING THE MOST MYSTERIOUS CLASSIC

And those that have translated [the Yi jing or Book of Changes] into Latine, who seem not to have understood the true design thereof: for both the Chinese and European Commentators assert it to be a Conjuring Book, or a Book to tell Fortunes by, and to be made use of by the Chinese for that purpose; whereas by the small Specimen I have seen of it, I conceive it to contain the whole Ground, Rule or Grammer, of their Character, Language and Philosophy. . . .
    ROBERT HOOKE, "SOME OBSERVATIONS AND CONJECTURES CONCERNING THE CHINESE CHARACTERS," *PHILOSOPHICAL TRANSACTIONS*, 1686

Coleridge says, in his strange language, speaking of the union of the human soul with the divine essence, that this takes place, "Whene'er the mist, which stands 'twixt

God and Thee, Defecates to a pure transparency"; and so, too, it may be said of
that union of the translator with his original, which alone can produce a good
translation, that it takes place when the mist which stands between them—the mist
of alien modes of thinking, speaking, and feeling on the translator's part—
"defecates to a pure transparency," and disappears.
        MATTHEW ARNOLD, *ON TRANSLATING HOMER,* 1861

The Mist of Alien Modes of Thinking

Beyond the wonderfully apposite transcultural symbolism of the presentations of the *Sacred Books* to Queen Victoria in London and a Chinese New
Testament to the dowager empress in Peking is the fundamental issue that
we are dealing first and foremost with translations and translators. The very
possibility of a truly "inter-national" or transcultural discourse depends on
the possibility of translating from one language to another—of achieving
some cultural transparency in the face of Coleridge's "mist of alien modes
of thinking." As suggested by George Steiner and others, translation "may
be one of the paradigms for human understanding and learning: for in understanding something new, isn't the first instinct to relate it to something
old and familiar? And when the false analogy between the 'new' and the
'old' has been discovered, hasn't one then begun to appreciate the new on
its own terms?"[43] Thus the volumes comprising the *Sacred Books of the East,*
perhaps more so than any other major cultural artifact of the late-Victorian
era, dramatize both the power and pathos of a translated, transformed, and
traduced knowledge of exotic civilizations.[44] Translation is—for nineteenth-
century Orientalists in particular—a way of knowing and deciphering that
is intrinsically comparative.

As Legge's fellow Congregationalist Andrew Martin Fairbairn put it,
"There is not a language on earth that is not capable of allowing translation
into every other language." But what is the "necessary condition" for translation? According to Fairbairn, who was following Müller's lead on these
matters, it is "that thought be in the language—no thought, no translation." It is then the "thought"—and the Logos, structure, or grammar of
thought—that is secretly written into the terms of man and nature. Thus
"man could not get natural science, could not get knowledge of nature, unless nature were the great speech, the great language, an articulate and
definite expression of thought." And so also, declares Fairbairn, God and
religion "is the definite expression of thought, wherein man, the individual,
places himself in relation to the universal—the intelligence in me to the intelligence that underlies all things."[45]

Contrary to Jacques Gernet's linguistic argument for the incommensu-
rable nature of the Chinese and Indo-European cultures, translation (or

comparison) cannot be, always and only, a manipulative conceit of the agency ostensibly controlling the process of philological and cultural transfer. For all of the inevitable distortions associated with the power differential in translation, whether of the matching concepts variety associated with the Buddhist adaptation to China or the term question mode of Protestant Christianity, some authentically alien and potentially transformative meaning reciprocally filters through the best efforts at transcultural linguistic exchange. Whatever the failures of Christianity in translating itself into Chinese tradition in the nineteenth century (and it should be remembered that the transferral is still taking place), it must be appreciated that Buddhism—which is certainly no less exotic, and even more linguistically Indo-European, than Christianity—was in the course of time able to transform China, just as it was itself sinified in the overall process of translation from Sanskrit to Chinese.

The power of translation is seen in the "comparativistic" ability of these linguistically refracted works to move and transform someone emotionally, intellectually, and imaginatively (say, a Scotsman or a Chinese) in relation to an alien point of view, even to convert someone (which is always partial and syncretistic in an intracultural context)—a translator or reader—to another system of meaning and value. At the same time, this power is relativized and often pathetically (and unconsciously) subverted by the fact that the difficult work of translation is naturally, but all too uncritically, regulated by preexisting epistemological assumptions associated with a particular theory of translation and a set of prescribed terms controlling the linguistic transfer.

Translation as expressive of the understanding and actions of the translator is, therefore, always transgressive and transformatively syncretistic in its relation to the source text. At the same time, translation can carry over, or trans-port, some of the foreignness of the other culture. As seen so vividly in the case of both Legge and Müller (and as also was the case for Kumarajiva, the great fifth-century Buddhist translator and missionary to China), it is the cultural history of translation—or, more particularly, of the translator and the reader-receiver of a translation—that modulates the nature and degree of the cross-cultural power of any translation. It is necessary, in other words, to know the particular social and political history of translators to arrive at some understanding of the why and how of their translations.

A Great and Good Translator

The important point is that Legge's lasting cultural significance, like that of Kumarajiva, is largely to be found in his greatness as a translator.[46] Admittedly, he was not a systematic thinker, creative theorist, or elegant writer as an Orientalist—nor, for that matter, was he a particularly great preacher, a conventionally effective missionary, or a completely successful educator.[47] The special bane of anyone identified primarily as a translator is the common assumption that, by the very self-effacing nature of the work, the translator must aspire to a perfect invisibility in relation to his source material— the ideal being that the translator's own personality and intentionality should be completely masked by the mist, or what the Chinese would call the vaporous *qi*, of alien modes of thinking. A great translator is in this idealized sense a Daoist who seemingly does nothing *(wuwei)*, and should do nothing, that meddles with the integrity and originality of the source document.

Notwithstanding the practical and philosophical impossibility of this principle, the result is often, as it is in the case of Legge, that the product is remembered and valorized while the producer and his transformative character and personal history that shape the work of translation are forgotten and depreciated. The implication of these considerations is that the greatness—or perhaps more in the moral and aesthetic sense of the goodness—of a translation (i.e., its cultural and intertextual reverberations through time and space) can only be fully understood in relation to the contextualized cultural significance of the translator. Unfortunately, however, both translation and translators have been sorely neglected in the history of world scholarship and literature.[48]

James Legge was a great and good man who produced great and good translations. Both aspects of the equation—that is, his own character and the character of his work—are ritually reciprocal functions. Most of all as a great translator, he was able to communicate in a carefully chosen and richly annotated, if not always syntactically graceful or stylistically beautiful, English the authentic transformative power of some ancient Chinese books to a Western audience. Despite the animadversions of many Victorian and twentieth-century commentators, great translators are never just mere translators. They are, as Legge certainly was, "real decipherers," mediators, transformers, and transgressors of both the foreign (or source-language) and familiar (target-language) cultural and linguistic codes that they are manipulating. As Louis Kelly—along with George Steiner, one of the very few serious historians of translation—has put it, it is the translator who is the "true interpreter" of culture and is a crucial, though most often overlooked, agent in the development of both Western and Eastern civilizations.[49]

The ability of Legge's major translations of the Ruist, or Confucian, tradition to perdure (they have continued to be remembered, used, reissued for more than a century and a half) as standard versions is a sure sign of their greatness—even though recognition of the translator himself has languished. This kind of endurance has surely not been the case for most other specimens of Victorian Chinese-to-English translation, which have been—and in most cases, rightly so—rapidly superseded, blithely forgotten, or violently repudiated (e.g., the *Shu jing* [Book of historical documents] by Walter Medhurst, the *Yi jing* [Book of changes] by Canon McClatchie, the *Shi jing* [Book of poetry] by William Jennings, the *Daode jing* [Book of the *dao* and its characteristics] by John Chalmers, the *Zhuangzi* [Book of the Master Zhuangzi] by Herbert Giles, and so on). French translations of the nineteenth century have generally fared better than English works, yet, here again, no French scholar—even the truly great, but more eclectic, Julien (or his student Edouard Biot)—can be credited with producing a corpus of lasting translations on the heroic scale of Legge's *Chinese Classics* and *Sacred Books*.

Appropriation and Size

It has been said that no modern scholar has the special kind of help necessary to cope with such a massive collection of texts. In this regard, it is sometimes maliciously, but often quite ignorantly, insinuated that it is really all a matter of Victorian scholars resident in China having ready access to a cheap native amanuensis capable of doing all the philological drudge work, and perhaps even the actual translation. The noted European sinologue enters the picture only when it is time to polish up a final version and make it suitable for publication under his name alone in the *China Review*. There were surely instances of this kind of plagiarism (and forgery, Edmund Backhouse being the most notorious) among various self-styled European sinologues living in China during the nineteenth (and twentieth) century and Legge did make extensive use of native scholarly assistants such as Wang Tao and others.[50] But scholars of intelligence, integrity, and hard work, such as Legge and most of the other better-known China-coast missionary and lay scholars, were accomplished sinologists and translators in their own right and cannot legitimately be charged with the false appropriation of another's work. Legge may even be seen to be an innovator in the ethics of cross-cultural scholarly attribution. He was always careful in his published works to acknowledge the help he received from native assistants such as Wang Tao. Some other well-known Orientalists (e.g., Max Müller) seem not to have been so conscientious.[51]

Another angle on these issues is related to the massiveness of Legge's production—work that was, moreover, mostly advanced by hand and by candle (later in Oxford by gaslight) while he was carrying on a separate full-time and active career as a missionary. It is the awareness of these incredibly difficult circumstances that underscores Legge's great industry, if not his theoretical sophistication, as a translator. We cannot help but notice how Legge's accomplishment, granting all of its deficiencies, contrasts with the timidity and narrowly specialized achievements of many modern scholars possessing all the marvels of modern academic technology.

Apprehending the Goodness of Translation

The greatness of Legge's accomplishment is also connected with what can be called, in a rather Confucian or Mencian manner, the goodness, rightness, or ripeness of his translations. I refer to the question of Legge's faithfulness or fidelity as a translator in terms of Mengzi's method of "apprehending the scope" of ancient classical works such as the *Book of Poetry*. This is a principle that, as the Chinese equivalent to Müller's romantic emphasis on a symbolic "sense by sense" translation of the *Sacred Books of the East*, Legge notably takes as the "motto, figure-head, and flag" for all of his translations of the Confucian classics and describes in a passage from *Mengzi* (see the first epigraph on page 336).

Legge's translations were not, or are not, necessarily the best, the most definitive, the most philologically accurate, the most historically critical, the most philosophically refined, the most psychologically sensitive, or the most stylistically expressive and elegant. Nevertheless, at the time they appeared in the nineteenth century, his translations came closer to these ideals, except perhaps in literary style, than any other comparable works did.[52] It might be said that Legge's translations were superior simply because they were the only complete Western-language versions of the classics available in the nineteenth century. But this observation is relevant only to a few works (such as the *Spring and Autumn Annals [Chunqiu]* and *Zuo's Commentary [Zuozhuan]*) because almost all of the Five Classics and Four Books were available in eighteenth- or nineteenth-century translations—sometimes in several Latin, French, English, German, or Russian versions. Legge's work was truly the best in its time, whatever the criteria of evaluation.

Timbre and Taste

The oft-stated charge of Legge's "woodenness" as a translator by both nineteenth-century and modern-day commentators often has more to do with matters of literary taste and academic politics than it does with questions about his faithfulness or general accuracy as a translator. It has long been recognized, for example, that, because they seem to follow the original text so closely, Legge's translations are excellent schoolboy cribs for those studying classical Chinese. His translations clearly follow Chinese semantics and syntax closely, but they are not slavishly literal or "word by word" renditions. The problem is really more of an illusion of stolid literality created by twentieth- and twenty-first-century readers reacting to Legge's Victorian diction and classical Latinate cadence.

Sweepingly dismissive judgments about Legge's translations (and I am thinking more of his Confucian, than his Daoist, translations here)—that they are hopelessly stilted and datedly Victorian in tone, too awkwardly literal, and hopelessly distorted by a Christian missionary bias—are often misguided.[53] At present, when politically correct fashion tends to rule academic discourse even more rigidly than it did in the Victorian era, criticism of Legge's rendering of the Confucian classics often disguises an abiding prejudice against Victorian cultural and stylistic forms and a bias against missionaries and all forms of religious belief. Legge's hearty earnestness and pious seriousness—expressed by the sober tone of his translations, his elaborate commentarial notes, and especially his long-winded prolegomena replete with apologetic observations—are simply not self-consciously ironic enough for contemporary scholastic taste.

Weighing Waley

Arthur Waley, the great twentieth-century sinologist and translator who carried on the British tradition of the independent gentleman scholar, is perhaps the best example of these issues of latter-day, both modern and postmodern, opinion concerning Legge's work as a translator and sinologist.[54] In particular, Waley found that Legge too slavishly followed Zhu Xi and that Legge's *Mencius* consequently contained "numerous passages" that were "certainly wrong." Here I want only to attend to another dimension of a broader Waleyesque critique of Legge. For many scholars and lay readers, Waley's translations became the accepted standard of faithfully accurate and elegantly literate Chinese-to-English translation in the twentieth century, and, when compared with Waley's translations, Legge's work appears even more frightfully Victorian and ridiculously wooden than it really is. But this response is clearly conditioned by the fact that Waley's Bloomsbury set sensibility, anthropological methods, and limpid poetic style were very much in keeping with the Lytton Stracheyian post–First World War revulsion toward all things stiffly and piously Victorian.[55] Since Waley shaped many of our modern Anglo-American attitudes regarding a translator's style in rendering classical Chinese, it is no wonder that we have difficulty with Legge's Latinate classicism, Old Testament diction and syntax, term question pieties, Evangelical earnestness, and preacher's long-windedness. After reading Legge's *Book of Poetry*—whether in its prose or metric incarnation—a reader today longs for Waley's spry sprung-rhythm version, with its renditions that read like surprisingly good English verse seasoned with an exotic subject matter and a strangely archaic and rueful folk quality.[56] Waley's wry, and anthropologically sensitive, translations of Chinese poetry sound so elusively and allusively modern that Legge's work can only be found portentously dull and deficient—that is to say, hopelessly Victorian.[57]

But the question of whether or not Waley's translations are really better—more faithful, more accurate, or more in keeping with the archaic meaning of the Chinese text—than Legge's work is a moot point.[58] As much, if not more, of a case could be made for the appropriateness of rendering ancient Chinese poetry with the rhyming rhythms of Scottish highland dialect as with the sprung meter popularized by Gerard Manley Hopkins.[59] Our aesthetic preference for one or the other today does not mean that either is not, in its own transgressive way, a very good and faithful translation. Waley would say that the crucial difference is that he translated with a critical eye toward capturing the original meaning of the ancient text whereas Legge was too uncritically smitten by Zhu Xi and later Ching-dynasty interpretations of the ancient classics. For example, Zhao Qi/Chao Ch'i, of the second century C.E., was closer to Mencius's time than Zhu Xi, who flourished in the twelfth century, was, and, because Legge mostly seemed to follow Zhu, Legge's translation is "certainly wrong."

Waley is mostly wrong here.[60] I refer both to his assumptions about Legge's indebtedness to Zhu Xi and to Waley's own confidence that, by following a native commentator closer in time to the text in question, he can approximate more of the original meaning.[61] The difficulty with this last conviction is that, as Legge recognized, Zhu Xi's own theory of commentary or interpretive translation emphasized the need to understand, or to "apprehend the scope" of, a text in its own terms. These terms were most often moral in nature, but also included a consideration of the earlier commentarial tradition associated with the text. Incongruously, Waley's view may imply that his own twentieth-century understanding comes closer to the original Chinese text of the *Mengzi* than do Zhao's second-century, Zhu's twelfth-century, or Legge's nineteenth-century versions. Most problematic of all is the assumption that a scholar can capture some singular original meaning, whatever the text or commentary used.

In the Commentarial Stream

In keeping with the loose postmodernist implications of some forms of traditional Chinese literary hermeneutics, it may be possible to say that the meaning of an ancient Chinese text emerges only within, and as a part of, the totality of the continuously evolving intertextual tradition of commentary—or that a Chinese text is authoritative, canonical, or classical *(jing)* only if it has a commentarial tradition *(zhuan)* associated with it. A native Chinese commentary is a running lexical transcription, or paraphrased translation, of a source text. It is in this sense, especially since his annotated translations participate in the *totum scribile* of Chinese commentarial tradition more than almost any other Western sinological works of his own or other ages do, that Legge's translations may be said to be both faithful and good. As Gabelentz, Edkins, and Chalmers all astutely observed in response to Legge's *Book of Changes,* we may legitimately disagree with different aspects of his translations but, to do so, we must also go behind and contend with the whole native Chinese tradition of textual commentary.[62]

Given the fact that he was constantly reworking his translations even after they were published, Legge clearly never considered any of his work definitive or finished. But his published works, in both their original and various revised forms, were very good translations as translations go. For all the partial validity of accusations about his stiff style and Christian bias, Legge was nevertheless able to convey much of the authentic Qing-dynasty Chinese sense of the texts he was translating. Furthermore, he did this in a way that was quite reflective of the manner and form of a traditional Chinese commentary (which were often structurally intermingled with the classical text).[63] In the original Hong Kong edition of the classics, there is even an interesting attempt (which, for reasons of expense and accessibility, was not continued in the *Sacred Books* edition) to emulate in a hybrid way the interlinear, and vertical/right-to-left, glossing format of a traditional Chinese text and commentary, while incorporating a horizontal/left-to-right structure along with other Western biblical and classical conventions of prefatory comment and "footed" annotation.

The overall design, physical layout, and actual printing of the first set of the *Chinese Classics* were personally supervised by Legge. In this way, his versions of the Confucian classics graphically reveal their translator's deep literary, philological, and historical awareness of the native tradition of commentary. Even at the level of typographical structure and form, Legge's original English versions of the Confucian classics participate in the intertextual stream of printed Chinese commentarial tradition during the late Qing period. As Benjamin Elman has shown in his masterful study of late-Qing scholarship, this was mostly a neo-Confucian commentarial stream, a tradition that was still largely intact despite various iconoclastic Chinese and Western disruptions of the current.[64] In some ways, therefore, Legge's work is traditional and commentarial, but—by virtue of its philological, comparative, and historical concerns—also exhibits much of the transitional nature (caught between old-fashioned and modern attitudes) of native Chinese commentary and criticism toward the end of the nineteenth century.

Related to this identification of Leggian translation and a traditional commentarial form is the important fact that, in the nineteenth century, scholarship in *both* Western and Chinese tradition was turning away from the old commentarial conviction in the undisturbed authority of ancient classical or sacred books to a contextualized critical, academic, or secular focus on a text's historicity. This was a method inherently destructive of an ancient work's traditional "author-ity." As John Henderson remarks, "[F]or nineteenth-century German historians," as well as for various maverick Qing scholars such as Qian Daxian/Ch'ien Ta-hsien and Pi Xirui/P'i Hsi-jui (and Wang Tao could also be included here), "the main loci of profound meaning in the past were not classical texts, but the historical eras that these texts and other source materials illuminated."[65] As Müller also constantly reminded his audience, the *Sacred Books of the East* were primarily interesting and valuable as historical documents—not because of their own intrinsic profundity or sacredness.

Now it is this very transition—or "shift in hermeneutical focus from the classics to the classical era, 'from the *chefs-d'oeuvre* of mankind to the historical interconnection which supports them' "—that was, as Henderson says, "one of the most momentous" transformations "in the history of the human sciences."[66] This transition in the theory and practice of professionalized and secularized scholastic understanding (that is, freedom from sectarian Zhu Xi–style hermeneutics in the case of Qing scholarship), as embodied in the West in the work of Victorian figures such as Legge and Müller, is what I am trying to trace in this study. This effort is complicated by the realization that the emergent historiographical mode of academic discourse was itself used to devalue both traditional commentary and mere translation. Legge's significance in relation to these changes is problematic because only fitfully does he participate, both in the biblical and Chinese sense, in the newer, secular, or historical methods of the higher criticism while holding onto what Henderson calls an old-fashioned "commentarial mentality" that prefers the still reverent, dutiful, and ritual marginality of a gloss or translation.[67]

The Dutiful Sweat of Translation

Legge's incredibly diligent and prolonged effort in acquiring a familiarity with the Chinese commentarial tradition in the manner both of a native scholar and of an Evangelical biblical exegete gives his English translations a special fidelity and commentarial authority.[68] Some of Legge's ability to participate in the rich Chinese traditions of commentary in an almost native Chinese way has to do with his Victorian preacher's and Mandarin scholar's devotion to the hard work of a ritualized daily routine of constant reading, regular memorization, continuously refined annotation, and numerous draft translations and revisions. Sweated copybook repetition and rote transcription—dutiful iteration done with the expense of much intense intellectual and physical labor over the course of many months and years—were at the heart of this traditional Western and Chinese method for learning. Like Master Kong, Legge was forever a student dedicated to the duty of learning. This kind of hard work is also another dimension of what, in the previous chapter, was called the "whole duty" of transcultural understanding. These are activities that depend as much on the body as on intellectual cleverness. As Legge himself said, the work of translation was pretty much like the arduous physical labor of slowly and methodically, step by step, climbing a forbiddingly lofty mountain, sometimes with, but often without, the sturdy help of native coolies or pundits. Even though the peak always seems just beyond one's grasp, there comes that moment, attained by sheer persistence and the discipline of the climb, when the summit is reached and, in the ecstasy, all else down below fades away into insignificance. The sublimity that came from this kind of achievement was what linked Wordsworth's poetic labors with Legge's scholarly work of a translator.

This epiphanic elevation is soon tempered by the intimidating realization (as emphasized by Mark Pattison and Matthew Arnold) that one has attained only the foothills of a much more vast range of jagged mountains or has landed on only one small island of an extensive archipelago—that is, where the whole monstrous body of Chinese literature fades away into an eternal mist beyond the horizon. Legge's dawning awareness of the overwhelming depth and breadth of Chinese literature was in this way fundamentally akin to the recently deceased Mark Pattison's darkly alarming vision of the *totum scribile* of all European literature. One important difference was that, whereas for Pattison the vision of the immense ocean of literature was both depressing and debilitating, Legge reacted more positively and productively by accepting, and methodically addressing, the immensities unfolding before him.

When he was in China, Legge's early morning ritual always involved some biblical memorization and exegesis and a concentrated period of Chinese study and translation regularly supplemented by consultation with a knowledgeable native scholar. Even when he was back in England without the availability of any informed native assistance,[69] Legge continued his ritual routine of writing out several copies of his translations and Chinese lessons, going from Chinese to English and vice versa—version-making methods that he had cultivated from the very beginning of his life as a student of the Latin classics in Aberdeen and then continued as a scholar of the Chinese classics. In Oxford, ensconced in his Keble Terrace study and surrounded by his extensive library of Chinese books and Western sinological and Oriental scholarship, Legge's methods of translation habitually involved the determination of the best possible critical editions; long hours reading dynastic histories and the repeated writing out of the Chinese text and commentaries; and finally the preparation of an English version and annotations that would typically go through many different complete drafts. His preparation of a prolegomenon or introduction, and preface, would come only after the hard work of protracted study and repeated translation was accomplished.

Transparent Defecation

The ability to understand a foreign work deeply and to translate it faithfully and well, if not literally or photographically, is not some mysterious intuitive power or sixth sense involving, in Coleridge's "strange words," the "union of the human soul with the divine essence." Rather, as Legge demonstrates in his inimitable Evangelical way, the dissipation of the "mist of alien modes of thinking," the "transparent defecation" of translated meaning comes about through the sweat and experiential insight of laborious and dutifully prolonged work: repeated study, physical exertion, mental strain, imaginative stimulation, and the regular passing of time "well spent." Good translation has this in common with any process of productive learning—or for that matter with any kind of carefully rehearsed and repeatedly performed ritual activity that produces meaning both, to borrow from Catholic terminology, *ex opere operantis* and *ex opere operatus*.

The other factor that is crucial for a good, effective, or lasting translation is a general openness to, and a respect for, the real and potentially threatening meaningfulness of alien texts—even if that meaning is largely invented and the terms of transfer sound suspiciously familiar (Legge's equation of Shangdi, Tian, and the Christian God most obviously comes to mind). This is the factor that I have been calling the constructive comparativist temper of sympathetic comprehensiveness. To assume too quickly the complete unintelligibility of the Chinese meaning of texts such as the *Book of Changes*, as Legge's nemesis, Lacouperie, does, is to rely on an ostensibly higher and more scientific method of comparative interpretation that tended to believe that no actual translation of archaic Chinese as Chinese was really possible.

Regardless of my reservations, Coleridge's organic image for translation is an apt metaphor for the earthiness of the transformative activities of translation well done. The achievement of a transferable understanding of an alien text, the gradual attainment of an empathetic union characteristic of a good translation or of any form or dialogical communication, is, both rhetorically and practically speaking, a matter of an eventual "defecation" involving the mixed digested excreta of a mind and body at a particular time and place. Like a satisfying bowel movement, a translation is good when it has carnal substance as well as aesthetic form and temporal consummation.[70]

Recognizing a translation that is precipitously good for both the translator and the reader-receiver is, to borrow from Douglas Robinson's neoromantic reflections on these issues, a matter of a ritualized experiential or somatic feeling rather than a mystical flash of spirituality. So Robinson argues that the "self-projection" into the body of a native speaker or text is a "more crucial requirement for the good translator than a comprehensive cognitive understanding of the SL [source-language]"—adding the important parenthetical qualification that this primarily obtains "if one could only have one or the other." This is admittedly a dangerous line of thought to follow since it allows Robinson, for example, to defend Ezra Pound's fourth-hand quasi translation, or mutated transcription, of "Ernest Fennollosa's crib" of Chinese poetry, which was itself based on Japanese translations.[71]

Silver Sincerity

Robinson's observations should not be taken as the golden rule for all translation. It seems that his wonderfully playful reflections have more to do with the ambiguous implications of what Michael Polyani has called the "tacit knowledge" of mind and body that is always built into any practical human encounter with the different, the unknown, or the other—whether a person, a bicycle, or a text. This is intrinsically related to the fundamentally moral question of the faithfulness or fidelity of a translation, which is too often taken to mean the impossible determination of exact equivalents for the terms of the source text (whether in a literal or spiritual sense of *sense*). Faithfulness or transactional sincerity is a two-way relationship and can never attain to a perfect equivalence, an unsullied union of terms, or a wholly harmonious meeting of minds; there is always something left over or out—something compromised, transformed, and traduced on both sides of the equation. The difficulty here is the problem in all comparative acts, the nature, method, and degree of equivalence achieved in the dynamic human process of understanding. The acts of knowing and translation, as Müller put it, are, after all, dependent on a relational "dyad"—that is, the progressively deeper appreciation of sameness *and* difference.

In a way that has some real bearing on Legge's significance as a translator, Robinson helpfully draws out more of the somatic and dialogical— what Steiner calls the "reciprocal," or what could appropriately be called here the comparativist or silver Confucian principle of proper ritual relations—factors in the profoundly human act of good translation or any good social transaction. What counts in translation and the "feel of equivalence," as in human affairs, is the ability to respect the integrity of the other text or person, an attitude of "sympathetic comprehensiveness" that possesses the honest mercurial mutability and mutuality of silver more than the hypocritical perfection and stasis of gold. As Robinson says about "good translation":

> Translation succeeds best not when the translator has obeyed every cognitive
> rule—performed a painstaking textual analysis and planned his or her re-

structuring out carefully in advance—but when he or she is most sensitive to the feel of both the SL [source-language] and the TL [target-language] words. To the extent that it makes sense to talk of translational equivalence at all, in fact, it is a matter not so much of minds—analytical correspondences—as it is of bodies, of feel. Equivalence between an SL and a TL word or phrase is always primarily somatic: the two phrasings feel the same.[72]

The problem here, of course, is that feelings change and Robinson (even though he says that he intends otherwise) tends too much to imply that "good feelings" about translation are largely independent of "painstaking textual analysis."[73] Legge would agree that it is the translator's "feeling" of being *"en rapport"* that is crucial to the transaction, but he would also want to affirm the precept, in keeping with principles articulated by Matthew Arnold, Benjamin Jowett, and Max Müller, that right feelings result only from a long and grueling process of intellectual and physical "construal" (requiring commentarial breadth, scholarly analysis, and interpretive deduction). Even though I would like to maintain that some of Robinson's ideas about the somatic dimension of translation help us to understand the nature of Legge's achievement as a translator, Legge himself—given the hermeneutical assumptions of the Victorian period and his own Scottish common sense upbringing—would probably be inclined to find such theories more bemusing than beguiling.

For Legge—influenced by various biblical, Aristotelian, Coleridgian, Arnoldian, Jowettian, and Müllerian theories about translation[74]—the translator's construing of a Chinese text is romantically idealized in the manner of a mind-to-mind operation that involves a process of acute observation and decipherment, a careful sifting through the evidence and, after an intellectual reenactment of the modus operandi, a dawning apprehension of the hidden meaning. Good translation is like the good detective work of that great decipherer and eccentric genius Sherlock Holmes, first described by Arthur Conan Doyle in the 1880s (*A Study in Scarlet* appeared in *Beeton's Christmas Annual* of 1887). This was a method that required a careful and repeated examination of all the evidence that, if the observational or detective process were thorough and rationally empirical enough, would eventually—in a rather typically British intuitive-empirical, and amateurishly professional, Sherlockian way—reveal the hidden clues that illuminate the secrets of murder, mayhem, and meaning. It is a method not so much of the "dog in the nighttime" (which was significant because it did nothing) but of the "Hound of the Baskervilles," the beastly meaning of which is uncovered only after the layers of fearfully distorting legend are exposed and developmentally deconstructed—only after true history is distinguished from tradition and myth. It is in this sense that Legge's mature ideas about translation come closest to Müller's romantic theory of symbolic decipherment articulated in the first volume of the *Sacred Books.*

Translation from this perspective depends on the interpretive unveiling of an original or essential meaning secreted beneath layers of linguistic distortion and historical development. Behind the racial and temporal deformations of grotesque savage and cunning Oriental traditions, there is a universal human nature waiting only to be known by those who can sympathetically see that history reveals the secret homologies of languages and religions.[75]

The Secrets of the Book of Changes

This preamble about the theory and orthopraxis of translation sets the necessary context for appreciating the significance of Legge's rendition of the enigmatic *Book of Changes (Yi jing),* which appeared in 1882 as volume 26 of the *Sacred Books of the East.* This translation of the most mysterious of the Chinese classics represents a milestone both in Legge's continuing growth as a scholar-translator and in the overall history of nineteenth-century Orientalism. It is in his long and convoluted attempt to understand this incredibly puzzling text that Legge first came to some explicit understanding of his own theory of translation—albeit a theory that was largely, if not entirely, reflective of Müller's ideas. While generally following a Song-style commentarial line of moralistic decipherment, he also for the first time critically challenged (in a modern sense) some of the pious native theories about the extreme antiquity, textual integrity, and Confucian authorship of the text.

Legge was the first Western scholar to produce an intelligible rendition of the complete work, clearly disentangling the ancient core Text (made up of the six-line figures, or *hexagrams,* a term that seems to be Legge's invention, with short explanatory statements and terse comments on individual lines) and the later, symbolically interpretive Appendixes.[76] Legge's translation of the *Book of Changes* is an extremely important way station in the application of historiographical methods to Chinese texts and in the popular Western cultural imagination concerning an occult China of cosmic lore and secret moral wisdom.[77] As a significant artifact within the impossibly diverse constellation of persons, texts, and objects included within the Western tradition of the so-called Mystic East, the *Book of Changes* comes into full-blown life only in the 1960s and 1970s with the English renderings of Richard Wilhelm's German scriptural translation and its attendant valorization as a guide to Jungian synchronicity. The reprinting of English-language editions of the text down to the present (many of these new editions are only slightly modified or modernized versions of Legge's 1882 public-domain translation) furthermore indicates that, while undergoing an ebb and flow, the thirst in the New Age for the Oriental mysteries continues unabated. Despite scholarly misgivings about such hermetic approaches, this is a text that, by its very nature as a repository of past and future secrets, invites puzzlement. We need to appreciate that a scholarly or historiographical approach can often be just as hermetic as a blatantly occult, Jungian, or moralistic interpretation of an archaic scripture. The notion that a scholar can return to the original historical context of an ancient Oriental text, Chinese or otherwise, and then understand it in relation to the linguistic and cultural standards that prevailed in the ancient period, is, to say the least, highly esoteric and problematic. It depends on a coupling of scholarly deduction and intuitive speculation that approximates a form of interpretive divination.

Divinatory Translation: Clues about Change

The *Book of Changes*—more than any other of the Chinese classics or *Sacred Books of the East*—is a cryptogram of both graphic and linguistic signs that requires some method of divination, decipherment, or symbolic translation. Divination (even though Legge prefers the rationalized and moralistic style of Song decipherment) is, after all, a form of translation that seeks to understand and communicate the sacred digital or yin-yang code of meaning written into the dynamically pulsating heart of the cosmos and human beings. Some twentieth-century sinologists, after more than a century of specialized scholarship, had the good sense to take the issue of divination more seriously than did Legge, but we are really no closer to the secret meaning of the *Changes* than Legge was back in 1882.[78] It seems to be the genius of this text to maintain its integrity by resisting any overly glib formulations of its meaning. This book defies any finality of translation or interpretation since its meaning always depends on a changing set of chance encounters involving the text, translator, and reader.

In his preface to the *Book of Changes*—written on March 16, 1882, only a few months before the work appeared in bookstores in London and Oxford—Legge revealingly discussed his long struggle to "get hold of a clue" that would guide him "to a knowledge of the mysterious classic." He mentions that he had actually written out a translation of the text and appendixes of the *Changes* in 1854 and 1855 at the beginning of his scholarly career, but that at that time—and even after this version was soaked in the Red Sea after a shipwreck in 1870—he admittedly knew "very little about the scope and method of the book."[79] It was only after his final return to England in 1874 that, realizing that his "toil of twenty years before was no service at all," he "got hold" of a "clue" that promised to "reveal" the "secrets" of the *Book of Changes*. Legge's discovery was his dawning historiographical apprehension that the Text of the classic had to be distinguished from the

Appendixes, the latter, traditionally said to have been written by Kongzi, having become, in the course of centuries, interspersed with the text portion of each graphic hexagram. As Legge says, and this realization represents a major advance toward a higher critical approach in sinological Orientalism (the preface is rather remarkable for the number of times Legge uses the term *sinologist* in a professional sense), "I now perceived that the composition of the Text and of the Appendixes, allowing the Confucian authorship of the latter, was separated by about 700 years, and that their subject-matter was often incongruous."[80]

Studying the Text "by itself and as complete in itself" was, for Legge, the needed breakthrough toward a "right understanding of the Yi."[81] A comparison of the linguistic "tone and style" of the book as related to historical periods also led to Legge's conclusion that, although the Text was composed by the semilegendary King Wen and the duke of Zhou (dating, says Legge, to the "twelfth century B.C."), there was, more iconoclastically, no real evidence for the Confucian or Ruist authorship of the Appendixes (dating "six and seven centuries later at least"). Using these critical philological and historical methods, supplemented by careful consideration of native views, Legge arrived at an understanding of the meaning of the Text of the *Book of Changes* that, as he notes, generally agreed with received commentarial opinion from the "Han dynasty down to the present" (especially the *Yuzhi rijiang yijing jieyi* of 1682).[82]

Symbolic Themes

What, then, was the secret meaning of the Text? Descriptively the *Changes* was a "text in explanation of certain lineal figures, and of appendixes to it." His understanding of the real or deeper meaning of the sixty-four enigmatic sets of lines and their "sixty-four short essays" (which constituted the Text as distinguished from explanations in the Appendixes) hinged on Legge's exegetical discovery that both the lines and essays "emblematically" or "symbolically expressed" various hidden but "important themes, mostly of a moral, social, and political character." For Legge it was important to maintain that, when King Wen and his son originally composed the lines and text, they "were not divining themselves"—even though both "were familiar with the practice of divination which had prevailed in China for more than a thousand years."[83]

The point seems to be—and it is interestingly in keeping with rationalistic and moralizing presuppositions of Song philosophy, as well as with Western Enlightenment and Reformation views on superstitious practices—that the "merely vulgar" (as Gabelentz said) magical belief in, and ritualized practice of, divination could not in its own right be meaningfully, authentically, or essentially religious and moral.[84] So, therefore, even though the

Book of Changes claimed to be a manual of divination or, as Robert Hooke said, a "conjuring book," such mere vulgarity could not be. Rather, the divinatory dimension was only a corrupt distortion of its true, though hidden or forgotten, meaning as a guidebook, or lesson book, of moral, social, and political behavior under certain specified, and generally universal, temporal and physical circumstances. From this point of view, the lesson of the *Book of Changes* was that change, the flow of cosmic and human time, had a mutable but recurrent structural pattern (a Logos or *dao*) harboring intrinsic moral and political implications for individuals and society.

The fascinating import of this from both a traditional Song Chinese and Western Romantic perspective is that all interpretation, translation, and knowing are never simply literal. Just as the meaning of the Christian Bible was increasingly being understood (especially in terms of moral and historical criteria) by academic scholars in its secularly symbolic rather than its literal supernaturalistic significance, so also was this kind of hermeneutics of the occult seen as the most powerfully objective and scientific form of human understanding. "Meaningfulness" was always fundamentally symbolic, representational, or metaphorical and was, therefore, always a matter of using an investigative method that saw behind the superficialities of lines and words to the secret inner (the pure, original, archaic, essential, moral) sense of things. Again, the fact that the most profound secret meaning of "sacred books" just so happened to turn out to be intrinsically moral and rationally idealistic in nature was hardly an accident for Ruist, Enlightenment, Romantic, or Victorian Evangelical interpreters. The fact that Song Ruist scholars were predisposed to both a moral and rationally idealistic perspective when dealing with their own ancient classics is a particularly telling point that necessarily conditions our evaluation of Legge's interpretive choices concerning this material. This confluence of interpretive choices also suggests much about why the modern rejection of these preferences in the twentieth and twenty-first centuries (both in the West and in China) has numbed some observers to the importance of Legge's work.

The Secrets of Mind-to-Mind Translation

Knowing the secret of the *Book of Changes* still left Legge with the quandary of how best to translate such an intrinsically occult text intelligibly for an English audience. Many sinologists, after all, wanted to maintain that it was merely a divination book and that the "oracles of divination were designedly wrapped up in mysterious phraseology." Most significant in this regard was Legge's realization that any attempt to emulate the incredible terseness of the Chinese text, as in the Regis-Mohl edition of 1834 (see page 693, note 76) and his own 1854 version, was doomed to utter unintelligibility. Much better was to follow the principle he had "unconsciously acted on" in all of his other translations of the classics: "namely, that the written characters of the Chinese are not representations of words, but symbols of ideas, and that the combination of them in composition is not a representation of what the writer would say, but of what he thinks."[85]

Legge goes on to emphasize that it is "vain" for "a translator to attempt a literal version." It is far better for the translator to follow Mengzi's "rule" of trying to "meet the scope of a sentence" with our thoughts. In this way a sensitive translator allows the symbolic Chinese characters to bring his mind *"en rapport"* with the "author" of the text. Legge does not say exactly how this rapport is achieved or what experientially it amounts to. Beyond the fact that this rapport is spiritually akin to the "sympathetic comprehensiveness" driving Müllerian comparison and involves much preparatory work and intensely repetitive study, Legge seems to understand it as an almost Coleridgian fecal epiphany. This is suggested by Legge's one attempt to explain the meaning of being *en rapport* with a text—that there is some kind of "participation" of the translator in the thoughts of the author. "There is," concludes Legge, "the seeing of mind to mind." Translating, like true knowing, is a matter of a meditative seeing with the inner eye of the mind into the secret scope, core, or root of things—even when there is no particular, or identifiable, author. Primarily a visual science and art (like Müller's comparative anatomy), it depends on the penetrating gaze of the translator, scholar, or sleuth, which is able to observe, detect, and enter into the original authorial intentionality of the text, classic, or crime.

Parenthetical Translation

The "mind to mind" method of translation does not give the translator unlimited license. Rather, it is a matter of expressing the "meaning of the original as exactly and concisely as possible," but with the careful parenthetical introduction of "a word or two now and then to indicate what the mind of the writer supplied for itself." While he is careful to put his interstitial interpolations in parentheses in his published text of the *Book of Changes,* Legge actually claims that, in keeping with his semimystical theory of authorial intentionality, he could have dispensed altogether with the typographical brackets. There was "nothing in the English version," he says, that was not "present in the writer's thought."[86]

Legge conscientiously notes that, for lack of space, he was prevented from appending supporting translations from Zhu Xi and other Song philosophers.[87] But he did include a copious "running commentary" that further drew out the "teachings of king Wan and his son" as related to the symbolic import of the linear figures and enigmatic words. Legge's full "symbolic" translation of the *Book of Changes* was, then, a typographical mosaic made up of the translation of the Text and his parenthetical inclusion of the Text's implicit connective tissue or "thoughts"—together with a fecal precipitation of Legge's own added commentarial exposition of the fuller "symbolic" meaning (in a commentarial, philological, historical, moral, social, and political sense) of the book. A glance at Legge's *Book of Changes* will show that it is the "running commentary" that takes up about two-thirds of most pages.

Discussing the other European translations of the *Book of Changes,* Legge notes that, while the Regis-Mohl edition suffered from "excessive literalness," the version by Canon McClatchie showed the "delirious" dangers of a symbolic approach by a translator blithely unaware of the structural, historical, and authorial problems with the text. Unfortunately, McClatchie was also ignorantly dismissive of native scholarship. In the grandly deluded spirit of Mr. Casaubon in George Eliot's *Middlemarch,* McClatchie sought to unlock the mysteries of the book by using a universal "Key of Comparative Mythology." But, according to Legge, the results were "not pleasant to look at or dwell upon." "Happily," says Legge, McClatchie's titillating discovery of a sexually dualistic cosmogony "never entered into the minds of Chinese scholars."[88]

Legge also mentions the appearance of two other translations in the early 1880s: a partial version in Latin by Angelo Zottoli and a promised edition by the London Orientalists Terrien de Lacouperie and Robert K. Douglas.[89] Noting that Lacouperie seemed basically ignorant of the actual "contents of the classic," Legge was less than sanguine about the "prospects for success" of a translation that "promised" to reveal the Babylonian or "Accadian" secrets of the *Book of Changes.*[90] Lacouperie's reaction to Legge's work actually led to a heated and protracted scholarly fracas over the occult meaning of this most mysterious of classics. This upsurge of interest in a book that was so blatantly enigmatic seems particularly expressive of a whole scholarly vogue in European culture at this time concerned with the uncovering, and the rational and historical explanation, of all manner of apparent Oriental mysteries (encompassing Buddhism and, for the first time, the Daoist classics; at a more popular level also embracing the then-current infatuation with theosophy, spiritualism, the Golden Dawn, and the occult novels of George Bulwer-Lytton and Rider Haggard). These were mysteries that were now being found to be largely "unconscious" and only partially fathomed by the native tradition itself.[91]

Only the higher critical prowess of Western Orientalistic scholarship was able to go behind the superficial meanings of the *Book of Changes* as a manual of divination and discover its hidden symbolic meaning as a repository of moral and political lessons (the European sinologue Legge more fully than the Song commentators) or, even more radically and historically, as a Babylonian lexicon (e.g., Terrien de Lacouperie). The methodological principle was really the same—that is, the driving desire to penetrate the veils of mystery, to prove in either a religious or secular sense that the essential meaning of Oriental texts was always something other than it superficially said itself to be. And if that symbolic, original, or archaic hidden meaning happened ultimately to have Western historical roots, so much the better for the obvious transcendental superiority of Western civilization, Western science, and the Western God.

The Nearest Analogue for God

The issue on Legge's mind as he was finishing up his preface to the *Book of Changes* was the old terminological terror engendered by his belief that certain Chinese classical words referred to a monotheistic god. This issue was for Legge not a matter of uncovering symbolic meanings as in his general theory of "mind to mind" decipherment and translation described in the main part of his preface. Rather, it was a straightforward matter of knowing what these classical terms actually meant to the ancient Chinese and to Chinese emperors down to the nineteenth century. There was nothing hidden about it (at least to Chinese emperors and Legge when worshiping at the Altar of Heaven): Di and Shangdi were simply the proper Chinese names for the monotheistic deity of all humankind. Even though it was a secret to most latter-day Chinese and Western scholars, the "Chinese fathers" intended "to express the same concept" that the Western biblical "fathers" expressed by "God."

According to Legge, *di* was not originally a symbolic term, but its monotheistic meaning was eventually, in the course of time (most likely, though he does not say so here, from the inevitable Müllerian "disease of language"), forgotten or confused by most Chinese. In this way, the original meaning of these special Chinese terms became sequestered or "symbolic" and could be known, or "properly" translated (and Legge seems to intend the ritualistic, Aristotelian, or Confucian sense of *proper* and *propriety* here), only by sinologists who had deciphered the ancient Chinese classics in comparative relation with other Oriental sacred books. The terminological problem of whether or not all religions must, by the very nature of human thought and historical experience, have some awareness of—some terms, metaphorical images, or proper names for—a universal and transcendental infinite or monotheistic deity is really the foundation upon which the hegemonic Western, or generically Protestant, idealistic episteme and analogical methodology of the human sciences were based.

Legge acknowledged that his previous discussion of such matters, and his rendering of *di* and *shangdi* as *God,* in volume 3 of the *Sacred Books* had given "offence to some of the missionaries in China and others." Legge here reasserts his conviction in the correctness of his views and says that he has translated *di* and *shangdi* (although these terms are not "so frequent" in the *Changes* as they are in the *Book of Poetry* and the *Book of Historical Documents*) as *God*. With the confidence that comes from the editorial support of Müller and the testimony of the "great majority of the Protestant missionaries in China," Legge says sardonically that he has no interest in provoking "controversy." However, he must act in the interests of "truth" and it was abundantly clear to him that *di* and *shangdi* were the nearest Chinese "analogue for God." After all, says Legge, "I am translating, and not giving a private interpretation of my own."

Modern and Destructive Criticism

It was John Chalmers's opinion that Legge's *Book of Changes* had the "spirit and manner" of, rather, a "new commentary by a somewhat rationalistic Confucianist than a translation by a European." Chalmers also notes that Legge's conception of the non-Confucian authorship of the Appendixes was especially provocative: "For a Chinaman to say this would be as dangerous as for a Christian to deny the Mosaic authorship of the Pentateuch." Concerning Legge's belief that the original Text was composed by King Wen and the duke of Zhou with "profound" symbolic meaning, Chalmers perceptively remarks that it was probably better to view it in terms of what it claimed itself to be—that is, a "handbook gradually framed by and for the professors of divination."[92] This mantic dimension was largely disregarded by sinologists until Richard Wilhelm's scriptural translation in the twentieth century brought the symbolic, moral, and divinatory dimensions together for a Western audience (the translation appeared first in German in 1924 and, with the Bollingen English translation accompanied by C.G. Jung's foreword, it became a publishing phenomenon in the 1960s).[93]

Several contemporaneous reviews of Legge's *Book of Changes* evoke some of the complexity of the intellectual climate in sinological Orientalism at this time. An interesting example of the more radically comparativist and Indo-Europeanist school of modern critical sinology is the article by Thomas Kingsmill, a geological engineer and amateur sinologist from the China coast. Kingsmill's review is noteworthy for drawing attention to the "more bracing atmosphere of Oxford" that allowed Legge, finally and "boldly," to overcome some of the "great errors of his previous work." For the first time, says Kingsmill quite inaccurately, Legge actually went beyond Zhu Xi and the Chinese commentaries and sifted "the historical evidence of their statements."[94] The only problem for Kingsmill was that the elderly Legge was still too needlessly wary of modern "destructive criticism" and trusted too much in traditional Chinese accounts that were "vapid and feeble" philosophically and clearly not "true history" (e.g., the legendary elements in the stories of King Wen and the duke of Zhou and the blatant myth of Fu Xi, which can be understood, according to Kingsmill, only by realizing its basis in Aryan mythology). On the one hand, from the perspective of twenty-first-century hindsight, we may agree with Kingsmill that Legge did not go far enough in questioning the historicity of figures such as Fu Xi, just as he had not fully accepted the more radical Wellhausian methods of biblical analysis directed against Moses and other Pentateuchal patriarchs.

On the other hand, Kingsmill's attempt to understand Chinese traditional history as no more than a philologically disguised rendition of Indo-European mythology is even more egregiously wrongheaded. Kingsmill's Aryan theories about Chinese tradition were one of Eitel's prime examples of unjustified comparativist silliness in sinology. In this light, the audacity of Kingsmill's criticism of Legge's new parenthetical method of translation was astonishing: "If a translator be at liberty to introduce, even within blackets [sic], matters altogether outside the text, there is no possibility of predicting the result, and, as in this case, an author's plain words may be made to bear any meaning whatever at the fancy of the manipulator."[95] What is so incredible about this is that it was Kingsmill who, while eschewing brackets or parentheses, felt compelled on comparative philological and mythological grounds to translate many key Chinese terms as only phonetically and monosyllabically altered versions of originally inflected Aryan words (e.g., "Fu-hi [Fu Xi]" was really equivalent to the Aryan mythic "Va-yu," meaning Wind).[96]

As Eitel so effectively showed in the 1870s, it was really Kingsmill, more than Legge, who—in the name of the semifashionable late-nineteenth-century methods of comparative mythology—had a penchant for producing wildly esoteric interpretive translations of a Chinese text's plain words. The incongruity of this situation toward the end of the century (the 1880s and 1890s rather than the 1870s) was that Kingsmill's general approach could be seen as modern, critical, and properly destructive, whereas Legge was sometimes criticized (by stylish younger comparativists such as Kingsmill and Lacouperie, by non-Aryan sinologists such as Herbert Giles, and by non-sinologists such as Legge's sometime Oxford friend and Congregationalist Andrew Fairbairn) for being out of touch with the latest historiographical theories and critical methodologies.

THE *RECORD OF RITES*:
AN EPOCH IN THE HISTORY OF SINOLOGY

I may be permitted to express my satisfaction that, with the two volumes of the Li Ki now published, I have done, so far as translation is concerned, all and more than all which I undertook to do on the Chinese Classics more than twenty-five years ago. When the first volume was published in 1861, my friend, the late Stanislas Julien, wrote to me, asking if I had duly considered the voluminousness of the Li Ki, and expressing his doubts whether I should be able to complete my undertaking. Having begun the task, however, I have pursued it to the end, working on with some unavoidable interruptions, and amidst not a few other engagements.

JAMES LEGGE, PREFACE TO THE *LI KI, THE SACRED BOOKS OF THE EAST*, VOL. 27, 1885

The completion of the translation of the Chinese Classics—the Four Books and the Five Ching—commenced nearly thirty years ago, by Dr. Legge, marks an epoch in the history of Sinology.

JOHN CHALMERS, "THE SACRED BOOKS OF THE EAST," *CHINA REVIEW*, 1886

Ceremonies of Closure

With the publication of the *Book of Changes* and the assurance that the *Sacred Books* would continue as a series till the end of the century, Legge in 1883 concentrated on completing his translation of the voluminous forty-six-section version of the *Li ji*, the *Record* (or *Records*) *of Rites* (rendered more elaborately on this occasion as *The Collection of Treatises on the Rules of Propriety or Ceremonial Usages*). In so doing he had the satisfaction of knowing that he was on the verge of quashing Stanislas Julien's doubts, expressed at the very outset of his labors in 1861, that anyone could complete such a monstrous undertaking. This, along with the fact that he was rapidly approaching three score and ten years on earth and was engaged in the culmination at last of a labyrinthine textual journey initiated more than a quarter century earlier, must have given a special emotional edge and a sense of solemn ceremonial closure to his work on the Chinese *Record* of ritual.[97] Legge carefully and reverently prepared for these scholarly rituals devoted to the Confucian canon. He tells us that, although he had actually written out the first six or more books of the classic before he left China in 1873, it was not until early in 1883 that he was able to give the text his full attention. This he did by working assiduously with two Chinese imperial editions (especially the 1322 *Liji jishou* with commentary by Chen Hao), an unpublished manuscript translation made by his old London Missionary Society colleague Alexander Wylie (who had by this time returned, blind and feeble, to Britain), a collection of commentaries compiled by Wang Tao, and the partial 1853 French translation by the Catholic missionary-scholar J.-M. Callery.[98] His "simple and only aim," he says, was "to understand the text" for himself and "then to render it in English, fairly and as well as [he] could" for his readers. Toward this end, he was impressively successful in that both his philological analysis of the text's history and his translation hold up extremely well when judged by the excellent later French and Latin version by Séraphin Couvreur and by the best contemporary sinological standards.[99]

Rites of Remembrance

The publication of the *Record of Rites* represents a moment of closure in the history of sinological Orientalism and deserves to be ritually remembered by later generations. This has not, however, been the typical fate of Legge's translation. Neither the substance of the text nor the overall tradition of state ceremonial practice has been remembered by later sinologists. It was much easier to focus on the quasi-Protestant moral perspicacity of the Four Books, the enigmatic secrets of the *Book of Changes,* and the esoteric wisdom of the Daoist classics. The various lists in the *Rites* of minutely defined ritual terms and the random descriptions of miscellaneous ceremonies of the ancient court traditions were largely spurned as corruptly religious or tedious and irrelevant ritual by later, especially Anglo-American, scholars concerned with political and social issues.[100] This is, to say the least, an unfortunate and debilitating state of affairs concerning the full scope of ancient Chinese literature and civilization.

For all his evangelical Protestantism (although Legge's Scottish Sabbatarianism is a partial offsetting factor) and what twentieth-century commentators saw as his old-fashioned methods and his irritating Christian bias, Legge was able to see the real moral significance and reverential religious and civilizational power of the individual "rules of propriety" and socially based "ceremonial usages" described in the *Record of Rites.* For this reason, the *Rites* deserves a place of honor in Legge's evolving understanding of Chinese tradition. In the case of the scholarship devoted to the ancient classics of ritual (what in the *Mengzi* was called the *Lijing* [The book of ritual] and traditionally includes, besides the *Li ji* [The record of rites], the *Yi li* [The rites of the Yi] and the *Zhou li* [The rites of the Zhou]) and the state religion, Legge's work was progressive even by twenty-first-century sinological standards. Rather than marking the end of an epoch, Legge's *Rites* could have been the beginning of a more complete and balanced study of the history of ancient Chinese religion at the state level. But the aura of the other more ancient, more immediately mesmerizing and pure, classics was too great and the study of important ancient Chinese texts such as the *Record of Rites* languished. Most astounding is that so much sinological scholarship in the nineteenth and twentieth centuries tended to avoid what was the obvious and overwhelming element of Chinese tradition—its fundamental ritual character.

Always and in Everything Let There Be Reverence

Legge's translation of the *Record of Rites* might seem to have been a relatively straightforward task since this text had none of the hoary antiquity and apparent theological suggestiveness of the *Book of Poetry* and *Book of Historical*

Documents. Nor did it have any of the ciphered moralistic secretiveness to be found in the *Book of Changes.* It was a text that seemed to be pretty much what its title claimed it to be: a miscellaneous, Han-period compilation of collections (*ji,* etymologically a "packet of cocoons") of proprietary ritual, ceremonies, and social customs (all connoted by *li*) associated with court practices dating to different times. What seems immediately curious about this situation is that Legge—the good Congregationalist and sometimes conventional Victorian antipapist—seems solemnly respectful toward a text so conspicuously a repository of mostly "superstitious" terminological definitions, anecdotal descriptions, and random prescriptions of court ritual. The strong liturgical focus of the *Record of Rites* was not so very unlike the emphasis on ecclesiastical ritual of the Roman Catholic (or to a lesser degree, the High Church Anglican) practice of Christianity.

The difference seems to rest on Legge's renewed affirmation of the Confucian key to ritual meaningfulness and moral worth: "Always and in everything let there be reverence."[101] Let there be (in an Evangelical and Scottish Sabbath-culture sense) personal feelings, religious conviction, and moral sensitivity in all proper acts of self-cultivation and social interaction. At the same time, and it has been hinted at before, there is Legge's growing comparativist appreciation in an almost sociological, Robertson Smith vein (and despite any Protestant squeamishness) of the universal role and social functionality of ceremony in human lives. The intricacies of Victorian social intercourse and the elaborate ceremonies of academic life in Oxford were as suggestive of the generalized human role of ritual as anything found in the Chinese *Record of Rites.*[102] It appears that Legge's understanding of the heathen Chinese religion was still evolving in even more sympathetic and comprehensive directions. With suspicions about ritual religion being expressed as recently as 1880 in the *Religions of China,* it is remarkable that only a few years later Legge would declare that a careful study of the "rules of propriety" and "ceremonial usages" of the *Record of Rites* had increased his "appreciation of the religion and general reach of thought of the ancient Chinese."[103]

Two Fundamental Ideas

For Legge an understanding of the *Record of Rites* hinged on a careful appreciation of the complex historical meanings associated with the highly resonant character of *li.* Based on an analysis of textual sources (including the *Mengzi* and the ancient dictionary known as the *Shuo wen*), Legge found that the character conveyed two "fundamental ideas." The first of these was, significantly enough in light of Legge's previous theorizing on symbolic decipherment, that *li*—made up of the radical *shi,* meaning "spiritual beings" and, by extension, "sacrifice" and "prayer," and the phonetic *li*, which also had the meaning of "a sacrificial vessel used in performing rites"—was basically "a symbol of religious import." What Legge means by this is that *li-*actions were religious because they were actions performed in relation to a belief in some kind of spiritual beings or being.[104]

The second fundamental meaning of the character was also symbolic, but as applied in traditional "moral and philosophical disquisitions," it was a "symbol" of the "feeling of propriety," which was one of the four "primary constituents of human nature" as set forth by the *Mengzi* (*ren, i, li, zhi*, or, in Legge's translation, "benevolence, righteousness, propriety, and understanding"). It is *li* as an inner moral sense of propriety that is "proved" by natural human "feelings of modesty and courtesy."[105] *Li* is not just a matter of superficially going through the motions of some socially prescribed action. In Master Kong's understanding, it had hidden depths of meaning because of its twin symbolic references to religious belief (worship of a spiritual being) and moral feeling.

Twofold Symbol and Mere Ritual

Li is thus doubly symbolic in a religious and moral sense. In the Victorian and in the Evangelical sense, it also amounts to a "very high ideal" of human life and character. Again it is the necessary, conjoined duality of "symbol" that is crucial to the realization of meaning: outer material form linked with inner spirit, essence, idea, or intention. The problem is that "never and nowhere" is it possible "to maintain this high standard of living" in which the "twofold" symbolism remains seamlessly and purely linked. Legge consequently suggests that there is a rule of moral depletion—roughly equivalent to Müller's principle of progressive semantic depletion, symbolic impoverishment, or linguistic contagion—that is operant in the history of "China and elsewhere."[106] In the course of history (particularly social history) the original linkage breaks down, is lost, or is infantilized by the uncontrolled addition of later more formal and literal, less original and pure, meanings. (Cf. Müller's theory of semantic depletion discussed in the preface to volume 1 of the *Sacred Books;* see pages 262–63.)

The customs and usages of any society "in its various relationships," its *li*, become in time and in varying degrees "matters of course" and "forms without the spirit." The spirit of social custom tends therefore to become progressively routinized, literal, or merely ritualistic. The original conjunction of religious and moral meaning is ruptured and the resulting practices have less of the original dual power. In this diminished context, such "rules and usages" in individual and social life can be translated with various kinds of terminology, not all of which may be perfectly equivalent or truly significant in the original dualistic symbolic sense. The impoverished sense of *li* is, in fact, suggested by the range of translations offered by the Catholic priest Callery: ceremony, customs, etiquette, politeness, urbanity, courtesy, good manners, *savoir-vivre,* decorum, decency, dignity, rights, social laws, social order, and especially rites or ritual.[107]

Fittingly enough in relation to what is known of his own ceremonial Protestant antipathy toward ritualism (tempered by the ritual context of his Scottish Sabbath-culture upbringing), Legge tells us that he purposely avoided the use of the formalistic words "rite" or "rites" (Father Callery having had no such qualms) and preferred to use "rules of propriety" or "ceremonial usages." This was admittedly awkward, but for Legge such expressions more accurately suggested the original dual nature of *li* as a religious and moral symbol.[108] Whatever creeping sympathy Legge had for quasi-Catholic and Anglican ritual, it is clear that he still felt compelled to pull back and carefully qualify such action with a symbolic reification of its performative meaning.

Questions of Comparative Hypocrisy

What was it about the *Record of Rites* that continued to broaden Legge's horizons regarding the ancient Chinese? As suggested by his introduction to the *Rites,* it was clearly his increased apprehension that ritual actions and truly reverential thought properly worked together in Chinese tradition—indeed, as action and thought, body and spirit, precept and practice should in any tradition claiming some degree of religious truth and moral sincerity. It is also notable that Legge is so little bothered by the manifest lack of specific or sustained reference to monotheistic belief in the *Record of Rites.* The crux of Legge's unexpected respect for the ceremonial way of religion and moral etiquette articulated in that text actually comes down, as it had so often in the past, to the haunting questions of comparative morality and the assumed supremacy of Christianity and the Christian nations. This issue was especially related to the disturbing question of opium and now it was more generally associated with the unequality of the treaties between the Western Christian nations and China. The problem with these treaties was the duplicity of those clauses designed to allow for the special "toleration of Chinese Christians," clauses premised, as Legge says, on the notion that "'the Christian religion, as professed by Protestants or Roman Catholics, inculcates the practice of virtue, and teaches man to do as he would be done by.'"[109]

The problem was that—over the years and both in China and in Great Britain—"scores of Chinese, officers, scholars, and others" had come to Legge to ask, bluntly and appropriately, about the manifest disparity between Christian moral doctrines (which sounded so promisingly close to traditional Chinese ideals of ritual reciprocity) and immoral actions. Legge says only that "as the creeds of men elsewhere are often better than their practice, so it is in China." But whether there was a closer approximation between Christian creed and actual Christian behavior back home in Britain, Legge says—somewhat sadly, but fairly—that this is a "point on which different conclusions will be come to, according to the knowledge and prejudices of the speculators."[110]

A Daoli *of Reason and Analogy*

Legge's growing empathetic ability to see and dispassionately speculate on such touchy matters through the eyes of the other is remarkable. This ultimately ambiguating issue of judging the practical morality of national behavior becomes more and more Legge's touchstone for understanding and translating the enduring human worth of Chinese tradition. To appreciate the transformative courage of Legge's position on this matter we need to recall that one of the most common condemnations of China—assumed by popular, diplomatic, and commercial, as well as missionary, interests— rested on the assurance that the Chinese people were devious and insincere hypocrites who ritualistically followed the letter rather than the spirit of religious and moral law.[111]

The *Record of Rites* is a moral and religious treatise that deserved special attention and respect: "[M]ore may be learned about the religion of the ancient Chinese from this classic than from all the others together." This text is more of a documentary collection, or undogmatic assemblage, of recorded religious and moral practices than it is an attempt at a systematized theology.[112] It is, then, for Legge a revealing portrait of the ancient religion. Furthermore, the difficult question of the absolute historical accuracy of all the descriptions of "ancient" ritual and religion (the sources for the *Rites* were most likely not as ancient as Chinese tradition, Callery, or Legge believed—the earliest dating only from the late Warring States period, i.e., ca. third century B.C.E.)[113] is offset by both Legge's and Callery's agreement that the "philosophical and moral ideas" in the *Record of Rites* are "'sound and profound.'" Although sometimes "eccentric" and "hedged about with absurd speculations," these ideas and practices most often "bring to light what Chinese scholars call a tao-li [*daoli*], a ground of reason or analogy, which interests and satisfies the mind."[114]

Ritual Responses to Legge's Daoli

Critical response to the appearance in April 1885 of Legge's *Record of Rites,* his last installment in the *Texts of Confucianism* volumes for the *Sacred Books,* was extensive for such a scholarly work and generally flattering.[115] What is worth noting is that most of the critics did not share Legge's largely favorable view of the ancient ritual tradition, preferring instead to fall back upon stock Orientalistic slander about the "formalistic" nature, "obstinacy," and "lying pride" of the Chinese.[116] These critical reactions often hint that the old translator was increasingly out of touch with the more progressive and modern assessments of humanistic scholarship at the end of the century. Thus an anonymous reviewer for the *Athenaeum* congratulated Legge for completing his "herculean" labors on the Confucian classics, but found the *Record of Rites* to be a "strange and grotesque" ritualistic attempt to reduce "man as far as possible to the level of a machine." Much of it, according to the self-styled Victorian standards of literary propriety upheld by the *Athenaeum,* would be distinctly "distasteful to English readers" unused to such "slavish forms" and "minute rules" of individual and social behavior![117]

In another substantive review, John Chalmers lavishly applauded Legge's sinological skills and his "fidelity as a translator." Obviously thinking of such "destructive" modern critics as Kingsmill, Giles, and Lacouperie, Chalmers says that if "sceptical critics" should seek to quibble with Legge on textual matters, they will have to contend with the "best Chinese commentators as well." Legge's rendition of the *Record of Rites* represents what the Chinese classics "have been to the Chinese themselves." For this reason, sinological upstarts of the future who might "succeed in proving that the Chinese classics are something quite different from what the people have taken them to be" (and Chalmers alludes to Lacouperie as a "man of the future" who was trying to show that the *Book of Changes* was an "Accadian vocabulary") will "not thereby invalidate Dr. Legge's work." Others may have more aptitude for "concocting theories," but there was no Western scholar then living, says Chalmers, who "should not sit at [Legge's] feet as a translator of Confucian Classics."[118]

Chalmers agreed with Legge that the *Record of Rites* was the "most instructive of all the Chinese Classics" concerning the "Confucian religion"— the "religion which was common to the Chinese people before the sects divided." Keeping in mind that the material in the *Rites* was "too recent" to give us the "best" picture of religion "at the dawn of history," Chalmers nevertheless finds that the "disjointed" and "unspeakably drivelling" nature of the records had much scholarly value: "[T]he student of folk-lore must take the folk as they are." For Chalmers, more so than for Legge, Chinese civilization "culminated" around the time of Confucius and had gone rapidly downhill ever since.[119] Despite these concerns, Chalmers concurred with Legge's comparative judgment that there was "glorious hope" for a nation that once knew the religious and moral meaning of *li.*

The key question was whether or not a revitalization of China's own ancient cardinal virtues can come about through the coercive assistance of a higher Christian civilization and religion. The moral, social, and political difficulties of any overly presumptuous answer to this question were painfully obvious to Legge and Chalmers. For both of them, a deep appreciation of the ambiguities of national religiosity and morality was the necessary basis for comparatively evaluating the *li* of all other forms of transcultural intercourse: "China takes the measure of us just as we take the measure of her; and it becomes us, as we prize the Christian religion above everything else, to commend it to the adoption of the Chinese not in word only but in deed and in truth" (alluding here to 1 John 3:18).[120]

RITUAL COMBAT IN THE BABYLONIAN ERA OF SINOLOGY

What unbiased mind can doubt, that as all heathendom has been "made drunk" by the apostate cup of idolatry handed down from Babylon, so has China amongst the rest.

THOMAS MCCLATCHIE, "PAGANISM," *CHINESE RECORDER*, 1877

We hope that this present Babylonian Era of Sinology, which succeeded a weary Indian and a mysterious Arian era, will soon be succeeded by some fresh discovery of a still more ancient source. One is apt to get tired of finding everything Chinese to have been derived from one and the same place, be it India or the Aryans or Accadians, and to become rather sceptic as to the Chinese having had no originality whatsoever, from the Chows down to the Mings, and having in their intercourse with Babylonia remained simply passive, receiving everything and never giving anything in return.

E. J. EITEL, EDITORIAL COMMENT ON JOSEPH EDKINS, *CHINA REVIEW*, 1888

Odium Sinologicum

Having witnessed the nightmarish fury and righteous indignation engendered by missionary disagreements about Chinese texts and religions, Legge saw his more impartial vocation as a university professor as a way to obviate any further sectarian fighting. Such a rosy outcome was not to be. If anything, the nineteenth century was both the age of the professionalization of secular academic careers and of the efflorescence of academic feuds rivaling any of the earlier theological battles. The bones of contention among missionaries and scholars were basically the same: It was either a matter of theological truth or scientific correctness using fundamentally similar weapons of scriptural exegesis or symbolic decipherment. It was the aura of transcendental, rational, or essential truth coupled with the public adulation coming from the discovery of hidden secrets that gave theological and academic modes of discourse a powerful potential for either pointless triumphalism or petty viciousness. To borrow from Edward Parker's colorful discussion of these matters, there is a shift from the stench of the *odium theologicum* to an equally rank *odium sinologicum.*[121]

The ferocious battles among the early Parisian academicians were but a prelude to the more generalized, and nationalistic, fighting among sinological Orientalists at the end of the century. Whether or not sinologists, in particular, were any worse than other kinds of Orientalists is unclear. Perhaps, however, it can be said that their special isolation and relative institutional impotence generated a distinctly heightened degree of pettiness and irrationality. Certainly the furious intensity of the scholarly disagreements provoked by Julien and Klaproth of the early French tradition and by Giles, Lacouperie, and Parker of the latter part of the century suggest as much. With the steady rise of academic careerism in the early twentieth century, these intellectual battles over texts and interpretations reached new heights of rhetorical duplicity, immoral vindictiveness, political pettiness, and personal nastiness—qualities that in many ways have come to characterize academic life forever more.[122] It was Legge's misfortune to be making the passage from missionary to professor just when, in Western tradition, the intellectual authority and emotional intensity of opinions about other texts and cultures were being definitively transferred from religious organizations to secular academic institutions that were no less hierarchical or domineering.

A representative instance of this fiercely trivial fighting is seen in the outbreak of sino-Babylonian Orientalism at the beginning of the 1880s. The Aryan school of sinology continued to some degree (witness the ongoing work of Kingsmill), but its thunder had mostly passed to those concerned with deciphering the philological and historical secrets of the apparent mother of all literate civilizations—that is, the Accadian or Babylonian tradition. Part of the reason for the surge of interest in Babylonian tradition was simply that it was the most spectacularly archaic and advanced literate tradition to be discovered and analyzed by the new science of archaeology in the mid to late nineteenth century. The Babylonians possessed a written script that was seemingly more ancient than those of the Indians, Egyptians, or Chinese.[123]

The well-known work of Austen Henry Layard (1817–1894) and Henry Rawlinson at midcentury on the excavations at Nimrud and the discovery of the cuneiform library at Ninevah came to fruition in the 1870s with the work of George Smith (1840–1876) of the British Museum, who translated the tablets "which gave the Chaldean account of the Biblical flood."[124] These Babylonian discoveries were in turn popularized by François Lenormant, Archibald Sayce, and others in the late 1870s. Along with the continuing influence of Darwinism (Darwin himself had died in 1882) and the pent-up pressure of the German higher criticism and the comparative science of religions as manifest in the *Sacred Books,* the Babylonian findings pushed British gentleman scholars, particularly academic intellectuals, in the direction of a more continental-style modern, secular, destructive, or even decadent approach to textual and historical scholarship.[125]

The Modern Scientific School of Orientalism

Who could be better in propagating the message of Babylon as the key to the secret of the ages—and to facilitate the inroads of a continental, critical, and fully professionalized scientific scholarship within British Orientalism— than Terrien de Lacouperie, an aggressively brilliant thirty-four-year-old Frenchman who settled in London in 1879? Born in Normandy, Lacouperie (1845–1894) was a businessman and scholar who became in 1884 the flamboyant professor of Indo-Chinese philology at University College, London. Having a distinct flair for numismatics and comparative philology, Lacouperie had learned some Chinese while living in Hong Kong and, upon returning to Europe, passionately took up the comparative study of the newly deciphered cuneiform script.[126] Becoming convinced (as prompted by Lenormant) that "numerous" and "striking" similarities in script and civilizational "ideology" indicated a clear relationship between Babylonian tradition and ancient Chinese tradition, Lacouperie maintained that this kind of affiliation could be explained only by the dependence of the latter on the former.[127]

Within many British academic circles at the end of the nineteenth century, Lacouperie's "quite fantastic" views represented the cutting edge of the progressive "modern scientific school" of Orientalistic scholarship (for Henri Cordier this meant a combination of English "practical knowledge" with French "scientific training").[128] Indeed, the basis for Lacouperie's reputation for fashionable scholarship was his "discovery" of the true secret of the *Book of Changes,* which he first hinted at an article in the London *Times* (April 20, 1880) and in lectures given in London at the Royal Asiatic Society (in May 1880) and at the Society of Arts (in July 1880). These preliminary reports of Lacouperie's self-proclaimed, breakthrough realization that the *Book of Changes* was actually a Babylonian syllabary and dictionary gave rise to the mild renunciation of Lacouperie in the preface to Legge's 1882 edition of the *Changes.*

Inasmuch as Legge was now being viewed by the younger scholarly generation as vaguely old-fashioned, his initial views did little to dampen the growing enthusiasm for Lacouperie and the whole idea of a Babylonian—rather than a biblical, Egyptian, or Aryan—monogenetic diffusionist interpretation of Oriental tradition. For many with either reverent or secular scholarly leanings, Babylonianism seemed to be the *Western* key that finally unlocked a whole host of Oriental mysteries and racist issues, including the much-debated questions of the real meaning of the biblical Land of Sinim and the

apparent unintelligibility of the *Book of Changes*.[129] Most of all for the still reverent school of missionaries and scholars such as Edkins and Sayce, these new
comparative discoveries suggested a critical and scientific basis for the biblical account of the Tower of Babel. The sino-Babylonian theories also had the
distinct advantage of being demurely asexual unlike the earlier sinological
eroticism of Canon McClatchie's Aryan theories about a phallic cult.

The excitement engendered by these developments was related to the
possibility that Lacouperie was on the verge of proving that the Babylonian
or Accadian language was the comparative philological key to understanding the Chinese language and civilization. This would constitute an intellectual breakthrough equal to the discovery that Sanskrit was the crucial key
for establishing the whole Indo-European family of languages.[130] Quickly
winning over that "respectable mediocrity," Robert K. Douglas, as an outspoken sinological disciple to his cause, Lacouperie also gained the initial
approval of various Near Eastern scholars such as Hyde Clarke, Lenormant,
and the Oxonian Archibald Sayce, as well as the Belgian sinologist Charles
de Harlez and even Legge's old friend Joseph Edkins. At the height of his
influence in the mid-1880s, Lacouperie twice received the Prix Julien and
in 1886 founded the consistently monomaniacal journal known as the *Babylonian and Oriental Record*. This periodical, although mostly an outlet for Lacouperie's own erratic and piecemeal articles, continued through nine volumes until the end of the century.[131]

Edkins became quite smitten with the sino-Babylonian thesis—doubtlessly
because it seemed to fit so nicely with monogenetic biblical theories of
Western origins and seemed to have the factual support of sciences such as
archaeology and astronomy. In his typically effusive way, Edkins produced
many articles and pamphlets throughout the 1880s and early 1890s arguing for the Babylonian origin of most things Chinese (especially the seemingly strange Daoist tradition, which could not be understood in terms of
the unimaginative practicality of Chinese or Confucian civilization).[132] The
high point of Edkins's contributions to sino-Babylonianism was reached
when he proposed in 1886 a startling new solution to the incredibly persistent problem of deciphering the "symbolic" terminological code in chapter
14 of the *Book of the Dao and Its Characteristics* (the words *i, xi, wei*). Julien,
Legge, and Müller held that this hoary riddle was simply a matter of "false
parallels." Edkins found that the "trinitarian" formula of words actually referred to the Babylonian cosmogonic trinity of the Heaven, Earth, and
Chaotic Abyss (the last of which was the Chinese term *hundun*).[133]

Round One in the Sino-Babylonian Age

I will not rehearse the whole complicated and amusing history of sino-
Babylonianism. Rather, I will focus on the now largely forgotten saga of

Legge's battles with Lacouperie and his acolytes over the secret sino-Babylonian meaning of the *Book of Changes.* The saga begins with Lacouperie's impassioned rejoinder, in the January 1882 issue of the influential and widely circulated weekly literary journal the *Saturday Review,* to Legge's prefatory comments for the edition of the *Changes* in the *Sacred Books.* In a short article, Lacouperie defends his "discovery" of sino-Babylonian parallels and proudly notes that he had won the support of the sinologue R. K. Douglas. Moreover, he argues that his views were based on many of the same principles that Legge based his findings on: that it is necessary to consider only the "oldest part of the book" and to take to heart, even more so than did Legge (who trusts too much to native commentary and the traditional role of King Wen and the duke of Zhou as authors), the radically symbolic and nonhomogeneous nature of the "primitive" text. Lacouperie says that he was forced to the more extreme or destructive application of the symbolic principle when he realized that many of the sixty-four different chapters or sections were only "lists of the meanings of the characters placed at the head of the chapter." The primitive text of the *Book of Changes* was therefore "like the syllabaries [i.e., ancient phonetic dictionaries] preserved in Cuneiform." For this reason, the book maintained its "absolute obscurity" and Legge's translation missed the more deeply hidden philological, historical, and non-Chinese truth of the matter. Lacouperie says that he will soon publish his own translation and the whole issue will be put to rest once and for all.[134]

Lacouperie then went on to publish in the *Athenaeum* a fuller attack on Legge's theory of symbolic translation. According to Lacouperie, Legge's only resort was to "make up" and "force" parenthetical meanings on the text while claiming the blessings of the native Song commentaries. It was far better, and oddly more scientific, to admit the real absurdity of any Chinese meaning and to recognize that the text was known only in relation to its original literal meaning as an ancient Babylonian syllabary or vocabulary. The strange outcome of Lacouperie's interpretation is that the symbolic secret of the *Book of Changes* is that it is not symbolic. The forgotten historical and linguistic connection with Babylonia hides a purely literal and philological meaning fundamentally unintelligible to either traditional Chinese commentators or most nineteenth-century sinologists.[135]

Loving War and Despising Letters

Later that same year Robert K. Douglas weighed into the battle with articles in the *Academy* and the *Quarterly Review.*[136] The more important of these is the *Quarterly* article, which, with feigned erudition (he claims to have considered the one hundred volumes of Ban Gu's *Qian Han Shu* and the five-thousand-volume Qing encyclopedia) and fairness, elaborately argues that

Chinese literature is especially characterized by "the want of those mental qualities which instigate independent research and the exercise of the imagination." The best examples of this trait are, according to Douglas, the "prosy and dosy" Chinese classics and the turgid encyclopedic "compendiums of ready-made knowledge gathered from writings of preceding authors." This is, above all, a manifestation of the desultory commentarial mode of Chinese literary tradition.[137]

It is the formalistic and narrow Chinese love of letters (the "narrow love of mechanical detail, in its want of scientific training and logical exactness, and in the conspicuous absence of the power of imagination") that, for Douglas, is "a sufficient answer to those who maintain an Aryan origin for the Chinese." In a way that sounds much like an idealized, warrior ethos description of the Scottish highlander, English amateur sportsman, British imperial administrator, aristocratic gentleman, entrepreneurial businessman, tough-minded but impartial scientist, indefatigable Orientalist scholar, or Victorian muscular Christian, Douglas makes the point that, "in all parts of the world the old Aryans loved war and despised letters. The warrior is the hero of romance and legend alike in Europe and India; and even at the present day the popular mind is more stirred by the valiant acts of an illiterate soldier in the field, than by the highest mental achievements in the 'schools' or in the study."[138]

"In China," says Douglas (as it was with all who spent too much time in the study instead of being on the playing field or participating in the hunt—in general, the new breed of overly effeminate professional academics), "this state of public opinion is exactly reversed. The successful scholar there wins the suffrages of all novel-readers, and in real life throws into the shade the doughtiest champion of a hundred fights." It is the sadly deficient fate of the Chinese people to be "peace-abiding and plodding and, above all, literary."[139] Or as Douglas said elsewhere, the Chinese are an "immature people" who are like smooth-cheeked young schoolboys rather than the bearded warriors of Aryan lore.[140]

For Douglas, it is the tough "riddle" of the *Book of Changes* and the innumerable and ineffectual native commentaries associated with it, that dramatize the poverty of native tradition and the amazing inability of the Chinese to interpret their own literature. Recent research by Terrien de Lacouperie showed that the mystery of the *Book of Changes* was "beyond the reach" of native Chinese scholars "who know no other language than their own." Now, however, Lacouperie has "opened the seals of the book which has been practically closed for upwards of thirty centuries"—and it is no accident that the choice of language here directly evokes the exegetical methods of deciphering the secrets of the biblical book of Revelation. According to Douglas, Lacouperie's work "shows beyond reasonable doubt an unmistakable affinity between the written characters of [Babylonia] and of ancient China."[141]

Douglas's article is full of the scientific language of "facts," "proofs," "inferences," "conclusive evidence," and "scholarly concurrence"—all of which is said to "accumulate upon us in all directions" when we consider the cogency of Lacouperie's sino-Babylonian theory of origins. Parading some of these ostensible proofs past his readers, Douglas mentions various bits of ill-digested linguistic, astronomical, geographical, calendrical, and mythological evidence. One example of this kind of mostly specious evidence is Lacouperie's triumphant conclusion that the "mythical Emperor Hwang-ti (B.C. 2697–2597) . . . may be identified with Nakhunta," the chief god of the Susian or Babylonian texts. According to both Douglas and Lacouperie, the ancient Chinese knew Huangdi as "Kon-ti" with the "distinctive name of Nak." Putting this together as "Nak-konti," Douglas says that we can easily see its derivation from the Babylonian Nakhunta.[142] Discussing Douglas's theory in a paper on "Chinese Chronology" delivered before the Royal Asiatic Society, Legge devastatingly notes that Douglas's (and Lacouperie's) attempt to link the Babylonian "Kon-ti" and "Nak" with the Chinese Huangdi actually seemed to be based on a mistaken transcription in *The Chinese Reader's Manual* by William Mayers! All such sino-Babylonian associations, says Legge, pass away "like the baseless fabric of a vision."[143]

Scholarly and Symbolic Unintelligibility

In September of 1882, Legge responded to Lacouperie's and Douglas's general criticism by publishing letters in the *Athenaeum* and the *Academy*. By this time Lacouperie's partial translation of the *Book of Changes* had appeared with less of a bang than a whimper ("The Oldest Book of the Chinese," 1882).[144] Nevertheless, Legge still felt compelled to set the record straight regarding his understanding of the *Changes*. In the *Athenaeum*, he questioned Lacouperie's sinological abilities—especially over the matter of the authorship of the "Wings" or Appendixes to the *Book of Changes*. In a later letter, Legge again doubted Lacouperie's technical competence in the classical Chinese language. According to Legge, only "hasty ignorance" could have led to Lacouperie's mistakes and seeming failure to have consulted the famous Kangxi dictionary. Legge freely admitted that he did not know any "Arcadian or the 'writing borrowed by the Chinese book,'" while at the same time leaving the impression that the real problem was that Lacouperie knew very little classical Chinese.

Legge's letter concerning Douglas is even more pointed than his response to Lacouperie.[145] Part of the reason for pummeling the disciple more than the master is probably that at one point Legge clearly considered Douglas (who had publicly argued for Legge's professorship at Oxford) a sympathetic academic colleague,[146] only to discover that he had quickly sold his soul to a mesmerizing Anglo-French scholar and the latest academic fad. Declaring that his own views were sanctioned by the best native commentarial opinion, Legge chides Douglas for going along with the notion that the text was totally "unintelligible" to the Chinese. But the proof of the matter was to investigate the sino-Babylonian translation of *Changes* by Lacouperie and Douglas and to discover that it was so "lame and impotent." Any examination of the matter, says Legge, would show that their version was fundamentally unrelated to the actual Chinese text. Legge concluded by saying that he "must grudge being drawn off from important inquiries to discuss views not commended by reason in themselves or analogy from without."[147]

The Cradle Lullaby of Terrien de Lacouperie

Legge was too courteous a scholarly gentleman to show the full extent of his frustration and anger over the often slipshod methods, faulty logic, chauvinistic arrogance, and surprising success of the dynamic duo of sino-Babylonianism. In China a younger consular official and sinologue by the name of Edward H. Parker had no such compunctions. He made no lasting contributions to sinological Orientalism, but Parker had already proven his mettle in the *China Review* in various ferocious fights over technical philological and textual issues with the rising star of pugnacious modern, scientific, or destructive criticism, Herbert Giles—an accomplished sinologist, polemicist, and eventual inheritor of Thomas Wade's chair of Chinese at Cambridge University.

Parker's critique, "M. Terrien de Lacouperie as a Sinologist," is worth documenting both for its marvelously hyperbolic rhetoric and its defense of Legge's old-fashioned and sometimes "too unimaginative," but good and steady, work as a sinologist.[148] It also suggests—as seen from Eitel's blasts at comparative mythologists such as Edkins and Kingsmill and Julien's frantic attacks on Pauthier—that one of the determinative factors in the later professionalization and specialization of sinological Orientalism was its pronounced avoidance of comparativistic methodologies and interpretive strategies. Especially after the turn of the century, it was far better to be accused of narrow overspecialization and a purposely exclusivistic focus on China than to court the professional mockery that often came with any sort of comparativistic approach to Oriental traditions.

Wonder-Mongering and an Old Tar

Parker begins his article by raising the question, which was then being bandied about by sinologues even within the coastal communities of China, as to just who the "mysterious Terrien de Lacouperie" was and how he had gained such rapid acclaim. For Parker it was obvious that Lacouperie was mostly a "specious wonder-monger" who was "maybe" an "Akkadian scholar." While "very clever and imaginative," Lacouperie was demonstrably "not a Sinologist," an assertion proved by his "rash generalizations," ridiculous "mistranslations," and "unusually imperfect knowledge of Chinese."[149] What was sad about Lacouperie's "tissue of mischievous rubbish from beginning to end" was that it attracted disciples like the "steady, respectable mediocrity" Robert Douglas. "Left alone with his dictionaries," says Parker, Douglas was quite capable of doing "routine work very passibly." Under the spell of the likes of Lacouperie, however, Douglas was prone to harmful mischief. For Parker, there were only three men in England who had attained "quasi-eminence in Sinology": the brilliant but now blind and retired Alexander Wylie, the aloofly unproductive Thomas Wade at Cambridge, and the prolific "giant" James Legge at Oxford.[150] Parker indicates that it was especially galling to find the vaunted *Saturday Review* "sneer[ing]" at the old master, Legge, and taking up the "flashy, flimsy" work of the "giddy trifling," but mellifluously named, Terrien de Lacouperie.[151] A decision about which is the more likely accurate translation and interpretation of the admittedly "obscure" *Book of Changes* comes down to a question of competence and trust. Is it better to have confidence in Lacouperie's "aerial car of triumph," which blithely soars over great obstacles of language and native commentary, or in the findings of Legge, who, "like an old Tar of many voyages," has repeatedly struggled and suffered with the text and the native tradition?[152]

Legge's Contested Recantation

One honored way of winning a losing scholarly battle is simply to declare victory and move on to other battles. This is more or less the tactic employed by Lacouperie and his followers after Parker's withering blast from China. Never responding directly to Parker, Lacouperie suddenly claimed in the *Academy* that Legge, at a reception at the Chinese ambassador's house in London, had confessed his "most honourable" conversion to the theory that the *Book of Changes* was fundamentally "unintelligible" as a Chinese text.[153] This incredible declaration provoked Müller to write his Oxonian colleague about his supposed "change of mind." Legge responded to Lacouperie and Müller a few weeks later in another letter to the *Academy,* in which he flatly stated that Lacouperie's statement was "incorrect." Differing with Lacouperie on nearly "every" point concerning the *Book of Changes,* Legge reiterated his position that "the version which I gave of the Yih King is correct, and that the interpretation of it which I gave as conveying moral, social, and political lessons under the guise of the style of divination is the true one."[154]

Legge's weary correction was hardly a deterrent to Lacouperie's continuing fixation on Legge's supposed admission that his translation was "decidedly erroneous." Saying that he was honor bound now to accept Legge's "repudiation of his change of view" concerning the *Book of Changes,* Lacouperie indicated that he was privately prepared to name those who overheard the conversation at the ambassador's house. Given every indication that Lacouperie was planning to prolong this petty bickering indefinitely, the editors of the *Academy* had the good sense to announce that "this controversy must now cease."[155] And so round one of the great debate between Lacouperie and Legge over the symbolic or literal "intelligibility" of the enigmatic *Book of Changes* came to an ignoble end.

Despite this flurry of public misunderstanding and carping debate, Lacouperie mostly preferred to ignore his enemies, especially if, like Parker, they were safely removed from the immediate field of battle in London and Oxford and commanded only the tiny audience reading a specialized publication, the *China Review,* circulated mostly in China. Legge had by this time moved on to other related, but more formidable, opponents, such as Herbert Giles. Toward the end of the decade Legge's scholarly concerns were primarily directed toward the contested translation and interpretation of the Daoist classics, especially the *Book of the Dao and Its Characteristics,* which in many ways was on the same level of symbolic mystery and meaning as the *Book of Changes.* In the mid and late 1880s Lacouperie's influence flourished and, while he continued to proselytize for the discoveries touted in his *Book of Changes,* he also moved on to other very eclectic sino-Babylonian topics (see, for example, the inventory of cultural parallels that he published in the *Babylonian and Oriental Record* and his major book, *The Languages of China Before the Chinese; Researches on the Languages Spoken by the Pre-Chinese Races of China Proper Previously to the Chinese Occupation,* 1887).[156]

Round Two: Lacouperie versus Schlegel

The death knell of sino-Babylonianism at the end of the nineteenth century was sounded in many respects by Gustave Schlegel (1840–1903), a formidable sinologist at the University of Leiden and the cofounder along with Henri Cordier of *T'oung Pao* (1890), the most thoroughly professional manifestation of academic sinological Orientalism and the revived French-Continental tradition at the end of the century.[157] Besides being a young and impressively skilled representative of the new Continental school of thoroughly "modern scientific" sinology, Schlegel was also a staunch defender of Legge against the charges of upstart comparativists such as Lacouperie. Despite his increasingly old-fashioned methods, Legge had the good sense to take the Chinese as they themselves claimed to be. More so than many of his younger and more flamboyant contemporaries, Legge always struggled with the Orientalist temptation to force the Chinese into categories that completely denied the integrity of their own otherness or accented their inability to understand the hidden historical meanings of their own tradition.

Schlegel's attack on Lacouperie in *T'oung Pao* signaled the final decline of diffusionistic Babylonianism in sinological Orientalism. At the same time, it is part of a larger shift—seen for example in the work of Otto Franke in Orientalism and Franz Boas in anthropology—away from overt monogenetic comparativism in the newly emerging humanistic and social scientific academic disciplines at the turn of the century.[158] Expressing what would become the dominant polygenetic mode of independent cultural invention favorable to an isolated area of specialization in Chinese studies, Schlegel is adamant in his rejection of any kind of significant "importation" from India, Chaldea, or any other Western country.

The evidence for Schlegel's view is especially plain in the case of the fledgling Lacouperie school of sino-Babylonian diffusionism identified with the *Babylonian and Oriental Record.* It is clear to Schlegel, for example, that Lacouperie's philological methods have no validity (his "method of dissecting ancient Chinese characters and giving each part a phonetic value," which allows them to be equated with polysyllabic Chaldean words, is impossible from the standpoint of the Chinese language). Furthermore, according to Schlegel, it still remained to be proven that "Elam, Chaldea, or Bactria" have "an older history" than does China.[159] But the most convincing reason that "no genuine Sinologue can admit to [Lacouperie's] conclusions" was simply that "even the latest Assyriological discoveries" were "dangerously uncertain and based on unstable foundations."[160] To explain the ambiguous origins of ancient Chinese civilization with the still more tenuous uncertainties of the Babylonian script and tradition was ill advised, to say the least. In the meantime, says Schlegel, it was far better to proceed in the sinological field of Orientalism with what seemed to be the more and more "firmly rooted conviction" of scholars in the "independent" origin and growth of Chinese civilization.[161]

Good and Proper Comparison

Despite Lacouperie's considerable sway in Orientalist circles, he was fated by temperament, accomplishment, and health to be a shooting star who would prematurely burn out in 1894 at the age of forty-nine. He left behind only a trail of rapidly fading sparks, although pan-Babylonianism would continue to sputter for several decades longer in various fields (the *Babylonian and Oriental Record* eventually expired with a whimper in 1901). Almost completely forgotten today, Lacouperie merits some attention as a significant representative of a certain kind of late-nineteenth-century Orientalistic hyperdiffusionism and scientifically disguised biblical monogenesis. This is not to say that everything related to a Babylonian explanation of Chinese tradition is a subject fit only for parody. One of the more interesting aspects of contemporary sinological discourse is the creeping reappearance of more sophisticated variations on some of the diffusionist themes concerning the linguistic and cultural origins of sinitic civilization. Examples of this are the important early-twentieth-century "Sino-Iranica" findings of Berthold Laufer, the "local cultures" approach of Wolfram Eberhard, the impressive panastronomical theories of Giorgio de Santillana and Hertha von Dechend, and, more recently, the specialized sinological, archaeoastronomical, and comparative philological perspectives of scholars such as David Pankenier and Victor Mair.[162]

More illustrative of what will become the dominant, even orthodox, strain of academic Orientalism and area-specific polygenetic comparativism at the end of the century are the views expressed by the brilliant Orientalist T.W. Rhys Davids.[163] Rhys Davids at University College in London played an important role in the scholarly popularization of Buddhist studies in late-Victorian Britain. He was a Hibbert Lecturer and contributor of the Buddhist sutras to the *Sacred Books* and was responsible in 1881 for founding the famed Pali Text Society, which stressed the priority of a "simpler, purer, and more intellectual Buddhism."[164] In many respects, Rhys Davids was to Buddhist studies in England what Legge was to Confucianism or Müller was to Hinduism. The full extent of their relationship is not clear, but Legge and Rhys Davids knew and respected each other as fellow British Orientalists and contributors to the *Sacred Books*. It may even be that Legge's growing interest in Buddhism was influenced by his association with Rhys Davids. Whatever the case, we know from a letter to Edkins that Legge had Rhys Davids read the proofs of the *Travels of Fa-Hien* (Legge's forthcoming translation of a Buddhist pilgrim's travelogue; 1886), noting only that they "agreed to differ" about certain aspects of Chinese Buddhism.[165]

Rhys Davids's long article in the *Quarterly Review* discussing the overall accomplishment of the first twenty-eight volumes of the *Sacred Books of the East* constitutes an intelligently balanced overview of the comparative historical sciences in the mid-1880s.[166] This article exemplifies the directions that Oriental scholarship—philological and historical in its methodology and increasingly specialized and particularistic with respect to cultural traditions—would take well into the next century. It cogently estimates the accomplishments and promise of the comparative science of religions and, more specifically, anticipates Legge's entry into other more specialized sacred realms associated with the Buddhists and the Daoists.

Ex Oriente Lux: *The Clear and Cold Light of Stern Historical Fact*

Rhys Davids's comments on the "progress of historical research" and "scientific discovery" concerning the Oriental scriptures showed the "increasing degree" of public interest in the comparative study of the "origin and development of religious belief throughout the world." The proof of this assertion was the renewal and continuing publication of Müller's *Sacred Books of the East,* even though these works appealed "much more to the scientific historian than to the general reader."[167] Reviewing the volumes published so far in the series, Rhys Davids called attention to the not always very "edifying" lessons found in the *Sacred Books.* Much of this discussion amounts to a less orotund paraphrase of points already trumpeted by Müller, but it also indicates the formative influence of historical methods on the evolving discourse of the humanistic sciences at this time. Rhys Davids concurred with Müller that the forgotten bibles of the world did not give rise to any new insights about the origins of religion. Rather, they dramatized the "slow and painful advance" and frequent "petrifaction" of religious development. The "real human interest" of the *Sacred Books* was the interest any adult takes in "watching the mind of a child unfold itself."[168]

Rhys Davids also seconded Müller's point about the authorless nature of the sacred books in a way that underscored differences with Legge's often more old-fashioned and reverential ideas.[169] With regard to other aspects of the "uniformity" of belief shown by the *Sacred Books,* Rhys Davids notes that the developmental linkage of religion and ethics—one of the most important steps in the history of religious "reform" and "advance"—was best exemplified "directly and clearly" by the Chinese *Record of Rites* as translated by Legge: "a religion without ethics seems a contradiction in terms."[170] Repeating Müller's elitist ideas about the ideal audience for the *Sacred Books,* Rhys Davids agreed that it "requires a kind of special training to be able to use them aright." And this was a professional academic training provided only in the great research universities of the Western world. He concluded that what was needed, then, was the creation of a new mandarinate of "professorships in the comparative study of the history of religious beliefs," especially at England's "two old universities." In the meantime, it was the public "edifice" of the *Sacred Books* that was attracting attention to the "scientific history" of religions.[171]

ENDS AND NEW BEGINNINGS:
THE BEARING OF OUR KNOWLEDGE OF COMPARATIVE RELIGIONS

> *The literature of a nation, if it is to be studied at all, must be studied systematically and as one connected whole, and not fragmentarily and without plan or order, as it has hitherto been done by most foreign scholars. "It is," says Matthew Arnold, ". . . through the apprehension, either of all literature,—the entire history of the human spirit,—or of a single great literature, or of a single great literary work, as a connected whole, that the real power of literature makes itself felt."*
> "CHINESE SCHOLARSHIP," *NORTH-CHINA HERALD,* 1883

What My Heart Desired

Legge's translation of the *Record of Rites* appeared in April of 1885 and, having turned seventy years of age and knowing what was proper and right, he spent the rest of that year and most of the next preparing, like Kongzi, to follow his heart's desire. While his transformative journey within the domain of Ruist literature would continue on an irregular basis, his primary energies would now be marshaled for his strategic exploration of the other worlds of Chinese literature—particularly those realms defined by the sacred books of the Buddhists and Daoists. He also found time for other heartfelt literary projects so that, during the summer of 1885, he wrote a first draft of his will and relaxed—as only he could—by versifying the Hebrew Psalms in a manner similar to his metric rendition of the Chinese *Book of Poetry*.[172] During this same period, and as a part of his ongoing response to a prolonged debate over his earlier article on Daoism for the 1883 *British Quarterly Review*, Legge redoubled his efforts to understand and translate the *Daode jing* for the new series of the *Sacred Books*. He also lectured on Buddhist and Daoist topics at Oxford and spent much of 1886 "hard at work" on a translation of the ancient Daoist classic known as the *Zhuangzi* (The book of the Master Zhuang).[173]

During this period in 1886, Legge gave an unusually frank talk at a Christian conference that retrospectively reviewed his lifelong experience with Chinese traditions and the Confucian classics and set forth his new concern for the fuller, and more diverse, Arnoldian universe of Chinese literature.[174] Equally important in this presentation is Legge's autobiographical approach to his understanding of the importance of "comparative religions" for missionary work. Related to his personal involvement in these issues is his confession that he was "reluctant" to give such an address at this time. He mentions by way of explanation that he was hesitant to take the podium ahead of someone like Andrew Fairbairn, who was generally "more competent" in matters of comparative religion and philosophy. The undertow to this talk also suggests that wounds from earlier sectarian battles about his views made him uncomfortable in accepting the invitation to speak before a church audience.

Whatever Legge's initial feelings, he warmed to his task and, drawing upon his considerable "field experience" going back some forty-seven years, he gives us a revealing statement about his understanding of comparative religions and the missionary enterprise at that time. Declaring that from the very beginning of his career he was fundamentally a "moderate Calvinist" with a "mind to work and an habit of working," Legge says that already in 1841 he was convinced that missionaries must investigate "the whole path of thought in which the Sages of China had ranged." These convictions led naturally to his just consummated translation project devoted to the Confucian classics. Interestingly enough, Legge mentions that it was his distaste for Frederick D. Maurice's protocomparative *Religions of the World and Their Relation to Christianity* (1842) that, after his first return to England in 1845, led him to a more sympathetic evaluation of his encounter with heathen religion. Legge says that he was "startled" to read of Maurice's strictly theoretical opinion that "the actual sight of a country wholly given to idolatry" must be incredibly "appalling." What was so disturbing about this was that Legge's own field experience in China—since the time of his very first "peep" of China—had the opposite effect on him. Instead of pity and loathing, he felt interest, curiosity, and an abiding thirst for learning. Furthermore, the more he saw of the Chinese, the better he thought of them both morally and socially.

Impure Thoughts

Legge straightforwardly declared to his audience that he was "increasingly struck" by the "simplicity and purity" of the Confucian books. The problems of Confucianism were fundamentally those of "defect" and not of "error." Furthermore, the "better acquainted" he grew with the Master Kong, the "more [he] liked him." It may even be, he intimates, that traditional Confucian moral education is actually better than the moral training given at Oxford. Instead of the all-too-typical missionary "scorn and defiance" directed toward Confucianism, it was far better to approach it "as a friend" who seeks only "to supply what it lacks." He adds that there was no doubt in his mind that the Confucian classics "compare favourably" with the books of the Hebrew Old Testament. Admitting that the "normal reader" of the Confucian classics often found them "insufferably prosy and dosy," Legge bluntly asserted that the Confucian books were often more appropriate for a family worship service than were some readings from the Old Testament! He reinforces this observation by almost casually mentioning that his study of the classics had "often brought [him] to the brink of acknowledging a Jewish element" in Chinese tradition. The reason for this astonishing statement had to do with the relative "purity"—sexual purity in this case—of the two sets of scriptures. The Confucian works were often "uninteresting," but they would never, as sometimes was the case with the Hebrew books, "awaken a blush on the cheek of the most delicate minded lady, or introduce an impure thought in the mind of the schoolboy or girl."[175]

It is in relation to his comparative perspective on scriptural and sexual purity that Legge finally bares his feelings about the conventional missionary enterprise in China. Commenting on his growing impatience with missionaries who all too often, he says, bore "false witness" against the Confucian tradition, he makes one of the most astonishing public confessions of his entire career. He now declares that he was "content for the most part to keep away from missionary meetings and run the risk of being stigmatized as having lost [his] interest in the great missionary work."[176] That this confession was more than mere words is shown later in 1888 by his decision not to attend a major missionary conference in London—even though his absence created something of a public furor at the time.

More Impure Thoughts

Jesus Christ was for Legge the one and only "Master and Lord" of the entire world and the New Testament provided Christianity with heights of religious and moral excellence unattainable by Confucianism or any other tradition. Nonetheless, Kongzi or Confucius was a reforming master if not a divine lord, and Legge had the temerity to suggest that the Daoist and Buddhist traditions, even if they were not as purely theistic as early Confucianism was, had much in them that was religiously and morally good. Laozi actually taught that "evil should be overcome by good" and Buddhism preached the virtues of a "self-sacrificing life" (using as an example the pilgrim Fa Xian) and the "vow of the Bodhisattva." Both Buddhism and Daoism—as well as the "atheopolitical" (defined as "akin to our Positive Philosophy or Comtism") Song Confucianism—teach the "second table of the Decalogue" and should be respected.

Perhaps the most surprising advance was Legge's revisionary opinion of the Buddha. I have already noted his progressively more favorable evaluation of Confucius and, as seen in the *Religions of China,* his relatively elevated opinion of Laozi, the Old Boy founder of Daoism. Legge's previous understanding of the Buddha was, however, not so favorable and it is remarkable to see how he has altered his views. Jesus was, without doubt, "a greater and better man" than any founder of an Oriental religion, but still we must admit, says Legge, that Buddha—like Kongzi and Laozi—was a "great and good man."

Facing Up to Heathenism

Legge concluded his remarks by strongly reasserting his belief that Christianity was the ultimate "religion of mankind." The only question was when, and how, the conversion of China and the world would take place. According to Legge, it was not given to us to know the time of consummation, but there was much that could, and should, be done in the meantime. In this postmillennialist sense, missionaries and scholars had an important role to play. And, for both, it was the "how" of moral, social, and political means that was the crucial question. Thus it is clear to Legge that missionaries in China, seemingly more than sinological scholars, must free themselves from "all prejudices and bigotries" concerning Chinese tradition. Most of all, they need to appreciate the "bearing" that the comparative study of religions has on the missionary approach to heathens. Echoing Müller's oration in Westminster Abbey, Legge says that it will be only through a "learned" body of more "highly endowed" missionaries, and especially through an "invigoration of piety at home," that Christians will be able to look a Confucian, Buddhist, and Daoist "in the face." Legge in this way inevitably comes back to the "whole duty of man" and the commandments of reciprocity. The right and proper human duty is to face up to an honest comparative assessment of the actual moral, social, and political behavior of different national and religious traditions. The problem is that, given the continuing moral deficiencies of both Christian and Oriental nations, authentic "face to face," or ritually dialogical, communication was exceedingly difficult and delayed. In this kind of ambiguous dialectical situation, there can be no immediate translation or transformation of China into Christian terms.

CHAPTER SEVEN

Ancestor Legge:
Translating Buddhism and Daoism,
1886-1892

The spirit of the age is . . . a spirit of enquiry into other men's beliefs, with the inevitable result that the enquirer finds there is much commendable, where he would once have been taught to believe all was beyond question condemnable. Audi alteram partem *["hear the other side"], is the motto of the day. . . . Fetischism may eventually find partisans, or at least apologists, for aught we can tell; at any rate Buddhism, Mahometanism, Confucianism and Taoism have their admirers, and with respect to all creeds, whether religious or philosophical, there is a general feeling growing up that we ought to understand before we condemn. . . . On the whole, ["enquirers of 'honest doubt'"] gain in Charity where they lose in Faith.*

G.M.H. PLAYFAIR, "AN EXPOUNDER OF DARK SAYINGS," *JOURNAL OF THE NORTH CHINA BRANCH OF THE ROYAL ASIATIC SOCIETY*, 1889–1890

ANCESTOR WORSHIP

Though frequently honored for his "supereminence" as the premier sinological Orientalist at the end of the century, James Legge was also coming under attack for being methodologically antiquated. Increasingly he was viewed as a great, though aging, representative of an earlier generation, someone who was unfortunately out of touch with the newer and higher—more skeptically destructive and radically secular—methods of modern historiographic and philological scholarship at the end of the century.[1] Even before his death in the late 1890s, Legge was being ceremoniously classified as an exalted ancestral figure (see figure 35) who represented a pioneering, but more naively reverent and simplistically uncritical, generation of humanistic scholarship. The funereal qualities of this increasingly ritualized praise are suggested by the recurrent designations of Legge as the Nestor of European sinology, a classical allusion that served only to affirm his ancestral status by testifying to his association with the sage, but aged and decrepit, Greek hero in the Trojan War.[2]

Figure 35. James Legge as a Victorian sage, ca. 1870s. Painting, oil on canvas (53 inches × 47 inches), by J. E. Christie. Reproduced courtesy of Corpus Christi College, Oxford.

Nestor's Blue Christmas

Legge had a highly cultivated appreciation for the rhetorical suggestiveness of Greek classical allusions and a fervent conviction that he had not yet passed from the realm of vital scholarship. He was therefore not insensitive to the premature and inaccurate implications of the ritualized tributes paid to him by his younger contemporaries. It is in this context that his actions a little before Christmas in the year 1886 take on a special pathos. At this time, Legge sent a letter (and book parcel) to the Permanent Secretary of the l'Académie française des inscriptions et belles-lettres in Paris.[3] In this brief but poignant epistle, Legge reminds the academy that he had the "honour to receive" the "first award of the Julien prize" and that he was hoping that he might be considered again for this great and special honor. Doubtlessly feeling neglected and put upon by the new generation of more scientifically trained, and continentally influenced, sinological Orientalists such as Cordier, Lacouperie, Schlegel, Gabelentz, and Giles, who did not bear the stigma of an earlier missionary career, Legge sadly found it necessary to plead his own case. He was in the awkward position of having personally to inform the academy that some of his most recent publications might again merit consideration for this most prestigious and lucrative trophy of professional sinological accomplishment.

Having won the inaugural Prix Julien in 1875 for his production of the *Spring and Autumn Annals,* Legge—despite his many scholarly achievements during the intervening years—had not published a complete translation of a new Chinese text until his 1882 rendition of the *Book of Changes* for the first series of Müller's *Sacred Books of the East.* As a result of the whole protracted Terrien de Lacouperie affair, this translation—whatever its considerable technical merits and interpretive sensitivity to a symbolic level of meaning—acquired the controversial aura of a work perhaps deficient in its application of a fully scientific and modern methodology. In his letter to the academy, Legge nowhere alludes to his rendition of the still "unintelligible" mysteries of the *Book of Changes* and refers only to the submission (by "separate parcel") of his less notorious translation of the "Li Ki or the Collection of Ceremonial Usages," which, as he puts it, was "certainly one of the most important of the Classical Works of China, forming two volumes of the Sacred Books of the East." Showing his newfound breadth as a comprehensive Orientalist concerned with all aspects of Chinese literature and very much in keeping with the growing popular and scholarly fascination with Buddhism, Legge also submitted his translation of "the Travels of Fahien, with notes, and accompanied with a revision of the Chinese text," as published in 1886 by the Clarendon Press.

What is pitiful about these overtures is the sense in which Legge seemed to feel the need to prove that he had "not ceased to pursue [his] Chinese studies" from the time he received the first Julien Prize. Now at the height of his career at Oxford but, as some would say, in his waning years as a scholar on the frontiers of sinological science, Legge was forced to become his own publicist by sending along his work to France and by plaintively "hoping again" that he might, as he put it, "obtain the distinction of [the Julien Prize] being awarded to me." Legge was still highly respected by the new continental arbiters of entrepreneurial sinology such as Gustave Schlegel and Henri Cordier, the cofounders in 1890 of *T'oung Pao,* a journal that quickly became the leading organ of a wholly professionalized (more narrowly specialized, highly technical, and critically irreverent) academic sinological Orientalism. But the unhappy truth seems to be that the movers and shakers of the newly resurgent French tradition, among them the influential Cordier, Schlegel, and Barthélemy-Saint-Hilaire, were no longer actively championing the prize-winning attributes of Legge's latest works among their academic colleagues in Paris.[4]

The Roar of Silence

Legge's demeaning entreaties to the French academy were met with silence. He never again received the Julien Prize, a fact that is made all the more politically revealing and disturbing by the simple fact that parvenus such as Lacouperie and Giles, and others such as Cordier, were receiving attention and recognition for works that, in the hindsight of later sinological history, have none of the lasting greatness of Legge's *Book of Changes*, *Record of Rites,* his Buddhist studies, or his translations of the Daoist classics for the *Sacred Books.* Legge was never given to bitterness about such slights to his scholarly achievements, but he must have felt some special pain at being silently branded as obsolete. No longer just a mere translator, he was now the esteemed, but aging and mostly irrelevant, Nestor of sinological Orientalism.

Another sign of this silent treatment combining formal respect with practiced neglect is perhaps seen from the fact that, although he was duly designated as a vice-president of the Royal Asiatic Society (along with the Sanskritist William Hunter) toward the end of his life, Legge never attained the honorific presidential office of this most prestigious learned society of Orientalists in London.[5] The reason for this was simply that, despite his Oxford professorship, Legge was still a Scottish Nonconformist who did not move in the higher orders of society. The effrontery of this is seen from the fact that the sinologically lightweight, but knighted and better bred and connected, Thomas Wade was given the presidency of the society in 1887 shortly after his retirement from the British diplomatic corps in China and right before his appointment (after the strategic donation of his Chinese library) to the first chair of Chinese at Cambridge in 1888.[6] Aside from his token chairmanship of the Chinese section at the congress at Florence in 1878, Legge also was never offered any of the highest honorary offices associated with the international Congress of Orientalists—positions attained by the likes of Müller, Cordier, Leon de Rosny, and even by such relative mediocrities as Robert Douglas and Samuel Beal.

The Dissidence of Dissent at Oxford

With his silvery thatch of hair and bushy muttonchops, Legge had started to take on the physical demeanor of a vaguely disheveled Old Testament prophet or a gauntly wizened Scottish bard. As seen by his periodic bouts of gout and an especially bothersome and persistently recurrent eczema, Legge was also starting to show the effects of his age and his lifetime routine of uncompromising hard work. But his sparkling blue eyes, retentive memory, seriousness of purpose, simple humor, and independent spirit still shone brightly. Often to the chagrin of his family, Legge only marginally modified his working habits by conducting his multifarious labors at a somewhat slower pace. Although it might take a bit longer to finish any particular project, he vigorously pursued his sinological scholarship, even moving into the new areas of Buddhist, Daoist, Tang dynasty (particularly the *guwen* writings of Han Yu), and poetic literature. He also held to a full schedule of university teaching and lecturing (his notable public lectures during this period dealing with the Nestorian Monument and the Daoist texts associated with the mysterious sages Laozi and Zhuangzi), and wrote several general articles for the 1888 *Chambers' Encyclopedia* ("Confucius" and "China") and for the 1890 supplement to the ninth edition of the *Encyclopedia Britannica* ("Lao Tzu" and "Confucius").[7] In addition to this, he continued to give talks to various religious and educational groups and kept up his energetic, though selective, involvement in the congregational affairs at his local church on George Street.

Ever concerned with the need to promote a spiritual and intellectual climate at Oxford sympathetically responsive to Dissenting culture, Legge was also anxious to advance, even beyond the largely successful efforts of the Nonconformists' Union, the greater fortunes of organized Nonconformist education at Oxford. Through his participation in various key committees, Legge was accordingly involved in the establishment and subsequent growth of the Congregationalist Mansfield College, the first Dissenting institution for graduate theological education in Oxford.[8] Opened on October 18, 1886, with nine students meeting in rented rooms, Mansfield College prospered under the energetic leadership of Andrew Martin Fairbairn—a "Nonconformist divine of commanding character, whose learning and piety," opined the London *Times*, "even Anglican Oxford must fain respect."[9] By the Michaelmas term of 1889, the college, with Jowett and other representatives of liberal Anglicanism at Oxford in benign attendance, was officially installed in a handsomely designed suite of newly constructed buildings in east Oxford.[10]

Although not officially a part of the university, Mansfield College by 1889 seemed to be tolerated, if not embraced, by the ruling Anglican elite of the university and city. Even such limited acceptance made a considerable difference in the still largely cloistered theological world of Oxford. The more visible and substantial "inclusion of Nonconformity" within the "charmed circle" of Oxonian culture was, said the *Times*, diminishing the more destructive forms of the "dissidence of dissent" and was ultimately hastening the secular revolution in Oxford intellectual and social life. This peculiarly virulent strain of Oxonian "dissidence" grew out of the "secular deposit in the Nonconformist mind of antagonisms excited by long generations of exclusion and of something very like contempt" on the part of Anglican Oxford, a posture that all too often resulted in a "peculiarly aggressive and not too urbane type of Nonconformity."[11] The founding of Mansfield College was a "happy omen" of religious freedom and social acceptance at Oxford. As an institution that called for intellectual and religious reconciliation rather than for more rancorous theological conflict, Mansfield College signaled the end of the kind of dissidence witnessed in the scandal occasioned by Robert Horton's nomination as examiner. From the perspective of the *Times,* these developments rightly alluded to an even greater process of religious conciliation and social secularization in the overall "national life" of England.[12]

Audi Alteram Partem

The advance of Nonconformity and the tempering of sectarian dissonance at Oxford are also seen in the role played by Dissenting scholars and colleges in furthering the study of Oriental languages and in introducing the study of comparative religions into the theological course of studies in English higher education.[13] Dr. Fairbairn at Mansfield was especially influential in the curricular introduction of comparative religions, but there were others, such as John Estlin Carpenter, who was based at the Unitarian Manchester College, which opened a few years after Mansfield College and was only a stone's throw away from it.[14] For all his glory as the reputed father of the comparative science of religions, Müller seems rarely, if ever, to have taught the subject in any extensive way at Oxford.[15] He had expounded eloquently on the science of religions at the Royal Institution in London, as the Hibbert and Gifford Lecturer in London and Glasgow, and in public forums in various other British cities. However, the distinction of being the first to teach a regular and ongoing series of courses on comparative religions at Oxford appears to belong to Fairbairn.[16]

Müller preferred the national fame and substantial remuneration that came from publishing books and accepting well-publicized lectureships over the tedium and obscurity of routine teaching. His inclination in these matters was particularly one-sided when it was associated with the special notability of inaugurating a new, and heavily endowed, invitational lectureship devoted to an approach to religion largely identified with his own reputation as the preeminent comparative scholar in the world. Such was the case with his acceptance of the inaugural Hibbert Lectures in 1878 and now, in the 1880s, with his acceptance of the invitation to give the first series of the new Gifford Lectures on "Natural Theology" in Glasgow. These lectures were presented as four successive sessions (1889–1892) of well-attended and controversial talks on "Natural, Physical, Anthropological, and Psychological" religion, which in their published form constitute Müller's culminating statement on religious development.[17]

The efforts by Legge, Fairbairn, Carpenter, and others associated with the Oxford Society for Historical Theology in the 1890s (which embraced both Nonconformists such as Fairbairn and Carpenter and Broad Church Anglicans such as Müller, Sayce, and Thomas Cheyne) indicate that there was a special, though still often unrecognized, connection with the struggle for the acceptance of Nonconformity within the Anglican bastions of English university life and the difficult emergence and spotty acceptance of the comparative study of religions in British higher education. This battle was but a handmaiden to the larger contest for a more impartial, more fully nonsectarian and secular, system of national education capable of disrupting the old sinecures of class and religion.

Curricular Charity before Sectarian Faith

The conciliatory climate at Oxford and willingness to put academic charity before a narrow sectarian faith in the Christian Bible and Mediterranean classics are also seen in a tiny victory for the greater disciplinary inclusiveness of the Oxford examination system. The establishment and bureaucratic administration of the universitywide examination system (since the 1850s) was the primary mechanism of curricular canonization and was consequently the key to significant intellectual change at Oxford, especially in the direction of an ostensibly more pluralistic, secular, scientific, and modern course of studies. Thus in March 1887 the Board of Oriental Studies of the University Examination Schools (which had already accepted Sanskrit out of concern for training young men for the Indian civil service) added Chinese to the languages that could be offered in the Honours School examinations.[18] Although the number of students taking Chinese remained extremely small and the British Foreign Office and missionary societies maintained their studied indifference toward recruits taking professional training in Chinese at Oxford, the study of Chinese, and by extension the emergent discipline of sinological Orientalism, found official recognition within the Oxonian curriculum.

At Oxford at the end of the century, exotic Oriental languages were generally allowed to supplement the standard curriculum (and examination system) of the Greek and Roman classics only to the degree that such literatures could be shown to be classical, authoritative, and moral in nature. Moreover, Oriental traditions had to have coherent bodies of literature in the Carlylian or Arnoldian sense. The crucial factor of classical sameness had already been demonstrated for Sanskrit literature by the regnant Indo-European theory, but the linguistic and cultural strangeness of China was a more difficult matter that required the combined canonical efforts of both Legge's *Classics* and Müller's *Sacred Books*.

THE VICTORIAN INVENTION OF BUDDHISM

Buddhism is for many reasons the religion that has attracted most attention. . . . Of all the Eastern religions [Buddhism] is the one that seems at first sight most alien to the spirit of the West; yet it is the one that has awakened in her the most deep and distinct echo. Our contemporary Pessimism not only owed its inception and earliest form to Buddhism, but owes it to-day most of its vitality, and much of its right to consideration and criticism. The similarities of its political organization or constitution, its ritual, observances, ethical and social ideals, with those distinctive of Roman Catholicism, open a large field at once of comparison and inquiry. . . . But of much greater scientific significance than [Buddhism's] relation to our speculative Pessimism on the one hand, and its institutional and ceremonial affinities with Catholicism on the other, are the questions connected with its origin, history, and interpretation.

A.M. FAIRBAIRN, "HISTORY OF RELIGIONS," *CONTEMPORARY REVIEW*, 1885

Deep and Distinct Echoes

Legge's talk, "The Bearing of Comparative Religions," shows that, by the mid-1880s, he had already started to extend his feelers of sympathetic comprehensiveness to the Buddhist tradition. Borrowing from Fairbairn's discussion of these matters, he acknowledged that Buddha was a "great and good man." Despite the "similarities" between Chinese Buddhism and the "holy mummeries" of Roman Catholicism, Buddhism generally expressed "deep and distinct echoes" with the "spirit of the West" during the waning years of the nineteenth century.[19] In Fairbairn's fin de siècle understanding of these matters, the growing fascination with Buddhism primarily resulted from its philosophical resonance with the darker currents of decadence and pessimism (e.g., the apparent annihilation of *nirvāṇa* and the denial of a creator god and a personal self).[20] For Legge and other Orientalists such as Müller (whose interest in Buddhism went back to the 1850s and 1860s), however, the curiosity about, and study of, Buddhism in the last quarter of the century often had a scientific orientation that was more positively charged with an appreciation of Buddha's Lutherlike reformation of Brahmanic sacerdotalism and a sympathy for some popular forms of later Mahayana Buddhist piety and morality.

Popular Buddhist morality seemed commendable because it was expressive of the basic religious needs of human nature as understood by most Victorians (particularly the affirmation of an afterlife as a recompense for one's behavior and the emphasis on the ideal of salvific or philanthropic compassion). In his lecture "The Purgatories of Buddhism and Taoism" (given at Oxford in May 1893), Legge said that Buddhism, despite its deficiencies, "taught an admirable morality, and an astonishing love of charity and an extensive amount of self-culture." It seems that the morbidly delineated punishments of the traditional ten hells of popular Buddhism and Daoism, which were illustrated in his public lecture, appealed to Legge's religious sensibilities. As an abstemious teetotaler living during a period of rising sentiment in Britain and America in favor of temperance, Legge was also impressed that Buddhism recommended the "total abstinence from all intoxicating drinks, which must awaken the admiration of total abstainers in our own and other Christian countries."[21]

By the 1870s, Buddhism was generally an object of popular infatuation (e.g., as filtered through Edwin Arnold's *Light of Asia*, first published in 1879 but extremely popular in Britain and America for the rest of the century), of occult dalliance (e.g., the wildly eclectic theosophical form of "esoteric Buddhism" promoted by Mme Blavatsky and Henry Steel Olcott), and of more serious scholarly attention (going back to Eugène Burnouf's *Introduction à l'histoire du Buddhisme indien* in 1844 and to influential comparativists and Orientalists such as Müller and Rhys Davids who emphasized the originary status of the Indian, non-Mahayana or pre-Chinese, canon of Pali texts).[22] Because of its Indo-European roots, Buddhism was invented as a taxonomic category as early as the 1830s in British tradition. And by midcentury—well before there was any similar Western interest in Daoism—Buddhism, in both its so-called pure and degenerate forms, was largely a textually defined object for Orientalists and a significant, though often contradictory, artifact of the general Victorian cultural imagination concerning the Orient.[23]

Throughout the late Victorian period, much of the special respect given to Buddhism was related to the tradition's status as the largest, most crossculturally successful and only missionary-style Oriental religion (in Müller's sense of the uniquely dynamic missionary religions). In light of the fantastic numbers often associated with the "swarming" populations in Asia, especially those based on extrapolated statistical estimates derived from questionable Chinese census figures, there was a creeping fear that Buddhism was actually the largest religion in the entire world. The apparent size and international sway of Buddhism conjured up the threatening possibility that Christianity could not maintain its claim to a divinely ordained dominion over all the nations of the earth.[24]

The Commendable and Condemnable

Because of its Indian origins, its heterodox status among many Ruist scholars in the Qing period, and its seemingly corrupt nature, Chinese forms of Mahayana Buddhism were slower to come under the scrutiny of Oriental scholars.[25] Well before Legge developed an interest in the subject, French academicians such as Julien, missionary-scholars such as Gützlaff and Edkins, and especially ex- or nonmissionary sinologues such as Eitel and Beal, were seriously exploring Buddhist tradition in China.[26] But these studies tended to focus on the purity of some hypothetical "original" Buddhism and were persistently textual, rationalistic, and essentialist in nature.[27] The living Buddhist traditions in China, such as the multifaceted Pure Land and Chan sects, were scrupulously overlooked.

The sinological understanding of Buddhism and Daoism in China was, moreover, strongly reinforced by the native Chinese condemnation of irrational and heterodox religion during the Ming and Qing periods (influenced by Han Yu and Zhu Xi and crystallized in Emperor Kangxi's Sacred Edict). The native Chinese polemic tended to merge sympathetically with the Western biblical apologetic directed against idolatry, with the Renaissance, Jesuit, and Enlightenment rational condemnation of superstition, and with the perspective of the new nineteenth-century comparativistic sciences. In no other form of Orientalism was there such a powerful coalescence of both Western and Eastern scholarly prejudices in the name of some higher so-called heavenly principle (God or Tian; Logos, Dao, or the Song Confucian *li* or *daoli*).

The Fixation on Chinese Buddhist Travel Literature

Even sinological scholars such as Legge, who found some commendable religious and moral values in the Mahayana tradition, paid an inordinate amount of attention to the Indian or Aryan sources of the Chinese tradition. It is this peculiar compulsion to study Chinese Buddhism in relation to almost anything that was not Chinese—coupled with the pressures for a monogenetic, Western, Indo-European, Babylonian, or biblical source for this dynamic, imaginative, philosophical, moral, and missionary manifestation of Oriental civilization—that partially explains the curiously disproportionate attention the early sinological Orientalists placed on Chinese Buddhist pilgrim and travel literature. The doctrinal, liturgical, and ethical sutra literature in Chinese was more technically demanding and conceptually esoteric (especially in relation to Buddhist cosmology and the Chinese transcription of Sanskrit names and terminology)—and hence more difficult to translate—than the travel literature was.[28] By the 1880s, however, these were only minor considerations since there was a growing body of Western Buddhist scholarship on the early and later forms of Buddhism and on the problems of Chinese transliteration (i.e., Julien's classic *Méthode pour déchiffrer et transcrire les noms sanscrits* [1861]; and Eitel's *Handbook for the Student of Chinese Buddhism* [1870]). The fact is that sinological Orientalism in the nineteenth century consistently emphasized the study of Buddhist travel narratives. This is seen not only in some of the earliest Buddhological studies by the French sinologues Rémusat and Julien,[29] but also in Legge's selection of the fifth-century Fa Xian's *Fuguo ji* (A record of Buddhist kingdoms) as his first major translation and annotation of a Buddhist text:

A Record of Buddhist Kingdoms: Being an Account by the Chinese Monk Fa-Hien of His Travels in India and Ceylon (A.D. *389–414*) *in Search of the Buddhist Books of Discipline* (referred to as *The Travels of Fa-Hien*).[30]

Beyond Legge in the Preparation of the Chinese Mind

By the time Legge was developing a strong interest in Buddhism and Daoism in the 1880s, other younger Protestant missionaries—especially influential liberal figures such as the British Baptist Timothy Richard (1845–1919) and the American Presbyterian W. A. P. Martin (1827–1916)—were starting to see the possibility of interpreting Buddhism, like Confucianism, as a kind of *praeparatio evangelica*.[31] Timothy Richard was prepared to go further than Legge was in promoting what amounted to a quasi-syncretistic method of evangelization that, depending on the circumstances and audience, drew upon either Confucian or Buddhist traditions (including an impassioned consideration of the gospel-like implications of the Pure Land sutra literature).[32] For the radically individualistic Richard, there was even the insinuation that the civilizational reformation and social salvation of China would come about through the efforts of the Chinese themselves, albeit as a result of the liberalized educational, medicinal, scientific, and religious social gospel mission of the Protestant missionaries.[33]

A brilliant American missionary and the first president of Peking Imperial University, W. A. P. Martin specifically connected the more positive appreciation of Chinese Buddhism with the increasing impact of the science of comparative religions on missionary policy and procedures.[34] He recommended that missionaries adopt the comparativist's motto of "impartial not neutral" in all further dealings with Oriental religions such as Confucianism and Buddhism. Along with Richard, Martin also suggested that, while the living traditions of Mahayana Buddhism displayed a disheartening degree of corruption, they nevertheless show—historiographically and scientifically—the popular triumph of theism over "atheistic Buddhism." In this way, popular Buddhism "prepares the Chinese mind for Christianity" and gives the Chinese a rich religious vocabulary concerning heavenly spheres and beings, ideas of sin and hell, the problems of eternal retribution, and the relation between faith and good works.[35]

Legge's Travels of Fa-Hien

Legge was not as formative a figure in the study of Chinese Buddhism as were others, among them Julien, Eitel, Edkins, and Beal. Nor was he as creative as Richard and Martin were in the appropriation of Buddhism for the evangelization of China. Moreover, because Daoism and Confucianism were perceived to share the same indigenous archaic roots, Legge showed a more sympathetic appreciation for early classical or philosophical Daoism than for the originally foreign import of Buddhism. Some small part of Legge's more highly cultivated regard for the Daoist classics may also be due to his singular responsibility for preparing them for the *Sacred Books,* whereas the Buddhist contributions were entrusted to other more Buddho-logically focused Orientalists such as Rhys Davids (volumes 13, 17, 19, 20, 35, and 36), Beal (volume 19, a Chinese translation of Asvaghosha's *Bud-dhakarita*), and Takakusu Junjiro (volume 49, part 2, Mahayana texts).[36] Legge was a follower of preordained scholarly fashion rather than a leader in the study of Buddhist texts—a state of affairs seen in his work on Fa Xian, in which he most often defers to the more extensive technical knowledge of scholars such as Eitel and Rhys Davids.[37] Certainly he was not an authorita-tive inventor of Chinese Buddhological discourse in the same way that he was for the Victorian understanding of Confucianism and Daoism. Never-theless, as the greatest living sinological Orientalist of his day and someone who was closely identified with the Confucian classics and with the Müller-ian comparativist project of the *Sacred Books,* Legge's entry into the field of Buddhist translation gave Chinese Buddhist studies a new prominence within Orientalism.

From the late 1870s until his death, Legge addressed Buddhist topics in various formats and forums, including periodic public lectures in Oxford (in 1878, 1885, and 1893),[38] course readings (especially throughout the 1880s and 1890s), including the polemical essays by Han Yu, and published articles and letters (such as his publication in 1887 of a review article in the *Athenaeum* on "The Image of Maitreya Buddha"). But Legge can really be credited with only two major scholarly works on Buddhism: *The Travels of Fa-Hien* and his translation of the thirteenth-century minor classic of Bud-dhist apologetic writings, "A Fair and Dispassionate Discussion of the Three Doctrines Accepted in China," published in 1893.[39]

Legge's version of Fa Xian's text is by far his most important Buddho-logical work, and is particularly interesting for the way in which it reflects his evolving views about non-Confucian Chinese religions and the grow-ing, but still elementary, sophistication of sinological scholarship con-cerning the difficult subject of Chinese Buddhism.[40] Legge himself cau-tiously notes that there were "many things in the vast field of Buddhistic literature which still require to be carefully handled." In keeping with the lower and higher criticism being applied to the Christian Scriptures, Legge remarks that, among other issues, difficult questions about the genuineness of the sutra literature and the comparative "similarities" be-tween the biographies of the Buddha and the gospel narratives, "which startle us so frequently," were yet to be sufficiently investigated by Orien-talists.[41]

Fa Xian's *Foguo ji,* as a transcultural narrative of a pilgrim cleric and missionary-translator, mirrors in some ways Legge's own transformative journey as a conscientious missionary agent and as a faithful scholar. In this sense, Fa Xian's account of his travels to India and beyond can almost be viewed as a fifth-century Chinese Buddhist exercise in the semianthropological observation of different cultures and the "impartial but not neutral" comparative study of religions. Fa Xian and Legge shared a dutiful devotion to "simple straightforwardness" when it came to the description of other nations and religions.[42] Legge probably did not view Fa Xian's narrative as a neat Chinese analogue to his own espousal of a comparativist methodology, but it is clear that he held the publication of this Buddhist work in high regard. This is seen, for example, in the care he lavished on its physical production at the Oxford University Clarendon Press and the obvious pride he took in making this small book the full equivalent to the original editions of the *Chinese Classics,* the production of which he supervised in Hong Kong. The *Travels of Fa-Hien* included a preface, introduction, full translation with copious notes using Chinese characters, numerous woodblock illustrations, and—something he regretted the absence of in his publications for the *Sacred Books*—the complete Chinese text of a Korean recension that was set with the two fonts of Chinese type he had acquired for the press.[43]

Statistical Size and Rhetorical Truth

In *The Travels of Fa-Hien,* Legge's increasingly sympathetic view of Buddhism and the "three religions" is, as it always was with Confucianism, carefully qualified in relation to his mostly impartial, but certainly not neutral, thesis regarding the ultimate Christian fulfillment of the three religions. This factor comes out infrequently and obliquely throughout the notes to the translation. More interesting in this regard is the general introduction in which, after briefly discussing the life of Fa Xian and various textual issues, Legge devotes most of his attention to the curiously controversial issue of the "number of Buddhists in the world." Because of its disturbing implications for the manifest destiny of Christianity and Western imperialism, the "number of Buddhists in the world" was a hotly debated question in both popular and scholarly Victorian circles. For this reason, Legge's treatment of the problem is interesting both for its scholarly appeal to reasoned analysis and, by finally affirming that the "smallest" of the estimates of the size of Buddhism was "much above what is correct," for its deeper rhetorical logic.[44]

Beginning with a review of some of the conflicting reports about the relative size of the various major world religions, Legge rehearses several of the more prominent estimates of the magnitude of Buddhism. He noted that some distinguished scholars, using mostly estimates of the size of the Chinese population, were finding that Buddhism was actually the largest religion in the world. He specifically refers to Müller's estimate in 1868 that Buddhism was "professed by 455 millions of human beings"; to Rhys Davids's more recent suggestion that the number of Buddhists amounted "in all to 500 millions," of which China contributed "414,686,974 millions to the total"; and to the influential seven-volume atlas by Hermann Berghaus, in which a disturbing statistical division of the world population by religion was proposed: "Buddhists 31.2 per cent, Christians 30.7, Mohammedans 15.7, Brahmanists 13.4, Heathens 8.7, and Jews 0.3."[45]

Legge was careful to record Müller's comment (seconded by Rhys Davids) that "truth" should not be "settled by majorities," but it is abundantly clear that size and truth were closely connected, discursively and psychologically, with Christianity's understanding of its own divinely prophetic mission to all the nations of the world (Matt. 28:18–20). Legge's attempt to correct the record concerning the number of Buddhists is noteworthy for its rightful criticism of "per-centages" based on unfounded estimates of the size of the Chinese population and on a questionable apportionment of the Chinese people among "Confucianists, Taoists, and Buddhists." His obsessive need to protect Christianity's status as the numerically greatest religion (Buddhism is "only entitled to occupy the fifth place, ranking below Christianity, Confucianism, Brahmanism, and Mohammedanism, and followed, some distance off, by Taoism") without questioning the apportionment and possible inflation of the number of Christians (and deflation of the number of Muslims) raises doubts about Legge's fairness in this matter.[46] Such pronouncements won him a number of questionable allies—such as the increasingly conservative and bitterly anti-Müllerian Boden professor, Monier-Williams—in the "which religion is biggest and best" sweepstakes.[47]

Eitel was on record for saying that "most Chinese are theoretically Confucianists, but emotionally Buddhists or Taoists." Legge found it hard to agree fully with Eitel's opinion because, in his experience as a missionary in China for thirty years, he had already discovered that, "as a whole," the Chinese people "sneer at Buddhist priests" and have "no respect for the Buddhist church." For Legge it could only be maintained, in accordance the edits of the Kangxi emperor and the Ruist bureaucrats (who upheld the "Ju Chiao [rujiao]" or "the Doctrines held by the Learned Class"), that Confucianism was "the orthodoxy of China."[48] The "great majority" of the Chinese are (and were) "Confucianists," even though most average Chinese would not be aware of any such explicit identity. The Chinese people thus become quantifiable members of an orthodox and exclusive Confucian religion or faith that was almost entirely constructed of various quantifiable religious terms, doctrines, and moral practices supposedly found in the ancient classics. The Chinese themselves, especially in the modern period and encompassing both the masses and the learned scholars, were mostly oblivious to any emotional and intellectual attachment to a classically divine Shangdi or an orthodox Confucian religion.[49]

Mitigated Sympathies

Reaction to the new translation of Fa Xian's *Travels* was generally respectful of Legge's supereminence as a sinological scholar. He was applauded by the *Athenaeum* for producing a work that, due to his own abilities and the "distinct advantage" of the cooperation of Professor Rhys Davids, was "superior to its predecessors."[50] Also basically congratulatory, the review by Thomas Pearce in the *China Review* is intriguing for its insightful criticism of Legge's overly simplified efforts to make the Chinese into "Confucianists" rather than "Buddhists." As the reviewer notes, the problem in China was "how much Buddhism must be in a man to constitute him a Buddhist 'emotionally' or 'intellectually.'" This issue is compounded by the fact that the Chinese, "within the limits of their religious knowledge and capacity," are "everything by turns."[51]

More in keeping with the opinion that Legge was losing touch with the critical methods and skeptical spirit prevailing at the end of the century are the reviews appearing in the *Saturday Review* and the *Journal of the North China Branch of the Royal Asiatic Society*. The Royal Asiatic Society review was by the increasingly notorious enfant terrible of the younger generation of British consular scholars in China, the pugnacious Herbert Giles. As described by one commentator, Giles was happy to slash away at the "critical" shortcomings of all other sinologues, whether of the stature of Legge or of the relative middling status of Edward Parker and John Chalmers.[52] By this time, Giles had already picked a major fight with Legge over the problem of the authenticity and authority of the *Book of the Tao and Its Characteristics,* but in this review he mainly complained about Legge's "cribbing" parts of Giles's earlier 1877 translation of Fa Xian's *Foguo ji.*[53]

The anonymous reviewer in the *Saturday Review* is even more provocative, taking Legge to task for injecting too much of a Christian apologetic into his scholarship.[54] Once condemned by missionary critics for being too liberal, too comparative, too impartial, too heretical, and too sympathetic toward Chinese religion, Legge is now found to be overly theological and Christian by more secular and skeptical critics. It is true that Legge was trying to be comparatively impartial in his study of Chinese tradition, but his approach was never just neutral or completely indifferent to the "evident" superiority of the Christian religion and civilization. This kind of approach was very much in the spirit of the still-reverent Müllerian school of comparativism that was often understood as an "adjunct to the study of Apologetics."[55]

According to the *Saturday Review,* which one contemporaneous wag described as the "organ of sceptical conservatism,"[56] Legge showed too much of "his training as a defender of the truths of Christianity *in partibus infidelium.*" It is this bias of an aging ex-missionary that has tended "to mitigate [Legge's] power of sympathy with alien faiths." The irony of this observation is that Legge's *Travels* is much less defensive and apologetic than was his first conscious application of the comparative method in the *Religions of China* and, for that matter, in his translations and annotations for the *Chinese Classics* and the *Sacred Books.* Enunciating an opinion that reflected more of the Arnoldian *Light of Asia* admiration for Buddhism or Oscar Wilde's newfound respect for the Chinese sage Zhuangzi, the *Review* chastised Legge for not showing more "respectful consideration" for a religion that had "removed mountains of iniquity in Asia."[57]

Betwixt and Between at the End of the Century

Legge had the misfortune of being caught betwixt and between rapidly changing religious and intellectual fashions in the waning years of the Victorian era, even though he had helped to bring about some of the liberal movements that were now turning against him. As a skepticism about all that was held reverent reached new heights among academics and intellectuals at the end of the nineteenth century, Legge found himself torn between the missionary and scholarly sides of his career. He was now often too conservative and trusting in the validity of a classic past and the authorial integrity of ancient texts for a younger generation of more progressive academic scholars and "less reverent" critical Orientalists. Yet as seen in the minor backlash among missionaries at the end of the century against the inroads of comparative religions, he was still too liberal and tainted with a wimpish indifferentism to satisfy the conservatives in the missionary movement in China. Legge would forever be identified as a hopelessly liberal comparativist by conservative missionaries and as a heroically diligent, but vaguely old-fashioned and excessively pious, ex-missionary scholar by critical academics and secular Orientalists. *Leggism* would come to be used by some younger sinologists as a label for old-fashioned and uncritical scholarship and by various conservative missionaries as an epithet for an unjustified sympathy for Chinese religions.

Toward the end of his life—as witnessed by his interest in the "comparative apologetics" of native critics such as the Buddhist Liu Mi and the Ruist Han Yu and his revision in 1893 of the prolegomena to volume 1 of the Oxford edition of the *Classics*—Legge gradually seemed to place more emphasis on the crucial "not neutral" addendum to the comparativist credo of impartiality. This was a wholly understandable development on Legge's part, but it led to considerable confusion in the evaluation of Legge's work by missionaries and Orientalists during the last years of the century. Legge's liminal status at the end of the Victorian era also suggests a reason for his being so quickly forgotten, overlooked, and trivialized by later missionaries, both conservative and liberal, and by the more highly specialized, noncomparative, area-specific, and secular sinologists.

Comparative Apologetics: Liu Mi and Han Yu

Legge's interests during his last years in Oxford suggest that he was seeking to refine his comparativist methods in a somewhat more apologetically sensitive and sinologically specific way. He seems to have been searching for a method that was both sympathetically comparative and resolutely apologetic—a method that did not capitulate to conservative missionary forces, but was also not dependent upon Müller's Indo-European-based science of religions or on some of the wilder monogenetic theories of Lacouperie, Edkins, and Kingsmill. It appears that he was seeking a new method of controlled comparison more carefully and exclusively focused on, and rooted in, the indigenous complexities of Chinese religion and literature.

What was this new method? This is a question that Legge never really answers. From all indications, it involved an approach to the study of Chinese religions that combined European Orientalist concerns for sympathetic comprehensiveness and developmental classification with the more hierarchical and authoritative models of comparative analysis associated with some forms of native Chinese tradition. These concerns for more of a transcultural comparative method were also very much in harmony with his lifelong habit of carefully considering native commentarial tradition on philological and interpretive questions. There was nothing new about this conservatively liberal strategy for Legge as a missionary or as a scholar, but there is a sense in which, during the twilight of his scholarly career, he was more assiduously trying to fashion a hybrid method uniquely appropriate to the Chinese tradition.

It is in this light that we should evaluate Legge's other major Buddhist work on the apologetics of the thirteenth- or fourteenth-century monk Liu Mi and his special interest in the writings of Han Yu—the Tang-dynasty Confucian, classical scholar-poet, and comparative critic.[58] Both Liu Mi's "Fair and Dispassionate Discussion of the Three Doctrines" and Han Yu's numerous polemical essays about Buddhism and Daoism (especially the famous "Buddha Bone" essay as well as other key writings) may be said to constitute a kind of Chinese "comparative apologetics" from either a Buddhist or Ruist point of view.

A Fair and Dispassionate Discussion

These native Chinese methods challenge—but also supplement, fulfill, and complete—Legge's own evolving synthesis of liberal postmillennial theology of the Pauline tradition, the secularly critical approach of professionalized academic Orientalism, and the Müllerian-style comparativism of the

Sacred Books. This synergy of Western and Eastern methods is seen in Legge's treatment of Liu Mi's influential comparative discussion of the "three religions of China"—a work that Müller's former student, Japanese Buddhist monk Bunyiu Nanjio, called "a very able exposition and defence of Buddhism" and "one of the most popular books in Japan."[59] Obviously curious about Liu Mi's "method of argument" and impressed by his "range of information," Legge says that this Buddhist monk, who too often "errs" by "exaggeration" or "defect," falls short of "what a scholar trained in the schools of the West would pursue." But it is interesting to see how much of a real spirit of sympathetic comprehensiveness there is in this medieval Buddhist exercise in comparative religions—an effort that was couched in the Yuan-Ming syncretistic tradition, the "three teachings are one."[60]

In many ways, this treatise is unusually "fair and dispassionate" when placed alongside similar thirteenth- or fourteenth-century Christian discussions of heathen religions. Only in the post-Enlightenment context, and especially with respect to the nineteenth-century emergence of the comparative sciences of man and the modern secular academy, does it makes sense to say that Liu Mi's Chinese Buddhist version of religious relativism does not live up to the methods of an Orientalist scholar "trained in the schools of the West."[61] And even in the context of latter-day studies of comparative cultures, it could be argued that the distinction really comes down to different logics of inference and disparate rhetorical strategies. Legge is particularly disdainful of Liu Mi's "dispassionate" comparative evaluations of the teachings of the Confucians. Part of his scorn stems from his chagrin that Liu Mi "misses or overlooks" the "most important doctrine of the literati." He is referring to his own great discovery of the ancient classical doctrine of a "Supreme Being," a "monotheistic faith" that "convert[s]" the "doctrines of the literati" into a "religion."[62] Even though Zhu Xi and later Ruist scholars of the Qing seemed innocent of any such monotheistic beliefs, Legge was amazed that Liu Mi was unable to see what Legge himself saw so clearly. "Perhaps," Legge says, Liu Mi's "familiarity with Buddhism, in which there is no such belief, made it easier for him to overlook or undervalue the evidence of it in all the orthodox literature of his country." Perhaps, in the same way, it was Legge's classicist textual emphasis, and his upbringing as a Victorian Protestant believing in the "first principle" of a patriarchal creator god, that made it easy to find the evidence for a "monotheistic faith" in the authoritative ancient scriptures of the Chinese.[63]

Sublime Benevolence and Drivelling Absurdity

Legge concludes his hardly dispassionate discussion with five general, and rather crotchety, "observations" about Liu Mi's syncretistic hierarchy of religions that placed Buddhism, like the sun, at the apex of the overall system.

There is no point in enumerating each of Legge's points, but we should notice his Victorian bewilderment over the chaotically "vast" Buddhist cosmology devoid of a Divine Creator, his "dissent" from Buddhism's pessimistic emphasis on the misery of human life, and his confusion about the meaning (was it a nihilistic extinction?) of the difficult doctrine of nirvana. At the same time, Legge does not hesitate to say that the Buddhist "inculcation of moral duties in the sphere of one's own character and life is both minute and grand." Moreover, Buddha's efforts to awaken, through sacrifice and self-denial, the "sentiment of compassion for the woes of others" are, for Legge, "very wonderful." He cannot, however, resist the temptation to add that "the association in Buddhism of what seems sublime benevolence and of drivelling absurdity of method is not to be paralleled in any other doctrine or religion." The unspoken footnote to this last statement was that, with regard to the "drivelling absurdity of method," or the whole "ridiculously foolish" issue of liturgical practice, Buddhism was most obviously paralleled by Roman Catholicism.[64]

Legge declares that he is not convinced by Liu Mi's arguments for the superiority of Buddhism. His conviction rests on his study of the Confucian classics and from his own experience in China, both of which prove that the "doctrine of the literati" is foundational for all that is good and great in Chinese tradition.[65] Like the effect of Romanism on the Christian tradition in Europe, Buddhism has been "in China but a disturbing influence, ministering to the element of superstition in our nature that plays so large a part in the world." The classical Ruist doctrines of the literati are far from "perfect," but nevertheless they have "kept the people of China together in national union" and are "still not without a measure of heart and hope." Again rehearsing the peculiar Victorian fetish for numerical statistics about Oriental religions, Legge is lastly concerned to quash the "prevalent error" about the exaggerated number of Buddhists in the world.[66]

A Christian-Confucian Comparative Apologetics

It is the Ruist-Confucian spirit of Han Yu that seems to animate Legge's efforts to criticize Liu Mi and to put Buddhism (and Daoism) back into the official imperial category of a "heterodox" *(i-duan)* tradition in China. This kind of dual orthodox-heterodox system of relativistic classification was traditionally judged in China in terms of whether or not a particular teaching was "injurious to the ways of the world and to the sentiments of man"—or, as a Nonconformist Christian such as Legge might say, "know them by their fruits," especially as these pertain to morality and social reform. This kind of perspective in Chinese tradition broadly derives from Han Yu's rationalistic and developmental evaluation of Chinese religious history (that is, the assumed progressive passage from magic and superstition to rationality and ethics). As appropriated and developed by the Song neo-Confucians, this approach is crystalized in the "Doctrines of the Ruists [*rujiao*]" and state policy during the Ming and Qing dynasties.[67]

In the last years of his life, Legge seemed to see a special connection between his own "comparative apologetics" and Han Yu's elegant "impartial but not neutral" comparativism. For both of them, it was a matter of showing the superstitious shortcomings of those heterodox traditions not focused on proper beliefs, personal moral cultivation, or social reform. Legge was able to incorporate Han Yu's views on Confucianism by asserting that Christianity was an authentic fulfillment of the once vital, but now largely moribund, "Teachings of the Ruists." Legge was, in this way, moving toward a China-based theory of comparison that meshed with many of the historiographical presuppositions of Müller's comparative science of religions.

Legge's appreciation of Han Yu goes back to the appearance of the first volume of the *Classics* in 1861; now, some thirty years later, it had taken on a new degree of thoroughness and conviction. From either Müller's or Han Yu's perspective, it seemed evident that the course of later historical development, especially the "disturbing influences" of Buddhism and Daoism, led to the corruption of the classically pure religion of Confucianism. The unstated inference for Legge is that the final reformation of these historical developments will come about through the devoted efforts of a new group of literati. These reformist mandarins are the reverent missionaries and rational scholars from the West whose worship of God, moral teachings, and formidable science of cosmic, social, and textual life, were divinely charged by a universal "Master and Lord." This suggests that Legge's prophetic sensitivity to the existential relativity of judging national traditions by their moral, social, and political fruits (whether Ruist China or Christian England) is always conditioned by his conviction in the inevitable triumph of a divine lord of all nations over an anachronistic Chinese master and sage.

Another way to view this renewed apologetic stance is to recognize that Legge typically distinguished between religious doctrinal issues and more general moral, social, and political problems. Religious comparisons primarily involved doctrinal claims analyzed conceptually. But moral, social, and political questions were not necessarily associated with religious institutions. In Legge's case, a moral claim against England (which for Evangelicals was only partly Christian, a fact that the census of 1851 statistically documented) would be consistent with other prophetic reforms Christianity would bring to English national life (e.g., concerning Sabbath policy, gambling, drinking, or opium). This kind of apologetic perspective could, therefore, be applied prophetically to both the Chinese and English nations. But the practical moral and political deficiencies of European and Oriental countries did not directly compromise the religious foundations of Legge's Evangelical faith—just as religious parallels seen in the Sacred Books did not diminish Müller's own Christian convictions.

THE WAY OF VICTORIAN DAOIST DISCOURSE

There are many who may be inclined to say, Confucianism we know and Buddhism we know, but what is Taoism?
REVIEW OF LEGGE'S *THE SACRED BOOKS OF CHINA*, THE TEXTS OF TAOISM, 1891

"The evil that men do lives after them; the good is oft interred with their bones."
The errors of Leggism live and fructify; the truths too often lie forgotten in the sepulchre.
T.W. KINGSMILL, *CHINA REVIEW*, 1899

Legge's Way and Other Byways

There is a strong case to be made for Legge's role in institutionalizing an authoritative discourse concerning China in general and, through the classification of certain ancient texts, the establishment of a particular Orientalist genre of scholarly opinion on the nature of Chinese religion and literature. Legge's *Chinese Classics* valorized the so-called Confucian texts as the authoritative classics, orthodox sacred books, or "forgotten bibles" of Chinese civilization. The validity of this kind of judgment seemed secure in the knowledge that these texts were specially privileged by native Chinese as well as by Western scholars.[68] It is in this significantly synergistic way that particular ancient Chinese texts—along with attendant Western and Qing Chinese scholarly attitudes and interests—were translated into the intertextual byways of the Western imagination.[69] Legge is a threshold figure for the late-Victorian development of an imperial logic of representation concerning the always problematic Chinese manifestations of an Orientalism most closely identified with the romantically racist Indomania of the early to mid-nineteenth century comparative philologists. Legge is the greatest of the nineteenth-century sinological Orientalists. He is, therefore, irrevocably identified with a "China of the Sinologues" image that focused on a timelessly classical Chinese civilization almost wholly defined by archaic texts associated with the founder-reformer known as Confucius, the orthodox Confucian tradition and moralistic religion, and the political teachings of the elite scholar-bureaucrats or Ruists of the imperial state.[70]

By the 1880s, however, Legge was cultivating a scholarly interest in Buddhist and Daoist literature that qualifies his exclusive identification with the Confucian classical tradition. His Buddhist studies are noteworthy, but much more sinologically substantial and discursively foundational are his works on philosophical Daoist classics such as the *Book of the Tao and Its*

Characteristics and the *Zhuangzi*. If Legge, by virtue of a lifetime of labor on behalf of the Confucian classics, may be thought of as the sinologue of Confucianism par excellence, he was also—roughly from the death of Julien until the turn of the century when de Groot and Chavannes were active— the leading Western scholar of "Taoism," which had, up until that time, been the "least known of the Oriental religions."[71] While only an interloper within the domain of sinological Buddhology, Legge was truly one of the inventors of the Daoist tradition in the West.

In the late-Victorian period in the Leggian understanding of the tradition, Daoism was primarily a reified entity located classically, essentially, and philosophically within two ancient "sacred books" associated with the shadowy religious founders known as Laozi and Zhuangzi. The initial emergence of *Taoism* (also spelled *Tauism* and *Taouism*) in English as a classifiable terminological construct within Victorian tradition is found by the *Oxford English Dictionary* to date to various articles from the 1880s (citing primarily the *Athenaeum*)—an etymology that alludes to Legge's *Religions of China* and to several other works appearing in the late 1870s and early 1880s.[72] But the full-blown crystalization of Daoism as a Victorian cultural artifact is more accurately dated to the appearance in 1891 of Legge's translations of the *Texts of Taoism* that made up volumes 39 and 40 of the *Sacred Books of the East*. With the appearance of these new classics sanctioned by the distinguished Oxford series of Oriental scriptures, Daoism for the first time in Western consciousness became a "world religion" or, more precisely, one of Müller's six Oriental book religions.

Beyond the Daoist volumes for the *Sacred Books of the East*, Legge's involvement with issues related to the translation, definition, classification, and interpretation of Daoist texts extended throughout his Oxford years and included a broad range of technical and semipopular books, essays, chapters, articles, reviews, and lectures.[73] Given the impressive breadth and imposing reputation of these materials at the time they were written or translated, it may be said that Legge's Daoist works consolidated the Victorian and Confucian-Ruist understanding of Daoism. In addition, and allowing for important qualifications, they set much of the underlying discursive agenda for the subsequent Western understanding of this tradition within sinology, the general history of religions, and popular culture. The power and persistence of the nineteenth-century Leggian image of classical Daoism—and its intertwined Protestant, Orientalist, and Ruist logic (especially as stemming from Wang Bi's commentarial tradition)—also indicates the reasons that the rich historical, textual, and social complexities of the sectarian Daoist tradition have only recently been appreciated by sinologists and historians of religion. A more accurately ambiguated picture of the Daoist tradition, particularly as related to the contested nature of the earliest texts, has only within the past few years started to filter down into a popular Western awareness still largely mesmerized by the "sublime mysteries" of the *Daode jing* and the philosophical rhapsodies of the *Zhuangzi*.[74]

Within the native Chinese context, as Kristofer Schipper notes, it was Wang Bi's third-century "philosophical interpretation of the *Tao-te ching*" that became "the only acceptable one." From that time on, the Ruist literati, who traditionally controlled the media of official commentarial discourse, "claimed to have the only true key" to the meaning of the *Daode jing*. Interestingly enough in terms of its eventual fit with the Western views traced here, this was primarily an essentialist key that, by its emphasis on "the separation of mind and body," showed the influence of Buddhist metaphysics on Wang Bi. By following Wang's hermeneutical characterization of Daoism, the Ruist scholars and bureaucrats of the elite tradition tended to perpetuate an illusory "distinction between a 'philosophical' Taoism that they claimed was noble and pure, and a 'religious' Taoism that was supposedly vulgar and materialistic, that is, the Taoism of the people."[75]

Naming the Way in the Early Nineteenth Century

Legge follows and builds upon a meager Western legacy of translation and interpretation of Daoism that goes back to the spotty and confused efforts of the Jesuit missionaries and to the more substantial endeavors of the remarkable French academic Orientalists of the early nineteenth century.[76] Abel Rémusat, the very first professional sinologue and a precocious physician-scholar (1788–1832) published several pioneering works on the School of the Rationalists (e.g., *Mémoire sur la vie et les ouvrages de Lao-tseu, Mélanges asiatiques*, 1832), as did also J.-P.G. Pauthier and Heinrich Klaproth. But the single most influential scholar during the early nineteenth century was Stanislas Julien, who took over Rémusat's chair in 1832 and, till his death in 1873, was the veritable dictator of academic sinology. It is especially Julien who, haltingly, and often with great personal animosity and pedantic fury directed at Pauthier, staked out the textual and intellectual terrain for a rudimentary consensus on the "school of Tao."

It was Julien's complete annotated translation of the *Daode jing* in 1842 (*Le Livre de la voie et de la vertu composé dans le vie siècle avant l'ère chrétienne par le philosophe Lao-tseu*) that became the benchmark for most later European translations as well as for much of the subsequent scholarly and popular speculation about the meaning of this alluring Oriental text, the obscurity of which was only rivaled by the *Book of Changes*. For the first time in Europe, the meaning of the Dao (then transcribed Tao) was established in relation to strict philological considerations and with regard to the testimony of the native commentarial tradition (Wang Bi in particular—a figure whose philosophy of being and nonbeing would appeal to the enlightened Jesuit academician). In stark contrast to Rémusat's judgment that the Dao was best understood as a Chinese variation on the Enlightenment principle of Rationality, Intelligence, or Logos, and to Pauthier's claim that its meaning was primarily rooted in ancient Vedic or Brahmanic philosophy, Julien simply and elegantly translated the term in its indigenous Chinese sense of Way (*voie*)—that is, the path or method of phenomenal reality.

Julien's work on the *Daode jing* is still an impressive model of precise philological research. *Le Livre de la voie et de la vertu* is distinctive for its "cool and dispassionate" avoidance of the fanciful exaggerations of some earlier Western opinion (e.g., Jesuit allegorical commentators and Rémusat) that found the meaning of the text in sources not only alien to the text itself but also to all of Chinese tradition (i.e., the Christian Trinitarian or Hebraic meaning of chapter 14 of the *Daode jing*).[77] Julien was, nonetheless, supremely confident that China as an Oriental civilization could be fully understood from the sanctuary of his library in Paris.[78] In this way, he especially epitomizes the "relentless domination of textuality" in Orientalism that operated on the principle that the fundamental meaning of an Oriental civilization, or some particular tradition or institution, could be fathomed only in relation to its ancient foundational literature or classics.[79] Exposure to the people of the villages and streets, to the vernacular, and to the actual social institutions and practices of the living tradition was largely irrelevant, or even misleading, in the scholarly quest to understand the definitive and essential meaning of Oriental civilization.

The early nineteenth-century consensus reached in the aftermath of the work of Rémusat, Pauthier, and Julien was that Daoism had attained the tentative status of a taxonomic object. It was identified almost exclusively with the single ancient text known as the *Daode jing* and said to be written by the wise sage, and older contemporary of Kongzi, called Laozi (or Laocius, Latinized as was Confucius).[80] The classification of all other later forms of the tradition fell naturally into a basic developmental distinction between some originally pure system of thought and morality (in Rémusat's estimation, a "sublime" philosophy that "breathes mildness and good-will") and its eventual corruption and superstitious decline as witnessed in the popular sectarian traditions.

These sentiments concerning the history of the newly named entity of Daoism, and the essential difference between its original and later forms, indicate that the fundamental paradigm of the "pure and the corrupt"— along with its attendant multifarious dichotomies of substance and accident, spirit and matter, transcendence and immanence, authentic and superstitious religion, monotheism and polytheism, true worship and false idolatry, civilized and savage, philosophical thought and ritual action, moral prudence and vulgar sexual licentiousness, written and oral, fixed and chaotic—had already entered into the European imagination of Oriental philosophy and religion.[81] As seen in the application of the essentialist paradigm to Confucianism and to other Oriental book religions, the power of this construct within sinological Orientalism was, first of all, related to the fact that it was so strongly reinforced by the elite commentarial tradition of the native Ruist scholars. Equally important was that this perspective could be assimilated (and sometimes unconsciously or surreptitiously) into the old biblical model of the Noachide dispersal and degeneration of ancient civilizations while maintaining its secular academic credibility by appealing to the documentary record of ancient texts and history.

The Way at Midcentury

During the 1840s and 1850s some limited discussion of Daoism in English was appearing for the first time among a few Protestant missionaries in China, such as Karl Gützlaff, Samuel Wells Williams, and Joseph Edkins.[82] But, aside from some desultory and random comments based on personal observation within the treaty port cities of China, these early missionary accounts were mostly deferential to the French sinologues who had the good fortune to be sequestered from the "horrid devil worshippers" of the living tradition and could focus their attention more fully upon the fascinating enigmas of the *Daode jing.* One rare early exception to the usual British dependence on French academic opinion, though basically coming to the same conclusions (keeping in mind that Julien's framework was more enlightenment-Jesuitical whereas Edkins's episteme was that of a Scottish enlightenment Evangelical), was an 1855 article, "Phases in the Development of Tauism," by Edkins.[83]

Edkins went beyond Julien's Chinese sources and examined the assessments of Ma Duanlin (ca. 1254–1323), the great Song-dynasty scholar, in order to work out a more precise understanding of the meaning and historical development of Daoism. The basic dualistic logic of the pure and the corrupt was intact so that, for example, the ancient sage Laozi was said to have preached a "religion of purity" wholly concerned with spiritual matters. The germ of corruption comes about through a process understood in terms of a Puritan analysis of the fleshy sinful nature of humankind and of the travails of Christianity during its Romanist degradation. The downfall of the originally pure Daoism (as seen in the "absurd" Daoist alchemy and other forms of superstitious magic) comes about, therefore, through the devilish allure of coarse physical nature and gross external ritual over the refinements of the pristine spiritual dimension. The history of Daoism thus recapitulates the history of Christianity: In both cases, the purity of the beginnings falls prey to base corruption.

Hardwick's School of the Fixed Way

More important for its general impact on Victorian tradition was the appearance, also in 1855, of the first popularly circulated and widely read synthetic treatment, in English, of "Tau-ism" within a comparative theological context. The work in question is the multivolume *Christ and Other Masters* written by the influential Anglican "Christian Advocate" of Cambridge University, Charles Hardwick.[84] This is a book, somewhat like F.D. Maurice's earlier and more speculative *Religions of the World* (1848), which did not discuss Daoism, that shows the growing influence of Orientalist scholarship on British theology at this time, and, by virtue of Hardwick's historical approach and generally tolerant stance, forecasts some of the later perspectives of Müller's comparative science of religions.

Hardwick's discussion takes up a whole chapter entitled "Tau-ism or the School of the Fixed Way"[85] and, although wholly dependent on the translations and specialized views provided by the French academicians, is notable for its careful application of the Aristotelian distinction between spirit and matter. From this perspective, Hardwick is impressed by the "soaring and contemplative" thought of Laozi, which, unlike the "materialistic genius of the Chinese nation," truly harbored the "spirit of religious sentiment." Proceeding to a comparative judgment, Hardwick declares that the Confucians were like the "sceptical and self-complacent Saducees," whereas the early Daoists were the "Chinese spiritualists" whose "mystic creed and fervid temperament" resembled the "sect of the Essenes among the ancient Jews."[86]

Although Hardwick was intrigued by earlier claims (made by the Jesuits and Rémusat) about Trinitarian and Hebraic codes hidden within the opening verses in chapter 14 of Laozi's treatise and cites the influence of this passage on various other theological works of the day, he had the good sense to adopt, no doubt due to Julien's influence, a circumspect attitude toward ideas of prefigured Christian doctrine and theories of foreign origin.[87] As an original contribution, he even volunteers the sensible suggestion that the way of the Dao seemed closest to the idea of Nature discussed by the "modern speculators" of his day. Given the mounting influence of Darwin in the coming decades, it is no wonder that this suggestion would prove especially popular in later, more secular Victorian evaluations of Daoism's surprisingly modern philosophy.[88] After devoting the greater part of his chapter to Laozi's "soaring" philosophy, Hardwick moves on to a brief concluding discussion of the so-called degeneracy witnessed in the later tradition. Hardwick asserts that the process was fundamentally analogous to the Roman Catholic corruption of Christ's doctrine or to the neo-Platonic debasement of Plato. Both forms of corruption ended up making the "great business" of religion the accumulation of merits and the cultivation of "theurgical magic."

As illustrated throughout Hardwick's book, one of the characteristics of mid-Victorian thinking was an inclination toward a "juster view of heathendom" built on the idealistic speculations of the "young Hegelians of Germany." This "juster view" was built on a methodological discrimination between the historical forms of a religion and its inner essence, expressed most fully by doctrines that "appease the moral and emotional wants of the human soul." This is a critical method that—when, for example, the scriptures are being studied to determine which parts are really divine and which merely accidental—depends on the possibility of detecting a moral dignity that "appeals to the 'pure instincts' of our spiritual nature."[89]

The Pure and the Corrupt after 1870

The larger cultural significance of Hardwick's book is that its methodological concern for a "juster view of heathendom" points directly to the more portentous and radical developments in the overall Victorian comparative assessment of other religions, civilizations, and races that occurred in the next few decades. For it is in the 1870s that Hardwick's tremulous "quick glance" at the "vastness of rational creation"—its bewildering evolutionary changes, historical complexity, and religious multiplicity—gave rise to the "establishment of truer canons both in verbal and historic criticism; profound researches into the structure and affinities of language" and "the more copious inductions of ethnology, elucidating the condition of the ancient world, and helping us to track the pre-historic wanderings of influential tribes."[90]

For Archdeacon Hardwick's generation, the "features of resemblance" uncovered by an inductive historical confrontation with the "unconscious prophecies of heathendom" could be "welcomed as so many testimonies to the truth of revelation." But these same inductions had by the 1870s produced the "bewildering evolutionary changes" of the new comparative "sciences of man"—especially the anthropological and social sciences associated with the Darwinian historicism of Edward Tylor, J.F. M'Lennan, and Herbert Spencer along with Müller's more idealistically inclined science of religion. Instead of confirming the "truth of revelation," these developments, for many, gave rise to a profound questioning of the absolute and eternal truth of Christianity, the unique distinction between "revealed" and "natural" religion, and the literal veracity of a single biblical model of historical development. In the last half of the century the "spirit of the age" had become an all-pervasive vogue for comparison.

A Juster View of Heathendom?

These changes in the 1870s—coupled with a growing popular fascination with the more exotic Oriental religions such as Buddhism—resulted in a sudden rush of interest in the still dimly understood subject of Daoism. This newly heightened attention, and shifting methodological context, is in many ways signaled by a long article on Daoism published in 1873 in the very first volume of the *China Review*.[91] This article, written by John Chalmers of the London Missionary Society, an old personal friend of

Legge, reflected Chalmers's growing fascination with the "pure and simple" philosophy of Laozi engendered by his earlier publication of the first complete English translation of the *Daode jing* as *The Speculations in Metaphysics, Polity, and Morality, of the Old Philosopher* (1868).[92] Applying the developmental logic of the "pure and the corrupt" to Daoist history, Chalmers concludes his article with a plea for continued Western intervention in China. Expressing a view not unlike Legge's emphasis on the selective reformation of China, Chalmers argues that "humanity demands of us that we should endeavour to the utmost to save the helpless myriads of this empire" from falling into "a state of scepticism in regard to religion and morality, which must inevitably, as all history teaches, lead to confusion, anarchy, and misery untold."[93]

Chalmers's work on Daoism coincides with a surge of new translations of the infinitely malleable *Daode jing*—an activity that, while subject to periodic lulls, continues unabated to this day and has resulted in this little work's peculiar status as the most frequently translated, or creatively mistranslated, of all Asian texts.[94] For the first time, the "marvelous literary beauty" and "surprisingly modern thought" of the *Zhuangzi* was discovered through a series of translations and appreciative expositions (by, for example, Frederic Henry Balfour, Herbert A. Giles, and Legge). In addition to all of this work on specific texts, there was a growing number of popular and semipopular discussions of the overall meaning and history of Daoism in various books devoted generally to China or to Chinese religions (such as Legge's *Religions of China* [1880]) and in general works by Edkins and Robert Douglas).[95]

Most of this new work on Daoism was self-consciously philological, critical, and scientific in approach and was increasingly produced by amateur scholars within the secular domain in China (e.g., Eitel, Thomas Watters, Balfour, Herbert Giles, T. W. Kingsmill, and Edward Parker) or by newly professionalized sinologues who had, upon retirement from missionary or civilian work in the field, secured for the first time in British tradition full-time positions in scholarly institutions (e.g., Legge at Oxford, Robert Douglas at King's College, London, and later in the century, Wade and Giles at Cambridge). Even among the still active, and most prolific and respected, missionary-scholars in China such as Chalmers and Edkins, it was clear that the scientific and comparative spirit was becoming the ruling principle for serious sinological study.

Legge's Right Course

The exemplary figure in the study of Daoism during the last quarter of the nineteenth century was the new professor of Chinese at Oxford, James Legge. I have already examined his pioneering discussion of Daoism in his popular book *Religions of China*. Three other works merit close attention for the way in which they directly contribute, in both a scholarly and popular sense, to the late-Victorian image of Daoism. The first of these is Legge's important overview article on the *Daode jing* for the *British Quarterly Review* of 1883; the second is his prolonged dispute with Herbert Giles in the late 1880s over critical questions of the Daoist classic's authorship and textual integrity; and the last, and most important, is his publication in 1891 of the Daoist volumes for the *Sacred Books of the East*.

The Bible of the Taoists

In the *Religions of China* Legge says that, because of his commitment to the *Sacred Books of the East*, he had already in 1879 made two translations of the *Daode jing* and was advancing on a third version. Giving some insight into his sinological methods and theory of translation, which were becoming progressively parenthetical, he says that only his laborious method of painstakingly copying out several complete translations, along with the "happiest portions of Chinese commentary," gave one a "mastery of the old books of China." While "waiting for more light" on Laozi's "philosophy," he felt that he had "attained to the practical drift and aim of the old moralist and mystic."[96]

This preliminary attainment of the enigmatic text's "drift and aim" was the basis for Legge's important article on the "Tao Teh King," which was itself a published version, with some minor though interesting changes, of an earlier lecture given at Oxford.[97] This article for the Congregationalist-sponsored *British Quarterly* was intended for a general readership but, as always the case with Legge, was based on a meticulous consideration of the text and the commentarial tradition. Legge opens his discussion by emphasizing, as he had in the *Religions of China*, Laozi's philosophical and moral significance as distinct from the later religion, which was "begotten by Buddhism out of the old superstitions of the country." Laozi's "Bible of the Taoists" may have some "little trace," or "soupçon," of those ancient superstitions, but on the whole there is really nothing in it "justifying or sanctioning" the "wildly absurd" practices of the later traditions.

The Discursive Way.   After a balanced survey of earlier Western scholarship, Legge moved on to a consideration of the authorship, terminology, and meaning of the text in a way that owed much to Julien's textual methods and to the overall comparative spirit of Samuel Johnson and Max Müller (both of whom he specifically mentions in this article). Taking up the perplexed terminological discussion about the best translation of Laozi's *dao* (variously rendered at this time as Rationality, Supreme Intelligence, Logos or Word, Way, Nature, or even God in the theosophical speculations of Victor von Strauss und Tornay), he concluded (on philo-logical, contextual, and commentarial grounds) that the term was best translated as the *Course* (i.e., a guiding channel such as a watercourse).[98] Straining to distinguish this somewhat awkward translation from Julien's "Way," he says that "Course" connotes a "course of action or way of living" together with (for Legge, unsurprisingly), the doctrinal idea of the "method or rule inculcating such a course."[99] In Legge's estimation, an ap-propriate translation of the title of Laozi's little book, the *Tao Teh King*, re-vealingly becomes the prolix "Sacred Text of the Right Course and Its Characteristics."[100]

Laozi's Thought Woven into Writing.   Legge noted that the Latin word *tex-tus* and the Chinese term *jing* both etymologically refer to the idea of "thought woven into writing"—that is, the fabric of ancient thought is given special authority and classical weight by being written down and system-atized by a great mind or author. In this sense, it was important for Müller and Legge to maintain that the sacredness of the forgotten Oriental bibles was a matter directly linked to their demonstrable antiquity, philosophical coherence, textual integrity, and authorial intentionality. So even though the early Confucianism of the Master Kong, because of the theistic presence of Shangdi/Tian in the Confucian classics, could be considered more fully religious than could Laozi's Daoism, which possessed only the religiosity of moral philosophy, both could be considered sacred traditions. The prob-lematic nature of these criteria as related to the authoritative significance of Laozi as an "author" and "founder" of Daoism, as well as the actual antiquity and integrity of the *Daode jing* as a "sacred book," will be seen in the furious debate over these issues provoked a few years later by Giles.[101]

Discussing Laozi's philosophy of the "right course," Legge first notes that the *dao* as applied to human behavior fundamentally involves the "inculca-tion of humility," which refers, unlike Kongzi's negative principle of reci-procity, to the Christlike return of injury with kindness (see the *Daode jing*, chapter 43, and compare chapter 67). In contrast with most Western com-mentators since the time of Julien, who were quick to seize upon the pas-sivity of Oriental religion and philosophy, Legge understood the principle of *wuwei* (literally, "not acting" or "no action") not as an "absolute qui-etude" or as an extreme asceticism in the manner of the Hindus or Bud-dhists, but rather as humbled natural action, which is "not acting with a pur-pose" or any kind of selfish concern.[102]

The possibility that some sections of the *Daode jing* allude to meditation techniques or trance conditions is only very obliquely considered by Legge or the other Victorian commentators. The preconceived purity and ideal-ized nature of the moral philosophy mostly precluded any such contami-nating considerations.[103] Legge consequently notes that the "gates of heaven" passage in chapter 49 is said by Chinese commentators to be the "nostrils and mouth," which played an important role in later "magical" attempts, "by the management of the breath," to "sublimate the body." This is taken by Legge as only an irrelevant "trace" of superstitious materialistic practices in ancient China that would later, through Buddhist agency, spawn the abominations of the Daoist religion. For Legge, the small number of suspiciously meditational and magical passages shows the essential spirituality of the philosophy and its resistance to the corrupting forces of superstitious belief and ritual practice.

Vain Dreams.   Legge next took up the "right course" for government. He was appreciative of Laozi's sentiments against war and capital punishment, but also felt that the ideal of a "purposeless government" and "primitive simplicity" was only a "vain dream" when compared to Kongzi's more pragmatic recommendations for conscious virtue in government. He then shifted his attention to the meaning of the *dao* in relation to the origin and course of nature. Although the *dao* may not be considered a cosmogonic Creator in the manner of the Victorian Watchmaker God or even in Victor von Strauss und Tornay's "theosophical" sense, Legge's investigation of the "vestiges of creation" in chapters 42 and 25 led him to the conclusion that the *dao* does pertain to some functional aspect of creation related to the "primeval chaos" *(hundun)*. In his estimation—which was, significantly, presented with little suggestion of theological condemnation—there was "something about that chaos" that the *dao* "is employed to designate" and that "something was the way or course by which, as along a path, there came from it, as out of a womb, heaven and earth and all things."[104] Just as the *dao* cannot be directly equated with the primeval chaos, so also according to Legge was it wrong to identify the *dao* with nature. To equate it with "Nature hides the scope of Lao-tsze" and misses the point that *dao* primarily refers to the dynamic course, method, or process of phenomenal reality.

Legge was left with the quandary as to whether God was present at all in the *Daode jing*. This issue obviously had a special poignancy for Legge given his convictions in an ancient Chinese monotheism and his need to account for the moral purity, if not the complete religious nature, of the "Old Master's" philosophy. He therefore struggled to a conclusion that he subsequently rejected. Here he says that God is at least implied by the five or six references to Heaven *(tian)* or the Way of Heaven *(tiandao)* that, as seen in the Confucian classics and as corroborated by Müller's comparative science of religions, document a special philological relation between the words for sky and the High God. It is with regard to this issue, as Legge says, that "we find the fathers of the Chinese race at one with those of the Aryan race."[105]

Despite the "very strange" aspects of Laozi's notion of the *dao* and its relationship to the doctrine of God, Legge was remarkably favorable in his overall estimation of ancient Daoism. In the lecture that was the basis for this article he even confessed that he had "long ceased to think of [Laozi] as . . . a Taomaniac." And he concluded both his lecture and his *British Quarterly* article by emphasizing, without any trace of apologetic censure, that the philosophical outlook of the Old Master was "that of an evolutionist . . . looking at nature." "We must," he says, finally pronounce that Laozi's "type of mind was very much akin to that of Charles Darwin."[106]

On the Cusp of Reverent and Irreverent Methods

The article on the *Tao Teh King* is another exemplification of Legge's still-reverent methods regarding the coherence of ancient classics and the integrity of sage authors. It is this factor, as it was also for Müller's own romantic conception of the "symbolic meaning" of sacred books and forgotten bibles, that distinguishes Legge's "parenthetical" methods of sinological translation, as well as his conception of Daoism, from the turn-of-the-century modern—more irreverent, critical, historical, and destructive—forms of sinological Orientalism. Legge is, accordingly, very much of a transformational and transitional figure in the history of sinology. He is someone who anticipates many of the larger interstitial tensions concerning religious belief, and the sources of textual intentionality and representational cultural meaning, seen in the establishment of the human sciences as academic disciplines.

What really distinguishes Legge's scholarship from the later more fully professionalized, academically specialized, and intellectually rationalized *T'oung Pao*–style sinology of Schlegel, Chavannes, and Pelliot of the revived French tradition of Orientalism, as also was the difference between Müller's comparative science of religion and the later more area-specific and fully secularized academic approaches of anthropology and the "history of religions," is a matter of two antagonistic, but not always clearly separable, forms of critical faith and ritual practice concerning the origin and development of ancient literatures and civilizational forms. Some of the crucial factors in this distinction have to do with the passage from a semiexegetical or commentarial mode of an idealistically inclined comparativism or "hermeneutics of trust" (exemplified by the innate religious, historical, and literary piety of Legge's sinology and Müller's humanistic science of religion) to a more fully historiographical, pluralistic, analytical, fragmented, academic, scientistic, rationalistic, naturalistic, polygenetic, noncomparative, relativistic, and secularly irreverent "hermeneutics of suspicion" concerning ancient civilizations, texts, and authors.

In keeping with the retarded and isolated development of sinological Orientalism throughout the last quarter of the nineteenth century, it is pos-

sible to think of a contrast between a hermeneutics of constructive reverence (rooted in a faith in a transcendent monotheism, ultimate monogenetic origins, or the hidden symbolic meaning of linguistic roots, racial
families, and the category of the infinite) and a hermeneutics of deconstructive irreverence (rooted in a naturalistic faith in an immanential polytheism and a multicentered processural cosmology of chaos and natural selection). The first is naturally conservative, mythological, doctrinal, textual,
symbolic, representational, authoritarian, spiritual, and essentialist; the
second is more fundamentally liberal, consensual, particularistic, contextual, polygenetic, processural, material, perspectival, discrete, and empirical. Legge has a larger commitment to the more reverent position, but,
more accurately, falls somewhere between both categories. Moreover, this
kind of betwixt-and-between methodology may in the final analysis (as a
liminal comparativism for the twenty-first century) be the best modality for
finding human meaning in texts and persons.

This issue comes down to a difference between those holding onto the
transcendental ideal of the purity, sacredness, authenticity, essence,
meaning, coherence, integrity, and truth of ancient texts, history, and traditions and those (meaning in this case those academic elites controlling
the sources of textual information and production) holding a higher and
less reverent critical attitude that parcels out ancient authority, sacred
books, civilizations, and religions into so many disparate historical
phases, different racial strains, unique cultural entities, and discrete
philological families. This deconstructive approach does not deny the singularity of ultimate origins, but affirms, in the spirit of "all the king's
horses and all the king's men," the impossibility of ever putting Humpty
Dumpty back together again. Scholars and other people of humanistic
science are left to forever rearrange the pieces of their various cultural-
historical puzzles, jigsaw fashion, into patterns of their own divining.
Legge is interesting because he stands on the cusp of this transition to
modern humanistic discourse on both the Western academic study of
China and the study of religion. This is a situation that is, moreover, directly illustrated by Legge's further involvement with studies of the nature and authorship of ancient Daoist texts and the overall historical
meaning of Daoism—as either an integral system of purely rarefied spiritual philosophy or as an "absurd" sectarian collection of corrupt materialistic and superstitious practices.

The Remains of Lao Tzu or Lao Tzu Remains?

The pivotal event with regard to the tense dialectical passage from a
method of constructive reverence to one of deconstructive irreverence
(along with a related transition in scholarly rhetoric and the heightened
"psychology of the specialist") is witnessed in the protracted debate—or

"grand Taoist war" as Parker described it—that took place over the biographical authenticity of Laozi as a contemporary of Confucius and the integrity and coherence of the book either named after him or called the "Classic of the Tao and Its Te." This dispute was provoked by the young British counselor official and part-time scholar Herbert A. Giles, who in 1885 published a "very controversial" article on "the Remains" of Laozi for the *China Review*.[107]

In the most radical spirit of Germanic higher criticism and what after the turn of the century was to become the "doubting antiquity" movement among native Chinese scholars, the "always pugnacious" Giles combatively rejected the views of Chalmers, Balfour, and Legge on the impressively pure system of ancient Daoist thought. There was simply, said Giles, no real evidence for a sixth-century historical personage named Laozi. For Giles, even the account of Laozi by Sima Qian, the great Han-dynasty historian, could hardly be considered a "biography" since, according to Sima's own testimony, he was really only compiling legendary materials. Furthermore, Giles maintained, the text supposedly composed by the Old Master was best understood as a late-Han-dynasty forgery patched and padded together with various authentic early "remains" (as determined by excerpts from the *Zhuangzi*, *Han Feizi*, and *Huainanzi*) interspersed with an unknown editor's much later and very "feeble" and "inane" ideas.

The battle that ensued from Giles's initial blast at some of the cherished sinological pieties of the time engaged most of the European sinologues having any interest in early Daoism and lingered on until after the turn of the century. By that time, Giles's deconstructive approach had been absorbed into the mainstream assumptions of modern twentieth-century scholarship. Giles had challenged one strain of a prevailing Orientalist faith that, in a way strangely immune to the already widely circulated lessons of higher biblical criticism, continued to affirm the integral truth of ancient documents—especially those texts traditionally given some classical, canonical, sacred, or authoritative status with respect to the meaning of certain Oriental systems or schools of thought. Giles also contested the pretense of a tradition of translation that operated with the romantic idea that it was possible—through a repeatedly deepened empathy with the author's mind as expressed in the text—to decipher an ancient document's hidden meaning and to reproduce an originally coherent system of thought.

The fact that in these charges Giles—who did not identify Legge in this article—was primarily attacking him was made explicit by Thomas Kingsmill, who said that it was the "pretended renderings of Dr. Legge and his school" that had naively given the "cobbled up and dreamy philosophy of the Taoist school" an "importance altogether out of proportion to its actual merits." Striking at the heart of Legge's reputation as a master translator and supereminent sinologist, Kingsmill found Legge's work (because it was *too* intelligible) to be often only a "paraphrase or sometimes a parody of the original." For Kingsmill and Giles, Legge was admittedly a "monument of great and wholesome energy," but he was not adept at "literary criticism" and had consequently "failed signally" as a translator.[108]

Legge's Unshaken Convictions. In 1888, Legge published a lengthy rejoinder to Giles.[109] This article is fascinating from several standpoints, but it generally reads as a poignant reiteration of Legge's scholarly faith in the integrity of the ancient Chinese documents and his "unshaken" conviction in traditional native Chinese testimony that Laozi had, in fact, "written the book" known as the *Daode jing.* It is quite probable, as Giles subsequently remarks, that Legge was especially "annoyed" at the impact the debate might have on his promised translation of Laozi's book for the *Sacred Books of the East.*[110] Despite the dismissive criticism and personal insinuations of Giles, Legge characteristically proceeded with his response in an exceedingly modest and methodical way. Discussing Sima Qian and what he takes as the corroborating implications of the "many" authentic citations found in the *Han Feizi,* the *Huainanzi,* and other early texts not considered by Giles, Legge goes on to a long and detailed, passage by passage, critique of Giles's retranslated "Remains" of Laozi. Most revealing is the restatement of Legge's translator's credo, which prompts him to first appeal to the old Horacian principle derived from his Latin classical scholarship. He consequently invokes the saying *Quandoque bonus dormitat Homerus:* "when Homer nods," even his epic verse may seem "feeble" and "absurd."[111] Such typical lapses in ancient texts do not necessarily call into question the overall integrity of authorship, until, as Legge puts it, "a fuller sympathy with the writer is established in the mind of the student."

Even more important for Legge, though showing his resistance to the higher biblical criticism and the implications of David Friedrich Strauss's *Lebens Jesu Forschung,* is his fascinating thought experiment based on gospel parallels. "Casting things over in his mind," he reasons that if the received Gospel of Mark had been made up of eighty-one paragraphs as was the *Daode jing* and seventy of those were found to be present in texts certainly dating to the third and fourth century, then the result for "all critical students of the New Testament" would be to "confirm their faith in the whole of the old Gospel and not to destroy it." Toward the end of this article Legge restates his "typical procedure" as a translator, which he had developed early in life when, as a college student in Scotland, he was working on the Latin and Greek classics and, most recently, had perfected in his work on the *Book of Changes.* This is a "symbolic" method that depends on the "slow progress" of entering into the thought of an ancient author with "one's own mind." From this testimony, it is clear that Legge's impatience with Giles stems from the latter's reliance on the quick and dirty methods of critical demolition rather than on the hard work of slowly mastering the ancients by becoming *"en rapport"* with their thought. The hidden implication is that this principle applies especially to those works such as the *Daode jing* and the *Book of Changes* that are seemingly incoherent or "absurd."

The issue comes down to the fact that Giles's "most unmeasured abuse" of both Laozi and of Legge's own sinological predecessors should have been more "civil" and concerned to "correct" rather than to "chastise." This rhetorical invocation of a Victorian and Confucian propriety is particularly telling in that it brings out Legge's inability to adjust to a new critical climate and faith that was so resolutely—uncivilly, immorally, and irreverently—premised on a systematic methodological mistrust of the past.

The Shallowness of Dr. Legge's Logic.   Giles's response to Legge, appearing in the same issue of the *China Review,* acerbically stressed that, in the spirit of "accurate" translation and critical scholarship, "there should be no respect of persons." Going to what he saw as the heart of the matter, Giles called attention to the "shallowness of Dr. Legge's logic," which was too trusting of questionable authoritative dicta that gave the "benefit of doubt" to ancient authors such as Laozi, Homer, and Mark. Pointing out that the integrity of Homer had already been challenged by modern Greek classicists in Germany and at Cambridge, he especially chided Legge for his "unhappy" appeal to parallels with the Gospels.[112] As he says, "[T]here is not one particle of evidence, save faith, that [the Gospels] were in existence until 120 years after the Crucifixion of Christ." Moreover, and here is the rub, "many people who lack faith" had already found the Gospels to be documents compiled in the second century from traditional and fragmentary sayings of Jesus.

Seizing upon another kind of methodological faith—that of Legge's belief that his special translator's rapport with the mind of Laozi had given him a "key" to the symbolic meaning of the *Daode jing's* philosophy—Giles attacks not only Legge's own presumption, but also some of the basic assumptions undergirding the production of the *Sacred Books of the East.* He thereby indirectly chastises Müller for his inclusion of the *Book of Changes* among the so-called sacred books in a translation by Legge that "is a byword of reproach to a great scholar and an object of derision to the world at large." Turning the screws of his criticism, Giles concludes by observing that the *Daode jing* is a work that is "unknown to the masses" of the Chinese people and is "widely unread by native scholars who one and all regard it as a spurious production of the Hans." An obvious forgery that is not genuinely ancient, authoritative, or religious, the *Daode jing* cannot be considered a "sacred book" or to have anything "to do with the Taoist religion of China."

The Texts of Taoism

Believing he had "rebutted every attempt of Mr. Giles" to cast doubt on the "genuineness" of ancient classical Daoism, Legge steadfastly proceeded with his culminating contribution to Daoist studies. This came about in 1891 when, after fifteen years of labor, he finally completed his contractual obligations to Müller by publishing the two-volume *Texts of Taoism* for the *Sacred Books of the East* series.[113] These volumes, which represent the definitive summation of nineteenth-century Daoist scholarship, include a complete annotated translation of the *Daode jing,* the *Zhuangzi,* and the oddly ubiquitous twelfth-century popular tract the *Ganying pian* (called by Legge the *Tractate on Actions and Their Retributions*), which exhibited the "practical" side of the mostly grotesque living religion.[114] In addition to these key works of the Daoist system, Legge appended a few short, randomly assorted, "vague and shadowy" specimens of the "mysticism" of the later Daoist religion.[115]

Legge's preface and introduction to these volumes, as well as his annotations and commentary on the actual translations, reiterate many of his earlier views. The real significance of this work, aside from the translations themselves, is that it reveals, both in content and rhetorical nuance, a number of interestingly subtle and overt modifications of Legge's evaluation of the "system of Taoism." It is also obvious that, although he refers to Giles as "one of the ablest Chinese scholars living," Legge had been stung by the criticism of his methods. The preface and introduction conspicuously pay special attention to enumerating the Chinese sources for the translations and to bolstering the case for the "authenticity and genuineness" of the ancient Daoist "books" and "authors." Although he was vaguely aware of a so-called Daoist canon *(Daozang),* which had been catalogued in 1626, Legge discusses the textual history of the "shadowy" texts of the "corrupt" later tradition only in a very cursory and second-hand manner.

Two Classics and a Single Scheme of Thought.   Legge's discussion is complicated by his inclusion of the *Zhuangzi,* which, even more than the *Laozi (Daode jing),* raised difficult questions of textual provenance and authorship. With his confidence in such matters unshaken, Legge found that these two classics of ancient Daoism express a single "scheme of thought" originally devised in written form by Laozi in the sixth century B.C.E. Zhuangzi is therefore taken as a disciple of Laozi who, in the fourth century B.C.E., contributes "little more" than an "ingenious defense of his master's speculations." Moreover, while Zhuangzi's literary abilities are impressive, his "charmingly composed" illustrative narratives are "in themselves" largely "unbelievable, often grotesque, and absurd." Most of all, the purely speculative system of these two ancient works must be kept distinct from the more "ordinary sense" of religion found in the later tradition. By "ordinary," Legge explains that he is referring to those developments after the first century C.E. when, as a "degraded adjunct of Buddhism," Daoism began to "organize itself as a Religion" and, in a manner similar to the Roman Catholic transformation of Christianity, grafted onto itself "monasteries and nunneries . . . images and rituals."[116]

These views are basically congruent with his earlier conclusions. However, a curious theory is advanced that was only hinted at before. This concerns Legge's understanding of the defining historical relation, or classificatory distinction, between the early speculative system and the later ordinary religion. It seems, in other words, that the purity and integrity of the beginnings have been somewhat diluted; as Legge says, much "prolonged study and research" had led him to the "conclusion that there was a Daoism earlier than [Laozi]; and that before he wrote his Tao Teh King, the principles taught in it had been promulgated." Because of the stories about, or fabulous allusions in Laozi, Zhuangzi, and Kongzi to an earlier more perfect civilization, he finds grounds for believing that "to Taoism, as well as to Confucianism, we ought to attribute a much earlier origin than the famous men whose names they bear."[117]

Legge's exact historical conception at this point is not entirely clear. He seems to be struggling, not very cogently, toward the application to China of Müller's Herderian notions of an oral—"fabulous" or "mythic"—tradition that predates, surrounds, and dangerously compromises the purity of "written down" thought and feeling found in classics or sacred books. The implication is that it is the truly primordial, fundamentally ahistorical and chaotic oral tradition, unbounded by the systematizing genius of a creative author and the stable authority of a written book, that represents the matrix of all Chinese thought and institutions—whether in their elevated literary distillations in the systems of Laozi and Kongzi or in the base material instincts and superstitious ritual practices of ordinary religion.

The power of this vague theoretical perspective for Legge is that it allows for an almost Dao-like simultaneity of unity and diversity between the posited two Taoisms. It also constitutes another line of defense against Giles's argument that various "feeble absurdities" in the *Daode jing* demonstrate its fragmentary and spurious character. Thus Laozi's book represented a creative, systematic, and Protestant-like reformation of the oral and ritual primordium in terms of its higher, spiritual, metaphysical, author[itative], and moral aspirations while the later tradition, under the pernicious influence of Buddhism, drew upon only the coexisting primeval materialistic practices and fabulous instincts. The fact that there are certain small "hints" of the base "religious" sentiments in Laozi and Zhuangzi (such as various allusions to the superstitious beliefs and practices of longevity) only indicate the existence of a common preliterary primordial source, not that the philosophical system could have given rise to the later superstitions or that the ancient text itself was a later forgery. For Legge, then, some suspicious passages may be found in the early texts, but both of the great ancient Daoist philosophers "discountenanced the use of superstitious practices" and "endeavoured to give the doctrine a higher character."[118]

Daoist Metaphysics.   Proceeding to an exposition of the ancient Daoist "scheme of thought," Legge reversed the order of his *British Quarterly* discussion and starts with what he now refers to as the "metaphysical" aspects of Laozi and Zhuangzi. Beginning with a standard retrospective review of Western scholarship on the meaning of the *dao,* Legge retreated somewhat from his earlier preference for translating the term as the "Course." The idea of *dao* is now primarily seen as a descriptive metaphor meaning "road" or "way" used in a manner similar to the use of "Way" in the Revised Version of the New Testament. Whatever its various shades of meaning, Legge concludes that the *dao,* unlike Tian in the Confucian classics, is "not a positive being." Rather, it is an evolutionary "mode of being," which also indicates for Legge that there can be "no idea of creation in Taoism." The *dao* is an impersonal "operation" rather than a Creator who caused and accounts for phenomenal reality. As to what explains the *dao*'s own spontaneous and "sudden appearance in the field of non-existence," Legge frankly admits that this is beyond his comprehension. Given all of these metaphysical ambiguities and in keeping with his original inclinations in 1879, Legge sensibly says that it is impossible to find an "exact equivalent" for the *dao* and that the "best way of dealing with it in translating is to transfer it to the version, instead of trying to introduce an English equivalent for it."[119]

Legge also significantly qualified his earlier views on the use and meaning of Heaven or *tian* in the *Daode jing.* He finds that this is a term "never once," in either the *Laozi* or the *Zhuangzi,* "used in the sense of God, the Supreme Being." This finding allows him to scold Giles, who had previously agreed that the Daoists had "no idea of a personal God," yet erratically translated *tian* as God in his 1889 version of the *Zhuangzi.* Clearly assuaging his own wounded dignity as a translator, Legge remarks that it was bad enough for Giles to have violated the critical principle of using only "strict equivalents" in translating from one language to another, but the constant appearance of the "great name 'God'" in his rendition of *Zhuangzi* was a "blot" on the translation "more painful" to his "eyes and ears than the use of 'Nature' for Tao by Mr. Balfour."[120]

The Practical Lessons of Daoism.   Legge concluded his introduction with an abbreviated, and somewhat less tolerant, restatement of his 1883 views on the "practical lessons" of the Daoist system as it pertained to individuals and to the administration of government. It is almost as if some small glimmer of the "Taomaniac" had crept back into Legge's conception of Laozi and Zhuangzi. He tones down his earlier appreciation of the Daoist virtue of humility and the "yet to be developed" principle of the "returning of good for evil," and stresses more than ever before the "opposition to the increase of knowledge" seen in Daoism. This is a fatal flaw that is especially dramatized by Zhuangzi's appeal to the "curious" story of Hundun as personified Chaos since, above all else, the Daoists refused to see that "it was better that the Chaos should give place to the Kosmos."[121] Reflecting his own deep predilections for a Divine Order of fixed imperial design and traditional moral civility—as well as, perhaps, his identification with an academic cosmos that sought to "increase knowledge" by disciplining the undifferentiated and unruly condition of ancient Oriental texts—Legge invokes the rhetorically and ideologically potent Victorian principle that "man exists under a law of progress." In contrast to what he recognized as Laozi's harmonizing "law of contraries," Legge says that "good and evil, truth and error" have "to fight out the battle on the field of the world, and in all the range of time." In the march toward higher civilization, morality, and religion, there can be "no standing still for the individual or for society."[122]

A Taste for Translation.   In rendering the texts of the *Daode jing* and *Zhuangzi*, Legge followed his careful *"en rapport"* method of parenthetical translation first clearly enunciated in his version of the mysterious *Book of Changes.* He also attempts, somewhat in the spirit of his metrical versions of the classical *Book of Poetry*, to reproduce in English rhyme the rhymed passages in the *Daode jing*, a procedure that sometimes creates awkward English locutions that are unmarked by parentheses (e.g., the opening verse of the "enigmatic" chapter 6 is rendered as "The valley spirit dies not, aye the same; / The female mystery thus do we name").[123]

Schipper comments that, "compared to his rendering of the Confucian classics," Legge's translations of the "texts of Taoism are not always very accurate."[124] "Neither were they always felicitous" when, for example, Legge rendered some rhymed passages in the *Daode jing* in Wordsworthian doggerel (e.g., chapter 21: "The grandest form of active force, / From Tao came their only source. / Who can of Tao the nature tell? / Our sight it flies, our touch as well").[125] Our retrospective stylistic taste recoils from the quaint Victorian stiffness of Legge's Daoist translations, but his general philological scholarship, granting the reverential suppositions and rhetorical tropes of the Victorian tradition, is an advance over anything else produced at that time. Even in matters of style, it may be said that Legge's translations are considerably more in keeping with the imaginatively poetic spirit of the early Daoist texts than, for example, is Giles's overly lush Edwardian version of *Zhuangzi*.[126]

Unintelligible and Un-Chinese

For Giles, the *Daode jing* was manifestly an incoherent collection of absurd sayings from different historical periods. The implication of this kind of perspective was that it was always best to adopt a skeptical attitude toward the possibility of deciphering the symbolic intentionality of ancient texts, authors, and philosophies. And it was Giles's agnostic methodological spirit, if not his actual procedures and interests, that came to define academic sinology. At the end of the nineteenth century, as seen in the case of Kingsmill, young sinologists were favoring Giles's methods of challenging the integrity and intelligibility of the ancient Daoist texts. In a somewhat similar manner, there was a whole other group of diffusionist scholars who remained convinced that the Daoist classics were unintelligible to the Chinese because the root meaning was so obviously foreign (coming either from distant Babylon or, more typically, from India). The problem with Legge's translations of the *Daode jing* and *Zhuangzi* for the *Sacred Books* was that he relied too heavily on Chinese commentators who were "quite unable to understand much of what Lao-tsze tries to convey." The reason for this is that, as one of Legge's reviewers put it, the "teachings of Lao-tsze" are "nothing more or less than the doctrines of Brahminism."[127]

For other reviewers, Laozi "would appear not to have been a Chinaman" and, when his alien Hindu metaphysics were imported into China, they "found an inhospitable welcome in the minds of the Chinese." This supposition of foreign origins based on claims that the Chinese could not have imagined such a purely spiritual philosophy became the thin reed upon which was built a whole theory of religious development. The discursive power of this theory is simply that it helped to explain the obvious "absurdities" of the tradition: "A Chinaman has no taste for metaphysics, and just as the seed of a garden flower, when sown in an unprepared and uncongenial soil, is apt to reproduce a wild and deteriorated species of the plant, so the doctrines of Tao, falling by the wayside in China, speedily lost their original shape and original features."[128] Note particularly the allusion to the "wild and deteriorated," or carelessly cross-bred, plants that give rise to monstrous and unintelligible offspring. The significance of this kind of rhetorical trope is seen in the aggressive condemnations by the missionaries of an overly compromising comparativistic or Leggian approach to Chinese religions, which could potentially result in some kind of grotesque syncretistic hybrid of heathenism and Christianity.

Colonizing the Past

Many of the modifications in substance and tone observed in the *Texts of Taoism* reflect not just specific sinological reconsiderations in Legge's response to Giles, but also generally relate to shifting attitudes toward Oriental traditions. One aspect of these changes that may have some bearing on Legge's cooler and more modulated attitude toward the purity of Daoism was simply, as Müller put it in response to public criticism engendered by the new science of religion and the appearance of the Oriental bibles, the need for a "more scholarlike spirit" that did not bow to the unfounded fears or foolish enthusiasms of the nonacademic public about so-called Oriental Wisdom. Even though the *Sacred Books* were intended for the general public, it was probable that "no one but the historian will be able to understand the important lessons which they teach." Müller was referring, of course, to the lessons of historical development that—in keeping with commonplace imperialistic assumptions of the period—document, despite all fearful resemblances and comparative homologies, the advanced nature of Western civilization, the higher superiority of the Christian religion, and the objective power of the Western humanistic sciences.[129]

Even if the public ignored or feared the tediously accomplished productions of scholars, it was still the mission of the academy to appropriate, define, classify, translate, and publish all such textual objects. There can be "no standing still for the individual or for society." The method is, as Müller suggests, one of compiling and controlling the literary history of Oriental tradition for science the way a museum collects, classifies, and displays the material artifacts of history. The essential task of Oriental scholarship was, in effect, "to colonize the past" just as Western civilization was progressively domesticating the globe.[130]

This "rhetoric of domination" concerning the methods of apprehending and representing the textual products of non-Western civilizations—as well as a whole martial vocabulary and strategy of battle—suggested by Müller was largely shared by nineteenth-century missionaries, comparativists, and Oriental specialists. This is aptly illustrated for the case of China and early sinology by E.J. Eitel, who, as the restless editor of the *China Review,* always emphasized the need for a more fully professionalized sinological science.[131] According to Eitel, the real advantage in the use of a specialized philological and historical methodology was that it gave Western sinologists the means to understand China better than the Chinese themselves did. Once the sinologist was armed with the critical methods that gave him the historical facts and *Quellen* of ancient Chinese texts, he would be "more than a match" for "the native scholars." After all, as Eitel says, the struggle that is enjoined with Oriental civilizations will be won "not with shot and shell only or by feats of engineering skill, but also with the more subtle weapons of Western science, on the battle field of practical, speculative and critical philosophy." Here a muscular missionary Christianity has been translated into a brawny and pugnacious, though "subtle," scientific scholarship.[132]

The issue of Daoism at the end of the nineteenth century was twofold. On the one hand, it could be carefully defined, classified, and tamed as a textual object or sacred book religion by Müller and Legge's relatively reverent and civil methods of comparison. Yet in the sense suggested by Giles's more overtly suspicious, combative, and noncomparative approach, it could be made to disappear altogether as a religion by being reduced to other fragmented, though ostensibly more objective and natural, philological and historical categories. For both methods, the fundamental question was really the matter of the self-interested control of the past through varying intellectual strategies of representation that often, in the final analysis, produced similar ideological results—the dominion over the Other in the interest of some preconceived Same. As to which of these methods, rhetorical strategies, or faiths is more true to the complex otherness of the Chinese traditions collectively called Daoism is still, relatively speaking, a moot question.

Daoism after Leggism

The end of the nineteenth century was a turning point in the history of sinological Orientalism that is marked in several important ways. This changing situation can be associated with the death of Legge in 1897, but it is also marked by Giles's assumption in 1898 of the chair of Chinese first held by Thomas Wade at Cambridge University. Even more pivotal, and a sure sign of the demise of the brief Leggian epoch, was the powerful renewal of French sinology after the turn of the century. The significance of these changes as related to the sinological evaluation of the ancient Daoist texts is that, during his lifetime, Legge had temporarily won the particular battle over Laozi's sacred integrity, but, by the end of the century, Giles had triumphed in the disciplinary war over the kind of academic faith, or lack thereof, that was proper toward early Chinese documents.

The triumph of an irreverent methodological agnosticism reflected broader professional developments within the increasingly specialized, historically discrete, and rationally secular human sciences—as well as the gradual demise of the nineteenth-century passion for various supererogated types of boundless cross-cultural comparison. For all his bluster over critical standards, Giles's scholarship, aside from his Chinese dictionary, is manifestly dilettantish when compared with the work of Chavannes, Pelliot, and Maspero on Daoism and Chinese literature in general—or, in the final analysis, even when it is compared with Legge's amazingly exhaustive concern for primary sources, if not his literary and historical acumen.[133] Giles's leadership in modern sinological matters was quickly eclipsed after the turn of the century by the resurgent French sinological tradition. After his assumption of Wade's chair at Cambridge, Giles retreated into a kind of Edwardian aestheticism noted primarily for its luxuriant contributions to the "gems of literature" style of scholarship and is today mostly remembered only in relation to a partially antiquated English system of Chinese romanization (the so-called Wade-Giles system of transcription).[134]

The Errors of Leggism

This changing state of affairs with regard to "modern sinology and Taoism" is aptly and comically shown by an article in 1899 by Giles's old comrade in arms Thomas Kingsmill, who succeeded in transforming Legge into an essentialized entity or system of scholarship called Leggism. Defined by its credulous and outdated historical faith in the "stupid patchwork" of Laozi, the "errors of Leggism" grew out of the fact that neither Legge's "early education nor his bent of mind fitted him for the task" of "criticism."[135] Kingsmill, though hardly a critical paragon himself, elsewhere went on in an even more apoplectic vein to explicate Legge's mistaken ways concerning the "ridiculous pot pourri" of Daoism. According to Kingsmill, Legge's essential problem as a "pioneer in untrodden paths" was that he was too "content to take the assurances of his 'teacher,' and instead of himself going to the original text for his information, blindly wrote down the patter of the simple-minded siensheng." Even worse was that this hypothetical "simple-minded" teacher had in turn "equally innocently been made the recipient of the rubbish of that arch humbug Chuhi [Zhu Xi], further bemuddled through being handed down along seven hundred years of incapables, not one of whom, had he even ventured to harbour an independent thought, dared publicly confess that he held an opinion of his own."[136]

As laughable as Kingsmill's analysis of Leggism is, it is nevertheless the case that after the turn of the century Legge's reputation had suffered because of his faith in the purity of the past. It is also true that Legge's erstwhile attempt, in the spirit of a cautious sinological Orientalism and by virtue of his participation in the *Sacred Books of the East* project, to bring China into the purview of the comparative science of religions was largely abortive. Some of the reasons for this have to do with the changing sinological evaluation of the purity of Daoism—that is, the assumption that classical Daoism was more purely philosophical than it was religiously sacred. These changes indicate that after the turn of the century the whole notion of an authentic ancient Chinese religion rooted in the classical affirmation of a monotheistic High God was being severely questioned by sinologists. At the same time, historians of religion and anthropologists were demolishing much of the degenerationist "primordial High God" theory championed by Müller on comparative philological grounds and by others, such as Andrew Lang and Wilhelm Schmidt, on ethnographic (and as many would say regarding Schmidt, on "crypto-Catholic") grounds.[137]

China's Unique Nonreligious Nature

This situation represents a fascinating reversal of Legge's position since, whereas before as a missionary his discovery of a Chinese High God was viciously attacked by other more conservative missionaries on theological grounds, he was now as a scholar assaulted for the same findings by professional sinologists who were profoundly disturbed by the ambiguity and fragmentary nature of the textual evidence. These more modern specialists were operating with another kind of critical, and secularly irreverent, scholarly faith that was fundamentally convinced of the unique nonreligious "difference" of ancient China and were overwhelmingly suspicious of any kind of ancient Chinese God, religion, or transcendence. These developments suggest a hidden transposition or affinity of faiths that, though couched in different terminology, strangely enough both ended up affirming the total otherness of China regarding religion. For nineteenth-century conservative missionaries and twentieth-century professional sinologists a conclusion such as Legge's was logically and evidentially impossible. Putting aside any further discussion of the intriguing and hardly closed question of an ancient Chinese High God, we may say that mainstream academic sinology after Leggism was mostly satisfied with what was taken as the manifest secularity, rationality, and agnosticism of Confucius and the classical Confucian canon.

The Way That Was Trodden

It is not possible, in considering the way that was trodden with respect to Daoism as a classified and classical entity—like a Buddhism that was "grounded in the past, ideally conceived, and textually constructed"[138]—to document fully how much of the old nineteenth-century image, appropriately updated and disguised, continues within the churning *Daode jing* translation factory. It is found, for example, within various scholarly and semipopular traditions still concerned with some kind of essential Oriental mysticism, perennial philosophy, mythic paradigm, or wisdom of Pooh Bear. It also has vigorous life within many textbooks and anthologies of what has been called World Religion, Asian Philosophy, and East Asian Tradition still widely used today.[139] Rather in the spirit of the inevitable Daoist premise that in changing the *dao* stays fundamentally the same, it is more interesting and revealing to focus on those who should have been among the first to know better. Thus despite the increased "doubting of the past" and a concern for compilations and editors rather than for sacred books and authors, the old Orientalist logic of the "pure and the corrupt" regarding Daoism, most powerfully and scholastically articulated by Legge, was still intact within sinology until very recently. The tenacity of this kind of logic can be observed throughout most of the twentieth century—both directly and indirectly in Western sinology and, even more blatantly, within the academic tradition of the general history of religions. The terms were changed to protect the innocent, but the results were in many ways the same.

Within academic sinology, the special religiosity or mystic sacrality of the early Daoist texts was dropped in favor of an apparently more critical view that stressed the uniquely secular and nonreligious character of Chinese tradition. While known by sinologists only through fragmentary texts and shards of turtle shells, Chinese civilization was still primarily understood through an essentializing Orientalist filter that focused on the ancient Confucian, classical, and traditional foundations of China. This kind of emphasis tended to mean that Taoism/Daoism, however defined or romanized, was often ignored as peripheral and irrelevant to the elite Ruist civilization. At best, Daoism was considered only in terms of its marginal philosophical, literary, or sociological impingement on the development of the Confucian Great Tradition. In the latter sense, even the anonymous fragments of ancient Daoism were distinctly privileged over the later sectarian religious traditions that were, perhaps, no longer corrupt precisely in Leggian terms, but were surely civilizationally deficient as a manifestation of the little, popular, or mass aspects of Chinese history.

The beguiling power of this construct was that it seemed objectively consistent with the traditional native Chinese scholarly distinction between the intriguingly sublime literary and philosophical fragments of the ancient teachings *(daojia)* and the heterodox beliefs and liturgical practices of the village religion *(daojiao)*. For all of these reasons, the later Daoist sectarian tradition was neglected both in relation to the study of the Daoist canon *(Daozang)* and with regard to any extensive ethnographic investigations. Very much in keeping with Legge's old predisposition, a fundamental distinction was made between what was safely, anciently, intellectually, and textually pure and what was most often viewed as the superstitiously popular, ambiguously historical, esoterically textual, and chaotically ritualized sectarian traditions.

Stereotypes such as this persisted in Western sinology down to the 1970s when Kristofer Schipper's groundbreaking work on the sectarian tradition was first becoming known.[140] This is poignantly indicated by the testimony of John Lagerwey, an American sinologist who had gone to Paris in 1975 to study with Schipper. As Lagerwey says, he thought at the time, as some sinologists still do, that "Chinese history belonged to an 'agnostic' Confucian elite, and Chinese society to the 'superstitious' masses." "Lov[ing] Taoist philosophy," Lagerwey confesses that he fundamentally "believed the scornful judgment of others concerning Taoist religion." It therefore came "with the force of revelation" for him to learn from Schipper's courses that what he believed about Daoism was a particularly powerful fiction of sino-logical science: "It is not so. What you believed is false. The truth is. . . ."[141]

An Elliptic Truth

The truth is, perhaps, always a matter of the elusive ellipsis written into the heart of all cultural discourse. In this sense, the truth is that Daoism remains a fascinating and meaningful imaginary construct precisely because it re-sists all easy Western definitions and essentializing classifications. Both con-cretely as a living aspect of Chinese religious tradition and more philosoph-ically as a fragmentary repository of ancient beliefs, it forces us to reconsider what reverses, and harmonizes, all such abstract yin-yangish di-chotomies as the "pure and corrupt," "great and little," or "mind and body." Daoism has always been a tradition, whether expressed in anonymous an-cient texts or within current liturgical ritual, that invites, and even encour-ages, its own deconstruction.

The Way that was trodden and written by James Legge in the nineteenth century was certainly not the "enduring and unchanging Tao." But as seen from the perspective of Legge's own lifelong capacity for transformative change, it is possible that he would see the meaningful irony in what the *dao* has represented for the Western imagination. Today those sinologists who have trodden the path and know about the Way say different and sometimes contradictory things.[142] Nathan Sivin, for example, has, along with Forrest Gump, suggested that in Chinese tradition Daoism is as Daoism does,[143] whereas Lagerwey, now knowing, says it is the "religion of the people of the land." Kristofer Schipper knows that it is the Body that knows. Notwith-standing this expert testimony, Zhuangzi has articulated the best, and most darkly and faithfully intimated, metagloss on both Eastern and Western ways of knowing Daoism. If reality is but the twilight play of light and dark, then finally—in the words of Zhuangzi's Penumbra—it is the Shadow that knows!

INDIFFERENTISM AND THE VICISSITUDES OF MISSION

With deep intuition and mythic rite
We worship the Absolute-Infinite,
The Universe-Ego, the Plenary-Void,
The Subject-Object Identified,
The great Nothing-Something, the Being-Thought,
That mouldest the mass of Chaotic Nought,
Whose beginning unended and end begun
Is the One that is All, and the All that is One,
    Hail Light with Darkness joined!
    Thou Potent Impotence!

> *Thou Quantitative Point*
> *Of all Indifference!*
>
> NINETEENTH-CENTURY STUDENT DITTY, *THE OXFORD BOOK OF OXFORD*, 1978

Light with Darkness Joined

For Giles and Kingsmill, Legge's deficiencies as a scholar were often associated with his blind faith in the Chinese commentarial tradition, but were also seen as a result of his "early education and bent of mind" as an ex-missionary with too much belief in an ancient Chinese monotheism and a Confucian tradition that was authentically religious. Legge's scholarly work, no matter how pioneering it once was, emitted too much of the sickly sweet aroma of the *odium theologicum* for younger sinological Orientalists at the end of the century. In contrast, many missionaries found Legge and the methods of Leggism to represent the dangerously modern attitudes of the comparative science of religions. What was alarming among conservative missionaries in China about Legge's work on Confucianism—and even worse, his later work on abominations such as Buddhism and Daoism—was the comparativist's weak liberal tolerance, jellyfish sympathy, limp charity, or effeminate indifferentism that perverted the manly spirit of Christianity bent on conquering the world for Christ. This revival of the triumphalistic theology of the muscular Christianity genre was a backlash against the increasingly influential methods of comparative religions and the liberal postmillennialist theology among missionaries and, even more generally, an offshoot of the heightened imperialistic feelings and belligerent tensions among Western nations toward the end of the Victorian era.[144]

These developments resulted in a flurry of attacks by missionaries on those identified too closely with comparativists such as Müller and Legge. These circumstances also seemed to promote Legge's effort to bring scholarly impartiality and theological aggression, charity and faith, together in the form of some kind of still-reverent "comparative apologetics." While he never developed it in any theoretical way, Legge's last works and revisions (especially his final revision for the Oxford University Press of the first volume of the *Classics* in 1893) indicate that this method consciously sought to respect the religiosity and greatness of the Chinese heathen past (especially as symbolized by the elite state tradition of Ruism or Confucianism). But this method also selectively and unashamedly asserted, in the prophetic spirit of Legge's postmillennialist theology, the need for a radical Christian reformation of the decrepit Chinese civilization of the Qing dynasty.

Not Deserving to Do Its Work

Despite the vicissitudes of his own missionary career and his satisfaction with his secular identity as a professor, Legge passionately believed in the divine rightness of the Protestant missionary movement in China. He was, nonetheless, averse to getting involved in organized missionary activities because he was, as he put it, all too often "stigmatized" as an overly tolerant and independent enemy of missions. As known from his "reluctant address" on the "Bearing of Comparative Religions" in 1886, he was also sorely disturbed by the average missionary's "false witness" and lack of charity toward Confucianism and Confucians and the best aspects of Buddhism and Daoism. A significant example of his reluctance to get overly involved in organized missionary activities at home was his widely publicized refusal to speak at the centennial conference of all foreign missions held during the summer of 1888 in London. In a private letter, Legge says only that he decided "not to go at all" to the conference, "partly" because of health and "partly" because he was more interested, at that time, in working on his translation of the *Zhuangzi* for the *Sacred Books* ("the hardest nut to crack in all Chinese literature").[145]

Another reason for Legge's not even attending such an important meeting was the way in which it must have conjured up the nightmarish memories of the sectarian rivalries and his own preemptory treatment at the Shanghai missionary conference back in 1877. This factor was publicly acknowledged by William Hunter—the distinguished Sanskrit scholar, long-time resident of India, and vice-president, along with Legge, of the Royal Asiatic Society—who wrote a long, and generally favorable, account of the conference for the widely read periodical *Nineteenth Century*.[146] Hunter dramatically concluded his article with the startling observation (based, it seems, on some personal communication) that, whatever the great need for the missionary movement, James Legge, the distinguished ex-missionary and world-famous professor of Chinese at Oxford, had actually made a special point of not attending the conference in order to draw attention to some of the problems in the overall missionary enterprise. Legge holds, says Hunter, that "as long as Christianity presents itself infected with the bitter internal animosities of the Christian sects, and associated with the habits of drunkenness and the Social Evil conspicuous among Christian Nations, it will not do its work, because it does not deserve to do its work, in the non-Christian world." Hunter explained that when Legge was officially asked to take part in the conference, he responded by saying that "he [Legge] would have to clearly put forward his convictions—with the result that he did not take part in it at all." Hunter's final comment on the scandal of Legge's absence was that "it may be that some of the ground which he would have occupied lay beyond [the conference's] scope, and could not be satisfactorily dealt with by it." "But incidents like these, although perhaps isolated ones," concludes Hunter, "tend to weaken the authority of such an assemblage, and to create a suspicion among fair-minded men that they have not been placed in full possession of the facts."[147]

The Aggressive Genius of the English Race

The paradox of Legge's inaction (*wuwei*, perhaps) is suggested in Hunter's portrait of the conference as a missionary movement ready at last to embrace the liberal methods of postmillennialist evangelical theology and even some of the perspectives of the comparative science of religions. "During the last twenty-five years the study of the science of religion" had, according to Hunter, "profoundly modified missionary methods." "Between the missionary conceptions of the beginning of the century and of the present day there is all the difference between St. Peter at Joppa and St. Paul on Mars' Hill." Equally important is that the comparative method, which is sympathetically prepared "to acknowledge the good in other faiths," is nevertheless not any less aggressive in promoting the Christian mission to the world. If anything, the missionary is "armed" with "new weapons" by the science of religion and is able to "wield the sharp blade of historical criticism" to further the inevitability of the Christian triumph.[148]

Hunter firmly declared that, in "controversial combats," the study of comparative religions will enable the missionary to wield the weapons of "historical criticism" with "an effectiveness hitherto unknown." Moreover, "in popular appeals," these new methods combining sympathy and strength will give the missionary "the means of accurately and powerfully pressing home the claims of the religion which he advocates as against those which he would supersede." Hunter specifically links the religious and intellectual battle of the missionary, armed with the new and more powerful findings of the science of religions and the *Sacred Books,* with the British imperial mission to the world. He has these scientific and prophetic sentiments because, as Hunter says in a way that could have been uttered by Legge, he "honestly" believes "the missionary instinct forms the necessary spiritual complement of the aggressive genius of [the] English race." Missionary work in this sense is seen to be "an expiation of national wrong-doing in the past" and, even more important, "an aid to national right-doing in the future."[149]

The Ambiguities of Orthodoxy

Only a few months after his avoidance of the Centennial Missionary Conference, Legge was asked to help adjudicate the case of the aggressive Baptist missionary maverick Timothy Richard, whose orthodoxy was being questioned by his missionary colleagues in Shandong. Legge was put in the curious position of being asked to evaluate Richard in relation to issues somewhat similar to those raised by the paper on Confucianism and Christianity Legge himself had written for the missionary conference in Shanghai in 1877. In 1888 the Baptist Missionary Society home office became suspicious, on the basis of reports from the field in Shandong, that Richard, using a Chinese pamphlet he had prepared as a course of study for native evangelists and "devout Confucianists," was teaching something other than the "essential theology" of the "Gospel of Christ." In the pamphlet, Richard made no reference to Christ or atonement and stressed the Confucianistic importance of character building and moral cultivation.[150] The Baptist Missionary Society in England attempted to arbitrate the issue while, at the same time, keeping the whole affair private. Having only the versions of Richard's Chinese publications made by one of his accusers (J. J. Turner), the society decided to turn to Legge for an independent translation of the offending documents. Legge affirmed the accuracy of Turner's version and commented that, while he found Richard's optimistic ideas about "'national reform'" among the Chinese themselves to be mostly "'utter dreams and foolish fancies,'" there was "little evidence in the submitted writings of theological error." Interestingly, given his own problems with secretive accusations about possible heresy, Legge adds that Richard's works showed no cause for alarm because they primarily dealt with secular "educational" matters having no significant theological import. Legge admits that if such topics were all that he taught the Chinese then there would be "reason for serious complaint." But he doubted that Richard was deficient in this regard.[151]

There are several haunting dimensions to this unusual event. One of these is related to the largely successful efforts of the London Missionary Society, the organizers of the missionary conference in Shanghai, and the Baptist Missionary Society to keep such internal dissent hidden from the greater public. There is reason to wonder whether or not the Baptist Society was fully aware that its "independent" authority in Oxford had some ten years earlier been accused in Shanghai of similar theological impertinences. But it is even more difficult to understand why Legge—given all the strains in his own career as a missionary—would agree to join in a proceeding that seems so inquisitional.[152] Legge was able to attest to the non-threatening nature of Richard's works and to prevent any further bearing of "false witness" by missionaries against one of their own brethren. Nevertheless, his willingness to participate in this affair perhaps shows another side of his betwixt-and-between character at the end of the century. His involvement in the proceedings seems to draw upon the mixed sentiments of an old, but still orthodox, evangelical liberal whose carefully circumscribed fulfillment theories were being superseded by the views of a younger generation of missionaries such as Richard. These younger missionaries more radically and secularly trusted in China's own capacity for civilizational reform. Old missionary and scholarly soldiers such as Legge held onto the prophetic and progressivist notion that, however religious and moral the Chinese were in the classical period, contemporary Confucianism was fundamentally incapable of self-generated reform civilizationally or religiously.

We are back to the question of the galvanic battery and the kind of electrical charge that was necessary to get things moving again in Chinese civilization. Was it a matter of Dr. Frankenstein's secular science, which would reanimate the massive Oriental corpse once the Chinese were attached to the electrodes of a modern education? Or was it a matter of God's grace channeled to every nation—whether antagonistically by the total replacement of heathenism or more sympathetically, though not unaggressively, by the selective fulfillment of native religions—by the Bible and the progressive actions of missionaries and scholars? Or was it some other combination of reverent and irreverent methods? Such was the spectrum of methods and questions emerging at this time in the history of the Western imperial engagement with China. What is curious is that at the extreme poles of this spectrum there is a paradoxical convergence of the conservative Christian and radical secular positions—namely, a basic agreement that native Chinese religion should be aggressively obliterated and replaced by something higher, truer, and purer. Both are fundamentalist methods that depended upon, to paraphrase William Hunter, the "aggressive genius of the Aryan race." Only the ambiguous middle ground inhabited by assorted hyphenated missionary-scholars, pedantically impartial Western Orientalists, resolute Chinese Christians, and reformist Ruist scholars—such as Legge, Richard, Hong Rengan, Wang Tao, and Kang Youwei—provides the kind of impartial cultural space necessary for some honest intellectual and moral reciprocity.

A Monument to Mission

Legge published his culminating statement on Christian missions in 1888. This is his long monograph entitled *The Nestorian Monument of Hsi-an Fu in Shen-hsi, China Relating to the Diffusion of Christianity in China in the Seventh and Eighth Centuries.* Containing a typically meticulous translation of the relatively brief Nestorian paleographic text, this work, as indicated by the full title of the published pamphlet,[153] also represents a notable summation of his overall understanding of the Christian missionary experience in China and his complex relationship with that movement.

The engraved stone tablet known as the Nestorian Monument of the Xi'an prefecture, which in the eighth century was erected in the city of Chang'an, was important to Roman Catholic and Protestant missionaries as proof of the great antiquity of the Christian missionary movement to China. But by the eighteenth and nineteenth centuries, the monument had become notorious among enlightenment *philosophes* (e.g., Voltaire), Orientalist scholars (e.g., Julien), and some Protestant missionaries as a probable seventeenth-century forgery by early Jesuits in China. Because of the work of Alexander Wylie (whose translation of the Nestorian inscription appeared in 1854) and others such as Alexander Williamson (who visited Chang'an in 1866), the weight of testimony was siding in favor of the monument's authenticity. It was even suggested in the London *Times* by the infamous Terrien de Lacouperie that the monument, like the Elgin Marbles or Rosetta Stone, should quickly be acquired for the British Museum and made available to the comparative sciences.[154] It was important for Legge to corroborate judgments about the monument's genuineness, but also, and even more portentously within the context of the general Christian experience in China, to analyze missionary history for clues as to the best and most effective methods of evangelization. In addition to this, Legge's sweeping assessment of the overall history of the China missions was clearly intended as a defense of his own fulfillment theories of accommodationist mission policy. It also seems designed to show that, although a liberal and a comparativist, he himself was both aggressive and orthodox.

Nestorian and Romanist Methods

Legge suggests that at first the success of Nestorianism, or the Illustrious Religion *(jingjiao)* as it was known in China, was due to the general Chinese openness to foreigners and foreign religion in the seventh century C.E. (just as China was hospitable to Buddhism in the first century C.E.). The gradual acceptance and modest efflorescence of Nestorianism was due to the religion's wisely tolerant decision to draw upon some of the terminology and teachings of Confucianism and Daoism (more so than from Buddhism). As Legge notes, the monument (see figure 36) "says nothing against any of the three systems" already present in China and thus programmatically avoided an antagonistic method.[155]

The demise of Nestorianism only came about during the religious turmoil evoked with the proscription against Buddhism by the emperor Wu Zong in the ninth century. Reflecting on the causes of its failure, Legge drew some lessons for the latter-day Protestant missionary movement—lessons that just happened to coincide with what Legge had been recommending over the years as a missionary and professor. The first point was the importance of a sophisticated intellectual and rhetorical education for missionaries to enable them to command the attention and respect of the highly trained Confucian scholars. A second issue concerned the Nestorian attempt to "propitiate and conciliate the emperors as the Powers that were, [rather] than to enlighten and convert the people." This was also the method of the Jesuits. But instead of condemning such an elitist strategy, as was the wont of nineteenth-century Protestants bent on converting the masses, Legge strongly implied that the Nestorians and Jesuits were only taking advantage of circumstances peculiar to their immediate situation. Legge's third point was more disparaging in that he found the Nestorians

Figure 36. The Nestorian Tablet. Engraving from A. Williamson, *Journeys in North China, Manchuria, and Eastern Mongolia; With Some Accounts of Corea* (London: Smith, Elder, 1870), 1: facing page 381.

strikingly deficient in an "evangelical" focus for their teachings. They were much "too passionless" and lacking in a "vigorous propagandism."[156]

Legge then takes up the period of the Roman Catholic missions and, despite the antipapist elements in his own and Müller's comparativist approach to religious history, does not hesitate to side with the great Matteo Ricci's "liberal" methods, which sought to accommodate the use of some Chinese "religious terms" and "ritual practices." It is clear that the failure of the Romanists was due both to the insensitive stupidity and sectarian politics of the pope in siding with the Dominicans and Franciscans, coupled with the nonevangelical emphasis on proselytizing from the top down. Even though the Catholics, like the Nestorians, "sought the imperial favour too much, and made doubtful concessions to obtain it, . . . what else could they have done in their circumstances?"[157]

The Aggressive Sympathy of Protestant Evangelism

When reflecting on the nineteenth century in light of the early history of missions, Legge is careful to say that he tried very much to avoid "Protestant prejudice" in his treatment of the Nestorians and Catholics. Surveying Protestant missionary history from the time of Robert Morrison, Legge characteristically stresses moments of suffering perseverance in the name of intercultural communication (e.g., Morrison's dictionary, Samuel Dyer's movable metallic types, the Delegates' translation of the Bible), leaving undeclared, but obvious, his own contribution of the *Chinese Classics* to the effort. Legge was optimistic about the future hopes of the mission and is even driven to mention the favorable statistics of missionary progress since the very conference of missionaries that had censured him back in 1877 in Shanghai. The "increase" was great in the intervening years and Chinese "communicants" now numbered "hardly fewer than 20,000" and, together with their children and dependents, amounted to probably more than "100,000 souls as well deserving to be called Christian as the inhabitants of any parish in this country."[158]

Legge was particularly proud that the Chinese empire was being "covered with a network of small churches, gathered from among the middle classes and the poor." Even more heartening, and showing the wisdom of the evangelical approach over the elitist methods of old, was the effect of these "small churches" of the common people on the "higher classes of Chinese society and the members of the government, many of whose prejudices are passing away." Most promising was that, according to Legge, the signs of the times at the end of the century were pointing to an even more dramatic reformation and modernization of the government: "[T]he government itself has its school or college in Peking for teaching other languages; a considerable staff of foreign and native scholars engaged in the translation of scientific Works; its arsenals under foreign superintendence at several places; its embassies in Europe and the United States."

All of this, suggests Legge, came about not in spite of, but because of, the reforming leaven of Protestant Christianity among the people.[159] There is, to be sure, a necessary aggressive element associated with this process but, as Legge says in his conclusion, missionaries must avoid sectarian "striving among themselves" and, most of all, seek to be inclusive, multifaceted, and "many-hued" in their methodology. Aggression need not be antagonistic, but Paulinely measured and craftily appropriate to the circumstances. Whatever the method, there should be "forebearance and sympathy" toward native traditions and an accommodating readiness "to acknowledge the elements of good that are to be found, not only in Confucianism, but also in Taoism and Buddhism."[160]

When will it come to pass that China is figured among the nations of Christendom? This, intimates Legge, cannot be told. Alluding to his "calling" while a callow student, Legge ends by saying in the spirit of his brother George's postmillennialist theology that the prophetic uncertainty of knowing the hour of the final triumph does not preclude the immediate need for self-sacrifice among practicing missionaries, printers, teachers, physicians, engineers, and scholars. It is the life of mission as a evangelist,

scholar, or politician—the sagely giving of one's life to others so that all
may share the universal truth of God, morality, history, and science (not the
life of profit, however philanthropic)—that should be the noblest aim of
the "educated youth of Christendom."[161]

Fears of Emasculation

The underlying tone of Legge's dissertation on missions and traditional
evangelical policy was conciliatory or even slightly retrogressive when compared with some of his earlier work. Legge had not really changed any of
his views as expressed in the *Religions of China,* but at the same time the progressive, and even vaguely daring, spirit of that work seems somewhat truncated and diminished. There appears to be less of a willingness to deal with,
and existentially face up to, the real ambiguities of comparative moral judgments that prophetically call into question the whole edifice of European
superiority and the theological basis of the missionary movement. This kind
of partial retrenchment is understandable as a seventy-three-year-old man's
response to the increasing attacks on his faith and methods by both missionary and scholarly critics. Given everything known about Legge's character, we can surmise that the questions about his toughness as a Scottish
Evangelical Christian, and his commitment to the aggressive, "impartial not
neutral" prosecution of the missionary cause, were profoundly disturbing
to him.

What is important about Legge's declarations in the *Nestorian Monument*
is not that he was inconsistently trying to be honest to himself and conciliatory to some of the more conservative-minded missionaries. Rather, it has
to do with how this work was interpreted by his critics and friends. For many
conservative missionaries, Legge had already been identified too closely
with heretical comparativist attitudes and methods. Not satisfied with
finding some good in Confucianism, Legge was even prepared to find positive attributes in Buddhism and Daoism. This kind of reaction was to be expected among Legge's more righteously orthodox missionary critics, but
even some of his hyphenated scholarly defenders questioned his toughness
of resolve toward reforming Chinese traditions. Most disturbing of all must
have been that his old missionary and sinological colleague Eitel actually
joined the reactionary missionaries in leveling admonitions about the danger of "accommodating" native religions such as Confucianism, Daoism,
and Buddhism. The lesson that Eitel drew from Legge's brief history of the
rise and fall of Nestorian Christianity was that it was eventually "emascu-
lated and swamped" by Confucianism, Daoism, and that "despicable hybrid
thing" of Buddhism. Legge was ignoring the dual "imperial" and "imperious" nature of Christianity (as well as the humanistic and naturalistic sciences): "Of all religions the Christian religion is both the most imperial and

the most imperious, and admitting absolutely of no accommodation, no compromise, no half-measures, no half-hearted allegiance, or else the candlestick is removed and heathen darkness replaces the light."[162]

No Deference to Indifferentism

Many Protestant missionaries in the field in China were fearfully suspicious of overly impartial comparative methods, especially if these methods risked a dangerous depletion of Christian truth in the name of accommodation, completion, or fulfillment. These fears were only magnified when manifestly corrupt religions or "excrescences" such as Buddhism and Daoism—which focused willy-nilly on asceticism, mystical passivity, magical superstitions, and ritual excesses—were praised along with more morally conscious traditions like Confucianism.[163] Here again the rhetoric critical of a comparative approach to missions was rooted in a nested set of metaphors alluding not just to a lack of masculinity and aggressiveness, but also to the spiritual and biological degeneration coming from the careless mixing of religions, cultures, and races.

During the last few decades of the Victorian period, there was a gradual shift in missionary circles toward more liberal and selectively tolerant approaches to Chinese tradition. These developments are most powerfully dramatized in the Parliament of Religions, held in Chicago in 1893, a spectacular outgrowth of the "impartial not neutral" spirit of comparativism. Even before the parliament, the Second General Conference of Missionaries in China, held in Shanghai in 1890, gave evidence of the inroads of the liberal trends in the evolution of Protestant missionary policy. In arguing for a second general conference, Alexander Williamson, Legge's old missionary comrade in Peking, emphasized that the spectacular material and intellectual changes in the world (steamships, telegraph, the railroad, mass circulation periodicals, etc.) foretold a coming "revolution" in China. But there was "no hope" for the "permanent elevation of China" except through "religious knowledge and the sanctions of religion." It was the "higher civilization" made possible by Christianity that was needed by China. Thankfully, said Williamson, China had "much to build on"—especially in relation to Legge's old litany of the Confucian "knowledge of God," "moral code," "paternal government," and tradition of "ancestral worship." In this light, the "great duty" of missionaries was "supplementary" in the liberal Leggian sense.[164]

During this same period, there was also a partial translation of the concept of "Christian salvation and life" into social-gospel terms that were more overtly civilizational, secular, and scientific. One fascinating example of this, and something that is the ultimate iteration of the general missionary squeamishness about Oriental "filthiness" (both James and Hannah Mary

Legge had commented on it), was a movement of "sanitary salvation" evident in the mid-1880s. In the evangelical spirit of the temperance movement that was sweeping Victorian Britain and America at that time, it was strongly suggested to missionaries that the rule of cleanliness being next to godliness (implying "neatness, order, physical comfort" and related to "temperance, Sunday rest, and the influence of faith and hope") needed to be strictly enforced among Chinese Christians.[165]

Muscular Christianity Revisited

Whatever the liberal inroads toward a more sympathetic appreciation, and strategic supplementary use, of native traditions such as Confucianism, there was still a strong conservative missionary contingent that was increasingly disturbed by compromising tendencies (among such missionaries as Williamson, Martin, Faber, Edkins, Richard, Candlin, Ross, and others) that were broadly associated with the methods of Leggism. These reactionary feelings reached a peak after the dubious success of the Parliament of Religions in 1893, but already in the mid- to late 1880s there was a noticeable movement among some (often American) missionaries to reject indignantly the new methods of the comparative religions and to be highly suspicious of the unmanly weaknesses of accommodationism and indifferentism. In the words of one of the most outspoken conservative missionaries in China, D. Z. Sheffield, the liberal comparativists too often forgot that Christianity was primarily a "religion of conquest" that could never be party to a "dangerous compromise between truth and falsehood." Especially dangerous in this regard was the appeal of Confucianism, which superficially (or ideally) seemed to have such an elevated moral system. All such attempts at building upon heathen tradition were doomed to failure. Just as Christianity could not be "blended" with Judaism, and just as Roman Catholicism was the arch religion of compromise with paganism, so should the pure Protestant Christianity avoid any "degenerate" compromise with Confucianism.[166]

Other missionaries variously opposed any attempt "to graft the pure religion of Christ on to Confucianism" or to "baptise paganism like the Romanists."[167] Gilbert Reid railed against the compromising "limp leniency" of the overly "goody-goody" and too "genial" liberal missionaries who make use of "dim parallels" and diminish the "zeal of the gospel." The perceived "vogue to be conciliatory in preaching" to the Chinese by using the Confucian classics and the "lore of the people" was likewise condemned.[168] Most of all, said Arthur H. Smith (who would go on to write the extremely influential *Chinese Characteristics,* published in 1894), a missionary should "not be too much of a scholar" in the battle with heathens. To make it absolutely clear who he was referring to, Smith went on to identify Legge as someone who upheld an impossibly "high ideal" for the "average mission-ary." After all, says Smith, "not ever [*sic*] one" can or should "become a Sinologue." Is "not the ultimate and the legitimate tendency of such ample and minute scholarship" more "in the direction of Professorships than of Mission chapels?"[169]

Monier-Williams's Change of Heart

The backlash against comparativism seen within the China mission reflected more general developments within both missionary and scholarly circles. A provocative example of this is seen from the actions of the Boden professor of Sanskrit at Oxford, Sir Monier Monier-Williams. For many years broadly identified with the vaguely liberal evangelical fulfillment thesis of missionary policy, Monier-Williams was suddenly motivated in 1887 to unleash the ag-gressive masculine spirit of the Bible against the flabby sentiments, and "jelly-fish tolerance," engendered by the *Sacred Books of the East*.[170] Part of Monier-Williams's conversion experience in this regard was no doubt caused by his gnawing bitterness over the slights large and small rendered by his old neme-sis Max Müller. He was also voicing broadly based sentiments of anger and frustration over the progressive inroads of liberal attitudes throughout Vic-torian religion and society. "Every library," Monier-Williams said, "teems with infidel publications; false criticism and carping scepticism are in the air."[171]

The immediate reasons for his outburst at this time are not known, but the occasion became a celebrated instance of the late-Victorian reaction against the *Sacred Books* and all "degenerate" and "unmanly" forms of Mül-lerian comparativism. Addressing the annual meeting of the Church Mis-sionary Society in 1887 (and repeating his remarks in London at the an-niversary meeting of the British and Foreign Bible Society), Monier-Williams delivered the lecture that was published as a pamphlet entitled *The Holy Bible and the Sacred Books of the East*. The lecture itself is another marvelous specimen of exaggerated Victorian rhetoric that in many ways is the quin-tessential distillation of pent-up conservative resentment. To heighten the dramatic effect of his change of heart that had come about through his more "mature reflection" on the supplementary or fulfillment thesis, Monier-Williams piled up the *Sacred Books* in an immense stack on one side of a table in front of the speaker's podium; on the other side, he placed a lone Bible. This graphic demonstration of the might of the Holy One over and against the Sacred Multitude was not lost on his sympathetic missionary audience for, as reported, his actions were met with a "roar of delight."[172] The lecture itself was no less graphic or simplistic, as Monier-Williams basi-cally expressed his conviction that the "limp tolerance" of the *Sacred Books* was "incompatible with the 'fibre and backbone that ought to characterize a manly Christian.'" The Bible is never "flabby" and brooks no "milk and water" compromise or craven impartiality. Between Christianity and all other religions there is, then, a "bridgeless chasm" that no theory of evolution or science of religion "can ever span."[173]

Max Müller was the primary target of Monier-Williams's stern application of the birch rod of reprimand to the soft dimpled hindside of British comparativism. But inasmuch as he was closely identified at Oxford with the *Sacred Books* and Müller's patronage, Legge may certainly be numbered among the fellow travelers of religious indifference and flaccid toleration. As illustrated in the pages of the *Chinese Recorder,* Legge was so perceived by conservative missionaries in China. Neither Müller nor Legge's responses to Monier-Williams's wildly excessive charges are recorded. However, as a proud ex-missionary and faithful evangelical defender of the civilizational mission of the West, Legge would have felt acutely the exaggerated unfairness and blind distortion of attacks of this kind. Legge's last years were, in fact, devoted to a quietly measured response to such overheated and artificially polarized accusations.

CHAPTER EIGHT

Teacher Legge:
Upholding the Whole Duty of Man,
1893-1897

*Let us hear the conclusion of the whole matter: Fear God, and keep his command-
ments: for this is the whole duty of man. For God shall bring every work into judgment, with every secret thing, whether it be good or whether it be evil.*

ECCLESIASTES 12:13-14

THE CONCLUSION OF THE WHOLE MATTER

In 1893, at the age of seventy-eight, twenty years after his departure from
China and four years before his death, James Legge published his final
testimony concerning the Chinese master and sage Kongzi. Legge was as
he always was: a good Evangelical Christian and an earnest scholar. Yet
everything—missions, religion, scholarship, the Orient, and the world—
had changed forever. He had by this time done his heartfelt duty to the
Buddhist and Daoist sacred books and nostalgically knew that he should
come back to more familiar and godly realms of Chinese literature. As a devoted Victorian-Confucian transmitter and decipherer, he returned therefore to his original sinological passions and prepared a final version, or climactic revision, of his translations of the Chinese classics initiated thirty-two
years earlier in Hong Kong. With these last modifications of his beloved
Confucian-Ruist texts, Legge brought full closure to the *Chinese Classics*—an
enterprise that even his old nemesis Herbert Giles called the "greatest existing monument of Anglo-Chinese scholarship."[1]

Legge's revisions truly represented the culmination of his lifelong involvement with the classics, since it was only now—after the publication of
his *Book of Changes* and the *Record of Rites* for the *Sacred Books,* the publication of Edouard Biot's translation of the *Zhou Li* (The rites of the Zhou) in
1851, and the appearance, in 1892, of Charles de Harlez's version of the *I li*
(The rituals of the I)—that all the works of the Tang collection of the Thirteen Classics, except for the lexical *Er ya,* were made available to a Western
audience. Legge was proud to note that he had translated ten of those texts,
more than any other Westerner. He was, moreover, pleased to have the opportunity to make various improvements in his earlier versions of this

canonical literature, and to have a final say as to how his translations and interpretations of these ancient Oriental documents—now indelibly identified as the Confucian classics associated with the foundational sage known to the West as Confucius—would be remembered.[2]

It was fitting that Legge's final version of the *Chinese Classics* started to appear in 1893. This was a transitional year similar to the fateful year of 1873 when he left China. Things were "on the turn" again so that, for example, the end of the nationalizing and liberalizing era at Oxford University came about in 1893 with the death of the redoubtable Benjamin Jowett.[3] Even more momentous with regard to changes in the conduct and national identity of sinological Orientalism is that this year, which witnessed Legge's final revision of the greatest product of nineteenth-century sinology, was the year that a young French sinological scholar by the name of Édouard Chavannes began his ascendancy. After spending time on language study and research in China, Chavannes returned to France in 1893 to assume (at the age of twenty-eight!) the famous chair of Chinese at the Collège de France once held by the founding fathers of academic European sinology, Abel Rémusat and Stanislas Julien. No longer bound to the confines of the library in the habit of earlier Parisian sinologues, Chavannes joined Julien's analytical passion with a Leggian dedication to translation and an anthropologist's concern for fieldwork. Already in 1895 the first volume of Chavannes's uncompleted masterwork as a translator had appeared, *Les Mémoires historiques de Se-ma Ts'ien*. Somewhat later, he published a meticulous interpretive analysis of the cult associated with the sacred pilgrimage mountain of Taishan (*Le T'ai Chan; Essai de monographie d'un culte chinois; appendice, Le Dieu du sol dans la Chine antique* [1910]), a study (somewhat like J.J.M. de Groot's *Religious System of China* [six volumes, 1892–1910]) that impressively combined a deft sense of ethnographic description with a historian's skill in using ancient documents (textual and paleographic) and a philologist's mastery of the language.[4] Chavannes was a scholar who eschewed the unfettered philological and historical comparativism of Lacouperie or Kingsmill, yet could never be accused, as Legge was, of being a missionary, old-fashioned in his methodology, or merely a translator. These events, along with the creation of *T'oung Pao* by Henri Cordier and Gustave Schlegel in 1890, the establishment of the École française d'Extrême-Orient in 1898, and the emergence of the polymath Paul Pelliot after the turn of the century, signaled the revival of the glorious French-Continental tradition, which had remained mostly fallow during the twentysome years of the Leggian epoch of sinological Orientalism.[5]

A Very Great Man

The most prodigious single-handed contribution of British scholarship to sinology is unquestionably Legge's five-volume "second edition, revised" set of the *Chinese Classics* published at the Oxford University Clarendon Press between 1893 and 1895. The first of these volumes was, appropriately enough, the very first of the original volumes—that is, the one devoted to three of the Four Books: the *Lunyu* (Analects), the *Daxue* (Great learning), and the *Zhongyong* (Doctrine of the mean). Volume one of this new edition, along with volume two, containing *The Works of Mencius,* was meticulously amended with occasional, and relatively minor, alterations in the translation, notes, dating, nomenclature (e.g., "kingdom" rather than "empire" in reference to the clannish Zhou period), and romanization system (a combination of Thomas Wade's system and the system used in the *Sacred Books*). But only the first volume, the translation of Confucius and the first three of the Four Books, received an extensive new preface. And only in the prolegomena to the first volume do we witness a series of subtle, but critical, changes in Legge's overall interpretation of Kongzi as the originary master and foundational sage of the Confucian tradition. The other three volumes (3: the *Shoo King* [The book of historical documents], 4: the *She King* [Book of poetry], and 5: the *Ch'un Ts'ew* [Spring and autumn annals], with the *Tso Chuen* commentary) were exact reprints of the 1865–1872 editions (or, perhaps, a rebinding of printed sheets from the original editions).[6]

It is in the 1893 revised edition of the first volume of the *Chinese Classics* that Legge, in significant though modulated contrast with the 1861 version, concludes his prolegomena by flatly declaring Confucius to have been a great man. The full revised passage deserves citation:

> But I must now leave the sage. I hope I have not done him injustice; the more I have studied his character and opinions, the more highly have I come to regard him. He was a very great man, and his influence has been on the whole a great benefit to the Chinese, while his teachings suggest important lessons to ourselves who profess to belong to the school of Christ.[7]

As the episode of Legge's shoeless worship at the Altar of Heaven in Peking reverberated powerfully throughout his life, so does his revised judgment of Confucian "greatness" hark back to that other prophetically poignant scene in North China in 1873—that is, Legge's reverie, while standing in front of the ancient master's burial mound in Qufu, about the comparative "greatness" of Napoleon and Confucius. Clearly his moral and scholarly conscience concerning a possible injustice to Confucius had motivated these important alterations.

Gone is the sour chorus from the original Hong Kong edition of the *Chinese Classics.* Legge had dramatically altered his evaluation of the Chinese master, but unfortunately the niggling refrain from the 1861 edition was too often remembered as his definitive judgment—especially by those unaware of, or purposefully oblivious to, the full scope of his revisionary life and transformative vision. For Legge himself, however, he had forever banished these words published in the 1861 edition: "He [Kongzi/Confucius] threw no new light on any of the questions which have a world wide interest. He gave no impulse to religion. He had no sympathy with progress. His influence has been wonderful, but it will henceforth wane. My opinion is that the faith of the nation in him will speedily and extensively pass away."[8]

Dutifulness and Decadence

After his refining pilgrimage of thirty-odd years and his evangelical Christian sojourn in the "houses" of John Bunyan's "straight and narrow" Interpreter and Max Müller's more diversionary science of comparative religions, Legge's understanding of the ancient Chinese master's "character and opinions" had greatly altered. Legge's moral judgment of the man, Kongzi, and his system had significantly changed over the years, but such changes also served to underscore some continuing apologetic and prophetic themes. His views had changed so much that the things that stayed the same stood out in bold relief. It seems that, at the end of his life, Legge tried to preserve some final antagonistic and sympathetic tension concerning Confucius and Confucianism. In the conservatively liberal spirit of both his Oriental mentor, Han Yu, and his Oxonian paragon, Müller, Legge was in this way able to maintain his hyphenated integrity as a missionary-scholar and apologetic-comparativist.

Part of the reason for the change in 1893 concerning the greatness of Kongzi was simply that in the past thirty years the faith of the Chinese nation in Confucius had not, as predicted in 1861, "speedily and extensively" passed away.[9] It had also become clear to Legge that the ancient Chinese master did enlighten various moral "questions of world wide interest." Furthermore, a nationalistic Protestant-style faith in a reform Confucianism was becoming an increasingly self-conscious factor among some liberal-minded Ruist scholar-bureaucrats in China (e.g., the modernizing faction exemplified by Li Hongzhang politically and Kang Youwei and Liang Qichao more philosophically). These Chinese were responding to the disastrous humiliation of China by the westernized Japanese in 1895 (the Treaty of Shimonoseki ending the Sino-Japanese War). Even more generally, they were reacting to the aggressive religious, political, and economic "missionary" onslaught of the Christian nations and the dynamically progressive, prophetic (either in terms of Christian postmillennialism or secular modernism), but always unpredictable, cross-cultural intercourse of Westerners and Chinese.

The waning years of the Victorian period witnessed a tense polarization between the old demands of duty and stability and a new aesthetic of anarchistic depletion and decadence. This was an era in Britain broadly defined ideologically by the rousing imperial rhetoric of Rudyard Kipling's tales of the white man's God-given burden to elevate the lesser races. At the same time, the 1890s were bounded by Oscar Wilde's decadent fascination with the radical Chinese sage Zhuangzi and by increasing anxieties about racial pollution and alien invasion.[10] At the terminus of the decade, there was the abortive One Hundred Days Reform at the Chinese court in Peking and the radically transgressive, anti-Christian and anti-Western, Boxer Rebellion in northeastern China—spasmodic events that brought an end to overly optimistic assumptions about Chinese modernization at the dawn of the new century.

The undergraduate climate at Oxford had also changed in the direction of a more publicly pronounced display of decadent indifference, scoffing skepticism, and fashionable agnosticism (seen as a "hall-mark of intellectuality").[11] What Mrs. Humphry Ward, the famous author of *Robert Elsmere*, called the "unsettlement of religion" in the 1880s had become even more pronounced at Oxford in the 1890s.[12] According to contemporary accounts, Oxford had itself lost much of the revolutionary intellectual vigor of the previous decades and was once again, as Andrew Lang put it, an "eminently discontented place" seeking new intellectual and spiritual directions. It was an institution on the verge of becoming the "vast learning machine" of the modern research university. Professors, with few exceptions, were "merely an ornamental order of beings" devoted to pure scholarship and to bringing notoriety to the university.[13]

Through the thick and thin of these ambiguous years, Legge held on to the conviction that Confucius's "teachings" suggested "important lessons." Never content to be merely a translator or a scholarly ornament, he was always dedicated to an educational mission that involved both pure scholarship and applied teaching. At the heart of this pragmatic faith was a devotion to edifying lessons learned and taught, lessons that were rooted in the sacred and classical literature of the whole world. In the case of the instruction coming from the ancient Chinese master, Kongzi, this involved "practical lessons" (thinking here of the discussion in the *Religions of China;* see pages 303–5) that would profit all honest scholars and students, even those who professed "to belong to the school of Christ."[14]

Revisionary Lessons

What were these lessons for the school of Christ in 1893? The answer, as it happens, is not spelled out in any exact terms. Nonetheless, there is little doubt, as was said in the *Religions of China* in 1880, that Christian professors, as well as preachers and missionaries, must "personally" and "untiringly" exhibit "Christ-like attributes" of character and work. In his revision of the first volume of the *Classics* and almost by way of a belated but direct response to criticism in the 1869 *Edinburgh Review* (see pages 78–80) Legge only hints that it is a matter of trying "not" to do an "injustice" to the Chinese master. Interestingly enough, this is a concern that resonates more with Kongzi's negative principle of moral reciprocity ("what you do not want done to yourself, do not do to others," *Analects* XV.xxiii) and his silver rule of returning injury with justice than with the sometimes overly presumptuous and aggressive enthusiasm of Evangelical Christian love. In keeping with the comparative lessons of the *Religions of China* there are also the universal religious (Christian *and* Chinese involving Confucian, Daoist, and Buddhist elements) and natural (humanistic and secular) lessons of an idealized intracultural morality involving a methodical and methodological humility, tolerance, sympathy, fairness, and impartiality.

A kind of Confucian justice (*zhi*, meaning an interpersonal straightness, directness, honesty, uprightness, frankness) actually seems to create the possibility for Christian love (understood by Legge in a pietistic Evangelical sense—i.e., the sentimental golden glow of "gushings of a loving heart responsive to the promptings of Heaven"), not the other way around.[15] The fact that Kongzi did not express himself with the "gushing" enthusiasm and pious sentimentality of a Sabbath culture Scots Dissenter is hardly surprising, but it is interesting to see that, while he was mostly unconscious of this perspectival disparity, Legge was nonetheless capable of granting the moral relevance of Confucius's cold justice. Legge's revised judgment of Master Kong indirectly suggests, therefore, the importance of a ritually structured openness to learning from a cultural Other, an undeclared realization on Legge's part that dialectical self-revision is a necessary aspect of character building and understanding. This principle of transcultural morality was as troubling and tacit for nineteenth-century Ruist scholars in China as it was for Western Orientalists such as Legge.

These lessons were especially pertinent for all those Westerners inhabiting a privileged position of power (whether religious, commercial, political and social, or intellectual) in relation to Orientals. And if the school of Christ were to fulfill or complete the Chinese school of Confucius, professors and politicians, in both a Christian missionary and Orientalistic academic sense, must be prepared first of all to listen to the universal lessons of religion and morality taught by even heathen traditions such as Confucianism. The unstated extension of this Protestant postmillennialist and academic comparativist ideal of inclusive accommodation is that even Christianity, as well as other values, methods, and institutions of Western civilization, must be open to meaningful change and developmental renovation. This idea of revisionary reciprocity was recognized in different ways by both Müller and Legge. For Müller, it was mostly a matter of the progressive improvement of human civilization and the concomitant evolution of Christianity as the universal religion of the future; for Legge, the historical reformation of human civilization and society depended more on a

Protestant Christianity already complete in its God-given biblical commandments and intentionality. The Protestant reformation of Christianity was pure and absolute in essence, but not, to be sure, in its practice by professing individuals and nations.

The possibility of a comparative revision of all that was known and believed about Chinese persons, the Turanian language, Oriental civilization, and heathen religions is at the transgressive and transformative heart of an approach to other traditions based on some form of sympathetic comprehensiveness, whether warmly "gushing" and sentimental or coldly scientific and rational. These emerging revisionary views based on the "science of comparison" were in their own way often only more radically secularized versions of the liberal Protestant worldview and civilizing mission. James Legge's and Max Müller's methods and interests differed in many ways, but both agreed with the basic proposition that finally one God, or more secularly one Universal Truth, was originally, progressively, philologically, and ultimately revealed in the multiple languages, cultures, and texts of world history. The comparativist's movement in the direction of pausing, amid the sweaty work of administering a global empire or editing a library of the world's sacred books, to listen to the Other was at least a step in the right direction—that is, a step that led eventually to a more existentially relativistic, albeit sometimes nihilistic, questioning of the epistemological and value-free universality of the human sciences. By a reciprocal extension of the relational equation implied by the intrinsically dynamic and ambiguous transactions with Oriental people, it was possible that Christian and Western cultural and moral presuppositions could be reformed as much as any Confucian and Chinese suppositions. But given the radically skewed gradient of power involved in this calculus of understanding, it was all too often the case that, among both Christian missionaries and Western Orientalist scholars at the end of the nineteenth century, the actual expectation of change and revolutionary revision was conspicuously slanted in one direction.

Sentimentally Selective Revision

At the end of his life Legge was not very revolutionary in the application of his own self-taught lessons about the need for a constant revisionary transformation of all conclusions drawn from encounters with Oriental texts and persons. He was, it seems, somewhat weary in body, mind, and soul—as was only to be expected after such a long career of diligent duty and intense conviction. Moreover, as his highly selective revision of the first volume of the *Classics* suggests to a greater degree than did the more overtly apologetic *Religions of China*, Legge did not want to be thought of as practicing (whether by his newly militant Evangelical Oxonian colleague, Monier-Williams, or by missionaries still active in China) an overly indifferent and compromising approach to Confucianism or any other Oriental religion. Legge's own existential dilemma at this time was that the method known as Leggism was too liberal for many practicing missionaries in China and too conservative for the younger generation of sinologists. No wonder, then, that Legge himself, as he approached his eighth decade, seemed increasingly prone to reiterate and qualify old positions and to avoid controversial topics.

For the cosmopolitan worlds of Oxford and London in the 1890s, Legge was often too reverently pious, even old-fashioned, in his Christianity, comparativism, and sinological scholarship. In the waning years of the nineteenth century, when middle-class Victorian religious culture was becoming militantly defensive in the face of an elite society that was increasingly decadent and an academic culture that was increasingly secular and often antireligious, Legge seemed less inclined to revise his evaluations of Oriental tradition. Part of this hesitancy simply has to do with the fact that Legge had always viewed the transformations in his life as fundamentally consistent with his original Evangelical Christian vision of the pilgrim's progress. Given the general postmillennialist liberality of his Scottish Nonconformity, Legge's religious and scholarly views were not necessarily new or inherently radical.

Whatever his precise thoughts and emotions at this time, Legge was old and tired. Some of his fatigue came about because of the passage of time, but there also seems to be an emotional (as well as moral and intellectual) weariness or chill affecting his very being at this time. Not only was he publicly reviled by some of the more conservative missionaries, but also, and more important, he was becoming marginalized in scholarly and Orientalist circles in Oxford, London, Leiden, and Paris. Sadly some of the devaluing of Legge as an academic sinologist at the end of the century was connected with old misgivings that his scholarly detachment—as a former missionary—was "not complete."[16] The "long nightmare" of his earlier efforts as a hyphenated missionary-scholar seemed to be haunting him yet again like a cold gray specter.

During the last decade of his life, Legge appears to pull back from texts and topics directly having to do with heathen religions and morals and even seems to gloss over, or retreat, from some of the more radical comparative and political implications of his earlier works. This newfound placidity as a scholar and teacher seems particularly manifest in his increased focus on more purely literary and historical projects—that is, his speaking, writing, and teaching on Chinese poetry, belles lettres, and the dynastic histories. Despite Müller's continued skirmishes with critics over the results of his comparative approach to religions, Legge was not given to any further disruptive public speculation about his more provocative findings concerning an archaic and modern Chinese monotheism, the greatness of Confucius and the impressive principles of Confucian morality, or the surprising purity of the ancient Daoist philosophy. Interestingly enough, it is Müller, rather than Legge himself, who writes, at the turn of the century, a last summing up of a quasi-Leggian position on the Chinese religions.

Legge's restraint during his waning years, even to the point of engendering some creative misconceptions about his views, is graphically illustrated by revisions made for the 1893 edition of the first volume of the *Classics* on Confucius. A close reading of this revisionary text, especially the significantly altered prolegomena to volume 1, shows that Legge operated with a very discrete, and often sentimentally nostalgic, principle of revision in the years immediately before his death. The result is that, regardless of the special revisionary drama of the concluding paragraph on Kongzi as a "very great" man, we are left with the feeling that the ancient Chinese master's enduring national importance, authentic religiosity, and significant morality were, in the end, contestable, even contradictory, issues for Legge.

Certainly the 1893 edition of the *Chinese Classics*—which is the version of the *Analects* that was most commonly reprinted and used by succeeding generations—can lend itself to multiple, and often conflicting, interpretations of Confucius as a religious figure. This confusing situation is especially disconcerting when Legge's comments in the *Classics* are compared with his more effusive views in the *Religions of China*. The revised volume has most commonly been used by twentieth- and twenty-first-century missionaries and sinologists to document the case for Confucius and Confucianism's *obvious* agnostic, nonreligious, irreligious, a-religious, antireligious, or (as Legge himself put it) "unreligious" nature.[17] The problem is that both missionaries and sinologists often lack any historical appreciation of the issues involved in the nineteenth-century definition and comparative discussion of religion (from either a Western or Chinese point of view), any contextual awareness of Legge's actual revisions, especially the overall historical and methodological significance of the culminating paragraph on Confucius's greatness (discussed above), or much understanding of their own cultural and methodological embeddedness.

Missionaries at the end of the nineteenth century were particularly puzzled over Legge's final position on Confucius. Some, among them the liberal German missionary Paul Kranz, a disciple of Ernst Faber, appreciated that Legge could not be "accused of having been prejudiced" one way or another about the Chinese sage. Legge acknowledged the "many good doctrines" of the tradition while at the same time pointing out the "serious defects of Confucianism in comparison with Christianity." Elsewhere Kranz drew attention to the "remarkable change of view" represented by Legge's revised estimation of Confucius's greatness, but also stressed that this change was for "Christian soldiers" to be able to "use" Confucianism more effectively "as an ally" in the Christianization of China. For Kranz, Faber, and Legge, the key to the transformation of the Chinese was always a utilitarian matter of education. In this sense, the teaching of the idealistic morality of the *Classics* led naturally to the higher metaphysical ground of the Gospels.[18]

The conservative camp of missionaries greatly feared the compromising implications of the Leggian position and, in the expression of the American Absalom Sydenstricker, found it "repugnant" to think that Christianity could in any way be compared or allied with Confucianism. Such a liberal approach showed the danger of taking Saint Paul's views too far—especially his conciliation with idolaters and his use of the heathen classics. According to Sydenstricker, more attention should be given to the complete failure of Paul's conciliatory approach to the Athenians and to the fact that Paul himself, after his arrival in Corinth, put aside forever all such liberal procedures. Christianity must always avoid building upon the "rotten materials" of an "essentially agnostic and largely atheistic Confucianism." But whatever the contested "agnostic and atheistic" nature of Confucianism itself, Sydenstricker was truly prescient when—in 1898, the year of the abortive but anticipatory One Hundred Days Reform in Peking—he forecast that revolutionary elements in Confucianism would ultimately "combine with European and American agnosticism and with natural science to oppose Christianity."[19]

Camouflaged Greatness

Beyond a simple benign neglect of Legge as a typical Victorian missionary and translator, there has been much uninformed misconception about Legge's intellectual pilgrimage as a sinological Orientalist and his final evaluations of Confucius and the Confucian tradition. This situation is made all the worse by the realization that Legge brought some of these problems upon himself. A large part of the confusion stems from Legge's own apparent timidity in the 1893 revision of the *Chinese Classics,* or perhaps more accurately and fairly, from his overly camouflaged and subtle changes in the text and tenor of the prolegomena and annotations to the translations. The meagerness of the revisions was probably due largely to the restrictions placed on Legge by the Delegates of the Oxford University Press, who were always concerned with the expense of producing such a complicated volume (Legge seemed to be working within the limited parameters of photolithographically reproduced plates of the original Hong Kong edition). But Legge conspicuously does not call attention to his alterations, whether of the minor sort or of the more remarkable kind seen in his recasting of his closing sentences on Kongzi's greatness.

All the more problematic is that Legge frequently, and apparently inconsistently, does not modify or ameliorate many one-sided passages criticizing Kongzi's religiosity and morality.[20] Part of this inconsistency is more apparent than real and depends on the unfair vantage of our own anachronistic hindsight and sensibilities. Be that as it may, there is a clear residue of ambiguity and strain in Legge's later opinions about Confucius. His very reticence about what he fastidiously maintained, discretely qualified, or radically changed in the 1893 prolegomena and translation, suggests the ambiguity of his fin de siècle position on these matters. Legge most likely felt that he was being completely consistent in his revision; a closer reading reveals a more complicated situation that is as baffling today as it must have been in the 1890s.

Legge leaves intact many of the conclusions he reached in 1861, conclusions that, for many nineteenth-century Protestant missionary and scholarly commentators (e.g., Muirhead in his *China and the Gospel* of 1870 or Butcher in the 1869 *Edinburgh Review*), could be used in different ways to support either the conservative theological belief in Confucius's heathen depravity (as seen in the antagonistic conviction of many China missionaries that Confucius was rotting in hell!) or the old Enlightenment notion that Confucius, and the Confucian tradition, was uniquely nonreligious, naturally moralistic, rationalistic, atheistic, or agnostic. The *Zhongyong* (The doctrine of the mean) is, for instance, still portrayed by Legge in 1893 as a Confucian text that sadly "exalted sages over God" and was clearly "antagonistic to Christianity."[21]

Another example of Legge's curiously selective principle of revision is that, although in both his paper on the relation of Confucianism and Christianity and in his *Religions of China* there was a strong suggestion of Kongzi's prophetic relationship with Heaven or God, Legge in 1893 stays with his original melancholy deduction that Kongzi "may" have harbored thoughts of serving "his generation by the will of God, but [upon his deathbed] he gave no sign." Legge's depiction of Kongzi's deathbed despondency (based on the account in the *Record of Rites* II.I.ii.20) has all the earmarks of a typical Victorian dissenter's expectation of some testimonial sign of pious reliance upon God at the end of earthly life. Legge knew that Kongzi's *overall* life and character were collectively and cumulatively the most meaningful sign of some special association with Heaven (whether understood as a theistic or moral principle), but he could not help but fall back on more melodramatic presumptions about the pietistic importance of a dying declaration of religious faith (the *Record of Rites* says nothing about signs or testimonials). In death, therefore, Confucius reveals himself to have been merely a "great philosopher," not a truly great religious figure, founder, or crypto-Christian.[22]

Confucius's Unreligion

There are numerous instances where Legge actually softened aspects of the critical portrait of Confucius published in 1861. One notable example comes in his standardized Victorian discussion of the Confucian underpinnings of Chinese duplicity. In 1861, he confidently asserted that "foreigners, and with reason, charge a habit of deceitfulness upon the nation and its government." In 1893, however, he notably amends this to say that "foreigners charge a habit of deceitfulness upon the nation and its government;—on the justice or injustice of this charge I say nothing."[23] The alteration is tiny, but a pointed reminder of Legge's increasingly acute sensitivity to the ambiguity of judging the relative practical morality of England and China. In the twilight of his life, it was seemingly best and most just for him to say nothing definitive, or nothing at all, about such equivocal matters.

Regardless of these ameliorating modifications, the cumulative effect of reading the 1893 prolegomena remains decidedly critical. Like the 1861 prolegomena, the 1893 revision often reads as an aggressively antagonistic and hyperconscientious cataloguing of the ancient master's "very defective" and "cold" views on religion and morality. Though Legge tones down the charge of Confucius's "doubting" or "sceptical" nature (Legge "was inclined to think that [Confucius] doubted more than he believed"), there remains the vaguely anti-Semitic suggestion that Confucius was incomplete or overly aloof in his religious beliefs just as certain ancient Jews, the Sadducees, were.[24] Thus Confucius's basic shortcoming was that, although he made "frequent references to Heaven," he failed to follow the explicit theistic "phraseology of the older sages" (i.e., in the books of *Historical Documents* and *Poetry*). By so doing, he gave license "to many of his professed followers to identify God with a principle of reason and the course of nature." So also does Legge thereby give occasion for many of his sinological followers to affirm Confucius's fundamental "unreligion." Legge here seems to change very little in his early sternly disapproving opinions about Confucius and the Chinese. One result of this is that the impact of the last altered paragraph on the master's greatness is considerably weakened and blurred.

In contrast with his confident declaration about the authentic religiosity of the Master Kongzi and what I have called his theory of "primordial 'Confucianism' " in the *Religions of China,* Legge pointedly does not in 1893 excise some of his strongest statements about Confucius's coldly "unreligious" if not "irreligious" views. Kongzi was still found to be too "aloof"—too much "of the earth earthy" and not heavenly or spiritual enough. Legge was, in effect, accusing Confucius of not being evangelically "gushing," pietistically "ardent," or metaphysically Protestant enough. As Legge says both in 1861 and 1893: "I would say that he was unreligious rather than irreligious; yet by the coldness of his temperament and intellect in this matter, his influence is unfavourable to the development of ardent religious feeling among the Chinese people generally; and he prepared the way for the speculation of the literati of medieval and modern times, which have exposed them to the charge of atheism."[25] Legge did not exactly deny conclusions like these in 1880, but the tone of the *Religions of China* regarding the religiosity of Confucius and Confucianism was significantly different at that time.

Divine Dissolution

The context for these reiterated views is Legge's rousing reaffirmation of the Frankensteinian need for Christianity to recharge China's civilizational batteries. Again this is but an unrevised reassertion of his original postmillennialist declaration (a statement that was written during the Taiping upheaval in 1861): "Of the earth earthy, China was sure to go to pieces when it came into collision with a Christianly-civilized power. Its sage [Kongzi/Confucius] had left it no preservative or restorative elements against such a case. . . . Disorganization will go on to destroy it more and more, and yet there is hope for the people, with their veneration for the relations of society, with their habits of industry and sobriety."[26] Legge grants that there is some small ember of indigenous hope for such glowing middle-class Victorian qualities as social propriety, earnest industry, and resolute sobriety. But he also makes it abundantly clear that the purifying fires of civilizational salvation among the Chinese can only be fanned into full life by a "look[ing] away from *all* [my emphasis] their ancient sages" and "turn[ing]" to the capital-H "Him." For it is the One God of the Jews and Christians who has truly and prophetically sent the Chinese "the dissolution of their ancient state" so that they may have "the knowledge of Himself, the only living and true God, and of Jesus Christ whom He hath sent."[27]

The blunt presumptuousness of this only barely tempered triumphalist theology is retrospectively troubling and becomes even more so when we appreciate that Legge, despite his growing sympathetic comprehensiveness, was still accusing the "Chinese government and people" of a "contemptuous arrogance" in their dealings with the West. Such tough talk about China's need to reject "all" of her ancient sages, along with the unholy assertion about the divine blessedness of China's "dissolution," is especially jarring when encountered after the seemingly more liberal inclusivism of Legge's earlier works (e.g., his paper on Confucianism and Christianity, the *Religions of China*, and various comparativist essays and talks from the 1880s). To be fair to Legge it must be said that, even if in 1893 his moral courage seems to be flagging and his Christian assertiveness somewhat more antagonistic, his political vision of the coming dissolution of imperial China was in the end prophetically correct.

Creative Ambivalence and Comparative Perspectives

Legge's renewed criticism of Confucius's "unreligion" and modern China's woeful vanity and civilizational backwardness is curious not only in the light of some of his earlier, more sympathetic writings, but also in relation to views he was expressing at the same time, or right after, he prepared his revision of the *Chinese Classics.* The best example of this apparent ambivalence, if not outright contradiction, is Legge's long review of Robert K. Douglas's book *Society in China.*[28] In this unusually polemical article, published in 1894, Legge expresses his repugnance for the unfairness and superficiality of Douglas's derogatory portrait of Confucius and his relentlessly biased condemnation of the retarded, "make-believe" material and moral condition of the Chinese government and people. As Legge suggests in this review, comparative judgments about other nations are always perspectivally conditioned. The "great defect" of Englishmen like Douglas who comment so confidently and disparagingly on China was that they all too often failed to analyze with any kind of reciprocal or comparative "justice." In opposition to Douglas, Legge declares his agreement with a certain Archdeacon Gray of Canton who made a simple but powerful point about issues of comparative national morality: "Were a native of China, with a view of acquiring a thorough knowledge of the English people, to make himself familiar with the records of our police and other law courts, the transactions that take place in what we call 'the Commercial world,' and the scandals of what we term 'Society,' he would probably give his countrymen at home a very one-sided and depreciatory account of this nation."[29]

As known from the unflattering accounts of the British in diaries of the Chinese ambassadors to England during the previous decade, this was very much the case. Even more so than Legge or the Archdeacon Gray, however, these "natives of China with a view of acquiring a thorough knowledge of the English people" were much more willing to apply the practical lessons of comparative morality to issues of comparative religions. Therefore in a diary record for the "15th day of the third moon, 1890," Minister Xue [Hsüeh] rightly notes that "those in the West who follow the Christian religion aim at cultivating virtue and loving men, not very different from Confucianists." But he goes on to note that the Christians' "allegories and stories of the gods," as found in their "Old and New Testaments," are generally "not equal [in allegorical fantasy] to such Chinese novels as the *Canonisation of the Gods* [*Fengshen yenyi*] and *Record of Travel to the West* [*Xiyou ji*]." Xue only observes, dryly and comparatively, that "[e]very three-foot child knows that these stories are not true. When occasionally meeting men of learning of the West they seem to know this well [about their Bible] but are unwilling to say it out plainly."[30]

Deferential and Differential Aggression

The directness of Legge's censorship of Douglas's "defects" and "bias" is certainly exacerbated by Legge's own acute sensitivity to Douglas's identification with the aggressively "destructive" methods of modern sinologists such as Lacouperie and also by Douglas's insinuation that Legge was too much of a Whiggish "sentimentalist," evangelical "enthusiast," and Chinese apologist when it came to difficult political matters such as the Christian missions and the opium question.[31] Legge was, for example, opposed to Douglas's overly sweeping condemnation of the Ruist or Mandarin Confucian scholars whose "bigotry, violence, and corruption" were said to be responsible for instigating the increasingly frequent "outrages" against Christian missionaries in China. Legge argues that a distinction must be made between reputable native Ruist scholars—who, in his intimate acquaintance with "hundreds" of them, were "gentlemanly, courteous, and generally well-behaved"—and various "disappointed students" or "stickit mandarins" who had dishonorably incited mob action against missionaries. In a judicious and temperate application of Rhys Davids's concern for the "aggressive genius of the English race," Legge strongly recommended appropriate punishments for all such native Chinese agents of violent action against missionaries. At the same time, however, he emphasized that "there should be no recourse to the 'gunboat' or other hostilities of war, in which the guilty are likely to escape and many innocent parties are sure to be victims."[32]

Bringing Every Work into Judgment

Legge's intellectual and practical experience in China and at Oxford had led him to challenge overly glib, and sometimes hypocritical, conclusions about the obvious moral superiority of "Christianly-civilized" powers. In his 1893 revision of the first volume of the *Classics*, however, he seems to withdraw from his Christian duty to raise such far-reaching questions about the comparative morality of nations and races, saying only as he had in 1861 that he did "not feel called to judge or to pronounce" on such matters of "justice and injustice." Yet, at the same time, Legge chastises Douglas for precisely this failure to judge cross-cultural matters fairly and justly. For Legge, these practical issues of comparative moral justice are directly related to the "whole duty of man," whether the human beings in question be Christian or Confucian. God will truly judge "every secret thing," as the Preacher in Ecclesiastes indicates, but after "all has been heard" about Confucian and Chinese defects, it is incumbent upon a Christian professor to "fear God and keep his commandments" by clearly judging what is right and wrong. More than a "hope," it was a Christian's duty, "at the conclusion of the whole matter," to judge forthrightly questions of Confucius's and China's "greatness."

There is no sure way to read Legge's heart regarding the ambivalent revisionary strategy he adopted for his Oxford edition of the *Chinese Classics*. In many ways, he does not retreat from the difficult practical lessons of comparative moral judgment that he had learned during his long career as both a Christian and an academic professor. Nonetheless, there is a difference in emphasis and an evident decision on his part to avoid the difficult responsibility of comparative pronouncements about Confucian religion and morality that might leave the wrong impression about his own strongly abiding commitment to the Christian reformation of China. Some of Legge's actions at this time were conditioned by the heightened belligerence among conservative missionaries in China, a situation that became even more emotionally heated in the face of increasingly violent attacks by the natives on missionaries and in response to the "indifferent" methods of comparativists often associated with the controversial success of the Parliament of Religions in 1893. Especially after the military defeat of Confucian China by a modernized and Westernized Japan in 1895, there was a newly aggressive imperialistic scramble among Western nations for political and commercial "spheres of influence" in China accompanied by a rekindled triumphalism among many Orientalist scholars and Evangelical missionaries. The signs of the time all seemed to indicate that traditional China was teetering on the brink of impending "dissolution," to use Legge's prophetic terminology, and would shortly submit itself to the galvanic batteries of Western civilization and religion.

THREE PROPHETIC CONFERENCES

England had realized, and more than realized, the dream of Alexander, the marriage of the East and West, and has drawn the principal nations of the world together more closely than they have ever been before. But to conquer and rule is one thing, to understand them is quite another.

MAX MÜLLER, ADDRESS TO THE NINTH INTERNATIONAL CONGRESS
OF ORIENTALISTS, 1892

A Mission to Understand and Conquer

Whatever the precise reasons for Legge's muted reassertion of a more aggressive Christian and comparative approach to Confucius and Confucianism, the decade of the 1890s was manifestly a time for condemning material and spiritual indifferentism and for avowing, in the pugnacious language of Monier-Williams and Kipling, the "manly spirit" of the Anglo-Aryan race. These tendencies, particularly as they impinge upon Legge's emotional and intellectual sensibilities, are powerfully illustrated by three different, but ultimately interrelated and representative, conferences during the first part of the decade. The first of these is the second general conference of Protestant missionaries held in Shanghai in May of 1890. The second is the controversial Ninth Congress of Orientalists in London presided over by Max Müller in 1892. The third—and, in some important ways, the culminating—event was the unique Parliament of Religions held in 1893 as a part of the World Columbian Exhibition in Chicago. What is interesting to observe is that, while there are superficial conservative and liberal differences, each of these movements is emotionally committed to the proposition that it was the divine or Darwinian destiny of the Western powers to advance aggressively the reformation of Oriental civilizations. In this light, Legge's views were in no way recidivistic, but were in keeping with the more assertively progressive attitudes of the period.

The Second General Conference of Protestant Missionaries

The second conference, in Shanghai, in 1890, was, like the first in 1877, broadly expressive of the various complicated and conflicting forces affecting the missionary movement in China. Even more than in the 1870s, the tenor of the times in the 1890s involved a mounting fear of and disgust with the more frequent and brutal Chinese assaults against missionaries and foreigners together with a prophetic sense of an impending political revolution in China. Protestant missionaries in China also had to contend with continuing problems of denominational and national unity, an evermore contentious internal debate over practical missionary methods (whether antagonistic, accommodating, or more secularly scientific and social in focus), and an increasingly vocal public criticism of the whole "ghastly failure" of the missionary movement.[33] Despite all of these problems, the decade of the 1890s witnessed both a reawakened interest in evangelical religion at home and a general renewal of the missionary spirit in foreign lands such as China (e.g., the China Inland Mission, the "salvation army" of the Young Men's Christian Association, the evangelical student volunteer movement in the United States and Britain, and the growing American ascendancy in the missionary movement accompanied by the rise of the social-gospel tradition).[34]

As a result of these factors, the conference of missionaries in Shanghai in May 1890 was at times a contentious event that, in some surprisingly déjà vu ways, recalled the scandal involving Legge at the conference in May 1877. The most celebrated of these incidents in 1890 was the heated debate over W. A. P. Martin's accommodationist lecture on "The Worship of Ancestors," which led to J. Hudson Taylor's public condemnation of Martin and to the collective decision to leave Martin's paper "out of the printed proceedings of the conference."[35] More often, there was considerable agreement on most major issues, especially the need for a more militant approach to missionary matters and an evangelical revival of confidence in the divine rightness of the missionary movement.

The Committee of Arrangements for the conference actually included a number of prominent liberal missionary-scholars such as Ernst Faber and

Alexander Williamson. They put together a program that, while focusing on issues of unity (e.g., agreement on common Chinese versions of the Christian Bible, and on problems of denominational and national cooperation),[36] also dealt with a whole slate of practical methodological problems broadly associated with a Leggian inclusivist and comparative agenda. The schedule for the conference consequently included sessions on the "Native Church," the role of "ladies' auxiliaries" and "medical work," the "place of the Confucian Classics in Christian schools and colleges," the question of "how far" current Chinese literature was "antagonistic to Christianity," the "comity of mission work and relations to the government," "how China views Christianity," "the relation of Christian missions to foreign residents," and, perhaps most important at this time, the "relation of Christianity to Universal Progress" (an evening presentation under the aegis of Legge's old nemesis Bishop John Shaw Burdon).[37]

Satanic Comparison.   Certain topics, such as the "place of the Confucian Classics" in missionary educational work, were especially identified with Legge's legacy and were also generally connected with the touchy subject of the inclinations of the comparative science of religions toward compromise. The educational use of the classics was an issue that, like other related questions of method and policy, took on a life of its own and was hotly debated for the rest of the decade. Some conservatives and liberals agreed that the Chinese classics were, on the whole, the "purest heathen classics that the world has produced."[38] Yet even liberals such as Faber recommended the teaching of the Confucian classics in the mission schools only in editions "expurgated" in relation to the historical and critical "light of Christian culture."[39]

One of the leaders of the strictly antagonistic conservative forces at this time, the combative American William Ashmore, argued volubly and repeatedly that there should be no educational compromise at all with the Chinese classics. Neither should there be any diminishment of a completely antagonistic condemnation of the whole demonic tradition of Confucianism.[40] As Ashmore contended in one of his more memorably hyperbolic articles, the issue of the classics—which was, of course, the quintessential Leggian issue—came down to a question of whether or not missionaries were "getting ready to believe that God is the Architect of Heathenism." What is so telling in Ashmore's formulation of this pithy rhetorical question is his abrupt retort of "God Forbid!"—an emotional exclamation immediately qualified by his sad realization that "nowadays there is a drift in that direction." This is a tendency of the times that, as Ashmore says, is most closely and logically identified with the "teaching on 'Comparative Religion.'" The pernicious teaching of "comparative religions" is, after all, "much dilated

upon in [the] halls of learning" in America and Europe and was even affecting missionary practices in China.[41]

Especially disturbing for Ashmore was the "new turn" in comparativism
that moved away from a legitimate concern with knowing the enemy to an
argument for the kinship between Christianity and heathenism. Far better,
according to Ashmore, is the realization that the only authentic textbook in
comparative religion is the Bible. It is Jehovah himself who shows the divine
right of a sternly "antagonistic" attitude to all other religions. Moreover, the
"New Testament proposes no alliances, blending, compromise," or any sort
of "common platform" upon which to "establish universal religion."[42] Playing on Monier-Williams's old fears concerning the wishy-washy indifferentism of comparison, Ashmore notes that "[i]n some sort of vague ill defined
way, by some half and half procedure, it is intimated that God has had
much to do with the make up and the moulding of heathen religions. After
the same general style of working, though not with equal flow of efficiency,
He has had a hand in heathenism just as He had in Judaism and Christianity." Hidden behind all the talk about impartiality and justice, there is a
frightening satanic duplicity. The great failure of all comparative methods
is, then, that they fail to recognize the double nature of heathenism: "it is
partly of men" and "it is partly of Satan who has taken advantage of the situation and has manipulated the movement for the perpetuation of his own
reign of darkness."[43]

Manfully Going Forth to War.   The conference in Shanghai saw more
than four hundred and thirty missionaries in attendance (only one of
whom was a native Chinese Christian—which was, however, a 100 percent
improvement in indigenization over the previous conference!), representing forty different denominational and national societies that collectively
ministered to some thirty-seven thousand native communicants. All in all,
the statistics of the movement seemed mildly encouraging and, if the conference appeal for at least a thousand more male and female "workers for
Christ" in China were honored, there was every confidence that the final
triumph would surely be swift in coming.[44] There was even a strong sense
that, with the special assistance of modern Western technology, it would be
possible for relatively small numbers of missionaries to evangelize, more so
than before, a large percentage of the vast horde of Chinese. So therefore
in the aftermath of the Shanghai conference, the *Chinese Recorder* seriously
discussed the pros and cons of using a phonograph in evangelization, the
danger being that the Chinese might see it as a kind of Buddhist prayer
wheel.[45] The *Recorder* was also pleased to report that, according to "recent
computations," the living population of the entire world at that time (said
to be "about 1,400,000,000") could "find standing room in a field ten miles

square" and "by aid of telephone could be addressed by a single [mission-ary] speaker"![46] Given the Chinese "thirst for secular knowledge," W.A.P. Martin even recommended that missionaries make special use of various "scientific toys" (i.e., "magic lanterns, phonograph, optical, electrical, steam" devices) in their educational efforts.[47]

Notwithstanding spirited quarrels among the antagonistic and accom-modating camps of missionaries at the conference (in addition to the lib-eral missionary-scholars favoring comparative methods, the accommodat-ing or uniting camp included members of the China Inland Mission, who often affected Chinese dress with a "conspicuous lack of throat gear"—an issue that did not go uncriticized by conservative conference partici-pants),[48] there was overall agreement among both conservatives and liber-als on the need for a more aggressive apologetic explication of, and final bold confrontation with, the enervating defects of Confucianism and the Chinese nation. It is in this context that supporters of what were perceived to be effeminately indifferent comparativist methods were criticized and mocked, a situation that reached a fever pitch at the Parliament of Reli-gions (discussed below). It is also possible to understand some of the am-bivalence, and renewed aggression, in Legge's new Oxford edition of the *Analects.* Conservatively exclusive and liberally inclusive missionaries all shared the sharpened martial language of imperialism in the 1890s and "sought to 'conquer the heathen' on behalf of Christ." In this sense, the re-ally unifying spirit of the conference was most accurately expressed by A.J.H. Moule, who ostentatiously asked: "Is Christ's Church militant indeed on earth? Are we all bound to fight manfully under His banner against sin, the world and the devil? Has the Son of God indeed gone forth to war? And is our lot cast, whether missionaries or foreign residents, in this advanced post in an enemy's country?"[49]

The answer to all of these rhetorical queries by Moule and by the other conference participants—as well as by such intellectually impartial ex-missionaries as Legge and Eitel—was unhesitatingly in the affirmative. What should be appreciated is that such an aggressively martial stance not only characterizes conservative and liberal missionary discourse at this time, but was also an abiding force within Western Orientalist scholarship and the Müllerian comparative sciences. All come together by sharing in the nineteenth-century imperialistic will to power, that driving inner com-pulsion and pietistic enthusiasm for classifying, conquering, controlling, and civilizing all the world. To save, to study, to interpret, to do business with, to minister to, and to love the Orient on the West's own higher divine, superior moral, or more progressive scientific terms—even when that significant Other was not interested in, or actively opposed to, such a smothering embrace—was the underlying transcendental imperative for much of the swaggering imperialistic bravado of the 1890s.

The righteous intensity at the end of the Victorian era unleashed counter-sentiments of agnostic self-doubt and chthonian fear in the Western psyche. At the popular level, such contrapuntal manifestations are seen in a whole dark genre of gothic fantasy novels that dwell on themes of a horridly de-structive or polluting alien invasion from a symbolic Orient of, or beyond, the earth. Examples of this trend are the archetypal precursor of science fiction tales of extraterrestrial invasion, H. G. Wells's *War of the Worlds,* and the undy-ing novel of a foul blood lust that knew no bounds of time or space, Bram Stoker's *Dracula.*[50] Both of these narratives of an aggressively malignant op-position to the progress of Western religion and civilization appeared, it is worth remarking, in 1897—the year of Legge's death at Oxford, the time of the revolutionary Sun Yat-sen's departure from London and Oscar Wilde's in-carceration for homosexuality, and the diamond jubilee year of Queen Vic-toria's reign over the greatest empire in the history of the world.

The Ninth International Congress of Orientalists

The meeting in London in 1892 was the largest Congress of Orientalists ever held (more than five hundred members, along with other interested parties were in attendance) and an emphatic acknowledgment of Britain's stature as the premier imperial power in the world at that time. This congress also testified to Max Müller's privileged position as the grand old man of Orien-talism. In the winter of 1892, Müller had just finished giving the last of his cel-ebrated Gifford Lectures in Glasgow (on "Psychological Religion") and was pleased, after all the controversy engendered by his talks in Scotland,[51] to ac-cept the great honor of the presidency of the ninth Congress of Orientalists meeting in London in September. With the advance of the British empire throughout the far and near Orient (Egypt was acquired in 1882), Oriental studies were increasingly regarded with interest and appreciation by a large public throughout Britain. Furthermore, even though at the age of sixty-nine he was in his waning years and had repeatedly suffered the bitter attacks of ec-clesiastical and academic critics, Müller was hailed as a giant of Victorian scholarship and was certainly—in terms of accomplishment, reputation, and influence—the greatest of all living Orientalists. Müller was, as one Oriental-ist colleague put it without exaggeration, "a household word in every country where the English language is spoken."[52] During the late 1890s, Müller was also, for much of the younger generation of scholars and the general public, mostly famous for being famous. By the time of his death in 1900, it would even be reported that most of "young Oxford" found Müller to be less than intellectually fashionable or stimulating.[53] Nevertheless, Müller was undeni-ably the most internationally acclaimed advocate of Orientalism and com-parativism at the end of the Victorian age and his talk at the Congress of Ori-entalists stands as an eloquent epitome of the discipline at that time.

The importance of his presidential address to the ninth Congress of Orientalists is that, along with a related talk delivered at the Royal Asiatic Society in 1891, Müller uses the occasion to summarize his thoughts about Orientalism as an academic tradition crucial to international understanding and worldwide civilizational progress.[54] As with much of the rationale for the Protestant missionary movement, Müller treats us to a triumphant dissertation on the higher "aggressive genius" of the Aryan people. In like manner, he emphasized the intellectual battles being waged successfully by the Western historiographical and comparative sciences within all of the various domains of Orientalism. Most indicative of the overall tone of Müller's presidential address was his ritualistic, and grandly effusive, praise for the British royal patronage of the congress. "Completely identified with all that is good and noble in the aspirations of science and art" and unfailingly conscientious in its rule over the Indian empire, the British Crown magnificently shows itself, says Müller, to be an agent of "Divine Providence."[55] After this fawning prologue and a brief and sanitized allusion to some of the academic "misunderstandings and personal jealousies" that broke out after the previous congress in Stockholm,[56] Müller hurried on to his primary concern to explicate and justify the seemingly arcane ways of Orientalists to a general audience.

Prehistoric Homogeneity and Multiple Historical Unities.   The very reason for the existence of Orientalism was "to bring the East" near again to the West, to overcome the boundary of the Mediterranean Sea, which, by way of unfortunate inheritance from Greek and Roman tradition, had come to physically distinguish two artificially polarized domains: "West and East, white and dark, Aryan and Semite." Müller counts it as one of the "greatest achievements of Oriental scholarship" to have shown "by irrefragable evidence, in harmony with Darwin's general conclusions, that the complete break between East and West did not exist from the beginning; that in prehistoric times language formed really a bond of union."[57] However, the recognition of the ultimate prehistoric "homogeneousness of the human species" was only of academic import as historically there was a division of humankind by language and civilization. It was also one of the "glories" of comparative Oriental scholarship to demonstrate the continuation of some degree of unity at the level of several different language "families." Most important in this regard was the Aryan grouping, which dramatically reunited the East and West in terms of their original "bonds of a common language, law, and gods."[58] These are, says Müller, "stern immovable facts, just like Mont Blanc—though from a distance we must often be satisfied with seeing its gigantic outline only." As to the hotly debated issue concerning the original "home of the Aryans," Müller says only that it was "somewhere in Asia" that the "ancient consolidations took place." And then, rather defensively to avoid some of the more racist overtones of the Indo-European theory, he adds that "Aryan," the word *ārya* itself, meaning noble or tillers of the soil, refers "only to language" and not to "skulls."[59]

The Deepest Mysteries of the Beginnings.   No doubt because of the attacks on an unfettered pan-Aryanism or a willy-nilly search for the ultimate origins of the different language families (as seen in the work of Edkins) and the increasing skepticism about the comparative method, Müller firmly declares that the comparative philological and historiographical sciences must relearn the old lesson that "our mind was not made to grasp beginnings." As he says in the spirit of the growing anthropological emphasis on cultural polygenesis, "[W]e know the beginnings of nothing in this world, and the problem of the origin of language, which is but another name for the origin of thought, evades our comprehension quite as much as the problem of the origin of our planet." Whatever the human capacity to unveil some of the most profound symbolic secrets of history, we cannot and should not "venture to pierce into the deepest mysteries of the actual creation or cosmic beginnings."[60]

The determination of ultimate beginnings was futile, but Müller does indicate that, by the reconstruction of thought based on certain root words, some "mosaic picture of the Aryan civilization before separation" was possible. This is not to say that the original Aryans were either "savages or sages." A study of the Indian *Vedas,* which revealed the "earliest phases" of "natural religion," showed that the Aryans were not "mere idolaters or niggers" and must "be recognized as our brothers in language and thought." Taking up, then, Terrien de Lacouperie's popular Babylonian theory of linguistic and civilizational origins, which was used by Edkins and others to reestablish the biblical priority of the Semitic family of languages over the Aryan and Chinese, Müller notes only that the Semitic cuneiform of Babylonia "must have come from the earlier non-Semitic Sumerians or Accadians" and that the supposed "connection between Chinese and Babylonian writing" was "extremely doubtful."[61] Even in the most ancient historical past, Semitic peoples in the Near East, such as the Babylonians, the Egyptians, and the Hebrews, were already greatly mixed up, in terms of words and thought, among themselves and with other language families. This means, according to Müller, that the two most "absolutely isolated" countries in the world, India and China, have a special value for the comparative sciences since the traditions of these countries preserve in their sacred books, more than do the syncretistically intermixed Semitic traditions, linguistic and cognitive elements associated with the earliest emergence of the Aryan and Turanian language groups.[62]

This discussion of several, mostly isolated and pure, linguistic centers reinforced the growing scholarly consensus on the polygenesis of human culture. Gustave Schlegel, in reviewing Müller's discussion of India and China as "perfectly isolated countries during the ancient period," made the polyge-netic implications of this situation explicit. He noted that, contrary to older biblical ideas of monogenesis, there was not "any serious objection against the hypothesis of two, three, or more independent centres of culture, and no reason whatever for the necessity of a forced imposition upon these centres of civilization by one single culture" such as Egypt or Babylonia.[63]

The Special Isolation of China.   Despite the scientific parity of their civi-lizational and literary "isolation," India was privileged over China. This is both because of India's common Aryan brotherhood with the West and also because China must finally be seen as *too* completely and perfectly isolated. The special problem was always the matter of China's overwhelming lin-guistic and cultural singularity, its incomparable "formidable solitude." Therefore, even after the fledgling efforts of the newly professionalized sci-ence of sinological Orientalism, the study of Chinese language and litera-ture was not as advanced philologically or comparatively as was either In-dological or Semitic Orientalism. In his talk to the Asiatic Society Müller noted that the problem with the study of China was that it was still "confined to a very small number of scholars." Unlike the situation with the Aryan or Semitic traditions, which were connected to Europe by a common language and a single holy scripture, there were "no intellectual bonds that unite [the West] with ancient China."[64]

Even more dramatically, Müller proclaimed that "we have received noth-ing from the Chinese. There is no electric contact between the white and the yellow race. It has not been brought near to our hearts. China is simply old, very old—that is, remote and strange." By way of an indirect criticism of Legge's efforts both in the *Chinese Classics* and in his own *Sacred Books,* Müller indicates that the problem of solitude would be alleviated if only "Chinese scholars would bring the ancient literature near to us, if they would show us something in it that really concerns us, something that is not merely old but eternally young." Saying moreover that there was "no reason why China should remain so strange, so far removed from our common interests," Müller was in effect suggesting that such an unfortunate situation was pri-marily a failure of the current generation of sinological Orientalists.[65] It was almost as if Legge had not labored for half a century to produce the Confu-cian and Daoist classics or that he had never written the *Religions of China.* Legge had seemingly become so totally old-fashioned and hapless as an aging ex-missionary that Müller felt he had the license to suggest that the subject of "Chinese religion" had never really received "serious attention." Müller even implies that, contrary to Legge's findings, the "very contrast" be-tween Western tradition and Chinese religion and philosophy "might teach us at least that one useful lesson that there is more to be learnt even there than is dreamt of in our philosophy."[66] There is no extant record of what

Legge made of these barbed comments, but we may well imagine that the aged Scotsman must have felt some special degree of hurtful dismissal.[67]

Understanding to Conquer and Rule.   The prophetic edge of Müller's congressional address is indicated in his finale: after noting the precedent of Alexander's "triumphant progress" in attempting to "re-establish the union between East and West," he declares that it was now the divinely given role of England to stand at the "centre of the whole world." "England has proved," trumpeted Müller, that "she knows not only how to conquer but how to rule." England has "realized, and more than realized, the dream of Alexander, the marriage of the East and [the] West, and has drawn the principal nations of the world together more closely than they have ever been before." But, says Müller with a crescendo of rhetoric, "to conquer and rule is one thing, to understand" Oriental nations "is quite another."[68] Müller's whole career, as well as the underlying thesis of this congressional address, tended to show, of course, that conquering, ruling, and understanding were quite the same thing.

At this time, Oriental studies began to play a crucial role in England's militantly divine political mission. For it was incumbent upon all Westerners, especially the English, to "become Orientalized-lovers of the East." Unfortunately, England had been "deficient in providing basic instruction" in Oriental languages and literatures and should follow the lead of Queen Victoria who recently "devoted some of her very precious leisure to the study of the language and literature of India." It is most likely that Müller was himself the queen's "very precious" tutor in her Oriental studies, but he says only that an "intimacy of knowledge" is needed to achieve a peaceful relationship between "rulers and ruled."[69] If such practical accommodation and understanding had been the case earlier, there "would have been no Indian Mutiny" and, no doubt, fewer violent attacks on missionaries in China.

Müller more generally declared that Oriental scholarship should foster the coming reunion of East and West by marshaling "historical facts" rather than by "a priori reasoning."[70] This will help to "remove old prejudices" between the white and colored races. There is always the danger of findings coming from "dabblers, babblers, and half-scholars," but, says Müller, the real "conquests" of Oriental knowledge are "massive and safe." All self-sacrificing and hard-working Orientalists have finally shown themselves to be "bold generals" in the battle for human understanding and unity.[71]

The First Parliament of Religions

The "bold generals" of understanding and unity were not only to be found among Orientalists in Europe. Among the boldest generals of all were two heretofore obscure Protestant churchmen living in the burly and brash new

American metropolis of Chicago—namely, Charles Carroll Bonney, a visionary Chicago lawyer and Swedenborgian layman, and John Henry Barrows, the dynamic head of Chicago's First Presbyterian Church. These two men were the primary organizers of the unique and boldly prophetic World's Parliament of Religions held in association with the 1893 Columbian Exposition in Chicago. Hailed as the "quintessential event" of late-nineteenth-century American history, the Columbian Exposition exemplified the aggressively optimistic spirit of the age and symbolized the newfound maturity of America as a future custodian of Western civilization.[72]

One of the surest signs of impending American leadership was in the area of religion and education, so that the Parliament of Religions was, as a "higher and nobler" expression of the Columbian spirit of progress and the most important event marking the "dawn of religious pluralism," a direct precursor of the Christian ecumenical movement in the twentieth century and a harbinger of the increased "comparative" study of "world religions" in universities, colleges, and seminaries throughout the United States and Europe.[73] The impact of the parliament is suggested by the fact that, though only an auxiliary activity, it was the most popular and newsworthy single event of the entire Columbian Exposition (it attracted more than one hundred fifty thousand spectators, more than any other of the exposition's many different congresses and auxiliary events).[74] Even Müller, who was not given to praising American ventures, admitted in hindsight that it was an immensely important historical event.[75]

Running for more than two weeks in September at the downtown Art Institute building far removed from the main Columbian exposition fairgrounds to the south of the city, the parliament became an exotic spectacle attracting hundreds of official speakers and a standing-room-only audience. The vast majority of the speakers were aggressively stalwart champions of evangelical Protestant Christianity (including missionaries and various other lay and ministerial churchmen together with a small but impressive group of women speakers) accompanied by a smaller, but no less imperious, contingent of scholarly comparativists (e.g., Müller, C.P. Tiele, August and Jean Réville, and J. Estlin Carpenter; like Müller, most of these distinguished European Orientalists avoided any personal contact with the American "dabblers, babblers, and half-scholars" and only sent papers to be read).[76] For the first time anywhere in the world, the parliament also brought together living representatives of many of the non-Protestant book religions of the world, Roman Catholicism, Judaism, Islam, Hinduism, Buddhism, Parsiism, and Jainism, as well as the relatively more obscure and non-Aryan Far Eastern traditions of Confucianism, Daoism, and Shintoism. So-called savage nonscriptural traditions, including native Amerindian traditions, were generally excluded or relegated to the material displays of lower forms of cultural life set up in the Midway exhibition area of the exposition.

The parliament was indicative of a growing liberal modernist element, or "cosmopolitan habit," in American Protestant theology that was generally associated with the ecumenical and the social-gospel developments in the missionary movement.[77] The parliament was in this sense founded upon, and dedicated to, the advance of civilizational unity under Western leadership, an "impartial but not neutral" comparativist understanding of the Oriental and non-Protestant world, and an increased appeal to a nonsectarian and scientific secularism.

A Fellowship with Twilight.   Instead of the oft-repeated conservative refrain that "light can brook no association with darkness," John Henry Barrows emphasized an accommodationist rationale for the parliament—that "light does have" a creative and effective "fellowship with twilight." Barrows contended that a "fraternal" meeting of the "historic faiths" of the world would dramatize once and for all the essential Pauline message to all missionaries that, while "there is a certain unity in religion," there is finally no doubt that "Christianity is to supplant all other religions." This is because Christianity alone "contains all the truth there is in [other religions] and much besides, revealing a redeeming God."[78] Such a parliamentary approach to religion would not, as many conservative missionaries were claiming, "foster the bigotry of 'indifferentism,'" but would rather open up a "grand field for Christian apologetics" where the "distinctive truths" of Christianity could be triumphantly confirmed (that "Christianity alone shows . . . a mediator").[79] Most of all, it was the progressive civilizing power of Christianity that would be definitively established by such a meeting. Citing the support of illustrious Victorian figures from Britain such as the politician William Gladstone, the poet Alfred Tennyson, and the religious educator Andrew Fairbairn, Barrows emphasized that religion must be considered "one of the chief forces of progress" and that, clearly, it was the "light and religion of Christ" that had "led to the chief and noblest development of modern civilization."[80]

The driving motivation for the parliament was a version of the liberal form of comparativism and missionary inclusivism I have been tracing in relation to both Müller and Legge. The connection with the mission of the comparative science of religions as identified with Müller runs throughout Barrows's promulgation of the parliament ideal, but Legge was also expressly invoked as a kind of patron saint of the comparativist spirit in education and the missionary movement. In contrast with his later opinion about Legge's views concerning Confucius's "unreligiousness," Barrows at this time approvingly refers to "Professor Legge of Oxford" on the "intricate, delicate, and thorny" matter of comparative religions.[81] For Legge the issue was always a straightforward matter of Christian duty because, as he is quoted by Barrows, "the more Christian a man is . . . the more anxious he will be to do justice to every system of religion."[82] It is this liberal but militant accommodationism of the Parliament of Religions that most closely characterizes the spirit of Legge's 1893 revision of the *Classics*. In this sense, Legge's views in the 1890s may be considered not so much contradictory but consistently illustrative of this particular genre of comparative discourse at the end of the nineteenth century. The only jarring element is that the presumptive "impartial but not neutral" militancy that was always behind the rhetoric of accommodation, unity, love, and justice was especially accentuated at this time by parliamentarians such as Barrows and scholars such as Legge and Müller.

Anxious Justice. The suspicion among more conservative Christians was that "the very discussion of [the non-Christian] religions in the parliament would seem to put them almost on a par with Christianity and provide pulpits for their teachers."[83] As it turned out, the parliament did in the long run lend itself to more of a pluralistic belief in the parity of all religions than it did to the realization of Barrows's desire for a hastened Christianization of the world. The origins of a reverse mission of Oriental religions to the West (especially Hinduism and Buddhism) begins, in fact, with the popular effect in Chicago of heathen spokesmen such as Swami Vivekananda, Anagarika Dharmapala, and Shaku Soyen (who was assisted by a young D. T. Suzuki).[84] But these results had more to do with the intelligence of the Asian participants and the ultimate success of secular modernity in the early twentieth century than they did with any kind of ignorant naivete or demonic duplicity on the part of the parliament organizers in 1893. The aggressive toleration of late-nineteenth-century Protestant ecumenical inclusivism and scientific comparativism encouraged an active opposition to Christianity or even a denigration of religion altogether.[85] Especially in postimperial China, where highly refined native traditions of rationality seemed more and more to mesh with the radical secularity and modern unreligiousness of the West, it was relatively easy to dismiss the claim that religion was the essential spark necessary to recharge the batteries of civilizational progress.

An Immensely Dignified Chinese Doll. Like the reaction to the inherent unfairness and hypocrisy of the "equal but separate" justifications for segregation in the post–Civil War United States, the anxious justice of the impartial but not neutral strategy of late-nineteenth-century comparativism actually led to an uppity presumption among the "colored" representatives of Oriental religions about their own moral and religious equality with Christians. If the discussion is limited to only those examples pertaining to China and the fortunes of Kongzi and Confucianism, the Parliament of Religions may

be recognized as the first public Western forum for native Chinese statements about the relative merits of Confucianism and Christianity.[86] There
were several presentations at Chicago by native Chinese delegates, but the
most provocative was entitled simply "Confucianism." This address was
given by the Honorable Pung Kwang Yu, who was the first secretary of the
Chinese Legation in Washington, D.C. A public talk in Chicago by a representative of the imperial Chinese government takes on added significance
if we recall that it was being given at a time of extreme uncertainty among
Confucian reformers in China and in the tense aftermath of blatant racial
prejudice against the immigration of Chinese to the United States.[87]

Described as "a mandarin of the red button" who sat "bolt upright,
squarely facing" the parliament audience with "immense dignity and looking somewhat like a huge Chinese doll with a round and moonlike face,"
Pung offered an overly rambling presentation notable for its confident assertion of the distinctly undoll-like virtues of Confucianism and its respectful, but sometimes slyly sarcastic, unwillingness to concede the moral and
religious superiority of Christianity.[88] Pung's lecture really amounts to a dissertation on the deficiencies of the Christian missionary movement in
China, which too often failed to respect Chinese customs, particularly the
practices of filial piety and ancestral sacrifice. It was Pung's strong recommendation that missionaries should be better educated and should "set a
higher value upon scientific knowledge" and "be less zealous in religious
matters." Expressing the elitist perspective of a Ruist scholar-official, Pung
adds that missionaries should also "turn away from the low and vulgar" and
by so doing the "wicked will disappear" and "those that had in former times
avoided the sight of a missionary and had resisted his efforts to the utmost
will turn around and vie with one another in inviting him to teach them."[89]

Pung goes on to mention W.A.P. Martin as the best example of his ideal
missionary, an identification that Martin may not have wholly appreciated.
Pung's audacious recommendation of Martin by name also generally impli-
cated the manifestly liberal, comparativist, and secular methods represented in varying degrees by Candlin and Faber of the younger generation
and most famously by Legge of the older generation.[90] Pung even had the
brazenness to take up an old Leggian comparative technique that argued
for the validity of the Chinese ideal of filial piety in relation to the Fifth
Commandment "given by Moses and Christ": "Thou shall honor thy father
and thy mother."[91] Most disconcerting of all was that Pung had no qualms
about overturning the key assumption shared by both liberals and conservatives on the relationship of Christianity and civilizational progress. Pung
shrewdly notes that while "missionaries in China . . . often contend in their
controversial writings that the Christian nations of the West owe their material well-being and political ascendancy to their religion," it is really
"difficult to see upon what this argument is based." Subjecting his American

Christian audience to a miniature lecture on the necessary separation of religion and politics, Pung justly comments that "when teachers of religion speak of material prosperity and political ascendancy in such commendable terms, they, in fact turn away from teaching religion to propagating . . . theories of government." Pung even had the droll impertinence to suggest that Christ himself "proposes an entirely different end, which is to seek the Kingdom of Heaven. He certainly did not hold up the foreign masters that were exercising supreme political control over his own country at the time as an example worthy of imitation."[92]

This kind of presumptuous heathen assertion of the comparative principles of perspectival understanding and reciprocal justice was an outcome that, for many anxious conservative missionaries, only confirmed the extreme dangers of the liberal methods, no matter how aggressively militant or impartial but not neutral such methods claimed to be. The problem was that these methods—whether of the more radically secularizing variety of Martin and Candlin or the more guarded methods of Faber and Legge—left the door open for overly brazen heathens to mount their own Occidentalist hobby horses of comparative impartiality and equality. To be confronted with, and mildly taunted by, the doll-like, but distressingly clever, Pung must have severely rattled the confident composure of both conservative and liberal parliamentarians.

In the Wake of the Parliament.   The Honorable Pung's table-turning presentation was paralleled, and bettered, by several other charismatic Oriental spokesmen, among them, Swami Vivekananda and Anagarika Dharmapala. Not only did they speak fluent English, but also they were extremely persuasive public speakers for the Aryan religions of Hinduism and Buddhism. The unexpectedly challenging impact of these representatives of the major Oriental religions indicates that the parliament would be strikingly controversial. This was so much the case that, for years afterward, there was a spirited debate as to whether the parliament was prophetic of the coming postmillennialist triumph or the future humiliation of Christianity. In the simplest sense, the parliament's quest for religious unity ended up only dramatizing the real plurality of religions.[93]

This "wide divergence of opinion in the matter of the outcome of the parliament" was specifically noted in the pages of the *Chinese Recorder*.[94] Ultraliberal missionary participants in the parliament, such as the Chinese-garbed George Candlin, impulsively claimed that the meeting was of a "mountainous order of greatness" and a turning point in the "religious history of the world." Instead of fearing some "compromise of creeds" or "cheap moderation," missionaries should cherish the "charity and truth" that comparative methods brought to mission work. Above all else, missionaries should not be too proud to recognize the "great principle of reciprocity" that is at the heart of Confucius's system. For if Master Kong were to return to earth and see that the "West [was] in advance of the rest of the world," he, more than some overly antagonistic missionaries, would only emphasize that we "should learn the good and correct the evil."[95]

Barrows's Parliamentarian Sinecure.   The greatest defender of the unmitigated success of the parliament was none other than the hardly disinterested John Henry Barrows. Once an obscure Presbyterian churchman in the wilds of Chicago, Barrows had become famous as the primary organizer and leading spokesman of the parliament. Having become the leading American proselytizer of the parliamentary message of ecumenical unity and the comparative study of world religions, Barrows effectively dedicated the rest of his life to these causes. He went on to be both a peripatetic lecturer on "comparative theology" throughout the world and an innovative figure in American higher education.

His own retrospective assessment of the "results of the Parliament of Religions" was mostly a reiteration of the self-serving claim that the event was the "crowning work of the nineteenth century" and an inflated restatement of the well-known liberal inclusivist position on the postmillennialist "preparation for a Christianized world." The only really new element was his proud announcement of several pioneering efforts to bolster the study of comparative religions at all levels of American education. He referred specifically to a proposal to produce a manual of comparative religions for Sunday schools and to the efforts of the young immigrant intellectual Paul Carus to organize a parliament extension in Chicago. He also commended Mrs. Caroline E. Haskell's donation of funds to establish the Haskell Lectureship in Comparative Religions (Barrows was himself the first lecturer) and to construct an Oriental Institute building at the new University of Chicago.[96]

Parliamentarian Devil-opment.   The polarization of views on these issues was dramatically evident in the rebuttal to Barrows's talk written by Arthur F. Pierson, the editor-in-chief of the widely circulated *Missionary Review of the World,* and published in the next issue of the *Chinese Recorder.*[97] Pierson's presentation was a bluntly inelegant, but effectively argued statement of the old antagonistic thesis—namely, that the parliament's "attempted amalgamation of the one and only true faith and saving Gospel with the imperfect iniquitous, idolatrous systems of so-called 'religion'" was an especially evil "devil-opment" of recent missionary history. Pierson emotionally reported that he was particularly disgusted by the unseemly scene of "supposedly Christian" American women who went "wild with delight" and "scrambled over chairs" to get close to exotic speakers like Vivekananda. In the case of a Shinto priest "who threw mud at Christianity," these harpies actually ran forward after his lecture and "kissed him!" Such actions, combined with the effeminate "milk and water" compromise of the liberal position and the "false bombast" and skillful insulting of Christianity by Vivekananda and other Orientals (such as Pung), amounted to an abomination paralleled only by "Israel's dance with Baal."[98]

Pierson's discussion of egregious parliamentarian "mistakes" is a mostly conventional catalogue of familiar conservative complaints against the unmanly "indifferentism" of the liberal position (e.g., a "false leveling of all faiths to a common plane"; such events create a "bad precedent" and lead to further "devil-opment"; the damnable "substitution of laxity for liberality" and a failure to appreciate that "charity is not tolerance of error"; "too much presentation of an ideal heathenism" without any reference to such obscenities as the Kali cult or the "filthy holy men" of India; the "blasphemous" implication that "salvation is not in Christ alone"; and so on). By far the most serious charge was that the parliament, as in the case of the "lionized" Vivekananda or the "dignified" Pung Kwang Yu, had only given Orientals a forum for slander against Christianity and for "the propagation of false religions." Especially pernicious were the reports that the Japanese delegates to Chicago returned home with the "arrogant and boastful" claim that the parliament had actually documented the "weakness and folly of Christianity" and the "superiority of Buddhism." "Pray God," says Pierson, "that such a gathering may never again give occasion to the enemies of the Lord to blaspheme!"[99]

The Real Significance of the Parliament of Religions.   It is appropriate that Max Müller get the last word on these matters.[100] Given his general disdain for American dilettantes and his decision not to attend in person, Müller disingenuously lamented that the parliament organizers, Bonney and Barrows, did not make the "real purpose and scope" of the event "sufficiently clear." "At first glance," says Müller, it looked as if the parliament would be a "mere show," and, if anything, a sideshow to the greater "show of industry and art" at the Columbian Exposition. Instead, as a gathering of "representatives of the principal religions of the world" and a veritable "museum of faiths," it was a uniquely important event. Falling into his usual hyperbolic mode, Müller declares the parliament to have been "one of the most memorable events in the history of the world."[101]

After a brief discussion of the history of related meetings and councils, Müller raised the issue of the "real significance" of the parliament.[102] He indicates that the very possibility of a Parliament of Religion at the end of the nineteenth century hinged, first of all, on the simple fact of the increased "intercourse between Christians and Non-Christians," and, secondly and more importantly, on the growing search for some universal commonality among religions. Related to both of these developments was the gradual emergence of "respectful toleration" for "what is peculiar to each [religion], unless it offended against reason or morality." It was the influence of "honest missionaries" (such as Legge, although he is not mentioned by name here) and sensitive travelers that helped to "soften" the "feeling of aversion toward and misrepresentation of other religions."[103] The implication is that "honest" churchmen and laymen—such as those tolerant dilettantes and dabblers in Chicago—have a role to play in the spread of universal religious and moral values. But it is a preliminary and ancillary role that is completed only by an elite professional corps of trained Oriental scholars.

Not surprisingly, Müller claimed that the "publication of the *Sacred Books of the East*" contributed most "powerfully" to the "spread" of a "feeling of toleration" throughout the world. This new attitude is further described in terms of what Candlin called the Confucian ideal of reciprocal justice so that toleration of the other is seen primarily to be a matter of "honest" feelings of "kindliness for and the desire to be just to non-Christian religions." With paternalistic pride, Müller noted that his "parliament in type" (the *Sacred Books of the East*) had an advantage over the Chicago parliament. Even though the meeting in Chicago involved "living witnesses," it was only Müller's textual parliament that had the special authority of history: "[I]n the end what remains of the world of deeds is the world of words, or, as we call it, History." Books weigh more than living persons in the assessment of the real or universal significance of religions. "No religion," declares Müller, "has ever recognized an authority higher than that of its sacred book, whether for the past or the present or the future." Müller says that it was the absence of any appeal to inscribed and tested historical documents, and hence the "impossibility of checking the enthusiastic descriptions of the supreme excellence of every single religion," that interfered with the "usefulness" of the Parliament in Chicago.[104]

The "real significance" of the parliament was, consequently, that it called attention to the need for the careful study of the sacred books and the overall history of religions, a pursuit only properly and fully conducted by Oriental scholars. Too often, as seen in Chicago, the shared emotions of "respectful toleration" toward other religions engendered a false, even gushing, enthusiasm for a religious unity not subject to any certain documentary standards of significance. Only the more rigorous translation and comparative analysis of religious scriptures by Orientalists can establish a meaningful historical hierarchy of religious truth. From this higher academic point of view, then, the essential meaning, or "real significance," of a religion was often better understood by an unbelieving scholar versed in the language and ancient holy books of the tradition than by an actual living exponent of the religion.[105] Müller's underlying assumption was that, once historical evidence about religious beliefs and practices was properly assembled from the sacred books, it would be possible to prove definitively the actual superiority, and higher truth, of one religion over another. Needless to say, this higher, if not final, religion would prove to be Protestant Christianity.

Bold Generals of Understanding

Here the rhetoric and images of the biblical "whole duty of man" are interpreted in a more secular, but no less prophetic or provocative, impartial but not neutral way. From Müller's vantage, the imperial mission of finding universal truth was founded upon the privileged methods of a fully professionalized scholarship duty-bound and impartially dedicated to the difficult translation of alien texts and the comparative deciphering of historical categories and civilizational hierarchies. As argued in Müller's address to the Congress of Orientalists, it is this kind of specialized academic battalion that provides the boldest generals in the heroic struggle for universal understanding. More effectively, aggressively, progressively, and dutifully than the well-meaning but dilettantish churchmen and laymen of old, Oriental scholars prophetically assist in the creation of what Müller calls here the "universal communion of mankind" under the special "shared blood" leadership of Englishmen and Americans.[106]

By virtue of his active participation in the *Sacred Books of the East* project and his professorial identity as a sinologist during the last two decades of his life, Legge in the 1890s could surely count himself among Müller's "bold generals" of Orientalism. Given his Scottish and evangelical humility, however, he probably would have accepted only the rank of a sinological colonel in an Orientalist army of Aryan generals, but the point is basically the same. This does not mean that Legge would have agreed with all aspects of Müller's martial strategy concerning a final universal religion or even with his suggestion that the secular methods of scholars had completely replaced the theological procedures of missionaries. Legge's changing understanding of Confucius and Confucianism—that is, his movement to an appreciation of Kongzi's historical and moral "greatness," if not his full religious significance—underscores this common ground with the aggressive comparativism exemplified by Müller. In 1893, Legge retreated somewhat from his views on Confucian religiosity roughly sketched out in the *Religions of China*, but his final position on these matters was in keeping with his own postmillennialist theology, as well as the prophetic tone and assertive tolerance espoused at this time by academic Orientalism and the comparative science of religions.

EVERY SECRET THING AT THE END OF THE CENTURY

"The great mountain must crumble; / The strong beam must break; / And the wise man wither away like a plant" [Li ji II.I.ii. 20]. . . . Such is the account which we have

of the last hours of the great philosopher of China. His end was not unimpressive, but it was melancholy. He sank behind a cloud.... No wife... was by to do the kindly offices of affection for him.... He uttered no prayer, and he betrayed no apprehensions. Deep treasured in his own heart may have been the thought that he had endeavoured to serve his generation by the will of God, but he gave no sign.

. . .

[Confucius/Kongzi] was a Chinese of the Chinese; he is also represented as, and all now believe him to have been, the beau ideal *of humanity in its best and noblest estate.... Confucius cannot be thought to speak of himself... more highly than he ought to do.... He was conscious that personally he came short in many things, but he toiled after the character, which he saw, or fancied that he saw, in the ancient sages whom he acknowledged.... Emphatically he was a "transmitter and not a maker." It is not to be understood that he was not fully satisfied of the truth of the principles which he had learned. He held them with the full approval and consent of his own understanding. He believed that if they were acted on, they would remedy the evils of his time.... If in anything he thought himself "superior and alone," having attributes which others could not claim, it was in his possessing a divine commission as the conservator of ancient truth and rules.*

JAMES LEGGE, PROLEGOMENA, *THE CHINESE CLASSICS,* VOL. 1, 1893

Fear God and Keep His Commandments

In the years after the appearance of the revised edition of the *Chinese Classics,* Legge clearly preferred the quiet life of teaching and lecturing at Oxford to the more aggressive intellectual battles still being waged by the bold scholar-generals of Orientalism. In stark contrast with Legge, Müller maintained his usual frantic pace of professional activity and public engagement. Though he once in later life confessed to an acquired taste for reading superficial novels, Müller continued right up to the time of his death to edit (working on the *Sacred Books* as well as editing and revising various earlier books and articles), write, lecture, pontificate, quarrel, and indulge his penchant for academic politics. Even wracked with painful shingles and within a fortnight of his death in 1900, Müller felt compelled to dictate extensive galley corrections for a series of popular journal articles—interestingly enough, a three-part series on the "Chinese Religions," still the least appreciated of the major Oriental religious traditions even after the best efforts of Legge.[107] The one activity that Müller stood imperiously aloof from was teaching, especially from the time of his editorship of the *Sacred Books* in the mid-1870s and the creation of his special sinecure at Oxford. Müller saw himself as one of the glittering ornaments of scholarly research at Oxford and, aside from a few specialized graduate students (such as the two Japanese Buddhists), he avoided any regular teaching commitments at Oxford.

Legge maintained his own ornamental scholarship and continued a steady, if less prolific and glamorous, schedule of lectures and publications during his last years. But unlike Müller, Legge was wholly content to teach both beginning and advanced students and, twice during the academic year, to deliver his professorial lectures to all interested parties. In June 1894, for example, Legge wrote his stepdaughter Marian to complain about the eczema that had lodged amid his "bushy eyebrows." It was bothersome that this condition caused him to sleep longer than usual and thus lose many of his best working hours in the early morning. Despite these difficulties, he reports that, above all, he was "working very hard with [his] students"—an odd lot that, in addition to his elementary Chinese pupils (Mr. and Mrs. Kenmore from the Bible Society as well as, no doubt, his Davis Scholarship students), included several advanced students such as Arthur von Rosthorn (who had returned to Oxford after ten years of study in China) and a brilliant Japanese Buddhist scholar, Takakusu Junjiro. Legge was especially proud of Takakusu, who went on to be the first Oxford Honors School candidate in both Sanskrit and Chinese. In this same letter, Legge mentions that he was also preparing his two public lectures for the coming academic year on the "very strange and troublesome Chinese poem of the 2nd or 3rd century B.C. called the Li Sao."[108]

To the very end of his days at Oxford and in distinction from the elevated Pattison-Müller model of pure research, Legge upheld an ideal of the scholar-teacher very much in keeping with both the Jowettian liberal arts tradition and the Confucian emphasis on study and service. The life of the scholar-teacher may not have been as exciting as the exploits of the bold generals of scholarship like Müller, but it is clear that for someone like Legge "fearing God and keeping his commandments" primarily implied a relatively anonymous dedication to the basics of learning and education. This difference is aptly illustrated by the situations surrounding the deaths of these two great Orientalists. Müller, as noted, was engaged in editing various articles and dictating his autobiography while on his deathbed. Legge was more prosaically and dutifully involved with the teaching of his regular Friday class in elementary Chinese. Legge's diligent commitment to the routine fundamentals of scholarship and teaching at the end of his life in fact harks back to his earnest dedication to these same tasks at the very beginning of his career as a missionary in Malacca and Hong Kong.

Legge was never overly concerned with creating a public persona as a warrior-scholar who constantly fought in the great academic battles of the day.[109] It seems that, after he had finished with his contractual commitments to the *Sacred Books* (and after his hopes for several additional volumes on Zhu Xi and Song Confucianism failed to materialize), he spent very little time, if any, in collegial intercourse with Müller. Moreover, aside from maintaining his scholarly correspondence and taking care of various duties in connection with his ceremonial vice presidency of the Royal Asiatic Society in London, he was only minimally involved in professional activities outside Oxford during the last half decade of his life.[110]

This relative lack of interest in actively promoting his academic visibility and fame was not as a result of any diminished mental or physical prowess, since, aside from some increasingly irritating bouts with eczema and chronic partial deafness, he was remarkably hale and hearty almost right up to the hour of his death. As Legge himself noted during his eighty-first year, "my eye is not dim, nor is my natural force much abated."[111]

Also indicative of Legge's partial withdrawal from the scholarly battlements is the simple fact that, after 1893, he chose to focus his attention on topics of general Chinese literature and history (i.e., lectures and articles on poetry, novels, literary allusions such as the legendary Fusang tree, the philosopher and poet Han Yu, certain ancient emperors, the Ban family, and the Han dynasty).[112] These topics were mostly far removed from the aggressively controversial issues of archaic Chinese theism, the greatness and religiosity of Confucius, or the contemporary moral, educational, and political relevance of Confucianism. Given his growing appreciation of Zhu Xi and the Song Ruists, and the fact that he had started to work on these materials for Müller's series, it is truly remarkable that there is no further mention of these or similarly controversial texts during the last part of his life. According to Legge at the time he was proposing these writings for the *Sacred Books,* the Song materials raised important issues about the moral and metaphysical relevance of Ruism-Confucianism. Furthermore, as Legge said in 1893 in the preface to volume 1 of the revised *Chinese Classics,* Zhu Xi, the "Old Man of the Cloudy Valley," was someone whose views about the meaning of the classics "generally coincided" with his own.[113]

In the years from 1893 to 1897, Legge's image is one of an "old, simple, kind, and true" professor living out his years in quiet dedication to his educational duties. This is the hagiographical image created by Helen Edith Legge that I have amended throughout the discussion of Legge's career as a missionary and a scholar. Here, however, it fits with what is known of Legge's last days as the professor of Chinese at Oxford—that is, a routine of steadfast teaching and calm literary scholarship instead of any further public tilting at religious, intellectual, and political windmills.[114] Legge, as a Scots Nonconformist professor of an exotically irrelevant language, was always to some degree on the margins of university life, but there is reason to believe that in his waning years, in contrast with his earlier outspoken challenges to the accepted order, he gradually came to accept his respected, but peripheral, status within the cold bosom of Oxford.

The whole area of personal life and family intrigue is missing from this portrait and some indirect evidence leads us to believe that things were not always so perfectly placid. Legge's final years were clearly marked by frequent and loving intercourse with his large and growing brood of six children and fifteen grandchildren. These exchanges were certainly happy and rewarding for the old scholar and patriarch, but there is also a hint of darker stresses involving some sporadic rivalry (and money matters) among the off-spring of his two different marriages and jealousies related to the amount of affection and attention extended to his stepdaughter Marian and her family living in the vicinity of Oxford. From hearsay testimony one infers that there was also the powerful assimilationist allure of Oxonian-style Anglicanism and educated English middle-class society for many of the children, as well as the minor vexations of a widower's home-life seemingly dominated by the overly protective ministrations of his unmarried daughter, Helen Edith (affectionately called Edie). Several of these factors emerged openly after the great scholar's death (particularly the assimilationist trends concerning religion and Helen Edith's selfishly manipulative control of the old man's legacy) and continue to simmer down to the present.[115]

His End Was Not Unimpressive, But It Was Melancholy

Legge's last years were not "unimpressive," but—to draw upon his poignant portrait of the death of the teacher-scholar Confucius—it seems that they were somewhat clouded and chilled by the traces of a vague "melancholy." This sense of wistful sadness is especially suggestive of the attitude of someone who had honorably accomplished much in life but was in the end content to be ignored and surpassed by the greater, and more resolutely hypocritical, world. There is no reason to believe that Legge's last few years were filled with the kind of extreme "disappointment" and "bitterness" he attributes to Kongzi. His previous bouts of severe despondency understandably came about after the premature deaths of his two wives, and there is nothing here that suggests the dark depth of those feelings. Nevertheless, there are signs that in his final years he wearily felt periodic pangs of diminished usefulness, nostalgic sorrow, and bleak loneliness. At one point, for instance, he says that he frequently felt helplessly "feckless" in keeping up with his work and berates himself for "how little" he had accomplished. Interestingly, in this same revealing letter to Marian Hunt, he confesses that, while reminiscing about his childhood, he often had regretful thoughts about not having had a "wise and cultured mother or elder sister" to watch over "the development of [his] mental and moral development."[116]

Most of all, Legge tells us that he often felt physically and emotionally cold. Several times he remarks on the "bitterly cold" weather during winters in Oxford but, even more suggestively, he reports that in the spring of 1896 he was experiencing a kind of constant mistlike cold hanging about his person. This was, moreover, a feeling that "always increased" whenever he was away from his Keble Road home in Oxford and the ministrations of his caretaker daughter, Helen Edith. While starting his never finished "Notes of My Life" at around this same time in 1896, Legge also comments that he was frequently reminded of the lines from the *Book of Poetry* (*Chinese Classics*

[1860], 4:406; *Shi jing* II.vii.ix) about an old horse that vainly tries to run like a young colt.[117] These images of the plaintive chill and diminished abilities of old age recall Legge's favorite biblical passage, from Ecclesiastes (12:13–14), where the eponymous Hebrew teacher, sage, and preacher knew that at "the conclusion of the whole matter" there was only the "whole duty" of fearing God and keeping his commandments. All else is vanity, especially for those of "grasshopper gait and white haired" old age who foolishly try to keep up with the young (Eccles. 12:1–8). Whatever one's greatness as a scholar, the reality is that in the end all mortal life is brought low by itching patches of eczema and the putrid woes of death.

Fallen into Sorrow

There is another factor that has a bearing on Legge's emotions at this twilight of his life. I refer to his single major scholarly project at this time. This was Legge's work on the ancient anthology of miscellaneous verse known as the *Chuci/Ch'u Tz'u*, translated by Legge as *The Compositions of the [Southern State of] Chu*. Legge focused his attention on the longest poetic composition in this collection—the famous elegy to remorse and suicide know as the *Li sao*, or, as Legge renders the title, *Fallen into Sorrow*, attributed to the slandered Chu statesman Qu Yuan. It is not at all clear why Legge devotes so much time and energy to this single, rather Daoistically esoteric, poem after he had finished with the *Classics* and the *Sacred Books*. Whatever his reasons, he worked singlemindedly on this one poem for several years. It became a subject for his teaching and lecturing, and ultimately he produced a long three-part article analyzing and translating the poem. These published articles are interesting in their own right because they display Legge's typically fastidious approach to translation and even suggest a new concern for the folkloric context of meaning (i.e., the traditional dragon-boat festival associated with the drowning of Qu Yuan). The translations themselves were stylistically awkward and mockly archaic in the Victorian manner, but their technical accuracy, as recognized by Gustave Schlegel in the pages of *T'oung Pao*, was superior to earlier efforts by August Pfizmaier and the marquis d'Hervey de Saint-Denys.[118]

The mystery of this fixation on Qu Yuan and the poem *Fallen into Sorrow* is deepened when it is known that Legge agreed with d'Hervey's observation that "the Chinese have little aptitude for the composition of poems of great extent, requiring method and invention." According to Legge, the native "admiration" for a poem such as the *Li sao* is "a proof" of the Chinese "inferiority" regarding epic-length poetry.[119] With such "obvious contempt" for the content of the *Li sao* (not that Legge "had no feeling for poetry of any kind," as David Hawkes, the most proficient twentieth-century translator of the *Chuci*, unfairly says),[120] why did he spend so much time and energy on it? Part of the answer was unquestionably a matter of Legge's sense of scholarly duty: traditional Chinese commentators deemed this poem to be an important foundational literary work. After his work on the Confucian and Daoist classics, Legge entered into the whole ocean of "polite" Chinese literature and naturally sought out the ancient sources of Chinese poetry and belles lettres. In the case of historical romances, therefore, he refers back to the Yuan origins of *Sanguozhi Yenyi* (The romance of the three kingdoms). With regard to the more ancient and substantive tradition of poetry, he goes first (having already dealt with the classic of poetry) to the most famous poem in the Chu anthology of the second and third centuries B.C.E.

These methodological considerations do not entirely answer the question about the reason for this project's becoming so obsessive for Legge at this time. There is a degree of emotional attachment with Qu Yuan that goes beyond Legge's simple scholarly desire to produce a definitive English edition of this single obscure poem by a suicidal Chinese statesman. Legge actually admits as much when he declares that the *Li sao* may not be a "great poem" but nevertheless "awakens in the mind no small amount of sympathy with its author." There is, then, an almost autobiographical identification with the trajectory of Qu Yuan's life, especially his lifelong dedication to a course of "self-culture" and the disillusionment of his later years. Putting aside the "queer and absurd notions" of "Taoist fairy-lore," Legge characteristically says that he "admir[ed]" most of all Qu Yuan's sense of resolute duty—"his devotion to service, and his inflexible conviction of his own honesty and honour."[121]

Without being able to say so directly, Legge clearly felt a degree of special understanding and emotional sympathy with the sorrow and disillusionment at the end of Qu Yuan's life. Although there is no single dramatic instance of Legge's being slandered as was the Chinese poet, this study of Legge's often transgressive life shows us that he assuredly felt the cumulative effect of a whole series of small slights running throughout his career (e.g., by the London Missionary Society board and conservative missionaries, his intellectual mentor Müller, the Oxford University Press, the Nonconformist Union, his George Street church, the university honors examination committee, the Anglican overseers of Holywell cemetery, his fair-weather friend Fairbairn, sinological vituperators such as Giles and Lacouperie, and so on). In this way, Qu Yuan's plaintive disillusionment resonates with the vague disappointments of Legge's last years.

As the epitome of John Bunyan's good Christian, Legge does not sympathize with the fantastic Daoist wanderings of Qu Yuan's forlorn spirit or with the suicidal solution to his sorrows. Nonetheless, there is a sense in which Legge's partial identification with this ancient poet, like his evident sensitivity to the melancholy surrounding Confucius's last days, underscores his ability to find important lessons throughout a broad range of heathen Chinese literature—even for those "who profess to belong to the school of Christ." It is likely that Legge was not entirely conscious of the full implications of his own empathetic imagination, but even a qualified appreciation of the edifying significance of Qu Yuan and Kongzi's lives is remarkable. Whatever the extent of these conscious and unconscious identifications with heathen exemplars, we are given some important clues about Legge's own emotional state of mind during this final phase of his lifelong pilgrim's passage.

The Strong Beam Must Break

Recovering from unspecified ailments that caused him to cancel some of his public lectures during the academic year of 1896–1897, Legge reports that in March of 1897 he was under the medical care of his son-in-law, William Collier. His recovery was prolonged and, while he had the energy to work, he could only write in his study at home by supporting himself with his left hand and reclining across two specially arranged chairs.[122] By the coming of the Easter vacation and the beginning of April, he was better. With the prompting of his sons (James Granville and Thomas Morison) who were reacting to the recent intimations of their father's mortality, he was even able to begin his autobiographical "Notes of My Life." Writing with obvious relish and an engaging anecdotal charm, he hoped to finish the story of his life by the end of the month. Sadly this was never to come to pass since, for some unknown reason (most likely having to do with protracted health complications), he forever broke off his narrative in mid-sentence while describing his arrival in Malacca in the late 1830s.

Legge was mostly back to normal and, as he happily reports, in "good spirits" toward the end of the academic year and the arrival of summer. He actually rejoiced in the hope that, after more than three years, he was almost "entirely free" from his troublesome eczema, which had recently settled into the skin of his right ankle. He also mentions that, although he was able to travel about again, he had no great desire to go into London to witness the Diamond Jubilee procession of the "dear old lady," Queen Victoria. There was no need for such exertion since he was well acquainted with the majesty of the queen—after all, he was present at her coronation and had actually had a "private interview with Prince Albert and her in 1848."[123] For the present, he was more interested in preparing his courses and lectures scheduled for the forthcoming Michaelmas term.[124]

Beginning in October, the Michaelmas term of 1897 would encompass James Legge's last few months of life. The year of Legge's death is also notable for embracing various other events of significant transition and portentous anticipation. This was the year of the queen's Diamond Jubilee, an event that both marked the incredible imperial accomplishments of Victoria's long reign and, at the same time, pointed to the moral uncertainties

and terrible disasters of the coming Edwardian age.[125] The curious propin-
quity of death and anticipation in the year 1897 is additionally suggested by
such aforementioned occurrences as the publication of both the *War of the
Worlds* and *Dracula* as stories of a reverse imperialism. This was, moreover,
the year that Müller, at the age of seventy-four and a year after the singular
honor of being appointed to the royal Privy Council, attempted to settle old
scores by publishing his revisionary two-volume work on the *Science of
Mythology*. Perhaps the strangest of all Müllerian events at this time, however, was the presentation of a set of the *Sacred Books of the East* to the pope
in Rome.[126]

Three other events in 1897 display a noteworthy synchronicity with the
death of James Legge as the oldest of the second generation of Protestant
missionaries to China. Remarkably, the year of 1897 was the ninetieth anniversary of the Protestant missionary movement inaugurated by Robert Morrison's arrival in Canton in 1807.[127] This year also saw the return of the Congress of Orientalists to Paris, where these scholarly meetings first began in
1873, the year of Legge's final return from China. Most extraordinary is that
1897 turns out to be the year of Wang Tao's death in China at the age of sixty-
nine. Since his days as Legge's classical mentor and colleague, Wang had
gone on to a distinguished career as a reforming journalist in China. To some
degree because of his association with Legge and the School of Christ, Wang
was actively engaged in applying a revisionary understanding of Confucius's
"practical lessons" to the situation in China. Even though he died in obscurity, Wang's work and influence lived on in the coming revolutionary
changes in his country, changes that, as variously exemplified by Kang
Youwei and Sun Yat-sen, drew upon a reformist understanding of Confucianism and a socially conscious interpretation of Protestantism.[128] The linkage
of the transformative values expressed in the careers of Legge and Wang—
representing the combined lessons of liberal Evangelical Christianity, a
revisionary and enlightened Confucianism, and modern science and
technology—was especially embodied in the life of the young revolutionary
and future creator of Republican China, Sun Yat-sen. Sun met Wang in 1894
and then, in 1896 and 1897, lived in London where the aging Oxford sinologist introduced Sun to the dynamic young missionary Timothy Richard.[129]

He Sank Behind a Cloud

Appropriately enough, Legge's final pilgrim's passage would occur while
he was engaged in his life-defining occupation as a teacher and scholar at
Oxford. At the start of the term, he felt that he had overcome his difficulties from the year before. He uncomplainingly began his regular three-days-
a-week course in basic Chinese and, on October 28, publicly lectured on
"The Pan Family of Our 2nd Century" (devoted to the later Han dynasty

and Ban Zhao, the "authoress" and sister of the historian Ban Gu). At first his old vigor as the indomitable Scotsman and robust "gentleman farmer" seemed almost to return, but by the middle of November he became perceptibly more feeble. Suddenly after his regular class on Friday, November 26, he experienced what was described as a "paralytic shock." At some point before he became entirely incapacitated, Legge seems to have found the strength to rise from what would prove to be his deathbed and greet a "Chinese youth of humble origin and rank" (Sun Yat-sen?) who happened to be visiting Oxford at that time.[130] But later the same day, Legge fell into unconsciousness and his family was notified to gather ritually around his bedside in his Keble Road home. Speechless and in a coma for a day and a half, Legge had "passed behind a cloud" from which he would never reappear. To paraphrase what he had said of Confucius's death, the ailing professor went to his couch and after two days expired.[131]

The end came on Monday, November 29, which was only twenty-one days before his eighty-third birthday. There is no elaborate Victorian deathbed description of his demise by immediate family members, but Robert Troup, the Huntly churchman and historian, piously reports (doubtlessly based on family testimony) that toward the very end Legge's breath became "unusually fast and laboured." After a few moments, his breathing was quieter and slower. And "then it ceased" altogether. Troup assures us that the old scholar "died without the slightest spasm and without even a sigh." Those in attendance "looked sad to lose the presence of one they loved so well," but felt that it was a "blessing" to witness him "pass away so peacefully." All family members agreed that their beloved Papa and Grandpapa "simply fell asleep." In the best evangelical sense of the "pure of heart" who have done their duty and "shall see God," James Legge passed on to his heavenly reward.[132]

He Gave No Sign

Very much like Confucius, Legge remarkably "gave no sign" when he "passed through the dark valley." He gave no explicit audible signal of having dramatically achieved his higher destiny: "[h]e uttered no prayer" and "he betrayed no apprehensions." Just as in the case of the Chinese master, those in attendance were forced to rely on more subtle signs of a final blessedness. The implied sense of this style of quiet passage was that, even though he did not have a chance to give his dying testimony audibly, Legge's silent peacefulness at the end was sign enough of the righteousness of his life and the transformational nature of his last moments on earth. Here, in contrast with the imagined circumstances surrounding Kongzi's death, there was every "expectation of another life." Regardless of this difference and the sad fact that neither the Chinese sage nor the Scottish scholar gave any definite sign of what was finally and secretly in their hearts, both had diligently done their heavenly duties and both had willingly served their respective generations.[133]

No matter what is made of the piously routinized observations about the peaceful circumstances and triumphant Christian meaning of the old professor's death, the important point is that Legge himself provides us with the material for a more Confucian interpretation of all those who treasure humility, who are "fond of antiquity and are earnest in seeking knowledge there," and who constantly strove to attain the moral character of a "superior man." For both the classical Chinese master and the Victorian Oxford professor, death was made meaningful if, as the outcome of the whole course of life, one had honestly performed one's duty to Heaven by sympathetically teaching others the meaning and methods of moral cultivation found in ancient texts. Both seemed to feel that they were in possession of a "divine commission" to be the transmitters and transformers of ancient truth and rules. And both were able to live up to these commandments despite the "unsettlement in religion" and the "prevailing lawlessness" of their respective ages.[134] Both men, it must be said, were engaged in a lifelong educational mission. Both were, more than anything else, teachers.

Legge's Last Blackboard

Legge's last actions were in keeping with the whole course of his life. From his beginnings as a missionary in Malacca to his end as a professor at Oxford, he was forever the dedicated scholar-teacher. How fitting that he spent his last conscious hours teaching a few hardy students what he himself had started to learn with Samuel Kidd in London almost sixty years earlier—that is, the rudiments of the written Chinese language. To pass through the "dark valley" of death in this way was a perfect summation of his long pilgrim's journey. It is in this sense that, even though there are no firsthand accounts of Legge as a teacher in China or Oxford, we are fortunate in having some wonderfully suggestive graphic evidence concerning his methods as an elementary language instructor. The evidence in question is a photograph of the blackboard as Legge left it after his very last class on Friday, November 26 (see figure 37).

Robert Troup reports that the image of Legge's last blackboard was preserved because the pupils in Legge's last class (both of them!), upon hearing of his stroke after their class, wanted to have a permanent record of their distinguished teacher's ability to write Chinese characters "beautifully."[135] This is hardly the best conclusion to draw as the photograph shows the work of someone with a competent, but certainly not a perfectly fluid or near-native, calligraphic hand. Chalk or other Western writing implements were no substitute for a Chinese brush (allowing for the shaky hand of the aged). It is obvious, from other scratchy samples of his writing throughout his career (see his copybook, figure 38), that Legge—who was not known

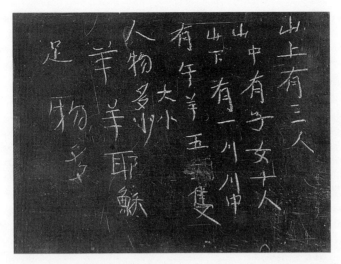

Figure 37. James Legge's last blackboard, Oxford, November 26, 1897. Photograph by Hills and Saunders, Oxford. University of Oxford, Bodleian Library, Legge Archive. Reproduced courtesy of the Legge Family Collection.

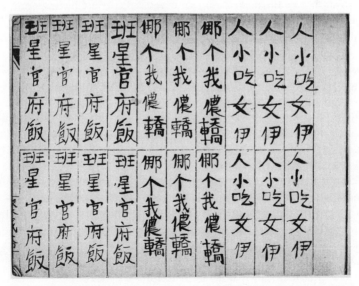

Figure 38. James Legge's Chinese practice book, 1878. Reproduced with permission of the Pitts Theology Library, Emory University (Atlanta, Georgia).

for "bardic talent," "oratory graces," or the perfect fluency of his spoken Cantonese vernacular—had never fully mastered the structural aesthetics of the Chinese script. This is not to say that he had not mastered Chinese; it is just that, in keeping with the classical themes defining his overall career as a London Missionary Society missionary-scholar and as an Oxford professor, he was primarily an expert in the archaic, artificial, and essentialized classical language found inscribed in ancient texts, in traditional commentaries, and in the writings and speech of the Chinese literati. Legge read, wrote, and spoke various kinds of classical and modern Chinese with varying degrees of proficiency.[136] It seems, however, that he was only a true master of the language as a reader-translator-decipherer of the classical written idiom of Chinese. To keep this in perspective it should be appreciated that, whatever Legge's shortcomings in writing characters and in speaking different vernacular forms of dialectical Chinese, no other Westerner of his generation in the nineteenth century could equal his expertise in the classical textual tradition.[137]

More interesting than Legge's calligraphic deficiencies is that this image of his last classroom blackboard gives us some unique insight into Legge's pedagogical methods in teaching basic Chinese, as well as some sense of his favorite illustrative examples and digressive topics. It is worth observing, therefore, that the blackboard records no quotations from the *Analects* or the *Book of Poetry*. Rather, what is seen (reading the eight columns of characters from the right to the left) is a series of very simple sentences and words designed to illustrate basic aspects of classical Chinese composition and grammar. For example, the first four columns telling of people and animals at different points on a mountain were clearly intended to demonstrate various simple aspects of sentence structure, word order, number, and form. The next columns display more random character groups showing such principles as reduplication (*yang-yang*, meaning several lambs or sheep) and the construction of generalized concepts from compounded opposites (*da-xiao*, big-small, for size; *duo-shao*, many-few, for quantity).[138]

Perhaps most curious is that, amid all of these prosaic linguistic issues, Legge has written down a compound word made up of *ye* and *su* (although *su* seems to be miswritten with an extra stroke). *Yesu* was one of the traditional Protestant missionary transliterations for "Jesus" and the fact that it has suddenly appeared in the middle of a general discussion of classical Chinese composition (the divine shepherd perhaps being suggested by the "sheep" of the previous characters) shows that, for Legge, even the simplest aspects of a heathen language such as Chinese could be used to communicate a higher religious purpose. Perhaps Legge was simply illustrating some of the grammatical and historical principles of transliteration first elaborated for the Chinese translation of Buddhist texts (the elucidation of which was one of Julien's major sinological contributions) or, more likely, he was reminiscing about some of the issues related to the translation of the New Testament into Chinese. Ever the good Evangelical Christian pilgrim, it seems that he could not help but think of Jesus in the middle of his elementary discourse on Chinese composition.

At the very end of his life, it was the principle of linguistic transliteration and religious "translatability" that gave meaning to Legge's career as a missionary, scholar, and teacher.[139] Whatever the explanation for Yesu's sudden digressive appearance within the context of this class on introductory classical Chinese, we are given some poetic license to see it as an unexpectedly ideal symbol for the transformational nature of Legge's overall career as the nineteenth century's greatest translator-teacher of things Chinese. For real transmission and transformation to take place in China (whatever the educational, religious, or political sense of mission), a transliterated Jesus/Yesu would have to be made present among the heathen otherness of the Turanian languages. So also would the British need to understand that the translations of the Chinese classics revealed universal moral and religious values. For in the Romantic and Protestant sense of Müllerian comparativism, the strange two-headed science of translation-deciphering was always secretly a matter of symbolic transliteration—forever a matter of the eternal phonetic permutations, marked by the arbitrary shuffle of written glyphs, of one spoken Word or Logos.

LAST RITES

The Master said: "If a man in the morning hear the right way, he may die in the evening without regret."
EPITHET FROM THE *ANALECTS* OF CONFUCIUS USED FOR JAMES LEGGE'S MEMORIAL
SERVICE, DECEMBER 3, 1897

By faith Abel offered to God a more acceptable sacrifice than Cain, through which he received approval as righteous, God bearing witness by accepting his gifts; he died, but through his faith ["the assurance of things hoped for"] he is still speaking.
HEBREWS 11:4

A Double Internment

In the best Anglican and Confucian sense, Oxford was a corporate believer in the importance of ritual, especially the richly emotional ceremonies associated with initiation and termination. The last rites for and burial of Dr. Legge in Oxford's Wolvercote cemetery constitute in this way an event that requires our mindful attention. Some twenty-one years earlier Legge was inaugurated into the office of professor on the floor of the Sheldonian Theatre. In the intervening years he had a respectful, but sometimes circumspect, relationship with his honorary alma mater. Now it was necessary to bring proper closure to the career of Oxford's first professor of Chinese, and this called forth the full pomp and circumstance of a major university funeral. It was almost as if the university, in belated rectification of earlier slights, had finally accepted the stubborn old Nonconformist. Only in death was it possible for the Scottish sinologist to become a full member of the university community.

The most powerful sign of this ultimate reconciliation is that the burial rites on December 3 involved an extraordinary double internment that finally corrected the most profound moment of alienation in Legge's career at Oxford. In keeping with her husband's last wishes and with the special permission of the vicar of Saint Giles and the Home Secretary, Hannah Mary Legge's moldering remains were exhumed from their resting place in Saint Sepulchre's cemetery. After sixteen years of dishonor, her still-intact oak coffin was raised and then conducted to Wolvercote, "where it was placed in the grave prepared for the remains of the Late Professor Legge," whose funeral was to take place in the afternoon. As the *Oxford Times* reported, this exhumation was a "somewhat unusual incident."[140] This was particularly the case for a community so hyperconscious of ritual proprieties, but in the end the intrinsic rightness of this postmortem reunion of a distinguished Dissenting professor and his spiritually fastidious wife overwhelmed all ecclesiastical and legal objections. Hannah Mary's internment with her husband was both an appropriate gesture of Christian justice and a fitting act of Confucian familial piety. Legge's wife was again by his side, now ready to perform "the kindly offices of affection for him."

In Memoriam

In death, Legge's Nonconformity was no longer a bone of contention for the Anglican establishment of the university and most of Oxford's collegiate and professorial ornaments turned out for the memorial service and funeral procession. Not one of the most elaborate of Oxonian funerals, it still involved a notably substantial five-carriage procession that, beyond the members of the family and university, included representatives from the Royal Asiatic Society (interestingly, Müller chose to march in this capacity), the London Missionary Society, the Religious Tract Society, the Congregational Union, the Oxford Union of Free Churches, and the Anti-Opium Society. This litany of organizations especially brings to mind the role of the London Missionary Society, which, somewhat like the university, was concerned with setting the record straight on its relationship with the deceased and to declare its undying "sense of obligation to him for the valuable linguistic service he had rendered in translating the Chinese Classics into English." Our awareness that this ringing affirmation was made only in hindsight helps to put the society's "high esteem" for the "missionary devotion" and "marked ability" of the deceased professor into perspective.[141] At the time of his death, Legge's international celebrity (somewhat similar to that of another transgressive Scottish agent for the London Missionary Society, David Livingstone) as the translator of the *Chinese Classics* and as a major contributor to the *Sacred Books of the East* really brought more honor to the society than the other way around.[142]

The university memorial service was conducted by Legge's old colleague and fellow churchman Andrew Fairbairn in the chapel of the Congregationalist Mansfield College. Fairbairn, like other of Legge's sometimes fair-weather associates, had misgivings about the aging sinologist's philosophical sophistication and his ability to keep up with the latest developments in Oriental scholarship.[143] But Fairbairn's critical concerns were never very serious, and the brief eulogy he delivers is a sincerely felt and poignantly insightful meditation on Legge's long career. Fairbairn opened with words that sound the proper chords of funereal recollection and praise. Legge was said to be distinguished by the "dignity which never fails to adorn the single-minded man." With a flourish of Victorian evangelical sentimentality, Legge is remembered to have been outstandingly "upright" yet "as gentle as a child." While "severely conscientious," he was gracefully "saved by his delightful humour from being either fierce or fanatical." A ritual litany of common attributes then follows. This may be most efficiently recounted here in list form, along with similar invocations from other eulogies.

> Fairbairn: [He was a man] . . . of fine presence, pure purpose, and courageous speech . . . whose high spirit a small school and imperfect sympathy could not break, whose wide and lofty aims a circumscribed sphere could neither narrow nor lower. . . . [He was] honest, childlike, manly, clean in soul, true in word, incapable of crookedness in policy or duplicity in speech, upright yet kindly in nature, charitable as only the just in conduct and the pure in heart can be, often homely, but never commonplace in conversation. . . .
>
> Troup: [He was someone of] sound sense, calm and clear judgment, practical wisdom, moral and spiritual worth, indomitable perseverance, sturdy independence of thought, thorough uprightness and straightforwardness and a genial and kindly disposition.
>
> Edkins and Parker: [In religious matters, he was marked by] the earnestness of his religious faith and his fairness to other religionists, . . . [and was always] broad minded, tolerant, charitable and utterly free from sanctimoniousness. . . .
>
> Parker: [In sum, he was a] stout, warm-hearted, hard-headed industrious Scotchman . . . [of] indefatigable zeal which led him, for more than fifty years, to raise habitually at 3 A.M. and work at his desk from three till eight o'clock.[144]

An Eminent Victorian?

This is an inventory of praise that cries out for some Lytton Stracheyish debunking of what seems to be the insufferable Victorian emphasis on an impossible goodness. While making allowances for the excessive rhetoric and pious "clean of soul" tone of the genre, we are struck by the general accuracy of these ritual tabulations of Legge's public persona. Except for some hints about his "independence," his flaws as a long-winded preacher and self-centered patriarch, and the possibility that he "thought too well" of the Chinese, the darker and more transgressive dynamics of his righteously patriarchal relations with his family and his Chinese associates, as well as with various religious, educational, and political institutions, must remain the hidden subtext of all such funereal discourse.[145] Be that as it may, a basic listing of Legge's most characteristic features would include traits in keeping with the above litany—especially his scholarly industry and early-morning working habits; his straightforwardness and simplicity of demeanor (which seems to be a coded reference to his general lack of Oxonian pretension and London urbanity); his sympathetic comprehensiveness regarding Christianity and other religions; his outspoken moral integrity; and his personal geniality and "pawky" humor.[146]

What really needs to be appreciated is that a Stracheyish debunking of such eminent Victorian virtues depends on the fact that, by the end of the nineteenth century, many of these evangelical attributes marked Legge as hopelessly out of touch with the prejudices and jaded attitudes of a certain secularized intelligentsia in London and Oxbridge. Later, after the extreme disillusionment of the First World War, Victorians found to be overly "clean of soul" were particularly susceptible to the denigration of a "Bloomsbury chic" bohemianism and a Freudian analysis of darker psychological forces and deceptive evasions.[147] But it also needs to be recognized that these were the same features (especially the sense of pious duty to both God and society) that often bothered and bemused many of Legge's younger contemporaries from both the missionary and academic sectors of Victorian society. These were the features that defined Legge's conventionalized and conservative Victorian image after the turn of the century and yet, at the same time, were foundational elements in his quiet challenges to various aspects of the established Victorian order of religion and education. Unfortunately, because many of these transgressive factors were muted even in his own lifetime, later commentators have either ignored Legge altogether or have, all too easily, fit him into the equally misleading categories of insipid evangelical scholar-saint or minor Victorian missionary-hypocrite.

Vincible Ignorance

It is to Fairbairn's credit that, for all of his ritual panegyrics, he focuses on some of Legge's transformative qualities as a religious and scholarly pilgrim. Very much a nonconforming religious maverick and scholarly pretender himself, Fairbairn is quick to acknowledge the courage of Legge's work on the Chinese classics and his open love of the Chinese people. From the very beginning of his missionary career, Legge was known for his moral indignation over wrongs done to the Chinese in the name of commerce, politics, or religion. Fairbairn also had the insight of a true comparativist by suggesting that the lesson of this was the universal one of Confucian ritual reciprocity. This was because in the mission field Legge was ever ready, even at the expense of murmurs of scandal, to teach his compatriots the meaning of not doing to a "Chinaman" what they would not want done to themselves.[148] In the spirit of Robert Morrison in Canton, Legge recognized that "English ignorance was as invincible and as mischievous as Chinese exclusiveness" and worked tirelessly to rectify these problems in the new colony of Hong Kong. Never just an "obscure" and politically irrelevant missionary or a mere translator and Oriental scholar, Legge embodied the best of a Christian loving conscience and a Scottish-Confucian dedication to education. Fairbairn rightly notes that in the early part of Legge's career he was very much a "genuine statesmen" who "impressed his mind and character on the infant colony." Legge, says Fairbairn, was "almost like an embodied conscience to the English merchants, and added to his pastoral office the attributes and functions of a moral judge."[149]

A Mission without Regret

The distinctiveness and power of Legge's scholarly views were likewise related to the "simple integrity" of his Christian love for the Chinese and his respect for "all that was good and true"—and seemingly theistic—in their ancient texts. Something of a Müllerian comparativist himself, Fairbairn was able to see that it was Legge's rare sympathetic comprehensiveness as a man and scholar that made him emphasize the "whole duty" of understanding others in relation to both the head and the heart—to know that "the primary condition of making the West influential in the East was to make the East intelligible to the West." This splendidly inclusive "dream of humanity and religion" was the basis for the overriding sense of a transcultural mission that progressively colored Legge's life as a Christian missionary in China and as a sinological Orientalist in Oxford. But recognition of Legge's scholarly significance did not go much further than this cautious acclaim during the waning years of the Victorian era. Thus the sinological evaluation of Legge toward the end of the century was already guarded in the "Nestor of Sinology" mode—an estimation ratified by Gustave Schlegel's careful obituary in the new quasi-official standard of sinology, *T'oung Pao*.[150]

Taking up the Oxford years, Fairbairn finished his comments by alluding to the "crowning sorrow" of the premature death of Hannah Mary and the way this event "mellowed" Legge's last years at the university. How fitting it was that "spirits so long parted" were "now one for evermore." Fairbairn finally could not help but indulge in a pietistic reverie about Legge's silent passage into blissful death: "Sleep sweetly, tender heart, in peace. / Sleep, holy spirit, blessed soul, / While the stars burn, the moons increase, / And the great ages onward roll." The salvation of Fairbairn's conclusion is that the tenderhearted Christian poetry of "sweet sleep" is nicely tempered by a very last quotation taken from Legge's translation from the heathen *Analects* of Confucius: "If a man in the morning hear the right way, he may die in the evening without regret."[151] God, the Right Way, and the *dao* all come together sweetly in death.

CONCLUSION

Darker Labyrinths:
Transforming Missionary Tradition, Sinological Orientalism, and the Comparative Science of Religions after the Turn of the Century

Historians don't want to write a history of historians. They are quite happy to plunge endlessly into limitless historical detail. But they themselves don't want to be counted as part of the limitless historical detail. They don't want to be part of the historical order. It's as if doctors didn't want to fall ill and die.

CHARLES PÉGUY, *L'ARGENT*, QUOTED BY PIERRE BOURDIEU, *HOMO ACADEMICUS*, 1988

Let us take the old saying, Divide et impera, and translate it somewhat freely by "Classify and conquer," and I believe we shall then lay hold of the old thread of Ariadne which has led the students of many a science through darker labyrinths even than the labyrinth of the religions of the world. All real science rests on classification, and only in case we cannot succeed in classifying the various dialects of faith, shall we have to confess that a science of religion is really an impossibility.

MAX MÜLLER, *LECTURES ON THE SCIENCE OF RELIGION*, 1870, 1873

DARKER ACADEMIC LABYRINTHS

By the end of the First World War, James Legge and Max Müller were forgotten Victorian sages. Both had passed behind the dark clouds of physical and intellectual conflict that had arisen so suddenly after the turn of the century. Each of them had become vaguely embarrassing antecedents to Pierre Bourdieu's *Homo Academicus,* who, in the dismal aftermath of the Great War, was more fully and faithlessly imbued with a critical *habitus*—a system of thought and action that was broadly secular, scientistic, specialized, historicistic, positivistic, and frequently nonreligious or even antireligious.[1] Academic life had become aggressively rationalistic and often agnostic—or, to adopt the growing consensus among professional sinologists during the early twentieth century, quite "Confucian" in its concerted efforts to keep the spirit of religious belief and the subject of religion at a distance from the practicalities of moral learning.[2] In this climate, Legge and Müller too obviously epitomized an earlier transitional era in which a personal Christian faith, however liberal and transformative, and scholarly interests focused on religion, however exotic, Oriental, and comparative, ruled intellectual life.

In the "darker labyrinths" of the early twentieth century, academic discourse increasingly classified religion as an epiphenomenon of the more foundational material and social realities of cultural development. Religion seemed to be only a powerful, but waning, illusion generated by the earlier superstitious stages of "savage tradition" and sustained by the retarded history of the Orient. Furthermore, sectarian theological attitudes toward and methods of knowing other traditions, especially as embodied by Protestant missionaries in Oriental and Savage Lands, were commonly branded as hopelessly backward and narrow. Religion however defined, sacred books of whatever ilk (including the heretofore sacrosanct Christian Bible), and overly demonstrative affirmations of religious belief and theological method were all felt to be largely antithetical to the rational and progressive forces animating the rapid development of the natural and human sciences within European and especially American universities.[3]

In many instances within the burgeoning learning factories of higher education in the Western world, religion disappeared as a distinct and integral subject of significant academic interest. The scientific concerns of the new humanistic disciplines turned toward the observable realities of cultural life to the point where, allowing for some important national differences, the specialized study of religion was mostly left to a few isolated professorships in universities and, more commonly, to those increasingly marginalized theological scholars who inhabited church-related colleges, seminaries, and divinity schools. After the success of Müller's *Sacred Books,* the public notoriety of the Parliament of Religions in Chicago in 1893, and the first efforts toward international disciplinary organization immediately after the turn of the century (the first international congress for the academic study of religion was held in Paris in 1900, the second in Geneva in 1904, and the third in 1908 in Oxford, administered by John Estlin Carpenter, Legge's and Müller's young Unitarian colleague), the great promise of a general academic discipline known as the "comparative science of religions" or *Religionswissenschaft* languished at the fringes of mainstream university discourse.[4] In answer to Müller's famous lectures of 1870 setting out the agenda for a brave new comprehensive discipline focused on the nontheological study of religion (see the epigraph on page 511), the greater academic world of the early twentieth century generally concluded that the erstwhile "science of religion" really was an oxymoronic and hopelessly biased impossibility.

The academic vitality and popularity of the nineteenth-century science of religion was dissipated both by the withering of the comparative method and by the growing secular climate within universities.[5] This meant that, if the professionalized academic study of religion continued at all within universities, it was generally subsumed under other, more established historiographic and social science disciplines or came under the purview of a few chairs devoted to the study of particular religious traditions (many of which were still conducted in an apologetic manner). These changes were dramatized by a decided shift away from the increasingly discredited and unfashionable rubric of comparative religions to a delimited and less ostentatious label, the "history of religions"—a revealing alteration of nomenclature that signaled a sea change in the overall cultural discourse associated with religion.[6]

Throughout most of the first half of the twentieth century in both Europe and North America, therefore, religion was generally trivialized in relation to the greater academic concerns of the university. The study of religion that persisted within the walls of academe was reductionistically left to those within the departments of history (Raffaele Pettazzoni), psychology (Sigmund Freud), economics (Karl Marx), sociology (Emile Durkheim, Max Weber), and ethnographic anthropology (Arnold van Gennep, Franz Boas), who claimed to deal with the actual constituent aspects of human experience.[7] In this kind of intellectual and institutional climate, the scholarly contributions of missionaries (or ex-missionaries) and the study of missionary history were simply beyond the pale. It was one thing to be tainted by association with comparativism or Müllerian humbug; even worse was the disreputable matter of individual missionaries and missionary tradition. These were subjects best left to the parochial assessment and apologetic debate conducted within the seminary. To be sure, ex-missionaries and sons of missionaries continued to populate the ranks of many Oriental disciplines (especially sinology) roughly down to the Second World War. However, unlike the Victorian Indologist Monier-Williams and the sinologist Legge, who directly or indirectly sought to further the Christian missionary enterprise, this newer generation of missionary descendants found that it was necessary to maintain some explicit demarcation between their personal commitments and their professional academic lives. This boundary line wavered considerably, but nonetheless became increasingly rigid throughout the first half of the century.

Legge is a prime example of the general fate of many missionary-scholars who crossed over to an academic career. Not too long after the turn of the century, his significance for the liberal transformation of the Protestant missionary enterprise, the professionalization of sinological Orientalism, the reform of Oxford University, and the development of a comparative science of Chinese religions was almost completely obscured. Throughout most of the twentieth century he was usually remembered, if at all, as merely an ex-missionary and translator—all in all, a distinctly minor Victorian figure. Furthermore, when measured against the highly technical philological expertise of Édouard Chavannes, Paul Pelliot, and Bernhard Karlgren, the ethnographic, sociological, and historical sophistication of J.J.M. de Groot, Marcel Granet, and Henri Maspero, or the avant-garde literary style and Bloomsbury sensibility of Arthur Waley, Legge was no longer considered much of a sinological pioneer or even a very good translator of the Chinese classics. In this way, Legge was largely stereotyped as an indefatigable, though quaint and stilted, Victorian translator with an irritating missionary bias.

French Dismissal and Yang's Assessment

With the resurgence of the French-Continental sinological tradition after the turn of the century, there was a growing scholarly tendency to dismiss Legge's interpretive conclusions about Chinese tradition as hopelessly antiquated—particularly because they tended to promote a biased missionary conviction about archaic high gods and the religiosity of the Confucian tradition. It was preferable to put him back into the category of a mere translator without any significant hermeneutical insight.[8] In the more highly professionalized and specialized disciplinary context of academic sinological Orientalism emerging in the 1890s and after the First World War, it became more or less the orthodox scholarly position that Confucianism, and the Chinese elite "great tradition" generally, was uniquely rationalistic, agnostic, nontheistic, nonmythological, and nonreligious.[9] The irony of this situation was that, by way of extending Absalom Sydenstricker's prediction about turn-of-the-century Ruist scholars in China embracing an agnostic scientism from the West (i.e., their appropriation of the Enlightenment agenda of their fellow European literati), Western sinological scholars were simultaneously and synergistically coming to the same kind of overtly secular conclusions about the "greatness" of Chinese tradition. Western sinological discourse in the early twentieth century basically returned to the position that China was a special case, a position staked out centuries before by anti-Jesuit Dominican clerics and by the anticlerical French Enlightenment *philosophes*. The strangeness of this position is that it also relied upon a selective interpretive appropriation of Legge's translations and opinions on Chinese tradition, as well as the views of native Ruist scholars imbued with a modern Western Enlightenment perspective on religion.[10]

The fulfillment of these developments came about after the Second World War when, as an artifact of strategic military and political interests during the war, Oriental scholars tended to identify with regional areas, the modern period, and specific social scientific disciplines (political science, sociology, history, economics, anthropology, etc.). In this sense, sinologists (as well as other Oriental scholars) were often no longer aware of, or concerned with, their own disciplinary history and found mock solace in the universal rationality and quasiobjectivity of their particular academic methodologies. Needless to say, the significance of an antiquated missionary scholar such as Legge, the role of Kongzi and religion in China (especially in a modern China, which had become officially, and perhaps naturally, Marxist and atheistic), and the overall nature of sinological Orientalism were mostly extraneous issues for professional academics doing some version of Chinese studies.

The long-term effects of the confusion over Legge's evaluation of Kongzi-Confucius and the revitalization of the old Jesuitical French *philosophe* tradition of sinology are aptly illustrated by the brilliant Chinese American sociologist of religion C.K. Yang. It was Yang who rightly observed, in his pioneering work on *Religion in Chinese Society* (1961), that Legge, in particular, and Giles (and, I may add, the revived French-Continental tradition imbued with Enlightenment sentiments, the secular attitudes of the modern academy, and new Durkheimian and Weberian sociological perspectives) were responsible for foisting an image of the "agnostic character" of Confucius and Confucianism upon later generations of European and American scholars. More accurately, it was the often distorted interpretation of Legge's position that was influential in shaping later sinological discourse, but Yang's general point is well taken. These factors, as well as an overweening emphasis on nonreligious or purely humanistic classical philological studies (to the exclusion of the Leggian-Müllerian *Sacred Books* coloration given to the Chinese classics) and the views of the Chinese educated class, meant that sinological Orientalists after Legge commonly "assigned a relatively unimportant place to religion in Chinese society."[11] In this way, several generations of Western and native Chinese sinologists in the twentieth century simply trivialized or blithely ignored "the universal presence of religious influence" at all levels of Chinese tradition.[12] It was not until these views were challenged in the 1960s and 1970s by Yang and others that the whole crucial, but sorely neglected, issue of Chinese religious history, in all its multifaceted cultural complexity, was rediscovered. These developments were aided at this time by a broad cultural fascination with religious experience and Oriental religions and by the revival of the academic or scientific study of world religions in American and European universities.[13]

These considerations indicate the difficulty of placing and judging Legge in the late-nineteenth- and early-twentieth-century history of the human sciences. Given his evolving approach to transcultural translation and comparative interpretation, it may be said that he was poised between an old theological hermeneutics of trust and a more thoroughly suspicious, destructive, and modern method of shifting symbolic sands. It is exactly because he teetered upon this methodological cusp that he has been so difficult to classify. Because Legge was typecast primarily as a missionary translator and seemed, in terms of his scholarly methods and comparativism as an Oxford professor, to be neither wholly old-fashioned nor newfangled, it has been convenient to simply ignore him.

Missions Secularized and Ignored

This drastic turn of events concerning the intellectual and cultural relevance of a hyphenated missionary-scholar such as Legge and missionary tradition in general was conditioned by attitudes already present toward the end of the nineteenth century among academics with both liberal religious and reformist educational commitments. Like Legge, many of these professional scholars came out of a missionary or clerical background and were affected by the comparativist spirit emerging both in the missionary movement and in academic life. Ordained dons such as Benjamin Jowett at Oxford recognized, for example, that new methods of knowledge and conversion were necessary in the larger, and more recalcitrant, world of Oriental nations, methods that were "safer and less liable to abuse" than were the proselytizing techniques of the old missionary movement. The modern world had entered a new, more secular age of civilizational transformation and progress powerfully promoted by a mission of government, science, and education "rather than of churches or individuals." Instead of fearing that such a secularized mission based on comparative, moral, and social principles might diminish "some of the distinctive marks of Christianity," Jowett emphasized that "the increase of justice and mercy, the growing sense of truth, even the progress of industry, are in themselves so many steps towards the kingdom of heaven."[14] This was, as we have seen, a dutiful methodological and moral truth that Legge came to embody in the long course of his pilgrim's encounter with Chinese tradition.

The problem was that, regardless of the increase of sympathetic comprehensiveness and the expected realization of God's design, such liberal and comparative perspectives of mission and sectarian religion too easily lent themselves to governmental, scientific, and academic agendas that had very little faith in God's providence or in a future "kingdom of heaven." It is in this sense, particularly after the great cataclysm of the First World War had smashed most pious assumptions about the progressive realization of God's kingdom, that the rapidly expanding research universities of the early twentieth century imperiously preferred to emphasize their educational and civilizing mission over any continuing association with the old Protestant mission to convert the heathen nations of the world. Moreover, whatever evangelical missionary interests persisted within the academy at this time were mostly of the transformed comparativistic, Leggian, and social gospel varieties that were appearing at the end of the nineteenth century. The enthusiasm for such a transformed missionary enterprise was, however, primarily among students rather than among university faculties concerned with furthering their own specialized professional and disciplinary interests. The fact is that, until recent revisionary efforts in the 1980s and 1990s, the cultural history of missionary institutions and personalities was ignored within the secular academy. This state of affairs is not so much a "mystery," as one observer put it, but rather another aspect of the overall secularization of the forms and institutions of knowledge in the twentieth century.[15]

The underlying irony of these academic developments, particularly in America, is that in many respects the modern research university was born and bred by liberal transformations within Protestant evangelical tradition. However much the academic institutions of the early twentieth century embraced a manifestly secularist agenda and shied away from "heavenly kingdoms" and the study of religion, it is evident that these same institutions were still being covertly driven by much of the same evangelical fervor and disguised Protestant rhetoric that characterized the nineteenth-century missionary movement. Although the coming of God's "heavenly kingdom" was no longer an issue, there was still a compelling utopian need to build a more perfect earthly empire. We have already witnessed the submerged presence of a Protestant strategy of interpretation, and its attendant anti-Catholic and anti-Semitic rhetoric, in Legge's sinology and in Müller's science of religions. Thus the interpretive procedures in many of the human sciences often presuppose only a transposed variation (in either its late-nineteenth-century "comparative" guise or in the more strictly secularized and specialized twentieth-century form) of the Protestant essentialist paradigm of the singularly "pure" (embracing such common nineteenth-century tropes as early or original, philosophical or mystical, poetic or mythological, classical, written, prophetic, spiritual, and moral) and the syncretistically "corrupt" (with the associated metaphors of late or degenerate, religious, prosaic or ritual, popular, vulgar, oral, priestly, materialistic, and moralist). There are other examples of the hidden religious foundations of nonreligious, and often stridently irreligious, forms of academic discourse, but let me only note additionally that the early history of sociology in the modern American university often reveals a deeply repressed indebtedness to postmillennialist evangelical Protestantism.[16]

Consumptive Comparisons

Another important factor in these developments at the turn of the century concerns the dramatic rise and undignified fall of comparativism in the Müllerian philological-historical and the Tylorian evolutionary-speculative modes. By the end of the nineteenth century, the old—and almost all-pervasive—comparative spirit was on the defensive. Comparativism, which grew out of the global encounters with other prehistoric and historical cultures, religions, and languages, had, in all of its immense excess and overblown confidence, turned back on itself and, like the alchemical Ouroborous, had started to consume itself as the privileged method of the human sciences. In addition to this, the confusing clashes between the Müllerian and Tylorian comparative methods seemed to swallow up religion (whether historic or prehistoric) as an independently meaningful datum of human experience.

Language and culture survived this autophagous operation in their continuing association with more regionally discrete and speculatively limited philological, historical, and functional methodologies. The study of religion was left without flesh and bone, substance and discipline, and seemed to evaporate into the shifting mists of various psychological, social, and historical forces. Operating with the fundamental principle of "classifying and conquering," the comparative method had reached a point where its surprising linguistic classifications and brash evolutionary explanations could no longer be sustained. The popular success of the comparative method in all its nineteenth-century guises was its own undoing. The self-devouring nature of the comparative method during the first part of the twentieth century, like the self-destructive conflict among the great imperial nations of the world, is an aspect of intellectual history that is too far-reaching and convoluted to be analyzed in any depth here. Furthermore, much of the disciplinary and institutional history related to different kinds of Orientalism and the study of religion is yet to be written or even fully appreciated.[17] I would maintain here only that the fledgling disciplines known as sinology and the science of religions had, in particular, a special relationship with the changing fortunes of comparative attitudes and methods. It is this special, and at times peculiar, association with comparativism that accounts for much of these disciplines' strangeness—that is, their status as the most forlorn and orphaned offspring of the established humanistic disciplines.

Instead of a quixotic quest for linguistic roots or evolutionary principles linking traditions into various cross-cultural families and developmental schema (or even some grander monogenetic primordium that mirrored the biblical account), there was a growing awareness that many of the linguistic and cultural categories (this included the Semitic group, but also especially the so-called Turanian family typically used to classify Chinese) were without the substantial linguistic and historical foundations established for the Aryan family. Moreover, the lack of any real evidence for the more aggressive evolutionary suppositions (especially those associated with Edward Tylor, Herbert Spencer, and James Frazer) led influential anthropological commentators such as Franz Boas at the end of the Victorian era to insist upon a strictly limited form of comparison restricted to particular regional units where causal connections among different cultural phenomena could be demonstrated temporally and spatially.[18]

The effect of this kind of timely and judicious criticism was to sever philological and historical methods from both Müllerian and Tylorian comparativism. This more limited, regionally discrete, polygenetic, and agnostic approach to cultural explanation represents a naturalization and secularization of the hidden religious implications of the old comparative search for the ultimate biblical taproot of all families, races, languages, and religions. From this point on, humanistic methodology and disciplinary identity within the university were best limited to fields or subject matters associated with discrete cultural or geographical regions. In emulation of the natural sciences, Boas and others argued that comparative interpretation had significance for phenomena only when, as a kind of biological reproductive link, there were clear historical, or homologous, causal relations.[19] Needless to say, it was not easy to prove cross-cultural homologies and, in the special case of sinology, various pan-Egyptian, pan-Aryan, and pan-Babylonian explanations of Chinese linguistic and cultural origins collapsed in the face of such critical demands. The dismissal of any sort of cross-cultural comparative concerns and revived convictions about China's unique linguistic and cultural heritage and general lack of any significant religiosity and mythology became, in fact, the hallmarks of sinology throughout much of the twentieth century.

SINOLOGICAL STRANGENESS

Because of its loftiness, and its sheer size, Chinese thought remained the most difficult peak for Europe to scale. China's linguistic instrument appeared in a formidable solitude, bewildering the mental habits of the West, rendering the problem of equivalences among languages almost absurd, and refusing to allow its closed system to be drawn into the comparative school.

RAYMOND SCHWAB, *THE ORIENTAL RENAISSANCE*, 1950

The Most Difficult Peak

More than other forms of Orientalism at the end of the nineteenth century, sinology wholeheartedly embraced the movement away from comparative speculation and tended to remain a closed disciplinary system singularly proud of its subject's cultural uniqueness and classical sophistication, as well as its own heroic mastery of an utterly incomparable language. In keeping with Charles Péguy's observation quoted at the head of this chapter, sinologists were on the whole methodologically shy and were most often content "to plunge endlessly" into the limitless historical and literary detail of the Chinese *totum scribile*. The isolated and insular nature of sinology down to the time of the Second World War may even be seen as the underlying source for a certain kind of outsider's psychology that, as powerfully exemplified by both Stanislas Julien in the nineteenth century and Paul Pelliot in the twentieth, characterized some professional sinologists—that is, a defensively erudite philological persona coupled with an arrogant pedantry and a prickly aversion to interdisciplinary interlopers.

This combativeness often led to highly ritualized battles among sinological specialists (e.g., the fights between Julien and Pauthier, Legge and Giles) that strangely rehearsed earlier Protestant term question theological debates over missionary methods and biblical translation. It appears that the secular combat was significantly different because it was ostensibly more intellectually open and publicly accountable than were the fights among missionaries. Yet at a deeper level of discourse, it may simply be that the essential issues and emotions were only being ritually transferred from one esoteric and sectarian elite to another more secular, though no less hermetic, academic clergy. Whether one or the other is really more public, open, or disinterested is often methodologically and morally ambiguous. In either the sectarian religious or secular academic case, the outcome seemed to hinge as much on the discursive faith of the particular learned community—implying commitment to a particular orthodoxy of method and meaning and the pronouncements of authoritative spokesmen such as Pope Gregory, Bishop Burdon, the London Missionary Society, Max Müller, Franz Boas, the French Academy, or Édouard Chavannes— as it does on a careful consideration of the textual evidence and putative facts.

When comparative and interdisciplinary insights were sporadically brought to bear on sinological questions, as they are in J.J.M. de Groot's ethnographic perspectives, Marcel Granet's Durkheimianism, and Arthur Waley's use of anthropology, China maintained its special aura of difference and diffidence. The comparative implications of such findings were often devalued as only erratic or insignificant deviations from those scholars' true brilliance as sinological translators and historians. Supportive of this disciplinary isolation and obsessive concern for precise philological procedures, the translation of basic texts associated with the elite tradition, and profound but regionalized historical analysis (in the manner of Chavannes, Pelliot, Maspero, the École française d'Extrême-Orient, and *T'oung Pao*) was the fact that attacks on Müllerian methods as applied to China were even more pointed and personal than was Boas's rejection of Tylorian evolutionary comparativism.

As Ernst Eitel was showing as early as the 1870s in the pages of the *China Review*, the shortcomings of the comparative method were especially obvious in studies of Chinese language, culture, and religion. For Dr. Eitel, who was educated in Germany, the difference was a matter of a fully professionalized sinological Orientalism devoted to specialized research as distinguished from the amateur dabbling in facts and theories by various kinds of hyphenated and part-time sinological comparativists. It would not be wrong to detect here a whiff of an old nationalistic disparagement of the British tradition of the amateurish gentleman scholar compared with the more professional methods of continental, especially German and French, scholarship. By the end of the century, neither Joseph Edkins and Terrien de Lacouperie's wild sino-Babylonian speculations, nor Legge's much more modest Müllerian suggestions about religion (as outlined in his *Religions of China*), provided any convincing evidence for the relevance of comparative methods in the understanding of Chinese tradition. If anything, the seeming absurdity of many of Edkins's and Lacouperie's ideas served only to hasten the demise of comparativism in relation to China.

The culmination of the attacks on comparative approaches to Chinese tradition came at the end of the Victorian era and were reinforced at this time by Boas's rejection of anthropological comparativism and by the continuing controversies over Müller's methods and conclusions. Gustave Schlegel mounted the first of these definitive assaults on Chinese comparativism and on Lacouperie in 1891, and a young German sinologist, Otto Franke (1863–1946), continued the attack with an influential article in the *China Review* in 1893. Franke emphasized that the "misty" and "hasty" theories of the Chinese philological comparativists (such as Edkins, John Chalmers, and Thomas Kingsmill) had completely failed to win the respect of the "real science of language" established by Franz Bopp and August Schleicher. Müller was conspicuously absent from the list of scholars associated with the so-called real science of comparative philology, and Franke drives his point home by calling attention to Müller's faulty assessment of Chinese linguistic matters (that is, his idea based on the authority of Stanislas Julien that many Chinese words were actually roots). Most of all, Franke strongly rejected Edkins's quasi-theological theorizing about the "common origin" of all languages and the significance of Chinese as a kind of monosyllabic "primeval speech." For Franke, all such theories were hopelessly flawed and should forever be abandoned.[20] Some six years later, another, more senior German sinologist, Paul Georg von Möllendorff (1847–1901), underscored Franke's misgivings and argued against the "premature comparison" of different linguistic and cultural families. Pleading, like Boas, for a "limited" philological and historical approach to such matters, Möllendorff supported the agnostic and polygenetic principle that it was impossible to know anything at all about the "ultimate origins" of languages, cultures, and religions. It was far better, particularly regarding the special case of China, to restrict one's purview to the specific circumstances of Chinese classical literature and history.[21]

Unfortunately, Müller became Legge's most vocal champion on the perplexing matter of comparative approaches to Chinese religion.[22] It is almost as if Müller's praise of ("my friend") Legge's "important discoveries" about Confucianism at the turn of the century led to their more rapid dismissal by later sinologists who greatly preferred a Confucius without any religion or comparative associations at all.[23] Certainly it was better for professional sinologists to remember Legge as the great translator and scholar of classical Confucianism rather than as an early practitioner of the comparative science of Chinese religions and as a disciple of the increasingly discredited solar mythologist, philological charlatan, and alleged plagiarist Müller.[24] Published in the widely read periodical the *Nineteenth Century*, Müller's articles on "The Religions of China" too triumphantly stressed that Legge's findings concerning an ancient Chinese sky god or High God (Shangdi, Tian) fundamentally verified Müller's own theories about the linguistic and "naturalistic" origin of religious beliefs. By the time of the Second World War, High God theories of this nature were easily attributable by secularly inclined scholars to the conscious or unconscious bias of religiously oriented interpreters such as the Kantian Romantic Müller, the Evangelical Legge, or (in the most elaborate sense in the twentieth century) the Catholic priest Father Wilhelm Schmidt.[25] It was preferable for sinologists, with the powerful validation of native Chinese scholarship, to fall back on the real ambiguities of the classical texts and to adopt an agnostic attitude toward all such unwieldy and theologically suspicious issues. After all, it was this nonreligious, if not atheistic, position that seemed to fit so neatly with the general humanistic and secular assumptions of the Great Tradition promulgated by many Ruist scholars past and present (e.g., C.K. Yang's views on these matters). These sentiments, which corresponded so well with the attitudes of the Western literati in the twentieth century, came to a head in 1919 with the revolutionary May Fourth student movement, fostered by Chinese intellectuals and students who vigorously rejected all religion (Chinese and Western) as outdated superstition and passionately embraced "Mr. Science" and a Western-style modernization.

The Scholarly Synergy of Chinese Singularity

The turn toward hyperspecialized regional concerns and its accompanying philological and cultural particularism was seized upon both by chauvinistic native scholars and by sinologists embarrassed by the methodological shortcomings of their nineteenth-century predecessors. This meshing of Western and native scholarship meant that the agnostic singularity and philological isolation of sinology in relation to other forms of Orientalism was maintained well into the twentieth century. Corroboration of these convictions about China's linguistic, historical, and cultural particularity was apparently forthcoming when, shortly after the First World War, the archaeological remains and archaic script of the Shang dynasty were uncovered. These important discoveries seemed to show conclusively that China was an ancient nuclear civilization independent from Western centers in Egypt and Sumer.[26] All of these factors—archaeological, philological, and especially the conspicuous absence of any imaginative mythology or lush religious ideology in the Semitic, Babylonian, or Indo-European sense—fortified China's formidable "prosaic solitude" in relation to all other Oriental nations.

With regard to China, it was much more than a simple matter of deferred comparative connections or the possibility of setting China within a broader historical and cultural framework. By the turn of the century and in light of the impressive successes of Chavannes's and Pelliot's more delimited philological concerns and their more controlled historical methods of analysis, it was rather a matter of sinology's confidently retreating into its own closed world of meaning and analysis, a world founded on both a distorted appropriation of Legge's classical, Confucian, archaic, and textual vision of China and on the official Chinese self-image fostered by the embattled Ruist literati at the end of the Qing dynasty. At the heart of this vision was the mesmerizing conviction that China was a unique "special case" in the history of world civilizations.

The outcome of this was to continue with the assumption of China's exceptional linguistic and cultural singularity and, as shown by the Great Tradition of Confucianism, its lack of any significant mythology or theistic religious belief. With regard to religion it was often not just the relative lack of religious belief but, more positively from the standpoint of the twentieth-century academy in the West, the surprisingly early emergence of wisely humanistic and a-religious attitudes. China was not just prosaically or placidly a-religious but precociously agnostic and progressively antireligious. In this sense, China became again in the early twentieth century, as it had been for many eighteenth-century Enlightenment *philosophes,* the great example of religion's vestigial nature and significance. As a turnabout of Legge's ideas on fulfillment, which depended on classical Chinese traces of theistic religion and morality, China's passage into modernity would come about precisely because it was hindered less than any other Oriental tradition was by such superstitious religious matters.

Aspects of Sinological Singularity

As a way to summarize these developments, I conclude with a partial inventory of some specific traits that in differing degrees contribute to the sinological condition of disciplinary strangeness. I have already discussed the general historical and methodological context for this state of affairs, so that in what follows I am concerned only with various habitual practices and rhetorical strategies that tend to characterize sinological Orientalism during the late nineteenth and early twentieth centuries. These points are especially characteristic of the Leggian epoch of sinology at the end of the Victorian era, but they also constitute some fundamental axioms of Western sinological discourse that persist down to the present time.

First of all, it is exceedingly important to reiterate the basic point that China generally remained a stranger to the larger Orientalist enterprise. Throughout the nineteenth century, there was never any successful attempt to determine China's place in philology and the sinological field was always peripheral to the organized international congresses of Orientalism. This situation was reinforced in British sinological tradition by the fact that philological science was late in coming to England and was distorted once it arrived (in part because of Müller).[27] As long as sinology lacked the "higher methods" and "depth of interpretation" found in comparative philology, Indo-European, and biblical studies, it would not attract the attention of the critical research scholars who were fomenting an Oriental Renaissance of learning in Germany and on the continent.[28]

Second, sinology was retarded in finding a place within the established academic institutions of Orientalism in the late nineteenth century.[29] This was especially true for the British university tradition, but was also the case in America and in most of Europe aside from France. Even in Paris, where academic sinology had been created in 1815, there was a certain imperious insularity of method and a haughty nationalistic attitude that did not lend itself to the cultivation of this discipline in other countries. Emblematic of this was Julien's "impossible character" and odious personality (what Schwab called his "touchy, jealous, and irascible" nature), which led to "an interminable series of disputes between Orientalists" during the forty years of his hegemonic rule over European academic sinology.[30] However, by the 1870s the "inadequacies of the philological method" of the Parisian armchair sinologues had become evident.[31] Much of this was caused by a growing French resistance to some of the more romantic forms of German-style comparative philology. But even the amateur or hyphenated sinology practiced by Anglo-American missionaries, diplomats, and merchants was showing the advantages of having direct access to the living tradition and native helpers. This was, in fact, the urgent message brought back to Paris from the field among Asians, British, and Americans by the ever-observant and industriously ambitious internationalist Henri Cordier.

The symbolism of Legge's first encounter with Julien in Paris is also indicative of the shift away from a book-bound approach that prided itself on its ignorance of spoken Chinese and any direct acquaintance with the native tradition. In a letter dating to 1867, when he was passing through Paris on his penultimate trip home, Legge remarks that he met both Julien and

Julius von Mohl, a German expatriate Persianist, "literary celebrity," and chronicler of European Orientalism. Legge describes Julien as a "stoutish, nervous old man—a Frenchman of the French, with a large head of long hair and a short neck, lion-like." Most suggestive of the changing of the guard in academic sinology is Legge's evocative observation that, while Julien received him with "much *empressement* [solicitous attention]," he could not help but feel that they "acted like a couple of prize-fighters, who come together in the ring for the first time, and take or attempt to take the measure of each other's strength and prowess."[32] Julien's atypical solicitousness and wariness toward his British visitor are a sure sign that, in his old age, he was no longer so confident in the proposition that his approach was more scientific precisely because he spoke no Chinese and had no actual experience of China.[33]

In this context it is also worth recognizing that, somewhat like Julien in his heyday and very much unlike Legge, who had actually visited the Altar of Heaven as well as having read about it in the classics, Müller firmly believed in the scientific superiority of a relentlessly textual approach to the study of the Orient. When invited to India in the early 1870s, Müller remarked to A.P. Stanley that his "curiosity to see India [was] not great." The reason for his utter lack of curiosity about the tradition he had been studying for most of his life was a classic enunciation of essentialist Orientalism: "It is the inner life, not the outward that I care for—and I can see more of the former from reading books, newspapers, letters, from seeing the men who come to see me, than from fireworks and Durbarr."[34]

Despite his difficult behavior, Julien's character reflects a moral purity and Jansenist asceticism that often criticized colonial policies and upheld the Enlightenment ideal of a "new universalism of scholarship" that looked beyond national affiliation.[35] This kind of scholarly essentialism was, however, more theory than practice. During much of the nineteenth century there were still important distinctions among different national styles in the production of scholarly knowledge. These nationalistic distinctions seem particularly pronounced in sinology, where the "amateur" aspects of the Anglo-American style (along with related rural, gentlemanly, evangelical, empirical, inductive, local, experimental, practical, and individualistic thematic tropes) seemed to clash with the "professional" pretensions of the French-Continental approach (with its associated urban, academic, Jesuitical, rational, centralized, bureaucratic, deductive, authoritarian, and synthetic themes).

French academic tradition tended to emphasize a post–French Revolution rational order that radiated out to the world from the metropolitan center of Paris, whereas the British amateur approach, in keeping with the colonial dispersion of its empire and the rural location of Cambridge and Oxford in relation to the political metropolis of London, was content to gather and classify individual artifacts and translate various useful texts without some overarching synthetic focus or theory.[36] This difference is illustrated during much of the nineteenth century by the centralized bureaucracy of French intellectual life associated with a few specialized and synthetic Oriental journals published in Paris (e.g., *Journal asiatique, Journal des savants, Revue des Deux-Mondes*) and the more diffuse and vital field activities of various British, but locally based, learned groups each publishing its own rather eclectic periodical (e.g., *Asiatic Researches, Journal of the North China Branch of the Royal Asiatic Society, Journal of the Hong Kong Branch of the Royal Asiatic Society, China Review*, and so on).[37]

The work of Eitel and others strongly recommended the adoption of various critical academic methods, but sinology was "slow to respond to the growth of the historical and social sciences in the nineteenth century."[38] Despite his broadly comparativist and developmental sensibility in the Müllerian mold, Legge never was able to approach his materials in a fully historical and critical manner. His scholarship was surprisingly original and critical at times, but it also tended to trust too reverently the testimony of ancient tradition. As Eitel said, Legge never really practiced his sinological scholarship in the complete historiographical spirit of *Quellenstudium*. In many ways, Legge's (and Müller's) inability to achieve a complete modernist break with an older biblical hermeneutics of trust is most dramatically, and ironically, seen in the debate with Herbert Giles over the authority and historicity of Laozi and the *Daode jing*. As Arthur Wright says, a major change in sinology took place when Chavannes "began to lecture on the *history* of China."[39]

It seems that sinology, more so than other Orientalist fields in the nineteenth century, remained focused on the translation of primary texts accompanied only by basic philological and explanatory commentary. Comparative, or speculative philological and historical, discussion remained largely underdeveloped or, when attempted, was ridiculed and spurned in the interests of preserving the singularity of the Chinese tradition. As seen characteristically (if not entirely) in Legge's work, the tendency in sinology was to follow an exegetical mode that eschewed cross-linguistic or cross-civilizational "conjectural-emotional" interpretation. As his prolegomena show, Legge was nonetheless quite concerned with broad philological and historical issues in both the Germanic lower and higher senses of technical academic scholarship. In a general way, however, there was a lingering commentarial mode among many late-nineteenth-century and early-twentieth-century sinologists that, although powerfully sanctioned and supported by the dominant currents of native Chinese literary tradition, became increasingly old-fashioned in the eyes of the comparative philologists and critical historians.[40] The real issue here is that mere translation retained its prestige much longer in sinology than it did in other Orientalist disciplines. Part of this was, no doubt, because of the assumption that there was so much more to translate and so much less to speculate about comparatively.

The number of available texts in Chinese was relatively greater than in all other Oriental fields. Moreover, to a degree even greater than seen in the Indian and Islamic traditions, Chinese literature was richly supplemented by a highly developed native tradition of commentarial exegesis and even, within some more progressive Ruist circles, a higher or truly critical philological scholarship.[41] For example, the editorial work in verifying texts in relation to variant manuscripts that was so central to the philological and historical labors of Müller and other Sanskritists was never as much of a factor for those working on Chinese classical texts. Much of this work had already been accomplished by native scholars.

China, unlike India, was never colonized by any Western power and in an intellectual sense may even be said to have impressed a certain self-image of its own essential uniqueness and ancient integrity—that is, its classical, imperial, bureaucratic, monolithic, and Ruist/Confucian nature—upon Western sinological scholarship. This reflexive and refractive process is something that goes back to the time of the Jesuits, but was also continued, ratified, and expanded by nineteenth-century sinologues such as Julien and Legge. The "Confucian" and "classical" image implanted in Western sinology had the approval of native scholars (in both the traditional commentarial and newer evidential sense of the Qing dynasty) and reinforced some already existing Orientalist methods concerning Asia (e.g., the importance of understanding a tradition in terms of its ancient classical sources, the essential purity of the origins, the changeless relevance of certain key principles, and the privileging of elite texts and the literate tradition over the oral and popular tradition).[42] The Chinese bureaucratic self-image of a Ruist or Confucian China and the emerging humanistic science of Western sinology converged in the overpowering conviction that China was unique in the world history of languages and civilizations. After the turn of the century, China's existence as a civilizational singleton (e.g., culturally and linguistically isolated, epic-less, unimaginative, religionless, prosaic, and mythless) meant that it was never comfortably included within the comprehensive history of world cultures.

There are some important differences (and similarities) between the sinological and Indological evaluation of traditional commentaries. As seen in the case of Rudolf von Roth (along with Otto Böhtlingk, the translator of the definitive Sanskrit lexicon, 1852–1875) and Müller's scholarship, there was a pronounced tendency in Indological Orientalism to depreciate the importance of traditional native Indian commentary because it failed to preserve the so-called original or pure sense of ancient texts such as the *Vedas*.[43] Even though Müller's major work of Indological scholarship was his critical edition of the *Rig-Veda* in relation to the traditional Sanhita commentary (undertaken ostensibly to please his first Oxford mentor, the Boden Sanskritist H. H. Wilson), he actually devalued the importance of his own work. In the preface to this edition of the *Rig-Veda,* he says that Sanhita gives only the "traditional" sense of the *Veda,* which suffers from "'the gradual corruption of simple truth [the original sense] into hierarchical dogmatism and hallucination [the traditional sense]'"—a process caused by the inevitable "disease of language" and by machinations of Brahmanic "priestcraft."[44]

Müller's Indological mode and Legge's sinological mode in dealing with native commentaries must therefore be distinguished. Both were convinced of the purity, authority, and sacrality of the most ancient classical texts, and both in varying degrees believed in the developmental degeneration of the ancient Indian and Chinese traditions. Legge, at times, also criticized the obfuscation of traditional commentaries (especially of the Han and Song schools) and employed the more modern critical views of the Ming-Qing scholars. Nevertheless, there is a sense in which the Confucianism of the Chinese tradition was less subject to reinterpretation and corruption than was the Hinduism of India. It seems that this is a result of the absence of a priestly class in China and because the Ruist tradition depended less on the vagaries of oral tradition. In contrast with a priestly group like the Roman Catholics entirely focused on religious ritual, the Ruists or Confucian elite were literate scholars, mandarins, political ministers, bureaucratic officials, or cultural experts who (like Protestant ministers charged primarily with scriptural exegesis and moral prescription) partially defined and credentialed themselves by their editorial and commentarial maintenance of an ancient corpus of authoritative texts.[45] Ancient texts about the core rituals of harmonious social interaction, supplemented by a constantly evolving critical commentary on those texts, were the cultural, moral, and intellectual focal points of Ruist tradition.

Last, and for all the reasons discussed in this book, it is worth emphasizing that sinology peremptorily set itself apart from other specialized scholarly disciplines studying Asia and has thereby tended to deny the label and implications of a "sinological Orientalism." Ever righteous about the seeming singularity and difficulty of its subject matter, sinologists have commonly denied any close association with either the epistemological regime or methods of Orientalism, whether understood in Müllerian or Saidian terms. That this is unfortunately an ongoing state of affairs is indicated by a "prominent" sinologist who was recently quoted as declaring haughtily that "there is no Orientalism in Chinese studies" since China is best seen as "a world in itself and no sinologist in his right mind would deem himself a general 'Orientalist.' "[46]

MISSION AT THE TURN OF THE MILLENNIUM

God will be His own interpreter. China, separated from the rest of the world, and without the light of revelation, has played its part, and brought forth its lessons, which will not, I trust, be long without their fitting exposition.
JAMES LEGGE, PROLEGOMENA TO THE *SHU JING, THE CHINESE CLASSICS*, VOL. 3, 1865

Every Secret Thing

I return to some last reflections on James Legge's pilgrim's life and the elusive symbolic sympathy we have found in the lives of the ancient Chinese transmitter known as Confucius and the nineteenth-century Scottish translator. This curious sympathetic resonance depends to a great extent on the construction of a certain standardized biography of the Chinese sage, a mythic and rhetorical edifice that was the work of countless Chinese commentators and, in the West, by learned Jesuits, various Enlightenment *philosophes*, French academicians, and especially James Legge, along with all of their later sinological and comparative epigones. What we have learned is that Legge's ambiguous and constantly evolving representation of Master Kong's greatness was manifestly an interpretive act creatively drawing upon all of the inherent biases of the nineteenth-century Protestant missionary mentality. At the same time, this exposure to alien traditions and persons, no matter how they were imaginatively manipulated, dynamically and reciprocally affected Legge's own applied morality of intracultural intercourse and his "comparative" understanding of himself, the Christian religion, and British imperial tradition.

It is the "head and heart" transactional nature of Legge's project of self-transformation and cross-cultural understanding through the translation and deciphering of Oriental texts, tempered by his encounters with Oriental persons, that qualifies the important but somewhat misleading insight that the "construction of identity" involves "establishing opposites and 'others' whose actuality is always subject to the continuous interpretation and reinterpretation of their differences from 'us.' "[47] As seen in Legge's journey to the East and back, the processural construction of a pilgrim's identity depends on the constantly contested discovery of comparative similarities, homologous parallels, and universal essences in response to the ever-shifting category of difference. Depending on the emphasis given to sympathetic similarity and antagonistic difference, there can be significant modulations in the imperialistic mission of understanding and conquering. One can approach the Orient as a judge or a guest, as an aggressive transformer or a careful translator, as a bold general or a cautious pilgrim.

Bold Generals and Cautious Pilgrims

There is good reason to say that Legge's career as both a hyphenated missionary-scholar and sinologist-teacher is a powerful instance of Edward Said's contrite observation about certain Orientalists who went against the grain of Oriental-*ism* and achieved some partial transcendence of their own religious and cultural context. Said's own example of the fragmented nature of Orientalists and Orientalism is his contrast between the antagonistic and judgmental Islamic Orientalism of Ernest Renan (1823–1892) and the sympathetic Orientalism of Louis Massignon (1883–1962). Both took for granted the French mission to the Muslim world and both assumed that scholarship can "dissolve all obstacles" and "represent anything." However, a crucial difference was the ameliorating influence of Massignon's Christian compassion, which allowed him to approach Islam with a spirit of reciprocal instruction and ultimate rapprochement. In this way, Said says that Massignon's empathetic methods strongly contrast with the "philologist as judge" approach of Renan, who surveyed all "lesser religions like Islam with disdain." Massignon more cautiously and quietly approached the Orient as a guest—as a "spiritual traveler extraordinary."[48]

Unfortunately there are some serious historical and cultural deficiencies in Said's typological comparison of Renan's and Massignon's styles of Orientalism. Renan was very much a creature of the nineteenth century, whereas Massignon (who possessed a modernist Catholic concern for mystical spirituality quite distinct from Renan's sensibility) was the product of the first half of the twentieth century, which, even within the French cultural context, was significantly different from the earlier era. To contrast the two in such a straightforward manner is to fall prey to what Müller would call the easy temptation of a "false parallel." To stay within the confines of the nineteenth century and to link Renan and Müller as exemplary representatives of Semitic and Sanskritic Orientalism would yield a better and more nuanced comparison. From this vantage point, the sinological Orientalist Legge becomes interesting precisely because of his comparative difference, his otherness, and his marginality in relation to the two "bold generals" of the mainstream disciplines of Orientalism. The distinction then becomes one of a contrast between the Orientalist as Leggian pilgrim and educator and the more rigorously imperious, impartial, entrepreneurial, and martial Orientalist exemplified by Müller and Renan.

But even this contrast is not simple and only hints at the microanalytic work that still needs to be done to appreciate the real differences among Orientalists and Orientalisms—or, for that matter, the similarities and differences among figures such as Legge the Scottish Nonconformist missionary sinologist, Renan the ex–Roman Catholic priest Semiticist, Müller the Lutheran-Anglican-Kantian Indologist, and Massignon the modern, quasi-mystic Catholic Islamicist. Not only is the story of the native resistance to, and transformation of, imperialistic institutions still too often left out of the history of Orientalism, but so also is there a failure to distinguish fully the different nationalistic and disciplinary styles of Orientalism, the interplay of different Western Orientalisms and various forms of Asian Occidentalism, and the particular transgressive and transformative qualities of individual Orientalists.[49]

The Assurance of Things Hoped For

Legge, for all his relative obscurity, still speaks to us about the special contradictions and sly ambiguities, negative distortions and positive contributions, of that "impossibly huge generalization" of Orientalism. He is an outstanding example of the difficult nineteenth-century passage from religious discourse to what Edward Said calls the "secular criticism" of the modern world. For Legge—as variously for some other significant, though also neglected, Victorian figures such as Max Müller, Benjamin Jowett, Andrew Lang, William Robertson Smith, A.M. Fairbairn, J. Estlin Carpenter, and James Hastings—liberal religion and the pietistic pilgrim's faith were not party to the antagonistic closing off of human investigation. Instead, in strategic alliance with more secular academic attitudes and comparative methods, such forms of liberal Evangelical faith were often the underlying motivation and mechanism leading to an increased sympathy for Oriental persons and to a more expansive view of history as a human production best known through a study of the ancient classical and holy books of the whole world.[50]

The underlying realization was that a dutiful understanding of people and of civilization in the broadest historical sense hinged on an encounter with the dynamic sacred and profane pluralities of world literature rather than on an unbending conviction about the static finality of the one and only Christian Bible. The obverse of this principle was, to draw upon Jowett's careful formulation, that the Hebrew and Christian Bibles themselves could and "should be read like any other book."[51] In this regard, it is also worth noting that liberal, but more conventionally pious, religious figures such as Legge and Massignon were sometimes more sensitive to the intellectual and moral integrity of other persons and religions than were the more boldly secularized and professionally judgmental generals of Orientalism such as Müller and Renan.

It was the postmillennialist faith in the "assurance of things hoped for" (Heb. 11:1) through human effort in the existing world that was often at the core of this transformative vision in the nineteenth century. The missionary, scholarly, and educational work of evangelical figures such as James Legge, Ernst Faber, W.A.P. Martin, Young John Allen, and Timothy Richard thus played a role in the very emergence, and ultimate success, of native Chinese forces of resistance to the old imperial Chinese order and to various prevailing forms of Western imperialism. In China it was the accommodating moral, social, and comparative conscience of liberal Protestant Christianity that sowed the seeds of its own dissolution. Ironically, it accomplished this radical kenosis by promoting both a revisionary appreciation of Confucianism and a more critical, secularly agnostic and scientific, approach to social reform among Chinese intellectuals.[52]

God Will Be His Own Interpreter

After all is said and done, Legge's conservative critics were in the short term correct in their suspicions about the compromising methods of sympathetic comprehension. It may also be said, after the passage of more than one hundred years, that Legge was symbolically and prophetically correct in his prediction that a more complicated, even contradictory, syncretistic mixture of the lessons of a compassionate Christianity, a revisionary Confucianism, and a secular sociopolitical ideology is crucial for the future of the Chinese nation. Curiously enough, at the start of the twenty-first century, in a severely disillusioned post-Tiananmen Marxist China plunging pell-mell into the worst excesses of materialistic capitalism, the interrelated term questions of faith, duty, moral values, religion, intellectual freedom, human rights, and sociopolitical reformation are again in the air.[53] Most haunting of all is that Leggian issues about a new economically adept Pacific Rim Confucianism and the possibility of Chinese forms of Christianity and democratic liberalism have reappeared in all their ambiguous glory. At the beginning of the twenty-first century the implementation of the "whole duty of man" throughout all the nations of the world remains as confused as ever.

CONCLUDING COMPARISONS

I will try
to fasten into order enlarging
grasps of disorder, widening
scope, but enjoying the freedom
that

> *Scope eludes my grasp, that*
> *there is no finality of vision,*
> *that I have perceived nothing*
> *completely,*
> *that tomorrow a new walk*
> *is a new walk.*
>
> A.R. AMMONS, *CORSONS INLET,* 1965

Studying Religion and China Religiously

This is not the forum in which to expand on the diminished and compromised status of the academic study of religion during the first half of the twentieth century. Nor will I address the surprising popular interest in, and important institutional renaissance of, the study of religion in the 1960s and 1970s. Schizophrenically pulled between romantic and rationalistic, confessional and reductionistic, comparative and particularistic, historical and anthropological concerns, the academic study of religion throughout the twentieth century was a defensive and residual activity that showed a degree of disciplinary strangeness even greater than that described for sinology. I have focused on the development and nature of sinological Orientalism during and immediately after the Leggian era, but it is worth underscoring again how significantly intertwined are the shifting fortunes and marginal status of these two curious disciplines (along with the missionary movement). It is no accident that at the same time in the 1960s and 1970s that the academy (which since the Second World War was especially affected by developments in North America) was revalorizing the nontheological study of religions as a legitimate humanistic discipline, sinologists, with the important interdisciplinary and comparative assistance of religionists and social scientists, were rediscovering the crucial role of religion throughout all periods and social divisions of Chinese history.[54]

This renewed appreciation of Chinese religion was, incongruously, a transformative event that took place when China had entered into its Marxist, Maoist, and atheistic Cultural Revolution—the darkest hour for traditional Chinese culture and all things having to do with old and so-called superstitious religious matters. In the decades since the death of Mao Zedong and especially after the unsuccessful democratic spasm of Tiananmen in 1989, China itself, though holding onto the trappings of communism, has radically changed and the younger generation no longer seems to believe in anything beyond the rapid accumulation of financial capital. A profound crisis of faith—religious, moral, and social—prevails within China at present.[55] It may well be that the Chinese people at the start of what appears to be a new Asian millennium will be left with only McDonalds, Coca-Cola, MTV, and a Disneyfied theme park of former religions—the simulacra of a consumerist global culture that allows for only voyeuristic belief and virtual

participation. But recent developments involving the Falun Gong movement suggest alternative and more interesting possibilities of real political and
spiritual reformation. Despite the Falun Gong's adept use of the Internet,
there is nothing that is merely virtual about the effect this syncretistic religious
movement is having on the ruling communist elite in Bejing.[56] Recent
events—somewhat in the spirit of Müller's comparative principle that "everything new is old"—suggestively recall the Taiping rebellion in the nineteenth
century, an earlier eclectic religious protest movement (branded "heretical"
and "superstitious") that dramatically challenged the government's right to
claim the Mandate of Heaven. The cataclysmic events associated with the
Taiping movement, together with all the other transformative foreign and indigenous agents traced in this book, did, after all, lead to the demise of the imperial regime and to the continuing, if sporadic, reform of Chinese tradition.

It is not without some significance that, during this same period of
chaotic economic development and rampant cynicism, the history of Chinese religious practices, and of the Christian missionary movement in
China, has become one of the most exciting and revisionary fields of sinological scholarship. As a flood of new articles and monographs from different disciplinary perspectives demonstrates, China eventually, after the
abortive efforts of Müller and Legge in the *Sacred Books of the East* at the end
of the nineteenth century, shows signs of being incorporated into the general history of world religions. This is a scholarly renaissance that is still intimately wedded to particular Western regimes of knowing, not the least of
which are the deceptively universal or phenomenological categories of sacred books, religion, world religions, and such things as origins, terms, and
beliefs. Nevertheless, some more expansive and multicultural perspectives
on the diverse complexity of non-Western traditions have emerged, perspectives that in the case of China strive to acknowledge and incorporate the
meaningful differences of the Chinese cultural and religious experience.
Moreover, with the postmodernist and postcolonialist deconstruction of all
totalizing categories of knowing, it is becoming increasingly likely that a
younger generation of international scholars will drastically reform our understanding of that shifting assemblage of cultural practices described as "religious." As in the case of James Legge, these practices of academic knowing
should be conducted with a "sympathetic comprehensiveness" that honors
the distinctiveness and moral complexity of those activities concerned with
the human imagination of, and response to, a radical Other.[57] These are
pursuits that are never value free or wholly objective. Rather, the crux of the
matter has to do with the ritualized exercise of knowing and respecting the
real otherness of others. This is the whole duty of men and women.

Especially important is that the rediscovery and reassessment of Chinese
religious tradition are now, after a long hiatus, being taken up by a new generation of native scholars in Taipei, Beijing, Nanjing, and a repatriated

Hong Kong. These young Chinese intellectuals of the post-Mao era are increasingly empowered to take questions of religious experience and action seriously, to study such matters openly and comparatively, to work in collaboration with Western colleagues, and to put forward approaches and categories more appropriate to Chinese cultural history. The old essentialist certainties about religion and philosophy, superstition and science, or "Confucianism" and "Taoism" (as well as the so-called purity and impurity of those categories) no longer dominate the academic study of religions in either the West or China.[58] All such commonplace distinctions have been blurred in recognition of the historical, political, and philosophical undertow of these categories. But in keeping with the postmodernist emphasis on religious practice over ideology (ritual orthopraxis over mythological and conceptual orthodoxy—a state of affairs that seems particularly descriptive of many Chinese traditions and texts), and the embeddedness of religious actions and symbols within all aspects of culture, it may be that a more fully comprehensive, international, comparative, and China-centered discourse about Chinese religious traditions will emerge.[59] The universalizing category of religion is rightly in question these days, but it is exactly the interesting difference of Chinese practices (especially the inclusive emphasis on a performative ritual ethos as distinguished from closed systems of terminological belief), as well as the contributions of a native Chinese scholarship now self-consciously aware of its own chauvinistic Occidentalism and its postimperial appropriation of Western forms of knowing (whether Marxist or scientific), that will help to reconfigure our approach to the always ambiguous issues of behavior and belief best called religious. At the very least, these new efforts at retrieving, preserving, reinterpreting, and reforming many of the forgotten records of the traditional Chinese imagination will provide the younger generation of Chinese with some of the resources necessary for constructing (and reconstructing) religious and moral practices meaningful for the new millennium.

The Scope of Comparison

At the conclusion of our long journey, perhaps it is permissible to say that Müller, for all of his intellectual folly and academic bluster, was right about one very basic issue. This concerns the infinitely corruptible—but simple and important—insight that it is the fundamental cross-cultural act, or "disciplined exaggeration" of comparison, the creative and transformative juxtaposition of "this and that" and "other and it" (Müller's dyad) to establish a metaphorical similarity *and* difference, that is at the heart of human imagination, knowledge, and morality.[60] It was Müller's entrepreneurial genius to promulgate the wisdom and method of comparison for the human sciences, if not its most appropriate and controlled application. It was Legge's transformative greatness to make the comparative principle the fulfillment of his Christian duty as a missionary pilgrim and as a scholarly translator.

In keeping with the ambiguous spirit of these observations, I end my reflections with a translation from an ancient Chinese text on the elusive but necessary practice of comparison: "the sorting which evens things out." This is not, I hasten to say, a translation from the Confucian classics by our stalwart companion James Legge. Rather, I refer to the rendering of the title to the second section *(Qi wu lun)* of the Daoist classic known as the *Zhuangzi* by the brilliant maverick A.C. Graham—a modern-day Welsh scholar whose work, like that of the Scotsman Legge, belies the charge that "listlessness" is a congenital aspect of British sinology. In many respects, the Daoist musings of the *Zhuangzi* constitute one of the earliest meditations in world literature on the methods of comparatively analyzing or sorting out the hidden judgments implied by different forms of conventional discourse. The Daoist sage known as Zhuangzi might indeed be thought of as an outsider to the conventional order, a playful comparativist, who delighted in juxtaposing the typical and the strange, butterflies and persons, to get at the "transformations of things." He was, in this sense, very much of an ancient Chinese pilgrim of sympathetic comprehensiveness and interpretive practicality, someone who approached the this and the that of life with a view to its infinite comparative possibilities.

I conclude this long comparative study, therefore, with Graham's rendering of Zhuangzi's marvelously perplexing ruminations on comparison, otherness, and meaning:

> What is It is also Other, what is Other is also It. There they say, "That's it, that's not" from one point of view, here we say, "That's it, that's not" from another point of view. Are there really It and Other? Or really no It and Other? Where neither It nor Other finds its opposite is called the axis of the Way. When once the axis is found at the centre of the circle there is no limit to responding with either, on the one hand no limit to what is *it*, on the other no limit to what is not. Therefore I say: "The best means is Illumination." Rather than use the meaning to show that "The meaning is not the meaning," use what is not the meaning.[61]

It is doubtful that Master Kong, James Legge, or Max Müller would agree with such a whimsically agnostic rendition of the comparative principle, but they might find some general agreement in the hermeneutical proposition that illumination, translation, transformation, and understanding all depend on the ever-changing relationship between this and that, the imaginatively manufactured meaning and not-meaning of things. So does the circle of knowing and translating—as well as the biographical circumambulation of a human life—turn back on itself and go forward.

APPENDIX A

Max Müller's Motto
for the *Sacred Books of the East*

For the epigraph of the first volume of the *Sacred Books of the East,* Müller chose the following passages from *Private Thoughts on Religion, In Two Parts Complete,* written by Bishop William Beveridge (1637–1708):

> The general inclinations which are naturally implanted in my soul to some religion, it is impossible for me to shift off: but there being such a multiplicity of religions in the world, I desire now seriously to consider with my self which of them all to restrain these my general inclinations to. And the reason of this my enquiry is not, that I am in the least dissatisfied with that religion I have already embraced; but because 'tis natural for all men to have an overbearing opinion and esteem for that particular religion they are born and bred-up in. That, therefore, I may not seem biassed by the prejudice of education, I am resolved to prove and examine them all; that I may see and hold fast to that which is best. . . .

> Indeed, there was never any religion so barbarous and diabolical, but it was preferred before all other religions whatsoever, by them that did profess it; otherwise they would not have professed it. . . .

> And why, say they, may not you be mistaken as well as we? Especially when there is, at least, six to one against your Christian religion; all of which think they serve God aright; and expect happiness thereby as well as you. . . . And hence it is that in my looking out for the truest religion, being conscious to my self how great an ascendant Christianity holds over me beyond the rest, as being that religion wherinto I was born and baptized, that which the supreme authority has enjoined and my parents educated me in; that which every one I meet withal highly approves of, and which I my self have, by a long continued profession, made almost natural to me: I am resolved to be more jealous and suspicious of this religion, than of the rest, and be sure not to entertain it any longer without being convinced by solid and substantial arguments, of the truth and certainty of it. That, therefore, I may make diligent and impartial enquiry into all religions and so be sure to find out the

best, I shall for a time, look upon my self as one not at all interested in any particular religion whatsoever, much less in the Christian religion; but only as one who desires, in general, to serve and obey Him that made me, in a right manner, and thereby to be made partaker of that happiness my nature is capable of.

APPENDIX B

James Legge's Oxford Lectures and Courses, 1876-1897

Source: Helen Edith Legge compilation, Council for World Mission archives, China/Personal/Legge/Box 9, School of Oriental and African Studies, University of London.

PUBLIC LECTURES

1876:	10/27	Inaugural Lecture
	11/16	"Nature and History of Chinese Written Characters"
	12/7	"Nature and History" continued; "Introduction to the Laws of Chinese Composition"
1877:	1/31	"Confucius"
	3/15	"Mencius"
	5/11	"Imperial Confucianism I"
	5/22	"Imperial Confucianism II"
	6/6	"Imperial Confucianism III"
	11/28	"Imperial Confucianism IV"
1878:	5/15	"War versus Conference and Covenant as Argued and Tried in China in the 7th Century B.C."
	11/20	"Principles of Composition in Chinese or Grammar without Inflections I"
	11/23	"Principles of Composition II"
1879:	5/21	"Ch'in Shih Hwang-Ti, First Emperor of Ch'in Who Brought the Feudal System to an End"
1880:	2/11	"Taoism"
1881:	5/11	"Yi King I"
	5/18	"Yi King II"

1882:	11/1	"Tao Teh King I"
	11/4	"Tao Teh King II"
1883:	11/7	"Chronology of China"
	11/14	"Feudal Period"
1884:	2/13	"Chau Dynasty I"
	2/20	"Chau Dynasty II"
	11/12	"Ch'in Dynasty I" [not given due to illness]
	11/19	"Ch'in Dynasty II" [not given due to illness]
1885:	11/4	"Fa Hsien and His Travels in India with the State of Buddhism in Our Fifth Century"
	11/?	"Rise of the Dynasty of Ch'in and Its Superseding of the Feudal States"
1886:		[unrecorded]
1887:		[unrecorded]
1888:	5/3	"Nestorian Monument of Hsi-an Fu"
1889:	11/13	"Taoism, Lao Tze and Chwang-tze I"
	11/20	"Taoism, Lao Tze and Chwang-tze II"
1890:		[unrecorded]
1891:		[unrecorded]
1892:		[unrecorded]
1893:	5/23	"Purgatories of Buddhism and Taoism"
1894:	5/22	"The Li Sao Poem and Its Author I"
	5/29	"The Li Sao Poem and Its Author II"
1895:	10/21	"Fu-sang, Was It in America and Thus That Continent Discovered by the Chinese More than 1,000 Years before Columbus?"
	10/28	"Chinese Poetry"
1896:		[unrecorded]
1897:	3/11	"China before the Time of Emperor Yao"
	10/28	"The Pan Family of Our 2nd Century, Especially Pan Chao, the Authoress"
	11/20	"The First Emperor of the Han Dynasty and the Empress Lu" [announced but never given]

COURSES

| 1877: | 1/24 | "Elements of Chinese and Confucian Analects" [on Monday, Wednesday, Friday] |
| | 4/18 | "Elements of Chinese Grammar and History; Confucian Analects, and Chinese Version of the Gospel of John" |

	10/24	"Chinese Grammar, Confucian Analects and Mencius" [on Monday, Wednesday, Friday]
1878:	1/25	"Elements of Chinese, Confucian Analects, Works of Mencius; Julien's 'Syntaxe Nouvelle de la Langue Chinoise' " [on Monday, Wednesday, Friday]
	5/1	"Elements of Chinese Grammar and Composition; the Four Books; Chinese History" [on Monday, Wednesday, Friday]
	10/16	"The Four Books; The Kan Ying P'ien or 'Actions and Their Recompenses'; and Chinese Grammar"
1879:	1/28	"The Four Books; the Kan Ying P'ien; Chinese History and Composition"
	4/22	"The Four Books, Khang-hsi Edict; Chinese History and Composition" [three days a week]
	10/21	"The Four Books, the Sze Chi; and Analysis of Characters and Composition" [three days a week]
1880:	1/22	"The Principle of Chinese; the Four Books and the Ts'iu Wang T'ing"
	4/16	"Elements of Composition in Chinese; the Four Books; Sir T. Wade's Tsze Chih" [three days a week]
	10/21	"The Four Books; the Sermon on the Mount, Delegates Version; Principles of Composition, History, Geography of China"
1881:	1/27	"The Works of Mencius; Travels of Fa-hsien; Old Toper's Pavilion; History and Geography of China"
	4/27	"Chinese Principle; the Four Books; and the Historical Record"
	10/20	"History of Ts'in Dynasty; Chinese Poetry; the Khang-hsi Edict; and the Four Books" [on Monday, Wednesday, Friday]
1882:	1/25	"The Four Books; the Tao Teh King; and Chinese Poetry"
	4/19	"Tao Teh King; the Sacred Edicts; Chinese Poetry; and the Elements of Composition" [on Monday, Wednesday, Friday]
	10/20	"Elements of Composition in Chinese; the Four Books; and the Historical Records"
1883:	1/12	"The Rules of Composition; Works of Mencius; the Historical Records; and Chinese History" [three days a week]
	4/18	"Chinese History and Composition; the San Tsze King; 11th Book of Confucius Analects; and 1st and 4th Books of Mencius"
	10/7	"Elements of Chinese; 4th Book of Mencius; and Han Yu's Memorial against Buddhism" [three days a week]
1884:	1/24	"The Elements in Chinese Composition; 5th Book of Mencius; Khang-hsi Precepts and Their Amplification"

4/23   "5th and 6th Books of Mencius, Texts and Commentary;
            Historical Records/History of the Ch'in Dynasty; 7th of
            Khang-hsi Precepts; Chinese Letter Writing"

10/15   [Elementary instruction] "Historical Records—Ch'in Dynasty;
            Precepts of Sacred Edicts; and Chinese Letter Writing" [three
            days a week]

1885:   1/20   [Elementary instruction if necessary] "San Tsze King; Histori-
                cal Records—Ch'in Dynasty; Portraits of the Four Books; Fa
                Hsien's Account of His Visit to India; and Chinese Letter and
                Official Writing" [three days a week]

        4/21   [Elementary instruction if necessary] "San Tsze King;
                Phonetic Elements of the Characters; Fa Hsien's Account of
                His Visit to India; Portions of the Four Books; and History of
                the Three Kingdoms" [three days a week]

        10/21   [Elementary instruction if necessary] "Phonetic Element;
                History of the Three Kingdoms; Portions of the Four Books;
                on Chu Fu-tsze's Philosophical Work" [three days a week]

1886:   1/29   [Elementary instruction] "Chu Fu-tsze's Philosophy; the Hao
                Chiu Chwan; the Shih King; and Chinese Poetry; Portions of
                the Four Books" [three days a week]

        4/5   [Elementary instruction] "Chu Fu-tsze; Hao Chiu Chwan; the
                Shih King; Hsuan-Chwang's Hsi Yu Chi, or Records of the
                Western Regions" [three days a week]

        5/18   [Announcement that the lectures/classes for the rest of May
                are suspended due to Legge's ill health]

        10/19   [Elementary instruction if necessary] "San Tsze King; Chu Fu-
                tsze; Hsi Yu Chi; and Selected Portions of Chinese History"

1887:   1/19   [Elementary instruction] "Portions of the Four Books; for Se-
                niors: Hsuan-chwang's Hsi Yu Chi; and Passages of Ku Wan"

        4/22   [Elementary instruction] "Portions of the Four Books; the
                Chien Tsze Wan; for Seniors: Hsi Yu Chi; and Ku Wan"

        October [Elementary instruction] "For Juniors: San Tsze-wan, Ch'ien
                Tsze-wan, and Portions of Four Books; for Seniors: Hsi Yu
                Chi; Shih King Part I, Bk XV; and Passages of Ku Wan"

1888:   1/18   [Elementary instruction] "Ch'ien Tsze Wan; the Four Books;
                Hsi Yu Chi; and the History of the Han Dynasty" [three days
                a week]

        4/24   [Elementary instruction] "Ch'ien Tsze Wan; the Four Books;
                Hsi Yu Chi; and the History of the Han Dynasty" [three days
                a week]

        10/17   [Elementary instruction] "San Tsze King and Ch'ien Tsze
                Wan; for Seniors: the Principles of Confucianism—the She
                Shu and Khang-hsi Precepts; and the Narrative of Fa-hsien"

1889:   1/23   [Elementary instruction] "San Tsze King, Ch'ien Tsze Wan; for Seniors: the Principles of Taoism; Tao The King and Chwang-tsze Shu; Shu King, Part I and II" [three days a week]

         5/1   [Elementary instruction] "San Tsze King and Principles of Composition in Chinese; for Seniors: Principles of Buddhism; the San Chiao Phing Sin Lun; 1st and 2nd Books of the Shu and Shih; and Portions of the Four Books" [three days a week]

         10/16   "Class for Juniors: Elementary Instruction; Various Classes of the Characters; 1st Lessons in Composition. For Seniors: History of the Chau Dynasty in the Historical Records; Fa-hsien's Travels; Confucianism, Taoism, and Buddhism Compared; and Chinese Composition" [three days a week]

1890:   1/22   [Elementary instruction if necessary] "Portions of the Four Books; the Ch'ien Tsze Wan; and Chinese Composition" [three days a week]

         4/22   [Elementary instruction] "On Structure of Sentences; Portions of the Four Books; Ming Hsin Pao Chien; Khang-hsi Precepts, Amplified and Colloquial" [three days a week]

         10/14   "Confucius Analects; Selections from Khang-hsi Shang Yu Kwang Hsun; and Composition in Chinese" [three days a week]

1891:   1/20   [Elementary instruction if necessary] "The Four Books; Ta Hsiao; the Mencius Chap 6; the Historical Records; the History of Confucius; Exercises in Composition" [three days a week]

         4/21   [Elementary instruction if necessary] "Cheong Yung; the Mencius Book 6; Li Sao, or Lamentations of Chu Yuan" [three days a week]

         10/20   [Elementary instruction if necessary] "The Confucius Analects Book 12; Life of Ch'u Yuan by Sze-ma Chun; Lamentations and Songs of Ch'u Yuan; and Composition in Chinese" [three days a week]

1892:   2/10   [Elementary instruction] "Li Sao; Specimens of Ku Wan and of Poetry from Tang Dynasty; Pieces of the Shi King Part III Book II, Odes 1 and 6; and Exercises in Chinese Composition" [three days a week]

         4/26   [Elementary instruction if necessary] "Lamentations of Ch'u Yuan; Specimens of Ku Wan from Han Yu; Odes I, Bk II, Part III of the Shi-king; and Exercises in Chinese Composition" [three days a week]

         10/20   [Elementary instruction if necessary] "A Buddhist View of the Three Doctrines, or Religion of China; Lamentations and Songs of Ch'u Yuan; and Exercises in Chinese Composition" [three days a week]

1893:   1/24   [Elementary instruction if necessary] "Liu Mi on the Three Doctrines; Han Yu on the Idea of the Tao; Works of Ch'u Yuan; and the Rise of the Han Dynasty" [three days a week]

4/25   [Elementary instruction if necessary] "Liu Mi, Ch'u Yuan, Han Yu's Expulsion of Crocodiles from the Waters of Chao-chau; and the Memorial against Buddhism" [three days a week]

10/17   [Elementary instruction if necessary] "Li Sao and Other Writings of Ch'u Yuan; and Specimens of Ku Wan" [three days a week]

1894:   1/16   [Elementary instruction if necessary] "Li Sao and Others of Ch'u Yuan; Essays of Ku Wan; Rise of Han Dynasty; the San Tsze King; the Confucius Book I, II with Commentaries; and the Three Supplements to Ch'un Ch'iu" [three days a week]

4/24   [Elementary instruction if necessary] "The Confucius Book II, III; History of the Han Dynasty; and the Shan Tao of Japan" [three days a week]

10/16   "For Juniors: San Tsze King; for Seniors: the Elegies of Chu, the Confucius Book V; and Sacred Edict IX" [three days a week]

1895:   1/18   [Elementary instruction] "San Tsze King; 1st Book of the Confucius; the Composition of Easy Sentences and the Chinese Characters; Colloquial Speech in the Mandarin Dialect" [three days a week]

4/29   "Juniors: Elementary Instruction, the San Tsze King; for Seniors: the Confucian Analects Book III; the Mencius Book VI, Part I; Portions of Hao Ch'iu Ch'wan and Chinese Composition" [three days a week]

6/18   "Juniors: Elementary Instruction, the San Tsze King; for Seniors: the Confucian Analects Book XII; the Mencius Book VI; Sacred Edict with Amplification and Paraphrase, Precept I; and Chinese Composition" [three days a week]

1896:   1/28   "Juniors: Elementary Instruction, San Tsze King; 1st Book of the Confucian Analects and Composition; for Seniors: the Mencius Book VI, Part I; Shi-king Part II, Book I; Shang Yu Kwang Hsun Precept XV; and Composition" [three days a week]

4/27   "Juniors: Elementary Instruction, San Tsze King; the Metaphysics of Chu-hsi; and Chinese Composition" [three days a week]

10/20   "Juniors: Elementary Instruction, San Tsze King; and Ming Hsin Pao Chien; Composition in Chinese; for Seniors: the Mencius Book I, Both Parts; Histories of the Han and Sui; and Composition" [three days a week]

1897:   1/26   "Juniors: Elementary Instruction, Classifiers or Radicals, and the Composition in Chinese of Easy Sentences; for Seniors: Ta Hsiao and the Mencius Book I, Both Parts" [three days a week]

5/4   "Juniors: Elementary Instruction, Classifiers or Radicals and
           the Phonetic Elements; the Geography of China; and
           Composition of Easy Sentences; for Seniors: the Confucian
           Analects Book I, Both Texts and Commentary; History of the
           Han Dynasty; Sacred Edict, Precept II; Expansions, Classical
           and Colloquial; and Composition" [three days a week]

10/19   [Juniors: elementary instruction,] "Classifiers and Phonetic
           Elements; the Geography of China; and Composition of Easy
           Sentences; for Seniors: the Sixfold Divisions of Characters;
           the Confucius Analects Book V, Both Text and Commentary;
           First Two Reigns of the Han Dynasty; History of Wang Mang;
           and Composition" [last class, never completed]

Principal Publications
of James Legge and Max Müller

JAMES LEGGE

1841: *A Lexilogus of the English, Malay, and Chinese Languages; Comprehending the Vernacular Idioms of the Last in the Hok-keen and Canton Dialects.* Malacca.

1843: *The Rambles of the Emperor Ching Tih in Keang Nan: A Chinese Tale.* 2 vols. London: Longmans, Green.

1850: *An Argument for Shang-te As the Proper Rendering of the Words Elohim and Theos, In the Chinese Language; with Strictures on the Essay of Bishop Boone in Favour of the Term Shin, etc., etc.* Hong Kong.

The Ordinance of the Sabbath. Three Sermons on the Institution of the Sabbath, the Christian Sabbath, the Sabbath in the Colonies. Hong Kong.

1852: *The Notions of the Chinese Concerning God and Spirits: with an Examination of the Defense of an Essay on the Proper Rendering of the Words Elohim and Theos, into the Chinese Language by William Boone, D.D.* Hong Kong: Hong Kong Register Office.

1859: *The Land of Sinim: A Sermon Preached in the Tabernacle, Moorfields, at the Sixty-Fifth Anniversary of the London Missionary Society.* London: John Snow.

1861– *The Chinese Classics: with a Translation, Critical and Exegetical Notes,*
1872: *Prolegomena, and Copious Indexes.* Hong Kong: At the Author's, and London: Trübner. Volume 1, 1861: *The Confucian Analects; The Great Learning; The Doctrine of the Mean.* Volume 2, 1861: *The Works of Mencius.* Volume 3, part 1, 1865: *The First Parts of the Shoo-King, Or the Books of T'ang; The Books of Yu; The Books of Hea; The Books of Shang; the Prolegomena* [*The Book of Historical Documents; The Bamboo Annals*]. Volume 3, part 2, 1865: *The Fifth Part of the Shoo-King, Or the Books of Chow; Indexes.* Volume 4, part 1, 1871: *The First Part of the She-King, Or the Lessons of the States; the Prolegomena.* Volume 4, part 2, 1871: *The Second, Third, and Fourth Parts of the She-King, Or the*

Minor Odes of the Kingdom, The Greater Odes of the Kingdom, The Sacrificial Odes and Praise-Songs; Indexes. Volume 5, part 1, 1872: *Dukes Yin, Hwan, Chwang, Min, He, Wan, Seuen, and Ch'ing* [*of The Spring and Autumn Annals*]; *the Prolegomena.* Volume 5, part 2, 1872: *Dukes Seang, Ch'aou, Ting, and Gae, With Tso's Appendix; the Indexes.*

1872– "The Colony of Hong Kong." *The China Review* 1: 163–76.

1873: "Two Heroes of Chinese History." *The China Review* 1: 370–80.

1876: "Inaugural Lecture on the Constituting of a Chinese Chair in the University of Oxford." Pamphlet. London: Trübner.

She-King; or The Book of Ancient Poetry, translated into English Verse, With Essays and Notes. London: Trübner.

1877: "Confucianism in Relation to Christianity. A Paper Read Before the Missionary Conference in Shanghai, On May 11th, 1877." Pamphlet. Shanghai: Kelly and Walsh, 1877; London: Trübner.

1877– "Imperial Confucianism." 4 parts. *The China Review* 6: 147–58,
1878: 223–35, 299–310, 363–74.

1879– Contributions to *The Sacred Books of the East,* ed. Max Müller. Oxford:
1891: Clarendon Press. *The Texts of Confucianism*—volume 3, 1879: *The Book of History;* "the religious portions of" *The Book of Poetry;* volume 16, 1882: *The Book of Changes;* volumes 27 and 28, 1885: *The Record of Rites; The Book of Filial Piety. The Texts of Taoism*—volumes 39 and 40, 1891, *The Book of the Way and Its Power; The Zhuangzi; The Taishang* [*Tractate of Actions and their Retributions*]; miscellaneous other texts of "religious Taoism." Various later editions.

1880: "A Letter to Professor Max Müller Chiefly on the Translation into English of the Chinese Terms Ti and Shang in Reply to a Letter to Him by 'Inquirer' in the Chinese Recorder and Missionary Journal for May–June, 1880." Pamphlet. London: Trübner.

Memorials of John Legge. With a Memoir by James Legge. London: J. Clarke.

The Religions of China: Confucianism and Taoism Described and Compared with Christianity. London: Hodder and Stoughton.

1883: "Christianity and Confucianism Compared in Their Teaching on the Whole Duty of Man." Pamphlet. London: Religious Tract Society.

"The Tao Teh King." *British Quarterly Review* (July): 41–59.

1886: *A Record of Buddhist Kingdoms: Being an Account by the Chinese Monk Fa-hien of His Travels in India and Ceylon (A.D. 389–414) in Search of the Buddhist Books of Discipline.* Oxford: Clarendon Press.

1888: *Christianity in China: Nestorianism, Roman Catholicism, Protestantism/Christianity in China: A Rendering of the Nestorian Tablet at Si-an-fu to Commemorate Christianity.* London: Trübner.

"A Critical Notice of 'The Remains of Lao Tsze, Retranslated,' by Mr. Herbert A. Giles." *The China Review* 16: 195–214.

1893– *The Chinese Classics: with a Translation, Critical and Exegetical Notes,*
1895: *Prolegomena, and Copious Indexes.* 2d. rev. ed. Oxford: Clarendon

Press, vols. 1 and 2; London: Henry Frowde/Oxford University Press Warehouse, vols. 3–5. Volume 1, 1893: *The Confucian Analects, The Great Learning, The Doctrine of the Mean.* Volume 2, 1895: *The Works of Mencius.* Volume 3, 1895: *The Book of History or the Book of Historical Documents; The Bamboo Annals.* Volume 4, 1895: *The She King or The Book of Poetry* . Volume 5, 1895: *The Ch'un Ts'eu with the Tso Chuen.*

1894–
1895:   "The Li Sao Poem and Its Author." 3 parts. *Journal of the Royal Asiatic Society of Great Britain and Ireland:* 77–92, 571–99, 839–64.

1960:   *The Chinese Classics.* Hong Kong: Hong Kong University Press. This is the most important of various editions published since 1895.

MAX MÜLLER

1869:   *Rig-Veda-sanhita: The Sacred Hymns of the Brahmans.* London: Trübner.

1873:   *Introduction to the Science of Religion.* London: Longmans, Green.

1879–
1902:   *The Sacred Books of the East,* 50 vols. Oxford: Clarendon Press. Various later editions.

1881:   *Immanuel Kant's Critique of Pure Reason.* Translation. London: Macmillan.

1883:   *India: What Can It Teach Us?* New York: J. W. Lowell.

1884:   *Biographical Essays.* New York: Charles Scribner's Sons.

            "Forgotten Bibles." *The Nineteenth Century* 15: 1004–22.

1885:   "The Savage." *The Nineteenth Century* 17: 109–32.

1887:   *The Science of Thought.* London: Longmans, Green.

1890:   *Natural Religion.* London: Macmillan.

1891:   *Lectures on the Origin and Growth of Religion as Illustrated by the Religions of India.* New York: Charles Scribner's Sons.

            Physical Religion. London: Longmans, Green.

            "On the 'Enormous Antiquity' of the East." *The Nineteenth Century* 29: 796–810.

1892:   *Anthropological Religion.* London: Longmans, Green.

1893:   *Theosophy; or, Psychological Religion.* Longmans, Green.

1894:   "The Real Significance of the Parliament of Religions." *The Arena* 11: 1–7.

1895–
1910:   *Chips from a German Workshop.* 5 vols. New York: Charles Scribner's Sons.

1897:   *Contributions to the Science of Mythology.* 2 vols. London: Longmans, Green.

1898:   *Auld Lang Syne.* New York: Charles Scribner's Sons.

            "The Science of Religion: A Retrospect." *Living Age* 219: 909–13.

1900:   "Religions of China: I. Confucianism." *The Nineteenth Century* 48: 373–84.

1901:   *My Autobiography: A Fragment.* New York: Charles Scribner's Sons.

1910:   *Sacred Books of the East,* vol. 50: *A General Index to the Subject-Matter of the Sacred Books of the East,* compiled by M. Winternitz. Oxford: Clarendon Press.

Genealogy of the Legge Family

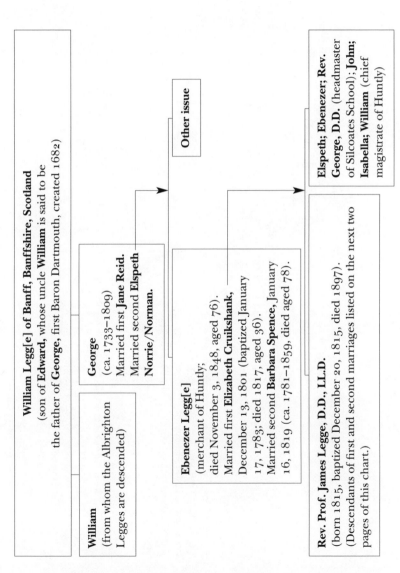

LEGGE OF HUNTLY, ABERDEENSHIRE

William Legg[e] of Banff, Banffshire, Scotland
(son of **Edward**, whose uncle **William** is said to be
the father of **George**, first Baron Dartmouth, created 1682)

William
(from whom the Albrighton
Legges are descended)

George
(ca. 1733–1809)
Married first **Jane Reid**.
Married second **Elspeth
Norrie/Norman.**

Other issue

Ebenezer Legg[e]
(merchant of Huntly;
died November 3, 1848, aged 76).
Married first **Elizabeth Cruikshank,**
December 13, 1801 (baptized January
17, 1783; died 1817, aged 36).
Married second **Barbara Spence,** January
16, 1819 (ca. 1781–1859, died aged 78).

Rev. Prof. James Legge, D.D., LL.D.
(born 1815, baptized December 20, 1815, died 1897).
(Descendants of first and second marriages listed on the next two
pages of this chart.)

**Elspeth; Ebenezer; Rev.
George, D.D.** (headmaster
of Silcoates School); **John;
Isabella; William** (chief
magistrate of Huntly)

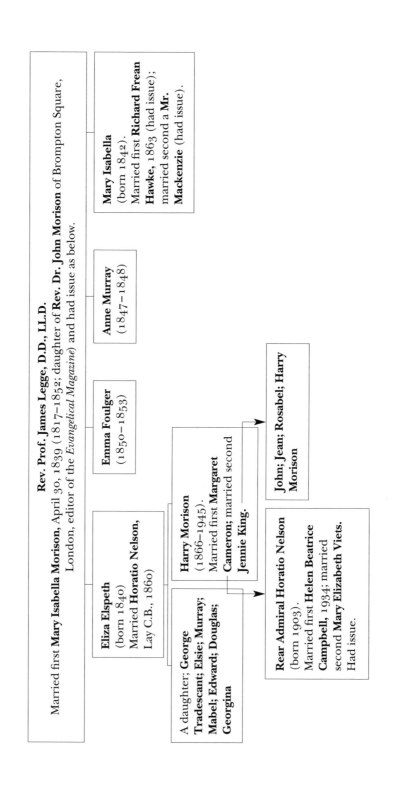

Rev. Prof. James Legge, D.D., LL.D.

Married first **Mary Isabella Morison**, April 30, 1839 (1817–1852; daughter of **Rev. Dr. John Morison** of Brompton Square, London, editor of the *Evangelical Magazine*) and had issue as below.

Mary Isabella
(born 1842).
Married first **Richard Frean Hawke**, 1863 (had issue); married second a **Mr. Mackenzie** (had issue).

Anne Murray
(1847–1848)

Emma Foulger
(1850–1853)

Eliza Elspeth
(born 1840)
Married **Horatio Nelson,** Lay C.B., 1860)

Harry Morison
(1866–1945).
Married first **Margaret Cameron;** married second **Jennie King.**

A daughter; **George Tradescant; Elsie; Murray; Mabel; Edward; Douglas; Georgina**

John; Jean; Rosabel; Harry Morison

Rear Admiral Horatio Nelson
(born 1903).
Married first **Helen Beatrice Campbell,** 1934; married second **Mary Elizabeth Viets.** Had issue.

Rev. Prof. James Legge, D.D., LL.D.

Married second **Hannah Mary Johnstone**, 1859 (1821–1881), daughter of **John Johnstone, Esq.**, of Hull.

James Granville
(1860–1940)
Married **Josephine Makins**, 1899 (daughter of Henry Francis Makins, Esq. [brother of **Sir William Makins Bart, MP**], by Keziah Elizabeth Hunt).

Sir Thomas Morison, Kt, CBE
(1863–1932)
Married **Norah Elizabeth Mack** (daughter of James Mack, Esq.).

Anna Georgina
Married **Lt. Col. Dr. William Collier** (1856–1935, son of Henry Collier Stapleford, Esq.). Descendants listed on page 555 of this chart.

Helen Edith
(1860–1940)
Died without descendants.

Cecilia Mireo
(1900–1963)
Died without descendants.

Prof. Mary Dominica, FBA
(1905–1986)
Died without descendants.

Beatrice Pompilia
(1906–1992)
Died without descendants.

Henry James Granville, OBE
(Descendants listed on the next page of this chart.)

Sylvia
(1909–1990)
Died without descendants.

Christopher Conlagh
(Descendants listed on the next page of this chart.)

Michael Morison
(Descendants listed on the next page of this chart.)

Henry James Granville, OBE
(1914–)
Married **Nancy Phipps-Osborne**, 1939 (1915– ; only daughter of **Stanley Phipps Osborne, Esq.**, by **Julia Munde Hodgson**).

Christopher Conlagh
Married **Jane.**

Michael Morison
(1913–1956)
Married **Gabriella Philipa Sowerly** (died 1956).

Christopher James
(1943–)
Married **Judith Mary Henrietta**, 1969 (1943– ; only daughter and heir of **Thomas Kenneth Carloss, Esq.**, by **Martha Mary Cecilia Camerer-Cuss**).

Anthony Phipps
(1948–)
Married **Christine Anderson-Tyrer,** 1981 (only daughter of **Adrian Anderson-Tyrer** by **Lesley Bishop**).

Thomas
(1951–)
Married **Bridget,** 1988 (1953–).

Jeremy Graham
(1949–1956)

Yolane Mary Zoe
(1949–1956)

Petra Amanda Cecilia
(1953–1956)

James Christopher Carloss Legge
(1974–)

Josephine Mary Carloss Legge
(1976–)

Annabel Miranda Venetia
(1983–)

Christopher Carra
(1988–)

Brian Thomas
(1989–)

Andrew Charles
(1992–)

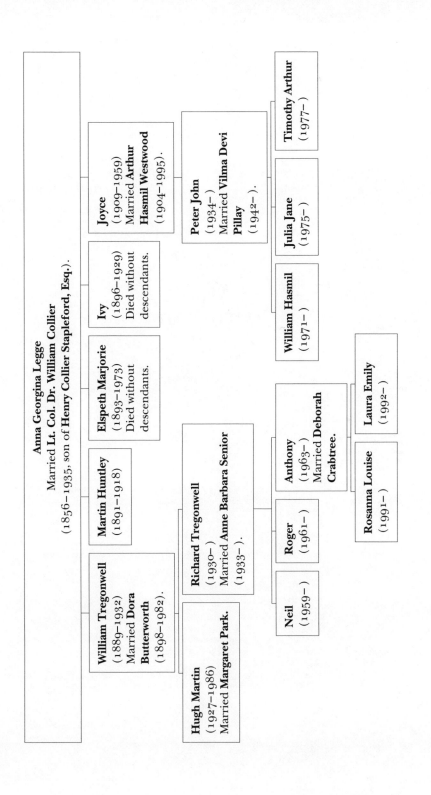

Anna Georgina Legge
Married **Lt. Col. Dr. William Collier**
(1856–1935, son of **Henry Collier Stapleford, Esq.**).

Joyce
(1909–1959)
Married **Arthur Hasmil Westwood**
(1904–1995).

Ivy
(1896–1929)
Died without descendants.

Elspeth Marjorie
(1893–1973)
Died without descendants.

Martin Huntley
(1891–1918)

William Tregonwell
(1889–1932)
Married **Dora Butterworth**
(1898–1982).

Hugh Martin
(1927–1986)
Married **Margaret Park.**

Richard Tregonwell
(1930–)
Married **Anne Barbara Senior**
(1933–).

Peter John
(1934–)
Married **Vilma Devi Pillay**
(1942–).

Neil
(1959–)

Roger
(1961–)

Anthony
(1963–)
Married **Deborah Crabtree.**

Rosanna Louise
(1991–)

Laura Emily
(1992–)

William Hasmil
(1971–)

Julia Jane
(1975–)

Timothy Arthur
(1977–)

NOTES

ABBREVIATIONS

Because this book does not contain a bibliography, full citations are supplied in the first instance in each chapter; thereafter, short titles are given. A few abbreviations have been used, including JL: James Legge.

In citing archival materials, the following abbreviations of the names of depositories have been used:

Bodleian: Oxford University, Bodleian Library

CWM: Council for World Mission archives

SOAS: University of London, School of Oriental and African Studies

PREFACE

1. See my *Myth and Meaning in Early Taoism: The Theme of Chaos (Hun-tun)* (Berkeley, Los Angeles, London: University of California Press, 1983, 1988); in particular, p. 309, where I highlight Legge's remark that he found the Daoist fascination with chaos "fantastic and unreasonable."

2. On my anticipation of the chaos theory of the 1980s, see the preface to the paperback edition, *Myth and Meaning* (1988), xi–xvii. See also Eugene Eoyang, "Chaos Misread: Or, There's Wonton in My Soup!" *Comparative Literature Studies* 26 (1989): 271–84.

3. The expressions "quite unimportant" and "formidably remote" are taken, respectively, from Max Müller and Raymond Schwab.

4. My strategic focus in this book is made all the more feasible by Lauren Pfister's published and unpublished articles, which deal extensively with the missionary and Hong Kong phase of Legge's life. Of Pfister's published studies on Legge, see especially his "Clues to the Life and Academic Achievements of One of

the Most Famous Nineteenth-Century European Sinologists—James Legge (A.D. 1815–1897)," *Journal of the Hong Kong Branch of the Royal Asiatic Society* 30 (1993): 180–218; idem, "Serving or Suffocating the Sage? Reviewing the Efforts of Three Nineteenth-Century Translators of the Four Books, with Special Emphasis on James Legge (A.D. 1815–1897)," *Hong Kong Linguist* 7 (1990): 25–55; idem, "Some New Dimensions in the Study of the Works of James Legge (1815–1897)," 2 parts, *Sino-Western Cultural Relations (16th–18th Centuries)* 12 (1990): 29–50 and 13 (1991): 45–48; idem, "The Failures of James Legge's Fruitful Life for China," *Ching Feng* 31 (December 1988): 246–71; and idem, "James Legge," in *An Encyclopedia of Translation: Chinese-English–English-Chinese,* ed. Chan Sin-wai and David E. Pollard (Hong Kong: Chinese University Press, 1995), 401–22.

5. See Richard D. Altick, "Eminent Victorianism: What Lytton Strachey Hath Wrought," *American Scholar* 64 (1995): 81–89.

6. Quoted by Gertrude Himmelfarb, "Manners into Morals," *American Scholar* 57 (1988): 228. "Friends," as Professor Benjamin Jowett said, "always think it necessary (except Boswell, that great genius) to tell lies about their deceased friend; they leave out all his faults lest the public should exaggerate them. But we want to know his faults,—that is probably the most interesting part of him." See F. Max Müller, *My Autobiography, A Fragment* (New York: Charles Scribner's Sons, 1901), 3–4.

7. Lytton Strachey, *Eminent Victorians* (London and New York: G. P. Putnam's Sons, 1918), viii.

8. Helen Edith Legge very briefly alludes to the term question and some of the related controversy, but generally neglects the issue of how this battle importantly transforms Legge. Other significant controversies in Legge's life are not mentioned. The one other early attempt at a substantial biographical portrait of Legge (aside from the more perfunctory obituary accounts and the entry in the *Dictionary of National Biography*) is Lindsay Ride's twenty-nine-page Biographical Note, published in the Hong Kong University Press 1960 reprinting of the *Chinese Classics.*

9. The quotations from Dominica Legge are from personal communications. She wrote (June 9, 1978) that her aunt, Helen Edith, "destroyed no end of correspondence etc., when she wrote the Life. Unfortunately, the house and contents were left to her." According to Dominica, Helen Edith did not "destroy anything deliberately" but was "desperately untidy and careless." My familiarity with the extant materials has led me to be somewhat more suspicious of Helen Edith's procedures in these matters. It is clear that Helen Edith's method for writing her biography involved going through whatever primary materials she had at hand and then typing out selected (and often severely truncated) excerpts. None of this would be particularly damning except for the fact that some of the original documents have disappeared (were mislaid or even, as it seems in the case of some crucial final pages from Legge's autobiographical "Notes of My Life," destroyed). It is worth noting that Helen Edith's portrait of her mother, Hannah Mary Legge, downplays Hannah's evident anxiety (and persistent debilitating dis-ease) about living in Hong Kong and in dealing with the "filthy" Chinese people and institutions.

10. For a collection of contemporaneous reviews of Helen Edith Legge's *James Legge Missionary and Scholar* (London: Religious Tract Society, 1905), see the clip-

pings in the Council for World Mission (hereafter cited as CWM)/China/Personal/ Legge/Box 7 (which includes advertising leaflets as well as reviews from the *Pall Mall Gazette*, the *Glasgow Herald*, and the *Presbyterian*).

11. See, for example, George Levine, "Victorian Studies," in *Redrawing the Boundaries: The Transformation of English and American Literary Studies*, ed. Stephen Greenblatt and Giles Gunn (New York: Modern Language Association of America, 1992), 130–53.

12. Altick, "Eminent Victorianism," 82–83.

13. See Janet Malcolm, *The Silent Woman: Sylvia Plath and Ted Hughes* (New York: Knopf, 1994), 8–10:

> Biography is the medium through which the remaining secrets of the famous dead are taken from them and dumped out in full view of the world. The biographer at work, indeed, is like the professional burglar, breaking into a house, rifling through certain drawers that he has good reason to think contain the jewelry and money and triumphantly bearing his loot away. The voyeurism and busybodyism that impel writers and readers of biography alike are obscured by an apparatus of scholarship designed to give the enterprise an appearance of banklike blandness and solidity. The biographer is portrayed almost as a kind of benefactor. He is seen as sacrificing years of his life to his task, tirelessly sitting in archives and libraries and patiently conducting interviews with witnesses. There is no length he will not go to, and the more his book reflects his industry the more the reader believes that he is having an elevating literary experience, rather than simply listening to backstairs gossip and reading other people's mail. The transgressive nature of biography is rarely acknowledged, but it is the only explanation for biography's status as a popular genre. The reader's amazing tolerance (which he would extend to no novel written half as badly as most biographies) makes sense only when seen as a kind of collusion between him and the biographer in an excitingly forbidden undertaking: tiptoeing down the corridor together to stand in front of the bedroom door and try to peep through the keyhole.
>
> Every now and then, a biography comes along that strangely displeases the public. Something causes the reader to back away from the writer and refuse to accompany him down the corridor. What the reader has usually heard in the text, what has alerted him to danger, is the sound of doubt—the sound of a crack opening in the wall of the biographer's self-assurance. As a burglar should not pause to discuss with his accomplice the rights and wrongs of burglary while he is jimmying a lock, so a biographer ought not to introduce doubts about the legitimacy of the biographical enterprise. The biography-loving public does not want to hear that biography is a flawed genre. It prefers to believe that certain biographers are bad guys.

14. Such ruses were certainly not Strachey's rhetorical inventions. As Altick notes ("Eminent Victorianism," 83):

> [The] ideal of calm objectivity had governed English history-writing since the mid-Victorian era [and, we may add, even earlier in the case of Scottish historiography], when the principles of the so-called scientific historiography, based on the assumption that truth could be told only if its teller stuck to the documented facts and eschewed artifice, had been imported from Germany. . . . Strachey's diatribes against the late Victorian and Edwardian monuments that passed for biographies simply meant that the "official" biographers had not learned from the historians,

or that the pressures of conformity were more compelling than the attractions of truth-telling.

15. Himmelfarb, "Manners into Morals," 223. Particularly interesting is her discussion of the interconnections of manners and morals, morals and laws, and laws and force.

16. Ibid.

17. See the revisionary work of David L. Hall and Roger T. Ames, *Thinking through Confucius* (Albany, N.Y.: State University of New York Press, 1987), which challenges conventional sinological notions about Confucian virtue.

18. On Antonio Gramsci's idea of hegemony, see especially the challenging views of Jean and John Comaroff as they relate to missionary tradition, at first blush the most obvious agents of a totalizing and delusional view of cultural conversion and progress (*Of Revelation and Revolution: Christianity, Colonialism, and Consciousness in South Africa,* vol. 1 [Chicago: University of Chicago Press, 1991]). See also Dorothy M. Figueira's *The Exotic: A Decadent Quest* (Albany, N.Y.: State University of New York Press, 1994) and *Translating the Orient: The Reception of Sakuntala in Nineteenth-Century Europe* (Albany, N.Y.: State University of New York Press, 1991), in which she intelligently discusses the problems in current Saidian-style discussions of Orientalism and cogently challenges the notion that the West's reception of the East was "solely in terms of hegemonic possession, power, and control."

19. See Figueira, *The Exotic,* 1–18.

20. Raymond Schwab, *La Renaissance orientale* (Paris: Éditions Payot, 1950). I have also loosely modeled my basic method on George Stocking's brilliant study of Victorian disciplinary history (anthropology in this case), which attempts "to be as interpretively suggestive as possible without knowingly doing violence to historical particulars." See George W. Stocking Jr., *Victorian Anthropology* (New York: Free Press, 1987), xii. Let me also acknowledge the influence of Jonathan Z. Smith's provocative reflections on the history of comparison and the academic study of religion, Andrew F. Walls's sensitive yet challenging approach to Protestant missionary history, Jean and John Comaroff's groundbreaking study of Victorian missionaries in South Africa, and Christopher Herbert's imaginative discussion of Victorian missionaries in the South Pacific: see Jonathan Z. Smith, *Imagining Religion: From Babylon to Jonestown* (Chicago: University of Chicago Press, 1982); idem, *To Take Place: Toward Theory in Ritual* (Chicago and London: University of Chicago Press, 1987); and idem, *Drudgery Divine: On the Comparison of Early Christianities and the Religions of Late Antiquity* (Chicago: University of Chicago Press, 1990); Andrew F. Walls, "The Nineteenth-Century Missionary as Scholar," in *Misjonskall og forskerglede,* ed. Nils E. Bloech-Hoell (Oslo: Universitetsforlaget, 1975), 209–21; idem, " 'The Best Thinking of the Best Heathen': Humane Learning and the Missionary Movement," in *Religion and Humanism,* ed. K. Robbins, Studies in Church History 17 (Oxford: Blackwood, 1981), 341–53; idem, "The Translation Principle in Christian History," in *Bible Translation and the Spread of the Church,* ed. Philip C. Stine (Leiden: E. J. Brill, 1990), 24–39; Comaroff and Comaroff, *Of Revelation and Revolution,* particularly pp. 1–48 and 49–85; and Christopher Herbert, *Culture and Anomie: Ethnographic Imagination in the Nineteenth Century* (Chicago: University of Chicago Press, 1991), 15.

21. Strachey, *Eminent Victorians,* viii.

INTRODUCTION

1. F. Max Müller, *My Autobiography, A Fragment* (New York: Charles Scribner's Sons, 1901), 14–15.

2. On the shared commentarial presuppositions of the lettered classes in traditional Western and Eastern traditions, see John B. Henderson, *Scripture, Canon, and Commentary: A Comparison of Confucian and Western Exegesis* (Princeton, N.J.: Princeton University Press, 1991). And on native Chinese traditions of textual scholarship in the Qing period (Hanxue [Han Studies] and Kaozhengxue [Evidential Research]), see especially Benjamin A. Elman, *From Philosophy to Philology: Intellectual and Social Aspects of Change in Late Imperial China* (Cambridge, Mass.: Council on East Asian Studies, Harvard University, 1984).

3. See the English translation of Schwab's magnum opus, *The Oriental Renaissance: Europe's Rediscovery of India and the East 1680–1880* (trans. by Gene Patterson-Black and Victor Reinking, with a foreword by Edward W. Said [New York: Columbia University Press, 1984]), 6: "China's linguistic instrument appeared in a formidable solitude, bewildering the mental habits of the West, rendering the problem of equivalences among languages almost absurd, and refusing to allow its closed system to be drawn into the comparative school." See also V. Barthold, *La Découverte de l'Asie*, trans. B. Nikitine (Paris: Payot, 1947), 153; Gustave Dugat, *Histoire des orientalistes de l'Europe du xiie au xixe siècles*, 2 vols. (Paris: Maisonneuve, 1868–1870); Jules Mohl, *Vingt-sept ans d'histoire des études orientales: Rapports faits à la Société asiatique de Paris de 1840 à 1867*, 2 vols. (Paris: Reinwald, 1879–1880); Francis Jullien, "Pour une sinologie occidentale: La Comparaison comme fiction et comme méthode. La Question de l'alterité," *Revue européene des sciences sociales* 24 (1986): 77–84; and Wilhelm Halbfass, *India and Europe: An Essay in Understanding* (Albany: State University of New York Press, 1988).

4. See Max Müller, "On the Enormous Antiquity of the East," *Nineteenth Century* 29 (1891): 808.

5. See Max Müller, *Address Delivered at the Opening of the Ninth International Congress of Orientalists Held in London Sept. 5, 1892, With the Replies of Prof. G. Bühler and Count Angelo de Gubernatis* (Oxford: Oxford University Press, 1892). For a full discussion of this address, which was published as a pamphlet, see chapter 8.

6. Zhang Longxi, "The Myth of the Other: China in the Eyes of the West," *Critical Inquiry* 15 (1992): 110. It is a curious fact that sinology is still resistant to the notion that it was affected by the distortions of "Orientalism" as discussed in Edward Said's *Orientalism*. See the discussion by Hans Hägerdal, "China and Orientalism," *International Institute for Asian Studies Newsletter* 10 (Autumn 1996): 31–32. I use the term *sinological Orientalism* both to indicate that sinology was not impervious to the forces affecting other kinds of disciplinary Orientalism and to distinguish it from the unfortunate monolithic implications of Said's original formulations. For further discussion of these issues, see the conclusion.

7. The literature on these developments is too immense to cite fully here. See, however, N. J. Girardot, "Chinese Religions: History of the Study Of," in *The Encyclopedia of Religion*, ed. Mircea Eliade (New York: Macmillan, 1986–1987), 3: 312–23; idem, " 'Very Small Books about Very Large Subjects': A Prefatory Appreciation of

the Enduring Legacy of Laurence G. Thompson's *Chinese Religion: An Introduction,*" *Journal of Chinese Religions* 20 (1992): 9–15; and Daniel Overmyer et al., "Chinese Religions—The State of the Field," *Journal of Asian Studies* 54 (1995): 124–60. For a more general historical perspective, see Paul A. Cohen, *Discovering History in China: American Historical Writing on the Recent Chinese Past* (New York: Columbia University Press, 1984).

8. See particularly the impressive, but controversial, work of Victor Mair, e.g., "Mummies of the Tarim Basin," *Archaeology* 48, no. 2 (March/April 1995): 28–35; the afterword to his translation of the *Tao Te Ching* (New York: Bantam, 1990); "Old Sinitic Mag, Old Persian Magus, and English 'Magician,'" *Early China* 15 (1990): 27–47; the notes on the "Heavenly Questions" in the *Columbia Anthology of Traditional Chinese Literature* (New York: Columbia University Press, 1994); and "The Bronze Age and Iron Age Peoples of Eastern Central Asia," *Early China News* 8 (1995): 1–10. See also, for example, Edward L. Shaughnessy, "Western Cultural Innovations in China, 1200 B.C.," *Sino-Platonic Papers* 11 (1989): 1–8; and Edwin G. Pulleyblank, "Chinese and Indo-Europeans," *Journal of the Royal Asiatic Society* (1966): 9–39.

9. Needless to say, these are now highly controversial issues. See, for example, the heated debate over Edwin G. Pulleyblank's "Early Contacts Between Indo-Europeans and Chinese," in the *International Review of Chinese Linguistics* 1 (1996): 1–50 (including comments by Victor Mair, David Keightley, Louisa Fitzgerald-Huber, Frederick Kortlandt, and Laurent Sagart). See also David N. Keightley's preface to *The Origins of Chinese Civilization,* ed. D. Keightley (Berkeley and Los Angeles: University of California Press, 1983), xix–xxix; and idem, "Archaeology and Mentality: The Making of China," *Representations* 18 (1987): 91–129. To take only one other example of these changes, it is worth noting that recent, and quite impressive, reevaluations of dynastic chronologies and ideological developments (especially the whole Mandate of Heaven or *Tianming* tradition) found in ancient texts by means of sophisticated applications of archaeoastronomical methods are not entirely unanticipated by nineteenth-century scholarship. See especially the work by David Pankenier: "Astrological Origins of Chinese Dynastic Ideology," *Vistas in Astronomy* 37 (1994); idem, "The *Bamboo Annals* Revisited: Problems of Method in Using the Chronicle as a Source for the Chronology of Early Zhou," 2 parts, *Bulletin of the School of Oriental and African Studies* 55 (1992): 272–97, 498–510; and idem, "The Cosmo-Political Background of Heaven's Mandate," *Early China* 20 (1995). Recent archaeoastronomical methods especially draw upon the multicultural and interdisciplinary insights of Giorgio de Santillana and Hertha von Dechend's *Hamlet's Mill: An Essay on Myth and the Frame of Time* (Boston, Mass.: David R. Godine, 1977). Legge himself made use of early astronomical methods developed by his missionary colleague John Chalmers, and even more impressively pioneered by a professional sinological associate, Gustave Schlegel. See the "Appendix on the Astronomy of the Ancient Chinese" by John Chalmers in James Legge, prolegomena to the *Book of History (Shu jing)* in *Chinese Classics* (1895), 3: 90–104; the astronomical chart of stars visible in China in 2300 B.C.E., prepared for Legge by his Oxonian colleague C. Pritchard in James Legge, introduction, *Sacred Books,* 3: 26–30; and Gustave Schlegel, *Uranographie chinoise, ou preuves directes que l'astronomie primitive est originaire de la Chine, et qu'elle a été empruntée par les anciens peuples occidentaux à la sphère chinoise* (Leiden: E. J. Brill, 1875).

10. By, among others, David Mungello, Paul Rule, Donald Lach, Jacques Gernet, Jonathan Spence, John D. Young, and Étiemble. On the history of French sinology, see especially Paul Demiéville, "Aperçu historique des études sinologiques en France," *Acta Asiatica* 11 (1966): 56–110; and Henri Maspero, "La Sinologie," in *Société asiatique. Le Livre de centenaire 1822–1922* (Paris: P. Geuthner, 1922), 261–83.

11. See, for example, John King Fairbank, "Introduction: The Place of Protestant Writings in China's Cultural History," in *Christianity in China, Early Protestant Missionary Writings,* ed. Suzanne Wilson Barnett and John King Fairbank (Cambridge, Mass.: Committee on American-East Asian Relations, Department of History, Harvard University, 1985), 7–18; Torben Christensen and William Hutchison, eds., *Missionary Ideologies in the Imperialist Era: 1880–1920* (Aros, Denmark: Christensens Bogtrykkeri, 1982), 2–6; Murray A. Rubinstein, "Christianity in China: One Scholar's Perspective on the State of Research in China Missions and Chinese Christian History, 1964–1986," *Newsletter for Modern Chinese History* 4 (September 1987): 111–43; and Paul William Harris, *Missionaries, Martyrs, and Modernizers: Autobiography and Reform Thought in American Protestant Missions,* 2 vols. (Ann Arbor, Mich.: University Microfilms International, 1986). I should note that Donald Treadgold's appraisal of missionary history is distinctive for its appreciation of Legge; see *The West in Russia and China: Secular and Religious Thought in Modern Times,* vol. 2 (Cambridge: Cambridge University Press, 1973). See also Daniel H. Bays, ed., *Christianity in China: From the Eighteenth Century to the Present* (Stanford, Calif.: Stanford University Press, 1996).

12. On the history of British sinology, see John Francis Davis, "The Rise and Progress of Chinese Literature in England" and "Observations on the Language and Literature of China," in *Chinese Miscellanies* (London: John Murray, 1865); and especially T. H. Barrett, *Singular Listlessness: A Short History of Chinese Books and British Scholars* (London: Wellsweep, 1989). For my disagreements with Barrett's evaluation of nineteenth-century British sinology as mostly "listless," see chapter 2. See also the discussion of Legge in Liu Cun-ren, "Cong Li Madou dao Li Yuese da Hanxue Daolu" (The ways of sinology from Matteo Ricci to Joseph Needham), *Ming Pao Monthly* 86 (July 1991): 85–87. The idea of "hyphenated" missionary-scholars I borrow from Andrew Walls; see his helpful study of the genre, "The Nineteenth-Century Missionary as Scholar," in *Misjonskall og forskerglede,* ed. Nils E. Bloch-Hoell (Oslo: Universitetsforlaget, 1975), 209–21. It should be noted that important German missionary-scholars such as Eitel and Faber worked largely within an Anglicized milieu. Both wrote extensively in English and were identified with communities dominated by the Americans and British. Henri Cordier can also, to a lesser extent, be included in this group since he had an English schooling and was at home in both English- and French-speaking communities of scholarship.

13. See, for example, Arthur Wright, "The Study of Chinese Civilization," *Journal of the History of Ideas* 21 (1960): 233–55. Orientalist contemporaries indeed recognized Legge's formative impact on sinology at the end of the century, so that, for example, his staunch nemesis, the sino-Aryan comparativist-engineer Thomas Kingsmill, following the lead of the outspoken and methodologically modern consular-scholar Herbert Giles, condemned what he considered to be the shamefully outdated "errors of Leggism." See T. W. Kingsmill, "Dr. Machlagan and the

Taoteh King," *China Review* 23 (1899): 265. For a fuller discussion of Kingsmill's views (and those of Herbert Giles) concerning Legge, see below, pages 431–43.

14. See Marcel Granet, *Festivals and Songs of Ancient China,* trans. E. D. Edwards (New York: E. P. Dutton, 1932), 15. On Granet, see N. J. Girardot, "Granet, Marcel," in *The Encyclopedia of Religion,* ed. Mircea Eliade (New York: Macmillan, 1986–1987), 4: 94–95.

15. See James Legge, "Notes of My Life" (1897).

16. On these issues, see, for example, Susan Bassnett-Mcguire, *Translation Studies* (London: Methuen, 1980). Totally forgotten in the mists of prejudice were Legge's more modern English translations (1867, 1872, 1876) of the *Analects, Mencius,* and *Poetry,* which show his literary playfulness and general sensitivity to particular audiences.

17. Charles Hardwick, *Christ and Other Masters: An Historical Inquiry into Some of the Chief Parallelisms and Contrasts Between Christianity and the Religious Systems of the Ancient World. With Special Reference to Prevailing Difficulties and Objections,* 4 parts (Cambridge: Macmillan, 1855–1859).

18. *Analects* VII. i, *Chinese Classics* (1893), 1: 195.

19. The electronic WorldCat bibliographical listing of editions of Legge's works runs to over two hundred entries and includes multiple Asian and Western reprintings of the *Chinese Classics.*

20. Earlier theologians such as Frederick Maurice (*The Religions of the World and Their Relations to Christianity* [London: John W. Parker, 1847]) and Charles Hardwick (*Christ and Other Masters,* 1855) had identified "Confucianism" (Maurice and Hardwick) and "Tau-ism" (only Hardwick) for the English-speaking tradition, but it was only the combined Orientalist expertise and academic authority of Legge and Müller that definitively linked these movements with sacred books and defined them as world religions.

21. Lauren Pfister first drew my attention to Legge's special interest in Han Yu.

22. Among other studies that challenge the monolithic tenor of Said's theory, see Dorothy M. Figueira, *Translating the Orient: The Reception of Sakuntala in Nineteenth-Century Europe* (Albany, N.Y.: State University Press of New York, 1991), and Lisa Lowe, *Critical Terrains: French and British Orientalisms* (Ithaca, N.Y., and London: Cornell University Press, 1991).

23. I am thinking here of a joint announcement by the Yale University Press and the American Council of Learned Societies about a long-term venture to publish the Chinese basic texts. Also under way are several other efforts to produce new versions of important Chinese texts.

PROLOGUE

1. See JL, "Notes of My Life" (1897). I used Helen Edith Legge's 160-page typed and edited version that was in Dominica Legge's possession at the time of my first research trip to England in the early 1980s. This version is now deposited in the Bodleian Library, Oxford University. Legge's original handwritten copybook is found in the Council for World Mission (CWM) archive at the School of African and Oriental Studies, University of London. This document can be fruitfully sup-

plemented by Legge's earlier autobiographical reflections published at the death of his older brother and theological confidant, George. See James Legge, "Memoir of the Rev. George Legge, LL.D.," in George Legge's posthumously published *Lectures on Theology, Science, and Revelation* (London: Jackson, Walford and Hodder, 1863). As to why the autobiography (which Legge says he hoped to complete by the end of April 1896) was never completed, I can only surmise that it was due to ill health during the rest of the year. He also did not give his regular public lectures at Oxford during the 1896 academic term. Helen Edith Legge may have destroyed some sections of the original "Notes." See, for example, the original handwritten copybook, which shows evidence of five pages having been removed (CWM/China/Personal/Legge/Box 10).

2. See William Raeper, *George Macdonald* (Batavia, Ill.: Lion Publishing, 1987), 37.

3. See Lauren Pfister's articles (see pages 557–58, note 4) for the details of Legge's career as a missionary.

4. JL, "Notes of My Life," 1. It should be noted that the spelling of the family name was variable: in records dating to the early part of the nineteenth century, the common form was Legg.

5. See Paul Johnson, *Birth of the Modern World Society, 1815–1830* (New York: HarperCollins, 1991).

6. The expression "well-off" is Legge's own description of his family's status in Huntly. See JL, "Memoir of the Rev. George Legge," xxi. For a description of the town of Huntly at the time of Legge's youth, see especially Raeper, *George Macdonald*, 18–26.

7. On the history and nature of the Missionar Kirk in Huntly, see George Gray, *Recollections of Huntly as It Was Seventy Years Ago* (Banff, Scotland: Banffshire Journal Office, 1892), and Robert Troup, *The Missionar Kirk of Huntly* (Edinburgh and Glasgow: John Menzies, 1901). The Reverend John Hill was minister of the church during the time of Legge's upbringing. Raeper notes (*George Macdonald,* 35) that the Missionar Kirk "comprised the most energetic men in the locality—men remarkably alike for their religious zeal and activity in business. Although not a numerous body, they exercised greater influence on the community than did any other of the religious denominations."

8. JL, "Notes of My Life," 43.

9. Concerning the romantic cult of the Scottish clan hero in the nineteenth century, see H. J. Hanham, "Mid-Century Scottish Nationalism: Romantic and Radical," in *Ideas and Institutions of Victorian Britain,* ed. Robert Robson (New York: Barnes and Noble, 1967), 143–79. See also Eric Hobsbawm and Terence Ranger, eds., *The Invention of Tradition* (Cambridge: Cambridge University Press, 1984).

10. Robertson Smith was born at New Farm in the parish of Keig, a dozen or so miles from Huntly. See the entries on both Robertson Smith and Hastings in the *Dictionary of National Biography.* For a insightful discussion of Robertson Smith that brings out the associations with Legge, see Andrew F. Walls, "William Robertson Smith and the Missionary Movement," in *William Robertson Smith,* ed. William Johnstone (Sheffield, England: Sheffield Academic Press, 1995), 101–17. On the Scottish and Aberdonian context for Legge, Hastings, and Robertson Smith, see James Thrower, "Aberdeen University and the Study of Religions," in *But Where Shall Wisdom Be Found?* (Aberdeen, Scotland: Aberdeen University Press, 1995), 81–92.

11. I borrow the expression "comparativist mentality" from G. W. Trompf, who uses it to trace the gradual unfolding of Max Müller's scholarly sensibility with respect to his scientific study of religion. See Trompf's *Friedrich Max Mueller as a Theorist of Comparative Religion* (Bombay: Shakuntala Publishing House, 1978), 3.

12. Müller himself makes a helpful (though clearly self-interested) distinction between "historical" comparison (as in his own science of religions and comparative linguistics, which are "inductive") and "speculative" or "philosophical" comparison, which relied on deductive conclusions (such as he attributes to Tylor and his epigones).

13. Concerning the emergence of the science of comparative religions and English intellectual history in the last half of the nineteenth century, see especially Marjorie Wheeler-Barclay, "The Science of Religion in Britain, 1860–1915" (Ph.D. diss., Northwestern University, 1987).

14. On Robertson Smith, see T. O. Beidelman, *W. Robertson Smith and the Sociological Study of Religion* (Chicago and London: University of Chicago Press, 1974); and the discussion in Wheeler-Barclay, "Science of Religion in Britain."

15. On the missionary movement in Britain during the nineteenth century, see, among other works, James Miller McCutcheon's "The American and British Missionary Concept of Chinese Civilization in the Nineteenth Century" (Ph.D. diss., University of Wisconsin, 1959) and Laurence Kitzan's "The London Missionary Society in India and China, 1798–1834" (Ph.D. diss., University of Toronto, 1965).

16. On George Legge's theology, see his *Lectures on Theology* and his pamphlet, *The Range and Limitations of Human Knowledge: A Sermon* (Leicester, England: J. & T. Spencer; London: Simpkin, Marshall, 1856).

17. See E. J. Sharpe's discussion of these issues in *Not to Destroy but to Fulfill: The Contribution of J. N. Farquhar to Protestant Missionary Thought in India* (Uppsala, Sweden: Gleerup, 1965). Farquhar was, like Legge, a graduate of King's College, Aberdeen.

18. Legge described his own understanding of Congregationalist independence in the following way (see JL to Mr. Walkinshaw, c. 1852–1853, CWM/China/Personal/Legge/Box 8):

> We are independents because we will allow no creeds, rituals, and forms of religious polity to come between us and our direct appeal to the word of God. . . . We are independent because among ourselves we hold each Church to be in itself in subjection to the Word of God, competent to manage all its own affairs and to be free from all authoritative interference from every other Church or body of Churches.

In nineteenth-century British church history, the labels "Dissenter," "Independent," and "Nonconforming" were roughly congruent in indicating a religious affiliation separate from the state churches of England and Scotland.

19. See JL, "Notes of My Life," 8. Legge notes that he learned to read and spell largely by memorizing the *Shorter Catechism*.

20. I borrow the helpful expression "Sabbath culture" from Lauren Pfister.

21. Raeper, *George Macdonald*, 35.

22. *Alec Forbes of Howglen*, as quoted and discussed by Raeper, *George Macdonald*, 37: The "missionars" in Huntly

> believed that Christ had died on the cross only for those who had been elected since before the foundation of the world—a limited number chosen capriciously

by God with no reference to merit. The thought that people could have a hand in their own salvation was both presumptuous and abhorrent—God chose some and he simply did not choose others. Believers, therefore, had to examine their lives for some measure of God's grace working in them, and if there was no evidence of this grace then they believed that they were doomed to hell—a real hell filled with eternal fire and torture.

23. JL, "Memoir of the Rev. George Legge," xxi. Legge is careful to emphasize that there was never "any dislike of religion" as a "consequence of the strictness of [the Sabbath] rule" (p. xxiv).

24. JL, "Notes of My Life," 15-17.

25. Legge, ibid., 2, dutifully records a family tradition that his mother, Elizabeth, "had been able to repeat all the Psalms 'without missing a word,' and that she had had a contrivance fitted to her spinning wheel, by means of which she could have her Psalm-book beneath her eye and available for reference, even when she was plying her work."

26. Ibid., 3-4. Legge says that his father's education had been "very defective; but by steady perseverance and strict integrity, he by and by won for himself a foremost standing in the community. Conscious . . . of his own disadvantages through the want of education, he was resolved that none of his sons should labour under the same."

27. Ibid., 10-11.

28. Ibid.

29. Ibid., 26.

30. Ibid., 26-27.

31. The significance of Buchanan's work for Legge's intellectual development is an insight that I owe to Lauren Pfister.

32. As Legge says ("Notes of My Life," 51), the Huttonian Prize was

the chief reward at that time of merit and success in the whole curriculum, and had been founded early in the present [nineteenth] century by an old alumnus of the College. Its pecuniary value was only £15, half in money, and the rest in books, but it was sought and worked for because of the honour and distinction which it conferred. In my notes of 1831 I have stated how I was told then, after I had gained the first bursary, that no first bursar had so far been also Huttonian Prizeman. I said nothing when the remark was made, but silently resolved that I would try to be the prizeman of 1835.

33. See his references to the Scottish philosophers of common sense, ibid., 44, 50. On Thomas Reid and Dugald Stewart, see William L. Davidson, "Scottish Philosophy," in The Encyclopedia of Religion and Ethics, ed. James Hastings (Edinburgh: T. and T. Clark, 1908-1921), 11: 261-71. Operating with the Aristotelian idea of "common sense" (i.e., the rational or "synthetic power of the human mind in the unifying experiences that come to us through the separate senses"), this tradition stressed the close association of the moral and religious tendencies of the human mind. Inasmuch as this philosophical tradition stressed the active role played by the mind in knowing, there was an affinity for Kant's more developed philosophy of consciousness.

34. JL, "Notes of My Life," 34. Legge also tells us that after his graduation in 1835 he spent some time studying French and Italian. His knowledge of Latin made

the learning of those two languages relatively easy, but as he says, his facility was more "literary" than practically useful (ibid., 59).

35. JL to George Legge, August 9, 1831. In other letters from this period, he bemoans his constant battle with "procrastination" (1834) and that "a life of struggling has always in my reveries to be my destiny" (March 3, 1833); CWM/China/Personal/Legge/Box 8. In 1837, George said of his younger brother that "study is with him a habit" (George Legge, "Letter to Highbury College Supporting James Legge's Entrance Examination," Leicester, March 7, 1837, Dr. Williams College Library Archive 383/10/3). As Legge said later, "assiduity certainly has an important place in my mental constitution" (CWM/China/Personal/Legge/Box 10). In his missionary career as he struggled to achieve a "thorough mastery" of the Chinese language, he emphasized that every difficult thing will "give way to perseverance" (JL, Journal, May 1847). These common evangelical themes of the self-made man engaged in the battle of life were echoed throughout Legge's life.

36. JL, "Notes of My Life," 38–39.

37. Ibid., 42–43.

38. JL, "Memoir of the Rev. George Legge," lxx.

39. JL, "Notes of My Life," 56–57.

40. Ibid., 57–58.

41. Ibid., 73–77.

42. Ibid., 60–69.

43. See Legge's description of Highbury College and his course of studies, ibid., 81–105.

44. George Legge, "Letter to Highbury College." George also observed that "in fluency of English speech—and familiarity of address as a speaker,—he has not a little to learn; . . . [he] only wants a little discipline and experience to make him a workman that needeth not to be ashamed."

45. JL, "Notes of My Life," 86–87. As Laurence Kitzan points out, most of the missionaries sent out by the London Missionary Society were not known for their educational achievements. See his "London Missionary Society," 15–16.

46. JL, "Notes of My Life," 102–3.

47. JL, Ordination Exam (CWM/China/Personal/Legge/Box 7). Reflecting on his answers almost sixty years later, Legge comments, in "Notes of My Life," that, in keeping with the independent spirit of Congregationalism, he was "happily" not asked "to sign any creed, old or new." Moreover, he proudly declares that "if such a requisition had been made," he would "not have obeyed it." It is worth comparing this ordination exam with his entrance examination for Highbury College, taken on March 7, 1837, which is preserved in the Dr. Williams College Library Archive 303/10/2. On both occasions, Legge's answers to the "usual queries" are basically congruent.

48. JL, "Notes of My Life," 105.

49. It is worth noting that this episode with his dead mother is also highlighted in his Highbury examination. As he said in 1837: "I do not date my conversion from the events of that morning, but the important impression which they made is still fresh upon my mind, and seldom could I afterwards engage in sin, without being startled at the time by the idea that her eye was upon me" (Dr. Williams College Library Archive 303/10/2).

50. JL, Ordination Exam, 4–10.

51. Ibid., 13–18.

52. Ibid., 26–30.

53. Livingstone is quoted in A. F. Walls, " 'The Best Thinking of the Best Heathen': Humane Learning and the Missionary Movement," in *Religion and Humanism,* ed. K. Robbins, Studies in Church History 17 (Oxford: Blackwood, 1981), 341. See also Sarah Potter, "The Social Origins and Recruitment of English Protestant Missionaries in the Nineteenth Century" (Ph.D. diss., University of London, 1974).

54. See A. F. Walls, "Nineteenth-Century Missionary as Scholar," in *Misjonskall og forskerglede,* ed. Nils E. Bloch-Hoell (Oslo: Universitetsforlaget, 1975), 209–10.

55. JL, "Notes of My Life," 116–17.

56. See the discussion of these issues in Kitzan, "London Missionary Society," 16–17.

57. JL, "Notes of My Life," 143–44.

58. Ibid., 122–33. It was Medhurst who first suggested to Legge that the Anglo-Chinese College in Malacca was largely unsuccessful.

59. See the discussion in Brian Harrison, *Waiting for China: The Anglo-Chinese College at Malacca, 1818–1843, and Early Nineteenth-Century Missions* (Hong Kong: Hong Kong University Press, 1979), 105–6. In November 1840 Evans wrote to the London Mission Society concerning his problems with Legge: "It has been for some time a matter of much grief to me to see a young person who has so recently joined me as a colleague, entirely ignorant of the manners and customs of the natives and quite inexperienced, not only desirous of introducing and setting up his own plans, but insisting on having them carried into effect." See also the corroborating discussion by R. L. O'Sullivan, "The Departure of the London Missionary Society from Malacca," *Journal of the Malaysian Historical Society* 23 (1980): 75–83.

60. JL, "Notes of My Life," 129–30.

61. James Legge and Tkin Shen, trans., *The Rambles of the Emperor Ching Tih in Keang Nan: A Chinese Fable,* 2 vols. (London: Longmans, 1843).

62. On Ho Tsun-sheen and his role as a pioneering Chinese Christian theologian, see the articles by Lauren Pfister listed on pages 557–58. Legge's first published work was his study-aid for Chinese, *A Lexilogus of the English, Malay, and Chinese Language, comprehending the vernacular idioms of the last in the Hok-keen and Canton dialects* (Malacca, 1841; Edinburgh: T. and T. Clark, 1908–1926).

63. JL, preface to the *Rambles of the Emperor Ching Tih,* v. Legge says that he "sketched" the "plan" of the *Classics* in 1841 (*Chinese Classics* [1893], 1: viii).

64. JL, Journal, 1846–1847, sixty-nine handwritten pages, Bodleian Library, Oxford University (hereafter cited as Bodleian), MS. Eng. Misc. E. 556. The passage in question is found on page 14.

65. There is a rich tradition of Protestant missionary commentary on the passage from Isaiah. Most famously in the 1840s was Walter M. Lowrie's long discussion of "The Land of Sinim" published in *The Chinese Repository* 13 (1844): 113–23. This was reissued in book form in the late 1840s and in 1850 (Philadelphia, Pa.: William S. Martien, 1850). Legge himself frequently preached on this passage; one of his more notable sermons on the theme was published as *The Land of Sinim: A Sermon Preached in the Tabernacle, Moorfields, at the 65th Anniversary of the London Missionary Society* (London: John Snow, 1859). For more recent discussions that discount

the equation of Sinim and China, see Paul S. Hsiang, "God in Ancient China," *Worldmission* (1956): 226; and Donald Leslie, "Japhet in China," *Journal of the American Oriental Society* 104 (1984): 404.

66. JL, sermon dating to the 1850s (CWM/China/Personal/Legge/Box 6). In this sermon Legge argued the thesis that the British had inherited the Jewish mantle of chosenness and were the primary agents of God's will in the nineteenth century.

67. Legge's reputation as a promising young scholar was ratified early in his career by his receipt of an honorary doctorate in the 1840s from the seminary at New York University in the United States. This award was most probably occasioned by the repute of his two published works (the *Lexilogus* and *Rambles of the Emperor Ching Tih*) among American missionaries. It is clear that he was very pleased to be able to use the title of Reverend Doctor.

68. Walter Medhurst, *A Dissertation on the Theology of the Chinese with a View to the Elucidation of the Most Appropriate Term for Expressing the Deity, In the Chinese Language* (Shanghae [Shanghai]: Mission Press, 1847). Prolific on this matter, Medhurst also wrote *An Inquiry into the Proper Mode of Rendering the Word God in Translating the Sacred Scriptures into the Chinese Language* (Shanghae: Mission Press, 1848) and *Of the Word Shin, As Exhibited in the Quotations Adduced under that Word, In the Chinese Imperial Thesaurus, Called the Pei-Wan-Yun Foo* (Shanghae: Mission Press, 1849).

69. On the overall term question, see Douglas G. Spelman, "Christianity in Chinese: The Protestant Term Question," *Papers on China* 22A (Cambridge, Mass.: Harvard University, 1969); and Jost Oliver Zetzsche, "The Bible in China: History of the Union Version or the Culmination of Protestant Missionary Bible Translation in China" (Ph.D. diss., University of Hamburg, 1997).

70. Concerning Legge's health at this time, see his letter to his brother John dated October 25, 1844, and another dated July 1845 (CWM/China/Personal/Legge).

71. See the anonymous article entitled "Chinese Youths," *Illustrated London News*, April 22, 1848, pp. 258–59.

72. Ibid., p. 259.

73. Ibid.

74. A fascinating account of one of these events is given by Legge's future second wife, Hannah Mary Johnston, in her diary dated January 20 (Lister Street) and 22 (Albion Chapel), 1848 (Helen Edith Legge, typescript, Bodleian Archive). She described them in the following way (p. 46; only Lee and Song were present):

> Attired in Chinese costume, their heads closely shaven (except for the crown which is plaited and hangs behind) and their contour perfectly Chinese, [they] contrast singularly with their English friends. [Lee] Kimlin the elder is the shorter of the two has a fine intelligent eye but otherwise is not attractive in appearance. It is not until his sweet and docile disposition has been developed, his mature piety and deep humility have been manifested, and his intelligence on general subjects has been elicited, that interest for him ripens into Christian affection. Song Hootkeam—a handsome young man—has a noble countenance and eyes thoroughly Chinese. They seem to go up into the organ of ideality. In the expression of his face you may read that nobility of nature and self-complacent superiority which characterize his countrymen in the vast empire of China.

75. See the account in "China: Reinforcement of the Missions," *Missionary Magazine and Chronicle* 13 (1848): 37.

76. Ibid., 41.

77. "Chinese Youths," p. 259. Legge understandably took this opportunity to "place in the hands of the Prince a memorial explanatory of the objects of his mission, and descriptive of the Theological Seminary at Hong-Kong, for the training of native evangelists." For Legge's own account of this meeting, see his letter to his brother John dated February 9, 1848 (CWM/China/Personal/Legge). In this letter he confesses that he has worries about his "meekness."

78. The original oil painting was done by Henry Room, a well-known portrait painter of the period. The engraving based on the painting was executed by J. Cochran. For background on this image, see "Room's Picture of Dr. Legge and the Three Chinese Youths," *Evangelical Magazine* (1848): 204–5.

79. Room's picture was specifically said to have "great moral" significance; ibid., 204.

80. Ibid.

81. For Legge's own assessment of the seminary, see his letter published under the title of "Missions in China" in the *China Mail*, no. 1220, May 1, 1867. See especially the balanced discussion of these issues in Carl T. Smith, "Dr. Legge's Theological School," *Chung Chi Bulletin* 50 (1971): 18–20. For a more general analysis of the fate of Chinese "coastal" converts, see Smith's *Chinese Christians: Elites, Middlemen, and the Church in Hong Kong* (Oxford: Oxford University Press, 1985).

82. JL, Journal for May 1848.

83. See William J. Boone, "Defense of an Essay on the Proper Rendering of the Words Elohim and Theos into the Chinese Language," which appeared in five parts in *The Chinese Repository* 19 (1850): 345 ff, 409 ff, 465 ff, 569 ff, 625 ff. *The Chinese Repository, The China Review,* and *The Chinese Recorder* are the journals of record for tracing out the vicissitudes of the term question debate.

84. Frederick D. Maurice, *The Religions of the World and Their Relations to Christianity* (London: John W. Parker, 1847). Maurice was a Broad Church Anglican cleric and scholar. Legge refers to Maurice in his 1886 sermon entitled "The Bearing of Our Knowledge of Comparative Religion on Christian Missions" (CWM/South China/Personal/Legge/Box 4). See pages 395–96 for the discussion of this sermon.

85. On Mary Isabella Legge's death, see the letters by Legge and Benjamin Hobson to John Morison, Mary's father. They were published in the *Evangelical Magazine* 31 (March 1853): 121–28. See also John Morison, "Sketches of the Life and Labours of the Late Mrs. Mary Isabella Legge, of Hong Kong," *Evangelical Magazine* (December 1853): 697–707, 757–61. Concerning the Victorian deathbed "sanctification of suffering," see Miriam Bailin, *The Sickroom in Victorian Fiction: The Art of Healing* (Cambridge: Cambridge University Press, 1994).

86. The "Specimen of the Chinese Classics" is found in CWM/South China/Personal/Legge/Box 6/Folder 1/Jacket B. Lauren Pfister notes that the model for Legge's layout of his edition of the classics was probably the work of the Ming scholar Deng Lin republished in 1779 by Du Dingji. It was entitled *Xinzeng si shu buzhu fukao beizhi* (translated by Legge as *The Four Books, with a Complete Digest of Supplements to the Commentary, and Additional Suggestions*).

87. See J. S. Gregory, "British Missionary Reaction to the Taiping Movement," *Journal of Religious History* 2 (1963): 205–12. Generally on the Taiping movement,

see Franz Michael and Chung-li Chang, *The Taiping Rebellion: History and Documents,* 3 vols. (Seattle: University of Washington Press, 1971).

88. Legge's increasingly disparaging evaluation of the Taiping movement is seen in his sermon *The Land of Sinim,* published in 1859. On Hong Rengan, see Shen Weibin's biography, *Hong Rengan* (Shanghai: People's Press, 1982).

89. See Legge's account of these developments in "Letters Chiefly on Pok-lo" (Helen Edith Legge typescript; twenty-seven pages; CWM/China/Personal/Legge/ Box 8); and his "Journal of a Missionary Tour along the East River of Canton Province," Supplement to the *Overland China Mail,* no. 238, June 28, 1861 (CWM/ China/Personal/Legge/Box 7).

90. Concerning educational policies in Hong Kong in the nineteenth century, see Gillian Bickley, *The Golden Needle: The Biography of Frederick Stewart (1836–1889)* (Hong Kong: David C. Lam Institute for East-West Studies, Hong Kong Baptist University, 1997). This publication is distributed by the Chinese University of Hong Kong Press.

91. See Jan Morris's spirited, though opinionated, *Hong Kong* (New York: Random House, 1989) and Michiko Kakutani's review of the book in the *New York Times,* 3 January 1989, p. 15. A more balanced approach that pays attention to the Chinese community is found in Jung-fang Tsai's *Hong Kong in Chinese History: Community and Social Unrest in the British Colony, 1842–1913* (New York: Columbia University Press, 1993). See also Frank Welsh's *A History of Hong Kong* (London: HarperCollins, 1993).

92. See "The Colony of Hong Kong. From a Lecture by the Rev. James Legge, D.D., LL.D. On Reminiscences of a Long Residence in the East, Delivered in the City Hall, November 5, 1872," *China Review* 1 (1872): 163–76.

93. The purported unhealthiness of the environment and climate of Hong Kong was a common theme in European writings in the 1840s and 1850s. As the pioneering photographer John Thompson noted, Hong Kong was often referred to as the "grave of Europeans" (see *Illustrations of China and Its People,* 4 vols. [London: Sampson Low, Marston, Low and Searle, 1873, 1874]). This condition was frequently described as a kind of deadly fever caused by a "marsh miasma derived from the oozy soil covered by rank vegetation" or by the "noxious exhalations from the large surface of new soil dug up," which generally gave rise to "excesses too powerful for the European constitution to bear." For corroboration of Legge's description, see "Review of Diseases in Hong Kong," *The Chinese Repository* (March 1846): 126; George Smith, *A Narrative of an Exploratory Visit to Each of the Consular Cities of China, and to the Islands of Hong Kong and Chusan on behalf of the Church Missionary Society in the Years 1844, 1845, 1846* (New York: Harper & Brothers, 1847), 447–48; and Robert Fortune, *Three Years' Wanderings in the Northern Provinces of China, Including a Visit to the Tea, Silk, and Cotton Countries: with an Account of the Agriculture and Horticulture of the Chinese, New Plants, etc.* (London: John Murray, 1847), 15–16. There is an Orientalist logic here that contrasts the "excess" and "poisonous opulence" of the Asian climate with the moderation and "temperate" nature of Europe. It is worth noting that in an early letter to his brother John recounting his first experience of the Orient, Legge makes a point of how dangerous the climate was and how the vegetation seems "painfully rapid in growth" and replete with "the pomp of barbarious luxuriance" (letter dated 31 March 1840; see Helen Edith Legge, *James Legge Missionary and Scholar* [London: Religious Tract Society, 1905], 14–15).

94. See the account given in the *North-China Herald,* October 15, 1898, p. 688. The introducer went on to say that Legge "had achieved another position not inferior to his position as a Sinologue. His judgment was considered most valuable in all the affairs relating to the Chinese of the colony. Governors had consulted him, and the public, though they did not always agree with him—it was only human nature that they should not agree with him sometimes—always attached great importance to his views."

95. For a revealing discussion of Chinese servants in Hong Kong, see Henry Knollys, *English Life in China* (London: Smith, Elder, 1885), 43–46.

96. See Hannah Mary Legge's letter dated 14 April 1860. From the description presented in this letter it would seem that the Legge household involved at least a half a dozen or more native servants; she specifically refers to a wet nurse, individual personal servants, and a cook with two assistants (CWM/China/Personal/Legge/Box 10). For a contemporaneous portrait of missionary opulence amid native squalor, see Knollys, *English Life in China.* Knollys describes the interior of one of these houses in a way that suggests the layout of the London Missionary Society Mission House (pp. 5–6):

> The interior of these houses . . . presents an aspect of luxury—I might almost say, of splendour—peculiarly characteristic of the East, and yet attainable at comparatively small expense. The shell, certainly, is exceedingly fragile, but every room and passage is of a magnificent size. . . . Then there is a profusion of lovely flowers and foliage which can never be out of place, while overhead, solemnly, gracefully, wave the white punkahs—huge oblong fans which stretch completely across the room. They move noiselessly by means of pulleys and ropes worked by a coolie outside, and set up regular waves of cool air, each puff of which gives a feeling of relief. . . . A broad, covered verandah lines the entire exterior length of the house, and, in fine, the combination of surroundings produces on a newcomer a strange, Arabian-night sensation.

Knollys's depiction is corroborated by Hannah Mary's own description; see her journal for June 13, 1859 (Helen Edith Legge, typescript of Hannah Mary Legge's journal for 1859, original lost, Christopher Legge family holdings). For a balanced discussion of some of these issues, see Jonathan J. Bonk, *The Theory and Practice of Missionary Identification 1860–1920* (Lewiston, N.Y.: Edwin Mellen Press, 1989), 37–90 (chapter 3 on "identification in the material-social sphere").

97. See especially the letter by Hannah Mary Legge, 16 May 1860 (CWM/China/Personal/Legge/Box 10). See also Hannah Mary's letter of 29 November 1864, which interestingly describes the Legge children playing at "Joss" with dolls and a miniature decorated "heathen temple."

98. Knollys, *English Life in China,* pp. 205–6. Knollys blithely goes on (pp. 206–7) to say that

> [i]n the course of a few years the missionary becomes tired of his work, or discovers a more attractive opening elsewhere. Apparently regardless of the fact that during the first part of his sojourn his services can have been little more than of an apprentice nature, he leaves the scene of his labours precisely when, by his indoctrination, he could be most useful, and hies him back to England, probably with a nice little accumulation of dollars wherewith to start in his new clearing. There he holds forth, on all possible public occasions, on the privations and toils, the

thrilling adventures and hair-breath escapes of a missionary's life. . . . He can scarcely fail to gain repute—especially among silly women little apt in weighing evidence—as a noble champion of Christianity, whereby he assumes a social status to which his birth and breeding have no means entitled him, and in many instances he will in some fashion reap much substantial advantage.

99. Lauren Pfister notes that all previous European editions of the Four Books followed the order set by Zhu Xi. This includes the Jesuit *Confucius Sinarum Philosophus* of the seventeenth century; F. Noël's *Les Livres classiques de l'empire de la Chine* (Paris: de Bure, Barrois aîné, S. Barrois jeune, 1784); David Collie's *The Chinese Classical Work Commonly Called the Four Books* (Malacca: Anglo-Chinese Press, 1828); and J.-P. Guillaume Pauthier's *Confucius et Mencius: Les Quatre Livres de philosophie morale et politique de la Chine* (Paris: Charpentier, 1854). I am indebted to Pfister for pointing out the unique ordering of the books making up Legge's *Chinese Classics.*

100. In 1858 Legge said that his plans involved the publication of "ten or twelve volumes" over a period of "six or seven years." See JL to Arthur Tidman, June 17, 1858 (CWM/South China/Personal/Legge/Box 6/Jacket B/Folder 2).

101. On Legge's sinological sources, see Lauren Pfister, "James Legge," in *An Encyclopedia of Translation: Chinese-English–English-Chinese*, ed. Chan Sin-wai and David E. Pollard (Hong Kong: Chinese University Press, 1995), 409–10.

102. JL, prolegomena, *Chinese Classics* (1861), vol. 1.

103. Ibid.

104. See Wang Tao's memorial to Legge translated in Lindsay Ride, Biographical Note, *Chinese Classics* (1961), 1: 16–17. Contrary to what is indicated in Ride's translation, this memorial dates to 1865.

105. JL to Hannah Mary Legge, December 3, 1867 (CWM/China/Personal/Legge/Box 10).

106. Ibid., June 24, 1866.

107. JL to the London Missionary Society Board, January 1867 (CWM/South China/Personal/Legge).

108. The reference to Legge's "special work" is found in a letter from F. Turner to Joseph Mullens, secretary of the London Missionary Society, 14 March 1870. As it is also said with respect to Legge's association with the London Missionary Society: "Being aware that his book is one important influence in drawing him back to us, I suppose he would prefer to have the printing office under his own control" (CWM/South China/Box 6/Folder 1/Jacket 8).

109. See Arthur Tidman to Legge, July 14, 1858; Helen Edith Legge typed excerpts (CWM/China/Personal/Legge/Box 8).

110. It seems that we have only Helen Edith Legge's typed excerpts of a letter dated July 21, 1858. It is possible that she destroyed the original documents.

111. See JL letter, exact 1858 date uncertain; Helen Edith Legge typed excerpts (CWM/China/Personal/Legge).

112. JL letter, February 26, 1864 (CWM/China/Personal/Legge).

113. JL to Mullens of the London Missionary Society, dated January 30, 1867 (CWM/China/Personal/Legge/Box 10).

114. See Mullens on behalf of the London Missionary Society Board of Directors, April 4, 1867 (CWM/China/Personal/Legge/Box 8). As far as I have been

able to determine, only Helen Edith Legge's typed excerpts (complete with tantalizing ellipses) remain of this important letter.

115. See John Legge, "Chinese Literature," *The Melbourne Review* (July 1876): 301–11 (CWM/China/Personal/Legge/Box 9).

116. See JL, prolegomena to the *Analects, Chinese Classics* (1893), 1: 84.

CHAPTER ONE. PILGRIM LEGGE
AND THE JOURNEY TO THE WEST, 1870–1874

1. See Jan Morris, *Hong Kong* (New York: Random House, 1989).

2. According to Wilfred Cantwell Smith (*The Meaning and End of Religion* [New York: Macmillan, 1963], 260 n. 63), the Latin transliteration of Confucius *(Cúm fu çù)* for Kongfuzi first appeared in 1662 in Prospero Intorcetta and Ignatio Costa Lusitano's *Sapientia Sinica*. This was reinforced by the influential work *Confucius Sinarum Philosophus* (1687). See Knud Lundbaek, "The Image of Neo-Confucianism in *Confucius Sinarum Philosophus,*" *Journal of the History of Ideas* 44 (1983): 19–30; and D. E. Mungello, *Curious Land: Jesuit Accommodation and the Origins of Sinology* (Honolulu: University of Hawaii Press, 1989), 247–99. The English term *Confucianism* already appears in Charles Hardwick's *Christ and Other Masters: An Historical Inquiry into Some of the Chief Parallelisms and Contrasts Between Christianity and the Religious Systems of the Ancient World. With Special Reference to Prevailing Difficulties and Objections,* part 3 (Cambridge: Macmillan, 1858), but receives special sanction from Legge's publication in 1861 of the *Analects* (the *Oxford English Dictionary* [*OED*], however, cites R. H. Patterson's *Essays in History and Art* [1862]. Legge's *Religions of China,* published in 1880, is a second citation in the *OED;* see Smith, *Meaning and End,* 261 n. 64). On these and related issues, see Wilfred Smith's *What Is Scripture? A Comparative Approach* (Minneapolis, Minn.: Fortress Press, 1993), 176–83. It is worth noting that the *OED* cites Legge as its source for documenting the Jesuit coinage of "Confucius" (i.e., in the 1687 *Confucius Sinarum Philosophus*). On the Jesuit invention of Confucius, see particularly Lionel M. Jensen, "The Invention of Confucius and His Chinese Other, 'Kong Fuzi,'" *Positions* 1 (1993): 414–49. Jensen's analysis is excellent, but he is mistaken in his view that Legge's "still-standard translations of the *Lunyu, Daxue,* and *Zhongyong* are based largely upon the original Latin translations of the same texts prepared by the Society of Jesus and published in 1687 in CSP [*Confucius Sinarum Philosophus*]" (p. 441 n. 6).

3. For an interesting discussion of Legge's "translation" from the standpoint of missionary tradition, see Lau Tze-yui, "James Legge (1815–1897) and Chinese Culture: A Missiological Study in Scholarship, Translation, and Evangelization" (Ph.D. diss., University of Edinburgh, 1994). Lau primarily relies upon Andrew F. Walls's theoretical development of the "translation principle" of acculturation. See also Andrew F. Walls, "The Translation Principle in Christian History," in *Bible Translation and the Spread of the Church,* ed. Philip C. Stine (Leiden: E. J. Brill, 1990), 24–39.

4. On Bishop J. W. Colenso (1853–1883) and the controversies surrounding him, see Owen Chadwick, *The Victorian Church* (New York: Oxford University Press, 1970), 2: 90–97. As Chadwick says (p. 90):

[Colenso] undertook a translation of the Bible into Zulu, and employed Zulu assistants. He liked his Africans and sought to learn from them. They began to perplex him with questions. While they were translating together the story of the flood, one of his Zulus asked, "Is all that true? Do you really believe that all this happened thus?" Colenso knew enough recent geology to be forced to confess to himself that he did not believe it. But he temporised; for he would not say so outright to the Zulu, lest he cast discredit on the general truthfulness of the Bible. Later he was much perturbed when his Zulu expressed moral revulsion against a brutal command of ancient Hebrew law (Exodus 21: 20–21).

5. See Moncure Conway, *Autobiography: Memories and Experiences* (Boston and New York: Houghton Mifflin, 1904), 2: 328. As Conway said:

Somehow, after knowing Colenso and listening to him, I found a certain felicity in the "nonsense verse" written when his heresies first appeared:—There was a My Lord of Natal / Who had a Zulu for a pal; / Said the Zulu, "Look here / Ain't the Pentateuch queer?" / Which converted My Lord of Natal. This learned and eloquent Englishman, with his superb head and figure, giving heed to the awakened doubt of the dark-skinned "heathen" he went out to convert, was a typical figure of the new generation. We were summoned by great scholars—even by some like Professor Legge who had been missionaries—to sit at the feet of those vulgarly called "heathen,"—Buddha, Zoroaster, Confucius,—through whom the genius of other races was expressed.

6. Hannah Mary Legge left China for good in 1866 because of various health problems (some of which seem to have been imagined or induced). For example, she describes various problems of painful boils, fainting, delirium, and a "great nervous irritability"; see Hannah's letters June 12, July 28, and November 30, 1864 (Council for World Mission [hereafter cited as CWM]/China/Personal/Legge/Box 10). Concerning Legge's mysterious sleepwalking and fall, see his letter to his wife, June 1872, in which he says, "of all this I remember nothing. How the thing took place I cannot tell. There are no signs of an apoplectic seizure." See also the account in his letter to his stepdaughter, Marian Willetts, August 28, 1872 (University of London, School of Oriental and African Studies, Legge Archive, ms. 380476). For Cordier's impressions, see "Les Études chinoises (1895–1898)," *T'oung Pao* 9 (1898): 4–18 (on Legge); and idem, "Half a Decade of Chinese Studies (1886–1891)," *T'oung Pao* 3 (1892): 532–57.

7. See JL, "Journey in North China and America," typescript, seventy-nine pages (CWM/China/Personal/Legge/Box 7).

8. JL to Joseph Mullens, secretary, London Missionary Society, April 15, 1870. Legge notes that, largely due to the shortcomings of a Rev. Morris (portrayed as an "old woman"), the attendance had dwindled to between only nine and twenty-five parishioners. By December 1871, Legge wrote that he had increased it back up to "two hundred plus children," which, as he says, was "not bad" (CWM/South China/Box 6/Folder 1/Jacket 8).

9. See JL, "Final Sermon" (CWM/China/Personal/Legge/Box 4). In his last sermon at the Union Church (also called the Union Chapel), Legge admitted to a "considerable emotion of sorrow and regret." In this sermon his sense of the finality of his departure is explicitly communicated along with his bittersweet emotions about the partial failure of his own ministry. He notes somberly that, while his ef-

forts have "not been all in vain," he nevertheless felt that the success of his ministry could "have been much greater." There is reason to believe that Legge—removed from his family and partially estranged from the London Missionary Society because of his commitment to his translation project—was truly struggling with various mixed feelings about his identity and methods as a missionary. He must even have had some questions about his effectiveness as a minister of the word of God, for he was not unanimously known as a great or eloquent preacher—see, for example, J. Edkins, "The Memory of the Just Is Blessed, Prov. x. 7." Sermon on James Legge preached at the Union Church, Shanghai, 1898, manuscript (CWM/China/Personal/Legge/Box 7).

10. JL, sermon, "Against Being Offended in Christ, Matt. II.6," July 24, 1870 (CWM/China/Personal/Legge/Box 4). Concerning his earlier prophetic triumphalism, see especially his Land of Sinim sermon given in 1859 at the sixty-fifth anniversary celebration of the London Missionary Society; see also *The Land of Sinim: A Sermon Preached in the Tabernacle, Moorfields, at the 65th Anniversary of the London Missionary Society* (London: John Snow, 1859). This sermon is also noteworthy for Legge's exegetical support of the equation of the biblical Sinim (Isa. 49:12) with the empire of China and his extended condemnation of what he called "popery." As he says, "Popery must fail" in China now that "churches of a purer faith" are called upon.

11. See JL, sermon, "The Privilege of the Gospel and the Free Offer of It," given in the Union Church, Hong Kong, January 15, 1871 (CWM/China/Personal/Legge/Box 4). For similar views about the uniquely inclusive nature of Christianity as a religion that "embraces all nations and languages and peoples," see also another of Legge's sermons, given in Hong Kong on July 23, 1871, and on September 8, 1872, and again at the parish school in Dollar, Scotland, in January 1874 (CWM/China/Personal/Legge/Box 5). Legge refers to the Jews, Jewish tradition, and the Old Testament in various, often anti-Semitic and sometimes contradictory ways. Thus, there are instances where Britain is positively identified as the prophetic inheritor of the Jewish covenant with God. At other times, Jews and Chinese are compared in terms of their "astonishing pride." See, for example, the untitled and undated, though clearly from the 1840s, talk (CWM/China/Personal/Legge/Box 6) wherein Legge says that the human mind in the East is "apathetic" and there is "so much less of individual mental energy." Even more astonishing in light of his later views is his defense of the Opium Wars, which opened China to free trade and the gospel, and his evaluation of the Chinese language: "you can neither be poetical in it—nor metaphysical. It consequently imposes a constraint upon a lively temperament." Most of all, Christianity should not make "any compromise with error." Christianity must therefore adopt a pugnacious approach toward the heathen religions so that "she will break and beat [them] into pieces, until they shall utterly disappear and the place of them no more be found."

12. JL, "Last Sermon in Hong Kong," March 23, 1873 (title given by Helen Edith Legge); scripture passage 1 Peter 5:10–11. Here Legge admits that at times his English preaching diverted him from his mission. One important theme involved the haunting question, especially amid both the heathen and secular temptations of Hong Kong, of why the progress of Christianity was so slow and limited among both Europeans and Chinese. See also his discussions of the "true Christian" in his

1847–1849 diary. For Legge, sham Christianity was especially shown by poor participation in the Lord's supper—see his "Sabbath in the Colonies," 1850 (CWM/China/Personal/Legge).

13. See George Smith, *A Narrative of an Exploratory Visit to Each of the Consular Cities of China, and to the Islands of Hong Kong and Chusan in behalf of the Church Missionary Society in the Years 1844, 1845, 1846* (New York: Harper & Brothers, 1847), 451. Smith indicates that Nonconformist missionaries were often looked upon as unwitting troublemakers and foolish meddlers in the affairs of China.

14. On the evolution of the English "man of letters" in the nineteenth century, see the important analysis by T. W. Heyck, *The Transformation of Intellectual Life in Victorian England* (New York: St. Martin's Press, 1982).

15. In the late 1860s Julien was writing Legge and praising his *Chinese Classics* (Julien's letters, said Legge, "bristle with compliments"). See, for example, the anonymous review of Legge's *Shi jing* (*Book of Poetry, Chinese Classics* [1871]) in the *Shanghai Budget,* clipping (CWM/China/Personal/Legge). The profession of sinologist or sinologue first achieves nominal existence and remunerative academic presence within the great French Orientalist tradition of Abel Rémusat (1815) and Stanislas Julien (who assumed Rémusat's chair at the Collège de France in 1828). As distinct from the already secularized French Enlightenment academic tradition of Rémusat and Julien, there was only a very meager and desultory establishment of Chinese professorships in Britain before 1876, when Legge's chair at Oxford was established. This difference is shown by the usage of the English and French terms *sinology/sinologie* and *sinologist/sinologue*. Whereas the French usage understandably coincides with the creation of the position at the Collège de France during the first part of the century, the English words do not enter active use until midcentury. It was not really until the 1870s that this technical terminology appeared regularly in popular English-language literary periodicals, as well as in sinological journals such as *The China Review.*

16. See E. J. Eitel, "The She King" (review of JL's *Chinese Classics,* vol. 4, 1871), *The China Review* 1 (1872): 2–12.

17. *The China Review* and the Shanghai-based *Journal of the North China Branch of the Royal Asiatic Society* (1858–1860, 1864–) were the first real sinological publications in English. Though both of these publications, which still included articles written by hyphenated amateur sinologists (from varying missionary, commercial, and governmental backgrounds), are sometimes hardly distinguishable from missionary-oriented journals such as *The Chinese Repository* (1832–1851) and *Chinese Recorder* (1867–1941), they—along with the pioneering *Journal asiatique* (1822–) in Paris—were the direct precursors of *T'oung Pao* (1890–), the most authoritative and professionally academic of the European sinological journals appearing at the turn of the twentieth century.

18. On Eitel, see T. W. Pearce, "Ernest John Eitel, Ph.D.—An Appreciation," *The Chinese Recorder* 40 (April 1909): 214–19.

19. Eitel, "She King" (review), 2.

20. Ibid., 4. Tischendorff was a prominent German scriptural scholar.

21. Ibid., 4–5. Eitel elaborated on this point by noting that, while capturing the "*meaning* of the original," the "*form*" of the *Book of Poetry* ("its style of diction, its rhythm, melody and rhyme") cannot be "preserved and transmitted in a prose trans-

lation." To attract "the interest of the general reader," therefore, some "Sinologue with music in his soul, must come forward, and we venture to say that with Dr. Legge's labours before him he will not find it impossible to produce a faithful metrical version of these ancient Odes." Since Legge was responsive to well-founded criticism, especially from respected colleagues like Eitel, it is quite probable that this review is the germ for Legge's later rhymed version of the *Poetry*. On these points, see Lauren Pfister, "A Forgotten Treasure: James Legge's Metrical Book of Poetry," in *Shijing Studies* (Tokyo: Waseda University, 1994), 11–18.

22. Eitel observed that the two Chinese schools deal with the *Book of Poetry* "somewhat after the manner in which the *Song of Solomon* is treated by the old and new schools of European theologians." Eitel, "She King" (review), 6.

23. Concerning Wang's views, see Lee Chi-fang, "Wang T'ao (1828–1897): His Life, Thought, Scholarship, and Literary Achievement" (Ph.D. diss., University of Wisconsin, 1973). Lee notes that in 1873 (or 1865) Wang

> commended Legge for his judicious eclecticism, saying: ". . . he threaded together, scrutinized, examined into sources, and analyzed. He maintained his own view and did not simply follow tradition. In his study of the Classics, he did not favour any one school or devote himself to any one theory, but he made wide and extensive his studies in order to reach a perfect comprehension. Generally speaking, he took his materials from Ma Yung and Cheng Hsuan, and blended them with the views of Chu Hsi. He was not partial either to the Han school or to the Sung school. . . ." (pp. 226–27).

Wang concurred with Legge's view that the *Shu jing* was authentic.

24. This process of composition was "more or less" comparable to the way "in which the compiler of the *Iliad* dealt with the ballads he collected, or in the fashion according to which Macpherson treated those ancient ballads, legends and ditties concerning Ossian's Fingal, which had wandered centuries before him from Ireland to the Scotch Highlands." Eitel, "She King" (review), 12.

25. See E. J. Eitel's "Protestant Missions of Hong Kong," *The Chinese Recorder* 7 (1876): 24–25. Eitel especially contrasts the "sober and practical" Legge with the flamboyant and controversial Gützlaff. Legge's translations, notes Eitel, were materials "best adapted to be forged into weapons of spiritual warfare." The fullest discussion of Wang's role is found in Lee, "Wang T'ao," and Paul Cohen, *Between Tradition and Modernity: Wang T'ao and Reform in Late Ch'ing China* (Cambridge, Mass.: Harvard University Press, 1974). See also Wong Man Kong, "A Pioneer at the Crossroads of East and West: James Legge" (Master's thesis, Chinese University of Hong Kong, 1993), 141–55.

26. See JL, prolegomena to the *Spring and Autumn Annals, Chinese Classics* (1872), 5: 189.

27. Even as he prepared to go home, Legge continued with draft renditions of, as he put it, the "so sui generis" *Book of Changes* and the "so very voluminous" *Record of Rites*, the remaining texts making up the traditional Five Classics. JL to Hannah Mary Legge, April 16, 1866 (CWM/China/Personal/Legge/Box 10).

28. See Eitel, "Protestant Missions of Hongkong," 34–35.

29. See preface, *Chinese Classics* (1872), vol. 5, pt. 1, p. v.

30. See JL, "Journey in North China and America," 1–5.

31. Smith, *Narrative of an Exploratory Visit*, 452. Henry Knollys (*English Life in China* [London: Smith, Elder, 1885], 17) observed that his first impression of the Chinese in Hong Kong (in the 1880s) was "displeasing." Moreover, as he became more fully acquainted with "their stupid ugly eyes, their air of stolid conceit, their fat, smooth faces, their shaven, pigtailed skulls, and their ceaseless discordant chatter," his feelings deepened "into absolute disgust."

32. JL, "Two Heroes of Chinese History," *The China Review* 1, no. 6 (1873): 370–81. This was originally given at the Hong Kong City Hall. See also JL, "Lecture on John Knox," 29 November 1871, Helen Edith Legge typescript, twenty-four pages (CWM/China/Personal/Legge/Box 7). In this talk he specifically refers to Carlyle's idea of the hero.

33. Ever responsive to criticism, Legge specifically, and rather defensively, refers to this review in his prolegomena for his translation of the *Spring and Autumn Annals*, published in 1872; see *Chinese Classics* (1893), 5: 51 (identical to the original 1872 edition). It seems that Legge did not know who wrote the article, which he refers to as "a review of my first volume, in the *Edinburgh Review*" in which he was "accused of being unjust to [Confucius], and of dealing with him inhumanely." The full passage is worth recording here.

> Others have said that I was partial to him, and represented his character and doctrines too favourably. The conflicting charges encourage me to hope that I have pursued the golden Mean, and dealt fairly with my subject. My conscience gives no response to the charge that I have been on the look-out for opportunities to depreciate Confucius. I know on the contrary that I have been forward to accord a generous appreciation to him and his teachings. But I have been unable to make a hero of him. My work was undertaken that I might understand for myself, and help others to understand, the religious, moral, social, and political condition of China, and that I might see and suggest the most likely methods of accomplishing its improvement. Nothing stands in the way of this improvement so much as the devotion of its scholars and government to Confucius. It is he who leads them that causes them to err and had destroyed the way of their paths.

34. [C. H. Butcher], review of JL's *Chinese Classics*, vol. 1 (1861), Wells Williams's *Middle Kingdom* (1861), and Alexander Wylie's *Notes on Chinese Literature* (1867), *Edinburgh Review* 129 (April 1869): 303–32. It is important to know that Butcher was one of the signers of a letter written by the Anglican bishop John Shaw Burdon in 1880 criticizing Legge's translations for Müller's *Sacred Books of the East*. My source for the identification of Butcher is Walter Houghton, ed., *The Wellesley Index to Victorian Periodicals 1824–1900* (Toronto: University of Toronto Press, 1966).

35. Though generally commending the "perspicuous" translation, Butcher also criticizes its stylistic crudities: "as it is, verbal anachronisms and impertinences often mar our enjoyment of the text." Interestingly, given Legge's appreciation of biblical cadence, it is suggested that the "best model" for the *Analects* would have been the "simple and vigorous diction of the English Bible" [Butcher], review, 303.

36. Ibid., 319–20. Despite his sympathy for Confucius, Butcher condemned Laozi as a "sour ascetic, who affected solitude, exercised himself with penances, and despised practical life." Butcher also says that, because Daoism appeals to the deity "Shang-te," Confucius does not use this name "with any expression of reverence" (p. 322).

37. Ibid., 330–31. Moreover, Confucius's own "grand deficiency" was his "inability to sympathize with the wants of minds constituted in moulds different from his own." He therefore left the Chinese nation "without safeguards against error simply because his own serene intellect saw no temptation to go astray" (p. 329). It was Confucius's "contradictory and imperfect conceptions of the loftiest truths" that "arrested the growth of the Chinese intellect, and thrust it into degrading superstitions [just as was the case for the Jews and Roman Catholics]" (p. 330).

38. Ibid., 332.

39. Ibid., 304.

40. See the notice of Legge's departure in the Hong Kong *China Mail,* 27 March 1873. It is significant that in this article Legge's "world-wide fame" is primarily associated with his scholarly achievements as a "Sinologue." There is no mention of his missionary work.

41. See, for example, the explanations offered in Legge's unpublished "Notes of a Tour Round the World," Helen Edith Legge typescript, twenty-four pages (CWM/China/Personal/Legge/Box 7). This was a talk originally given in Dollar, Scotland, shortly after his return home in 1873. Compare the explanations given by Helen Edith, who said that Legge had "his heart set on" seeing the "Five Great Sights" of China—i.e., the "tomb of Confucius, Altar of Heaven, Great Wall, Ming Tombs, and T'ae [Tai] Shan" (Helen Edith Legge, *James Legge Missionary and Scholar* [London: Religious Tract Society, 1905], 177). Jules Verne's novel *Tour du monde en quatre-vingt jours* was first published in 1873.

42. See "The Asiatic Society's Meeting," *North-China Herald,* June 7, 1873, p. 502.

43. His accounts of Japan and the United States are also mostly in the genre of tourist literature—e.g., his meandering overland route included stops at Yosemite, the Mormon Temple, and, most egregiously, Niagara Falls!

44. This kind of traveling for pleasure must be distinguished from travel in China undertaken by Westerners, for whom there was always a serious reason for the journey. Traveling, or touring as a tourist for the enjoyment of the itineration itself, seems to have some relation to the colonial sway of the British empire and its need to extend Victorian institutions of recuperative perambulation, romantic communion with nature, and the gathering of scientific information about exotic lands and peoples. For some discussion of these issues, see Mary Louise Pratt, *Imperial Eyes: Travel Writing and Transculturation* (New York: Routledge, Chapman and Hall, 1992); and David Spurr, *The Rhetoric of Empire: Colonial Discourse in Journalism, Travel Writing, and Imperial Administration* (Durham and London: Duke University Press, 1993).

45. Such an interpretive reading is made possible by the fact that we have several overlapping accounts of these travels in North China written by Legge himself and by his close associates, as well as several roughly contemporaneous descriptions of the same sites by other travelers and photographers. The accounts by Legge include the long, published article entitled "Notes from the Journal of a Tour in the North of China in the Months of April and May, 1873," *The Oriental* 3 (September–December 1874): 341–49, 403–12, 684–90; and 4 (January–June 1875): 48–58, 172–77, 289–94, 426–32, 667–75, as well as several other accounts: "Journey in North China and America," "Notes of a Tour Round the World," and copies of handwritten letters to Hannah Mary concerning the trip.

For all of the unpublished materials, see CWM/China/Personal/Legge/Box 7. See also *James Legge Missionary and Scholar,* chapter 13, "A Tour of North China"— a collage based on the materials described above. What is referred to as Legge's journal in the *Oriental* article appears to be the collection of detailed daily letters sent to Hannah Mary. The most important and complete source for these travels is the long typescript entitled "Journey in North China and America," which is a compilation of those letters. This material was evidently used for the articles published in the *Oriental.* Edkins provides us with his own account of the trip to Qufu: "A Visit to the City of Confucius," *Journal of the North China Branch of the Royal Asiatic Society* n.s. 8 (1874): 79–92. Other important contemporaneous accounts include especially John Thompson's hauntingly evocative images and text in his *Illustrations of China and Its People* (London: Sampson Low, Marston, Low and Searle, 1873, 1874); Alexander Williamson's *Journeys in North China, Manchuria, and Eastern Mongolia; With Some Account of Corea,* 2 vols. (London: Smith, Elder, 1870), which includes Joseph Edkins's account of Peking in volume 2, pp. 313–92; and A. P. Happer's "A Visit to Peking with Some Particular Notice of the Worship of Heaven, Earth, Sun, and Moon, etc.," *The Chinese Recorder* 10 (January–February 1879): 23–47. See also Ernst von Hesse-Wartegg's "China's 'Holy Land': A Visit to the Tomb of Confucius," *The Century Magazine* 60 (October 1900): 803–19.

46. See, for example, Williamson's itinerary as described in his *Journeys in North China.*

47. There are several published condemnations of Legge's shocking actions during his North China trip—especially his behavior at the Altar of Heaven. The American missionary and editor of the *Chinese Repository and Missionary Journal,* A. P. Happer, was Legge's most outspoken critic.

48. See JL's sermon, November 19, 1871 (Isa. 3:6), and sermons given November 26 and December 3, 10, 17, and 24, 1871 (CWM/China/Personal/Legge/Box 5). To borrow again from Legge's own language of change and transformation— that is, the evangelical language of conversion and the biblical sense of the "fourfold state of man"—it is well to note the fluidity and dynamic quality of any kind of conversion, religious or otherwise. JL's idea of the fourfold state of man (which follows Bishop Butler's ideas) involved: (i) the "natural state" as the vain pursuit of good; (ii) the "transitional state" as a mood of serious thought and a resorting to the means of change; (iii) the "regenerate state," which was the exercise of repentance and faith in Christ; and (iv) the "Christian state," which manifested "permanent security" and the "character and course of holy improvement and action."

49. JL, series of four sermons on the "fourfold state" given December 17 and 24, 1871, and January 14 and 24, 1872. In the fourth sermon, on the "Christian state," he says that he is enough of a Calvinist to cling to the "doctrine of the perseverance of Saints."

50. Thompson, introduction to *Illustrations of China.*

51. See JL, "Tour in the North of China," 3: 342.

52. See JL, "Tour Round the World," 10–12.

53. JL, "Tour in the North of China," 3: 403.

54. In "Journey in North China and America" Legge says: "I was amused by the contrast between Mr. Wade and the Russian Plenipotentiary; the former as reticent

in regard to public matters as the latter was or seemed to be open and communicative." There was always a barrier between the missionary Legge and the soldier-diplomat Wade, even after both of them became full-time scholars in England (Legge at Oxford and Wade at Cambridge).The friendly but tense relationship between these two sinologues goes back to the 1850s.

55. JL, "Tour in the North of China," 4: 53.

56. See JL, "Tour Round the World," 13.

57. Legge was accompanied by, among others, John Dudgeon and Mr. and Mrs. Meech. The Altar of Heaven should be distinguished from the more dramatically imposing, though less ritually significant, Temple of Heaven. For the quotation from Edkins, see Thompson, *Illustrations of China,* 4: plate xvi (the Open Altar of Heaven and the Temple of Heaven). The original discussion by Edkins is found in Williamson, *Journeys in North China,* 313–92.

58. Legge, *James Legge Missionary,* 177 ff.

59. Ibid., 180. Legge's characteristically Protestant emphasis on the aniconic nature of the imperial worship is noteworthy. See also E. T. Williams, "The State Religion of China during the Manchu Dynasty," *Journal of the North China Branch of the Royal Asiatic Society* 44 (1913): 11–45.

60. This was a comparative association he had already alluded to in his term question treatise, *The Notions of the Chinese Concerning Gods and Spirits: with an Examination of the Defense of an Essay on the Proper Rendering of the Words Elohim and Theos, into the Chinese Language by William Boone, D.D.* (Hong Kong: Hong Kong Register Office, 1852; reprint, Taipei: Ch'eng Wen, 1971).

61. For an excellent discussion of the altar and its religious symbolic significance, see Jeffrey F. Meyer, *The Dragons of Tiananmen: Beijing as a Sacred City* (Columbia: University of South Carolina Press, 1991), 79–120. As Meyer says, an understanding of the religious meaning of the altar is "not an easy task."

62. See A. P. Happer, "A Visit to Peking," 43–47. Happer further notes that, by holding onto the worship of the sky more than is seen presently in India, the state religion of China was in fact, in stark contrast with Legge's views, the "oldest form of false worship that now exists among men." It could even be thought of as the "form of worship which prevailed among men immediately after the deluge."

63. See JL, "Tour Round the World," 13.

64. See Owen Chadwick's discussion of Tennyson's faltering faith as expressed in *In Memoriam* (1850) in *The Victorian Church,* 1: 566–68. As Chadwick says: "Tennyson's faith, stumbling up the altar-stairs in darkness, marks an epoch in English religious life" (p. 567).

65. See JL, "Journey in North China and America," 27. A comparative description of Legge and Edkins in 1873 is given by H. Cordier, "Les Études chinoises (1895–1898)," 5. Like Legge, Edkins had his disagreements with the London Missionary Society and in 1880 resigned ("in consequence of some differences of opinion with his colleagues as to methods of work") to work for the imperial maritime customs (see S. W. Bushell, "Joseph Edkins," *Journal of the Royal Asiatic Society* [1906]: 270). Both Edkins and Legge shared a passion for "busy as a bee" early morning work habits.

66. See JL, "Journey in North China and America," 34. It may be noted that the "municipal management of affairs" was a fairly recent manifestation of the Victorian

middle-class passion for order and sanitation. Moreover, this ideal of ordered maintenance and cleanliness was realized more in the patriarchal family household than it was in English cities.

67. See Paul D. Bergen, "A Visit to T'ai Shan," *The Chinese Recorder* 19 (1888): 544–45; and Susan Naquin and Yu Chun-fang, eds., *Pilgrims and Sacred Sites in China* (Berkeley, Los Angeles, Oxford: University of California Press, 1992)—especially Glen Dudbridge's "Women Pilgrims to T'ai Shan: Some Pages from a Seventeenth-Century Novel," 39–64, and Wu Pei-yi, "An Ambivalent Pilgrim to T'ai Shan in the Seventeenth Century," 65–88. For an interesting description of Tai Shan today, see Fergus M. Bordewich, "Scaling the Heights of a Sacred Peak," *New York Times*, January 20, 1991, pp. 15–16.

68. See JL, "Journey in North China and America," 39.

69. Ibid., 42–44. It may be noted that in 1994, when I climbed Taishan, these temples were still dilapidated and filthy.

70. See the interesting article by Joseph Edkins giving his description of the trip to Qufu, "A Visit to the City of Confucius." This article is particularly valuable for its description of various Confucian rituals performed at that time. As Edkins, even more a budding comparativist than Legge, says (p. 88):

> I have been thus minute in the description of . . . the worship of Confucius, because it is a genuine relic of ancient life, and as such is adapted to cast light on the old world. The music and dancing of ancient nations were connected with their religion and have therefore a special interest attaching to them. They help us to understand the ceremonial of Babylon, Ninevah, Shushan the palace, and Memphis. So far as the Jews imitated the customs of the surrounding nations, these details may also illustrate the Old Testament.

71. They were not the first nineteenth-century European travelers to visit these sites. See the earlier visit, in 1865, to the "country of Confucius and Mencius" described by Williamson in *Journeys in North China,* 193 ff.

72. Typically, Helen Edith Legge's biography preserves only a truncated fragment of the comparison between Napoleon and Confucius, with none of the provocative implications concerning Legge's changing understanding of Kongzi. Far more sensitive to the real significance of these events was a certain correspondent in Hong Kong, identified only as H. Wicking, who wrote Legge in 1874 to "express the hope" that the "world will at some future time know something of the curious thoughts that must have arisen in your mind as you stood by the grave of Confucius." It is worth questioning whether or not Legge had any further "curious" thoughts about the provocative symbolism of the visit to Qufu. In keeping with the suspicions of Wicking, it seems probable that he did, but unfortunately extant documentation (especially in consideration of Helen Edith's editing of the record) gives us nothing more concerning Legge's response to Wicking. What is certain is that the whole issue is not just a matter of mere "curiosity," but directly bears on significant changes in Legge's career that allude to more profound alterations in the overall Protestant missionary attitude toward Chinese religion and civilization. It is also interesting that Wicking is quite convinced that Legge's true greatness will only be "fully appreciated after many generations." Should Legge happen to return

and die in China, Wicking says, "I think your remains would be placed by the side of that Sage [Confucius], and so share his temple and he your renown" (see H. Wicking to JL, February 25, 1874; CWM/China/Personal/Legge/Box 8).

73. Generally on this incident, see the descriptions in "Journey in North China and America," 47–51, and the articles in the *Oriental*. See also "The Asiatic Society's Meeting," 503.

74. See "Dr. Legge on Peking," *North-China Herald*, June 7, 1873, p. 496.

75. "Asiatic Society's Meeting," 503.

76. See JL's supplementary comments on the Japan trip found in his lecture given in 1894 entitled "The War Between China and Japan," typescript, eighteen pages (Bodleian Library, Oxford University, dep. c. 49). In this talk he specifically alludes to his earlier trips to Japan in 1865 and 1873, noting the civil "order" and absence of bound feet there.

77. See "Journey in North China and America," 75.

78. For an earlier account of feelings of sublimity related to an experience of nature, see page 25. See also JL's quasimystical description of the "dim heaving mass of the ocean," accompanied by various quasierotic memories, in a letter to his brother William, November 14, 1866 (CWM/China/Personal/Legge/Box 8):

> That minute [of viewing the ocean] was an era in my life. I could not have told what it was that I felt; but my nature received a sudden enlargement. . . . It was not fright which I felt but a consciousness of awe, and of some strange capacity within me, which was broader and deeper than the sea. I remember as distinctly when the beauty of nature first ravished me, years after, one day among the woods of Rothiemay; and about the same time the beauty of woman's face and reverence for female character took delicious possession of my whole being.

For a discussion of some of these themes in nineteenth-century theological tradition, see Lynn Poland, "The Idea of the Holy and the History of the Sublime," *Journal of Religion* (1992): 175–85.

79. The fullest account of his American travels is found in his unpublished lecture "Journey in North China and America."

80. The London Missionary Society Board of Directors was responding to Legge's letter of retirement dated November 29, 1873; see the Minute Book of the London Missionary Society Eastern Committee Board Meeting (J. A. Baynes in the Chair), held 8 January 1874 (CWM/Eastern Committee Minutes/Box 1/Book 2).

81. Legge attended the Eastern Committee board meetings, by invitation, on November 12, 1874, and February 11, 1875. From April 8, 1875, until June 8, 1876, he was listed as a member of the board and attended at least five meetings (see CWM/LMS Eastern Committee Minutes/Box 1/Book 2).

82. See the London Missionary Society Eastern Committee Board Meeting, January 8, 1874.

83. An anonymous Short Notice, appearing in *The China Review* 3 (1874–1875): 317, reported that the first number of a new publication called *Friend of China* was issued as the organ of the Anglo-Oriental Society for the Suppression of the Opium Trade and included Legge's name on the list of the founding committee. The *Review* notes that, although it is generally "approving" of the new publication, it finds

there "statements . . . apt to mislead" and says that local publications among foreign settlements in China have "criticized it rather freely."

84. See Jonathan J. Bonk's discussion of the financial arrangements of the London Missionary Society as set out in the *General Regulations* of the society: *The Theory and Practice of Missionary Identification, 1860–1920* (Lewiston, England: Edwin Mellen Press, 1989), 45–90.

85. From extant publisher's records it is not evident how much, if any, royalty income Legge was making at this time. See the Kegan Paul archives (incorporating Trübners) at University College, London. A poignant expression of Legge's relationship with his publishers is seen in one of his letters to Trübner on February 27, 1877. Discussing the sales of the (original edition of the) *Classics,* which he says were "not so very unsatisfactory," he notes that almost all of his meager profits were used to buy other books for his library. Nevertheless, he remarks that he is still owed £11. He laments that his new popular Trübner editions of *Mencius* and the *Book of Ancient Poetry* had yet to pay for the expense of publication, a situation that he says was "due to an undiscerning public." But the real point of the letter was to complain to Trübner that it charged him £8 to present a set of the *Classics* to Corpus Christi College. Besides the fact that Trübner had not actually published the original *Classics* (he himself had!), it was even more galling that the company did not even give him any kind of discount, treating him "just like a regular customer." He hoped that there would be some correction of this matter. There is, however, no record of any financial rectification.

86. Notable pirated editions include *Confucius and the Chinese Classics, or Readings in Chinese Literature,* edited and compiled by the Reverend A. W. Loomis (San Francisco: A. Roman, 1867), and *Mencius: The Life and Works of Mencius with Essays and Notes* (Philadelphia: J. B. Lippincott, 1874, 1875; in multiple editions).

87. See JL, *The Chinese Classics, Translated into English, With Preliminary Essays and Explanatory Notes (Reproduced for General Readers from the Author's Work Containing the Original Text, etc.),* vol. 1, *The Life and Teachings of Confucius* (London: Trübner, 1875). The fact that this is the fourth edition of this revision underscores the popularity of such classical or sacred Oriental works.

88. JL, *The She King; or, The Book of Ancient Poetry, Translated in English Verse, With Essays and Notes* (London: Trübner, 1876).

89. In addition to Eitel's review of the 1871 *Shi jing,* see C. H. Butcher's unsigned review in the *Phoenix* 3 (1872): 20. As Butcher says: "To grasp the meaning of these ancient songs is one thing, to reproduce them in English with spirit like the original is another. We miss the happy terseness of the original in the very faithful renderings of the translator."

90. See JL, "The Sphere of Labour" (an address in the Weighhouse Chapel at the Introduction of E. J. Dukes and his designation to the Mission at Amoy), October 5, 1874 (CWM/China/Personal/Legge/Box 6).

91. The quotation "things are on the turn" comes from Legge's lecture on Hong Kong: "The Colony of Hong Kong. From a Lecture by the Rev. James Legge, D.D., LL.D. On Reminiscences of a Long Resident in the East, Delivered in the City Hall, November 5, 1872," *China Review* 1 (1872): 163–76.

92. See George W. Stocking's discussion of the Crystal Palace exposition in London in 1851, *Victorian Anthropology* (New York: Free Press, 1987), 1–6.

93. For a penetrating discussion of many of these points, see Michael Adas, *Machines as the Measure of Men: Science, Technology, and Ideologies of Western Dominance* (Ithaca, N.Y., and London: Cornell University Press, 1989).

94. Concerning the museum phenomenon, which reached a peak of growth in the early 1870s, see David K. van Keuren, "Museums and Ideology: Augustus Pitt-Rivers, Anthropological Museums, and Social Change in Later Victorian Britain," in *Energy and Entropy: Science and Culture in Victorian Britain, Essays from Victorian Studies,* ed. Patrick Brantlinger (Bloomington and Indianapolis: Indiana University Press, 1989), 270–80.

95. See Richard D. Altick, *Victorian People and Ideas* (New York: Norton, 1973), 300.

96. See Patrick Brantlinger, *Rule of Darkness: British Literature and Imperialism, 1830–1914* (Ithaca, N.Y., and London: Cornell University Press, 1988), 228–32. See also the essay by Frank Turner, "The Victorian Crisis of Faith and the Faith That Was Lost," in *Victorian Faith in Crisis: Essays on Continuity and Change in Nineteenth-Century Religious Belief,* ed. Richard J. Helmsadter and Bernard Lightman (Stanford, Calif.: Stanford University Press, 1990).

97. See David Newsome, *Godliness and Good Learning: Four Studies on a Victorian Ideal* (London: John Murray, 1961), 26–27. For Legge's own reflections on "Christian manliness," see his "Sermon to Young Men and Women" given in the late 1860s and 1870s (CWM/South China/Personal/Legge/Box 4).

98. See Newsome, *Godliness and Good Learning,* 27. I discuss the transformations of the ancient English universities in the 1870s in chapter 2.

99. Concerning the problem of the meaning of *the secular* and *secularization* in the Victorian period, see Owen Chadwick, *The Secularization of the European Mind in the Nineteenth Century* (Cambridge: Cambridge University Press, 1975). At this time, secularization had something to do with changes and laxity in Christian doctrines (what Chadwick elsewhere called the problem of neology in Britain—i.e., the influence of Germanic higher criticism) and methods of studying and knowing religion (and religions). On the 1870s as a time of agnostic doubt, see Walter E. Houghton, *The Victorian Frame of Mind 1830–1870* (New Haven: Yale University Press, 1957), 10–13.

100. See E. J. Eitel, *Europe in China* (London: Luzac, 1895), 392. In 1856, Legge had closed the Anglo-Chinese College and "came forward as an educational reformer." With the support of the governor of the colony (at this time, Sir Hercules Robinson), he "set to work . . . to convert all the Government Schools, which had hitherto been conducted in the interest of religious education, into professedly secular institutions." Legge was, says Eitel, the "presiding spirit" of the Board of Education and "ruled it with the ease and grace of a born bishop." According to Shirley Mullen ("Freethought," in *Victorian Britain: An Encyclopedia,* ed. Sally Mitchell [New York and London: Garland, 1988]), the secularist and freethinking reform movements in Britain had particular associations with Nonconformity.

101. On the general issue of Victorian agnosticism, see, among many studies, Lance St. John Butler, *Victorian Doubt: Literary and Cultural Discourses* (New York: Harvester/Wheatsheaf, 1990); and Bernard Lightman, *The Origins of Agnosticism: Victorian Unbelief and the Limits of Knowledge* (Baltimore, Md.: Johns Hopkins University Press, 1987). See also the review of Lightman by Kevin Lewis in *Nineteenth-Century Studies* 3 (1989): 77–80.

102. Ibid., 77.

103. See Lightman's *Origins of Agnosticism*.

104. For Müller's understanding of Kant, see his translator's preface ("Why I Thought I Might Translate Kant's *Critique*") in *Immanuel Kant's Critique of Pure Reason*, translated into English by F. Max Müller (New York: Macmillan, 1881, 1896), xxvii–lxxix.

105. See the *Oxford English Dictionary*, s.v. Zeitgeist, which includes quotes from Matthew Arnold's *Literature and Dogma*.

106. See Willis B. Glover, *Evangelical Nonconformists and Higher Criticism in the Nineteenth Century* (London: Independent Press, 1954); and Marjorie Wheeler-Barclay, "Victorian Evangelicalism and the Sociology of Religion: The Career of William Robertson Smith," *Journal of the History of Ideas* 54 (1993): 59–78.

107. See R. apRoberts, *The Ancient Dialect: Thomas Carlyle and Comparative Religion* (Berkeley and Los Angeles, Calif.: University of California Press, 1988), 29.

108. Ibid. Legge, of course, described himself as a "moderate" Calvinist, a "new and milder" form of Calvinism promoted by his father-in-law, John Morison. On "moderate Calvinism," see W. B. Selbie, *The Life of Andrew Martin Fairbairn* (London: Hodder and Stoughton, 1914), 7–8.

109. apRoberts, *Ancient Dialect*, 102.

110. Ibid.

111. Ibid., 1.

112. Asa Briggs, quoted by Walter Arnstein et al. in "Recent Studies in Victorian Religion," *Victorian Studies* 32 (1989): 150, noted that "the religious climate was more exciting and important than anything else. The amount of pamphlet and periodical literature devoted to religious problems was far greater than that devoted to economic and social problems." It can be plausibly argued that even before the professionalization of the study of religion in the universities, the literary periodicals (the model in many ways being the *Edinburgh Review*) constituted an intellectual institution and a "primary historiographic source" often "overlooked in contemporary histories of the nineteenth-century study of religion." See Christina A. Banman, "The Study of Religion: Nineteenth-Century Sources and Twentieth-Century Misconceptions," *Method and Theory in the Study of Religion* 28 (1989): 160–85.

113. Frederick D. Maurice, *Religions of the World and Their Relations to Christianity* (London: John W. Parker, 1847), 7.

114. Samuel Johnson, *Oriental Religions and Their Relation to Universal Religion*, vol. 1, *India*, 2d ed. (Cambridge: John Wilson, 1873), 13.

115. On the problem of naming the new field, see Louis Henry Jordan, *Comparative Religion: Its Genesis and Growth* (New York: Charles Scribner's Sons, 1905), 7–8.

116. See Eric J. Sharpe, *Comparative Religion: A History*, 2d ed. (La Salle, Ill.: Open Court, 1986), 27–29. On the nineteenth-century history of comparative religions, see Jordan, *Comparative Religion*. Jordan discusses the relative significance of Müller, Cornelis Tiele, and Albert Réville. It may be noted that this book includes an introduction by A. M. Fairbairn, James Legge's fellow Congregationalist and first head of Mansfield College, Oxford.

117. See Sharpe, *Comparative Religion*, and also Banman's "The Study of Religion: Nineteenth-Century Sources," 160–85. Müller's actions are only part of a larger movement associated with the secular study of religion in the nineteenth cen-

tury—a movement that embraces the Reformation, the Enlightenment, Deism, American transcendentalism, changes in missionary policy, and so on. See Marjorie Wheeler-Barclay, "Science of Religion in Britain, 1860–1915" (Ph.D. diss., Northwestern University, 1987), and Peter Harrison, *'Religion' and the Religions in the English Enlightenment* (Cambridge: Cambridge University Press, 1990).

118. See Samuel Johnson's discussion of this in his *Oriental Religions; India,* 15–17. The Western "advantage over older civilizations" was due not to the "new force of Christian religion," but to the development of technology and scientific ways of knowing.

119. "Müller's intention in setting out to show that whatever the religion, there was only one religiosity, one intuition, one revelation, and one providential truth, became clear in the orders he gave to missionaries. The latter would be well advised, he wrote, to emphasize the similarities rather than the differences between various beliefs and cults. . . . For Max Müller declared unhesitatingly that Christianity was without a doubt vastly superior to all other religions. This conviction was used as a scientific argument in ratifying the role played by the 'comparative study of religions. The science of religion [would] for the first time assign to Christianity its right place among the religions of the world; it [would] show for the first time fully what was meant by the fullness of time; it [would] restore to the whole history of the world, in its unconscious progress towards Christianity, its true and sacred character' " (Maurice Olender, "The Indo-European Mirror: Monotheism and Polytheism," *History and Anthropology* 3 [1987]: 351–52; quoting Max Müller's introduction in *Chips from a German Workshop,* vol. 1 [New York: Charles Scribner's Sons, 1895]).

120. "As a token of gratitude and friendship," Müller dedicated volume 4 of *Chips from a German Workshop* (1907) to Stanley. On Stanley, see *Dictionary of National Biography,* s.v. Stanley, Arthur Penrhyn, 18: 931–35; and Rowland E. Prothero, *Letters and Verses of Arthur Penrhyn Stanley, D.D., Between the Years 1829 and 1881* (New York: Charles Scribner's Sons, 1895). Prothero comments (p. 291) that Müller "became one of Stanley's most intimate friends."

121. See Arthur Stanley, "The End and the Means of Christian Missions" (a Sermon Preached on the Day of Intercession for Missions, Wednesday, December 3, 1873), in Müller, *Chips,* 1: 276–77.

122. Stanley, "Christian Missions," 288.

123. Ibid., 292–93.

124. Ibid., 293–94.

125. Müller, "Lecture on Missions," *Chips,* 4: 239–41. For a more direct expression of his views on missions and the idea that "there is a Divine element in every one of the great religions of the world," see Müller to Sir Henry Acland, November 11, 1873, Georgina A. Müller, *The Life and Letters of the Right Honorable Friedrich Max Müller* (London: Longmans, Green, 1902), 2: 490–91.

126. Müller, "Lecture on Missions," *Chips,* 4: 242–43. Müller expanded on some of the ideas in this lecture in his article "Missionary Religions. A Note on the Preceding Article," *Fortnightly Review* 22 (July 1874): 68–75. For an analysis of Müller's ideas about missions, see especially E. J. Sharpe, *Not to Destroy but to Fulfill: Contributions of J. N. Farquhar to Protestant Missionary Thought in India* (Uppsala: Gleerups, 1965), 47–48. As Sharpe notes, Müller seemed to believe "that at some date in the future a new religion would arise . . . made up of the best of all religions . . . [and] a

fulfillment of all the religions of the past." This religion of the future "exists potentially in the heart of Christianity as the ethical and moral ideal which Jesus
taught . . . but [had been] overlain by accretions" (p. 48).

127. Müller, "Lecture on Missions," *Chips,* 4: 246–49.

128. Ibid., 151–52.

129. Ibid., 253.

130. Ibid., 255.

131. Ibid., 256.

132. Ibid., 260–61.

133. Concerning Müller's changing views on Keshub Chunder Sen, see his *Biographical Essays* (New York: Charles Scribner's Sons, 1884), 47–161 (this long essay
was originally written in 1883). For criticism of Müller's understanding of Hinduism and the problem of placing too much emphasis on a "comparative religions"
approach to missions, see the Reverend Dr. Caldwell's pamphlet *Relation of Christianity to Hinduism; Being a Reprint of a Paper on Foreign Missions, especially in relation to
the Oriental Systems of Religion; Read at the Church Congress held at Brighton in October,
1874* (London: Society for the Propagation of the Gospel in Foreign Parts, 1874).

134. Müller, "Lecture on Missions," *Chips,* 4: 261.

135. Ibid., 263–64.

136. Ibid., 265.

137. Ibid., 266.

138. Legge's evolving ideas about missionary policy on heathen religions are indicated by a lecture given between his return to Britain and his assumption of his
chair at Oxford. See JL, "The Relation Sustained by Missionaries to Existing Heathen Religions and the Use They May Make of Them," Helen Edith Legge typescript, twelve pages (CWM/China/Personal/Legge/Box 8). He begins with the observation that, despite native suspicions about ulterior motives, a missionary
primarily operates out of his "love of Christ" and his duty to fulfill Christ's charge to
go into the whole world to preach the gospel. Using a formula that he will greatly
expand upon, and modify, in his more overtly comparative writings, he maintains
that the missionary's relation to heathen religion is one that is best exemplified by
Saint Paul. It is a relationship of "opposition" but not, as he stresses here, "one of
hostility." However, he insists that his understanding of "opposition" will "not admit
of any compromise." His tough-minded insistence on this point is because there are
"some learned and powerful thinkers" who say that "the existing heathen religions
are the preparation, which has been made in providence, for the importation to
those who hold them of the fuller and more spiritual truth provided in Christianity." From their perspective, Christianity has not to "supersede [the heathen reli-
gions], but to purify them, striking an alliance with them, and producing an amal-
gam, which containing all that is good in the old religion, and that is most pleasing
to Christianity, shall be the some better thing which is yet in store for men in the future." No doubt Müller and Samuel Johnson are among the "learned and powerful
thinkers" Legge is alluding to here because he specifically mentions Müller at a later
point in this talk and will shortly review Johnson's magnum opus. The problem
Legge sees with this kind of reasoning is that it is too bookishly dependent upon the
ancient literature of the tradition without any "direct acquaintance with the existing
heathen religions." Too many of the scholars of this ilk, unlike the missionaries in

the field, "do not know how the leading principles which [the most ancient documents] contain have been obscured and overlaid by an ever-increasing mass of superstition and abominable idolatries." This is paralleled, Legge goes on to say, by the "system of Popery" in the West, which betrays the "melancholy" tendency of "what is best and truest to degenerate and become corrupt when committed to the keeping of men."

The relationship between "Popery and Protestantism" is therefore "like the relation of missionaries and heathen religion." It is a relation of "opposition" and not compromise. This kind of oppositional relationship requires that missionaries "use every means to become acquainted with those religions." Not surprisingly, the best and most successful missionaries were a lot like Legge himself—that is, those latter-day apostles of Saint Paul "whose command of the speech of the people was fluent and correct and whose research into literature had been deepest and most extensive." Missionaries who believed that simple preaching and not education was the best means of reaching the heathen Chinese ended up only making themselves "contemptible and inefficient." Even more significant for Legge is the need to affirm the purity of archaic Chinese religion, an affirmation that he specifically links here with Max Müller's Vedic studies. The "farther back one goes digging among the foundations of Chinese religion," he says, the more does one "find that it is in harmony with the living oracles of Revelation." He ends then by quoting from Müller's lectures on the *Vedas*: "Religions in their most ancient form, or in the minds of their authors, are generally free from many of the blemishes that attach to them in later times." What is noteworthy here is Legge's selective adoption of certain Müllerian principles of comparison.

139. For a general discussion of different forms of evangelical millennialism, see Timothy Weber, *Living in the Shadow of the Second Coming* (New York and Oxford: Oxford University Press, 1979).

140. See Stocking, *Victorian Anthropology*, 9-45.

141. See apRoberts, *Ancient Dialect*, 3, 17. As Olender says ("The Indo-European Mirror," 359-60), "[t]he paradox of the new science of religion was that in order to constitute themselves, they attempted first to place all religions on the same level in a secular manner, and then to prove the Christian meaning (identified with historic time) of this new comparative order."

142. See Chadwick, *Victorian Church*, 2: 17.

143. Max Müller, Address to the Aryan Section of the Second Congress, *Second Session of the International Congress of Orientalists, Held in London in September, 1874*, ed. Robert K. Douglas (London: Trübner, 1876), 184. Müller's address was reprinted in *Chips*, 4: 317-58.

CHAPTER TWO. PROFESSOR LEGGE
AT OXFORD UNIVERSITY, 1875-1876

1. Beyond archival materials in the Bodleian Library, the following contemporaneous sources were consulted: Edward A. Freeman, "Oxford after Forty Years," *Contemporary Review* 51 (1887): 609-23, 814-30; C. G. Brodrick, *A History of the University of Oxford* (London: Longmans, Green, 1886), and idem, "The University of

Oxford in 1898," *Nineteenth Century* 44 (July–December 1898); Algernon M. M. Steadman, *Oxford: Its Social and Intellectual Life. With Remarks and Hints on Expenses, the Examinations, the Selection of Books, etc.* (London: Trübner, 1878); Goldwin Smith, "Oxford Revisited," *Fortnightly Review* 55 (1894): 149–58, and idem, "A Glimpse at Oxford from the Inside," *Congregationalist* 8 (1879): 217–22; *The Student's Handbook to the University and Colleges of Oxford,* 5th ed. (Oxford: Clarendon Press, 1879); "Oxford and Its Professors," *Edinburgh Review* 348 (October 1889): 303–27; W. B. Selbie, "Fifty Years at Oxford," *Congregational Quarterly* (1938): 282–90; and Andrew Lang, *Oxford: Brief Historical and Descriptive Notes* (London: Seeley, 1890). The expression "castle of indolence" is taken from Lang. Helpful secondary discussions include Richard Symonds, *Oxford and Empire* (London: Macmillan, 1986); V. H. H. Green, *Religion at Oxford and Cambridge* (London: SCM Press, 1964), and idem, *History of Oxford University* (London: B. T. Batsford, 1974); Malcolm Graham, *Images of Victorian Oxford* (Oxford: Alan Sutton, 1992); Sheldon Rothblatt, *The Revolution of the Dons* (New York: Basic Books, 1968); Philip E. Smith II and Michael S. Helfand, *Oscar Wilde's Oxford Notebooks: A Portrait of Mind in the Making* (New York and Oxford: Oxford University Press, 1989); W. R. Ward, *Victorian Oxford* (London: Cass, 1965); Christopher Herbert, ed., *The Encyclopedia of Oxford* (London: Papermac, 1992); and Michael Sanderson, ed., *The Universities in the Nineteenth Century* (London and Boston: Routledge and Kegan Paul, 1975). As Symonds shows, Victorian Oxford (particularly Jowett's Balliol) was the school for the ruling classes. In this way, an Oxford education made formative contributions to the British "philosophy of and natural attitude to Empire." The teaching of the classics was especially important to this as the history of the Greek city states and the Roman governance of its dependents was often applied to Britain's imperial situation. At the time of the writing of this book the volume on Victorian Oxford had not been published in the multivolume series *The History of the University of Oxford* (Oxford: Clarendon Press, 2000).

2. Max Müller to Gladstone, January 12, 1873 (Georgina A. Müller, *The Life and Letters of the Right Honorable Friedrich Max Müller* [London: Longmans, Green, 1902], 2: 471–72). The full quotation is worth recording:

> Oxford wants new life. Both teaching and learning seem to me to be regarded as a burden, which ought not to be. . . . At a German university . . . a professor has a lab or institution supported by assistants where he works with his pupils [with fellowships] apart from his lectures . . . these institutions are the real secret of the success achieved by the German universities. . . . What I like in the German universities is the frankness with which everybody states the convictions at which he has arrived. Strauss' book has been very severely treated in Germany. Yet, there is a crisis going on there as in England; something is dying, whether we like it or not. To my mind Mansel's Bampton Lectures and the reception they met with were a sign of the times. They seemed to me far more irreligious than Herbert Spencer. They left religion as a mere cry of despair. Frederick Maurice saw the tendency of that school of thought . . . but he could not make himself understood. Mansel and Herbert Spencer seem to me at the present moment to rule at Oxford in the two opposite camps.

3. The expression "organized torpor," describing Oxford, is found in Brodrick, "The University of Oxford in 1898."

4. See, however, Peter Harrison, *'Religion' and the Religions in the English Enlightenment* (Cambridge: Cambridge University Press, 1990).

5. For a general discussion of these factors within British higher education in the nineteenth century, see T. W. Heyck, *The Transformation of Intellectual Life in Victorian England* (New York: St. Martin's Press, 1982). As Heyck shows, professionalism implies a kind of middle-class culture of achievement—i.e., a way of structuring society in relation to the values of progressively moving up in one's professional career. As Charles Derber, William Schwartz, and Yale Magrass note in *Power in the Highest Degree: Professionals and the Rise of a New Mandarin Order* (New York and Oxford: Oxford University Press, 1990), 33:

> The genius of professionalism was in creating a new paradigm that would mimic scientific rationality and extend it into the social world, uniting under one cognitive cloak physicists and professors of English literature. The inspiration for this was the university itself: the true institutional church of the professions. Heavily influenced by the scientific worldview, the university had defined a general commitment to rationality. Professionals embraced the university's more expansive paradigm, which claimed to distill many of science's essential principles, but proved elastic enough to encompass nonscientific viewpoints. Rational discourse melded the cultures of science, the university, and professional practice itself. It sanctified rational, theoretical, and reproducible knowledge, all in the service of objectivity.

An interesting, and thematically related, discussion of the nineteenth-century American situation as related to the naturalistic study of religion is Conrad Cherry's "Boundaries and Frontiers for the Study of Religion: The Heritage of the Age of the University," *Journal of the American Academy of Religion* 57 (1982): 807–27. In this context, it is also worth noting J. Pelikan's comment that "[t]here would be considerable merit to the thesis that the history of the process of secularization in the West can be traced more thoroughly through the history of education than through that of any other area of society (except perhaps family life)" (*The Idea of a University: A Rexamination* [New Haven, Conn.: Yale University Press, 1992], 46).

6. On German universities in the nineteenth century, see in particular Timothy Bahti, *Allegories of History: Literary Historiography after Hegel* (Baltimore and London: Johns Hopkins University Press, 1992). The idea of disinterested critical scholarship is especially argued by the Germanizer Matthew Arnold in his *Essays in Criticism*, 1st ser. (London: Macmillan, 1865)—it was a value founded on the Hellenic spirit of Greek humanism as opposed to a dour Hebraism focused on work and morality. On Arnold, see Ruth apRoberts, *Arnold and God* (Berkeley, Los Angeles, and London: University of California Press, 1983).

7. Richard R. Yeo, "Science," *Victorian Britain: An Encyclopedia,* ed. Sally Mitchell (New York and London: Garland, 1988), 695.

8. Max Müller, "Inaugural Lecture," in *Chips from a German Workshop* (New York: Charles Scribner's Sons, 1907), 4: 4–5.

9. Ibid., 41.

10. Ibid., 5.

11. Ibid., 7.

12. Ibid., 5–6. In addition to the promotion of research professorships, Müller proposed the creation of research-oriented "student-fellows" whose work would be

"properly organized" as it is "in the Institute of France or in the Academy of Berlin." The endowment of this kind of original research would come from the funds ordinarily used for "prize-fellowships" (pp. 8–10).

13. Ibid., 7.

14. Ibid., 6.

15. Ibid. Müller's discussion of academic scholarship is descriptively solipsistic. Professorships could not be "lucrative or even self-supporting" because, instead of being dedicated to teaching, professors were primarily concerned with their own specialized research and the promulgation of their findings through universitywide lectures (most often to small audiences) and technical articles published in specialized journals.

16. Ibid., 5.

17. See the firsthand account from a Nonconformist Congregationalist point of view in Goldwin Smith's "Glimpse at Oxford from the Inside." Smith discusses four trends at Oxford in the 1870s: Dandyism, Toryism, Sacerdotalism ("spectral Puseyisms" were outgrowths of the earlier Newmania), and Atheism, identifying the "thoughtful liberals" as Liddell, Liddon, Jowett, Pattison, Bradley, and Thorold Rogers. The danger was that "the charms of latitudinarianism in the hands of Mr. Jowett and Mr. Matthew Arnold must enervate the force of credos; the introduction of scientific teaching is ever the opening of the floodgate of shallow empiricism and ignorant denials." See also "Christian Oxford," *Congregationalist* 8 (1879): 307–13, by an anonymous "Oxonian" who discusses John Stuart Mill's autobiographical reflections on the "transitional period" when the "philosophic mind" can no longer believe in religion. According to Mill, this is a condition of "weak convictions, paralyzed intellects, and growing laxity of principle, which cannot terminate until a renovation has been effected in the basis of their belief, leading to the evolution of some faith, whether religious or merely human, which they really can believe" (p. 310).

18. Concerning Jowett's "typical liberal Protestant" views, see Peter Hinchliff, *Benjamin Jowett and the Christian Religion* (Oxford: Clarendon Press, 1987), 138. The last years (the 1880s) of "Jowett's life were . . . the period in which the 'scientific revolution' in the writing of history was taking place." On Pattison, see especially his autobiographical reflections, republished as *Memoirs of an Oxford Don: Mark Pattison, Late Rector of Lincoln College, Oxford,* ed. Vivian H. H. Green (London: Casswell, 1988). Especially haunting is the depiction of his own pilgrimage from being a disciple of Newman to a mostly secularized and cynical scholar in his later years as rector of Lincoln College. Equally significant is his portrait of the changing academic society at Oxford. In support of the liberal Müllerian position on professorial positions, he says (p. 133):

> In after years I became one of the most strenuous advocates for the endowment of professors. It was easy to suppose that I had simply changed my mind and gone round to the other side, because it was the popular liberal creed. Like other things in which change has been imputed to me, this was not an instance of shifting of opinion, but of development. I have never ceased to prize as highly as I did at that time the personal influence of mind upon mind,—the mind of the fully instructed upon the young mind it seeks to form. But I gradually came to see that it was impossible to base a whole academical system upon this single means of influence.

Teachers, it was plain, must know something of what they profess to teach and my own limited experience had shown me that a tutor could thoroughly master only a single branch of classical learning even; and then there was the whole field of knowledge outside classics to be furnished with teachers who could only be professors of the University.

19. This wonderfully graphic description comes from Vivian H. H. Green's introduction to his edition of Pattison's *Memoirs*, 10. For the other quotation, see J. Sparrow, *Mark Pattison and the Idea of a University* (London: Cambridge University Press, 1967), 3.

20. Sparrow, *Mark Pattison*, 128–30. Sparrow notes that the "vision of the totum scribile" comes from Pattison's 1885 *Sermons*.

21. See William S. Peterson, *Victorian Heretic: Mrs. Humphry Ward's Robert Elsmere* (Leicester: Leicester University Press, 1976). The novel portrays the destructive effect of biblical criticism on Christian orthodoxy in England in the last quarter of the nineteenth century. Ward's Mr. Grey was modeled on T. H. Green, the provost of St. Anselm's was clearly meant to be Jowett, and the embittered skeptic Squire Wendover was Mark Pattison. Pattison is portrayed as mordant, sarcastic, and encyclopedic; a person whose barren skepticism dominated his high intellect. Pattison has also been identified with Casaubon, George Eliot's antihero in *Middlemarch*—see Sparrow, *Mark Pattison*, 1, 9. Ward herself favored a *via media* of intellectual freedom and personal piety found only at Balliol with Jowett and Green. The Balliol tutor Thomas Hill Green renounced the dogmatic basis of Christianity but clung tenaciously to Christian morality. The problem with Green was (as Pattison put it) his metaphysical "puzzle-headedness" and a studied ambiguity that allowed Anglo-Catholics, Evangelicals, and Theists all to claim him. See also the discussion in Robert Lee Wolff, *Gains and Losses: Novels of Faith and Doubt in Victorian England* (New York and London: Garland, 1977).

22. Pattison, *Memoirs*, 163–64.

23. *Essays on the Endowment of Research* (London: Henry S. King, 1876). The essays, by various authors of the liberal, more Germanic, and less Jowettian, wing of Oxford, included, for example, Mark Pattison's "Review of the Situation," Archibald Henry Sayce's "Results of the Examination System at Oxford" and "Needs of the Historical Sciences," Henry Nettleship's "Present Relations Between Classical Research and Classical Education in England," Thomas Kelly Cheyne's "Maintenance of the Study of the Bible," and W. T. Thiselton Dyer's "Needs of Biology."

24. Thomas Kelly Cheyne, "Maintenance of the Study of the Bible," in *Essays on the Endowment of Research* (London: Henry S. King, 1876), 194. Cheyne was a fellow and lecturer at Jowett's Balliol College.

25. Archibald Henry Sayce, "The Needs of the Historical Sciences," in *Essays on the Endowment of Research*, 198–99. Sayce was the new deputy for Müller's chair in comparative philology and, at the time this essay was written, a fellow and tutor of Queen's College.

26. Ibid., 201.

27. Ibid., 208.

28. Ibid., 212.

29. Ibid., 221–22.

30. See Maurice Hutton, *Many Minds* (London: Hodder and Stoughton, 1928), 168. Refer also to Peter Hinchliff, *Benjamin Jowett and the Christian Religion,* who

depicts Jowett as the "chief inspirer of the predominant current of twentieth-century British 'liberal Christianity.'" See the discussion of Hinchliff in Walter Arnstein et al., "Recent Studies in Victorian Religion," *Victorian Studies* 32 (1989): 149–69. Especially helpful is William Peterson's discussion (*Victorian Heretic*, 73–75) of Jowett's center-of-the-road religious position, which was paralleled by A. P. Stanley and, implicitly, by Müller. All three were open-minded toward non-Christian religions. All three were also sometimes accused of "toadyism to the rich and well-born" (Hutton, *Many Minds*, 165). For Jowett it was clear that his engagement with the Greek classics (especially Plato) led to the broadening of his mind, just as Legge's involvement with the Chinese classics led to a more sympathetic position regarding Ruism. Jowett's study of Greek literature led him to rebel against the jealous sectarianism and petty ecclesiasticism of the established Church.

31. See Linda Dowling, *Language and Decadence in the Victorian Fin de Siècle* (Princeton, N.J.: Princeton University Press, 1986), 68.

32. A. C. de Vooys, *Andrew Lang: A Nineteenth Century Anthropologist* (Tilburg, The Netherlands: Zwijsen, 1968), 86. In all of Müller's publications, there was a religious Kantianism that affirmed the old adage *Nihil in fide quod ante fuerit in sensu* (There is nothing in faith anterior to what is found in the senses). In the words of E. E. Evans-Pritchard (*Theories of Primitive Religion* [Oxford: Clarendon Press, 1965], 21), "Max Müller did not wish to be understood as suggesting that religion began by men deifying grand natural objects, but rather that these gave him a feeling of the Infinite and also served as symbols for it."

33. Robert Forman Horton, *An Autobiography* (London: George Allen and Unwin, 1928), 30–34.

34. Ibid., 35–42.

35. "Oxonian," "Christian Oxford," 307–13. There is a strong possibility that the Oxonian in question was actually Robert Horton.

36. Ibid., 309.

37. See Müller's description of these students in his *Biographical Essays* (New York: Charles Scribner's Sons, 1884), 178–203 (on Bunyiu Nanjio) and 204–19 (on Kenjiu Kasawara). They arrived in London on August 11, 1876, to study English and in 1879 took up studies with Müller at Oxford. They studied in Oxford till 1884. Müller's *Essays* also include translated copies of letters and autobiographical reflections by the two Japanese.

38. Müller, "Inaugural Lecture," 5.

39. Ibid., 6.

40. Ibid., 13. The Boden chair was originally held by Müller's old mentor H. H. Wilson. Concerning the whole Boden controversy, see the balanced presentation in Nirad C. Chaudhuri, *Scholar Extraordinary: The Life of Professor the Rt. Hon. Friedrich Max Müller, P.C.* (London: Chatto and Windus, 1974), 221 ff. Chaudhuri notes that Monier-Williams's handbill for the position relied mainly on the "primary object" of the Boden endowment: "it is 'to enable his *Countrymen* [emphasis in the original] to proceed in the conversion of the Natives of India to the Christian Religion, by disseminating a knowledge of the Sacred Scriptures among them'" (p. 225).

41. Chaudhuri, *Scholar Extraordinary*, 221. Müller was one of the first of a certain kind of professional academic who would ultimately overwhelm university life—that

is, the smoothly eloquent academic entrepreneur and self-promoting master of the media (meaning public lectures, literary reviews and newspapers, and publishers) who was at home both in the academy and in society.

42. F. Max Müller, *My Autobiography: A Fragment* (New York: Charles Scribner's Sons, 1901), 12.

43. Ibid., 13.

44. See, for example, William Dwight Whitney (a professor of Sanskrit at Yale University), *Max Müller and the Science of Language: A Criticism* (New York: Appleton, 1892). Whitney's attacks had been going on for more than a decade and a half. On the battle between Darwin and Müller, see Chaudhuri, *Scholar Extraordinary*, 256–62.

45. See R. K. Douglas's discussion of the English apathy toward China except in the area of trade, *The Language and Literature of China: Two Lectures Delivered at the Royal Institution of Great Britain in May and June, 1875* (London: Trübner, 1875), 7.

46. University College, London, had a position going back to the 1830s that was originally held by the retired London Missionary Society agent and Legge's first Chinese teacher, Samuel Kidd. For a discussion of the British sinological situation in the mid-1870s, see Robert K. Douglas (who held the position at King's College at that time), *Language and Literature of China*. For Legge's own version of the history of British sinology, see pages 171–73.

47. Müller, "Inaugural Lecture," 2–3.

48. Ibid., 3.

49. Ibid., n. 1.

50. On Wang's lecture at Oxford, see Lee Chi-fang, "Wang T'ao (1828–1897): His Life, Thought, Scholarship, and Literary Achievement" (Ph.D. diss., University of Wisconsin, 1973), 119, a description based on Wang's *Manyu Suilu* [Random notes of travel], in *Xiaofanghu*, ser. 11, p. 542b.

51. Müller, "The Works of Confucius," a review of James Legge's *Chinese Classics*, which was first published in November 1861. Unfortunately, Müller does not say where this review first appeared. See Max Müller, *Chips from a German Workshop*, vol. 1, *Essays on the Science of Religion* (New York: Charles Scribner's Sons, 1895), 300–8. It is unclear whether or not Legge knew of this article when it was first published. It is possible that he learned of it only after it was reissued in the *Chips* collection—although Legge nowhere specifically mentions the review.

52. It is this kind of leisure-time science that is "bracing and invigorating" for the mind of the missionary—"keeping it from that stagnation which is the inevitable result of a too monotonous employment" (ibid., 300–1).

53. Ibid., 301–2.

54. Ibid., 307–8.

55. Ibid., 308.

56. See, for example, D. E. Mungello, *Curious Land: Jesuit Accommodation and the Origins of Sinology* (Honolulu: University of Hawaii Press, 1985, 1989); Jacques Gernet, *China and the Christian Impact*, trans. Janet Lloyd (New York: Cambridge University Press, 1985); Raymond Dawson, *The Chinese Chameleon: An Analysis of European Conceptions of Chinese Civilization* (London: Oxford University Press, 1967); Henri Cordier, "Les Études chinoises (1891–1894)," *T'oung Pao* 5 (1894): 421–57,

and idem, "Les Études chinoises (1895–1898)," *T'oung Pao* 9 (1898): 3–109; Kenneth Scott Latourette, "A Survey of the Work by Western Students of Chinese History," *Journal of the North China Branch of the Royal Asiatic Society,* n.s. 47 (1916): 103–14; John D. Young, *East-West Synthesis: Matteo Ricci and Confucianism* (Hong Kong: Centre of Asian Studies, University of Hong Kong, 1980); Elizabeth Te-chen Wang, "The Beginning of Chinese Studies in the English-Speaking World," *Chinese Culture* 17 (1976): 1–62; Edouard Chavannes, *Sinologie* (Paris: Larousse, 1915); P. Demiéville, "Études chinoises classiques," *Bulletin de la Société des études indochinoises,* n.s. 16 (1951): 511–17; John P. Martin, "A Critical Survey of French Sinology, 1870–1900" (M.A. thesis, Georgetown University, 1966); Donald F. Lach, *Asia in the Making of Europe,* 2 vols. (Chicago: University of Chicago Press, 1965–1977); Paul A. Cohen, *Discovering History in China: American Historical Writing on the Recent Chinese Past* (New York: Columbia University Press, 1984); Jerome Ch'en, *China and the West* (London: Hutchinson, 1979); *Deux Siècles de sinologies française* (Peking: Centre franco-chinois d'études sinologiques, 1943); Herbert Franke, *Sinologie* (Bern: A. Francke, 1953); José Frèches, *La Sinologie* (Paris: Presses Universitaires de France, 1975); Edward H. Schafer, *What and How Is Sinology?* (Boulder, Colo.: University of Colorado, 1982); and Zhang Longxi, *The Tao and the Logos: Literary Hermeneutics, East and West* (Durham and London: Duke University Press, 1992).

57. See T. H. Barrett, *Singular Listlessness: A Short History of Chinese Books and British Scholars* (London: Wellsweep, 1989), 22. See also the excellent work by David Honey, "Philology, Filiation, and Bibliography in the Textual Criticism of the Huainanzi: A Review Article," *Early China* 19 (1994): 161–92. Honey has recently published a general history of sinology, *Incense at the Altar: Pioneering Sinologists and the Development of Classical Chinese Philology* (New Haven, Conn.: American Oriental Society, 2001).

58. Sorely lacking is the kind of richly contextualized interpretive analysis Raymond Schwab achieved for nineteenth-century Indological Orientalism and Edward Said, more controversially, for nineteenth- and twentieth-century Islamic studies, although Arthur Wright made an interesting pre-Saidian attempt at briefly sketching some of the general cultural implications of sinological Orientalism. See Wright's several articles: "The Study of Chinese Civilization," *Journal of the History of Ideas* 21 (1960): 233–55; "On the Uses of Generalization in the Study of Chinese History," in *Generalization in the Writing of History,* ed. Louis Gotschalk (Chicago: University of Chicago Press, 1963), 36–58; "The Chinese Language and Foreign Ideas," in *Studies in Chinese Thought,* ed. Arthur F. Wright (Chicago: University of Chicago Press, 1953), 286–303; and "Chinese Studies Today," *Newsletter of the Association for Asian Studies* 10 (1965): 2–12. There are also, to be sure, several substantial but chauvinistic self-appreciations of the glories of the French academic tradition by Paul Pelliot, Henri Maspero, Paul Demiéville, and others. See, for example, Pelliot's "Les Études chinoises" (*Renaissance* 2–3 [1944–1945]: 258–64), Chavannes's *Sinologie,* Demiéville's "Études chinoises classiques," and Martin's *Critical Survey of French Sinology.*

59. See Michel Foucault, *The Order of Things: An Archaeology of the Human Sciences* (New York: Vintage Books, 1970).

60. On these issues, see especially Maurice Olender, *The Languages of Paradise: Race, Religion, and Philology in the Nineteenth Century* (Cambridge, Mass.: Harvard Uni-

versity Press, 1992), and idem, "Europe, Or How to Escape Babel," *History and Theory* 33 (1994): 5–25.

61. The letter in the *Academy* is discussed and quoted in Eitel's *China Review,* in the Notes and Queries section (*The China Review* 4 [1876]: 331). This letter also notes that the term "Chinese scholar" is overly ambiguous because it could refer to a native Chinese. The anonymous article "The Rising Generation of Sinologists," *The Celestial Empire,* November 23, 1876, pp. 577–78, included the comment that

> [t]here was probably never a time when the study of Chinese was pursued with greater vigour than at present, or when things looked more promising with regard to the future of Sinology. It is a healthy sign when the junior members of the Civil Services devote their energies to studying the language and literature of China. . . . Every publication in China of any standing . . . teems with proofs of the philological enterprise which is flourishing around us. If names are asked for, they are forthcoming at a moment's notice. One has only to take up a number of the *China Review,* for instance, to see how many scholars are already in the field . . .

(mentioning Medhurst, Bretschneider, Chalmers, Faber, Kingsmill, Eitel, Lister, von Möllendorff, and Fryer).

62. The first edition of the *Bibliotheca Sinica* appeared in eight volumes from 1878 to 1885; a supplement of three volumes was published in 1893–1895. Because of the "développement remarquable" of sinology in the last part of the nineteenth century, Cordier produced a second edition of this work, incorporating the earlier volumes and bringing everything up to date: Henri Cordier, *Bibliotheca Sinica: Dictionnaire bibliographique des ouvrages relatifs à l'empire chinois,* 2d ed., 5 vols. (Paris: Librairie orientale & américaine, E. Guilmoto; and Librairie orientaliste Paul Geuthner, 1904–1924). I used the second edition.

63. On Cordier, see Martin, *Critical Survey of French Sinology,* 66–69; and Zoe Zwecker's "Henri Cordier and the Meeting of East and West," in *Encounters and Exchanges from the Age of Explorations,* ed. Edwin J. van Kley and Cyriac K. Pullapilly (Notre Dame, Ind.: Notre Dame University Press, 1986), 309–26. As Martin notes, it was Cordier who became in the late 1870s (after the death of Julien and the ineffectualness of Hervey de Saint-Denys) the leader of French sinology. Cordier was a natural bridge between French and British sinology of the period because of his own multinational experience. As a boy he was sent to England to be trained for a career in Anglo-French commerce, and after his arrival at the age of twenty-one in Shanghai he had many British friends and colleagues, including Legge. He left China for Paris in 1876, never again to return to Asia.

64. Cordier, *Bibliotheca Sinica* (1924), 5: 4429–39. Ouvrages généraux, Géographie, Noms, Ethnographie et Anthropologie (including Ouvrages divers and Études comparées), Climat et Météorologie, Histoire naturelle, Population, Gouvernement, Jurisprudence, Histoire (which includes Chronologie and Histoire générale), Religion (including the subdivisions of Jou Kiao [*rujiao*], Tao Kiao [*daojiao*], Fo Kiao [*fojiao*], Judaisme, and Islamisme; only the category of Christianisme had its own distinct subdivisions), Sciences et Arts (involving Sciences morales et philosophiques, which includes Livres canoniques, *king* [*jing*]), Langue et Littérature (includes Études comparées), and Moeurs et Cotumes.

65. A very helpful historical account of sinology in the 1870s, including a detailed discussion of bibliographies, is Cordier's Préface de la première édition, *Bibliotheca Sinica* (1904), 1: vi–xvi.

66. In the second edition of the *Bibliotheca Sinica,* Cordier lists his accomplishments as "Professeur à l'École Spéciale des Langues Orientales Vivantes, membre du Comité des Travaux Historiques et Scientifiques, membre du conseil de la Société Asiatique, président de la commission centrale de la Société de Géographie, honorary member of the Royal Asiatic Society of Great Britain and Ireland, etc."

67. See Martin, *Critical Survey of French Sinology.*

68. Raymond Schwab, *The Oriental Renaissance: Europe's Rediscovery of India and the East 1680–1880,* trans. Gene Patterson-Black and Victor Reinking (New York: Columbia University Press, 1984), 8.

69. Edward Burnett Tylor, *Primitive Culture: Researches into the Development of Mythology, Philosophy, Religion, Language, Art, and Custom,* 2 vols. (London: John Murray, 1871); Herbert Spencer, *Principles of Sociology* (London: Williams and Norgate, 1877); Moncure Conway, coll. and ed., *The Sacred Anthology: A Book of Ethnical Scriptures* (London: Trübner, 1871; 5th ed., 1876); Freeman Clarke, *Ten Great Religions: An Essay in Comparative Theology* (Boston, Mass.: J. R. Osgood, 1871); and Samuel Johnson, *Oriental Religions and Their Relation to Universal Religion,* 3 vols. (Cambridge: John Wilson, 1872–1885).

For an excellent discussion of the significance of the American works, see Carl T. Jackson, *The Oriental Religions and American Thought: Nineteenth-Century Explorations* (Westport, Conn.: Greenwood Press, 1981). Müller's attitude toward Johnson is especially telling of the snobbish European attitude toward American intellectuals.

70. See Henri Cordier, "Half a Decade of Chinese Studies (1886–1891)," *T'oung Pao* 3 (1892). These developments are mirrored in French tradition by the emergence in 1878 of the École spéciale des langues orientales vivantes, which stressed the importance of a practical field experience in the Orient and a fluency in the living languages. This was coupled with the traditional French academic respect for scientific methods of observation and reporting (exemplified especially in the work of Camille Imbault-Huart [1857–1897] and Jean-Gabriel Deveria [1844–1899], who stressed practical language skills and the sciences of archaeology, epigraphy, numismatics, and ethnology). What needs to be recognized here is the influence of Cordier, and his experience with the more practical hyphenated British missionary- and consular-scholars in the field in China, on the establishment of the École spéciale des langues orientales vivantes.

71. Barrett, *Singular Listlessness.* In addition to the articles discussed in this chapter, see especially the following for contemporaneous discussions of nineteenth-century British sinology: the anonymously written "Review of the Facilities Existing for the Study of the Chinese Language, Especially as Regards England and America," *The Chinese Recorder* 7 (July 1838): 113–21; and Henri Cordier's detailed chronicle of developments in the 1890s published in *T'oung Pao.* Barrett correctly notes that "any rounded history of British studies of China would have to be concerned as much with attitudes or even the development of discourse on China as with the establishment of institutions" (p. 10). Martin is one of the few historians of sinology to recognize the "British leadership in Sinology" during this period (*Criti-*

cal Survey of French Sinology, 45): "Despite new Jesuit efforts and the revival of the École spéciale des langues orientales vivantes . . . the torch went to the Sinologists in England where Chinese studies experienced a great uplift under remarkable guidance. During these years England was just beginning to enjoy the fruits of the labors of her scholars, diplomats, and missionaries in China over the past fifty years."

72. The venerable *Journal asiatique* was founded by Rémusat in 1822 but, like the publications of other Oriental societies (*Journal of the Royal Asiatic Society,* established first as the *Transactions,* 1827–1833, then in 1834 as the *Journal,* and the *Journal of the American Oriental Society*), it tended to devote most of its pages to the more scientific Sanskritic and Semitic Orientalism. On French Orientalist publications, see, especially, Martin, *Critical Survey of French Sinology,* 62–66. The multilingual *T'oung Pao,* founded in 1890 by Cordier and Gustave Schlegel, is usually put forward as the first "modern"—that is, fully scientific, technical, and professional—sinological journal. *T'oung Pao* was preceded, however, by Cordier's *Revue de l'Extrême-Orient* (three volumes in 1882, 1883, 1884), which stressed the need to make sinology as scientific as other domains of Orientalism: "the scientific movement which characterizes our epoch has not involved the studies relative to the Far East with the other branches of research. It seems to us that a new impulsion can be given these studies and the methods of work which have not submitted to the modifications required urgently by the new conquests of science be transformed." See Henri Cordier, "À Nos Lecteurs," *Revue de l'Extrême-Orient* 1 (1882): 2. For publication details concerning the journals cited (as well as others), see Laurence G. Thompson, *Chinese Religion in Western Languages: A Comprehensive and Classified Bibliography of Publications in English, French, and German through 1980* (Tucson: University of Arizona Press, 1985), xix–xlix ("details concerning serial sources").

73. In the editor's introduction to the first issue of the *China Review,* the purpose of the journal is distinguished from the aims of the *Chinese Recorder,* which was "more especially intended for missionary readers." The basic desire of the editor was that the publication act as a general "repository" for scholarly papers on "arts and sciences, history, literature, mythology, manners and customs, natural history, religion, etc., etc., of China, Japan, Mongolia, Tibet, the Eastern Archipelago and the Far East generally." It is this duplicated etcetera that is so characteristic of the universal pretensions of this kind of imperialistic mode of Orientalist knowledge. See Introductory, *The China Review* 1 (July 1872): 1. Among the very few studies of the China-coast periodicals, see, especially, Kathleen Lodwick's introduction to her *The Chinese Recorder Index: A Guide to Christian Missions in Asia, 1867–1941,* 2 vols. (Wilmington, Del.: Scholarly Resources, 1986); and John Lang Rawlinson, *Rawlinson, The Recorder and China's Revolution,* 2 vols. (Notre Dame, Ind.: Cross Roads Books, 1990). It is particularly unfortunate that there is no index for the *China Review* along the lines of Lodwick's work on the *Recorder.*

74. See E. Bridgman, "Inaugural Address," *Journal of the Shanghai Literary and Scientific Society* 1 (June 1858): 1–16. This is a most revealing document, especially as it so explicitly and rhetorically connects intellectual and physical force in the imperialistic contest with China. It is also interesting for its implicit swipe at Legge's valorization of the Chinese classics, which, as Bridgman says here, are only their "most precious idols." The classics have a "high place" in the history of heathen literature

but they are "not pure, and lofty, and rich like the writings of Moses." Moreover, the Chinese classics show "a total absence of that wisdom and sound learning and true logic, so conspicuous, not only in the poetry and the prose of inspired seers, but in the select writings of most of our Christian philosophers" (p. 4).

75. Ibid., 5: "For those who love to extend their quiet and unobtrusive researches deep down beneath the surface, and who will bring up and out to light treasures hidden for ages, and so make the everlasting hills, the old rocks, bear their testimony to the power and wisdom of their great Creator and give in their evidence to the faithfulness of His Inspired Volume, our Holy Bible."

76. Barrett, *Singular Listlessness,* 75–76. Samuel Beal had been Anglican chaplain to the British fleet in the Far East.

77. The first two congresses are discussed here. There were ten other congresses down to the turn of the century: the third was in Saint Petersburg, the fourth in Florence, the fifth in Berlin, the sixth in Leiden, the seventh in Vienna, the eighth in Stockholm, the ninth again in London, the tenth in Geneva, the eleventh again in Paris, and the twelfth in Rome. Müller was either actively present at (often as section head or as overall president) or indirectly influential in all of these congresses. It appears that Legge attended only the meeting in Florence in 1878, the session in Berlin, and the meeting in London in 1891. In Florence and London, he gave papers. There are published proceedings for all of these congresses (a complete set is available at the New York Public Library).

78. On the first congress, see *Congrès international des orientalistes première session: Paris: Acts de comité national d'organisation* (Paris: Bureau de Congrés des Orientalistes, 1873).

79. See Robert K. Douglas, ed., *Second Session of the International Congress of Orientalists, Held in London in September, 1874* (London: Trübner, 1876).

80. Samuel Birch, Inaugural Address, *Second Session of the International Congress of Orientalists, Held in London in September, 1874,* ed. Robert K. Douglas (London: Trübner, 1876), 1–4.

81. On Julien's significance at the time of his death, see the anonymous article "Professor Stanislas Julien," *North-China Herald,* April 19, 1873, pp. 337–38.

82. Birch, Inaugural Address, 3–4.

83. Ibid. Birch says that a universal alphabet was prevented by "national amour-propre" among the major imperial nations of England, France, and Germany.

84. Ibid., 8–12.

85. See Walter Elliot, Address to the Turanian Section of the Second Congress, *Second Session of the International Congress of Orientalists, Held in London in September, 1874,* ed. Robert K. Douglas (London: Trübner, 1876), 53.

86. Max Müller, Address to the Aryan Section of the Second Congress, *Second Session of the International Congress of Orientalists, Held in London in September, 1874,* ed. Robert K. Douglas (London: Trübner, 1876): 177–204; reprinted in Müller, *Chips,* 4: 317–58.

87. Ibid., 177–80.

88. Ibid., 183.

89. Ibid., 183–84. On Müller's idea of comparison in the new "science of religion," see E. J. Sharpe, *Not to Destroy but to Fulfill: The Contribution of N. J. Farquhar to Protestant Missionary Thought in India* (Uppsala, Sweden: Gleerup, 1965), 45:

The term "the science of religion" was coined by Max Müller to describe the comparative method as applied to the study of religions. . . . Not only is all "higher knowledge" acquired by comparison; in the field of religion "he who knows one, knows none." He drew a sharp distinction between "comparative theology" (the study of the historical forms of religion) and "theoretic theology" (philosophy of religion and dogmatics), believing only the first of these to be scientifically relevant. In the comparative study of religion and theology, all religions must be treated as being on the same footing; it is not permissible to draw distinctions between "revealed" and "natural" religion, since that whole complex of problems belongs to "theoretic theology."

As Sharpe says, Müller's view of religion was basically "immanentist and rationalist."

90. Müller, Address to the Aryan Section, 185.

91. Ibid., 192.

92. For Müller's comments on missionaries in the address to the Aryan section, see ibid., 192–93.

93. On the relation of Oxford and empire in the nineteenth century, see especially Symonds, *Oxford and Empire*.

94. Samuel Johnson, *Oriental Religions; India* (1873), 30.

95. Joseph Edkins, *China's Place in Philology* (London: Trübner, 1871).

In an anonymous obituary for Edkins ("In Memoriam Rev. Joseph Edkins," *Journal of the North China Branch of the Royal Asiatic Society* 26 [1905]: 158), it was said that "in his philological theories Dr. Edkins stood almost alone, and that very little sympathy, sometimes even very little patience, was shown to them by other scholars whose study of the Chinese language itself had been perhaps more thorough than that of Dr. Edkins."

The author of this piece noted the "vast scope" of Edkins's languages (including Chinese, Mongolian, Sanskrit, Hebrew, Persian, etc.), but also added that his linguistic knowledge was sometimes "superficial."

Representative works of the early sinological folkloric and ethnographic tradition include Justus Doolittle, *Social Life of the Chinese*, 2 vols. (New York: Harper, 1865); N. B. Dennys, *The Folklore of China and Its Affinities with That of the Aryan and Semitic Races* (London and Hong Kong, 1876); and J. Dyer Ball, a series of articles on popular mythology appearing in *The China Review* (1880–1885). These works are the precursors of Arthur H. Smith's *Chinese Characteristics* (New York: Fleming H. Revell, 1894) and his *Village Life in China* (New York: F. H. Revell, 1899); and, most significantly, J. J. M. de Groot's *Les Fêtes annuellement célébrées à Emoui, Annales du musée guiment* 11, 12 (1886), and his six-volume *Religious System of China* (Leiden: E. J. Brill, 1892–1910). For discussions of the nineteenth-century folkloric school, see Maurice Freedman, "Sinology and the Social Sciences: Some Reflections on the Social Anthropology of China," *Ethnos* 40 (1975): 194–211; and Richard M. Dorson's foreword to *Folktales of China*, ed. Wolfram Eberhard (Chicago: University of Chicago Press, 1968).

The retarded nature of comparative philological studies in relation to China is interestingly corroborated by Hilderic Friend [pseud.], "Oriental Word-Lore," *The Chinese Recorder* 13 (January–February 1882): 48–55: "The general ignorance which prevails still in England relative to the Chinese and Turanian language and the forbidding appearance of the characters . . . sufficiently accounts for the want of interest generally manifested in studies other than Aryan." Friend goes on to praise

Legge's appointment at Oxford as a sign that a new age of Chinese philology was dawning, and concludes by noting that Legge's work on the etymology of *tian* for Heaven showed that "Chinese word-lore is as valuable and interesting as that of Sanskrit and may be made to yield similar results."

In a similar vein, the author of the editorial in *The Chinese Recorder* (12 [September–October 1881]: 385–86) says that "[s]cholars are prejudicial against China because of the claims of India and are impatient of any comparison being made between what relates to the heathen Chinese and what belongs to the refined Aryan, and then we have few if any who are able and willing to take up the subject from the Chinese stand-point and treat it fully and scientifically. Such work needs not only courage, but means."

96. There is a sizable bibliography of studies by both Edkins and T. W. Kingsmill illustrating this Aryan phase of sinology. Beyond Edkins's *China's Place in Philology*, see, for example, Kingsmill, "The Mythical Origin of the Chow or Djow Dynasty as Set Forth in the Shoo King," *Journal of the North China Branch of the Royal Asiatic Society*, n.s. 7 (1871–1872): 137–48; and Edkins, "On the Identity of Chinese and Indo-European Roots," *Phoenix* 3 (1872): 68–69. In this last article, Edkins states that languages of Eastern Asia "are now found to contain the very same mass of word-roots with which European philology has been so long familiar." Showing the controversy engendered by such theorizing, the article has an appended note by the journal editor: "We think it due to Mr. Edkins to suspend judgment regarding his theory as to China's place in philology, until the subject has been fully considered by philologists who have given some attention to Chinese." See also the general discussion of Edkins's philological theories in "Chinese Philology," *North-China Herald*, March 6, 1873, pp. 197–98; and the editorial in *The Celestial Empire*, January 25, 1877, pp. 88–89.

97. E. J. Eitel, "The She King," review of JL's *Chinese Classics*, vol. 4 (1871), *The China Review* 1 (1872): 6–7.

98. J. Edkins, "Chinese Philology," *The China Review* 1 (1872): 181–82. This is a response to T. Watters's "China's Place in Philology," *The China Review* (1872): 53–58. In an early article showing his growing interest in the possible Babylonian origins of Chinese tradition (wherein the Accadian language might be found to be the "Sanskrit of the Turanian languages of antiquity"), Edkins pointed to what he considered the deficiencies of the "Sanskritist school" of comparative philology. Hampered by the "assumption that gulfs between systems of language are impassable," this school—influenced by Wilhelm von Humboldt and in the modern period identified with Otto Böhtlingk, Max Müller, and August Pott—adhered to the "impossible doctrine of the necessary separation of linguistic families." Interestingly enough, given his own religious convictions, Edkins believed that the polygenetic theory of the modern Sanskritist school was "powerfully" determined by the "present state of physical science," especially the "doctrine of Darwin." See J. Edkins, "Present Aspects of Chinese Philology," *The China Review* 3 (1874): 125–27. Edkins notes that some of the "new interest in East Asian language" has come about "because of the recent progress in the decipherment of Accadian." Furthermore, the Oxford Assyriologist (and soon-to-be-appointed deputy to Müller's position in comparative philology) A. H. Sayce supported the affinity between Chinese and Accadian language and tradition. In this article, Edkins hints that Müller may be shifting

his opinion to a belief in the "unity of all language." Along with himself, Edkins mentions G. Schlegel (with his *Sinica Aryaca*), Chalmers, and Kingsmill as "heretical" monogenetic comparativists. On Darwin and the growing support of monogenesis among physical scientists and anthropologists after midcentury in Britain, see George W. Stocking Jr., *Victorian Anthropology* (New York: Free Press, 1987), 66–68. As Stocking points out (p. 68):

> The earlier hopes that comparative philology could be generalized beyond the Indo-European family to establish genealogical or morphological connections between all the languages of man were becoming somewhat tarnished. The French orientalist Renan now argued the absolute disparity between even the Aryan and the Semitic families; Müller's attempt to establish the unity of the Turanian tongues was being widely attacked; and some philologists, like August Pott, were now themselves embracing polygenism on purely linguistic grounds. In this context, the earlier alliance of linguistics and ethnology was greatly attenuated, and Müller himself came to insist that race was a purely physical category. Underlying the attack on monogenism and the linguistic view of race was a more fundamental issue: the extent to which it was appropriate to consider man in purely naturalistic terms.

99. See, for example, T. W. Kingsmill ("Mythical Origin of the Chow or Djow Dynasty"), who argues that China's "first step" toward civilization was certainly influenced by the "vigor and vitality of Aryan civilization." China did not possess the inner drive to create a dynamic civilization on its own because, unlike ancient Greece, it is not a nation of epic poets. In the "Aryan Origin of the Chinese" (*The China Review* 1 [1873]: 298–99), the anonymous author criticizes Kingsmill's theory by noting that, if China had Aryan origins, then it should show more of the special skills and imagination of the Aryan races (e.g., their aptitude for sciences and the belief in a future state). In the next issue (*The China Review* 2 [1873]: 62–63), Kingsmill responded to this criticism by reaffirming that "all research goes to prove that the religion and civilization, as well as the government and in great measure the language of China, owe their origin to Aryan sources." The Chinese failed to live up to their ancient Aryan heritage because their Aryan conquerors became "mingled in blood" with the Mongolian race. The underlying imperialistic appeal of this line of thought is clearly brought out in an article in the *North-China Herald* (September 7, 1878, p. 236) in which the parable of the sower is used to illustrate the point that, since the good seed of Aryanism fell on the poor soil of China, "no real progress has been effected, and no deep hold taken of the soil."

100. Eitel, "She King," 6–7.

101. Ibid.

102. E. J. Eitel, "Amateur Sinology," *The China Review* 2 (1873): 1–8.

103. Ibid., 3.

104. Ibid., 3–4.

105. See T. McClatchie, *Confucian Cosmogony* (Shanghai: American Presbyterian Mission Press, 1874). McClatchie was a canon of Saint John's Anglican cathedral of Hong Kong.

106. See also John Chalmers's review of McClatchie in *The China Review* 3 (1875): 342–54. Chalmers comments that McClatchie's work was obviously written

to "throw discredit on the excellent term *Shangti*, which it was his mistake, or misfortune, to reject when the best Chinese scholars [referring, of course, to Medhurst and Legge] adopted it some thirty years ago." See McClatchie's rejoinder in *The China Review* 4 (1876): 84–95, in which he says that Chalmers is too quick to "gloss over the filthy impurity of heathen phallic worship."

107. Eitel, "Amateur Sinology," 3–4. Kingsmill's rejoinder to Eitel is found in "Chinese and Hindoo Mythology," *The China Review* 2 (1873): 191–92. Kingsmill says that Eitel should be more careful in establishing his own position and that it "really" was possible to identify the figure of Yao in the Shujing with the Vedic Varuna. Thus Varuna comes from the root *Var,* meaning "to cover, surround, to choose," and in Chinese the word *yao* can mean "to cover." The article in reference here is T. W. Kingsmill, "Mythical Origin of the Chow or Djow Dynasty." See also Edkins's later discussion of some of these issues in his "Were Yau and Shun Historical Persons?" *The China Review* 6 (1878): 416–18. In this article, Edkins supports Legge over Kingsmill, saying that "Dr. Legge should be sustained in his representation of Yau and Shun as real Chinese sovereign chiefs. . . ."

108. See the unsigned article "Chinese Philology" in the *North-China Herald*, in which it is said that, when contrasted with Edkins, Legge is more reliable because he "has no special theory of the evolution of words to support."

109. Eitel, "Amateur Sinology," 5–6.

110. See John Chalmers, "Is Sinology a Science?" *The China Review* 2 (1873): 169–73. This article is a response to "Amateur Sinology."

111. Barthold Niebuhr was the influential German historian whose history of Rome was famous for its concern with origins. Franz Bopp's groundbreaking work on "comparative grammar" was foundational for the development of the tradition of comparative philology. As Hans Aarsleff says (*The Study of Language in England, 1780–1860* [Minneapolis: University of Minnesota Press, 1983], 159), Bopp's *Über das Conjugationssystem der Sanskritsprache in Vergleichung mit jenem der griechischen, lateinischen, persischen und germanischen Sprache,* published in 1816, was the work "which best serves to mark the beginning of comparative philology." See "Dr. Eitel on Amateur Sinology," *North-China Herald,* September 20, 1873, p. 230. This article is supportive of a comparative approach, remarking that "the canons of philological science are sufficiently well established to withstand [Eitel's] assaults, and whether they are handled by amateur or professional sinologues, they will not fail in the end to lead to conclusions undreamt of in his philosophy." The relation of Chinese to Aryan languages is still, it should be noted, an open issue. See, for example, Edwin G. Pulleyblank, "Chinese and Indo-Europeans," *Journal of the Royal Asiatic Society* (1966): 9–39, and much of the work of Victor Mair.

112. "Rising Generation of Sinologists"; this article refers to Wade, Edkins, Wylie, Muirhead, and Martin among the older generation, and Bretschneider, Faber, Kingsmill, Eitel, Lister, von Möllendorff, and Fryer among the younger. It is curious that Legge is not mentioned in this article (perhaps because he was no longer in China at this time).

113. Contrary to what has often been stated, Legge was receiving considerably more than £95 a year. One source for this figure (cited in Barrett's *Singular Listlessness*) is an obituary by Gustave Schlegel in which he reports that in a letter Legge mentioned his meager circumstances in Oxford. Under the heading "Chinese, Pro-

fessor of, Abroad," J. Dyer Ball's *Things Chinese* (London: John Murray, 1892; 5th ed., 1967) also mentions the sum of £95 a year. Concerning Legge's position, the *Historical Register of the University of Oxford: A Supplement to the Oxford University Calendar with an Alphabetical Record of University Honours and Distinctions Completed to the End of Trinity Term 1900* (Oxford: Clarendon Press, 1900) says (pp. 79–80) that the endowment ultimately amounted to £3,003 but does not indicate what Legge's per annum amount was. It does note, however, that in addition to the per annum amount coming from the basic endowment, he also received "the stipend of a fellowship" from Corpus Christi College (amount not given) and an additional £100 a year from the university. At the very least it is clear that Legge was receiving more than £95 a year in income related to the chair of sinology. As might be expected, Müller was receiving considerably more than Legge and, as the *Register* notes, the professorship of comparative philology founded in 1868 had a yearly stipend of £600 a year. After 1877, when the professorship was moved to Corpus Christi College, the position paid a stipend of £700 a year along with an additional £200 per year from a college fellowship.

114. See Joseph Edkins, review of *The Life and Works of Mencius* (London: Trübner, 1875), *Academy*, August 7, 1875, pp. 135–37; and idem, "Ancient Chinese Poetry" [review of Trübner's 1876 edition of *The She King*], *Pall Mall Gazette*, July 17, 1876, p. 220 (this article commends Oxford for appointing Legge to the new Chinese chair). Legge's first popular edition was his 1867 version of the *Analects*.

115. See the "President's [i.e., Reverend Richard Morris] Annual Address for 1875," which embodies the report by James Legge, "The History of Chinese Philology and Its Present State," *Journal of the Royal Asiatic Society* 7 (1875): 22–43.

116. Legge himself notes that the significance of Julien's *Syntaxe* is its full development of the basic Chinese philological principle, first noted in 1814 by Marshman in his grammar, that (quoting Marshman) "the whole of Chinese grammar depends on position." See Legge's report in ibid., 26.

117. Ibid., 23–24.

118. Ibid., 27.

119. Chalmers's work was entitled *The Origin of the Chinese; An Attempt to Trace the Connexion of the Chinese with Western Nations in Their Religion, Superstitions, Arts, Language, and Traditions* (Hong Kong: 1866).

120. JL, "President's Annual Address," 42.

121. Ibid., 42–43.

122. It seems reasonable to believe that Legge would have known of Müller's article in the *Edinburgh Review*, but Legge never, to my knowledge, mentions it. In 1879, the year that the first volumes of the *Sacred Books of the East* appeared, Legge wrote a fifteen-page essay entitled "Professor E. Max Müller" (Bodleian Library, Oxford University [hereafter cited as Bodleian], MS. Autogr. e. 11, *fols.* 53–54). The notes in Legge's *The Notions of the Chinese Concerning God and Spirits: with an Examination of the Defense of an Essay on the Proper Rendering of the Words Elohim and Theos, into the Chinese Language by William Boone, D.D.* (Hong Kong: Hong Kong Register Office, 1852; reprint, Taipei: Ch'eng Wen, 1971) show that he was already following philological debates at that time in the *Edinburgh Review*.

123. Max Müller to JL, February 13, 1875, Bodleian, MS. Top. Oxon. c. 528.

124. Chaudhuri says that this letter to Legge is notable for recording Müller's first reference to the *Sacred Books of the East* project. See Chaudhuri, *Scholar Extraordinary,* 349–50. This is, however, not accurate; we know that Müller already referred to the *Sacred Books* in his address to the Congress of Orientalists in 1874. Chaudhuri describes this letter as follows: "... he informed Legge that he was trying very hard to get a number of scholars together for making translations of the other sacred writings, but at the same time expressed the fear that it might not be an easy task."

125. See Dean Liddell to Sir Rutherford Alcock, November 5, 1875, Bodleian, MS. Top. Oxon. c. 528. In this letter, marked "private," Liddell asks for personal information on Legge—including his age, Christian name, what degrees he held, and whether he would be willing to live in Oxford.

126. See the notice appearing in the *Times* of London, February 10, 1876, p. 8. Taylor and Howell served as cosecretaries to the committee; both were former businessmen in Hong Kong. Taylor also served on the Legislative Council in Hong Kong. The manuscript "Documents relating to the Chinese Professorship at Oxford" are collected together: Bodleian, MS. Top. Oxon. c. 528. The best discussion of these matters is found in Wong Man Kong's "A Pioneer at the Crossroads of East and West: James Legge" (M.A. thesis, Chinese University of Hong Kong, 1993), 107–13. Interestingly, Alcock was opposed to missionaries meddling in matters concerning protection and opium. See his "Opium and Common Sense," *Nineteenth Century* 10 (1881): 854–68. On Alcock, see Alexander Michie, *The Englishman in China During the Victorian Era: As Illustrated in the Career of Sir Rutherford Alcock, K.C.B., D.C.L., Many Years Consul and Minister in China and Japan,* 2 vols. (London: William Blackwood, 1900).

127. Robert K. Douglas, *Language and Literature of China,* 8–9. See also the review of Douglas in the *Spectator* 44 (January 1, 1876): 19–20, in which the reviewer says that he is "glad" to hear that a committee had been formed to establish a Chinese chair at Oxford and that "Dr. Legge would probably be the first occupant." It is clear from this and other contemporaneous writings that there was a growing climate supporting efforts to overcome the "singular listlessness" in Chinese studies. It is also interesting that, inasmuch as the *Spectator* represented sophisticated and cosmopolitan public opinion, this article stresses the "immobility," "impassiveness," and "arrogance" of Chinese tradition and the possibility, reprising the French academician Joseph de Guines, that the Chinese language was connected with the Egyptian and Assyrian written languages.

128. By the time of the third meeting, the membership list included A. Howell, J. B. Taylor, R. Alcock, W. Walkinshaw, Arthur Smith, I. Macandrew, R. Jardine, the Reverend D. H. Snaith, and J. Davis. See Bodleian, MS. Top. Oxon. c. 528. Helen Edith Legge mentions also (in *James Legge Missionary and Scholar* [London: Religious Tract Society, 1905], 205–6) Vice Admiral Sir Charles Shadwell, W. T. Mercer, Esq., a former colonial secretary and acting governor of Hong Kong (who helped with the metrical *Shi jing*), Charles Winchester, a former consul to China and chargé d'affaires in Japan, and Archdeacon Gray.

129. Alcock wrote Liddell on October 11 to urge Oxford's support of a Chinese chair. Liddell's response to Alcock is dated October 16, 1875. Declaring his support

for the position, Liddell noted that the proposed endowment was too small and would result in "too shabby an income to offer a professor."

130. Bodleian, MS. Top. Oxon. c. 528. Legge was active in supporting his own cause, even to the extent of suggesting possible donors to the committee (see Legge to Howell, April 3, 1876, Bodleian, MS. Top. Oxon. c. 528).

131. See Müller to A. P. Stanley, dean of Westminster, November 6, 1875, and December 5, 1875; Bodleian, MS. Eng. d. 2346. In these missives, he refers to his "outrage" and "shock" over the Hebdomadal Council's proposal and Jowett's concurrence. In his November letter he remarks:

> I say nothing about [Monier-Williams's] claims [on the honorary degree], because ever since the election for the Sanskrit professorship I made up my mind that it would not be right for me, as Professor at Oxford, to express an opinion of his work as a Sanskrit scholar. Others have done it, and certainly no one has ever been able to point out any original work done by him which any university or academy could single out for its approval. . . . I felt that I could place but one interpretation on the measure proposed by the Council. It was meant as a notice to quit and therefore . . . I shall send in my resignation.

132. This is a quotation from one of Müller's letters to A. P. Stanley, August 22, 1875. The original is found in the Bodleian, MS. Eng. d. 2346. See Chaudhuri, *Scholar Extraordinary,* 231. See also the letters concerning this situation in Georgina Müller, *Life and Letters,* 1: 528–31.

133. Müller to George von Bunsen, son of Baron Bunsen, his old patron, January 7, 1876; see Chaudhuri, *Scholar Extraordinary,* 231, and Georgina Müller, *Life and Letters,* 2: 1.

134. Quoted in Georgina Müller, *Life and Letters,* 1: 527.

135. Strassburg promised him not only a distinguished professorial chair in Sanskrit with few duties other than research, but also complete support for the editing and publication of the *Sacred Books.* Chaudhuri, in *Scholar Extraordinary* (p. 350), remarks that at the same time that he was discussing Legge's possible involvement in the proposed *Sacred Books* project, Müller "received an invitation from the Austrian Government to transfer his services to Vienna and to publish a series of translations as envisaged by him under the auspices of the Imperial Academy. It was this proposal that, apart from personal reasons, lay behind his decision to resign from his chair at Oxford."

136. JL to Max Müller, December 13, 1875; Bodleian, Legge Dep. d. 172.

137. Max Müller to JL, December 14, 1875; Bodleian, MS. Autogr. e. 11, *fols.* 53–54b. In *James Legge Missionary,* Helen Edith Legge dates this letter to December 17, 1875 (p. 243). After the resolution of these matters and throughout the rest of 1876 (while Müller was on his eighteen-month leave in Europe), Müller and Legge corresponded mostly about technical details of the *Sacred Books* project. On March 10, 1876, for example, Müller wrote Legge to discuss the prospectus for the project and to reaffirm his desire to have complete translations of texts to be included in the series (Bodleian, MS. Autogr. e. 11, *fols.* 53–54b). On June 6, 1876, Müller wrote from Dresden to send along Legge's contract for his contributions to the first twenty-four-volume series of the *Sacred Books,* the first installment of three volumes to be out in 1879. Müller also warns Legge from afar to "keep a certain distance

from the Academic whirlpool" at Oxford. Other letters from Müller followed on June 14 and September 20, 1876, both of them discussing technical sinological matters and plans for the *Sacred Books*. In the September letter, no doubt because Legge was proposing an abridged translation of only the religious sections, Müller again emphasized that he would prefer complete translations of both *The Book of Historical Documents* and *The Book of Poetry:* "critics would at once lay hold of it, and say that we had left out things likely to throw discredit on the early Religions, etc." These words would come back to haunt both Müller and Legge. For these letters, see Bodleian, MS. Autogr. e. 11, *fols.* 53–54.

138. For Müller's letter of resignation, see Bodleian, Dep. d. 172, "Müller's Proposed Resignation of Professorship." Müller was supported by H. G. Liddell and, from afar, by A. P. Stanley and Lord Salisbury, the secretary of state for India. He was, moreover, championed by both Benjamin Jowett of Balliol and the leader of the High Church conservatives, Edward Pusey.

139. Because of Lord Salisbury's interest in these matters, the council of the governor general of India was prompted to cooperate with the university in the funding of the *Sacred Books* project. See Chaudhuri, *Scholar Extraordinary*, 233, and Georgina Müller, *Life and Letters*, 2: 4–6. Müller took an eighteen-month "absence and leave" from Oxford when this issue was resolved.

140. "Professor Max Müller and Oxford," London *Times*, February 16, 1876, p. 10. Charles Dodgson is reported as an obstructionist regarding the proposal to convocation to relieve Müller of his obligation to lecture. The decree in favor of the proposal carried by a vote of ninety-four to thirty-five.

141. Max Müller to A. P. Stanley, dean of Westminster, February 21, 1876, Bodleian, MS. Eng. d. 2346. For a description of the debate over Müller's new appointment, see the account in the *Oxford University Herald*, February 19, 1876, pp. 9–10.

142. Printed circular "Chinese Professorship at Oxford," see Bodleian, MS. Top. Oxon. c. 528.

143. In November 1876, a month after Legge was installed, subscription pledges were only £2,729. Finally, because of some money raised in Hong Kong, the total reached £3,105.10.4, which, after deducting £102.10.4 for advertising, left the £3,003 endowment sum noted by the Oxford *Historical Register;* see Bodleian, MS. Top. Oxon. c. 528.

144. "The Chinese Professorship at Oxford," *North-China Herald,* July 29, 1876, pp. 96–97.

145. The London *Times*, February 22, 1876, p. 11. The *Times* of February 10, 1876, reported that "[n]otice is given of the promulgation of a statute to provide for the appointment of James Legge, LL.D., of the University of Aberdeen, as Professor of Chinese in the University."

146. Liddell to Alcock, April 1, 1876; Bodleian, MS. Top. Oxon. c. 528.

147. Legge was given a fellowship in Corpus Christi College, but the college library holds no significant documents concerning this fellowship or Legge. On the issue of the permanent funding of the chair, see (Bodleian, MS. Top. Oxon. c. 528) the following: Alcock to Liddell, May 25, 1878; Legge to Howell, May 28, 1878 (reports that the president of Corpus Christi was supportive of its permanency); Sewell to Alcock, date uncertain (reports that the Hebdomadal Council has decided to let

the position expire at Legge's death); Alcock to Howell, June 8, 1878 (warns Howell to be cautious about handing the funds over to Oxford until the professorship was made permanent); Legge to Howell, July 8, 1878; and J. E. Sewell (warden of New College and, at this time, vice chancellor) to Legge, May 13 and 27, 1879 (says that Legge's protests will be brought to the Hebdomadal Council); Curators of the University to Legge, June 2, 1879 (reports that the council agrees that the endowment monies will be permanently invested).

148. Legge's own discussion of Davis and the fellowship is found in his lecture "On Chinese Poetry" (twenty-four pp. typescript, n.d., but probably early 1890s), New Bodleian Library, Oxford, Dep. c. 41. E. J. Eitel notes the establishment of the Davis scholarship in *The China Review* 5 (1877): 262. See also the discussion of the Davis scholarship in Wong Man Kong, "Pioneer at the Crossroads," 114–16.

149. At the time of Legge's death in 1897, the university "made a statute vesting the appointment of a Professor [of Chinese] in a board consisting of the Vice-Chancellor, the Regius Professor of Hebrew, the Laudian Professor of Arabic, the Boden Professor of Sanskrit, the Corpus Christi Professor of Comparative Philology, and the Readers in India History and India Law" (*Historical Register,* 80).

150. As late as 1892, Legge was still lamenting his difficulties in securing students, especially from the missionary societies. As he said (see his untitled address to a Baptist missionary breakfast, 1892, Helen Edith Legge typescript, eight pages, Council for World Missions [hereafter cited as CWM]/China/Personal/Legge/Box 7):

> The Chinese Chair at Oxford was intended by some of its promoters to be mainly a Chair of Research. I hailed my appointment to it very much in the hope that it would also give me the opportunity to lay in the minds of young men intended for Missionary work the foundation of a Chinese scholarship that would be useful to them in their future course, and make them able ministers of Christian truth in their several spheres. This hope has been realized to a considerable extent, but not so largely as I desire. . . . I must think also that the directors of Missionary Societies who do not insist on their accepted students doing so, are labouring under a sad mistake, and fall into serious error. I know well the excuses or apologies which are made for sending men out without the training which I recommend. The young men, it is said, are full of zeal, and eager to be in the field. So it is— happily, but not wisely. A young American missionary told me that after his conversion in a great revival movement, he would not rest to study at home, lest the work should be finished and all the Chinese converted before he could take any part in the work. Directors again have said to me, and very stupidly I submit to you, "the money comes to us for direct mission work, and not to prepare our candidates for it. The sooner we can send them into the field the better." My contention on the contrary is that the preliminary training will be a saving of time in the real missionary labour, and will promote its thoroughness and efficiency.

151. It has been reported by both nineteenth- and twentieth-century sources that Legge received only the tiny yearly sum of £95 (Dyer Ball and Timothy Barrett report this figure) as his professorial salary. No doubt this sum refers to the £100 contributed out of university funds; but the total yearly salary was made up of the endowment income, his fellowship at Corpus Christi, and the contribution from university coffers. The actual yearly total from all three sources is unclear. Moreover,

official university accounts are overly cryptic and other contemporary reports are often garbled (one says that the fellowship income was about £300 per annum, to which was added the endowment income and £100 from the university chest!). The *North-China Herald* of July 29, 1876, reported the total emoluments as £300 from Corpus Christi, £100 from the university, and an unspecified amount from the endowment. Legge himself wrote Professor Gustave Schlegel in 1894 that his yearly income was £220, made up of the chair endowment and the university contribution. It seems, however, that this amount does not include the income from his fellowship, which suggests that the actual total is still in doubt. Regardless of the confusion, several things can be deduced. One of these is simply that his salary was not the "mere pittance" often reported. On the other hand, his remuneration was modest when compared, for example, with the truly handsome income Müller was receiving from his chair (£600 a year); his All Souls fellowship, unreported; and his editorship, which seems, from Oxford University Press records, to have been about £200 a year, the £1,000 yearly income of the Boden professorship, or, for that matter, the reported incomes of Stanislas Julien (1,500 francs or £600 yearly) and Dutch sinologists such as Schlegel (6,000 guilders or around £560, and "living in Holland is cheaper than in England"). Even Archibald Sayce, the deputy holder of Müller's chair of comparative philology, was receiving £300 a year. See Schlegel's discussion in *T'oung Pao* 9 (1898): 59–63. An interesting comparative observation about university salaries at this time is found in one of Müller's letters (January 12, 1873) to Gladstone. He notes that in German universities, professors derive their income from the government and from fees paid by the students. The highest salary paid to a German professor "is only 4,000 thaler or £600 . . . yet even that is more than the average income of a professor at Oxford, with the exception of the Theological chairs." Sayce's salary, one-half of the £600 professorial salary, is reported by Chaudhuri, *Scholar Extraordinary,* 234.

152. Quoted in JL to Schlegel; see *T'oung Pao* 9 (1898): 60.

153. M. Dominica Legge makes this claim in her talk "James Legge," paper presented to the Sino-Scottish Society, University of Edinburgh, February 4, 1951.

154. See the "Eastern Sages," which is number 902 in the Falconer Madan set of Oxford Caricatures published by the booksellers Thomas Shrimpton and Sons between the late 1860s and the 1890s. The "Eastern Sages" (because of its placement in the series of caricatures) seems to date to around 1882; Bodleian, G.A. Oxon. 4° 412–18. I am grateful to Mr. Steven Tomlinson, assistant librarian at the Bodleian Library, for information concerning the Falconer Madan caricatures.

155. See William Dwight Whitney, *Max Müller and the Science of Language: A Criticism.*

156. JL, *Inaugural Lecture on the Constituting of a Chinese Chair in the University of Oxford; Delivered in the Sheldonian Theatre, October 27, 1876* (Oxford and London: James Parker, 1876), 3.

157. Ibid., 4.

158. JL, "Notes of My Life" (1897), 102–3.

159. JL, *Inaugural Lecture,* 4–5. This is understandable given Douglas's support for Legge's position at Oxford.

160. Ibid., 14.

161. Ibid., 6. After mentioning the chairs in Berlin, Munich, and Vienna, Legge remarks that Sanskrit "has hitherto had greater attractions for the scholars of Germany than Chinese."

162. Ibid., 9. This section of the lecture (pp. 9–13) addresses the reasons put forward by the endowment circular for the Chinese chair—that is, the aforementioned political, religious, and commercial interests of Britain in China. With regard to the first of these, Legge stresses the "contiguity of the British possessions in the East to China" (referring here to "Siam, Birmah, and Assam") and the complex set of entanglements (including, of course, the colony of Hong Kong) created by treaties between the two empires. Both of these political realities call for competent interpreters, and Legge expresses the hope that young men destined for the colonial or consular service in Hong Kong and China might, in a way similar to the proposal for those preparing for the Indian civil service, initiate their studies at Oxford (as they once did at King's College, London). Proceeding to a description of what he calls the "enormous" commercial interests of Britain, Legge quotes statistics to show the magnitude of the British balance of trade with China—for example, that, based on "tables" prepared for the Universal Exhibition of Vienna in 1873, British shipping was more than "one-half of the whole" of the value of the gross total of all commodities exported and imported into China for the years 1870, 1871, and 1872 (between £115 and £116 million). What was "astonishing" to Legge about this vast intercourse was that so much of it was conducted by means of "compradores and linguists" using the bastard "business" English known as "pidgin." In response, he presents the pragmatic case that mercantile interests will be furthered when such bastardized forms of communication pass away and men are properly prepared "to speak Chinese and translate Chinese documents." In this sense, the chair of Chinese can directly assist the training of young men embarking upon a commercial career in China by giving them "a practical acquaintance with one or more of the spoken dialects of the language."

163. The fact is that most missionary societies did not, at this time, have well-established language schools or language curricula for agents in the field in China; see Laurence Kitzan, "The London Missionary Society in India and China, 1798–1834" (Ph.D. diss., University of Toronto, 1965).

164. It is interesting that Legge spends considerably more time discussing political and commercial interests than religious and missionary concerns. Part of this is doubtlessly due to his appreciation for the support he had received from commercial sources (e.g., Jardine and the merchants associated with the Endowment Committee), but some of it also suggests Legge's sympathy for the more secular (i.e., less religiously sectarian) vantage point of a commercial perspective.

165. Ibid., 14–16.

166. Ibid., 14–25.

167. Ibid., 17–19.

168. Ibid., 19–25.

169. On the "ding-dong" theory, see Dowling, "Victorian Oxford and the Science of Language," 160–78. See also the discussion in G. A. Wells, *The Origin of Language: Aspects of the Discussion from Condillac to Wundt* (La Salle, Ill.: Open Court, 1987).

170. JL, *Inaugural Lecture,* 23.

171. Legge's prudence on these issues is no doubt influenced by Eitel's devastating ridicule of amateurish efforts at grandiose forms of philological comparison. But Legge's *festina lente* approach to the basic comparative question of parallels is also most probably influenced by an earlier, and even more celebrated, discussion of false analogies and Chinese texts by the master comparativist Max Müller. It is interesting to know, therefore, that in 1870 Müller published, first in the *Contemporary Review,* an article entitled "On False Analogies in Comparative Theology." Different from the "real similarities" to be found in nearly "all the religions of the world" are the false, strictly coincidental, or made-up analogies that are the bane of theological apologetic and any sort of comparative science (see Müller, "On False Analogies in Comparative Theology," in *Chips,* 5: 98–132).

In most of this article, Müller discusses instances of this problem seen in Indian religions but, significantly, ends with a consideration of the mysterious fourteenth chapter of the classical Daoist text known as the *Daode jing* [*Tao Te Ching*] (what Legge translated as *The Book of the Tao and Its Characteristics*), which—as early as the seventeenth century, and then repeatedly down to Müller's day—was said by Western sinological commentators to include a veiled reference to the triune God of the Bible. The three Chinese syllables *i-xi-wei* were found to be a cipher for the three persons of the trinity or were, according to Rémusat, an actual transliteration of Je-ho-vah. Müller says that "Rémusat goes on to remark that Lao-tse had really rendered this Hebrew name more accurately than the Greeks, because he had preserved the aspiration of the second syllable, which was lost in Greek" (ibid., 131). The amazing persistence, and changing contours, of this interpretive tradition is deserving of a monographic study, but in keeping with Müller's brief observations I want to note only that the "panic" created by Rémusat's discoveries was put to rest by the always cautious Julien, who relied on various native commentaries.

Even though discussions of the mysteries of chapter fourteen of the *Daode jing* continued after Julien's definitive criticism, more knowledgeable scholars such as Legge agreed with Julien and Müller that this case should serve as a "useful warning" against foolish comparisons in the history of religions. See Legge's discussion of chapter fourteen in his translation of the *Daode jing* published as volume 39 of the *Sacred Books of the East* (Oxford: Clarendon Press, 1891), 57–58. He notes that even after Julien, theologians such as Hardwick (*Christ and Other Masters: An Historical Inquiry into Some of the Chief Parallelisms and Contrasts Between Christianity and the Religious Systems of the Ancient World. With Special Reference to Prevailing Difficulties and Objections,* 4 parts [Cambridge: Macmillan, 1855–59] were still mesmerized by the earlier theories. Even worse was that sinological scholars who should have known better (such as Victor von Strauss und Tornay in 1870 and Edkins in 1884) continued to revive, in different ways, the idea that chapter fourteen was hiding deep secrets of grand unity. The best policy, says Müller, is to be "careful and honest" when dealing with such matters (Müller, "False Analogies," in *Chips,* 5: 132). This was a lesson more in evidence in Legge's work than in Müller's scholarship.

172. JL, *Inaugural Lecture,* 25. Legge notes: "I made the voyage with the first installment of those lads from China to San Francisco in 1873, and know well the Chinese gentlemen who have been the chief promoters of the scheme." His "faint hope" that his chair, and his contacts in China, might encourage students to study Chinese at Oxford was never realized.

173. Ibid., 26–27.

174. As was typical at the time, Legge's inaugural lecture was printed as a pamphlet and consequently had an audience that went well beyond the confines of the Sheldonian. Of special interest in this regard is a brief anonymous review in *The Chinese Recorder*, the leading Protestant missionary journal in China: "Inaugural Lecture on the Constituting of a Chinese Chair in the University of Oxford, London: Trübner & Co., 1876," *The Chinese Recorder* 8 (March–April 1877): 193–94. Given the reference to Trübner as publisher, it may be that there were several editions of the lecture in pamphlet form (the quotes are taken from the pamphlet published by James Parker and Company, also in 1876; see above, note 156). It is the tone rather than the substance that is notable here. Implicit in the effusive praise of this "auspicious event" and the observation that Oxford University is "honoured by the appointment of James Legge" is the understandable pride taken by the missionaries back in the field in the accomplishments of their former colleague. What is really remarkable is that, only a few months later, in May, opinions about Professor Legge would abruptly darken in the *Recorder* and among many missionaries in China as a result of events at the Missionary Conference in Shanghai.

Another representative review of the inaugural address appears in *The China Review*, E. J. Eitel's more secular and scholarly publication; see E. J. Eitel, "Short Notice. Inaugural Lecture Delivered Oct. 27, 1876 by Rev. James Legge," *The China Review* 5 (1877): 260–62. Eitel, as might be expected from his more professional sinological perspective, rejoices in Legge's chair because it shows that there are "higher reasons than those of commercial and political greatness" to be proud of Britain. Eitel was of German nationality but, while in Hong Kong, he married an Englishwoman, joined the London Missionary Society, and generally adopted an Anglicized point of view. On Eitel, see Wong Man Kong, "Protestant Missionaries' Images of Chinese Buddhism in Nineteenth-Century China; With Special Reference to Ernest John Eitel, Joseph Edkins, and James Legge, Missionaries of the London Missionary Society," paper presented at the University of Leeds, April 7–9, 1994; and Donald Leslie and Jeremy Davidson, *Author Catalogues of Western Sinologists* (Canberra: Department of Far Eastern History, Australian National University, 1966), 36. These "higher reasons" are based on the Germanic idea of the university, which encompasses the "learning of the whole universe" and the *ex oriente lux* truths of Orientalist scholarship. Sadly, when Britain is compared with other European nations, only "tardy and scanty justice" was done by Oxford's "almost reluctant" embrace of these principles. Remarking that Legge was "indeed the fittest and most deserving occupant" of this new position, Eitel commends the lecture for showing how the "practically useful" nature of the chair is not only related to various political, religious, and commercial reasons, but also is rooted in the importance of the study of literature and language "in themselves." Legge will be useful as a sinological Orientalist precisely because of his continued work on the classics and through his participation in the *Sacred Books of the East* project.

175. For a description (with illustrative material) of the Encaenia (as well as the overall academic year) in Victorian Oxford, see Graham, *Images of Victorian Oxford*, 53–72.

176. Müller was on an extended eighteen-month leave in Europe.

APPENDIX TO CHAPTER TWO. CARICATURES
OF MAX MÜLLER AND JAMES LEGGE AT OXFORD

1. See Jehu Junior, "Men of the Day.—No. 98. Frederick Maximilian Müller, L.L.D.," *Vanity Fair* (London), February 6, 1875, p. 75.

2. Ibid.; "Most of his books are of the high order which nobody will read . . . yet he is known to the Many, and indeed is one of the few of those who have trodden the higher and more thorny paths of science whose names command respect even from the vulgar."

3. Concerning the Grenfell family and Georgina Müller, see Chaudhuri, *Scholar Extraordinary,* 111–19.

4. On these mostly forgotten figures, see Justin Wintle, ed., *Makers of Nineteenth Century Culture, 1800–1914* (London: Routledge and Kegan Paul, 1982).

5. On the word *jehu,* see the *Oxford English Dictionary.*

6. See Jehu Junior, 75.

7. This caricature is Falconer Madan, no. 381. Bodleian, G.A. Oxon. 4º 412–418.

8. Although distorted, the symbols are close enough to actual characters to be tentatively identified as *sheng-ling,* meaning vigorous life. These characters had commercial associations, being used to write the Chinese name for the East India Company.

CHAPTER THREE. HERETIC LEGGE:
RELATING CONFUCIANISM AND CHRISTIANITY, 1877–1878

1. Helen Edith Legge, *James Legge Missionary and Scholar* (London: Religious Tract Society, 1905), 206–7, 228–29. Helen Edith quotes "a friend's" (unidentified) description of her father during his days at Oxford (p. 229):

> So honest, so healthy, so much of the open-air was in his aspect that he might have been anything rather than an Oxford don. One could have imagined his long life spent on Scottish hills in cold, pure air, tramping the heather all day long. How unlike the later years at Oxford, in his study, walled in by mysterious books, and absorbed in his strange learning to which scarcely any other man held his key.

2. See K. S. Elisabeth Murray, *Caught in the Web of Words: James A. H. Murray and the Oxford English Dictionary* (New Haven and London: Yale University Press, 1977), 247.

3. See Dominica Legge, "James Legge" (paper presented to the Sino-Scottish Society, University of Edinburgh, February 4, 1951), 13. The railway came to Oxford in the 1840s and the first train station was erected in 1850; see Malcolm Graham, *Images of Victorian Oxford* (Oxford: Alan Sutton, 1992), 13, 78–79.

4. Dominica Legge, "James Legge."

5. On the notable Oxford eccentrics of the Victorian period, see, for example, Graham, *Images of Victorian Oxford,* 37–51.

6. In a letter dated June 5, 1879, Legge mentions that he was suffering from "vile gout" in his foot (Bodleian Library, Oxford University [hereafter cited as Bodleian], MS. Top. Oxon. d. 528).

7. For Legge's very touching, and surprisingly revealing, views of his second wife, see *The Late Mrs. Legge: A Letter to Her Brother, The Reverend Joseph Johnston, of Fremantle, Western Australia, From Her Husband* (Oxford: E. C. Alden, 1881). This fascinating

family document is marked "For Private Circulation Only." For the quotations in this section, see pp. 27–37. On James Murray, see Elisabeth Murray, *Caught in the Web*. Murray (who died in 1915) and his wife, Ada, requested to be buried next to their old friends and fellow members of the George Street Congregational Church, Andrew Fairbairn and James Legge. Given the closeness of their association and their proximity at Oxford, there does not seem to be any extant written correspondence between Murray and Legge—at least, Murray's great-granddaughter, Elisabeth Murray, does not know of any materials (private communication).

Concerning Dodgson's acquaintance with the Legge family, see, especially, his invitation in purple ink to take pictures of "Miss Legge" (most probably Helen Edith): see C. L. Dodgson to Mrs. Legge, Bodleian, MS. Top. Oxon. d. 528. See also Morton N. Cohen, ed., *The Letters of Lewis Carroll* (New York: Oxford University Press, 1979), 1:343–44. The Legges entertained Dodgson at dinner on February 11, 1879, at which time "Dodgson 'arranged that they should bring Miss Willetts to be photographed in Japanese dress.'" On March 22, Mrs. Legge and Miss Willetts called, but "it was too dull to try any pictures." On Legge's possible influence on Dodgson's *Sylvie and Bruno* (1889)—Dodgson may have been aware, via Legge, of Zhuangzi's butterfly dream and the theme "life is but a dream"—see Raphael B. Shaberman, *George Macdonald: A Bibliographical Study* (Detroit: Omnigraphics, 1990), 125–26.

8. Murray, *Caught in the Web*, 248. Concerning the George Street Congregational Church, see the documents kept in the Oxford County Record Office: "Record of the Congregational Church Assembling at George Street Oxford 1858–1888" and "Records of the Congregational Church Assembling at George Street Oxford with the Declaration of Faith and Church Order 1887–1897" (Ox. C.C. I/ii/3). See also *Encyclopedia of Oxford*, S.V. Dissenters (London: Papermac, 1992), 121–23. James and Hannah Mary Legge, along with their daughter Marian Fitzgerald Willetts, joined the church on February 2, 1877. Helen Edith seems to have been admitted to the church on January 4, 1878. Legge was very active in the church—e.g., giving guest sermons, participating (along with Murray and later Andrew Fairbairn) on the Deacons' Committee, and regularly contributing to various charitable funds (interestingly, however, he did *not* give anything to the "LMS Collection").

9. Murray, *Caught in the Web*, 248.

10. Legge's love for his wife is, for example, charmingly expressed in a letter (dated June 8, 1877) to his stepdaughter, Marian Willetts, School of Oriental and African Studies, University of London (hereafter cited as SOAS), Legge archives.

11. JL, *The Late Mrs. Legge*.

12. Ibid., 36–37.

13. Ibid., 37. While admiring her "perfect Christian womanhood" and clearly loving and respecting her, Legge candidly admits to differences of religious opinion and temperament.

14. Ibid., 36.

15. Ibid.

16. Ibid., 27–28.

17. Legge, *James Legge Missionary*.

18. In a letter dated October 21, 1876, Legge discusses his recent participation in a meeting opposing the opium trade at which, along with "Mr. [Frederick Storrs] Turner and A-Choy," he was one of the principal speakers. Here he restates his

opinion that "the opium traffic is a thing of selfish devilish greed . . . and there is also cruelty and the arm of oppression about it, for the Chinese government protests against it and implores Great Britain to cease from it" (Council for World Mission [hereafter cited as CWM] China/Personal/Legge/Box 10). Those supporting the opium trade became increasingly indignant over the righteousness of missionary involvement in the opposition movement both at home and abroad. An example of this is found in the article "Missionaries and Opium" published in the *North-China Herald,* May 20, 1876, 477–78, in which the opposition publication known as the *Friend of China* is chastised for its "historical ignorance" and "misrepresentation of mercantile aims." This writer concludes by declaring:

> [I]t is to be regretted that, when dwelling so unctuously as they are prone to do, on the aggressiveness and iniquity of our relations with China, writers of the *Friend of China* stamp should forget that, for one dispute which arises in regard to merchants, ten occur about missionaries; and we will hazard a considerable wager that, if given the option of rejecting any particular feature of foreign intercourse—not only "missionaries or merchants" but "missionaries or opium"—the Chinese would say "missionaries."

19. See J.D. Frodsham, *The First Chinese Embassy to the West: The Journals of Kuo Sung-t'ao, Liu Hsi-hung, and Chang Te-yi* (Oxford: Clarendon Press, 1974), xlii. The original account is published in *Guo Songtao riji* (The diary of Guo Songtao) (Changsha, China, 1982). For the views of Zeng Jize (1839–1890, popularly known as Marquis Tseng in the nineteenth century), see Yu Yueheng, ed., *Zeng Jize yiji* (Changsha, China, 1983). Concerning Kuo's (Guo's) positive opinion of Western civilization, Frodsham says that "it must not be assumed that Kuo's opponents were unaware of the profoundly heretical nature of his views. On the contrary, it was precisely his praise of the moral, not the technological basis of Western civilization, which led them to burn the blocks of his diary, and demand his impeachment as a traitor." Despite the impressiveness of Western moral civilization and commerce, Kuo believed that "the Western religions" were clearly "inferior" to the teachings of their sages: "If one considers them from the point of view of profundity and perfection, there can be no comparison between the two. Only imbeciles would be deceived by Christianity. Intelligent people and wise men would never let themselves be taken in by such nonsense. Needless to say, all scholars and gentlemen detest the Christian religion." See also the interesting discussions of the Chinese ministers in "Kwoh Sung-Tao on the Christian Propaganda," along with a translation from Guo's journal, in the *North-China Herald,* January 3, 1878, pp. 6–7, 14; and "Chinese Minister's Views of England," in the *Celestial Empire,* January 17, 1879, pp. 52–53.

20. Frodsham, *First Chinese Embassy,* 17. It is also said by the Chinese that Legge, having lived in Kwangtung (Guandong) for many years, could speak Cantonese and had "completed" an English translation of the Four Books and the *Book of Poetry,* which "he hopes to use" to change "the customs of [Western] society." "We do not know," says Liu, whether Legge's translations "are free from mistakes."

21. See Legge, *James Legge Missionary,* 225–26.

22. See JL, "Education in China," Helen Edith Legge typescript, nine pages; n.d. but probably 1877, CWM/China/Personal/Legge/Box 7.

23. Ibid., 8–9. It is important to remember Legge's upbringing in the Sabbath culture of the Westminster Confession, which emphasized a belief in God and the conscientious practice of the Ten Commandments; he was already working out his educational logic in his early years. Legge's emphasis on "nondenominationalism" seems confusing because he criticizes Chinese education for teaching ethics and morality without the "sanction and obligation coming to them from religious and spiritual truths." This is only an apparent inconsistency, however, since for Legge a "nondenominational," "undenominational," or "secular" education does not mean that it is devoid of any "religious" content—meaning the teaching of a few basic truths such as belief in a monotheistic God and in a future life, both of which were documented in the Christian Bible and, according to Legge, in the *Chinese Classics*.

24. David Hawkes, *Classical, Modern and Humane: Essays in Chinese Literature,* ed. John Minford and Wong Siu-kit (Hong Kong: Chinese University Press, 1989), 6. On the difficulty of attracting students to Chinese studies at Oxford, Hawkes remarks (p. 3) that

> Chinese was first added to the Honour School of Oriental Studies in 1939. During the years 1939–49 only five candidates for Honours offered it; and though twenty-two, the corresponding number for the years 1950–60, represents a marked increase, it still cannot be said that the occupant of this Chair [i.e., the Oxford professorship of Chinese] gives instruction to multitudes. To be sure it may seem strange—to one unacquainted with British educational theory it will seem startling—that a language spoken by nearly a quarter of the world's inhabitants should be studied by only a score or so of people in one of the world's great universities. Such, however, is the case; and I cannot but feel some diffidence in venturing to talk to you about my subject and the problems of teaching it, when I reflect that it is studied by only one-fifth of one percent of the undergraduate members of this university.

It should be noted that these comments come from Hawkes's inaugural lecture upon assuming Legge's old position. What it shows is that the number of students Legge was working with in the nineteenth century was not so very much larger in the twentieth century; student listlessness reigned.

25. See "Knowledge of Chinese," *London and China Telegraph,* January 15, 1877, p. 50. See also the article "English Lack of Interest in China," *North-China Herald and South China and Coastal Gazette,* February 28, 1878, p. 206.

26. Algernon M. M. Steadman, *Oxford: Its Social and Intellectual Life. With Remarks and Hints on Expenses, the Examinations, the Selection of Books, etc.* (London: Trübner, 1878), 84, 86.

27. Ibid., 118. Steadman claims that the problem of mere "pass-men" at Oxford at this time was not as severe as it was sometimes said to be.

28. See A. M. M. Steadman, ed., *Oxford: Its Life and Schools* (London: George Bell, 1887). Commenting on "Oxford ladies" attending professorial lectures, Steadman says (p. 127):

> The . . . place [of undergraduates] is largely filled up by the Oxford ladies, who always throng in crowds to any public lecture of a popular character. Their presence is not always approved of. Ruskin once declared in a lecture that the undergraduates ought to be his only hearers, and the undergraduates present somewhat un-

gallantly applauded. But certainly Ruskin had some reason, for he could always draw crowds of men to his lecture-room, because all the space was taken up by ladies, who only attend by courtesy.

29. Max Müller, *Auld Lang Syne* (New York: Charles Scribner's Sons, 1898), 103.

30. Ibid. As Müller says, the "miserable scantiness" of attendance at lectures was a problem for even the most eloquent and renowned professors at that time— luminaries such as Goldwin, Smith, Freeman, and Stubbs. Müller comments that Dr. Stubbs sometimes delivered his college lectures on medieval and modern history "to two or three listless men."

31. "Chinese Studies at Oxford," *China Review* 6 (July 1877): 62. In this article it was also noted that Legge was hoping to secure the aid of a native teacher and was "in touch with the Foreign and Colonial Offices regarding his proposal that candidates for consular service (and the civil service in Hong Kong) should study at Oxford." Nothing came of either his hope for assistance or his proposal to the Foreign Office. On page 63 is a short notice to the effect that Yale had just appointed S. Wells Williams to the first American chair of Chinese and that Harvard was proposing to bring over natives for the teaching of Chinese.

32. "Oxford and Its Professors," *Edinburgh Review* 348 (October 1889): 308–22.

33. Ibid., 317–18. The author of this article sees the core problem with the professorate as its failure to promote "bread-winning subjects" like modern European languages instead of archaic Asian dialects. It may additionally be noted that the writer reports the income of the Chinese chair to be £500 and that the average professor's income, ranging from £1,500 to £50, was £525 a year. See also the discussion of professorial chairs in the *Encyclopedia of Oxford,* 75–76.

34. These figures are derived from the *Oxford University Gazette.*

35. "On the Davis Scholarship," London *Times,* March 16, 1877, p. 8. See also Bodleian, MS. Autogr. e. 11, *fols.* 53–54, for actual copies of the exams given. For an extensive listing of the exam questions, see Wong Man Kong, "A Pioneer at the Crossroads of East and West: James Legge" (M.A. thesis, Chinese University of Hong Kong, 1993), appendixes. In 1879, the candidates were expected to draw a map of China, showing the eighteen provinces with the names in Chinese; name the great feudal dynasties in Chinese; know the six classes of Chinese characters; show their familiarity with Chinese grammar and how the Chinese measured time; and to translate a passage and commentary from Chinese into English and a passage of text from English into Chinese.

36. See Lauren Pfister, "Some New Dimensions in the Study of the Works of James Legge (1815–1897), part 1," *Sino-Western Cultural Relations Journal* 12 (1990): 29–50.

37. Legge did everything possible to increase his student population by periodic, though usually unsuccessful, appeals to the Foreign Office and the missionary societies. See, for example, the testimonials recorded in Helen Edith Legge, *James Legge Missionary,* 224.

38. There are interesting tidbits in the Legge archives at the Bodleian that refer to his actual classroom teaching techniques. There is, for example, an extant copy of a mnemonic he composed to help his students remember the Chinese dynasties. See New Bodleian Library, Oxford University, Notebooks. It deserves to be recorded here for the light it throws on Legge as a teacher and sinologist (e.g., his

use of the new Wade romanization system and of Orientalist tropes: "The Manchu tartars last arose / Of whose decay we want the close").

> Backwards we go four thousand years,
> First Hsia, next Shang, through Chow appears,
> With Chow the feudal kingdoms passed.
> Lo! Despot rule that still doth last.
> First, Ts'in with fire and blood arose;
> Ere seventy years its sway did close.
> Three Hans four centuries and more
> Prevailed till A.D. 264;
> Through Chin, till A.D. 419
> Sung, Ch'i, Liang, and Ch'en combine,
> All in the south with Wei and Ch'i
> And Chow, that northward bore the decree.
> Till Sui obtained the sovereignty
> In 618 Sui bent to T'ang
> When learning through the Empire rang
> Three centuries gone to T'ang are due;
> And then for fifty years and two
> Then after Liang, T'ang, Chin, and Han,
> And Chow, each with brief rule we scan.
> The golden Sung, with learning's grace,
> For 319 years next we trace
> Then Yuan's Mongolian chiefs come on;
> Ere ninety years their course was done;
> And Ming the Bright 1368
> To 1643 ruled the state.
> The Manchu tartars last arose
> Of whose decay we want the close.

39. The fact that Legge clearly did pay some attention to grammar in his courses seems to contradict his comment to Gustave Schlegel: "I am much interested by what you say of your having learned Chinese yourself in the first place, and then taught it successfully for many years without using a grammar. So it was with myself from the time that I began to learn Chinese in 1837 or 1838, and when I came to the Chinese chair here in Oxford, I thought it better to carry on the instruction of my students without using any grammar" (JL to Schlegel, December 12, 1892; recorded in an obituary, G. Schlegel, "James Legge, M.A. Oxford, LL.D. Aberdeen," *T'oung Pao* 9 [1898]: 60). As a matter of fact, it appears that, while Legge started out paying some attention to abstract grammatical principles and analytical philological discussions (such as the use of Julien's *Syntaxe nouvelle de la langue chinoise*), he quickly (i.e., by the beginning of the 1880s) gave this up in favor of a more direct approach using native primers, such as the *Sanzi jing* (Three-character classic) and the *Qianzi wen* (Thousand-character classic) and primary sources. If his students knew German, he would have them read H. G. C. von der Gabelentz's *Aufgangs-grunde das Chinenischen Grammatik* (see CWM/China/Personal/Legge/Box 8). It is also worth remarking that, by the end of the 1870s, Legge had stopped using Chinese versions of Christian scriptures in his teaching.

40. "The Professorship of Chinese at Oxford," *North-China Herald,* July 28, 1877, p. 80. Concerning Oscar Wilde's taste for lilies and blue china ("Blue Pot"), see Richard Ellman, *Oscar Wilde* (New York: Vintage Books, 1987), 45.

41. Helen Edith Legge, *James Legge Missionary,* 224.

42. Ibid., 227–28. Helen Edith refers to an undated meeting at Oxford at which Legge presented an argument for encouraging missionaries to "intermeddle with existing heathen religions."

> In his answer [Legge] said, "The missionary has to open the eyes of the hea-
> then." He insisted on this because some learned and powerful thinkers maintain
> that heathen religions ought not to be interfered with. "Those who reason and
> speak in this way . . . can hardly have a direct acquaintance with existing heathen
> religions. They know them from a study of their most ancient documents, and
> do not know how the leading principles which these contain have been obscured
> and overlaid by an ever-increasing mass of superstitions and abominable idola-
> tries. Missionaries have to do with the systems which have grown up, and which
> contain many things so absurd and monstrous, so silly and so hideous, that I
> often found it difficult to quell the thought that some demoniac agency has been
> at work egging men on until their religion has become an insult to the high and
> Holy God."

What we see here is really the basic accommodationist thesis that the contemporary versions of Chinese religion (meaning especially "Confucianism") had become hopelessly corrupt and needed the righteous "meddling" of missionaries sensitive to its ancient religious purity and inherent moral capacity. There is no extant original text for this excerpt, not even one of Helen Edith Legge's typed and edited versions.

43. Even the arch Oxonian skeptic Mark Pattison was well aware of the significant difference between Legge's scholarly position and that of the run-of-the-mill missionary. For as Pattison put it in a letter (October 5, 1877) to Legge: "If all persons were as tolerant of differences of opinion as you are, and as able to distinguish the important from the trivial, missions ought to be more hopeful than they seem now to me to be" (CWM/China/Personal/Legge/Box 8).

44. JL, "Mencius," Bodleian, dep. c. 46. These two presentations were completely new addresses and not repetitions of earlier writings. It is important in particular to trace a line of development from 1861 through the popularized works of 1867–1875 down to these Oxford lectures. The popularized versions, though new translations, extensively repeated the 1861 prolegomena (only dropping the more technical sections). Kongzi was seen as a more insightful and influential "sage" *(shengren),* whereas Mengzi was seen as a less significant "philosopher."

45. See Léon Poliakov, *The Aryan Myth: A History of Racist and Nationalist Ideas in Europe,* trans. Edmund Howard (New York: Basic Books, 1974), 213–14. Poliakov believes that Müller was basically disingenuous in his retraction (especially in a talk given in 1872) of his earlier suggestions of a relation between language and race: "his self-criticism [was] . . . so timid as to be practically inaudible."

46. JL, "Mencius," Bodleian, dep. c. 46. The fact that in this lecture he identifies China as "Turanian" and elsewhere seemed to distinguish between them seems to hinge on his nonphilological use of the term here. That is, "Turanian" is being used here as an arbitrary generic label for a non-Aryan and non-Semitic civilization and without its technical (and mostly spurious) linguistic connotations.

47. Manuscript versions of these lectures are found in the Legge archive, Bodleian, dep. c. 46. The lectures were delivered on May 11 (part 1), May 22 (part 2), May 29 (part 3), and November 28, 1877 (part 4), and published in the *China Review* 6 (1877): 147–58, 223–35, 299–310, and 363–74. An interesting review of the overly goody-goody and insufficiently critical nature of these lectures (as printed in the *China Review*) appeared in the *North-China Herald,* June 1, 1878, pp. 561–62. It is worth giving the gist of this review here as it will reappear later in the century when Legge's old-fashioned and uncritical methods (and Leggism in a sinological rather than a missiological sense) come under fire by self-styled modernists such as Giles, Kingsmill, and others.

> Dr. Legge has evidently arrived at that stage when he can learn nothing and forget nothing. To him, Chinese criticism of today is as Chinese criticism of twenty-five years ago. Yaou, Shun, the "Mixed Court," and the Emperor Yung-cheng are all of equal substantiality, and come in for much the same treatment as use to befall patriarchs and heroes in the goody books of a generation ago, when the Golden Fleece, and the patriarch Joseph, and the Emperor Napoleon, all equally served as historical landmarks. It is a pity some more wholesome pabulum is not given to the students of Chinese at Oxford. We wonder at the want of interest taken in Chinese studies in Europe, but if Dr. Legge's lectures on Imperial Confucianism are to be considered as the standard to which a student may hope to attain, we need not wonder at the rising generation turning to more profitable fields of research.

See also the review of the printed lectures in *The Chinese Recorder* 9 (May–June 1878): 244. This reviewer found the lectures "disappointing," not so much because of Legge but because "imperial Confucianism itself is a disappointing thing . . . a weak, puerile, commonplace philosophy."

48. There were several translations of the Edict going back to Milne. See Victor Mair, "Language and Ideology in the Written Popularizations of the Sacred Edict," in *Popular Culture in Late Imperial China,* ed. David Johnson, Andrew J. Nathan, and Evelyn S. Rawski (Berkeley: University of California Press, 1985), 325–59. Of particular interest to missionaries was maxim number seven: "Discountenance and put away strange principles in order to exalt the correct doctrine." Here "strange principles" refers to Buddhism, Daoism, *and* Christianity (i.e., Roman Catholicism). The official explanation of the maxim is that it referred to those "corrupt and depraved principles" that "disrupt social relations"—a situation that Christianity could at that time in China be legitimately accused of.

49. See "The Chinese Ambassador at Oxford," *North-China Herald,* January 31, 1878, pp. 105, 116. Besides attending Legge's lecture, Guo met with Max Müller and was hosted at a luncheon at New College by J.E. Sewel, the vice-chancellor. After touring the colleges, the Clarendon Press, and the Bodleian Library, Guo went to a reception in the evening at Dr. Legge's house, "where many men of note were presented to His Excellency" (p. 116). Reflecting on the impact of Oxford on Guo, the reporter in the *Herald* remarks (p. 105):

> The actual sight of Oxford will probably make a far more lasting impression on the Chinese mind than all the deputations to whose oratory his Excellency Kwoh [Guo] has been compelled to listen with becoming gravity. . . . One cannot get down deep into the recesses of the Chinese mind. The inner chamber, which his thoughts inhabit, are *[sic]* mysteries to us; and as it is the fashion to interpret China

and the Chinese by the rule of contrary, we must suppose that Kwoh was perpetually making contrasts between the East and the West, largely to the disadvantage and disparagement of the latter. . . . The sight of an important city of learning like Oxford, with its colleges, libraries, chapels, and museums, must disabuse the Chinaman of this notion, and may perhaps induce him to place us on a higher platform of estimation than he had previously been in the habit of doing. At all events, the day of the Oxford visit must be regarded as a noteworthy day in Kwoh's sojourn in England, and the famous University may be sure that the sights she had to show will not be quickly forgotten by the grave and observant visitors from China.

50. It is probably a safe guess that Swasey was a foreign resident of one of the port cities, most probably Shanghai, and came from a secular or merchant background. *Some Observations upon the Civilization of the Western Barbarians* was published "for the proprietor" in London.

51. Ibid., 1.

52. Ibid., 6.

53. Ibid., 9.

54. Ibid., 39. It is interesting that Swasey's sarcasm fit into the mold of the "radical dissenter" and agnostic criticisms of Victorian life and belief.

55. See "Eastern and Western Superstitions," *North-China Herald,* June 1, 1878, p. 560.

56. On Chinese hostility toward foreigners and missionaries, see especially Paul Cohen, *China and Christianity: The Missionary Movement and the Growth of Chinese Antiforeignism, 1860–1870* (Cambridge, Mass.: Harvard University Press, 1963).

57. For documentation of the revived term debate, see especially the many different articles published in the pages of the *Chinese Recorder* during the 1870s and 1880s.

58. One of the most prominent and effective British critics at the time was Alexander Michie. See, for example, his *Missionaries in China,* 2d ed. (Shanghai, China: Kelly and Walsh, 1893). A good secondary discussion of these matters is found in Paul Cohen, "Christian Missions and Their Impact to 1900," *The Cambridge History of China* (Cambridge: Cambridge University Press, 1992), 1:553. See also Suzanne Wilson Barnett, "Protestant Expansion and Chinese Views of the West," *Modern Asian Studies* 6 (1972): 129–49. As Barnett says (p. 146): "Eventually Christianity became a focus for Chinese rejection of all Western influence. Far from winning Chinese approval of Christian culture, Protestant writings tended to support opposition to it." Moreover, it was the British who epitomized "foreign devils" for the Chinese. This was because they tended to "assume leadership in the foreign merchant community."

59. On Johnson and the generally poor reception of his work on Oriental religions, see Carl T. Jackson, *The Oriental Religions and American Thought: Nineteenth-Century Explorations* (Westport, Conn.: Greenwood Press, 1981) 132–33. As Jackson says, it was Johnson's misfortune to not find the right audience; he was "too scholarly for the general reader" and "not sufficiently so for professionals." Müller, for example, said that "a man who breaks stones on the road" of knowledge has not "always a very kindly feeling toward those who drive by in a carriage."

60. Samuel Johnson, *Oriental Religions and their Relation to Universal Religion,* vol. 2, *China* (Boston, Mass.: Houghton Mifflin, 1877), 837–55.

61. Ibid., 837.

62. Ibid., 849–50.

63. Ibid., 851–52.

64. Sensitive to American contributions, Johnson (ibid., 853) also names Samuel Wells Williams, Justus Doolittle, John Nevius, and Elijah Bridgman.

65. Ibid., 852–53.

66. Ibid., 855.

67. Quoting here from E.J. Eitel's review of Johnson's *Oriental Religions* (1877), *The China Review* 6 (1877): 125–28. While criticizing Johnson for seemingly knowing more about Confucianism than about Christianity, Eitel says that Johnson impressed him as "an authority on Chinese subjects." Coming from a sophisticated scholar like Eitel who was so impatient with "amateur" sinologists, this was truly a significant commendation of Johnson's China volume.

68. JL, review of Johnson's *Oriental Religions* volume on China, *Academy*, 1878, pp. 306–8.

69. See Johnson's discussion of these matters in *Oriental Religions*, 2:723–26. The fact of the matter is that Johnson clearly sees Legge's work as evidence for the universal religiosity of Chinese tradition. In contrast with those who deny that the Chinese have any religion at all, Johnson says (pp. 667–68):

> We are asked to believe that a quarter of the human race have achieved a vast and permanent civilization, while devoid of capacity for that which is asserted in the same breath to be the source of all personal and social good. More astounding than the statement itself, is the fact that its suicidal consequences should have escaped the notice of its authors. Where is the indispensableness of religion, if such effects are producible without it as the Chinese Empire exhibits? Benjamin Constant asserts broadly that religion in China is but a matter of usage, maintained by authority, all sentiment and conviction extinct; that the cultus of ancestors has nothing in common with the immortality of the soul; that rites addressed to Heaven are rendered to the Emperor by a people who have lost the faculty of believing and even of desiring. The reader of this volume is already aware that, while the evils of mechanical culture in China are too obvious for discussion, negations like the above can serve no other purpose than to prove the ignorance of the writers and their times. A more definite study of the inner life of this people will be necessary to show how exaggerated the picture is, not only in general outlines, but in every detail. But the inquiry has a larger scope; the phenomena will indicate the breadth of a demand in human nature that can assume forms so widely differing as the traditions of the Aryan, Semitic, and Chinese races.

Moving on to offer some "palpable" proof for Chinese "religion," Johnson clearly alludes to Legge's work (p. 723):

> Notwithstanding the long list of authorities for the "atheism" of the Chinese, from the Jesuit Father Longobardi to the recent "Edinburgh Reviewer," who describes them as "having a language without an alphabet and a religion without a God,"— a list including such names as Leibnitz, Bayle, Constant, Pauthier, Quinet, Abel Rémusat, and Barthélemy-Saint-Hilaire,—nothing can be now more palpable than that the Shang-te, or Te (Supreme Ruler), of the ancient Classics is represented as an intelligent Providence, hearing the prayers and knowing the hearts of men.

Although he does not say so in his review, Legge must also have been unhappy with Johnson's dismissal of the "fulfillment" or "precursor" theory popular with some liberal missionaries and many fledgling practitioners (among them Legge himself) of the new comparative science of religions. Johnson was particularly reacting against the American James Freeman Clarke's views as expressed in the very popular *Ten Great Religions: An Essay in Comparative Theology* (Boston, Mass.: J. R. Osgood, 1871). As Jackson (*Oriental Religions and American Thought,* 131–32) says: "Johnson believed that 'earlier beliefs are disparaged when they are made to point to it [i.e., Christianity] as their final cause. They stand, as *it* has stood, in their own right; justified, as it has been by meeting, each in its own day and on its own soil, the demands of human nature. . . . It is time the older religions were studied in light of their own intrinsic values.' "

70. JL, review of Johnson's *Oriental Religions,* p. 308.

71. This line of development was anticipated by Legge's reflections on Maurice in the late 1840s and his understanding of the imperial cultus in 1852; see JL, *The Notions of the Chinese Concerning God and Spirits: with an Examination of the Defense of an Essay on the Proper Rendering of the Words Elohim and Theos, into the Chinese Language by William Boone, D. D.* (Hong Kong: Hong Kong Register Office, 1852; reprint, Taipei: Ch'eng Wen, 1971).

72. "Is the Missionary Spirit Decaying?" *Congregationalist* 2 (1882): 443–53.

73. Ibid.

74. Ibid., 449.

75. See Leslie R. Marchant, "Ernst Faber's Scholarly Mission to Convert the Confucian Literati in the Late Ch'ing Period," Occasional Paper no. 8 (Centre for East Asian Studies, University of Western Australia, 1984). Seeing in Faber the emergence of a new type of "political reforming missionary" concerned to "redeem the world by saving nations rather than by saving individual souls" (p. 5), Marchant says (p. 9):

> The big turning point for the national reform evangelists came in 1876 and 1877 with the news of the Great Famine in China. This was viewed by missionaries as a heaven-sent sign that the Chinese people were, in fact, ruled by Pharaohs who lacked the knowledge and ability to produce sufficiently from the God-given bounteous resources for the people, and who consequently offered only years of "lean" marked by pestilence and plague.

I need to note that Legge translated a Chinese pamphlet on the great famine that was generally supportive of the collection of relief funds.

76. "The Proposed 'General Conference' of All the Missionaries in China," *The Chinese Recorder* 5 (November–December 1874): 355–59. Because Confucius was regarded as the supreme enemy of China's conversion, it was natural for missionaries to vent their frustrations, disappointments, and anger on the most immediate embodiment of Confucius's influence, the gentry-scholar class. "Under the outward show of politeness and refinement imparted to the educated Chinese chiefly by Confucianism," one missionary (John Chalmers) wrote, "there is almost nothing but cunning, ignorance, rudeness, vulgarity, arrogant assumption and inveterate hatred of everything foreign." Few missionaries in nineteenth-century China would have found this characterization excessive; Cohen, "Christian Missions and Their Impact," 1:565.

77. A. Williamson, letter of January 20, 1875 (concerning the article on the "General Conference,") *The Chinese Recorder* 6 (January–February 1875): 66–71.

78. For the operations of the Arrangements Committee, see the printed announcement brochure entitled "To the Protestant Missionaries in China," October 25, 1876. This document, along with other related materials, is found in the University of Birmingham Library, Church Missionary Society archive packet "Papers re 1877 Shanghai Missionary Conference," C CH/011.

79. Ibid.

80. See, for example, "The Shanghai Missionary Conference," *The Chinese Recorder* 8 (May–June 1877): 239–50; the *Recorder* was at the time edited by Legge's nemesis, the American Presbyterian A.P. Happer. Referring to Legge's essay on Confucianism, the publication reports, inaccurately, that "after full consultation," the paper was "withdrawn by common consent." The reason for this was that it brought "into discussion the vexed question of 'terms' contrary to the general understanding."

81. Of the several descriptions of the presentation and discussion of Legge's paper on the second day, see "The Missionary Conference," *Shanghai Courier,* several articles during the course of May 1877; and "Shanghai Missionary Conference," *China Review.* The *Courier* reported that "Dr. Legge seemed to be of the opinion that Confucianism is, or should be, just as suitable a preparation for Christianity, in one way, as Judaism was, in another."

82. *Records of the General Conference of the Protestant Missionaries of China, Shanghai, May 10–24* (Shanghai: Presbyterian Mission Press, 1878), 15.

83. Ibid., 20.

84. "Shanghai Missionary Conference," *The China Review,* 398.

85. Ibid., 400.

86. On the resolutions, see the *Records of the General Conference.*

87. See the printed pamphlet entitled *Resolution and Appeal Unanimously Adopted by the Conference of Protestant Missionaries at Shanghai May 16, 1877* (Shanghai: Presbyterian Mission Press, 1877); Birmingham University Library, Church Missionary Society archive, C CH/011.

88. Not much was done about producing the Union Bible till 1890. It was not until 1919 that there was a commonly agreed upon text (which used *Shangdi* for "true God" and *shen* for other gods).

89. See Cohen, "Christian Missions and Their Impact," or other standard missionary histories. Although mostly unrecognized in histories of the China mission during the nineteenth century, the early-twentieth-century liberal transformation of mainstream Protestant missionary tradition is directly indebted to the contested issue of Legge, Leggism, Confucianism, and comparativism in the late nineteenth century.

90. *Records of the General Conference.* One of the very few later historians who was aware of the dark side to the conference was Donald Treadgold, *The West in Russia and China: Secular and Religious Thought in Modern Times,* vol. 2 (Cambridge: Cambridge University Press, 1973).

91. Of course, there are most likely different reasons for this oversight. Helen Edith obviously made a conscious decision to go along with the silencing of the whole affair. In Ride's case, it more likely that, because of the manipulated record, he was simply unaware of the event and its significance.

92. See JL, *Confucianism in Relation to Christianity. A Paper Read Before the Mission-ary Conference in Shanghai, on May 11th, 1877* (Shanghai: Kelly & Walsh, 1877; and London: Trübner, 1877); CWM/China/Personal/Legge/Box 7. The foreword to this pamphlet says:

> In view of the author's reputation as the translator of the Chinese Classics, his zeal and success as a missionary for more than thirty years, the sympathy he still main-tains with the work of missions, and the intrinsic value of the essay itself, many of his friends, members of the Conference and others, have deemed it a duty to pub-lish it. They do this in the belief, that, as the result of nearly forty years' study of the Confucian books, it will be found most helpful to missionaries, and to students of the Confucian teachings generally.

93. E.J. Eitel, "Short Notice on the *Records of the General Conference of the Protestant Missionaries of China,* Shanghai 1878," *The China Review* 6 (1878): 337–38.

94. See E.R. Barrett, "Protestant Missions in China" [a review of the *Records of the General Conference of the Protestant Missionaries of China,* Shanghai, 1878], *Congre-gationalist* 7 (1878): 417–27. In a good example of the selective memory of the conference, Barrett makes no mention at all of the Legge affair, even though he was a resident of Shanghai and presumably knew what really transpired. In general the article is a defense of the missionary movement, quoting the *Records* to the ef-fect that the overall conference was "a complete success" and filled with a feeling of "perfect concord." Reinforcing the rosy picture promulgated by the conference *Records,* Barrett (p. 417) says that the meetings "were characterized throughout by the utmost harmony and by a spirit of intense and fervent devotion." It is true that there was much fervent intensity at the conference, but these emotions were often more a result of suppressed rancor than of harmonious devotion. See also the re-view of the *Records* in *The Chinese Recorder* 9 (March–April 1878): 156–57. This re-view, too, makes no mention of the Legge affair and emphasizes what it calls the "encouraging" statistics of missionary action in China (i.e., approximately thirteen thousand communicants, which "probably" amounts to some forty thousand souls saved).

95. For an excellent discussion of the Robertson Smith affair (running roughly from 1875 through 1881), see T.O. Beidelman, *W. Robertson Smith and the Sociologi-cal Study of Religion* (Chicago and London: University of Chicago Press, 1974), 13–22. It should be noted that Smith and Legge's views were both broadly comparativist, but with many differences. Perhaps the most important was that Smith was more of an antisupernaturalist practitioner of Germanic higher criticism than was Legge. It was this pivotal event in Smith's life that led eventually to his assumption of a professor-ship of Arabic at Cambridge University and to his pioneering contributions to the comparative sociology of religion (*Lectures on the Religions of the Semites,* Edinburgh: A. and C. Black, 1889).

96. For a discussion of the history of the fulfillment theory as it relates to Protes-tant missionary tradition in India, see E.J. Sharpe, *Not to Destroy but to Fulfill: The Con-tribution of N.J. Farquhar to Protestant Missionary Thought in India* (Uppsala, Sweden: Gleerup, 1965). Sharpe notes, for example, that the fulfillment theory especially develops among British, and to some degree American, missionaries. The new atti-

tude of sympathy toward Hinduism, says Sharpe, became almost the norm among missionaries in India in the 1920s—especially after the publication of J. N. Farquhar's *Crown of Hinduism* (London, New York: Oxford University Press) in 1915. Sharpe describes (p. 309) the basic apologetic view of the conservative Evangelical missionaries.

> The non-Christian religions (in this case Hinduism) were interpreted as being of the Evil One, hopeless corruptions of primeval revelation, to be attacked, destroyed and replaced by Biblical Christianity. This approach, which was traditional in Indian missions, and practically universal up to the turn of the century, has never been wholly abandoned, and in the years before 1914 was very far indeed from having been superseded by the more sympathetic approach of the "fulfillment" school.

It is clear that there are important differences in the introduction, period of debate, and nature of "sympathetic," or comparativist, approaches among China missionaries. Also, as Sharpe discusses (pp. 338–39), there are sometimes important variations in different versions of the so-called sympathetic, supplementary, conciliatory, and fulfillment theories. For Farquhar "fulfillment" meant:

> First, Hinduism is "fulfilled" by being replaced by Christianity: "fulfillment" therefore means "replacement." Secondly, the "truths" in Hinduism are "fulfilled" by reappearing in a "higher" form in Christianity. And thirdly, Christ "fulfills" the "questions" of Hinduism by providing an answer to its questions, a resolution of its problems, a goal for its religious strivings; in this third sense there need be no recourse to postulated "truths," since a genuine quest can reach an illegitimate goal and an adequate question receive a wholly wrong answer.

97. This is where Legge's Confucian tradition is becoming a full-fledged "ism" or religious ideology possessing a set of authentically religious doctrines or beliefs. Wilfred Cantwell Smith *(The Meaning and End of Religion* [New York: Macmillan, 1963], 254 n. 37), commenting on Legge's *Confucianism in Relation to Christianity,* says that "[t]he full title of this particular book is instructive, illustrating as it does the obvious and yet important point that the concepts being fashioned to present the Chinese religious situation to the West were (naturally) fashioned 'in relation to' the concepts already in use for the Western situation."

Legge was already in 1850 and 1852 coming to some appreciation of terminological parallels between Christianity and Chinese tradition. It is noteworthy that, on the title page of the printed version of *Confucianism in Relation to Christianity,* the "Rev. James Legge, D.D., LL.D.," is identified, first, in terms of his position as "Professor of the Chinese Language and Literature in Oxford University, England." Beneath this imposing credential is appended the phrase "Formerly Missionary of the London Missionary Society, Hongkong, China."

98. Sharpe, *Not to Destroy but to Fulfill,* 54–55, notes that in 1876 John Robson, a Free Church of Scotland missionary, published a pamphlet on *The Science of Religion and Christian Missions* in which "he accepted, virtually without reservation, the position of Max Müller." Sharpe, who is focusing on J. N. Farquhar and the mission to India, says that the missionaries' conflict with comparative religions was "delayed for years" and that "missionary opinion was not much influenced by the science of reli-

gion." In Sharpe's estimation of the Indian missionary situation, it was "only after the turn of the century" that missionaries started to draw upon a comparative religions perspective (Farquhar being one of the prime examples). Sharpe sees the change toward a new missionary apologetic starting in the 1890s and coming to fruition with Protestant efforts in higher education and Alexander Duff's work in India. Sharpe says (p. 23) that Farquhar in the years 1903–1913 adopted the "fulfillment theory" as an explanation of the relationship between Hinduism and Christianity; and he was drawing upon the earlier work of Müller and Monier-Williams (which had entered into the missionary debate in India through the efforts of T. E. Slater and F. W. Kellett). It would appear that, because of the work of Legge, and the events in 1877 in Shanghai, the whole mission and comparative religions debate in China was ahead of similar developments in India.

99. Legge says that "Mr. W" (most probably his old London Missionary Society colleague in North China, Alexander Williamson), on behalf of the Arrangements Committee officially invited him back on December 14, 1875. Legge completed the writing of the paper at Oxford on March 20, 1877. JL, *Confucianism in Relation to Christianity*, 1.

100. Ibid., 2.

101. See McClatchie's interesting letter to the Church Missionary Society secretary, dated July 8, 1876; University of Birmingham Library, Church Missionary Society archive, C CH/062/1-203. Regarding Legge, McClatchie says:

> The Yih King is the most difficult of the Chinese Classics and cost me years of hard study to master it. Dr. Legge's last communication to the London Mission here, states that he has not yet formed the key to it. The "key" as is evident from the book itself is comparative mythology, which subject unfortunately has no attractions for Dr. Legge. Dr. Legge has however laid all missionaries under a deep debt of gratitude to him for the translations he has made of the other classical books.

102. I may note here that the Council for World Missions archive copy of *Confucianism in Relation to Christianity* includes Legge's own penned corrections and emendations.

103. For an interesting nineteenth-century British discussion of the meaning of "lower" and "higher" criticism of Oriental texts, see A. H. Sayce, *The "Higher Criticism" and the Verdict of the Monuments*, 3d ed. (London: Society for Promoting Christian Knowledge, 1894), especially the introduction, 1–30. One of the Oxonian Eastern Sages (along with Müller and Legge), Sayce is appreciative of higher criticism, but is dismayed by its excesses and its failure to incorporate archaeological data. "By the 'lower criticism' is meant," says Sayce, "what we have been accustomed to call 'textual criticism,' a method of criticism which is wholly philological and palaeographical, busied with minute researches into the character and trustworthiness of the text, and the exact significance of its language" (pp. 3–4). Sayce then defines higher criticism: "By the 'higher criticism' is meant a critical inquiry into the nature, origin, and date of the documents with which we are dealing, as well as into the historical value and credibility of the statements which they contain."

104. Lauren Pfister ("Some New Dimensions," 48–49) sees a possible influence of the Epistle to the Hebrews on Legge's "confirming the good and supplementing the deficient" theory.

105. This expression was actually used in an article criticizing the supporters of *Shangdi*. See "The Term 'Shangti,'" *North-China Herald and South-China and Coastal Gazette*, December 14, 1878, p. 564. See also the discussion of "Shangti-ism" in the *North-China Herald*, August 12, 1879.

106. JL, *Confucianism in Relation to Christianity*, 4.

107. JL, *Chinese Classics* (1895), 3:320–44 (the Great Plan).

108. This involves a narrative paradigm that detects religious purity in authoritative writings describing an ancient time of patriarchal rectitude, an inevitable period of decline and corruption involving a proliferation of deities, and the need for a reformation. There is even a hint that China might be "purer" than Judaism or Roman Catholicism because the Chinese relied upon scholars, not priests.

109. See JL, *Chinese Classics* (1861), 2:65–74. In 1861 Legge says that Mengzi and Butler were "nearly . . . identical" yet Mengzi was defective for not dealing with the "whole duty" of man, especially his duty to God (p. 72).

110. A good example of prevailing anti-Semitism among missionaries in China is seen in a review of "a book by a Jew for Jews" in the *The Chinese Recorder* 13 (January–February 1882): 67–71. The book in question is *Jewish Life in the East* by Sydney M. Samuel (London: C. K. Paul, 1881). The pseudonymous reviewer ("Hilderic Friend") finds that the "book teems with proofs of the idleness, avarice, filth, and ignorance of Jews . . . a more thoroughly pauperized people scarcely ever existed. . . . We see the prejudice and bigotry of the Jew . . . no wonder some say 'if you will perish, you must.'"

Most telling, however, are the observations on the subject of Jewish monotheism and their "constant" adoption of idols. "The subject is full of interest, and especially so to those who have been following the recent discussions respecting the character of the ancient religion of China. . . . in many points the two cases are exactly analogous, in others widely different. . . . Jews also had many superstitious customs . . . [and are] not a whit better than Chinese."

111. JL, *Confucianism in Relation to Christianity*, 9.

112. See JL, *Chinese Classics* (1861), vol. 1, where Legge originally discusses the problem of the silver rule. In 1893 he changed his view on this.

113. JL, *Confucianism in Relation to Christianity*, 10. The important point that the Chinese classics possessed a quality that went beyond anything found in the Greek and Roman classics is ratified by a Legge sympathizer, R. H. Maclay, writing shortly after the conference. In "The Classical Literature of the Chinese," *The Chinese Recorder* 9 (January–February 1878): 49–62, Maclay agrees with Legge that in the Confucian view of human nature, "there is nothing contrary to the teachings of our Christian Scriptures. It does not cover what we know to be the whole duty of man, yet it is defective rather than erroneous." Moreover, the "general tendency" of the Chinese classics is "good" when compared with the "precepts of Greek and Roman sages." Thus the "works of Greek and Roman genius appear merely as monuments of literature, while these writings of China's sages are invested with an interest

which no book but the Bible can claim." Indeed, while the "classics of the Hindus, Greeks, and Romans teem with glowing narrations of amours and obscenities," the chaste "purity" of the Confucian classics "is most remarkable."

114. JL, *Confucianism in Relation to Christianity*, 10. For Legge, Confucius's problem as a historian refers especially to the "want of historical truth in the *Chunqiu* [Spring and autumn annals]."

115. Regarding this call for a "revolutionary" approach, see Cohen, "Christian Missions and Their Impact" (p. 544):

> A much smaller contingent of missionaries, mostly Protestant, were tolerant and even appreciative of certain facets of Chinese culture and defined their mission more in terms of the "fulfillment" of this culture than its destruction. Yet, oddly enough, the missionaries who went farthest in this direction were precisely those who were most insistent on the need for a comprehensive overhauling of Chinese ways. Thus, although some missionaries concentrated on attacking the old order in China while others placed more emphasis on the erection of a new order, all missionaries, by the very nature of their calling, posed a revolutionary challenge to the traditional culture. It is for this reason, more than any other, that so many Chinese felt so threatened.

Cohen feels that the threshold for change came about only in the 1890s with the rise of the "secular missionaries." My investigation of the record shows that these changes were already in evidence in the 1870s and 1880s (Legge being a symbol of this transition).

116. Interestingly, this phrase is the motto of the secular *North-China Herald* newspaper.

117. Faber is another good example of this approach. Quoted by the *North-China Herald* (May 20, 1879), he said, "Confucianism ought to become a most valuable ally to Christianity" or a kind of "detached fort of Christianity." The connection of all of this with Max Müller and the new comparative science of religions is made by the *Herald* (p. 485):

> Such men [i.e., Faber and Legge] are in the old and best sense pontiffs or bridge-builders, that is to say men occupied in removing the difficulties which lie between man and the appreciative study of that underlying mass of truth which exists in all religions. To quote the words of Max Müller, "No doubt the solid rock, the human heart, must be the same everywhere; some of the pillars even and the ancient vaults may be the same everywhere, wherever there is religion, faith, or worship."

118. Among the few modern commentators to appreciate the significance of these events, and Legge's special role in them, are Donald Treadgold, *The West in Russia and China;* James Miller McCutcheon, "The American and British Missionary Concept of Chinese Civilization in the Nineteenth Century" (Ph.D. diss., University of Wisconsin, 1959); and Lewis Strong Casey Smythe, "Changes in the Christian Message for China by Protestant Missionaries" (Ph.D. diss., University of Chicago, 1928). Though they were different in several important ways, Treadgold links Legge and Timothy Richard together as agents of progressive change in the missionary movement in the last quarter of the nineteenth century. He says (p. 68) that

> Timothy Richard was nowhere near the scholar Legge was but had the gift of influencing men as Legge did not. What happened to Richard was that, failing to gain the support he required for an apostolate to the learned elite, he turned

increasingly to the cause of secular reform for which the strength and prosperity of the Western powers were all the evidence needed to make converts. He did not become a theological "liberal" or "modernist" as the generation of missionaries after 1900 became; he retained his Protestant theology and tried to adapt the methods of its propagation to the Chinese culture from which his intended converts came. In retrospect it may be suggested that the task he, like Legge, undertook was too great. The evangelicals' suspicion of learning went too deep, their hostility to "heathen" culture was too strong, their sectarian pride and sense of self-sufficiency were too much a part of their identity to be diminished or eradicated. What Legge and Richard and their few supporters were asking of the overwhelming majority of evangelicals was that they cease to be what they were.

Smythe specifically identifies the conference in Shanghai in 1877 as the beginning of the debate over missionary attitudes toward Chinese religion and culture. He says that the "sympathetic" attitude went back to the time of that other Huntly missionary, William Milne, and was revived in 1877 by Legge's paper. The conciliatory group of missionaries exemplified by Legge included such important figures as Faber, Ross, Gilbert Reid, and W.A.P. Martin. This supplementary, completion, or fulfillment theory received validation in 1910 at the World Conference of Missionaries in Edinburgh. Smythe also identifies the late 1870s as the time when one sees the roots of the social gospel approach to missionary policy, which in the work of Richard, Turner, and Hill tended to stress educational and medical work. Social action was stressed by others such as Allen, Yates, Williamson, and Griffith John. It is important to see here that individual missionaries cannot always be identified as purely conservative or liberal-progressive in their attitudes and policies. Thus someone like Yates tended to agree with the attack on Legge on doctrinal grounds but was generally progressive when it came to social issues. At the 1877 conference, M.T. Yates, in direct contrast with Legge on Confucianism, condemned ancestor worship on the grounds that it was truly "idolatrous." By 1880, W.A.P. Martin was of the opinion that ancestor worship could be pruned of any idolatrous excess and Legge had suggested that some ancestral practices were really acts of worship.

McCutcheon also recognizes Legge's special role in the missionary movement because of his "sympathetic" approach to Chinese religion, especially Confucianism. He does, however, mistakenly identify Legge as a Presbyterian (as do others such as Eugene Chen Eoyang). He also fails to see how the "comparative religion" approach was already connected with Legge's paper in 1877, saying incorrectly that it was only in the "last decade of the century" that the new discipline of comparative religion started "to effect [sic] the thinking of some missionaries" (he uses the English Methodist G.T. Candlin as a primary example of these trends). Eventually, as McCutcheon points out, the "conciliatory" approach to Chinese culture "came to be the dominant approach of missionaries in the 20th century." He does appreciate that Legge, through his identification with Müller, can be linked with the comparative religions movement. It is McCutcheon's concluding judgment that, overall, the missionary response to the field of comparative religion was "small." This is not really an accurate assessment of the situation regarding comparative religions and the missionary movement, as I hope to show throughout the rest of this study.

119. Beyond materials cited earlier in this chapter, discussions of the Shanghai conference and related Legge affair are found in the following published sources: *The Chinese Recorder* 8 (1877): 184–91, 242–48, 411–26 (Happer), 351–59 (Nelson), 9 (1878): 74–75, 11 (1880): 161–86 (Happer), 12 (1881): 35–53; *The China Review* 5 (1877): 398–400, 6 (1877): 129–30, 202–3; *Revue critique* 42 (October 1877): 225–27. This list could be considerably expanded to include items dealing with the revival of the whole term question, an issue that was at this time directly related to the Legge affair. The secret history of the affair is found in the collection of manuscript letters written to Robert Nelson concerning his review of Legge's paper. These are held in the College of William and Mary, Earl Gregg Swem Library, Robert Nelson papers, 1845–1885; hereafter cited as Nelson papers.

120. Nelson several times says that missionaries should not be persuaded by Legge's stature as an Oxford scholar.

121. See Robert Nelson, review of James Legge's "Confucianism in Relation to Christianity," *The Chinese Recorder* 8 (May–June 1877): 351–59. The editor of the *Recorder* at this time was another of Legge's archenemies, the Presbyterian A.P. Happer. Descriptive reports, both titled "The Missionary Conference," are found in the Shanghai *North-China Herald,* May 19, 1877, pp. 494–96, and May 26, 1877, pp. 519–22. Contextual discussion (primarily letters to the editor pro and con) related to Nelson and the Legge affair includes "Dr. Legge and the Conference," *Celestial Empire,* June 30, 1877, pp. 756–59, and "The Conference Controversy," *Celestial Empire,* July 7, 1877, pp. 20–21.

122. See, for example, Happer's pseudonymous articles (both are signed as "Inquirer"): "Is Shangti of the Chinese Classics the Same Being as Jehovah?" *The Chinese Recorder* 8 (September–October 1877): 411–26; and idem, "The Theocratic Nature of the Chinese Government and the Principles of Its Administration as Stated in the Chinese Classics," *The Chinese Recorder* 9 (January–February 1878): 28–49. In the second of these articles, Happer tries to show that both Heaven and Earth, along with imperial ancestors, were the primary objects of worship in the contemporary state religion. In particular, Happer was adamant about Tian or Heaven being only a deification of the "physical heavens" and not a true monotheistic divinity. For a criticism of Happer's "Is Shangti . . . the Same Being as Jehovah," see E.J. Eitel's short review in *The China Review* 6 (1878): 202–3. Eitel says that he accepts the views of Legge, Chalmers, Edkins, and Faber on the classics.

123. See M.T. Yates, "Essay on Ancestral Worship," in *Records of the General Conference of the Protestant Missionaries of China, Shanghai, May 10–24* (Shanghai: Presbyterian Mission Press, 1878), 367–87.

124. See Eitel's discussion of this other distortion in Nelson's essay. Eitel's anonymous comments are found in the Short Notice review of the issue of the *Chinese Recorder* that carried Nelson's article; see *The China Review* 6 (1877): 129–30. Eitel says that Nelson tries to show Legge to be an "arch-heretic."

125. For Calvinist missionaries, the "issue of human nature was central." See McCutcheon, "American and British Missionary Concept," 136–37.

126. See D.Z. Sheffield, "A Discussion of the Confucian Doctrine Concerning Man's Nature at Birth. Do the Teachings of Confucianism on this Subject Conflict with the Teachings of Christianity?" *The Chinese Recorder* 9 (January–February 1878):

11–23. This paper is an extended attack on Legge's views as expressed in his conference paper—opinions that Sheffield says are "quite opposite to those reached by . . . a majority of his missionary brethren." Sheffield makes the valid point that it is "living Confucianism" that must be considered, not the ancient tradition. In this sense, Confucianism is a "system of self-culture starting from the basis of a perfect nature" without any "profound conception of the sinfulness of sin."

127. See D. Z. Sheffield, "The Condition and Hope of the Heathen," pt. 1, *The Chinese Recorder* 18 (March 1887): 89–98; pt. 2 (April 1887): 129–39; pt. 3 (May 1887): 188–98; pt. 4 (June 1887): 228–37. See also the rejoinder by "a German missionary" in *The Chinese Recorder* (August 1887): 305–17.

128. The expression is from the letter by the American Baptist (and later Congregationalist) D. Blodget, September 25, 1877—Nelson papers, folder 12, p. 3.

129. The reference to the English clergy is found in Nelson's appended note to this collection of letters, which was, apparently, put together by Nelson himself (Nelson papers, folder 12, p. 6).

130. Evidence for this assertion is found in a letter (dated September 15, 1876) by Alexander Wylie (one of Legge's staunch supporters during the Shanghai affair) to the Anglican bishop (and later Legge nemesis) J. S. Burdon. Wylie indicates that part of the increasing tension over the term question was related to the simple fact that the *Shangdi* group was "gaining in strength." In general, there was a polarization of factions in the different treaty ports, a division that "basically" concerned "Americans vs. English" and "Anglicans vs. Nonconformists." This letter is preserved in the University of Birmingham Library, Church Missionary Archives, C CH/03, 3d/1-46.

131. See the letters by the American Presbyterian Charles R. Mills, September 9, 1877, and by the American Southern Baptist T. P. Crawford, September 10, 1877 (Nelson papers, folder 12, pp. 1, 3).

Two letters (those by Crawford and S. L. Baldwin, an American Methodist) specifically make the charge of "heresy"; the others make essentially the same accusation but use various circumlocutions ("radically unsound theologically," "loose teachings," etc.).

132. See the letter by the American Presbyterian A. P. Happer, October 8, 1877, and the American Congregationalist D. Z. Sheffield, November 6, 1877 (Nelson papers, folder 12, pp. 3, 6).

133. R. H. Graves, September 28, 1877, and T. P. Crawford, September 10, 1877 (Nelson papers, folder 12, pp. 5, 1).

134. This is but another way of talking about changing states of belief or tendencies toward a reconceptualization of missionary policy and behavior regarding the otherness of China—tendencies that, as the passion of these letters also suggests, were attracting a considerable group of formidable supporters (especially among the hyphenated missionary-scholars such as Faber, Martin, Edkins, Wylie, and Chalmers) within the missionary movement. The best, and most Legge-like, example is perhaps the German Rhenish missionary Ernst Faber. With an impressive show of scholarly erudition, Faber published a series of articles on filial piety that directly challenged the paper ("Essay on Ancestral Worship") that Yates presented at the conference. Thus, Faber concluded that Chinese boys could not be considered any less filial than European Christian boys (he cites one disgraceful example of European impropriety when the Chinese delegation to Berlin had their queues pulled

by German boys). See Ernst Faber, "A Critique of the Chinese Notions and Practice of Filial Piety" (read before the Conference on Canton Missions, April 1878), *The Chinese Recorder* 9 (September–October 1878): 329–43; (November–December 1878): 401–19; (January–February 1879): 1–16; (March–April 1879): 83–96; (May–June 1879): 163–74; (July–August 1879): 243–53. For an excellent discussion of Faber, see Marchant, "Ernst Faber's Scholarly Mission." Marchant makes an important distinction between the Calvinist and the "Reforming" missionary evangelists. Reforming missionaries like the "mystical pietist" Faber believed (as did, to some degree, Legge as well) that (pp. 6, 21)

> mankind did not have to await the advent of the Messiah to achieve perfection on earth. They were convinced that Christian evangelical activists, equipped with correct spiritual beliefs, could lead men to perfectibility and could, by their own human efforts, recreate the lost paradise on earth. . . . Evangelists derived this belief from allusions in the Bible to a coming Kingdom of God or state of future perfectibility on earth. See especially Mark 1:14–15; 1 Corinthians 15:23–25; Revelation 20. Christian preachers and missionaries who did not accept the theological belief about the advent of the Messiah and the prophetic belief about a coming worked in separate and different missionary ways from the evangelists.

135. See the letter by the American Presbyterian Charles R. Mills, September 9, 1877 (Nelson papers, folder 12, p. 2). As far as I know, there is no extant copy of a Chinese version of Legge's essay.

136. See the letter by the American Episcopalian E. W. Syle, September 13, 1877 (Nelson papers, folder 12, p. 2). Syle reveals his allegiance to the Shin-ite position and his anti-Leggism in "Shin vs Shangti," *The China Review* 6 (1878): 367–87.

137. J. Edkins, September 24, 1877 (Nelson papers, folder 12, p. 3).

138. JL, October 18, 1877, written from 3 Keble Terrace, Oxford (Nelson papers, folder 12, p. 4).

139. See the "Editor's Corner" in *The Chinese Recorder* 9 (January–February 1878): 70–73, where it is announced that the term question will no longer be discussed in the pages of the journal. The reference to "sarcastic flings" is found in Edward Syle's "Shin vs Shangti." By the 1920s *Shangdi* seemed to have the upper hand among missionaries, but in many post–World War II discussions, particularly among both Chinese Christians and non-Christians, there has been a tendency to use *shen*.

140. See the "Short Notice" review of Chalmers's *The Question of Terms Simplified* (Hong Kong, 1876), *The China Review* 5 (1876): 135–37.

141. Ibid.,136.

142. See A. Wylie's review of Joseph Edkins's *Religion of China* (London: Trübner, 1878), *The Chinese Recorder* 9 (March–April 1878): 152–56. On the whole Edkins's book was less threatening than Legge's work was. One of the interesting aspects of Edkins's book was his discussion of the "compound" nature of Chinese religious belief, that is, the lack of exclusive adherence to any one Chinese religion. According to Edkins, the three Chinese religions were not contradictory but "supplementary" to one another. Each of the three originally came from one ancient national faith and later, after their division, represent the three basic aspects of human nature: the moral (Confucianism), material and physical (Daoism), and metaphysical (Buddhism).

CHAPTER FOUR. DECIPHERER LEGGE: FINDING THE SACRED
IN THE *CHINESE CLASSICS,* 1879–1880

1. See JL, *Chinese Classics* (1895), 4:509–10; he is actually quoting from his metrical version, JL, *The She King; or the Book of Ancient Poetry, Translated into English Verse, With Essays and Notes* (London: Trübner, 1876), 323, ode 1, stanza 8:

King Wan said, "Alas!
Alas! you [sovereign of] Yin-shang,
People have a saying,
'When a tree falls utterly,
While its branches and leaves are yet uninjured,
It must first have been unrooted.'
The beacon of Yin is not far-distant:—
It is the age of the [last] sovereign of Hëa."

2. This description is found in one of Legge's letters, dated November 1, 1877 (Helen Edith Legge typescript in group of materials labeled "From Papa's Letters to Members of the Family" [Council for World Mission (hereafter cited as CWM), China/Personal/Legge/Box 10]).

3. Already in his letters of 1850, in his Chinese renditions of biblical tales, and in the sermon delivered in 1869 in Huntly, Legge had cited passages from the Chinese classics as instances of methodological, moral, and anecdotal insight.

4. As Chadwick (*The Victorian Church* [New York: Oxford University Press, 1970], 2:59) says: "Between 1860 and 1900 . . . the new historical knowledge brought widespread agreement in the main study of the Old Testament, so widespread that it began to penetrate the minds of many educated people. This change was due not only to German criticism and to English scholarship but to the general growth of a historical consciousness and a more comparative attitude to early sources."

5. Müller's lectures were published as a book entitled *On the Origin and Growth of Religion as Illustrated by the Religions of India* (London: Longmans, Green, 1878). For a description of the excitement stirred by these lectures, see Nirad C. Chaudhuri, *Scholar Extraordinary: The Life of Professor the Rt. Hon. Friedrich Max Müller, P.C.* (London: Chatto & Windus, 1974), 357. On the Hibbert lectureship, see Jordan, *Comparative Religion: Its Genesis and Growth* (New York: Charles Scribner's Sons, 1905), 568–69.

6. See "The Hibbert Lectures," *North-China Herald,* June 15, 1878, pp. 613–14.

7. Ibid., 614.

8. See E. Renan's preface to his 1880 Hibbert Lectures published as *Lectures on the Influence of the Institutions, Thought, and Culture of Rome, on Christianity and the Development of the Catholic Church,* trans. Charles Beard (London: Williams and Norgate, 1880), v.

9. James Martineau first invited Müller to give the inaugural lectures for the Hibbert Trust in 1876, but delayed the start of the lectureship to 1878 because of Müller's eighteen-month sabbatical from Oxford. See Martineau to Müller, February 1876 in Georgina A. Müller, *The Life and Letters of the Right Honorable Friedrich Max Müller* (London: Longmans, Green, 1902), 2:4. As to the controversy over who

might legitimately be considered the father of the comparative science of religions, see Jordan, *Comparative Religion*, 521–23.

10. Ibid., 580–604 (chart 4: The Present Position of Comparative Religion in the World's Universities, Colleges, Etc.).

11. In a letter to Renan concerning the latter's agreement to give the third series of Hibbert Lectures, Müller says that, while there was "no chair yet in Comparative Theology in English universities," he believed that the Hibbert Lectures would have the same effect. Commenting on the creation of a new chair in comparative theology at the Collège de France, which will give "new sanction to a branch of study . . . long looked upon with very unreasonable suspicion," Müller says that the first holder of this position should be a "man of mature mind" who is a historian "able to sympathize with every effort of religious thought, however perverse and strange it may seem to the outside world." A comparativist requires, he says, "skill" and "fearlessness" in the face of the temptation to make the comparative science of religions "subservient to the theological theories of the day." Remarking that Professor Tiele, who held the chair of comparative theology at Leiden, is a good example of the kind of man required, Müller suggested Réville as someone "pre-eminently qualified" for the new French chair. Like Tiele, Réville began life as a pastor, but "never sacrificed his freedom of thought." In this same letter, Müller advises Renan against expecting Oxford to confer an honorary degree on him while he visits England for the Hibbert Lectures. Revealing much about the continuing political tension over religious matters at Oxford, Müller's wise counsel is that pushing for an honorary degree for the notorious religious liberal Renan would lead only to "opposition, controversy, strife, and anger; and for what?" See Müller to Renan, December 4, 1879, in Georgina Müller, *Life and Letters*, 2:73–74.

12. On the public interest in, and enthusiastic response to, Müller's first Hibbert Lecture, see Chaudhuri, *Scholar Extraordinary*, 357. One leading newspaper is quoted as saying:

> The place, the lecturer, and the occasion were all alike remarkable. Under the shadow of one of the noblest buildings ever raised by medieval Christianity, an Oxford Professor came forward to deal with the deepest problems of historical religion in the "dry light" of modern science, and in the name of a trust which was intended by its founder to promote "the unfettered exercise of private judgement in matters of religion."

13. Besides Müller, the "first among equals," the list of Hibbert Lecturers included Ernest Renan, T. W. Rhys Davids, Albert Réville, Otto Pfleiderer, John Rhys, Archibald Sayce, and Goblet d'Alviella. The Gifford roster consisted of such famous figures as Müller, Cornelis P. Tiele, John Caird, William James, Edward Tylor, Josiah Royce, Richard Haldane, and Andrew Lang. See Jordan, *Comparative Religion*, 568–71. The Bampton Lectures, established in 1779, were intended to be "sermons" given by a "graduate of Oxford or Cambridge," which, until the 1870s, meant that the lecturer was necessarily an ordained Anglican cleric; ibid., 562–63.

14. "Hibbert Lectures," p. 614.

15. Ibid.

16. See Müller to A. P. Stanley, December 7, 1878 (Bodleian Library, Oxford University [hereafter cited as Bodleian], MS. Eng. d. 2346). In this letter Müller is

discussing his Hibbert Lectures and the controversy they stirred: "Of course, I knew that many people [would] be angry with my lectures. If it were not so, I should not have written them, the more I see of the so-called heathen religions, the more I feel convinced that they contain germs of the highest truth."

17. Chaudhuri, *Scholar Extraordinary,* 358.

18. Ibid. Chaudhuri quotes Müller without identifying the source. See Müller's *Origin and Growth of Religion.*

19. See, for example, Müller to Legge, January 21, 1877, and December 7, 1878, on technical issues concerning Legge's translations of the *Documents* and *Poetry* for the *Sacred Books* (Bodleian, MS. Autogr. e. 11, *fols.* 53–54).

20. See JL to his stepdaughter, Marian Willetts, July 30, 1878 (University of London, School of Oriental and African Studies, Legge Archive, ms. 380476).

21. See JL, "Present State of Chinese Studies; What Is Still Wanted Towards a Complete Analytic Exhibition of the Chinese Language," in *Atti del IV Congresso internazionale degli orientalisti tenuto in Firenze (Florence) nel settembre 1878* (Florence: Coi Tipi dei successori le monnier, 1880), 1:255–67. This talk is only an expansion of certain points developed in his inaugural address at Oxford. Beginning with a brief history of Chinese studies, Legge discusses the accomplishments of the early Jesuits and then moves to the nineteenth century. Here he makes a point of noticing, in addition to important missionary contributions, the work of professional scholars and professors as well as the studies of many "unprofessional gentlemen" from diplomatic and commercial backgrounds.

He moves then to his real concern—that is, the "analytic exhibition of written characters, and what is still required in order to make it complete." Before entering into this discussion, however, he makes three preliminary points: (1) that there is really little difficulty in translating Chinese into a European language; (2) there has been a steady improvement in the manner of translation (it is "more exact and free from paraphrase" than before); and (3) the need to proceed slowly in translation and sinological research ("the mere work of translation is now not difficult; but to give an adequate exhibition of the mind of the author is often a difficult task"). Concerning his last point on the difficulty of translation it is interesting that he particularly mentions "such books as the Yih, Lao-tsze's Tao Teh King, the writings of Chwang-tsze and other authors of the Taoist school, and . . . the philosophical speculations of the Sung dynasty." As he says, "I for one have found the greatest difficulty in getting to see things from the stand point of my originals. Translations are in my drawers, made five and twenty years ago, to which I am not yet sure that I have found the clue."

Going on to a discussion of what was "still wanting" in the analysis of Chinese characters, Legge first makes the debatable point that, unlike language in general and the Aryan roots that are the "fruit of the tongue," the characters were the "work of the fingers" and were, at first, pictorial in nature. Presenting his theory of graphological representation, he states that Chinese written characters "were . . . artificial methods of representing the objects of men's senses and the subjects of men's thoughts. Their names indeed existed before their figures were made; but though their figures received those early names, they were yet independent of them, and can only be satisfactorily discussed by being still considered so."

After analyzing some of the unique features of the Chinese written language (the poverty of vocable sounds, the limited number of original pictorial symbols, the antiquity of the characters, the principles of developing new written symbols), Legge's real concern here was to make the point that the native system of the six classes of characters was still not sufficiently studied by foreign scholars. Legge then tried to show how any new analysis of Chinese characters needed to consider some of the work already done by native scholars. The results of such an analysis is that

> [w]e shall have before us all the elements of the Chinese characters, and under-stand how they grew up, and continue to the present day, not indeed without change of their pictorial and outward form, but without internal change, in the way of diminution or increase, such as happened to the root words of the Aryan and Se-mitic languages, without anything even that can properly be called agglutination; answering abundantly, however, all the purposes of the human mind, in narrating events, describing the scenes of nature, pursuing the current of philosophical spec-ulation, and expounding the processes of art and the researches of science.

Most of all, sinologues need to divert themselves from the misleading study of the so-called two hundred and fourteen radicals used in defining dictionaries and re-turn to the six classes as the "natural study of Chinese elements." He concludes with a consideration of the class of phonetic characters and the mysteries of the Chinese use of phonetic symbols.

22. Ibid., 267.

23. On the history of Chinese philology, see Bernhard Karlgren, *Philology and Ancient China* (Oslo: H. Aschehang, 1926); Paul L.-M. Serruys, "Philologie et lin-guistique dans le études sinologiques," *Monumenta Serica* 8 (1943): 167–219; Ed-ward H. Schafer, *What and How Is Sinology?* (Boulder, Colo.: University of Col-orado, 1982); and David Honey, *Incense at the Altar: Pioneering Sinologists and the Development of Classical Chinese Philology* (New Haven, Conn.: American Oriental Society, 2001).

24. See JL to Müller, September 29, 1878 (CWM/China/Personal/Legge/Box 7). Müller says that he knew Renan in Paris before he became famous, meeting him for the first time when Renan was an assistant librarian at the Bibliothèque Royale and Müller was collating Vedic manuscripts. Müller's description of the "foggy" Renan is found in a letter dated April 18, 1880 (Georgina Müller, *Life and Letters*, 2:91). The description of Renan as someone "clouded" by his language—though this "certainly produces beautiful colour effects"—could equally apply to Müller himself.

25. On Ernest Renan, see Chadwick, *Victorian Church*, 2:62–64. Of the "writer of genius" and his famous *Vie de Jésus* (first published in 1863), Chadwick says that

> [Renan] never got as far as being a sub-deacon [as a Catholic priest] and by the age of twenty-two rejected important Catholic doctrines. He was influenced by the German philosophers and by Strauss. Meanwhile he became one of the leaders of Semitic scholarship. . . . Though he lost his orthodox faith, Catholicism continued to fascinate him. In a famous epigram, he declared that to write the history of a re-ligion, it is necessary to have believed it—otherwise we should not understand; and it is necessary to have ceased to give a total assent to it, for total assent is in-compatible with the historian's detachment. . . . [In the *Vie*] Jesus was a sweet and enchanting person—in the English translation he kept appearing as "charming." Christianity was a pastoral idyll, and the portrait thus painted owed much to

Renan's wish. The Christianity which Jesus meant to teach was a pure worship, without priests or liturgies or external customs or a church.

On the English reaction to Renan, see Daniel L. Pals, *The Victorian "Lives" of Jesus* (San Antonio, Texas: Trinity University Press, 1982), 31–39.

26. *Somerville College Register, 1879–1959* (Oxford: Oxford University Press, 1961).

27. Ibid., 272. Two of Legge's granddaughters, Cecilia and Dominica (both daughters of James Granville Legge), graduated from Somerville College. Dominica Legge went on to become a well-known scholar of Anglo-Norman literature at the University of Edinburgh and a visiting professor at Somerville.

28. Müller's lack of support (if not active opposition) for women's colleges at Oxford is noted by Vera Brittain in *The Women at Oxford: A Fragment of History* (London: Harrap, 1960). Müller always maintained a cordial and cooperative relationship with Pusey, an association that clearly had much to do with their mutual respect for power politics at Oxford. Müller was, in fact, fondly appreciative of Pusey's support for the *Sacred Books* project. This side of their relation is brought out in Müller's letter to the London *Times* (September 25, 1882, p. 6) on the occasion of Pusey's death:

> Almost the last lines I had from him were meant to express his approval of "The Sacred Books of the East." No one would have been surprised if the editor of the "Library of the Fathers of the Christian Church" had objected to this new library of the founders and Fathers of all non-Christian churches being published by the University Press. Far from it. "I was very glad," he wrote, "to see the plan of translations in which your name appears. It must be of good service; but the older one grows, the narrower one's little pyramid becomes, if it is not too absurd to speak of a pyramid at all, except to say that in one's old age one has to add only little stones."

29. In an odd way the reforming zeal of many China missionaries to elevate the status of Chinese women (especially in light of the very real problems of footbinding and female infanticide) may have worked against the recognition of problems of equality and health among their own wives. See Wong Man Kong, "Hidden in History: The London Missionary Society Missionary Wives in Nineteenth-Century China (1807–1877)" (1995); and James Buzard, "Victorian Women and the Implications of Empire," *Victorian Studies* 36 (1993): 443–53.

30. JL, "Professor F. Max Müller" (1879), 15 pp., handwritten version in copybook (Bodleian MS. Autogr. e. 11, *fols.* 53–54, notebook numbered A).

31. Ibid. He notes that, for many of his details, he is indebted to the sketch of Müller found in volume 2 of Gustave Dugat's *Histoire des orientalists de l'Europe du xiie au xixe siècle* (Paris: Maisonneuve, 1870). It is worth commenting on the fact that in this essay Legge makes it clear that he has carefully read most of Müller's major works, among them his essay on false analogies, his review of Confucius, and a talk on missions.

32. Cf. Max Müller, preface, *Chips from a German Workshop* (New York: Charles Scribner's Sons, 1895), 1:xxiii (the text of this preface was initially given as a lecture in 1867).

> Whenever we can trace back a religion to its first beginnings, we find it free from many of the blemishes that offend us in its later phases. The founders of the an-

cient religions of the world, as far as we can judge, were minds of a high stamp, full of noble aspirations, yearning for truth, devoted to the welfare of their neighbors, examples of purity and unselfishness. What they desired to found upon earth was but seldom realized, and their sayings, if preserved in their original form, offer often a strange contrast to the practice of those who profess to be their disciples. As soon as a religion is established, and more particularly when it has become the religion of a powerful state, the foreign and worldly elements encroach more and more on the original foundation, and human interests mar the simplicity and purity of the plan which the founder had conceived in his own heart, and matured in his communings with his God. . . . If missionaries could show to the Brahmans, the Buddhists, the Zoroastrians, nay, even to the Mohammedans, how much their present faith differs from the faith of their forefathers and founders; if they could place in their hands and read with them in a kindly spirit the original documents on which these various religions profess to be founded, and enable them to distinguish between the doctrines of their own sacred books and the additions of later ages; an important advantage would be gained, and the choice between Christ and other Masters would be rendered far more easy to many a truth seeking soul.

33. It is worth remarking that in the introduction to this passage Müller mentions that "Comparative Theology is growing rapidly, particularly in America"—naming such figures as James F. Clarke, O.B. Frothingham, and Samuel Johnson; see Max Müller, *Introduction to the Science of Religion: Four Lectures Delivered at the Royal Institution in February and May, 1870* (London: Longmans, Green, 1873), ix.

34. Neglecting Legge's edition of the *Sacred Books of China,* Tsai Yen-zen makes the surprising claim that Legge's emphasis on the Confucian texts as classics resulted in a "legacy of prejudice" that became the "standard viewpoint towards Confucian holy books in the West." And it was this, says Tsai, that "helped generate and perpetuate the stereotyped impression that Confucianism is merely a humanist tradition. It divests the Confucian tradition of its religious dimension and, specifically, ignores how people living in this tradition respond to the transcendent through these texts." The record, as we are seeing, is much more complicated and ambiguous than Tsai would have it. See Tsai Yen-zen, "Ching and Chuan: Towards Defining the Confucian Scriptures in Han China (206 B.C.E.–220 C.E.)" (Ph.D. diss., Harvard University, 1992).

35. The fiftieth and last volume was a general index to the series that appeared ten years after Müller died. See Max Müller, *Sacred Books of the East,* vol. 50, *A General Index to the Names and Subject-Matter of the Sacred Books of the East,* comp. M. Winternitz (Oxford: Clarendon Press, 1910).

36. The original contingent included German and other continental scholars, along with some British scholars and a few token Indian scholars—such as R.G. Bhandarkar, who never completed his contribution, and Kashinath Trimbak Telang, who contributed volume 8, the *Bhagavadgita.* In the second series of volumes, a single Japanese scholar, J. Takakusu, produced volume 49 on Mahayana Buddhism. It is interesting to note that relatively few French scholars were invited to contribute to the *Sacred Books.* This situation reflects the relative, and temporary, impoverishment of French Orientalism in the last quarter of the nineteenth century (especially in Sanskrit and Aryan studies where, at this time, the best scholars were either German or English). Müller most likely would have invited Julien to con-

tribute the Chinese volumes were it not for his untimely death. As we know, Müller's first letter to Legge cites Julien's praise of Legge as an authoritative commendation of his sinological skills. Müller, Legge, Hermann Oldenberg, and T.W. Rhys Davids each contributed six volumes to the final collection of *Sacred Books;* Julius Eggerling and E.W. West, with five each, came next in terms of the number of volumes produced. All of this suggests that British scholarship, especially in Indological Orientalism, had been professionalized. On Müller's difficulties as an editor (the enormous correspondence, the dilatoriness and pettiness of the translators, the need for a heavy editing of the translations, etc.)—work that continued up to the last months of his life—see Georgina Müller, *Life and Letters,* 2:9-12.

37. On the complicated process and controversy over the revision of the English Bible, see Chadwick, *Victorian Church,* 2:44-75; and especially David Norton, *A History of the Bible as Literature,* vol. 2, *From 1700 to the Present Day* (Cambridge: Cambridge University Press, 1993). Concerning the *Oxford English Dictionary,* see K.S. Elisabeth Murray, *Caught in a Web of Words: James A.H. Murray and the Oxford English Dictionary* (New Haven, Conn., and London: Yale University Press, 1977); Susan Drain, "Oxford English Dictionary," in *Victorian Britain: An Encyclopedia,* ed. Sally Mitchell (New York and London: Garland, 1988), 566; John Willinsky, *Empire of Words: The Reign of the OED* (Princeton: Princeton University Press, 1994); and "Historical Introduction," *The Compact Edition of the Oxford English Dictionary* (Oxford: Oxford University Press, 1971), viii. On the involvement of the Oxford University Press with the Revised Version of the Bible and Murray's dictionary, see Peter Sutcliffe, *The Oxford University Press: An Informal History, 1478-1978* (Oxford: Clarendon Press, 1978), 48-50, 54-56.

38. On the *Encyclopedia Britannica,* see *Adam & Charles Black, 1807-1957: Some Chapters in the History of a Publishing House* (London: Adam & Charles Black, 1957), 7-22, 32-56, 68-69. Concerning the *Dictionary of National Biography,* see Mark Reger, "Dictionary of National Biography," in *Victorian Britain: An Encyclopedia,* ed. Sally Mitchell (New York and London: Garland, 1988), 219.

39. See Müller, statement to the Delegates of the Oxford University Press, handwritten, seven pages, 1878 (Oxford University Press archive).

40. Ibid.

41. In this brave new age, knowledge was no longer something possessed or known by some*one*, but a sifting, gathering, putting together of numerous facts and prodigious quantities of data from all over the world. It was this kind of situation that logistically required an organized bureaucratic and martial effort that privileged rational classification and statistical compilation. The comparative induction of hidden "meanings" from massive deposits of literary and cultural information from all "savage" times and "Oriental" places was the highest form of knowledge.

42. On the history of scriptural translations, see Norton, *History of the Bible as Literature,* vol. 2.

43. On biblical translatability, see Lamin Sanneh, "Global Christianity and the Re-education of the West," *Christian Century* 112 (1995): 715-18; idem, *Translating the Message: The Missionary Impact on Culture* (New York: Orbis, 1991); and Andrew Walls, "The Translation Principle in Christian History," in *Bible Translation and the Spread of the Church,* ed. Philip C. Stine (Leiden: E.J. Brill, 1990), 24-39. For an interesting discussion of the etymology of *jing,* see Isabelle Robinet, *Taoist Meditation:*

The Mao-shan Tradition of Great Purity, trans. Julian F. Pas and Norman J. Girardot (Albany, N.Y.: State University of New York Press, 1993), 19–21.

44. See, for example, R. D. Altick's discussion of "lower" and "higher" criticism in Victorian times in his *Victorian People and Ideas* (New York: Norton, 1973), 219.

45. See especially Thomas Coburn, "Scripture in India," in *Rethinking Scripture: Essays from a Comparative Perspective,* ed. Miriam Levering (Albany, N.Y.: State University of New York Press, 1989), 122.

46. Wilfred Cantwell Smith, "Scripture as Form and Concept," in *Rethinking Scripture: Essays from a Comparative Perspective,* ed. Miriam Levering (Albany, N.Y.: State University of New York Press, 1989), 35.

47. See William Graham, "Scripture" in *The Encyclopedia of Religion,* ed. Mircea Eliade (New York: Macmillan, 1986–1987), 13:133–45. For a fuller discussion of these issues, see Graham's *Beyond the Written Word: Oral Aspects of Scripture in the History of Religion* (Cambridge: Cambridge University Press, 1987). Graham notes that the shared attributes of scripture or sacred books were particularly power, authority, unicity, and divine inspiration.

48. Kendall Folkert notes that "one can read painstakingly the writings of F. Max Müller and his collaborators in the Sacred Books of the East without finding any degree of sustained reflection" on the meaning of "scripture" or the "question of sacredness as it applies to 'books.' . . . The existence of 'sacred books,' in short, seems to have needed no justification." As Folkert goes on to observe, the *Sacred Books* reveal an a priori notion of scripture based on a Protestant model—a model that is used both to define scripture and to privilege, in the Protestant manner of *sola scriptura,* a hermeneutical emphasis on the critical study of scriptural texts (and their embedded doctrines) in the overall study of religion. Folkert says that this relates "to general modes of historiography in Western academic circles," where there is an "unrelenting focus on textual documentation." Moreover, the "Christian, specifically Protestant, fascination with the Bible as a 'sacred book'—a fascination that is actually a dimension of Christian faith itself—provides another of the background sets for the problem of scripture in general." See Kendall Folkert, "Canons of Scripture," in *Rethinking Scripture: Essays from a Comparative Perspective,* ed. Miriam Levering (Albany, N.Y.: State University of New York Press), 171–72, 178.

49. See Miriam Levering's discussion of these issues in her introduction to *Rethinking Scripture: Essays from a Comparative Perspective,* ed. Miriam Levering (Albany, N.Y.: State University of New York), 16. The source of Müller's quote is not completely identified by Levering. Müller's canonical theory of the sacred books is first expressed in 1870 in his Lectures on the Science of Religion, Müller, *Introduction to the Science of Religion* (1873), 101–23.

50. Levering, introduction, *Rethinking Scripture,* 10. Miriam Levering rightly observes that "a mere statement that normativity characterizes sacred texts leaves undislodged many assumptions about the universality of attitudes that are in fact most especially Protestant" (ibid.).

51. Müller himself makes the distinction between classics and sacred books in his original prospectus for the *Sacred Books:*

Neither Greeks, nor Romans, nor Germans, nor Celts, nor Slavs have left us anything that deserves the name of Sacred Books. The Homeric Poems are national

Epics, like the Ramayana, and the Nibelunge, and the Homeric Hymns have never received that general recognition or sanction which alone can impart to the poetical effusions of personal piety the sacred or canonical character which is the distinguishing feature of the Vedic Hymns.

See Max Müller, *The Sacred Books of the East, Translated, with Introductions and Notes, By Various Oriental Scholars, and Edited by F. Max Müller* (hereafter cited as *Sacred Books* prospectus), original four-page printed circular in the Oxford University Press archive, *Sacred Books of the East 1877–1908*, packet 41. This also appears in the preface to the *Sacred Books of the East, Sacred Books,* 1:xl–xlv. There is a good deal of ambiguity surrounding Müller's criteria of sacredness. Another (and mostly unstated) level of distinction hinges on the degree to which a sacred text harbors a mostly pietistic Protestant doctrinal content (i.e., implicit or explicit monotheistic revelation; role of prophets or religious founders; prayerful worship of God; afterlife; moral retribution). Noticeably absent from the criteria for purity and sacredness is any real appreciation of ritual and material symbol and the role of priests—all of which are too Catholic and developmentally corrupt for Müller's Protestant sensibilities.

David Hawkes (*Classical, Modern, and Humane: Essays in Chinese Literature,* ed. John Minford and Wong Siu-kit [Hong Kong: Chinese University Press, 1989], 11–12, 75), an inheritor of Legge's chair at Oxford, makes the interesting, though not entirely defensible, observation (p. 11) that, "in the sense" that the so-called Confucian or Chinese classics are "the ancient texts of secular literature which were used to train countless generations of young men for positions of responsibility," these texts "may legitimately be compared with the Greek and Latin Classics of the West." However, "the analogy breaks down in that 'Classics' in the West refers in a general way to the literature of a period; whilst the Confucian books are only a small fraction of extant contemporary literature, and at that by no means the most valuable one, whether from a literary or a philosophical point of view." Concerning the "sacredness" or "religiousness" of these books, Hawkes remarks (p. 12) that,

> [a]lthough the Confucian books cannot be described as religious texts, they were thought of by Confucianists as in some way embodying the Truth. Even within living memory a few conservative Chinese scholars were still trying to find democracy, science, socialism, and all other "isms" and "ologies" of the West in these archaic writings on the grounds that all Truth had been revealed in them, however darkly, by the Sage. . . . In this sense the Confucian books, though they are secular texts, could more properly be compared with the Holy Scriptures than with the secular Classics of the West.

And elsewhere (p. 75):

> The Confucian Classics are not religious texts, but they resemble our own scriptures in being extremely heterogeneous. . . . It had to be assumed that Truth was concealed in these books, or expounded by them in some allegorical manner. Literature, then, must imitate the Classics in expounding Truth; it must exalt virtue and dispraise vice; in short, it must be didactic. This was the earliest Confucian view and continued, with some variations and modifications, to be the most commonly held view until comparatively recent times.

52. See, for example, the admittedly biased comments by Moncure Conway, *Autobiography, Memories and Experiences* (Boston and New York: Houghton Mifflin, 1904), 2:331.

53. Archibald Sayce, review of the first three volumes of the *Sacred Books, Nature* 21 (1879): 77–78.

54. See Max Müller, "Forgotten Bibles," *Nineteenth Century* 15 (1884): 1004–22; and idem, "On the Proper Use of Holy Scriptures," president's address, annual meeting, November 23, 1893, *Abstracts of the Society of Historical Theology,* Oxford University (1893): 5–26.

55. The Oxford University Press archive has only recently been professionalized. Years of neglect have taken their toll on the existence and condition of material. The records pertinent to Müller and Legge are extensive, but incomplete. There is, for example, a separate file on the *Sacred Books* and for Müller, and in each of these, along with the material in the Letter Books, is preserved valuable but sparse material. The *Sacred Books* file, in particular, is disappointing in this regard. There are, however, several important items relating to Müller's working relation with his contributors (e.g., a printed circular entitled "Regulations agreed upon between the Editor and Contributors to the Sacred Books of the East" and, in the Bodleian archives [MS. Eng. d. 2356], handwritten notes by Müller concerning his publishing agreement with the Oxford University Press [especially the terms of his payment]) and various documents concerning the sales of the series (but only for the years 1887–1908). Also interesting, and sometimes revealing (though terse), are the many copies of individual letters by Müller and Legge to the secretaries of the press found in the extant Letter Books. The actual contracts for the *Sacred Books* were found in 1995: the handwritten agreement with Müller as editor, dated October 19, 1877, and two printed contracts with Legge (one dated June 22, 1877, for the *Book of History* and the *Book of Poetry,* and the other dated July 31, 1884, for the *Book of Rites*). From these contracts, we see that Müller received £2,400 for the first set of twenty-four volumes and each author received £4 for "every printed sheet thereof containing sixteen pages" or about £112 per volume (at an average length of four hundred fifty pages). As we know from the figures for professors' salaries at Oxford, these were considerable sums of money at the time. It is also made clear that (to Legge's chagrin) "if expense of corrections shall exceed on the average of any volume 10 shillings per sheet of sixteen pages the amount of the excess shall be borne by the translator." The first edition of each volume involved a printing of fifteen hundred copies and "the whole of the profits thereof shall belong to the Delegates." Upon a second and subsequent printing, "four-tenths" of the net profits would be paid "to the translator by whom the volume was prepared, two-tenths to the Editor and four-tenths shall belong to the Delegates."

56. Müller refers to the project as his "opus magnum" in a letter to Georg von Bunsen, January 1, 1876 (Georgina Müller, *Life and Letters,* 2:1). From this letter it is also clear that, when he was threatening to leave Oxford (see pp. 163–65), Müller was using the "Bibliotheca Sacra" as an enticement in his negotiations with German universities for a position. Peter Sutcliffe *(Oxford University Press)* says only (p. 46) that

Max Müller's grand design for the *Sacred Books of the East* in twenty-four volumes was approved by the Delegates in 1875, after he had enlisted the help of Lord Salisbury, at one time Secretary of State for India [and then the chancellor of the University of Oxford], Sir Henry Maine [a member of the powerful council of the governor general of India], and perhaps most importantly Dean Liddell [of Christ Church College], to whom he had confided his intention of going to Vienna and publishing the books there if Oxford were not interested. The expenses of production were to be shared equally between the Press and the Government of India.

The Oxford University Press archives (i.e., contained in the separate *Sacred Books of the East* files) have no documents specifically relating to the approval and Delegates' vote on the *Sacred Books*. Based on my discussion of Oxford machinations involving Müller's threatened departure and Legge's position in the years 1875–1876, it seem probable that official press approval for the *Sacred Books* came toward the end of 1875. Final ratification, under Liddell's guidance, seems to have come only at the start of 1876 when Müller, under the new terms of his position, was persuaded to stay on at Oxford to work on the *Sacred Books*. This chronology is corroborated by a letter to the editor of the London *Times,* dated February 14, 1876, in which it was noted that "Professor Max Müller has undertaken to edit for the University Press all the sacred books of the world, except the Bible and the Chinese scriptures, which will be allotted to the eminent Sinologue, Dr. Legge." This correspondent (identified only as Bibliophilus), it is worth noting, was especially concerned that "the cost of printing the gigantic series would soon drain the University Press of its last penny, and absorb the rich endowments of all the Colleges. Instead of securing for Oxford the magnificent future predicted in the *Academy* as the result of this measure, it would, unless the programme were considerably reduced in its dimensions, involve the University in speedy bankruptcy."

57. Instrumental in final negotiations with the Oxford University Press was Dean Liddell of Christ Church College. The partial funding coming from British governmental sources in India was arranged through the efforts of Sir Henry Maine, who was a member of the council of the governor general of India, and especially through the influence of Lord Salisbury, who was the chancellor of Oxford University and formerly a secretary of state for India. Müller dedicated the *Sacred Books* to these three men who were so responsible for the project's approval and funding (Georgina Müller, *Life and Letters*).

58. See Max Müller, *Introduction to the Science of Religion* (1873), 101–23. He does not speak of any specific publishing plan, but the germ of the project is clearly suggested by the following (pp. 106–7):

With [the] eight religions the library of the Sacred Books of the whole human race is complete, and an accurate study of these eight codes, written in Sanskrit, Pali, and Zend, in Hebrew, Greek, and Arabic, lastly in Chinese, might in itself not seem too formidable an undertaking for a single scholar. Yet, let us begin at home, and look at the enormous literature devoted to the interpretation of the Old Testament, and the number of books published every year on controverted points in the doctrine or the history of the Gospels, and you may then form an idea of what a theological library would be that should contain the necessary materials for an accurate and scholar-like interpretation of the eight sacred codes.

59. Moncure Conway, coll. and ed., *The Sacred Anthology: A Book of Ethnical Scriptures* (London: Trübner, 1873). The popular success of this work is indicated by the fact that in 1876 it had already entered into a fifth edition.

60. Conway, *Autobiography,* 2:331.

61. Müller, preface, *Sacred Books,* 1:x.

62. Conway, *Autobiography,* 2:331. Concerning the costs of publication, Conway says: "My anthology was printed and bound at my own expense, Trübner selling it on commission; my outlay was covered by subscriptions, and my profits were good, though I gave many and contributed by royalties in the edition donated by Walter Thomson to India. I expressed to Max Müller my delight in his enterprise and willingness to help in obtaining subscriptions."

63. Ibid. It should perhaps be noted that Conway had a penchant for claiming to be the indirect cause of various significant reformative events in Victorian England. For example, he also says (p. 292) that "the first step towards a college at Oxford for women was made in the house of my heretical self in London, and the second [1876] in High Church Keble College." It is here that Conway notes Müller's "misgivings about the scheme" for women's education at Oxford. He does not mention Legge.

64. Schwab, *The Oriental Renaissance: Europe's Rediscovery of India and the East 1680–1880,* trans. Gene Patterson-Black and Victor Reinking (New York: Columbia University Press, 1984), 109. See also Jordan, *Comparative Religion,* on Pauthier as a precursor of comparative religion in France.

65. See Schwab, *Oriental Renaissance.*

66. Max Müller, "Review of *The Sacred Anthology: A Book of Ethnical Scriptures,* Collected and Edited by M.D. Conway, London: Trübner & Co., 1873," *Academy* 67 (October 1874): 476–77.

67. Ibid., 477.

68. The printed circular is found in the Oxford University Press archive, *Sacred Books of the East 1887–1908,* packet 41. This circular is identical with the printed version found in volume 1 of the *Sacred Books,* except for Müller's brief introductory comments, an appendix of the scholarly contributors to the first series of twenty-four volumes (set to be completed by 1884), and a list of the works "for the present" selected for translation.

69. The rules for the translators were, in fact, relatively few and, considering the honor and rather handsome remuneration involved, hardly onerous. See "Regulations agreed upon between the Editor and Contributors to the Sacred Books of the East" (Oxford University Press archive, *Sacred Books of the East 1887–1908,* packet 41). It is not clear whether this list of regulations was in existence for the first series of twenty-four volumes.

70. The letter making this point is found in Georgina Müller, *Life and Letters,* 2:12–13.

71. Müller, preface, *Sacred Books,* 1:xxxix.

72. Müller, *Sacred Books* prospectus, p. 1; and idem, preface, *Sacred Books,* 1:xl.

73. Müller, *Sacred Books* prospectus, p. 2; and idem, preface, *Sacred Books,* 1: xl–xli.

74. Müller, *Introduction to the Science of Religion* (1873), 103.

75. Interestingly, Müller uses a romanized transcription of the Chinese names rather than their artificial Latin names. It should be noted that the original printed circular does not make use of the special orthography Müller developed to transliterate Oriental languages; see the principles of transliteration discussed in Müller, preface, *Sacred Books,* 1:xlviii–lv.

76. Müller, *Sacred Books* prospectus, pp. 2–3; and idem, preface, *Sacred Books,* 1:xlii.

77. Müller, preface, *Sacred Books,* 1:xx–xxi. Müller says here that this principle of bowdlerization applied only to the most extreme examples of "coarseness."

78. Müller to JL, September 20, 1876 (Bodleian, MS. Autogr. e. 11, *fols.* 53–54). Earlier, on March 10, 1876, Müller stressed to Legge that he wanted "complete" translations.

79. Legge had already produced two separate complete versions of the *Book of Poetry* and felt strongly that only parts of this book had "professedly a religious character" (JL, "Introduction to the Shih King," *Sacred Books,* 3:278. In the title page (ibid., 273) to the section on the *Book of Poetry,* Legge qualifies his abridged translation as "The Shih King or Book of Poetry; All the Pieces and Stanzas in it Illustrating the Religious Views and Practices of the Writers and their Times." It was to some extent this decision to go against Müller's directions, with the resulting skewed emphasis on the theistic beliefs of the ancient Chinese, that led to the attack that engulfed both Legge and Müller in the term question yet again (see page 276ff.).

80. On the different "classes" of scholarship that a university should support, see Müller's 1868 inaugural address (pages 125–27) and his argument to the Delegates of the Oxford University Press (pages 246–47).

81. In addition to his earlier edition of the authoritative text of the *Rig-Veda,* Müller had begun to publish, with copious notes similar to those in Legge's *Chinese Classics,* a multivolume translation of the hymns: *Rig-veda-sanhita: The Sacred Hymns of the Brahmans, translated and explained,* vol. 1. *Hymns to the Maruts or the Storm Gods* (London: Trübner, 1869).

82. It is interesting to note that, in defining "Taoism," the *Oxford English Dictionary* cites Müller's reference to "Tao-ism" in his 1858 review of Charles Hardwick's *Christ and Other Masters.*

83. The expression "relentless dominance of textuality" is originally from Walter Ong. See the discussion by William Graham, "Scripture as Spoken Word," in *Rethinking Scripture: Essays from a Comparative Perspective,* ed. Miriam Levering (Albany, N.Y.: State University of New York Press, 1989), 142. Graham describes the "values of modern, 'scientific' scholarship" as:

> 1) suspension of subjectivity and visual verification . . . ; 2) observation and analysis of the data of sense perception rather than immersion in them—what George Steiner has summed up tellingly as "the cult of the positive, the exact, and the predictive," or "the mirage of mathematical exactitude and predictability"; and 3) rapid and easy access to "raw data"—the "growing thirst for quantitative information," which John U. Nef describes as a key element in the rise of industrial civilization.

84. See A. A. Macdonell's discussion of some of these figures in his preface to the last volume of the series, the index volume prepared by M. Winternitz. A former student of Müller, Macdonell was one of the great Indological Orientalists of his day and a holder of the Boden chair at Oxford. However, even after the turn of the century, he continued the "Indo-European" party line that *Sacred Books* "include all the most important works of the seven non-Christian religions that have exercised a profound influence on the civilization of the continent of Asia" (*Sacred Books,* 50:vii).

85. Müller, preface, *Sacred Books,* 1:xii.

86. Ibid.

87. Ibid., xiii–xvi.

88. Ibid., xxxvii–xxxviii.

89. Ibid., ix.

90. Ibid., xxi.

91. Ibid., xxiii–xxiv. Despite Müller's elaborate defense of the notion that a sensitive interpretation of the sacred books had to look to the meaning often buried in apparent unmeaning, some of the early reviews of the first volumes attacked Müller for finding merit in the "intrinsic absurdity" and "theosophic trash" of the *Upanishads*. Müller's problem in defending the intelligibility of *Om*, said the *Spectator*, was his mistaking of "om-nescience for omniscience." See the review of volumes 1–3 of *The Sacred Books of the East* in the *Spectator* (November 15, 1879). See also Archibald Sayce's much more positive evaluation of these same issues in his review of the first three volumes in *Nature* (1879). Neither of these reviews singles out Legge's volume for any special criticism or approbation. Sayce does, however, comment in passing that, compared with Müller's interpretive introduction to the *Upanishads*, Legge's introductions were "just description."

92. Ibid., xxvi.

93. Ibid., xxvi–xxvii.

94. Müller's reason for not translating *ātman* by "soul, mind, or spirit" is that it makes "the fundamental mistake of using words which may be predicated, in place of a word which is a subject only, and can never become a predicate" (ibid., xxviii). Legge articulated a similar principle concerning the translation of *shangdi, tian,* and *shen;* see pages 274–76.

95. Ibid., xxxii–xxxvi.

96. Ibid., xxxvi.

97. Ibid., xxxvii. This fits readily into the Scottish common sense philosophical tradition, which was based on a universalized claim about basic beliefs and the minds that observe and maintain them.

98. Ibid., xxxviii.

99. See Müller to Lady Welby, May, 16, 1879 (Georgina Müller, *Life and Letters,* 2:65). See also Müller to Lady Welby, July 27, 1879, in which he says that "this translation of the Sacred Books of the East which some of the good people here [i.e., Oxford] consider most objectionable, will do a great deal towards lifting Christianity into its high historical position. I look forward to the time when those who objected to my including the Old and New Testaments among the Sacred Books of the East will implore me to do so" (ibid., 70).

100. Ibid., 65. William Beveridge, *Private Thoughts on Religion, In Two Parts Complete* (London: J. Buckland, 1776).

101. See JL, *Sacred Books,* 3:xx, 449–63. In the "Introduction to the Hsiao King" (pp. 462–63), he tells us that his translation of the *Xiaojing* (the *Book of Filial Piety*) was based on four earlier versions—an unidentified version in the *Chinese Repository,* a version by the eighteenth-century Jesuit Cibot and two versions of his own (one as recent as "four years ago," when he was trying to deepen his knowledge of the "Confucian teaching on the subject of Filial Piety").

102. The Oxford edition of the *Confucian Analects* (*Chinese Classics* [1893], vol. 1) contains a new preface and a significantly revised prolegomena. Volumes 1

and 2 were revised editions with the imprint of the Clarendon Press; volumes 3, 4, and 5 were identified with the imprint "London: Henry Frowde" (the commercial division of the Oxford University Press) and seem to have been no more than a binding of sheets left over from the original Hong Kong printings of the *Book of Documents*, the *Book of Poetry*, and *Spring and Autumn Annals*. While there are some extant records from both Trübner's and the Oxford University Press concerning the publishing history of Legge's *Classics*, the exact circumstances are not clear. See, for example, the letter to Legge from the secretary of the press concerning the reprinting of volume 1 of the *Chinese Classics*, dated December 23, 1891 (Oxford University Press archive, Letter Book 54).

103. Legge seemed to cull his information from sinological Orientalists such as Samuel Beal, who was another of Müller's contributors to the *Sacred Books* (JL, preface, *Sacred Books*, 3:xiii). It is interesting to note that Legge was dismissive of the "statistics" attempting to show Buddhism to be the world's largest religion. See his discussion of the spurious use of such statistics in his review of "*Confucianism and Taouism* by Robert K. Douglas of the British Museum and Professor of Chinese at King's College," *Academy*, November 22, 1879, pp. 363–64. Legge primarily disagrees with the notion that China may be considered a Buddhist nation. Confucianism is "pre-eminently the religion of China." From this perspective, "Confucianism, perhaps, has the greatest following; then Christianity; then Hinduism; then Muhammadanism; and we would place Buddhism in the fifth place."

104. JL, preface, *Sacred Books*, 3:xxi–xxii.

105. Legge's interest in the Daoism of "Lao-tsze" at this time is indicated by his review of Douglas's *Confucianism and Taouism*, 363.

106. JL, preface, *Sacred Books*, 3:xxii.

107. Legge's description seems somewhat gratuitous here because of the connection he draws from the "name" to the Confucian tradition. It misleads by suggesting that the name is the key to the tradition while at the same time indicating that the tradition actually predates Master Kong. At the time Legge was writing it was more or less taken for granted among native scholars that the Ruist traditions (such as *rujiao* [teaching of the scholars] and *ruxue* [Ruist learning], as well as other Song-dynasty renderings such as *daoxue, lixue,* and the Song-Ming *lihsinxue*) were in fact very closely related to the ancient master Kongzi, especially because the Four Books heightened the importance of Kongzi and Mengzi as interpretive keys to all of the classics.

108. Ibid., xiv.

109. Ibid., xiv–xv.

110. Concerning the different canonical sets of Chinese classics, see the discussion by Steven Durrant, "Ching," in *The Indiana Companion to Traditional Chinese Literature*, ed. in chief William H. Nienhauser Jr. (Bloomington, Ind.: Indiana University Press, 1986), 309–15.

111. On Chinese eighteenth-century "evidential criticism," see especially Benjamin Elman, *From Philosophy to Philology: Intellectual and Social Aspects of Change in Late Imperial China* (Cambridge, Mass.: Council on East Asian Studies, Harvard University, 1984), 37–66. The work of Dai Zhen and Yan Ruoju (who showed that parts of the *Book of Poetry* were a forgery) is especially noteworthy.

112. JL, preface, *Sacred Books*, 3:xv; and idem, "Introduction to the Shu King," *Sacred Books*, 3:19, 15. In 1879 Legge includes newer information on astronomy, but

generally follows the results of his research from 1865. Legge was aware of the problem of forgeries (ibid., 11) but believed that the text used in the Qing dynasty was "substantially" the same as the one "in the collection of the Kau [Zhou] dynasty both before and after Confucius." In 1879, however, there is a more critical and analytical methodological approach to the text—even if the conclusions are roughly the same as those he reached in 1865.

113. Ibid., 4.

114. The point being that the astronomical events could not have been forged by a later compiler because, as Legge says here, the "procession of the equinoxes . . . was not known in China till more than 2500 years after the time assigned to Yao, so that the culminating stars at the equinoxes and solstices of his remote era could not have been computed back scientifically in the time of the Kau [Zhou] dynasty, during which the collection of the Shu existed" (ibid., 26). The problem with this theory is that the Yao sections were most likely forgeries of the third or fourth centuries A.D. when the procession of the equinoxes was known. See David Pankenier ("Astronomical Dates in Shang and Western Zhou," *Early China* 7 [1981–1982]: 2–37; and idem, "The Cosmo-Political Background of Heaven's Mandate," *Early China* 20 [1995]) on the contemporary application of archaeoastronomical methods when dealing with ancient texts. This raises important issues regarding the partial historicity and astronomical facticity of mythology. For the astronomical context for many types of world mythology, see Giorgio de Santillana and Hertha von Dechen, *Hamlet's Mill: An Essay on Myth and the Frame of Time* (Boston, Mass.: David R. Godine, 1977).

115. See JL, "Chinese Chronology," *Journal of the Royal Asiatic Society* (1893): 66–75.

116. In general, see Anne M. Birrell, "James Legge and the Chinese Mythological Tradition," *History of Religions* 83 (1999): 331–52. Two important overlapping documents give Legge's views on myth. The first of these, "An Argument for the Truth of the Gospel Narratives, and for the Inspiration of the New Testament Generally," was given as a sermon (referring to Luke 2:22–35) in Hong Kong on February 12, 1871 (CWM/China/Personal/Legge/Box 4). The other, which is a reworking of the first, is entitled "No Mythus in the Gospels. Illustrated by a Comparison of Christian and Buddhistic Narratives" and was given, no doubt after his permanent return to Britain, as a lecture for the Christian Evidence Society (nineteen pages typescript, CWM/China/Personal/Legge/Box 9). In the "No Mythus" lecture, Legge makes it clear that he follows the conservative Christian historian August Neander rather than the infamous David Friedrich Strauss. See Mark S. Fountain, *The Historiography of August Neander* (New York, Bern: Peter Lang, 1995).

In his "No Mythus" lecture, Legge first distinguishes two classes of myth or fable. The first of these he calls "religious myth" or that kind of fable that refers to nature and is properly studied by the Müllerian "science of mythology." The other type is "historical myth," including "historical legend" and "heroic legend," which is concerned primarily with the history of nations. The Gospels, Legge says, are related to the class of "historical myths" but are "genuine narratives" as evidenced by their dignified "propriety" and the fact that they do not "go against the stomach of our common sense." As to the supernatural element, or miracles, in the Gospels, Legge says that, unlike the supernatural in myths, this "marvelleous [*sic*]" (though not "fantastic" or "ridiculous") factor is verified by the eyewitness testimony of the apostles "who do not lie." With regard to the issue of whether or not the Gospels "glorify" Jesus as a mythological hero, Legge claims that the Christian records make use of "no vague, dreamy admiration." Compared with the "ridiculous" and exaggerated Buddhist biographies, the Gospels (even Saint John's) are "unique" as "unadorned narratives of fact." Legge's conclusion is that there is "something divinely conservative" about the "manner of the [Gospels'] composition"—a fact that "only revelation accounts for."

Let me comment only that Legge's analysis, an intriguing specimen of a certain kind of convoluted Victorian apologetic, is especially interesting for its defense of the Confucian and Evangelical notions that "propriety," "dignity," unimaginative conservatism, and sober historicity are the sure signs of divine revelation. The significant evidentiary role of eyewitness accounts by observers who "would not lie" as proof of the veracity of the gospel accounts of miracles is also a fascinating example of how the rhetoric of legal procedure influenced textual hermeneutics.

117. The uncontested contrast between a "critically constructed" life of a non-Christian religious founder (such as Buddha, Zoroaster, or Confucius) and an "uncritically constructed" life of Jesus was common in the late Victorian age. In this sense there was a tendency to "accept the miraculous element in the life of Jesus, but to reject it in the life of Buddha"—a judgment that was often made in terms of what was said to be the "appropriateness and modest dignity" of the gospel accounts as opposed to the "extravagance and childishness" of the Buddha stories. See Philip Almond, *The British Discovery of Buddhism* (Cambridge: Cambridge University Press, 1988), 67–68.

118. Concerning the mythology of Yao, Shun, and Yu, see especially the classic study by Henri Maspero, "Légendes mythologiques dans le Chou King," *Journal asiatique* 204 (1924): 1–100; and the more recent Lévi-Straussian analysis by Sarah Allan, *The Heir and the Sage: Dynastic Legend in Early China* (San Francisco, Calif.: Chinese Materials Center, 1981). In general on Chinese mythology, see Anne Birrell, *Chinese Mythology: An Introduction* (Baltimore and London: Johns Hopkins University Press, 1993); and Norman Girardot, "Chinese Religion: Mythology," in *The Encyclopedia of Religion*, ed. Mircea Eliade, vol. 3 (New York: Macmillan, 1986–1987).

119. For Legge, this was a matter of determining the relative number of fantastic or strictly imaginative elements in non-Christian myths compared with the Gospels' "realistic" and "dignified" elements that do not go against the "stomach of our common sense," a wonderful expression that is found both in JL, "Argument for the Truth of the Gospel Narratives" (CWM/China/Personal/Legge/Box 4) and "No Mythus in the Gospels" (CWM/China/Personal/Legge/Box 9).

120. See Norman Girardot, "The Problem of Creation Mythology in the Study of Chinese Religion," *History of Religions* 15 (1976): 289; and Anne Birrell, "Studies on Chinese Myth since 1970: An Appraisal," 2 parts, *History of Religions* 33 (1994): 380–93; 34 (1994): 70–94.

121. See JL, prolegomena, *The Chinese Classics*, vol. 3, pt. 1 (1865), 192–97.

122. JL, preface, *Sacred Books*, 3:xxx.

123. Some reviewers were less than convinced by Legge's case for the "religiousness" of these books. Noting his marked passages, the *Athenaeum* nevertheless confessed "to a degree of hesitation in accepting all we thus find as pertaining to religion." For the *Athenaeum*, and despite the references to *di* as "God," the problem

was the "strange anthropomorphizing element" in the *Book of Poetry.* This, more than anything else, shows their "absolute want of spiritual perception or faith in anything superhuman." See the review of "James Legge's Sacred Books of China, Part I, Shu King, Shih King, and Hsiao King," *Athenaeum,* September 18, 1880, pp. 360-61.

124. After the hints put forward in Legge's Shanghai paper, we are not astonished to discover that some readers of this Chinese bible will notice the parallels with the idea of God's covenant revealed in the Hebrew Old Testament. A "remarkable absence of the grosser forms of idolatry" is moreover evident in these Chinese sacred books and as one reviewer put it, there is wanting only the "installation" of the "purer and Diviner" system of the New Testament. See the *North-China Herald,* November 21, 1879, pp. 492-93. See also another positive review of volume 3 of the *Sacred Books* in the *North-China Herald,* October 24, 1879, pp. 402-3.

125. JL, prolegomena, *The Chinese Classics,* vol. 3, pt. 1 (1865), 197.

126. We also need to keep in mind, and this is a pattern throughout all of his many revisions, that Legge often seems to favor an understated, and sometimes overly subtle, system of signaling changes in his estimation of the nature and significance of Chinese religion. One indication of this is the tiny, but evocative, shift in the labeling of the ancient tradition so that in 1865 he subtitles his discussion of such matters as the "Religion and superstition of the early Chinese." See JL, prolegomena, *The Chinese Classics,* vol. 3, pt. 3 (1865), 192. In 1879, however, the pointedly pejorative term *superstition* as a way of immediately qualifying his understanding of the Confucian religion had mostly disappeared and is even less frequently used to classify and condemn the practices of "ancestor worship" and "divination."

127. JL, "Introduction to the Shih King," *Sacred Books,* 3:297-98. Cf. JL, prolegomena, *The Chinese Classics,* vol. 4, part 1 (1871), 23-33.

128. The discussion of the "religious portions" of the "Odes of the Temple and the Altar" shows considerable revision in the 1879 introduction. In 1871 Legge was referring to the whole book; in 1879 he focuses his attention on the fourth section (*Sacred Books,* 3:278). No similar introduction is given to the other sections (ibid., 3:347, 377). Unlike the prolegomena of 1871, which began with a discussion of the "worship paid to God" (cf. *The Chinese Classics,* vol. 4, pt. 1 [1871], 132-37), Legge now opens with a discussion of the royal "ancestral worship," which is found to have its own "professedly religious" character and, by ethical extension, to be "binding . . . on all" as seen in the *Book of Filial Piety*'s emphasis on filial piety (see JL, "Introduction to the Shih King," *Sacred Books,* 3:299). This appears to be a paragraph unique to the 1879 introduction.

129. Ibid., 301. Cf. *The Chinese Classics,* vol. 4, pt. 1 (1871), 136.

130. JL, "Introduction to the Shih King," *Sacred Books,* 3:302. Cf. *The Chinese Classics,* vol. 4, pt. 1 (1871), 134.

131. JL, preface, *Sacred Books,* 3:xvi.

132. Ibid., xvii.

133. Ibid.

134. Ibid., xix.

135. See, for example, Legge's note to chapter 16 of the *Book of Filial Piety (Xiaojing)*, where Heaven and Earth are referred to as two powers "taking the place of Heaven or God." This "development of filial piety into a religion" (which is "here as-

sumed and described") is, for Legge, the "pressing of this virtue too far." It was this process of forgetting the original divine sanction of virtue that "tended to deprave religion during the Kau [Zhou] dynasty" and "mingled with the earlier monotheism a form of nature-worship." These last ideas are presented as a rhetorical question that leaves little doubt as to Legge's own view of the matter (JL, "The Hsiao King," *Sacred Books*, 3:484–85 n. 3).

136. JL, preface, *Sacred Books*, 3:xx.

137. JL, "Introduction to the Hsiao King," *Sacred Books*, 3:462.

138. In 1850/1852, Legge (in *The Notions of the Chinese Concerning God and Spirits: with an Examination of the Defense of an Essay on the Proper Rendering of the Words Elohim and Theos, into the Chinese Language by William Boone, D. D.* [Hong Kong: Hong Kong Register Office, 1852; reprint, Taipei: Ch'eng Wen, 1971]) had specifically denied that *di* was a divinizing title for the Chinese ancestral leaders, desiring by this means to avoid Bishop Boone's terminological argument that naming "God" by *di* would invite confusions in meaning with the reigning emperor and, in the case of the First Commandment, advocate civil disobedience. Legge denied both the apotheosis and the political innuendo, but here he confirms the former without mentioning the latter. On the meaning of euhemerization, see Jan de Vries, *Perspectives in the History of Religions*, trans. Kees W. Bolle (Berkeley, Calif.: University of California Press, 1977); and Burton Feldman and Robert D. Richardson, *The Rise of Modern Mythology, 1680–1860* (Bloomington, Ind.: Indiana University Press, 1972).

139. JL, preface, *Sacred Books*, 3:xxix.

140. Ibid., xxiii. In fact there is evidence already in 1870 that Legge had embraced some of Müller's theories about the universality of some kind of "primaeval revelation" of God in all religions and a prior "religious sense in men prepared to receive the revelation." As he said in a sermon ("The Existence and Personality of God") given in Hong Kong on May 15, 1870 (CWM/China/Personal/Legge/Box 4):

> It does not affect the argument [of the universality of the God belief] that the idea of a God has been possessed—here very obscurely, and there more distinctly. A wide disparity unquestionably there has been between the holders of that idea; between the Fetish adorers, for instance, of barbarism and the polytheistic idolaters of refinement. But in this they have all agreed that there was a Power or that there were powers above them, that there was one God, or a dualistic principle or many deities to be owned and worshipped in such fashion as tradition enjoined or fancy prescribed. This, I say, is matter of fact derived from history and observation.

141. JL, preface, *Sacred Books*, 3:xxiv.

142. Ibid. and xxv. Legge's decipherment of a singular "God" in the Chinese sacred books became widely known in Victorian intellectual circles because of its inclusion in Müller's massively influential series of Oriental bibles. We can, for this reason, trace a thread of discussion in the early "sciences of man" concerning the problem of a primordial "high god" that makes frequent reference to the views of both Müller and Legge on the subject. We might even suggest that the academic debate over "savage" and civilizational "high gods" that raged among such latter-day "anthropological" luminaries as Edward Tylor and Andrew Lang (as well as down to the present day) constitutes a secularized continuation of the amazingly resilient Protestant term question.

Edward Tylor, the reputed father of anthropology and a fellow Oxonian, takes Legge to task for arguing, on the basis of ambiguous Chinese evidence, against the "usual course of theologic development" by which a "rude" mythological religion of the animated material "Heaven" rules before the rise of a personal monotheistic deity such as Shangdi (Edward Tylor, *Primitive Culture: Researches into the Development of Mythology, Philosophy, Religion, Language, Art, and Custom* [New York: G.P. Putnam's Sons, 1920], 2:352). More dramatic is Andrew Lang's famous recantation of his earlier Tylorian views of theistic development and his affirmation of a kind of primitive monotheistic belief. In this sense, Lang specifically rejects Tylor's overly cavalier dismissal of Legge concerning a Chinese conception of a supreme being. As Lang says:

> [I]t seems . . . probable that ancient China possessed a Supreme Personal Being, more remote and original than Heaven, just as the Zunis do. On the lower plane, Chinese religion is overrun, as everyone knows, by animism and ancestor-worship. This is so powerful that it has given rise to a native theory of Euhemerism. . . . On the highest plane is either a personal Supreme Being, Shang-ti, or there is Tien, Heaven (with Earth, parent of men), neither of them necessarily owing, in origin, anything to Animism. . . . Nothing shows or hints that Shang-ti is merely an imaginary idealized first ancestor. (Andrew Lang, *The Making of Religion* [London: Longmans, Green, 1898], 318–19.)

The situation is not as simple as Jacques Gernet or Michael Loewe would have it. Loewe, for example, writes as if the ancient Chinese understanding of *shangdi* and *tian* were simply a matter of determining what the Chinese *really* believed. So that (p. 189)

> [f]or the Chinese there could be no such implication of singularity [of God]. For them there was the age-old traditional worship of ti or shang-ti as the superior member of a group of spirits; he was the arbiter and the leader of a company in which the souls of deceased kings came to take part as equals. At a later stage the term ti was used in reference to five specific powers whose spheres of influence were limited to particular periods of time, or areas or phases of existence. Similarly, the Chinese concept of T'ien could hardly correspond with the God of Christianity. T'ien had started as a personified anthropomorphic godhead worshiped by some of the people of the west. In the hands of the philosophers, T'ien perhaps signified the mind that lay behind one of the three co-existing powers or states of the universe, the other two being earth and man. While in such a context T'ien could sometimes seem to be the source of creative processes, it had no personal relationship with the great majority of mankind. Finally, however, T'ien had assumed a central part in the imperial state cult, being a deity to whom the emperor alone was entitled to address communications. T'ien stood now in a specific relationship to the emperor, and was capable of authorizing his exercise of rule, or, alternatively, of withdrawing such support. The annual services performed at the majestic site of the Temple of Heaven served to strengthen the link between spiritual and temporal authority. Thus, while to Christians the worship of God was a duty imposed on all mankind, a relationship with T'ien was strictly reserved for one individual alone.

See M. Loewe, "Imperial China's Reactions to Catholic Missions," *Numen* 35 (1988): 179–212.

The terminological and phenomenological difficulty with the Chinese "high god" is not so much an argument over "God," but whether there is any one essential meaning hidden behind the words and texts. In the case of Chinese tradition, as Andrew Lang said, it seems to be a matter to be settled "purely" on the basis of "evidence." However, as we see in the furiously interminable term debate among different missionaries, such questions of fundamental discursive belief are always ambiguous and undecidable in terms of the "facts." The existence of a "high god" among tribal communities and in ancient civilizational traditions such as China's is still an open question.

143. John Chalmers, "Interminable Question," *The China Review* 9 (1880): 190–91. This article, dated December 28, 1880, was originally published in a Hong Kong newspaper and was republished in Müller's revised edition of the *Introduction to the Science of Religion* in 1882.

144. Inquirer [A.P. Happer], "A Letter to Prof. F. Max Müller on the Sacred Books of China, Part I the Shu King, Shih King, and the Hsiao King," *The Chinese Recorder* 11 (May–June 1880): 161–87.

145. This circular letter, dated June 25, 1880, was widely published in various newspapers in China. It is included, along with Müller's reply, in a response to Chalmers's article under the title of "The Interminable Question," *The China Review* 9 (1881): 228–33. For Burdon's general opinions about the Chinese religion and China, see "Bishop Burdon on the Religion of the Chinese" and "Why Foreigners Should Respect the Chinese," *North-China Herald,* September 18, 1880, pp. 270–72.

146. Chalmers, "Interminable Question," 190–91. The larger issues of the battle were also recognized in an editorial note (no doubt also by Happer) to the publication of Inquirer's "Letter to Müller." As this note says, the "real issue" is not terminological but a general matter of Chinese religious "beliefs and practice" (see the Editorial Note, *The Chinese Recorder* 12 [January–February 1881]: 35).

147. For Legge, Shangdi was "the true God" in the sense of the "true idea" of God, but this did not refer to the meaning of "self-existence" indicated by the Hebrew term of *Jehovah*. This idea is central to the Westminster Confession and underlies Legge's claims in 1850–1852 (JL, *Notions of the Chinese*).

148. Inquirer, "Letter to . . . Max Müller" (pamphlet edition), 1–5.

149. Ibid., 4, 20–24. Müller's views on "false" religions are found in his 1870 "Lectures on the Science of Religion" (Müller, *Introduction to the Science of Religion* [1873], 123–24.

150. This letter was drafted in Shanghai on June 25, 1880, and appeared in several China coast newspapers as well as in the *Chinese Recorder.* The identity of the author (or authors) of the letter is not made clear although, based on the listing of signatures, it may well be that Thomas McClatchie (here written as "M'Clatchie"), the Anglican canon of Hong Kong and Shanghai, was the primary writer. McClatchie was also someone who would most likely have consulted with his bishop, John Shaw Burdon, in the drafting of the letter. The version of the letter I am using here is that published, along with Burdon's introduction and Müller's response, in *The China Review* 9 (1881): 228–33. Besides McClatchie and Burdon, signatories to the letter included Legge's old American enemies from the Shanghai conference, Robert Nelson, A.P. Happer, and Matthew Yates. Others were Edward C. Lord, Frederick F. Gough, John L. Nevius, T.P. Crawford, H. Blodget, Samuel I.J.

Schereschewsky, Elliot Thompson, Charles Butcher, William J. Boone (a son of Legge's original debating partner, William Boone), Hunter Corbett, Charles Hills, John Wherry, James Bates, L.D. Chapin, Chauncey Goodrich, J.A. Leyenberger, and Henry V. Noyes.

151. For an official Church Missionary Society portrait of Burdon, see Eugene Stock, *The History of the Church Missionary Society, Its Environment, Its Men and Its Work* (London: Church Missionary Society, 1899–1916), 3:217–20. Known as the "pioneer of the North," Burdon was consecrated bishop of Victoria, Hong Kong, on March 15, 1874. The darker side of Burdon is seen in his suspicious behavior concerning a young missionary, A.B. Hutchinson, who was the secretary to the British and Foreign Bible Society in Hong Kong. This incident, which led to official proceedings against Burdon, was connected with the term question and Burdon's support of the Shin-ite position. As Hutchinson noted in parenthetical comments to Burdon's official defense, the bishop had a "violent temper" and was strongly opposed to the "Nonconformist bible" using the term of *shangdi*. Another incident that dramatized Burdon's problems of character involved three students who challenged his authority as head of Saint Paul's school in Hong Kong. On these matters, see the materials in the University of Birmingham Library, Church Missionary Society archive, C CH/03 3d/1-46.

152. *The China Review* 9 (1881): 229. The persons "as thoroughly qualified" as Legge "to form a judgment on the subject" are identified as Bishop Boone, Dr. Bridgman, Dr. Wells Williams, and the late Archimandrite Palladius—as well as, it would seem, many of those who signed the letter.

153. Ibid. Happer also agreed that the number of Protestants who agreed with Legge's position "may be counted on the *fingers of one hand* [original emphasis]" (Inquirer, "Letter to . . . Max Müller," 20). As to the contested number of Protestant missionaries supporting either position, it seems fairly clear that the Shangdi-ites were in ascendancy at this time.

154. Müller, *Introduction to the Science of Religion* (1873), 191. This suggests a slight difference with Legge. Legge still held that *shangdi* did mean "God," while Müller was more interested in the morphological symbols that projected the idea in various ways. Legge would be more reluctant than Müller would be to generalize. For Legge, the "one, true God" means the "true idea of God" gained through natural revelation. Legge was misinterpreted on this matter by Burdon and others who believed that Legge meant that *shangdi* was the equivalent of Jehovah. Legge explicitly denied this equation.

155. See, for example, Roger T. Ames, "Religiousness in Classical Confucianism: A Comparative Analysis," *Asian Cultural Quarterly* 12 (1984): 7–23. Ames concludes (p. 11) that, on the basis of his examination of the ancient documents, *shangdi* and *tian* have some anthropomorphic content, but "were never presented as a transcendent deity." See also Robert Eno, "Was There a High God Ti in Shang Religion?" *Early China* 15 (1990): 1–26. This is still a debatable issue.

156. Beyond Happer and Burdon's published criticism, there was also a long article in a German newspaper by the sinologist Victor von Strauss und Tornay on the "Controversy between the English Missionaries and Max Müller" and various private letters questioning Legge's translations. I have not located a copy of the original newspaper article, but I possess a copy of Legge's handwritten "Reply to Victor von

Strauss und Tornay," n.d., 8 pp. (CWM/China/Personal/Legge/Box 7). In this article, Legge mostly recounts points he makes in *A Letter to Professor F. Max Müller Chiefly on the Translation into English of the Chinese Terms Ti and Shang Ti in Reply to a Letter to Him by 'Inquirer' in the Chinese Recorder and Missionary Journal for May–June, 1880* (London: Trübner, 1880). Aware that "Inquirer" was A.P. Happer, Legge reiterates his conviction that the "proper meaning and translation" of shangdi is not "lord" but "God." This, he claims here, was his "own important discovery in the discussion of the 'term question.' " The term *tian* is, however, properly translated "Heaven" even though it can refer to God in the same way that Germans use *Himmel* to talk about God. For Legge, therefore, the Chinese "distinguish between the visible heavens and the God who dwells in heaven as clearly as the devout Christian."

Of the personal letters dealing with this subject, the most important is Legge's letter to Arthur Moule (brother of Bishop Moule), November 30, 1880 (CWM/China/Personal/Legge/Box 7), but see also the argument about "relative terms" in *Notions of the Chinese*. It is in the letter to Moule that he makes an interesting distinction between "generic" and "general" terms:

> You [i.e., Moule] say what we want for translational purposes is a generic term. I prefer in considering it, to use the grammatical term "general" or "common." God is an appellation name properly applicable only to one Being and the glory of nature. . . . What we want for translational purposes is a general term. A generic name . . . denies the first article of true religion that there is only one God. A general name (being a name, a generic name if you like, of quality or relation) is what we need. And such a name we have in Ti. The most common name for the scores of Taoist deities is this. All the state gods, the care of whose temples is committed to the Taoist monks, are Tis.

157. JL, *Letter to . . . Max Müller*, 6, 29.

158. JL to A. Wylie, December 1, 1880 (CWM/China/Personal/Legge/Box 7).

159. See the selections from Mori's letter in Georgina Müller, *Life and Letters*, 2:97–98. Even so, Mori did not completely endorse Legge's position.

160. Given the value Müller seemed to place on native evaluations of Legge's scholarship, it is worth noting that Legge says (p. 18 n. 1) that while writing his *Letter to . . . Max Müller*, he

> was interrupted by a visit from two of the gentlemen belonging to the Chinese legation in London,—the Charge d'Affaires in the absence of the marquis Tsang [marquis Tseng] on the continent, and one of the interpreters. I asked them their opinion about the meaning of Thien and Shang Ti. The Charge quoted Ku Hsi's [Zhu Xi's] account of Shang Ti, as "the Spirit of Heaven." The interpreter said, "If I may express my humble opinion, you in England say 'God,' we in China say 'Shang Ti.' There is no difference. God is Shang Ti, Shang Ti is God."

161. Ibid. Although he must have known of the circular letter of June 25, nowhere in this pamphlet does he mention it. He refers to it, however, in a letter to Alexander Wylie dated December 1, 1880, and in the previously cited letter to Arthur Moule dated November 30, 1880 (CWM/China/Personal/Legge/Box 7). In writing to Wylie, Legge makes the interesting observation that Thomas Wade

was acting "so mysterious and unaccountable that he may have assented to something from Bishop Burdon." In the *Letter to . . . Max Müller* there are several internal references to Legge's recently published *Religions of China: Confucianism and Taoism Described and Compared with Christianity* (London: Hodder and Stoughton, 1880).

162. JL, *Letter to . . . Max Müller*, 9.

163. In a letter dated February 22, 1880, to the duke of Argyll (Georgina Müller, *Life and Letters*, 2:84–85), Müller says:

> I also hold that our so-called Kantian categories are evolved; they are there potentially, but they want the objective world to become actual. What I call the Infinite is that which by its pressure calls forth that form of thought, that category, which Kant would call the category of substantiality. Without that category we should have nothing but predicates; i.e., thought would be impossible. . . . All names of God are predicates . . . but of what? Of that nameless Something which presses on us on all sides. . . . It was because I wanted a Substance for all Divine ideas that I traced the presence of the Infinite, or the Nameless, or the Unknown, as the antecedent though unconscious sine qua non of all later assertions about it.

164. JL, *Letter to . . . Max Müller*, 8–9.

165. Ibid., 10–16. Even where both Happer and Legge could be said to be authentic ethnographical observers—that is, with reference to the ritual and architectural significance of the Altar of Heaven in Peking—their interpretations depend almost entirely on the reading of the text of an inscribed tablet at the site (p. 16).

166. Ibid., 17.

167. Ibid., 18–19.

168. Ibid., 20.

169. Reaching an emotional crescendo in the revelation of his scholarly creed that had been evolving since the early 1850s, Legge uncontritely declares (ibid., 22) that, even though he has long been charged with holding unorthodox views,

> [t]he view of a primitive monotheism in China is more in accordance with the testimony of the Bible than any other, and that the usage of Thien and Ti, all along the course of history, struggling against the corruptions of that primitive monotheism, and occasionally succeeding, to a great extent, as during the Ming period, in casting them off, is most honouring to God, and shows how He has never left Himself without witness among the many millioned people of the Chinese empire.

170. The text of Müller's letter, which is dated December 19, 1880, is given in *The China Review* 9 (1881): 230–33. It was republished in the London *Times* of December 30, 1880. I should note that Happer was one of the signers of the June 25 circular letter, so Müller was also responding indirectly to Happer's letter. As suggested by a reference to a letter of December 12 (see Georgina Müller, *Life and Letters*, 2:95–98), there may also have been a separate letter to Happer, which I have not seen. Response to Müller's verdict is found in an article in the *North-China Daily News* dated February 17, 1881 (CWM/China/Personal/Legge/Box 9), and in a letter from A. Williamson to Legge (CWM/China/Personal/Legge/Box 8).

171. Müller tended to read his own Müllerian philosophy into Legge's carefully worked-out position. In this way, Müller was able to criticize the missionaries while promoting a misinterpretation of Legge's position that "Shangdi is God but not Jehovah."

172. See Müller's reply in *The China Review,* 230.

173. Ibid., 231. This position, it should be noted, was also confirmed by Legge on philological rather than on theological grounds as far back as 1850–1852 in *Notions of the Chinese.*

174. For the New Testament passage about Paul at Athens, see Acts 17:16–34. See also Müller's reply, *The China Review,* 232.

175. John Ross, "Our Attitude Towards Confucianism," *The Chinese Recorder* 18 (January 1887): 1–11.

176. See Ernst Faber's interesting discussion of the Pauline paradigm in his "Lessons from the Introduction of the Gospel to Europe," *The Chinese Recorder* 21 (April 1890): 170–79 and (May 1890): 193–200. Faber is especially concerned with what he considers the overly "sentimental" idea often extracted from the story of Paul at Athens—that is, "the idea of discovering even in idolatry something true, which should be acknowledged and taken as a basis to develop from it higher truths." While "pleasing" to "scholars in their studies," this perspective is "useless in practical work" among heathens. In his speech to the Athenians at Mars's Hill, Paul "really accuses them of ignorance and superstition." In this sense, one should not sentimentally appeal to the truth in the modern expression of heathenism; rather it is necessary to refer only to the ancient classics of the tradition.

CHAPTER FIVE. COMPARATIVIST LEGGE: DESCRIBING AND COMPARING THE RELIGIONS OF CHINA, 1880–1882

1. On many of these developments, see Walter De la Mare, ed., *The Eighteen-Eighties: Essays by Fellows of the Royal Society of Literature* (Cambridge: Cambridge University Press, 1930).

2. On the popularity of Arnold's *Light of Asia* (London: Trübner, 1879), see Philip Almond, *The British Discovery of Buddhism* (Cambridge: Cambridge University Press, 1988), 1–4. For contemporaneous comment, see especially Samuel H. Kellogg, *The Light of Asia and the Light of the World* (London: Macmillan, 1885); and William C. Wilkinson, *Edwin Arnold as Poetizer and as Paganizer* (New York: Funk and Wagnalls, 1884).

3. Müller was especially antagonistic to the ersatz "esoteric Buddhism" of Blavatsky and Olcott. See also Müller's introduction to Albert Réville's *Prolegomena of the History of Religions,* trans. A.S. Squire (London: Williams and Norgate, 1884), viii–ix. Noting that the interest in the science of religion was "spreading rapidly and widely," Müller says that the new science had to be especially wary of "indiscriminate admirers." Most of all, comparative religions should not be seen as "amusement for amateurs." It is the "conscience of a scholar" and a "true historical spirit" that should always prevail.

4. See especially the excellent study by Marjorie Wheeler-Barclay, "The Science of Religion in Britain, 1860–1915" (Ph.D. diss., Northwestern University, 1987).

5. See Sharpe, *Comparative Religion: A History,* 2d ed. (La Salle, Ill.: Open Court, 1986), 87–97, 133–36; and Robert Ackerman, *J. G. Frazer: His Life and Work* (Cambridge: Cambridge University Press, 1990).

6. Mrs. Humphry Ward, *Robert Elsmere* (London: Macmillan, 1888), 2:74.

7. Anthony S. Wohl, "The 1880s: A New Generation?" *Nineteenth-Century Studies* 4 (1990): 13. Wohl refers to a "new" kind of Christianity with a dominant social concern—e.g., the rise of the Salvation Army, the Christian Socialist movement, and the labor churches. It is interesting to see that these developments were paralleled by the emergence, in the China mission, of the social-gospel movement, which, it seems probable, was intertwined with habits of thought and practice associated with the comparative science of religions. On T.H. Green, see particularly Melvin Richter, *The Politics of Conscience: T.H. Green and His Age* (Cambridge, Mass.: Harvard University Press, 1964). Green promoted the uplifting message that the freedom of the individual "could be enhanced, rather than diminished by state action" and organized charitable activities. Legge seems to have had a cordial, if not a close, relationship with Green. See the letters and notes from Green to Legge in Bodleian Library, Oxford University (hereafter cited as Bodleian), MS. Top. Oxon. c. 528. In one letter, Green thanks Legge for reading his "not orthodox" essay on the Gospels.

8. For a contemporaneous discussion of T.H. Green as the "most potent intellectual influence in Oxford during the last fifteen years," see A.M.M. Steadman, ed., *Oxford: Its Life and Schools* (London: George Bell, 1887), 132–33, 156–57. Mark Pattison charged Green with bringing "Kant and Hegel to Oxford." As Steadman notes (pp. 156–57):

> Two great doctrines . . . formed the foundation of [Green's] teaching. . . . Neither nature nor man, he said[,] can be known by us, or made intelligible to us, without the assumption of a "Spiritual Principle," which gives unity and meaning to the one, and strives to realize itself ever more and more fully through the progressive ideals of the other. And, again, because God is thus revealed to us in the very fact of knowing, and in the very conditions of conduct, therefore we are not to think of Him as far away in some transcendental world, but as here, in our midst, accessible to our intelligence, working through our wills. For all pupils of Professor Green, to know God, meant to find the revelation of Him in their highest ideals, and to serve Him meant to make men Godlike. We need not now scan these propositions with the eye of a theologian or philosophical opponent; we can all see how profoundly they would affect the practical religion of young men who were, in any true sense, Christians. As a matter of fact, all parties in Oxford caught some echo of Green's meaning, and some measure of his enthusiasm. The best and most religious men of the present time are not content simply to go to their favourite church, to be more or less edified, and to come away again. They interest themselves in social questions.

9. Ward, *Robert Elsmere,* 2:71. The disingenuous student of comparative religions first isolates Christianity from all the other religious phenomena of the world, and then argues upon its details. You might as well isolate English jurisprudence, and discuss its details without any reference to Teutonic custom or Roman law! You may be as logical or as learned as you like within the limits chosen, but the whole result is false! You treat Christian witness and Biblical literature as you would treat no other witness, and no other literature in the world. And you cannot show cause enough. For your reasons depend on the very witness under dispute. And so you go on arguing in a circle, ad infinitum.

10. Ibid. At one point Grey addresses Elsmere's loss of faith:

"I see," said the tutor [Grey] at last, his hands in the pockets of his short gray coat, his brow bent and thoughtful. "Well, the process in you has been the typical process of the present day. Abstract thought has had little or nothing to say to it. It has been all a question of literary and historical evidence. I am old-fashioned enough"—and he smiled—"to stick to the a priori impossibility of miracles, but then I am a philosopher! You have come to see how miracle is manufactured, to recognize in it merely a natural inevitable outgrowth of human testimony, in its pre-scientific stages. It has been all experimental, inductive. I imagine"—he looked up—"you didn't get much help out of the orthodox apologists?"

There is a copy of a letter by T. H. Green to Legge that briefly alludes to their differences concerning miracles in the gospel narratives (Legge's views were more conventional). Helen Edith Legge, typed excerpts entitled "Letters to Dr. Legge," 32 pp. (Council for World Mission [hereafter cited as CWM] China/Personal/Legge/Box 8).

11. Max Müller, preface to *Introduction to the Science of Religion: Four Lectures Delivered at the Royal Institution in February and May, 1870* (London: Longmans, Green, 1873); quoted by JL in his essay "Professor F. Max Müller" (1879), 15 pp., handwritten version in copybook (Bodleian, MS. Autogr. e. 11, *fols.* 53–54, notebook numbered A). It is interesting that Victorians emphasized the silver *xiao* (filiality) over the golden *ren* (benevolence).

12. See De la Mare, *The Eighteen-Eighties*, xxiv. The edition used here is Walter Pater, *Marius the Epicurean: His Sensations and Ideas* (New York: Book League of America, 1929).

13. See especially Linda Dowling, *Language and Decadence in the Victorian Fin de Siècle* (Princeton, N.J.: Princeton University Press, 1986). Dowling sees the end of the Victorian age as a "post-philological moment" when language itself, as a representational system, became problematic. The "decadent" issue was no longer a matter of "symbol" or what was behind words, but a matter of surfaces and style.

14. The gradual bifurcation of different sciences at this time is suggested by Müller's remarks at the opening of the Mason Science College in Birmingham in October of 1880 (Georgina A. Müller, *The Life and Letters of the Right Honorable Friedrich Max Müller* [London: 1902], 2:93–94). Talking about the devotion of his "whole life to the science of man," Müller claimed that "a true college of science could not live if it were to exclude the science of man. Man is the measurer of all things, and what is science but the reflection of the outer world on the mirror of the mind."

On the late-nineteenth-century tradition of decadence as a revival of eighteenth-century empiricist epistemology, see Dowling, *Language and Decadence*, xiii.

15. Articles about Tylor are mostly deferential (e.g., *Oxford Magazine*, February 21, 1883, p. 88); those about Müller are increasingly dismissive and even chiding (e.g., *Oxford Magazine*, May 9, 1883, p. 217; May 18, 1887, pp. 215–16). See also the discussions of Müller and Tylor in Wheeler-Barclay, "Science of Religion."

16. Max Müller to von Strauss und Tornay, January 30, 1880 (Georgina Müller, *Life and Letters*, 2:81).

17. Müller refers to the "heavy burden" of the *Sacred Books* in a letter to his wife, January 20, 1881 (Bodleian, MS. Eng. d. 2344). In 1882, Müller prepared a revised edition of his "Lectures on the Science of Religion" (*Introduction to the Science of Religion: Four Lectures Delivered at the Royal Institution in February and May, 1870*, rev. ed.

[London: Longmans, Green, 1882]), which included copies of the letter from John Shaw Burdon, the Anglican bishop of Hong Kong, attacking Legge's volume and of Müller's reply; see page 276ff.

18. The correspondence between Müller and Renan over the latter's Hibbert Lectures in London are an excellent illustration of the strained climate in England at that time concerning the discussion of religious topics and the need to exercise cautious discretion in such matters. Advising him "to be careful" while in London, Müller nevertheless suggests that Renan should be "perfectly free" in his lecture and even recommends a topic that would show the "first deterioration which the personal teaching of Christ suffered." For Müller it would be interesting for Renan to discuss how "we, in our nineteenth century, are no more Christians than Constantine was; that by taking all that is metaphorical for real, and all that is real for metaphorical, we have produced a religion in many respects worse than the old heathen religions" (Georgina Müller, *Life and Letters,* 2:76–77). On January 15, 1880, Müller wrote Renan to say that he had had some correspondence with the editor of the *Times* about the forthcoming Hibbert Lectures (ibid., 80):

> Everything in England depends on the Times, everybody respects what the Times says. I am glad to say that the present editor is personally on our side, and that is of great importance . . . the difficulty in England is that few people read books, and form their own opinions; a clamor is raised and everybody joins in it. Now as to your position here [i.e., at Oxford], it will be, as you know, a difficult one, because the two strongest parties, the clerical and the materialistic, are opposed to you.

On Renan's stay in Oxford, Müller commented that "some of my friends refused to meet him at my house." Despite this and the fact that the Oxford papers treated the visit harshly, Müller says that "all went off well" (ibid., 90–91).

19. On Lang, see Wheeler-Barclay, "Science of Religion," and Philippa J. Baylis, "Andrew Lang and the Study of Religion in the Victorian Era, with Special Reference to His High God Theory" (Ph.D. diss., University of Aberdeen, 1987). On Whitney, see Dowling, *Language and Decadence,* 73–77.

20. See Max Müller, "The Savage," *Nineteenth Century* 17 (1885): 109–32.

21. Müller prefaces his translation with the question that his friends were asking him in 1880—that is, "How can you waste your time on a translation of Kant's *Critik der reinen Vernunft?*" See Max Müller, translator's preface ("Why I Thought I Might Translate Kant's *Critique*"), in *Immanuel Kant's Critique of Pure Reason,* translated into English by Max Müller (New York: Macmillan, 1891, 1896), xxvii. Kant's *Critique* was at that time (1881) already available in several English translations. It should also be noted that Müller's translation, with the prompting of his friend Ludwig Noiré, was undertaken in commemoration of the centenary of the *Critique*'s first publication.

22. Müller to Georgina Müller, January 20, 1881 (Bodleian, MS. Eng. d. 2344). Müller's translation of Kant's *Critique of Pure Reason* was first published in 1881 (and reprinted with alterations in 1896). In his translator's preface, Müller says that his reading of Kant as a schoolboy was a crucial factor in his intellectual growth (Müller, *Immanuel Kant's Critique,* xxxiv):

> Having once learnt from Kant what man can and what he cannot know, my plan of life was very simple, namely, to learn, so far as literature, tradition, and language

allow us to do so, how man came to believe that he could know so much more than he ever can know in religion, in mythology, and in philosophy. This required special studies in the field of the most ancient languages and literatures. But though these more special studies drew me away for many years towards distant times and distant countries, whatever purpose or method there may have been in the work of my life was due to my beginning life with Kant.

23. Ibid., xxxv. Müller's preface is also interesting for its elaboration of his theory of properly "construed" translation—see, especially, pp. xxvii–xxxiii.

24. Ibid., lxxviii.

25. Scottish common sense philosophy generally did not accept the a priori forms of reason that Kant took as fundamental. Therefore Thomas Brown criticizes Kant in one of the first issues of the *Edinburgh Review*. It is also well to remember that, aside from some general affinities between Müller's and Legge's positions on these matters, Germanic piety tended toward mysticism while the Scottish Dissenter tradition sought harmony with reason (e.g., see some of George Legge's sermons). Legge was less willing to appeal to universalized religious forms (as in Müller's neo-Kantianism), and was less critical of Christian religious texts and experiences. In their overall approach to understanding, Legge was more biblical, whereas Müller was more purely rational. Their most important similarities were the general Aristotelian moorings of their thought and the practical moral bent of their Protestant piety.

26. JL to Mr. Parry, June 20, 1879 (Bodleian, MS. Autogr. e. 11, *fols.* 53–54).

27. Ibid. The details on this incident are found in *The China Review* 8 (1879): 62–63 and 9 (1880): 118. As pointed out in the *China Review* (8: 62), the inscription (described by Heinrich Schliemann in his *Troy and Its Remains* [London: Murray, 1875]) was identified as Chinese by Émile Burnouf—and the Chinese envoy at Berlin and Robert Douglas in London tended to agree. Besides Legge's refutation in his letter to Parry, see also Archibald Sayce's rebuttal in the *Times* (June 11, 1879).

28. It is interesting to note that at this time A.P. Happer was explicitly applying a neo–Tower of Babel theory to the comparative issue of "how the knowledge of revealed truth was known by so many" (see his "On Post-Diluvians," *The Chinese Recorder* 11 [November–December 1880]: 395–411). Preferring the eighteenth-century Sanskritic Orientalist William Jones to his contemporary Legge, Happer says that, "if we accept the opinion of the late Sir William Jones, that Noah went with some of his descendants to China, this will account for the Chinese having preserved the knowledge of this early revelation to a greater extent and with greater purity than any other nation."

29. The George Street Congregational Church "Year Books" and "Records" are preserved at the Oxford County Record Office, Oxfordshire, England. The "Records" for 1879, 1880, and 1881 indicate that Legge was turned to for guidance in securing a new pastor (the previous pastor, David Martin, had resigned due to "severe mental prostration"), but his several suggestions (Thomas Jones from Australia and Robert F. Horton of Oxford) did not work out and, after the death of his wife, Legge ended his involvement in the search process. On November 4, 1881, Legge notified the deacons of his "intention not to attend the deacons meeting again, nor take any part in the Church meetings except as an individual member of

the church," assigning as his reason for this decision that it had been "forced upon his mind, though gradually, that this association with the deacons was hindering rather than promoting the settlement of a pastor" (Oxford County Record Office, Ox. C.C. I/ii/3). Legge did serve the church in a less administratively active, but concerned, way throughout the rest of his life in Oxford.

30. See also Legge's reference to the Altar of Heaven in his important pamphlet *Christianity and Confucianism Compared in Their Teaching of the Whole Duty of Man* (hereafter cited as *Whole Duty of Man*), Present Day Tract no. 18 (London: Religious Tract Society, 1883), 17.

31. A long section of the first part of the book is devoted to a detailed study of the solstitial practices associated with the Altar of Heaven (JL, *The Religions of China: Confucianism and Taoism Described and Compared with Christianity* [London: Hodder and Stoughton, 1880], 43–58).

32. Legge had already been reading an apologetic Buddhist work by the recluse monk Liu Mi (ibid., 59 n. A).

33. See JL, *Whole Duty of Man*. This was printed as a separate thirty-six page pamphlet and, in subsequent editions, together with essays on other religions. See also the review in "The Non-Christian Religions," *Spectator* 61 (September 22, 1888): 1294–96. The reviewer for the *Spectator* comments that Legge's tract on Confucianism was the "best in the volume" because it seemed "scrupulously careful not to deprecate but to make the best of everything that is good in the religion of the Chinese and the people themselves." See also JL, "Confucius the Sage and the Religion of China," in *Religious Systems of the World: A Contribution to the Study of Comparative Religion* (London: Swan Sonnenschein, 1908), 61–75; first edition 1889 and nine editions down to 1908. It is important to notice the extreme popularity of this contribution to the science of "comparative religions" and that Legge was willing to be popularly identified as a leading comparativist. The published essays were revisions of lectures given at the South Place Institute in London, where, say the editors of the volume, the lecturers spoke to "not always sympathetic" audiences and risked "offending their own co-religionists." With some small exceptions, these two essays basically quote, paraphrase, and condense the argument concerning "Confucianism" and "Confucius" presented in JL *Religions in China*.

34. Ernst Faber, *Introduction to the Science of Chinese Religion: A Critique of Max Müller and Other Authors* (Shanghai: Kelly & Walsh, 1879). In this work, the self-styled "practical missionary" Faber rejects the definition of religion proposed by Müller (a "faculty") and A. M. Fairbairn (a "relation"; a reference to Fairbairn's *Studies in the Philosophy of Religion and History* [New York: Lovell, Adam, Wesson, 1877]), but wants to apply a general Müllerian comparative "science" to the study of religions. Writing for a missionary conference in Canton, Faber is particularly concerned to counter the common view that the Chinese are a "people singularly deficient in the religious faculty . . . at least as Semitic and Indo-European peoples understand it" (p. vii). It is Faber's view that the Chinese are among "the most religious people of the world. Only we must not look for any symptoms of religion similar to those to which we are accustomed in Christian lands. There are however comparatively more temples and altars, more idols and more religious practices in China than in almost all other countries." These last sentiments are interestingly similar to C. K. Yang's twentieth-century rediscovery of Chinese religion in his *Reli-*

gion in Chinese Society (Berkeley and Los Angeles: University of California Press, 1961, 1967). Unfortunately, Faber was all anticipation in this work, with little actual analysis of the Chinese religions. See, for example, the critical reviews of Faber in the *North-China Herald,* February 26, 1880, pp. 160–61, and in *The Chinese Recorder* 11 (January–February 1880): 77–78.

35. As Jordan (*Comparative Religion: Its Genesis and Growth* [New York: Charles Scribner's Sons, 1905], x–xii) makes clear, there was nothing unusual in the apologetic application of comparativism, but he maintains that the comparative study of religions should not try to elevate "one Faith at the expense of another." In a touchingly disingenuous expression of classic Orientalist parochialism and mock impartiality, he goes on to say (pp. xi–xii) that,

> [u]nlike Christian apologetics of the older type, Comparative Religion holds no brief for the defence of Christianity. If, as the result of an unbiased comparison between that Faith and one or more other Religions, it should become manifest that the former must be pronounced more worthy than any of its competitors, that fact (and the proofs of it) will certainly be welcomed and recorded. . . . The demands of truth are paramount, and they must at all costs be respected.

Needless to say, it just so happened that the "facts" most often proved the superiority of Christianity.

36. JL, *Religions of China,* 278.

37. Ibid., and p. 242.

38. See the discussion for the evidence for the resurrection of Christ, i.e., that Christ foretold his death and resurrection; the testimony of eyewitnesses; and because of its acceptance by the early Church (ibid., 277–82). The crucial context for understanding Legge's views concerning Christian miracles is found in his sermon and lecture on "comparative" mythology; see pages 270–71.

39. In his memoirs Legge makes it clear that, even though he rejected its ethics and did not agree with all of the doctrinal positions, the Westminster *Shorter Catechism* was the shaping influence of his religious life. At eighty-two, Legge was still quoting the 107th, and last, question and answer (see "Notes of My Life" [1897], 8).

40. See JL, *Religions of China,* 247–48, for a discussion of his evidence for the supernatural:

> We dare not deny the possibility of God's supernatural, or rather extraordinary, interference both in nature and in providence. When any such interference is asserted, we dare not disbelieve without examination. Did it take place or not? The conclusion of our judgment allows its possibility; the yearning of our hearts suggests its probability. The question comes to be one of evidence, and we are not without sufficient tests of truth to guide us to a conclusion in which we feel assured our minds will be able to repose.

Müller, like Renan more than like David Friedrich Strauss, wanted to emphasize the "truly human character of Christ" over any supernatural elements or events. In a letter to his wife, June 25, 1880, he says, commenting on her attendance at the Oberammergau passion play (Bodleian, MS. Eng. d. 2344), "I feel sure just now nothing is more wanted than to be powerfully impressed with the truly human character of Christ. It has almost vanished under the extravagant phrasiology [*sic*] of hymns and creeds—and yet how much greater is the simple story of his unselfish life than all the superlatives of later theology."

For Müller's identification with Renan's understanding of Jesus, see his letter to Renan, July 3, 1880 (Georgina Müller, *Life and Letters,* 92–93).

41. JL, *Religions of China,* 287. Samuel Johnson's work is specifically referred to in a footnote to this quoted passage.

42. JL, *Notions of the Chinese Concerning God and Spirits: with an Examination of the Defense of an Essay on the Proper Rendering of the Words Elohim and Theos, into the Chinese Language by William Boone, D.D.* (Hong Kong: Hong Kong Register Office, 1852; reprint, Taipei: Ch'eng Wen, 1971).

43. JL, *Religions of China,* 248.

44. Ibid., 277.

45. Ibid., 308.

46. Ibid., 310. "So-called Christians" referred to divisions among the populace (as suggested by the newly administered censuses of the Victorian era) as much as it characterized different countries.

47. I am thinking here of his long transformative professional association, working partnership, and tentative transcultural friendship with Chinese such as Ho Tsun-sheen, Hong Rengan, and Wang Tao, as well as his encounter with the querulous Chinese father concerned about his son's moral development in Western lands (see page 78).

48. JL, *Religions of China,* 310.

49. Ibid., 4.

50. Ibid., 5.

51. Regardless of the popular nature of these lectures, Legge is not reluctant to display his awareness of the key methodological issues and to show that he has read the most important authors in the comparative sciences (especially Max Müller, but also Charles Hardwick, Samuel Johnson, James Freeman Clarke, Cornelis Tiele, and, by way of inference, Edward Tylor). In the published version of the lectures, Legge adds rather elaborate notes that inform his readers of his understandably broad acquaintance with scholars in sinological Orientalism (e.g., Regis, Edkins, McClatchie [which JL spells M'Clatchie], Morrison, Williams, Callery, Chalmers, Eitel, Doolittle, Douglas, Rémusat, Julien, and Giles) and in the native Chinese commentarial tradition (e.g., Xu Shan/Hsu Shan, Dai Dong/Tai Tung, Liu Mi, Zhu Xi/Chu Hsi, and Han Shan). See also JL to James Alston, October 13, 1884 (CWM/China/Personal/Legge/Box 8). Although he does not refer to Tylor by name, Legge indicates his Müllerian suspicions about the theory of animism in this letter: "Endeavours to account for the worship of God and of ancestors from an earlier animism and nature worship are mere speculations for which the reliable records of the people do not appear to afford any sufficient grounds."

52. JL, *Religions of China,* 6–7. Legge makes specific reference to Müller's "Essay on Comparative Mythology" here.

53. Ibid., 7.

54. Ibid., 8.

55. Ibid., 8–16.

56. Tiele, who, along with Müller, is often considered one of the founding fathers of the comparative study of religions, was professor of the philosophy and his-

tory of religion at Leiden. Legge specifically refers to Tiele's *Outlines of the History of Religion to the Spread of the Universal Religion,* trans. J. Estlin Carpenter (London: Trübner, 1877).

57. JL, *Religions of China,* 18. Throughout this section of his discussion of Tiele, Legge makes the point that the strong monotheistic convictions in ancient China "prevented the spiritual potencies" from "being regarded as independent and being elevated to the place of gods." Moreover, the wooden spirit tablets of Chinese ancestor worship could not be considered as fetishism or idolatry: "The table is not regarded as in itself either supernatural or sacred; and it has operated to prevent the rise of idolatry in the Confucian religion of China" (p. 22). Later on Legge observes that the inferior worship of nature spirits was "subordinate to the homage due to God," but no doubt "resulted from a mistaken idea of His government in creation" (p. 26).

58. Legge, in fact, notes that much of his discussion in this section (ibid., 27–29) was "taken almost verbatim" from his prolegomena to the Chinese classics (*Chinese Classics* [1861], 2:193–94; *Chinese Classics* [1865], 3:152). According to Legge, the expression "Heaven and Earth" was only a "new style of speech" that arose after the Zhou dynasty of the twelfth century B.C. It was not, however, originally a reference to dualistic deities but to the "two places" (i.e., the altars of heaven and earth) of worship of the one God. The danger was that such language could lead "to serious misconception concerning the oldest religious ideas and worship of the nation." As Legge was pleased to report, this was a danger that "Confucius himself happily came to avert" (see *Religions of China,* 30–31).

59. Ibid., 31.

60. There is evidence throughout the *Religions of China* that Legge was at that time hard at work on his translation of the *Record of Rites,* the work that would be his final contribution to his set of the Confucian classics (see, for example, ibid., 153 n. D).

61. Legge's discussion of the *Book of Changes* and McClatchie takes up eight pages (ibid., 35–43). On the results of using comparative methods, Legge says (p. 36): "I cannot admit that, as Chinese students, I, and others who think with me, have neglected comparative mythology. I have looked much into it, but I have looked more into the Yi itself. It would be passing strange if Confucius, with all his appendixes to it, had not been able to make its meaning sufficiently plain without our resorting to writings much more recent than itself, and whose authors had never heard of it."

62. Ibid., 38–39.

63. Ibid., 40–43. Legge tells us that he is thinking particularly of Confucius's appendix "Discourses on the Diagrams" *(guashuo/kua-shuo),* which reminds him of "Thomson's Hymn to the Seasons." This is an allusion to Ephesians 1:23, in which in the King James Version, the church is described as "his body, the fullnes of him that filleth all in all."

64. In 1852 in *Notions of the Chinese Concerning God and Spirits,* JL had given extended translations of these prayers. Pages 43–51 of *Religions of China* are specifically concerned with an elaborate description of the emperor's "special solstitial" prayers and services and need to be read with Legge's actions at the Altar of Heaven in mind. Clearly Legge had this in mind, as his participatory description of the services indicates: "But I hasten on. The selected day arrived, and we stand, with the emperor and his suite, at the round altar. We watch and listen to them while they engage in the different parts of their service . . . etc., etc." (p. 46).

65. On the Ming reforms, see Jeffrey F. Meyer, *The Dragons of Tiananmen: Being as a Sacred City* (Columbia, S.C.: University of South Carolina Press, 1991), 21–24.

66. JL, *Religions of China,* 53–55. In *The Notions of the Chinese Concerning God and Spirits,* Legge compared these rituals to the Solomonic temple rites and sacrifices, but did not distinguish the propitiatory sacrifices from other kinds.

67. JL, *Religions of China,* 58. Cf. "Confucius the Sage," 69–70. In this essay Legge makes the interesting observation (p. 70) that whatever the shortcomings of a religious worship restricted to the Chinese emperor, it was not as bad as the "separation" inherent in the Roman Catholic system of priests:

> The restriction of the direct, solemn worship of God to the Emperor has been unfortunate, excluding the people generally from that communion with Him which is the highest privilege of man and the most conducive to the beauty and excellence of his whole character; but better this even than a priestly class, claiming to stand between men and God, themselves not better than other men, and in no respect more highly gifted, and yet shutting up the way into the holiest that is open to all, and assuming to be able by rites and performances of theirs to dispense blessings which can only be obtained from the great God with Whom all have to do.

68. JL, *Religions of China,* 69–70.

69. Ibid., 70.

70. I know of no place where Legge refers to either Smith or McLennan. However, in 1889, in his essay "Confucius the Sage," Legge specifically, though critically, alludes to Herbert Spencer's social Darwinist views on the rise of ancestor worship (p. 71). "How this worship took its rise, I am unable to say. Herbert Spencer holds that 'the rudimentary form of all religion is the propitiation of dead ancestors who are supposed to be still existing, and to be capable of working good or evil to their descendants.' This view is open to the criticism which I made on the Confucian sacrifices generally,—that our idea of propitiation is not in them."

It almost seems that Legge retreats from the broad hints he made about the sociological functionality of Chinese religion in his 1877 paper. Why he was reluctant to pursue these earlier ideas, and whether it had anything to do with the Robertson Smith controversy (see pages 20–22, 219), is not clear.

71. JL, *Religions of China,* 73–80. It is worth noting that at one point Legge compares the practice of the ancient Chinese kings of carrying the tablets of the ancestors and spirits of the land with the "army of Israel" carrying around the "Ark of God" (p. 76). See also the complementary discussion in JL, *Whole Duty of Man,* 14–15.

72. JL, *Religions of China,* 87. Legge, it should be noted, altered his earlier view (*Chinese Classics* [1861], vol. 1) that the ceremonies to Master Kong at the ubiquitous "Confucian temples" were but another example of the corrupt elevation of ancestral figures or sages to the status of tutelary deities. He says that such practices concerning Kongzi displayed a "homage of gratitude" and "not" the more compromising "worship of adoration" (see JL, "Confucius the Sage," 72).

73. JL, *Religions of China,* 88. In his concluding section, Legge notes that the Christian "honour" of parents is "higher" than the mere Confucian "support" of parents (p. 256). It should be noted that Legge refers to the "full and graphic" account of this defect as presented in M.T. Yates's "Essay on Ancestral Worship" (*Records of the General Conference of the Protestant Missionaries of China, Shanghai, May 10–14* [Shanghai: Presbyterian Mission Press, 1878]), given at the 1877 missionary

, conference at Shanghai. As Legge says, "He unfortunately sees only its dark side" (p. 87 n. 1; see also note 1 on p. 88). Yates, we should recall, was one of those who condemned Legge's views. Moreover, the related practices of worshiping the departed great is not in itself anything shocking since "the memory of the just and the good is blessed all the world over." The danger here is the tendency to deify the exalted dead, building temples and offering sacrifices to them. It is at this point that Legge notes Confucius's warning that "to go beyond the circle of one's family and worship was nothing but flattery, a thing unauthorized, and done with a mercenary aim" (ibid.). See also Ernst Faber, "A Critique of the Chinese Notions and Practice of Filial Piety" (read before the Conference on Canton Missions, April 1878), *The Chinese Recorder* 9 (September–October 1878): 329–43; (November–December 1878): 401–19; (January–February 1879): 1–16; (March–April 1879): 83–96; (May–June 1879): 163–74; (July–August 1879): 243–53. Faber specifically argues against Yates and claims that "Chinese boys are not less filial than European Christian boys." One bit of evidence for this is Faber's observation that the Chinese ambassador to Berlin had his pigtail pulled by some German boys!

74. In *Whole Duty of Man* (p. 22) Legge says that the lack of any "glow of piety" in Confucius's utterances is one of the severe defects in Confucianism. It is worth comparing John Morison's writings on the duty of family members here. In many ways there was more reciprocity in Dissenter and Congregationalist family duties than might be expected. Important also is the relationship between the "glow of affection" and the "glow of piety." Many of these values are practically described in John Morison's Evangelical handbooks on marriage, which linked religious teachings and family devotions (especially day-by-day prayer and scriptural readings).

75. It may be noted that both of Legge's later comparative writings (i.e., the essays *Whole Duty of Man*, 1883, and "Confucius the Sage," 1889) indicate that the bedrock comparative issue in both an Evangelical and Confucian sense is the moral question of duty (which includes ideas of sacrifice).

76. JL, *Religions of China*, 103–4.

77. Legge observes (ibid., 107), for example, that the Chinese views on the "leading of the husband and the following of the wife" and the general direction of "outside affairs" by the husband and "all matters inside the family" by the wife are basically congruent with Western values; both also need to beware of the "strong-minded" wife who seeks to regulate "things outside as well as inside the family" (see also ibid., 107–12, 268). In his conclusion, Legge stresses that Christianity is higher than Confucianism because it "vindicates . . . a position of equality" for women. Because of her "feebler frame" she is rendered "subordinate" to the male head of the family. These were obviously very sensitive points for Legge and are found in both his *Whole Duty of Man* (pp. 26–28) and "Confucius the Sage." Moving on to another topic in this section of *Religions of China*, Legge next takes up the seeming paradox that, while the Chinese practice of ancestor worship obviously affirmed the afterlife existence of the dead, the "Confucian religion" generally said "very little, and nothing definite, as to the conditions of . . . future existence." Related to this is the problem of the apparent absence of any idea of future retribution in the afterlife and the eventual emergence of the theory of a retribution visited upon one's posterity. In this case Confucius himself only confirms "the existence of the soul after death" but says "nothing of the character of that existence" (ibid., 121–22).

78. Ibid., 123.

79. Ibid., 262.

80. Ibid., 149.

81. Ibid., 147–49.

82. Legge actually refers to his "pilgrimage to the tomb of the master outside the city of Chu-fau in Shan-tung" (ibid., 135).

83. Ibid., 136.

84. See also Legge's restatement of his credo of "dispassion" in *Whole Duty of Man,* 33.

85. See also JL, "Confucius the Sage," 66, where it is noted that Confucius's "greatest achievement" in his moral teaching was "his inculcation of the Golden Rule which he delivered at least five separate times" (referring to the principle of *shu* or reciprocity: "what you do not want done to yourself, do not do to others"). He adds that, despite this, Confucius "did not, or would not, appreciate the still higher rule" of returning kindness for hatred. The issue of what is silver and gold in morality is also stressed in the pamphlet *Whole Duty of Man,* 19–21. It is here (p. 19) that Legge emphasizes the defective, inverted, or silver way that Confucius's rule is stated: "What ye would not that men should do to you, do not ye do to them." It is also interesting that in this essay Legge is pained to point out that, contra Dr. Matheson's views, Confucius's rule could not have influenced the formulation of Christ's more positive principle (p. 21). The one place Legge does locate a positve rule is in a section of the *Doctrine of the Mean* (*Chinese Classics* [1861], 1:48–49, 109, 394–95), but this is questionably by Confucius (not even Zhu Xi would grant its authenticity). So it seems that Legge is stretching his academic precision in order to show a "comparativist sensibility."

86. JL, *Religions of China,* 139–40.

87. Ibid., 145. These issues are discussed in the prolegomena, *Chinese Classics* (1872), 5:12–16, 22, 38–49, 49–51.

88. Legge makes a special point of criticizing this point as promulgated by the American generalist scholar James Freeman Clarke in his best-selling *Ten Great Religions* (see *Religions of China,* 154–56).

89. JL, *Whole Duty of Man,* 22. In this essay (pp. 30–31), he says: "[Confucius] was a great man and a good man, and deserved well of his own country and of the world. Yet it is a true saying that 'the best of men are but men at the best.' He was not a perfect character." The contrast here is with the divine and "perfect Teacher and Exemplar," Christ.

90. JL, *Religions of China,* 149. Even in 1893 in the Oxford edition of the first volume of the *Classics,* Legge continues to charge Confucius with a lack of religious zeal that tended to lead others into an a-religious and even irreligious lifestyle.

91. See Herrlee G. Creel, *What Is Taoism?* (Chicago and London: University of Chicago Press, 1970). In fairness to Creel, I should note that his original essay on Daoism was written in 1956, only being revised and updated in the 1970 version. Creel exemplifies the last of the great traditional Anglo-American sinological Orientalists before the late-twentieth-century scholarly revolution in the Western study of Chinese religions, especially Daoism. A little bit like a twentieth-century reincarnation of Legge, Creel had a divinity school background that he put aside in favor of a more purely academic and aggressively secular career as a professor of sinology

at the University of Chicago. Also like Legge, but with his own twentieth-century twist, Creel was primarily known as a scholar interested in classical Chinese tradition. In Creel's case, this refers especially to his translations of oracle bone and bronze inscription texts as the primordial records of Chinese origins, his interpretive work on the spectacular archaeological discoveries of the earliest dynasties, and his secularized latter-day term question speculations concerning Shangdi and Tian as a mostly ancestral and totemistic ancestral High God. Creel's career shows a special concern for Confucius, albeit for his largely irreligious greatness as a rational moralist and political teacher, and a habit of teaching the Chinese language that, in the spirit of Legge's methods at Oxford, stressed the reading of classical texts such as the *Book of Filial Piety,* the *Mencius,* and the *Analects.* See H.G. Creel, *Confucius and the Chinese Way* (New York: Harper & Row, 1949, 1960). Aside from his rejection of the existence of an archaic Chinese monotheism, Creel's understanding of Kongzi is quite similar to Legge's view—an indebtedness not fully acknowledged.

92. JL, *Religions of China,* 159–60.

93. As Legge notes, the earlier name of Rationalism for the Daoist tradition was "admirably calculated to lead the mind astray as to what the religion is." The term *rationality* is primarily to be faulted for the suggestion that the *dao* is some kind of conscious being with the quality or faculty of reason (ibid., 160).

94. For the description of philosophical Daoism, see ibid., 229. For the discussion of the so-called corrupt Daoist religion, see ibid., 160–202. It is worth noting that, in addition to his own experience and the accounts of Western scholars such as Edkins, Eitel, and Chalmers, Legge primarily relies upon the *Tungjian gangmu* (The general mirror of history) for his information.

95. The use of the word *pope* to refer to the head of the Heavenly Masters sect of Daoism in China does not derive from Legge, but I have not tried to document the very first English usage (perhaps by either Gützlaff or Edkins). Regardless of the anti-Catholic bias, it is clear that Legge perceived the nature and history of the "popes of Taoism" to be a serious issue that deserved further study (ibid., 233–36).

96. Buddhism, especially the later more corrupt Mahayana Buddhism of China and Japan, was also often equated with Roman Catholicism. Buddhism could also be seen as a reformation of Hinduism and the Buddha compared with Luther! See, for example, Almond, *British Discovery of Buddhism,* 73–76, 123–26. Virulent anti-Catholicism was a problem throughout most of the Victorian period in Great Britain and America. See D.G. Paz, *Popular Anti-Catholicism in Mid-Victorian England* (Stanford, Calif.: Stanford University Press, 1992); J.H.S. Burleigh, *A Church History of Scotland* (London: Oxford University Press, 1960), 362 (on the antipapist movement of the 1840s and 1850s); and Gerald Parsons, ed., *Religion in Victorian England* (Manchester: Manchester University Press, 1988), 146–83.

97. One of the problems associated with Catholicism was the tendency to compromise itself syncretistically with heathenism. This was a recurrent theme in Protestant missionary writing—e.g., W.S. Ament, "Romanism in China," *The Chinese Recorder* 14 (January–February 1883): 47–55. For a general discussion of the element of anti-Catholicism in the rise of the comparative study of religions, see especially Jonathan Z. Smith, *Drudgery Divine: On the Comparison of Early Christianities and the Religions of Late Antiquity* (Chicago: University of Chicago Press, 1990).

98. JL, *Religions of China*, 255. From a native Chinese comparativist perspective it could just as well be argued that Protestantism was hardly a revival of some originally pure Christianity. Rather, it represented the emergence of a new, and strangely heterodox, religion (*jidu jiao* in Chinese) that had been syncretistically influenced by various social and political developments in sixteenth- and seventeenth-century Europe. At the very least it could be seen to be a grossly denatured transformation of the ancient or "classic" Christian religion *(tianzhu jiao)* bifurcated (in a way amazingly similar to Legge's understanding of archaic Confucianism) into the imperial-papal worship of the High God-Ancestor (Tianzhu, Shangdi, Tian) and the popular worship of ancestors and spirits. For a discussion of the Chinese perception of the religion of the early Catholic missionaries, see Jacques Gernet, *China and the Christian Impact*, trans. Janet Lloyd (New York: Cambridge University Press, 1985).

99. JL, *Religions of China*, 176. This stands in oppostion to the claim made by Legge in 1850–1852 that the imperial sacrifices were the monopoly of the emperor, but that worship and respect of Tian and Shangdi was common among the people. Part of the problem here with Daoism is that Legge identified the *sanqing* and multiple Shangdi figures in the Daoist religion as a "proper polytheism," in contrast with the "original monotheism" of "Confucianism."

100. Ibid., 164–67. There is, however, one difference from the Buddhist clergy that Legge is pleased to notice—that the Daoists have always refused "to submit to the yoke of celibacy" (ibid., 181). As a matter of fact, there are some celibate Daoist sects (see Isabelle Robinet, *La histoire du taoïsme des origines au xiv siècle* [Paris: Éditions du Cerf, 1991]).

101. JL, *Religions of China*, 168–69. Legge's discussion of religious Daoism really pertains only to one sectarian movement within a complex and diverse tradition—that is, the Heavenly Masters school. For a more informed and empathetic description of this tradition, see particularly K. Schipper, *The Taoist Body*, trans. Karen C. Duval (Berkeley and Los Angeles: University of California Press, 1993); see also N. J. Girardot's foreword to this book, "Kristofer Schipper and the Resurrection of the Taoist Body," ix–xviii. On the overall issue of the presence of "chaos" in Daoist tradition, see N. J. Girardot, *Myth and Meaning in Early Taoism* (Berkeley and Los Angeles: University of California Press, 1983).

102. JL, *Religions of China*, 182.

103. Ibid., 170. This statement should be compared with the revisionary portrait of the religious, intellectual, and aesthetic pleasures of the Heavenly Masters tradition seen in Schipper's *Taoist Body* and in John Lagerwey, *Taoist Ritual in Chinese Society and History* (New York: Macmillan, 1987).

104. Legge presents his discussion of the courts of purgatory as a new discovery of sinological scholarship based on the translation and work of the young councilor-scholar and later Legge's sinological nemesis, Herbert Giles. Legge had visited Daoist and Buddhist monasteries while in China and had actually translated a popular novel replete with ideas about postmortem purgatories, so it is curious that he presents this information here as something of a revelation. If a living religious belief such as this were not recorded in a scriptural text (in this case, the "Divine Panorama, published by the mercy of Yu-ti"), it seemed to be invisible (or at least unmemorable) to a missionary-scholar—even though its reality was mostly a phenomenological matter of what was iconographically imagined, ritually

spoken, and liturgically enacted. On Buddhist purgatories, see Stephen F. Teiser, *The Ghost Festival in Medieval China* (Princeton: Princeton University Press, 1988). On the "mercenary purposes" of the Daoist priests, see JL, *Religions of China*, 201.

105. Ibid., 200–2.

106. JL, "Confucius the Sage" (1889), 78. In 1883, in the pamphlet *Whole Duty of Man,* he argues that the aggressive side of Christian mission should be our own internal "struggle" to become true Christians. China will only be changed (p. 36) "[b]y our showing them, politically, commercially, and in other ways, we are ruled by the principles of love and righteousness, which blend together in 'the golden rule' of Christ, 'Whatsoever ye would that men should do unto you, even so do ye also unto them.'"

107. JL, *Religions of China*, 296–97. See also his discussion of the Daoist woman who became a convert to Christianity, pp. 275–76.

108. Ibid., 209.

109. Ibid., 209–12.

110. Ibid., 214–16.

111. Ibid., 216–24.

112. Ibid., 226.

113. Ibid., 227. Legge makes particular reference to Douglas's *Confucianism and Taouism,* a book that he had reviewed. The most problematic chapters in the *Daode jing* (i.e., those that seem to show the *dao* as preceding Heaven, *di,* or God) are chapters 1, 6, and especially 4. Legge's logic concerning chapter 4 is especially strained.

114. Ibid., 229.

115. In the best sense of the Reformation interpretation of Paul's Epistle to the Romans, the special genius of Christianity is found in its doctrines of the "propitiatory sacrifice" of Christ's atoning death for all humankind and in Christ's supernatural resurrection. On the doctrinal significance of "propitiatory sacrifice" and its supposed absence in Chinese religion, see ibid., 288–97. As Legge says (p. 297), "the sacrificial death of Christ is of the essence of Christianity."

116. Ibid., 242–43.

117. JL, *Whole Duty of Man,* 4–7.

118. JL, *Religions of China*, 242–43. It may be noted that the good *(kalos)* in the Pauline sense goes beyond the moral realm (see, for example, 1 Thess. 5:21 and Phil. 4:8).

119. JL, *Whole Duty of Man,* 23.

120. JL, "The Bearing of Our Knowledge of Comparative Religions on Christian Missions," a lecture given November 15, 1886 (CWM/South China/Personal/Legge/Box 4).

121. See JL, *Religions of China*, 283–86, on his argument concerning the special organic unity of the Old and New Testaments, which constitutes another "proof" of their special divine or revealed status—especially since "Jesus Christ is Himself the theme of them from the first to the last." The Confucian classics, in contrast, have (p. 284) "'no organic unity, no internal cohesion other than belongs to human writings produced in the same nation in the course of many centuries.'" Here Legge is quoting the views of the theologian Henry Rogers as expressed in Rogers's essay "The Superhuman Origin of the Bible, Inferred from Itself." In the *Whole Duty of Man* (pp. 23–24), Legge also refers to Rogers's *Eclipse of Faith.* On Rogers, see his

The Eclipse of Faith; Or, A Visit to A Religious Sceptic, 4th ed. (Boston: Crosby, Nichols, 1853).

122. JL, *Religions of China,* 287–88. This perspective can also be seen as an extension of principles learned at Highbury College in the 1830s, a heritage received from Reformation humanists.

123. The question of human and divine "duty" is also important in the essay "Confucius the Sage," 61.

124. JL, *Religions of China,* 33.

125. JL, *Whole Duty of Man,* 33–34, mentions that they are cheerful, temperate, industrious, kindly, faithful in engagements, and honest.

126. Ibid., 34. It may be noted that these passages recall the concluding section in the *Religions of China* discussing the moral quandary presented by Guo Songtao.

127. Legge's understanding of the failures of Confucianism were not only caused by his Christian bias, but also reflected popular eighteenth- and nineteenth-century native Chinese criticism of Ruist teachings and institutions (seen, for example, in the eighteenth-century novel *Zhulin waishi* [The unofficial history of the literati]).

128. Ibid., 35.

129. Ibid., 36, 33, 35.

130. Ibid., 36, 34.

131. JL to Marian Willetts Hunt, March 3, 1881. University of London, School of African and Oriental Studies, Legge Archive, MS. 380476/38. Marian, Hannah Mary's only child by her first marriage, had recently married and had given birth to a child, Colin.

132. See, for example, the anonymous reviews in the *North-China Herald,* November 11, 1880, pp. 441–42; the *China Review* 9 (1880): 42–44 (most probably written by Eitel); and the *Spectator* 54 (January 8, 1881): 48–50.

133. *China Review* 9 (1880): 42, 44. It is worth noting that the reviewer was happy to see that Legge did not change his views in response to the "rebuke administered to him" at the Shanghai Conference in 1877.

134. "The Religions of China," *Spectator* 54 (January 8, 1881): 48–50.

135. Ibid., 49. In this context, the reviewer remarks on the syncretistic fears of many missionaries—their concern that Christianity not be "grafted on the ancient stock of Chinese religion." It is also worth noting that for this reviewer (p. 49), "philosophical Taoism" represented the "quintessence of China": that is, a tradition without any "trace of a wholesome political life" and a focus on "humility and harmlessness, resignation, and an empty mind." It was this that "made Oriental despotism possible."

136. Ibid., 50.

137. See Inquirer [A.P. Happer], "The State Religion of China," *The Chinese Recorder* 12 (May–June 1881): 149–92. This is a review of Sir John Davis's *The Chinese: A General Description of the Empire of China and Its Inhabitants* (New York: Harper and Brothers, 1848), Walter Medhurst's *China* (Boston, Mass.: Crocker and Brewster, 1838), S. Wells Williams's *The Middle Kingdom: A Survey of the Geography, Government, Education, Social Life, Arts, Religion, etc., of the Chinese Empire and Its Inhabitants,* 2 vols. (New York: John Wiley, 1847), J. Edkins's *Religion in China* (London: Trübner, 1878), Robert K. Douglas's *Confucianism and Taouism* (London: Society for Promoting Christian Knowledge, 1879), and (especially) Legge's *Religions of China.* See

also William Muirhead's letter to the editor *(The Chinese Recorder)* 12 [May–June 1881]: 302–6) concerning Inquirer's lame attempt to revive the term question. Muirhead reasonably suggests that the Chinese should be left to settle the issue among themselves.

138. This is not to say that the *Chinese Recorder,* even during Happer's heyday, was not open to different points of view. The journal is so interesting precisely because there was so much real debate over these issues for the next two decades. For documentation of this debate, see my discussion in the next three chapters.

139. The emerging scholarly tradition of "comparative religions" at this time was by no means monolithic and encompassed a broad range of presupppositions and methods (as variously seen in the work of such leading practitioners as Müller, Tiele, Lang, Réville, Frazer, and Tylor).

140. "A Student," "The Sacred Books of the East, Translated by Various Oriental Scholars and Edited by F. Max Müller, Vol. I, Oxford, 1879," *The Chinse Recorder* 13 (January–February 1882): 17–30.

141. Ibid., 25.

142. On the ever-present danger of syncretism connected with the Leggian position, see, for example, A. Sydenstricker, review of *"Christianity the Completion of Confucianism,* Translated by the Author, Rev. Pastor P. Kranz," *The Chinese Recorder* 29 (December 1898): 614–16. Sydenstricker is incensed that Kranz still proposes the theory of Christianity's "completing" Confucianism. There is, he says (p. 615), something "so repugnant [in] the thought of blending the two that one recoils from the thought with the greatest dislike." In a reply to this article, Kranz (pp. 616–17 in the same issue) defends the "fulfillment" thesis that allows for the preservation of all that is good in the "old religion" of Confucianism. Furthermore, he finds solace in the good company of Legge, Faber, Edkins, and "many other Sinologues." It is noteworthy that by the end of the century Kranz could in good faith suggest that there were "many" sinologues who supported the Leggian position. But it is also Kranz who misuses Legge (citing only his *Chinese Classics* [1861] vols. 1 and 2 and often out of context) to show how "bad" Confucianism and Confucius were. See page 726, note 18, for a listing of Kranz's series of lectures, published in the *Chinese Recorder* in 1898.

143. See "Is the Missionary Spirit Decaying?" *Congregationalist* 2 (1882): 443–53. As this anonymous author says (p. 451) about the comparative view, "If the world does not need salvation, or if there be many possible saviours, of whom Christ is only one; or if His salvation is adapted only to a portion of the human family, an elect company, or men found in a certain plane of intelligence or civilization, then the wisdom of our procedure in sending the gospel to the heathen is open to question."

144. JL, *The Late Mrs. Legge. A Letter to Her Brother, The Reverend Joseph Johnston, of Fremantle, Western Ausralia, From Her Husband* (Oxford: E.C. Alden, 1881).

145. On Thomas and James Granville Legge, see the *Dollar Magazine* 24 (1925): 113–16; the *Dollar Magazine* for 1932, p. 91; and for 1940, pp. 23–24. Both sons were published authors and had relatively distinguished careers related to education. Thomas was the first Medical Inspector of Factories and Workshops and was knighted; James Granville (who had actually spent some time in London with the decadant literary set associated with Oscar Wilde) became an Inspector of Reformatory and Industrial Schools and, later, a well-known Director of Education for Liverpool.

146. Hannah Legge seemed to have a kind of constitutional morbidity, an aspect of her character that is underscored by her habit of writing "when I die" letters to her children and husband.

147. JL, *The Late Mrs. Legge*, 4. On Joseph Lister, see *Victorian Britain: An Encyclopedia*, ed. Sally Mitchell (New York and London: Garland, 1988), 455.

148. JL, *The Late Mrs. Legge*, 7–8.

149. Ibid., 9. We see the trappings here of a rather typical Victorian genre of the "death-bed scene"—see, for example, Elizabeth Longford, "Piety in Queen Victoria's Reign," pamphlet: Friends of Dr. Williams's Library, Twenty-seventh Lecture (London: Dr. Williams's Trust, 1973), 16–17.

150. JL, *The Late Mrs. Legge*, pp. 9–10. Because of uncertainty over the cause of her death and the degree to which the operation was a factor, an autopsy was performed by Lister and another doctor. The doctors wrote Legge to say that their postmortem examination showed that the perforation of the stomach due to peritonitis was accompanied by a "degeneration of the heart which was incompatible with the prolongation of life." Though they assured him that the "operation was in no way responsible" for her death, Legge was less than assured on this point. In his grief and guilt, he finally says that he came to be satisfied with the doctors' explanation of her death. "It is," he said (p. 12), "sufficient for me to know that before the appearance of that tumor, my darling carried two sentences of death in her system. And yet we were so unconscious of this, and so happy!" It is interesting that Lister's perfection of aseptic surgical techniques came about only toward the end of the 1880s (see *Victorian Britain,* 455).

151. In *The Late Mrs. Legge*, 16–17, Legge says that he specifically appealed to the vicar's higher "Christian regard" for "other Christians beyond the limits of [his] own communion." But this was to no avail and Legge even suspected that his bluntness about his Nonconformity may have soured the situation. Legge knew, for example, that "he had indeed given sites to bury one individual and another, connected with the University, who were not parishioners; but my case was different." The difference, Legge felt sure, was his and his wife's marginal status as Nonconformists.

152. As Legge declares after this last insult (ibid., 19–20):

> It was a great mistake in Osborne Morgan and others when carrying the Burial Laws' Amendment Act, that they did not expressly declare in it the right of all who buried their dead in any churchyard or parochial cemetery to the use of the mortuary chapel in it. The error will have to be remedied, and the sooner it is so the better. The clergy of the Established Church will yet find that they have committed a fault in trying to exclude Nonconformists from these buildings.

There is an interesting parallel here with Robert Morrison's burial of his wife in Macao outside the city gates (see JL, "Notes of My Life") that shows the ongoing battle throughout the nineteenth century between Nonconformists and the established religion.

153. As Legge says (*The Late Mrs. Legge*, 33): "I do not mean to say that either Hannah or myself considered it a matter of indifference what theological views the children became accustomed to hold concerning the facts of revelation; but it was

impressed on them that a religious life, essentially the same, might be found co-existing with different systems of ecclesiastical administration and doctrinal creed."

154. Ibid., 21–22. Helen Edith's reflections on her mother are also worth noting (undated letter to Marian [CWM/China/Personal/Legge/Box 10] and excerpts from notebook entitled "From Letters Written by Me and Family"):

> A full inward Renaissance never came to our Mother and yet in spite of it, how infinitely tender and more beautiful her spirit was than those of many modern enlightened women who have had all education and advantages. Put in the dungeon of Calvinism, dominated by the ideas that beauty is a snare, pleasure a sin, the world a fleeting show, man fallen and lost, death the only certainty, judgement inevitable, life everlasting, heaven hard to win—it is amazing how the tender grace of her should show through. . . .

CHAPTER SIX. TRANSLATOR LEGGE: CLOSING THE CONFUCIAN CANON, 1882–1885

1. See Helen Edith Legge to Marian Willetts Hunt, November 2, 1881, and January 6, 1882 (Council for World Mission [hereafter cited as CWM] China/Personal/Legge/Box 10; Helen Edith Legge, notebook, "From Letters Written by Me and Family"). It seems that Legge only attended the congress in Berlin and did not give a paper. This congress was tarnished by the spectacle of Monier-Williams and Müller showing off their prize Orientals (see R. N. Cust, "The International Congresses of Orientalists," *Asiatic Quarterly Review,* 3d ser., 4 [1897]: 79–98). Cust's descriptions of this affair are worth recording.

> One great blot must be recorded as a warning to future congresses. The grotesque idea was started of producing natives of oriental countries as illustrations of a paper: thus the Boden professor of Sanskrit at Oxford produced a real live Indian pandit, and made him go through the ritual of Brahmanical prayer and worship before a hilarious assembly: this shocks the religious sense of all thoughtful men. Prof. Max Müller of Oxford produced two rival Japanese priests [Bunyiu Nanjio and Kenjiu Kasawara], who exhibited their gifts; it had the appearance of two showmen exhibiting their monkeys. . . . In the Aryan section Prof. Max Müller occupied a good deal of time . . . his object was to note the shortcomings and want of liberality of Great Britain in the matter of Oriental Studies. It was surprising to hear these charges from one, who had received so much in grants from the Indian Government. . . . Prof. Monier Williams and Pandit Shamaji Krishna-Varma, gave what appeared to me an improper exhibition of the modes of religious worship of the Hindu, holding them up to ridicule. If the Hindus in their towns were to exhibit Anglican Ritual, we should feel offended.

2. Jowett, regardless of his intellectual and religious liberality, is a good example of the continuing social coolness toward Nonconformists on the part of the Anglican establishment at Oxford. With regard to university affairs, however, Jowett was a

prominent and influential supporter of the small but growing group of Nonconformist dons such as Legge, Green, Murray, and Horton. For Jowett's often contradictory attitudes toward Nonconformists, see Evelyn Abbott and Lewis Campbell, *The Life and Letters of Benjamin Jowett,* 2 vols. (London: John Murray, 1897).

3. It is interesting that after Legge's death, some of his children and grandchildren gravitated to the Anglican Church.

4. Concerning the question of Green's actual religious identity and affiliation, see Melvin Richter, *The Politics of Conscience: T. H. Green and His Age* (Cambridge, Mass.: Harvard University Press, 1964), 84–89, 115–18.

5. There are several different canonical groupings of ancient authoritative Ruist texts in traditional China (involving, variously, collections of five, six, seven, nine, twelve, and thirteen texts), but the most revered of these is the Han collection of Five Classics (*Shu jing* [The book of historical documents], *Shi jing* [The book of poetry], *Chunqiu* [Spring and autumn annals], *Yi jing* [The book of changes], and *Li ji* [The record of rites]; sometimes there is reference to a certain *Lijing* [The book of ritual], which is an assemblage of three ritual texts: the *Zhou li, Yi li,* and *Li ji*) and—added after the Song dynasty—the Four Books (*Lunyu* [The Confucian analects], *Mengzi* [The works of Mencius], *Daxue* [The great learning], and *Zhonyong* [The doctrine of the mean], the last two of which are found in one of the versions of the *Li ji*. As is seen in Legge's 1861 prolegomena to the *Chinese Classics,* it was always afterward his intention to translate the Five Classics and Four Books and it is this, along with miscellaneous other classics of the Confucian and other religious traditions, that he brings to fruition at this time. For up-to-date discussions of the current state of sinological scholarship concerning these and other early classical texts, see Michael Loewe, ed., *Early Chinese Texts: A Bibliographical Guide* (Berkelely, Calif.: Society for the Study of Early China and the Institute of East Asian Studies, University of California, 1993). It is worth recognizing that the individual discussions, in *Early Chinese Texts,* of texts treated by Legge acknowledge the technical competence, if not always the stylistic felicity, of his translations and commentaries. For a balanced discussion of the complexities of the canonic history and fluid content of the Confucian classics, see Stephen Durrant, "Ching," in *The Indiana Companion to Traditional Chinese Literature,* editor in chief William H. Nienhauser Jr. (Bloomington, Ind.: Indiana University Press, 1986), 309–15. Legge's own discussion of these matters of canonicity is found in *Chinese Classics* (1861), 1: 1–11. Although Legge did not translate the *Zhou li* or the *Yi li,* I should note that in the course of translating the core texts for his English-language set of the Confucian classics (embracing both the original *Chinese Classics* and the later *Texts of Confucianism* in the *Sacred Books* series), he included supplementary translations of various other classical and commentarial texts (i.e., significant portions of *Xunzi, Han Yu, Yangzhu* [or *Liezi*], and *Mozi* in *Chinese Classics* [1861], vol. 2; all of the Shenyue text and commentary of the *Zhushu* in *Chinese Classics* [1865], vol. 3; substantial parts of the *Gushi yuan,* a Shi Deqian eighteenth-century collection of ancient poetry, the *Da* and *Xiaoxu* [The great and small prefaces to the *Shi jing*], and Hanying's Han-period *Hanshi waizhuan* in *Chinese Classics* [1871], vol. 4; sections of the *Gungyang* and *Guliang,* all of the *Zuo,* commentaries on the *Chunqiu,* and an eighteenth-century letter by Yuanmei in *Chinese Classics* [1872], vol. 5; all of the *Xiaojing* [The book of filial piety] in *Sacred Books,* vol. 3; and all of the traditional ten appendixes to the *Yi jing* in *Sacred Books,* vol. 49).

6. I should note that Legge's November lectures for 1884 were not given because of illness—see the "List of Lectures by Dr. Legge Delivered at Oxford," compiled and typed by Helen Edith Legge (CWM/China/Personal/Legge/Box 9). Legge's classes during this period included the Four Books, the "Tao Teh King," the Emperor Kangxi's Sacred Edict, composition, *Mencius, Analects, The Book of Historical Documents (Shu jing)*, the writings of the Tang essayist and Confucian apologist Han Yu, and the accounts of the Buddhist pilgrim Fa Xian.

7. The January 30, 1884, edition of the *Oxford Magazine* mentions, for example, that the Davis Chinese Scholarship was awarded to Mr. Colin Campbell Brown, with honorary mention to Mr. Henry Groghegan. Both were unattached to colleges, which gives some indication of the status of Chinese as a desirable course of study among undergraduates at the colleges.

8. Legge made various efforts in the early 1880s to win over the missionary societies, mostly to little avail. See, for example, his proposals to the London Missionary Society (CWM/China/LMS Eastern Committee Minutes [September 8, 1881, and February 9, 1882] Box 1/Book 3); to the Anglican Church Missionary Society, Letter Books, November 21, 1882, University of Birmingham Library, Church Missionary Society archive, C CH/L3 1876–1882; a letter to the Church Missionary Society, October 12, 1882 (Bodleian Library, Oxford University [hereafter cited as Bodleian], MS. Autogr. e. 11, *fols.* 53–54); and a letter to the Wesleyan Methodist Missionary Society, October 12, 1882 (Bodleian, MS. Autogr. e. 11, *fols.* 53–54). As Legge put it to the secretaries of the Wesleyan Methodist Society (October 12, 1882): "let them have a year or two's study with me, they will have laid a foundation for a knowledge of Chinese that will be of immense service to them in all their future career." He did receive a few missionary students from the societies (e.g., he refers to two students [a Mr. Bannister and a Mr. Ost] from the Church Missionary Society and a certain Mr. G. Griffiths from the London Missionary Society), but the opinion of the societies tended to be that the "feelings and intellectual character of the men themselves" dictated against Legge's proposal. As the Church Missionary Society put it (November 21, 1882):

> They [men preparing for a missionary career in Asia] think it possible that the plan may be practicable in some cases, perhaps in the case of those who have already labored in the mission field and are at home on furlough. University men . . . with the zeal that has made them desirous to take up the missionary life . . . often however mistakenly dislike the delay; while an unwitting student would not perhaps derive much advantage from the course.

9. Rosthorn eventually went on to an accomplished, if not an outstandingly brilliant, career in sinology in his homeland. On Rosthorn, see Gerd Kaminski and Else Unterrieder, *Von Österreichern und Chinesen* (Vienna: Euporaverlag, 1980), 330–31. See also Lauren Pfister, "Some New Dimensions in the Study of the Works of James Legge (1815–1897), part 1," *Sino-Western Cultural Relations Journal* 12 (1990): 29–50.

10. For a description of this, see "A Short Account of the Life of Bunyiu Nanjio, by Himself (1849–1884)," in Max Müller, *Biographical Essays* (New York: Charles Scribner's Sons, 1884), 193–94. See also the notice on Bunyiu Nanjio appearing in the London *Times* (March 1884). The Chinese type matrices were acquired in 1881

from the Chinese government and still exist at the Oxford University Press—see "A Ms. Synopsis of 6060 Copper Drives (Matrices) for Chinese Types on a Two-Line Pica Body, No. 1," Oxford University Press archive.

11. *Oxford Magazine,* November 12, 1884, p. 401. On Kasawara, see Müller, *Biographical Essays,* 204–19.

12. For background and materials on the procession, see the archive on the tercentenary at the Edinburgh University Library. For the description of the procession, see *Oxford Magazine,* May 7, 1884, pp. 218–19. The descriptions of Pasteur and Lesseps come from Helen Edith Legge's letter to her stepsister, Marian, April 22, 1884, excerpts from a small notebook entitled "From Letters Written by Me and Family" (CWM/China/Personal/Legge/Box 10). Helen Edith also reports that the procession did not include the "horrible Prince of Wales."

13. These figures on Nonconformist students and faculty at Oxford in the early 1880s are given in Albert Peel and J. A. R. Marriot, *Robert Forman Horton* (London: G. Allen and Unwin, 1937), 110–15.

14. Meetings of the Nonconformists' Union are sporadically noted in the *Oxford Magazine* (e.g., January 23, 1884, p. 4; March 5, 1884, p. 139; March 7, 1884, p. 211; May 7, 1884, p. 211; etc.); details on the history of the union are provided by the extant minute book of the Oxford University Nonconformists' Union, handwritten, 69 pp., Mansfield College Library archive. Copies of Legge's talks seem to no longer exist. The talk on "Social Wreckage" was given by Samuel Smith of New College and was described by the *Oxford Magazine,* January 23, 1884, p. 4.

> Beginning with a careful examination of the economic facts of the century, he showed that the condition of the mass of the people had immensely improved, especially since 1846. In spite of this he did not deny the degradation and squalor of the lowest classes. There were probably two or three millions of people who were paupers in name or in reality. While all other classes had steadily progressed, the lowest had remained stationary. The causes of this, he, after twenty years' close personal contact with the very poor, believed to be rather moral than material. Nothing could be done till the character of these people was changed.

15. On Fairbairn, see E. J. Sharpe, *Not to Destroy but to Fulfill: The Contribution of N. J. Farquhar to Protestant Missionary Thought in India* (Uppsala, Sweden: Gleerup, 1965), 126–30. As Sharpe says (p. 128):

> Fairbairn was not primarily a biblical critic. His main field of interest and competence was the history of doctrine, in which he had read widely, and on which he wrote at great length. It is true that he specialized to some extent in New Testament theology, but he was never in any sense creative in the biblical field. Indeed, it has been pointed out that in Old Testament criticism he remained at the pre-Wellhausen stage, while in theology generally he made no attempt to understand Ritschl. . . . Fairbairn was nevertheless well aware of the importance of biblical criticism for the study of theology.

See also Willis B. Glover (*Evangelical Nonconformists and Higher Criticism in the Nineteenth Century* [London: Independent Press, 1954]) on Fairbairn's stature as a theologian. Glover is critical of Fairbairn, saying (pp. 139–40) that he was a "mediocre theologian" who was also "pompous and verbose." He was primarily a "transitional figure" whose work has had little "lasting worth" (p. 140). More important for my purposes is the fact that Fairbairn was, as Sharpe puts it (p. 130), a "pioneer among Christian theologians in the importance he attached to the comparative study of religion." This role is verified by Fairbairn's teaching of what may be the first regular courses on "comparative religions" at Oxford—i.e., his periodic courses at Mansfield College (see the College Registers in the Mansfield College Library). Sharpe traces Fairbairn's probable influence on Farquhar's comparativist views of Indian religion. From their close association at the George Street Church, the Nonconformists' Union, and the establishment of Mansfield College, it is also probable that Fairbairn and Legge reinforced each other's comparativist perspective while affirming an active Evangelical faith. Although Fairbairn sometimes expressed reservations about some of Legge's views on Chinese religions, the depth of their relationship is indicated by Fairbairn's eulogy in 1897.

16. Minute book of the Oxford University Nonconformists' Union for November 21, 1882.

17. See, for example, Elizabeth Longford, "Piety in Queen Victoria's Reign," Twenty-Seventh Lecture, Friends of Dr. Williams's Library (London: Dr. Williams's Trust, 1973), 13–14. Dominica Legge observes that her grandfather, while at Oxford, was noted for the extreme sincerity and earnestness of his "extempore prayers," which often included "odd and unexpected things." See Dominica Legge, "James Legge" (paper presented to the Sino-Scottish Society, University of Edinburgh, February 4, 1951), 13. The extreme length of services was especially characteristic of the kind of evangelical religion Legge grew up with in Scotland, something that is graphically portrayed in George MacDonald's novel *Robert Falconer.*

18. On the Horton affair, see Peel and Marriott, *Robert Forman Horton,* 110–12; Horton's *Autobiography* (London: George Allen and Unwin, 1928), 57–58; Letters to the Editor, *Oxford Magazine,* January 23, 1884, p. 1, and February 6, 1884; and "A Letter, Dec. 8, 1883, seeking support to negate the nomination of R. F. Horton as examiner in the Rudiments of Faith and Religion," Bodleian G.A. Oxon. b. 140 (49a).

19. There are no extant sales figures for the *Sacred Books of the East* during the late 1870s and early 1880s in the Oxford University Press archive. My estimate of the best-sellers is based on later, end-of-the-century figures in the archives (see Oxford University Press archive, *Sacred Books of the East 1887–1908,* packet 41). "Best-selling" for an expensive scholarly work such as the *Sacred Books* generally seems to have meant between fifty and a hundred, up to several hundred, copies sold per year, sustained over a substantial period of time.

20. JL to Müller, November 18, 1881 (Bodleian, MS. Autogr. e. 11, *fols.* 53–54). Concerning publishing details of Legge's volumes for the *Sacred Books of the East,* see also Müller to JL, December 18, 1882 (makes the point that the Chinese volumes are more expensive than other works in the *Sacred Books of the East* because the Indian government specifically excluded them from its subscription to the series), March 30, 1885 (problems over the length of the MS for the *Record of Rites;* Müller stresses that JL should condense his notes and index) (Bodleian, MS. Autogr. e. 11, *fols.* 53–54).

21. There is no extant documentation about the missing fourth Confucian volume in the *Sacred Books* series, but it may be that the revision of the Four Books published in two volumes in the 1893–1895 Oxford edition (including the prolegomena, text, and notes) was originally undertaken with Müller's series in mind. None

of the other classics published in the Oxford edition was revised at all from the earlier versions (1865–1872).

22. Müller to Henry Liddell, dated only 1882 (Bodleian, MS. Autogr. e. 11, *fols.* 53–54). Dean Liddell was the one most responsible for securing his editorship back in 1876. I should note that an extended excerpt from Legge's November 18 letter is included in Müller's letter.

23. Because of the popularity of Buddhism, Müller makes it clear that he hoped that this religion would be "presented as fully as possible in its different phases." One of the problems in fulfilling this plan was the prolonged illness of Samuel Beal.

24. See Bartholomew Price to JL, April 19, 1882, notifying Legge of his payment (£118) for *The Book of Changes,* volume 21 of the *Sacred Books of the East* (Oxford University Press archive/Letter Book).

25. See press secretary to JL, January 30, 1886, on corrections to *The Book of Changes* volume (ibid., 39); Oxford University Press to Max Müller, April 26, 1886, charging Legge £12/7- for correction overruns (ibid.); and press secretary to JL, May 19, 1886, thanking Legge for his check for corrections and promising to communicate Legge's complaint about the cost of corrections to the Delegates (ibid., 40).

26. Max Müller, "Forgotten Bibles," *Nineteenth Century* 15 (1884): 1004–22.

27. Ibid., 1005.

28. See also Müller's "The Savage," *Nineteenth Century* 17 (1885): 109–32.

29. See Marjorie Wheeler-Barclay, "The Science of Religion in Britain, 1860–1915" (Ph.D. diss., Northwestern University, 1987), 144–226.

30. Müller, "Forgotten Bibles," 1006–7.

31. Ibid., 1007–8. Müller was always careful to point out that he believed generally in the evolution or development of religions. His German romantic historical ideal (e.g., Herder's *Entwicklung* and Goethe's *Das Werden,* "becoming") was obviously rooted in such an idea. Müller could therefore accept many aspects of Darwin's approach, but could not accept his overly theoretical "enthusiasm" for believing that "man genealogically descended from an animal" (p. 1015): "As language had been pointed out as a Rubicon which no beast had ever crossed, Darwin lent a willing ear to those who think that they can derive language, that is, real *logos,* from interjections and mimicry, by a process of spontaneous evolution, and produced himself some most persuasive arguments." But, says Müller, the "barrier of language remains as unshaken as ever."

32. Ibid., 1011.

33. Ibid., 1008.

34. The "bow-wow" and "pooh-pooh" theories amusingly referred to the idea that human language originated in the spontaneous imitation of animal sounds (bow wow) or in instinctual ejaculations called forth by bodily sensations (pooh pooh). See Otto Jespersen, *Language: Its Nature, Development, and Origin* (New York: Norton, 1964), 413–16. See also Linda Dowling, "Victorian Oxford and the Science of Language," *PMLA* 97 (1982): 160–78. For Müller (in the "ding-dong" sense) it was a "law of nature" that "'everything which is struck rings . . . each substance has its peculiar ring . . .'" (p. 174). This was a "creative faculty or instinct," or "mystic nexus between mind and matter," which "supplied each new idea 'as it thrilled for the first time through the brain' with its own distinctive sound." As

Dowling says, Müller "retreated from this almost at once, . . . always offering modifications but without really disavowing it. . . . To see Müller's theory of linguistic roots as a function of his belief in the *logos* is finally to understand that Müller's rhetorical conduct of his lectures is the very enactment of that belief. Quite simply, Müller entrusted . . . much of his argument to wordplay and metaphor and rhapsodic repetition . . ." (ibid.).

35. Müller, "Forgotten Bibles," 1010.

36. Ibid.

37. The unstated implication was often that the illiterate masses in literate civilizational traditions were essentially equivalent to savages or children. Use of the word *masses* to suggest a mindless, childish, barbaric, and emotional mob is a Victorian phenomenon. Human beings in large groups lose their individuality and reason and revert to an uncivilized or savage state. The *Oxford English Dictionary*, for example, notes that the term *masses* for the lower orders was a Victorian invention. The reformer's antithesis of "the classes" and "the masses" is attributed to Gladstone in the 1880s.

38. Ibid.

39. Ibid., 1022. The comparison of the science of religions with comparative anatomy is frequently encountered in methodological discussions at the end of the nineteenth century. See, for example, further instances in this chapter and also the revealing article by A. M. Fairbairn, "What Is Religion?" *Congregationalist* 13 (1884): 275–91. As Fairbairn says (pp. 282–83): "The historical question [is] . . . the comparative question. . . . It puts the actual, extant, existing religions together, and compares them; and comparing them, proceeds on the same scientific principle that comparative anatomy recognizes when it may start with the structure of the leaf and culminate in the glorious anatomy of a man. And so you find running through the religions a structural principle."

40. Thomas Jones Barker's painting *Queen Victoria Presenting a Bible in the Audience Chamber at Windsor* (ca. 1861) is currently in the National Portrait Gallery, London. I am indebted to Steven Moore for this citation.

41. This event must have taken place some time in 1886; it is mentioned by Edkins in *The Chinese Recorder* 17 (September 1886): 325. See also R. Lechler, "Opium and Missions, the Twin Plagues of China," *The Chinese Recorder* 16 (December 1885): 454–56, who refers to the picture of the queen of England reading the Bible with the caption "The Secret of England's Greatness." I have not been able to locate this image. A set of the *Sacred Books* was presented to the pope in 1897.

42. See Timothy Richard, "Presentation Testament to the Empress Dowager of China," *The Chinese Recorder* 26 (April 1895): 151–61. This presentation was made in honor of the dowager empress's sixtieth birthday (November 1894). Especially revealing was Richard's cover letter to the empress: "We Christians in your empire constantly and fervently pray that your Highness and all the members of the Imperial Household may also get possession of this secret [the New Testament] of true happiness to the individual and prosperity to the nation, so that China may not be behind any nation on earth."

On November 11 the casket was presented to two imperial ministers and on November 12 it was sent to the dowager empress, who asked for the names of the presenters.

Lee Chi-fang ("Wang T'ao [1828–1879]: His Life, Thought, Scholarship, and Literary Achievement" [Ph.D. diss., University of Wisconsin, 1973]) supports the contention that Wang Tao was the main aide in the translation, between 1849 and 1851, of the Delegates' Version of the Bible. This may be an overstated claim, especially in light of the methods of the Delegates. In Shanghai this involved a committee of translation made up of (up to) eight native Chinese "teachers" along with five designated missionary translators.

43. See George Steiner, *After Babel: Aspects of Language and Translation* (New York: Oxford University Press, 1975). Here I am quoting from Eugene Eoyang, *The Transparent Eye: Reflections on Translation, Chinese Literature, and Comparative Poetics* (Honolulu: University of Hawaii Press, 1993), 187.

44. See also J. Z. Smith, "Differential Equations: On Constructing the Other," Thirteenth Annual University Lecture in Religion, Arizona State University, 1992 (pamphlet). As Smith says (p. 14):

> It is the issue of translation, that "this" is never quite "that," and, therefore, that acts of interpretation are required which marks the Human Sciences. It is thought about translation, an affair of the in-between that is always relative and never fully adequate; it is thought about translation across languages, places, and times, between text and reader, speaker and hearer, that energizes the Human Sciences as disciplines and suggests the intellectual contributions they make.

45. Fairbairn, "What Is Religion?" 285.

46. Arthur Wright, in a rare moment of hyperbole, described Kumarajiva as "perhaps the greatest translator of all time"—see *Buddhism in Chinese History* (Stanford, Calif.: Stanford University Press, 1959), 62. I do not want to suggest that Legge rivals Kumarajiva as the "greatest translator of all time," but certainly, Legge was the greatest sinological translator of the nineteenth century. On Kumarajiva, see also Kenneth Ch'en, *Buddhism in China: A Historical Overview* (Princeton, N.J.: Princeton University Press, 1972), 81–83; and Kogen Mizuno, *Buddhist Sutras: Origin, Development, Transmission* (Tokyo: Kosei, 1982), 49–50, 58–63.

47. It might, in fact, be said that Legge's second area of greatness was his career as a reforming educator both in Hong Kong and at Oxford. On the Hong Kong side of this, see, particularly, Wong Man Kong, "A Pioneer at the Crossroads of East and West: James Legge" (M.A. thesis, Chinese University of Hong Kong, 1993), 66–105.

48. See Louis Kelly, *The True Interpreter: A History of Translation Theory and Practice in the West* (Oxford: Basil Blackwell, 1979); and, with reference to China and James Legge, see Eugene Eoyang, *Transparent Eye*, 25–28. Concerning the English tradition of translation, see J. M. Cohen, *English Translators and Translations*, Writers and Their Work No. 142 (London: Longmans, Green, 1962).

49. Kelly, *True Interpreter*, 1–2.

50. Ironically Backhouse attempted to bribe Oxford into appointing him to the Chinese chair after Legge's death. On the notorious Backhouse, see Hugh Trevor-Roper, *Hermit of Peking: The Hidden Life of Sir Edmund Backhouse* (New York: Knopf, 1977); and D. L. McMullen, "The Backhouse File. 'Glorious Veterans,' 'Sinologists de chambre' and Men of Science: Reflections on Professor Hugh Trevor-Roper's Life of Sir Edmund Backhouse (1873–1944)," *New Lugano Review* 1 (1979): 78–83.

51. Charges (especially by Otto Böhtlingk and William Whitney) that Müller did not really edit all of his *Rig-Veda* were circulating in the 1870s and until after his death; see the material gathered in Bodleian, MS. Eng. c. 2809; and also Nirad C. Chaudhuri, *Scholar Extraordinary: The Life of Professor the Rt. Hon. Friedrich Max Müller, P.C.* (London: Chatto & Windus, 1974), 260–62.

52. Legge himself was acutely sensitive to the problem of stylistic form, although his one major experiment in the interest of a more exactly congruent emotive and poetic translation, his metric translation of the *Book of Poetry*, was largely unsuccessful.

53. See also the disappointing discussion of Legge's "biased translations" of the "highly secular Confucian Classics" (Li Xiansheng, "On James Legge's Translation of Confucian Texts," [M.A. thesis, Indiana University, 1984]). Li's own contemporary secular assumptions are more interesting than his simplistic, and sometimes uninformed, discussion of Legge's methods is. Much more sophisticated is Li's mentor, Eugene Eoyang, who has considered many of these issues in *The Transparent Eye*. Although impressively insightful and helpful in many ways, Eoyang's portrait of Legge as the "maladjusted messenger" of Chinese culture to the West who could not escape his Christian bias misses much of the complexity and progressive transformation of the man and his work. The story of Legge, from the very beginning of his career to the end, is of his continuous struggle to see and understand the Chinese from their own point of view.

54. See Arthur Waley, "Notes on Mencius," *Asia Major,* n.s. 1 (1949): 99–108; and reprinted in *Chinese Classics* (University of Hong Kong edition, 1960 and 1970), vol. 2.

55. See Ruth Perlmutter, "Arthur Waley and His Place in the Modern Movement between the Two Wars" (Ph.D. diss., University of Pennsylvania, 1971). See also Wong Siu Kit and Chan Man Sing, "Arthur Waley," in *An Encyclopaedia of Translation: Chinese-English–English-Chinese,* ed. Chan Sin-wai and David E. Pollard (Hong Kong: Chinese University Press, 1995), 423–28. Contrast this with Lauren Pfister's "James Legge," also in *An Encyclopaedia of Translation,* 401–22.

56. See Arthur Waley, *The Book of Songs* (New York: Grove Press, 1960). It is worth noting that in his introduction to his version of the songs, Waley actually connects the folkloric quality of the Chinese songs with Western folk songs, including Burnsian Scottish ballads. It seems that Waley was not aware of Legge's metric version.

57. Eoyang says, for example (*Transparent Eye,* 106–7):

The presentation of Chinese literature during the Victorian period introduced uncounted distortions that have bedeviled the study of Chinese in the English-speaking West. The Victorian period was, arguably, the worst era in which to introduce Chinese literature into English: its ornate and verbose style, its weighty and portentous tone, its lumbering, often inverted syntax—nothing could be further from the quicksilver, mercurial, and allusive nature of much traditional Chinese literature. The rhetoric of Victorian language aside, the gospel of colonization, blending peculiarly Western notions of material progress with Christian meliorism, could not be more inhospitable to a clear and unobstructed view of certain Chinese ways of thinking.

And for Eoyang the dead hand of Victorianism is, understandably enough, epitomized by Legge:

The nineteenth century was dominated by the masterly but misguided translations of James Legge, an English missionary whose view of China and the Chinese was tinted (if not tainted) by his failure to see them on their own terms; this short-coming was especially evident in his definitive and influential renderings of the Confucian canon, which emerged from his translation as highly civilized but fatally secular versions of Christian dogma.

The arguable problem here is that Eoyang's understanding of Victorianism is too much of a caricature that misses much of the complex allusive and changing nature of both the period and a man like Legge.

58. See Wong Siu-kit and Li Kar-shu, "Three English Translations of the Shi-jing," *Renditions* (November 1987): 113–39. Waley's disparagement of Zhu Xi, as Wong and Li point out, is really reflective of post–May 4th revolutionary attitudes in Chinese criticism that rejected the traditional moralistic interpretation. John M. Minford, "Moonlight and Water—Sunlight and Wine, Herbert Allen Giles (1845–1935)" (1991), discusses Waley's influence on sinological taste (especially concerning the preference for sprung rhythm over rhyming quatrains). See also Eoyang (*Transparent Eye,* 190–209), who shrewdly discusses the impossible, and intrinsically rhetorical and moral, question of "who is the better translator of Chinese poetry—Pound or Waley?" It is better to ask: "What is the persona of the intelligence behind the inquiry?" On Giles and Legge, see pages 431–39.

59. On his theory of translation and his use of a Hopkinslike sprung rhythm ("to have one stress to each Chinese syllable"), see Waley's article on Chinese poetry in the November 1958 *Atlantic Monthly*. On Waley and Legge as translators, see especially Wong Siu Kit and Chan Man Sing, "Arthur Waley," and Lauren Pfister, "James Legge."

60. David Nivison, for example, comments that Legge's version of Mencius is "old fashioned and awkward" but also displays an "extraordinary conscientiousness" that "refuses to smooth over a spot in the text when the translator feels the sense to be difficult to ascertain." Legge's "awkwardness," continues Nivison, is therefore "actually a virtue, and it is not his only virtue" (Nivison, "On Translating Mencius," *Philosophy East and West* 30 [1980]: 93–122). Interesting but simplistic is Lewis Gen's "Legge's Translation of Mencius," *Eastern World* (1955): 36–37. Gen is appreciative of Legge's "outstanding" work, but lists six areas needing "improvement."

61. As both Wang Tao and E.J. Eitel recognized, Legge drew eclectically on both Han and Song commentary. Wang Tao's opinion of Legge's "judicious eclecticism" in using Chinese commentary is more accurate than Waley's view on these matters. See Lee Chi-fang's discussion of this matter ("Wang T'ao [1828–1897]"). On Wang's and Legge's eclecticism, see also Cohen, *Between Tradition and Modernity: Wang T'ao and Reform in Late Ch'ing China* (Cambridge, Mass.: Harvard University Press), 59. Legge's own statement on his indebtedness to Zhu Xi is found in his preface to the Oxford edition of the classics (*Chinese Classics* [1893], 1: x–xi), written in 1892:

> He [i.e., Legge himself] has seen it objected to his translations that they were modelled on the views of the great critic and philosopher of the Song dynasty, the well-known Chu Hsi. He can only say that he commenced and has carried on his labours with the endeavour to search out the meaning for himself, independent of all commentators. He soon became aware, however, of the beauty and strength of Chu's style, the correctness of his analysis, and the comprehension and depth of his

thought. That his own views of passages generally coincide with those of "The Old Man of the Cloudy Valley" should be accepted, he submits, as complimentary to him rather than the reverse.

On Western interpretations of Zhu Xi, see Wing-tsit Chan, "The Study of Chu Hsi in the West," *Journal of Asian Studies* 35 (1976): 555–77. See also Knud Lundbaek, "The First European Translations of Chinese Historical and Philosophical Works," in *China and Europe: Images and Influence in Sixteenth to Eighteenth Centuries,* ed. Thomas H.C. Lee (Hong Kong: Chinese University Press, 1991), 29–44. Not surprisingly (ever since the time of Ricci and Longobardi), much of the issue comes down to whether Zhu Xi was "theistic" or not.

62. In a letter to Legge, April 12, 1882 (CWM/China/Personal/Legge/Box 8), Gabelentz, who had read the page proofs for the *Book of Changes,* commended Legge for having done his work "from the standpoint of a native scholar." Lindsay Ride (Biographical Note, *Chinese Classics* [1960], 1: 20) approvingly noted Edkins's judgment about Legge's "thorough-going fidelity as a translator":

> This does not mean as a rule he has translated verbatim. Sometimes he may have done so in defiance of English idiom. But more frequently, especially in the later volumes, he has expanded a single Chinese word into a whole line of English, thus giving the resultant of endless Chinese speculations on Classic enigmas. If, hereafter, skeptical critics should seek to go behind Dr. Legge, they will find that they must go for the most part behind the best Chinese commentators as well. We have therefore represented to us in these translations what their Classics have been to the Chinese themselves.

Concerning Legge's *Book of Changes,* John Chalmers, observing (in "The Sacred Books of China," typed draft of a review [CWM/China/Personal/Legge/Box 9]) that Legge writes from the standpoint of a native scholar, and, to one who has been accustomed to the habits of thought of Chinese commentators, commented that "this work in its spirit and manner seems more like a new commentary by a somewhat rationalistic Confucianist than a translation by a European. We may be surprised sometimes that the translator is not more rationalistic, but then, if he had been much more so, it seems very doubtful if he would have had the patience to produce such an exhaustive work." See note 118, page 698, below, for citation of the published review.

63. On the whole complicated issue of the nature and history of Chinese commentarial tradition as related to the classics, see the impressive study by John B. Henderson, *Scripture, Canon, and Commentary: A Comparison of Confucian and Western Exegesis* (Princeton, N.J.: Princeton University Press, 1991), 62–88. As Henderson says (p. 70):

> Although opinions differ on when commentaries began to be commonly interspersed with classical Confucian texts in the form of a running gloss, most trace the origins of this form to the Latter Han at the earliest. Even after this became a common practice, however, the use of special commentarial terminologies, typographical distinctions (after the invention of printing), and the emphasis on lexical problems in much pre-Song commentary tended to keep commentary distinct from the classical texts.

Though it was important to distinguish between classic works and commentaries, the meaning of a classic was communicated to a later audience by the commentarial translational gloss of the archaic terminology. This is more true for Legge's Confucian classics than for his Daoist or Buddhist works, certainly more so than for his synthetic works such as *Religions of China*.

64. See Benjamin A. Elman, *From Philosophy to Philology: Intellectual and Social Aspects of Change in Late Imperial China* (Cambridge, Mass.: Council on East Asian Studies, Harvard University, 1984). Legge's work was not in the spirit of the New Text mold of native Chinese criticism, which deconstructed most orthodox assumptions.

65. Henderson, *Scripture, Canon, and Commentary,* 214–15. On the emergence of a Chinese critical scholarship in the nineteenth century, see especially Elman, *From Philosophy to Philology*.

66. Henderson, *Scripture, Canon, and Commentary,* 214. Henderson is partially quoting Paul Ricoeur, "The Task of Hermeneutics," in *Paul Ricoeur, Hermeneutics, and the Human Sciences: Essays on Language, Action, and Interpretation,* ed. and trans. John B. Thompson (Cambridge: Cambridge University Press, 1985), 48.

To explain this "transition from commentarial forms and modes of discourse to modern scholarship and criticism," Henderson suggests (pp. 201–2) that

> the reasons why such movements did arise [and only in the "Christian biblical, Homeric, and Confucian" traditions] . . . probably have less to do with any special intellectual qualities they might have than with such developments as the differential impact of the printing revolution in early-modern Europe and China, as opposed to the Near East and India (where printing was not introduced until the nineteenth century). By making large selections of ancient writings widely available, printing helped foster examinations of the relationships between the classics or scriptures and the general intellectual and social milieus of the eras in which they were composed. The result of these examinations, of this historical recontextualization of the classics, frequently challenged some of the basic commentarial assumptions [i.e., comprehensiveness, coherence, self-consistency, morality, profundity, universal meaningfulness, and clarity]. . . . Challenges to traditional commentarial assumptions in early-modern Europe and China may be traced to the accelerated development of the philological sciences in those areas as well as to the printing revolution. First of all, by applying the critical methods and standards used in the study of profane texts to the classics or scriptures, philologists at least implicitly questioned the latter's claim to such special qualities or attributes as cosmic comprehensiveness or unfathomable profundity. More specifically, philologists' increasingly expert investigations of the grammatical structures and vocabularies of sacred and canonical texts such as the Bible revealed "lacunae, errors, ambiguities, and even contradictions in the canon" (quoting here Anna-Ruth Löwenbrück, "Johann David Michaelis et les débuts de la critique biblique," in *Le Siècle des lumières et la Bible,* eds. Yvon Belaval and Dominique Bourel [Paris: Editions Beauchesne, 1986], 114).

67. Henderson, *Scripture, Canon, and Commentary,* p. 221:

> Such commentarial confinement is not necessarily a mark of pedantry or of a lack of originality. Great ideas and insights may be presented in commentarial forms and formats, just as great music may take the form of the fugue. The commentary

itself may become a new classic, as has happened repeatedly in the history of canons. Indeed, many (or much) of the classics or scriptures were originally conceived as commentaries.

It may be mentioned that there is an important sense in which Legge's Victorian and Evangelical sensibilities would be naturally drawn to Zhu Xi's moralistically interpretive commentary on the classics. In this way also it is significant to notice that Legge begins his lifelong work by translating the Four Books, the most obviously ethical of the classics. As Henderson says (making allowances for the nebulous category of neo-Confucianism, p. 129):

> The Confucian classics, particularly the Neo-Confucian Four Books, are unusual, perhaps even sui generis, in the degree to which they are primarily concerned with moral issues and in the extent to which ethical systems can be convincingly extracted from them without obvious commentarial contortions. The Confucius of the Analects probably merits the mantle of moralist more than his counterparts in any other major classical or scriptural tradition. On the other hand, it was after all the Neo-Confucians who canonized the Four Books, including the Analects, and who de-emphasized the study of those established books of the Confucian canon which could not be so easily accommodated to their moral philosophy. In this respect they resembled medieval Christian exegetes who commented most extensively on those books of the Bible that lent themselves most readily to moralization, including the Psalms, the Song of Solomon, and the Gospels.

Let me only add that this last litany of biblical texts could largely be taken as a list of Legge's own favorite scriptures (which as seen from his sermons and John Morison's *Family Prayers* [1838] included Genesis, Psalms, Exodus, Isaiah, Jeremiah, Matthew, and the Pauline Epistles). I am indebted to Lauren Pfister for the information regarding John Morison.

68. Henderson speaks of what he calls a "universal commentarial mentality"— see *Scripture, Canon, and Commentary*, 221.

69. JL in "Notes of My Life" says that he kept the "early mornings" for study. As Lee Chi-fang points out ("Wang T'ao [1828–1897]"), Legge had the use of Wang's collected commentaries for the *Book of Changes* and *Record of Rites*. Cohen notes that, in 1877, Legge invited Wang to return to England to help him but that Wang had already embarked on a new career and declined (*Between Tradition and Modernity*, 60). So also does Legge make "frequent reference to Wang's textual interpretations" in the notes to the *Record of Rites*.

70. This principle is also an age-old Chinese theme best expressed in the *Zhuangzi*'s parable of the fish and the net; see Tu Wei-ming, *Neo-Confucian Thought in Action: Wang Yang-ming's Youth (1472–1509)* (Berkeley: University of California Press, 1976), 138. The acquiring of "an experiential understanding of the intentionality of a classic," notes Tu, is like trying to catch a fish with a net. "To equate the words of the Classics with the intentionality of the sages" is to make the mistake of identifying the "net with the fish." The basic principle of understanding and translation is therefore the following: "As one cannot find any fish in the net without actually involving oneself in fishing, so one cannot grasp the intentionality of the sages without really becoming engaged in an experiential understanding of the words of the classics." Once that is done, however, one can then "lay the net aside."

71. Douglas Robinson, *The Translator's Turn* (Baltimore and London: Johns Hopkins University Press, 1991), 17. See also Eoyang's discussion of Pound as a "translator" of Chinese, *Transparent Eye*, 184–87, 190–209.

72. Robinson, *Translator's Turn*, 17–18.

73. I tend to agree with Steiner's views on these matters (see *After Babel*, 301–3) as much as with Robinson's. However, it is worth noting Robinson's respectful modification of Steiner's observation that "fidelity is not literalism or any technical device for rendering 'spirit.'" As Robinson says (*Translator's Turn*, 19):

> Exactly, I want to go on: it is a technical device for rendering not spirit but "body." Body, somatic response, is the "substance" Steiner looks for in meaning. But Steiner is not talking about somatics, here, despite all his suggestive hints in that direction; he is talking about a mysterious ideal of "reciprocity" or "equalization," the notion that the ideal translation is one that gives back to the original as much as it took from it:
>
> > The whole formulation [of fidelity], as we have found it over and over again in discussions of translation, is hopelessly vague. The translator, the exegetist, the reader is *faithful* to his text, makes his response responsible, only when he endeavours to restore the balance of forces, of integral presence, which his appropriative comprehension has disrupted. Fidelity is ethical, but also, in the full sense, economic. By virtue of tact, and tact intensified is moral vision, the translator-interpreter creates a condition of significant exchange. The arrows of meaning, of cultural, psychological benefaction, move both ways. There is, ideally, exchange without loss. In this respect, translation can be pictured as a negation of entropy; order is preserved at both ends of the cycle, source and receptor (*After Babel*, 302).

Continuing, Robinson comments (pp. 20, 21):

> If Steiner's theory of disruption and reciprocity is to have any reference to reality at all, it seems to me that he must be talking not about texts but about our somatic responses to them. The disruptive effect of a translation is not on the original, but on the receptor's response to the original: having read an appropriative translation, the receptor may come to feel differently about the original. It may begin to feel like a different sort of text. . . .
>
> The point that I am trying to make is that all talk of "equivalence," "fidelity," or even "reciprocity" in the abstract is, and must remain, philosophically vague because the reality underlying it is a constantly shifting and therefore ultimately unsystematizable human response. Or rather, a series of human responses.

74. Other than what we see in his preface to the *Book of Changes*, Legge does not discuss nineteenth-century theories of translation. However, he was obviously aware of Müller's ideas as stated in the introduction to the *Sacred Books of the East* and, by virtue of his association with Oxford and interest in classical matters, most likely knew of both Matthew Arnold's and Benjamin Jowett's theories. Concerning Arnold's theories, see his polemical *On Translating Homer* (1861; reprint New York: Chelsea House, 1983), which takes up the problem of faithfulness in translation. For Arnold this can only properly mean (and here we see the academic mind of the "intelligent scholar" at work) that the translator's aim must be (p. 29)

> [t]o reproduce on the intelligent scholar, as nearly as possible, the general effect of Homer. Except so far as he reproduces this, he loses his labour, even though he

may make a spirited Iliad of his own, like Pope, or translate Homer's Iliad word for word, like Mr. Newman. If his proper aim were to stimulate in any manner possible the general public, he might be right in following Pope's example; if his proper aim were to help schoolboys to construe Homer, he might be right in following Mr. Newman. But it is not: his proper aim is, I repeat it yet once more, to reproduce on the intelligent scholar, as nearly as he can, the general effect of Homer.

Arnold (and Müller would certainly agree) sees the problem of English translators, and English literature, as a typical failing of the English intellect, which is amateurish ("eccentric" and "arbitrary") when compared with the "critical" and professionally academic methods of the French and German intellect (p. 59).

Regarding Jowett, see Lesley Higgins, "Jowett and Pater: Trafficking in Platonic Wares," *Victorian Studies* 37 (1993): 43–72. It is interesting to note G. G. Alexander's comments on Legge's middle-course principles of translation (*Lao-Tsze The Great Thinker, With a Translation of His Thoughts on the Nature and Manifestations of God* [London: Kegan Paul, Trench, Trübner, 1895], vii):

> [Legge, "our greatest Chinese scholar,"] in the preface to his translation of the Yih-King, . . . says: "The written characters of the Chinese are not representations of words but symbols of ideas, and the combination of them in composition is not a representation of what the writer would say, but of what he thinks. It is vain, therefore, for a translator to attempt a literal version. When the symbolic characters have brought his mind en rapport with that of his author, he is free to render his ideas in his own, or any other speech, in the best manner he can attain to. . . . In the study of a Chinese classical book there is not so much an interpretation of the character employed by the writer as a participation of his thoughts; there is the seeing mind to mind." Legge does not stand alone [in] . . . this mode of translation clearly laid down by Dr. Jowett in his preface to the second and third editions of the Dialogues of Plato. He says:—"An English translation ought to be idiomatic and interesting, not only to the scholar but to the unlearned reader. Its object should not simply be to render the words of one language into the words of another, or to preserve the construction and order of the original; this is the ambition of a schoolboy, who wishes to show that he has made a good use of his dictionary and grammar; but is quite unworthy of the translator who seeks to produce on his reader an impression similar, or nearly similar, to that produced by the original. To him the feeling should be more important than the exact word. . . . He must carry in his mind a comprehensive view of the whole work, of what has preceded, and of what has to follow, as well as of the meaning of particular passages. His version should be based, in the first instance, on an intimate knowledge of the text; but the precise order and arrangement of the words may be left to fade out of sight, when the translation begins to take shape."

75. As may be seen in the popular fiction of Bulwer-Lytton, Rider Haggard, and Conan Doyle, the late-Victorian era was awash with a lush tradition of occult secrets—hidden, deciphered, and revealed.

76. Until the publication of Legge's version of the *Book of Changes* there were only two European translations, Julius von Mohl's edition (Stuttgart and Tübingen: vol. 1, 1834, and vol. 2, 1839) of Jean-Baptiste Regis's early eighteenth-century translation, and McClatchie's controversial version of 1876; see the preface and introduction to *Sacred Books,* vol. 26 (1882). The 1880s and 1890s were,

however, a period that lusted after occult secrets and at that time a sudden flurry of interest in the text resulted in at least three or four more partial or complete translations.

77. For a generally knowledgeable discussion of the "inadequacies of Western *I Ching* scholarship," see Iulian K. Shchutskii, *Researches on the I Ching,* trans. William L. MacDonald and Tsuyoshi Hasegawa with Hellmut Wilhelm (Princeton, N.J.: Princeton University Press, 1979) and the long introduction to Shchutskii's work by Gerald Swanson, pp. vii–xlviii. It was Shchutskii's opinion (pp. 28–29) that Legge's *Book of Changes* was the "best for the period" and "continues to have significance." As Swanson says (p. xi), both Legge and Richard Wilhelm used the *Zhou I Zhezhong* edition of the text (with compiled commentaries), but the influence of Wilhelm's teacher gave rise to essential differences from Legge. Oddly, however, Swanson says (pp. xi–xii) that "James Legge translated what the text said, while Wilhelm translated what the text meant; that is, Legge was primarily a translator while Wilhelm was more of an interpreter."

78. For a thorough discussion of the *Book of Changes* as a divination manual, see Richard A. Kunst, "The Original 'Yijing': A Text, Phonetic Transcription, Translation, and Indexes, with Sample Glosses" (Ph.D. diss., University of California, Berkeley, 1985). For an approach that attempts to be sensitive to both a rationalistic historiographic approach and a "meaning behind the meaning" traditionalist approach, see Edward L. Shaughnessy, "Marriage, Divorce, and Revolution: Reading between the Lines of the Book of Changes," *Journal of Asian Studies* 51 (1992): 587–99.

79. JL, *Sacred Books,* 26: xiii.

80. Ibid., viii.

81. This operation was facilitated, as Legge says (ibid., xiv), by the 1715 imperial edition of the *Book of Changes,* which "keeps the Text and the Appendixes separate."

82. Ibid.

83. Ibid., 9–10.

84. In a letter (April 12, 1882) to Legge (CWM/China/Personal/Legge/Box 8), Gabelentz says that, after reading the page proofs of Legge's *Book of Changes,* "No disciple of Confucius and Mencius could have sought more devotedly to extract from the 'text' everything in the shape of a moral or political lesson, and to take away the reproach from the sages of being mere vulgar diviners than you have done."

For Legge's discussion of divination as related to the *Book of Changes,* see *Sacred Books,* 26: 40–42. Legge, not surprisingly given his general Müllerian thesis of religious developmental degeneration, claims that the actual mantic practice of divination was more a phenomenon of the later Appendixes than it was of the earlier, and purer, Text (lines and words) of King Wen and Duke Zhou. In this same vein, the presence of a mythology of sexual dualism so important for Canon McClatchie is primarily a corrupt result of the Appendixes (ibid., 50–51). By the same token, Legge finds that references to *di* or "God" are often clouded by overly mythologized or poetic allusions to God's action in the changing seasonal round of cosmic time (ibid., 51–52).

85. Ibid., xv. The notion that an idea was the causal origin of words (which, by their very concrete phonetic nature, could never express the spiritual fullness of the

originating thought) is, of course, a basic theme behind Müller's Kantian romanticism about symbolic interpretation. It is the focal point for Müller's science of thought in the late 1880s and, to some degree, is suggested by Legge's philological position on language in the early phase of the term question.

86. Ibid., xvi. One of the interesting implications here is that all textual meaning is in the end parenthetical—or made up between the lines, so to speak. It is in this way also that the Chinese *Book of Changes* can be taken as a postmodernist laboratory for theories of translation and interpretation.

87. JL (ibid., xvi) notes that the Song philosophy did not grow out of the "Yi proper" but from the Appendixes, especially the third Appendix (which "is more Taoistic than Confucian").

88. Ibid., xvii. We may well imagine that it must have been especially disturbing for Legge to encounter McClatchie's contention that the classical Shangdi was primarily symbolic of a gigantic phallus!

89. These developments indicate that the *Book of Changes* was suddenly capturing the fancy of educated circles on the Continent and in England. In 1883, a year after Legge's *Book of Changes*, volume 1 of Paul-Louis-Felix Philastre's *Tsheou Yi: Le Yi King ou Livre des changements de la dynastie des Tsheou* was published (volume 2 appeared in 1893), and later in the decade Charles Joseph de Harlez's translation appeared (*Le Yih-King: Texte primitif rétabli, traduit et commenté*, 1889). Regarding translations of the *Book of Changes*, and reviews, see the annotated bibliography by Hellmut Wilhelm, *The Book of Changes in the Western Tradition: A Selective Bibliography*, parergon 2 (Seattle, Wash.: Institute for Comparative and Foreign Area Studies, University of Washington, 1975).

90. JL, *Sacred Books*, 26: xix. On Terrien de Lacouperie's "most fantastic" approach to the *Book of Changes*, see Shchutskii, *Researches on the I Ching*, 24–25. As Shchutskii notes, Lacouperie's theories about the text as a kind of dictionary influenced the work of both de Harlez and Auguste Conrady.

91. It is an odd but interesting point that the self-styled Satanist and magician Aleister Crowley (1875–1947) became fascinated as a small boy with Legge's translation of the *Book of Changes*. See John Symonds and Kenneth Grant, eds., *The Confessions of Aleister Crowley: An Autobiography* (New York: Hill and Wang, 1969).

92. Chalmers, "The Sacred Books of China" (draft).

93. For the publishing history of Richard Wilhelm's translation of the *Book of Changes*, see Hellmut Wilhelm, *The Book of Changes in the Western Tradition*, 8–11.

94. T.W. Kingsmill, "The Sacred Books of China, Part II. The Yi King of James Legge," *The China Review* 11 (1882): 86–92.

95. Ibid. Kingsmill actually says that, because they could "frustrate the entire intention of the promoters of the *Sacred Books*," his comments on the deficiencies of Legge's new method of translation should be forwarded to the "editor of the series" (p. 92). See also the "editorial notice" of Kingsmill's review (in the *Chinese Recorder* 13 [November–December 1882]: 478), which laconically says that "most students will prefer to agree with Dr. Legge."

For further discussion of Legge's method of *en rapport* translation, see the pseudonymous criticism by "A Student," "A Study of the Yih King (a review essay of Yi King by James Legge, 1882; Mutationum Liber, Cursus Litteraturae Sinicae, vol. III, p. 520–619 by P. Angelo Zottoli S.J., Chang-hai, 1880; A Translation of the Confucian Yih King, or the 'Classic of Change' by Canon McClatchie, M.A., Shanghai, 1882; the Quarterly Review July 1882 article on Chinese Literature)," *The Chinese Recorder* 14 (1883): 13–32. This self-styled student says that both Legge and native scholars failed to understand the "true nature" of the "riddle" work of the *Book of Changes*. Now, however, the "Babylonian" secret was revealed by Terrien de Lacouperie. More astutely, the student also notes (pp. 31–32):

> A translation made on such a principle *[en rapport]* does not give the reader what is written in the original but the conception which the translator has of the meaning of the enigmatical and symbolical language. . . . Translations made with the view of giving the meaning of the enigmas will be different, the one from the other, because each translator has a different understanding of the enigmas. Readers will accept or reject the several meanings according to their own conceptions of the original.

96. Kingsmill, "The Sacred Books," 88. Despite his findings, like McClatchie's, that the Chinese originally worshiped "dual powers" as did the Aryans, Kingsmill remarks (ibid.) that the Chinese "were never led to orgies which disgrace other Asiatic natives."

97. Helen Edith Legge, *James Legge Missionary and Scholar* (London: Religious Tract Society, 1905), 212, quotes an unidentified source who describes a meeting with Legge in 1884 just as he was finishing up his manuscript translation of the *Record of Rites:* "You have come to me at the very moment at which my life has culminated. I have just finished correcting the proofs of my translation of the Sacred Books of China, on which I have been engaged for 25 years." On Julien's doubts about Legge's ability to finish the *Li ji,* see JL, *Sacred Books,* 27: xi.

98. See JL, *Sacred Books,* 27: xi–xiv. J. M. Callery's work is entitled *Li Ki, ou Mémorial des rites, traduit pour la première fois du chinois, et accompagné de notes, de commentaires, et du texte original* (Paris: B. Duprat, 1853). On Callery, see D. Marceron, *Bibliography du Taoism, suivie d'une biographie des principaux Sinologues, Japonistes et autres savants à donnés à l'étude de l'Extrême-Orient* (Paris: Ernest Leroux, 1898), 156–57. Legge also mentions some minor help derived from Father Angelo Zottoli's *Cursus Litteraturae Sinicae,* vol. 3 (1880) and Carlo Puini's *Li-Ki, institutioni, usi e costumanze della Cina antica; traduzione, commento e note* (1883).

99. See Séraphin Couvreur, *Li Ki ou Mémoires sur les bienséances: Texte chinois avec une double traduction en français et en latin,* 2 vols., 2d. ed. (Ho Kien Fou: Mission catholique, 1913). See Jeffrey K. Riegel, "Li chi," in *Early Chinese Texts: A Bibliographical Guide* (Berkeley, Calif.: Society for the Study of Early China and the Institute of East Asian Studies, University of California, 1993), 293–97.

100. See, for example, the description, by Jeffrey Riegel (ibid.), of the desultory studies of the *Li ji* (Record of rites). Exceptions to the general neglect of the ancient state religion are the two-volume work by Lester Bilsky, *The State Religion of Ancient China* (Taipei: Orient Cultural Service, 1975); and Laurence G. Thompson, "Confucian Thought: The State Cult," in *The Encyclopedia of Religion,* ed. Mircea Eliade (New York: Macmillan, 1986–1987), 4: 36–38. See also the often-overlooked article by E. T. Williams, "The State Religion of China during the Manchu Dynasty," *Journal of the North China Branch of the Royal Asiatic Society* 44 (1913): 11–45. French scholarship (a result of the Durkheimian focus on ritual) as seen in work of Granet and Maspero is much more respectful of the ritual context of meaning.

101. JL, *Sacred Books,* 27: 12. This is, as Legge says, "the first sentence of our classic."

102. It is worth noting, therefore, that Legge even defends (ibid.) the authentic religious and moral spirit of Chinese ceremony in the face of the Roman Catholic Callery's criticism that the "Chinese spirit" was too exclusively, rigidly, and formally ceremonial.

103. See the quoted words of Legge taken from a letter to Edkins, February 1886, "A Word from Dr. Legge," *The Chinese Recorder* 17 (April 1886): 161–62.

104. JL, *Sacred Books,* 27: 9–10.

105. Ibid., 10.

106. Ibid., 10–11.

107. Ibid., 11.

108. Ibid.

109. Ibid., 13. Legge is quoting from the eighth article of the 1858 treaty with Great Britain.

110. Ibid.

111. One classic expression of this is Arthur H. Smith's frequently reprinted work entitled *Chinese Characteristics* (New York: Fleming H. Revell, 1894). There is a sense in which we witness a growing realization that charity and tolerance toward others, whether fellow Christians or heathens, should come before faith and doctrinal beliefs.

112. JL, *Sacred Books,* 27: 13.

113. See Durrant, "Ching," 312–13.

114. JL, *Sacred Books,* 27: 14.

115. Besides the articles specifically discussed, see J. Edkins's "The Li Ki Translated by James Legge, D.D.," *The Chinese Recorder* 17 (September 1886): 325–28 (generally favorable, with some praise for Legge's refusal to indulge in the fashionable "post-dating of Chinese books by foreign authors" such as Herbert Giles); and a review in the *Indian Antiquary* (April 1887): 140 (clipping included in CWM/China/Personal/Legge/Box 7), noting Legge's "fair and judicious" estimate of the "social ideal" of the ancient Chinese and contrasting that with the "dead formalism of modern China." See also the anonymous review of Legge's work and several other books on China in the *Quarterly Review* 163 (July and October 1886): 65–85 (noteworthy for its praise of missionaries such as Legge and Edkins as "interpreters between the thought of the East and that of the West" and the missionary movement, "regarded on its purely secular side," as "one of the most powerful and most beneficent civilizing forces now at work" in China).

116. See, for example, the anonymous two-part review "Chinese Scholarship," *North-China Herald,* October 31, 1883, pp. 496–97, and November 7, 1883, pp. 524–35. Commenting (p. 524) that Chinese literature was often portrayed as "excessively over moral" yet "at the same time" the Chinese were called "a nation of liars," the reviewer pointed out rightly that this perception was a problem deriving from an overemphasis on the Chinese classics. Concerning Legge's work, the reviewer notes (p. 497) that

> [t]he quantity of work done [on the Chinese classics] is certainly stupendous, whatever may be thought of the quality. In presence of these huge volumes we feel almost afraid to speak. . . . [But it] must be confessed that the work does not altogether satisfy us. . . . Mr. Balfour justly remarks that in translating these classics a

great deal depends upon the terminology employed by the translator. Now we feel that the terminology employed by Dr. Legge is harsh, crude, inadequate, and, in some places, almost unidiomatic. So far for the form. As to the matter, we will let the Rev. Mr. Faber of Canton speak for us. . . . "[It is] extraordinary that neither in his notes nor in his dissertations has Dr. Legge let slip a single phrase or sentence to show what he conceived the teaching of Confucius really to be, as a philosophic whole.". . . Dr. Legge's judgment on the value of these works cannot by any means be accepted as final, and the translator of the Chinese Classics is yet to come. . . . Nothing shows that Chinese scholarship has reached an important turning point.

117. "Sacred Books of the East—The Texts of Confucianism," *Athenaeum,* July 24, 1886, p. 104.

118. John Chalmers, "'The Sacred Books of the East,' Edited by F. Max Müller, Vols XXVII and XXVIII.—The Sacred Books of China. The Texts of Confucianism, Translated by James Legge. Parts III and IV. The Le Ki. Oxford, Clarendon Press, 1885. Lane, Crawford, & Co., Hongkong and Shanghai," *The China Review* 15 (1886): 1.

119. Ibid., 3–4.

120. Ibid., 11–12.

121. See the editorial discussion in the *Chinese Recorder* 16 (January–February 1885): 75, which comments on E. H. Parker's use of the term *odium sinologicum* to refer to the absurdly vituperative fights between Julien and Pauthier back in the 1840s. Parker's discussion had appeared in the September–October 1884 issue of the *China Review.*

122. See William H. Honan, "Ode to Academic Nastiness," *New York Times Educational Supplement,* August 7, 1994, p. 38. Honan notes that, according to one popular theory about academic nastiness, "as scholars learn more and more about less and less they condemn themselves to a life that is the psychological equivalent of that of a caged rat. 'Pressed in against one another, perhaps for decades at a time, professors grow to despise one another.'"

123. It needs to be recognized that the nomenclature used of a so-called Babylonian tradition is notoriously variable and fluid at this time. There is, therefore, an abundance of generally synonymous terms such as Accadia, Akkadia, Susiana, Elam, Chaldeo-Elamite, Bak, and others.

124. See Laura Novo, "Archaeology," in *Victorian Britain: An Encyclopedia,* ed. Sally Mitchell (New York and London: Garland, 1988), 32–33. See also E. A. Wallis Budge, *The Rise and Progress of Assyriology* (London: Martin Hopkinson, 1925).

125. The label "Babylonian" is no more than a convenient umbrella term—albeit with a biblical ring—for an extremely complex historical and cultural situation; see Thorkild Jocobsen, "Mesopotamian Religions," in *The Encyclopedia of Religion,* ed. Mircea Eliade (New York: Macmillan, 1986–1987), 9: 447–66.

126. Lacouperie became a professor of Indo-Chinese philology at University College, London, in 1884. He seems to have disappeared from the professoriate there in 1890, four years before his premature death in 1894, but biographical details are sparse. See the *Annual Reports* for University College, London, for the years 1884–1890. For further information on Lacouperie, see R. K. Douglas, "Terrien de Lacouperie," *Journal of the Royal Asiatic Society* (1895): 214–16; Henri Cordier, "Half a Decade of Chinese Studies (1886–1891)," *T'oung Pao* 3 (1892): 532–63; and

idem, "Les Études Chinoises (1891–1894)," *T'oung Pao* 5 (1894): 428–40; and G. Schlegel, "Terrien De Lacouperie," *T'oung Pao* 5 (1894): 360; and Terrien de Lacouperie, "The Land of Sinim, Not China," *Babylonian and Oriental Record* 1 (1887): 183–91.

Though at first favorably disposed to Lacouperie's so-called scientific approach, Cordier took a less sanguine view in 1894 at the time of Lacouperie's death: "The weakness of his method is in trying to make all the facts conform to a preconceived theory, in place of deducing logically from his discoveries the conclusions that naturally emerge"; see *T'oung Pao* 5 (1894): 440. Inasmuch as Cordier became the arbiter of sinological discourse in the late nineteenth century, Lacouperie was effectively ignored from this point on.

127. This is R. K. Douglas's characterization in his "Terrien de Lacouperie," 215.

128. The description of Lacouperie and the "modern scientific school" is found in an unsigned article, "Sacred Books of the Chinese," published in the fashionable *Saturday Review*, June 30, 1883, p. 841. On this article, see pages 386ff. The criticism of Lacouperie views as "quite fantastic" is by Shchutskii in *Researches on the I Ching*, 14.

129. Lacouperie, "Land of Sinim, Not China."

130. The most triumphalistic claims along these lines are found in R. K. Douglas's "Origin of Chinese Culture and Civilization," *Lippincott's Monthly* 46 (1890): 850–55. In this article Douglas especially praises the Reverend C. J. Ball's work (especially as seen in the *Proceedings of the Society of Biblical Archaeology*) as verifying much of Lacouperie's early speculations. These were, according to Douglas, the "most remarkable philological discoveries of modern times." For Douglas it was Ball's "phonetic laws" that connected Accadian and Chinese in the same way that Sanskrit was related to Indo-European languages. Lacouperie and Ball were therefore pioneers in the sino-Babylonian hypothesis as William Jones and Franz Bopp were in Indo-European philology.

131. The roster of scholars who published in the *Babylonian and Oriental Record* includes, besides Lacouperie himself, Charles de Harlez, T. K. Cheyne of Oxford, the Reverend C. J. Ball (a leader of the later, end-of-the-century phase of sino-Babylonianism), Archibald Sayce, A. K. Glover, R. K. Douglas, and W. St. C. Boscowen. Charles de Harlez was perhaps the most distinguished scholar of this group. R. K. Douglas mentions Lacouperie's receipt of the Prix Julien, but does not indicate for which of his works.

132. For Edkins and sino-Babylonianism, see, among other works, J. Edkins, "Early Connections of Babylon with China," *The China Review* 16 (1887–1888): 371 (quoting Sayce for support); idem, *Ancient Symbolism* (London: Trübner, 1889), which argues that "Lau Tsi's . . . system is essentially Babylonian, but tinged with Hindoo thought. . . . It was because Lau Tsi seized on the scattered rays of Western thought and boldly adopted them, that he became the greatest of Chinese philosophers"; idem, "Primeval Revelation," *The Chinese Recorder* 21 (January 1891): 22–23 (according to the Book of Genesis Mesopotamia is the region of the primal revelation); and idem, *The Early Spread of Religious Ideas* (London: Religious Tract Society, 1893), in which he states that recent archaeological discoveries were "proof" of the "primaeval revelation" of Genesis; a "practical" nation like China which lacked the "imaginative faculty" could never have originated the Daoist philosophy.

133. See J. Edkins, "On the Three Words 'I Hi Wei' in the Tau Te King," *The Chinese Recorder* 17 (August 1886): 306–9. See also idem, "The Tau Te King," *The China Review* 13 (1884–1885): 10–19 (he refers here to the influence of Lacouperie); and idem, "The Foreign Origin of Taoism," *The China Review* 19 (1891): 397–99 (the distinctive Daoist cosmology and cosmogony show their foreign or Babylonian origins: "It is only in this way that Tauism, a highly ideal philosophy springing up among such a practical nation as the Chinese, can be accounted for"). For criticism of this theory, see the "Notices of New Books" in the *China Review* 15 (1886–1887): 315 ("We have had a time, now far behind us, when everything obscure to be found in China was derived from India. Dr. Edkins now labours to trace back everything peculiarly Chinese to a Babylonian source").

Edkins's views are a representative (and generative) example of the dominant sinological bias against the notion that there was any kind of indigenous cosmogonic mythology in ancient China. For a discussion of this problem in sinological discourses, see Norman Girardot, "The Problem of Creation Mythology in the Study of Chinese Religion," *History of Religions* 15 (1976): 289–318, and Anne Birrell, "Studies on Chinese Myths since 1970: An Appraisal," 2 parts, *History of Religions* 33 (1994): 380–93, and 34 (1994): 70–94.

With regard to Daoism and the *Daode jing*, Kingsmill continued to support the Aryan theory of origins. In "The Tao Teh King, A Translation with Notes," *The China Review* 24 (1899–1900): 147, Kingsmill argued that "both the form [like Indian sutra literature of an "enigmatic string"] and the doctrines [of Daoism] are so essentially Indian . . . [that we] must assume the writer or writers had considerable knowledge of the Indian schools." Daoism was therefore "essentially Buddhistic" with a dose of Sankhya philosophy.

134. Terrien de Lacouperie, "Yh King," *Saturday Review,* January 1882.

135. Terrien de Lacouperie, *Athenaeum,* September 5, 1882.

136. See Robert K. Douglas, "A New Interpretation of the 'Yi King,'" *Academy,* August 12, 1882, pp. 121–22 (". . . fortunately to the discerning eye of M. Terrien de La Couperie the secret . . . has become apparent. . . . The sentences of the text which yield such strange results when interpreted by the commentators now stand revealed—some as vocabularies, some as ephemerides, some as geographical or ethnological enumerations, etc."); idem (but written anonymously), "Chinese Literature (a review of The Sacred Books of China, Vols. III and XVI; the Chinese Classics, 3 vols., 1875, 1876 by J. Legge)," *Quarterly Review* 154 (July 1882): 124–50; and Alexander Wylie, *Notes on Chinese Literature* (Shanghai: American Presbyterian Mission Press, 1867).

137. Douglas, "Chinese Literature," 124. About the commentarial mode of Chinese literature Douglas says, "Instead of thinking for themselves, they have studied only how to reproduce the thoughts of others, and instead of seeking new fields of knowledge, they have been content to add commentary to commentary on the ancient texts, in which they have been reduced to criticizing every word and weighing every sentence."

138. Ibid., 133.

139. Ibid. Douglas suggests that, inasmuch as Susiana invented "letters," this is but another indication of the Chinese indebtedness to ancient Babylonian tradition.

140. R. K. Douglas, "Society and Religious Ideas of the Chinese," *Journal of the Anthropological Institute* 22 (1892–1893): 159–72. In this article, Douglas describes the Chinese as (p. 159) "an immature people and just as their eyes are infants' eyes, so far as the absence of the coruncula lachryinalis and the heavy fold of the upper lid are concerned, and their cheeks, the smooth cheeks of young boys, so their characters represent an arrested stage in the mental development of the people."

Douglas also notes that the evidence for the *Book of Changes* as a Babylonian syllabary was "stronger than ever" (p. 172).

141. Douglas, "Chinese Literature," 127–28.

142. Ibid. 129–30.

143. See JL, "Chinese Chronology," *Journal of the Royal Asiatic Society* (1893): 55–82. This paper was delivered as a lecture in May of 1892 (the ten-year hiatus shows that the sino-Babylonian controversy persisted for more than a decade, dying out only after the death of Lacouperie in 1894). In the discussion that followed this lecture, Thomas Wade agreed with Legge's attempt to argue for the general historicity of ancient Chinese figures such as "Fu Hsi, Shan Nang, and Hwang Ti," saying, "The ages assigned to the individual men are to us, who believe in the patriarchal ages, in no instance astonishing" (p. 79). As Legge put it: "The existence of Yao, Shun, and Yu is not to be doubted. I could as soon doubt the existence of Abraham and the other Hebrew patriarchs in our Sacred Scriptures" (p. 66). Wade does, however, make it clear that he does not believe that the ancient Chinese "were acquainted with God." See William Frederick Mayers, *The Chinese Reader's Manual: A Handbook of Biographical, Historical, Mythological, and General Literary Reference* (Shanghai: American Presbyterian Mission Press, 1874).

144. Terrien de Lacouperie, "The Oldest Book of the Chinese (the Yh-King) and Its Author," *Journal of the Royal Asiatic Society* 14 (1882): 798–815. A second installment was published in the *Journal of the Royal Asiatic Society* in 1883. Lacouperie's translation was published in book form as *The Oldest Book of the Chinese: The Yih-king and Its Authors*, vol. 1, *History and Method* (London: Nutt, 1892). No second volume ever appeared.

145. See Legge's letter to the editor, *Academy*, September 19, 1882. Here Legge is specifically responding to Douglas's "A New Interpretation of the 'Yi King.'"

146. JL, "*Confucianism and Taouism*, by Robert K. Douglas of the British Museum and Professor of Chinese at King's College," *Academy*, November 22, 1879, pp. 363–64. See also the argument over Maitreya Buddha initiated by Robert K. Douglas in "Fa-Hien's Description of the Image of Maitreya Buddha," *Athenaeum*, March 12, 1887, p. 359.

147. Legge specifically mentions four points against the "reasonableness" of Lacouperie and Douglas's translation: the issue of unintelligibility, the illegitimacy of breaking up the text as given, the overemphasis on phonetic principles, and the non sequitur of arguing that such syllabaries can be found in other traditions such as the Babylonian.

148. E. H. Parker, "M. Terrien de Lacouperie as a Sinologist," *The China Review* 13 (1884): 301–5.

149. Ibid., 301. Parker includes a list of obvious mistranslations.

150. Ibid., 302.

151. The "sneering" article mentioned here is no doubt the anonymous "Sacred Books of the Chinese" (*Saturday Review,* June 30, 1883, pp. 841–43), in which Legge is denigrated as an able scholar "of the missionary type" who has been surpassed by the sinologists of the "modern scientific school" like Lacouperie (p. 841).

152. Parker, "Terrien de Lacouperie," 304–5. For "serious" sinologists the answer should have been obvious, but Parker was astute enough to acknowledge the power of a siren's call in the fields of Orientalism. The reference to "serious" sinologists is found in the discussion of Parker's article in the *North-China Herald,* June 5, 1885, p. 646.

153. See letter to the editor, *Academy,* September 4, 1886, p. 156. The detail (*Academy,* August 7, 1886) that this conversation took place at the residence of the Chinese ambassador Zeng Jize (Marquis Tseng, 1839–1890) is especially fascinating in that Zeng fancied himself a decipherer of the modern secrets of the *Book of Changes* (see Yu Yueheng, ed., *Zeng Jize yiji* [Changsha, China, 1983], 377).

154. For a copy of Müller to Legge, August 7, 1886, and a copy of Legge to the editor of the *Academy,* August 21, 1886, see CWM/China/Personal/Legge/Box 8.

155. Terrien de Lacouperie, "The Yih King" (letter to the editor), *Academy,* September 4, 1886, p. 156. The editorial note concerning the cessation of the debate is found on the same page as Lacouperie's letter.

156. On the title page to the *Languages of China Before the Chinese* (London: David Nutt, 1887), Lacouperie is identified as "Doctor of Philosophy and in Letters; Professor of Indo-chinese Philology University College, London; member of the Royal Asiatic Society and Philological Society; corresponding member of the Académie de Stanislas of Nancy, the Peking Oriental Society, etc." In that book (p. 8) Lacouperie is concerned to overcome the "inveterate and unjustifiable prejudice of the Aryan school of philology" (especially concerning the "permanence of grammar"; cf. his "Comparative Ideology" in the *Academy,* September 4, 1886, pp. 155–56). See also R. K. Douglas's congratulatory review of this book in the *Academy,* October 22, 1887, pp. 271–72 ("a monument of scholarly instinct and of patient research").

In the article "Babylonia and China" (*Academy,* August 7, 1886, pp. 91–92), Lacouperie restated his theories and added that new evidence continued to support his position (e.g., the names of the Chinese duodenary cycle were very similar to the twelve names of the Babylonian months; *Shangdi* was clearly derived from the Babylonian god *Shamash;* and so on). He also was glad to see that Edkins was now arguing for a Western origin of Chinese civilization.

Besides Douglas's continuing accolades, favorable appraisals of Lacouperie's work were published in the *Saturday Review,* June 30, 1883, pp. 841–43, and in a pseudonymous article, "A Student," "A Study of the Yih King."

157. G. Schlegel, "China or Elam," *T'oung Pao* 2 (1891). Schlegel's most famous sinological work was his *Uranographie chinoise, ou preuves directes que l'astronomie primitive est originaire de la Chine, et qu'elle a été empruntée par les anciens peuples occidentaux à la sphère chinoise* (Leiden: E.J. Brill, 1875). On Schlegel, see H. Cordier, "Nécrologie. Dr. Gustave Schlegel," *T'oung Pao* 4 (1903): 407–15. Schlegel was the teacher of J. M. M. de Groot and, according to K. Schipper (*The Taoist Body,* trans. Karen C. Duval [Berkeley and Los Angeles: University of California Press, 1993], 5), a "convinced comparatist."

158. See Otto Franke, "China and Comparative Philology," *The China Review* 20 (1893): 310–27; Franz Boas, "The Limitations of the Comparative Method of An-

thropology," *Science* 4 (1896): 901–8. See also Parker's other articles, "The Chinese Language," *The Chinese Recorder* 15 (May–June 1884): 151–64 (contra Edkins and Kingsmill); and "The Ancient Language of China," *The Chinese Recorder* 16 (May 1885): 161–74 (contra Kingsmill and Lacouperie). For the relation to the comparative science of religions, see P. Borgeaud, "Le problème du comparatisme en histoire des religions," *Revue européens des sciences sociales* 24 (1986): 59–75; Jonathan Z. Smith, "Adde Parvum Parvo Magnus Acervus Erit," *History of Religions* 11 (1971): 67–90; and Henry M. Hoenigswald, "On the History of the Comparative Method," *Anthropological Linguistics* 5 (1963): 1–11.

159. Schlegel, "China or Elam," 245–46.

160. Archibald Sayce, who was at first a supporter of Lacouperie, eventually started to qualify his support. See, for example, A. H. Sayce, "Old Babylonian and Chinese Characters," *Nature* 38 (1888): 122–23. He suggests here that, although Lacouperie has nothing to fear from Assyrian scholars, he must await the verdict of sinologists. See the comment on Sayce's position in the Editorial Note, *The Chinese Recorder* 20 (January 1889): 43–44.

Interestingly enough, this is still largely the situation in the study of ancient Mesopotamia. As Thorkild Jacobsen said ("Mesopotamian Religions," 446–69), there are still "grave problems with the script and language of ancient Mesopotamia." Moreover, "no translation of Akkadian texts prior to the twentieth century can safely be taken at face value" (p. 469). With regard to the earliest Sumerian tradition, there is "no certainty at all" and "extreme caution is thus indicated" (ibid.).

161. Schlegel, "China or Elam," 246. It is this strongly antidiffusionist and polygenetic position that became the orthodox perspective on cultural genesis and development within sinology, a view only reinforced by the spectacular archaeological discoveries of Shang Chinese oracle bones at the end of the century.

162. It is not that the named perspectives do not have merit, but that there is need for extreme caution. The problem is exacerbated by the ideological position of sinitic singularity argued by both traditional and modern native Chinese scholars. An extreme of this is seen in Ping-ti Ho's chauvinistic *The Cradle of the East: An Inquiry into the Indigenous Origins of Techniques and Ideas of Neolithic and Early Historic China, 5000–1000 B.C.* (Hong Kong and Chicago: Chinese University of Hong Kong and University of Chicago Press, 1975). The most balanced appraisal of these issues as they relate to the origins of Chinese civilization is found in David Keightley, ed., *The Origins of Chinese Civilization* (Berkeley and Los Angeles: University of California Press, 1983). See, in particular, Keightley's preface to this volume, pp. xix–xxix, on the "historiographical and epistemological problems" of sinological studies. For developments favoring more of a diffusionist perspective, see Jerry H. Bentley, "Cross-Cultural Interaction and Periodization in World History," *American Historical Review* 101 (1996): 749–70.

Concerning the checkered career of pan-Babylonianism in other fields of Orientalistic and comparativistic disciplines, see Jan de Vries, "Panbabylonianism," in *The Study of Religion: A Historical Approach,* trans. Kees W. Bolle (New York: Harcourt, Brace & World, 1967), 95–98; and Wilhelm Schmidt's classic discussion in his *Origin and Growth of Religion: Facts and Theories,* trans. H. J. Rose (London: Methuen, 1931), 91–102.

163. On T.W. Rhys Davids, see Philip Almond, *The British Discovery of Buddhism* (Cambridge: Cambridge University Press, 1988). In the late nineteenth century, it could certainly be said that the London University colleges—with Rhys Davids, Lacouperie, and Samuel Beal at University and R.K. Douglas at King's—had the most impressive record of Oriental studies of any British institution.

164. Ibid., 28.

165. See JL to Edkins, February 1886, quoted in "A Word from Dr. Legge," *The Chinese Recorder* 17 (April 1886): 161–62. See also the references to Rhys Davids in JL, *A Record of Buddhist Kingdoms, Being An Account by the Chinese Monk Fa-Hien of His Travels in India and Ceylon (A.D. 389–414) in Search of the Buddhist Books of Discipline* (Oxford: Clarendon Press, 1886), ix, and throughout the notes.

166. See [T.W. Rhys Davids], "Sacred Books of the East, Translated by Various Oriental Scholars, and Edited by F. Max Müller," *Quarterly Review* 163 (1886): 180–203. It may be noted that the *Quarterly Review* was generally considered to be a journal of highbrow Toryism.

167. Ibid., 180–81.

168. Ibid., 182. Deviating from the Müllerian aversion to the theoretical school as expressed in "Forgotten Bibles," Rhys Davids subscribed to the notion that the new theory of animism (Edward Tylor is not named) was deserving of "attention" and "respect" in relation to the question of origins (ibid., 196).

169. Rhys Davids's comments (ibid., 187, 188) on the pseudoauthority of authorship are worth noting:

> A book to a modern mind implies an author. It was not so then. No one of them can be properly said to have had an author. . . . In those early times a book was seldom or never composed originally in the shape in which it has come down to us. It was not made, it grew. . . . The books lived, or rather were kept alive, not for the sake of the author, but for the sake of their contents. Hence it is that, though certain of the wise sayings or verses it contains may have authors assigned to them, no really ancient book claims to have an author—a human author. It is only later that the tendency is felt, to satisfy the natural craving for a cause by assigning books to individual hands . . . more likely to that of some old and famous teacher of the particular school than that of the real compiler of the "book." . . . These "sacred books" differ in many ways from what would be implied by such an expression in its modern connotation. They were not written when first composed; they were put together after a method entirely unknown among later books; they grew different as they grew older, and they contain older strata intermixed with, covered over by later accretions. Old as they are, there is a long past lying behind them. . . . They are not only much later than the origin of religion, but also later than the rise of the special forms of belief they represent, and they carry within them the evidence of their gradual growth and of their strange history.

170. Ibid., 188–89.

171. Ibid., 203.

172. The first version of Legge's will is dated July 7, 1885, the last added codicil dating to 1890.

173. See "Dr. Legge's Translations," *The China Review* 14 (1886): 294 (reference to his Daoist work); and "A Word from Dr. Legge," *The Chinese Recorder* 17 (April 1886): 161–62.

174. JL, "The Bearing of Our Knowledge of Comparative Religions on Christian Missions" (CWM/South China/Personal/Legge/Box 4). This important document can be dated to 1886 from internal evidence even though the handscript date on the first page seems to read "November 15, 1866."

175. It is worth remarking on the fact that Legge says he was also brought to the brink of acknowledging a "Jewish element" in the Christian New Testament: The writers were, after all, Jews! It may also be noted that Legge's reference to family worship recalls the recommendations of his father-in-law, John Morison's, *Family Prayers*, which emphasized readings from the Old Testament (especially Genesis, Exodus, the Psalms, Isaiah, and Jeremiah). This comparison is also a perfect example of the congruence of Victorian and classical Confucian prudishness. This assumed purity is, moreover, something that only heightens the often hypocritical possibilities of sexual propriety and repression, and the contradictions of an overly fastidious general morality, closeted in both traditions.

176. JL, "The Bearing of Our Knowledge."

CHAPTER SEVEN. ANCESTOR LEGGE:
TRANSLATING BUDDHISM AND DAOISM, 1886–1892

1. Legge's "supereminence as a translator of the Chinese Classics" is referred to in an editorial note in *The China Review* 16 (1887–1888) (in which Giles's attacks on Legge are discussed). The references to Nestor are numerous, but let me refer only to the use of the expression by Henri Cordier and G. Schlegel, "James Legge, M.A. Oxford, LL.D. Aberdeen," *T'oung Pao* 9 (1898): 59–63. For an example of the kind of carping criticism being rendered by more thoroughly professionalized younger sinologists, see Paul Georg von Möllendorff's discussion of Legge's failure to appreciate the importance of Manchu for the translation of Chinese, *A Manchu Grammar, With Analysed Texts* (Shanghai: American Presbyterian Mission Press, 1892), v.

2. See, for example, Friedrich Hirth, "Über Sinologische Studien," *T'oung Pao* 6 (1895).

3. JL, December 17, 1886, Council for World Mission (hereafter cited as CWM)/China/Personal/Legge/Box 7.

4. This is to some extent detectable in Cordier's retrospective appraisals of sinology at the end of the century—especially those published in *T'oung Pao*.

5. Social connections were as important as scholarship for appointment to the presidency of the Royal Asiatic Society (private communication, Michael Pollack, secretary to the Royal Asiatic Society). Legge's association with the society was minimal. He gave presentations at the general meetings in 1879, 1893, and 1895; and he participated in the society's council only on January 17, 1893, and April 10, 1894 (at which time he was serving as an honorary vice-president). It is interesting to note that Müller's involvement with the society was also very rudimentary. More active on the society's council were Lacouperie, Douglas, Wade, Henry Rawlinson, and Monier-Williams. For details concerning participation in the meetings and council, see Royal Asiatic Society Minutes of General Meetings and the Minutes of Council, Royal Asiatic Society archive, London. See also the *Centenary Volume of the Royal Asiatic Society*, ed. F.E. Pargiter (London: Royal Asiatic Society, 1923).

6. See James C. Cooley, *T.F. Wade in China: Pioneer in Global Diplomacy, 1842–1882*, monographies du T'oung Pao, vol. xi (Leiden: E.J. Brill, 1981).

7. On Legge's courses and lectures during this period, see appendix B. During the period from 1886 to 1892, Legge continued to teach from his favorite Four Books and continued to use various Chinese primers for grammar and composition. Most notably, he supplemented these materials with an extremely broad range of other texts—e.g., Buddhist (especially travel and pilgrimage literature) and Daoist texts, historical readings from the Han dynasty, poems from the *Chuci* (*Ch'u Tz'u*), and especially (in the late 1880s and early 1890s) the Tang-dynasty writings of the Confucian "comparativist" critic and stylist, Han Yu.

8. For documentation of the founding of Mansfield College and Legge's participation, see the *Report of the Committee of Management of Mansfield College Oxford for the Session 1886–87*, for *Session 1887–88*, and for *Session 1888–89*. These materials are available in the archive at the Mansfield College Library, Mansfield College, Oxford.

9. See the article on the dedication of Mansfield College in the *Times* (October 15, 1889), available in the Mansfield College Library archive, News Cuttings, Book 2, p. 3. On Fairbairn, see also "The Story of Principal Fairbairn's Career," in the Mansfield College Library archive, News Cuttings, Book 4, pp. 20–24. For the arguments in favor of establishing a new Nonconformist College at Oxford, see A.M. Fairbairn, "Nonconformity and the Universities. The Free Churches and a Theological Faculty. I," *British Quarterly Review* 79 (1884): 372–390.

10. See the *Times* article and articles in the *Inquirer* (October 19, 1889) and *Vanity Fair* (October 19, 1889). All of these are available in Mansfield College Library archive, News Cuttings, Book 2, pp. 3, 17.

11. Ibid., p. 3.

12. Ibid. See also Hugh W. Strong, "Modern Oxford and Nonconformity," *London Quarterly and Holborn Review*, no. 2 (1899): 279–290.

13. See J.S. Reynolds, "The Evangelicals at Oxford 1735–1871: A Record of an Unchronicled Movement with the Record Extended to 1905," in *The Evangelicals at Oxford*, ed. J.S. Reynolds (Oxford: Marcham Manor Press, 1975). As Reynolds notes (pp. 30–31), evangelicals at Oxford had a special affinity for Oriental learning (e.g., the Arabists Macbride, Gandell, and David Margoliouth; the Syriac scholar Payne Smith; Legge in Chinese; and Monier-Williams in Sanskrit).

14. On Joseph Estlin Carpenter, see the material in the archive at Manchester College, Oxford. For Carpenter's views on the science of comparative religion, see his *Comparative Religion* (London: Williams and Norgate, 1913).

15. One minor exception to this was Müller's presidential address given at the annual meeting of the Oxford Society of Historical Theology on November 23, 1893. See Müller, "On the Proper Use of Holy Scriptures," *Abstracts of the Society of Historical Theology* (Oxford University), 1893, pp. 5–26.

16. Already in the second session of the college (1887–1888), Fairbairn was teaching a course devoted to the "History of Religions," which included consideration of the religions of the "Further East" (China and India) and the "Nearer East" (Egyptian, Semitic, and Islamic). See the *Report of the Committee of Management of Mansfield College Oxford for the Session 1887–88*, p. 14.

17. Becoming even more celebrated than the Hibbert Lectures, the Gifford Lectureships (established as a permanent endowment in each of the Scottish universi-

ties) were created in 1888 by Adam Gifford, a distinguished and wealthy senator in the College of Justice in Scotland. In his will he stipulated that the lectures were for "promoting, advancing, teaching, and diffusing the study of Natural Theology" in the "widest sense of the term." For Gifford this implied the rejection of any reliance on "special revelation" and that "no religious test of any kind" was to be "prescribed." The lecturers could therefore "be of no religion, or they may be so-called sceptics, or agnostics, or free-thinkers." Most of all, the "study of Natural Theology" stressed the need to study religion scientifically, "like astronomy or chemistry." See Morris Jastrow, *The Study of Religion* (1901; reprint, Chico, Calif.: Scholars Press, 1981), 51.

18. See the "Notice of the Board of Oriental Studies" (CWM/China/Personal/Legge/Box 8). It is said that the exams would cover Chinese composition and grammar, aspects of Chinese history and geography, the familiarity with texts such as the Four Books and traditional Chinese primers such as the *Sanzi jing* and the *Qianzi wen*, and the ability to translate Chinese into English and English into Chinese. In this batch of odd documents dating to roughly this time, there is a letter from Legge to the secretary of state for foreign affairs in which Legge pleads, yet again, with the Foreign Office to consider sending young trainees destined for China to Oxford for language study. Again Legge's plea fell on deaf ears and he registers his "sore discouragement." "Surely," as he says, this failure to take advantage of language training in England was a grave "defect which should be remedied."

19. On the comparisons of Buddhism and Catholicism, see E.J. Eitel, "Buddhism versus Romanism," *The Chinese Recorder* 3 (November 1870): 142–43; and, more generally, see Philip Almond, *The British Discovery of Buddhism* (Cambridge: Cambridge University Press, 1988), 123 (Almond uses the expression "holy mummeries").

20. A.M. Fairbairn, "History of Religions," *Contemporary Review* 47 (1885): 436. The categorization of the original, "pure," and "atheistic" pre-Mahayana forms of Buddhism (as well as the early Daoism of Laozi and Zhuangzi) as primarily "philosophical" in nature was a pronounced tendency throughout the nineteenth century—see Almond, *British Discovery of Buddhism*, 93–96.

21. JL, "The Purgatories of Buddhism and Taoism," handwritten original and Helen Edith Legge typescript, 13 pp. (Bodleian Library, Oxford University [hereafter cited as Bodleian] Dep. c. 38). This lecture is at one point described as an "illustrated lecture," but the illustrations (no doubt native Chinese depictions of the ten hells) have not been preserved. Although Buddhist notions of "future punishment" and an afterlife had a special appeal for the Calvinist sensibilities of many Victorian commentators such as Legge, the doctrine of *karma* was often viewed, as he said in the lecture, as "merely an absurdity."

22. By the late 1880s there was a conservative Christian backlash against Edwin Arnold's work and its propagation of misconceptions about the "likeness" of Buddhism and Christianity, a situation that is best exemplified by S.H. Kellogg's book *The Light of Asia and the Light of the World* (London: Macmillan, 1885). See, for example, D.Z. Sheffield's review of Kellogg in *The Chinese Recorder* 19 (August 1888): 349–58. Especially bothersome to these critics was the notion that somehow Buddhist teachings were sympathetic to the teachings of Darwin and modern naturalistic science (see the discussion in *The Chinese Recorder* 24 [February 1893]: 92–93).

For Müller's increasingly disparaging evaluation of Blavatsky's Buddhism, see the review of Müller's lectures in the *Oxford Magazine,* May 25 and June 1, 1892, pp. 388, 404. See also the discussion of the "Buddhist cult" in Boston and New York City by the new professor of comparative religions at New York University, F.F. Ellinwood, "Shall We Study the False Religions?" *The Chinese Recorder* 20 (November 1889): 519–24. On Müller's views, see his "Buddhism" (1862), "Buddhist Pilgrims" (1857), and "The Meaning of Nirvana" (1857) in *Chips from a German Workshop* (New York: Charles Scribner's Sons, 1895), 1: 179–231, 232–75, 276–87. In "Buddhism" (p. 196), Müller noted that it was Burnouf's *Histoire du Buddhisme* (1844) that "laid the foundation for a systematic study of the religion of Buddha." On the whole issue of the Victorian "invention" of Buddhism, see especially Almond's excellent overview, *British Discovery of Buddhism.* See also Thomas A. Tweed, *The American Encounter with Buddhism, 1844–1912: Victorian Culture and the Limits of Dissent* (Bloomington and Indianapolis: Indiana University Press, 1992). Tweed's discussion of Müller's Buddhist studies (pp. 14–15) is particularly helpful:

> [Müller] suggested . . . that the Buddha's philosophy was atheistic and nihilistic, but the later tradition, acting from the deepest inherent impulses of human nature, had moved toward theism and immortality and hopefulness. In his 1862 essay, Müller offered another argument from "human nature," and this time he went further. He defended even the Buddha against the usual criticisms and brought the founder's thinking into line with the dominant Western conceptions of humans' innate religious inclinations. Arguing from human nature, such as we find it in all times and countries, Müller confessed that—whatever the other great scholars had suggested—he simply could not believe that so great a moral teacher and social reformer could have "thrown away one of the most powerful weapons in the hands of every religious teacher—the belief in a future life." Because it would be contrary to human nature to be motivated by a desire for the "annihilation" of all individuality in nirvana, Buddha could not have been so deluded as to have believed that. At least, Müller asserted, he could not have been foolish enough to teach that!

23. See especially Almond, *British Discovery of Buddhism.*

24. See, for example, the discussion in "The Number of Buddhists in the World," *The Chinese Recorder* 14 (November–December 1883): 453–63.

25. See D. Brear, "Early Assumptions in Western Buddhist Studies," *Religion* 5 (1975): 136–159. Brear notes (p. 149) that Chinese Mahayana was seen as a "degeneration" of the purer Pali Buddhism.

26. Eitel and Edkins were the two most notable missionary scholars of Chinese Buddhism. Both were acutely critical of Buddhism, but both tended to suggest that, however it had degenerated from the earlier austerities of primal Buddhism, Chinese Buddhism at least allowed for the more human development of religious needs and aspirations (e.g., compassion, salvation, afterlife). The twist here was that early Buddhism was too cold and too pessimistic to satisfy basic "religious instincts." See Brear, "Early Assumptions," p. 149. For Edkins's views, see his *The Religious Condition of the Chinese with Observations on the Prospects of Christian Conversion amongst that People* (London: Routledge, Warnes, and Routledge, 1859). See Eitel's *Handbook for the Student of Chinese Buddhism* (Hong Kong: Lane, Crawford, 1888), which Legge cites as an especially valuable aid; and idem, *Buddhism: Its Historical, Theoretical and Popular Aspects* (Shanghai: Kelly & Walsh, 1884).

27. See Griffith John, "The Ethics of the Chinese," *Journal of the North China Branch of the Royal Asiatic Society* (1859): 185–87. This article is singled out by Legge in his 1861 edition of the Four Books. Throughout his 1880s and early 1890s Legge had a growing interest in Han Yu as both a Ruist critic of heterodox traditions such as Buddhism and Daoism and as an important literary stylist. It seems clear that, inasmuch as Legge preferred to do the work of translation within a native Chinese commentarial stream, his interest in Han Yu's polemics and Confucian methodology increased as his interest in the heterodox traditions of Buddhism and Daoism increased.

28. Buddhist travel literature had its own special problems associated with the identification of details of geography, flora, and fauna.

29. Julien produced the *Histoire de la vie à Hiouen-thsang et de ses voyages dans l'Inde* (Paris, 1853) and *Mémoires sur les contrées occidentals* (Paris, 1857–1858), a translation of the original by Xuan Zang (ca. 600–664).

30. JL, *A Record of Buddhist Kingdoms: Being an Account by the Chinese Monk Fa-Hien of His Travels in India and Ceylon (A.D. 389–414) in Search of the Buddhist Books of Discipline* (hereafter cited as *The Travels of Fa-Hien*) (Oxford: Clarendon Press, 1886).

Legge (ibid., viii) refers to the translation of Fa Xian by Rémusat and Klaproth (Paris, 1836). He mentions (ibid., vii) that he first attempted to read Fa Xian's texts when he was living in Hong Kong, but had little success because of the difficult matter of deciphering Chinese phonetic renderings of Sanskrit names and terminology. Legge indicates that Eitel's *Handbook* (1870) alleviated the problem of working with the Chinese transliteration of Sanskrit, but it was not until 1878 that he went back to his Buddhist studies and worked on the Fa Xian narrative. The work was done with his Davis scholar that year, who was also a Boden Sanskrit scholar; Legge does not identify this person, but perhaps it was A. A. Macdonald. It does not appear to have been one of Müller's Japanese Buddhist students because they did not arrive in Oxford until 1879 and would surely not have been eligible for the Davis Scholarship. After lecturing on Fa Xian at Oxford in 1885 and making another translation, and then receiving a "good and clear" Chinese text from his "friend," the Japanese Buddhist Bunyiu Nanjio, Legge says that he was ready to publish his version of the text.

31. See W. Gluer, "Encounter Between Christianity and Chinese Buddhism in the 19th and 20th Centuries," *Ching Feng* 11 (1968): 39–57; and Ralph R. Covell, *Confucius, the Buddha, and Christ: A History of the Gospel in Chinese* (Maryknoll, N.Y.: Orbis Books, 1986). See also Eric J. Sharpe, *Karl Ludvig Reichelt: Missionary, Scholar, and Pilgrim* (Hong Kong: Tao Fong Shan Ecumenical Centre, 1984), 7–21.

32. See, for example, Timothy Richard, "The Influence of Buddhism in China," *The Chinese Recorder* 21 (February 1890): 49–64. Donald Treadgold identifies him as "syncretistic" (*The West in Russia and China: Secular and Religious Thought in Modern Times* [Cambridge: Cambridge University Press, 1973], 2: 186).

33. On Richard's "radical" proposals, see Treadgold's *West in Russia and China*, 2: 185–87; Gluer's "Encounter," 45–46; and Covell's *Confucius, the Buddha, and Christ*, 125–27. Instead of the emphasis that Legge and Edkins placed on fulfillment or completion that builds on, but replaces the "defects" of indigenous systems such as Confucianism and Buddhism, Richard suggested that Mahayana Buddhism, as a kind of Chinese New Testament, needed only some "quantitative 'additions' to be fulfilled"

(see especially Covell's helpful discussion of these points). Richard was an evangelical with a strong leaning toward Socialist political teachings (especially after the 1898 reform). In this sense, he was not a social-gospel religious reductionist, but a strong advocate of a broad range of social agencies to help the Chinese people. Covell (p. 127) makes it clear that Richard read the Christian gospel into Buddhist literature (Mahayana), and argued that Saint Thomas had passed the message of Christ to Asvaghosha (Covell).

34. W.A.P. Martin, "Is Buddhism a Preparation for Christianity?" *The Chinese Recorder* 20 (May 1889): 193–203. In this article, Martin refers to the recent appointment of F.F. Ellinwood, the secretary of the American Presbyterian Missionary Society, to the new chair of comparative religions at New York University. "Fairness" rather than any "renunciation of the claims of Christianity" was the qualification for the duties of this new chair, a qualification that Martin also recommends to his missionary brethren.

35. See the critical discussion of Martin's article, "Is Buddhism a Preparation," in *The China Review* 18 (1889–1890): 199–201.

36. On the Japanese Buddhologist Takakusu Junjiro (1866–1945), see Shinsho Hanayama, *Bibliography on Buddhism* (Tokyo: Hokuseido Press, 1961), 735–38.

37. JL, *Travels of Fa-Hien*, x, notes that they have agreed to disagree about some aspects of Buddhism.

38. Besides the lecture on "Purgatories" mentioned above, Legge also discussed Buddhism in at least one other public lecture, "On Future Punishment as Conceived by Confucianists and Other Chinese Religionists" (Bodleian, Dep. c. 61; ca. 1890s). It is worth noting that, on June 14, 1879, Legge wrote Müller a four-page letter outlining his gleanings on Buddhism from various dynastic histories (Bodleian, MS. Autogr. e. 11, *fols.* 53–54).

39. JL, "A Fair and Dispassionate Discussion of the Three Doctrines Accepted in China: From Liu Mi, a Buddhist Writer," in *Transactions of the Ninth International Congress of Orientalists, London* (London: Printer for the Committee of the Congress, 1893), 2: 563–82.

40. Using four recensions of the Chinese text (a Korean and a Japanese edition, along with Song and Ming editions), Legge's textual scholarship was of the highest standards for the period. See JL, *Travels of Fa-Hien*, 4–5.

41. Ibid., x.

42. Ibid., 4.

43. As an ex-superintendent of the Hong Kong Missionary Press, Legge was always careful about the details and difficulties of Oriental typesetting. As he points out (ibid., x–xi):

> The two fonts of Chinese types in the Clarendon Press were prepared primarily for printing the translation of our Sacred Scriptures [in Hong Kong] and then extended so as to be available for printing also the Confucian Classics; but a Buddhist work necessarily requires many types not found in them, while many other characters in the Corean recension are peculiar in their forms, and some are what Chinese dictionaries denominate "vulgar." That we have succeeded so well as we have done is owing chiefly to the intelligence, ingenuity, and untiring attention of Mr. J.C. Pembrey, the Oriental Reader.

The Korean text was sent from Japan by the Buddhist monk-scholar Bunyiu Nanjio, who had been a student of both Legge and Müller.

44. Ibid., 5. The whole distorted debate over the relative size of the major world religions underscores the rhetorical nature of the nineteenth-century science of statistics; ibid., 7–8. On the special interest of Victorians in the whole issue of statistics, see *Victorian Britain: An Encyclopedia,* Sally Mitchell, ed. (New York and London: Garland, 1988), s.v. "statistics."

45. JL, *Travels of Fa-Hien,* 5–6. See Hermann Berghaus, *Berghaus' physikalischer Atlas,* 7 vols. (Gotha, Germany: J. Perthes, 1887). It is interesting to know that, as early as October 8, 1877, Legge was writing to Mark Pattison to the effect that "the adherents of Buddhism are often egregiously exaggerated" (Bodleian, MS. Pattison 57).

46. It is interesting to see that Legge's ranking is essentially the system graphically depicted in the frontispiece to Jordan's *Comparative Religion, Its Genesis and Growth* (New York: Charles Scribner's Sons, 1905); the colored chart carries the legend "A Comparative View of the Present Numerical Strength of The Principal Religions of the World."

47. Monier-Williams wrote Legge on January 12, 1889 (after his infamous attack on the *Sacred Books;* see pages 457–58), praising his discussion about the statistics concerning the size of Buddhism ("my idea is that even reckoning laymen, we ought not to put down true Buddhists as exceeding 156 million"). Other letters from Monier-Williams to Legge, as well as Legge's attendance of the inauguration of the Indian Institute in Oxford, suggest that there was a cordial if not close relationship between the two scholars. The significance of this is that Legge was closely identified with Müller and, after 1887, Monier-Williams declared himself to be the most outspoken evangelical Christian opponent of the *Sacred Books* and of a comparative approach to the study of religion. Whether or not this is another indication of Legge's more conservative turn toward the end of his life is unclear. For Monier-Williams's letters to Legge, see CWM/China/Personal/Legge/Box 8.

48. JL, *Travels of Fa-Hien,* 7.

49. Ibid. In fact, the sense of a Confucian orthodoxy was heightened in the Qing period because of the Manchurian concern to accommodate Han customs and yet overcome Ming dynastic syncretisms (which incorporated Buddhist and Daoist traditions). A kind of Zhu Xi or Ruist orthodoxy with explicit political overtones was strongly supported. The religious dimensions of this Qing orthodoxy were most probably not explicit intellectual and emotional convictions (particularly beliefs related to a classical Shangdi) at the court or among the common people. Even the distinction of a religion *(zongjiao)* in opposition to the more generic term *jiao* (teaching, doctrine) would have been difficult to maintain throughout the nineteenth-century Qing period. On the Qing conservative swing toward Zhu Xi–style Ruist thought, see Jonathan Spence and John E. Wills, Jr., *From Ming to Ch'ing: Conquest, Reform, and Continuity in 17th-Century China* (New Haven: Yale University Press, 1979); and Lynn Strove, *The Southern Ming, 1644–1662* (New Haven: Yale University Press, 1984).

50. *Athenaeum,* October 23, 1886.

51. Thomas Pearce, "Review of James Legge's Travels of Fa-Hien," *The China Review* 15 (1886–1887): 213.

52. See, for example, the characterization of Giles, and his constant need for scholarly confrontation, in the *North-China Daily News,* June 18, 1886, clipping, n.p. (CWM/China/Personal/Legge/Box 9).

53. H. Giles, review of Legge's *Travels of Fa-Hien, Journal of the North China Branch of the Royal Asiatic Society* (1886): 319–20. Legge did, of course, duly acknowledge Giles's earlier translation, as well as others, but makes it clear that his version is entirely his own. Giles cavalierly says that it "would have been a cheap and graceful compliment from an old Sinologue to the early effort of a young student to admit that he had borrowed my renderings and served it up in different words" (p. 319). See the discussion of Giles's "characteristic philippics" in editorial comment in *The China Review* 16 (1887–1888).

54. Anonymous, review of Legge's *Travels of Fa-Hien, Saturday Review,* February 19, 1887, pp. 270–71.

55. Jordan, *Comparative Religion,* p. x. It is worth quoting Jordan's entire statement (pp. x–xi):

> Viewed as a department of study, Comparative Religion aspires to obtain, and doubtless will ultimately secure, the status of a separate theological discipline. In the meantime it is generally regarded as being, at most, a useful adjunct to the study of Apologetics; and the many questions which it raises are usually investigated, more or less fully, in connection with that subject. This arrangement, though only temporary, has admittedly borne good fruit; for, as the result of this alliance, the scope of modern Apologetics has been immensely and permanently widened. Take Christian Apologetics, for example. That branch of instruction, as formerly understood, was practically limited to a defence and vindication of the tenets of Christianity; but it is now widely recognised that no one can expound the real significance of that Faith until he has made himself acquainted with its relationships to the various non-Christian Faiths. Accordingly, it is one of the notable achievements of Comparative Religion that, even already, it has broadened the outlook of that important domain of learning with which it at present stands associated. Christian Apologetics has still, undoubtedly, a great and urgent mission to fulfil: its task, moreover, has been rendered tenfold more arduous and more critical by the vigorous propagandism of modern Christian Missions; and yet, largely because of the movement just referred to, it is now commonly conceded that a fuller and more exact study of Comparative Religion has been rendered simply imperative. Much, therefore, as this new Science has been esteemed hitherto, it is certain to grow in favour as men come to appreciate better its rare worth as the ally and handmaid of every competent Apologetic.

56. For the description of the *Saturday Review,* see Evelyn Abbott and Lewis Campbell, *The Life and Letters of Benjamin Jowett* (London: John Murray, 1897), 1: 294–95.

57. Anonymous, review of JL's *Travels of Fa-Hien, Saturday Review,* p. 270. On Oscar Wilde's interest in the Daoist sage Zhuangzi ("the Chinese philosopher became a Victorian Sage with a dialectical and Darwinian philosophy"), see his essay "A Chinese Sage" (1890), a sympathetic review of Giles's translation. See Philip E. Smith II and Michael S. Helfand, eds., *Oscar Wilde's Oxford Notebooks: A Portrait of Mind in the Making* (New York: Oxford University Press, 1989), 158–61.

58. See the printed version of the "Fair and Dispassionate Discussion," which appeared in *Transactions of the Ninth International Congress of Orientalists,* 563–82. There is

also a thirty-eight-page typescript version of this article (Bodleian, Dep. c. 41). Already in *Chinese Classics* (1861), 2: 89–91, Legge had published some translations of Han Yu on human nature along with some commentary (see pp. 120–22). There are no published versions of Legge's translations of, and writings about, Han Yu from this later Oxford period, but there is an extensive collection of manuscript material that testifies to his strong and prolonged interest during the 1880s and 1890s (or during the period that Legge was preoccupied in making sense out of Buddhism and Daoism). See, for example, the preserved manuscripts (often both the handwritten and typescript versions) in Bodleian, Dep. c. 55 (four handwritten and typescript essays by Han Yu) and c. 66 (including a seventy-two-page handwritten notebook containing, among other items, "The Buddha Bone Memorial of Han Yu," "An Inquiry into the Nature of the Course [Dao]," "A Warning to Crocodiles to Make Themselves Scarce," "The Nature of Morality," and "A Sacrificial Offering to the Spirit of a Nephew").

59. Because it was prepared for delivery to the Ninth Congress of Orientalists in London in 1893, Legge's work is necessarily condensed and represents only a partial translation and paraphrase of the Chinese text with an running interpretive commentary. JL, "Fair and Dispassionate Discussion," 563–64. Bunyiu Nanjio is cited by Legge.

60. On the "three religions are one" tradition, see Judith Berling, *The Syncretic Religion of Lin Chao-en* (New York: Columbia University Press, 1980).

61. JL, "Fair and Dispassionate Discussion," 564.

62. Ibid., 507.

63. It can also be said that Legge's classicist, Nonconformist Protestant, and Victorian perspective was less attuned to the Song Ruist development of an explicit "Confucianistic" metaphysics that did not rely on monotheistic assumptions or on religious worship as a means to express respect and mature social engagement. This development is especially witnessed in Zhu Xi's shift away from the ancient classics toward an emphasis (via the Four Books) on a more experientially based self-cultivation method that redeveloped metaphysics not along historical lines (as in the *Book of Historical Documents* and the *Book of Poetry*) but along the synchronic moralistic lines of the commentaries to the *Book of Changes*.

64. JL, "Fair and Dispassionate Discussion," 577–79. In many ways, the language used here is particularly reminiscent of Legge's early dismissals of Buddhism during his missionary days—e.g., his characterization of Buddhists during his trips (in the 1850s and 1860s) along the East and West Rivers (where on Mount Lofu the monks were "vulgar and ignorant"; at a monastery by the West River, the monks "seemed verging on idiocy" and the monastery itself was a "place for imbeciles"). In these accounts, Legge notes the "curious resemblance" to Roman Catholicism. In his journal written while on the East River, Legge also carefully notes that "[b]ad as Buddhism and Taoism are, it may be questioned whether they do not keep before the people some moral lessons which it would be a pity to take from them violently. The systems must pass away gradually, as they are supplanted by the higher and completer teaching of the Gospel" (JL, "Journal of a Missionary Tour along the East River" [CWM/China/Personal/Legge/Box 7] and Helen Edith Legge, *James Legge Missionary and Scholar* [London: Religious Tract Society, 1905], 143, 146). See also Holmes Welch, *The Practice of Chinese Buddhism, 1900–1950* (Cambridge, Mass.: Harvard University Press, 1967).

65. It is worth commenting on the fact that in this article Legge consistently uses Liu Mi's terminology of "*Ju Chiao* [*rujiao*]" or the "Doctrines held by the Literati" rather than his own favorite construct of "Confucianism."

66. JL, "Fair and Dispassionate Discussion," 579–80. For a comparative perspective of Indian tradition, see Arjun Appadurai, "Number in the Colonial Imagination," in *Orientalism and the Postcolonial Predicament: Perspectives on South Asia,* ed. Carol A. Breckenridge and Peter van der Veer (Philadelphia: University of Pennsylvania Press, 1993), 314–40; and Bernard Cohn, "The Census, Social Structure and Objectification in South Asia," in *An Anthropologist among the Historians and Other Essays* (Delhi and London: Oxford University Press, 1987).

67. On Han Yu, see Charles Hartman, *Han Yu and the T'ang Search for Unity* (Princeton: Princeton University Press, 1986); and Paul Cohen, *China and Christianity: The Missionary Movement and the Growth of Chinese Antiforeignism, 1860–1870* (Cambridge, Mass.: Harvard University Press, 1963), 9–10, 13. I am indebted to William LaFleur for some of these ideas concerning Han Yu.

68. On the official Confucian bias toward Daoism, especially during the Qing dynasty, see K. Schipper, *The Taoist Body,* trans. Karen C. Duval (Berkeley and Los Angeles: University of California Press, 1993), 16–19.

69. One of the ironies here, despite surface appearances to the contrary, is that the old attitudes of a triumphalistic muscular Christianity are only transposed into the muscularly aggressive science of the Orientalist scholar who seeks, on the battlefield of historical and philological truth, to classify, define, and control the cultural products of other peoples. It is interesting to see how martial metaphors and an imperialistic rhetoric color the affairs of professional sinologues as much as they did for the missionaries waging "Christ's holy battle with the heathen Chinee." When E. J. Eitel calls for the professionalization of sinology ("Amateur Sinology," *The China Review* 2 [1873]: 1–8), he cannot help but fall into a rhetorical mode of martial metaphors that stress the "scientific" superiority and control of Western scholarship over Chinese modes of understanding their own tradition. So also does Eitel suggest that an imperious Western critical "science" will decisively arm the sinological scholar in the struggle to determine the hidden truths, or historical "facts" and *Quellen,* of ancient texts: "we [i.e., sinologists] are more than a match for [the native scholars], not with shot and shell only or by feats of engineering skill, but also with the more subtle weapons of western science, on the battle field of practical, speculative and critical philosophy." Muscular Christianity has here been translated into a brawny scholarship; the terms have changed but the transcendental logic and triumphalist agenda is fundamentally congruent.

70. On the "China of the Sinologues" image, see especially Arthur Wright, "The Study of Chinese Civilization," *Journal of the History of Ideas* 21 (1960): 233–55.

71. See Carl T. Jackson, *The Oriental Religions and American Thought: Nineteenth-Century Explorations* (Westport, Conn.: Greenwood Press, 1981), 95. Traditions such as Shintoism, Chan or Zen Buddhism, and Tibetan Buddhism were mostly unknown in the nineteenth century.

72. In French the terminology for *taoisme* came about through the pioneering work of Rémusat during the first part of the century. The very earliest English uses of "Taoism" were found in an article appearing in the 1839 *Chinese Repository.* See also the earlier English-language review of Pauthier's work on Daoism in the un-

signed (but probably by Karl Gützlaff) article "The Taou Sect of China," *Asiatic Journal*, n.s. 5 (1831): 97–104.

73. From the time of his earliest textual explorations of the *Daode jing* in the late 1870s, Legge's Daoist works include such notable efforts as the long section devoted to both early and later Daoism in his popular book *The Religions of China: Confucianism and Taoism Described and Compared with Christianity* (London: Hodder and Stoughton, 1880); the important long review-essay "The Tao Teh King" (*British Quarterly Review*, July 1883, pp. 41–59); various influential book reviews on assorted definitional, philological, dating, and methodological topics concerning the early texts, with reference especially to the infamous "remains of Lao Tzu" debate sparked by the young and "always pugnacious" counselor-scholar Herbert Giles; several formal professorial lecture series at Oxford in 1880, 1882, 1889, and 1893 on the *Daode jing*, Laozi, Zhuangzi, and Daoist purgatories; and discussions, for a general audience, of Lao Tzu, as the single entry on "Taoism," in the ninth, tenth, and eleventh editions of the *Encyclopedia Britannica*. See also the short discussion in 1879 in his preface to his first contribution to the *Sacred Books of the East*. In his autobiographical "Notes of My Life," Legge mentions that he first experienced Daoism in 1839 at a Chinese temple in Batavia, where he witnessed a service to "Thien Hau (Queen of Heaven), a famous Tauist goddess worshipped by sailors." This event reminded him of the idolatrous worship of a "Queen of Heaven" in Jerusalem condemned in chapter 44 of Jeremiah. Legge mentions that Dr. Medhurst, who was with him at the temple, was disturbed by the "folly" of the service and tried to cause a "commotion" ("Notes of My Life" [1897], 8).

74. On the ambiguities of Daoism in Chinese tradition, see Nathan Sivin, "On the Word 'Taoist' as a Source of Perplexity," *History of Religions* 17 (1978): 303–30. On the problems of Western scholarship concerning Daoism, see N.J. Girardot, "Part of the Way: Four Studies on Taoism," *History of Religions* 11 (1972): 319–37.

75. Schipper, *Taoist Body*, 193–94.

76. At first the great Jesuit pioneers such as Matteo Ricci seemed unaware of the existence of any truly ancient or classical Daoist texts and quickly dismissed the living tradition as devilishly "idolatrous." Eventually a loose group of Jesuit scholars known as the figurists discovered the enigmatic "mysteries" of the *Daode jing*, said to be written by a certain Laocius whose hermetic wisdom rivaled that of the classical West. By the mid-eighteenth century, therefore, there were already several Latin versions of the *Daode jing*, in which was found—especially in reference to the triply evocative description of the Dao in chapter 14—an amazingly convincing prefiguration of the Christian trinitarian concept of God (see Joseph Dehergne, "Les Historiens jesuites du Taoisme," *Actes du Colloque international de sinologie, La Mission française de Pekin aux xviie et xviiie siècles* [Paris: Belles Lettres, 1976], 59–67). Generally on nineteenth-century scholarship, see the fascinating contemporaneous bibliography by D. Marceron, *Bibliographie du taoisme* (Paris: Ernest Leroux, 1898).

77. Quoted from Legge, "Tao Teh King," p. 43. Legge also remarks that "most readers have thought, probably, that the translator [Julien] had not sufficient sympathy with his original, and failed in consequence to do justice to it."

78. Julien also exemplifies a certain psychological typology among the great Orientalists. In Raymond Schwab's estimation, this was an uncompromising "moral purity" and "asceticism" that was often "touchy, jealous, and irascible." Sinologists like

Julien display the "psychology of the specialist" in an especially intense fashion, since, by virtue of their unique subject matter, they were largely insulated from the romantic license and comparative largesse of their Orientalist colleagues focused on India. To his legendary battles with all sinological interlopers (especially Pauthier), Julien "brought the jealous fury of a proprietor to bear on the preserve of Chinese studies."

79. I borrow the expression "relentless domination of textuality" from Almond, *British Discovery of Buddhism.*

80. The *Zhuangzi* was largely unknown, although Julien did promise a translation. This was never completed. The other text was surprisingly the *Ganying pian* (The tractate of actions and their retributions).

81. See Almond, *British Discovery of Buddhism,* on dichotomized methodological approaches.

82. For the earliest writings in English on Daoism, see "The Taou Sect of China"; and Karl Gützlaff's "Remarks on the Religion of the Chinese," *Chinese Repository* 4 (1835): 271–76. See also S. Wells Williams's account in his popular book *The Middle Kingdom: A Survey of the Geography, Government, Education, Social Life, Arts, Religion, etc., of the Chinese Empire and Its Inhabitants,* 2 vols. (New York: John Wiley, 1847).

83. J. Edkins, "Tauism. The Phases in the Development of Tauism," *Transactions of the North China Branch of the Royal Asiatic Society* 5 (1855): 83–99.

84. Charles Hardwick, *Christ and Other Masters: An Historical Inquiry into Some of the Chief Parallelisms and Contrasts Between Christianity and the Religious Systems of the Ancient World. With Special Reference to Prevailing Difficulties and Objections,* 4 parts (Cambridge: Macmillan, 1855–1859).

85. Ibid., 55–76.

86. Ibid., 56.

87. Ibid., 66–67.

88. For Legge's views, see page 430; the Darwinian and Spencerian implications of early Daoist thought were especially provoked by the discovery of the *Zhuangzi.*

89. Hardwick, *Christ and Other Masters,* 21.

90. Ibid., 5–6.

91. J. Chalmers, "Tauism," *The China Review* 1 (1872–1873): 209–20. In this article, Chalmers takes it for granted that his audience will accept his qualified praise for Laozi and the *Daode jing.* Though Laozi recommended the principle of "inertia" and indulged in an "abstruse metaphysics" wherein the "Tau is chaotic," Daoism, if "not a religion in the highest sense," is nevertheless a fundamentally "pure and simple" speculative philosophy with many "beautiful moral precepts." His real concern in this article was to trace a four-part developmental scheme to account for the degradation of Daoism's original purity. After the foundational "speculative" stage comes the "dreamy" stage represented in the works of Zhuangzi and Liezi, where "philosophy becomes wedded to myth and fables," followed by an "adventurous stage" seen in the deluded efforts of various Han emperors to find the "fairy lands" conjured up by the earlier stage. Finally there is the "extremely absurd . . . occult stage" of later Daoism, the extreme absurdity of which is seen especially in the beliefs and practices of alchemy. Concluding in the spirit of Carlyle with respect to the difficulty of understanding how any "sane men" could continue to believe and live by the

"jungle of delusions" represented by the living tradition of Daoism, Chalmers finds it impossible to accept that, while the "commerce, civilization, and the comity of nations" may be "forced upon this people," their religion should be left alone.

92. It is worth noting that Chalmers's translation of the *Daode jing* was dedicated to Legge.

93. Chalmers, "Tauism."

94. See Kurt Walf, *Westliche Taoismus-Bibliographie* (Essen, Germany: Die Blaue Eule, 1989). Before the turn of the century, there were translations by Chalmers, Watters, Balfour, Giles, Legge, Maclaglan, and Kingsmill in English; Planckner and Strauss und Tornay in German; and de Harlez and de Rosny in French.

95. See, for example, Robert K. Douglas, *Confucianism and Taouism* (in the series "Non-Christian Religious Systems") (London: Society for Promoting Christian Knowledge, 1879); and Joseph Edkins, *The Religious Condition of the Chinese.*

96. JL, "The Tao Teh King."

97. Ibid.

98. Ibid.

99. In his preface to his first volume for the *Sacred Books* (1879), Legge mentioned that he felt that Julien's "Way" was "too materialistic to serve the purpose of a translation" (*Sacred Books,* 3: xxi). Inasmuch as the term *dao* can also mean talking or speech, Legge's translation lends itself nicely to associations with the idea of a linguistic and cultural "discourse."

100. JL, "Tao Teh King," 46–47.

101. Ibid., 46.

102. Ibid., 47–48.

103. On the Victorian failure to see meditative allusions in Buddhism, see Almond, *British Discovery of Buddhism,* 122. In general, mysticism was not a category for Victorian comparative analysis.

104. For a discussion of the problem of cosmogonic myth in Chinese tradition and the theme of chaos *(hundun),* see N.J. Girardot, *Myth and Meaning in Early Taoism* (Berkeley and Los Angeles: University of California Press, 1983).

105. The only perplexing aspect of these considerations is the "very strange" nature of chapter 4, which seems to suggest that the *dao* is prior to *di,* or Shangdi, the word Legge had already established as the "personal name" for the Heavenly Divinity. Legge offered an interesting speculative explanation of the "Old Master's" possible reasons for placing the *dao* before *di,* but it is a rationalization that he eventually dropped in his later discussion for the *Sacred Books of the East.*

106. JL, "Tao Teh King," 59.

107. Herbert A. Giles, "The Remains of Lao Tzu Retranslated," *The China Review* 14 (1885–1886): 231–81.

108. See T.W. Kingsmill, "Review. The Remains of Lao-tzu, Retranslated by Mr. H.A. Giles," *Journal of the North China Branch of the Royal Asiatic Society,* n.s. 21 (1886): 116–20; and idem, "Modern Sinology and the Tao Teh King," *Journal of the North China Branch of the Royal Asiatic Society* 37 (1906): 192–95.

109. JL, "A Critical Notice of 'The Remains of Lao Tsze, Retranslated,' by Mr. Herbert A. Giles," *The China Review* 16 (1888): 195–214.

110. H.A. Giles, "Dr. Legge's Critical Notice of the Remains of Lao Tzu," *The China Review* 16 (1888): 238–41.

111. For a discussion of Horace's notion that "the good Homer sometimes nods," see Matthew Arnold, *On Translating Homer* (1861; reprint, New York: Chelsea House, 1983), a work that was most likely familiar to Legge.

112. On the overall issue of reading Homer in the Victorian period as related to the interpretation of the Bible and the higher forms of Germanic criticism (especially the relation between the pioneering biblical scholar Julius Wellhausen and the classicist Ulrich von Wilamovitz-Moellendorff), see Frank M. Turner, "The Reading of Homer," in *The Greek Heritage in Victorian Britain* (New Haven: Yale University Press, 1981), 135–86.

113. JL, *The Sacred Books of China: The Texts of Taoism*, pt. 1, 2, *Sacred Books*, vols. 39, 40.

114. As Legge said in 1879, the *Ganying pian*, which he then translated as *Tractate of Actions and Their Retributions*, though associated with the later "system of grotesque beliefs and practices," does generally inculcate "a morality of a high order in some respects" (*Sacred Books*, vol. 3).

115. These minor works of the later religious tradition included *Chang qingjing miaojing* (The classic of purity); *Yinfunjing* (The classic of the harmony of the seen and unseen); *Yushujing* (The classic of the pivot of jade, an abstract); *Riyungjing* (The classic of the directory for a day); Lin Yunming's seventeenth-century study of the *Zhuangzi;* and two stone inscriptions (the "Stone Tablet in the Temple of Lao-zse" and "Record for the Sacrificial Hall of Kwang-zse"). See K. Schipper, "The History of Taoist Studies in Europe" (paper presented at the symposium on the History of European Sinology, Chiang Ching-kuo Foundation, Taipei, 1992). On most of these works, see Judith M. Boltz, *A Survey of Taoist Literature: Tenth to Seventeenth Centuries* (Berkeley: Institute of East Asian Studies, University of California, 1987).

116. JL, *Sacred Books*, 39: xi–xii.

117. Ibid., 1–4.

118. Ibid.

119. Ibid., 15.

120. Ibid., 17.

121. Ibid., 30.

122. Ibid., 29.

123. Ibid., 51.

124. Schipper, "History of Taoist Studies," 4.

125. Ibid.

126. Legge's renditions of the Daoist classics are less the continuing standard of translation than his Confucian classics are largely because, in terms of time and inclination, he always had much more sympathy for Kongzi than for Laozi. It may also be that Legge's Daoist translations have not had the lasting impact of his Confucian works simply because there are so many rival editions of the much shorter and more vaguely mystical Daoist texts. The protean beauty of an incredibly terse and allusive text such as the *Daode jing* is that every generation can have a transformative version appropriate to its own peculiar tastes and interests (even if many of these versions are only pseudotranslations of the Chinese original). It is doubtful that there will ever be another Western scholar willing to undertake a complete translation of the classical nine books associated with the authoritative Ruist tradition.

127. Anonymous, review of "*The Sacred Books of China—The Texts of Taoism.* Translated by James Legge" (clipping, CWM/China/Personal/Legge/Box 9).

128. Anonymous, review of Legge's *Texts of Taoism.* See also the review in the *North-China Daily News,* July 8, 1892; a defense of Legge's nondiffusionist view of the early Daoist texts is found in the review entitled "Tao-teh-ching: The Course of Nature, Or the Way of Heaven. The Classic Work of Laotsze, Translated by the Rev. Dr. Legge" (clippings, CWM/China/Personal/Legge/Box 9). After discounting associations with either Babylonian or Hindu philosophy, this last reviewer says, "The Tao-teh-ching appears rather to be the natural emanation of a contemplative mind, constituted, it is true, in a peculiar manner, but not without many parallels in the history of the world, on the part of men whether living in solitude or in the midst of public and social life."

129. Max Müller, introduction to the *Sacred Books,* vol. 1., and idem, "Program of Translation of the Sacred Books." See above, pages 257-62.

130. On the theme of "colonizing the past," see Gauri Viswanathan, *Masks of Conquest: Literary Study and British Rule in India* (New York: Columbia University Press, 1989).

131. See Eitel, "Amateur Sinology," 1-8.

132. Ibid.

133. While Giles was still composing semipopular literary pastiches on Daoism and other bellettrisc literary topics (such as his *Gallery of Chinese Immortals*), Chavannes and Pelliot were already (by 1913) using the *Daozang* in their research (an incomplete copy of the canon arrived in Paris in 1912, a complete photo-offset copy becoming available in 1929). By the 1930s, Henri Maspero was engaged in the first extensive Western exploration of this massive storehouse of sectarian Daoist literature. Most of the rest of the sinological world ignored these groundbreaking Daoist studies until the late 1960s when K. Schipper's "participant observer" discoveries concerning the living tradition began to be circulated. See T.H. Barrett, introduction to *Taoism and Chinese Religion,* by Henri Maspero, trans. Frank A. Kierman Jr. (Amherst: University of Massachusetts Press, 1981), vii-xxiii. In terms of their respective abilities as translators of the Daoist classics, it is worth noting Burton Watson's opinion (*Chuang Tzu: Basic Writings* [New York: Columbia University Press, 1964], 21-22) that

> Giles, who produced the first complete English translation [of the *Zhuangzi*], is very free in his rendering, and again and again substitutes what strike me as tiresome Victorian cliches for the complex and beautiful language of the original. In spite of his offensively "literary" tone, however, he generally gets at what appears to me to be the real meaning of the text. Legge is far more painstaking in reproducing the literal meaning, and for the most part, uses a simple, unaffected English that can still be read with pleasure today. But, perhaps because of his long years of work on the Confucian texts, he seems to miss Chuang Tzu's point rather often, and to labor to make common sense out of paradox and fantasy.

134. See D.L. McMullen, "The Backhouse File. 'Glorious Veterans,' 'Sinologists de chambre,' and Men of Science: Reflections on Professor Hugh Trevor-Roper's Life of Sir Edmund Backhouse (1873-1944)," *New Lugano Review* 1 (1979): 78-83. As McMullen says with regard to Giles:

Almost all Giles' work has dated badly. His approach was often anecdotal and sentimental; he believed in selecting "literary gems." His translations of Chinese poetry were forced into English rhyming verse sometimes of irritating triteness. . . . Giles' translations were by no means infallible, and when in 1920 he charged the young Arthur Waley with mis-translations, Waley accused him in return of "hurling his courteous and learned stones . . . from a very glassy house indeed."

It may also be noted that, unlike Legge, Giles had no interest at all in teaching. McMullen recounts that Giles was famous for his disdain for teaching at Cambridge and actively chased "prospective students away with a walking stick."

135. T. W. Kingsmill, "Dr. Maclagan and the Tao Teh King," *The China Review* 23 (1898–1899): 265–70. In an even more frantic vein, Kingsmill elsewhere ("Modern Sinology and the Tao Teh King," 192–95) digresses on "modern Sinology" as distinguished from the "errors of Leggism."

136. Ibid., 192–93.

137. See Philippa J. Baylis's discussion of "The Subsequent Fate of the High God Theory" in "Andrew Lang and the Study of Religion in the Victorian Era, with Special Reference to His High God Theory" (Ph.D. diss., University of Aberdeen, 1987), 331–49. From the standpoint of late-twentieth-century sinology, see Robert Eno, "Was There a High God Ti in Shang Religion?" *Early China* 15 (1990): 1–26.

138. Almond, *British Discovery of Buddhism*, 12–13.

139. See the discussion of these issues by Norman Girardot, "Visualizing Taoism: Isabelle Robinet and the Mao-shan Revelations of Great Purity," in Isabelle Robinet, *Taoist Meditation: The Mao-shan Tradition of Great Purity,* trans. Julian F. Pas and Norman J. Girardot (Albany, N.Y.: State University of New York Press, 1993), xvii–xxvi.

140. See Norman Girardot, "Kristofer Schipper and the Resurrection of the Taoist Body," in Schipper, *Taoist Body,* ix–xviii.

141. John Lagerwey, *Taoist Ritual in Chinese Society and History* (New York: Macmillan, 1987), xvii–xviii.

142. Today there is an ironic reversal of these positions. So therefore Michel Strickmann would argue that the only authentic Daoism is the later "self-conscious" traditions springing from the lineage of Zhang Daoling at the end of the Han dynasty. The so-called classical tradition of the *Daode jing* and *Zhuangzi* evaporates as an identifiable "movement" or "tradition." See some of the preliminary discussion in Michel Strickmann, *Le taoisme du Mao-Chan* (Paris: Collège de France, Institut des hautes études chinoises, 1981).

143. As Sivin says ("On the Word 'Taoist,'" 316):

By "Taoist" a Sinologist may mean a mystical author; a hereditary priest, whether or not ordained by the Celestial Master or the head of another orthodox sect; a monk; a lay member of a sect dedicated to worship of the Tao and its emanations; an initiate, whether isolated or a member of a coterie; any priest, operator, healer, medium, shaman, or supporter of popular liturgies; anyone who took seriously or practiced occult disciplines, even fakes and swindlers who merely claimed mastery of them; anyone who lived a nonconformist life outside Buddhist circles; or anyone who harbored anti-feudal feelings as certain historians define them today.

144. On the conservative premillennial advocates among missionaries, who reacted strongly to any attempt to reduce the Christian gospel to social action, see the

evangelical historian Brian Stanley, *The Bible and the Flag: Protestant Missions and Imperialism in the Nineteenth and Twentieth Centuries* (Leicester, England: Apollos, 1990).

145. See the excerpt of Legge's letter, typed by Helen Edith Legge, in CWM/China/Personal/Legge/Box 8.

146. W.W. Hunter, "Our Missionaries," *Nineteenth Century* 24 (July 1888): 14–29.

147. Ibid., 28. Legge's actions did not go unnoticed by conservative missionaries back in China. See, for example, the comment on Hunter's article in "Editorial Note" (the editor at this time was Luther H. Gulick), *The Chinese Recorder* 19 (September 1888): 443.

148. Hunter, "Our Missionaries," 21–22.

149. Ibid., 16, 21. It is worth noting that these themes are echoed in George Legge's *Aberdeen Address* in 1859. For George Legge, missionary expiation of "national wrong-doing" is an anticipation; for Hunter it is a foregone conclusion.

150. See Brian Stanley's account of this incident in *The History of the Baptist Missionary Society 1792–1992* (Edinburgh: T&T Clark, 1992), 193.

151. Ibid. For Legge's comments, see Legge to Baynes (secretary of the committee), September 27, 1888, Baptist Missionary Society, China and Japan Sub-Committee Minute Book, 1: 246–48. The committee's verdict was rendered on December 18, 1888. The committee expressed "confidence in Richard's fidelity to central truths of the gospel" but criticized "many of his missionary aims and methods . . . particularly his estimate of the proportion which efforts to promote the social and material welfare of the people should bear to 'direct Gospel teaching and work'" (see Stanley, *History of the Baptist Missionary Society*, p. 193).

152. There is no extant account of Legge's private views on this incident.

153. The full title was *The Nestorian Monument of Hsi-an Fu in Shen-hsi, China Relating to the Diffusion of Christianity in China in the Seventh and Eighth Centuries with the Chinese Text of the Inscription, a Translation, and Notes and a Lecture on the Monument with a Sketch of Subsequent Missions in China and Their Present State* (London: Trubner, 1888). This was originally given as a public lecture at Oxford.

154. Terrien de Lacouperie, "The Nestorian Tablet," letter to the editor, *Times* (London), February 4, 1886, p. 14.

155. JL, *Nestorian Monument*, 46.

156. Ibid. Legge's conclusion from these factors is that it was the combination of the shortsightedness of the appeal to emperors and the Confucian elite combined with the lack of evangelicalism that led to the Nestorian downfall.

157. Ibid., 58–59.

158. Ibid., 64.

159. Ibid., 63–64.

160. Ibid., 65.

161. Ibid.

162. E.J. Eitel, "Notes on New Books" (*Christianity in China. Nestorianism, Roman Catholicism, Protestantism.* By James Legge, Professor of the Chinese Language and Literature in the University of Oxford, London: Trubner & Co., 1888), *The China Review* 16 (1888): 384–86. *Christianity in China* appears to have been a reprinting in pamphlet form of the *Nestorian Monument* monograph without the translation, notes, and Chinese text. See also William Muirhead's favorable review in *The Chinese Recorder* 20 (January 1889): 39–40.

163. Even the generally liberal Alexander Williamson described Buddhism and Daoism as "excrescences" (see "Shall the Next General Conference of Missionaries be Held in 1887 or 1890?" *The Chinese Recorder* 16 [December 1885]: 475–78). See also Almond, *British Discovery of Buddhism,* 46–49, where he contrasts the "indolence" of Buddhism with the "Victorian ideal of work and activity." It was the "effeminacy or unmanliness of the Oriental mind" that was opposed to the "vigorous, aggressive, and progressive" European mind. In particular, it was the Buddhist doctrine of *nirvāṇa* as a "passionless, emotionless rest" that contrasted with Christian ideas.

164. Williamson, "Shall the Next General Conference."

165. ["M"], "Sanitary Salvation," *The Chinese Recorder* 17 (September 1886): 352–53.

166. See D.Z. Sheffield, "The Relation Between Christianity and Heathen Systems of Religions," *The Chinese Recorder* 14 (March–April 1883): 93–107; and idem, "The Ethics of Christianity and Confucianism Compared," *The Chinese Recorder* 17 (October 1886): 365–79.

167. See M.T. Yates, "Letter in Response to A. Williamson," *The Chinese Recorder* 17 (January 1886): 34–36 (Williamson's rejoinder is found on pp. 77–78); and W.W. Royall, "China's Need—Conversion or Regeneration?" *The Chinese Recorder* 17 (April 1886): 141–44.

168. See Gilbert Reid, "Spiritual Life of Missionaries," *The Chinese Recorder* 17 (September 1886): 338–44; A. Sydenstricker, "Preaching to the Chinese by Similarities and Contrasts," *The Chinese Recorder* 20 (July 1889): 327–30; and Chauncey Goodrich, "How to Be a Missionary and Convert No One," *The Chinese Recorder* 20 (June 1889): 254–62.

169. Arthur H. Smith, "The Best Method of Presenting the Gospel to the Chinese," *The Chinese Recorder* 14 (September–October 1883): 394–409.

170. Concerning Monier-Williams's initial espousal of the fulfillment theory, see Sharpe, *Not to Destroy but to Fulfill: The Contribution of N.J. Farquhar to Protestant Missionary Thought in India* (Uppsala, Sweden: Gleerup, 1965), 49–52.

171. Quoted here from Richard Symonds, *Oxford and Empire* (London: Macmillan, 1986), 111. For the full text, see Sir M. Monier-Williams, *The Holy Bible and the Sacred Books of the East: Four Addresses; To which is Added a Fifth Address On Zenana Missions* (London: Seeley, 1887).

172. See the descriptions of the meeting in Reynolds, *Evangelicals at Oxford,* 30–31; and Sharpe, *Not to Destroy but to Fulfill,* 52.

173. The eyewitness description of Monier-Williams's talk is found in Luther H. Gulick, "Sacred Books of the East," *The Chinese Recorder* 18 (August 1887): 325–26.

CHAPTER EIGHT. TEACHER LEGGE: UPHOLDING THE WHOLE DUTY OF MAN, 1893–1897

1. Herbert A. Giles, *A History of Chinese Literature* (New York: Appleton-Century, 1937), 441.

2. JL, preface, *Chinese Classics* (1893), 1: ix–x. It is this Oxford edition that has been most frequently reprinted and constitutes the basis of Legge's authoritative status as the translator par excellence of the Confucian classics.

3. On Jowett, see, for example, "In Memoriam, Benjamin Jowett," *Oxford Magazine,* October 18, 1893, pp. 5–6:

> As we saw him, he had descended into the cave. His interest in metaphysical speculation had largely settled down into its manipulation for practical purposes. He seemed of this world rather than of any other. In this sphere as a ruler he was full of ideas and aims, but they seemed immediate and utilitarian. His great desire was to make the University national, and, it may be added, apparently Balliol cosmopolitan. Whatever would make Oxford comprehensive had his sympathy, especially anything that would bring it into relation with the great practical professions, Law, Medicine, Engineering, the Civil Service at home or in India. He appeared too careless of abstract speculations, of learning for its own sake, too careful of success, of results.

4. See Chavannes's review of de Groot in *Revue de l'histoire des religions* 37 (1898): 81–89.

5. See Paul Pelliot, "Les Études chinoises," *Renaissance* 2–3 (1944–1945): 258–64. Pelliot says (pp. 258–59):

> En fait, Édouard Chavannes est le premier qui, ayant reçu à l'École normale supérieure une préparation de philosophe et d'historien, alla ensuite en Chine pendant plusieurs années et combina ainsi le double avantage d'une bonne technique universitaire et de la connaissance pratique du pays. Chavannes a été le premier sinologue complet.

See also Martin's discussion of Chavannes and the state of French sinology at the end of the century ("A Critical Survey of French Sinology" [M.A. thesis, Georgetown University, 1966], 77–79). At the time of his election to the Collège de France chair, Chavannes was a consul at the French legation in Peking; his previous scholarly training had been at the University of Paris and at the École spéciale des langues orientales vivantes. It was, in fact, the extension of Chavannes's rigorous sinological ideas that led to the creation of the highly specialized École française d'Extrême-Orient.

It should be noted that the forerunner of *T'oung Pao* was Cordier's *Revue de l'Extrême-Orient,* which appeared in three volumes in 1882, 1883, and 1887. On the global Orientalist vision of these journals, see the "Avertissement de Directeurs," *T'oung Pao* 1 (1890): i–iv.

6. It is not entirely clear why Legge revised only the first two volumes of the *Classics,* but it was most likely determined by the Oxford University Press. Legge had already worked upon the revision of the Four Books for Müller's *Sacred Books of the East,* and it seems that some decision was made simply to revise (by "photographic process") the original "author's" edition of the first two volumes of the *Classics* rather than publish new editions of these works. Moreover, this arrangement meant that the press would not have to pay Legge "at the rate paid for works in the Sacred Books of the East series" (see Oxford University Press secretary to JL, December 23, 1891, Oxford University Press archive, Letter Book 54). The reluctance to undertake a revised reprinting of the rest of the *Classics* was no doubt dictated by the poor sales of works other than the Four Books. Even the revised volumes did not sell very well: Oxford University Press records indicate that, of the 1,000 copies printed in 1893 and 1895, there were 222 copies of volume 1 left and 536 copies of volume 2 left (see memo, "Legge's Chinese Classics," 1925, Oxford University Press, Letter Book 968).

It is obvious that Legge was very happy to have the chance to publish a new edition of the original *Chinese Classics*. Part of the reason for his delight was simply that, in this way, he was again able to include the complete Chinese texts, something that was not possible in the *Sacred Books* series.

In a letter published in the *Chinese Recorder* 24 (January 1893): 34–35, Legge noted that the reprints of volumes 1 and 2 would no longer be "his property" and he hoped that the Oxford University Press would "make some allowance for missionaries" in the pricing of these works. After all, the original sales of the *Classics* were never "remunerative" to Legge and he "never realized from sales the amount of [his] original outlay." In his "advertisement" for the 1895 revision of volume 2 of the *Classics* (on Mengzi), Legge draws attention to the new circumstances by referring to the "generosity" of the late John Dent, who, like Joseph Jardine, a famous "merchant-prince" of China, subsidized the price of the volumes for missionaries (see *Chinese Classics* [1895], 2: v). Needless to say, Oxford University Press made no such allowance.

7. JL, prolegomena, *Chinese Classics* (1893), 1: 111.

8. Ibid., 113. Legge's dramatic reevaluation of Confucius was recognized by contemporaries such as Paul Kranz and by later commentators such as G. Mason (*Western Concepts of China and the Chinese, 1840–1876* [New York: Russell and Russell, 1939], 204) and S.C. Miller (*Unwelcome Immigrant* [Berkeley: University of California Press, 1969], 66–67). Miller says:

> Later in the nineteenth century the reputation of Confucius appears to have recovered considerable lost ground. Very late in his life, Emerson reversed his opinion, praising Confucius as "the singular genius the Asiatics seem to have had for moral revelation," and some admirers were picked up among the American Humanists. But nowhere is this shift more dramatically revealed than in the revised judgment of Legge in the second edition of his translations, published in 1893.

Paul Cohen, in his study of Legge's assistant, Wang Tao, seems unaware of the revisionary changes in the 1893 edition of the *Classics* (e.g., in *Between Tradition and Modernity: Wang T'ao and Reform in Late Ch'ing China* [Cambridge, Mass.: Harvard University Press, 1974], p. 63, Cohen stresses Legge's typical attempt, despite some "generous appreciation of [Confucius] and his teaching," to keep him "at arm's distance"). Raymond Dawson (*Confucius* [New York: Hill and Wang, 1981], 1–2) also seems to know only Legge's opinion of Confucius as expressed in the 1861 edition of the *Classics*. See Lauren Pfister, "Some New Dimensions in the Study of the Works of James Legge (1815–1897): part 2," *Sino-Western Cultural Relations Journal* 13 (1991): 45–48.

9. Writing in 1900, Legge's old nemesis, Herbert Giles, observed (in "Confucianism in the Nineteenth Century," *North American Review* 171 [1900]: 370) that "[f]orty years have passed since these words were penned [i.e., Legge's 1861 comments on Confucius], yet the hold of this wonderful influence seems to-day as strong as ever. And this in spite of the fact that . . . little or nothing has been done by the Emperors of the nineteenth century to stimulate zeal in the cause."

10. See, for example, the discussion in Patrick Brantlinger, *Rule of Darkness: British Literature and Imperialism, 1830–1914* (Ithaca, N.Y., and London: Cornell University Press, 1988), 233. Noting the connections between the new science

fiction of H. G. Wells's *War of the Worlds* and the gothic romance formulas of Bram Stoker's *Dracula* (both published in 1897), Brantlinger remarks:

> A similar connection is evident between imperial gothic and the romance fictions of the decadent movement, as seen in Oscar Wilde's *Picture of Dorian Gray,* which traces an atavistic descent into criminal self-indulgence as mirrored by a changing portrait. Both Stoker's and Wells's romances can be read, moreover, as fanciful versions of yet another popular literary form, invasion-scare stories, in which the outward movement of imperialist adventure is reversed. . . . *Dracula* itself is an individual invasion or demonic possession fantasy with political implications. Not only is Stoker's bloodthirsty count the "final aristocrat," he is also the last of a "conquering race."

11. See Anthony C. Deane, "The Religion of the Undergraduate," *Nineteenth Century* 38 (1895): 673–80. This article indicates that the situation was largely the fault of the dons who stupidly enforced compulsory attendance at college chapels and maintained the use of Paley's outdated *Evidences* in exams. It was, after all, "the sign of 'culture' to ridicule by cheap jests any allusion to Christianity" and to "scoff at ancient beliefs." For a rejoinder, see H. Legge (no relation), "A Reply from Oxford," *Nineteenth Century* 38 (1895): 861–69, who points out that Deane was, after all, only a visitor from Cambridge who confused "indifferentism with agnosticism."

12. See Mrs. Humphry Ward, *A Writer's Recollections* (New York and London: Harper, 1918), 1: 224–26.

13. Andrew Lang, *Oxford, Brief Historical and Descriptive Notes* (London: Seeley, 1890), 245–71.

14. JL, *Chinese Classics* (1893), 1: 111.

15. I am thinking here of the famous saying from the *Analects:* "Some one said: 'What do you say concerning the principle that injury should be recompensed with kindness?' The Master said, 'With what will you recompense kindness? Recompense injury with justice [*zhi*], and recompense kindness with kindness'" (JL, *Analects* XIV.xxxviii, *Chinese Classics* [1893], 1: 288). In his annotation, Legge is careful to comment: "How far the ethics of Confucius fall below our Christian standard is evident from this chapter." In his prolegomena, Legge says that Confucius's principle of moral reciprocity relied too much on the publicly acknowledged relational structures of straightness *(zhi)* and propriety *(li)*. The problem was, according to Legge, that (p. 110) "this 'propriety' was a great stumbling-block in the way of Confucius. His morality was the result of the balancing of his intellect, fettered by the decisions of men of old, and not the gushings of a loving heart, responsive to the promptings of Heaven, and in sympathy with erring and feeble humanity."

16. See Edward H. Parker, *China and Religion* (New York: Dutton, 1905), ix–x. Parker makes a special point of saying that, by the turn of the century, it was clear that most "authorities" regarded Chavannes "as the soundest and most industrious of living Sinologists."

17. See especially H. G. Creel's revealing discussion of Confucian agnosticism and Legge's dramatic revisionary assessment of Confucius in "Was Confucius Agnostic?" *T'oung Pao* 29 (1935): 55–99. See also Cheuk-woon Taam, "On Studies of Confucius," *Philosophy East and West* 3 (1953): 147–66. Taam notes that by the 1950s there were more than thirty translations of the *Analects* into Western languages. However, among all these translations, Legge's version was formative

(p. 150): "this pioneer work [i.e., Legge's translation of the *Analects*] laid the foundation for later studies of Confucius and Legge's translations have furnished the basic source materials for the study of Chinese philosophy by Westerners ever since." For a more recent analysis of these questions, see Thomas H. Kang, "A Bibliographic Survey on Confucian Studies in Western Languages: Retrospect and Prospect," *Synthesis Philosophica* 8 (1989): 699–710.

18. See Paul Kranz, "Some of Professor J. Legge's Criticisms on Confucianism," *The Chinese Recorder* 29 (June 1898): 273–82, (July 1898): 341–45, (August 1898): 380–88, (September 1898): 440–45. See also Kranz's subsequent article, "Professor J. Legge's Change of Views Concerning Confucius," *The Chinese Recorder* 35 (1904): 93–94. On Faber, see especially Leslie R. Marchant, "Ernst Faber's Scholarly Mission to Convert the Confucian Literati in the Late Ch'ing Period," Occasional Paper no. 8 (Centre for East Asian Studies, University of Western Australia, 1984). Like Legge, Faber was a reforming postmillennialist who believed that "mankind did not have to await the advent of the Messiah to achieve perfection on earth. [The postmillennialists] were convinced that Christian evangelical activists, equipped with correct spiritual beliefs, could lead man to perfectibility and could, by their own human efforts, recreate the lost paradise on earth" (p. 6). Marchant makes the important point about Faber's views (which could be applied equally to Legge) that the postmillennialist view of Confucianism sometimes seemed contradictory since, while willing to use Confucianism as a strategic ally in Christianization, it was often deeply pessimistic about the real effects of Confucianism in contemporary China. These views were generally in keeping with the prophetic beliefs of the liberal evangelical missionaries of the period.

19. See A. Sydenstricker's review of "*Christianity the Completion of Confucianism,* Translated by the Author, Rev. Pastor P. Kranz," *The Chinese Recorder* 29 (December 1898): 614–16. See also the rejoinder by Kranz in the same issue of the *Recorder,* 616–17. Kranz specifically identifies his liberal position with the pioneering approach of Faber and Legge (particularly the views in the *Religions of China*). See also the anti-Leggian discussion by D. Z. Sheffield, "Christianity and the Ethnic Religions," *The Chinese Recorder* 34 (March 1903): 105–18.

20. Examples include the discussion (JL, prolegomena, *Chinese Classics* [1893], 1: 105) of Confucius's "very defective" views on moral self-cultivation. He placed too much stress on external dress and propriety and "never recognized a disturbance of the moral elements in the constitution of man." Elsewhere (p. 110), Legge says that "Confucius falls short of standards of Christian benevolence" because of the "stumbling block" of propriety *(li)* and that his moral system was "too much the result of the balancing of his intellect, fettered by the decisions of men of old and not the gushings of a loving heart, responsive to the promptings of Heaven, and in sympathy with erring and feeble humanity." Let us remember that, in the *Religions of China*, *li* was a much more positive, and authentically moral, principle (see page 378).

21. Ibid., 55.

22. Ibid., 87–88.

23. Ibid., 101; and ibid. (1861), 1: 102. On this same page, Legge, in discussing Confucius's "un-religion" and lack of "true piety," notes only that he does not "set [the Chinese] against dissimulation." In 1861, Legge said that Confucius actively "encourages them to act, to dissemble, to sin."

24. Ibid. (1893), 1: 100.

25. Ibid., 99; and ibid. (1861), 1: 100. These views are reinforced in the discussion in volume 2 (in both the 1861 and 1895 editions), in which Legge says (*Chinese Classics* [1895], 2: 73):

> [The] absence from Mencius's ideal of our [human] nature of the recognition of man's highest obligations [to God] is itself a striking illustration of man's estrangement from God. His usage of the term Heaven has combined with the similar practice of his Master [Kongzi] to prepare the way for the grosser conceptions of the modern literati, who would often seem to deny the divine personality altogether, and substitute for both God and Heaven a mere principle of order and fitness of things. It has done more: it has left the people in the mass to become an easy prey to the idolatrous fooleries of Buddhism. Yea, the *unreligiousness* [JL's emphasis] of the teachers has helped to deprave still more the religion of the nation, such as it is, and has made of its services a miserable pageant of irreverent forms.

26. JL, prolegomena, *Chinese Classics* (1861), 1: 108.

27. Ibid. (1893), 1: 108.

28. JL, review of R. K. Douglas's *Society in China, Journal of the Royal Asiatic Society,* October 1894, pp. 851–65.

29. Ibid., 855. Legge also favorably quotes (pp. 855–56) an apposite statement by a "resident of Peking to his old teacher in England": "Here [in China] I find a morality, or at worst a most excellent substitute, free from all trammels of faith or dogma, and, as far as I can see, a real living power amongst 400 millions of people. For all their self-complacent ignorance and for all their dirtiness, the Chinese, as a moral people, compare favourably with most European nations."

30. See "Chinese Ministers on Christian Missions; I—Minister Kwoh [Guo Songtao], II—Marquis Tseng [Zeng Jize], III—Minister Hsueh [Xue]," *North-China Herald,* October 6 and 31, 1893, pp. 536–47, 580–81.

31. JL, review of Douglas, 859–60, 860–63.

32. Ibid., 863.

33. See the discussion in "The Coming General Conference," *The Chinese Recorder* 21 (January 1890): 1–7.

34. On many of these general issues concerning the missionary movement in China during the 1890s, see Mary Jane Conger, "Missionary Views of China and Japan, 1890–1899" (M.A. thesis, University of Virginia, 1975).

35. See the description of the incident in "The Missionary Conference at Shanghai," *The Chinese Recorder* 21 (September 1890): 409–12.

36. Although there was still much passionate rancor over the issue of preparing several different versions of the Chinese Bible, the term question debate had generally died down. Many were loath to admit that any final resolution of the debate had been reached, but there were growing signs that a grass-roots consensus was emerging. In April of 1894 the editor of *The Chinese Recorder* sent out six hundred circulars to all of the Protestant missionaries in China asking them to indicate "what term or terms they used for God and the Holy Spirit." The results documented the overwhelming preference for Shangdi (173 responses) over shen (65 responses), with some minor support for other variations such as Tianzhu, Shangzhu, both Shangdi and shen, or both Shangdi and Tianzhu, etc. As the editor pointed out, the results clearly showed "a trend of usage and general opinion" that could be used to

settle the question once and for all (see *The Chinese Recorder* 25 [November 1894]: 553).

37. See the anonymous article "The Proposed Missionary Conference of 1890," *The Chinese Recorder* 20 (January 1889): 27–31, in which the plans for the conference were outlined. In general, most of the recommendations of the Arrangements Committee were carried out in the actual conference—see *Records of the General Conference of the Protestant Missionaries of China Held at Shanghai, May 7–20, 1890* (Shanghai: American Presbyterian Mission Press, 1890).

38. See C. Hartwell, "To What Extent Should We Teach the Chinese Classics in Our Mission Schools?" *The Chinese Recorder* 24 (December 1893): 569.

39. See the discussion of Faber's views in Hartwell, "To What Extent," 567–74. For many, Legge and Faber were the two primary exemplars of the liberal position. See, for example, Huberty F. James, "The Theism of China," *The Chinese Recorder* 28 (October 1897): 481–87, 516–24; and especially Paul Kranz, "Some of Professor J. Legge's Criticisms on Confucianism." Kranz was one of the few contemporary commentators to draw attention to Legge's revised conclusion about Kongzi's "greatness." It was Kranz's concern, however, to show that Legge's ameliorated conclusion did not detract from his elaborate catalogue of Confucius's "defects" or his opinion that the Confucian books were "not adapted for youthful minds" in primary and secondary missionary schools.

40. Among other articles by William Ashmore, see "Note on the Classics," *The Chinese Recorder* 26 (March 1895): 138. See also J.C. Hoare, "God and Man in the Chinese Classics," *The Chinese Recorder* 26 (May 1895): 201–10; C.F. Kupfer, "Our Attitude to the Literature of China," *The Chinese Recorder* 28 (June 1897): 284–87; and "Inquirer's" letter, *The Chinese Recorder* 28 (March 1897): 135–36, with the query, "In order to set forth the fallacies which arise out of the study of Comparative Religion should a public effort be made to explain the facts of the case to people at home?"

41. William Ashmore, "Are We Getting Ready to Believe That God Is the Architect of Heathenism?" *The Chinese Recorder* 23 (November 1892): 517–18.

42. See also Ashmore's discussion of these issues in "The First Text Book in Comparative Religion," *The Chinese Recorder* 27 (February 1896): 53–61.

43. William Ashmore, "Are We Getting Ready to Believe," 517–18. It may be noted that this article provoked an extended debate in the pages of the *Recorder*. Ashmore's chief antagonist in this exchange was a Rhenish missionary by the name of J. Genähr, who defended the proposition that missionaries had nothing to fear, and everything to gain, from the study of comparative religions. See J. Genähr, "Is He Not the God of Gentiles Also? Rom. ii.29," *The Chinese Recorder* 24 (May 1893): 229–40. Genähr was, however, careful to condemn those who fell into "emotional raptures" over heathen religions such as Buddhism, and he rejected Müller's belief in a "genetic connection" between Christianity and pagan religions. Genähr, like Legge, upheld an "impartial not neutral" approach to Confucianism. In this regard, it is important to notice that Genähr actually identifies Legge with this kind of comparativist methodology (p. 239), even going so far as to identify a so-called uniting school of missionaries upholding the "impartial not neutral" position (besides Legge, he named Faber, John Ross, W.A.P. Martin, G.T. Candlin, G. Owen, and

Timothy Richard). On this exchange, see also Ashmore's "Response to Rev. Genahr," *The Chinese Recorder* 24 (August 1893): 391–93; Genähr's letter concerning Ashmore's letter on "God's Own Estimate of Heathenism," *The Chinese Recorder* 24 (October 1893): 484–86, and Genähr's "Deepest Cause of the Anti-Foreign Riots in China," *The Chinese Recorder* 25 (March 1894): 112, where he provocatively suggests a connection between Ashmore's antagonistic methods and the violence in China against foreigners. Better, says Genähr, would be a Pauline principle of accommodation and a Leggian use of the Chinese classics "to show commonalities and differences" with Christianity.

44. See "Missionary Conference at Shanghai," *The Chinese Recorder*.

45. See "Editorial Comment," *The Chinese Recorder* 25 (November 1894): 554.

46. See "Editorial Comment," *The Chinese Recorder* 21 (March 1891): 140.

47. See W.A.P. Martin, "Western Science as Auxiliary to the Spread of the Gospel," *The Chinese Recorder* 28 (March 1897): 111–16.

48. See B.C. Henry, "Chinese Dress in the Shanghai Conference," *The Chinese Recorder* 21 (December 1890): 550–52. Henry reports that "almost a fourth of those in attendance" at the conference, both men and women, wore native dress so that they might "become Chinese to the Chinese." But Henry pointed to the questions of the "healthfulness" of such practices, especially regarding the "conspicuous lack of throat gear." Moreover, going native usually meant the acceptance of a Chinese house, which would be much "too trying" for missionaries.

49. Moule is quoted in the "Missionary Conference at Shanghai," 411–12. See also Joseph W. Esherick, *The Origins of the Boxer Uprising* (Berkeley: University of California Press, 1987), 92. It is worth noting that Esherick (p. 68) defends the notion that "the initial and primary target of the Boxer movement was not foreign economic imperialism, but the 'foreign religion'—the missionaries and their Chinese converts."

50. See Brantlinger, *Rule of Darkness*, 233.

51. After his third Gifford Lecture on "Anthropological Religion" in 1891, Müller was accused of blasphemous "atheism under the guise of pantheism" by some of his more vociferous critics. As Müller's wife said: "Those who know Max Müller's firm faith in a personal God ruling and directing all things in love and wisdom, and in Christ's own teaching (not, indeed, as shown in the teaching of Roman Catholic priests, or Calvinistic ministers), will hardly believe that such attacks could have been made upon him" (Georgina A. Müller, *The Life and Letters of the Right Honorable Friedrich Max Müller* [London: 1902], 2: 276–77).

52. Quoting G. Bühler's comments in *Proceedings of the Ninth International Congress of Orientalists*, 71–77. See also the obituary in the *Oxford Magazine*, October 31, 1900, pp. 43–44:

> "Max Müller." The very name is significant. It is a household word, and has been so not only in Oxford, but throughout England, and indeed the "civilized world," for some forty years. . . . He was, like all the greatest specialists, no mere specialist. His aspiration had been . . . "to attract the attention not only of the scholar, but of the philosopher, the historian, and the theologian to a science which concerns them all." And he had spoken to all, and with a voice that had arrested. He became now even more the man of letters and of the world. He lived on in Oxford

as the distinguished scholar, the example of a European savant, when we had perhaps fewer savants of world-wide repute than to-day. Friends, men and women of mark, notabilities from all sides, came to visit him. He had always been a persona gratissima in the highest circles. His cosmopolitan and courtly training, and his command of the leading modern languages, helped him here.

53. See the obituary "Professor Max Müller," *Jackson's Oxford Journal,* November 11, 1900.

54. See Max Müller, "On the Enormous Antiquity of the East," *Nineteenth Century* 29 (1891): 791–810. This lecture was originally given as the inaugural address at the Royal Asiatic Society on March 4, 1891. Many of the themes in this lecture are similar to those in his address to the congress—both of which reiterate and expand on ideas first expressed in his introduction to the *Sacred Books of the East* back in 1879. Müller argues for modesty when dealing with the "mysterious" charm of the East. This applies especially to the supposed "enormous antiquity" of the Orient, which is then used to justify all sorts of inflated conclusions. For Müller the important thing is that Oriental scholarship should not pander to the false charm, unfounded mystery, and stereotypical images ("the Jew a prophet, the Hindu a dreamer, the Chinaman a joke") of the Orient, but should rather more transcendentally emphasize the "higher sympathies" that directly bear on the "great questions of humanity." In this sense, it is necessary for the Orientalist to distinguish between "authentic and constructive history." Authentic history refers, therefore, to records that include the "testimony of a contemporary" to the events described. From this perspective, Indian history "does not begin before the third century B.C." and authentic Chinese history, despite the "constructive" claims of the *Classics* and Legge's arguments for the eighth century B.C.E. (Müller does not, however, mention Legge here), seems to date only to the third century "burning of the books" and the early Han dynasty. The important issue is not just age but "what is ante"—that is, what is historically and logically antecedent. It is in this light that the study of comparative philology demonstrates the Indo-European antecedents, or original Aryan unity, of many apparently different European languages. Working himself into a fit of quasi-racist exclamation, Müller says, "Think what the synthesis of these two words, India and Europe implies! It implies that the people who migrated into India thousands of years before the beginning of our era spoke the same language which we speak in England . . . [which unites us] into the nobility of the ancient Aryan brotherhood!"

55. Max Müller, *Address Delivered at the Opening of the Ninth International Congress of Orientalists Held in London Sept. 5, 1892, With the Replies of Prof. G. Bühler and Count Angelo de Gubernatis* (Oxford: Oxford University Press, 1892), 5–6.

56. See G. W. Leitner ("The Healing of the Schism among Orientalists," *Asiatic Quarterly Review* 10 [1890]: 212–18), who discusses the debate over the site for the ninth congress. It is clear from this and from R. N. Cust's discussion ("The International Congresses of Orientalists," *Asiatic Quarterly Review,* 3d ser., 4 [1897]: 79–98) that there was some dissatisfaction with Müller's role in the Stockholm and London meetings. As Leitner said: "German scholarship must ever be honoured, but it will not again be allowed to override the genius of French savants or the practical experience of English and Russian orientalists." It was Müller's position that the congress should meet only where there were likely to be real Orientalists—that is, scholars

who were "at least able to publish texts that have never been published before and to translate texts."

57. Müller, *Address [to the] Ninth . . . Congress*, 15–16.

58. Ibid., 29–30.

59. Ibid., 19–20.

60. Ibid., 27–28.

61. Ibid., 44–45.

62. Ibid., 51–53. Needless to say, a monogenesis theorist such as Edkins would not be happy with Müller's comments on this point—see, therefore, Joseph Edkins's evaluation of Müller's address (presented to an audience that included Kingsmill, Möllendorff, Faber, and Franke) in "Proceedings," *Journal of the North China Branch of the Royal Asiatic Society* 27 (1893): 231–46. Edkins continued to hold that "Aryan roots are identical with Semitic and Turanian roots." Moreover, an "English School of Chinese philology" was "springing up" (p. 236) "[a]nd if to the study of Chinese be added the comparative study of Tibetan and Mongol, the issue does not appear doubtful. Philology will accept the view that the vocabularies of all the Asiatic systems of language are ultimately identical." Edkins also notes (p. 241) that, upon the presentation of C. J. Ball's paper connecting Babylonian and Chinese, "Dr. Legge opposed him" and "Sir Thomas Wade spoke moderately, as if the theory were possible but not as if he were fully convinced." As for Edkins himself, "I spoke decidedly in favour of the identification of Chinese primitive characters with those of the Accadians . . . convinced a quarter of a century ago by the fact that the Chinese have the ten signs of the denary cycle and the twelve signs of the duodecimal cycle, as well as by the native astronomy being Babylonian."

63. See G. Schlegel, "The International Congress of Orientalists," *T'oung Pao* 3 (1892): 511–12. Schlegel, the mentor of J. J. M. de Groot, did at times argue (in the 1870s) for the common roots of Chinese and Western civilization—see Maurice Freedman's discussion in "Sinology and the Social Sciences: Some Reflections on the Social Anthropology of China," *Ethnos* 40 (1975): 198.

64. Max Müller, "Enormous Antiquity of the East," 808.

65. Ibid.

66. Ibid.

67. Legge was, at this time, a vice-president of the Asiatic Society and might have been in attendance on Wednesday, March 4, 1891, when Müller gave this inaugural address.

68. Müller, *Address [to the] Ninth . . . Congress*, 67.

69. In 1896 Müller received the special honor of being named as the only non-political member of the queen's Privy Council. This appointment was exceptional and indicates the rare intimacy of Müller 's relationship with the British crown. See Nirad Chaudhuri, *Scholar Extraordinary: The Life of Professor the Rt. Hon. Friedrich Max Müller, P. C.* (London: Chatto & Windus, 1974), 366–67.

70. Müller, *Address [to the] Ninth . . . Congress*, 67.

71. Ibid., 65–66.

72. See Eric J. Ziolkowski, "Heavenly Visions and Worldly Intentions: Chicago's Columbian Exposition and World's Parliament of Religions (1893)," *Journal of American Culture* 13 (1990): 9–15.

73. Ibid.; and Richard Hughes Seager, ed., introduction, in *The Dawn of Religious Pluralism: Voices from the World's Parliament of Religions, 1893* (La Salle, Ill.: Open Court, 1993), 3–4. Seager's volume reprints a representative selection of the parliament papers, but for the original versions of these papers, see John Henry Barrows, ed., *The World's Parliament of Religions, An Illustrated and Popular Story of the World's First Parliament of Religions, Held in Chicago in Connection with the Columbian Exposition of 1893*, 2 vols. (Chicago: Parliament Publishing Company, 1893); and Walter R. Houghton, *Neely's History of the Parliament of Religions* (Chicago: Neely, 1894). Ziolkowski ("Heavenly Visions," 11), following Alan Race, defines *pluralism* in this context as an attitude that accepts that "all faiths, including Christianity" possess only "partial knowledge of God."

Increased academic interest in comparative religions in the United States is discussed in Robert S. Shepard, *God's People in the Ivory Tower: Religion in the Early American University* (Brooklyn, N.Y.: Carlson, 1991).

74. See Ziolkowski, "Heavenly Visions," 10–11.

75. Max Müller, "The Real Significance of the Parliament of Religions," *The Arena* 11 (1894): 1.

76. Müller's paper was an odd appeal for a return to a "pure" or ante-Nicene Christianity that, in the spirit of Alexandrine theology, rejected the "vulgar mythological" understanding of Christ's nature. See Max Müller, "Greek Philosophy and the Christian Religion," in Barrows, ed., *World's Parliament of Religions*, 2: 935–36.

77. The expression "cosmopolitan habit in theology" is taken from Martin Marty's discussion in his *Modern American Religion*, vol. 1, *The Irony of It All* (Chicago: University of Chicago Press, 1986). It may also be noted that the China mission was increasingly dominated by Americans after the turn of the century.

78. John Henry Barrows, "The Religious Possibilities of the World's Fair," *The Chinese Recorder* 23 (December 1892): 547–56.

79. Barrows was responding to an "Editorial Comment" in *The Chinese Recorder*. In a wary discussion of the proposed parliament of religion as a "new sort" of "ecumenical move," the *Recorder* warned of the "singular peril" that "any serious attempt to cultivate a spirit of brotherhood among the religions of the world" might only "foster a spirit of indifferentism" and "compromise" the Christian gospel. Can anyone really "imagine Jesus Christ sitting in council with Buddha, Brahmin, and other false gods?" (*The Chinese Recorder* 23 [July 1892]: 345–46). All true Christians must always ask themselves: "What communion hath light with darkness?" Barrows's retort to this was "though light has no fellowship with darkness, light does have fellowship with twilight" ("Religious Possibilities," 552).

80. Ibid., 549–50.

81. See George Candlin, "What Should Be Our Attitude toward the False Religions?" *The Chinese Recorder* 23 (March 1892): 99–110. As Candlin says, the missionary movement "has nothing to fear and everything to hope" from comparative religions. The proper attitude was one of "vigilant conciliation" and not "compromise"—of "contrast" not "contradiction." See the support for Candlin and the comparative approach in Hope W. Gill, "The Study of Comparative Religions," *The Chinese Recorder* 23 (October 1892): 482–83. Elegantly and ostentatiously dressed in Chinese garb, Candlin gave three talks at the Chicago parliament: "The Future Religious Unity of Mankind," "Criticism and Discussion of Missionary Meth-

ods," and "The Bearing of Religious Unity on the Work of Christian Missions." Along with W.A.P. Martin and Ernst Faber, the English Methodist George Candlin became one of the leading voices of liberal comparativism among the missionaries in China. Martin and Faber were also speakers at the Chicago parliament. On the "impartial but not neutral" comparative method specifically associated with Legge, see also Martin Schaub, "Heathenism: A Scriptural Study," *The Chinese Recorder* 24 (August 1893): 353–61.

Perhaps most incredible is that some contemporaneous nineteenth-century figures, who should have known better, relied on the original 1861 edition of the *Classics* and consequently identified Legge with those who saw no vital and progressive religious "impulse" *at all* in Confucius and Confucianism. One surprising instance of this is seen in the generally progressive theological views of Barrows himself. Writing in 1899 in expectation of the coming "Christian conquest of Asia," Barrows commented that he had to take exception to the opinions of Legge, "who, after his long study of the character and opinions of the Chinese sage, refused to regard him as a great man." The reason for this, and here we see Barrows's uncritical reliance on the 1861 edition of the *Classics*, is that, according to Legge, "Confucius threw no new light on any questions which had a world-wide interest, gave no impulse to religion, and had no sympathy with progress." Oblivious to the changes in Legge's comparative judgment of Confucius, Barrows is content to repeat in Emersonian terms what Legge had already learned decades before through the annealing power of his own dissenting Christianity and the liberating influence of figures such as Burns, Reid, Carlyle, and Müller. In ratification of his own self-styled higher view of Confucius, Barrows says only that he was "taught by Emerson to regard him as great who represents in himself a great people, who absorbs and remoulds what may belong to an age or a race" (John Henry Barrows, *The Christian Conquest of Asia: Studies and Personal Observations of Oriental Religions* [New York: Charles Scribner's Sons, 1899], 199–200).

It is Barrows's style of progressive Protestantism, informed by the tolerant spirit of the comparative science of religions, that most obviously merges into the full-blown social-gospel form of Protestantism that was especially characteristic of American missionary movements after the turn of the century. As Barrows put it in the preface to the *Christian Conquest of Asia* (pp. ix–x):

> Until Protestant missionary work, with its schools, its hospitals, its purer ideals and its aggressive energy, made its way into Western Asia, and into the lands of the East and Far East, the Asiatic world may almost be said to have missed any accurate knowledge of that apostolic type of the Christian religion which is pure and vigorous enough to command the world's future. The results already achieved [may be seen] not only [in] the making of converts, but particularly in the improvement of social conditions, the lifting up of new ideals, etc.

82. Barrows, "Religious Possibilities," 553.

83. Quoting from "Missionary News," *The Chinese Recorder* 23 (September 1892): 440. In this article it is noted that, after a presentation by Barrows, the International Missionary Union meeting at Clifton Springs, New York, voted down a resolution approving the Parliament of Religions. See also the account of the Clifton Springs meeting by John C. Ferguson, "A Notable Meeting," *The Chinese Recorder* 23 (October 1892): 465–68. Ferguson noted the "wide division" at the meeting, with the

larger group fearful that a parliament would "lower the Christian religion by calling it only 'one' of the world's religions."

84. On these and related issues, see the introduction and various articles in Eric Ziolkowski, ed., *A Museum of Faiths: Histories and Legacies of the 1893 World's Parliament of Religions* (Atlanta, Ga.: Scholars Press, 1993). See also Robert H. Sharf, "The Zen of Japanese Nationalism," *History of Religions* 33 (1993): 1–43.

85. The classic statement of this position is by J.R. Levenson, "Western Religion and the Decay of Traditional China. The Intrusion of History on Judgments of Value," *Sinologica* 4 (1954): 14–20. See also his fuller discussion in *Modern China and Its Confucian Past: The Problem of Intellectual Continuity* (Garden City, N.J.: Anchor Books, 1964).

86. This was very much unlike an anonymous "prize essay" on Daoism, which essentially apologized for the religion's deterioration; see Seager, *Dawn of Religious Pluralism*, 361–63.

87. There were two other native Chinese representatives in Chicago. One (Kung Hsien Ho) spoke for orthodox Zhu Xi philosophy and metaphysics; the other was the Reverend Y.K. Yen, a Chinese Protestant pastor of second-generation religious affiliation who spoke on "What Has Christianity Done for the Chinese?"

Despite prejudice against Chinese immigrants, Pung indicates (Seager, *Dawn of Religious Pluralism*, 341) that "[i]n regard to the character of the foreign missionaries in China, Americans are on the whole more desirable than Englishmen, and Englishmen are more desirable than Frenchmen. Such is the general opinion in China. I am not influenced in any way by my residence in this country in making this statement."

88. See Pung's talk in ibid., 341–44, 375–82. The sarcastic edge of Pung's presentation is indicated, for example, by his comments on the problems with the Chinese versions of the Christian Bible: "It is a great pity that the Christian Scriptures have been translated into Chinese thus far only by men evidently deficient in doctrinal knowledge as well as in lingual requirements, so that the best version of the Christian Bible is far inferior to the versions of the Buddhistic scriptures. There is no Chinese scholar, after reading a few lines of it, but lays it aside."

89. See Pung's presentation in ibid., 341–42. It was reported by Chicago newspapers that Pung did not speak English and that an English version of his paper was read for him on the parliament platform.

90. Legge neither attended nor sent a paper to the parliament, and I know of no published or unpublished materials in which Legge discusses the event. Leggian sinological "comparativism" was, however, represented at the Parliament by Ernst Faber's paper "Genesis and Development of Confucianism" and by George Candlin's several presentations. Concerning Faber's presentation, which was printed only in digest form in Barrows's edited collection of parliament papers, see E. Faber, "Confucianism," *The Chinese Recorder* 33 (April 1902): 159–75, a reprint of the original draft version of the paper (notable for its argument that Daoism was closest to the original archaic religion of China).

91. Pung in Seager, *Dawn of Religious Pluralism*, 343.

92. Ibid., 376.

93. See especially Richard Hughes Seager, *The World's Parliament of Religions: The East/West Encounter, Chicago, 1893* (Bloomington and Indianapolis: Indiana University Press, 1995), 139–48.

94. See the "Editorial Note" attached to John Henry Barrows's "Results of the Parliament of Religions," *The Chinese Recorder* 26 (March 1895): 101–13. In "Missionary News" (*The Chinese Recorder* 25 [February 1894]: 98–99), it was reported that some think of the parliament as "the climax of modern religious development" while others see "it as letting down of Christianity and a humiliation." Especially galling was the fact that some Japanese observers were saying that the "Parliament was called because the West realized the weakness and folly of Christianity and wanted to learn what was the best religion."

95. See George T. Candlin, "The Parliament of Religions," *The Chinese Recorder* 25 (January 1894): 35–38; and idem, "Bearing of Religious Unity upon the Work of Missions," *The Chinese Recorder* 24 (December 1893): 553–57. Candlin was a British Methodist. For support of Candlin's position, see Isaac T. Headland's review of Barrows's *World's Parliament of Religions*, *The Chinese Recorder* 25 (May 1894): 249–51. Criticism of Candlin is found in "C.L's" letter to the editor of *The Chinese Recorder* 25 (March 1894): 138–42. More general condemnation of the dangers of the comparative method and the "fallacies which gave birth to the 'Parliament of Religions'" is found in John C. Gibson's review of Charles George Sparham's *Christianity and the Religions of China: A Brief Study in Comparative Religions* (London: John Snow, 1897), *The Chinese Recorder* 28 (1897): 597–99. As Gibson says (p. 598), "But how much writing on 'comparative religions' is of [a] careless and impressionistic character. . . . They find an agreeable zest in friendly if superficial contact with strangeness. Then they go to write of the gloom and failure of Christianity and of the brighter and happier life produced by natural religions in summer lands beyond the sea."

96. Barrows, "Results of the Parliament," 102, 107. On the Haskell Lectureship, see Shepard, *God's People in the Ivory Tower*, 97 n. 149.

97. A.F. Pierson, "The Parliament of Religions: A Review," *The Chinese Recorder* 26 (April 1895): 161–75.

98. Ibid., 162, 173. Pierson specifically quotes William Ashmore's truculent defense of the antagonistic position here.

99. Ibid., 173.

100. Müller's article actually appeared before Barrows's defense and Pierson's condemnation. See also the attack on the parliament by the American Presbyterian missionary S.I. Woodbridge, "The Pan-Religious Convention. A Retrospect," *The Chinese Recorder* 28 (1897): 18–21. (Woodbridge was particularly incensed by the failure of heathens to call a similar parliament in their own countries and the fact that they "have covered up their defects.")

101. Max Müller, "Real Significance of the Parliament," 1.

102. Müller discussed the councils associated with the Buddhist king Asoka, the Christian patriarchs of Nicea, and the Islamic emperor Akbar—all of which were shown to be severely wanting when compared with Chicago.

103. Ibid., 7–8.

104. Ibid., 11.

105. Ibid., 13.

106. In his conclusion, Müller waxed eloquent on the need for a global unity of all religions and nations under the leadership of the English and Americans. Blood being thicker than water, these two great nations must stand "shoulder to shoulder"

in the great work of creating for the first time a league of nations, a "great parliament of the world," where the universal communion of mankind comes before party, country, and creed (ibid., 13).

107. See Georgina Müller, *Life and Letters*, 2: 292–93 (cf. Müller's comments on novel reading in old age: "tales meant for entertainment form generally the last stages of the literature of the great nations of the world") and pp. 438–40 (on his activities at the time of his death). With a great deal of insight, the London *Times*, October 29, 1900, wrote at the time of Müller's death that, whereas Oxford lost "one of its chief ornaments," the whole "world of letters" was "poorer by the disappearance of a sympathetic intelligence." Over the years, as the *Times* recognized, Müller's critics had tarnished his luster as an intellectual celebrity and had even questioned his monumental work on the *Rig-Veda*. He was not therefore of the stature of a Humboldt, Grimm, or Bopp, but he was "unsurpassed as a scientific expositor, possessing, as he did, a certain attractive vivacity, a power of breathing human interest into dry bones, a curiously sympathetic intelligence, and a rare mixture of the talents of the poet and the savant. He loved great things and great conceptions, and it was his delight to build, often a little hastily, stately arches spanning large gulfs and chasms." More than anything else, he would be remembered for the "service he rendered to the East and the West by the series 'The Sacred Books of the East.'"

108. JL to Marian Hunt, June 3, 1894 (University of London, School of Oriental and African Studies [hereafter cited as SOAS], Legge archive, MS. 380476, no. 44). On Takakusu (1866–1945), who went on to become a prominent and widely published Buddhist scholar, see Donald Leslie and Jeremy Davidson, *Author Catalogues of Western Sinologists* (Canberra: Department of Far Eastern History, Australian National University, 1966), 165.

109. Edward Parker's obituary comments on Legge are quite revealing in this regard (*Asiatic Quarterly Review*, 1898). As Parker says, Legge at the end of his scholarly life seems "never" to have made a "literary enemy." If anything, Legge was "too considerate and courteous" to his "rash and presumptuous critics" (and Parker is certainly thinking of both Giles and Lacouperie here). He was quite capable in private conversation, says Parker, of cracking a "humorous joke at the expense of imposters," but he "never wrote a harsh word." A "gentleman" and teacher to the core, he "made no mystery of his craft" and always was prepared "to help others."

110. Even at Oxford, Legge seems to have retreated from activities that would have attracted him in his earlier years. An example of this is Legge's apparent lack of involvement in the Oxford Society for Historical Theology, a group of liberal Oxonian scholars devoted to the discussion of generally liberal and comparativist religious topics. This mostly Anglican group met from 1891 to 1898 and included Müller, A. M. Fairbairn, J. Estlin Carpenter, T. K. Cheyne, and A. Sayce. Honorary members included such notable liberals as James Martineau, Count Goblet d'Alviella (Brussels), A. Harnack (Berlin), O. Pfleiderer (Berlin), and Cornelis Tiele (Leiden). See the bound volume of papers from the *Society of Historical Theology*, 1891–1898 (Oxford University, Radcliff Camera Library, S. Th. Per 17, Soc. Oxon 8 525).

111. JL to G. Schlegel, April 1, 1896; see G. Schlegel, "James Legge, M.A. Oxford, LL.D. Aberdeen," *T'oung Pao* 9 (1898): 62.

112. For JL's lectures and courses during this period, see appendix B. His publications included articles for the *Journal of the Royal Asiatic Society* on chronology

(1893) and "The Late Appearance of Romances and Novels" (1893, pp. 799–822). Most important during this period was his extensive three-part series, "The Li Sao Poem and Its Author" (1895, 1: 77–92, 2: 571–99, 3: 839–64)—see pages 497–99. Most are minor works, but some of them raise interesting methodological and personal questions. For example, in discussing Chinese chronology, he rather conservatively argues for the historical existence of the ancient emperors Yao and Shun (in stark contrast with the views of extreme sino-Aryan and sino-Babylonian comparativists such as Edkins, Lacouperie, and Kingsmill). The accounts of Yao and Shun are said to be not like the "silly fables" of mythology. The historical veracity of these Chinese tales is therefore fundamentally similar to the truth of the biblical stories of Abraham (a conclusion that, it is noted, Thomas Wade concurs with). On these issues, see also Legge's lecture on "The Emperor Yao" (Oxford University, Bodleian Library dep. c. 32). It is worth noting that his discussion of Chinese historical romances (first appearing in the Yuan-dynasty *Sanguozhi Yenyi* [The romance of the three kingdoms]) is an interesting, but inconclusive, essay on comparative "coincidences in narratives" (p. 821). More than anything else, Legge's analysis highlights the increased questioning in the 1890s of extreme comparative methods.

113. JL, preface, *Chinese Classics* (1893), 1:x–xi.

114. See Helen Edith's description of her father at this time (Helen Edith Legge, *James Legge Missionary and Scholar* [London: Religious Tract Society, 1905], 227–28). She makes a point of noting that, health permitting, he maintained his habit of rising in the early morning to the very end of his life. No longer so actively involved in Nonconformist causes at Oxford, Legge tells us in a letter (to his stepdaughter Marian Hunt, October 22, 1893; SOAS MS. 380476, no. 42) that he "shrank from" attending too many of the opening services for the new Unitarian Manchester College. Part of his reluctance had to do with his theological difficulties with Unitarianism, but it also seems indicative of his broader withdrawal from university activities.

115. Information about Helen Edith Legge's protective (and sometimes destructive) guardianship of the Leggian legacy comes from personal communications from Dominica Legge in 1983. Some other insights into family matters came from communications in 1993 with Christopher Legge and his son, James Legge. Legge's will was dated July 24, 1885, and includes later codicils. There is nothing peculiar about the will. Aside from various odds and ends divided up among family members (e.g., his sons were given the "silver plate" and Helen Edith received his gold watch), it is clear that the estate had no extraordinary monetary value. The only possession that had some worth was his Chinese library and it was stipulated that this be sold.

116. JL to Marian Hunt, February 2, 1892 (SOAS MS. 380476, no. 40). Marian was by this time married to Bertram Hunt, M.D., and had three children (Colin, Jack, and Mary). It often seems as if Legge were particularly close to Marian. His letters to her during this period seem unusually revealing and personal.

117. For his comments on the weather, see JL to Bertram Hunt, January 1, 1894 (SOAS MS. 380476, no. 43). The reference to "the cold that hangs about me" is found in JL to Marian Hunt, March 17, 1896 (SOAS, MS. 380476, no. 45). The allusion to the writing of "Notes of My Life" (1897) and the *Book of Poetry* is found in Legge to Schlegel, April 1, 1896, "In Memoriam," 62.

118. See G. Schlegel's review of "The Li Sao Poem and Its Author," *T'oung Pao* 7 (1896): 91–94. See also Henri Cordier's praise in a letter to Legge, November 17, 1895 (Council for World Mission [hereafter cited as CWM]/China/Personal/Legge/Box 7).

119. JL, "Li Sao and Its Author," pt. 2: 571.

120. See David Hawkes, *Ch'u Tz'u. Songs of the South* (Boston: Beacon Press, 1959), 215–17.

121. JL, "Li Sao and Its Author," pt. 2: 598–99.

122. JL to Schlegel, March 23, 1897, in Schlegel, "In Memoriam," 62. In a contemporary portrait appearing in *The Christian*, March 11, 1897, it was reported that, even in his eighty-second year, Legge was "working hard at writing."

123. See JL to Marian Hunt, June 20, 1897 (SOAS MS. 38046, no. 48). Legge mentions that he was being treated by Dr. Collier who was giving him a "new application" for his eczema.

124. Besides the "composition of easy sentences," Legge's junior and senior classes for the Michaelmas term were devoted to such topics as the geography of China; philological aspects of Chinese characters; the *Analects*, book V, with text and commentary; and aspects of Han history, including a consideration of Wang Mang; see appendix B.

125. For a contemporary discussion of the Diamond Jubilee, see the account in *The Chinese Recorder* 28 (June 1897): 297. See also Dorothy Thompson, *Queen Victoria: The Woman, the Monarchy, and the People* (New York: Pantheon Books, 1990), 132–33.

126. Georgina Müller, *Life and Letters*, 2: 378. Müller himself was in Rome but did not meet with the pope. Müller comments: "I am proud to think that my collection will have a place in the Papal Library, and go to the Propaganda with the implied approval of the Pope." On the two-volume *Science of Mythology*, see Chaudhuri, *Scholar Extraordinary*, 362–64. Müller was the only nonpolitical member of the Privy Council (an appointed body that constituted the queen's closest advisers). On the Privy Council announcement of his appointment by Lord Salisbury, see the London *Times*, May 20, 1896.

127. See, for example, the "Nonagesimal of Protestant Missions in China," *The Chinese Recorder* 28 (September 1897): 403–9. It was estimated that in 1897 there were about eighty thousand Protestant Christians in China. Hoping for one hundred thousand by the turn of the century, the anonymous author of this article opined that there were still problems of "union and cooperation" among the different denominations, as well as a continuing lack of "harmony of Christian terminology." This article also mentions that "Legge in England and Hepburn [not identified further] in the US" were at that time the "oldest living missionaries."

128. On Wang's death, see especially Cohen, *Between Tradition and Modernity*, 3–4 and 279–80 n. 3, which gives the relevant bibliography.

129. On Sun Yat-sen in London, see J. Y. Wong, *The Origins of a Heroic Image: Sun Yat-sen in London 1896–1897* (New York: Oxford University Press, 1986). See also Jonathan D. Spence, *The Search for Modern China* (New York: Norton, 1990), 224–26; and Donald Treadgold, *The West in Russia and China: Secular and Religious Thought in Modern Times* (Cambridge: Cambridge University Press, 1973), 2: 70–98.

In the Council for World Mission archive there is passing reference to Legge's introducing Timothy Richard to Sun Yat-sen in London on February 12, 1897.

130. This incident is recounted by his Nonconformist colleague Andrew Fairbairn (see A. M. Fairbairn, *In Memoriam Rev. Professor James Legge, December 20, 1815– November 29, 1897*, Mansfield College Chapel address, December 3, 1897, pamphlet, Mansfield College archive, 7).

131. JL, prolegomena, *Chinese Classics* (1893), 1: 87.

132. See Robert Troup, "The Late Professor Legge," *Huntly Express,* December 11, 1897, p. 8 (clipping, CWM/China/Personal/Legge/Box 9). The allusion to the Sermon on the Mount ("Blessed are the pure of heart, / For they shall see God") is the motto for Andrew Fairbairn's eulogy, *In Memoriam.*

133. For Legge's description of Kongfuzi's death, see his prolegomena, *Chinese Classics* (1893), 1: 87–88.

134. Ibid., 94–95.

135. Troup, "Late Professor Legge," 8. See also Dominica Legge's description in "James Legge" (paper presented to the Sino-Scottish Society, University of Edinburgh, February 4, 1951), 14.

136. References to Legge's linguistic shortcomings sometimes surfaced in obituaries by missionaries. Muirhead, for example, says that because he tried "several dialects at once," he was "without perfect speech" of any single Chinese vernacular. Moreover, he spoke Chinese with an Aberdonian brogue. See W. Muirhead's obituary in *The Chinese Recorder* 39 (1898): 113–14. Joseph Edkins (clipping of sermon, CWM/China/Personal/Legge/Box 7) makes the interesting point that it was Legge's exceedingly "powerful" memory that naturally inclined him to textual study over speaking. Edkins described Legge's remarkable memory as "a great aid in the study of Chinese words which consist of many thousands. He could store in his mind with ease the singular complicated forms by the Chinese pencil in enormous variety. These same characters freighted many persons by their difficulty. To him they were attractive because he could so readily remember them." This restricted sense of mastering Chinese was deeply inculcated within sinological Orientalism in the West and it was only during and after World War II that the study of the spoken vernacular was emphasized.

137. See especially Schlegel's assessment of Legge's technical sinological abilities, "James Legge," 60–63. From a scholarly standpoint, see also the *Oxford Journal,* December 4, 1897, which quotes Legge's old nemesis, and now inheritor of Wade's chair at Cambridge, Herbert Giles; and the *Athenaeum,* December 1898, p. 788.

138. In the fourth column from the right, it seems that he mistakenly wrote *wu* (the seventh symbol of the Earthly Branches' computational system for time) for *niu* (cow).

139. On the principle of "translatability" as related to the Protestant missionary movement, see Lamin Sanneh, *Translating the Message: The Missionary Impact on Culture* (New York: Orbis, 1991); and idem, "Global Christianity and the Re-education of the West," *Christian Century* 112 (1995): 715–18.

140. See the *Oxford Times,* December 11, 1897.

141. The directors of the London Missionary Society essentially reiterated the declaration made at the time of Legge's retirement from the society in 1874. For

the resolution of December 4, 1897, see CWM/China/Personal/Legge/Box 9. It should be noted, however, that at the end of the century the London Missionary Society was generally considered a liberal organization—socially, politically, and religiously. On some of these issues involving the society, see Susan Elizabeth Thorne, "Protestant Ethics and the Spirit of Imperialism: British Congregationalists and the London Missionary Society, 1795–1925" (Ph.D. diss., University of Michigan, 1990).

142. Jay Pridmore, reviewing Jean and John Comoroff's *Of Revelation and Revolution: Christianity, Colonialism, and Consciousness in South Africa,* vol. 1 (Chicago: University of Chicago Press, 1991) for the *University of Chicago Magazine,* August 1991, p. 20, notes that Livingstone was one of the few to understand the irony of missionary work. He was "too much of a relativist to convert anybody." His problem, like Legge's, was that "he kept seeing virtues in the arguments of the other."

143. See, for example, W. B. Selbie, *The Life of Andrew Martin Fairbairn* (London: Hodder and Stoughton, 1914), 308. Selbie reports that Fairbairn's Gifford Lectures in Aberdeen were especially criticized because his Chinese material, which relied on Legge, was not "up-to-date." Fairbairn's uncertainty about Legge's views was apparently one of the primary reasons the publication of the lectures was delayed. Fairbairn also had his own debate with Herbert Giles and must have known of his strong criticism of Legge. See Fairbairn's letter to the editor of the *Daily Free Press,* 1894 (clipping, CWM/China/Personal/Legge/Box 7).

144. For these quotations, see Fairbairn, *In Memoriam,* 3–4; Troup, "Late Professor Legge," 8; Parker, *Asiatic Quarterly Review,* 1898; *Oxford Magazine,* December 8, 1897, p. 142; and Edkins, "Sermon on Dr. Legge" (clipping in CWM/China/Personal/Legge/Box 7).

145. Troup (ibid.) is harshly revealing about Legge's ability as a speaker:

The Doctor was a good but not a great preacher. He did not stand in the first rank, as could scarcely be expected in one whose mind was so absorbed in Chinese missions and the study, translation, and interpretation of ancient Chinese books. He had few or none of the graces of oratory, nor had he its passion, fervour or fluency. He did not enchant you by vivid pictures of the imagination nor charm you by flashes of wit or humour, nor awe you by stern denunciations of divine wrath, nor lift you up as by a heavenly inspiration. He was slow of speech, but always sensible and reasonable, scriptural in doctrine, weighty in argument, careful in the selection of words, accurate in all his statements, never in any way exaggerating.

Concerning Legge's sympathetic views of the Chinese people, it is interesting that this quotation comes from a spokesman for the London Missionary Society—see Norman H. Smith, "In Memoriam. The Late Rev. Professor Legge, M.A., D.D., LL.D., pt. 2, Professor Legge in Oxford," *Chronicle of the London Missionary Society,* 1898, p. 8.

146. Legge's good humor is frequently commented on, but for this reference to his unsophisticated or *pawky* humor, see Fairbairn, "In Memoriam," 9 ("able by his pawky yet genial humour to brighten dismal things, illumine things that were dark, soften harsh things"). It should be noted that in Scottish dialect *pawky* connotes not just simple good humor, but a "tricky, artful, cunning, and crafty" demeanor (see the *Oxford English Dictionary*).

147. See Richard D. Altick, "Eminent Victorianism: What Lytton Strachey Hath Wrought," *American Scholar* 64 (1995): 81–89.

148. Fairbairn, "In Memoriam," 5.

149. Ibid., 6–8.

150. Schlegel, "James Legge," 59. There is no testimony from Müller except the rather lame report that Legge was always punctual in his commitments to the *Sacred Books*—see Mrs. Max Müller to the Legge family (Helen Edith Legge, typed excerpts, Council for World Mission/China/Personal/Legge/Box 9).

151. Fairbairn, "In Memoriam," 9–11.

CONCLUSION

1. Pierre Bourdieu defines *habitus* as "a system of shared social dispositions and cognitive structures which generates perceptions, appreciations, and actions." See his *Homo Academicus,* trans. Peter Collier (Stanford: Stanford University Press, 1988), 279 n. 2.

2. Despite Legge's best efforts to salvage some kind of religiosity for Confucius, most later commentators preferred to emphasize his a-religious or agnostic character, a condition that came to characterize the overall elite Chinese tradition. Even critics sympathetic to the comparativist point of view saw "nothing religious" at all about Confucius. As the anonymous reviewer of the forty-nine volumes of the *Sacred Books* for the *Quarterly Review* (195 [April 1902]: 327–61) noted (p. 353), Confucius was the "supreme representative of the Mongolian mind, which is the very antithesis of the Indian—prosaic, practical, unimaginative, and altogether averse from metaphysical speculation." On the standard agnostic interpretation of Confucius, see H.G. Creel, "Was Confucius Agnostic?" *T'oung Pao* 29 (1935): 55–90.

3. For a discussion of these issues from various nationalistic and disciplinary perspectives, see George M. Marsden and Bradley J. Longfield, eds., *The Secularization of the Academy* (New York, Oxford: Oxford University Press, 1992).

4. For a discussion of the success and promise of comparative religions at the turn of the century, see the review of the forty-nine volumes of the *Sacred Books* in the *Quarterly Review.* For developments in France, see Jean Baubérot et al., *Cent Ans de sciences religieuses en France* (Paris: Éditions du Cerf, 1987). See also Robert S. Shepard, *God's People in the Ivory Tower: Religion in the Early American University* (Brooklyn, N.Y.: Carlson, 1991); and Eric J. Sharpe, *Comparative Religion: A History,* 2d ed. (La Salle, Ill.: Open Court, 1986). Sharpe's work is a pioneering and important overview of many of these issues, but is too often a genealogical history of ideas. What is needed is a full cultural history of the academic study of religions. Although more up to date, Walter H. Capps, in *Religious Studies: The Making of a Discipline* (Minneapolis: Fortress Press, 1995), also fails to contextualize the history of the study of religion sufficiently. Works by Jacques Waardenburg (*Classical Approaches to the Study of Religion: Aims, Methods and Theories of Research,* vol. 1 [The Hague: Mouton, 1973]) and Frank Whaling (*Contemporary Approaches to the Study of Religion,* 2 vols. [New York: Mouton, 1983–1984]) are helpful but also disappointing. Older, and still useful, surveys of the field are the works by Louis Henry Jordan (*Comparative Religion: Its Genesis and Growth* [New York: Charles Scribner's Sons, 1905]), Morris Jastrow (*The Study of Religion* [reprint, Chico, Calif.: Scholars Press, 1981]), and Pinard de la Boullaye (*L'Étude comparée des religions* [Paris: G. Beauchesne,

1922–1925]). For a recent postmodernist approach to these issues, see Willi Braun and Russell T. McCutcheon, eds., *Guide to the Study of Religion* (London and New York: Cassell, 2000).

5. Secularization was always a relative matter within modern universities and society at large. So, while faculties were conspicuously secular as a matter of academic discipline, compulsory chapel for students continued well into the twentieth century at many older universities in Europe and America.

6. See Sharpe, *Comparative Religion,* 119–43 ("The Quest for Academic Recognition"). Müller himself discussed some of these problems in his "Science of Religion: A Retrospect," *Living Age* 219 (1898): 909–13. Müller always maintained that his comparative approach depended entirely on historical methods. For this reason, the problem with those who spoke of "religion in general" was their overly speculative and nonhistorical attempt to link "all historic religions" with some "common pre-historic religion." The "leaders of the philosophic and generalizing movement" were Schelling and Hegel, whose work resulted in "many theories" but with "few well-established facts." At the same time Müller makes it clear that he includes anthropological scholars such as Tylor among the generalists who mistakenly attempt to treat "religion as one, and trying to recognize in the rationale of one [e.g., Tylor's theory of animism] the rationale of all religions" (p. 912). In this article Müller actually prefers the disciplinary name of "science of religion" to that of "comparative religion." Comparison, he says here (p. 913), "must always" be restricted to the comparison of "homogeneous or organically related religions." Despite Müller's protestations and the existence of different comparative methods, many critics came to identify the very idea of comparison with Müller.

7. See Mircea Eliade, "The History of Religions in Retrospect: 1912 and After," in *The Quest: History and Meaning in Religion* (Chicago: University of Chicago Press, 1969), 12 ff.

8. See, for example, Marcel Granet, *Festivals and Songs of Ancient China,* trans. E. D. Edwards (New York: E.P. Dutton, 1932), 15–16. This work was originally published in French in 1919. Granet's complete assessment of Legge should be noted:

> Legge appears to work upon the Classics rather with ancient China in view, but it must be admitted that his outlook on them is extraordinarily narrow. Often he seems to have no end in view beyond that of making an inventory of the literary labours of Confucius and deciding whether or not he was really a great man. A rather brief review which does not appreciate the real problems; a too-industrious scholarship with, apparently, no rules to guide it; a desire to show at times the absurdity of the commentaries and at others to include in his translation injudiciously selected notes, all these factors combine to detract from the value of his work, notwithstanding the fact that it was done under the most favourable material conditions. The faults indicated are especially evident in his treatment of the Odes of the States.

9. For documentation of this perspective in early-twentieth-century sinology, see Creel's discussion, "Was Confucius Agnostic?" 55–64.

10. A prefiguring of the dominant position espoused by the revived French-Continental sinological establishment is seen in Barthélemy-Saint-Hilaire's elabo-

rate four-part review in 1894 of Legge's Chinese contributions to the *Sacred Books of the East* for the Parisian *Journal des savants*. His conclusions attacked the very heart of Legge's case for the archaic monotheistic basis of Confucianism (as argued most overtly in the *Religions of China* and in his contributions to the *Sacred Books*) because, according to the French academician, the classical figure of Shangdi could not be convincingly equated with the Christian creator God. Furthermore, as shown by the a-causal and nontheistic cosmology of the *Book of Changes*, educated Chinese were fundamentally atheistic and neither Confucius nor Confucianism could be considered religious in any meaningful way. (Jules Barthélemy-Saint-Hilaire, "The Sacred Books of China, The Texts of Confucianism, trans. by James Legge, Part I, Oxford 1879," *Journal des savants*, 4 pts. [February 1894]: 65–78; [June 1894]: 321–31; [July 1894]: 381–92; [September 1894]: 511–20.) See also Lauren Pfister, "Clues to the Life and Academic Achievements of One of the Most Famous Nineteenth-Century European Sinologists—James Legge (A.D. 1815–1897)," *Journal of the Hong Kong Branch of the Royal Asiatic Society* 30 (1993): 180–218.

11. See C. K. Yang, *Religion in Chinese Society* (Berkeley and Los Angeles: University of California Press, 1961, 1967). See also Arthur Wright, "The Study of Chinese Civilization," *Journal of the History of Ideas* 21 (1960): 233–55; and Maurice Freedman, "Sinology and the Social Sciences: Some Reflections on the Social Anthropology of China," *Ethnos* 40 (1975): 198, who identifies the "China of the Sinologues"—i.e., "early China and the normative culture associated with the Classics"—with "the world of Legge." Yang's definition of religion is manifestly sociological but, interestingly enough, stems from the liberal Protestant theological views of his mentors Joachim Wach and Paul Tillich; as Yang says (p. 1):

> For purpose of this study [*Religion in Chinese Society*], the structural viewpoint of Joachim Wach has been combined with the functional viewpoint of Paul Tillich in defining religion as the system of beliefs, ritualistic practices, and organizational relationships designed to deal with ultimate matters of human life such as the tragedy of death, unjustifiable sufferings, unaccountable frustrations, uncontrollable hostilities that threaten to shatter human social ties, and the vindication of dogmas against contradictory evidences from realistic experience.

I should note the exclusion of any monotheistic element in this understanding of religion.

12. See Yang, *Religion in Chinese Society*, p. 3 (quoting the 1967 paperback edition). Yang is evidently unaware of the significant differences between Legge and Giles concerning Kongzi and Confucianism. See, for example, Giles's article "Confucianism in the Nineteenth Century," *North American Review* 171 (1900): 359–74. Yang also corroborates the important point that Chinese intellectuals reinforced their own self-image among Western scholars and also tended to go beyond their Western mentors regarding rationalistic, antireligious, and naturalistic attitudes. As Yang says (p. 6):

> It is quite natural for modern Chinese intellectuals, who have followed the West in exalting science, to catch the spirit of the times and to shun religion. But perhaps an even stronger motivation for the assumption of an "unreligious" or "rationalistic" society for China lies in the Chinese intellectual's necessity of emphasizing the

dignity of Chinese civilization in the face of the political and economic superiority of the nationalistically oriented Western world.

13. See particularly N.J. Girardot, "Chinese Religions, History of the Study of," *The Encyclopedia of Religion*, ed. Mircea Eliade, vol. 3 (New York: Macmillan, 1986–1987), 312–23. Herrlee Creel, Arthur Waley, and D.C. Lau may be taken as the most important Anglo-American commentators on Confucius in the first half of the twentieth century. Of these three, only Creel confronted the question of a Confucian "religious impulse" ambiguously raised by Legge (see Creel's "Was Confucius Agnostic?"). Recent revisionary appreciations of Confucius by Herbert Fingarette, Laurence Thompson, Rodney Taylor, Julia Ching, John Berthrong, and Tu Wei-ming have emphasized the religiosity of the tradition, if not any particular theistic or monotheistic element. It may also be said that these more contemporary views still perpetuate a protestantized vision of Confucian "self-cultivation." The recent postmodernist rethinking of the *Analects* by Roger Ames and David Hall (*Thinking through Confucius* [Albany, N.Y.: State University of New York Press, 1987]) has not privileged the category of religion, but has nevertheless effectively shown the contested nature of most earlier sinological understandings of the Chinese master.

14. Benjamin Jowett, "Essay on Natural Religion," in *The Epistles of St. Paul, To the Thessalonians, Galatians and Romans*, ed. Lewis Campbell (London: John Murray, 1894), 197. Jowett, like Legge and Müller, recognized that the encounter with the Oriental traditions of China and India especially called for a more secular understanding of the missionary enterprise (p. 196):

> To restore life to those countries [India and China] is a vast and complex work, in which many agencies have to co-operate—political, industrial, social; and missionary efforts, though a blessed, are but a small part; and the Government is not the less Christian because it seeks to rule a heathen nation on principles of truth and justice only. Let us not measure this great work by the number of communicants or converts. Even when wholly detached from Christianity, the true spirit of Christianity may animate it.

15. See John King Fairbank, "Introduction: The Place of Protestant Writings in China's Cultural History," in *Christianity in China: Early Protestant Missionary Writings*, ed. Suzanne Wilson Barnett and John King Fairbank (Cambridge, Mass.: Committee on American–East Asian Relations, Department of History, Harvard University, 1985), 7–18. Fairbank recognized, as something of an afterthought, that the neglect of missionary tradition within universities may actually be due to the (p. 15) "secular bent of the modern social sciences." As Laurence Sullivan noted (*Religious Regimes in Contact: Christian Missions, Global Transformations, and Comparative Research: A Bibliography* [Cambridge, Mass.: Harvard University Center for the Study of World Religions, 1993]), "the avoidance of Christian missions as a subject matter has played a constitutive, unacknowledged role in the formation of academic discourse about culture and society, although many scholars of language, culture, society, and religion have been personally affected by missionary experiences and perceptions." See also the discussion by Claude Stipe, "Anthropologists versus Missionaries: The Influence of Presuppositions," *Current Anthropology* 21 (1980):

165–79. As Stipe says, most anthropologists and social scientists during the first half of the twentieth century were convinced of the "meaninglessness of religious beliefs." Also helpful in a revisionary approach to the importance of missionary tradition are the works by Jean and John Comaroff *(Of Revelation and Revolution: Christianity, Colonialism, and Consciousness in South Africa* [Chicago: University of Chicago Press, 1991]); Christopher Herbert (*Culture and Anomie: Ethnographic Imagination in the Nineteenth Century* [Chicago: University of Chicago Press, 1991], especially chapter 3); and Paul William Harris, *Missionaries, Martyrs, and Modernizers: Autobiography and Reform Thought in American Protestant Missions,* 2 vols. (Ann Arbor, Mich.: University Microfilms International, 1986).

16. See, for example, Susan Henking, "Placing the Social Sciences: Cases at the Intersection of the Histories of Disciplines and Religions," *Religious Studies Review* 19 (1993): 116–24; and Arthur J. Vidich and Stanford M. Lyman, *American Sociology: Worldly Rejections of Religion and Their Directions* (New Haven, Conn.: Yale University Press, 1985). To borrow from Jonathan Smith's perspective on these matters (*Drudgery Divine: On the Comparison of Early Christianities and the Religions of Late Antiquity* [Chicago: University of Chicago Press, 1987], 34), "Protestant anti-Catholic apologetics" are not just an "antiquarian concern." The "same presuppositions" and the "same rhetorical tactics" are continued in much of the "present-day research" in the academic study of religion.

17. See Jonathan Z. Smith's study of comparativism, "Adde Parvum Parvo Magnus Acervus Erit," *History of Religion* 11 (1971): 67–90. There are, of course, exceptions to the general retreat of comparativism during the first part of the twentieth century. The most notable of these are various German diffusionist schools (e.g., Leo Frobenius's tradition of *Kulturkreise*).

18. See Franz Boas, "The Limitations of the Comparative Method of Anthropology," *Science* 4 (1896): 901–8.

19. Ibid., 907–8. See also Smith's discussion, "Adde Parvum," 88–90.

20. Otto Franke, "China and Comparative Philology," *China Review* 20 (1893): 310–27. As Franke suggests, the odd thing was that Edkins's own work on Chinese dialects showed that the Chinese language was hardly primordial and that it had "clearly undergone a long process of decay." On these issues relating to the mythology of the language origins and problems with Müller's comparative philology, see Maurice Olender, *The Languages of Paradise: Race, Religion, and Philology in the Nineteenth Century* (Cambridge, Mass.: Harvard University Press, 1992), 90–92; and G.A. Wells, *The Origin of Language: Aspects of the Discussion from Condillac to Wundt* (La Salle, Ill.: Open Court, 1987). It is worth noting that Franke's philological hero, Schleicher, believed that languages began as monosyllabic roots and that Chinese remained at that stage (ibid., 61). By the end of the nineteenth century, it was clear that the Chinese radicals were certainly not roots in the linguistic sense (something already recognized by Legge) and that ancient Chinese words were not, properly speaking, monosyllabic.

21. See P.G. von Möllendorff, "On the Limitations of Comparative Philology," *Journal of the North China Branch of the Royal Asiatic Society* 31 (1896): 81–101.

22. On the deficiencies of Müller's approach, see Olender, *Languages of Paradise,* 90–92.

23. See Max Müller, "The Religions of China: I. Confucianism," *Nineteenth Century* 48 (September 1900): 373–84. As Müller wrote (p. 375):

> The religion of the Chinese seemed to have left the mythological stage long before the time of Confucius. It seemed to be a prosaic and thoroughly unpoetical religion—full of sensible and wise saws, but a system of morality and of worldly wisdom rather than of religious dogmas and personal devotion. If it was full of eternal verities, it was also full of truisms. Again, if we mean by religion a revelation of the Deity, of its existence, its acts and its qualities, miraculously imparted to inspired seers and prophets, Confucius and those who followed him knew of none of these things, and hence they were even accused of having had no religion at all, or of having been Atheists in disguise. Against such a charge however, as Professor Legge has clearly shown, the Chinese language, nay, even the Chinese system of writing protests most strongly.

24. Toward the end of his life Müller was still being attacked by Andrew Lang for his solar mythology theories and by William Whitney for his philological mistakes. Even worse were the charges that he plagiarized or falsely took credit for parts of his magnum opus on the *Rig-Veda*. See, for example, various "Letters on Controversies" in Bodleian Library, Oxford University (hereafter cited as Bodleian), MS. Eng. c. 2810. See, in particular, the letters having to do with the accusations concerning Müller's editorship of the *Rig-Veda* (charges started by the *New York Nation* and the *Academy* of November 24, 1900). By the time of his death, there was a growing consensus that Müller was something of a has-been or, at the very least, that his scholarship was "unprogressive" and that "he sacrificed too much time to the production of merely popular books." Müller was also found to be too "uncompromising" to the "anthropological school" and that, generally, "his attitude towards fellow scholars left something to be desired." Most tellingly in this regard, it was seen that Müller "dearly loved a lord" and "liked to dedicate his works to royalties" (see "Newspaper Notices of the Death of F. Max Müller," Bodleian, MS. Eng. C. 2814).

25. On Schmidt, see Ernest Brandewie, *Wilhelm Schmidt and the Origin of the Idea of God* (Lanham, Md.: University Press of America, 1983).

26. On the Shang-period civilization, see, for example, Herrlee Glessner Creel, *The Birth of China: A Study of the Formative Period of Chinese Civilization* (New York: Frederick Ungar, 1937). For a chauvinistic discussion of these matters from a native Chinese point of view, see Ping-ti Ho, *The Cradle of the East: An Inquiry into the Indigenous Origins of Techniques and Ideas of Neolithic and Early Historic China, 5000–1000 B.C.* (Hong Kong and Chicago: Chinese University of Hong Kong and University of Chicago Press, 1975). For a more up-to-date appraisal of Chinese archaeological matters, see David Keightley, ed., *The Origins of Chinese Civilization* (Berkeley and Los Angeles: University of California Press, 1983).

27. See Hans Aarsleff, *The Study of Language in England, 1780–1860* (Minneapolis: University of Minnesota Press, 1983).

28. In general, see the magisterial work of Raymond Schwab, *The Oriental Renaissance: Europe's Rediscovery of India and the East 1680–1880,* trans. Gene Patterson-Black and Victor Reinking (New York: Columbia University Press, 1984); and also more particularly on China, see H. Franke, *Sinology at German Universities* (Weisbaden, Germany: Franz Steiner, 1968), 1–2. Franke comments that "as long as

sinology was not an academic subject with requirements of exactitude and depth of interpretation like the established disciplines [i.e., Orientalist fields such as Indology, Islamics, Turkish, and Iranian studies], it lagged below the level of its older sister-subjects."

29. On the "founding of the first academic chairs" in Orientalism, see Schwab, *Oriental Renaissance*, 78–80.

30. John P. Martin, "A Critical Survey of French Sinology" (M.A. thesis, Georgetown University, 1966), 37.

31. Ibid.

32. JL letter, Paris, May 29, 1867, Helen Edith Legge, typed excerpt (Council for World Mission/China/Personal/Legge/Box 7).

33. See Henri Cordier, "Half a Decade of Chinese Studies (1886–1891)," *T'oung Pao* 3 (1892): 532–57.

34. Max Müller to A. P. Stanley, dean of Westminster, August 13, 1875 (Bodleian, MS. Eng. d. 2346).

35. Schwab, *Oriental Renaissance*, 87.

36. The role and status of the British Museum in London, exemplifying as it does the progressive inroads of centralized and rationalized professionalization in English tradition in the nineteenth century, is a partial exception to this principle in Britain.

37. On British and French modes of cultural production, see for example Edward Said, *The World, the Text, and the Critic* (Cambridge, Mass.: Harvard University Press, 1983), 272–74. On the Jesuitical aspects of the French tradition of bureaucratic rationality, see the controversial study by John Ralston Saul, *Voltaire's Bastards: The Dictatorship of Reason in the West* (New York: Vintage Books, 1992). On the French sinological tradition, see (among other works already cited) Paul Demiéville, "Aperçu historique des études sinologiques en France," *Acta Asiatica* 11 (1966): 56–110; and José Frèches, *La Sinologie* (Paris: Presses Universitaires de France, 1975).

38. Wright, "The Study of Chinese Civilization," 246.

39. Ibid. See also H. Maspero, "Edouard Chavannes," *T'oung Pao* 21 (1922): 43–56.

40. See especially John B. Henderson, *Scripture, Canon, and Commentary: A Comparison of Confucian and Western Exegesis* (Princeton, N.J.: Princeton University Press, 1991).

41. Ibid.

42. On this point, see Hans Hägerdal, "China and Orientalism," *International Institute for Asian Studies Newsletter* 10 (autumn 1996): 31.

43. See Herman W. Tull, "F. Max Müller and A. B. Keith: 'Twaddle,' the 'Stupid' Myth, and the Disease of Indology," *Numen* 38 (1991): 38–39; and Dorothy M. Figueira, *The Exotic: A Decadent Quest* (Albany, N.Y.: State University of New York Press, 1994), 141–43. The claim by Roth that "a conscientious European interpreter may understand the Veda far better and more correctly than Sayana" appears to be, says Tull (p. 40):

at least in part, based on the supposition that the European shared a cultural heritage with the Vedic people, and that this ancient tradition had been lost to the Indians in the post–Rg Vedic period. Thus, Sayana's commentary merely represented the culmination of the loss of the ancient tradition. Although, of course,

Europeans such as Roth were themselves far removed from the Ṛg Vedic tradition, their vision was not, like that of the Hindus, obfuscated by the myths, rites, and mumbo-jumbo of an all-powerful priestly caste, but was clearly focused through their "scientific" understanding of the Vedic language itself. Understanding the Veda "better and more correctly" thus seems to be born of the notion that the European interpreter had open to him, through the science of language, a channel to this ancient cultural heritage that had long ago been shut off to the Hindus.

In commenting on his translation of the *Upanishads* for the *Sacred Books*, Müller said that

if, as has been pointed out, my translation often differs so widely from previous translations as to seem hardly based on the same original text, this is due chiefly to my venturing to steer a course independent of native commentators. I have little doubt that future translators of the Upanishads will assert their independence of Sankara's commentary still more decidedly. Native commentators though indispensable and extremely useful, are so much under the spell of the later systematic Vedanta philosophy that they often do violence to the simplest thoughts of ancient poets and philosophers.

See Nirad C. Chaudhuri, *Scholar Extraordinary: The Life of Professor the Rt. Hon. Friedrich Max Müller, P.C.* (London: Chatto & Windus, 1974), 354, on Müller's defense of his translation of the *Upanishads* for the *Sacred Books of the East*.

44. See Tull, "F. Max Müller and A.B. Keith," 39–42.

45. For a discussion of the term *ru*, see Robert Eno, *The Confucian Creation of Heaven: Philosophy and the Defense of Ritual Mastery* (Albany, N.Y.: State University of New York, 1990), 6–7.

46. See Hägerdal, "China and Orientalism," 31. The "prominent" sinologist is not identified.

47. See Edward Said, "East Isn't East," *Times Literary Supplement*, February 3, 1995, pp. 3–6.

48. Idem, *The World, the Text*, 268–92.

49. See the interesting criticism by Dorothy M. Figueira, *Translating the Orient: The Reception of Sakuntala in Nineteenth-Century Europe* (Albany, N.Y.: State University of New York Press, 1991), and *The Exotic*. As Figueira says (*The Exotic*, pp. 3–4):

[The] gravest criticism against Said and company is that it imposes an authorial intention upon the text, disregarding the testimony of a work's language, reception, and character as narrative, poetry, translation, scholarship. . . . By consigning to a secondary position the work of individual artists [or scholars or translators] a text becomes a commentary on a political situation rather than an expression of the motivations and desires that inspire the individual artist or scholar. . . . [There is a] need for more of a microanalysis of individual Orientalists and discrete styles of Orientalism.

On nationalistic differences in Orientalistic traditions and the heterogenity of Orientalism, see Lisa Lowe, *Critical Terrains: French and British Orientalisms* (Ithaca, N.Y., and London: Cornell University Press, 1991). Concerning Chinese "Occidentalism," see Xiao-mei Chen, *Occidentalism: A Theory of Counter-Discourse on Post-Mao China*, 2d ed. (Lanham, Md.: Rowman and Littlefield, 2000).

50. See Edward Said, *The World, the Text*, 290–92.

51. See the discussion in James Barr, "Jowett and the Reading of the Bible 'Like Any Other Book,'" *Horizons in Biblical Theology* 4/5 (1982–1983): 1–44. In fact, Jowett's position on the *historical* criticism of ancient texts was quite similar to Legge's still-reverent approach to textual matters.

52. See, for example, the discussion by Suzanne Wilson Barnett, "National Image: Missionaries and Some Conceptual Ingredients of Late Ch'ing Reform," in *Reform in Nineteenth-Century China*, ed. Paul A. Cohen and John E. Schrecker (Cambridge, Mass.: East Asian Research Center, Harvard University, 1976), 160–69.

53. See William Theodore de Bary, "The New Confucianism in Beijing," *American Scholar* 64 (1995): 175–89. These changes have been the subject of popular articles in various newspapers and magazines—for example, William Rees-Mogg, "What He Says Still Goes: Modern China Is More Influenced by Confucius Than by Mao," London *Times*, December 30, 1993; Richard Reeves, "More Than Confucius Needed to Save China from Itself, History," *Allentown Morning Call*, August 11, 1995; "Christianity Growing Fast in China," *Easton Express-Times*, May 23, 1996; and Steve Crawshaw, "Seven Years after Tiananmen No One Mentions the Massacre: Fear of Chaos Rules," *Independent* (London), June 4, 1996.

54. These developments are exemplified by the international Society for the Study of Chinese Religions, an interdisciplinary group founded in 1974 at a meeting of the American Academy of Religion. On many of these issues related to the recent history of the study of Chinese religions, see Girardot, "Chinese Religions, History of the Study of," 312–23; and idem, "'Very Small Books about Very Large Subjects': A Prefatory Appreciation of the Enduring Legacy of Laurence G. Thompson's *Chinese Religion: An Introduction*," *Journal of Chinese Religions* 20 (1992): 9–15.

55. See the series of articles collectively entitled "China on the Edge . . . of What?" *New York Times Magazine*, February 18, 1996, pp. 25–54.

56. See, for example, Danny Schechter, *Falun Gong's Challenge to China: Spiritual Practice or "Evil Cult"?* (New York: Akashic Books, 2000).

57. On some of these theoretical developments, see, for example, Russell T. McCutcheon's "The Category 'Religion' in Recent Publications: A Critical Survey," *Numen* 42 (1995): 284–309; Jonathan Z. Smith, "'Religion' and 'Religious Studies': No Difference at All," *Soundings* 71 (1988): 231–44; and especially David Chidester, *Savage Systems: Colonialism and Comparative Religion in Southern Africa* (Charlottesville and London: University Press of Virginia, 1996).

58. On some of these newer approaches to the study of Chinese religions, see, for example, Daniel Overmyer et al., "Chinese Religions—The State of the Field," 2 parts, *Journal of Asian Studies* 54 (1995): 124–60, 314–95; Catherine Bell, "Religion and Chinese Culture: Toward an Assessment of 'Popular Religion,'" *History of Religions* 29 (1989): 35–57; David Johnson, Andrew J. Nathan, and Evelyn S. Rawski, eds., *Popular Culture in Late Imperial China* (Berkeley: University of California Press, 1985); Jordan Paper, *The Spirits Are Drunk: Comparative Approaches to Chinese Religion* (Albany, N.Y.: State University of New York Press, 1995); and Donald S. Lopez Jr., ed., *Religions of China in Practice* (Princeton, N.J.: Princeton University Press, 1996).

59. As Smith says (*Drudgery Divine*, 34), comparison does not directly tell us about things, but, "like models and metaphors, [it] tells us how things might be conceived, how they might be redescribed." A comparison is a "disciplined exaggeration in the interests of knowledge."

60. A.C. Graham, *Chuang Tzu: The Inner Chapters* (London: George Allen & Unwin, 1981), 53. On the Daoist method of "sorting out [*lun*]," see ibid., 48, and Graham's *Disputers of the Tao: Philosophical Arguments in Ancient China* (La Salle, Ill.: Open Court, 1989), 189, 192–94.

61. For Legge's views on section two of the *Zhuangzi*, see *Sacred Books* (1891), 39:128–30. Here Legge actually says that Zhuangzi's methods in this chapter are expressive of "agnosticism" (p. 129). Legge's translation of this passage is as follows (p. 183):

> This view is the same as that, and that view is the same as this. But that view involves both a right and a wrong; and this view involves also a right and a wrong:—are there indeed, or are there not the two views, that and this? They have not found their point of correspondency which is called the pivot of the Tao. As soon as one finds this pivot, he stands in the centre of the ring (of thought), where he can respond without end to the changing views;—without end to those affirming, and without end to those denying. Therefore I said, "There is nothing like the proper light (of the mind)." By means of a finger (of my own) to illustrate that the finger (of another) is not a finger is not so good a plan as to illustrate that it is not so by means of what is (acknowledged to be) not a finger.

BIBLIOGRAPHICAL NOTE

In the best of all possible worlds, this long and complicated book should conclude with a complete bibliographical listing of all the primary and secondary materials consulted. Because of obvious problems of length and expense, however, it has been necessary to forgo such a full-scale bibliography. It seemed best to maintain the chapter notes in full rather than to accept a diminished set of notes *and* a truncated bibliography. The unusually rich published and unpublished sources for this work are found in the profuse backnotes. I can only hope that those interested in tracing particular materials will not be overly troubled by the extra time required to dig out specific citations and archival references. Scholarly excavation, though tedious, often has its own pleasures and sometimes even the thrill of discovery.

Despite the absence of a proper bibliography, I would like to mention some of the archives and research aids that I found especially helpful in the writing of this book. One reason for attaching this brief guide to my Legge work (and a short bibliography of bibliographies) is simply that the research encompassed a number of different disciplinary realms and various bodies of (sometimes arcane) information. Moreover, these are sources and methods that cannot easily be reconstructed by just perusing my backnotes. I thought it wise, therefore, to provide the reader with a basic road map to some of the paths I followed when exploring these various cultural worlds.

JAMES LEGGE AND MAX MÜLLER: PRIMARY SOURCES

The first of these worlds concerns James Legge and Max Müller. Fortunately, the extant primary sources by and about Legge and Müller are abundant and are concentrated in archives in Oxford and London. The most important collections of material on the life and work of James Legge are found in the School for Oriental and African Studies Library (abbreviated as SOAS in the notes) at the University of London, and in the Bodleian Library, Oxford University. The SOAS materials include the voluminous Council for World Mission archive (abbreviated as CWM), which incorporates the papers from the London Missionary Society. Legge's correspondence with the London Missionary Society is found in *(a)* CWM/Ultra-Ganges/China-Malacca/Incoming Letters/Box 3 (1839–1843) and *(b)* CWM/South China/Incoming Letters/Boxes 4–7 (1843–1873). Miscellaneous Legge papers, sermons, journals, cuttings, family documents, etc., are found in CWM/China/Personal/Legge/Boxes 4–10. There are many other materials related to Legge's missionary career dispersed throughout the CWM archive, which is now available on microfiche through IDC Microform Publishers, The Netherlands. The SOAS Library also has a separate collection of letters and materials dating to Legge's later career, bound collections of the *North-China Herald* and other China-coast periodicals, and the library of the London Missionary Society (still not catalogued). In London another valuable source of primary and contextual material on Legge is the Dr. Williams Library, which has extraordinary holdings in British evangelical history. Other small collections of material are located in the library of the Royal Asiatic Society, London, and in the archive of the Council for World Mission, London (where there is a copy of the original oil painting by Henry Room, *Dr. Legge and the Three Chinese Converts*). Rare printed materials can be found at the British Library and at the University College Department of Special Collections, University of London (e.g., having to do with Terrien de Lacouperie and the Oriental publishers Trübner & Company, the records of which are included in the Kegan Paul archive). On the University of London materials, see Janet Percival, ed., *A Guide to Archives and Manuscripts in the University of London* (London: University of London, 1984).

The other great deposit of Legge materials (especially those having to do with his academic career and association with Max Müller) is found in various libraries in Oxford, especially the Bodleian Library, Oxford University. Some of Legge's writings in Chinese (especially his Christian tract writings), as well as letters from Wang Tao, are found in the Oriental Special Collections division of the Bodleian. See David Helliwell, "List of Chinese Protestant Missionary Publications by James Legge in the Bodleian Library" and the "Collection of Pamphlets by James Legge at the Oriental Institute Library" (as well as some other materials, including the Wang Tao memorial to Legge) in the Chinese Institute, Oxford University. The Bodleian collection now includes many of the papers originally held by Dominica Legge (who inherited them from Helen Edith Legge). When Dominica Legge died, some of her materials were incorporated into the collection of papers, photos, and artifacts privately held by Christopher Legge and family, in London. Other primary sources and much contextual material are located variously at the Somerville College Library, the Mansfield College Library, and the Taylorian Institution Library, all at Oxford University. Also valuable with respect to Legge's relationship with Müller and the *Sacred Books of the East* project are the materials in the Oxford University Press archive. Some interesting personal information is found in the George Street Congregational Church materials held in the Oxford County Records Office, Oxford.

Other materials pertinent to Legge's career are held at the Aberdeen University library (his school records), the Edinburgh University libraries, and in Huntly, Scotland (newspaper and a few library materials). In the United States, there are some interesting papers and letters at the American Bible Society in New York, the New York University Library, and the College of William and Mary Library, Virginia (the Robert Nelson papers, folder 12, concerning Legge's so-called heresy in 1877). Related documents are found in the archives at the Cambridge University Library (i.e., papers concerning Thomas Wade, Herbert Giles, the Jardine-Matheson Company, and the Church Missionary Society). Materials concerning Legge's nemesis, John Shaw Burdon, are found in the University of Birmingham library. Some municipal records, as well as rare local newspapers and periodical literature dating to Legge's missionary career, are found in Hong Kong at the Government Records Office, Hong Kong University, and Hong Kong Baptist University.

Lauren Pfister is to be commended for tracking down Legge's personal library. This collection of Chinese- and Western-language books and materials, many with Legge's own marginalia, was catalogued and auctioned after Legge's death. See the *Bibliotheca Orientalis. III. Being a Catalogue of Books on China. Being the Chinese Part of the Library of the Late Rev. Prof. J. Legge, M.S., etc.* (London: Luzac, 1899). Interestingly, Legge's library went to the United States at the turn of the century, ending up at the New York Public Library and the Hartford Seminary Library, Hartford, Connecticut. Subsequently, most of the Hartford collection was sold to the Pitt Theological Library at Emory University in Atlanta, Georgia. The largest portion of these books is held in the Oriental Collections at the New York Public Library.

Beyond the substantial published articles by Lauren Pfister (see the listing on pages 557–58), there are two dissertations on Legge that give valuable suggestions for research. One of these (originally an M.A. thesis for the Department of History, Chinese University of Hong Kong) has now been published: Wong Man Kong, *James Legge: A Pioneer at the Crossroads of East and West* (Hong Kong: Hong Kong Educational Publishing Co., 1996). The other work is Lau Tze-yui's "James Legge (1815–1897) and Chinese Culture: A Missiological Study in Scholarship, Translation, and Evangelization" (Ph.D. diss., Centre for the Study of Christianity in the Non-Western World, University of Edinburgh, 1994).

The largest deposit of Müllerian materials is found at the Bodleian Library, Oxford University. See Elizabeth Turner, comp., "Catalogue of the Papers of Friedrich Max Müller, 1823–1900" (Oxford: Bodleian Library, 1992). Elsewhere in Oxford, there are other primary materials on Müller at All Souls College Library, the Mansfield College Library, the Manchester College Library, and the Taylorian Institution Library. For a guide to the Taylorian holdings, see "A Small Collection of Pamphlets and Press Cuttings Relating to the Life and Work of F. Max Müller" (Fiedler L 370), Taylorian Institution Library. There are also some materials at the British Library, London. See also the meager listings in the National Register of Archives in London. An interesting collection of Müller's letters to the American Unitarian Moncure Conway is held in the special collections division of the University of Oregon Library.

VICTORIAN STUDIES AND RELIGIOUS HISTORY

A second disciplinary world crucial to this study was the whole complex area of Victorian studies and nineteenth-century British religious history (especially the history of Nonconformist traditions). For general approaches to Victorian studies, see, for example, the convenient listing in Sally Mitchell, ed., *Victorian Britain: An Encyclopedia* (New York and London: Garland, 1988), s.v. "Research Materials for Victorian Studies"; J. Don Vann and Rosemary T. VanArsdel, *Victorian Periodicals: A Guide to Research* (New York: Modern Language Association of America, 1989); Lionel Madden, ed., *The Nineteenth-Century Periodical Press in Britain: A Bibliography* (New York: Garland, 1976); and Walter Houghton, ed., *The Wellesley Index to Victorian Periodicals 1824–1900* (Toronto: University of Toronto Press, 1966). Particularly useful for getting at the intellectual and academic culture associated with Legge and Müller was periodical literature such as the *Edinburgh Review*, the *British Quarterly*, the *Saturday Review*, the *Academy*, the *Athenaeum*, the *Pall Mall Gazette*, the *Spectator*, the *Contemporary Review*, and the *Nineteenth Century*, as well as the more popular *Times* of London, *Vanity Fair*, and the *Illustrated London News*. Fortunately for my research, the Lehigh University library has an excellent collection of nineteenth-century British periodical literature. For a discussion of recent methodological developments, see George Levine, "Victorian Studies," in *Redrawing the Boundaries: The Transformation of English and American Literary Studies,* ed. Stephen Greenblatt and Giles Gunn (New York: Modern Language Association of America, 1992), 130–53. For an orientation to research in the history of nineteenth-century Nonconformity, especially Congregationalism, see the discussion of primary and secondary bibliographical materials in Mark D. Johnson, *The Dissolution of Dissent 1850–1918* (New York: Garland, 1987),

329–38. Also useful is Susan Elizabeth Thorne, "Protestant Ethics and the Spirit of Imperialism: British Congregationalists and the London Missionary Society, 1795–1925" (Ph.D. diss., University of Michigan, 1990).

MISSIONARY HISTORY

Thirdly, there is the vast area having to do with Protestant missionary history in general and the China mission in particular. Although much significant work has been done recently on missionary tradition, this is still an underutilized body of material—especially in terms of the way in which the missionary movement relates to broad cultural developments in the Victorian period. For a general perspective on the overall missionary movement as it relates to Western discourse on religion, see the guide published by the Center for the Study of World Religions at Harvard University: *Religious Regimes in Contact: Christian Missions, Global Transformations, and Comparative Research: Bibliography* (Cambridge, Mass.: Center for the Study of World Religions, 1993). A good starting point for missionary research as it relates to China is R. G. Tiedeman, "A Brief Guide to Archival and Manuscript Sources Relating to Protestant and Roman Catholic Missions to China, 1800–1865" (1985); Gerald Anderson, *A Bibliography of the Theology of Missions* (New York: Missionary Research Library, 1966); Jonathan T'ien-en Chao, *A Bibliography of the History of Christianity in China* (Waltham, Mass.: China Graduate School of Theology, 1970); and the indispensable Archie Crouch et al., eds., *Christianity in China: A Scholars' Guide to Resources in the Libraries and Archives of the United States* (Armonk, N.Y.: M. E. Sharpe, 1989). In addition to various other research tools, this last work has an exhaustive listing of dissertations on the China missions. Regarding British materials on the China missions, see the older research aids: Leslie R. Marchant, *A Guide to the Archives and Records of Protestant Christian Missions from the British Isles to China, 1796–1914* (Perth: University of Western Australia Press, 1966), and Stuart C. Craig, ed., *The Archives of the Council for World Mission (Incorporating the London Missionary Society): An Outline Guide* (London: School of Oriental and African Studies, 1973). More up-to-date is Rosemary Seton and Emily Naish, comps., *A Preliminary Guide to the Archives of British Missionary Societies* (London: School of Oriental and African Studies, University of London, 1992); Robert Bickers and Rosemary Seton, eds., *Missionary Encounters: Sources and Issues* (Richmond, England: Curzon, 1996); and Murray A. Rubinstein, *The Origins of the Anglo-American Missionary Enterprise in China, 1807–1840* (Lanham, Md., and London: Scarecrow Press, 1996). Now available on microfilm is "China through Western Eyes: Manuscript Records of Traders, Travellers, Missionaries & Diplomats, 1792–1942" (Marlborough, England: Adam Matthew, 1998). Material found only in China-coast journals such as the *Chinese Repository* (Canton, 1832–1851), the *China Review* (Hong Kong, 1872–1900), and the *Chinese Recorder and Missionary-Journal* (Shanghai, 1868–1938) has still not been sufficiently explored. One excellent guidebook to this literature is Kathleen Lodwick, comp., *The Chinese Recorder Index: A Guide to Christian Missions in Asia, 1867–1941*, 2 vols. (Wilmington, Del.: Scholarly Resources Inc., 1986).

SINOLOGY AND ACADEMIC HISTORY

Lastly, there are the overlapping areas dealing with the increasingly secularized and professionalized world of academic life in the nineteenth century—particularly the history of Oxford University, the emergence of British sinological Orientalism, the rise of the comparative science of religions, and the history of academic publishing. Generally on academic history in the nineteenth century, see Michael Sandeson, ed., *The Universities in the Nineteenth Century* (London and Boston, Mass.: Routledge and Kegan Paul, 1975). Concerning Oxford sources, see E. H. Cordeaux and D. H. Merry, eds., *A Bibliography of Printed Works Relating to the University of Oxford* (Oxford: Clarendon Press, 1968), and the bibliographies in the individual volumes making up the series *The History of the University of Oxford,* appearing under the auspices of the Oxford University Press. In addition to the comprehensive unpublished holdings in the Bodleian Library and individual college libraries in Oxford, see also the research collection at the Centre for Oxfordshire Studies at the Oxford city library. The Centre, with its complete runs of nineteenth-century city newspapers and the *Oxford Magazine,* as well as working copy machines, greatly facilitates research on many aspects of Oxford history.

For general research on nineteenth-century China, see Andrew J. Nathan, *Modern China, 1840–1972: An Introduction to Sources and Research Aids* (Ann Arbor: University of Michigan Press, 1973). Regarding sinology and its relation to the study of religion, see Laurence G. Thompson's invaluable compendium of secondary literature, *Studies of Chinese Religion: A Comprehensive and Classified Bibliography of Publications in English, French, and German through 1970* (Encino, Calif.: Dickenson, 1976). Later volumes by Thompson cover material down to the 1990s. The literature on Orientalism has grown prodigiously ever since the groundbreaking monograph by Edward Said, but there are very few studies that touch on the sinological dimension of Orientalism. No balanced historical appraisal of sinology is yet available, although there are worthwhile studies on individual periods, themes, and national traditions (the work of David Mungello is notable). See David B. Honey's *Incense at the Altar: Pioneering Sinologists and the Development of Classical Chinese Philology* (New Haven, Conn.: American Oriental

Society, 2001). Concerning sinological Orientalism in Britain, there is Timothy Barrett's acerbic *Singular Listlessness: A Short History of Chinese Books and British Scholars* (London: Wellsweep, 1989), which is suggestive for research topics. Useful as a research guide to British sinologists is Joseph Ting, comp., "British Contributions to Chinese Studies" (London: School of Oriental and African Studies, University of London, 1951). See also Noel Matthews and M. Doreen Wainwright, comps., J. D. Pearson, ed., *A Guide to Manuscripts and Documents in the British Isles Relating to the Far East* (Oxford: Oxford University Press, 1977).

I know of no general guides to primary research on the history of the ademic study of religion. However, useful suggestions are given for the United States in Robert S. Shepard's *God's People in the Ivory Tower: Religion in the Early American University* (Brooklyn, N.Y.: Carlson, 1991), and for Britain in Philip Almond's *The British Discovery of Buddhism* (Cambridge: Cambridge University Press, 1988) and especially in Marjorie Wheeler-Barclay's "The Science of Religion in Britain, 1860–1915" (Ph.D. diss., Northwestern University, 1987). In addition to the Müller papers mentioned above, the J. Estlin Carpenter Library on Comparative Religions at Manchester College, Oxford, and the papers of Andrew Fairbairn at Mansfield College Library, Oxford, are notable collections of published and unpublished materials related to the nineteenth-century British history of the science of religion. See also insightful work on the history of the history of religions by Jonathan S. Walters, "Rethinking Buddhist Missions" (Ph.D. diss., University of Chicago, 1992). For both the history of comparative religions and sinological Orientalism in the nineteenth century, much remains to be done with early journal literature and the published proceedings from various international conferences or congresses. Lastly, the history of publishing as related to various monumental nineteenth-century projects such as the *Sacred Books of the East* needs to be examined. The archive at the Oxford University Press in Oxford has recently been organized and is congenial to research on many of these issues.

INDEX

Page numbers in italics indicate figures. Abbreviations: JL: James Legge; MM: F. Max Müller.

Text: 10/12 Baskerville
Display: Baskerville
Compositor: Impressions Book and Journal Services, Inc.
Printer and Binder: Thomson-Shore, Inc.